中国统计年鉴

CHINA STATISTICAL YEARBOOK

2001

(总第20期 No.20)

中华人民共和国国家统计局　编

Compiled by

National Bureau of Statistics of China

中国统计出版社
China Statistics Press

（京）新登字 041 号

图书在版编目（CIP）数据

中国统计年鉴. 2001/ 国家统计局 编
—北京：中国统计出版社, 2001. 9
ISBN 7-5037-3487-6

Ⅰ. 中 …
Ⅱ. 国 …
Ⅲ. 社会经济统计-统计资料-中国-2001-年鉴
Ⅳ. C832-54

中国版本图书馆 CIP 数据核字（2001）第 26280 号

中国统计年鉴-2001

作　　者/ 中华人民共和国国家统计局
责任编辑/ 叶礼奇　陈悟朝
封面设计/ 张　冰
E-mail: yearbook@stats.gov.cn
出版发行/ 中国统计出版社
通信地址/ 北京市西城区三里河月坛南街 75 号　　邮政编码/ 100826
办公地址/ 北京市丰台区西三环南路甲 6 号
电　　话/（010）63459084、63266600-22500（发行部）、63262276（编辑部）
印　　刷/ 中国科学院印刷厂
经　　销/ 新华书店
开　　本/ 890 × 1240 毫米　　1/16
字　　数/ 148 万字
印　　张/ 58.75
版　　别/ 2001 年 9 月第 1 版
版　　次/ 2001 年 9 月第 1 次印刷
书　　号/ ISBN 7-5037-3487-6/C · 1861
定　　价/ 298.00 元　　PRICE/ 149.95 USD

本书附同版本 CD-ROM 一张，光盘内容以书面文字为准。
中国统计版图书，如有印装错误，本社发行部负责调换。

《中国统计年鉴－2001》

编委会和编辑出版人员

China Statistical Yearbook-2001

EDITORIAL BOARD AND STAFF

编者说明

一、《中国统计年鉴—2001》是一部全面反映中华人民共和国经济和社会发展情况的资料性年刊。本书收录了全国和各省、自治区、直辖市2000年经济和社会各方面大量的统计数据，以及历史重要年份和近二十年的全国主要统计数据。

二、全书内容分为26个部分，即：1.行政区划和自然资源；2.综合；3.国民经济核算；4.人口；5.从业人员和职工工资；6.固定资产投资；7.能源生产和消费；8.财政；9.物价指数；10.人民生活；11.城市概况；12.农业；13.工业；14.建筑业；15.运输和邮电；16.国内贸易；17.对外经济贸易；18.旅游；19.金融和保险；20.教育和科技；21.文化、体育和卫生；22.其他社会活动及环境保护；23.香港特别行政区主要社会经济指标；24.澳门特别行政区主要社会经济指标。另附：台湾省主要社会经济指标；我国经济、社会统计指标同世界主要国家比较。各篇前设《简要说明》对本篇章的主要内容、资料来源、统计范围、统计方法以及历史的变动情况作简要概述，篇末附有《主要统计指标解释》。

三、书中所涉及的全国性统计数据，除行政区划、国土面积和森林资源外，均未包括香港、澳门特别行政区和台湾省数据。

四、香港特别行政区和澳门特别行政区的统计是构成国家统计总体的一部分。但根据中华人民共和国"香港特别行政区基本法"和"澳门特别行政区基本法"的有关原则，香港、澳门与内地是相对独立的统计区域，根据各自不同的统计制度和法律规定，独立进行统计工作。本年鉴中香港和澳门特别行政区统计资料分别由香港特别行政区政府统计处、澳门特别行政区政府统计暨普查局提供，国家统计局进行编辑。

五、资料中所使用的度量衡单位均采用国际统一标准计量单位。

六、本年鉴的资料来源大部分来自年度统计报表，一部分来自抽样调查。台湾省统计资料来自其编印的《统计月报》。主要国家和地区统计资料来自联合国出版的有关统计资料。

七、本年鉴部分数据合计数或相对数由于单位取舍不同而产生的计算误差均未作机械调整。

八、本年鉴各表中，有关对全表的注解均在该表上方，对表中部分指标的注解则在该表下方。凡带续表的资料，对部分指标的注解一律在最后一张续表的下方。

九、本年鉴表中的符号使用说明："-"表示数据不足本表最小单位数；"空格"表示该项统计指标数据不详或无该项数据；"#"表示其中的主要项；"*"或"①"表示本表下有注解。

PREFACE

I. *China Statistical Yearbook 2001* is an annual statistics publication, which covers very comprehensive data in 2000 and some selected data series in historically important years and the most recent twenty years at national level and local levels of province, autonomous region, and municipalities directly under the central government and therefore, reflects various aspects of China's social and economic development.

II. The book contains the following twenty-six parts, l. Division of Administrative Areas and Natural Resources; 2. General Survey; 3. National Accounts; 4. Population; 5. Employment and Wages; 6. Investment in Fixed Assets; 7. Production and Consumption of Energy; 8. Government Finance; 9. Price Indices; 10. People's Livelihood; 11. General Survey of Cities; 12. Agriculture; 13. Industry; 14. Construction; 15. Transport, Post and Telecommunication Services; 16. Domestic Trade; 17. Foreign Trade and Economic Cooperation; 18. Tourism; 19. Banking and Insurance; 20. Education, Science and Technology; 21. Culture, Sports and Public Health; 22. Other Social Activities and Environment Protection; 23. Main Social and Economic Indicators of Hong Kong Special Administrative Region (SAR); 24. Main Social and Economic Indicators of Macao Special Administrative Region (SAR). In the appendices listed are Main Social and Economic Indicators of Taiwan Province and a Comparison of Economic and Social Indicators among the People's Republic of China and Other Countries. In brief introduction at the beginning of each part, mainly coverage of this chapter, data sources, statistical coverage, statistical methods and historical changes are concerned. In addition, Explanatory Notes on Main Statistical Indicators are provided at the end of each part.

III. The national data in this book do not include that of Hong Kong Special Administrative Region, Macao Special Administrative Region and Taiwan Province except for divisions of administrative areas, territory and forest resources.

IV. Statistics of Hong Kong Special Administrative Region and Macao Special Administrative Region constitute an integral part of the national statistics of China. According to the principles set forth in *the Basic Law of Hong Kong Special Administrative Region*, and *the Basic Law of Macao Special Administrative Region* statistically Hong Kong, Macao and the mainland of China are three mutually independent regions, and follow their own and different statistical systems in carrying out independent statistical operation. Statistics on Hong Kong Special Administrative Region and Macao Special Administrative Region as included in this yearbook are provided by the Department of Census and Statistics of the Government of Hong Kong Special Administrative Region, the Department of Census and Statistics of the Government of Macao Special Administrative Region, and edited by National Bureau of Statistics. Users are alerted to the difference in the concepts, definitions and coverage of statistics when using and comparing data of the mainland of China, Hong Kong and Macao.

V. The units of measurement used in this book are internationally standard measurement units.

VI. The major data sources of this publication are obtained from annual statistical reports, and some from sample surveys. Data of Taiwan Province are collected from *Monthly Statistics Bulletin*. Data for major countries and territories are collected from various statistical publications published by the United Nations.

VII. Statistical discrepancies due to rounding are not adjusted in this yearbook.

VIII. The notes concerning the whole table are placed at the upper part of the table, while the notes concerning individual indicators are placed at the lower part. If the table is a continued one, the footnotes are placed in the last page.

IX. Notations used in this yearbook:

" ... " indicates that the figure is not large enough to be measured with the smallest unit in the table;

" (blank) " indicates that the data not available;

" # " indicates the major items of the total;

" * "or " ① " indicated " see footnotes below ".

目　录

CONTENTS

一、行政区划和自然资源
Divisions of Administrative Areas and Natural Resources

二、综合
General Survey

三、国民经济核算
National Accounts

四、人口
Population

五、从业人员和职工工资
Employment and Wages

六、固定资产投资
Investment in Fixed Assets

七、能源生产和消费
Production and Consumption of Energy

八、财政
Government Finance

九、物价指数
Price Indices

十、人民生活
People's Livelihood

十一、城市概况
General Survey of Cities

十二、农业
Agriculture

十三、工业
Industry

十四、建筑业
Construction

十五、运输与邮电
Transport, Post and Telecommunication Services

十六、国内贸易
Domestic Trade

十七、对外经济贸易
Foreign Trade and Economic Cooperation

十八、旅游
Tourism

十九、金融和保险
Banking and Insurance

二十、教育和科技
Education, Science and Technology

二十一、文化、体育和卫生
Culture, Sports and Public Health

二十二、其他社会活动及环境保护
Other Social Activities and Environment Protection

二十三、香港特别行政区主要社会经济指标
Main Social and Economic Indicators of Hong Kong Special Administrative Region

二十四、澳门特别行政区主要社会经济指标
Main Social and Economic Indicators of Macao Special Adminstrative Region

附录一、台湾省主要社会经济指标
Main Social and Economic Indicators of Taiwan Province

附录二、我国经济、社会统计指标同世界主要国家比较
A Comparison of Indicators of Economy and Society among the People's Republic of China and Other Countries

一、行政区划和自然资源

Divisions of Administrative Areas and Natural Resources

简要说明

本篇主要包括我国行政区划、自然状况以及自然资源的开发和利用情况等内容，由国家统计局综合司根据有关部门资料进行整理和编辑。

1．“全国行政区划”来自民政部提供的《全国县级以上行政区划变更情况》。

2．自然状况包括国土、山脉、河流、海洋、气象等状况。国土、山脉、河流的资料来自农业部1984年“农业资源区划”资料；海洋资料摘自国家海洋局编辑的《中国海洋统计年鉴》综合部分；气象资料由中国气象局整理提供。

3．自然资源包括土地、气候、林木、水、矿产等资源情况。气候资源数据来自农业部1984年“农业资源区划”资料；林木资源数据来自国家林业局1994−1998年调查公报数据；水资源数据由水利部提供；矿产资源数据由国土资源部提供。

Brief Introduction

This chapter mainly covers the data on China's divisions of administrative areas, natural conditions and the exploitation and utilization of the natural resources. Data in this chapter are compiled by the Department of Integrated Statistics of the National Bureau of Statistics using information from relevant ministries and agencies.

1) Data on *"Divisions of Administrative Areas in China"* are prepared in accordance with the *"Changes in the Divisions of Administrative Areas at and Above County Level in China"* provided by the Ministry of Civil Affairs.

2) Natural conditions cover land area, mountain ranges, rivers, ocean and meteorological phenomena. Data on land area, mountain ranges and rivers are prepared in accordance with the data on "The Divisions of Agricultural Resources" compiled by the Ministry of Agriculture in 1984. Data on ocean are taken from the *"China Oceanic Statistics Yearbook"* of complied by the State Oceanic Administration, and the meteorological data are provided by China Meteorological Bureau.

3) Natural resources cover land, climate, forest, water conservancy and mineral resources. Climate data are prepared in accordance with the data on *"The Divisions of Agricultural Resources"* compiled by the Ministry of Agriculture in 1984. Data on forest are prepared according to data in the communiqué of the surveys conducted by the National Bureau of Forestry in 1994-1998. Data on water conservancy are provided by the Ministry of Water Conservancy. Data on mineral resources are provided by the Ministry of Land and Resources.

1-1 全国行政区划(2000年底)

Divisions of Administrative Areas in China (End of 2000)

单位：个 (unit)

省级区划名称 Provinces, Municipalities and Autonomous Regions		地级区划数 Number of Prefectures	#地级市 Cities at Prefectural Level	县级区划数 Number of Counties	#县级市 Cities at County Level	地县级市个数 Number of Cities at All Levels	市辖区数 Districts Under the Jurisdiction of Cities
全国	**National Total**	**333**	**259**	**2074**	**400**	**659**	**787**
北京市	Beijing			5			13
天津市	Tianjin			4			14
河北省	Hebei	11	11	138	23	34	35
山西省	Shanxi	11	10	97	12	22	22
内蒙古自治区	Inner Mongolia	12	5	84	15	20	17
辽宁省	Liaoning	14	14	44	17	31	56
吉林省	Jilin	9	8	41	20	28	19
黑龙江省	Heilongjiang	13	12	66	19	31	64
上海市	Shanghai			3			16
江苏省	Jiangsu	13	13	58	28	41	51
浙江省	Zhejiang	11	11	62	24	35	26
安徽省	Anhui	17	17	61	5	22	45
福建省	Fujian	9	9	60	14	23	25
江西省	Jiangxi	11	11	80	10	21	19
山东省	Shandong	17	17	92	31	48	47
河南省	Henan	17	17	110	21	38	48
湖北省	Hubei	13	12	66	24	36	35
湖南省	Hunan	14	13	88	16	29	34
广东省	Guangdong	21	21	77	31	52	45
广西壮族自治区	Guangxi	14	9	81	10	19	29
海南省	Hainan	2	2	17	7	9	3
重庆市	Chongqing			26	4	4	14
四川省	Sichuan	21	18	140	14	32	40
贵州省	Guizhou	9	4	78	9	13	9
云南省	Yunnan	16	4	120	11	15	8
西藏自治区	Tibet	7	1	72	1	2	1
陕西省	Shaanxi	10	9	87	4	13	20
甘肃省	Gansu	14	5	76	9	14	10
青海省	Qinghai	8	1	39	2	3	4
宁夏回族自治区	Ningxia	4	3	17	2	5	7
新疆维吾尔自治区	Xinjiang	15	2	85	17	19	11
香港特别行政区	Hong Kong Special Administrative Region						
澳门特别行政区	Macao Special Administrative Region						
台湾省	Taiwan						

1-2 自　然　状　况

Natural Conditions

项　目	Item	2000
国土	**Territory**	
国土面积　(万平方公里)	Area of Territory　(10 000 sq.km)	960
海域面积　(万平方公里)	Area of Sea　(10 000 sq.km)	473
海洋平均深度　(米)	Average Depth of Sea　(m)	961
海洋最大深度　(米)	Maximum Depth of Sea　(m)	5377
岸线总长度　(公里)	Length of Coastline　(km)	32000
大陆岸线长度　(公里)	Mainland Shore　(km)	18000
岛屿岸线长度　(公里)	Island Shore　(km)	14000
岛屿个数　(个)	Number of Islands	5400
岛屿面积　(万平方公里)	Area of Islands　(10 000 sq.km)	3.87
气候	**Climate**	
热量分布　(积温≥0℃)	Distribution of Heat　(Accumulated Temperature≥0℃)	
黑龙江北部及青藏高原	Northern Heilongjiang and Tibet Plateau	2000-2500
东北平原	Northeast Plain	3000-4000
华北平原	North China Plain	4000-5000
长江流域及以南地区	Changjiang (Yangtze) River Drainage Area and the Area to the south of it	5800-6000
南岭以南地区	Area to the South of Nanling Mountain	7000-8000
降水量　(毫米)	Precipitation　(mm)	
台湾中部山区	Mid-Taiwan Mountain Area	>=4000
华南沿海	Southern China Coastal Area	1600-2000
长江流域	Changjiang River Valley	1000-1500
华北、东北	Northern and Northeastern Area	400-800
西北内陆	Northwestern Inland	100-200
塔里木盆地、吐鲁番盆地和柴达木盆地	Tarim Basin, Turpan Basin and Qaidam Basin	<=25
气候带面积比例　(国土面积=100)	Percentage of Climatic Zones to Total Area of Territory	
湿润地区　(干燥度<1.0)	Humid Zone　(aridity<1.0)	32
半湿润地区　(干燥度=1.0-1.5)	Semi-Humid Zone　(aridity 1.0-1.5)	15
半干旱地区　(干燥度=1.5-2.0)	Semi-Arid Zone　(aridity 1.5-2.0)	22
干旱地区　(干燥度>2.0)	Arid Zone　(aridity>2.0)	31

注：1．气候资料为多年平均值。

2．岛屿面积未包括香港、澳门特别行政区和台湾省。

a) The climate data refer to the average figures in many years.

b) Island area does not include that of Hong Kong Special Administrative Region, Macao Special Administrative Region and Taiwan Province.

1-3 自　然　资　源

Natural Resources

项　目	Item	2000
土地资源　(万公顷)	**Land Resources　(10 000 hectares)**	
耕地面积	Area of Cultivated Land	13004
荒地面积	Area of Undeveloped Land	10800
#宜农荒地	Useable for Agricultural Production	3535
林业用地面积	Area of Afforestated Land	26330
#宜林荒山荒地	Undeveloped Land Usable for Afforestation	6303
草地面积	Grassland	40000
#可利用草地	Utilizable	31333
林木资源	**Forest Resources**	
活立木总蓄积量　(亿立方米)	Total Standing Stock Volume　(100 million cu.m)	124.9
森林面积　(万公顷)	Forest Area　(10 000 hectares)	15894
森林蓄积量　(亿立方米)	Stock Volume of the Forest　(100 million cu.m)	112.7
森林覆盖率　(%)	Forest-coverage Rate　(%)	16.55
水利资源	**Water Resources**	
大陆	Land	
地表水资源总量　(亿立方米)	Surface Water Volume　(100 million cu.m)	28124
地表径流	Surface Runoff	27115
#冰川融水量	Melt-Water Volume of Glaciers	560
地下(浅层)水量	Shallow Ground Water Volume	8287
水力资源蕴藏量　(亿千瓦)	Hydropower Resources　(100 million kw)	6.76
#可开发量	Developable Resources	3.79
内陆水域总面积　(万公顷)	Inland Water Area　(10 000 hectares)	1747
#可养殖面积	Cultivatable Area	675
#已养殖面积	Cultivated Area	467
海洋	Sea	
海洋能源理论蕴藏量　(亿千瓦)	Theoretical Sea-energy Reserves　(100 million kw)	6.3
海岸带面积　(万平方公里)	Coastal Area　(10 000 sq.km)	28
滩涂面积　(万平方公里)	Sea-beach Area　(10 000 sq.km)	2.08
海水可养殖面积　(万公顷)	Cultivatable Area in Marine Areas　(10 000 hectares)	260.01
#已养殖面积　(万公顷)	Cultivated Area　(10 000 hectares)	109.49
浅海滩涂可养殖面积　(万公顷)	Cultivable Area in Shallow Sea and Sea-beaches　(10 000 hectares)	242
#已养殖面积　(万公顷)	Cultivated Area　(10 000 hectares)	89.37
矿产资源(保有储量)　(亿吨)	**Mineral Resources (Ensured Reserves)　(100 000 000 ton)**	
煤	Coal	10063
铁矿石	Iron Ore	458.1
磷矿石	Phosphate Ore	132.5
钾盐	Sylvite	4.6
盐	Salt	4048.3

注：1.土地、水利资源为以前清查数，有待进一步勘测；耕地面积为1996年农业普查数据（下表同）。
　　2.森林资源为1994—1998年调查数；矿产资源为1999年数据。

a)Figures on land and water resources in this table were obtained from surveys in pervious years. The figures are subject to further verification. Figures on area of cultivated land were taken from the 1996 's agricultural census. The same as in the following table.

b)Figures on forest resources were taken from the Third Forest Census (1994-1998). Figures on mineral resources were taken in 1999.

1-4 土 地 状 况

Land Characteristics

项 目	Item	面 积 Area	占总面积(%) Percentage to Total Area
总面积 （万平方公里）	**Total Land Area (10 000 sq.km)**	**960**	**100.00**
按地形分： （万平方公里）	**By Topographic Feature (10 000 sq.km)**		
山地	Mountains	320	33.33
高原	Plateaus	250	26.04
盆地	Basins	180	18.75
平原	Plains	115	11.98
丘陵	Hills	95	9.90
按地高分： （万平方公里）	**By Altitude (10 000 sq.km)**		
500米以下	Under 500m	241.7	25.18
500-1000米	500-1000m	162.5	16.93
1000-2000米	1000-2000m	239.9	24.99
2000-3000米	2000-3000m	67.6	7.04
3000米以上	Above 3000m	248.3	25.86
按特征分： （万公顷）	**By Land Use (10 000 hectares)**		
耕地	Cultivated Land	13004	13.54
森林	Forests	15894	16.56
内陆水域面积	Water Area in Land	1747	1.82
草地	Area of Grassland	40000	41.67
#可利用草地	Useable Area	31333	32.64
其他	Others	25355	26.41

注：本表数字多为过去清查数。

a)Most figures in this table were obtained from surveys in previous years.

1-5 主 要 山 脉 基 本 情 况

Main Mountain Ranges

名 称	Mountain Range	山峰高程（米） Height of Mountain Peak (m)	雪线高程（米） Height of Snow Line (m)	冰川面积（平方公里） Glacier Area (sq.km)
阿尔泰山	Altay Mountains	4374	3000--3200	287
天山	Tianshan Mountains	7435	3600--4400	9548
祁连山	Qilian Mountains	5826	4300--5240	2063
帕米尔	Pamirs	7579		2258
昆仑山	Kunlun Mountains			11639
喀喇昆仑山	Karakorum Mountain	8611	5100--5400	3265
唐古拉山	Tanggula Mountains	6137		2082
羌塘高原	Qiangtang Plateau	6596		3566
念青塘古拉山	Nyainqentanglha Mountain	7111	4500--5700	7536
横断山	Hengduan Mountains	7556	4600--5500	1456
喜玛拉雅山	The Himalayas	8848	4300--6200	11055
冈底斯山	Gangdise Mountains	7095	5800--6000	2188

1-6 主要河流基本情况
Major Rivers

名称	River	流域面积（平方公里）Drainage Area (sq.km)	河长（公里）Length (km)	年径流量（亿立方米）Annual Flow (100 million cu.m)
长江	Changjiang River (Yangtze River)	1808500	6300	9513
黄河	Huanghe River (Yellow River)	752443	5464	661
松花江	Songhuajiang River	557180	2308	762
辽河	Liaohe River	228960	1390	148
珠江	Zhujiang River (Pear River)	453690	2214	3338
海河	Haihe River	263631	1090	228
淮河	Huaihe River	269283	1000	622

1-7 河流流域面积
Drainage Area of Rivers

流域名称	River	流域面积（平方公里）Drainage Area (sq.km)	占外流河、内陆河流域面积合计 Percentage to Total(%)
合计	**Total of Out-flowing Rivers and Inland Rivers**	**9559370**	**100.00**
外流河	**Out-flowing Rivers**	**6114728**	**63.97**
黑龙江及绥芬河	Heilongjiang River and Suifenhe River	875342	9.16
辽河、鸭绿江及沿海诸河	Liaohe, Yalujiang and Related Coastal Rivers	345207	3.61
海滦河	Haihe River and luanhe River	318161	3.33
黄河	Huanghe River (Yellow River)	752443	7.87
淮河及山东沿海诸河	Huaihe and Related Coastal Rivers in Shandong Province	329211	3.44
长江	Changjiang River (Yangtze River)	1808500	18.92
浙闽台诸河	Rivers in Zhejiang, Fujian and Taiwan Provinces	239803	2.51
珠江及沿海诸河	Zhujiang River (Pear Rive) and Related Coastal River	580640	6.07
元江及澜仓江	Yuanjiang River and Lancang River	240652	2.52
怒江及滇西诸河	Nujiang River and West Yunnan Rivers	157156	1.64
雅鲁藏布江及藏南诸河	Yarlung Zangbo River and Southern Tibet Rivers	396258	4.15
藏西诸河	Western Tibet Rivers	57340	0.60
额尔齐斯河	Ertix River	50000	0.52
内陆河	**Inland Rivers**	**3408659**	**35.66**
内蒙内陆河	Rivers in Inner Mongolia	300067	3.14
河西内陆河	Rivers in Huanghe Upper Reach Area	488301	5.11
准噶尔内陆河	Rivers in Zhunger Basin	316530	3.31
中亚细亚内陆河	Rivers in Central Asia	93130	0.97
塔里木内陆河	Rivers in Tarim Basin	1074810	11.24
青海内陆河	Rivers in Qinghai Province	316285	3.31
羌唐内陆河	Rivers in Qiangtang	721182	7.54
松花江、黄河、藏南闭流区	Blind Drainage Areas of Songhua River, Huanghe River and Southern Tibet	90353	0.95

注：本表所列面积系水利部门量算初步汇总数，有待进一步核实。

a)Figures in the table are obtained from preliminary measurements and tabulated data by water conservancy departments, and are subject to

1-8 全国内陆水面面积

Inland Water Area

单位：千公顷 (1 000 hectares)

水域	Water Area	总水面 Total Water Area	可养殖水面 Cultivatable Area	已养殖水面 Cultivated Area	尚可利用水面 Utilizable Area
总计	**Total**	**17471**	**6749**	**4669**	**2080**
池塘	Pool	1922	1922	1858	64
湖泊	Lake	7524	2151	824	1327
水库	Reservoir	2302	1884	1516	368
河沟	Brook	5278	766	347	419
其他	Others	445	26	124	

注：已养殖水面中其他养殖面积是指工厂化养殖和非养殖水面中的网箱养殖等面积。

a)Other cultivated area refer to factory cultivated and box cultivated area.

1-9 海区海域及渔场面积

Sea Area and Areas of Fishing Ground

名称	Sea	海域总面积（千公顷）Sea Area (1 000 hectares)	大陆架渔场面积（千公顷）Area of Fishing Ground of Continental Shelf (1 000 hectares)	深度（米）Depth (m) 平均 Average	最大 Maximum
总计	**Total**	**472700**	**280000**		
渤海	Bohai Sea	7700	7700	18	70
黄海	Huanghai Sea	38000	35300	44	140
东海	Donghai Sea	77000	54900	370	2719
南海	Nanhai Sea	350000	182100	1212	5559

1-10 浅海滩涂海湾可养殖面积

Seashore Land Area for Cultivation

单位：千公顷 (1 000 hectares)

地区	Region	海水可养殖面积 Cultivatable Marine Area	浅海 Shallow Sea	滩涂 Sea-beach	港湾 Harbor
全国	**National Total**	**2600.11**	**1622.56**	**797.00**	**180.55**
北京	Beijing	0.44		0.44	
天津	Tianjin	18.49	10.00	8.49	
河北	Hebei	111.37	49.66	61.70	
辽宁	Liaoning	725.84	590.44	92.45	42.95
上海	Shanghai	3.22		3.22	
江苏	Jiangsu	139.00	7.87	130.96	0.17
浙江	Zhejiang	101.46	36.30	57.39	7.77
福建	Fujian	184.94	77.39	100.76	6.79
山东	Shandong	358.21	131.68	173.41	53.12
广东	Guangdong	835.67	664.00	120.00	51.67
广西	Guangxi	31.95	6.78	22.09	3.08
海南	Hainan	89.52	48.43	26.09	15.00

1-11 主要城市平均气温（2000年）

Monthly Average Temperature of Major Cities (2000)

单位：摄氏度 （℃）

城市	City	1月 Jan.	2月 Feb.	3月 Mar.	4月 Apr.	5月 May	6月 June	7月 July	8月 Aug.	9月 Sept.	10月 Oct.	11月 Nov.	12月 Dec.	年平均 Annual Average
北　京	Beijing	-6.4	-1.5	8.0	14.6	20.4	26.7	29.6	25.7	21.8	12.6	3.0	-0.6	12.8
天　津	Tianjin	-6.5	-1.9	7.7	14.8	20.4	26.3	28.8	26.3	22.0	13.2	3.7	-0.4	12.9
石家庄	Shijiazhuang	-4.3	0.4	10.1	16.7	21.8	26.7	28.6	26.6	21.9	13.2	4.2	1.2	13.9
太　原	Taiyuan	-7.1	-1.5	6.9	12.8	20.3	22.1	24.7	22.4	17.5	9.9	1.6	-1.0	10.7
呼和浩特	Hohhot	-13.4	-8.2	2.6	9.1	17.4	22.6	25.0	21.8	16.8	7.5	-3.6	-7.1	7.5
沈　阳	Shenyang	-15.7	-9.1	2.2	10.1	18.3	24.9	26.5	25.4	19.3	8.9	-1.8	-9.1	8.3
大　连	Dalian	-6.4	-2.6	5.1	10.9	15.7	23.6	25.2	25.4	21.9	13.3	5.0	0.2	11.4
长　春	Changchun	-18.1	-13.2	-0.8	7.3	16.8	23.4	25.2	23.4	17.9	6.5	-5.8	-15.0	5.6
哈尔滨	Harbin	-20.0	-14.4	-2.3	7.0	16.2	23.5	24.9	23.1	17.0	5.9	-7.2	-18.4	4.6
上　海	Shanghai	5.1	4.3	10.7	16.1	21.3	24.8	29.1	28.3	24.3	19.9	13.2	9.1	17.2
南　京	Nanjing	2.3	4.0	11.1	16.9	22.3	25.3	28.8	27.9	23.5	18.0	10.1	6.9	16.4
杭　州	Hangzhou	4.3	4.7	11.2	17.1	22.7	25.3	29.4	28.3	24.3	19.1	11.5	8.7	17.2
合　肥	Hefei	1.5	4.4	12.0	17.9	23.4	26.2	29.9	27.8	23.6	17.4	9.4	7.2	16.7
福　州	Fuzhou	12.3	10.1	15.1	18.5	24.0	26.3	28.6	27.6	26.5	23.6	18.0	15.0	20.5
南　昌	Nanchang	5.1	6.0	12.7	17.6	24.1	25.8	30.1	28.3	25.0	19.3	11.9	8.9	17.9
济　南	Jinan	-3.3	0.6	10.6	16.7	21.6	26.6	28.5	26.4	22.1	14.5	6.4	3.7	14.5
青　岛	Qingdao	-1.2	0.3	6.9	12.2	16.4	21.4	25.4	26.1	22.6	16.1	8.2	4.2	13.2
郑　州	Zhengzhou	-1.7	2.6	11.5	17.4	23.1	26.1	27.6	26.1	21.5	14.5	6.9	4.3	15.0
武　汉	Wuhan	2.7	6.3	13.7	18.8	24.3	27.2	31.1	28.7	24.4	17.7	9.9	7.5	17.7
长　沙	Changsha	3.7	6.0	12.6	17.3	23.0	26.0	30.2	27.8	23.3	17.7	10.2	7.9	17.1
广　州	Guangzhou	14.6	14.0	19.0	22.7	26.1	28.4	28.9	28.2	27.1	24.9	19.0	16.5	22.5
南　宁	Nanning	14.4	11.9	17.1	22.6	25.3	27.2	28.5	28.5	26.3	23.0	17.2	15.7	21.5
海　口	Haikou	18.7	18.3	21.7	26.4	27.3	28.7	28.7	28.7	27.2	26.2	22.0	20.3	24.5
桂　林	Guilin	8.3	7.7	13.9	18.5	23.8	26.2	29.1	28.1	25.1	20.2	13.5	11.6	18.8
重　庆	Chongqing	7.7	9.1	14.1	17.8	23.7	25.2	28.5	26.5	23.2	19.6	13.0	9.7	18.2
成　都	Chengdu	5.6	7.3	12.8	17.1	23.3	24.0	26.1	24.6	21.6	17.7	11.0	7.8	16.6
贵　阳	Guiyang	3.8	3.0	9.8	13.8	19.1	20.5	22.9	21.9	19.2	15.6	9.5	6.9	13.8
昆　明	Kunming	9.0	10.7	13.9	17.8	18.2	19.5	20.4	20.4	18.7	16.7	12.0	10.2	15.6
拉　萨	Lhasa	-0.5	1.8	4.6	9.1	12.5	17.2	15.1	14.1	12.8	9.4	4.6	-0.2	8.4
西　安	Xi'an	-0.5	3.4	12.0	16.4	23.0	24.9	28.1	24.6	20.1	13.5	5.6	2.8	14.5
兰　州	Lanzhou	-3.4	-1.4	6.8	12.8	20.3	21.4	26.0	21.0	16.5	10.0	2.5	-0.9	11.0
西　宁	Xining	-7.1	-6.0	1.6	7.5	13.6	15.2	19.6	15.6	11.2	5.8	-2.3	-5.7	5.8
银　川	Yinchuan	-8.8	-4.1	4.5	11.5	19.6	21.2	25.7	22.0	17.1	9.2	0.1	-2.6	9.6
乌鲁木齐	Urumqi	-13.9	-9.5	-0.5	13.1	19.1	21.9	24.7	23.0	17.8	3.1	-4.8	-7.0	7.3

1-12 主要城市平均相对湿度（2000年）

Average Relative Humidity of Major Cities (2000)

单位：%　　　　　　　　　　　　　　　　　　　　　　　　　　　(%)

城市	City	1月 Jan.	2月 Feb.	3月 Mar.	4月 Apr.	5月 May	6月 June	7月 July	8月 Aug.	9月 Sept.	10月 Oct.	11月 Nov.	12月 Dec.	年平均 Annual Average
北　京	Beijing	55	40	36	40	57	53	61	76	64	62	59	48	54
天　津	Tianjin	73	64	53	42	59	58	69	80	71	71	67	66	64
石家庄	Shijiazhuang	64	56	39	40	57	55	71	73	68	75	71	61	61
太　原	Taiyuan	57	47	33	37	41	61	72	75	69	71	63	51	56
呼和浩特	Hohhot	65	56	32	27	38	42	53	61	52	53	60	61	50
沈　阳	Shenyang	73	68	54	51	58	56	70	76	66	57	58	67	63
大　连	Dalian	62	56	51	51	68	62	80	82	66	60	59	61	63
长　春	Changchun	75	76	59	53	58	51	66	79	63	55	61	73	64
哈尔滨	Harbin	80	78	60	54	58	49	69	81	65	55	63	78	66
上　海	Shanghai	77	73	72	68	72	79	77	81	79	80	79	79	76
南　京	Nanjing	79	72	64	62	67	76	76	81	75	81	81	80	75
杭　州	Hangzhou	80	77	72	68	67	77	72	79	75	82	85	82	76
合　肥	Hefei	81	72	63	59	63	73	70	81	74	84	82	82	74
福　州	Fuzhou	74	83	72	80	70	81	76	81	67	75	77	76	76
南　昌	Nanchang	80	82	79	79	76	82	72	82	76	83	80	82	79
济　南	Jinan	68	55	36	38	53	56	70	76	68	75	69	62	61
青　岛	Qingdao	67	61	64	58	75	80	84	82	71	72	69	71	71
郑　州	Zhengzhou	69	63	46	47	54	62	80	80	76	79	73	68	66
武　汉	Wuhan	80	77	67	66	67	73	69	78	74	84	80	85	75
长　沙	Changsha	87	87	82	81	78	81	72	83	82	88	84	88	83
广　州	Guangzhou	70	74	78	85	79	78	79	83	71	77	70	72	76
南　宁	Nanning	76	82	85	82	83	80	79	80	74	82	73	74	79
海　口	Haikou	87	87	88	84	85	79	82	82	81	84	78	82	83
桂　林	Guilin	73	75	81	81	79	81	74	77	72	80	68	69	76
重　庆	Chongqing	83	75	76	80	73	81	77	82	83	83	82	86	80
成　都	Chengdu	85	77	75	74	64	79	83	82	82	81	79	80	78
贵　阳	Guiyang	85	87	82	85	73	84	79	83	80	87	79	85	82
昆　明	Kunming	63	61	59	61	70	78	78	78	72	77	71	71	70
拉　萨	Lhasa	31	25	30	37	48	51	70	73	63	44	34	30	45
西　安	Xi'an	67	58	47	50	49	65	67	78	76	83	81	76	66
兰　州	Lanzhou	51	50	44	35	34	52	45	61	67	70	62	53	52
西　宁	Xining	50	49	52	48	49	68	61	69	78	72	63	57	60
银　川	Yinchuan	61	43	39	31	37	62	56	66	67	64	58	54	53
乌鲁木齐	Urumqi	82	75	68	37	41	45	42	44	39	74	80	76	59

1–13 主要城市降水量（2000年）

Monthly Precipitation of Major Cities (2000)

单位：毫米 (millimeters)

城市	City	1月 Jan.	2月 Feb.	3月 Mar.	4月 Apr.	5月 May	6月 June	7月 July	8月 Aug.	9月 Sept.	10月 Oct.	11月 Nov.	12月 Dec.	全年 Annual total
北京	Beijing	11.9		8.8	18.3	37.7	19.0	61.5	150.5	18.4	35.2	9.7	0.1	371.1
天津	Tianjin	7.8	1.3	3.2	16.4	53.2	2.7	181.3	154.1	13.5	19.5	5.3	0.5	458.8
石家庄	Shijiazhuang	19.2		0.3	1.7	22.9	41.0	299.4	44.1	92.0	68.5	6.8		595.9
太原	Taiyuan	13.7	0.1	0.1	5.0	6.0	66.0	118.4	84.3	62.3	58.3	5.1		419.3
呼和浩特	Hohhot	8.3	0.8	3.9	3.7	50.3	40.6	83.8	56.2	29.5	32.1	6.3	1.3	316.8
沈阳	Shenyang	27.5	3.7	25.1	54.2	25.9	34.0	87.1	113.9	23.7	51.5	30.1	24.8	501.5
大连	Dalian	13.2	1.0	2.2	10.9	33.7	50.8	134.0	87.2	20.3	42.6	15.0	8.3	419.2
长春	Changchun	15.9	1.4	3.8	18.5	45.3	29.8	85.6	135.9	32.4	4.9	25.1	17.7	416.3
哈尔滨	Harbin	12.9	4.6	4.9	27.2	50.1	49.4	84.8	157.9	31.4	38.0	13.1	13.7	488.0
上海	Shanghai	108.9	52.8	102.2	63.1	142.5	172.3	72.5	235.6	113.5	151.2	105.3	11.8	1331.7
南京	Nanjing	73.8	33.5	25.3	39.7	90.4	181.5	110.2	141.3	103.7	125.5	76.2	28.5	1029.6
杭州	Hangzhou	126.9	88.7	110.9	90.3	82.6	168.2	108.9	128.3	47.1	97.8	118.6	30.0	1198.3
合肥	Hefei	69.6	23.7	12.7	27.4	51.2	216.5	51.4	142.4	96.6	108.4	79.6	22.4	901.9
福州	Fuzhou	57.3	97.4	28.7	230.0	35.7	420.2	171.0	260.6	19.6	45.5	121.5	72.7	1560.2
南昌	Nanchang	120.8	75.6	172.5	163.0	113.0	352.5	49.8	99.5	37.9	100.8	136.6	14.0	1436.0
济南	Jinan	17.2	17.0	0.3	25.8	40.3	138.4	90.3	218.6	40.4	103.9	28.8	0.2	721.2
青岛	Qingdao	39.5	7.3	1.6	10.9	59.9	99.8	74.9	276.8	99.5	68.9	46.4	2.7	788.2
郑州	Zhengzhou	26.3	1.8		8.6	20.1	43.5	243.1	88.2	105.0	73.5	22.1	4.9	637.1
武汉	Wuhan	107.7	28.6	28.5	22.9	170.9	178.7	44.7	150.1	201.6	149.9	56.7	39.5	1179.8
长沙	Changsha	71.5	67.7	171.0	126.2	148.2	290.5	66.8	160.3	192.4	111.2	77.0	25.0	1507.8
广州	Guangzhou	10.6	29.7	27.7	418.7	202.9	197.4	288.9	185.0	56.7	304.3	34.0	43.0	1798.9
南宁	Nanning	1.7	47.7	37.0	66.5	154.9	37.7	248.7	68.8	69.6	159.2	10.8	2.4	905.0
海口	Haikou	16.5	23.9	45.2	121.2	263.8	87.5	319.8	245.4	189.5	770.2	38.7	42.0	2163.7
桂林	Guilin	41.4	53.3	178.8	273.5	384.9	432.4	67.5	228.5	201.4	147.3	28.0	19.1	2056.1
重庆	Chongqing	13.9	6.2	33.7	115.2	95.5	96.1	229.8	123.5	174.6	61.0	40.0	21.4	1010.9
成都	Chengdu	16.6	21.0	21.3	48.7	18.2	80.0	250.3	207.7	76.3	32.2	9.5	1.5	783.3
贵阳	Guiyang	24.6	24.9	52.2	94.4	174.1	314.9	164.1	304.4	127.3	100.3	38.6	21.4	1441.2
昆明	Kunming	35.1	23.0	44.5	16.0	188.6	118.5	162.0	164.1	54.5	59.9	19.8		886.0
拉萨	Lhasa	3.5	0.1	9.2	8.9	39.9	60.2	170.4	164.5	71.3	1.7			529.7
西安	Xi'an	9.2	4.9	5.4	18.6	38.0	106.3	54.4	128.9	62.9	73.6	26.2	10.6	539.0
兰州	Lanzhou	0.3	6.4	5.0	6.1	6.2	77.3	22.0	111.5	65.7	55.5	3.9		359.9
西宁	Xining	1.6	4.2	3.5	17.1	27.1	52.1	46.9	62.2	87.7	21.7	17.7	1.2	343.0
银川	Yinchuan	4.0			0.6	0.2	31.4	11.7	52.0	31.6	2.3			133.8
乌鲁木齐	Urumqi	30.3	20.6	13.7	20.6	25.5	58.2	19.1	42.1	16.2	49.8	27.6	8.6	332.3

1-14 主要城市日照时数（2000年）

Monthly Sunshine Hours of Major Cities (2000)

单位：小时　　(hours)

城市	City	1月 Jan.	2月 Feb.	3月 Mar.	4月 Apr.	5月 May	6月 June	7月 July	8月 Aug.	9月 Sept.	10月 Oct.	11月 Nov.	12月 Dec.	全年 Annual total
北京	Beijing	170.9	230.8	275.5	248.8	304.8	275.2	232.3	186.9	239.3	170.0	159.5	173.2	2667.2
天津	Tianjin	132.4	194.2	220.3	220.2	262.6	252.2	208.8	155.7	209.4	143.7	129.3	119.0	2247.8
石家庄	Shijiazhuang	114.3	149.6	214.6	233.6	240.1	188.5	183.6	176.7	218.1	119.2	79.3	90.2	2007.8
太原	Taiyuan	159.7	216.4	262.2	268.5	290.8	205.1	215.7	184.7	202.6	145.0	130.7	157.3	2438.7
呼和浩特	Hohhot	118.3	193.1	275.2	273.2	296.7	300.0	266.2	225.3	253.1	201.9	171.9	166.2	2741.1
沈阳	Shenyang	116.0	197.6	234.1	216.2	225.8	263.7	241.4	188.4	222.8	196.1	149.3	115.3	2366.7
大连	Dalian	182.7	220.3	279.2	272.9	263.3	290.5	219.4	213.7	273.4	186.7	148.2	154.2	2704.5
长春	Changchun	159.0	218.0	248.3	218.0	267.4	293.5	236.8	222.3	247.0	230.9	196.0	174.3	2711.5
哈尔滨	Harbin	99.2	180.6	202.5	210.9	224.4	309.1	278.3	229.8	242.7	230.0	168.1	130.9	2506.5
上海	Shanghai	87.8	121.6	146.8	154.3	180.7	129.3	213.4	172.0	142.5	96.4	99.6	105.1	1649.5
南京	Nanjing	89.4	148.0	179.9	204.6	220.4	173.7	256.4	181.3	157.1	92.2	120.1	110.2	1933.3
杭州	Hangzhou	61.9	65.4	119.7	150.9	197.3	138.0	238.6	184.2	124.4	64.6	72.6	96.2	1513.8
合肥	Hefei	70.1	127.9	166.8	212.9	209.2	161.2	242.5	122.1	127.7	72.9	100.8	90.4	1704.5
福州	Fuzhou	87.1	21.4	96.0	86.1	188.0	174.1	202.1	153.7	200.1	89.8	57.3	93.8	1449.5
南昌	Nanchang	65.3	26.6	82.7	86.6	213.9	197.2	298.2	202.1	201.9	104.6	123.6	109.6	1712.3
济南	Jinan	129.1	183.7	239.5	236.9	245.5	205.3	192.3	198.3	208.3	120.1	140.7	134.2	2233.9
青岛	Qingdao	140.8	212.6	242.1	241.5	215.0	212.8	199.9	185.7	210.6	177.4	142.2	180.0	2360.6
郑州	Zhengzhou	85.8	141.7	222.1	232.3	237.6	196.9	152.7	154.2	135.9	95.7	113.4	112.1	1880.4
武汉	Wuhan	69.5	78.4	148.7	158.4	198.3	171.4	256.2	199.6	156.7	102.1	117.1	95.8	1752.2
长沙	Changsha	46.1	26.9	71.9	58.1	157.8	148.7	279.0	148.2	117.7	52.9	114.1	74.5	1295.9
广州	Guangzhou	109.2	62.2	93.2	49.3	106.7	179.4	203.6	130.5	185.1	137.6	139.2	213.2	1609.2
南宁	Nanning	56.5	22.1	43.2	71.6	126.6	135.3	228.1	211.0	175.3	118.5	163.6	126.4	1478.2
海口	Haikou	64.9	77.4	143.0	154.9	170.4	233.7	235.2	209.5	188.7	147.7	93.0	81.6	1800.0
桂林	Guilin	52.8	21.7	35.5	66.6	135.5	133.3	243.2	213.3	197.2	110.0	136.9	126.8	1472.8
重庆	Chongqing		30.2	75.6	79.2	183.9	82.4	168.4	80.7	76.3	90.2	59.9	34.3	961.1
成都	Chengdu	6.0	33.6	83.7	91.5	179.3	86.2	134.0	117.3	82.0	61.3	62.2	73.1	1010.2
贵阳	Guiyang	35.6	3.7	61.4	56.3	157.6	109.4	164.9	113.2	119.2	73.6	117.1	56.2	1068.2
昆明	Kunming	193.0	222.8	217.0	208.1	156.7	79.4	133.2	117.0	132.2	117.8	226.8	191.5	1995.5
拉萨	Lhasa	221.4	232.7	267.0	214.5	220.1	227.6	154.4	144.5	209.7	274.4	248.8	257.8	2672.9
西安	Xi'an	39.8	54.5	144.6	124.6	178.3	97.2	128.1	157.9	80.2	24.4	22.5	39.8	1091.9
兰州	Lanzhou	186.3	189.5	245.5	255.3	301.9	229.5	326.0	263.4	152.8	162.5	157.2	187.4	2657.3
西宁	Xining	185.1	188.2	210.7	227.8	259.0	213.5	286.1	244.4	133.3	197.9	192.1	196.1	2534.2
银川	Yinchuan	175.5	205.6	227.1	245.3	284.9	222.9	321.3	279.8	200.0	190.0	202.1	204.8	2759.3
乌鲁木齐	Urumqi	112.1	173.5	230.4	287.4	307.3	268.4	277.6	282.9	266.3	167.3	99.8	97.5	2570.5

主 要 统 计 指 标 解 释

行政区划　指国家对行政区域的划分。根据宪法规定，我国的行政区域划分如下：⑴全国分为省、自治区、直辖市；⑵省、自治区分为自治州、县、自治县、市；⑶自治州分为县、自治县、市；⑷县、自治县分为乡、民族乡、镇；⑸直辖市和较大的市分为区、县；⑹国家在必要时设立的特别行政区。

国土　指中华人民共和国国家管辖下的领土、领海和领空。

气候　指地球与大气之间长期能量交换与质量交换所形成的一种自然环境状态，它是多种因素综合作用的结果。气候既是人类生活和生产的环境要素之一，又是供给人类生活和生产的重要资源。气温、降水、湿度等气象要素的多年平均值是用来描述一个地区气候状况的主要参数，而各种气象要素某年、某月的平均值（或总量）则可以反映出该时期天气气候状况的重要特征。

自然资源　指人类可以直接从自然界获得，并用于生产和生活的物质资源。自然资源一般可以分成可再生资源和非再生资源两大类。可再生资源指在较短时间内可以再生、可以循环利用的资源，包括土地资源、水资源、气候资源、生物资源和海洋资源等。非再生资源指在使用后不能再生的资源，包括矿产资源和地热能源。

土地资源　土地指陆地的表层部分，它主要由岩石、岩石的风化物和土壤构成。土地资源按利用类型可以分为农用地、建筑用地和未利用地。农用地包括耕地、园地、林地、牧草地和水面。建筑用地包括居民点及工矿用地、交通用地和水利设施用地。未利用地指农用地和建筑用地以外的土地，包括滩涂、荒漠、戈壁、冰川和石山等。

耕地面积　指经过开垦用以种植农作物并经常进行耕耘的土地面积。包括种有作物的土地面积、休闲地、新开荒地和抛荒未满三年的土地面积。

林业用地面积　指生长乔木、竹类、灌木、沿海红树林等林木的土地面积，包括有林地、灌木林、疏林地、未成林造林地、迹地、苗圃等。

草地面积　指牧区和农区用于放牧牲畜或割草，植被盖度在5%以上的草原、草坡、草山等面积。包括天然的和人工种植或改良的草地面积。

森林资源　指森林、林木、林地以及依托森林、林木、林地生存的野生动物、植物和微生物。林木指树木和竹子。森林指以乔木为主体的植物群落，是集生的乔木及与共同作用的植物、动物、微生物和土壤、气候等的总体。

活立木总蓄积量　指一定范围内土地上全部树木蓄积的总量，包括森林蓄积、疏林蓄积、散生木蓄积和四旁树蓄积。

森林面积　指由乔木树种构成，郁闭度0.2以上（含0.2）的林地或冠幅宽度10米以上的林带的面积，即有林地面积。森林面积包括天然起源和人工起源的针叶林面积、阔叶林面积、针阔混交林面积和竹林面积，不包括灌木林地面积和疏林地面积。

森林蓄积量　指一定森林面积上存在着的林木树干部分的总材积。它是反映一个国家或地区森林资源总规模和水平的基本指标之一，也是反映森林资源的丰富程度、衡量森林生态环境优劣的重要依据。

森林覆盖率　指一个国家或地区森林面积占土地总面积的百分比。森林覆盖率是反映森林资源的丰富程度和生态平衡状况的重要指标。在计算森林覆盖率时，森林面积包括郁闭度0.2以上的乔木林地面积和竹林地面积，国家特别规定的灌木林地面积、农田林网以及四旁（村旁、路旁、水旁、宅旁）林木的覆盖面积。计算公式为：

森林覆盖率（%）＝森林面积／土地总面积×100%

水资源　水在自然界中以固体、液体和气态三种聚集状态存在，分布于海洋、陆地（包括土壤）以及大气之中，通过水循环形成水资源。水资源包括经人类控制并直接可供灌溉、发电、给水、航运、养殖等用途的地表水和地下水，以及江河、湖泊、井、泉、潮汐、港湾和养殖水域等。水资源是发展国民经济不可缺少的重要自然资源。

地表水和地下水　陆地上的水因空间分布不同，分为地表水和地下水。地表水指分别存在于河流、湖泊、沼泽、冰川和冰盖等水体中水分的总称，又称陆地水。地下水指储存在地面以下饱和岩土孔隙、裂隙及溶洞中的水。

内陆水域总面积　指江、河、湖泊、池塘、塘堰、水库等各种流水或蓄水的水面占地面积。

海洋　是海和洋的统称。洋为地球表面上相连接的广大咸水水体的主体部分。海为地球表面相连接的广大咸水水体被陆地、岛礁、半岛包围或分隔的边缘部分。

海水可养殖面积　指利用滩涂、浅海、港湾进行鱼、虾、蟹、贝、藻等海水经济动植物的人工养殖的水面面积。

径流　指陆地上接受降水后扣除损耗外，从地表和地下向流域出口断面汇集的水流。径流可分为地表径流、地下径流和壤中流。地表径流指沿地表向河流、湖泊、沼泽、海洋等汇集的水流；地下径流指沿潜水层或隔水层间的含水层，向河流、湖泊、沼泽、海洋等汇集的地下水水流。

径流量　指在一定时段内通过河流某一过水断面的水量，用以反映一个国家或地区水资源的丰歉程度。计算公式为：

径流量＝降水量－蒸发量

矿产资源　矿产指由地质作用形成，富集于地壳中或出露于地表达到工农业利用要求的有用矿物。矿产是一种重要的自然资源，是社会发展的重要物质基础。

矿产保有储量 指探明的矿产储量（包括工业储量和远景储量），扣除已开采部分和地下损失量后的年末实有储量。

流域 每条河流都有自己的干流和支流，干支流共同组成这条河流的水系。每条河流都有自己的集水区域，这个集水区域就称为该河流的流域。

外流河 指直接或间接流入海洋的河流。供给外流河河水的区域称为外流区域。

内陆河 指在陆地内部干燥地区，河水沿途消失于沙漠或注入内陆湖泊的河流。供给内陆河河水的区域称为内陆区域。

大陆架 指沿海国家的领海以外，依其陆地领土的全部自然延伸，扩展到大陆边缘的，其宽度依据《联合国海洋法公约》规定的海底区域的海床和底土。大陆架海区水产资源丰富，海底多蕴藏石油、天然气以及其他矿产资源，这些自然资源属沿海国家所有。我国的大陆架为我国领海以外依本国陆地领土的全部自然延伸，扩展到大陆边外缘的海底区域的海床和底土；如果从测算领海宽度的基线量起至大陆边外缘的距离不足200海里，则扩展到200海里。

浅海养殖 指在可养殖的浅海中进行海水经济动植物养殖。

滩涂养殖 指利用位于海边潮间带的软泥或砂泥地带加以平整，筑堤、建坝等进行海水养殖。

港湾养殖 指利用港、湾，或在海边、河口附近的滩涂、洼地拦闸筑堤进行海水养殖。

气温 指空气的温度，我国一般以摄氏度（℃）为单位表示。气象观测的温度表是放在离地面约1.5米处通风良好的百叶箱里测量的，因此，通常说的气温指的是离地面1.5米处百叶箱中的温度。其统计计算方法为：

月平均气温是将全月各日的平均气温相加，除以该月的天数而得。

年平均气温是将12个月的月平均气温累加后除以12而得。

相对湿度 指空气中实际所含水蒸气密度和同温度下饱和水蒸气密度的百分比值。其统计方法与气温相同。

降水量 指从天空降落到地面的液态或固态（经融化后）水，未经蒸发、渗透、流失而在地面上积聚的深度。其统计计算方法为：

月降水量是将全月各日的降水量累加而得。

年降水量是将12个月的月降水量累加而得。

日照时数 指太阳实际照射地面的时间。其统计方法与降水量相同。

Explanatory Notes on Main Statistical Indicators

Administrative Division refers to the division of administrative areas by the state. The Constitution of the People's Republic of China stipulates that the administrative areas in China are divided as: 1) The whole country is divided into provinces, autonomous regions and municipalities directly under the central government; 2) Provinces and autonomous regions are divided into autonomous prefectures, counties, autonomous counties and cities; 3) Autonomous prefectures are divided into counties, autonomous counties and cities; 4) Counties and autonomous counties are divided into townships, nationality townships and towns; 5) Municipalities and large cities are divided into districts and counties, 6) The state shall, when necessary, establish special administrative regions.

Territory refers to territorial land, sea and air space under the administration of the People's Republic of China.

Climate refers to the natural environmental status formed by the long-term exchange of energy and mass between the earth and the air, and is the results of interaction of many factors. Climate is both one of the environment factors and the important resources for the living and production activities of the human being. The average values across several years of meteorological factors such as temperature, rainfall and humidity are used as important parameters to describe the climate of a region, while the average values (or total values) of a given year or month of meteorological factors reflect the key characteristics of climate for that period of time.

Natural Resources refer to material resources that could be obtained from the nature by human being and used for production and living. Natural resources in general can be classified as renewable resources and non-renewable resources. Renewable resources refer to resources that could be renewed and recycled during a relatively short period of time, including land resource, water resource, climate resource, biology resource and marine resource. Non-renewable resources include resources that could not be renewed, such as minerals and geothermal resource.

Land Resource Land refers to the surface of the earth, consisting of mainly rocks and its whethering and earth. Land resource can be classified, by its utilization, as land for agriculture, land for construction and unused land. Land for agriculture includes cultivated land, plantation land, forestland, grassland and waters. Land for construction includes land for residential purpose, for manufacturing and mining, for transportation and for water-conservancy projects. Unused land refers to land other than land for agriculture and construction, including beaches, deserts, Gobi, glaciers and rock mountains.

Area of Cultivated Land refers to area of land reclaimed for the regular cultivation of various farm crops, including crop-cover land, fallow, newly reclaimed land and land laid idle for less than 3 years.

Area of Afforested Land refer to land for trees bamboo, bushes and mangrove, including forest-cover land, bush-covered land, sparse forest land, land planned for afforestation and nurseries of young trees.

Area of Grassland refers to areas of grassland, grass-slopes and grass-covered hills with a vegetation-covering rate of over 5% that are used for animal husbandry or harvesting of grass. It includes natural, cultivated and improved grassland areas.

Forest Resource refers to forests, trees, forestland and wild animals, plants and microorganism that live on forest and trees. Trees include trees and bamboo. Forest refers to the population of clusters of trees and other plants, animals and microorganism as well as the earth and climate that have interactions with the trees.

Total Standing Stock Volume refers to the total stock volume of trees growing in land, including trees in forest, tress in sparse forest, scattered trees and trees planted by the side of farm houses and along the roads, rivers and fields.

Forest Area refers to the area of forest land where trees and bamboo grow with canopy density above 0.2, including land of natural woods and planted woods, but excluding bush land and thin forest land. It reflects the total areas of afforestation.

Stock Volume of Forest refers to total stock volume of wood growing in forest area, which shows the total size and level of forest resources of a country or a region. It is also an important indicator illustrating the richness of forest resource and the status of forest ecological environment.

Forest Coverage Rate refers to the ratio of area of afforested land to total land area. It is a very important indicator that reflects the status of abundance of forest resource and ecosystem balance. Forest area includes the area of trees and bamboo grow with canopy density above 0.2, the area of shrubby tree according to regulations of the government, the area of forest land inside farm land and the area of trees planted by the side of farm houses and along the roads, rivers and fields. The formula for calculating forest coverage rate is as follows:

Forestry coverage rate (%)= (Area of Afforested Land/Area of Total Land) × 100%

Water Resource Water exists in the nature in solid, liquid and gaseous states, is distributed in the ocean, land (including earth) and air, and constitutes the water resource through the circulation of water. Water resource includes the surface water and underground water that is controlled by the human being for irrigation, power-generation, water supply, navigation and cultivation. It also includes rivers, lakes, wells, springs, tides, gulf and water area for cultivation. Water resource as an important natural resource is indispensable for the development of the national economy.

Surface Water and Underground Water Water on earth can be divided into surface water and underground water according to its distribution. Surface water refers to moisture exists in rivers, lakes, swamps, glaciers, icecaps and so on. It is also called land water. The underground water refers to water deposited underground in the cranny and the hole of saturated rock soil and in the water-eroded cave.

Inland Water Area refers to water area of rivers, lakes, ponds, reservoir, etc.

Ocean is the general name for sea and ocean. Ocean refers to the main body of large salt water connected with the earth. Sea refers to the edge areas of the salt water on the earth that are comparted or surrounded by land, island, reef or peninsula.

Marine Cultivatable Areas refer to water areas in beach, shallow sea and lough that are used to breed marine cash propagation, such as fish, shrimp, crab, shellfish, alga and so on.

Runoff refers to the water gathered at the way out of the cross section of drainage area either from the surface or underground after deducting the wastage of the precipitation on the land. Runoff can be divided into surface runoff, underground runoff and within soil runoff. Surface runoff refers to water flow to the rivers, lakes, swamps, and seas on the surface of the earth. Underground runoff refers to water flow to rivers, lakes, swamps, and seas through the water-bearing stratum of confined layer or unconfined layer.

Volume of Runoff refers to the total volume of water running through a certain cross section of a river during a certain period of time, reflecting the water resource condition in a country or a region. The formula for calculating volume or runoff is as follows:

Runoff =Precipitation-Evaporation

Mineral Resources refer to useful minerals that can be used for industrial or agricultural purposes enriched in lithosphere or on earth due to the geological process. Minerals are important natural resources, and important material base for social development.

Ensured Mineral Reserves refer to the actual mineral reserves, which equal to the proven mineral reserves (including industrial reserves and prospective reserves) minus extracted parts and underground losses.

Drainage Area Each river has its own main stream and branches to form the water system of the river. Each river has its own catchment area, which is also called as the drainage area of the river.

Out-flowing Rivers refer to rivers directly or indirectly flowing into the sea. The area providing water to the out-flowing rivers is called as out-flowing area.

Inland Rivers refer to rivers in inland dry areas that die away in desert on the way or infuse into inland lakes. The area providing water to the inland rivers is called as inland area.

Continental Shelf refers to seabed and subsoil of sea floor area that beyond the marginal sea of the coastal countries which stretches naturally of its land territory to continent edge, and its width is defined by the nited Nations Marine Convention. The continental shelf area is rich in aquatic products, and its seabed contains petroleum, natural gas and other mineral resources, which belong to the coastal countries. The continental shelf of our country is the natural stretch of its land territory to the continent edge besides the marginal sea of our country. It expands to the seabed and subsoil of the sea floor area to the edge of the continent. If the distance from the baseline of the marginal sea to the continent edge is less than 200 sea miles, it can be expanded to 200 sea miles.

Shallow Sea Cultivation refers to the breeding of marine cash propagation in the cultivatable shallow sea.

Sea-breaches Cultivation refers to the level off the ooze and mud in tideland to bank up and build dam to conduct marine cultivation.

Lough Cultivation refers to marine cultivation conducted in harbors, bends, or the sea-beaches or marshes around seaside and bayou by blocking the gate and banking up the dam.

Temperature refers to the air temperature. China uses centigrade as the unit. The thermometry used for weather observation is put in a breezy shutter, which is 1.5 meters high from the ground. Therefore, the commonly used temperature refers to the temperature in the breezy shutter 1.5 meters away from the ground. The calculation method is as follows:

Monthly average temperature is the summation of average daily temperature of one month divided by the actual days of that particular month.

Annual average temperature is the summation of monthly average of a year divided by 12 months.

Relative Humidity refers to the ratio of actual water vapor pressure to the saturation water vapor density under the current temperature. The statistical method is the same as that of temperature.

Volume of Precipitation refers to the deepness of liquid state or solid state (thawed) water falling from the sky to the ground that has not been evaporated, infiltrated or run off. The calculation method is as follows:

Monthly precipitation is the summation of daily precipitation of a month.

Annual precipitation is the summation of 12 months precipitation of a year.

Sunshine Hours refer to the actual hours of sun irradiating the earth. The calculation method is the same as that of the precipitation.

二、综合

General Survey

简要说明

一、本篇包括国民经济综合资料和民族自治地方社会经济发展情况等内容。

二、国民经济综合资料中的“各部门机构数”，除地质勘探机构数由国土资源部提供、运输机构数由铁道部、交通部和民航管理局提供外，均来自本年鉴各篇；国民经济总量、速度、结构、比例和效益指标的数据也均来自本年鉴各篇。

三、民族自治地方及少数民族统计资料由两部分组成：

一是以地域为主体进行的统计调查。根据国家民委和国家统计局联合布置的民族自治地方国民经济和社会发展主要指标综合报表制度，由有民族自治地方的20个省、自治区民委和统计局共同组织实施。统计范围是民族自治区、自治州、自治县辖区内的全部单位，全国汇总时不重复计算。另外，全国民族自治地方卫生情况由卫生部提供。民族自治地方行政区划资料是根据民政部编辑的《年度行政区划简册》汇总整理的。

二是以民族成分为主体进行的统计调查，主要反映少数民族社会发展情况。其中全国少数民族教职员工、学生数据由教育部提供；全国少数民族优秀运动员、教练员数据由国家体育总局提供；全国少数民族文字出版物数据由新闻出版署提供。

四、1992年国家统计局与国家工商行政管理局联合制定了《关于经济类型划分的暂行规定》，它对于反映我国的所有制结构及其变化情况发挥了积极的作用，但这一规定已不适应我国现阶段的经济情况。为了更好地贯彻落实党的十五大精神，全面反映以公有制为主体，多种所有制经济共同发展，调整和完善所有制结构的进展情况，为各级党政领导和有关部门进行决策和管理提供依据，1998年国家统计局和国家工商行政管理局以我国工商行政管理部门对企业登记注册的实际类型为基础，共同制定了《关于划分企业登记注册类型的规定》，并从1998年年报开始执行此规定。

Brief Introduction

I. This chapter covers the summary data on the national economy and data on the social and economic development of the minority national autonomous areas.

II. In the summary data on the national economy, the data on "the number of grassroots units in various sectors" are extracted from the concerned data in other chapters in this yearbook with the exception that the number of geological survey and prospecting teams is provided by the Ministry of Land and Resources; the number of transport grassroots units are provided by the Ministry of Railways, Ministry of Communication and the Civil Aviation Administration of China.

III. Data on the minority nationality autonomous areas and the minority nationalities are composed of two parts:

(1) The data collected from the surveys mainly on the areas. A statistical reporting scheme on the economic and social development in the minority nationality autonomous areas has been assigned jointly by the State Ethnic Affairs Commission and the National Bureau of Statistics and implemented by the ethnic affairs commissions and the statistical bureaus of 20 provinces and autonomous regions. The statistical coverage includes all the units under the jurisdiction of the minority nationality autonomous regions, autonomous prefectures and autonomous counties. There is no duplicated computation in the national tabulation. In addition, the data on the public health of the minority nationality autonomous areas are provided by the Ministry of Public Health. The data on the divisions of administrative areas of the minority nationality autonomous areas are tabulated and prepared in accordance with the *"Annual Concise Edition of the Divisions of Administrative Areas"* edited by the Ministry of Civil Affairs.

(2) The data collected from the surveys mainly on the minority nationalities. They chiefly show the social development of the minority nationalities. Among them, the data on the students and teaching staff of the minority nationalities are provided by the Ministry of Education; the data on the excellent athletes and coaches are provided by the State Sports Administration; and the data on the publications of the minority nationality languages are provided by the Press and Publication Administration.

IV. In 1992, the National Bureau of Statistics (then State Statistical Bureau) and the State Administration for Industry and Commerce jointly formulated *Interim Regulation of the Classification of Economic Ownership,* which played an positive role in reflecting the ownership structure and its change in China. However, this classification was no long appropriate to the economic situation of China. In order to give a full reflection of the current economic structure where the public ownership retains the dominant position while developing diversified forms of ownership in the light of the spirit of the 15th National Congress of the Chinese Communist Party, and to better depict the progress of the adjustment and improvement of the ownership structure, the National Bureau of Statistics and the State Industry and Commerce Administration jointly developed in 1998 the *Regulation on the Classification of the Registration Status of Enterprises*, which has put into effect and used in compiling the annual statistics since 1998.

2-1 各部门机构数

Grassroots Units in Various Sectors

部门	Sector	机构数 Grassroots Units		2000年比上年增长(%) Increase Rate in 2000 over 1999
		1999	2000	
农村基层单位 （万个）	**Rural Grassroots Units (10 000 units)**			
基层组织	Basic Units			
乡政府	Township Governments	2.56	2.40	-6.3
镇政府	Town Governments	1.92	1.97	2.6
村民委员会	Village Committees	73.74	73.47	-0.4
乡村户数	Numbers of Rural Households	23811	24149	1.4
乡镇企业	Township Enterprises	2070.9	2084.7	0.7
国营农场	**State-owned Farms**	**0.21**	**0.20**	**-4.8**
国有及规模以上非国有工业企业 （万个）	**State-owned and Non-state-owned above Designated Size Industrial Enterprises (10 000 units)**	**16.20**	**16.29**	**0.5**
内资企业	Domestic Funded Enterprises	13.52	13.44	-0.6
国有企业	State-owned Industry	5.07	4.24	-16.2
集体企业	Collective-owned Industry	4.26	3.78	-11.1
股份合作企业	Cooperative Enterprises	1.01	1.09	6.9
联营企业	Joint Ownership Enterprises	0.28	0.25	-9.4
有限责任公司	Limited Liability Corporations	0.97	1.32	36.0
股份有限公司	Share Holding Enterprises	0.45	0.51	13.5
私营企业	Private Enterprises	1.46	2.21	51.6
其他企业	Other Enterprises	0.02	0.04	55.9
港澳台商投资企业	Enterprises with Funds from Hong Kong, Macao and Taiwan	1.58	1.65	4.5
外商投资企业	Foreign Funded Enterprises	1.11	1.20	8.2
建筑业企业 （个）	**Construction Enterprises and Units (unit)**	**96648**	**97263**	**0.6**
国有企业	Construction Enterprises	9394	9030	-3.9
城镇集体企业	Affiliated Construction Units	25443	22905	-10.0
农村建筑队	Rural Construction Teams	49414	49745	0.7
邮电业 （个）	**Establishments of Postal and Telecommunication Services (unit)**			
邮电局所	Post and Telecommunications Offices	66649	70968	6.5
卫生事业 （个）	**Health Care (unit)**	**310996**	**324771**	**4.4**
#医院、卫生院	Urban and Township Hospitals	66935	66509	-0.6
疗养院	Sanatoriums	503	471	-6.4
门诊部、所	Clinics	226588	240934	6.3
专科防治所、站	Specialized Prevention & Treatment Stations	1877	1839	-2.0
卫生防疫站	Sanitation and Antiepidemic Stations	4023	4065	1.0
妇幼保健所、站	Maternity and Childcare Centers	2630	2598	-1.2
社会福利 （个）	**Social Welfare Establishments (unit)**			
社会福利事业单位	Social Welfare Institutions	99569	101222	1.7
#收养性福利事业单位	Adopting Social Welfare Institutions	40430	40491	0.2
社会福利企业	Social Welfare Enterprises	44628	40670	-8.9
社区服务单位	Community Services Units	7623	12674	66.3

2-1 续表 1 Continued

部门	Sector	机构数 Grassroots Units 1999	2000	2000年比上年增长 % Increase Rate in 2000 over 1999
教育事业	**Education**			
普通高等学校 （所）	Regular Institutions of Higher Education (unit)	1071	1041	-2.8
普通中等学校 （万所）	Secondary Schools (10 000 units)	9.53	9.39	-1.5
#普通中学	Regular Secondary Schools	7.72	7.73	0.1
小学 （万所）	Primary Schools (10 000 units)	58.23	55.36	-4.9
幼儿园 （万所）	Kindergartens (10 000 units)	18.11	17.58	-2.9
特殊教育 （所）	Special Schools (unit)	1520	1539	1.3
科技机构 （个）	**Science and Technology Institution (unit)**	**22223**	**28461**	**28.1**
艺术事业 （个）	**Art Institutions (unit)**	**5131**	**5120**	**-0.2**
#艺术表演团体	Art Performance Troupes	2632	2630	-0.1
艺术表演场所	Art Show Centers	1911	1912	0.1
#剧场、影剧院	Theaters	1875	1877	0.1
公共图书馆 （个）	**Public Libraries (unit)**	**2767**	**2677**	**-3.3**
群众文化事业 （个）	**Mass Cultural Establishments (unit)**	**45837**	**45321**	**-1.1**
群众艺术馆	Mass Art Centers	389	390	0.3
文化馆	Cultural Centers	2905	2907	0.1
文化站	Cultural Stations	42534	42024	-1.2
#乡镇文化站	Township Cultural Centers	39719	39348	-0.9
艺术教育事业	**Arts Education Establishments (unit)**	**238**	**220**	**-7.6**
其他文化事业	**Other Cultural Establishments (unit)**	**272983**	**225972**	**-17.2**
艺术创作机构	Art Creation Institutions	414	407	-1.7
艺术研究机构	Art Research Institutions	184	185	0.5
艺术展览机构	Art Exhibition Institutions	47	49	4.3
文化艺术经纪与代理业	Brokers and Agents for Cultural and Arts Activities	242	264	9.1
出版、发行事业 （个）	**Publishing and Distribution Establishments (unit)**	**14407**	**14499**	**0.6**
书刊出版社	Publishing Houses	530	565	6.6
国家定点书刊印刷厂	Pointed Printing Houses	304	301	-1.0
书店	Book Stores	13573	13633	0.4
文物事业 （个）	**Cultural Relic Establishments (unit)**	**3553**	**3618**	**1.8**
博物馆	Museums	1364	1392	2.1
文物机构	Cultural Relic Agencies	2068	2109	2.0
文物商店	Cultural Relic Shops	121	117	-3.3
广播电视台站 （座）	**Broadcasting and Television Stations (unit)**			
广播电台	Radio Stations	296	304	2.7
电视台	Television Stations	357	354	-0.8
县级广播电视台	Number of Wire Broadcasting and Television Stations in County Level	1562	1446	-7.4
金融、保险业 （个）	**Banking and Insurance (unit)**	**120858**	**138998**	**15.0**
银行系统合计	Sub-total of Banking System	112141	130170	16.1
保险系统合计	Sub-total of Insurance System	8717	8828	1.3

注：广播电台和电视台未包括县级数。

a) Number of broadcasting and television stations excludes that in county level.

2-2 平均每天主要社会经济活动

Selected Indicators on Average Daily Social and Economic Activities

指标	Item	1985	1990	1995	2000
每天创造的财富	**Daily Production**				
国内生产总值 (亿元)	Gross Domestic Product (100 million yuan)	24.6	50.8	160.2	244.9
第一产业	Primary Industry	7.0	13.7	32.9	38.9
第二产业	Secondary Industry	10.6	21.1	78.2	124.6
#工业	Industry	9.4	18.8	67.7	108.4
建筑业	Construction	1.1	2.4	10.5	16.2
第三产业	Tertiary Industry	7.0	15.9	49.2	81.4
#交通运输仓储和邮电通信业	Transport, Storage, Post & Telecommunication Services	1.1	3.1	8.4	13.5
批发和零售贸易餐饮业	Wholesale and Retail Trade & Catering Services	2.4	3.9	13.5	20.0
财政收入 (亿元)	Government Revenue (100 million yuan)	5.5	8.0	17.1	36.7
财政支出 (亿元)	Government Expenditures (100 million yuan)	5.5	8.4	18.7	43.5
粮食 (万吨)	Grain (10 000 tons)	103.9	122.3	127.8	126.6
棉花 (万吨)	Cotton (10 000 tons)	1.1	1.2	1.3	1.2
油料 (万吨)	Oil-bearing Crops (10 000 tons)	4.3	4.4	6.2	8.1
肉类 (万吨)	Meat (10 000 tons)				16.8
水产品 (万吨)	Aquatic Products (10 000 tons)	1.9	3.4	6.9	11.7
布 (万米)	Cloth (10 000 m)	4019	5173	7129	7589
原煤 (万吨)	Coal (10 000 tons)	238.4	295.9	372.6	273.4
发电量 (亿千瓦小时)	Electricity (100 million kwh)	11.3	17.0	27.6	37.1
原油 (万吨)	Crude Oil (10 000 tons)	34.2	37.9	41.1	44.7
钢 (万吨)	Steel (10 000 tons)	12.8	18.2	26.1	35.2
成品钢材 (万吨)	Steel Products (10 000 tons)	10.1	14.1	24.6	36.0
水泥 (万吨)	Cement (10 000 tons)	40.0	57.5	130.3	163.6
每天消费量	**Daily National Consumption**				
最终消费 (亿元)	Final Consumption Expenditure (100 million yuan)	15.8	31.1	92.2	149.6
居民消费	Resident Consumption	12.6	25.0	73.8	117.6
农民	Peasants Consumption	8.0	14.1	36.3	53.1
非农业居民	Non-agricultural Residents' Consumption	4.6	10.9	37.5	64.5
政府消费	Government Consumption Expenditure	3.2	6.2	18.3	32.1
能源消费量 (万吨标准煤)	Energy Consumption (10 000 tons of SCE)	210.1	270.4	359.4	350.7
社会消费品零售总额 (亿元)	Total Retail Sales of Consumer Goods (100 million yuan)	10.4	19.9	56.5	93.6
每天其他经济活动	**Other Daily Economic Activities**				
资本形成总额 (亿元)	Gross Capital Formation (100 million yuan)	9.3	17.7	65.4	88.4
固定资产形成	Fixed Capital Formation	7.2	13.0	55.6	89.4
存货增加	Changes in Stock	2.0	4.7	9.8	-1.0
城镇新建住宅面积(万平方米)	Residential Buildings Completed in Urban Areas (10 000 sq.m)	51.5	47.4	102.7	150.1
农民个人新建住宅面积 (万平方米)	Private Residential Buildings Completed in Rural Areas (10 000 sq.m)	190.5	185.8	181.5	218.4
货运量 (万吨)	Freight Traffic (10 000 tons)	2043	2659	3383	3721
客运量 (万人)	Passenger Traffic (10 000 persons)	1699	2117	3213	4051
沿海主要港口货物吞吐量(万吨)	Cargo Handled at Principal Seaports (10 000 tons)	85.4	132.4	219.6	344.1
邮电业务总量 (亿元)	Business Volume of Postal and Telecommunications Services (100 million yuan)	0.2	0.4	2.7	13.1
进出口总额 (亿美元)	Total Value of Imports and Exports (USD 100 million)	1.9	3.2	7.7	13.0
出口总额	Total Exports	0.7	1.7	4.1	6.8
进口总额	Total Imports	1.2	1.5	3.6	6.2
实际利用外资额 (亿美元)	Foreign Capital Actually Used (USD 100 million)	0.1	0.3	1.3	1.6
来华旅游人数 (万人)	Number of Tourists from Abroad (10 000 persons)	4.9	7.5	12.7	22.9
居民新增储蓄额 (亿元)	Outstanding Amount of Savings Deposit (100 million yuan)	1.1	5.3	22.3	13.6
每天人口变动和婚姻	**Daily Population Changes and Marriages**				
出生 (万人)	Births (10 000 persons)	6.1	6.5	5.7	
死亡 (万人)	Deaths (10 000 persons)	2.0	2.1	2.1	
结婚 (万对)	Marriages (10 000 couples)	2.3	2.6	2.5	2.3
离婚 (对)	Divorces (couples)	1255	2192	2891	3323

注:1.本表价值指标除邮电业务总量按1990年不变价格计算外，其余均按当年价格计算。
2."城镇新建住宅面积"从1990年起包括城镇及工矿区个人新建住宅面积。

a) Figures in value terms in this table are at current prices, except that on the business transaction of post and telecommunications service which is at 1990 constant prices.

b) Since 1990, residential buildings completed in urban areas included private residential buildings completed in towns, cities, industrial and mining areas.

2-3 国民经济和社会发展总量与速度指标

指　标	Item	1985
人口与就业	**Population and Employment**	
人口　(万人)	**Population**　(10 000 persons)	
年底总人口	Population at the Year-end	105851
市镇人口	Urban	25094
乡村人口	Rural	80757
男性人口	Male	54725
女性人口	Female	51126
就业　(万人)	**Employment**　(10 000 persons)	
从业人员数	Employment	49873
#职工人数	Staff and Workers	12358
城镇登记失业人数	Registered Unemployed in Urban Areas	239
宏观经济	**Macroeconomic Indicator**	
国民核算　(亿元)	**National Accounting**　(100 million yuan)	
国民生产总值	Gross National Product	8989
国内生产总值	Gross Domestic Product	8964
第一产业	Primary Industry	2542
第二产业	Secondary Industry	3867
第三产业	Tertiary Industry	2556
支出法国内生产总值	Gross Domestic Expenditures	8792
#最终消费	Total Consumption	5773
居民消费	Resident Consumption	4589
政府消费	Public Consumption	1184
资本形成总额	Total Investment	3386
固定资本形成	Fixed Assets	2641
存货增加	Stock	745
固定资产投资　(亿元)	**Investment in Fixed Assets**　(100 million yuan)	
全社会固定资产投资总额	Total Investment in Fixed Assets	2543.2
#国有单位	State-Owned Units	1680.5
集体单位	Collective-Owned Units	327.5
个体经济	Individuals	535.2
财政　(亿元)	**Public Finance**　(100 million yuan)	
国家财政收入	Government Revenue	2004.8
中　央	Central Government	769.6
地　方	Local Governments	1235.2
国家财政支出	Government Expenditures	2004.3
中　央	Central Government	795.3
地　方	Local Governments	1209.0
物价总指数　(上年=100)	**Price Indices**　(preceding year=100)	
商品零售价格总指数	General Retail Price Index	108.8
居民消费价格总指数	General Consumer Price Index	109.3
农产品收购价格总指数	General Farm and Sideline Products Purchasing Price Index	108.6
利用外资　(亿美元)	**Utilization of Foreign Capital**　(USD 100 million)	
签订利用外资协议额	Amount of Foreign Capital for Utilization Through Signed Contracts or Agreements	98.7
实际利用外资额	Amount of Foreign Capital Actually Utilized	46.5
能源生产与消费　(万吨标准煤)	**Production and Consumption of Energy**　(10 000 tons of SCE)	
能源生产总量	Total Energy Production	85546
能源消费总量	Total Energy Consumption	76682

Principal Aggregate Indicators on National Economic and Social Development and Their Related Indices and Growth Rates

总量指标 Aggregate Data				速度指标(%) Indices and Growth Rates						
				指数 Index（2000为以下各年） (2000 as percentage of the following years)				平均增长速度 Average Annual Growth Rate		
1990	1995	1999	2000	1985	1990	1995	1999	1986-1990	1991-1995	1996-2000
114333	121121	125909	126583	119.6	110.7	104.5	100.5	1.6	1.2	0.9
30191	35174	38892	45844	182.7	151.8	130.3	117.9	3.8	3.1	5.4
84142	85947	87017	80739	100.0	96.0	93.9	92.8	0.8	0.4	
58904	61808	64189	65355	119.4	111.0	105.7	101.8	1.5	1.0	1.1
55429	59313	61720	61228	119.8	110.5	103.2	99.2	1.6	1.4	0.6
63909	67947	70586	71150	142.7	111.3	104.7	100.8	5.1	1.2	0.9
14059	14908	11773	11259	91.1	80.1	75.5	95.6	2.6	1.2	
383	520	575	595	249.5	155.3	114.5	103.5	9.9	6.3	2.7
18598	57495	80579	88190	377.1	257.8	149.2	108.3	7.9	11.6	8.3
18548	58478	82068	89404	383.0	262.3	148.8	108.0	7.9	12.0	8.3
5017	11993	14472	14212	178.2	145.3	118.5	102.4	4.2	4.2	3.5
7717	28538	40558	45488	547.6	356.4	159.9	109.6	9.0	17.4	9.8
5814	17947	27038	29704	372.6	238.0	148.1	107.8	9.4	10.0	8.2
18320	58511	82673	89113							
11365	33635	49723	54617							
9113	26945	39334	42912							
2252	6691	10388	11705							
6444	23877	30702	32255							
4732	20301	29476	32624							
1712	3577	1226	-369							
4517.0	20019.3	29854.7	32917.7	1294.3	728.8	164.4	110.3	12.2	34.7	11.2
2986.3	10898.2	15947.8	16504.4	982.1	552.7	151.4	103.5	12.2	29.6	9.9
529.5	3289.4	4338.6	4801.5	1466.1	906.8	146.0	110.7	10.1	44.1	8.0
1001.2	2560.2	4195.7	4709.4	879.9	470.4	183.9	112.2	13.3	20.7	14.0
2937.1	6242.2	11444.1	13395.2	668.2	456.1	214.6	117.0	7.9	16.3	16.5
992.4	3256.6	5849.2	6989.2	908.2	704.3	214.6	119.5	5.2	26.8	16.5
1944.7	2985.6	5594.9	6406.1	518.6	329.4	214.6	114.5	9.5	9.0	16.5
3083.6	6823.7	13187.7	15886.5	792.6	515.2	232.8	120.5	9.0	17.2	18.4
1004.5	1995.4	4152.3	5519.9	694.1	549.5	276.6	132.9	4.8	14.7	22.6
2079.1	4828.3	9035.3	10366.7	857.5	498.6	214.7	114.7	11.5	18.4	16.5
102.1	114.8	97.0	98.5							
103.1	117.1	98.6	100.4							
97.4	119.9	87.8	96.4							
120.9	1032.1	520.1						4.1	53.6	
102.9	481.3	526.6	593.6	1276.6	576.9	123.3	112.7	17.2	36.1	4.3
103922	129034	109126	109000	127.4	104.9	84.5	99.9	4.0	4.4	
98703	131176	130119	128000	166.9	129.7	97.6	98.4	5.2	5.9	

2-3 续表 1

指　标	Item	1985
产　业	**Industry**	
农业	**Agriculture**	
耕地面积 (千公顷)	Cultivated Areas (1 000 hectares)	96846
农林牧渔业劳动力 (万人)	Labor Force of Farming, Forestry, Animal Husbandry and Fishery (10 000 persons)	30352
农林牧渔业总产值 (亿元)	Gross Output Value of Farming Forestry, Animal Husbandry and Fishery (100 million yuan)	3619.5
主要农产品产量 (万吨)	Output of Major Farm Products (10 000 tons)	
粮　食	Grain	37911
棉　花	Cotton	414.7
油　料	Oil-bearing Crops	1578.4
甘　蔗	Sugar Cane	5154.9
甜　菜	Beet Roots	891.9
茶　叶	Tea	43.2
水　果	Fruits	1163.9
肉　类	Meat	
水产品	Aquatic Products	705.2
工业	**Industry**	
主要工业产品产量	Output of Major Industrial Products	
布 (亿米)	Cloth (100 million m)	146.7
机制纸及纸板 (万吨)	Machine-Made Paper and Paperboards (10 000 tons)	911
糖 (万吨)	Sugar (10 000 tons)	451
家用电冰箱 (万台)	Household Refrigerators (10 000 units)	145
彩色电视机 (万台)	Color Television Sets (10 000 units)	435
家用洗衣机 (万台)	Household Washing Machines (10 000 units)	887
房间空气调节器 (万台)	Room Air-conditioning (10 000 units)	12
原　煤 (亿吨)	Coal (100 million tons)	8.7
原　油 (万吨)	Crude Oil (10 000 tons)	12490
发电量 (亿千瓦小时)	Electricity (100 million kwh)	4107
钢 (万吨)	Steel (10 000 tons)	4679
成品钢材 (万吨)	Steel Products (10 000 tons)	3693
水　泥 (万吨)	Cement (10 000 tons)	14595
国有及限额以上非国有工业企业主要指标	Principal Indicators of Industrial Enterprises of State Ownership and Non-state-owned Above Designated Size	
工业总产值 (亿元)	Gross industrial Output Value (100 million yuan)	
固定资产原价 (亿元)	Original Value of Fixed Assets (100 million yuan)	6926
固定资产净值年平均余额 (亿元)	Annual Average Balance of Net Value of Fixed Assets (100 million yuan)	4725
利润总额 (亿元)	Profits (100 million yuan)	
建筑业	**Construction**	
建筑业企业人数 (万人)	Number of Employed Persons (10 000 persons)	1701
建筑业总产值 (亿元)	Gross Output Value (100 million yuan)	985.1
施工房屋面积 (万平方米)	Floor Space of Buildings under Construction (10 000 sq.m)	35492
竣工房屋面积 (万平方米)	Floor Space of Buildings Completed (10 000 sq.m)	17073
交通运输	**Transportation**	
货运量 (万吨)	Freight Traffic (10 000 tons)	745763
铁　路	Railways	130709
公　路	Highways	538062
水　运	Waterways	63322
管　道	Pipelines	13650
空　运	Civil Aviation	20
客运量 (万人)	Passenger Traffic (10 000 persons)	620206
铁　路	Railways	112110
公　路	Highways	476486
水　运	Waterways	30863
空　运	Civil Aviation	747
沿海主要港口货物吞吐量 (万吨)	Volume of Freight Handled at Major Coastal Ports(10 000 tons)	31154

Continued

总量指标 Aggregate Data				速度指标(%) Indices and Growth Rates						
				指数 Index (2000为以下各年) (2000 as percentage of the following years)				平均增长速度 Average Annual Growth Rate		
1990	1995	1999	2000	1985	1990	1995	1999	1986-1990	1991-1995	1996-2000
95673	94971									
33336	32335	32912	32798	108.1	98.4	101.4	99.7	1.9		
7662.1	20340.9	24519.1	24915.8	242.3	192.0	134.1	103.6	4.8	7.4	6.0
44624	46662	50839	46218	121.9	103.6	99.0	90.9	3.3	0.9	
450.8	476.8	382.9	441.7	106.5	98.0	92.6	115.4	1.7	1.1	
1613.2	2250.3	2601.2	2954.8	187.2	183.2	131.3	113.6	0.4	6.9	5.6
5762.0	6542.0	7470.3	6828	132.5	118.5	104.4	91.4	2.3	2.6	0.9
1452.5	1398.4	863.9	807.3	90.5	55.6	57.7	93.4	10.2		
54.0	58.9	67.6	68.3	158.1	126.5	116.0	101.0	4.6	1.8	3.0
1874.4	4214.6	6237.6	6225.1	534.8	332.1	147.7	99.8	10.0	17.6	8.1
		5820.7	6125.4				105.2			
1237.0	2517.2	4122.4	4278.5	606.7	345.9	170.0	103.8	11.9	15.3	11.2
188.8	260.2	250.0	277.0	188.8	146.7	106.5	110.8	5.2	6.6	1.3
1372	2812	2159	2487	273.0	181.3	88.4	115.2	8.5	15.4	
582	559	861	700	155.2	120.3	125.2	81.3	5.2		4.6
463	919	1210	1279	882.1	276.2	139.2	105.7	26.1	14.7	6.8
1033	2058	4262	3936	904.8	381.0	191.3	92.4	18.9	14.8	13.8
663	948	1342	1443	162.7	217.6	152.2	107.5		7.4	8.8
24	683	1338	1827			267.5	136.5			21.7
10.8	13.6	10.5	10.0	114.9	92.6	73.5	95.2	4.4	4.7	
13831	15005	16000	16300	130.5	117.9	108.6	101.9	2.1	1.6	1.7
6212	10070	12393	13556	330.1	218.2	134.6	109.4	8.6	10.1	6.1
6635	9536	12426	12850	274.8	193.8	134.8	103.5	7.2	7.5	6.2
5153	8980	12110	13146	356.0	255.1	146.4	108.6	6.9	11.7	7.9
20971	47561	57300	59700	409.0	284.7	125.5	104.2	7.5	17.8	4.7
		72707	85673.7				116.9			
14390	44989	71847	78646	1135.5	546.5	174.8	109.5	15.7	25.6	11.8
10139	32287	47281	51792	1096.1	510.8	160.4	109.5	16.5	26.1	9.9
560	1635	2288	4393		784.5	268.7	192.0		23.9	21.9
1717	2512	2766	2741	161.1	159.6	109.1	99.1	0.2	7.9	1.8
1947.6	9505.0	15151.5	16780.9	1703.5	861.6	176.5	110.8	14.6	37.3	12.0
37923	89863	147263	160141	451.2	422.3	178.2	108.7	1.3	18.8	12.2
19553	35666	73925	80715	472.8	412.8	226.3	109.2	2.7	12.8	17.7
970602	1234810	1292650	1358124	182.1	139.9	110.0	105.1	5.4	4.9	1.9
150681	165855	167196	178023	136.2	118.1	107.3	106.5	2.9	1.9	1.4
724040	940387	990444	1038813	193.1	143.5	110.5	104.9	6.1	5.4	2.0
80094	113194	114608	122391	193.3	152.8	108.1	106.8	4.8	7.2	1.6
15750	15274	20232	18700	137.0	118.7	122.4	92.4	2.9		4.1
37	101	170	197	985.0	532.4	195.0	115.9	13.1	22.2	14.3
772682	1172596	1394413	1478573	238.4	191.4	126.1	106.0	4.5	8.7	4.7
95712	102745	100164	105073	93.7	109.8	102.3	104.9		1.4	0.4
648085	1040810	1269004	1347392	282.8	207.9	129.5	106.2	6.3	9.9	5.3
27225	23924	19151	19386	62.8	71.2	81.0	101.2			
1660	5117	6094	6722	899.9	404.9	131.4	110.3	17.3	25.3	5.6
48321	80166	105162	125603	403.2	259.9	156.7	119.4	9.2	10.7	9.4

2-3 续表 2

指　　标	Item	1985
邮电通信业	**Post and Telecommunication Services**	
邮电业务总量　(亿元)	Total Business Revenue　(100 million yuan)	62.2
函　件　(亿件)	Number of Letters Delivered　(10 000 pieces)	46.8
报刊期发数　(万份)	Number of Newspapers and Magazines Distributed(10 000 copies)	30172
局用交换机容量　(万门)	Capacity of Office Telephone Exchanges　(10 000 lines)	613
中央国有	Central State-owned	337
地方国有	Local State-owned	277
电话机　(万部)	Number of Telephone Sets　(10 000 units)	626
中央国有	Central State-owned	476
地方国有	Local State-owned	150
移动电话用户　(万户)	Number of Mobile Telephone Subscribers(10 000 subscribers)	
国内商业	**Domestic Trade**	
社会消费品零售总额　(亿元)	Total Retail Sales of Consumer Goods　(100 million yuan)	3801
对外经济贸易	**Foreign Trade**	
进出口总额　(亿美元)	Total Exports and Imports　(USD 100 million)	696.0
出口额	Exports	273.5
进口额	Imports	422.5
国际旅游	**International Tourism**	
来华旅游人数　(万人)	Number of Tourists from Abroad　(10 000 persons)	1783
旅游外汇收入　(亿美元)	Foreign Exchange Earnings from Tourism　(USD 100 million)	12.5
金融保险	**Finance and Insurance**	
金融机构各项存款　(亿元)	Deposits of National Banking System　(100 million yuan)	
金融机构各项贷款　(亿元)	Loans of National Banking System　(100 million yuan)	
中外资保险公司保险金额　(亿元)	Insurance Coverage of Domestic and Foreign Funded Insurance Companies (100 million yuan)	
中外资保险公司保费　(亿元)	Insurance Premium of Domestic and Foreign Funded Insurance Companies (100 million yuan)	
中外资保险公司赔款及给付　(亿元)	Indemnity Expenditure and Payment of Domestic and Foreign Funded Insurance Companies (100 million yuan)	
教育、科技、文化	**Education, Science and Technology and Culture**	
教育	**Education**	
专任教师数　(万人)	Full-time Teachers　(10 000 persons)	
普通高等学校	Institutions of Higher Education	34.4
中等学校	Secondary Schools	296.7
小　学	Primary Schools	537.7
在校学生数　(万人)	Students Enrollment　(10 000 persons)	
普通高等学校	Institutions of Higher Education	170.3
中等学校	Secondary Schools	5092.6
小　学	Primary Schools	13370.2
教育经费支出　(亿元)	Government Expenditures on Education　(100 million yuan)	
科技	**Science and Technology**	
科学家、工程师数　(万人)	Number of Scientists and Engineers　(10 000 persons)	
研究与发展经费支出　(亿元)	Expenditures on Research and Development(100 million yuan)	
技术市场成交额　(万元)	Volume of Transaction in Technical Markets　(10 000 yuan)	
文化	**Culture**	
出版数量	Publications	
图　书　(亿册.张)	Number of Books Published　(100 million copies)	66.7
杂　志　(亿册)	Number of Magazines Issued　(100 million copies)	25.6
报　纸　(亿份)	Number of Newspapers Issued　(100 million copies)	246.8
故事影片产量　(部)	Production of Feature Films　(film)	127
电视节目制作时间　(小时)	Time for TV Programs Production　(hours)	38056

Continued

总量指标 Aggregate Data				速度指标(%) Indices and Growth Rates						
				指数 Index (2000为以下各年) (2000 as percentage of the following years)				平均增长速度 Average Annual Growth Rate		
1990	1995	1999	2000	1985	1990	1995	1999	1986-1990	1991-1995	1991-2000
155.5	988.9	3330.8	4792.7	7704.1	3081.3	484.7	143.9	20.1	44.8	37.1
54.9	79.6	60.5	77.71	166.0	141.5	97.6	128.4	3.2	7.7	
20078	21689	25035	20090	66.6	100.1	92.6	80.2		1.6	
1232	7204	15346	17826	2908.0	1446.9	247.4	116.2	15.0	42.4	19.9
826	5456	11094	13306	3948.4	1610.9	243.9	119.9	19.6	45.9	19.5
406	1747	4252	4519	1631.4	1113.1	258.7	106.3	7.9	33.9	20.9
1233	5762	17567	25607	4090.6	2076.8	444.4	145.8	14.5	36.1	34.8
1026	4346	9505	12634	2654.2	1231.4	290.7	132.9	16.6	33.5	23.8
205	1152	3732	4519	3012.7	2204.4	392.3	121.1	6.4	41.2	31.4
1.8	362.9	4329.6	8453.3		461929.0	2329.1	195.2		188.1	87.7
7250	20620	31135	34153	898.5	471.1	165.6	109.7	13.8	23.3	10.6
1154.4	2808.6	3606.3	4742.9	681.5	410.9	168.9	131.5	10.6	19.5	11.0
620.9	1487.8	1949.3	2492	911.2	401.4	167.5	127.8	17.8	19.1	10.9
533.5	1320.8	1657.0	2250.9	532.8	421.9	170.4	135.8	4.8	19.9	11.3
2746	4639	7280	8344	468.0	303.9	179.9	114.6	9.0	11.1	12.5
22.2	87.3	141.0	162.2	1296.0	729.7	185.6	114.9	12.2	31.5	13.2
		108779	123804				113.8			
		93734	99371				106.0			
		666427	508579				76.3			
		1406	1598				113.6			
		508	526				103.5			
39.5	40.1	42.6	46.3	134.6	117.2	115.5	108.7	2.8	0.3	2.9
349.2	388.3	459.6	473.4	159.6	135.6	121.9	103.0	3.3	2.1	4.0
558.2	566.4	586.1	586.0	109.0	105.0	103.5	100.0	0.8	0.3	0.7
206.3	290.6	413.4	556.1	326.5	269.6	191.4	134.5	3.9	7.1	13.9
5105.4	6191.5	8002.7	8518.5	167.3	166.9	137.6	106.4	0.1	3.9	6.6
12241.4	13195.2	13548.0	13013.3	97.3	106.3	98.6	96.1		1.5	
	1878.0	3349.0								
	155.4	159.5	200.4			129.0	125.6			5.2
125.4	348.7	678.9	897.7		715.9	257.4	132.2		22.7	20.8
750969	2683447	5234123	6507519		866.5	242.5	124.3		29.0	19.4
56.4	63.2	73.2	62.7	94.0	111.2	99.2	85.7		2.3	
17.9	23.4	28.5	29.4	114.8	164.2	125.6	103.2		5.5	4.7
211.3	263.3	318.4	329.3	133.4	155.8	125.1	103.4		4.5	4.6
134	146	82	91	71.7	67.9	62.3	111.0	1.1	1.7	
91572	383513	526483	585007	1537.2	638.8	152.5	111.1	19.2	33.2	8.8

2-3 续表 3

指　　标	Item	1985
家庭、生活、环境	Family, People's Livelihood and Environment	
家庭	Family	
家庭总户数 (万户)	Total Number of Households (10 000 households)	23804
城镇居民平均每户家庭人口 (人)	Average Household Size in Urban Areas (person)	3.9
农村居民平均每户家庭人口 (人)	Average Household Size in Rural Areas (person)	5.1
婚姻	Marriages and Divorces	
结婚数 (万对)	Number of Marriages (10 000 couples)	829.1
离婚数 (万对)	Number of Divorces (10 000 couples)	45.8
居住	Housing	
城市居民人均使用面积 (平方米)	Per Capita Gross Floor Space of Urban Residents (sq.m)	
城市居民人均居住面积 (平方米)	Per Capita Net Floor Space of Urban Residents (sq.m)	5.2
农村居民人均居住面积 (平方米)	Per Capita Net Floor Space of Rural Residents (sq.m)	14.7
生活	People's Livelihood	
城镇居民人均可支配收入 (元)	Per Capita Annual Disposable Income of Urban Households (yuan)	739
农村居民人均纯收入 (元)	Per Capita Net Income of Rural Residents (yuan)	398
城乡储蓄存款余额 (亿元)	Outstanding Amount of Saving Deposits in Urban and Rural Areas (100 million yuan)	1622.6
工资	Wages and Welfare	
工资总额 (亿元)	Total Wages (100 million yuan)	1383
职工平均工资 (元)	Average Wage of Staff and Workers (yuan)	1148
离休、退休、退职费 (亿元)	Pensions for Retired Staff and Workers (100 million yuan)	145.6
卫生	Health Care	
医院、卫生院 (个)	Number of Hospitals	59614
医生 (万人)	Number of Doctors (10 000 persons)	141.3
医院、卫生院床位数 (万张)	Number of Hospital Beds (10 000 units)	222.9
市政建设	City Construction	
自来水供应量 (亿吨)	Volume of Tap Water Supply (100 million tons)	128.0
下水道长度 (公里)	Length of Sewer Pipelines (km)	31556
城市煤气和天然气供气量(万立方米)	Volume of Coal Gas and Natural Gas Supply in Urban Areas (10 000 cu.m)	411853
公共汽(电)车总数 (辆)	Total Number of Public Buses and Trolley Buses (unit)	45155
铺装道路长度 (公里)	Length of Paved Roads (km)	38282
绿地面积 (公顷)	Areas of Green Land (hectare)	159291
环境、灾害	Environment and Disaster	
污染治理项目本年完成投资额(亿元)	Actual Investment in Implementation of the Project for Pollution Treatment in the Year (100 million yuan)	22.2
环境污染与破坏事故次数 (起)	Number of Pollution Accidents (times)	2716
环境污染直接经济损失 (万元)	Losses Converted into Cash (10 000 yuan)	
环境污染事故赔罚款金额 (万元)	Amount of Reparations and Fines (10 000 yuan)	
火灾发生数 (起)	Number of Fire Disasters	34996
火灾损失 (万元)	Fire Loss (10 000 yuan)	28422
交通事故发生数 (起)	Number of Traffic Accidents	97573
交通事故损失 (万元)	Loss of Traffic Accidents (10 000 yuan)	6599

注:1.本表价值指标除邮电业务总量按1990年不变价格计算外，其余均按当年价格计算。
2.本表速度指标中，国民生产总值、国内生产总值及三次产业、物价指数、农林牧渔业总产值、工业总产值、邮电业务总量、城乡居民收入和平均工资指标均按可比价格计算。
3.2000年人口数和家庭总户数均为第五次人口普查快速汇总数(下表同)。
4.1999年及以后职工人数为在岗人数，1995年及以前为全部职工人数，故不可比。

Continued

总量指标 Aggregate Data				速度指标(%) Indices and Growth Rates						
				指数 Index（2000为以下各年） (2000 as percentage of the following years)				平均增长速度 Average Annual Growth Rate		
1990	1995	1999	2000	1985	1990	1995	1999	1986-1990	1991-1995	1996-2000
27738	31676	34153	34837	146.3	125.6	110.0	102.0	3.1	2.7	1.9
3.5	3.2	3.1	3.1	79.5	88.6	96.9	100.0			-0.6
4.8	4.5	4.3	4.2	82.4	87.5	93.3	97.7			-1.4
948.7	929.7	879.9	842.0	101.6	88.8	90.6	95.7	2.7		-2.0
80.0	105.5	120.2	121.3	264.8	151.6	115.0	100.9	11.8	5.7	2.8
9.9	11.8	14.2	14.9		150.5	126.3	105.0		3.6	4.8
6.7	8.1	9.8	10.3	198.1	153.7	127.2	105.3	5.2	3.9	4.9
17.8	21.0	24.2	24.8	168.7	139.3	118.1	102.4	3.9	3.4	3.4
1510	4283	5854	6280	239.2	193.7	132.2	106.4	4.3	7.9	5.7
686	1578	2210	2253	179.8	155.4	126.0	102.1	3.0	4.3	4.7
7119.8	29662.3	59621.8	64332.4	3964.8	914.6	216.9	107.9	34.1	33.4	16.7
2951	8100	9876	10656	770.5	361.1	131.6	107.9	16.4	22.4	5.6
2140	5500	8346	9371	229.8	204.0	153.6	111.4	2.4	5.8	9.0
396.2	1305.6	2420.9	2733.3	1877.3	689.9	209.4	112.9	22.2	26.9	15.9
62454	67807	66935	66509	111.6	106.5	98.1	99.4	0.9	1.7	-0.4
176.3	191.8	204.5	207.6	146.9	117.8	108.2	101.5	4.5	1.7	1.6
262.4	283.6	292.8	294.8	132.3	112.3	103.9	100.7	3.3	1.6	0.8
382.3	496.6	467.5	469.0	366.4	122.7	94.4	100.3	24.5	5.4	-1.1
57787	110293	134486	141758	449.2	245.3	128.5	105.4	12.9	13.8	5.1
2389354	1940248	2121481	2345091	569.4	98.1	120.9	110.5	42.1		3.9
62215	136821	209884	225993	500.5	363.2	165.2	107.7	6.6	17.1	10.6
94820	130308	152385	159617	417.0	168.3	122.5	104.7	19.9	6.6	4.1
474613	678310	778161	865295	543.2	182.3	127.6	111.2	24.4	7.4	5.0
45.4	98.7	152.7	239.4	1078.4	527.3	242.6	156.8	15.4	16.8	19.4
3462	1966	1614	2411	88.8	69.6	122.6	149.4	5.0		4.2
	9938	5711	17808			179.2	311.8			12.4
	4260	2116	3683			86.5	174.0			-2.9
57302	37136	179955	189185	540.6	330.2	509.4	105.1	10.4		38.5
51182	107777	143394	152217	535.6	297.4	141.2	106.2	12.5	16.1	7.1
250244	271843	412860	616971	632.3	246.5	227.0	149.4	20.7	1.7	17.8
35362	152267	212402	266890	4044.4	754.7	175.3	125.7	39.9	33.9	11.9

a) Figures in value terms in this table are at current prices, except that on the business transaction of post and telecommunications service which is at 1990 constant prices.

b)The indices and growth rates of the follow indicators are calculated at comparable prices: GNP, GDP, price indices, gross output value of farming, forestry, animal husbandry and fishery, gross output value of industry,business volume of post and telecommunications total retail sales, per capita income of urban and rural residents, wages and welfare.

c)Total population and household number in 2000 are from the fast report of 5th National Population Census. Similarly in the following tables.

d)figures since 1998 on workers and staff refer to fully employed workers and staff, while figures for previous years refer to total workers and staff. Therefore, they are not comparable.

2-4 国民经济和社会发展结构指标

Structural Indicators on National Economic and Social Development

单位：%　　　　　　　　　　　　　　　　　　　　　　　　　　　　　　　(%)

指　标	Item	1985	1990	1995	2000
人口与就业	**Population and Employment**				
人口	**Population**				
城乡结构	Urban and Rural Structure				
城镇	Urban	23.7	26.4	29.0	36.2
乡村	Rural	76.3	73.6	71.0	63.8
性别结构	Sexual Structure				
男	Male	51.7	51.5	51.0	51.6
女	Female	48.3	48.5	49.0	48.4
就业	**Employment**				
产业结构	Industrial Structure				
第一产业	Primary Industry	62.4	60.1	52.2	50.0
第二产业	Secondary Industry	20.9	21.4	23.0	22.5
第三产业	Tertiary Industry	16.7	18.5	24.8	27.5
宏观经济	**Macro Economy**				
国民核算	**National Accounting**				
国内生产总值产业结构	Industrial Structure				
第一产业	Primary Industry	28.4	27.1	20.5	15.9
第二产业	Secondary Industry	43.1	41.6	48.8	50.9
第三产业	Tertiary Industry	28.5	31.3	30.7	33.2
投资	**Investment**				
全社会固定资产投资结构	Structure of Total Investment in Fixed Assets				
基本建设	Capital Construction	42.2	37.7	37.0	40.8
更新改造	Innovation	17.7	18.4	16.5	15.5
房地产开发	Real Estate Development	–	5.6	15.7	15.1
其他投资	Other Investment	40.1	38.3	30.8	28.6
资金来源结构	Structure of Funded Sources				
国家预算内资金	State Budgetary Appropriation	16.0	8.7	3.0	6.4
国内贷款	Domestic Loans	20.1	19.6	20.5	20.3
利用外资	Foreign Investment	3.6	6.3	11.2	5.1
自筹和其他投资	Fundraising and Others Investment	60.3	65.4	65.3	68.2
财政	**Government Finance**				
财政收入结构	Structure of Government Revenue				
中央	Central Government	38.4	33.8	52.2	52.2
地方	Local Governments	61.6	66.2	47.8	47.8
财政支出结构	Structure of Government Expenditures				
中央	Central Government	39.7	32.6	29.2	34.7
地方	Local Governments	60.3	67.4	70.8	65.3
利用外资	**Utilization of Foreign Capital**				
实际利用外资结构	Structure of Foreign Capital Actually Utilized				
对外借款	Loans from Abroad	57.8	63.5	21.5	16.8
外商直接投资	Direct Investment by Foreign Entrepreneurs	35.7	33.9	77.9	68.6
外商其他投资	Other Investment by Foreign Entrepreneurs	6.4	2.6	0.6	14.6
能源生产与消费	**Energy Production and Consumption**				
能源生产总量结构	Structure of Total Energy Production				
原煤	Coal	72.8	74.2	75.3	67.2
原油	Petroleum Crude Oil	20.9	19.0	16.6	21.4
天然气	Natural Gas	2.0	2.0	1.9	3.4
水电	Hydropower	4.3	4.8	6.2	8.0
能源消费总量结构	Structure of Total Energy Consumption				
煤炭	Coal	75.8	76.2	74.6	67.0
石油	Petroleum Oil	17.1	16.6	17.5	23.6
天然气	Natural Gas	2.2	2.1	1.8	2.5
水电	Hydropower	4.9	5.1	6.1	6.9

2-4 续表 1 Continued

单位：%　　(%)

指　标	Item	1985	1990	1995	2000
产　业	**Industrial**				
农业	**Agriculture**				
农林牧渔业产值结构	Structure of Gross Output Value of Agriculture				
农业	Farming	69.3	64.7	58.4	55.7
林业	Forestry	5.2	4.3	3.5	3.8
牧业	Animal Husbandry	22.1	25.7	29.7	29.7
渔业	Fishery	3.5	5.4	8.4	10.9
工业	**Industry**				
工业总产值规模结构	Structure of Gross Output Value of Industry				
大型企业	Large Enterprises	28.1	33.2	39.7	44.7
中型企业	Medium-sized Enterprises	18.9	18.9	16.5	12.5
小型企业	Small Enterprises	53.0	47.8	43.8	42.8
建筑业	**Construction**				
建筑业总产值结构	Structure of Gross Output Value of Construction Industry				
土木工程建筑业	Civil Engineering Construction			86.8	87.8
线路管理设备安装业	Line and Equipment Installation			11.0	8.7
建筑物装修装饰业	Building Decoration			2.2	3.4
交通运输业	**Transportation**				
货运量结构	Structure of Freight Traffic				
按运输方式分	By Means of Transportation				
铁　路	Railways	17.5	15.5	13.4	13.1
公　路	Highways	72.1	74.6	76.2	76.5
水　运	Waterways	8.5	8.3	9.2	9.0
民用航空	Civil Aviation	...	...	...	...
管道输油(气)	Pipelines	1.8	1.6	1.2	1.4
国内商业	**Domestic Trade**				
社会消费品零售总额构成	Composition of Retail Sales of Consumer Goods				
市	Cities	49.3	53.6	60.0	61.8
县	Counties	19.4	18.4	14.2	12.3
县以下	Below Counties	31.3	28.0	25.8	25.8
对外经济贸易	**Foreign Trade**				
出口商品结构	Structure of Exports				
初级产品	Primary Goods	50.6	25.6	14.4	10.2
工业制成品	Manufactured Goods	49.4	74.40	85.6	89.8
进口商品结构	Structure of Imports				
初级产品	Primary Goods	12.5	18.5	18.5	20.8
工业制成品	Manufactured Goods	87.5	81.5	81.5	79.2
国际旅游	**International Tourism**				
来华旅游人数结构	Structure of Tourists				
外国人	Foreigners	7.7	6.4	12.7	12.2
华侨	Overseas Chinese	0.5	0.3	0.2	0.1
港澳台同胞	Compatriots form Hong Kong, Macao and Taiwan	91.8	93.3	87.1	87.7
金融保险业	**Finance and Insurance**				
金融机构资金来源结构	Structure of Sources of Funds in State Banks				
各项存款	Deposits				91.4
金融债券	Bonds				...
对国际金融机构负债	Liability to International Finance Institutions				0.3
货币流通量	Currency in Circulation				10.8
其他	Others				-2.5
金融机构资金运用结构	Structure of Fund Uses in State Banks				
各项贷款	Loans				73.3
有价证券及投资	Securities and Investment				14.5
在国际金融机构资产	Capital in International Finance Institutions				0.4
金银占款	Purchase of Gold and Silver				...
外汇占款	Purchase of Foreign Exchanges				10.5
财政借款	Government Debt				1.2
教育、科技、文化	**Education, Science and Culture**				
教育	**Education**				
在校学生结构	Structure of Student Enrollment				
大学生	College and University Students	0.9	1.2	1.5	2.5
中学生	Secondary School Students	27.3	29.1	31.5	38.6
小学生	Primary School Students	71.8	69.7	67.1	58.9

2-4 续表 2 Continued

单位：% (%)

指标	Item	1985	1990	1995	2000
专任教师结构	Full-time Teachers by Type				
大学	College and Universities	4.0	4.2	4.0	4.2
中学	Secondary Schools	34.2	36.9	39.0	42.8
小学	Primary Schools	61.9	59.0	56.9	53.0
科技	**Science and Technology**				
科技经费筹集额结构	Structure of Funding for Scientific and Technological Outlay				
#政府资金	Government Fund			25.8	25.1
企业资金	Enterprises Fund			44.2	55.7
银行贷款	Loans from Banks			13.2	8.2
科技经费内部支出结构	Structure of Internal Expenditures on Scientific and Technological Activities				
#劳务费	Service Fees			21.0	23.1
固定资产购建	Purchases of Fixed Assets			28.5	30.0
#研究与发展经费支出	Research and Development Expenses			41.3	43.5
生活、环境	**Family, People's Livelihood and Environment**				
生活	**People's Livelihood**				
城镇居民消费结构	Consumption Structure of Urban Residents				
食品类	Food	52.2	54.2	49.9	39.2
衣着类	Clothing	14.6	13.4	13.5	10.0
用品及其他	Articles for Daily Use and Others	28.4	27.6	29.5	40.8
居住	Residence	4.8	4.8	7.1	10.0
农村居民消费结构	Consumption Structure of Rural Residents				
食品类	Food	57.8	58.8	58.6	49.1
衣着类	Clothing	9.7	7.8	6.9	5.8
用品及其他	Articles for Daily Use and Others	14.2	16.1	20.6	29.6
居住	Residence	18.2	17.3	13.9	15.5
福利	**Social Welfare**				
离退休退职人员结构	Structure of Retired and Resigned Persons				
离休人员	Retired Veterans		7.9	6.4	4.4
退休人员	Retired Persons		88.5	90.6	93.4
退职人员	Resigned Persons		3.6	3.0	2.2
离退休退职人员保险福利费结构	Structure of Insurance Contribution and Welfare Funds of Retired and Resigned Persons				
离休金	Pensions for Retired Veterans		7.4	8.0	6.6
退休金	Pensions for Retired Persons		51.5	64.8	75.8
退职生活费	Resignation Allowances for Living Expenses		1.1	1.0	1.0
医疗卫生费	Expenses for Medical Care		16.4	15.5	11.4
其他	Others		23.6	10.7	5.2
卫生	**Health Care**				
医生结构	Doctors by Types				
中医	Doctors of Traditional Chinese Medicine	23.8	20.9	18.7	16.2
西医师	Doctors of Western Medicine	42.6	60.0	61.8	64.1
西医士	Paramedics of Western Medicine	33.5	18.8	19.0	19.0
医院床位结构	Hospital Beds by Area				
市医院	Hospitals at City Level	43.2	52.9	61.3	64.9
县医院	Hospitals at County Level	56.8	47.1	38.7	35.1
环境、灾害	**Environment and Disasters**				
治理污染资金使用结构	Uses of Funds in Pollution Treatment				
治理废水	Waste Water Treatment	44.6	47.6	46.2	45.8
治理废气	Waste Gas Treatment	32.4	32.6	33.6	38.0
治理固体废物	Solid Wastes Treatment	9.0	11.2	14.2	4.8
治理噪声	Noise Abatement	2.3	2.6	2.2	2.5
其他	Others	11.7	6.0	3.8	9.0
火灾事故损失额结构	Structure of Fire Losses Converted into Cash				
特大	Extraordinarily Serious Fires	41.4	35.1	35.8	13.1
重大	Serious Fires	33.4	27.8	38.3	10.9
一般	Ordinary Fires	25.2	37.2	25.9	75.9
交通事故损失额结构	Structure of Losses of Traffic Accidents Converted into Cash				
特大	Extraordinarily Serious Accidents	18.0	12.5	11.8	8.9
重大	Serious Accidents	14.6	19.8	22.0	17.2
一般	Ordinary Accidents	67.4	67.7	66.2	73.9

2-5 国民经济和社会发展比例和效益指标

Indicators on Proportions and Efficiency in National Economic and Social Development

指标	Item	1985	1990	1995	2000
人口与就业	**Population and Employment**				
人口	**Population**				
出生率 (‰)	Birth Rate (‰)	21.04	21.06	17.12	
死亡率 (‰)	Death Rate (‰)	6.78	6.67	6.57	
自然增长率 (‰)	Natural Growth Rate (‰)	14.26	14.39	10.55	
就业	**Employment**				
就业者负担人口	Dependency Ratio	1.12	0.79	0.78	0.56
三次产业从业者比例(以第一产业为100)	Employment Ratio by Type of Industry (Employment in primary industry=100)				
第一产业	Primary Industry	100	100	100	100
第二产业	Secondary Industry	33.5	35.5	44.1	45.0
第三产业	Tertiary Industry	26.8	30.8	47.5	55.0
城镇失业率 (%)	Unemployment Rate in Urban Areas (%)	1.8	2.5	2.9	3.1
宏观经济	**Macro Economy**				
国民核算	**National Accounting**				
三次产业增加值比例(以第一产业为100)	Ratio of Value-added by Type of Industry (Value added in primary industry=100)				
第一产业	Primary Industry	100	100	100	100
第二产业	Secondary Industry	152.1	153.8	238.0	320.1
第三产业	Tertiary Industry	100.6	115.9	149.6	209.0
全社会劳动生产率 (元/人)	Overall Labor Productivity (yuan/person)	1797	2902	8606	12566
第一产业	Primary Industry	817	1306	3381	3995
第二产业	Secondary Industry	3711	5652	18261	28414
第三产业	Tertiary Industry	3061	4915	10651	15181
人均国内生产总值 (元)	Per Capita GDP (yuan)	853	1634	4854	7078
固定资产投资	**Investment in Fixed Assets**				
全社会固定资产投资相当于国内生产总值比例 (%)	Proportion of Investment in fixed Assets to GDP (%)	20.2	24.4	34.2	36.8
全社会房屋建筑面积竣工率 (%)	Rate of Total Floor Space of Buildings Completed in Construction (%)	82.0	78.6	67.7	68.6
基本建设固定资产交付使用率 (%)	Rate of Fixed Assets Completed in Capital Construction and Put into Use (%)	68.2	80.0	63.7	77.7
基本建设项目建成投产率 (%)	Rate of Projects Completed in Capital Construction and Put into Use (%)	50.7	53.8	57.0	57.7
财政	**Finance**				
国家财政收入相当于国内生产总值比例(%)	Proportion of Government Revenue to GDP (%)	22.4	15.8	10.7	15.0
国家财政支出相当于国内生产总值比例 (%)	Proportion of Government Expenditures to GDP (%)	22.4	16.6	11.7	17.8
地方收入相当于中央财政收入比例 (%)	Proportion of Local Government Revenue to Central Government Revenue (%)	160.5	196.0	91.7	91.7
地方支出相当于中央财政支出比例 (%)	Proportion of Local Government Expenditure to Central Government Expenditure (%)	152	207	242	188
预算外资金收入相当于国家财政收入比例 (%)	Proportion of Extra-budgetary Receipt to Government Revenue (%)	76.3	92.2	38.6	
物价指数	**Price Index**				
工农商品综合比价(1978=100)	Overall Industrial and Farm Products Price Parity Index (use 1978=100 index)	66.6	62.8	52.0	67.8
利用外资	**Utilization of Foreign Capital**				
实际利用外资额相当于签订利用外资额比例 (%)	Proportion of Foreign Capital Actually Used to Total Amount of Foreign Capital for Utilization by Signed Contracts or Agreements (%)	47.1	85.1	46.6	114.1
能源生产与消费	**Production and Consumption of Energy**				
能源生产弹性系数	Elasticity Ratio of Energy Production	0.73	0.58	0.83	
能源消费弹性系数	Elasticity Ratio of Energy Consumption	0.60	0.47	0.66	
每万元国内生产总值消耗的能源 (吨)	Energy Consumption per 10 000 yuan GDP(ton)	8.6	5.2	2.2	1.4

2-5 续表 1 Continued

指 标	Item	1985	1990	1995	2000
产 业	**Industries**				
农业	**Agriculture**				
人均耕地面积 (公顷)	Per Capita Cultivated Land (hectare)	0.09	0.08	0.08	
农业从业者人均耕地面积 (公顷)	Cultivated Land per Agricultural Laborer(hectare)	0.33	0.29	0.29	
每公顷耕地农业机械总动力(千瓦)	Total Power of Agricultural Machinery per Hectare of Cultivated Land (kw)	2.09	3	3.8	
每公顷耕地用电量 (千瓦小时)	Electric Power Consumption per hectare of Cultivated Land (kwh)	510	883	1743	
每公顷耕地化肥施用量 (公斤)	Chemical Fertilizer Consumption per Hectare of Cultivated Land (kg)	178	271	378	
每公顷耕地生产的农业产值 (元)	Agricultural Output Value per Hectare of Cultivated Land (yuan)	2510	5178	12514	
农业从业者人均农产品产量(公斤)	Output of Farm Products per Agricultural Laborer (kg)				
粮食	Grain	1222	1357	1435	1405
棉花	Cotton	13.4	13.7	14.7	13.4
油料	Oil-bearing Crops	50.9	49.1	69.2	89.8
肉类	Meat				186.2
水产品	Aquatic Products	22.7	37.6	77.4	130.1
每公顷播种面积农产品产量(公斤)	Output of Farm Crops per Hectare of Sown Area (kg)				
粮食	Grain	3483	3933	4240	4261
棉花	Cotton	810	810	879	1093
油料	Oil-bearing Crops	1338	1480	1572	1919
工业企业效益	**Economic Efficiency of Industry**				
总资产贡献率 (%)	Ratio of Total Assets to Industrial Output Value (%)			9.19	9.00
资产负债率 (%)	Assets-Liability Ratio (%)			65.31	60.81
成本费用利润率 (%)	Ratio of Profits to Industrial Cost (%)			3.21	5.56
流动资产周转次数 (次/年)	Number of Times of Annual of Turnover Circulating Funds (times/year)			1.58	1.62
全员劳动生产率 (元/人.年) (按增加值计算)	Overall Labor Productivity (yuan/person-year) (in terms of value-addedper employee)			18477	45679
建筑业	**Construction**				
技术装备率 (元/人)	Value of Machinery per Laborer (yuan/person)		2467	4264	6304
产值利税率 (%)	Ratio of Per-tax Profits to Gross Output Value (%)		5.4	4.2	4.6
全员劳动生产率 (元/人) (按总产值计算)	Overall Labor Productivity (yuan/person) (in terms of gross output value per employee)		13109	38680	59585
交通运输业	**Transportation**				
客运量弹性系数	Elasticity of Passenger Traffic	1.26	–	0.69	0.75
货运量弹性系数	Elasticity of Freight Traffic	0.3	–	0.44	0.63
铁路网密度 (公里/万平方公里)	Railway Density (km/10000 sq.km)	57.3	60.2	62.2	71.6
公路网密度 (公里/万平方公里)	Highway Density (km/10000 sq.km)	982	1071	1205	1461
铁路货运密度 (吨/公里)	Railway Freight Traffic Density (ton/km)	23765	26069	27781	25913
公路货运密度 (吨/公里)	Highway Freight Traffic Density (ton/km)	5709	7041	8128	7406
平均每一沿海港口泊位货物吞吐量 (万吨)	Cargo Handled at Seaports per Berth (10 000 tons)	84	50	63	86
邮电通信业	**Post and Communication Services**				
邮电业务总量弹性系数	Elasticity of Postal and Telecommunications Services	1.35	33.15	4.16	5.49
全国电话普及率 (部/百人)	Access to Telephones, National (set/100 persons)	0.6	1.1	4.7	20.1
城市电话普及率 (部/百人)	Access to Telephones, Urban (set/100 persons)	3.2	6.4	15.8	39.2
国内商业	**Domestic Trade**				
批零和餐饮业人均消费品零售额(元)	Per Capita Retail Sales of Consumer Goods (yuan)	17681	25852	50213	72380
对外经济贸易	**Foreign Trade**				
进出口总额相当于国内生产总值比例 (%)	Proportion of Total Imports & Exports to GDP (%)	23.1	30.0	40.2	43.9
国际旅游	**International Tourism**				
每一来华游客花费 (美元)	Expenditure per International Tourist in China (USD)	70	81	188	194

2-5 续表 2 Continued

指　　标	Item	1985	1990	1995	2000
金融保险	**Finance and Insurance**				
金融机构存款相当于国内生产总值比例 (%)	Bank Deposits as Percentage of GDP (%)				138.5
金融机构贷款相当于国内生产总值比例 (%)	Bank Loans as Percentage of GDP (%)				111.1
金融机构现金支出相当于收入比例 (%)	Proportion of Cash Outlay to Cash Receipt in Bank (%)				100.4
教育、科技、文化	**Education, Science and Technology and Culture**				
教育	**Education**				
学龄儿童入学率 (%)	Rate of School-age Children Enrollment (%)	96.0	97.8	98.5	99.1
小学升学率 (%)	Rate of Graduates of Primary Schools Entering Junior Secondary Schools (%)	68.4	74.6	90.8	94.9
初中升学率 (%)	Rate of Graduates of Junior Secondary Schools Entering Senior Secondary Schools (%)	41.7	40.6	48.3	51.1
学校教师负担系数 (%)	Student-teacher Ratio(in percentage) (%)				
高等学校	Colleges and Universities	5.0	5.2	7.2	12.0
中等学校	Secondary Schools	17.2	14.6	15.9	18.0
小学学校	Primary Schools	24.9	21.9	23.3	22.2
科技	**Science and Technology**				
研究与开发经费支出相当于国内生产总值比例 (%)	R&D Expenditures as Percentage of GDP (%)		0.71	0.60	1.00
文化	**Culture**				
每百万人有艺术表演团体 (个)	Number of Troupes per Million Persons	3.13	2.45	2.21	2.08
每百万人有公共图书馆 (个)	Number of Public Libraries per Million Persons	2.21	2.21	2.16	2.11
每百万人有博物馆 (个)	Number of Museums per Million Persons	0.67	0.89	0.99	1.10
家庭、生活、环境	**Family, People's Livelihood and Environment**				
家庭	**Family**				
负担少儿系数 (%)	Dependency Ratio of Children (%)	43.73*	41.52	40.16	32.64
负担老年系数 (%)	Dependency Ratio of the Aged (%)	8.33*	8.37	10.06	9.92
婚姻	**Marriages and Divorces**				
离婚率 (‰)	Divorce Rate (‰)	0.88	1.38	1.75	1.91
生活	**People's Livelihood**				
城镇与农村居民收入增长率比例 (以农村居民收入指数为1) (1978=100)	Proportion of Growth Rate of Annual Income of Urban Residents to the Growth Rate of Annual Net Income of Rural Residents (1978=100)	0.36	0.46	0.67	0.74
福利	**Welfare**				
离退休退职费相当于工资总额比例(%)	Pensions for Retired Veterans, Retired and Resigned Persons as Percentage of Total Wages (%)	10.5	13.4	16.1	25.6
离退休退职相当于在职人数比例(%)	Proportion of the Number of Workers Who Have Retired or Resigned to the Number of Employed Ones (%)	13.2	16.4	20.8	34.4
卫生	**Health Care**				
每万人医院数 (个)	Number of Hospitals per 10 000 Persons (unit)	0.56	0.55	0.56	0.53
每万人医生数 (人)	Number of Doctors per 10 000 Persons (unit)	13.3	15.4	15.8	16.8
每万人医院床位数 (张)	Number of Hospital Beds per 10 000 Persons (unit)	21.1	23	23.4	23.8
医院病床使用率 (%)	Utilization Rate of Hospital Beds (%)	82.7	80.9	66.9	60.8
市政建设	**City Construction**				
城市自来水普及率 (%)	Percentage of Households with Access to Tap Water(%)	81.0	89.2	93.0	96.7
城市用气普及率 (%)	Percentage of Households with Access to Tap Gas (%)	22.4	42.2	70.0	84.2
每万人绿地面积 (公顷)	Public Green Areas per 10 000 Persons(hectare)	13.7	32.2	36.7	41.3
环境、灾害	**Environment and Disasters**				
平均每起火灾损失 (元)	Average Loss of per Fire Disaster (yuan)	8121	8932	29022	8046
平均每起交通事故损失 (元)	Average Loss of per Traffic Accident (yuan)	676	1413	5601	4326
平均每起环境污染事故直接经济损失 (元)	Average Loss per Pollution Accident (yuan)			50549	73861

注：1."*"负担少儿和老年系数为1987年数。

2.预算外资金收入自1993年开始不含国有企业和主管部门收入。

a)Figures of dependency ratio of children and the aged with (*) were data in 1987.

b)Since 1993, data on extrabudgetary receipt excluded the revenue of state-owned enterprises and their responsible departments.

2-6 人均主要工农业产品产量

Per Capita Output of Major Industrial and Agricultural Products

年份 Year	粮食（公斤） Grain (kg)	棉花（公斤） Cotton (kg)	油料（公斤） Oil-bearing Crops (kg)	糖料（公斤） Sugar Crops (kg)	茶叶（公斤） Tea (kg)	水果（公斤） Fruits (kg)	猪牛羊肉（公斤） Pork, Beef and Mutton (kg)	水产品（公斤） Aquatic Products (kg)
1978	318.74	2.27	5.46	24.91	0.28	6.87		4.87
1979	342.74	2.28	6.64	25.40	0.29	7.24		4.45
1980	326.69	2.76	7.84	29.67	0.31	6.92		4.59
1981	327.02	2.99	10.27	36.25	0.35	7.85		4.64
1982	351.47	3.57	11.72	43.22	0.39	7.65		5.12
1983	378.46	4.53	10.31	39.40	0.39	9.27		5.34
1984	392.84	6.04	11.49	46.11	0.40	9.50		5.97
1985	360.70	3.95	15.02	57.53	0.41	11.07		6.71
1986	367.00	3.32	13.82	54.86	0.43	12.63		7.72
1987	371.74	3.92	14.09	51.20	0.47	15.39		8.81
1988	357.72	3.77	11.98	56.17	0.49	15.12		9.63
1989	364.32	3.39	11.58	51.88	0.48	16.38		10.30
1990	393.10	3.97	14.21	63.55	0.48	16.51		10.90
1991	378.26	4.93	14.24	73.16	0.47	18.91		11.74
1992	379.97	3.87	14.09	75.61	0.48	20.95		13.37
1993	387.37	3.17	15.31	64.70	0.51	25.55		15.47
1994	373.46	3.64	16.69	61.63	0.49	29.36		17.98
1995	387.28	3.96	18.67	64.96	0.49	34.98		20.89
1996	414.39	3.45	18.16	68.66	0.49	38.21	30.35	23.10
1997	401.74	3.74	17.54	76.31	0.50	41.37	34.55	29.28
1998	412.42	3.62	18.63	78.82	0.54	43.90	37.02	31.45
1999	405.55	3.05	20.75	66.48	0.54	49.76	37.99	32.88
2000	365.90	3.50	23.39	60.45	0.54	49.28	38.30	33.87

2-6 续表 1 Continued

年份 Year	布（米） Cloth (m)	机制纸及纸板（公斤） Machine-made Paper and Paperboard (kg)	纱（公斤） Yarn (kg)	原煤（吨） Coal (ton)	原油（公斤） Crude Oil (kg)	发电量（千瓦小时） Electricity (kwh)	钢（公斤） Steel (kg)	水泥（公斤） Cement (kg)
1978	11.54	4.59	2.49	0.65	108.82	268.36	33.24	68.23
1979	12.54	5.09	2.72	0.66	109.55	291.02	35.58	76.26
1980	13.73	5.45	2.98	0.63	107.98	306.35	37.83	81.39
1981	14.36	5.43	3.19	0.63	101.84	311.20	35.82	83.41
1982	15.22	5.84	3.33	0.66	101.25	324.90	36.84	94.39
1983	14.54	6.46	3.20	0.70	103.65	343.40	39.11	105.78
1984	13.21	7.29	3.10	0.76	110.54	363.61	41.93	118.65
1985	13.96	8.67	3.36	0.83	118.83	390.76	44.52	138.86
1986	15.44	9.36	3.73	0.84	122.51	421.36	48.93	155.66
1987	15.96	10.53	4.03	0.86	123.74	458.75	51.92	171.81
1988	17.06	11.53	4.23	0.89	124.41	494.90	53.95	190.75
1989	16.92	11.92	4.26	0.94	123.04	522.78	55.05	187.99
1990	16.63	12.08	4.07	0.95	121.84	547.22	58.45	184.74
1991	15.79	12.85	4.00	0.94	122.52	588.77	61.70	219.51
1992	16.37	14.81	4.31	0.96	121.97	647.18	69.47	264.57
1993	17.23	16.24	4.26	0.98	123.25	712.34	76.00	312.18
1994	17.73	17.94	4.11	1.04	122.57	778.72	77.70	353.39
1995	21.59	23.34	4.50	1.13	124.54	835.81	79.15	394.74
1996	17.17	21.67	4.21	1.15	129.22	888.10	83.15	403.42
1997	20.23	22.22	4.55	1.12	130.68	923.16	88.57	416.02
1998	19.40	17.11	4.36	1.01	129.61	939.48	93.05	431.50
1999	19.94	17.22	4.52	0.83	127.63	988.60	99.12	457.09
2000	21.93	19.69	5.20	0.79	129.04	1073.20	101.73	472.63

2-7 民族自治地方自然资源

Natural Resources in Minority Nationality Autonomous Areas

项　　目	Item	2000	占全国% Percentage to National Total
总面积　（万平方公里）	**Total Area　(10 000 sq.km)**	**611.73**	**63.72**
牧区、半农半牧区草原面积（万公顷）	Area of Grasslands in Pastoral and Semi-pastoral Areas　(10 000 hectares)	30000.00	75.0
森林面积　（万公顷）	Area of Forest　(10 000 hectares)	5648.00	42.2
森林蓄积量　（亿立方米）	Stock Volume of the Forest (100 million cu.m)	52.49	51.8
水力资源蕴藏量　（亿千瓦）	Hydropower Resources　(100 million kw)	4.46	66.0

注：除总面积外，其它资源为以前清查数，有待进一步勘测。

a)The figures of resources, except total area, were obtained from surveys in previous year, and are subject to further verification.

2-8 民族自治地方行政区划和人口（2000）

Administrative Division and Population of Minority Nationality Autonomous Areas (2000)

省级单位名称	Provinces and Autonomous Regions	地级区划数（个）Number of Prefectures	#地级市 Cities at Prefectural Level	县级区划数（个）Number of Counties	#县级市 Cities at County Level	总人口（万人）Total Population in Minority Areas (10 000 persons)	#少数民族人口 Minority Population	少数民族人口占自治地方总人口比重(%) Minority Population as Percentage to Total Population in Minority Areas (%)
全　国	**National Total**	**77**	**20**	**699**	**70**	**16673.15**	**7725.93**	**46.34**
河　北	Hebei			6		191.60	109.53	57.17
内蒙古	Inner Mongolia	12	5	101	15	2376.00	493.00	20.75
辽　宁	Liaoning			8		334.27	173.88	52.02
吉　林	Jilin	1		11	6	329.29	114.94	34.91
黑龙江	Heilongjiang			1		24.58	5.16	20.99
浙　江	Zhejiang			1		17.68	1.75	9.88
湖　北	Hubei	1		10	2	441.68	232.76	52.70
湖　南	Hunan	1		15	1	472.62	332.17	70.28
广　东	Guangdong			3		46.19	17.21	37.26
广　西	Guangxi	14	9	110	10	4489.00	1721.00	38.34
海　南	Hainan			6		148.56	74.51	50.15
重　庆	Chongqing			4		244.44	169.77	69.45
四　川	Sichuan	3		50	1	606.11	334.26	55.15
贵　州	Guizhou	3		46	4	1512.33	882.44	58.35
云　南	Yunnan	8		78	7	2068.76	1122.22	54.25
西　藏	Tibet	7	1	73	1	262.00	246.00	93.89
甘　肃	Gansu	2		21	2	311.62	174.33	55.94
青　海	Qinghai	6		35	2	309.42	183.90	59.43
宁　夏	Ningxia	4	3	24	2	562.00	194.11	34.54
新　疆	Xinjiang	15	2	96	17	1925.00	1143.00	59.38

2-9 民族自治地方国民经济和社会发展主要指标

指　标	Item	1985
人口与就业	**Population and Employment**	
人口（万人）	**Population (10 000 persons)**	
年底总人口	Population at the Year-end	13548
#少数民族人口	Minority Population	5853
就业	**Employment**	
从业人员数（万人）	Employment (10 000 persons)	5965.34
宏观经济	**Macroeconomic Indicator**	
国内生产总值（亿元）	**Gross Domestic Product(100 million yuan)**	
第一产业	Primary Industry	
第二产业	Secondary Industry	
第三产业	Tertiary Industry	
固定资产	**Investment in Fixed Assets**	
全社会固定资产投资总额（亿元）	Total Investment in Fixed Assets (100 million yuan)	
#国有单位	State-owned Units	161.9
财政	**Government Finance**	
地方财政收入（亿元）	Local Governments Revenue (100 million yuan)	63.5
地方财政支出（亿元）	Local Governments Expenditures (100 million yuan)	157
产业	**Industry**	
农业	**Agriculture**	
耕地面积（万公顷）	Cultivated Areas (10 000 hectares)	1747
灌溉面积（万公顷）	Irrigated Areas (10 000 hectares)	686
农林牧渔总产值（亿元）	Gross Output Value of Farming Forestry, Animal Husbandry and Fishery (100 million yuan)	
主要农产品产量	Output of Major Farm Products	
粮食产量（万吨）	Grain Output (10 000 tons)	4006
棉花产量（万吨）	Cotton Output(10 000 tons)	19
油料产量（万吨）	Oil-bearing Crops Output (10 000 tons)	193
大牲畜年底头数（万头）	Large Domestic Animals (10 000 heads)	4749
羊年底头数（万只）	Goats and Sheep (10 000 heads)	9757
猪年底头数（万头）	Hogs (10 000 heads)	4533
工业	**Industry**	
工业总产值（亿元）	Gross Industrial Output Value (100 million yuan)	771.7
主要工业产品产量	Output of Major Industrial Products	
布（亿米）	Cloth (100 million m)	5.4
机制纸及纸板（万吨）	Machine-Made Paper and Paperboards(10 000 tons)	59.2
糖（万吨）	Sugar (10 000 tons)	126.9
原煤（亿吨）	Coal (100 million tons)	0.9
原油（万吨）	Crude Oil (10 000 tons)	805
发电量（亿千瓦小时）	Electricity (100 million kwh)	389.0
钢（万吨）	Steel (10 000 tons)	232.5
生铁（万吨）	Pig Iron (10 000 tons)	258.1
水泥（万吨）	Cement (10 000 tons)	1222.1
木材（万立方米）	Timber (10 000 cu.m)	1826

Principal Aggregate Indicators on National Economic and Social Development of Minority Nationality Autonomous Areas

总量指标 Aggregate Data				速度指标(%) Indices and Growth Rates						
				指数 Index (2000比以下各年) (2000 as percentage of the following years)				平均增长速度 Average Annual Growth Rate		
1990	1995	1999	2000	1985	1990	1995	1999	1986-1990	1991-1995	1996-2000
15296	16044	16678	16673							
6880	7232	7571	7726							
7406.44	7869.62	7983.22	8308.89	139.3	112.2	105.6	104.1	4.4	1.2	1.1
	4901.14	6886.17	7496.15			154.2	107.9			9.0
	1628.55	2007.83	2022.30			131.4	101.7			5.6
	1746.52	2528.18	2834.00			168.4	109.2			11.0
	1526.07	2350.16	2639.41			160.8	111.8			10.0
	1444	2231	2477			171.5	111.1			11.4
259	983	1412	1553	959.0	598.5	158.0	110.0		30.5	9.6
167	248	437	476	748.9	285.3	191.7	108.8	21.3	8.3	13.9
304	595	1004	1173	747.1	385.3	197.1	116.8	14.2	14.3	14.5
1763	1508	2096	2086	119.4	118.3	138.4	99.5	0.2	-3.1	6.7
764	838	918	936	136.4	122.5	111.7	101.9	2.2	1.9	2.2
	2536.6	3156	3200	246.8	182.4	131.0	101.9	6.2	6.9	5.5
5373	5801	6874	6381	159.3	118.8	110.0	92.8	6.0	1.5	1.9
47	95	136	146	769.7	311.1	154.6	107.4	19.9	15.0	9.1
208	264	333	353	183.0	169.8	133.8	106.1	1.5	4.9	6.0
5286	5618	5689	5566	117.2	105.3	99.1	97.8	2.2	1.2	-0.2
11362	11906	13036	13076	134.0	115.1	109.8	100.3	3.1	0.9	1.9
5668	7240	7292	8201	180.9	144.7	113.3	112.5	4.6	5.0	2.5
1295.1	4248.4	5450.4	5940.9	547.8	302.3	137.5	102.3	12.6	17.1	6.6
7.4	6.9	5.2	5.0	92.8	67.7	72.6	96.3	6.5	-1.4	-6.2
94.1	191.2	153.1	175.5	296.4	186.5	91.8	114.6	9.7	15.2	-1.7
222.6	239.5	567.2	498.2	392.6	223.8	208.0	87.8	11.9	1.5	15.8
1.2	1.7	1.5	1.5	170.0	120.8	88.1	95.0	7.1	6.5	-2.5
1265	1610	2058	2292	284.7	181.2	142.3	111.4	9.5	4.9	7.3
738.8	1186.5	1428.9	1712.5	440.2	231.8	144.3	119.8	13.7	9.9	7.6
368.3	699.6	643.3	647.1	278.3	175.7	92.5	100.6	9.6	13.7	-1.5
417.0	554.7	696.4	724.8	280.8	173.8	130.7	104.1	10.1	5.9	5.5
1957.8	4295.9	5271.4	5703.1	466.7	291.3	132.8	108.2	9.9	17.0	5.8
1761	3257	1230	1052	57.6	59.8	32.3	85.6	-0.7	13.1	-20.2

2–9 续表 1

指　　标	Item	1985
建筑业	**Construction**	
建筑业企业人数（万人）	Number of Employed Persons (10 000 persons)	
建筑业总产值（亿元）	Gross Output Value (100 million yuan)	
施工房屋面积（万平方米）	Floor Space of Buildings Under Construction	
竣工房屋面积（万平方米）	Floor Space of Buildings Completed (10 000 sq.m)	
邮电运输	**Transportation,Post and telecommunication**	
铁路营业里程（万公里）	Railways in Operation (10 000 km)	1.25
公路通车里程（万公里）	Highways (10 000 km)	25.41
邮电业务总量（亿元）	Total and Telecommunications Services	
邮路及农村投递线路总长度（万公里）	Postal Routes (10 000km)	90.0
国内商业	**Domestic Trade**	
社会消费品零售总额（亿元）	Total Value of Retail Sales (100 million yuan)	370.5
对外经济贸易	**Foreign Trade**	
进出口总额（亿美元）	Total Exports and Imports(USD 100 million)	
出口额	Exports	
进口额	Imports	
国际旅游	**International Tourism**	
国际旅游人数（万人次）	Number of Foreign Tourists(10 000 persons)	
旅游外汇收入（亿美元）	Foreign Exchange Earning from tourism(USD 100 million yuan)	
金融	**Finance**	
金融机构各项存款（亿元）	Deposits of National Banking System(100 million yuan)	
金融机构各项贷款（亿元）	Loans of National Banking System(100 million yuan)	
教育、文化、卫生	**Education,Technology and Culture**	
教育	**Education**	
在校学生数　（万人）	Students Enrollment (10 000 persons)	2420.6
高等学校	Institutions of Higher Education	10.4
中等学校	Secondary Schools	573.3
小学	Primary Schools	1836.9
各类专任教师数（万人）	Full-time Teachers(10 000 persons)	95.7
高等学校	Institutions of Higher Education	2.2
中等学校	Secondary Schools	33.5
小学	Primary Schools	60.0
文化	**Culture**	
出版数量	Publications	
图书（万册）	Number of Books Published(10 000 copies)	35906.9
杂志（万册）	Number of Magazines Issued(10 000 copies)	7818.8
报纸（万份）	Number of Newspapers Issued(10 000 copies)	76847.2
卫生	**Health Care**	
卫生机构（万个）	Number of Health Institutions(10 000 units)	3.0
卫生机构床位（万张）	Number of Hospitals and Sanatorium Beds	31.21
卫生技术人员（万人）	Medical Personnel (10 000 persons)	42.37

注：2000年铁路营业里程为国家铁路营业里程。

Continued

总量指标 Aggregate Data				速度指标(%) Indices and Growth Rates							
				指数 Index (2000比以下各年) (2000 as percentage of the following years)				平均增长速度 Average Annual Growth Rate			
1990	1995	1999	2000	1985	1990	1995	1999	1986-1990	1991-1995	1996-2000
		133.8	131.6				98.3			
		639.7	754.3				117.9			
		12105	9232				76.3			
		8573	5326				62.1			
1.31	1.70	1.75	1.43							
29.37	33.21	40.26	42.36	166.7	144.2	127.6	105.2	2.9	2.5	5.0
88.0	106.8	106.1	109.5	121.7	124.5	102.5	103.2	-0.4	3.9	0.5
681.8	1692.3	2378.2	2569.8	693.6	376.9	151.9	108.1	13.0	19.9	8.7
		62.2	85.6				137.7			
		37.7	49.7				131.8			
		24.5	36.0				146.8			
		285.1	348.2				122.1			
		6.26	7.55				120.6			
		6918.3	7905.8				114.3			
		6738.4	6548.0				97.2			
2476.1	2629.2	2872.3	2940.0	121.5	118.7	111.8	102.4	0.5	1.2	2.3
13.6	18.6	26.0	33.6	323.5	247.4	180.9	129.4	5.5	6.5	12.6
609.6	721.1	918.8	978.3	170.6	160.5	135.[illegible]	106.5	1.2	3.4	6.3
1852.9	1889.5	1927.5	1886.0	102.7	101.8	99.8	97.8	0.2	0.4	...
129.1	138.4	147.3	176.2	184.1	136.5	127.3	119.6	6.2	1.4	4.9
2.8	3.7	3.1	3.6	165.4	130.0	98.4	117.4	4.9	5.7	-0.3
41.5	48.9	54.3	54.5	162.7	131.3	111.5	100.4	4.4	3.3	2.2
84.8	85.8	89.9	115.7	192.9	136.5	134.9	128.7	7.2	0.2	6.2
30166.3	42275.0	48394.5	42309.5	117.8	140.3	100.1	87.4	-3.4	7.0	...
7866.4	7881.0	8069.5	8332.4	106.6	105.9	105.7	103.3	0.1	...	1.1
79119.6	94984.8	111943.9	123276.9	160.4	155.8	129.8	110.1	0.6	3.7	5.4
3.2	2.9	1.7	1.6	52.7	50.0	55.2	95.9	1.0	-1.9	-11.2
35.94	38.71	37.91	38.20	122.4	106.3	98.7	100.8	2.9	1.5	-0.3
48.87	52.74	48.27	35.53	83.8	72.7	67.4	73.6	2.9	1.5	-7.6

a)The length of railway in operation in 2000 is national railways.

2-10 全国少数民族分布的主要地区

Geographic Distribution of Minority Nationalities

人口数为1990年人口普查资料。

Figures of population are obtained from the Population Census in 1990.

民族	Nationality	分布的主要地区	Main Geographic Distribution	人口数(人) Population (person)
蒙古族	Mongolian	内蒙古、辽宁、吉林、河北、黑龙江、新疆	Inner Mongolia,Liaoning,Jilin,Hebei, Heilongjiang and Xinjiang	4802407
回族	Hui	宁夏、甘肃、河南、新疆、青海、云南、河北、山东、安徽、辽宁、北京、内蒙古、天津、黑龙江、陕西、贵州、吉林、江苏、四川	Ningxia,Gansu,Henan,Xinjiang,Qinghai, Yunnan,Hebei,Shandong,Anhui,Liaoning, Beijing,Inner Mongolia,Tianjin, Heilongjiang,Shaanxi,Guizhou,Jilin, Jiangsu and Sichuan	8612001
藏族	Tibetan	西藏、四川、青海、甘肃、云南	Tibet,Sichuan,Qinghai,Gansu and Yunnan	4593072
维吾尔族	Uygur	新疆	Xinjiang	7207024
苗族	Miao	贵州、湖南、云南、广西、重庆湖北、四川	Guizhou,Hunan,Yunnan,Guangxi,Chongqing, Hubei and Sichuan	7383622
彝族	Yi	云南、四川、贵州	Yunnan,Sichuan and Guizhou	6578524
壮族	Zhuang	广西、云南、广东	Guangxi Yunnan and Guangdong	15555820
布依族	Bouyei	贵州	Guizhou	2548294
朝鲜族	Korean	吉林、黑龙江、辽宁	Jilin,Heilongjiang and Liaoning	1923361
满族	Man	辽宁、河北、黑龙江、吉林、内蒙古、北京	Liaoning,Hebei,Heilongjiang,Jilin, Inner Mongolia and Beijing	9846776
侗族	Dong	贵州、湖南、广西	Guizhou,Hunan and Guangxi	2508624
瑶族	Yao	广西、湖南、云南、广东	Guangxi,Hunan,Yunnan and Guangdong	2137033
白族	Bai	云南、贵州、湖南	Yunnan,Guizhou and Hunan	1598052
土家族	Tujia	湖南、湖北、重庆、贵州	Hunan,Hubei,Chongqing and Guizhou	5725049
哈尼族	Hani	云南	Yunnan	1254800
哈萨克族	Kazak	新疆	Xinjiang	1110758
傣族	Dai	云南	Yunnan	1025402
黎族	Li	海南	Hainan	1112498
傈僳族	Lisu	云南、四川	Yunnan and Sichuan	574589
佤族	Va	云南	Yunnan	351980
畲族	She	福建、浙江、江西、广东	Fujian,Zhejiang,Jiangxi and Guangdong	634700
高山族	Gaoshan	台湾、福建	Taiwan and Fujian	2877
拉祜族	Lahu	云南	Yunnan	411545
水族	Shui	贵州、广西	Guizhou and Guangxi	347116
东乡族	Dongxiang	甘肃、新疆	Gansu and Xinjiang	373669
纳西族	Naxi	云南	Yunnan	277750
景颇族	Jingpo	云南	Yunnan	119276
柯尔克孜族	Kirgiz	新疆	Xinjiang	143537
土族	Tu	青海、甘肃	Qinghai and Gansu	192568
达斡尔族	Daur	内蒙古、黑龙江	Inner Mongolia and Heilongjiang	121463
仫佬族	Mulam	广西	Guangxi	160648
羌族	Qiang	四川	Sichuan	198303
布朗族	Blang	云南	Yunnan	82398
撒拉族	Salar	青海	Qinghai	87546
毛南族	Maonan	广西	Guangxi	72370
仡佬族	Gelo	贵州	Guizhou	438192
锡伯族	Xibe	辽宁、新疆	Liaoning and Xinjiang	172932
阿昌族	Achang	云南	Yunnan	27718
普米族	Primi	云南	Yunnan	29721
塔吉克族	Tajik	新疆	Xinjiang	33223
怒族	Nu	云南	Yunnan	27190
乌孜别克族	Uzbek	新疆	Xinjiang	14763
俄罗斯族	Russian	新疆、黑龙江	Xinjiang and Heilongjiang	13500
鄂温克族	Ewenki	内蒙古	Inner Mongolia	26379
德昂族	Deang	云南	Yunnan	15461
保安族	Baoan	甘肃	Gansu	11683
裕固族	Yugur	甘肃	Gansu	12293
京族	Jing	广西	Guangxi	18749
塔塔尔族	Tatar	新疆	Xinjiang	5064
独龙族	Derung	云南	Yunnan	5825
鄂伦春族	Oroqen	黑龙江、内蒙古	Heilongjiang and Inner Mongolia	7004
赫哲族	Hezhen	黑龙江	Heilongjiang	4254
门巴族	Monba	西藏	Tibet	7498
珞巴族	Lhoba	西藏	Tibet	2322
基诺族	Jino	云南	Yunnan	18022

主 要 统 计 指 标 解 释

可比价格 指计算各种总量指标所采用的扣除了价格变动因素的价格，可进行不同时期总量指标的对比。按可比价格计算总量指标有两种方法：一种是直接用产品产量乘某一年的不变价格计算；另一种是用价格指数进行缩减。

不变价格 指以同类产品某年的平均价格作为固定价格，用于计算各年的产品价值。按不变价格计算的产品价值消除了价格变动因素，不同时期对比可以反映生产的发展速度。新中国成立后，随着工农业产品价格水平的变化，国家统计局先后五次制定了全国统一的工业产品不变价格和农业产品不变价格。从1952年到1957年使用1952年工（农）业产品不变价格，从1957年到1970年使用1957年不变价格，从1971年到1980年使用1970年不变价格，从1981年到1990年使用1980年不变价格，从1991年开始使用1990年不变价格。

平均增长速度 我国计算平均增长速度有两种方法：一种是习惯上经常使用的“水平法”，又称几何平均法，是以间隔期最后一年的水平同基期水平对比来计算平均每年增长（或下降）速度； 另一种是“累计法”，又称代数平均法或方程法，是以间隔期内各年水平的总和同基期水平对比来计算平均每年增长（或下降）速度。在一般正常情况下，两种方法计算的平均每年增长速度比较接近；但在经济发展不平衡、出现大起大落时，两种方法计算的结果差别较大。

本《年鉴》内所列的平均增长速度，除固定资产投资用“累计法”计算外，其余均用“水平法”计算。从某年到某年平均增长速度的年份，均不包括基期年在内。如建国四十三年以来的平均增长速度是以1949年为基期计算的，则写为1950－1992年平均增长速度，其余类推。

企业（单位）登记注册类型 是以在工商行政管理机关登记注册的各类企业为划分对象，以工商行政管理部门对企业登记注册的类型为依据，将企业登记注册类型分为内资企业、港澳台商投资企业和外商投资企业三大类。内资企业包括国有企业、集体企业、股份合作企业、联营企业、有限责任公司、股份有限公司、私营公司和其他企业；港澳台商投资企业和外商投资企业分别包括合资经营企业、合作经营企业、独资经营企业和股份有限公司。对不在工商行政管理部门进行登记注册的行政机关、事业单位和社会团体，主要按其经费来源和管理方式进行划分。

国有企业 指企业全部资产归国家所有，并按《中华人民共和国企业法人登记管理条例》规定登记注册的非公司制的经济组织。不包括有限责任公司中的国有独资公司。

集体企业 指企业资产归集体所有，并按《中华人民共和国企业法人登记管理条例》规定登记注册的经济组织。

股份合作企业 指以合作制为基础，由企业职工共同出资入股，吸收一定比例的社会资产投资组建，实行自主经营，自负盈亏，共同劳动，民主管理，按劳分配与按股分红相结合的一种集体经济组织。

联营企业 指两个及两个以上相同或不同所有制性质的企业法人或事业单位法人，按自愿、平等、互利的原则，共同投资组成的经济组织。联营企业包括国有联营企业、集体联营企业、国有与集体联营企业和其他联营企业。

有限责任公司 指根据《中华人民共和国公司登记管理条例》规定登记注册，由两个以上、五十个以下的股东共同出资，每个股东以其所认缴的出资额对公司承担有限责任，公司以其全部资产对其债务承担责任的经济组织。有限责任公司包括国有独资公司以及其他有限责任公司。

股份有限公司 指根据《中华人民共和国公司登记管理条例》规定登记注册，其全部注册资本由等额股份构成并通过发行股票筹集资本，股东以其认购的股份对公司承担有限责任，公司以其全部资产对其债务承担责任的经济组织。

私营企业 指由自然人投资设立或由自然人控股，以雇佣劳动为基础的营利性经济组织。包括按照《公司法》、《合伙企业法》、《私营企业暂行条例》规定登记注册的私营有限责任公司、私营股份有限公司、私营合伙企业和私营独资企业。

其他企业 指上述企业之外的其他内资经济组织。

与港澳台商合资经营企业 指港澳台地区投资者与内地企业依照《中华人民共和国中外合资经营企业法》及有关法律的规定，按合同规定的比例投资设立、分享利润和分担风险的企业。

与港澳台商合作经营企业 指港澳台地区投资者与内地企业依照《中华人民共和国中外合作经营企业法》及有关法律的规定，依照合作合同的约定进行投资或提供条件设立、分配利润和分担风险的企业。

港澳台商独资经营企业 指依照《中华人民共和国外资企业法》及有关法律的规定，在内地由港澳台地区投资者全额投资设立的企业。

港澳台商投资股份有限公司 指根据国家有关规定，经外经贸部依法批准设立，其中港、澳、台商的股本占公司注册资本的比例达25% 以上的股份有限公司。凡其中港、澳、台商的股本占公司注册资本的比例小于25%的，属于内资企业中的股份有限公司。

中外合资经营企业 指外国企业或外国人与中国内地企业依照《中华人民共和国中外合资经营企业法》及有关法律的规定，按合同规定的比例投资设立、分享利润和分担风险的企业。

中外合作经营企业　指外国企业或外国人与中国内地企业依照《中华人民共和国中外合作经营企业法》及有关法律的规定，依照合作合同的约定进行投资或提供条件设立、分配利润和分担风险的企业。

外资企业　指依照《中华人民共和国外资企业法》及有关法律的规定，在中国内地由外国投资者全额投资设立的企业。

外商投资股份有限公司　指根据国家有关规定，经外经贸部依法批准设立，其中外资的股本占公司注册资本的比例达25%以上的股份有限公司。凡其中外资股本占公司注册资本的比例小于25%的，属于内资企业中的股份有限公司。

行政机关、事业单位和社会团体　参照企业登记注册类型，主要按其经费来源和管理方式划分。具体规定如下：

⑴行政机关：包括国家机关和政党机关，原则上均列为"国有"。但有特殊规定的，如供销社等，则列为"集体"。

⑵事业单位：包括经国家机构编制部门和有关业务主管部门批准成立的各类事业单位，不包括实行企业化管理的事业单位。事业单位的划分办法如下：

①由国家财政预算拨款或列入财政预算外资金管理以及经费主要来源于国有主管部门或国有上级单位的事业单位，列为"国有"。

②经费主要来源于集体单位的事业单位，列为"集体"。

③公民个人（或个人合伙）开办的事业单位，列为"私营"。

④上述以外的其他事业单位，如果其经费来源不明确，按管理方式进行归类。

⑶社会团体：包括经民政部门批准成立以及未纳入社会团体管理条例范围的工会、妇联等各类社会团体。社会团体的划分办法如下：

①未纳入民政部社会团体管理条例范围的工会、妇联、共青团、青联、工商联、科协、侨联等社会团体，国家拨款设立的基金会或基金管理组织以及经费主要来源于国有业务主管部门或国有上级单位的社会团体，列为"国有"。

②经费主要来源于集体单位的社会团体，列为"集体"。

③公民个人（或个人合伙）开办的社会团体，划为"私营"。

④上述以外的其他社会团体，如果其经费来源不明确，改按管理方式进行归类。

Explanatory Notes on Main Statistical Indicators

Comparable Prices refer to prices that are used to remove the factors of price change in calculating economic aggregates, so as to facilitate comparison of aggregates over time. Two methods are used for calculating economic aggregates at comparable prices: 1. Multiplying the output of products by their constant prices of certain year; 2. Deflation of data at current prices by relevant price index.

Constant Price refers to the average price of a given product in certain year, which is used for comparison of output value over time. As the output value at constant prices removes the factor of price changes, it reflects the trend of production development over time. Since 1949, with the changes in general price level, National Bureau of Statistics has issued nationally unified constant prices five times: the 1952 constant prices for 1949-1957; the 1957 constant prices for 1957-1971; the 1970 constant prices for 1971-1981; the 1980 constant prices for 1981-1990; and the 1990 constant prices have been used since 1991.

Average Annual Growth Rate Two methods for calculating average annual growth rate are applied in China, one is often called "level approach", or the method of calculating geometric average, which is derived by comparing the level of the last year of the interval with that of the beginning year; the other is called "accumulative approach" or algebraic average or equation method, which is derived by the summation of the actual figure of each year in the interval divided by the figure in the base year.

Usually the results calculated by the two methods are fairly close, but they differed sharply when uneven economic development occurred with striking fluctuations in growth.

The average annual growth rates listed in this statistical yearbook are calculated by "level approach" except for the growth rate of investment in fixed assets. The base years are not listed when the years are listed for average annual growth rates. For instance, the average annual growth rate of 43 years since 1949 is listed as average annual growth rate of 1950-1992 without listing the base year 1949. And the analogy of this is also the same for the rest of the years.

Registration Status of Enterprises Enterprises are classified into 3 categories, namely domestic-funded enterprises, enterprises with investment from Hong Kong, Macau and Taiwan, and enterprises with foreign investment, in the light of the registration status of an enterprise in industrial and commercial administration agencies. Domestic-funded enterprises include state-owned enterprises, collective-owned enterprises, cooperative enterprises, joint ownership enterprises, limited liability corporations, share-holding corporations Ltd., private enterprises and other enterprises. Included in the enterprises with investment from Hong Kong, Macau and Taiwan and enterprises with foreign investment are joint-venture enterprises, cooperative enterprises, sole investment enterprises and share-holding corporations Ltd. For government agencies, institutions and social organizations which are not requested to be registered in industrial and commercial administration agencies, they are classified mainly by their sources of funds and way of management.

State-owned Enterprises refer to non-corporation economic units where the entire assets are owned by the state and which have registered in accordance with the *Regulation of the People's Republic of China on the Management of Registration of Corporate Enterprises*. Excluded from this category are sole state-funded corporations in the limited liability corporations.

Collective-owned Enterprises refer to economic units where the assets are owned collectively and which have registered in accordance with the *Regulation of the People's Republic of China on the Management of Registration of Corporate Enterprises*.

Cooperative Enterprises refer to a form of collective economic units (enterprises) where capitals come mainly from employees as their shares, with certain proportion of capital from the outside, where production is organized on the basis of independent operation, independent accounting for profits and losses, joint work, democratic management, and a distribution system that integrates remuneration according to work with dividend according to capital share.

Joint Ownership Enterprises refer to economic units established by two or more corporate enterprises or corporate institutions of the same or different ownership, through joint investment on the basis of equality, voluntary participation and mutual benefits. They include state joint ownership enterprises, collective joint ownership enterprises, joint state-collective enterprises, other joint ownership enterprises.

Limited Liability Corporations refer to economic units established with investment from 2-50 investors and registered in accordance with the *Regulation of the People's Republic of China on the Management of Registration of Corporations*, each investor bearing limited liability to the corporation depending on its share of investment, and the corporation bearing liability to its debt to the maximum of its total assets. Limited liability corporations include exclusive state-funded limited liability corporations and other limited liability corporations.

Share-holding Corporations Ltd. refer to economic units registered in accordance with the *Regulation of the People's Republic of China on the Management of Registration of Corporations*, with total registered capitals divided into equal shares and raised through issuing stocks. Each investor bears limited liability to the corporation depending on the holding of shares, and the corporation bears liability to its debt to the maximum of its total assets.

Private Enterprises refer to profit-making economic units invested and established by natural persons, or controlled by natural persons using employed labour. Included in this category are private limited liability corporations, private share-holding corporations Ltd., private partnership enterprises and private-funded enterprises registered in accordance with the *Corporation Law*, *Partnership Enterprises Law* and *Interim Regulations on Private Enterprises* .

Other Domestic-funded Enterprises refer to domestic-funded economic units other than those mentioned above.

Cooperative Enterprises with Funds from Hong Kong Macau and Taiwan established by investors from Hong Kong, Macau and Taiwan with enterprises in the mainland of China in accordance with the *Law of the People's Republic of China on Sino-foreign Cooperative Enterprises* and other relevant laws, where the investment or provision of facilities, and the share of profits and risks is stipulated in the cooperative contract.

Enterprises with Sole (exclusive) Investment from Hong Kong, Macau and Taiwan refer to enterprises established in the mainland of China with exclusive investment from investors from Hong Kong, Macau and Taiwan in accordance with the *Law of the People's Republic of China on Foreign-Funded Enterprises* and other relevant laws.

Share-holding Corporations Ltd. with Investment from Hong Kong, Macau and Taiwan refer to share-holding corporations Ltd. established with the approval from the Ministry of Foreign Trade and Economic Relations in line with relevant state regulations, where the share of investment from Hong Kong, Macau or Taiwan businessmen exceeds 25% of the total registered capital of the corporation. In case the share of investment from Hong Kong, Macau or Taiwan is less than 25% of the total registered capital, the enterprise is to be classified as domestic-funded share-holding corporation Ltd.

Joint-venture Enterprises with Foreign Investment refer to enterprises jointly established by foreign enterprises or foreigners with enterprises in the mainland of China in accordance with the *Law of the People's Republic of China on Sino-foreign Joint Venture Enterprises* and other relevant laws, where the share of investment, profits and risks is stipulated in the contract.

Cooperation Enterprises with Foreign Investment refer to enterprises jointly established by foreign enterprises or foreigners with enterprises in the mainland of China in accordance with the *Law of the People's Republic of China on Sino-foreign Cooperative Enterprises* and other relevant laws, where the investment or provision of facilities, and the share of profits and risks is stipulated in the cooperative contract.

Enterprises with Sole (exclusive) Foreign Investment refer to enterprises established in the mainland of China with exclusive investment from foreign investors in accordance with the *Law of the People's Republic of China on Foreign-Funded Enterprises* and other relevant laws.

Share-holding Corporations Ltd. with Foreign Investment refer to share-holding corporations Ltd. established with the approval from the Ministry of Foreign Trade and Economic Relations in line with relevant state regulations, where the share of investment from foreign investors exceeds 25% of the total registered capital of the corporation. In case the share of foreign investment is less than 25% of the total registered capital, the enterprise is to be classified as domestic-funded share-holding corporation Ltd.

Government Agencies, Institutions and Social Organizations are classified into following categories by source of funds and way of management taking reference of the registration status of enterprises:

(1) Government agencies: include state and party agencies, classified in principle as "state-owned". There are exceptions, such as supply and marketing cooperatives which are classified as "collective-owned".

(2) Institutions: include institutions of various types established with the approval by organization and staffing departments of the government, but exclude institutions where enterprise management system is introduced. Institutions are further classified as follows:

(a) Institutions whose main budget is listed in the government budget appropriations or extra-budget funds, or allocated from the budget of their competent government agencies. Such institutions are classified as "state-owned".

(b) Institutions whose budget mainly comes from collective units. Such institutions are classified as "collective-owned".

(c) Institutions other than those mentioned above whose source of budget is not clear. Such institutions are classified by way of management.

(3) Social organizations: include social organizations established with the approval from the Ministry of Civil Affairs, and organizations that are not covered by social organization management regulations such as trade unions, women's federations etc.. Social organizations are further classified as follows:

(a) Social organizations that are not covered by social organization management regulations of the Ministry of Civil Affairs such as trade unions, women's federations, communist youth leagues, youth associations, industrial and commerce associations, scientists associations, overseas Chinese associations, etc., foundations and fund management organizations established with funds from the state, and social organizations whose funds mainly come from the budget of their competent government agencies. Such institutions are classified as "state-owned".

(b) Social organizations whose budget mainly comes from collective units. Such institutions are classified as "collective-owned".

(c) Social organizations established by individual or a group of citizens, which are classified as "private".

(d) Social organizations other than those mentioned above whose source of budget is not clear. Such organizations are classified by way of management.

三、国民经济核算

National Accounts

简要说明

国民经济核算资料主要包括国内生产总值、投入产出表、资金流量表及国际收支概况四个部分。

一、国内生产总值

国内生产总值数据是由国家统计局国民经济核算司根据不同产业部门、不同支出构成的特点和资料来源情况而采用不同方法计算的。国民生产总值是在国内生产总值的基础上加上来自国外的净要素收入求得的。

本年鉴公布的国民经济核算资料，最后一年数据不是最终数，还会发生变动；如果遇到普查年，在能够获得更详细的基础资料的情况下，国内生产总值的历史数据也会发生变动。1995年，根据第一次全国第三产业普查结果，对国内生产总值的历史数据做了调整，年鉴中的数据是调整以后的数据。

本年鉴所列分地区的数据来自各省、自治区、直辖市统计局的国民经济核算资料，各地区数据相加不等于全国总计。

二、投入产出表

中国1997年投入产出表是由国家统计局国民经济核算司编制的。

投入产出表也称部门联系平衡表或产业关联表，它是根据国民经济各部门生产中的投入来源和使用去向纵横交叉组成的一张棋盘式平衡表。它可以用来揭示部门间经济技术的相互依存、相互制约的数量关系。

三、资金流量表

我国资金流量表表式与国际上通用的表式相似，是机构部门与交易项目的矩阵表式。主栏为交易项目，主要反映分配方式和融资工具；宾栏按机构部门分类。机构部门分类是根据机构单位具有的基本特征所进行的部门分类。资金流量表把参与资金活动的主体分为非金融企业、金融机构、一般政府、住户和国外五个部门。每一部门下设资金来源与资金运用两栏。现行的资金流量表分为两大部分，上半部分为实物交易部分，由国家统计局国民经济核算司编制；下半部分为金融交易部分，由中国人民银行调查统计司编制。

四、国际收支平衡表(国际收支概况)

国际收支平衡表(国际收支概况)由国家外汇管理局国际收支司编制。

依据国际货币基金组织编写的《国际收支统计手册》第五版，并按其要求编制国际收支平衡表。

Brief Introduction

Statistics on national accounts include mainly four components, namely, gross domestic product, input-output table, flow of fund table and balance of payment.

I. Gross Domestic Product

The data on GDP are calculated by the Department of National Economic Accounting, National Bureau of Statistics (NBS) with various approaches in the light of the features of various sectors, various expenditure structures and the data sources. The gross national product can be calculated on the base of GDP and the net factor income from abroad.

Data on the national accounts of the latest year published in the yearbook are not final and are subject to changes. When it happens to be a census year, the data of GDP of the past years may also be revised. In 1995, the GDP figures of the past years were adjusted in accordance with the result of the first tertiary industry census. Data published in this yearbook are the adjusted data.

Regional data in this yearbook are prepared according to the data of national accounts provided by the statistical bureaus of the provinces, autonomous regions and municipalities directly under the central government. The sum of the regional data is not equal to the national total.

II. Input-output Table

The 1997 input-output table of China included in this chapter are compiled by the Department of National Accounts of the National Bureau of Statistics.

Reflecting the sources of the input into, and the utilization of the output from production by various industries of the national economy. It is used to reveal, in quantitative terms, the interrelated and mutually dependent economic and technological relations between industries.

III. Flow of Fund Table

Similar to internationally accepted format, the flow of fund table of China constitutes a matrix of institutional sectors by transactions. Items of transactions are expressed as row headings representing forms of distribution and methods of financing. Institutional sectors are shown as column headings, grouped by the characteristics of the transactors. There are 5 groups of institutional sectors in the flow of fund table, namely, nonfinancial corporations, financial institutions, general governments, households, and the rest of the world. Under each sector there are 2 headings: source of fund and utilization of fund. The current flow of fund table is composed of two parts: the first part is the physical (real) transaction compiled by the National Accounts Department of the National Bureau of Statistics, and the second part is the financial transactions compiled by the Survey and Statistics Department of the People's Bank of China.

IV. Balance of Payment Table

The balance of payment table was compiled by the Balance of Payment Department of the State Administration of Foreign Exchanges. The methodology and standards in the 5th edition of the *Manual on Balance of Payment* were fully adopted in compiling balance of payment statistics since 1997.

3-1 国内生产总值

Gross Domestic Product

本表按当年价格计算。

Data in value terms in this table are calculated at current prices.

单位：亿元 (100 million yuan)

年份 Year	国民生产总值 Gross National Product	国内生产总值 Gross Domestic Product	第一产业 Primary Industry	第二产业 Secondary Industry	工业 Industry	建筑业 Construc-tion	第三产业 Tertiary Industry	#交通运输仓储邮电通信业 Transport, Post and Telecommuni-cation Services	#批发和零售贸易餐饮业 Wholesale, Retail Trade & Catering Services	人均国内生产总值(元) Per Capita GDP (yuan)
1952	679.0	679.0	342.9	141.8	119.8	22.0	194.3	29.0	80.3	119
1953	824.0	824.0	378.0	192.5	163.5	29.0	253.5	35.0	115.5	142
1954	859.0	859.0	392.0	211.7	184.7	27.0	255.3	38.0	120.3	144
1955	910.0	910.0	421.0	222.2	191.2	31.0	266.8	39.0	119.8	150
1956	1028.0	1028.0	443.9	280.7	224.7	56.0	303.4	46.0	131.4	165
1957	1068.0	1068.0	430.0	317.0	271.0	46.0	321.0	49.0	133.0	168
1958	1307.0	1307.0	445.9	483.5	414.5	69.0	377.6	71.0	136.6	200
1959	1439.0	1439.0	383.8	615.5	538.5	77.0	439.7	94.0	145.7	216
1960	1457.0	1457.0	340.7	648.2	568.2	80.0	468.1	104.0	133.1	218
1961	1220.0	1220.0	441.1	388.9	362.1	26.8	390.0	69.2	110.8	185
1962	1149.3	1149.3	453.1	359.3	325.4	33.9	336.9	57.4	80.5	173
1963	1233.3	1233.3	497.5	407.6	365.6	42.0	328.2	55.0	76.1	181
1964	1454.0	1454.0	559.0	513.5	461.1	52.4	381.5	58.4	94.0	208
1965	1716.1	1716.1	651.1	602.2	546.5	55.7	462.8	77.4	118.3	240
1966	1868.0	1868.0	702.2	709.5	648.6	60.9	456.3	85.1	148.1	254
1967	1773.9	1773.9	714.2	602.8	544.9	57.9	456.9	72.3	153.5	235
1968	1723.1	1723.1	726.3	537.3	490.3	47.0	459.5	70.5	138.9	222
1969	1937.9	1937.9	736.2	689.1	626.1	63.0	512.6	84.9	163.6	243
1970	2252.7	2252.7	793.3	912.2	828.1	84.1	547.2	100.2	178.1	275
1971	2426.4	2426.4	826.3	1022.8	926.6	96.2	577.3	108.4	178.3	288
1972	2518.1	2518.1	827.4	1084.2	989.9	94.3	606.5	118.0	194.3	292
1973	2720.9	2720.9	907.5	1173.0	1072.5	100.5	640.4	125.5	211.0	309
1974	2789.9	2789.9	945.2	1192.0	1083.6	108.4	652.7	126.1	206.6	310
1975	2997.3	2997.3	971.1	1370.5	1244.9	125.6	655.7	141.6	175.8	327
1976	2943.7	2943.7	967.0	1337.2	1204.6	132.6	639.5	139.6	147.2	316
1977	3201.9	3201.9	942.1	1509.1	1372.4	136.7	750.7	156.9	213.8	339
1978	3624.1	3624.1	1018.4	1745.2	1607.0	138.2	860.5	172.8	265.5	379
1979	4038.2	4038.2	1258.9	1913.5	1769.7	143.8	865.8	184.2	220.2	417
1980	4517.8	4517.8	1359.4	2192.0	1996.5	195.5	966.4	205.0	213.6	460
1981	4860.3	4862.4	1545.6	2255.5	2048.4	207.1	1061.3	211.1	255.7	489
1982	5301.8	5294.7	1761.6	2383.0	2162.3	220.7	1150.1	236.7	198.6	526
1983	5957.4	5934.5	1960.8	2646.2	2375.6	270.6	1327.5	264.9	231.4	582
1984	7206.7	7171.0	2295.5	3105.7	2789.0	316.7	1769.8	327.1	412.4	695
1985	8989.1	8964.4	2541.6	3866.6	3448.7	417.9	2556.2	406.9	878.4	855
1986	10201.4	10202.2	2763.9	4492.7	3967.0	525.7	2945.6	475.6	943.2	956
1987	11954.5	11962.5	3204.3	5251.6	4585.8	665.8	3506.6	544.9	1159.3	1103
1988	14922.3	14928.3	3831.0	6587.2	5777.2	810.0	4510.1	661.0	1618.0	1355
1989	16917.8	16909.2	4228.0	7278.0	6484.0	794.0	5403.2	786.0	1687.0	1512
1990	18598.4	18547.9	5017.0	7717.4	6858.0	859.4	5813.5	1147.5	1419.7	1634
1991	21662.5	21617.8	5288.6	9102.2	8087.1	1015.1	7227.0	1409.7	2087.0	1879
1992	26651.9	26638.1	5800.0	11699.5	10284.5	1415.0	9138.6	1681.8	2735.0	2287
1993	34560.5	34634.4	6882.1	16428.5	14143.8	2284.7	11323.8	2123.2	3090.7	2939
1994	46670.0	46759.4	9457.2	22372.2	19359.6	3012.6	14930.0	2685.9	4050.4	3923
1995	57494.9	58478.1	11993.0	28537.9	24718.3	3819.6	17947.2	3054.7	4932.3	4854
1996	66850.5	67884.6	13844.2	33612.9	29082.6	4530.5	20427.5	3494.0	5560.3	5576
1997	73142.7	74462.6	14211.2	37222.7	32412.1	4810.6	23028.7	3797.2	6159.9	6054
1998	76967.2	78345.2	14552.4	38619.3	33387.9	5231.4	25173.5	4121.3	6579.1	6307
1999	80579.4	82067.5	14472.0	40557.8	35087.2	5470.6	27037.7	4460.3	6910.3	6547
2000	88189.6	89403.6	14212.0	45487.8	39570.3	5917.5	29703.8	4918.6	7306.9	7078

注：1980年以后一、二、三产业之和与国民生产总值的差额为国外净要素收入。

a)Since 1980, the difference between the total of primary, secondary & tertiary industries and the gross national product has been the net factor income from abroad.

3-2 国内生产总值构成
Composition of Gross Domestic Product

本表按当年价格计算。

Data in value terms in this table are calculated at current prices.

单位：% (%)

年份 Year	国内生产总值 Gross Domestic Product	第一产业 Primary Industry	第二产业 Secondary Industry	工业 Industry	建筑业 Construction	第三产业 Tertiary Industry	#交通运输仓储邮电通信业 Transport, Post and Telecommunication Services	#批发和零售贸易餐饮业 Wholesale, Retail Trade & Catering Services
1952	100.0	50.5	20.9	17.6	3.2	28.6	4.3	11.8
1953	100.0	45.9	23.4	19.8	3.5	30.8	4.2	14.0
1954	100.0	45.6	24.6	21.5	3.1	29.7	4.4	14.0
1955	100.0	46.3	24.4	21.0	3.4	29.3	4.3	13.2
1956	100.0	43.2	27.3	21.9	5.4	29.5	4.5	12.8
1957	100.0	40.3	29.7	25.4	4.3	30.1	4.6	12.5
1958	100.0	34.1	37.0	31.7	5.3	28.9	5.4	10.5
1959	100.0	26.7	42.8	37.4	5.4	30.6	6.5	10.1
1960	100.0	23.4	44.5	39.0	5.5	32.1	7.1	9.1
1961	100.0	36.2	31.9	29.7	2.2	32.0	5.7	9.1
1962	100.0	39.4	31.3	28.3	2.9	29.3	5.0	7.0
1963	100.0	40.3	33.0	29.6	3.4	26.6	4.5	6.2
1964	100.0	38.4	35.3	31.7	3.6	26.2	4.0	6.5
1965	100.0	37.9	35.1	31.8	3.2	27.0	4.5	6.9
1966	100.0	37.6	38.0	34.7	3.3	24.4	4.6	7.9
1967	100.0	40.3	34.0	30.7	3.3	25.8	4.1	8.7
1968	100.0	42.2	31.2	28.5	2.7	26.7	4.1	8.1
1969	100.0	38.0	35.6	32.3	3.3	26.5	4.4	8.4
1970	100.0	35.2	40.5	36.8	3.7	24.3	4.4	7.9
1971	100.0	34.1	42.2	38.2	4.0	23.8	4.5	7.3
1972	100.0	32.9	43.1	39.3	3.7	24.1	4.7	7.7
1973	100.0	33.4	43.1	39.4	3.7	23.5	4.6	7.8
1974	100.0	33.9	42.7	38.8	3.9	23.4	4.5	7.4
1975	100.0	32.4	45.7	41.5	4.2	21.9	4.7	5.9
1976	100.0	32.8	45.4	40.9	4.5	21.7	4.7	5.0
1977	100.0	29.4	47.1	42.9	4.3	23.4	4.9	6.7
1978	100.0	28.1	48.2	44.3	3.8	23.7	4.8	7.3
1979	100.0	31.2	47.4	43.8	3.6	21.4	4.6	5.5
1980	100.0	30.1	48.5	44.2	4.3	21.4	4.5	4.7
1981	100.0	31.8	46.4	42.1	4.3	21.8	4.3	5.3
1982	100.0	33.3	45.0	40.8	4.2	21.7	4.5	3.8
1983	100.0	33.0	44.6	40.0	4.6	22.4	4.5	3.9
1984	100.0	32.0	43.3	38.9	4.4	24.7	4.6	5.8
1985	100.0	28.4	43.1	38.5	4.7	28.5	4.5	9.8
1986	100.0	27.1	44.0	38.9	5.2	28.9	4.7	9.2
1987	100.0	26.8	43.9	38.3	5.6	29.3	4.6	9.7
1988	100.0	25.7	44.1	38.7	5.4	30.2	4.4	10.8
1989	100.0	25.0	43.0	38.3	4.7	32.0	4.6	10.0
1990	100.0	27.1	41.6	37.0	4.6	31.3	6.2	7.7
1991	100.0	24.5	42.1	37.4	4.7	33.4	6.5	9.7
1992	100.0	21.8	43.9	38.6	5.3	34.3	6.3	10.3
1993	100.0	19.9	47.4	40.8	6.6	32.7	6.1	8.9
1994	100.0	20.2	47.9	41.4	6.4	31.9	5.7	8.7
1995	100.0	20.5	48.8	42.3	6.5	30.7	5.2	8.4
1996	100.0	20.4	49.5	42.8	6.7	30.1	5.1	8.2
1997	100.0	19.1	50.0	43.5	6.5	30.9	5.1	8.3
1998	100.0	18.6	49.3	42.6	6.7	32.1	5.3	8.4
1999	100.0	17.6	49.4	42.7	6.7	33.0	5.4	8.4
2000	100.0	15.9	50.9	44.3	6.6	33.2	5.5	8.2

3-3 国内生产总值指数

Indices of Gross Domestic Product

本表按可比价格计算。

The indices in this table are calculated at comparable prices.

(上年=100) (preceding year=100)

年 份 Year	国民生产总值 Gross National Product	国内生产总值 Gross Domestic Product	第一产业 Primary Industry	第二产业 Secondary Industry	工 业 Industry	建筑业 Construction	第三产业 Tertiary Industry	#交通运输仓储邮电通信业 Transport, Post and Tele-communication Services	#批发和零售贸易餐饮业 Wholesale, Retail Trade & Catering Services	人均国内生产总值 Per Capita GDP
1953	115.6	115.6	101.9	135.8	135.7	136.4	127.3	124.1	138.0	113.1
1954	104.2	104.2	101.7	115.7	119.3	96.7	99.4	110.8	101.8	101.8
1955	106.8	106.8	107.9	107.6	106.6	113.8	104.6	102.5	99.9	104.5
1956	115.0	115.0	104.7	134.5	128.6	170.0	114.1	121.8	108.5	112.7
1957	105.1	105.1	103.1	108.0	111.4	92.9	104.8	107.2	98.9	102.4
1958	121.3	121.3	100.4	152.9	153.4	150.0	117.9	146.7	103.6	118.3
1959	108.8	108.8	84.1	125.8	129.1	105.7	115.2	131.0	105.9	106.7
1960	99.7	99.7	83.6	105.6	106.1	101.4	104.8	110.4	91.2	99.5
1961	72.7	72.7	101.4	57.9	61.0	34.6	74.3	65.0	73.0	73.4
1962	94.4	94.4	104.5	89.2	86.7	123.8	90.8	81.1	96.0	93.6
1963	110.2	110.2	111.3	114.5	113.3	125.9	104.4	98.4	108.2	107.5
1964	118.3	118.3	112.9	125.6	125.6	125.6	115.5	105.4	113.2	115.5
1965	117.0	117.0	109.7	124.2	125.8	110.6	115.8	134.5	99.5	114.3
1966	110.7	110.7	107.2	122.4	123.8	109.4	98.2	110.3	120.4	107.7
1967	94.3	94.3	101.9	85.7	84.9	95.0	100.5	86.0	104.1	91.9
1968	95.9	95.9	98.4	90.8	91.8	81.1	100.6	97.7	90.7	93.4
1969	116.9	116.9	100.8	133.1	133.0	134.5	113.3	122.7	119.2	113.7
1970	119.4	119.4	107.7	134.8	135.2	130.4	107.1	116.8	109.4	116.1
1971	107.0	107.0	101.9	112.3	112.3	112.1	105.8	108.3	99.9	104.1
1972	103.8	103.8	99.1	106.7	107.6	97.9	105.0	109.6	108.8	101.2
1973	107.9	107.9	109.0	108.3	108.8	103.4	105.5	106.3	109.0	105.4
1974	102.3	102.3	104.1	101.4	101.0	106.2	101.6	100.3	98.0	100.2
1975	108.7	108.7	102.0	115.8	116.0	113.8	104.9	111.4	99.9	106.8
1976	98.4	98.4	98.2	97.5	96.9	104.3	100.4	98.4	96.3	96.9
1977	107.6	107.6	97.8	113.3	114.4	101.7	109.5	112.6	113.4	106.2
1978	111.7	111.7	104.1	115.0	116.4	99.4	113.7	108.9	123.1	110.2
1979	107.6	107.6	106.1	108.2	108.7	102.0	107.8	107.7	108.8	106.1
1980	107.8	107.8	98.5	113.6	112.7	126.7	105.9	105.7	98.7	106.5
1981	105.2	105.2	107.0	101.9	101.7	103.2	110.4	101.9	130.0	103.9
1982	109.3	109.1	111.5	105.6	105.8	103.4	113.0	111.7	103.9	107.5
1983	111.1	110.9	108.3	110.4	109.7	117.1	115.2	110.0	121.9	109.3
1984	115.3	115.2	112.9	114.5	114.9	110.9	119.4	115.0	121.5	113.7
1985	113.2	113.5	101.8	118.6	118.2	122.2	118.3	113.5	128.9	111.9
1986	108.5	108.8	103.3	110.2	109.6	115.9	112.1	112.8	110.6	107.2
1987	111.5	111.6	104.7	113.7	113.2	117.9	114.4	110.0	113.5	109.8
1988	111.3	111.3	102.5	114.5	115.3	108.0	113.2	113.3	114.3	109.5
1989	104.2	104.1	103.1	103.8	105.1	91.6	105.4	104.7	91.7	102.5
1990	104.2	103.8	107.3	103.2	103.4	101.2	102.3	108.6	95.2	102.3
1991	109.1	109.2	102.4	113.9	114.4	109.6	108.8	111.2	104.5	107.7
1992	114.1	114.2	104.7	121.2	121.2	121.0	112.4	110.5	113.1	112.8
1993	113.1	113.5	104.7	119.9	120.1	118.0	110.7	112.4	106.6	112.2
1994	112.6	112.6	104.0	118.4	118.9	113.7	109.6	109.5	107.7	111.4
1995	109.0	110.5	105.0	113.9	114.0	112.4	108.4	112.0	105.9	109.3
1996	109.8	109.6	105.1	112.1	112.5	108.5	107.9	111.4	105.4	108.4
1997	108.6	108.8	103.5	110.5	111.3	102.6	109.1	110.8	108.5	107.7
1998	107.8	107.8	103.5	108.9	108.9	109.0	108.3	110.6	107.7	106.8
1999	107.2	107.1	102.8	108.1	108.5	104.3	107.7	111.3	107.2	106.2
2000	108.3	108.0	102.4	109.6	109.9	106.2	107.8	109.4	108.4	107.1

3-4 国内生产总值指数

Indices of Gross Domestic Product

本表按可比价格计算。

The indices in this table are calculated at comparable prices.

(1978=100)

年 份 Year	国民生产总值 Gross National Product	国内生产总值 Gross Domestic Product	第一产业 Primary Industry	第二产业 Secondary Industry	工 业 Industry	建筑业 Construc-tion	第三产业 Tertiary Industry	#交通运输仓储邮电通信业 Transport, Post and Tele-communications Services	# 批发和零售贸易餐饮业 Wholesale, Retail Trade & Catering Services	人均国内生产总值 Per Capita GDP
1978	100.0	100.0	100.0	100.0	100.0	100.0	100.0	100.0	100.0	100.0
1979	107.6	107.6	106.1	108.2	108.7	102.0	107.8	107.7	108.8	106.1
1980	116.0	116.0	104.6	122.9	122.4	129.2	114.2	113.8	107.4	113.0
1981	122.0	122.1	111.9	125.2	124.5	133.3	126.2	116.0	139.6	117.5
1982	133.3	133.1	124.8	132.1	131.7	137.9	142.6	129.5	145.1	126.2
1983	148.2	147.6	135.1	145.8	144.5	161.4	164.3	142.5	176.8	137.9
1984	170.9	170.0	152.6	166.9	166.0	179.0	196.1	163.8	214.8	156.8
1985	193.5	192.9	155.4	197.9	196.2	218.7	231.9	185.9	276.8	175.5
1986	209.9	210.0	160.5	218.2	215.2	253.4	260.0	209.7	306.1	188.2
1987	234.1	234.3	168.1	248.1	243.6	298.7	297.4	230.7	347.3	206.6
1988	260.5	260.7	172.3	284.1	280.8	322.5	336.7	261.5	396.9	226.3
1989	271.5	271.3	177.6	294.8	295.0	295.3	354.8	273.8	363.8	231.9
1990	283.0	281.7	190.7	304.1	304.9	298.8	363.0	297.2	346.5	237.3
1991	308.8	307.6	195.2	346.3	348.8	327.4	395.0	330.5	362.1	255.6
1992	352.2	351.4	204.4	419.5	422.6	396.2	444.0	365.2	409.4	288.4
1993	398.4	398.8	214.0	502.8	507.5	467.5	491.3	410.5	436.4	323.6
1994	448.7	449.3	222.6	595.2	603.5	531.5	538.3	449.5	469.9	360.4
1995	489.1	496.5	233.7	677.7	688.2	597.4	583.4	503.4	497.6	394.0
1996	536.8	544.1	245.6	759.8	774.3	648.2	629.4	561.1	524.3	427.1
1997	582.9	592.2	254.2	839.4	861.9	665.2	687.1	621.4	568.8	460.3
1998	628.4	638.5	263.1	914.2	938.6	725.2	744.1	687.5	612.7	491.5
1999	673.5	684.1	270.5	988.6	1018.6	756.2	801.6	765.0	656.9	521.8
2000	729.6	738.8	277.0	1083.7	1119.9	802.9	864.1	836.9	712.2	558.7

3–5 第三产业增加值

Value-added of the Tertiary Industry

本表按当年价格计算。

Data in value terms in this table are calculated at current prices.

单位：亿元 (100 million yuan)

行业	Sector	1991	1992	1993	1994	1995	1996	1997	1998	1999
总计	**Total**	**7227.0**	**9138.6**	**11323.8**	**14930.0**	**17947.2**	**20427.5**	**23028.7**	**25173.5**	**27037.7**
农、林、牧、渔服务业	Farming, Forestry, Animal Husbandry and Fishery	53.6	66.6	76.5	101.3	115.8	129.6	177.3	199.6	221.9
地质勘查业水利管理业	Geological Prospecting and Water Conservancy	76.8	98.0	134.5	191.2	253.3	280.2	302.3	302.1	316.2
交通运输、仓储及邮电通信业	Transport, Storage, Post and Telecommunication Services	1409.7	1681.8	2123.2	2685.9	3054.7	3494.0	3797.2	4121.3	4460.3
交通运输和仓储业	Transport and Storage	1261.7	1488.0	1823.5	2204.3	2378.0	2626.6	2689.6	2886.2	3058.1
邮电通信业	Post and Telecommunications	148.0	193.8	299.7	481.6	676.7	867.4	1107.6	1235.1	1402.2
批发和零售贸易餐饮业	Wholesale and Retail Trade and Catering Services	2087.0	2735.0	3090.7	4050.4	4932.3	5560.3	6159.9	6579.1	6910.3
金融、保险业	Finance and Insurance	1288.1	1601.0	2057.0	2767.2	3482.8	4017.4	4534.6	4672.6	4847.3
房地产业	Real Estate	368.2	521.1	640.7	870.3	1058.6	1149.3	1258.8	1452.6	1528.4
社会服务业	Social Services	447.3	599.7	899.2	1200.5	1546.4	1717.7	2177.9	2649.3	2893.7
卫生体育和社会福利业	Health Care, Sports and Social Welfare	215.2	264.0	333.7	433.8	483.2	564.2	617.1	687.2	742.7
教育、文化艺术及广播电影电视业	Education, Culture and Arts, Radio, Film and Television	454.9	547.7	709.9	977.6	1124.5	1354.9	1573.2	1823.9	2098.0
科学研究和综合技术服务业	Scientific Research and Polytechnic Services	97.5	125.0	151.8	213.4	277.1	335.7	434.1	470.8	556.6
国家机关、政党机关和社会团体	Government Agencies, Parties Agencies and Social Organizations	662.1	809.7	986.4	1279.1	1438.0	1615.3	1763.9	1969.1	2201.2
其他行业	Others	66.6	89.0	120.2	159.3	180.5	208.9	232.4	245.9	261.2

3-6 第三产业增加值构成

Composition of Value-added of the Tertiary Industry

本表按当年价格计算。

Data in value terms in this table are calculated at current prices.

单位：%

(%)

行业	Sector	1991	1992	1993	1994	1995	1996	1997	1998	1999
总 计	**Total**	**100.0**	**100.0**	**100.0**	**100.0**	**100.0**	**100.0**	**100.0**	**100.0**	**100.0**
农、林、牧、渔服务业	Farming, Forestry, Animal Husbandry and Fishery	0.7	0.7	0.7	0.7	0.6	0.6	0.8	0.8	0.8
地质勘查业水利管理业	Geological Prospecting and Water Conservancy	1.1	1.1	1.2	1.3	1.4	1.4	1.3	1.2	1.2
交通运输、仓储及邮电通信业	Transport, Storage, Post and Telecommunication Services	19.5	18.4	18.7	18.0	17.0	17.1	16.5	16.4	16.5
交通运输和仓储业	Transport and Storage	17.5	16.3	16.1	14.8	13.2	12.9	11.7	11.5	11.3
邮电通信业	Post and Telecommunications	2.0	2.1	2.6	3.2	3.8	4.2	4.8	4.9	5.2
批发和零售贸易餐饮业	Wholesale and Retail Trade and Catering Services	28.9	29.9	27.3	27.1	27.5	27.2	26.7	26.1	25.6
金融、保险业	Finance and Insurance	17.8	17.5	18.2	18.5	19.4	19.7	19.7	18.6	17.9
房地产业	Real Estate	5.1	5.7	5.7	5.8	5.9	5.6	5.5	5.8	5.7
社会服务业	Social Services	6.2	6.6	7.9	8.0	8.6	8.4	9.5	10.5	10.7
卫生体育和社会福利业	Health Care, Sports and Social Welfare	3.0	2.9	2.9	2.9	2.7	2.8	2.7	2.7	2.7
教育、文化艺术及广播电影电视业	Education, Culture and Arts, Radio, Film and Television	6.3	6.0	6.3	6.5	6.3	6.6	6.8	7.2	7.8
科学研究和综合技术服务业	Scientific Research and Polytechnic Services	1.3	1.4	1.3	1.4	1.5	1.6	1.9	1.9	2.1
国家机关、政党机关和社会团体	Government Agencies, Parties Agencies and Social Organizations	9.2	8.9	8.7	8.6	8.0	7.9	7.7	7.8	8.1
其他行业	Others	0.9	1.0	1.1	1.1	1.0	1.0	1.0	1.0	1.0

3-7 第三产业增加值指数

Indices of Value-added of the Tertiary Industry

本表按可比价格计算。

The indices in this table are calculated at comparable prices.

(上年=100) (preceding year=100)

行 业	Sector	1991	1992	1993	1994	1995	1996	1997	1998	1999
总 计	**Total**	**108.8**	**112.4**	**110.7**	**109.6**	**108.4**	**107.9**	**109.1**	**108.3**	**107.7**
农、林、牧、渔服务业	Farming, Forestry, Animal Husbandry and Fishery	110.7	110.4	102.2	110.3	108.7	105.8	132.5	113.4	106.3
地质勘查业水利管理业	Geological Prospecting and Water Conservancy	110.9	115.1	111.2	116.3	105.4	105.1	104.3	100.7	106.2
交通运输、仓储及邮电通信业	Transport, Storage, Post and Telecommunication Services	111.2	110.5	112.4	109.5	112.1	111.4	110.8	110.6	111.3
交通运输和仓储业	Transport and Storage	108.6	107.9	105.9	107.1	105.0	103.8	105.3	102.0	105.6
邮电通信业	Post and Telecommunications	135.5	130.3	153.3	120.1	139.0	134.1	123.1	127.4	120.1
批发和零售贸易餐饮业	Wholesale and Retail Trade and Catering Services	104.5	113.1	106.6	107.7	105.9	105.4	108.5	107.7	107.2
金融、保险业	Finance and Insurance	102.3	108.0	110.9	109.4	108.5	107.5	108.5	104.9	104.8
房地产业	Real Estate	112.0	134.7	110.8	112.0	112.4	104.0	104.1	107.7	105.9
社会服务业	Social Services	126.8	119.3	118.9	108.3	105.8	105.0	107.9	110.6	108.1
卫生体育和社会福利业	Health Care, Sports and Social Welfare	114.9	109.4	111.8	108.2	106.4	110.3	108.1	107.8	104.6
教育、文化艺术及广播电影电视业	Education, Culture and Arts, Radio, Film and Television	107.8	108.0	114.9	115.0	108.0	113.9	114.8	110.2	107.2
科学研究和综合技术服务业	Scientific Research and Polytechnic Services	112.0	115.3	106.9	117.9	110.5	114.0	112.1	110.8	110.5
国家机关、政党机关和社会团体	Government Agencies, Parties Agencies and Social Organizations	114.5	108.6	107.7	108.3	106.0	106.2	107.0	108.3	108.6
其他行业	Others	114.8	119.5	117.9	110.6	108.6	109.5	110.2	108.1	106.5

3-8 各地区国内生产总值和指数

Gross Domestic Product and Its Indices by Region

本表绝对数按当年价格计算，指数按可比价格计算。

Absolute figures in this table are calculated at current prices while indices are calculated at comparable prices.

地区	Region	国内生产总值（亿元） Gross Domestic Product (100 million yuan)				指数（上年=100） Indices (preceding year=100)			
		1997	1998	1999	2000	1997	1998	1999	2000
北京	Beijing	1810.09	2011.31	2174.46	2478.76	109.6	109.8	110.2	111.0
天津	Tianjin	1235.28	1336.38	1450.06	1639.36	112.1	109.3	110.0	110.8
河北	Hebei	3953.78	4256.01	4569.19	5088.96	112.5	110.7	109.1	109.5
山西	Shanxi	1480.13	1486.08	1506.78	1643.81	110.5	109.0	105.1	107.8
内蒙古	Inner Mongolia	1099.77	1192.29	1268.20	1401.01	109.7	109.6	107.8	109.7
辽宁	Liaoning	3582.46	3881.73	4171.69	4669.06	108.9	108.3	108.2	108.9
吉林	Jilin	1446.91	1557.78	1660.91	1821.19	109.2	109.0	108.1	109.2
黑龙江	Heilongjiang	2708.46	2798.89	2897.41	3253.00	110.0	108.3	107.5	108.2
上海	Shanghai	3360.21	3688.20	4034.96	4551.15	112.7	110.1	110.2	110.8
江苏	Jiangsu	6680.34	7199.95	7697.82	8582.73	112.0	111.0	110.1	110.6
浙江	Zhejiang	4638.24	4987.50	5364.89	6036.34	111.1	110.1	110.0	111.0
安徽	Anhui	2669.95	2805.45	2908.58	3038.24	112.7	108.5	108.1	108.3
福建	Fujian	3000.36	3286.56	3550.24	3920.07	114.5	111.4	110.0	109.5
江西	Jiangxi	1715.18	1851.98	1853.65	2003.07	111.5	108.2	107.8	108.0
山东	Shandong	6650.02	7162.20	7662.10	8542.44	111.2	110.8	110.1	110.5
河南	Henan	4079.26	4356.60	4576.10	5137.66	110.4	108.7	108.0	109.4
湖北	Hubei	3450.24	3704.21	3857.99	4276.32	113.0	110.3	108.3	109.3
湖南	Hunan	2993.00	3118.09	3326.75	3691.88	110.8	109.1	108.3	109.0
广东	Guangdong	7315.51	7919.12	8464.31	9662.23	110.6	110.2	109.5	110.8
广西	Guangxi	1817.25	1903.04	1953.27	2050.14	108.1	109.1	107.7	107.3
海南	Hainan	409.86	438.92	471.23	518.48	106.7	108.3	108.6	108.8
重庆	Chongqing	1350.10	1429.26	1479.71	1589.34	111.0	108.4	107.6	108.5
四川	Sichuan	3320.11	3580.26	3711.61	4010.25	110.2	109.1	105.6	109.0
贵州	Guizhou	792.98	841.88	911.86	993.53	109.0	108.5	108.3	108.7
云南	Yunnan	1644.23	1793.90	1855.74	1955.09	109.4	108.0	107.2	107.1
西藏	Tibet	76.98	91.18	105.61	117.46	111.3	110.2	109.6	109.4
陕西	Shaanxi	1300.03	1381.53	1487.61	1660.92	109.2	109.1	108.4	109.0
甘肃	Gansu	781.34	869.75	931.98	983.36	108.5	109.2	108.3	108.7
青海	Qinghai	202.05	220.16	238.39	263.59	109.0	109.0	108.2	109.0
宁夏	Ningxia	210.92	227.46	241.49	265.57	107.6	108.5	108.7	109.8
新疆	Xinjiang	1050.14	1116.67	1168.55	1364.36	111.0	107.3	107.1	108.2

3-9 各地区国内生产总值（2000年）

Gross Domestic Product by Region (2000)

本表绝对数按当年价格计算，指数按可比价格计算。

Absolute figures in this table are calculated at current prices while indices are calculated at comparable prices.

单位：亿元 (100 million yuan)

地区	Region	国内生产总值 Gross Domestic Product	第一产业 Primary Industry	第二产业 Secondary Industry	工业 Industry	建筑业 Construction	第三产业 Tertiary Industry	农林牧渔服务业 Farming, Forestry, Animal Husbandry and Fishery Services	地质勘查业水利管理业 Geological Prospecting and Water Conservancy
北京	Beijing	2478.76	89.97	943.51	745.32	198.19	1445.28	2.25	5.33
天津	Tianjin	1639.36	73.54	820.17	747.28	72.89	745.65	1.68	9.17
河北	Hebei	5088.96	824.55	2559.96	2246.73	313.23	1704.45	7.12	21.61
山西	Shanxi	1643.81	179.86	827.59	706.39	121.20	636.36	7.67	12.97
内蒙古	Inner Mongolia	1401.01	350.80	556.28	455.21	101.07	493.93	4.68	6.27
辽宁	Liaoning	4669.06	503.44	2344.40	2114.89	229.51	1821.22	14.01	8.29
吉林	Jilin	1821.19	398.73	800.28	655.68	144.60	622.18	3.41	4.21
黑龙江	Heilongjiang	3253.00	357.00	1868.55	1664.35	204.20	1027.45	10.06	13.93
上海	Shanghai	4551.15	83.20	2163.68	1956.66	207.02	2304.27	4.55	8.55
江苏	Jiangsu	8582.73	1031.17	4435.89	3848.52	587.37	3115.67	37.17	22.90
浙江	Zhejiang	6036.34	664.16	3183.47	2883.37	300.10	2188.71	6.40	7.16
安徽	Anhui	3038.24	732.19	1296.31	1100.45	195.86	1009.73	9.76	12.35
福建	Fujian	3920.07	640.57	1711.16	1470.07	241.09	1568.34	6.14	6.18
江西	Jiangxi	2003.07	485.14	700.76	539.78	160.98	817.17	7.23	8.22
山东	Shandong	8542.44	1268.57	4244.40	3737.38	507.02	3029.47	15.52	17.85
河南	Henan	5137.66	1161.58	2413.78	2078.94	334.84	1562.30	6.10	30.30
湖北	Hubei	4276.32	662.30	2123.70	1903.28	220.42	1490.32	5.38	8.89
湖南	Hunan	3691.88	784.92	1461.86	1230.71	231.15	1445.10	9.12	15.00
广东	Guangdong	9662.23	1000.06	4868.75	4295.03	573.72	3793.42	18.97	25.19
广西	Guangxi	2050.14	538.69	748.00	619.84	128.16	763.45	5.21	4.30
海南	Hainan	518.48	196.56	102.45	65.76	36.69	219.47	1.05	2.69
重庆	Chongqing	1589.34	283.00	657.51	527.48	130.03	648.83	4.83	3.07
四川	Sichuan	4010.25	945.58	1700.49	1393.84	306.65	1364.18	13.43	11.24
贵州	Guizhou	993.53	270.99	387.85	314.73	73.12	334.69	3.44	1.93
云南	Yunnan	1955.09	436.26	843.24	697.69	145.55	675.59	8.08	6.65
西藏	Tibet	117.46	36.32	27.21	10.13	17.08	53.93	2.23	1.30
陕西	Shaanxi	1660.92	279.12	731.90	549.58	182.32	649.90	6.32	11.86
甘肃	Gansu	983.36	193.36	439.88	328.41	111.47	350.12	5.08	9.53
青海	Qinghai	263.59	38.53	114.00	80.55	33.45	111.06	1.59	4.11
宁夏	Ningxia	265.57	45.95	120.04	93.00	27.04	99.58	1.59	2.75
新疆	Xinjiang	1364.36	288.18	586.84	422.08	164.76	489.34	5.83	13.12

3-9 续表 1

单位：亿元

地　区	Region	交通运输仓储及邮电通信业 Transport, Storage, Post and Telecommunication Services	批发零售贸易及餐饮业 Wholesale, Retail Trade and Catering Services	金融、保险业 Finance and Insurance	房地产业 Real Estate	社　会服务业 Social Services	卫生体育和社会福利业 Health Care, Sports and Social Welfare	教育、文化艺术及广播电影电视业 Education, Culture, Arts, Radio, Film and Television	科学研究和综合技术服务事业 Scientific Research and Polytechnic Services
北　京	Beijing	190.12	218.54	378.89	77.37	191.18	43.19	148.42	102.87
天　津	Tianjin	178.83	158.56	55.80	69.35	104.98	29.08	61.90	25.54
河　北	Hebei	415.79	459.00	183.77	99.53	115.47	47.79	113.93	19.25
山　西	Shanxi	146.01	135.19	103.59	29.39	43.36	17.33	47.25	7.31
内蒙古	Inner Mongolia	142.59	133.45	24.27	17.63	43.20	17.39	40.35	5.87
辽　宁	Liaoning	350.46	631.64	127.91	103.56	237.97	75.34	111.75	40.19
吉　林	Jilin	119.10	153.74	62.15	45.83	52.60	24.27	53.43	30.30
黑龙江	Heilongjiang	203.13	320.00	32.04	104.70	104.35	41.90	74.43	16.21
上　海	Shanghai	315.42	485.30	685.03	251.70	221.45	62.94	137.66	58.88
江　苏	Jiangsu	557.37	857.57	430.68	351.92	265.25	92.16	203.85	30.42
浙　江	Zhejiang	428.30	827.78	209.25	116.90	220.20	80.89	135.76	16.28
安　徽	Anhui	179.85	315.00	100.00	114.29	98.19	35.11	72.59	8.43
福　建	Fujian	444.13	384.17	187.85	118.02	159.83	41.82	100.96	11.75
江　西	Jiangxi	194.98	181.96	98.84	89.76	52.76	20.44	57.58	6.50
山　东	Shandong	553.17	785.68	450.94	309.99	174.51	111.41	209.50	28.75
河　南	Henan	391.88	380.66	125.30	154.71	119.72	67.37	110.86	16.40
湖　北	Hubei	256.94	442.82	205.99	87.75	146.79	71.24	106.67	26.58
湖　南	Hunan	277.69	348.10	140.70	97.14	82.87	77.11	154.16	17.38
广　东	Guangdong	908.45	968.99	371.53	515.52	477.01	94.36	183.81	32.15
广　西	Guangxi	160.87	277.73	20.42	46.12	54.16	37.33	69.33	6.14
海　南	Hainan	46.97	68.97	33.56	9.32	23.68	5.14	14.89	1.56
重　庆	Chongqing	98.19	154.46	68.62	51.92	101.67	23.40	51.09	27.49
四　川	Sichuan	249.39	381.59	170.46	105.49	130.14	56.58	97.02	20.26
贵　州	Guizhou	64.59	77.62	33.12	27.58	26.71	17.88	33.71	4.09
云　南	Yunnan	119.77	199.63	69.00	71.09	44.00	35.50	60.45	10.00
西　藏	Tibet	2.12	14.15	2.45	2.18	3.96	3.46	6.89	0.85
陕　西	Shaanxi	156.18	113.21	29.51	35.85	65.61	24.55	71.68	15.39
甘　肃	Gansu	50.07	114.24	55.87	24.77	14.92	11.43	22.36	9.17
青　海	Qinghai	19.19	21.37	16.20	4.06	6.26	4.07	11.98	1.58
宁　夏	Ningxia	19.31	21.60	15.49	5.46	5.43	3.77	9.64	1.23
新　疆	Xinjiang	121.79	118.08	42.23	15.00	43.90	14.08	54.17	5.44

continued

(100 million yuan)

国家机关、政党机关和社会团体 Government Agencies, Party Agencies and Social Organizations	其他行业 Others	构成% Composition			指数 Indices 1999=100				人均国内生产总值（元） Per Capita GDP (yuan)
		第一产业 Primary Industry	第二产业 Secondary Industry	第三产业 Tertiary Industry	国内生产总值 Gross Domestic Product	第一产业 Primary Industry	第二产业 Secondary Industry	第三产业 Tertiary Industry	
70.01	17.11	3.6	38.1	58.3	111.0	104.0	111.4	111.1	22460
46.27	4.49	4.5	50.0	45.5	110.8	103.7	111.5	110.5	17993
169.25	51.94	16.2	50.3	33.5	109.5	105.1	110.1	110.4	7663
83.26	3.03	10.9	50.3	38.7	107.8	110.7	107.9	106.7	5137
45.48	12.75	25.0	39.7	35.3	109.7	102.6	112.1	111.8	5872
107.01	13.09	10.8	50.2	39.0	108.9	98.4	110.7	109.6	11226
56.15	16.99	21.9	43.9	34.2	109.2	97.0	113.4	111.7	6847
84.02	22.68	11.0	57.4	31.6	108.2	96.8	109.8	111.8	8562
64.71	8.08	1.8	47.5	50.6	110.8	103.4	109.8	112.9	34547
235.08	31.29	12.0	51.7	36.3	110.6	103.9	111.6	111.2	11773
126.71	13.08	11.0	52.7	36.3	111.0	104.5	111.7	111.9	13461
59.51	4.65	24.1	42.7	33.2	108.3	101.2	109.9	110.3	4867
98.21	9.28	16.3	43.7	40.0	109.5	102.6	111.2	110.2	11601
82.50	16.40	24.2	35.0	40.8	108.0	106.8	106.7	110.4	4851
243.84	128.31	14.9	49.7	35.5	110.5	103.8	112.4	110.3	9555
146.54	12.46	22.6	47.0	30.4	109.4	104.5	111.7	109.3	5444
129.52	1.75	15.5	49.7	34.9	109.3	102.5	110.8	110.6	7188
203.67	22.16	21.3	39.6	39.1	109.0	103.9	110.6	110.6	5639
162.23	35.21	10.4	50.4	39.3	110.8	102.4	111.7	111.8	12885
65.86	15.98	26.3	36.5	37.2	107.3	100.2	109.0	111.5	4319
11.29	0.35	37.9	19.8	42.3	108.8	110.2	107.5	108.2	6894
63.08	1.01	17.8	41.4	40.8	108.5	101.5	110.5	109.5	5157
116.97	11.61	23.6	42.4	34.0	109.0	103.3	111.1	110.2	4784
38.41	5.61	27.3	39.0	33.7	108.7	103.6	110.3	110.5	2662
44.51	6.91	22.3	43.1	34.6	107.1	105.7	105.7	109.7	4637
14.29	0.05	30.9	23.2	45.9	109.4	102.1	114.1	112.9	4559
66.36	53.38	16.8	44.1	39.1	109.0	104.5	109.7	110.3	4549
23.21	9.47	19.7	44.7	35.6	108.7	101.5	110.8	109.6	3838
19.14	1.51	14.6	43.2	42.1	109.0	96.0	111.5	111.3	5087
9.15	4.16	17.3	45.2	37.5	109.8	98.0	114.5	110.3	4839
51.24	4.46	21.1	43.0	35.9	108.2	104.8	109.0	110.3	7470

3-10 各地区国内生产总值项目结构(2000年)

Structure of Gross Domestic Product by Region (2000)

本表按当年价格计算。

Data in value terms are calculated at current prices.

地　　区	Region	国内生产总值(亿元) Gross Domestic Product (100 million yuan)	劳动者报酬 Compensation of Employees	固定资产折旧 Depreciation of Fixed Assets	生产税净额 Net Taxes on Production	营业盈余 Operating Surplus
北　京	Beijing	2478.76	1131.02	430.93	304.04	612.77
天　津	Tianjin	1639.36	765.87	269.58	281.14	322.77
河　北	Hebei	5088.96	2693.00	717.61	446.02	1232.33
山　西	Shanxi	1643.81	853.44	213.50	186.70	390.17
内蒙古	Inner Mongolia	1401.01	875.67	172.95	156.84	195.55
辽　宁	Liaoning	4669.06	2099.17	776.07	670.78	1123.04
吉　林	Jilin	1821.19	1044.82	325.76	176.09	274.52
黑龙江	Heilongjiang	3253.00	1395.03	422.94	513.74	921.29
上　海	Shanghai	4551.15	1592.48	635.73	1107.50	1215.44
江　苏	Jiangsu	8582.73	4262.60	1303.16	1026.24	1990.73
浙　江	Zhejiang	6036.34	2982.39	767.78	872.66	1413.51
安　徽	Anhui	3038.24	1629.00	433.07	430.06	546.11
福　建	Fujian	3920.07	1884.85	496.00	391.12	1148.10
江　西	Jiangxi	2003.07	1218.95	351.41	210.94	221.77
山　东	Shandong	8542.44	4082.21	1616.66	1207.64	1635.93
河　南	Henan	5137.66	3104.51	708.22	677.28	647.65
湖　北	Hubei	4276.32	2528.86	669.88	676.49	401.09
湖　南	Hunan	3691.88	2287.45	578.46	465.18	360.79
广　东	Guangdong	9662.23	4648.59	1641.14	1744.10	1628.40
广　西	Guangxi	2050.14	1318.95	215.33	225.15	290.71
海　南	Hainan	518.48	299.08	83.49	59.63	76.28
重　庆	Chongqing	1589.34	861.91	261.39	212.12	253.92
四　川	Sichuan	4010.25	2263.21	642.46	468.83	635.75
贵　州	Guizhou	993.53	604.60	128.72	183.60	76.61
云　南	Yunnan	1955.09	867.04	287.11	482.15	318.79
西　藏	Tibet	117.46	79.80	28.85	6.14	2.67
陕　西	Shaanxi	1660.92	992.52	267.26	248.17	152.97
甘　肃	Gansu	983.36	579.33	186.02	100.01	118.00
青　海	Qinghai	263.59	159.50	59.91	29.57	14.61
宁　夏	Ningxia	265.57	156.64	49.73	37.82	21.38
新　疆	Xinjiang	1364.36	685.57	231.30	162.52	284.97

3-11 支出法国内生产总值

Gross Domestic Product by Expenditure Approach

本表按当年价格计算。

Data in value terms in this table are calculated at current prices.

年份 Year	支出法国内生产总值(亿元) Gross Domestic Product by Expenditure Approach (100 million yuan)	最终消费 Final Consumption Expenditure	资本形成总额 Gross Capital Formation	货物和服务净出口 Net Export of Goods and Services	资本形成率(投资率)(%) Capital Formation Rate (%)	最终消费率(消费率)(%) Final Consumption Rate (%)
1978	3605.6	2239.1	1377.9	-11.4	38.2	62.1
1979	4074.0	2619.4	1474.2	-19.6	36.2	64.3
1980	4551.3	2976.1	1590.0	-14.8	34.9	65.4
1981	4901.4	3309.1	1581.0	11.3	32.3	67.5
1982	5489.2	3637.9	1760.2	91.1	32.1	66.3
1983	6076.3	4020.5	2005.0	50.8	33.0	66.2
1984	7164.4	4694.5	2468.6	1.3	34.5	65.5
1985	8792.1	5773.0	3386.0	-366.9	38.5	65.7
1986	10132.8	6542.0	3846.0	-255.2	38.0	64.6
1987	11784.7	7451.2	4322.0	11.5	36.7	63.2
1988	14704.0	9360.1	5495.0	-151.1	37.4	63.7
1989	16466.0	10556.5	6095.0	-185.5	37.0	64.1
1990	18319.5	11365.2	6444.0	510.3	35.2	62.0
1991	21280.4	13145.9	7517.0	617.5	35.3	61.8
1992	25863.7	15952.1	9636.0	275.6	37.3	61.7
1993	34500.7	20182.1	14998.0	-679.4	43.5	58.5
1994	46690.7	26796.0	19260.6	634.1	41.3	57.4
1995	58510.5	33635.0	23877.0	998.5	40.8	57.5
1996	68330.4	40003.9	26867.2	1459.3	39.3	58.5
1997	74894.2	43579.4	28457.6	2857.2	38.0	58.2
1998	79003.3	46405.9	29545.9	3051.5	37.4	58.7
1999	82673.1	49722.7	30701.6	2248.8	37.1	60.1
2000	89112.5	54617.2	32255.0	2240.3	36.2	61.3

注：支出法国内生产总值不等于国内生产总值是由于计算误差的影响。

a)The gross domestic production by expenditure approach is not equal to gross domestic product due to statistical discrepancies.

3-12 支出法国内生产总值结构

Structure of Gross Domestic Product by Expenditure Approach

本表按当年价格计算。

Data in value terms in this table are calculated at current prices.

年份 Year	最终消费 Final Consumption Expenditure								资本形成总额 Gross Capital Formation			
	绝对数（亿元） Absolute Figure (100 million yuan)				构成 Composition				绝对数（亿元） Absolute Figure (100million yuan)		构成（资本形成总额=100） Composition (Gross Capital Formation=100)	
					最终消费=100 Final Consumption Expenditure=100		居民消费=100 Household Consumption=100					
	居民消费 Household Consumption Expenditure	农村居民 Rural Households	城镇居民 Urban Households	政府消费 Government Consumption Expenditure	居民消费 Household Consumption Expenditure	政府消费 Government Consumption Expenditure	农村居民 Rural Households	城镇居民 Urban Households	固定资本形成总额 Gross Fixed Capital Formation	存货增加 Changes in Inventories	固定资本形成总额 Gross Fixed Capital Formation	存货增加 Changes in Inventories
1978	1759.1	1092.4	666.7	480.0	78.6	21.4	62.1	37.9	1073.9	304.0	77.9	22.1
1979	2005.4	1259.7	745.7	614.0	76.6	23.4	62.8	37.2	1151.2	323.0	78.1	21.9
1980	2317.1	1427.3	889.8	659.0	77.9	22.1	61.6	38.4	1318.0	272.0	82.9	17.1
1981	2604.1	1630.8	973.3	705.0	78.7	21.3	62.6	37.4	1253.0	328.0	79.3	20.7
1982	2867.9	1826.5	1041.4	770.0	78.8	21.2	63.7	36.3	1493.2	267.0	84.8	15.2
1983	3182.5	2063.4	1119.1	838.0	79.2	20.8	64.8	35.2	1709.0	296.0	85.2	14.8
1984	3674.5	2385.7	1288.8	1020.0	78.3	21.7	64.9	35.1	2125.6	343.0	86.1	13.9
1985	4589.0	2921.5	1667.5	1184.0	79.5	20.5	63.7	36.3	2641.0	745.0	78.0	22.0
1986	5175.0	3210.0	1965.0	1367.0	79.1	20.9	62.0	38.0	3098.0	748.0	80.6	19.4
1987	5961.2	3630.1	2331.1	1490.0	80.0	20.0	60.9	39.1	3742.0	580.0	86.6	13.4
1988	7633.1	4473.2	3159.9	1727.0	81.5	18.5	58.6	41.4	4624.0	871.0	84.1	15.9
1989	8523.5	4919.8	3603.7	2033.0	80.7	19.3	57.7	42.3	4339.0	1756.0	71.2	28.8
1990	9113.2	5129.1	3984.1	2252.0	80.2	19.8	56.3	43.7	4732.0	1712.0	73.4	26.6
1991	10315.9	5639.8	4676.1	2830.0	78.5	21.5	54.7	45.3	5940.0	1577.0	79.0	21.0
1992	12459.8	6571.6	5888.2	3492.3	78.1	21.9	52.7	47.3	8317.0	1319.0	86.3	13.7
1993	15682.4	7867.2	7815.2	4499.7	77.7	22.3	50.2	49.8	12980.0	2018.0	86.5	13.5
1994	20809.8	10308.3	10501.5	5986.2	77.7	22.3	49.5	50.5	16856.3	2404.3	87.5	12.5
1995	26944.5	13247.1	13697.4	6690.5	80.1	19.9	49.2	50.8	20300.5	3576.5	85.0	15.0
1996	32152.3	16398.0	15754.3	7851.6	80.4	19.6	51.0	49.0	23336.1	3531.1	86.9	13.1
1997	34854.6	17436.8	17417.7	8724.8	80.0	20.0	50.0	50.0	25154.2	3303.4	88.4	11.6
1998	36921.1	17667.3	19253.9	9484.8	79.6	20.4	47.9	52.1	27630.8	1915.1	93.5	6.5
1999	39334.4	18147.6	21186.8	10388.3	79.1	20.9	46.1	53.9	29475.5	1226.1	96.0	4.0
2000	42911.9	19382.4	23529.5	11705.3	78.6	21.4	45.2	54.8	32623.8	-368.8	101.1	-1.1

3-13 各地区支出法国内生产总值（2000年）

Gross Domestic Product by Expenditure Approach by Region (2000)

本表按当年价格计算。

Data in value terms in this table are calculated at current prices.

地 区	Region	支出法国内生产总值（亿元）Gross Domestic Product by Expenditure Approach (100 million yuan)	最终消费 Final Consumption Expenditure	资本形成总额 Gross Capital Formation	货物和服务净出口 Net Export of Goods and Services	资本形成率（投资率）(%) Capital Formation Rate (%)	最终消费率（消费率）(%) Final Consumption Rate (%)
北 京	Beijing	2478.76	1221.33	1517.38	-259.95	61.22	49.27
天 津	Tianjin	1639.36	804.71	817.15	17.50	49.85	49.09
河 北	Hebei	5088.96	2240.68	2364.03	484.25	46.45	44.03
山 西	Shanxi	1638.03	946.04	746.23	-54.24	45.56	57.75
内蒙古	Inner Mongolia	1391.88	787.21	613.68	-9.00	44.09	56.56
辽 宁	Liaoning	4669.06	2587.52	1471.61	609.93	31.52	55.42
吉 林	Jilin	1854.61	1174.91	686.58	-6.88	37.02	63.35
黑龙江	Heilongjiang	3209.48	1871.54	993.54	344.40	30.96	58.31
上 海	Shanghai	4551.15	1947.10	2117.94	486.11	46.54	42.78
江 苏	Jiangsu	8482.79	3710.72	3944.78	827.29	46.50	43.74
浙 江	Zhejiang	6040.00	2774.65	2673.60	591.75	44.26	45.94
安 徽	Anhui	3041.24	1947.78	1094.97	-1.50	36.00	64.05
福 建	Fujian	3894.17	2052.41	1798.27	43.49	46.18	52.70
江 西	Jiangxi	1982.17	1269.58	718.29	-5.70	36.24	64.05
山 东	Shandong	8542.44	4099.74	4200.61	242.09	49.17	47.99
河 南	Henan	5137.66	2758.60	2169.04	210.02	42.22	53.69
湖 北	Hubei	4153.90	2146.54	1952.36	55.00	47.00	51.68
湖 南	Hunan	3691.88	2383.27	1274.94	33.67	34.53	64.55
广 东	Guangdong	9662.23	5336.22	3487.86	838.15	36.10	55.23
广 西	Guangxi	2050.14	1443.17	676.12	-69.15	32.98	70.39
海 南	Hainan	517.73	284.51	240.66	-7.44	46.48	54.95
重 庆	Chongqing	1597.53	994.39	690.58	-87.44	43.23	62.25
四 川	Sichuan	4010.25	2522.87	1485.43	1.95	37.04	62.91
贵 州	Guizhou	993.53	775.25	495.89	-277.61	49.91	78.03
云 南	Yunnan	1955.09	1481.81	724.70	-251.42	37.07	75.79
西 藏	Tibet	119.67	66.16	45.51	8.00	38.03	55.29
陕 西	Shaanxi	1660.92	956.45	851.69	-147.22	51.28	57.59
甘 肃	Gansu	986.29	579.21	439.28	-32.20	44.54	58.73
青 海	Qinghai	253.05	167.31	160.46	-74.72	63.41	66.12
宁 夏	Ningxia	265.57	186.63	167.59	-88.65	63.11	70.28
新 疆	Xinjiang	1364.36	899.90	590.68	-126.22	43.29	65.96

3-14 各地区资本形成总额及构成(2000年)

Gross Capital Formation and It's Composition by Region (2000)

本表按当年价格计算。

Data in value terms in this table are calculated at current prices.

地区	Region	资本形成总额 (亿元) Gross Capital Formation (100 million yuan)	固定资本形成总额 Gross Fixed Capital Formation	存货增加 Changes in Inventories	构成(资本形成总额=100) Composition (Total=100) 固定资本形成总额 Gross Fixed Capital Formation	存货增加 Changes in Inventories
北京	Beijing	1517.38	1376.98	140.40	90.75	9.25
天津	Tianjin	817.15	695.10	122.05	85.06	14.94
河北	Hebei	2364.03	1963.65	400.38	83.06	16.94
山西	Shanxi	746.23	657.60	88.63	88.12	11.88
内蒙古	Inner Mongolia	613.68	430.42	183.26	70.14	29.86
辽宁	Liaoning	1471.61	1293.92	177.69	87.93	12.07
吉林	Jilin	686.58	627.74	58.84	91.43	8.57
黑龙江	Heilongjiang	993.54	926.70	66.84	93.27	6.73
上海	Shanghai	2117.94	1933.01	184.93	91.27	8.73
江苏	Jiangsu	3944.78	3125.42	819.36	79.23	20.77
浙江	Zhejiang	2673.60	2267.20	406.40	84.80	15.20
安徽	Anhui	1094.97	928.09	166.88	84.76	15.24
福建	Fujian	1798.27	1258.89	539.38	70.01	29.99
江西	Jiangxi	718.29	605.54	112.75	84.30	15.70
山东	Shandong	4200.61	3200.77	999.84	76.20	23.80
河南	Henan	2169.04	1659.58	509.46	76.51	23.49
湖北	Hubei	1952.36	1451.85	500.51	74.36	25.64
湖南	Hunan	1274.94	1082.00	192.94	84.87	15.13
广东	Guangdong	3487.86	3175.93	311.93	91.06	8.94
广西	Guangxi	676.12	670.65	5.47	99.19	0.81
海南	Hainan	240.66	196.40	44.26	81.61	18.39
重庆	Chongqing	690.58	633.43	57.15	91.72	8.28
四川	Sichuan	1485.43	1349.69	135.74	90.86	9.14
贵州	Guizhou	495.89	458.84	37.05	92.53	7.47
云南	Yunnan	724.70	701.43	23.27	96.79	3.21
西藏	Tibet	45.51	38.26	7.25	84.07	15.93
陕西	Shaanxi	851.69	796.21	55.48	93.49	6.51
甘肃	Gansu	439.28	336.23	103.05	76.54	23.46
青海	Qinghai	160.46	156.97	3.49	97.83	2.17
宁夏	Ningxia	167.59	160.82	6.77	95.96	4.04
新疆	Xinjiang	590.68	648.12	-57.44	109.72	-9.72

3-15 各地区最终消费及构成(2000年)

Final Consumption Expenditure and It's Composition by Region (2000)

本表按当年价格计算。

Data in value terms in this table are calculated at current prices.

地区	Region	最终消费(亿元) Final Consumption Expenditure (100 million yuan)	居民消费 Household Consumption	农村居民 Rural Households	城镇居民 Urban Households	政府消费 Government Consumption	最终消费=100 Final Consumption Expenditure=100: 居民消费 Household Consumption	最终消费=100 Final Consumption Expenditure=100: 政府消费 Government Consumption	居民消费=100 Household Consumption Expenditure=100: 农村居民 Rural Households	居民消费=100 Household Consumption Expenditure=100: 城镇居民 Urban Households
北京	Beijing	1221.33	808.53	125.92	682.61	412.80	66.20	33.80	15.57	84.43
天津	Tianjin	804.71	557.34	129.91	427.43	247.37	69.26	30.74	23.31	76.69
河北	Hebei	2240.68	1682.76	974.53	708.23	557.92	75.10	24.90	57.91	42.09
山西	Shanxi	946.04	651.84	283.48	368.36	294.20	68.90	31.10	43.49	56.51
内蒙古	Inner Mongolia	787.21	578.67	248.84	329.83	208.54	73.51	26.49	43.00	57.00
辽宁	Liaoning	2587.52	1867.36	535.84	1331.52	720.16	72.17	27.83	28.70	71.30
吉林	Jilin	1174.91	899.31	236.47	662.84	275.60	76.54	23.46	26.29	73.71
黑龙江	Heilongjiang	1871.54	1394.21	343.16	1051.05	477.33	74.50	25.50	24.61	75.39
上海	Shanghai	1947.10	1521.05	213.74	1307.31	426.05	78.12	21.88	14.05	85.95
江苏	Jiangsu	3710.72	2815.51	1338.46	1477.05	895.21	75.88	24.12	47.54	52.46
浙江	Zhejiang	2774.65	1957.85	1134.31	823.54	816.80	70.56	29.44	57.94	42.06
安徽	Anhui	1947.78	1615.43	964.49	650.95	332.34	82.94	17.06	59.70	40.30
福建	Fujian	2052.41	1496.20	1020.49	475.71	556.21	72.90	27.10	68.21	31.79
江西	Jiangxi	1269.58	989.20	574.63	414.57	280.38	77.92	22.08	58.09	41.91
山东	Shandong	4099.74	3099.76	1546.85	1552.91	999.98	75.61	24.39	49.90	50.10
河南	Henan	2758.60	2084.08	1216.60	867.48	674.52	75.55	24.45	58.38	41.62
湖北	Hubei	2146.54	1699.45	757.18	942.27	447.09	79.17	20.83	44.55	55.45
湖南	Hunan	2383.27	1782.77	1038.80	743.97	600.50	74.80	25.20	58.27	41.73
广东	Guangdong	5336.22	3754.80	1471.03	2283.77	1581.42	70.36	29.64	39.18	60.82
广西	Guangxi	1443.17	1019.36	578.22	441.14	423.81	70.63	29.37	56.72	43.28
海南	Hainan	284.51	218.38	123.81	94.57	66.13	76.76	23.24	56.69	43.31
重庆	Chongqing	994.39	760.02	335.94	424.08	234.37	76.43	23.57	44.20	55.80
四川	Sichuan	2522.87	2059.20	1254.76	804.44	463.67	81.62	18.38	60.93	39.07
贵州	Guizhou	775.25	600.07	357.99	242.08	175.18	77.40	22.60	59.66	40.34
云南	Yunnan	1481.81	1066.77	717.29	349.48	415.04	71.99	28.01	67.24	32.76
西藏	Tibet	66.16	46.97	23.90	23.07	19.19	70.99	29.01	50.88	49.12
陕西	Shaanxi	956.45	743.07	333.69	409.38	213.38	77.69	22.31	44.91	55.09
甘肃	Gansu	579.21	444.22	206.07	238.15	134.99	76.69	23.31	46.39	53.61
青海	Qinghai	167.31	116.82	46.00	70.82	50.49	69.82	30.18	39.38	60.62
宁夏	Ningxia	186.63	125.69	54.54	71.15	60.94	67.35	32.65	43.39	56.61
新疆	Xinjiang	899.90	585.69	182.05	403.64	314.21	65.08	34.92	31.08	68.92

3-16 居 民 消 费 水 平

Household Consumption

本表绝对数按当年价格计算，指数按可比价格计算。

Absolute figures in this table are calculated at current prices, while indices are calculated at comparable prices.

地区 Region / 年份 Year	绝对数(元) Value (yuan)			城乡消费水平对比(农村居民=1) Urban/Rural Consumption Ratio (Urban Households=1)	指数（上年=100) Index(Preceding year=100)			指数(1978=100) Index (1978=100)		
	全国居民 All Households	农村居民 Rural Households	城镇居民 Urban Households		全国居民 All Households	农村居民 Rural Households	城镇居民 Urban Households	全国居民 All Households	农村居民 Rural Households	城镇居民 Urban Households
1978	184	138	405	2.9	104.1	104.3	103.3	100.0	100.0	100.0
1979	207	158	434	2.7	106.5	106.1	105.2	106.5	106.1	105.2
1980	236	178	496	2.8	108.7	108.8	106.3	115.8	115.5	111.9
1981	262	199	562	2.8	108.0	108.4	110.6	125.1	125.2	123.8
1982	284	221	576	2.6	106.5	109.1	100.4	133.2	136.6	124.3
1983	311	246	603	2.5	107.8	110.4	102.5	143.6	150.8	127.4
1984	354	283	662	2.3	111.6	113.0	107.0	160.2	170.4	137.8
1985	437	347	802	2.3	113.1	114.1	108.2	181.3	194.4	147.5
1986	485	376	920	2.4	104.4	102.5	107.3	189.3	199.3	158.3
1987	550	417	1089	2.6	105.6	104.3	108.7	200.0	207.9	172.0
1988	693	508	1431	2.8	107.4	106.0	108.9	214.9	220.4	187.3
1989	762	553	1568	2.8	99.5	99.2	98.4	213.8	218.8	184.4
1990	803	571	1686	3.0	103.4	100.3	107.5	221.0	219.5	198.1
1991	896	621	1925	3.1	108.3	106.7	109.3	239.4	234.2	216.6
1992	1070	718	2356	3.3	112.9	109.8	115.4	270.3	257.2	249.9
1993	1331	855	3027	3.5	108.1	106.1	108.9	292.2	272.8	272.1
1994	1746	1118	3891	3.5	104.3	104.6	101.7	304.8	285.4	276.7
1995	2236	1434	4874	3.4	107.5	108.2	104.6	327.7	308.7	289.6
1996	2641	1768	5430	3.1	109.1	114.0	102.5	357.5	351.9	296.7
1997	2834	1876	5796	3.1	104.2	103.3	103.5	372.4	363.6	307.0
1998	2972	1895	6217	3.3	105.5	101.8	108.3	393.1	370.2	332.4
1999	3138	1927	6796	3.5	107.9	104.7	111.3	424.1	387.6	370.1
2000	3397				108.3			459.4		
北京 Beijing	7326	3601	9054	2.5	126.7	113.7	128.6			
天津 Tianjin	6117	3414	8056	2.4	110.2	110.6	109.7			
河北 Hebei	2534	1816	5554	3.1	109.6	107.6	110.4			
山西 Shanxi	2037	1209	4312	3.6	111.1	111.0	109.7			
内蒙古 Inner Mongolia	2425	1609	3930	2.4	106.4	107.5	104.4			
辽宁 Liaoning	4490	2403	6903	2.9	108.8	108.8	108.4			
吉林 Jilin	3381	1593	5639	3.5	107.4	104.9	107.3			
黑龙江 Heilongjiang	3669	1665	6046	3.6	106.9	104.5	107.4			
上海 Shanghai	11546	6296	13369	2.1	111.8	107.3	111.9			
江苏 Jiangsu	3862	2651	6589	2.5	107.5	103.6	105.6			
浙江 Zhejiang	4366	3229	8478	2.6	112.6	115.4	106.2			
安徽 Anhui	2588	1922	5323	2.8	102.6	99.1	106.8			
福建 Fujian	4428	3815	6757	1.8	108.9	108.9	108.0			
江西 Jiangxi	2396	1793	4488	2.5	116.5	111.6	120.8			
山东 Shandong	3467	2352	6572	2.8	108.5	107.5	108.5			
河南 Henan	2208	1587	4902	3.1	116.1	115.3	116.3			
湖北 Hubei	2857	1760	5719	3.2	106.1	103.7	108.0			
湖南 Hunan	2723	1981	5705	2.9	105.0	101.9	107.9			
广东 Guangdong	5007	2855	9737	3.4	105.2	100.4	108.4			
广西 Guangxi	2147	1478	5277	3.6	103.3	101.3	105.8			
海南 Hainan	2904	2215	4900	2.2	106.4	107.6	104.2			
重庆 Chongqing	2466	1380	6544	4.7	105.6	102.2	105.7			
四川 Sichuan	2456	1833	5236	2.9	112.1	113.8	107.4			
贵州 Guizhou	1608	1120	4517	4.0	104.2	103.5	104.2			
云南 Yunnan	2530	2007	5444	2.7	108.1	106.5	110.4			
西藏 Tibet	1823	1144	4737	4.1	109.2	111.0	103.4			
陕西 Shaanxi	2035	1186	4891	4.1	108.0	100.5	108.2			
甘肃 Gansu	1734	993	4890	4.9	105.1	104.3	106.0			
青海 Qinghai	2255	1260	4630	3.7	104.9	104.1	105.6			
宁夏 Ningxia	2290	1393	4523	3.2	113.7	107.4	118.6			
新疆 Xinjiang	3207	2002	4402	2.2	109.2	106.2	110.4			

注：城乡消费水平对比，没有剔除城乡价格不可比的因素。

a)The effect of price differentials between urban and rural areas has not been removed in the calculation of the urban/rural consumption ratio.

3-17 1997年投入产出基本流量表(中间使用部分)

Intermediate Use Part of 1997 Input-Output Table

按当年生产者价格计算。

Data are calculated at producers' prices of 1997.

单位：万元　　(10 000 yuan)

产出 Output / 投入 Input	农业 Agriculture	采掘业 Mining and Quarrying	食品制造业 Foodstuff	纺织、缝纫及皮革产品制造业 Textile, Sewing Leather and Furs Products	其他制造业 Other Manufacturing
总投入合计 Total Input	**246773827**	**68283887**	**137925948**	**153665629**	**98848920**
中间投入合计 Intermediate Input	**99357988**	**32596402**	**99668550**	**108530266**	**64056866**
农业 Agriculture	39641456	675345	59227841	13766692	5121334
采掘业 Mining and Quarrying	512276	5189811	638067	404519	1626660
食品制造业 Foodstuff	16368977	19193	17661566	2424849	93490
纺织、缝纫及皮革产品制造业 Textile, Sewing, Leather and Furs Products	706277	586373	318942	62034310	7209598
其他制造业 Other Manufacturing	1043260	1050214	3899115	1904950	21650594
电力及蒸汽、热水生产和供应业 Production and Supply of Electric Power, Steam and Hot Water	1805193	3335467	1094571	932638	2413096
炼焦、煤气及石油加工业 Coking, Gas and Petroleum Refining	2088501	1526676	311343	250143	527875
化学工业 Chemical Industry	18257172	3323577	3483962	11768560	7641355
建筑材料及其他非金属矿物制品业 Building Materials and Non-metal Mineral Products	627725	813500	937385	203651	823945
金属产品制造业 Metal Products	768793	2666788	1058482	481970	4623987
机械设备制造业 Machinery and Equipment	3947123	5977909	1162357	1967437	2440373
建筑业 Construction	489538	151682	73883	94121	86535
运输邮电业 Transportation, Post and Telecommunications	2938150	2960339	1722914	2016013	2085389
商业饮食业 Commerce and Catering Trade	4474912	2086388	5556990	7977096	5535757
公用事业及居民服务业 Public Utilities and Resident Services	1084031	774349	1612580	1100203	1032915
金融保险业 Banking and Insurance	1157123	836806	755732	1065063	849957
其他服务业 Other Services	3447479	621986	152819	138050	294005
增加值合计 Total Value-added	**147415839**	**35687485**	**38257398**	**45135363**	**34792054**
固定资产折旧 Depreciation of Fixed Assets	5847862	7287726	5182806	6496572	3652824
劳动者报酬 Compensation for Laborers	129786622	16499480	10604835	21120006	14319783
生产税净额 Net Taxes on Production	4329970	3635071	13072630	7466536	3913428
营业盈余 Operating Surplus	7451384	8265209	9397127	10052250	12906020

3-17 续表 1

单位：万元

产出 Output / 投入 Input	电力及蒸汽、热水生产和供应业 Production and Supply of Electric Power, Steam and Hot Water	炼焦、煤气及石油加工业 Coking, Gas and Petroleum Refining	化学工业 Chemical Industry	建筑材料及其他非金属矿物制品业 Building Materials and Non-metal Mineral Products	金属产品制造业 Metal Products
总投入合计 Total Input	**39087093**	**32376889**	**152122332**	**88074034**	**127583044**
中间投入合计 Intermediate Input	**22205940**	**25174545**	**111267717**	**60249007**	**100112375**
农　业 Agriculture	5131	272	7064054	258180	44363
采掘业 Mining and Quarrying	7823817	17238884	7179760	9967089	12930346
食品制造业 Foodstuff	0	0	1928944	70711	0
纺织、缝纫及皮革产品制造业 Textile, Sewing, Leather and Furs Products	150590	91778	6160921	1251885	570381
其他制造业 Other Manufacturing	501075	239985	3436184	5381129	5842582
电力及蒸汽、热水生产和供应业 Production and Supply of Electric Power, Steam and Hot Water	1359811	707988	5820387	3857306	5785481
炼焦、煤气及石油加工业 Coking, Gas and Petroleum Refining	2055738	1605821	2889692	2463300	3304255
化学工业 Chemical Industry	290250	689330	55577051	5048999	2907159
建筑材料及其他非金属矿物制品业 Building Materials and Non-metal Mineral Products	305215	284985	1511766	12485245	3053889
金属产品制造业 Metal Products	270662	204512	1998710	4692560	45536301
机械设备制造业 Machinery and Equipment	4573294	1270428	3815086	3926578	5954860
建筑业 Construction	107570	38902	133936	66657	109855
运输邮电业 Transportation, Post and Telecommunications	1270322	930573	3521590	3701908	4871233
商业饮食业 Commerce and Catering Trade	2069164	1231608	6472986	5032198	4564053
公用事业及居民服务业 Public Utilities and Resident Services	441565	243816	1807090	743412	1387441
金融保险业 Banking and Insurance	792128	324307	1627719	1151446	2850889
其他服务业 Other Services	189608	71356	321842	150405	399289
增加值合计 Total Value-added	**16881153**	**7202344**	**40854615**	**27825027**	**27470669**
固定资产折旧 Depreciation of Fixed Assets	5226651	1133550	6466886	4336511	4863252
劳动者报酬 Compensation for Laborers	4315793	1737068	15324744	13248777	13387503
生产税净额 Net Taxes on Production	2978902	2900162	9364034	4718972	5720111
营业盈余 Operating Surplus	4359807	1431564	9698951	5520767	3499803

continued

(10 000 yuan)

机械设备制造业 Machinery and Equipment	建筑业 Construction	运输邮电业 Trans-portation, Post and Telecommuni-cations	商业饮食业 Commerce and Catering Trade	公用事业及居民服务业 Public Utilities & Resident Services	金融保险业 Banking and Insurance	其他服务业 Other Services	中间使用合计 Total Intermediate Use
255466116	**173855000**	**70251899**	**132988462**	**75005204**	**35952759**	**110181277**	**1998442320**
183445498	**123880172**	**31017292**	**68626933**	**38494913**	**14007704**	**58709439**	**1241401607**
87531	720592	111895	5836096	465986	0	1095289	134122054
2064525	4556902	433718	185867	474238	18632	843953	72089064
3895	111106	407549	9684161	1846867	6325	641018	51268650
2005356	571970	459632	1905099	1640951	88252	1306299	87058615
5976565	4538579	1331464	5554532	4198349	1437858	7003008	74989443
2799201	1219631	1154518	1135994	777927	192304	1880014	36271526
1823841	4976394	5585580	1797425	1649959	126414	1002957	33985916
18540227	3636574	1080006	2443682	2319909	88468	8317496	145413775
5377706	47055800	293977	1070552	1258972	52158	1240752	77397224
38924664	21294423	427799	640325	687268	62038	1232107	125571389
84493857	14018761	10031861	11045545	8278096	1749497	7135734	171788795
299583	100902	1362719	578260	1964188	664985	3961777	10285093
4968275	6373168	3116229	3287578	3084330	1321098	7425467	55594576
9456432	8315085	1473558	11913663	2805690	784895	5152530	84903004
3112737	3502911	2163407	6718287	4837674	4078783	6150654	40791855
2754770	1071355	1106938	4266460	1475869	3120636	1734350	26941550
756333	1816020	476442	563406	728640	215361	2586034	12929076
72020618	**49974828**	**39234607**	**64361529**	**36510291**	**21945055**	**51471838**	**757040713**
8860452	2869086	11462638	6485812	13150824	1710435	8088308	103122194
30857379	34578592	15385376	32194689	15281357	6569014	40192494	415403512
11568865	4073778	3217431	13507238	2758762	8310619	912582	102449091
20733922	8453373	9169162	12173789	5319348	5354987	2278453	136065916

3-18 1997年投入产出基本流量表(最终使用部分)

按当年生产者价格计算。

单位：万元

产出 Output / 投入 Input	最终使用 Final Use				
	最终消费 Final Consumption Expenditure				
	居民最终消费 Household Consumption Expenditure			政府消费 Government Consumption Expenditure	合计 Total Consumption
	农村居民 Agricultural Households	城镇居民 Non-agricultural Households	小计 Subtotal		
总投入合计 Total Input					
中间投入合计 Intermediate Input	**177983003**	**179806594**	**357789597**	**87248700**	**445038297**
农业 Agriculture	67413084	36196125	103609210	0	103609210
采掘业 Mining and Quarrying	613818	300718	914537	0	914537
食品制造业 Foodstuff	36624475	39334145	75958619	0	75958619
纺织、缝纫及皮革产品制造业 Textile, Sewing, Leather and Furs Products	11064578	19532632	30597209	0	30597209
其他制造业 Other Manufacturing	4415358	7694009	12109368	0	12109368
电力及蒸汽、热水生产和供应业 Production and Supply of Electric Power, Steam and Hot Water	1589524	2608939	4198463	0	4198463
炼焦、煤气及石油加工业 Coking, Gas and Petroleum Refining	226944	1057613	1284557	0	1284557
化学工业 Chemical Industry	6082942	4244879	10327820	0	10327820
建筑材料及其他非金属矿物制品业 Building Materials and Non-metal Mineral Products	1479375	3808972	5288347	0	5288347
金属产品制造业 Metal Products	1386980	1582250	2969230	0	2969230
机械设备制造业 Machinery and Equipment	10404037	12499630	22903666	0	22903666
建筑业 Construction	0	0	0	0	0
运输邮电业 Transportation, Post and Telecommunications	3914186	5622458	9536644	0	9536644
商业饮食业 Commerce and Catering Trade	12883060	16744352	29627412	0	29627412
公用事业及居民服务业 Public Utilities and Resident Services	10919728	11107654	22027381	6271330	28298712
金融保险业 Banking and Insurance	3614603	5629294	9243897	0	9243897
其他服务业 Other Services	5350312	11842923	17193236	80977370	98170606

Final Use Part of 1997 Input-Output Table

Data are calculated at producers' prices of 1997

(10 000 yuan)

最终使用 Final Use					进口 Import	其他 Other	总产出 Total Output
资本形成总额 Capital Formation			出口 Export	最终使用合计 Total of Final Use			
固定资本形成总额 Gross Fixed Capital Formation	存货增加 Changes in Inventories	资本形成总额 Subtotal					
251542000	**33034300**	**284576300**	**165432047**	**895046644**	**-127590693**	**-10415239**	**1998442320**
5937880	4696120	10634000	4082649	118325859	-3999547	-1674540	246773827
0	224225	224225	3897712	5036473	-7685119	-1156532	68283887
0	5404753	5404753	7331464	88694836	-4706434	2668895	137925948
0	8179756	8179756	38675714	77452679	-12051113	1205448	153665629
1970480	1947877	3918357	13795546	29823271	-6874073	910279	98848920
0	0	0	381953	4580416	-1906	-1762942	39087093
0	715258	715258	1779496	3779311	-3945330	-1443009	32376889
0	4199937	4199937	15143683	29671440	-21130161	-1832722	152122332
0	3193696	3193696	2995152	11477196	-1062219	261833	88074034
1703365	-1358927	344438	11354202	14667870	-11566144	-1090071	127583044
68737964	2925923	71663887	38761119	133328672	-47932420	-1718930	255466116
167473028	0	167473028	244603	167717631	-501160	-3646564	173855000
583581	367879	951460	5853928	16342032	-1094934	-589774	70251899
3267003	2537803	5804806	12892969	48325186	-431179	191451	132988462
1868700	0	1868700	7551824	37719236	-3672074	166186	75005204
0	0	0	169241	9413138	-440742	38813	35952759
0	0	0	520793	98691398	-496138	-943060	110181277

3-19 投入产出直接消耗系数表（1997年）

产出 Output / 投入 Input	农业 Agriculture	采掘业 Mining and Quarrying	食品制造业 Foodstuff	纺织、缝纫及皮革产品制造业 Textile, Sewing Leather and Furs Products	其他制造业 Other Manufacturing
总投入合计 Total Input	**1.0000000**	**1.0000000**	**1.0000000**	**1.0000000**	**1.0000000**
中间投入合计 Intermediate Input	**0.4026277**	**0.4773659**	**0.7226236**	**0.7062755**	**0.6480280**
农业 Agriculture	0.1606388	0.0098903	0.4294177	0.0895886	0.0518097
采掘业 Mining and Quarrying	0.0020759	0.0760035	0.0046262	0.0026325	0.0164560
食品制造业 Foodstuff	0.0663319	0.0002811	0.1280511	0.0157800	0.0009458
纺织、缝纫及皮革产品制造业 Textile, Sewing, Leather and Furs Products	0.0028620	0.0085873	0.0023124	0.4036967	0.0729355
其他制造业 Other Manufacturing	0.0042276	0.0153801	0.0282696	0.0123967	0.2190271
电力及蒸汽、热水生产和供应业 Production and Supply of Electric Power, Steam and Hot Water	0.0073152	0.0488471	0.0079359	0.0060693	0.0244120
炼焦、煤气及石油加工业 Coking, Gas and Petroleum Refining	0.0084632	0.0223578	0.0022573	0.0016278	0.0053402
化学工业 Chemical Industry	0.0739834	0.0486729	0.0252597	0.0765855	0.0773034
建筑材料及其他非金属矿物制品业 Building Materials and Non-metal Mineral Products	0.0025437	0.0119135	0.0067963	0.0013253	0.0083354
金属产品制造业 Metal Products	0.0031154	0.0390544	0.0076743	0.0031365	0.0467783
机械设备制造业 Machinery and Equipment	0.0159949	0.0875449	0.0084274	0.0128034	0.0246879
建筑业 Construction	0.0019838	0.0022213	0.0005357	0.0006125	0.0008754
运输邮电业 Transportation, Post and Telecommunications	0.0119062	0.0433534	0.0124916	0.0131195	0.0210967
商业饮食业 Commerce and Catering Trade	0.0181337	0.0305546	0.0402897	0.0519120	0.0560022
公用事业及居民服务业 Public Utilities and Resident Services	0.0043928	0.0113401	0.0116916	0.0071597	0.0104494
金融保险业 Banking and Insurance	0.0046890	0.0122548	0.0054793	0.0069310	0.0085985
其他服务业 Other Services	0.0139702	0.0091088	0.0011080	0.0008984	0.0029743
增加值合计 Total Value-added	**0.5973723**	**0.5226341**	**0.2773764**	**0.2937245**	**0.3519720**
固定资产折旧 Depreciation of Fixed Assets	0.0236973	0.1067269	0.0375767	0.0422773	0.0369536
劳动者报酬 Compensation for Laborers	0.5259335	0.2416306	0.0768879	0.1374413	0.1448653
生产税净额 Net Taxes on Production	0.0175463	0.0532347	0.0947801	0.0485895	0.0395900
营业盈余 Operating Surplus	0.0301952	0.1210419	0.0681317	0.0654164	0.1305631

Direct Input Coefficient of Input-Output Table (1997)

电力及蒸汽热水生产和供应业 Production and Supply of Electric Power, Steam and Hot Water	炼焦、煤气及石油加工业 Coking, Gas and Petroleum Refining	化学工业 Chemical Industry	建筑材料及其他非金属矿物制品业 Building Materials and Non-metal Mineral Products	金属产品制造业 Metal Products	机械设备制造业 Machinery and Equipment	建筑业 Construction
1.0000000	**1.0000000**	**1.0000000**	**1.0000000**	**1.0000000**	**1.0000000**	**1.0000000**
0.5681144	**0.7775468**	**0.7314358**	**0.6840723**	**0.7846840**	**0.7180815**	**0.7125488**
0.0001313	0.0000084	0.0464367	0.0029314	0.0003477	0.0003426	0.0041448
0.2001637	0.5324441	0.0471973	0.1131672	0.1013485	0.0080814	0.0262109
0.0000000	0.0000000	0.0126802	0.0008029	0.0000000	0.0000152	0.0006391
0.0038527	0.0028347	0.0404998	0.0142140	0.0044707	0.0078498	0.0032899
0.0128194	0.0074122	0.0225883	0.0610978	0.0457943	0.0233947	0.0261055
0.0347893	0.0218671	0.0382612	0.0437962	0.0453468	0.0109572	0.0070152
0.0525938	0.0495978	0.0189958	0.0279685	0.0258989	0.0071393	0.0286238
0.0074257	0.0212908	0.3653445	0.0573268	0.0227864	0.0725741	0.0209173
0.0078086	0.0088021	0.0099378	0.1417585	0.0239365	0.0210506	0.2706612
0.0069246	0.0063166	0.0131388	0.0532797	0.3569150	0.1523672	0.1224838
0.1170027	0.0392387	0.0250791	0.0445827	0.0466744	0.3307439	0.0806348
0.0027521	0.0012015	0.0008804	0.0007568	0.0008610	0.0011727	0.0005804
0.0324998	0.0287419	0.0231497	0.0420318	0.0381809	0.0194479	0.0366579
0.0529373	0.0380397	0.0425512	0.0571360	0.0357732	0.0370164	0.0478277
0.0112970	0.0075305	0.0118792	0.0084408	0.0108748	0.0121845	0.0201485
0.0202657	0.0100166	0.0107001	0.0130736	0.0223454	0.0107833	0.0061623
0.0048509	0.0022039	0.0021157	0.0017077	0.0031296	0.0029606	0.0104456
0.4318856	**0.2224532**	**0.2685642**	**0.3159277**	**0.2153160**	**0.2819185**	**0.2874512**
0.1337181	0.0350111	0.0425111	0.0492371	0.0381183	0.0346835	0.0165028
0.1104148	0.0536515	0.1007396	0.1504277	0.1049317	0.1207885	0.1988933
0.0762119	0.0895751	0.0615559	0.0535796	0.0448344	0.0452853	0.0234320
0.1115408	0.0442156	0.0637576	0.0626833	0.0274316	0.0811611	0.0486231

3-19 续表 1 continued

产出 Output / 投入 Input	运输邮电业 Transportation, Post and Telecommunications	商业饮食业 Commerce and Catering Trade	公用事业及居民服务业 Public Utilities & Resident Services	金融保险业 Banking and Insurance	其他服务业 Other Services
总投入合计 Total Input	**1.0000000**	**1.0000000**	**1.0000000**	**1.0000000**	**1.0000000**
中间投入合计 Intermediate Input	**0.4415153**	**0.5160367**	**0.5132299**	**0.3896142**	**0.5328441**
农　业 Agriculture	0.0015928	0.0438842	0.0062127	0.0000000	0.0099408
采掘业 Mining and Quarrying	0.0061738	0.0013976	0.0063227	0.0005182	0.0076597
食品制造业 Foodstuff	0.0058013	0.0728196	0.0246232	0.0001759	0.0058178
纺织、缝纫及皮革产品制造业 Textile, Sewing, Leather and Furs Products	0.0065426	0.0143253	0.0218778	0.0024547	0.0118559
其他制造业 Other Manufacturing	0.0189527	0.0417670	0.0559741	0.0399930	0.0635590
电力及蒸汽、热水生产和供应业 Production and Supply of Electric Power, Steam and Hot Water	0.0164340	0.0085420	0.0103716	0.0053488	0.0170629
炼焦、煤气及石油加工业 Coking, Gas and Petroleum Refining	0.0795079	0.0135156	0.0219979	0.0035161	0.0091028
化学工业 Chemical Industry	0.0153733	0.0183751	0.0309300	0.0024607	0.0754892
建筑材料及其他非金属矿物制品业 Building Materials and Non-metal Mineral Products	0.0041846	0.0080500	0.0167851	0.0014507	0.0112610
金属产品制造业 Metal Products	0.0060895	0.0048149	0.0091629	0.0017255	0.0111825
机械设备制造业 Machinery and Equipment	0.1427984	0.0830564	0.1103670	0.0486610	0.0647636
建筑业 Construction	0.0193976	0.0043482	0.0261874	0.0184961	0.0359569
运输邮电业 Transportation, Post and Telecommunications	0.0443579	0.0247208	0.0411216	0.0367454	0.0673932
商业饮食业 Commerce and Catering Trade	0.0209754	0.0895842	0.0374066	0.0218313	0.0467641
公用事业及居民服务业 Public Utilities and Resident Services	0.0307950	0.0505178	0.0644978	0.1134484	0.0558230
金融保险业 Banking and Insurance	0.0157567	0.0320814	0.0196769	0.0867982	0.0157409
其他服务业 Other Services	0.0067819	0.0042365	0.0097145	0.0059901	0.0234707
增加值合计 Total Value-added	**0.5584847**	**0.4839633**	**0.4867701**	**0.6103858**	**0.4671559**
固定资产折旧 Depreciation of Fixed Assets	0.1631648	0.0487697	0.1753322	0.0475745	0.0734091
劳动者报酬 Compensation for Laborers	0.2190030	0.2420863	0.2037373	0.1827124	0.3647852
生产税净额 Net Taxes on Production	0.0457985	0.1015670	0.0367809	0.2311538	0.0082826
营业盈余 Operating Surplus	0.1305184	0.0915402	0.0709197	0.1489451	0.0206791

3-20 投入产出完全消耗系数表（1997年）

Total Input Coefficients of Input-Output Table (1997)

产出 Output / 投入 Input	农业 Agriculture	采掘业 Mining and Quarrying	食品制造业 Foodstuff	纺织、缝纫及皮革产品制造业 Textile, Sewing Leather and Furs Products	其他制造业 Other Manufacturing
农业 Agriculture	0.2637992	0.0439736	0.6417691	0.2447338	0.1413611
采掘业 Mining and Quarrying	0.0402350	0.1620645	0.0493851	0.0533891	0.0941056
食品制造业 Foodstuff	0.1048177	0.0155109	0.2082444	0.0668050	0.0322586
纺织、缝纫及皮革产品制造业 Textile, Sewing, Leather and Furs Products	0.0279523	0.0452378	0.0354919	0.7137695	0.1912631
其他制造业 Other Manufacturing	0.0312424	0.0607627	0.0732780	0.0624677	0.3260199
电力及蒸汽、热水生产和供应业 Production and Supply of Electric Power, Steam and Hot Water	0.0262071	0.0821687	0.0335099	0.0364646	0.0647083
炼焦、煤气及石油加工业 Coking, Gas and Petroleum Refining	0.0242809	0.0517360	0.0245600	0.0248168	0.0347221
化学工业 Chemical Industry	0.1802896	0.1532671	0.1630155	0.2755285	0.2455304
建筑材料及其他非金属矿物制品业 Building Materials and Non-metal Mineral Products	0.0141050	0.0342418	0.0229673	0.0175181	0.0313613
金属产品制造业 Metal Products	0.0380975	0.1412369	0.0562844	0.0553091	0.1510592
机械设备制造业 Machinery and Equipment	0.0760616	0.2301838	0.0902848	0.1100796	0.1456266
建筑业 Construction	0.0055613	0.0076601	0.0056814	0.0057510	0.0064900
运输邮电业 Transportation, Post and Telecommunications	0.0342579	0.0816880	0.0451192	0.0522869	0.0654869
商业饮食业 Commerce and Catering Trade	0.0544698	0.0833907	0.0963845	0.1391373	0.1352811
公用事业及居民服务业 Public Utilities and Resident Services	0.0200673	0.0361045	0.0349331	0.0363334	0.0409253
金融保险业 Banking and Insurance	0.0164847	0.0331132	0.0230525	0.0299465	0.0336722
其他服务业 Other Services	0.0204824	0.0153535	0.0136190	0.0087910	0.0107884

3-20 续表1

产出 Output / 投入 Input	电力及蒸汽、热水生产和供应业 Production and Supply of Electric Power, Steam and Hot Water	炼焦、煤气及石油加工业 Coking, Gas and Petroleum Refining	化学工业 Chemical Industry	建筑材料及其他非金属矿物制品业 Building Materials and Non-metal Mineral Products	金属产品制造业 Metal Products
农业 Agriculture	0.0324796	0.0407908	0.1483512	0.0549643	0.0459445
采掘业 Mining and Quarrying	0.3090029	0.6786512	0.1605432	0.2436206	0.2756783
食品制造业 Foodstuff	0.0160575	0.0175746	0.0509644	0.0232602	0.0201654
纺织、缝纫及皮革产品制造业 Textile, Sewing, Leather and Furs Products	0.0377092	0.0443316	0.1383676	0.0748429	0.0578417
其他制造业 Other Manufacturing	0.0614135	0.0627464	0.0875420	0.1414980	0.1424805
电力及蒸汽、热水生产和供应业 Production and Supply of Electric Power, Steam and Hot Water	0.0734606	0.0811756	0.0921420	0.0955236	0.1146250
炼焦、煤气及石油加工业 Coking, Gas and Petroleum Refining	0.0854043	0.0934892	0.0593320	0.0698408	0.0793817
化学工业 Chemical Industry	0.1053286	0.1521871	0.6733935	0.2039703	0.1608742
建筑材料及其他非金属矿物制品业 Building Materials and Non-metal Mineral Products	0.0326798	0.0384012	0.0368996	0.1898010	0.0675359
金属产品制造业 Metal Products	0.1148322	0.1238348	0.1006939	0.1846480	0.6577748
机械设备制造业 Machinery and Equipment	0.2939370	0.2335203	0.1675827	0.2107191	0.2497265
建筑业 Construction	0.0087875	0.0082980	0.0073430	0.0074309	0.0089337
运输邮电业 Transportation, Post and Telecommunications	0.0777225	0.0916315	0.0760634	0.0984839	0.1110217
商业饮食业 Commerce and Catering Trade	0.1127009	0.1108959	0.1285860	0.1376981	0.1275358
公用事业及居民服务业 Public Utilities and Resident Services	0.0404884	0.0409218	0.0468917	0.0421856	0.0522655
金融保险业 Banking and Insurance	0.0444627	0.0389110	0.0394506	0.0425756	0.0634293
其他服务业 Other Services	0.0124548	0.0133905	0.0110571	0.0100120	0.0133529

continued

机械设备制造业 Machinery and Equipment	建筑业 Construction	运输邮电业 Trans-portation, Post and Telecommuni-cations	商业饮食业 Commerce and Catering Trade	公用事业及居民服务业 Public Utilities & Resident Services	金融保险业 Banking and Insurance	其他服务业 Other Services
0.0486593	0.0500341	0.0317881	0.1374388	0.0625975	0.0242635	0.0605956
0.1267431	0.1772352	0.1046078	0.0537821	0.0762873	0.0365138	0.0763700
0.0214903	0.0222810	0.0195834	0.1118701	0.0480536	0.0134209	0.0280987
0.0655481	0.0556122	0.0389344	0.0576657	0.0755249	0.0313751	0.0640665
0.1074419	0.1163593	0.0635424	0.0968962	0.1181215	0.0880928	0.1285922
0.0657581	0.0657548	0.0440483	0.0329544	0.0398698	0.0228712	0.0488637
0.0485828	0.0753888	0.1074129	0.0358898	0.0493497	0.0224395	0.0396591
0.2556968	0.1625328	0.1033483	0.1150167	0.1402236	0.0605400	0.2047217
0.0639880	0.3436842	0.0305298	0.0287711	0.0483084	0.0224817	0.0445853
0.4164735	0.3126108	0.1055156	0.0806642	0.1081638	0.0605050	0.1018267
0.6213684	0.2707979	0.3003297	0.2107208	0.2620953	0.1536108	0.2052665
0.0080110	0.0079335	0.0250304	0.0108118	0.0332323	0.0269605	0.0438533
0.0806027	0.1013294	0.0800949	0.0587538	0.0801906	0.0663310	0.1087387
0.1266873	0.1372092	0.0712703	0.1466140	0.0968076	0.0608019	0.1080644
0.0506447	0.0564471	0.0557550	0.0816133	0.0950479	0.1472556	0.0877643
0.0460164	0.0391578	0.0352364	0.0541120	0.0417080	0.1087199	0.0382993
0.0116239	0.0189549	0.0125182	0.0110264	0.0164116	0.0112732	0.0307001

3-21 资金流量表(实物交易,1998年)

单位：亿元

机构部门	Institutional Sector	非金融企业部门 Non-financial Enterprises		金融机构部门 Financial Institutions		政府部门 Governments	
交易项目	Transaction	运用 Utilization	来源 Source	运用 Utilization	来源 Source	运用 Utilization	来源 Source
1.净出口	Net Exports						
2.增加值	Value Added		45510.20		1861.83		7649.10
3.劳动者报酬	Compensation of Laborers	17052.80		716.40		6860.10	
(1)工资及工资性收入	Wages and Related Income						
(2)单位社会保险付款	Employer's Contribution of Social Securities						
4.生产税净额	Taxes on Production, Net	10856.58		782.64		59.02	12724.34
(1)生产税	Taxes on Production						
(2)生产补贴	Subsidies to Production						
5.财产收入	Income from Properties	7304.04	2586.01	6545.26	6789.00	721.28	249.80
(1)利息	Interest	5870.33	2568.86	6515.03	6774.21	721.28	249.80
(2)红利	Dividend	1433.71	7.29	0.00	14.79	0.00	0.00
(3)土地租金	Rent on Land Use						
(4)其他	Others		9.86	30.23			
6.初次分配总收入	Total Income from Primary Distribution		12882.79		606.53		12982.84
7.经常转移	Current Transfer	2559.80	282.10	460.46	326.20	2911.21	3484.24
(1)收入税	Taxes on Income	905.50		133.26			1377.41
(2)社会保险付款	Payment to Social Security					1574.71	1562.63
(3)社会补助	Allowances	90.00		1.00		883.38	
(4)其他	Others	1564.30	282.10	326.20	326.20	453.12	544.20
8.可支配总收入	Total Disposable Income		10605.09		472.27		13555.87
9.最终消费	Final Consumption Expenditure					9484.80	
(1)居民消费	Household Consumption						
(2)政府消费	Government Consumption					9484.80	
10.总储蓄	Savings		10605.09		472.27		4071.07
11.资本转移	Capital Transfer		2133.05		1.00	2134.05	
(1)投资性补助	Investment Allowances						
(2)其他	Other						
12.资本形成总额	Gross Capital Formation	22201.66		188.16		2721.71	
(1)固定资本形成总额	Gross Fixed Capital Formation	20976.56		188.16		2721.71	
(2)存货增加	Changes in Inventories	1225.10					
13.其他非金融资产获得减处置	Minus Items from Other Non-financial Capital						
14.净金融投资	Net Financial Investment	-9463.52		285.11		-784.69	
15.统计误差	Statistical Discrepancy	1016.94		-7.96		-313.24	
16.净金融投资	Financial Investment, Net	-8446.58		277.15		-1097.93	

3-22 资金流量表(金融交易,1998年)

单位：亿元

机构部门	Institutional Sector	非金融企业部门 Non-financial Enterprises		金融机构部门 Financial Institutions		政府部门 Governments	
交易项目	Transaction	运用 Utilization	来源 Source	运用 Utilization	来源 Source	运用 Utilization	来源 Source
净金融投资	Net Financial Investment	-8446.58		277.15		-1097.93	
资金运用合计	Total Utilization	5096.85		14663.53		3720.07	
资金来源合计	Total Sources		13543.44		14386.38		4818.00
通货	Currency in Circulation	96.68			1026.54	19.37	
存款	Savings Deposits	3847.63		141.70	14173.85	1312.31	
贷款	Loans		10148.50	11375.42			
证券	Securities		876.82	5159.38	1637.73	13.22	4918.07
保险准备金	Reserves for Insurance Business	14.12			336.57		
结算资金	Settlement Funds	-419.76			-419.76		
金融机构往来	Flow Between Financial Institutions			790.00	797.06		
准备金	Reserve Funds			-1742.94	-1523.42		-24.19
库存现金	Cash			64.22	65.53		
中央银行贷款	Loans from the Central Bank			-1976.51	-1993.32		
其他（净）	Other(net)	-1493.79			538.52	2375.19	
直接投资	Foreign Investment	218.06	3622.26				-75.88
其他对外债权债务	Other Claims or Liabilities on Abroad	2833.92	268.20	320.25	-252.93		
国际储备资产	Assets in International Serves			532.01			
国际收支错误与遗漏	Errors and Omission of Balance of Payment		-1372.35				

Flow of Funds Table (Physical Transaction, 1998)

(100 million yuan)

住户部门 Households		国内合计 Total of Domestic Sectors		国外部门 Rest of the World		合计 Total	
运用 Utilization	来源 Source	运用 Utilization	来源 Source	运用 Utilization	来源 Source	运用 Utilization	来源 Source
					-3051.40		-3051.40
	23324.07		78345.20				78345.20
21378.40	45998.84	46007.70	45998.84	8.03	16.89	46015.73	46015.73
1026.10		12724.34	12724.34			12724.34	12724.34
30.75	3607.49	14601.33	13232.30	454.36	1823.39	15055.69	15055.69
30.75	3527.96	13137.39	13120.83	447.07	463.63	13584.46	13584.46
0.00	59.16	1433.71	81.24	7.29	1359.76	1441.00	1441.00
	20.37	30.23	30.23			30.23	30.23
	50495.15		76967.31				76967.31
2498.38	4691.79	8429.85	8784.33	386.10	31.62	8815.95	8815.95
338.65		1377.41	1377.41			1377.41	1377.41
1562.63	1574.71	3137.34	3137.34			3137.34	3137.34
	974.38	974.38	974.38			974.38	974.38
597.10	2142.70	2940.72	3295.20	386.10	31.62	3326.82	3326.82
	52688.56		77321.79				77321.79
36921.20		46406.00				46406.00	
36921.20		36921.20				36921.20	
		9484.80				9484.80	
	15767.36		30915.79		-2027.99		28887.80
3.89		2137.94	2134.05		3.89	2137.94	2137.94
4434.37		29545.90				29545.90	
3744.37		27630.80				27630.80	
690.00		1915.10				1915.10	
11329.10		1366.00		-2024.10		-658.10	
297.06		992.80		-334.71		658.09	
11626.16		2358.80		-2358.81		-0.01	

Flow of Funds Table (Financial Transaction, 1998)

(100 million yuan)

住户部门 Households		国内合计 Total of Domestic Sectors		国外部门 Rest of the World		合计 Total	
运用 Utilization	来源 Source	运用 Utilization	来源 Source	运用 Utilization	来源 Source	运用 Utilization	来源 Source
11626.16		2358.80		-2358.80		0.00	
12465.74		35946.20		1604.12		37550.33	
	839.58		33587.40		3962.93		37550.33
850.75		966.79	1026.54	59.75		1026.54	1026.54
9257.12		14558.75	14173.85	-437.77	-52.86	14120.99	14120.99
	839.58	11375.42	10988.08	-270.49	116.85	11104.92	11104.92
2179.27		7351.87	7432.62	63.34		7415.21	7432.62
298.26		312.38	312.38			312.38	312.38
		-419.76	-419.76			-419.76	-419.76
		790.00	797.06			790.00	797.06
		-1742.94	-1523.42			-1742.94	-1523.42
		64.22	65.53		-1.31	64.22	64.22
		-1976.51	-1993.32			-1976.51	-1993.32
-119.66		761.74	538.52		-3.98	761.74	534.54
		218.06	3622.26	3622.26	218.06	3840.32	3840.32
		3154.17	-60.61	-60.61	3154.17	3093.56	3093.56
		532.01			532.01	532.01	532.01
			-1372.35	-1372.35		-1372.35	-1372.35

3-23 国际收支平衡表(2000年)

Balance of Payments (2000)

单位：千美元 (USD 1000)

项目	Item	差额 Balance	贷方 Credit	借方 Debit
经常帐户	**Current Account**	**20519248**	**298972814**	**278453565**
货物	Goods	34473606	249130638	214657032
出口	Exports		249130638	
进口	Imports			214657032
服务	Service	-5600122	30430487	36030608
运输	Transportation	-6725148	3670967	10396115
旅游	Tourism	3117313	16231000	13113687
通讯服务	Communication Service	1103482	1345452	241970
建筑服务	Construction Service	-392131	602313	994444
保险服务	Insurance Service	-2363620	107802	2471422
金融服务	Financial Service	-19637	77804	97441
计算机和信息服务	Computer and Information Service	90934	355947	265013
专有权利使用费和特许费	Fee for Patent or Royalty	-1200624	80348	1280972
咨询	Consultation	-284016	355716	639732
广告、宣传	Advertisement and Publicity	21018	223436	202418
电影、音像	Movies and Audio-video Products	-26122	11302	37424
其他商业服务	Other Commercial Service	966651	7083865	6117214
别处未提及的政府服务	Government Service not Elsewhere	111778	284535	172757
收益	Income and Profit	-14665541	12550854	27216395
职工报酬	Compensation of Staff and Workers	-477490	201871	679361
投资收益	Profit from Investment	-14188051	12348983	26537034
经常转移	Current Transfer	6311305	6860835	549530
各级政府	Governments	53573	147418	93845
其他部门	Other Departments	6257732	6713417	455685
资本和金融账户	**Capital and Finance Account**	**1922224**	**91986392**	**90064168**
资本账户	Capital Account	-35283	0	35283
金融账户	Financial Account	1957507	91986392	90028885
直接投资	Direct Investments	37482887	42095575	4612688
我国在外直接投资	Chinese Direct Investments Abroad	-915777	1323575	2239352
外国在华直接投资	Foreign Direct Investments in China	38398664	40772000	2373336
证券投资	Securities	-3990732	7814483	11805215
资产	Assets	-11307470	54915	11362385
负债	Liabilities	7316738	7759568	442830
其他投资	Other Investments	-31534648	42076334	73610982
资产	Assets	-43863491	4643518	48507009
贸易信贷	Trade Credit	-12959875	0	12959875
贷款	Loans	-18429647	91075	18520722
货币和存款	Currencies and Deposits	-6048944	1428243	7477187
其他资产	Other Assets	-6425024	3124200	9549224
负债	Liabilities	12328843	37432816	25103973
贸易信贷	Trade Credit	18232379	18232379	0
贷款	Loans	-2391224	12200369	14591593
货币和存款	Currencies and Deposits	-53564	8782	62347
其他负债	Other Liabilities	-3458748	6991286	10450033
储备资产变动	**Change in Reserve Assets**	**-10548400**	**407000**	**10955400**
货币黄金	Gold Reserves	0	0	0
特别提款权	Foreign Exchange	-57000	0	57000
在基金组织的储备头寸	SDR (Special Drawing Rights)	407000	407000	0
外汇	China's Reserve in IMF (International	-10898400	0	10898400
其他债权	Monetary Fund)	0	0	0
净误差与遗漏	**Net Error and Omission**	**-11893073**		**11893073**

注：1. 本表贸易数据来自海关统计。

2. 本表直接投资贷方数据来自外经贸部统计和间接申报中的“与土地有关的土地批租和租赁”；借方数据来自间接申报统计。

3. 本表其余数据来自间接申报统计。

a)Trade data in the table are from customs statistics.

b)Credit data on direct investment in the table are from statistics and from "Approved Leasing of Land" in indirect reporting, both collected by the Ministry of Foreign Trade and Economic Cooperation, and debit data are from indirect reporting.

c)Other data in the table are from indirect reporting.

主 要 统 计 指 标 解 释

国民生产总值（GNP） 指一个国家（或地区）所有常住单位在一定时期内收入初次分配的最终结果。一国常住单位从事生产活动所创造的增加值在初次分配中主要分配给该国的常住单位，但也有一部分以生产税及进口税（扣除生产和进口补贴）、劳动者报酬和财产收入等形式分配给非常住单位；同时，国外生产所创造的增加值也有一部分以生产税及进口税（扣除生产和进口补贴）、劳动者报酬和财产收入等形式分配给该国的常住单位，从而产生了国民生产总值的概念。它等于国内生产总值加上来自国外的净要素收入。与国内生产总值不同，国民生产总值是个收入概念，而国内生产总值是个生产概念。

国内生产总值（GDP） 指一个国家（或地区）所有常住单位在一定时期内生产活动的最终成果。国内生产总值有三种表现形态，即价值形态、收入形态和产品形态。从价值形态看，它是所有常住单位在一定时期内生产的全部货物和服务价值超过同期中间投入的全部非固定资产货物和服务价值的差额，即所有常住单位的增加值之和；从收入形态看，它是所有常住单位在一定时期内创造并分配给常住单位和非常住单位的初次收入分配之和；从产品形态看，它是所有常住单位在一定时期内最终使用的货物和服务价值与货物和服务净出口价值之和。在实际核算中，国内生产总值有三种计算方法，即生产法、收入法和支出法。三种方法分别从不同的方面反映国内生产总值及其构成。

三次产业 是根据社会生产活动历史发展的顺序对产业结构的划分，产品直接取自自然界的部门称为第一产业，对初级产品进行再加工的部门称为第二产业，为生产和消费提供各种服务的部门称为第三产业。它是世界上较为通用的产业结构分类，但各国的划分不尽一致。

我国的三次产业划分是：

第一产业： 农业（包括种植业、林业、牧业和渔业）。

第二产业： 工业（包括采掘业，制造业，电力、煤气及水的生产和供应业）和建筑业。

第三产业：除第一、第二产业以外的其他各业。由于第三产业包括的行业多、范围广，根据我国的实际情况，第三产业可分为两大部分；一是流通部门，二是服务部门。具体又可分为四个层次：

第一层次：流通部门，包括交通运输、仓储及邮电通信业，批发和零售贸易、餐饮业。

第二层次：为生产和生活服务的部门，包括金融、保险业，地质勘查业、水利管理业，房地产业，社会服务业，农、林、牧、渔服务业，交通运输辅助业，综合技术服务业等。

第三层次：为提高科学文化水平和居民素质服务的部门，包括教育、文化艺术及广播电影电视业，卫生、体育和社会福利业，科学研究业等。

第四层次：为社会公共需要服务的部门，包括国家机关、政党机关和社会团体以及军队、警察等。

支出法国内生产总值 指一个国家(或地区)所有常住单位在一定时期内用于最终消费、资本形成总额，以及货物和服务的净出口总额，它反映本期生产的国内生产总值的使用及构成。

最终消费 指常住单位在一定时期内对于货物和服务的全部最终消费支出，也就是常住单位为满足物质、文化和精神生活的需要，从本国经济领土和国外购买的货物和服务的支出；不包括非常住单位在本国经济领土内的消费支出。最终消费分为居民消费和政府消费。

居民消费 指常住住户对货物和服务的全部最终消费支出。居民消费按市场价格计算，即按居民支付的购买者价格计算。购买者价格是购买者取得货物所支付的价格，包括购买者支付的运输和商业费用。居民消费除了直接以货币形式购买货物和服务的消费之外，还包括以其他方式获得的货物和服务的消费支出，即所谓的虚拟消费支出。居民虚拟消费支出包括以下几种类型：单位以实物报酬及实物转移的形式提供给劳动者的货物和服务；住户生产并由本住户消费了的货物和服务，其中的服务仅指住户的自有住房服务；金融机构提供的金融媒介服务；保险公司提供的保险服务。

政府消费 指政府部门为全社会提供公共服务的消费支出和免费或以较低价格向住户提供的货物和服务的净支出。前者等于政府服务的产出价值减去政府单位所获得的经营收入的价值，政府服务的产出价值等于它的经常性业务支出加上固定资产折旧；后者等于政府部门免费或以较低价格向住户提供的货物和服务的市场价值减去向住户收取的价值。

资本形成总额 指常住单位在一定时期内获得的减去处置的固定资产加存货的变动，包括固定资本形成总额和存货增加。

固定资本形成总额 指常住单位购置、转入和自产自用的固定资产，扣除固定资产的销售和转出后的价值，分有形固定资产形成总额和无形固定资产形成总额。有形固定资产形成总额包括一定时期内完成的建筑工程、安装工程和设备工器具购置（减处置）价值，以及土地改良、新增役、种、奶、毛、娱乐用牲畜和新增经济林木价值。无形固定资产形成总额包括矿藏的勘探、计算机软件、娱乐和文学艺术品原件等获得减处置。

存货增加 指常住单位存货实物量变动的市场价值，即期末价值减期初价值的差额。存货增加可以是正值，也可以是负值；正值表示存货上升，负值表示存货下降。它包括生产单位购进的原材料、燃料和储备物资等存货，以及生产单位生产的产成品、在制品等存货等。

货物和服务净出口 指货物和服务出口减货物和服务进口的差额。出口包括常住单位向非常住单位出售或无偿转让的各种货物和服务的价值；进口包括常住单位从非常住单位购买或无偿得到的各种货物和服务的价值。由于服务活动的提供与使用同时发生，因此服务的进出口业务并不发生出入境现象，一般把常住单位从国外得到的服务作为进口，非常住单位从本国得到的服务作为出口。货物的出口和进口都按离岸价格计算。

劳动者报酬 指劳动者因从事生产活动所获得的全部报酬。包括劳动者获得的各种形式的工资、奖金和津贴，既包括货币形式的，也包括实物形式的；还包括劳动者所享受的公费医疗和医药卫生费、上下班交通补贴和单位支付的社会保险费等。对于个体经济来说，其所有者所获得的劳动报酬和经营利润不易区分，这两部分统一作为劳动者报酬处理。

生产税净额 指生产税减生产补贴后的余额。生产税指政府对生产单位生产、销售和从事经营活动以及因从事生产活动使用某些生产要素（如固定资产、土地、劳动力）所征收的各种税、附加费和规费。生产补贴与生产税相反，指政府对生产单位的单方面收入转移，因此视为负生产税，包括政策亏损补贴、粮食系统价格补贴、外贸企业出口退税收入等。

固定资产折旧 指一定时期内为弥补固定资产损耗按照核定的固定资产折旧率提取的固定资产折旧，或按国民经济核算统一规定的折旧率虚拟计算的固定资产折旧。它反映了固定资产在当期生产中的转移价值。各类企业和企业化管理的事业单位的固定资产折旧是指实际计提并计入成本费中的折旧费；不计提折旧的政府机关、非企业化管理的事业单位和居民住房的固定资产折旧是按照统一规定的折旧率和固定资产原值计算的虚拟折旧。原则上，固定资产折旧应按固定资产的重置价值计算，但是目前我国尚不具备对全社会固定资产进行重估价的基础，所以暂时只能采用上述办法。

营业盈余 指常住单位创造的增加值扣除劳动者报酬、生产税净额和固定资产折旧后的余额。它相当于企业的营业利润加上生产补贴，但要扣除从利润中开支的工资和福利等。

直接消耗系数 指某一个部门生产单位总产出需要直接消耗各部门产品和服务的数量，也称为投入系数。它反映该部门与其他部门之间直接的技术经济联系和直接依赖关系。

完全消耗系数 指增加某一个部门单位总产出需要完全消耗各部门产品和服务的数量。完全消耗系数等于直接消耗系数和全部间接消耗系数之和，它是全面揭示国民经济各部门之间技术经济的全部联系和相互依赖关系的主要指标。

机构单位 指能以自己的名义拥有资产、发生负债、从事经济活动并与其他实体进行交易的经济实体。根据机构单位在生产、消费、融资活动中所起的不同作用，资金流量核算将常住单位区分为如下四类机构单位：非金融企业、金融机构、政府单位、住户和国外。

机构部门 将相同性质的机构单位归并在一起，就形成机构部门。资金流量核算中区分了如下几类机构部门：非金融企业部门、金融机构部门、政府部门、住户部门。

非金融企业与非金融企业部门 非金融企业指主要从事市场货物生产和提供非金融市场服务的常住企业，它主要包括各类法人企业。所有非金融企业归并在一起，就形成非金融企业部门。

金融机构与金融机构部门 金融机构指主要从事金融中介以及与金融中介密切相关的辅助金融活动的常住单位，它主要包括中央银行、商业银行和政策性银行、非银行信贷机构和保险公司。所有金融机构归并在一起，就形成金融机构部门。

政府单位与政府部门 政府单位指在我国境内通过政治程序建立的、在一特定区域内对其他机构单位拥有立法、司法和行政权的法律实体及其附属单位。政府单位的主要职能是利用征税和其他方式获得的资金向社会和公众提供公共服务。通过转移支付，对社会收入和财产进行再分配。它主要包括各种行政单位和事业单位。所有政府单位归并在一起，就形成政府部门。

住户与住户部门 住户指共享同一生活设施、部分或全部收入和财产集中使用、共同消费住房、食品和其他消费品与消费服务的常住个人或个人群体。所有住户归并在一起，就形成住户部门。

非常住单位与国外部门 所有不具有常住性的机构单位都是非常住单位。将所有与我国常住单位发生交易的非常住单位归并在一起，就形成国外部门。

初次分配总收入 初次分配指以劳动者报酬、固定资产折旧、生产税及财产收入等形式对增加值进行的分配。初次分配形成的收入余额为初次分配总收入。

经常转移 指部门间以实物和资金方式实现的单方面转让。包括社会保险付款、社会补助、侨汇、无偿捐赠、赔偿等。

可支配总收入 指各机构部门在初次分配总收入基础上通过经常转移后所获得的收入。这部分收入用于最终消费和储蓄。

总储蓄 指可支配总收入扣除最终消费后的余额。

资本转移 指一个部门无偿地向另一个部门支付用于资本形成的资金，是一种不从对方获取任何对应物作为回报的交易。资本转移具有不同于经常转移的两个特征，一是转移的目的是用于投资，而不是用于消费；二是资产所有权的转移，而不仅仅是使用权的转移。资本转移包括投资性补助和其他资产转移，根据我国目前的实际情况，投资性补助是指财政投资性拨款，即财政拨款中用于基本建设、更新改造和其他固定资产投资的部分。

净金融投资 从实物交易角度看，它是指总储蓄加资本转移收入减资本转移支出减资本形成总额后的余额。从金融交易角度看，它是金融资产的增加额减金融负债的增加额之后的余额。

通货 指以现金形式存在于市场流通领域中的货币，包括辅币和纸币。

存款 指以各种形式存在的所有存款，包括活期存款、定期存款、住户储蓄存款、财政存款、外汇存款和其他存款。

贷款 指金融机构向非金融部门提供的各种形式的所有贷款，包括短期贷款、中长期贷款、财政贷款、外汇贷款和其他贷款。

证券 包括债券和股票。

保险准备金 指对人寿保险准备金和养恤基金的净权益、保险费预付款和未结索赔准备金。

结算资金 指银行的汇兑在途资金。

金融机构往来 指各机构之间的资金往来，包括同业存放款和同业拆借款。

准备金 指各金融机构在中央银行的存款及缴存中央银行的法定准备金。

中央银行贷款 指中央银行向各金融机构的贷款。

经常项目 包括货物、服务、收益及经常性转移。

货物 指通过我国海关进出口的货物，以海关进出口统计资料为基础，并根据国际收支统计口径的要求，出口、进口都以商品所有权变化为原则进行调整。出口和进口金额均按离岸价格统计。

服务 包括运输、旅游、通讯、建筑、保险、国际金融服务、计算机和信息服务、专有权力使用费和特许费、各种商业服务、个人文化娱乐服务以及政府服务。

收益 包括职工报酬和投资收益。投资收益包括直接投资、证券投资和其它投资的收益和支出以及直接投资收益的再投资。

资本项目 包括移民转移、债务减免等资本性转移。

金融项目 包括直接投资、证券投资和其它投资。

直接投资 指外国、港澳台地区在我国和我国在外国、港澳台地区以独资、合资、合作及合作勘探开发方式进行的投资。

证券投资 指外国、港澳台地区购买(或我国买回)我国(包括地方政府和企业)发行的股票、债券等有价证券和我国(政府、企业、私人)买卖外国、港澳台地区发行的股票、债券等有价证券。

其它投资 包括外国提供给我国和我国提供给外国的贸易信贷、贷款、货币和存款以及其它资产。

储备资产增减额 指我国在黄金储备、外汇储备、在国际货币基金组织的储备头寸、特别提款权、使用基金信贷等方面本年末与上年末余额之间的差额。储备资产增加用负号表示。

Explanatory Notes on Main Statistical Indicators

Gross National Product (GNP) refers to the final result of the primary distribution of the income created by all the resident units of a country (or a region) during a certain period of time. The value-added created by the resident units of a country engaged in production activities is mainly distributed to the resident units of that country while a part of it is distributed to the non-resident units in the form of production tax and import duties (minus subsidies to production and import), remuneration for the labourers and property income. At the meantime, a part of the value-added created abroad is distributed to the resident units of the country in the form of production tax and import duties (minus subsidies to production and import), remuneration for the labourers and property income. Thus the concept of gross national product is formed, which equals to gross domestic product plus net factor income from abroad. Unlike gross domestic product which is a concept of production, gross national product is a concept of income.

Gross Domestic Product (GDP) refers to the final products of all resident units in a country (or a region) during a certain period of time. Gross domestic product is expressed in three different forms, i.e. value, income, and products respectively. The form of value refers to the total value of all products and services produced by all resident units during a certain period of time minus total value of intimidate input of materials and services of the nature of non-fixed assets or the summation of the value-added of all resident units; the form of income includes all the income created by all resident units and distributed primarily to all resident and non-resident units; the form of products refers to the value of all final goods and services for final use by all resident units plus the value of net exports of goods and services during a given period of time. In the practice of national accounting, gross domestic product is calculated with three approaches, i.e. production approach, income approach, and expenditure approach, which reflect gross domestic product and its composition from different aspects.

Three Industries Industry structure has been classified according to the historical sequence of development. Primary industry refers to extraction of natural resources; secondary industry involves processing of primary products; and tertiary industry provides services of various kinds for production and consumption. The above classification is universal although it varies to some extent form country to country. Industry in China comprises:

Primary industry: agriculture (including farming, forestry, animal husbandry and fishery).

Secondary industry: industry (including mining and quarrying, manufacturing, production and supply of electricity, water and gas) and construction.

Tertiary industry: all other industries not included in primary or secondary industry.

Due to the fact that tertiary industry involves in a large variety of industries in China, it is divided into two sectors: circulation sector and service sector and further into four levels:

The first level: circulation sector, including transportation, storage, postal and telecommunications, wholesale and retail trade, and catering trade.

The second level: service sector providing services for production and consumption, including banking, insurance, geological survey, water conservancy management, real estates, service for residents, service for agriculture, forestry, animal husbandry, fishery, subsidiary services for transportation and communications, comprehensive technical services, etc.

The third level: service sector for upgrading scientific, educational and cultural level of the people, including education, culture and arts, broadcasting, movies, television, public health, sports, social welfare and scientific research, etc.

The fourth level: sector providing services for public needs, including government agencies, political parties, social organizations, military and police service.

GDP Calculated with Expenditure Approach refers to total expenditure on final consumption, total capital formation and net export of goods and services by resident units of a country in a certain period of time. It reflects the composition of GDP by its use.

Final Consumption refers to the total expenditure of resident units on final consumption of goods and services in a certain period, namely the expenditure of the resident units for purchases of goods and services from domestic economic territory and abroad to meet the requirements of material, cultural and spiritual life. It excludes the expenditure of non-resident units on consumption in the economic territory of the country. The final consumption is classified into household consumption and government consumption.

Households Consumption refers to the total expenditure of resident households on the final consumption of goods and services. The households consumption is calculated at market prices, namely the purchaser's prices which the households pay; the purchasers' prices of goods are the prices the households pay when they obtain the goods, including the transport and commercial expenses paid by the households. In addition to the consumption of goods and services bought by the households directly with money, the expenditure on goods and services obtained by the households in other ways, i.e. the so-called imputed expenditure on consumption, is also included in the households consumption. The imputation expenditure of the households on consumption includes the following types: (a) the goods and services provided to the households by the units in the form of payment in kind and transfer in kind; (b) the goods and services produced and consumed by the households themselves, in which the services refer only to the services provided by the residential buildings owned by the households; (c) the services of financial intermediary provided by the financial institutions; (d) the insurance services provided by the insurance companies.

Government Consumption refers to the expenditure on the consumption of the public services provided by the government to the whole society and the net expenditure on the goods and services provided by the government to the households at free charge or lower prices. The former equals to the output value of the government services minus the value of operating income obtained by the government departments. (The output value of the government services equals to its current operating expenditure plus depreciation of fixed assets). The latter equals to the market value of the goods and services provided by the government free of charge or at low prices to the households minus the value received by the government from the households.

Total Capital Formation refers to the fixed assets acquired minus those disposed and the change in inventory, including the total fixed assets formation and the increase in inventory.

Total Fixed Capital Formation refers to the value of fixed assets purchased, transferred in by the resident units and those produced and used by themselves deducting the value of fixed assets sold and transferred out. It can be classified into total tangible assets formation and total intangible assets formation. The total tangible assets formation include the value of the construction projects, installation projects completed and the equipment, apparatus and instruments purchased as well as the value of land improved, the value of draught animals, breeding stock, milk, wool and recreational animals and the newly increased economic forest in a certain period. The total intangible assets formation includes the prospecting of minerals, the acquisition of computer software, the originals of recreational works and works of literature and arts minus the disposal of them.

Increase in Inventory refers to the market value of the change in inventory, i.e. the difference of value between the beginning and the end of the period. The increase in inventory can be positive or negative. A positive value indicates the increase in inventory while a negative value indicates the decrease in stock. The inventory includes the raw materials, fuels and reserve materials purchased by the production units as well as the inventory of finished products, semi-finished products, work-in-progress, etc.

Net Export of Goods and Services refers to the difference of the exports of goods and services minus the imports of goods and services. The imports include the value of various goods and services sold or gratuitously transferred by the resident units to the non-resident units. The imports include the value of various goods and services purchased or gratuitously acquired by the resident units from the non-resident units. Because the provision of services and the use of them happen simultaneously, the import and export of services do not appear to have the phenomena of crossing the border of the country. The acquisition of services by the resident units from abroad is usually treated as import while the acquisition of services by non-resident units in this country is usually treated as export. The export and import of goods are calculated at FOB.

Labourers' Remuneration refers to the whole payment of various forms earned by the labourers from the productive activities they are engaged in. It includes wages, bonuses and allowances the labourers earned in monetary form and in kind. It also includes the free medical services provided to the labourers and the medicine expenses, traffic subsidies and social insurance fee paid by the labourers' working units for them. As the individual economy is concerned, since the labourers' remuneration is not easily distinguished from the operating profit, both are treated as labourers remuneration.

Net Taxes on Production refers to the residual of the taxes on production minus the subsidies on production. The taxes on production refers to the various taxes, extra charges and fees levied on the production units on their production, sale and business activities as well as on some factors of production, such as fixed assets, land and labour force, used in the production activities they are engaged in. In contrast to the taxes on production, the subsidies on production refer to the unilateral transfer of part of the government's revenue to the production units and is therefore regarded as negative taxes on production. They include subsidies on the loss due to implementation of government policies, price subsidies to the grain institutions, foreign trade corporations' receipts from drawback, etc.

Depreciation of Fixed Assets refers to the depreciation of fixed assets of a given period, drawn in accordance with the stipulated depreciation rate for the purpose of compensating the wear loss of the fixed assets or the depreciation of fixed assets calculated in a fictitious way in accordance with the stipulated unified depreciation rate in the national economic accounting system. It reflects the value of transfer of the fixed assets in the production of the current period. The depreciation of fixed assets in various enterprises and institutions managed as enterprises refers to the depreciation expenses actually drawn and calculated as part of the cost. In government agencies and institutions not managed as enterprises which do not draw the depreciation expenses, as well as for the houses of residents, the depreciation of fixed assets is the imputed depreciation, which is calculated in accordance with the stipulated unified depreciation rate. In principle, the depreciation of fixed assets should be calculated on the basis of the re-purchased value of the fixed assets. However, there is no actual condition to re-evaluate all the fixed assets in China. Therefore, the above-mentioned methods are temporarily adopted at present.

Operating Surplus refers to the balance of the value added created by the resident units deducting the labourers' remuneration, net taxes on production and the depreciation of fixed assets. It is equivalent to the business profit of the enterprises plus subsidies on production, but the wages and welfare expenses paid from the profits should be deducted.

Direct Input Coefficient refers to the volume of products and services of all sectors consumed directly by a certain sector's productive units, which are needed for their total output. It is also named as technical coefficient. It represents the direct technical economical ties and direct interdependence between the sector and other sectors.

Total Input Coefficient refers to the volume of products and services of all sectors needed for a certain sectors productive units to increase their total output. Total input coefficient is equal to the sum of direct input coefficient and total indirect input coefficient. It is a major indicator to disclose the technical economical ties and interdependence between sectors of the national economy.

Institutional Units refer to economic entities that are in a position to own assets and incur liabilities in their own name, and to engage in economic activities and conduct transactions with other entities. Depending on their different role in production, consumption and financing, 4 groups of resident institutional units are identified in the flow of fund tables, namely, non-financial corporations, financial institutions, governments, households and the rest of the world.

Institutional Sectors refer groups of institutional units that are classified by their nature. Following groups (or institutional sectors) are identified in the flow of fund accounts: the sector of non-financial corporations, the sector of financial institutions, the sector of governments and the sector of households.

Non-Financial Corporations and the Sector of Non-Financial Corporations Non-financial corporations refer to resident corporations that are engaged in the production of goods and the provision of non financial services in the market, mainly covering corporate enterprises of various types. All non-financial corporations make up the sector of non-financial corporations.

Financial Institutions and the Sector of Financial Institutions Financial institutions refer to resident institutions that are engaged in the financial services or auxiliary financial activities, mainly covering central banks, commercial banks, policy-related banks, non-banking credit institutions and insurance companies. All financial institutions make up the sector of financial institutions.

Government Units and the Sector of Governments Government units refer to legal entities and their auxiliary units within the territory of China that are established through political process and are empowered with legislative, administrative or judicial rights over other institutional units in a given region. The main function of government units is to acquire funds through taxation or other means, to provide public services to the society and households, and to conduct redistribution of income and properties of the society through transfer payment. Government units cover mainly administrative and institutional units of various types. All government units make up the sector of governments.

Households and the Sector of Households Households refer to resident individuals or groups of resident individuals who share common living facilities, pool together entire or part of their income and properties at their common disposal, and share their housing, food and other consumer goods and services. All households make up the sector of households.

Non-resident Units and the Sector of the Rest of the World Non-resident units refer to of units that are of a non-resident nature. All non-resident units that have transactions with resident units make up the sector the rest of the world.

Total Income of Primary Distribution Primary distribution refers to the distribution of value-added in the form of compensation for labours, depreciation of fixed assets, production taxes and property income. The sum of income obtained through primary distribution is called the total income of primary distribution.

Current Transfers include 4 parts: income tax, payment to social securities, social allowances and other current transfers.

Total Disposable Income refers to income received by institutional sectors on the basis of total income of primary distribution and through current transfers. This is the income that is used for final consumption and savings.

Total Savings is the difference between total disposable income and the final consumption.

Capital Transfer refers to the free payment from one sector to another sector for capital formation, and is a transaction that seeks no return from the recipient. The capital transfer differs from the current transfer in 2 aspects. Firstly, the objective of the transfer is investment rather than consumption. Secondly, capital transfer features the transfer of the ownership of the capital rather than the utilization right of the capital. Capital transfer includes investment subsidies and other capital transfers. Under the current situation in China, investment subsidies refer to investment allocations from government finance, i.e. the financial allocations that are used for capital construction, updating and transformation projects and other investment in fixed assets.

Net Financial Investment refers to total savings plus the net income from capital transfer minus the gross capital formation from the point of view of physical transaction. In terms of monetary transaction, it is the increased value of financial assets minus the increase of the financial liabilities.

Currency in Circulation refers to currency that is in circulation in the market, including notes and fractional currency.

Savings Deposit refers to deposits of all types, including current deposit, fixed deposit, household savings deposit, government deposit, foreign exchange deposit and other deposits.

Loans refer to loans of all forms provided by financial institutions to non-financial sectors, including short-term loans, medium and long-term loans, government loans, foreign exchange loans and other loans.

Securities include bonds and stocks.

Insurance Reserve Funds refer to reserve fund for life insurance, the net pension fund, advance payment of premium and non-claimed reserves.

Settlement Fund refers to bank fund that is in the process of remittance.

Transactions Between Financial Institutions refer to flow of capital between financial institutions, including interbank deposits and loans.

Reserve Funds refer to savings of financial institutions in the central bank and designated reserves to the central bank.

Loans from the Central Bank refer to loans from the central bank to financial institutions.

Current Account includes goods, services, earnings and current transfers.

Goods refer to imported or exported goods through Chinese customs. Figures in the Yearbook are based on customs statistics, adjusted in line with the concepts and definitions of the balance of payment statistics and with the change in the ownership of commodities. Statistics on both exports and imports are valued at f.o.b. prices.

Services include transportation, tourism, communications, construction, insurance, international financial services, computer and information service, royalty for patent, trademarks and other special rights, commercial services, personal cultural and recreational services and government services.

Earnings include compensation of employees and earnings from investment (including earnings from and expenses on direct investment, security investment and other investment, as well as reinvestment of earnings from direct investment).

Capital Account includes capital transfers such as immigration transfer, reduction or exemption of debts, etc..

Financial Account includes direct investment, security investment and other investments.

Direct Investment refers to investment, made in forms of exclusive investment, joint investment, contracted operation and cooperative development, by foreign investors or investors from Hong Kong, Macao and Taiwan in China, or by Chinese investors in foreign countries or in Hong Kong, Macao and Taiwan.

Security Investment refers to the purchase of stocks and securities issued by central and local governments and enterprises in China by institutions or individuals of foreign countries or from Hong Kong, Macao and Taiwan (and the re-purchase by Chinese institutions), and the purchase and selling of stocks and securities issued in foreign countries and in Hong Kong, Macao and Taiwan by Chinese governments, enterprises and individuals.

Other Investment includes trade credits, loans, currency, savings and other assets, provided by foreign countries to China and by China to foreign countries.

Reserve Assets, Net Increase refers to the net balance between the end of the reference year and the end of the previous year, in the gold reserve, foreign exchange reserve, special drawing rights in the International Monetary Fund, and the use of the Fund's credits. The increase in the reserve assets is expressed as a negative figure.

四、人口

Population

简要说明

一、本篇资料反映2000年11月1日人口普查及历年人口方面的基本情况，包括全国及31个省、自治区、直辖市的主要人口统计数据，如：全国历年人口总数、城镇人口、乡村人口；第五次全国人口普查快速汇总的数据，有分地区总人口增长情况、汉族和少数民族人口、人口负担系数、家庭户规模及人口受教育程度等。另外，我们还对建国以来进行的五次人口普查主要数据进行了比较。

二、本篇的12张表均由国家统计局人口和社会科技统计司整理提供。其中表4－1、4－2中1982－1989年数据是根据1982年、1990年两次人口普查数据调整的；1990－1999年的数据是根据人口变动抽样调查数据推算的；2000年数据为第五次全国人口普查快速汇总的11月1日零时数；其余年份数据为户籍统计数。表4－4为五次人口普查主要数据。其他表均为2000年第五次全国人口普查快速汇总的数据。

三、2000年人口普查的对象是：具有中华人民共和国国籍，并在中华人民共和国境内常住的人。人口普查采用按常住人口登记的原则，每个人必须在常住地进行登记，一个人只能在一个地方进行登记。普查登记的标准时间是2000年11月1日零时，2000年人口普查数据均为这个时点的常住人口数据。

2000年人口普查数据中的全国总计，如不做特殊说明，均指大陆31个省、自治区、直辖市以及解放军现役军人的合计(还包括105万常住地待定的人)，分省数据不包括解放军现役军人(也不包括前述的105万常住地待定的人)。全国总计是按快速汇总资料直接计算的，个别省对快速汇总的城乡人口和文盲人口数据进行了调整，因此部分表中分省合计不等于全国总计。

2000年人口普查数据中的绝对数取到万位，由于四舍五入原因，表内数据略有不平，编辑时未做调整。全国总计的相对数是按登记资料直接计算的，分省的相对数保持与各地人口普查公报相一致。

Brief Introduction

I. Data in this chapter show the basic condition of population at the 5th National Population Census, with zero hour of November 1, 2000 as the reference time, and at the previous censuses, including the main data of population of the whole nation and of 31 provinces, autonomous regions and municipalities directly under the central government, such as the national population, urban population and rural population over the years, and data of the advance tabulation of the 5th national population census, such as population growth rate by regions, Han nationality and various national minorities population, dependency ratio, family household size and the educational level of population, etc.. In addition, a comparison is made among the main data of the five population censuses undertaken after the founding of the People's Republic of China.

II. The 12 tables in this chapter are prepared and provided by the Department of Population, Social and Science Statistics of the National Bureau of Statistics. Among them, figures for 1982-1989 in tables 4-1 and 4-2 have been adjusted in accordance with the data from the population censuses of 1982 and 1990, figures for 1990-1999 are estimated on the basis of the annual national sample surveys on population changes, figures for 2000 are obtained from the advance tabulation of the 5th national population census, with zero hour of November 1, 2000 as the reference time, and figures for other years are collected from the residence registration. Data in Table 4-4 present results from the five national population censuses. Data in other tables are obtained from the advance tabulation of the 5th National Population Census.

III. Population enumerated in 2000 national population census refers to people with citizenship of the People's Republic of China and with permanent residence on the mainland of the country. The principle of de jure population was adopted in the population census, that is everyone should be enumerated at his/her permanent residence and one person is enumerated only at one place. The reference time of the census is zero hour of November 1, 2000. Data of 2000 national population census are the data of de jure population at the reference time.

Unless otherwise specified, the national total population of 2000 national population census refers to the total population of the 31 provinces, autonomous regions and municipalities and of military personnel of the mainland of China (including 1.05 million persons with their household registration unsettled), and population by regions excludes the military personnel (also excluding 1.05 million persons with their household registration unsettled). The national total is obtained from the advance tabulation. Data for the urban/rural population and for illiterate population have been adjusted in several provinces, so the sum of figures by province is not equal to the national total in some tables.

Figures in the tables may be not balanced slightly and have not adjusted at the compilation since the absolute figures of 2000 national population census are rounded by 10,000. The relative figures of national total are calculated from the enumeration and the relative figures by regions are kept in accordance to the communiqué of each province, autonomous region or municipally.

4-1 人口数及构成

Population and Its Composition

本表各年人口包括中国人民解放军现役军人数据，未包括香港、澳门特别行政区和台湾省的人口数据。

Data in this table include the military personnel of Chinese People's Liberation Army, but exclude the population of Hong Kong, Macao and Taiwan.

单位：万人 (10 000 persons)

年 份 Year	年底总人口 Total Population (year-end)	按性别分 By Sex				按城乡分 By Residence			
		男 Male		女 Female		城镇总人口 Urban		乡村总人口 Rural	
		人口数 Population	比重（%） Proportion	人口数 Population	比重（%） Proportion	人口数 Population	比重（%） Proportion	人口数 Population	比重（%） Proportion
1978	96259	49567	51.49	46692	48.51	17245	17.92	79014	82.08
1979	97542	50192	51.46	47350	48.54	18495	18.96	79047	81.04
1980	98705	50785	51.45	47920	48.55	19140	19.39	79565	80.61
1981	100072	51519	51.48	48553	48.52	20171	20.16	79901	79.84
1982	101654	52352	51.50	49302	48.50	21480	21.13	80174	78.87
1983	103008	53152	51.60	49856	48.40	22274	21.62	80734	78.38
1984	104357	53848	51.60	50509	48.40	24017	23.01	80340	76.99
1985	105851	54725	51.70	51126	48.30	25094	23.71	80757	76.29
1986	107507	55581	51.70	51926	48.30	26366	24.52	81141	75.48
1987	109300	56290	51.50	53010	48.50	27674	25.32	81626	74.68
1988	111026	57201	51.52	53825	48.48	28661	25.81	82365	74.19
1989	112704	58099	51.55	54605	48.45	29540	26.21	83164	73.79
1990	114333	58904	51.52	55429	48.48	30191	26.41	84142	73.59
1991	115823	59466	51.34	56357	48.66	30543	26.37	85280	73.63
1992	117171	59811	51.05	57360	48.95	32372	27.63	84799	72.37
1993	118517	60472	51.02	58045	48.98	33351	28.14	85166	71.86
1994	119850	61246	51.10	58604	48.90	34301	28.62	85549	71.38
1995	121121	61808	51.03	59313	48.97	35174	29.04	85947	70.96
1996	122389	62200	50.82	60189	49.18	35950	29.37	86439	70.63
1997	123626	63131	51.07	60495	48.93	36989	29.92	86637	70.08
1998	124810	63629	50.98	61181	49.02	37942	30.40	86868	69.60
1999	125909	64189	50.98	61720	49.02	38892	30.89	87017	69.11
2000	126583	65355	51.63	61228	48.37	45844	36.22	80739	63.78

注：1.1981年以前数据为户籍统计数，1982—1989年数据根据1982年、1990年两次人口普查数据有所调整，1990—1999年数据是人口变动抽样调查推算数（下表同），2000年数据为第五次全国人口普查快速汇总的11月1日零时数。

2.总人口和城镇人口中包括中国人民解放军现役军人。

a)Data before 1982 were taken from the annual reports of the Ministry of Public Security. Data in 1982-1989 were adjusted on the basis of the 1982 and 1990 national population censuses. Data in 1990-1999 have been estimated on the basis of the annual national sample surveys on population changes (the next table is the same), Data of 2000 are obtained from the advance tabulation of the 5th national population census, with zero hour of November 1, 2000 as the reference time.

b)Urban Population include the military personnel of Chinese People's Liberation Army.

4-2 人口出生率、死亡率、自然增长率

Birth Rate, Death Rate and Natural Growth Rate of Population

单位：‰ (‰)

年 份 Year	全国 National			市镇 City			县 County		
	出生率 Birth Rate	死亡率 Death Rate	自然增长率 Natural Growth Rate	出生率 Birth Rate	死亡率 Death Rate	自然增长率 Natural Growth Rate	出生率 Birth Rate	死亡率 Death Rate	自然增长率 Natural Growth Rate
1978	18.25	6.25	12.00	13.56	5.12	8.44	18.91	6.42	12.49
1979	17.82	6.21	11.61	13.67	5.07	8.60	18.43	6.39	12.04
1980	18.21	6.34	11.87	14.17	5.48	8.69	18.82	6.47	12.35
1981	20.91	6.36	14.55	16.45	5.14	11.31	21.55	6.53	15.02
1982	22.28	6.60	15.68						
1983	20.19	6.90	13.29						
1984	19.90	6.82	13.08						
1985	21.04	6.78	14.26						
1986	22.43	6.86	15.57						
1987	23.33	6.72	16.61						
1988	22.37	6.64	15.73						
1989	21.58	6.54	15.04	16.73	5.78	10.95	23.27	6.81	16.46
1990	21.06	6.67	14.39	16.14	5.71	10.43	22.80	7.01	15.79
1991	19.68	6.70	12.98	15.49	5.50	9.99	21.17	7.13	14.04
1992	18.24	6.64	11.60	15.47	5.77	9.70	19.09	6.91	12.18
1993	18.09	6.64	11.45	15.37	5.99	9.38	19.06	6.89	12.17
1994	17.70	6.49	11.21	15.13	5.53	9.60	18.84	6.80	12.04
1995	17.12	6.57	10.55	14.76	5.53	9.23	18.08	6.99	11.09
1996	16.98	6.56	10.42	14.47	5.65	8.82	18.02	6.94	11.08
1997	16.57	6.51	10.06	14.52	5.58	8.94	17.43	6.90	10.53
1998	16.03	6.50	9.53	13.67	5.31	8.36	17.05	7.01	10.04
1999	15.23	6.46	8.77	13.18	5.51	7.67	16.13	6.88	9.25

4-3 各地区总人口和性别比

Total Population and Sex Ratio by Region

本表是2000年全国人口普查快速汇总的11月1日零时数。

Data in this table are obtained from the advance tabulation of the 5th national population census, with zero hour of November 1, 2000 as the reference time.

地区	Region	总人口 (万人) Total (10 000 persons)			占总人口比重 (%) % to Total		性别比 (女性=100)
		合计 Total	男 Male	女 Female	男 Male	女 Female	Sex Ratio (Female=100)
全国总计	**National Total**	**129533**					
大陆31个省、自治区、直辖市和解放军现役军人合计	Mainland Total of the 31 Provinces, Autonomous Regions and Municipalities and of Military Personnel	126583	65355	61228	51.63	48.37	106.74
北　京	Beijing	1382	721	661	52.15	47.85	108.97
天　津	Tianjin	1001	510	491	50.98	49.02	103.99
河　北	Hebei	6744	3433	3311	50.90	49.10	103.67
山　西	Shanxi	3297	1706	1591	51.76	48.24	107.28
内蒙古	Inner Mongolia	2376	1229	1147	51.73	48.27	107.17
辽　宁	Liaoning	4238	2161	2077	50.99	49.01	104.04
吉　林	Jilin	2728	1397	1331	51.20	48.80	104.92
黑龙江	Heilongjiang	3689	1886	1803	51.12	48.88	104.60
上　海	Shanghai	1674	860	814	51.39	48.60	105.74
江　苏	Jiangsu	7438	3766	3672	50.64	49.36	102.58
浙　江	Zhejiang	4677	2402	2275	51.35	48.65	105.57
安　徽	Anhui	5986	3089	2897	51.60	48.40	106.61
福　建	Fujian	3471	1789	1682	51.54	48.46	106.36
江　西	Jiangxi	4140	2153	1987	52.00	48.00	108.31
山　东	Shandong	9079	4596	4483	50.63	49.37	102.53
河　南	Henan	9256	4775	4481	51.59	48.41	106.58
湖　北	Hubei	6028	3138	2890	52.06	47.94	108.59
湖　南	Hunan	6440	3359	3081	52.16	47.84	109.02
广　东	Guangdong	8642	4402	4240	50.94	49.06	103.82
广　西	Guangxi	4489	2378	2111	52.98	47.02	112.68
海　南	Hainan	787	412	375	52.33	47.67	109.77
重　庆	Chongqing	3090	1605	1485	51.93	48.07	108.04
四　川	Sichuan	8329	4305	4024	51.69	48.31	106.98
贵　州	Guizhou	3525	1847	1678	52.40	47.60	110.10
云　南	Yunnan	4288	2247	2041	52.41	47.59	110.11
西　藏	Tibet	262	133	129	50.65	49.35	102.62
陕　西	Shaanxi	3605	1875	1730	52.02	47.98	108.42
甘　肃	Gansu	2562	1328	1234	51.83	48.17	107.59
青　海	Qinghai	518	268	250	51.70	48.30	107.06
宁　夏	Ningxia	562	288	274	51.29	48.71	105.28
新　疆	Xinjiang	1925	996	929	51.75	48.25	107.27
解放军现役军人	Military Personnel	250	236	14			
香港特别行政区	Hong Kong Special Administrative Region	678					
澳门特别行政区	Macao Special Administrative Region	44					
台湾省和福建省的金门、马祖等岛屿	Taiwan Province and Jinmen, Mazu and a few Other Islands of Fujian Province	2228					

注：1.全国总计为大陆31个省、自治区、直辖市和中国人民解放军现役军人、常住地待定以及香港特别行政区，澳门特别行政区，台湾省和福建省的金门、马祖等岛屿人口的合计。

2.各省、自治区、直辖市和中国人民解放军现役军人的人口合计与祖国大陆总人口之差，为常住地待定的人口。

a)The national total population is total of the 31 provinces, autonomous regions, municipalities, the military personnel and of household unsettled, and of Hong Kong SAR, Macao SAR, Taiwan province and Jinmen, Mazu and a few other islands of Fujian province.

b)The difference between the total population on the mainland of China and the sum of population of the 31 provinces, autonomous regions and municipalities and of military personnel is the population with their household registration unsettled.

4-4 五次全国人口普查人口基本情况

Basic Statistics on National Population Census in 1953, 1964, 1982,1990 and 2000

本表未包括香港、澳门特别行政区及台湾省数据。

Data in this table excluded the population of Hong Kong , Macao and Taiwan.

指标	Item	1953	1964	1982	1990	2000
总人口(万人)	**Total Population (10 000 persons)**	**59435**	**69458**	**100818**	**113368**	**126583**
男	Male	30799	35652	51944	58495	65355
女	Female	28636	33806	48874	54873	61228
性别比	Sex ratio	107.56	105.46	106.30	106.60	106.74
家庭户规模(人/户)	**Average Family Size (person/household)**	**4.33**	**4.43**	**4.41**	**3.96**	**3.44**
各年龄组人口(%)	**Population by Age Group (%)**					
0-14岁	Age 0-14	36.28	40.69	33.59	27.69	22.89
15-64岁	Age 15-64	59.31	55.75	61.50	66.74	70.15
65岁及以上	Age 65 and Over	4.41	3.56	4.91	5.57	6.96
民族人口(万人、%)	**Nationality Population (10 000 persons, %)**					
汉族	Han Nationality	54728	65456	94088	104248	115940
占总人口比重	% to Total Population	93.94	94.24	93.32	91.96	91.59
少数民族	Minority Nationalities	3532	4002	6730	9120	10643
占总人口比重	% to Total Population	6.06	5.76	6.68	8.04	8.41
每十万人拥有的各种受教育程度人口(人)	**Population with Various Education Attainment Per 100 000 from Population Censuses (person)**					
大专及以上	Junior College and Above		416	615	1422	3611
高中和中专	Senior Secondary/Secondary Technical School		1319	6779	8039	11146
初中	Junior Secondary School		4680	17892	23344	33961
小学	Primary School		28330	35237	37057	35701
文盲人口及文盲率	**Illiterate Population and Illiterate Rate**					
文盲人口(万人)	Illiterate Population (10 000 persons)		23327	22996	18003	8507
文盲率(%)	Illiterate Rate (%)		33.58	22.81	15.88	6.72
城乡人口(万人)	**Population By Residence (10 000 persons)**					
城镇人口	Urban Population	7726	12710	21082	29971	45844
乡村人口	Rural Population	50534	56748	79736	83397	80739

注：1.历次普查总人口数据中包括了中国人民解放军现役军人。在城乡人口中，中国人民解放军现役军人列为城镇人口统计。

2.1953年总人口数据中包括了间接调查人口，而民族人口、城乡人口中未包括。

3.1964年文盲人口为13岁及13岁以上不识字人口，1982、1990、2000年文盲人口为15岁及15岁以上不识字或识字很少的人。

a) Total population from population censuses includes the military personnel. Military personnel is listed in urban population in population by residence.

b)Total population of 1953 census includes the population from indirect survey, but excludes in the nationality population and urban/rural population.

c)Illiterate population of 1964 census referred to people of 13 years old and over who could not read. Illiterate population of 1982,1990 and 2000 censuses referred to people of 15 years old and over who could not read or could read very little.

4-5 各地区家庭户与集体户的总户数和总人口

Family Households and Collective Households and Their Population by Region

本表是2000年全国人口普查快速汇总的11月1日零时数。

Data in this table are obtained from the advance tabulation of the 5th national population census, with zero hour of November 1, 2000 as the reference time.

地　区	Region	总人口（万人）Total Population (10 000 persons)	家庭户 Family Households 户数（万户）Family Households (10 000 Households)	家庭户 Family Households 人口数(万人) Population (10 000 persons)	集体户人口数（万人）Population of Collective Households (10 000 persons)	家庭户人口占总人口比重（%）% of Family Households Population to Total	平均每个家庭户人口（人）Average Size of Family Households (persons)
全　国	**National Total**	**126333**	**34837**	**119839**	**6494**	**94.86**	**3.44**
北　京	Beijing	1382	418	1215	167	87.92	2.91
天　津	Tianjin	1001	303	937	64	93.63	3.09
河　北	Hebei	6744	1822	6503	241	96.43	3.57
山　西	Shanxi	3297	882	3192	105	96.82	3.62
内蒙古	Inner Mongolia	2376	696	2304	72	96.99	3.31
辽　宁	Liaoning	4238	1306	4114	124	97.07	3.15
吉　林	Jilin	2728	800	2654	74	97.29	3.32
黑龙江	Heilongjiang	3689	1119	3610	79	97.86	3.23
上　海	Shanghai	1674	539	1508	166	90.08	2.80
江　苏	Jiangsu	7438	2184	7065	373	94.98	3.23
浙　江	Zhejiang	4677	1445	4322	355	92.41	2.99
安　徽	Anhui	5986	1667	5853	133	97.78	3.51
福　建	Fujian	3471	885	3124	347	90.00	3.53
江　西	Jiangxi	4140	1052	3950	190	95.42	3.76
山　东	Shandong	9079	2701	8678	401	95.58	3.21
河　南	Henan	9256	2479	9056	200	97.84	3.65
湖　北	Hubei	6028	1592	5587	441	92.69	3.51
湖　南	Hunan	6440	1805	6218	222	96.55	3.44
广　东	Guangdong	8642	1915	7068	1574	81.79	3.69
广　西	Guangxi	4489	1141	4349	140	96.88	3.81
海　南	Hainan	787	184	749	38	95.13	4.06
重　庆	Chongqing	3090	929	2984	106	96.56	3.21
四　川	Sichuan	8329	2404	7976	353	95.76	3.32
贵　州	Guizhou	3525	932	3459	66	98.13	3.71
云　南	Yunnan	4288	1100	4097	191	95.55	3.73
西　藏	Tibet	262	53	253	9	96.61	4.77
陕　西	Shaanxi	3605	959	3421	184	94.90	3.57
甘　肃	Gansu	2562	623	2474	88	96.56	3.97
青　海	Qinghai	518	126	497	21	95.98	3.95
宁　夏	Ningxia	562	144	547	15	97.29	3.80
新　疆	Xinjiang	1925	503	1852	73	96.22	3.68

注：本表数据未包括中国人民解放军现役军人。

a) Data in the table exclude the military personnel of Chinese People's Liberation Army.

4-6 各地区年龄结构

Age Composition by Region

本表是2000年全国人口普查快速汇总的11月1日零时数。

Data in this table are obtained from the advance tabulation of the 5th national population census, with zero hour of November 1,2000 as the reference time.

地区	Region	总人口（万人） Total Population (10 000 persons)	年龄别人口（万人） Population by Age Group(10 000 persons)			占总人口比重（%） % to Total Population		
			0-14岁 Age 0-14	15-64岁 Age 15-64	65岁及以上 Age 65+	0-14岁 Age 0-14	15-64岁 Age 15-64	65岁及以上 Age 65+
全国	**National Total**	**126583**	**28979**	**88793**	**8811**	**22.89**	**70.15**	**6.96**
北京	Beijing	1382	188	1078	116	13.60	78.04	8.36
天津	Tianjin	1001	168	750	83	16.75	74.93	8.33
河北	Hebei	6744	1539	4742	463	22.82	70.32	6.86
山西	Shanxi	3297	851	2242	204	25.80	68.00	6.20
内蒙古	Inner Mongolia	2376	506	1743	127	21.28	73.37	5.35
辽宁	Liaoning	4238	749	3157	332	17.68	74.49	7.83
吉林	Jilin	2728	517	2051	160	18.96	75.19	5.85
黑龙江	Heilongjiang	3689	697	2792	200	18.90	75.68	5.42
上海	Shanghai	1674	204	1277	193	12.19	76.28	11.53
江苏	Jiangsu	7438	1462	5325	651	19.65	71.59	8.76
浙江	Zhejiang	4677	845	3418	414	18.07	73.09	8.84
安徽	Anhui	5986	1528	4012	446	25.52	67.03	7.45
福建	Fujian	3471	799	2445	227	23.02	70.44	6.54
江西	Jiangxi	4140	1076	2811	253	25.99	67.90	6.11
山东	Shandong	9079	1893	6457	729	20.85	71.12	8.03
河南	Henan	9256	2401	6211	644	25.94	67.10	6.96
湖北	Hubei	6028	1379	4269	380	22.87	70.82	6.31
湖南	Hunan	6440	1428	4543	469	22.17	70.54	7.29
广东	Guangdong	8642	2089	6030	523	24.17	69.78	6.05
广西	Guangxi	4489	1178	2991	320	26.24	66.64	7.12
海南	Hainan	787	216	519	52	27.47	65.95	6.58
重庆	Chongqing	3090	678	2168	244	21.93	70.17	7.90
四川	Sichuan	8329	1887	5822	620	22.65	69.90	7.45
贵州	Guizhou	3525	1068	2253	204	30.29	63.92	5.79
云南	Yunnan	4288	1116	2915	257	26.02	67.98	6.00
西藏	Tibet	262	82	168	12	31.20	64.30	4.50
陕西	Shaanxi	3605	902	2490	214	25.01	69.06	5.93
甘肃	Gansu	2562	692	1742	128	27.00	68.00	5.00
青海	Qinghai	518	138	358	22	26.62	69.05	4.33
宁夏	Ningxia	562	160	377	25	28.38	67.15	4.47
新疆	Xinjiang	1925	526	1312	87	27.30	68.17	4.53

注：全国数据包括中国人民解放军现役军人，分省数据未包括。

a)National total population include the military personnel of Chinese People's Liberation Army, but population by regions exclude that.

4-7 各地区每十万人拥有的各种受教育程度人口比较

Comparison of Population with Various Education Attainment Per 100 000 Persons by Region

单位：人 (persons)

地区	Region	大专及以上 Junior College and Above		高中和中专 Senior Secondary / Secondary Technical School		初中 Junior Secondary School		小学 Primary School	
		1990	2000	1990	2000	1990	2000	1990	2000
全国	**National Total**	**1422**	**3611**	**8039**	**11146**	**23344**	**33961**	**37057**	**35701**
北京	Beijing	9301	16843	18974	23151	30551	34391	22577	16956
天津	Tianjin	4668	9007	15908	20851	29379	34590	29635	25031
河北	Hebei	955	2698	7429	10717	24689	39075	36805	33760
山西	Shanxi	1384	3423	8820	11562	29237	38928	35713	31761
内蒙古	Inner Mongolia	1475	3803	10056	13760	25473	34798	33397	31134
辽宁	Liaoning	2596	6182	10933	13205	32321	40082	34270	29771
吉林	Jilin	2154	4926	12701	15076	26308	35687	35327	33598
黑龙江	Heilongjiang	2139	4797	11729	13866	28460	38863	34089	31253
上海	Shanghai	6534	10940	19532	23018	31592	36803	22683	18934
江苏	Jiangsu	1474	3917	8670	13039	26426	36372	34791	32881
浙江	Zhejiang	1170	3189	7006	10758	23741	33336	39664	36622
安徽	Anhui	883	2297	5035	7625	19967	32780	34685	37342
福建	Fujian	1227	2967	6979	10602	16867	33708	43238	38317
江西	Jiangxi	991	2576	7097	9819	18841	33219	40672	38902
山东	Shandong	975	3331	7140	11036	25182	36634	36260	32736
河南	Henan	848	2674	7069	10031	26545	39392	34729	33196
湖北	Hubei	1566	3898	8862	12595	23164	34311	35832	35416
湖南	Hunan	1138	2927	8010	11125	22567	35656	42071	38328
广东	Guangdong	1338	3560	8928	12880	23041	36690	40451	33145
广西	Guangxi	791	2389	6804	9554	19141	32339	45041	42176
海南	Hainan	1244	3167	10345	12491	22528	32502	34583	34404
重庆	Chongqing	1070	2802	6230	8596	22860	29413	45000	43386
四川	Sichuan	925	2470	5071	7587	21243	29358	43439	42960
贵州	Guizhou	777	1902	3927	5626	14645	20480	37336	43595
云南	Yunnan	807	2013	4095	6563	13795	21233	37905	44768
西藏	Tibet	574	1262	2122	3395	3850	6136	18597	30615
陕西	Shaanxi	1672	4138	9255	12246	24359	33203	31130	34475
甘肃	Gansu	1104	2665	7825	9863	16851	23925	29127	36907
青海	Qinghai	1490	3299	8275	10431	17761	21661	26489	30944
宁夏	Ningxia	1609	3690	8000	10910	20274	27830	29384	31770
新疆	Xinjiang	1845	5141	10372	12089	20662	27528	36423	37950

注：1.1990年数据取自国务院人口普查办公室编的《中国第四次人口普查主要数据》（手工汇总资料）。2000年数据是第五次人口普查快速汇总的11月1日零时数。

2.全国数据包括中国人民解放军现役军人，分省数据未包括。

a) The data on 1990 are obtained from *Major Figures on 4th Population Census of China (manual tabulation)*,edited by the National Population Census Office. The data on 2000 are obtained from advance tabulation of the 5th national population census, with zero hour of November 1,2000 as the reference time.

b) National total population include the military personnel of Chinese People's Liberation Army, but population by regions exclude that.

4-8 各地区按城乡分的文盲人口

Illiterate Population by Urban, Rural Residence and Region

本表是2000年全国人口普查快速汇总的11月1日零时数。

Data in this table are obtained from the advance tabulation of the 5th national population census, with zero hour of November 1,2000 as the reference time.

地 区	Region	文盲人口（万人） Illiterate Population (10 000 persons)			文盲率（%） Illiterate Rate(%)	
		合计 Total	城镇 Urban	乡村 Rural	城镇 Urban	乡村 Rural
全 国	**National Total**	**8507**	**1842**	**6665**	**4.04**	**8.25**
北 京	Beijing	59	34	25	3.13	8.22
天 津	Tianjin	49	30	19	4.12	6.88
河 北	Hebei	448	43	405	2.47	8.13
山 西	Shanxi	138	33	105	2.87	4.89
内蒙古	Inner Mongolia	217	52	164	5.15	12.07
辽 宁	Liaoning	202	78	124	3.38	6.39
吉 林	Jilin	125	45	80	3.29	5.84
黑龙江	Heilongjiang	188	77	111	4.07	6.20
上 海	Shanghai	90	65	25	4.43	12.75
江 苏	Jiangsu	469	143	326	4.65	7.48
浙 江	Zhejiang	330	115	215	5.06	8.95
安 徽	Anhui	602	114	489	6.83	11.31
福 建	Fujian	250	75	175	5.20	8.63
江 西	Jiangxi	214	39	175	3.36	5.85
山 东	Shandong	768	169	599	4.89	10.65
河 南	Henan	543	79	465	3.66	6.54
湖 北	Hubei	431	110	321	4.53	8.91
湖 南	Hunan	299	49	251	2.55	5.54
广 东	Guangdong	332	135	197	2.84	5.07
广 西	Guangxi	170	35	136	2.73	4.20
海 南	Hainan	55	14	41	4.46	8.67
重 庆	Chongqing	215	40	175	3.95	8.45
四 川	Sichuan	636	89	547	4.02	8.96
贵 州	Guizhou	490	55	435	6.53	16.20
云 南	Yunnan	488	60	429	5.95	13.05
西 藏	Tibet	85	9	76	17.94	35.90
陕 西	Shaanxi	263	44	218	3.82	8.95
甘 肃	Gansu	367	32	336	5.14	17.25
青 海	Qinghai	93	14	79	7.85	23.45
宁 夏	Ningxia	75	10	65	5.55	17.17
新 疆	Xinjiang	107	26	81	3.95	6.38

注：分城乡文盲率，中国人民解放军现役军人未参加计算。

a) The calculation of illiterate rate by urban and rural residence excludes the military personnel of Chinese People's Liberation Army.

4-9 各地区文盲人口比较

Comparison of Illiterate Population by Region

地 区	Region	文盲人口（万人）Illiterate Population (10 000 persons)		文盲率（%）Illiterate Rate (%)		
		1990	2000	1990	2000	降低百分点 Down
全 国	**National Total**	**18003**	**8507**	**15.88**	**6.72**	**9.16**
北 京	Beijing	94	59	8.70	4.23	4.47
天 津	Tianjin	78	49	8.92	4.93	4.00
河 北	Hebei	929	448	15.21	6.65	8.56
山 西	Shanxi	325	138	11.30	4.18	7.12
内蒙古	Inner Mongolia	330	217	15.39	9.12	6.27
辽 宁	Liaoning	348	202	8.81	4.76	4.06
吉 林	Jilin	259	125	10.49	4.57	5.92
黑龙江	Heilongjiang	383	188	10.87	5.10	5.77
上 海	Shanghai	147	90	11.04	5.40	5.64
江 苏	Jiangsu	1156	469	17.23	6.31	10.93
浙 江	Zhejiang	724	330	17.46	7.06	10.40
安 徽	Anhui	1373	602	24.43	10.06	14.37
福 建	Fujian	470	250	15.63	7.20	8.43
江 西	Jiangxi	612	214	16.22	5.16	11.05
山 东	Shandong	1423	768	16.87	8.46	8.41
河 南	Henan	1381	543	16.15	5.87	10.28
湖 北	Hubei	852	431	15.79	7.15	8.64
湖 南	Hunan	734	299	12.10	4.65	7.45
广 东	Guangdong	656	332	10.45	3.84	6.61
广 西	Guangxi	448	170	10.61	3.79	6.82
海 南	Hainan	92	55	13.97	6.98	6.99
重 庆	Chongqing	405	215	14.02	6.95	7.07
四 川	Sichuan	1336	636	17.05	7.64	9.41
贵 州	Guizhou	786	490	24.27	13.89	10.38
云 南	Yunnan	941	488	25.44	11.39	14.05
西 藏	Tibet	98	85	44.43	32.50	11.93
陕 西	Shaanxi	579	263	17.62	7.29	10.33
甘 肃	Gansu	625	367	27.93	14.34	13.59
青 海	Qinghai	123	93	27.70	18.03	9.67
宁 夏	Ningxia	103	75	22.06	13.40	8.66
新 疆	Xinjiang	193	107	12.75	5.56	7.20

注：1.1990年数据取自国务院人口普查办公室编的《中国第四次人口普查主要数据》（手工汇总资料）。2000年数据是第五次人口普查快速汇总的11月1日零时数。

2.全国数据包括中国人民解放军现役军人，分省数据未包括。

a) The data on 1990 are obtained from *Major Figures on 4th Population Census of China (manual tabulation)*, edited by the National Population Census Office. The data on 2000 are obtained from advance tabulation of the 5th national population census, with zero hour of November 1,2000 as the reference time.

b)National total population include the military personnel of Chinese People's Liberation Army, but population by regions exclude that.

4-10 各地区总人口增长情况

Growth of Total Population by Region

单位：万人

(10 000 persons)

地　区	Region	1990年普查总人口 Population at 2000 Census	2000年普查总人口 Population at 1990 Census	2000年与1990年比较 Comparison between 2000 and 1990		
				增加人数 Growth in Persons	增长率（%） Growth Rate (%)	年均增长率（%） Annual Growth Rate (%)
全　国	**National Total**	**113368**	**126583**	**13215**	**11.66**	**1.07**
北　京	Beijing	1082	1382	300	27.73	2.40
天　津	Tianjin	879	1001	122	13.94	1.27
河　北	Hebei	6108	6744	636	10.41	0.96
山　西	Shanxi	2876	3297	421	14.64	1.33
内蒙古	Inner Mongolia	2146	2376	230	10.73	0.99
辽　宁	Liaoning	3946	4238	292	7.40	0.69
吉　林	Jilin	2466	2728	262	10.63	0.98
黑龙江	Heilongjiang	3521	3689	168	4.76	0.45
上　海	Shanghai	1334	1674	340	25.47	2.22
江　苏	Jiangsu	6706	7438	732	10.92	1.01
浙　江	Zhejiang	4145	4677	532	12.85	1.18
安　徽	Anhui	5618	5986	368	6.55	0.62
福　建	Fujian	3005	3471	466	15.51	1.41
江　西	Jiangxi	3771	4140	369	9.78	0.91
山　东	Shandong	8439	9079	640	7.58	0.71
河　南	Henan	8551	9256	705	8.25	0.77
湖　北	Hubei	5397	6028	631	11.69	1.08
湖　南	Hunan	6066	6440	374	6.17	0.58
广　东	Guangdong	6283	8642	2359	37.55	3.13
广　西	Guangxi	4225	4489	264	6.26	0.59
海　南	Hainan	656	787	131	20.02	1.78
重　庆	Chongqing	2886	3090	204	7.07	0.66
四　川	Sichuan	7836	8329	493	6.29	0.59
贵　州	Guizhou	3239	3525	286	8.83	0.82
云　南	Yunnan	3697	4288	591	15.98	1.44
西　藏	Tibet	220	262	42	19.31	1.72
陕　西	Shaanxi	3288	3605	317	9.63	0.89
甘　肃	Gansu	2237	2562	325	14.52	1.32
青　海	Qinghai	446	518	72	16.22	1.47
宁　夏	Ningxia	466	562	96	20.72	1.84
新　疆	Xinjiang	1516	1925	409	27.01	2.34

注：1.1990年数据取自国务院人口普查办公室编的《中国第四次人口普查主要数据》（手工汇总资料）。2000年数据是第五次人口普查快速汇总的11月1日零时数。

2.全国数据包括中国人民解放军现役军人，分省数据未包括。

a) The data on 1990 are obtained from *Major Figures on 4th Population Census of China (manual tabulation)*, edited by the National Population Census Office. The data on 2000 are obtained from advance tabulation of the 5th national population census, with zero hour of November 1,2000 as the reference time.

b) National total population include the military personnel of Chinese People's Liberation Army, but population by regions exclude that.

4-11 各地区汉族和各少数民族人口

Population of Han and Minority Nationalities by Region

本表是2000年全国人口普查快速汇总的11月1日零时数。

Data in this table are obtained from the advance tabulation of the 5th national population census, with zero hour of November 1,2000 as the reference time.

单位：万人 (10 000 persons)

地区	Region	总人口 Total Population	汉族 Han		各少数民族 Minority Nationalities	
			人数 Sub-total	占总人口比重（%） % to Total	人数 Sub-total	占总人口比重（%） % to Total
全国	**National Total**	**126583**	**115940**	**91.59**	**10643**	**8.41**
北京	Beijing	1382	1323	95.74	59	4.26
天津	Tianjin	1001	975	97.36	26	2.64
河北	Hebei	6744	6453	95.69	291	4.31
山西	Shanxi	3297	3287	99.71	10	0.29
内蒙古	Inner Mongolia	2376	1883	79.24	493	20.76
辽宁	Liaoning	4238	3560	83.98	678	16.02
吉林	Jilin	2728	2482	90.97	246	9.03
黑龙江	Heilongjiang	3689	3504	94.98	185	5.02
上海	Shanghai	1674	1664	99.40	10	0.60
江苏	Jiangsu	7438	7413	99.67	25	0.33
浙江	Zhejiang	4677	4637	99.15	40	0.85
安徽	Anhui	5986	5948	99.37	38	0.63
福建	Fujian	3471	3413	98.33	58	1.67
江西	Jiangxi	4140	4129	99.73	11	0.27
山东	Shandong	9079	9017	99.32	62	0.68
河南	Henan	9256	9143	98.78	113	1.22
湖北	Hubei	6028	5766	95.66	262	4.34
湖南	Hunan	6440	5782	89.79	658	10.21
广东	Guangdong	8642	8519	98.58	123	1.42
广西	Guangxi	4489	2768	61.66	1721	38.34
海南	Hainan	787	651	82.71	136	17.29
重庆	Chongqing	3090	2892	93.58	198	6.42
四川	Sichuan	8329	7914	95.02	415	4.98
贵州	Guizhou	3525	2191	62.15	1334	37.85
云南	Yunnan	4288	2855	66.59	1433	33.41
西藏	Tibet	262	16	5.93	246	94.07
陕西	Shaanxi	3605	3587	99.51	18	0.49
甘肃	Gansu	2562	2339	91.31	223	8.69
青海	Qinghai	518	282	54.49	236	45.51
宁夏	Ningxia	562	368	65.47	194	34.53
新疆	Xinjiang	1925	782	40.61	1143	59.39

注：全国数据包括中国人民解放军现役军人，分省数据未包括。

a) National total population include the military personnel of Chinese People's Liberation Army, but population by regions exclude that.

4-12 各地区城乡人口分布

Population Distribution by Urban, Rural Residence and Region

本表是2000年全国人口普查快速汇总的11月1日零时数。

Data in this table are obtained from the advance tabulation of the 5th national population census, with zero hour of November 1,2000 as the reference time.

单位：万人 (10 000 persons)

地区	Region	总人口 Total Population	城镇人口 Urban Population	乡村人口 Rural Population	占总人口比重(%) % to Total 城镇 Urban	乡村 Rural
全 国	**National Total**	**126583**	**45844**	**80739**	**36.22**	**63.78**
北 京	Beijing	1382	1072	310	77.54	22.46
天 津	Tianjin	1001	721	280	71.99	28.01
河 北	Hebei	6744	1759	4985	26.08	73.92
山 西	Shanxi	3297	1151	2146	34.91	65.09
内蒙古	Inner Mongolia	2376	1014	1362	42.68	57.32
辽 宁	Liaoning	4238	2299	1939	54.24	45.76
吉 林	Jilin	2728	1355	1373	49.68	50.32
黑龙江	Heilongjiang	3689	1901	1788	51.54	48.46
上 海	Shanghai	1674	1478	196	88.31	11.69
江 苏	Jiangsu	7438	3086	4352	41.49	58.51
浙 江	Zhejiang	4677	2277	2400	48.67	51.33
安 徽	Anhui	5986	1665	4321	27.81	72.19
福 建	Fujian	3471	1443	2028	41.57	58.43
江 西	Jiangxi	4140	1146	2994	27.67	72.33
山 东	Shandong	9079	3450	5629	38.00	62.00
河 南	Henan	9256	2147	7109	23.20	76.80
湖 北	Hubei	6028	2424	3604	40.22	59.78
湖 南	Hunan	6440	1916	4524	29.75	70.25
广 东	Guangdong	8642	4753	3889	55.00	45.00
广 西	Guangxi	4489	1264	3225	28.15	71.85
海 南	Hainan	787	316	471	40.11	59.89
重 庆	Chongqing	3090	1023	2067	33.09	66.91
四 川	Sichuan	8329	2223	6106	26.69	73.31
贵 州	Guizhou	3525	841	2684	23.87	76.13
云 南	Yunnan	4288	1002	3286	23.36	76.64
西 藏	Tibet	262	50	212	18.93	81.07
陕 西	Shaanxi	3605	1163	2442	32.26	67.74
甘 肃	Gansu	2562	615	1947	24.01	75.99
青 海	Qinghai	518	180	338	34.76	65.24
宁 夏	Ningxia	562	182	380	32.43	67.57
新 疆	Xinjiang	1925	651	1274	33.82	66.18

注：全国总人口和全国城镇人口包括解放军现役军人，分省人口未包括。

a) National total population and urban population include the military personnel of Chinese People's Liberation Army, but population by regions exclude that.

主 要 统 计 指 标 解 释

人口数 指一定时点、一定地区范围内的有生命的个人的总和。

年度统计的年末人口数指每年12月31日24时的人口数。年度统计的全国人口总数内未包括台湾省和港澳同胞以及海外华侨人数。

城镇人口和乡村人口 其定义有三种口径：

第一种口径（按行政建制）

城镇人口是指市辖区内和县辖镇的全部人口；

乡村人口是指县辖乡人口。

第二种口径（按常住人口划分）

城镇人口是指设区的市的区人口和不设区的市所辖的街道人口以及不设区的市所辖镇的居民委员会人口和县辖镇的居民委员会人口；

乡村人口是除上述人口以外的全部人口。

第三种口径

城乡人口的划分是按照国家统计局1999年发布的《关于统计上划分城乡的规定（试行）》计算的。

1952–1980年数据为第一种口径的数据，1982–1999年的数据为第二种口径的数据。2000年人口普查数据的城乡人口的划分是第三种口径。

出生率(又称粗出生率) 指在一定时期内(通常为一年)一定地区的出生人数与同期内平均人数(或期中人数)之比。一般用千分率表示。本资料中的出生率指年出生率，其计算公式为：

出生率＝年出生人数／年平均人数×1000‰

式中：出生人数指活产婴儿，即胎儿脱离母体时(不管怀孕月数)，有过呼吸或其他生命现象。年平均人数指年初、年底人口数的平均数，也可用年中人口数代替。

死亡率(又称粗死亡率) 指在一定时期内(通常为一年)一定地区的死亡人数与同期内平均人数(或期中人数)之比，一般用千分率表示。本资料中的死亡率指年死亡率，其计算公式为：

死亡率＝年死亡人数／年平均人数×1000‰

人口自然增长率 指在一定时期内(通常为一年)人口自然增加数(出生人数减死亡人数)与该时期内平均人数(或期中人数)之比，一般用千分率表示。计算公式为：

人口自然增长率＝（本年出生人数－本年死亡人数）／年平均人数×1000‰＝人口出生率－人口死亡率

总负担系数 指被抚养人口（0–14岁和65岁以上人口）与15–64岁人口的比例。计算公式为：

总负担系数＝被抚养人口／15–64岁人口×100%

负担老年系数 指老年人口（65岁以上人口）与15–64岁人口的比例。计算公式为：

负担老年系数＝老年人口／15–64岁人口×100%

负担少年系数 指少年儿童与15–64岁人口的比例。计算公式为：

负担少年系数＝少年儿童人口／15–64岁人口×100%

Explanatory Notes on Main Statistical Indicators

Total Population refers to the total number of people alive at a certain point of time within a given area.

The annual statistics on total population is taken at midnight, the 3lst of December, not including residents in Taiwan province, Chinese compatriots in Hong Kong and Macao and overseas Chinese.

Urban Population and Rural Population There are three definitions.

The first definition (by the administrative system):

Urban Population refers to total population under the jurisdiction of city and the population of towns under the jurisdiction of counties.

Rural Population refers to total population of townships under the jurisdiction of counties.

The second definition (by the permanent residence):

Urban Population refers to total population of districts under the jurisdiction of a city with district establishment, the population of street committees under the jurisdiction of a city without district establishment, population of resident-committees of towns under the jurisdiction of a city without district establishment, and the of resident-committees of towns under the jurisdiction of a county.

Rural Population refers to total population except urban population.

The third definition (based on the statistical classification)

Urban Population/ Rural Population are classified according to *the Regulation of Statistics Classification on Urban and Rural Population (Draft)*, formulated by the National Bureau of Statistics in 1999.

Data from 1952 to 1980 are the figures according to the first definition. Data from 1982 to 1999 are the figures according to the second definition. Urban/rural population in 2000 is the figure according to the third definition.

Birth Rate or (Crude Birth Rate) refers to the ratio of the number of births to the average population (or mid-period population) during a certain period of time (usually a year) which is often expressed in ‰. Birth rate in the chapter refers to annual birth rate. The following formula is used:

Birth Rate = Number of Births/Average Number of Population × 1000‰

Number of births refers to live births i.e. the births when babies had showed any vital phenomena regardless of the length of pregnancy.

Annual Average Number of Population is the average of the number of population at the beginning of the year and that at the end of the year. Sometimes it is substituted for with the mid year population.

Death Rate (or Crude Death Rate) refers to the ratio of the number of deaths to the average population (or mid-period population) during a certain period of time (usually a year) which is often expressed in ‰. Death rate in the chapter refers to annual death rate. The following formula is used:

Death Rate= Number of Deaths/Annual Average Number of Population × 1000‰

Natural Growth Rate of Population refers to the ratio of natural increase in population (number of births minus number of deaths) in a certain period of time (usually a year) to the average population (or mid-period population) of the same period which is often expressed in ‰. The following formulas are applied:

Natural Growth of Population = (Number of Births−Number of Deaths)/Average Number of Population × 1000‰

Natural Growth Rate of Population = Birth Rate-Death Rate

Total Dependency Ratio refers to the ratio of number of dependents to the total population aged 15-64, the number of dependents being population aged 0-14 and population aged 65 and over. The total dependency ratio is calculated as follows:

Total Dependency Ratio = Number of Dependents/Population Aged 15-64 × 100%

The Aged Dependency Ratio refers to the ratio of the number of the aged population to the total population aged 15-64, the aged being population aged 65 and over. The aged dependency ratio is calculated as follows:

The Aged Dependency Ratio = Number of the Aged Population/ Population Aged 15-64 × 100%

The Juvenile and Children Dependency Ratio refers to the ratio of the number of the juvenile and children to the total population aged 15-64, the juvenile and children being population aged 0-14. The juvenile and children dependency ratio is calculated as follows:

The Juvenile and Children Dependency Ratio = Number of Juvenile and Children/ Population Aged 15-64 × 100%

五、从业人员和职工工资

Employment and Wages

简要说明

一、本篇资料反映我国劳动经济方面的基本情况，包括31个省、自治区、直辖市的主要劳动统计数据。如：从业人员及职工人数，城乡私营企业和个体工商业从业人数，城镇登记失业人数，职工工资总额，平均工资及指数变化情况等。

二、本篇资料来源主要有以下三个方面：

1.就业基本情况及分组资料(5-1至5-14表)及在岗职工工资总额等资料(5-19至5-28表)，根据国家统计局《劳动综合统计报表制度》及《乡村社会经济调查方案》搜集汇总的资料，由国家统计局人口和社会科技统计司整理提供。

2.职业介绍服务机构及劳动力交流情况(5-29表)，根据劳动和社会保障部的《培训、就业统计报表制度》搜集汇总的资料，由劳动和社会保障部提供。

3.私营企业及个体工商业从业人员(5-15至5-18表)，根据国家工商行政管理局的城乡私营企业基本情况统计表及城乡个体工商业基本情况统计表搜集汇总的资料，由国家工商行政管理局提供。

三、统计范围和调查方法

1.统计范围：《劳动综合统计报表制度》的调查范围为全部独立核算单位；《乡村社会经济调查方案》的调查范围为全国乡镇以下农村地区；《培训、就业统计报表制度》的调查范围为全国的城镇人口；私营企业及个体工商业统计范围为全部在私营企业和个体工商业就业的从业人员。

2.调查方法：劳动综合统计采用全面调查方法，由各级统计部门逐级上报；培训、就业统计及私营企业和个体工商业统计利用行政登记资料加工整理。

四、自1989年始，国家统计局与劳动部联合出版《中国劳动统计年鉴》，提供了比本篇更为详细的资料。

Brief Introduction

I. The data in this chapter show the basic conditions of China's labour economy, including the main data of labour statistics of the whole country and 31 provinces, autonomous regions and municipalities under the direct leadership of the central government, such as the economically active population, number of the employed persons and staff and workers, number of persons employed in the urban and rural private enterprises and self-employed persons in industry and commerce, number of registered unemployed persons in urban areas, total wages and average wages of the staff and workers and the changes in index, etc.

II. There are three main sources for the data published in this chapter:

(1) Data on basic conditions of employment (tables 5-1 to 5-14), total wage bill of fully employed workers and staff (tables 5-19 to 5-28) are collected and tabulated in accordance with the *Comprehensive Labour Statistics Reporting System*, and *Rural Social and Economic Survey* of the National Bureau of Statistics. They are prepared and provided by the Department of Population, Social and Science Statistics, NBS.

(2) Data on the career services and the exchanges of labour force (tables 5-29) are collected in line with the *Statistical Reporting System on Training and Employment* and provided by the Ministry of Labour and Social Security.

(3) Data on the number of persons employed in the urban and rural private enterprises and self-employed persons in industry and commerce (tables 5-15 to 5-18) are collected through *Statistical Reports on Basic Conditions of Urban and Rural Private Enterprises* and *Statistical Reports on Basic Conditions of Urban and Rural Individual Industrial and Commercial Business* and provided by the State Administration for Industry and Commerce.

III. Coverage of statistics and survey methods:

(1) Coverage of statistics: The *Comprehensive Labour Statistics Reporting System* covers all independent accounting units. The *Rural Social and Economic Survey* covers all rural areas below township level in China. The *Statistical Reporting System on Training and Employment* covers all urban population of China. The *Statistical Reports on Basic Conditions of Urban and Rural Private Enterprises and on Basic Conditions of Urban and Rural Individual Industrial and Commercial Business* cover all employed persons in private enterprises and self-employed individuals of the whole society.

(2) Survey methodology: A complete enumeration and reporting from lower levels to higher levels is used in the *Comprehensive Labour Statistics Reporting System.* Statistics on training, employment, private enterprises and self-employed individuals are collected compiled on basis of administrative records.

IV. Since 1989, *"China Labour Statistical Yearbook"* has been jointly published by the National Bureau of Statistics and the Ministry of Labour and Social Security, which provides more detailed data than those in this chapter.

5-1 就业基本情况

Employment

项　目	Item	1996	1997	1998	1999	2000
从业人员合计　(万人)	**Total Number of Employed Persons (10 000 persons)**	**68850**	**69600**	**69957**	**70586**	**71150**
第一产业	Primary Industry	34769	34730	34838	35364	35575
第二产业	Secondary Industry	16180	16495	16440	16235	16009
第三产业	Tertiary Industry	17901	18375	18679	18987	19566
从业人员构成(合计=100)	**Composition of Employed Persons (total=100)**					
第一产业	Primary Industry	50.5	49.9	49.8	50.1	50.0
第二产业	Secondary Industry	23.5	23.7	23.5	23.0	22.5
第三产业	Tertiary Industry	26.0	26.4	26.7	26.9	27.5
按城乡分从业人员(万人)	**Number of Employed Persons by Urban and Rural Areas (10 000 persons)**					
城镇从业人员	Urban Employed Persons	19815	20207	20678	21014	21274
#国有单位	State-owned Units	11244	11044	9058	8572	8102
城镇集体单位	Urban Collective-owned Units	3016	2883	1963	1712	1499
股份合作单位	Cooperative Units	-	-	136	144	155
联营单位	Joint Ownership Units	49	43	48	46	42
有限责任公司	Limited Liability Corporations	-	-	484	603	687
股份有限公司	Share-holding Corporations Ltd.	363	468	410	420	457
私营企业	Private Enterprises	620	750	973	1053	1268
港澳台商投资单位	Units with Funds from Hong Kong, Macao & Taiwan	265	281	294	306	310
外商投资单位	Foreign Funded Units	275	300	293	306	332
个体	Self-employed Individuals	1709	1919	2259	2414	2136
乡村从业人员	Rural Employed Persons	49035	49393	49279	49572	49876
#乡镇企业	Township and Village Enterprises	13508	13050	12537	12704	12820
私营企业	Private Enterprises	551	600	737	969	1139
个体	Self-employed Individuals	3308	3522	3855	3827	2934
职工人数　(万人)	**Number of Staff and Workers (10 000 persons)**	**14845**	**14668**	**12337**	**11773**	**11259**
国有单位	State-owned Units	10949	10766	8809	8336	7878
城镇集体单位	Urban Collective-owned Units	2954	2817	1900	1652	1447
其他单位	Units of Other Types of Ownership	942	1085	1628	1785	1935
城镇单位女性从业人员(万人)	**Number of Female Employment in Urban Units (10 000 persons)**	-	-	-	**4613**	**4411**
城镇登记失业人数(万人)	**Number of Registered Unemployed Persons in Urban Areas (10 000 persons)**	**553**	**570**	**571**	**575**	**595**
城镇登记失业率　(%)	**Registered Unemployment Rate in Urban Areas (%)**	**3.0**	**3.1**	**3.1**	**3.1**	**3.1**

注：1.1990年以后，经济活动人口、从业人员总计、城镇和乡村从业人员小计资料根据人口变动情况抽样调查调整，因此分地区、分经济类型、分行业的资料相加不等于总计。(下表同)。

2.1998年及以后城镇单位从业人员、职工人数统计口径有调整，详见本篇末指标解释。

a)Since 1990 data on economically active population, the total employed persons and the sub-total of employed persons in urban and rural areas have been adjusted in accordance with the data obtained from the sample surveys on population changes. As a result, the sum of the data by region, by ownership or by sector is not equal to the total. The same as in the following tables.

b)Statistical coverage of staff and workers employed in urban units has adjusted since 1998. Please refer to the explanatory notes at the end of this chapter.

5-2 按三次产业分的年底从业人员数

Number of Employed Persons at the Year-end by Type of Industry

年 份 Year	经济活动人口（万人）Economically Active Population (10 000 persons)	从业人员（万人）Total (10 000 persons)				构成（合计total=100）Composition in Percentage		
			第一产业 Primary Industry	第二产业 Secondary Industry	第三产业 Tertiary Industry	第一产业 Primary Industry	第二产业 Secondary Industry	第三产业 Tertiary Industry
1952	21106	20729	17317	1531	1881	83.5	7.4	9.1
1957	23971	23771	19309	2142	2320	81.2	9.0	9.8
1962		25910	21276	2059	2575	82.1	7.9	9.9
1965		28670	23396	2408	2866	81.6	8.4	10.0
1970		34432	27811	3518	3103	80.8	10.2	9.0
1975		38168	29456	5152	3560	77.2	13.5	9.3
1978	40682	40152	28318	6945	4890	70.5	17.3	12.2
1979	41592	41024	28634	7214	5177	69.8	17.6	12.6
1980	42903	42361	29122	7707	5532	68.7	18.2	13.1
1981	44165	43725	29777	8003	5945	68.1	18.3	13.6
1982	45674	45295	30859	8346	6090	68.1	18.4	13.4
1983	46707	46436	31151	8679	6606	67.1	18.7	14.2
1984	48433	48197	30868	9590	7739	64.0	19.9	16.1
1985	50112	49873	31130	10384	8359	62.4	20.8	16.8
1986	51546	51282	31254	11216	8811	60.9	21.9	17.2
1987	53060	52783	31663	11726	9395	60.0	22.2	17.8
1988	54630	54334	32249	12152	9933	59.4	22.4	18.3
1989	55707	55329	33225	11976	10129	60.0	21.6	18.3
1990	64483	63909	38428	13654	11828	60.1	21.4	18.5
1991	65399	64799	38685	13867	12247	59.7	21.4	18.9
1992	66184	65554	38349	14226	12979	58.5	21.7	19.8
1993	67033	66373	37434	14868	14071	56.4	22.4	21.2
1994	67879	67199	36489	15254	15456	54.3	22.7	23.0
1995	68737	67947	35468	15628	16851	52.2	23.0	24.8
1996	69665	68850	34769	16180	17901	50.5	23.5	26.0
1997	70580	69600	34730	16495	18375	49.9	23.7	26.4
1998	71407	69957	34838	16440	18679	49.8	23.5	26.7
1999	71983	70586	35364	16235	18987	50.1	23.0	26.9
2000		71150	35575	16009	19566	50.0	22.5	27.5

5−3 各地区按三次产业分的年底从业人员数（2000）

Number of Employed Persons at the Year-end by Type of Industry and Region (2000)

地 区	Region	从业人员（万人）Number of Employed Persons (10 000 persons)	第一产业 Primary Industry	第二产业 Secondary Industry	第三产业 Tertiary Industry	构成（合计total=100）Composition in Percentage 第一产业 Primary Industry	第二产业 Secondary Industry	第三产业 Tertiary Industry
全 国	**National Total**	**71150.0**	**35575.0**	**16009.0**	**19566.0**	**50.0**	**22.5**	**27.5**
北 京	Beijing	622.1	72.7	201.6	347.9	11.7	32.4	55.9
天 津	Tianjin	406.7	80.9	166.8	159.0	19.9	41.0	39.1
河 北	Hebei	3441.2	1678.2	874.2	888.9	48.8	25.4	25.8
山 西	Shanxi	1419.1	662.7	353.4	402.9	46.7	24.9	28.4
内蒙古	Inner Mongolia	1016.6	553.7	167.4	295.5	54.5	16.5	29.1
辽 宁	Liaoning	1812.6	683.3	476.9	652.3	37.7	26.3	36.0
吉 林	Jilin	1078.9	541.6	206.3	330.9	50.2	19.1	30.7
黑龙江	Heilongjiang	1635.0	808.5	347.3	479.1	49.5	21.2	29.3
上 海	Shanghai	673.1	88.0	288.3	296.8	13.1	42.8	44.1
江 苏	Jiangsu	3558.8	1502.7	1057.3	998.8	42.2	29.7	28.1
浙 江	Zhejiang	2700.5	1021.0	833.6	845.8	37.8	30.9	31.3
安 徽	Anhui	3372.9	2017.9	532.4	822.6	59.8	15.8	24.4
福 建	Fujian	1660.2	778.2	407.0	475.0	46.9	24.5	28.6
江 西	Jiangxi	1935.3	1004.4	279.1	651.8	51.9	14.4	33.7
山 东	Shandong	4661.8	2473.7	1101.7	1086.3	53.1	23.6	23.3
河 南	Henan	5571.7	3569.0	977.1	1025.5	64.1	17.5	18.4
湖 北	Hubei	2507.8	1204.8	459.6	843.4	48.0	18.3	33.6
湖 南	Hunan	3462.1	2104.4	507.5	850.2	60.8	14.7	24.6
广 东	Guangdong	3861.0	1588.5	1011.8	1260.7	41.1	26.2	32.7
广 西	Guangxi	2530.4	1574.5	257.1	698.8	62.2	10.2	27.6
海 南	Hainan	333.7	204.4	32.0	97.2	61.3	9.6	29.1
重 庆	Chongqing	1636.5	925.2	251.1	460.2	56.5	15.3	28.1
四 川	Sichuan	4435.8	2643.4	641.9	1150.5	59.6	14.5	25.9
贵 州	Guizhou	2045.9	1377.9	189.4	478.6	67.3	9.3	23.4
云 南	Yunnan	2295.4	1695.9	210.4	389.2	73.9	9.2	17.0
西 藏	Tibet	123.4	91.0	7.2	25.2	73.8	5.8	20.4
陕 西	Shaanxi	1812.8	1010.2	299.1	503.6	55.7	16.5	27.8
甘 肃	Gansu	1182.1	706.1	163.3	312.7	59.7	13.8	26.5
青 海	Qinghai	238.6	145.3	31.9	61.4	60.9	13.4	25.7
宁 夏	Ningxia	274.4	158.6	49.7	66.1	57.8	18.1	24.1
新 疆	Xinjiang	672.5	387.9	92.7	191.9	57.7	13.8	28.5

5-4 按城乡分的年底从业人员数

单位：万人

年份 地区	Year Region	合计 Total	城镇 小计 Sub-total	#国有单位 State-owned Units	#集体单位 Collective-owned Units	#股份合作单位 Cooperative Units	#联营单位 Joint Ownership Units	#有限责任公司 Limited Liability Corporations	#股份有限公司 Share Holding Corporations Ltd.
	1978	40152	9514	7451	2048				
	1979	41024	9999	7693	2274				
	1980	42361	10525	8019	2425				
	1981	43725	11053	8372	2568				
	1982	45295	11428	8630	2651				
	1983	46436	11746	8771	2744				
	1984	48197	12229	8637	3216				
	1985	49873	12808	8990	3324		38		
	1986	51282	13293	9333	3421		43		
	1987	52783	13783	9654	3488		50		
	1988	54334	14267	9984	3527		63		
	1989	55329	14390	10108	3502		82		
	1990	63909	16616	10346	3549		96		
	1991	64799	16977	10664	3628		49		
	1992	65554	17241	10889	3621		56		
	1993	66373	17589	10920	3393		66		164
	1994	67199	18413	11214	3285		52		292
	1995	67947	19093	11261	3147		53		317
	1996	68850	19815	11244	3016		49		363
	1997	69600	20207	11044	2883		43		468
	1998	69957	20678	9058	1963	136	48	484	410
	1999	70586	21014	8572	1712	144	46	603	420
	2000	71150	21274	8102	1499	155	42	687	457
北京	Beijing	622.1	456.3	266.2	48.3	8.5	4.0	34.2	14.0
天津	Tianjin	406.7	238.6	108.3	25.8	1.1	2.3	23.0	5.8
河北	Hebei	3441.2	734.1	426.0	60.1	5.8	0.5	26.2	17.9
山西	Shanxi	1419.1	430.5	286.3	49.8	5.0	0.3	29.4	8.4
内蒙古	Inner Mongolia	1016.6	385.1	201.1	25.6	2.9	0.6	26.0	8.2
辽宁	Liaoning	1812.6	846.6	418.4	93.1	5.9	0.7	31.0	21.7
吉林	Jilin	1078.9	437.9	250.5	42.8	1.9	0.3	13.0	17.1
黑龙江	Heilongjiang	1635.0	721.8	411.4	76.2	8.4	0.9	22.4	29.1
上海	Shanghai	673.1	417.5	198.6	31.6	5.0	3.0	25.8	22.3
江苏	Jiangsu	3558.8	870.8	421.7	117.9	17.8	5.5	47.1	30.7
浙江	Zhejiang	2700.5	592.1	202.5	54.0	17.2	1.8	53.7	25.0
安徽	Anhui	3372.9	575.1	276.0	68.3	6.1	0.9	28.7	17.0
福建	Fujian	1660.2	416.1	170.8	34.2	3.6	3.4	12.1	9.3
江西	Jiangxi	1935.3	388.1	238.7	33.5	2.5	0.2	16.4	3.9
山东	Shandong	4661.8	1022.2	555.1	105.3	12.1	2.7	43.3	37.4
河南	Henan	5571.7	859.3	463.7	143.2	6.5	1.6	68.8	34.7
湖北	Hubei	2507.8	726.1	417.4	64.8	5.3	1.5	14.1	31.0
湖南	Hunan	3462.1	606.0	372.5	56.3	2.7	0.7	8.5	11.0
广东	Guangdong	3861.0	1075.9	425.5	106.0	10.6	6.7	36.1	28.2
广西	Guangxi	2530.4	385.0	234.5	28.4	1.4	0.3	15.1	8.8
海南	Hainan	333.7	109.7	66.9	4.4	0.4	0.6	1.4	2.4
重庆	Chongqing	1636.5	283.9	149.3	30.3	3.6	0.7	13.5	10.5
四川	Sichuan	4435.8	646.8	381.5	71.6	5.4	1.0	32.3	29.9
贵州	Guizhou	2045.9	243.3	160.0	19.8	1.4	0.5	14.9	2.9
云南	Yunnan	2295.4	346.5	224.6	26.0	3.9	0.3	12.7	9.2
西藏	Tibet	123.4	22.6	16.4	0.9	...	0.1	0.1	0.4
陕西	Shaanxi	1812.8	469.6	272.4	30.2	3.3	0.4	17.3	10.6
甘肃	Gansu	1182.1	247.6	169.4	25.8	3.9	0.1	3.7	1.5
青海	Qinghai	238.6	66.6	41.7	4.6	0.3	...	0.5	0.4
宁夏	Ningxia	274.4	76.5	51.0	5.0	1.1	0.1	4.0	1.7
新疆	Xinjiang	672.5	318.4	223.4	15.6	1.4	0.3	12.3	5.9

Number of Employed Persons at the Year-end by Residence in Urban and Rural Areas

(10 000 persons)

Urban Area				乡　村 Rural Area			
#私营企业 Private Enterprises	# 港澳台商投资单位 Units with Funds from Hong Kong, Macao and Taiwan	#外商投资单位 Foreign Funded Units	#个　体 Self-employed individuals	小　计 Sub-total	#乡镇企业 Township and Village Enterprises	#私营企业 Private Enterprises	#个　体 Self-employed Individuals
			15	30638	2827		
			32	31025	2909		
			81	31836	3000		
			113	32672	2970		
			147	33867	3113		
			231	34690	3235		
			339	35968	5208		
		6	450	37065	6979		
	1	12	483	37990	7937		
	1	20	569	39000	8805		
	2	29	659	40067	9545		
	4	43	648	40939	9367		
57	4	62	614	47293	9265	113	1491
68	69	96	692	47822	9609	116	1616
98	83	138	740	48313	10625	134	1728
186	155	133	930	48784	12345	187	2010
332	211	195	1225	48786	12017	316	2551
485	272	241	1560	48854	12862	471	3054
620	265	275	1709	49035	13508	551	3308
750	281	300	1919	49393	13050	600	3522
973	294	293	2259	49279	12537	737	3855
1053	306	306	2414	49572	12704	969	3827
1268	310	332	2136	49876	12820	1139	2934
4.3	14.2	23.8	20.2	165.8	101.4	4.8	14.3
27.5	10.7	24.6	9.4	168.1	120.4	10.5	11.7
44.0	5.0	6.9	141.3	2707.1	849.6	157.5	568.7
22.5	1.7	0.9	26.2	988.6	287.4	16.1	30.6
28.6	1.7	2.2	88.2	631.5	405.0	12.8	71.5
83.3	10.2	20.9	161.0	966.0	464.5	41.6	118.4
21.5	2.4	5.9	81.9	641.0	250.9	7.0	70.9
40.5	3.5	3.4	126.0	913.2	154.3	13.2	118.2
58.2	23.3	40.3	9.3	255.6	144.1	92.7	15.3
96.6	20.0	31.4	81.2	2688.0	855.8	137.8	200.5
110.6	15.9	13.9	97.1	2108.4	880.4	189.9	175.3
37.6	2.1	3.6	134.8	2797.8	479.8	27.6	201.6
44.4	51.5	40.3	45.7	1244.1	555.6	23.5	48.2
27.1	2.6	1.4	61.6	1547.2	307.2	20.1	78.4
105.3	11.9	38.7	110.0	3639.6	1311.6	108.8	165.5
27.9	9.6	5.5	97.4	4712.4	889.2	29.1	184.3
52.9	4.1	4.7	129.5	1781.7	629.7	26.7	114.3
33.5	2.7	2.9	115.0	2856.1	938.9	12.7	112.8
151.7	102.7	43.0	164.9	2785.1	928.3	65.8	143.9
21.9	3.0	3.8	67.9	2145.4	353.2	8.7	71.6
16.6	1.7	1.7	13.6	224.0	28.2	2.0	7.4
35.5	2.0	2.6	35.6	1352.6	151.0	13.2	52.4
49.5	2.6	3.3	68.5	3789.0	610.1	32.0	99.8
16.4	0.6	1.2	25.5	1802.6	140.6	9.2	27.9
22.9	1.7	1.3	43.5	1948.9	270.8	11.9	50.1
0.7	...	...	4.1	100.8		0.1	2.2
40.3	1.3	1.6	92.2	1343.2	401.0	43.1	122.6
16.1	0.3	0.9	25.5	934.5	157.0	6.2	24.7
8.1	0.1	...	10.5	172.0	23.4	3.1	5.3
4.8	0.3	1.0	7.6	197.9	49.8	5.8	5.7
17.1	0.9	0.5	40.9	354.1	80.6	5.2	19.8

5-5 分行业年底从业人员数

单位: 万人

年份 地区	Year Region	合计 Total	农、林、牧、渔业 Farming, Forestry, Animal Husbandry and Fishery	采掘业 Mining and Quarrying	制造业 Manufacturing	电力、煤气及水的生产和供应业 Production and Supply of Electricity Gas and Water	建筑业 Construction	地质勘查业水利管理业 Geological Prospecting and Water Conservancy
	1978	40152	28318	652	5332	107	854	178
	1979	41024	28634	670	5516	112	916	185
	1980	42361	29122	697	5899	118	993	188
	1981	43725	29777	728	6122	125	1028	188
	1982	45295	30859	747	6329	128	1142	191
	1983	46436	31151	758	6508	131	1282	193
	1984	48197	30868	767	7029	134	1660	197
	1985	49873	31130	795	7412	142	2035	197
	1986	51282	31254	809	8019	152	2236	197
	1987	52783	31663	819	8359	164	2384	200
	1988	54334	32249	832	8652	177	2491	204
	1989	55329	33225	842	8547	180	2407	199
	1990	63909	34117	882	8624	192	2424	197
	1991	64799	34956	905	8839	203	2482	199
	1992	65554	34795	898	9106	215	2660	202
	1993	66373	33966	932	9295	240	3050	144
	1994	67199	33386	915	9613	246	3188	139
	1995	67947	33018	932	9803	258	3322	135
	1996	68850	32910	902	9763	273	3408	129
	1997	69600	33095	868	9612	283	3449	129
	1998	69957	33232	721	8319	283	3327	116
	1999	70586	33493	667	8109	285	3412	111
	2000	71150	33355	597	8043	284	3552	110
北京	Beijing	622.1	72.7	2.6	130.1	4.0	64.9	1.5
天津	Tianjin	406.7	80.9	7.1	130.6	4.9	24.2	1.9
河北	Hebei	3441.2	1678.2	32.6	586.5	14.5	240.7	8.0
山西	Shanxi	1419.1	662.7	52.4	216.0	10.9	74.1	3.1
内蒙古	Inner Mongolia	1016.6	553.7	28.5	89.9	8.5	40.5	3.1
辽宁	Liaoning	1812.6	683.3	32.6	321.6	17.6	105.1	5.5
吉林	Jilin	1078.9	541.6	31.8	123.6	7.7	43.2	2.8
黑龙江	Heilongjiang	1635.0	808.5	77.5	185.7	14.4	69.7	5.7
上海	Shanghai	673.1	88.0	0.1	250.6	5.7	32.0	0.9
江苏	Jiangsu	3558.8	1502.7	18.4	740.2	12.6	286.0	5.3
浙江	Zhejiang	2700.5	1021.0	2.5	664.0	9.0	158.2	1.6
安徽	Anhui	3372.9	2017.9	29.6	294.1	8.3	200.4	4.9
福建	Fujian	1660.2	778.2	5.5	289.9	7.1	104.4	1.3
江西	Jiangxi	1935.3	1004.4	14.3	179.1	9.3	76.3	3.0
山东	Shandong	4661.8	2473.7	64.4	692.5	19.8	325.1	4.7
河南	Henan	5571.7	3569.0	48.1	572.0	21.3	335.8	8.7
湖北	Hubei	2507.8	1204.8	13.2	298.4	12.0	136.0	7.5
湖南	Hunan	3462.1	2104.4	16.4	324.1	10.7	156.3	4.9
广东	Guangdong	3861.0	1588.5	6.1	732.4	19.3	253.9	4.5
广西	Guangxi	2530.4	1574.5	6.3	143.6	8.1	99.2	2.7
海南	Hainan	333.7	204.4	1.9	16.0	2.1	12.0	0.6
重庆	Chongqing	1636.5	925.2	10.4	134.5	5.2	101.0	1.2
四川	Sichuan	4435.8	2643.4	25.5	335.5	14.6	266.2	4.8
贵州	Guizhou	2045.9	1377.9	10.1	118.7	5.1	55.5	1.4
云南	Yunnan	2295.4	1695.9	10.8	118.1	6.8	74.8	2.8
西藏	Tibet	123.4	91.0	0.4	2.7	0.6	3.5	0.2
陕西	Shaanxi	1812.8	1010.2	19.6	172.2	8.0	99.3	6.5
甘肃	Gansu	1182.1	706.1	9.5	89.9	7.2	56.6	4.6
青海	Qinghai	238.6	145.3	1.9	17.0	1.4	11.5	2.0
宁夏	Ningxia	274.4	158.6	6.0	24.9	2.0	16.9	1.1
新疆	Xinjiang	672.5	387.9	11.3	47.8	5.1	28.5	3.4

Number of Employed Persons at the Year-end by Sector

(10 000 persons)

交通运输仓储和邮电通信业 Transport, Storage, Post & Telecommunication Services	批发零售贸易和餐饮业 Wholesale and Retail Trade & Catering Services	金融、保险业 Finance and Insurance	房地产业 Real Estate	社会服务业 Social Services	卫生体育和社会福利业 Health Care, Sports & Social Welfare	教育、文化艺术和广播电影电视业 Education, Culture and Arts, Radio, Film and Television	科学研究和综合技术服务业 Scientific Research and Polytechnic Services	国家机关、政党机关和社会团体 Government Agencies, Party Agencies and Social Organizations	其他 Others
750	1140	76	31	179	363	1093	92	467	521
781	1232	86	34	210	386	1131	100	505	527
805	1363	99	37	276	389	1147	113	527	588
844	1491	107	38	305	375	1095	127	556	819
878	1576	113	38	322	399	1128	132	611	702
936	1732	117	37	367	415	1151	133	646	879
1122	1994	127	36	439	435	1204	137	743	1305
1279	2306	138	36	401	467	1273	144	799	1319
1376	2413	152	38	466	482	1324	152	873	1338
1453	2576	170	39	501	496	1375	158	925	1502
1521	2743	194	42	534	508	1403	161	971	1655
1522	2770	205	43	550	518	1426	165	1022	1709
1566	2839	218	44	594	536	1457	173	1079	1798
1617	2998	234	48	604	553	1497	179	1136	1910
1674	3209	248	54	643	565	1520	183	1148	2313
1688	3459	270	66	543	416	1210	173	1030	3740
1864	3921	264	74	626	434	1436	178	1033	4155
1942	4292	276	80	703	444	1476	182	1042	4484
2013	4511	292	84	747	458	1513	183	1093	4563
2062	4795	308	87	810	471	1557	186	1093	4862
2000	4645	314	94	868	478	1573	178	1097	5118
2022	4751	328	96	923	482	1568	173	1102	4969
2029	4686	327	100	921	488	1565	174	1104	5643
32.2	78.2	7.1	12.3	66.8	15.9	41.7	32.7	24.7	34.7
24.7	46.7	3.9	2.4	14.9	6.9	19.4	5.0	12.1	21.3
132.3	285.8	16.1	2.3	39.0	21.2	86.3	4.8	64.5	228.7
79.8	114.0	10.4	1.3	17.6	13.5	47.7	4.1	42.1	69.4
40.9	92.0	7.8	1.7	22.9	10.6	36.1	2.8	29.7	47.9
97.5	226.1	18.3	8.1	62.3	23.2	58.1	8.4	40.4	104.5
43.2	105.7	9.6	3.4	24.6	14.3	41.2	4.6	25.1	56.3
67.8	164.5	11.5	4.8	43.3	18.2	50.7	4.4	39.1	69.1
31.8	87.9	9.8	8.0	43.0	15.7	31.3	9.1	15.1	44.3
136.9	278.9	17.9	6.1	47.9	29.9	87.1	8.1	46.4	334.3
96.4	269.2	16.3	4.0	43.7	20.9	51.1	4.4	34.8	303.6
95.5	246.1	10.4	2.5	40.6	16.6	60.3	3.6	40.9	301.3
55.4	130.0	10.1	3.1	23.5	10.8	46.4	2.8	28.9	162.6
45.6	111.8	8.6	1.7	16.6	13.5	47.3	3.2	34.4	366.1
153.6	342.3	22.2	4.3	47.1	33.5	111.5	6.2	78.2	282.8
154.8	323.3	21.0	3.8	39.1	30.2	107.0	7.6	80.8	249.2
91.8	225.9	13.5	3.5	45.3	26.2	72.6	7.0	52.8	297.4
91.8	211.0	14.6	2.4	33.3	23.0	73.9	5.4	53.3	336.4
130.7	384.5	27.4	10.6	77.3	33.5	93.3	6.8	69.7	422.6
58.8	132.3	8.4	1.9	22.4	14.6	59.9	3.5	34.4	359.8
11.9	29.9	2.1	0.9	9.9	2.9	9.1	1.3	8.8	19.9
36.0	88.1	6.2	1.8	15.0	8.7	32.1	5.5	19.8	246.0
85.9	220.5	16.6	3.2	32.8	26.3	83.4	9.5	59.9	607.8
30.0	73.0	5.2	1.3	10.9	8.8	35.6	1.9	27.4	283.0
55.8	99.4	7.5	1.4	19.7	12.8	49.7	5.3	36.1	98.8
3.5	5.9	0.6		1.5	1.2	3.2	0.2	5.7	3.0
67.3	152.9	9.2	1.2	27.4	13.4	51.0	9.0	38.3	127.5
32.3	64.8	5.3	0.9	11.2	7.5	30.5	3.2	23.1	129.1
8.5	17.3	1.7	0.2	3.6	2.3	6.6	0.7	6.2	12.0
11.8	18.7	2.1	0.4	3.3	2.5	8.3	0.7	6.3	11.1
25.0	59.1	5.3	0.9	15.4	9.3	33.5	2.6	25.1	12.2

5-6 分行业年底职工人数

单位：万人

年份 地区	Year Region	合计 Total	农、林、牧、渔业 Farming, Forestry, Animal Husbandry and Fishery	采掘业 Mining and Quarrying	制造业 Manufacturing	电力、煤气及水的生产和供应业 Production and Supply of Electricity Gas and Water	建筑业 Construction	地质勘查业水利管理业 Geological Prospecting and Water Conservancy
	1978	9499	830	652	3595	107	623	178
	1979	9967	799	670	3754	112	682	185
	1980	10444	788	697	3947	118	710	188
	1981	10940	797	728	4130	125	730	188
	1982	11281	797	747	4240	128	762	191
	1983	11515	801	758	4316	131	798	193
	1984	11890	787	767	4442	134	845	197
	1985	12358	777	795	4620	142	900	197
	1986	12809	784	809	4820	152	922	197
	1987	13214	792	819	4988	164	946	200
	1988	13608	789	832	5149	177	955	204
	1989	13742	782	842	5206	180	900	199
	1990	14059	780	882	5304	192	896	197
	1991	14508	769	905	5443	203	940	199
	1992	14792	758	898	5508	215	995	202
	1993	14849	708	925	5469	232	1153	144
	1994	14849	680	904	5434	244	1072	137
	1995	14908	660	914	5439	257	1053	134
	1996	14845	617	886	5293	272	1035	128
	1997	14668	612	851	5083	282	1004	128
	1998	12337	546	702	3769	281	846	115
	1999	11773	519	650	3496	283	778	110
	2000	11259	494	581	3240	282	744	109
北　京	Beijing	397.9	2.8	2.6	89.6	3.9	48.7	1.5
天　津	Tianjin	193.3	1.1	6.6	78.6	4.8	11.9	1.9
河　北	Hebei	539.4	10.4	31.5	155.4	14.4	33.1	8.0
山　西	Shanxi	370.2	4.2	52.1	94.7	10.9	19.4	3.1
内蒙古	Inner Mongolia	263.9	26.6	27.2	54.1	8.5	13.9	3.1
辽　宁	Liaoning	587.0	29.9	31.7	198.4	17.4	42.8	5.5
吉　林	Jilin	329.9	16.7	31.1	88.5	7.7	19.7	2.8
黑龙江	Heilongjiang	531.5	46.3	77.1	122.1	14.3	39.1	5.6
上　海	Shanghai	307.0	2.2	0.1	119.1	5.5	14.4	0.9
江　苏	Jiangsu	673.3	21.5	18.1	251.4	12.5	29.2	5.3
浙　江	Zhejiang	373.0	4.8	2.2	113.4	8.9	42.6	1.6
安　徽	Anhui	392.7	13.7	29.0	104.7	8.2	22.9	4.7
福　建	Fujian	318.0	8.6	5.3	127.9	7.1	21.9	1.2
江　西	Jiangxi	291.6	19.5	13.5	75.1	9.2	14.2	3.0
山　东	Shandong	790.1	9.6	64.2	281.0	19.7	32.6	4.7
河　南	Henan	718.2	9.7	47.2	196.2	21.2	51.2	8.6
湖　北	Hubei	529.4	40.7	11.6	154.2	11.9	26.7	7.3
湖　南	Hunan	441.3	32.0	15.6	105.2	10.6	23.8	4.9
广　东	Guangdong	747.7	17.0	5.7	251.8	19.2	53.7	4.4
广　西	Guangxi	283.1	16.6	5.7	65.9	8.0	13.1	2.6
海　南	Hainan	77.8	24.8	1.6	7.8	2.1	3.2	0.6
重　庆	Chongqing	208.9	3.4	10.2	61.4	5.2	18.1	1.2
四　川	Sichuan	515.4	11.6	24.5	138.0	14.6	47.3	4.7
贵　州	Guizhou	194.0	5.0	9.6	46.0	5.1	18.0	1.4
云　南	Yunnan	273.4	20.0	10.1	54.7	6.7	18.4	2.8
西　藏	Tibet	16.2	0.6	0.3	0.9	0.6	1.0	0.2
陕　西	Shaanxi	327.6	6.7	18.3	93.6	7.9	20.0	6.5
甘　肃	Gansu	201.2	8.1	9.4	54.3	7.2	13.4	4.4
青　海	Qinghai	46.9	2.6	1.9	8.3	1.4	4.4	1.9
宁　夏	Ningxia	62.7	5.3	5.9	14.4	2.0	4.1	1.1
新　疆	Xinjiang	255.8	72.5	11.0	32.7	5.1	21.5	3.4

注：1998年及以后为在岗职工数(以下各表同)。

Number of Staff and Workers at the Year-end by Sector

(10 000 persons)

交通运输仓储和邮电通信业 Transport, Storage, Post & Telecommunication Services	批发零售贸易和餐饮业 Wholesale and Retail Trade & Catering Services	金融、保险业 Finance and Insurance	房地产业 Real Estate	社会服务业 Social Services	卫生体育和社会福利业 Health Care, Sports & Social Welfare	教育、文化艺术和广播电影电视业 Education, Culture and Arts, Radio, Film and Television	科学研究和综合技术服务业 Scientific Research and Polytechnic Services	国家机关、政党机关和社会团体 Government Agencies, Party Agencies and Social Organizations	其他 Others
669	1079	65	31	166	247	736	92	430	
699	1161	75	34	191	269	769	100	468	
714	1239	89	37	218	287	817	105	490	
741	1337	97	38	239	302	857	111	520	
761	1388	102	38	253	311	868	118	577	
771	1424	106	37	268	322	878	121	591	
793	1454	115	36	276	335	915	125	669	
823	1518	126	36	271	342	962	131	718	
846	1544	138	38	289	354	1008	137	770	
860	1578	154	39	304	365	1059	142	805	
874	1643	174	42	318	375	1091	144	843	
874	1675	184	43	327	382	1117	147	885	
895	1715	195	44	344	392	1143	152	929	
916	1786	208	48	369	410	1181	156	974	
921	1844	223	54	386	421	1212	159	996	
826	1796	239	66	422	416	1205	166	1030	55
835	1833	261	72	447	428	1249	174	1017	63
824	1828	273	77	449	438	1291	178	1027	66
830	1807	288	82	458	451	1345	176	1075	103
824	1774	298	84	480	464	1403	179	1080	125
701	1256	301	89	451	469	1451	168	1084	108
682	1110	300	90	453	473	1480	165	1088	96
659	977	294	93	457	476	1500	164	1091	99
17.5	42.6	7.0	10.3	55.4	13.4	39.5	28.4	24.3	10.5
12.5	16.0	3.5	2.2	9.6	6.8	18.8	4.5	11.6	2.9
28.6	48.3	15.0	2.3	16.6	21.0	82.7	4.7	64.2	3.0
23.5	33.2	8.9	1.2	12.0	13.3	44.0	4.0	41.8	3.7
18.8	14.7	7.3	1.7	7.6	10.5	34.7	2.8	29.4	3.0
38.9	38.3	16.4	7.5	29.1	22.8	55.8	8.1	39.7	4.9
23.8	26.1	8.8	3.4	13.9	14.2	40.4	4.6	25.0	3.3
34.9	40.0	10.5	4.6	22.3	18.0	49.3	4.3	38.8	4.1
21.8	31.1	8.5	5.9	28.1	14.2	29.0	8.3	13.4	4.6
42.5	74.7	15.3	5.8	23.4	29.1	85.5	7.8	45.5	5.8
21.1	30.7	14.4	3.7	17.9	20.3	49.9	4.1	34.0	3.3
21.5	43.3	9.1	2.5	13.3	16.2	58.0	3.5	40.2	2.0
14.9	19.3	8.8	2.8	10.3	10.6	45.3	2.7	28.7	2.7
17.9	26.4	7.9	1.6	6.5	13.2	44.7	3.2	34.2	1.4
33.6	70.2	19.3	4.2	23.0	33.1	104.1	6.0	77.9	6.9
37.5	76.6	18.9	3.7	22.3	29.8	102.5	7.4	80.1	5.3
34.7	52.0	12.9	3.4	18.7	25.9	67.0	6.8	52.4	3.2
28.0	36.4	11.8	2.4	13.4	22.7	72.7	5.3	52.9	3.6
46.4	69.0	26.2	10.3	37.6	32.8	90.3	6.6	69.4	7.4
16.8	24.5	8.0	1.8	11.0	14.4	54.9	3.4	34.0	2.5
3.8	4.9	2.0	0.9	4.2	2.9	8.7	1.3	8.7	0.3
15.4	15.6	5.0	1.7	6.1	8.6	31.5	5.4	19.7	0.4
25.5	40.4	13.8	3.1	14.1	25.6	81.4	9.3	59.3	2.2
9.1	16.4	5.0	1.2	4.5	8.4	33.6	1.9	26.7	1.8
17.0	24.3	7.3	1.3	9.4	12.6	48.5	3.5	35.5	1.2
1.1	0.8	0.6	...	0.7	1.0	2.9	0.2	5.4	...
21.4	25.2	7.9	1.2	9.8	13.2	47.4	8.9	37.9	1.7
11.8	16.0	5.0	0.9	6.0	7.4	28.7	3.2	22.9	2.5
3.6	3.2	1.5	0.2	1.6	2.3	6.4	0.7	6.1	0.6
3.3	4.1	1.9	0.4	1.9	2.5	8.3	0.7	6.2	0.8
11.4	12.5	5.1	0.9	6.7	9.2	33.2	2.6	25.1	2.9

a)Data since 1998 are on-post staff and workers figures. (The same as in the following tables).

5-7 分登记注册类型和细行业年底职工人数（2000年）

Number of Staff and Workers at the Year-end by Status of Registration and Sector in Detail (2000)

单位：万人 (10 000 persons)

项　目	Item	合　计 Total	国有单位 State-owned Units	城镇集体单位 Urban Collective-owned Units	其他单位 Units of Other Types of Ownership
全国总计	**National Total**	**11258.5**	**7877.5**	**1446.5**	**1934.5**
按企、事业和机关分组	**Grouped by Enterprises, Institutions and Agencies**				
企业	Enterprises	7507.8	4265.4	1310.9	1931.6
事业	Institutions	2689.1	2555.0	131.2	2.9
机关	Agencies & Organizations	1061.6	1057.1	4.4	
按国民经济行业分组	**Grouped by Sector**				
农、林、牧、渔业	**Farming, Forestry, Animal Husbandry and Fishery**	**494.4**	**474.5**	**13.7**	**6.1**
农业	Farming	270.3	265.2	2.8	2.2
林业	Forestry	75.4	74.5	0.6	0.3
畜牧业	Animal Husbandry	33.2	30.5	0.8	2.0
渔业	Fishery	11.4	9.5	0.7	1.2
农、林、牧、渔服务业	Services	104.1	94.9	8.8	0.4
采掘业	**Mining and Quarrying**	**580.9**	**448.3**	**34.5**	**98.0**
制造业	**Manufacturing**	**3239.5**	**1415.1**	**518.9**	**1305.5**
电力、煤气及水的生产和供应业	**Production and Supply of Electricity, Gas and Water**	**281.8**	**232.5**	**9.2**	**40.1**
建筑业	**Construction**	**744.2**	**371.9**	**260.9**	**111.4**
土木工程建筑业	Civil Engineering	642.7	322.1	228.2	92.4
线路管道和设备安装业	Circuit, Pipelines and Equipment Installation	84.6	46.6	26.1	11.9
装修装饰业	Buildings Fitting up and Decoration	17.0	3.2	6.5	7.2
地质勘查业水利管理业	**Geological Prospecting and Water Conservancy**	**108.9**	**106.8**	**1.9**	**0.2**
地质勘查业	Geological Prospecting	51.2	50.6	0.5	0.1
水利管理业	Water Conservancy	57.7	56.1	1.4	0.1
交通运输、仓储及邮电通信业	**Transport, Storage, Post and Telecommunication Services**	**658.5**	**548.6**	**56.1**	**53.8**
铁路运输业	Railway Transport	187.1	178.3	3.3	5.4
公路运输业	Highway Transport	120.0	77.4	23.4	19.2
管道运输业	Pipeline Transport	2.2	2.0	0.1	0.1
水上运输业	Water Way Transport	38.8	21.6	12.0	5.2
航空运输业	Air Transport	11.7	9.0	0.1	2.6
交通运输辅助业	Transport Supporting and Auxiliary Services	147.7	124.8	12.8	10.0
其他交通运输业	Other Transport	1.9	1.0	0.6	0.4
仓储业	Storage	36.0	31.6	1.9	2.4
邮电通信业	Post and Telecommunication Services	113.2	102.8	1.8	8.6
批发和零售贸易餐饮业	**Wholesale and Retail Trade & Catering Services**	**977.1**	**531.0**	**284.8**	**161.3**
食品、饮料、烟草和家庭日用品批发业	Wholesale Trade of Food, Beverages, Tobacco and Household Goods	320.1	225.5	60.0	34.6
能源、材料和机械电子设备批发业	Wholesale Trade of Energy, Materials and Electronic Equipment	124.9	80.7	23.1	21.1
其他批发业	Other Wholesale Trade	74.7	29.7	38.2	6.9
零售业	Retail Trade	399.0	170.0	151.5	77.4
商业经纪与代理业	Commercial Brokerage and Agencies	4.1	2.7	0.3	1.0
餐饮业	Catering Services	54.3	22.4	11.7	20.3
金融、保险业	**Finance and Insurance**	**293.5**	**199.9**	**68.0**	**25.5**
金融业	Finance	271.5	183.4	68.0	20.2

5-7 续表 1 continued

单位：万人 (10 000 persons)

项　目	Item	合　计 Total	国有单位 State-owned Units	城镇集体单位 Urban Collective-owned Units	其他单位 Units of Other Types of Ownership
保险业	Insurance	22.0	16.6	...	5.4
房地产业	**Real Estate Trade**	**93.1**	**60.3**	**6.3**	**26.4**
房地产开发与经营业	Real Estate Development and Operation	42.7	21.7	4.3	16.6
房地产管理业	Real Estate Management	48.0	36.8	1.8	9.4
房地产代理与经纪业	Real Estate Brokerage and Agencies	2.4	1.8	0.2	0.4
社会服务业	**Social Services**	**457.1**	**313.7**	**60.6**	**82.9**
公共设施服务业	Public Facilities Services	204.2	172.2	15.6	16.4
居民服务业	Resident Services	32.8	15.5	14.0	3.3
旅馆业	Hotels	115.8	69.5	12.0	34.3
租赁服务业	Leasing Services	2.9	1.2	0.5	1.2
旅游业	Tourism	12.2	8.4	0.7	3.2
娱乐服务业	Recreational Services	6.6	1.8	0.8	3.9
信息、咨询服务业	Information and Consultative Services	22.1	12.3	2.5	7.4
计算机应用服务业	Computer Application Services	9.3	1.8	0.5	7.0
其他社会服务业	Other Social Services	51.2	31.0	14.0	6.2
卫生体育和社会福利业	**Health Care, Sports and Social Welfare**	**476.1**	**419.1**	**55.8**	**1.2**
卫生	Health Care	448.4	392.8	54.9	0.7
体育	Sports	8.4	8.0	...	0.4
社会福利保障业	Social Welfare	19.3	18.3	0.9	0.1
教育、文化艺术及广播电影电视业	**Education, Culture and Arts, Radio, Film and Television**	**1499.5**	**1447.2**	**49.2**	**3.2**
教育	Education	1393.3	1345.3	46.0	1.9
#普通高等学校	Regular Institution of Higher Education	108.9	108.8	...	0.1
普通中学	Regular Secondary Schools	469.0	467.3	1.3	0.4
小学校	Primary Schools	634.6	593.3	40.5	0.8
文化艺术业	Culture and Arts	60.2	57.3	2.2	0.7
广播电影电视业	Radio, Film and Television	46.1	44.5	0.9	0.6
科学研究和综合技术服务业	**Scientific Research and Polytechnic Services**	**164.3**	**146.6**	**5.4**	**12.2**
科学研究业	Scientific Research	69.8	69.4	0.2	0.2
自然科学研究	Natural Science Research	54.4	54.0	0.2	0.2
社会科学研究	Social Science Research	3.2	3.2	...	...
其他科学研究	Other Science Research	12.2	12.1	...	...
综合技术服务业	Polytechnic Services	94.5	77.2	5.2	12.0
#气象	Meteorology	5.1	5.1	...	...
地震	Seismology	1.4	1.4	...	...
测绘	Survey and Mapping	4.1	4.0	0.1	...
技术监督	Technological Supervision	15.5	14.9	0.2	0.3
海洋环境	Oceanic Environment	0.5	0.5	...	...
环境保护	Environmental Protection	7.6	7.3	0.2	0.1
技术推广和科技交流服务业	Technology Application & Dissemination, Science and Technology Exchange Services	10.1	6.2	2.2	1.6
工程设计业	Engineering Design	27.9	26.2	0.8	0.9
其他综合技术服务业	Other Polytechnic Services	22.1	11.4	1.7	9.0
国家机关、政党机关和社会团体	**Government Agencies, Party Agencies and Social Organizations**	**1090.8**	**1086.0**	**4.7**	
#国家机关	Government Agencies	1022.1	1018.7	3.4	
政党机关	Party Agencies	51.9	51.9	...	
其他	**Others**	**98.8**	**75.8**	**16.4**	**6.6**
#企业管理机构	Enterprise Management Organizations	51.4	36.6	12.1	2.7

5-8 国有单位分行业年底职工人数

单位：万人

年份 地区	Year Region	合计 Total	农、林、牧、渔业 Farming, Forestry, Animal Husbandry and Fishery	采掘业 Mining and Quarrying	制造业 Manufacturing	电力、煤气及水的生产和供应业 Production and Supply of Electricity Gas and Water	建筑业 Construction	地质勘查业水利管理业 Geological Prospecting and Water Conservancy
	1978	7451	774	588	2449	102	447	177
	1979	7693	747	600	2502	106	463	184
	1980	8019	740	621	2601	112	475	187
	1981	8372	745	649	2720	119	475	187
	1982	8630	742	666	2794	122	481	190
	1983	8771	739	674	2833	125	497	192
	1984	8637	732	680	2862	127	518	196
	1985	8990	726	706	2975	134	545	196
	1986	9333	736	715	3096	144	557	196
	1987	9654	744	722	3209	155	566	200
	1988	9983	743	735	3327	167	568	204
	1989	10109	736	757	3344	172	541	199
	1990	10346	737	786	3395	183	538	194
	1991	10664	727	797	3482	193	557	196
	1992	10889	717	792	3526	203	577	199
	1993	10920	672	834	3444	220	663	142
	1994	10890	653	820	3321	230	629	135
	1995	10955	634	834	3326	237	605	132
	1996	10949	592	809	3218	250	595	126
	1997	10766	588	772	3011	257	577	125
	1998	8809	525	596	1883	242	444	113
	1999	8336	500	525	1648	239	399	108
	2000	7878	475	448	1415	233	372	107
北京	Beijing	255.8	2.3	2.5	48.0	3.1	24.4	1.4
天津	Tianjin	105.2	1.0	1.4	23.4	4.1	5.3	1.8
河北	Hebei	419.5	10.1	27.1	85.3	12.8	20.4	7.9
山西	Shanxi	276.6	4.0	39.2	49.1	9.6	13.5	3.1
内蒙古	Inner Mongolia	197.3	25.6	23.2	13.7	7.0	6.2	3.0
辽宁	Liaoning	409.0	29.1	23.6	99.7	13.1	21.2	5.4
吉林	Jilin	247.0	16.4	28.0	39.7	6.8	11.2	2.7
黑龙江	Heilongjiang	390.2	44.1	56.9	57.2	12.7	18.1	5.2
上海	Shanghai	181.0	2.0		48.3	4.5	7.7	0.9
江苏	Jiangsu	411.4	20.5	15.2	88.5	9.4	14.1	5.0
浙江	Zhejiang	196.7	4.3	1.9	23.5	6.6	5.7	1.5
安徽	Anhui	269.1	13.0	14.6	50.0	7.4	11.9	4.7
福建	Fujian	166.8	8.0	4.2	16.5	5.7	8.4	1.2
江西	Jiangxi	231.8	19.3	12.4	41.4	8.3	6.5	3.0
山东	Shandong	542.1	8.0	58.1	118.5	17.7	16.5	4.7
河南	Henan	455.1	8.7	21.3	81.8	18.3	27.4	8.5
湖北	Hubei	406.2	39.9	9.8	86.6	10.0	17.0	7.3
湖南	Hunan	360.8	30.8	15.1	68.0	9.7	13.7	4.7
广东	Guangdong	417.7	15.6	4.8	47.6	14.1	19.0	4.2
广西	Guangxi	225.1	16.1	5.0	36.9	7.2	5.2	2.6
海南	Hainan	65.4	24.6	1.5	3.9	1.4	1.8	0.6
重庆	Chongqing	146.9	2.5	8.9	34.1	3.5	6.3	1.2
四川	Sichuan	371.7	9.3	19.3	67.5	10.5	24.6	4.5
贵州	Guizhou	153.6	5.0	6.2	26.7	4.7	10.8	1.4
云南	Yunnan	220.6	19.4	8.5	32.5	4.6	11.7	2.8
西藏	Tibet	15.0	0.6	0.2	0.4	0.6	0.6	0.2
陕西	Shaanxi	264.6	6.3	16.5	59.2	6.8	14.2	6.4
甘肃	Gansu	165.3	8.0	7.3	39.0	5.6	7.4	4.4
青海	Qinghai	40.8	2.6	1.7	6.1	1.3	2.8	1.9
宁夏	Ningxia	49.9	5.3	5.1	6.7	1.8	2.5	1.1
新疆	Xinjiang	219.4	72.3	8.8	15.4	3.5	15.9	3.3

Number of Staff and Workers in State-owned Units at the Year-end by Sector

(10 000 persons)

交通运输仓储和邮电通信业 Transport, Storage, Post & Telecommunications Services	批发零售贸易和餐饮业 Wholesale and Retail Trade & Catering Services	金融、保险业 Finance and Insurance	房地产业 Real Estate	社会服务业 Social Services	卫生体育和社会福利业 Health Care, Sports & Social Welfare	教育、文化艺术和广播电影电视业 Education, Culture and Arts, Radio, Film and Television	科学研究和综合技术服务业 Scientific Research and Polytechnic Services	国家机关、政党机关和社会团体 Government Agencies, Party Agencies and Social Organizations	其他 Others
465	907	42	28	107	183	674	91	417	
480	960	50	30	114	200	707	99	451	
498	1005	63	33	130	217	757	104	476	
522	1063	71	33	141	233	797	110	507	
537	1094	74	33	150	242	825	117	563	
549	1112	77	32	157	253	835	120	576	
559	780	84	31	165	264	873	124	642	
585	800	93	32	181	272	925	129	691	
604	824	101	34	193	283	973	135	742	
618	851	113	34	203	296	1025	140	778	
636	900	128	37	214	306	1059	142	817	
640	923	136	38	221	314	1086	144	859	
660	947	145	40	236	323	1112	148	903	
682	993	154	43	251	340	1151	151	946	
693	1037	166	48	269	356	1183	153	969	
664	1014	182	55	293	356	1180	153	1014	34
677	1054	196	59	308	368	1227	165	1007	40
677	1061	203	61	315	379	1265	167	1019	42
684	1055	208	63	329	390	1322	166	1068	74
681	1037	210	64	345	402	1362	167	1074	95
584	694	208	63	322	410	1408	155	1079	84
568	608	205	61	319	415	1433	153	1084	72
549	531	200	60	314	419	1447	147	1086	76
15.4	18.8	4.8	4.5	28.7	12.3	38.1	18.6	24.2	8.6
9.5	6.4	2.4	1.4	6.2	6.6	18.3	3.3	11.6	2.4
26.3	30.6	9.7	2.1	14.3	19.7	82.4	4.7	64.0	2.3
20.9	18.4	5.9	0.9	9.1	11.2	43.4	3.9	41.7	2.8
17.4	9.7	5.3	1.6	6.3	9.1	34.7	2.8	29.4	2.4
31.7	20.0	11.1	5.7	20.9	20.7	55.4	7.7	39.7	4.1
21.1	16.5	5.6	2.4	11.3	13.0	40.2	4.4	24.9	2.8
32.0	25.5	7.1	3.7	16.2	17.2	49.0	4.0	38.6	2.5
15.7	12.0	5.8	3.2	17.4	11.9	28.6	7.9	13.3	1.8
31.2	35.0	10.5	4.1	16.7	20.2	83.7	7.6	45.1	4.8
15.3	11.3	8.7	2.2	10.0	16.6	49.2	3.7	34.0	2.2
14.7	22.8	6.4	1.8	8.2	10.9	57.6	3.5	39.8	1.7
11.8	10.9	6.5	1.1	6.5	7.8	45.1	2.5	28.5	2.0
16.2	16.6	5.8	1.4	5.3	12.5	44.7	3.2	34.0	1.2
29.2	36.8	12.7	3.2	17.5	27.7	102.9	5.8	77.7	4.9
32.0	45.8	11.8	2.1	16.1	28.6	61.6	7.3	79.8	3.9
29.0	27.5	9.3	2.6	14.2	24.9	66.7	6.5	52.1	2.8
22.7	22.9	7.6	1.9	11.0	19.2	72.6	5.2	52.6	3.1
32.9	35.6	17.1	5.2	20.8	31.1	89.4	6.0	68.6	5.5
14.6	14.3	5.8	1.2	8.2	14.3	54.4	3.4	33.9	2.0
3.0	3.3	1.5	0.4	2.2	2.6	8.5	1.2	8.6	0.3
12.0	8.3	3.4	1.0	4.5	6.6	31.4	3.4	19.6	0.2
20.1	21.9	9.2	2.2	11.3	20.1	81.1	9.2	59.0	2.0
8.5	10.8	3.7	0.5	3.5	8.3	33.5	1.9	26.7	1.3
15.3	13.3	5.2	0.8	6.1	12.5	48.4	3.3	35.4	1.0
1.1	0.8	0.6		0.5	1.0	2.9	0.2	5.4	
20.2	14.8	5.6	1.0	7.1	11.8	47.0	8.8	37.7	1.2
11.1	9.3	4.0	0.9	4.8	7.0	28.7	2.9	22.8	2.2
3.5	2.1	1.2	0.2	1.2	2.2	6.4	0.7	6.0	0.6
3.3	2.6	1.6	0.2	1.6	2.4	8.3	0.7	6.2	0.7
10.9	6.6	3.9	0.7	5.7	9.0	33.1	2.5	25.0	2.7

5-9 城镇集体单位分行业年底职工人数

单位: 万人

年份 地区	Year Region	合计 Total	农、林、牧、渔业 Farming, Forestry, Animal Husbandry and Fishery	采掘业 Mining and Quarrying	制造业 Manufacturing	电力、煤气及水的生产和供应业 Production and Supply of Electricity Gas and Water	建筑业 Construction	地质勘查业水利管理业 Geological Prospecting and Water Conservancy
	1978	2048	56	64	1146	5	176	0.5
	1979	2274	52	70	1252	6	219	0.7
	1980	2425	48	76	1346	6	235	1.0
	1981	2568	52	79	1410	6	255	1.0
	1982	2651	55	81	1446	6	281	1.0
	1983	2744	62	84	1483	6	301	1.0
	1984	3216	55	87	1547	7	326	1.0
	1985	3324	51	89	1608	8	354	1.0
	1986	3421	48	93	1680	8	364	0.7
	1987	3488	47	96	1724	8	379	0.3
	1988	3527	45	96	1745	9	385	0.2
	1989	3502	45	84	1754	7	357	0.4
	1990	3549	42	95	1773	8	357	3.3
	1991	3628	41	107	1782	9	380	3.4
	1992	3621	39	105	1747	10	414	3.2
	1993	3393	34	89	1595	8	479	2.1
	1994	3211	24	81	1515	9	427	2.0
	1995	3076	23	77	1417	9	427	2.0
	1996	2954	22	72	1346	11	412	2.0
	1997	2817	20	72	1244	11	393	3.0
	1998	1900	16	49	742	11	311	2.0
	1999	1652	14	42	622	10	278	1.9
	2000	1447	14	35	519	9	261	1.9
北京	Beijing	41.7	0.1	...	7.9	0.1	15.3	...
天津	Tianjin	23.4	...	...	10.5	...	2.9	...
河北	Hebei	58.2	0.3	0.3	24.3	0.1	9.7	0.1
山西	Shanxi	48.2	0.2	3.6	17.8	0.4	4.2	...
内蒙古	Inner Mongolia	25.3	0.5	1.5	9.3	0.1	5.2	...
辽宁	Liaoning	90.5	0.5	3.7	41.1	1.3	18.2	0.1
吉林	Jilin	42.3	0.2	1.2	20.4	0.2	6.8	0.1
黑龙江	Heilongjiang	75.0	1.8	5.2	28.6	0.5	16.9	0.3
上海	Shanghai	26.6	0.1		8.5	0.2	2.0	
江苏	Jiangsu	114.9	0.6	1.3	47.9	0.6	10.7	0.2
浙江	Zhejiang	52.5	0.3	0.1	15.5	0.3	15.0	0.1
安徽	Anhui	66.1	0.5	3.6	21.1	0.1	9.1	...
福建	Fujian	33.2	0.1	0.1	10.9	0.2	8.8	...
江西	Jiangxi	33.0	0.2	0.7	11.1	0.1	7.1	...
山东	Shandong	103.9	1.2	4.1	44.3	0.3	12.6	...
河南	Henan	137.3	0.8	1.6	35.8	0.3	17.2	0.1
湖北	Hubei	63.6	0.7	1.3	26.8	0.1	7.9	
湖南	Hunan	53.7	1.1	0.3	18.4	0.2	9.5	0.2
广东	Guangdong	104.6	0.5	0.5	38.6	1.6	24.3	0.2
广西	Guangxi	26.2	0.1	0.4	8.7	0.1	4.3	
海南	Hainan	4.3	0.1	...	0.7	...	1.0	...
重庆	Chongqing	29.7	0.9	0.4	9.6	0.2	7.1	...
四川	Sichuan	69.7	2.2	1.3	20.3	0.2	18.0	0.2
贵州	Guizhou	19.0		0.2	5.4	0.1	5.9	...
云南	Yunnan	23.7	0.3	0.5	7.7	0.2	3.9	...
西藏	Tibet	0.8		0.1	0.4		0.2	
陕西	Shaanxi	29.0	0.3	0.3	10.9	...	5.1	...
甘肃	Gansu	25.4	0.1	1.0	8.4	1.4	5.9	0.1
青海	Qinghai	4.5	...	0.1	1.4	...	1.5	
宁夏	Ningxia	4.8	...	0.7	1.6	0.1	0.9	
新疆	Xinjiang	15.3	0.1	0.4	4.9	0.1	3.8	...

Number of Staff & Workers in Urban Collective-owned Units at the Year-end by Sector

(10 000 persons)

交通运输仓储和邮电通信业 Transport, Storage, Post & Telecommunication Services	批发零售贸易和餐饮业 Wholesale and Retail Trade & Catering Services	金融、保险业 Finance and Insurance	房地产业 Real Estate	社会服务业 Social Services	卫生体育和社会福利业 Health Care, Sports & Social Welfare	教育、文化艺术和广播电影电视业 Education, Culture and Arts, Radio, Film and Television	科学研究和综合技术服务业 Scientific Research and Polytechnic Services	国家机关、政党机关和社会团体 Government Agencies, Party Agencies and Social Organizations	其他 Others
204	172	23	3	59	64	62	1	13	
219	201	25	4	77	69	62	1	17	
216	234	26	4	88	70	60	1	14	
219	274	26	5	98	69	60	1	13	
224	294	28	5	103	69	43	1	14	
222	312	29	5	111	69	43	1	15	
233	672	31	5	111	71	42	1	27	
237	716	33	4	87	70	37	2	27	
241	718	37	4	91	71	35	2	28	
241	722	41	5	93	69	34	2	27	
237	738	45	4	94	69	32	2	26	
232	748	49	4	94	68	32	3	26	
232	762	51	4	93	69	32	3	26	
232	786	54	5	98	70	30	4	28	
226	796	57	4	96	65	28	5	27	
154	744	55	5	101	60	24	9	15	20
149	716	62	6	102	59	21	7	9	22
138	693	67	6	94	59	26	8	8	23
134	667	73	7	86	60	22	7	7	27
125	637	76	7	87	62	40	8	6	27
79	414	71	7	68	58	41	7	5	20
67	345	70	7	65	57	45	6	5	18
56	285	68	6	61	56	49	5	5	16
0.6	7.7	0.7	0.3	6.1	1.0	0.5	1.1	...	0.4
1.2	5.3	0.4	0.1	1.8	0.2	0.2	0.5	...	0.4
1.4	13.3	4.4	0.1	1.6	1.4	0.4	...	0.2	0.7
1.4	11.6	2.6	0.1	2.5	2.1	0.6	0.2	0.1	0.9
0.7	3.2	2.0	...	0.9	1.4	...	...	0.1	0.4
3.2	10.4	3.5	0.3	5.0	1.9	0.4	0.2	...	0.8
2.1	5.2	2.5	0.1	1.6	1.2	0.1	0.1	0.1	0.5
2.3	9.3	2.0	0.5	4.7	0.8	0.2	0.2	0.2	1.5
1.2	7.8	0.4	0.3	2.1	2.3	0.3	0.1	0.1	1.3
6.9	26.6	3.3	0.8	4.1	8.8	1.7	0.1	0.5	0.7
1.7	7.8	3.6	0.2	2.7	3.6	0.5	0.2	0.1	0.8
4.6	14.7	2.3	0.2	3.7	5.2	0.4	...	0.4	0.2
1.4	5.1	1.7	0.2	1.3	2.6	0.1	0.1	0.1	0.3
1.4	8.6	1.8	0.1	0.8	0.7	...	...	0.2	0.1
2.3	23.2	5.1	0.3	2.0	5.4	1.0	0.1	0.2	1.9
3.6	24.5	6.1	0.3	4.0	1.2	40.7	0.1	0.2	1.0
4.0	16.4	2.7	0.1	1.8	0.9	0.2	...	0.2	0.4
3.9	11.1	3.4	0.1	1.0	3.4	0.2	0.1	0.3	0.5
3.9	18.3	5.8	1.3	5.5	1.5	0.7	0.2	0.7	1.0
1.2	7.9	1.8	0.1	0.8	0.1	0.1	...	0.1	0.4
0.1	1.1	0.4	0.1	0.3	0.3	0.1	...	...	0.1
1.9	4.5	0.7	...	0.4	2.0	0.1	1.7	0.1	0.2
2.9	12.6	4.1	0.2	1.4	5.5	0.2	0.1	0.3	0.3
0.3	4.5	1.0	0.2	0.7	0.1	0.1	...	...	0.5
0.7	6.9	1.7	0.1	1.2	0.1	0.1	0.1	0.1	0.1
...	...			0.1		...			...
0.5	6.6	1.7	0.1	1.0	1.4	0.4	...	0.2	0.5
0.6	5.0	1.0	...	0.9	0.4	...	0.2	0.1	0.3
0.1	0.7	0.2	...	0.3	...	...		0.1	...
	1.0	0.3	...	0.1	...	...	...		0.1
0.1	4.1	0.8	0.1	0.5	0.2	...	...	0.1	0.1

5-10 其他单位分行业年底职工人数

Number of Staff and Workers in Units of Other Types of Ownership at the Year-end by Sector

单位：万人 (10 000 persons)

登记注册类型及行业	Registration Status and Sector	1995	1996	1997	1998	1999	2000
总　计	**Total**	**876.95**	**941.67**	**1085.53**	**1627.63**	**1785.38**	**1934.49**
按登记注册类型分组	**Grouped by Registration Status**						
股份合作单位	Cooperative Units				132.77	139.96	150.39
联营单位	Joint Ownership Units	51.71	48.51	42.61	46.17	43.92	39.90
有限责任公司	Limited Liability Corporations				474.68	588.08	665.75
股份有限公司	Share-holding Corporations Ltd.	311.65	357.28	460.15	401.35	408.85	441.71
其他	Others	10.78	8.84	17.53	8.43	18.72	23.43
港澳台商投资单位	Units with Funds form Hong Kong, Macao and Taiwan	267.34	259.10	274.85	284.29	295.08	298.89
外商投资单位	Foreign Funded	235.47	267.94	290.39	279.94	290.77	314.42
按国民经济行业分组	**Grouped by Economic Sector**						
农、林、牧、渔业	Farming, Forestry, Animal Husbandry and Fishery	3.16	3.87	4.14	5.06	4.63	6.14
采掘业	Mining and Quarrying	3.97	4.34	6.79	56.96	82.78	98.02
制造业	Manufacturing	696.02	728.37	826.71	1143.57	1225.25	1305.49
电力、煤气及水的生产和供应业	Production and Supply of Electricity, Gas and Water	10.25	10.71	13.83	28.68	34.80	40.08
建筑业	Construction	20.96	28.20	33.72	91.49	101.38	111.43
地质勘查、水利管理业	Geological Prospecting and Water Conservancy	0.08	0.05	0.05	0.10	0.18	0.24
交通运输、仓储及邮电通信业	Transport, Storage, Post and Telecommunication Services	9.67	11.78	17.09	37.73	47.81	53.83
批发和零售贸易餐饮业	Wholesale and Retail Trade & Catering Services	74.42	84.95	100.06	148.88	157.02	161.26
金融、保险业	Finance and Insurance	3.80	7.72	12.48	21.90	25.14	25.54
房地产业	Real Estate Trade	9.32	11.21	12.80	19.26	22.15	26.37
社会服务业	Social Services	39.70	44.13	48.89	61.02	69.14	82.89
卫生体育和社会福利业	Health Care, Sports and Social Welfare	0.41	0.51	0.53	0.98	1.05	1.16
教育、文化艺术和广播电影电视业	Education, Culture and Arts, Radio, Film and Television	0.89	1.15	1.25	1.52	2.02	3.19
科学研究和综合技术服务业	Scientific Research and Polytechnic Services	2.90	3.24	4.60	6.43	6.37	12.24
其他	Others	1.40	1.43	2.59	4.04	5.66	6.63

5-11 分行业城镇单位年底女性从业人员

Number of Female Employed in Urban Units at the Year-end by Sector

单位：万人 (10 000 persons)

行 业	Sector	1995	1996	1997	1999	2000
总 计	**Total**	**5889.0**	**5883.3**	**5824.8**	**4613.4**	**4411.3**
农、林、牧、渔业	Farming,Forestry,Animal Husbandry and Fishery	252.6	237.8	238.4	201.5	195.6
采掘业	Mining and Quarrying	238.9	233.4	222.5	173.6	152.8
制造业	Manufacturing	2482.1	2391.7	2286.3	1541.9	1425.3
电力、煤气及水的生产和供应业	Production and Supply of Electricity, Gas and Water	81.1	86.3	90.3	91.6	91.0
建筑业	Construction	207.1	208.1	203.6	150.8	144.0
地质勘查业水利管理业	Geological Prospecting and Water Conservancy	33.5	32.2	32.6	29.4	29.5
交通运输、仓储及邮电通信业	Transport, Storage, Post and Telecommunication Services	221.5	227.9	232.1	197.2	193.3
批发和零售贸易餐饮业	Wholesale and Retail Trade and Catering Services	858.3	855.3	841.2	528.0	461.2
金融、保险业	Finance and Insurance	111.3	120.1	128.1	140.4	141.2
房地产业	Real Estate Trade	26.6	28.9	30.4	32.6	34.2
社会服务业	Social Services	215.2	221.6	230.4	211.5	210.4
卫生体育和社会福利业	Health Care, Sports and Social Welfare	247.5	257.0	265.6	274.4	278.2
教育、文化艺术和广播电影电视业	Education, Culture and Arts, Radio, Film and Television	588.0	622.1	650.3	680.6	689.3
科学研究和综合技术服务业	Scientific Research and Polytechnic Services	61.4	61.8	62.7	57.1	57.9
国家机关、政党机关和社会团体	Government Agencies, Party Agencies and Social Organizations	238.3	258.6	257.9	266.1	268.8
其他	Others	25.6	40.5	52.4	36.7	38.5

注：不含城镇私营个体从业人员。

a) Data do not include the Urban private self-employed individuals.

5-12 分登记注册类型和细行业女性年底从业人员（2000年）

Number of Female Employed by Registration Status and Sector in Detail at the Year-end (2000)

单位：万人 (10 000 persons)

项目	Item	合计 Total	国有单位 State-owned Units	城镇集体单位 Urban Collective-owned Units	其他单位 Units of Other Types of Ownership
全国总计	**National Total**	**4411.3**	**2952.5**	**605.8**	**853.0**
按企、事业和机关分组	**Grouped by Enterprises, Institutions and Agencies**				
企业	Enterprises	2944.2	1552.0	540.8	851.4
事业	Institutions	1205.7	1140.8	63.4	1.6
机关	Agencies Organizations	261.4	189.5	1.7	
按国民经济行业分组	**Grouped by Sector**				
农、林、牧、渔业	**Farming, Forestry, Animal Husbandry and Fishery**	**195.6**	**189.5**	**3.9**	**2.2**
农业	Farming	118.9	116.5	1.3	1.1
林业	Forestry	30.0	29.6	0.3	0.1
畜牧业	Animal Husbandry	12.8	11.8	0.3	0.7
渔业	Fishery	3.4	3.0	0.2	0.2
农、林、牧、渔服务业	Services	30.5	28.6	1.8	0.1
采掘业	**Mining and Quarrying**	**152.8**	**114.8**	**12.7**	**25.3**
制造业	**Manufacturing**	**1425.3**	**552.5**	**259.9**	**612.9**
电力、煤气及水的生产和供应业	**Production and Supply of Electricity, Gas and Water**	**91.0**	**75.5**	**3.0**	**12.5**
建筑业	**Construction**	**144.0**	**79.7**	**47.6**	**16.7**
土木工程建筑业	Civil Engineering	117.9	67.3	37.6	13.0
线路管道和设备安装业	Circuit, Pipelines and Equipment Installation	22.5	11.6	8.5	2.4
装修装饰业	Buildings Fitting up and Decoration	3.5	0.7	1.5	1.3
地质勘查业水利管理业	**Geological Prospecting and Water Conservancy**	**29.5**	**28.9**	**0.5**	**0.1**
地质勘查业	Geological Prospecting	14.4	14.2	0.2	...
水利管理业	Water Conservancy	15.1	14.7	0.3	...
交通运输、仓储及邮电通信业	**Transport, Storage, Post and Telecommunication Services**	**193.3**	**157.7**	**18.1**	**17.5**
铁路运输业	Railway Transport	44.3	41.3	1.8	1.2
公路运输业	Highway Transport	38.8	25.9	6.8	6.1
管道运输业	Pipeline Transport	0.7	0.6	...	0.1
水上运输业	Water Way Transport	7.7	3.2	3.5	1.0
航空运输业	Air Transport	3.8	2.9	0.1	0.9
交通运输辅助业	Transport Supporting and Auxiliary Services	39.3	32.5	4.0	2.9
其他交通运输业	Other Transport	0.6	0.3	0.2	0.1
仓储业	Storage	12.5	10.9	0.9	0.7
邮电通信业	Post and Telecommunication Services	45.5	40.1	0.9	4.5
批发和零售贸易餐饮业	**Wholesale and Retail Trade & Catering Services**	**461.2**	**237.3**	**133.0**	**90.9**
食品、饮料、烟草和家庭日用品批发业	Wholesale Trade of Food, Beverages, Tobacco and Household Goods	135.8	91.6	27.1	17.2
能源、材料和机械电子设备批发业	Wholesale Trade of Energy, Materials and Electronic Equipment	47.1	29.3	9.8	8.0
其他批发业	Other Wholesale Trade	31.2	12.8	15.6	2.8
零售业	Retail Trade	212.1	89.6	73.3	49.2
商业经纪与代理业	Commercial Brokerage and Agencies	1.7	1.1	0.2	0.5
餐饮业	Catering Services	33.2	13.1	7.1	13.1
金融、保险业	**Finance and Insurance**	**141.2**	**94.2**	**29.7**	**17.3**
金融业	Finance	122.5	82.2	29.7	10.6

5-12 续表 1 continued

单位：万人 (10 000 persons)

项目	Item	合计 Total	国有单位 State-owned Units	城镇集体单位 Urban Collective-owned Units	其他单位 Units of Other Types of Ownership
保险业	Insurance	18.8	12.0	...	6.7
房地产业	**Real Estate Trade**	**34.2**	**21.9**	**2.3**	**10.0**
房地产开发与经营业	Real Estate Development and Operation	15.4	7.8	1.5	6.1
房地产管理业	Real Estate Management	17.8	13.3	0.7	3.7
房地产代理与经纪业	Real Estate Brokerage and Agencies	1.1	0.8	0.1	0.2
社会服务业	**Social Services**	**210.4**	**143.1**	**29.1**	**38.2**
公共设施服务业	Public Facilities Services	88.2	76.4	7.1	4.7
居民服务业	Resident Services	15.4	6.9	6.6	1.8
旅馆业	Hotels	67.1	40.1	7.7	19.3
租赁服务业	Leasing Services	1.1	0.5	0.2	0.3
旅游业	Tourism	5.7	3.9	0.3	1.5
娱乐服务业	Recreational Services	3.6	0.9	0.5	2.2
信息、咨询服务业	Information and Consultative Services	9.3	4.7	1.0	3.5
计算机应用服务业	Computer Application Services	3.5	0.7	0.2	2.6
其他社会服务业	Other Social Services	16.6	8.9	5.5	2.2
卫生体育和社会福利业	**Health Care, Sports and Social Welfare**	**278.2**	**247.5**	**30.0**	**0.7**
卫生	Health Care	266.1	236.3	29.2	0.5
体育	Sports	2.9	2.7	...	0.2
社会福利保障业	Social Welfare	9.2	8.4	0.8	...
教育、文化艺术及广播电影电视业	**Education, Culture and Arts, Radio, Film and Television**	**689.3**	**663.3**	**24.2**	**1.8**
教育	Education	646.8	622.7	22.9	1.2
#普通高等学校	Regular Institution of Higher Education	44.4	44.3	...	...
普通中学	Regular Secondary Schools	193.8	192.9	0.6	0.3
小学校	Primary Schools	318.6	299.0	19.2	0.4
文化艺术业	Culture and Arts	26.0	24.6	1.0	0.3
广播电影电视业	Radio, Film and Television	16.6	16.0	0.3	0.3
科学研究和综合技术服务业	**Scientific Research and Polytechnic Services**	**57.9**	**51.3**	**2.3**	**4.2**
科学研究业	Scientific Research	25.1	24.9	0.1	0.1
自然科学研究	Natural Science Research	19.5	19.4	0.1	0.1
社会科学研究	Social Science Research	1.2	1.2	...	...
其他科学研究	Other Science Research	4.4	4.4	...	...
综合技术服务业	Polytechnic Services	32.8	26.4	2.3	4.1
#气象	Meteorology	1.8	1.8	...	...
地震	Seismology	0.4	0.4	...	...
测绘	Survey and Mapping	1.2	1.2	...	...
技术监督	Technological Supervision	5.1	4.9	0.1	0.1
海洋环境	Oceanic Environment	0.1	0.1	...	...
环境保护	Environmental Protection	3.0	2.9	0.1	...
技术推广和科技交流服务业	Technology Application & Dissemination, Science and Technology Exchange Services	3.7	2.3	0.8	0.6
工程设计业	Engineering Design	9.5	8.9	0.3	0.3
其他综合技术服务业	Other Polytechnic Services	8.0	4.0	1.0	3.1
国家机关、政党机关和社会团体	**Government Agencies, Party Agencies and Social Organizations**	**268.8**	**266.7**	**2.1**	
#国家机关	Government Agencies	250.6	249.4	1.1	
政党机关	Party Agencies	11.3	11.3	...	
其他	**Others**	**38.5**	**28.5**	**7.3**	**2.7**
#企业管理机构	Enterprise Management Organizations	18.2	12.0	5.2	1.0

5-13 分登记注册类型和细行业年底女性从业人员占全部从业人员比重(2000年)

Proportion of Female Employed at the Year-end to Total by Registration Status and Sector in Detail (2000)

以本类型从业人员为100。

Total Number of This Item Employed = 100.

单位：% (%)

项目	Item	合计 Total	国有单位 State-owned Units	城镇集体单位 Urban Collective-owned Units	其他单位 Units of Other Types of Ownership
全国总计	**National Total**	**38.0**	**36.4**	**40.4**	**42.4**
按企、事业和机关分组	**Grouped by Enterprises, Institutions and Agencies**				
企业	Enterprises	37.9	35.3	39.8	42.4
事业	Institutions	43.4	43.2	46.1	43.9
机关	Agencies & Organizations	24.3	38.2	36.3	
按国民经济行业分组	**Grouped by Sector**				
农、林、牧、渔业	**Farming, Forestry, Animal Husbandry and Fishery**	**37.9**	**38.2**	**27.7**	**34.9**
农业	Farming	41.3	41.2	45.9	45.1
林业	Forestry	39.0	38.9	43.0	28.8
畜牧业	Animal Husbandry	37.4	37.7	32.0	34.8
渔业	Fishery	29.3	30.9	30.0	17.2
农、林、牧、渔服务业	Services	28.8	29.6	20.1	33.8
采掘业	**Mining and Quarrying**	**26.1**	**25.4**	**36.3**	**25.6**
制造业	**Manufacturing**	**43.2**	**38.6**	**48.9**	**45.8**
电力、煤气及水的生产和供应业	**Production and Supply of Electricity, Gas and Water**	**32.1**	**32.3**	**31.9**	**30.9**
建筑业	**Construction**	**18.5**	**20.3**	**17.5**	**14.4**
土木工程建筑业	Civil Engineering	17.5	19.8	15.8	13.6
线路管道和设备安装业	Circuit, Pipelines and Equipment Installation	25.7	24.1	31.2	19.5
装修装饰业	Buildings Fitting up and Decoration	19.1	19.4	22.6	16.3
地质勘查业水利管理业	**Geological Prospecting and Water Conservancy**	**26.8**	**26.8**	**28.1**	**23.4**
地质勘查业	Geological Prospecting	27.8	27.7	46.4	21.9
水利管理业	Water Conservancy	25.9	25.8	21.9	24.8
交通运输、仓储及邮电通信业	**Transport, Storage, Post and Telecommunication Services**	**28.4**	**27.8**	**31.0**	**31.5**
铁路运输业	Railway Transport	22.9	22.4	52.4	21.8
公路运输业	Highway Transport	31.9	33.0	28.2	31.3
管道运输业	Pipeline Transport	30.4	30.0	39.8	37.7
水上运输业	Water Way Transport	19.5	14.7	28.1	19.1
航空运输业	Air Transport	32.5	32.2	50.4	33.6
交通运输辅助业	Transport Supporting and Auxiliary Services	26.0	25.6	28.7	28.0
其他交通运输业	Other Transport	30.0	30.0	25.8	30.1
仓储业	Storage	34.2	34.2	43.7	28.8
邮电通信业	Post and Telecommunication Services	37.3	36.1	50.8	49.2
批发和零售贸易餐饮业	**Wholesale and Retail Trade & Catering Services**	**45.7**	**43.6**	**45.5**	**52.5**
食品、饮料、烟草和家庭日用品批发业	Wholesale Trade of Food, Beverages, Tobacco and Household Goods	41.4	39.9	44.1	47.0
能源、材料和机械电子设备批发业	Wholesale Trade of Energy, Materials and Electronic Equipment	36.3	35.3	40.7	35.2
其他批发业	Other Wholesale Trade	40.4	42.0	39.7	38.9
零售业	Retail Trade	51.5	51.2	47.2	60.0
商业经纪与代理业	Commercial Brokerage and Agencies	37.8	39.3	49.6	38.4
餐饮业	Catering Services	57.0	57.0	57.9	57.0
金融、保险业	**Finance and Insurance**	**43.2**	**42.2**	**42.2**	**52.6**

5-13 续表 1 continued

单位：%　　　　(%)

项　目	Item	合　计 Total	国有单位 State-owned Units	城镇集体单位 Urban Collective-owned Units	其他单位 Units of Other Types of Ownership
金融业	Finance	42.7	42.0	42.2	50.8
保险业	Insurance	46.9	43.0	32.8	55.6
房地产业	**Real Estate Trade**	**34.1**	**34.6**	**33.9**	**33.0**
房地产开发与经营业	Real Estate Development and Operation	33.5	34.2	32.8	32.7
房地产管理业	Real Estate Management	34.3	34.5	35.7	32.9
房地产代理与经纪业	Real Estate Brokerage and Agencies	44.0	42.1	44.3	51.5
社会服务业	**Social Services**	**43.5**	**43.8**	**45.3**	**41.2**
公共设施服务业	Public Facilities Services	41.4	43.0	42.9	25.4
居民服务业	Resident Services	44.3	43.1	43.9	49.5
旅馆业	Hotels	55.5	55.7	61.6	52.9
租赁服务业	Leasing Services	35.5	38.5	42.6	26.8
旅游业	Tourism	45.2	45.9	46.8	43.4
娱乐服务业	Recreational Services	50.0	47.4	52.6	50.6
信息、咨询服务业	Information and Consultative Services	36.0	34.8	35.2	37.7
计算机应用服务业	Computer Application Services	32.7	35.0	32.7	31.4
其他社会服务业	Other Social Services	29.9	26.4	37.9	30.5
卫生体育和社会福利业	**Health Care, Sports and Social Welfare**	**57.0**	**57.9**	**50.6**	**49.9**
卫生	Health Care	58.2	59.0	52.0	59.3
体育	Sports	33.0	32.9	51.7	35.1
社会福利保障业	Social Welfare	41.6	44.4	24.3	51.3
教育、文化艺术及广播电影电视业	**Education, Culture and Arts, Radio, Film and Television**	**44.0**	**44.0**	**45.4**	**44.0**
教育	Education	44.4	44.4	45.8	45.8
#普通高等学校	Regular Institution of Higher Education	40.0	40.0	41.7	35.8
普通中学	Regular Secondary Schools	40.4	40.4	44.9	46.0
小学校	Primary Schools	46.9	47.1	43.7	45.1
文化艺术业	Culture and Arts	41.9	41.7	42.0	43.0
广播电影电视业	Radio, Film and Television	35.2	35.2	32.2	38.5
科学研究和综合技术服务业	**Scientific Research and Polytechnic Services**	**33.2**	**33.9**	**29.8**	**27.6**
科学研究业	Scientific Research	35.0	35.0	35.5	37.4
自然科学研究	Natural Science Research	34.9	35.0	35.6	38.4
社会科学研究	Social Science Research	36.4	36.4	35.3	48.0
其他科学研究	Other Science Research	34.9	34.9	35.2	30.8
综合技术服务业	Polytechnic Services	31.9	33.0	29.6	27.4
#气象	Meteorology	34.6	34.6	40.6	27.7
地震	Seismology	26.7	26.7		20.0
测绘	Survey and Mapping	29.3	29.3	39.8	23.0
技术监督	Technological Supervision	31.3	31.8	29.3	17.6
海洋环境	Oceanic Environment	20.0	20.0		14.3
环境保护	Environmental Protection	39.0	39.7	43.4	29.4
技术推广和科技交流服务业	Technology Application & Dissemination, Science and Technology Exchange Services	34.6	35.9	34.4	28.4
工程设计业	Engineering Design	32.4	32.6	32.4	29.1
其他综合技术服务业	Other Polytechnic Services	29.3	32.8	25.2	27.5
国家机关、政党机关和社会团体	**Government Agencies, Party Agencies and Social Organizations**	**24.4**	**24.3**	**42.7**	
#国家机关	Government Agencies	24.2	24.2	32.8	
政党机关	Party Agencies	21.6	21.6	75.0	
其他	**Others**	**37.3**	**36.2**	**42.9**	**36.7**
#企业管理机构	Enterprise Management Organizations	34.4	31.9	41.7	36.8

5-14 分地区分行业专业技术人员年末人数（2000年）

单位：万人

地区	Region	合计 Total	农、林、牧、渔业 Farming, Forestry, Animal Husbandry and Fishery	采掘业 Mining and Quarrying	制造业 Manufacturing	电力、煤气及水的生产和供应业 Production and Supply of Electricity Gas and Water	建筑业 Construction	地质勘查业水利管理业 Geological Prospecting and Water Conservancy
全国总计	**National Total**	**3060.2**	**79.8**	**86.3**	**462.7**	**62.2**	**142.8**	**32.0**
北京	Beijing	119.2	0.7	0.3	17.4	0.9	11.5	0.6
天津	Tianjin	53.4	0.3	2.2	11.1	1.2	3.2	0.8
河北	Hebei	154.7	2.3	4.7	21.5	3.3	7.2	2.3
山西	Shanxi	87.8	1.2	7.0	13.5	2.6	4.2	0.9
内蒙古	Inner Mongolia	71.3	4.7	4.7	7.7	2.0	2.3	1.0
辽宁	Liaoning	148.8	3.6	3.9	29.3	3.6	6.6	1.3
吉林	Jilin	94.2	3.5	5.6	12.8	2.0	3.6	0.9
黑龙江	Heilongjiang	114.6	4.0	12.4	16.7	3.4	4.8	0.8
上海	Shanghai	80.3	0.5		19.7	1.1	4.1	0.3
江苏	Jiangsu	168.3	3.2	2.5	33.7	2.9	6.8	1.4
浙江	Zhejiang	109.9	1.4	0.4	15.0	2.3	6.9	0.6
安徽	Anhui	107.0	2.7	3.2	13.7	1.9	4.5	1.2
福建	Fujian	83.1	1.3	1.1	11.2	1.7	4.2	0.4
江西	Jiangxi	83.8	2.3	2.1	11.5	2.0	2.5	0.9
山东	Shandong	231.9	3.2	7.6	40.1	5.0	7.4	1.8
河南	Henan	184.4	1.8	7.9	25.1	3.9	8.7	2.9
湖北	Hubei	119.2	3.8	1.2	18.7	2.0	5.8	2.0
湖南	Hunan	130.4	2.5	2.2	17.9	2.2	4.7	1.1
广东	Guangdong	191.3	2.3	0.8	29.2	3.9	9.8	1.0
广西	Guangxi	93.1	3.4	1.0	9.9	1.8	3.1	0.7
海南	Hainan	17.0	2.9	0.3	0.8	0.3	0.4	0.1
重庆	Chongqing	60.3	1.3	1.3	11.4	0.9	3.2	0.4
四川	Sichuan	160.5	4.9	3.5	23.5	3.3	7.8	1.7
贵州	Guizhou	58.1	1.8	2.1	8.0	1.2	3.2	0.5
云南	Yunnan	87.2	5.0	1.8	9.1	1.6	3.5	1.2
西藏	Tibet	3.5	0.1	...	0.1	0.1	0.1	0.1
陕西	Shaanxi	95.3	2.3	2.5	17.5	1.6	4.4	1.8
甘肃	Gansu	53.3	1.7	1.3	8.7	1.4	2.5	1.3
青海	Qinghai	13.3	0.7	0.2	1.3	0.4	0.9	0.5
宁夏	Ningxia	17.3	0.9	0.9	2.0	0.5	0.9	0.3
新疆	Xinjiang	67.6	9.5	2.0	4.6	1.1	4.0	1.2

Number of Professional Personnel by Sector and Region at the Year-end (2000)

(10 000 persons)

交通运输仓储和邮电通信业 Transport, Storage, Post & Telecommunication Services	批发零售贸易和餐饮业 Wholesale and Retail Trade & Catering Services	金融、保险业 Finance and Insurance	房地产业 Real Estate	社　会服务业 Social Services	卫生体育和社会福利业 Health Care, Sports & Social Welfare	教育、文化艺术和广播电影电视业 Education, Culture and Arts, Radio, Film and Television	科学研究和综合技术服务业 Scientific Research and Polytechnic Services	国家机关、政党机关和社会团体 Government Agencies, Party Agencies and Social Organizations	其　他 Others
106.0	**152.6**	**167.1**	**24.1**	**60.8**	**337.2**	**1145.6**	**89.7**	**90.5**	**20.8**
3.3	8.6	5.4	2.5	9.7	9.4	27.4	13.2	6.0	2.3
2.7	3.1	2.5	0.6	1.7	5.4	14.7	2.7	0.7	0.5
4.5	7.7	8.6	0.6	2.4	14.4	65.2	2.6	6.6	0.7
2.6	4.4	4.9	0.3	1.2	9.4	32.1	2.3	0.3	0.7
2.4	2.2	4.1	0.3	1.0	7.7	26.7	1.7	2.2	0.5
6.7	7.9	10.5	1.8	3.9	16.5	45.9	5.0	1.4	0.9
3.0	4.5	5.6	0.8	2.0	10.6	33.0	2.8	2.5	1.1
3.9	5.5	5.4	0.8	2.9	12.1	35.9	2.3	3.0	0.9
4.9	4.5	4.7	1.6	2.6	10.2	20.2	4.5	0.4	1.0
6.6	8.7	9.1	1.6	2.9	19.9	60.1	4.6	3.1	1.4
4.1	6.3	9.1	1.4	3.1	14.9	40.4	2.7	0.5	0.9
2.8	5.1	4.6	0.7	1.5	11.4	46.2	2.0	5.0	0.5
2.8	2.9	5.1	0.8	1.3	7.6	37.6	1.6	3.0	0.5
2.5	4.1	4.5	0.3	0.8	9.6	36.2	1.6	2.8	0.3
6.9	13.3	11.8	1.7	4.0	25.8	86.8	3.9	10.8	1.6
4.5	9.1	8.1	0.8	2.4	19.3	76.1	3.9	9.0	0.9
6.3	6.7	4.5	0.7	1.8	15.8	42.7	3.4	3.4	0.5
4.2	6.3	6.4	0.6	1.8	16.8	55.1	2.7	5.0	0.9
8.8	12.3	14.7	2.7	4.8	22.5	72.3	3.8	0.9	1.4
2.6	4.3	4.6	0.6	1.5	10.4	42.5	1.8	4.2	0.6
0.7	0.5	1.0	0.2	0.4	2.0	6.3	0.4	0.7	0.1
2.4	2.4	2.8	0.5	0.6	6.1	23.5	2.2	1.3	0.1
4.0	6.6	8.0	0.7	1.5	19.0	65.3	5.1	5.4	0.4
1.3	1.8	2.8	0.4	0.4	6.0	24.4	1.2	2.7	0.3
3.2	4.1	5.2	0.4	1.2	9.3	36.7	2.3	2.2	0.3
0.1	0.1	0.5		...	0.5	1.4	0.1	0.3	...
3.4	3.9	4.9	0.3	1.2	9.3	34.0	5.3	2.6	0.3
1.5	1.7	2.6	0.1	0.7	5.1	21.2	1.6	1.4	0.3
0.6	0.5	1.0	0.1	0.2	1.6	4.6	0.5	0.2	0.1
0.5	0.7	1.2	0.1	0.2	1.9	6.6	0.4	...	0.1
2.1	2.6	3.0	0.2	1.0	6.8	24.4	1.7	2.8	0.6

5-15 分地区分行业私营企业和个体从业人数

Number of Employed Persons in Private Enterprises and Self-employed Individuals by Sector and Region

单位：万人　　　　(10 000 persons)

年份 地区	Year Region	合计 Total	农、林、牧、渔业 Farming, Forestry, Animal Husbandry & Fishery	采掘业 Mining and Quarrying	制造业 Manufacturing	建筑业 Construction	交通运输仓储和邮电通信业 Transport, Storage, Post & Telecommunication Services	批发零售贸易和餐饮业 Wholesale & Retail Trade & Catering Services	社会服务业 Social Services	其他 Others
	1989	2142.0	2.6		441.4	24.8	165.0	1272.6	214.3	21.3
	1990	2274.3	0.6		469.2	23.3	182.0	1321.0	251.9	26.3
	1991	2491.5	0.4		549.9	27.3	200.5	1446.2	244.4	22.7
	1992	2699.5			578.8	26.9	207.1	1592.2	283.9	10.6
	1993	3312.0		35.7	691.4	35.0	254.6	1926.6	334.4	34.3
	1994	4424.2	57.0		1003.6	50.5	360.9	2481.0	412.2	59.1
	1995	5569.5	119.5	61.4	1253.5	69.5	419.4	3020.4	552.3	73.5
	1996	6188.2	183.5	66.5	1388.3	77.5	468.6	3300.0	612.6	91.2
	1997	6791.1	255.0	68.1	1518.5	85.9	501.2	3585.6	680.6	96.3
	1998	7823.5	362.1	80.6	1774.7	115.3	559.9	4013.5	795.0	122.4
	1999	8262.5	416.2	78.7	1932.3	129.3	564.7	4161.6	853.8	125.9
	2000	7476.5	339.0	69.2	1932.9	144.8	445.7	3621.7	776.0	147.1
北　京	Beijing	43.6	0.4	0.1	6.7	0.6	1.3	28.8	5.0	0.7
天　津	Tianjin	59.0	0.2		17.5	1.2	2.2	26.7	6.1	5.0
河　北	Hebei	911.5	68.2	13.7	293.4	19.7	65.1	372.2	67.2	12.0
山　西	Shanxi	95.4	0.8	1.5	20.9	1.7	6.7	53.9	8.5	1.4
内蒙古	Inner Mongolia	201.1	17.1	3.0	30.2	4.6	16.5	99.8	23.4	6.6
辽　宁	Liaoning	404.3	43.0	4.8	79.9	7.5	38.3	183.6	40.0	7.1
吉　林	Jilin	181.4	51.4	1.8	18.4	1.7	11.3	76.7	14.3	5.7
黑龙江	Heilongjiang	297.8	55.6	1.4	46.6	3.5	21.3	136.5	28.7	4.3
上　海	Shanghai	175.5	0.5		49.7	7.1	1.9	89.9	18.3	8.0
江　苏	Jiangsu	516.1	16.6	1.1	184.5	8.4	23.9	227.8	47.5	6.2
浙　江	Zhejiang	572.9	4.8	3.2	296.9	7.7	24.0	189.2	43.7	3.3
安　徽	Anhui	401.6	7.7	2.2	71.4	6.1	27.3	227.7	53.8	5.4
福　建	Fujian	161.9	3.1	0.9	44.9	2.8	6.0	82.4	19.0	2.9
江　西	Jiangxi	187.1	6.3	3.6	45.1	1.6	10.1	94.0	20.0	6.4
山　东	Shandong	489.6	15.7	2.0	171.2	12.4	19.4	219.3	45.3	4.4
河　南	Henan	338.6	5.5	4.0	68.5	5.2	28.7	185.5	36.0	5.3
湖　北	Hubei	323.5	11.7	2.9	55.2	6.7	25.2	169.5	42.3	10.0
湖　南	Hunan	274.0	1.8	2.1	52.1	4.3	21.1	151.4	37.1	4.2
广　东	Guangdong	526.4	2.1	2.1	146.2	5.6	15.2	276.4	56.0	22.7
广　西	Guangxi	170.0	3.7	1.5	25.7	1.8	12.6	103.2	19.1	2.3
海　南	Hainan	39.6	2.5	0.5	2.6	1.3	3.0	20.9	6.7	2.0
重　庆	Chongqing	136.6	1.6	1.9	29.1	8.5	3.8	73.8	15.8	2.1
四　川	Sichuan	249.8	1.5	3.9	53.0	4.4	12.9	133.6	35.7	4.9
贵　州	Guizhou	79.0	1.9	2.3	15.0	1.6	4.2	42.8	9.5	1.7
云　南	Yunnan	128.3	1.9	2.3	24.9	5.5	8.1	69.5	15.1	1.2
西　藏	Tibet	7.1	0.1		0.3	0.1	0.6	4.8	1.0	0.1
陕　西	Shaanxi	298.2	10.1	4.8	50.3	8.1	23.9	157.8	36.0	7.4
甘　肃	Gansu	72.6	1.0	0.5	11.7	1.6	1.6	46.9	8.2	1.2
青　海	Qinghai	27.0	0.7	0.5	5.1	2.1	1.4	14.1	2.6	0.6
宁　夏	Ningxia	23.9	0.6	0.2	4.6	0.8	1.5	13.2	2.6	0.4
新　疆	Xinjiang	83.1	0.9	0.6	11.3	0.8	6.6	49.7	11.6	1.7

注：1993年以前城镇私营和个体从业人数来源于国家统计局(下同)。

a) Number of employed persons in private enterprises and self-employed individuals before 1993 came from National Bureau of Statistics. The Same as in the following tables.

5-16 分地区分行业城镇私营企业和个体从业人数

Number of Employed Persons in Urban Private Enterprises and Self-employed Individuals at the Year-end by Region and by Sector

单位：万人 (10 000 persons)

年份 地区	Year Region	合计 Total	农、林、牧、渔业 Farming, Forestry, Animal Husbandry and Fishery	采掘业 Mining and Quarrying	制造业 Manufacturing	建筑业 Construction	交通运输仓储和邮电通信业 Transport, Storage, Post & Telecommunication Services	批发零售贸易和餐饮业 Wholesale & Retail Trade and Catering Services	社会服务业 Social Services	其他 Others
	1978	15.0			3.0	1.0	1.0	9.0	1.0	
	1979	32.0			6.0	1.0	1.0	18.0	6.0	
	1980	81.4	0.2		9.5	0.4	0.8	57.1	13.4	
	1981	113.0			11.0	1.0	2.0	79.0	20.0	
	1982	147.0			16.0	1.0	2.0	105.0	23.0	
	1983	231.0			24.0	1.0	4.0	172.0	30.0	
	1984	339.0	1.0		38.0	4.0	12.0	242.0	42.0	
	1985	450.1	1.9		51.4	5.1	22.3	325.0	44.4	
	1986	483.1	1.9		60.0	5.1	24.4	336.7	55.0	
	1987	568.8	1.7		74.3	6.5	30.6	390.7	65.0	
	1988	659.3	4.2		90.3	9.7	39.5	442.9	72.7	
	1989	648.2	2.6		84.5	4.9	34.1	443.1	79.0	
	1990	670.5	0.6		91.3	4.6	36.4	431.2	106.4	
	1991	759.5	0.4		128.0	7.9	46.1	489.0	78.2	9.9
	1992	837.9			129.6	5.9	47.5	550.7	93.6	10.6
	1993	1115.7		6.7	175.4	10.8	62.3	714.9	132.8	12.8
	1994	1557.4	5.4		271.8	17.9	95.7	973.5	167.2	26.0
	1995	2045.0	13.4	10.2	339.0	28.1	111.0	1265.8	241.9	35.6
	1996	2328.8	17.7	10.3	400.1	33.9	131.8	1419.1	274.5	41.4
	1997	2669.0	31.8	10.8	450.6	38.8	153.6	1617.7	315.7	50.1
	1998	3231.9	43.4	13.9	563.9	55.2	190.3	1896.2	397.2	71.8
	1999	3466.9	44.0	12.4	601.7	64.9	202.3	2024.7	447.2	69.7
	2000	3404.0	40.5	12.3	632.7	79.7	178.4	1924.3	438.5	97.6
北　京	Beijing	24.5	0.1		2.1	0.2	0.6	17.9	3.4	0.2
天　津	Tianjin	36.8	0.1		6.4	0.8	1.6	18.5	4.6	4.9
河　北	Hebei	185.3	2.3	1.0	41.3	3.4	11.1	101.9	22.1	2.2
山　西	Shanxi	48.7	0.1	0.1	5.5	0.6	1.9	34.3	5.4	0.8
内蒙古	Inner Mongolia	116.8	2.5	1.3	17.5	3.4	10.3	62.3	15.3	4.3
辽　宁	Liaoning	244.3	2.2	0.8	42.1	4.4	20.1	136.8	32.0	5.8
吉　林	Jilin	103.4	8.0	0.5	13.1	1.3	5.5	59.9	10.3	4.7
黑龙江	Heilongjiang	166.4	4.8	0.3	25.5	2.7	14.0	96.5	19.4	3.3
上　海	Shanghai	67.5	0.1		12.6	3.0	1.3	36.6	9.0	4.9
江　苏	Jiangsu	177.7	0.4	0.2	45.9	3.8	4.1	97.1	23.2	3.0
浙　江	Zhejiang	207.7	1.3	0.3	73.9	4.0	5.8	95.9	24.7	1.8
安　徽	Anhui	172.4	1.9	0.4	26.4	4.3	12.0	98.3	27.0	2.2
福　建	Fujian	90.2	0.6	0.2	19.4	2.3	3.3	49.4	12.8	2.3
江　西	Jiangxi	88.6	0.8	0.6	18.1	1.1	4.6	51.3	9.8	2.5
山　东	Shandong	215.3	1.5	0.2	56.7	6.2	6.5	117.8	23.3	3.2
河　南	Henan	125.3	0.7	0.7	19.5	2.1	8.9	74.8	16.3	2.3
湖　北	Hubei	182.5	4.2	0.7	26.2	4.2	11.8	100.8	26.1	8.4
湖　南	Hunan	148.5	0.4	0.3	24.7	3.3	9.9	88.1	19.3	2.6
广　东	Guangdong	316.7	1.0	0.4	59.1	4.0	7.0	185.0	39.2	20.9
广　西	Guangxi	89.7	0.8	0.5	11.2	1.4	7.2	55.7	11.2	1.6
海　南	Hainan	30.2	1.9	0.3	1.5	1.2	2.0	15.8	5.6	1.9
重　庆	Chongqing	71.1	0.3	0.2	13.0	7.0	1.7	38.8	8.8	1.3
四　川	Sichuan	118.0	0.6	0.8	20.7	3.2	5.2	66.0	18.3	3.2
贵　州	Guizhou	41.9	0.6	0.5	7.2	1.2	2.0	23.0	6.2	1.1
云　南	Yunnan	66.3	0.8	0.6	10.8	2.9	2.6	37.9	10.0	0.9
西　藏	Tibet	4.8	0.1		0.3	0.1	0.5	3.0	0.8	0.1
陕　西	Shaanxi	132.5	1.3	1.0	15.7	3.7	9.2	79.7	17.4	4.6
甘　肃	Gansu	41.7	0.4	0.1	5.2	0.9	1.0	28.1	5.0	0.8
青　海	Qinghai	18.6	0.2	0.1	2.5	1.9	1.0	10.5	1.9	0.4
宁　夏	Ningxia	12.5	0.1		2.2	0.4	0.7	7.2	1.4	0.3
新　疆	Xinjiang	58.1	0.5	0.2	6.2	0.7	5.3	35.6	8.5	1.1

5-17 各地区私营企业年底从业人员数（2000年）

Number of Employed Persons in Private Enterprises at the Year-end by Region (2000)

单位：万户、万人 (10 000 enterprises,10 000 persons)

地区	Region	合计 Total 户数 Number of Enterprises	合计 Total 从业人数 Number of Employed Persons	合计 Total #投资者 Employers	城镇 Urban Areas 从业人数 Number of Employed Persons	城镇 Urban Areas #投资者 Employers	乡村 Rural Areas 从业人数 Number of Employed Persons	乡村 Rural Areas #投资者 Employers
全国	**National Total**	**176.2**	**2406.5**	**395.3**	**1267.9**	**246.9**	**1138.6**	**148.5**
北京	Beijing	10.3	9.1	1.1	4.3	0.6	4.8	0.5
天津	Tianjin	3.4	38.0	7.8	27.5	6.0	10.5	1.9
河北	Hebei	8.9	201.5	23.1	44.0	5.5	157.5	17.6
山西	Shanxi	2.5	38.6	5.9	22.5	3.9	16.1	2.0
内蒙古	Inner Mongolia	2.7	41.4	7.8	28.6	5.6	12.8	2.2
辽宁	Liaoning	7.4	124.9	13.8	83.3	10.8	41.6	3.0
吉林	Jilin	2.7	28.5	5.0	21.5	4.0	7.0	1.1
黑龙江	Heilongjiang	4.2	53.7	8.4	40.5	6.9	13.2	1.4
上海	Shanghai	13.8	150.9	28.3	58.2	11.8	92.7	16.4
江苏	Jiangsu	17.4	234.3	39.8	96.6	19.4	137.8	20.4
浙江	Zhejiang	17.9	300.5	45.1	110.6	21.7	189.9	23.4
安徽	Anhui	4.7	65.2	11.0	37.6	7.2	27.6	3.8
福建	Fujian	4.9	68.0	11.6	44.4	8.0	23.5	3.6
江西	Jiangxi	2.6	47.2	7.0	27.1	4.7	20.1	2.3
山东	Shandong	14.1	214.1	34.8	105.3	21.6	108.8	13.2
河南	Henan	4.8	57.0	12.6	27.9	8.7	29.1	3.9
湖北	Hubei	5.3	79.6	13.1	52.9	9.7	26.7	3.4
湖南	Hunan	2.5	46.2	7.1	33.5	5.4	12.7	1.6
广东	Guangdong	18.4	217.5	41.1	151.7	34.1	65.8	7.0
广西	Guangxi	2.1	30.6	5.6	21.9	4.2	8.7	1.4
海南	Hainan	2.0	18.6	5.2	16.6	4.8	2.0	0.4
重庆	Chongqing	3.1	48.6	8.1	35.5	6.6	13.2	1.4
四川	Sichuan	5.5	81.5	13.7	49.5	9.7	32.0	4.0
贵州	Guizhou	2.0	25.6	5.7	16.4	4.1	9.2	1.6
云南	Yunnan	2.0	34.7	5.0	22.9	4.0	11.9	1.0
西藏	Tibet	0.1	0.8	0.1	0.7	0.1	0.1	
陕西	Shaanxi	6.1	83.4	14.3	40.3	7.5	43.1	6.8
甘肃	Gansu	1.7	22.4	4.2	16.1	3.3	6.2	0.9
青海	Qinghai	0.5	11.2	1.6	8.1	1.4	3.1	0.3
宁夏	Ningxia	0.7	10.6	1.9	4.8	1.0	5.8	0.9
新疆	Xinjiang	1.9	22.4	5.6	17.1	4.6	5.2	1.0

5-18 各地区个体年底从业人员数 （2000年）

Number of Self-employed Individuals at the Year-end by Region (2000)

单位：万户、万人 (10 000 households,10 000 persons)

地区	Region	合计 Total 户数 Number of Households	合计 Total 从业人数 Number of Employed Individuals	城镇 Urban Areas 从业人数 Number of Employed Individuals	乡村 Rural Areas 从业人数 Number of Employed Individuals
全国	**National Total**	**2571.4**	**5070.0**	**2136.1**	**2933.9**
北京	Beijing	24.5	34.5	20.2	14.3
天津	Tianjin	14.3	21.1	9.4	11.7
河北	Hebei	292.4	710.1	141.3	568.7
山西	Shanxi	29.9	56.7	26.2	30.6
内蒙古	Inner Mongolia	80.7	159.7	88.2	71.5
辽宁	Liaoning	145.2	279.4	161.0	118.4
吉林	Jilin	99.7	152.8	81.9	70.9
黑龙江	Heilongjiang	119.0	244.1	126.0	118.2
上海	Shanghai	20.1	24.5	9.3	15.3
江苏	Jiangsu	149.1	281.7	81.2	200.5
浙江	Zhejiang	158.9	272.4	97.1	175.3
安徽	Anhui	148.9	336.4	134.8	201.6
福建	Fujian	45.6	93.9	45.7	48.2
江西	Jiangxi	59.5	140.0	61.6	78.4
山东	Shandong	132.0	275.5	110.0	165.5
河南	Henan	140.2	281.7	97.4	184.3
湖北	Hubei	100.7	243.9	129.5	114.3
湖南	Hunan	95.0	227.8	115.0	112.8
广东	Guangdong	152.2	308.9	164.9	143.9
广西	Guangxi	96.8	139.4	67.9	71.6
海南	Hainan	11.2	21.0	13.6	7.4
重庆	Chongqing	41.1	88.0	35.6	52.4
四川	Sichuan	121.1	168.3	68.5	99.8
贵州	Guizhou	36.9	53.4	25.5	27.9
云南	Yunnan	62.6	93.6	43.5	50.1
西藏	Tibet	4.2	6.3	4.1	2.2
陕西	Shaanxi	104.7	214.8	92.2	122.6
甘肃	Gansu	27.3	50.2	25.5	24.7
青海	Qinghai	8.7	15.9	10.5	5.3
宁夏	Ningxia	8.1	13.3	7.6	5.7
新疆	Xinjiang	40.7	60.8	40.9	19.8

5-19 职工工资总额和指数
Total Wages of Staff and Workers and Related Index

年份 地区	Year Region	工资总额（亿元）Total Wages (100 million yuan)				指数（上年=100）Indices (preceding year=100)			
		合计 Total	国有单位 State-owned Units	城镇集体单位 Urban Collective-owned Units	其他单位 Units of Other Types of Ownership	合计 Total	国有单位 State-owned Units	城镇集体单位 Urban Collective-owned Units	其他单位 Units of Other Types of Ownership
	1978	568.9	468.7	100.2		110.5	110.1	112.5	
	1979	646.7	529.5	117.2		113.7	113.0	117.0	
	1980	772.4	627.9	144.5		119.4	118.6	123.3	
	1981	820.0	660.4	159.6		106.2	105.2	110.4	
	1982	882.0	708.9	173.1		107.6	107.3	108.5	
	1983	934.6	748.1	186.5		106.0	105.5	107.7	
	1984	1133.4	875.8	254.0	3.6	121.3	117.1	136.2	
	1985	1383.0	1064.8	312.3	5.9	122.0	121.6	123.0	163.9
	1986	1659.7	1288.5	362.8	8.4	120.0	121.0	116.2	142.4
	1987	1881.1	1459.3	409.1	12.6	113.3	113.3	112.8	151.2
	1988	2316.2	1807.1	487.6	21.5	123.1	123.8	119.2	169.3
	1989	2618.5	2050.2	534.4	33.9	113.1	113.5	109.6	157.7
	1990	2951.1	2324.1	581.0	46.0	112.7	113.4	108.7	135.7
	1991	3323.9	2594.9	658.6	70.4	112.6	111.7	113.4	153.0
	1992	3939.2	3090.4	743.2	105.6	118.5	119.1	112.8	150.0
	1993	4916.2	3812.7	849.9	253.6	124.8	123.4	114.4	240.2
	1994	6656.4	5177.4	1023.3	455.6	135.4	135.8	120.4	179.7
	1995	8100.0	6080.2	1182.0	637.8	121.7	117.4	115.5	140.0
	1996	9080.0	6792.7	1241.0	761.4	112.1	111.7	105.0	119.4
	1997	9405.3	7211.0	1253.4	940.8	103.6	106.2	101.0	123.6
	1998	9296.5	6812.5	1021.6	1462.4	100.2	95.8	83.1	156.9
	1999	9875.5	7160.8	962.7	1752.0	106.2	105.1	94.2	119.8
	2000	10656.2	7612.9	919.0	2124.3	107.9	106.3	95.5	121.3
北京	Beijing	663.9	437.5	42.8	183.7	115.0	108.3	108.3	137.2
天津	Tianjin	244.5	136.4	18.4	89.6	108.4	105.9	93.2	116.6
河北	Hebei	427.2	346.0	31.9	49.4	107.3	107.2	95.7	117.9
山西	Shanxi	256.1	200.9	20.1	35.1	111.8	112.7	106.8	109.8
内蒙古	Inner Mongolia	186.0	144.3	12.5	29.2	104.5	104.6	88.5	112.6
辽宁	Liaoning	525.1	383.0	53.7	88.4	103.4	102.9	90.8	116.2
吉林	Jilin	265.0	203.8	23.5	37.7	104.6	103.5	96.9	117.5
黑龙江	Heilongjiang	421.5	308.2	35.0	78.3	103.6	95.1	91.1	176.9
上海	Shanghai	587.7	355.1	34.3	198.3	104.8	100.8	89.0	116.7
江苏	Jiangsu	705.4	463.6	83.0	158.8	105.9	104.6	90.3	121.2
浙江	Zhejiang	490.6	288.5	55.3	146.8	110.0	107.5	86.1	129.4
安徽	Anhui	275.5	201.6	31.7	42.2	103.2	102.1	99.0	112.2
福建	Fujian	334.6	188.1	26.6	119.9	111.0	108.2	102.9	117.8
江西	Jiangxi	204.7	168.2	15.2	21.4	99.5	100.3	89.0	101.3
山东	Shandong	695.1	524.4	58.8	111.9	112.1	110.2	98.0	133.0
河南	Henan	495.7	338.4	66.4	90.8	111.2	110.2	106.6	119.3
湖北	Hubei	405.3	328.2	32.9	44.3	101.3	101.9	86.4	110.8
湖南	Hunan	358.1	303.1	31.9	23.1	107.5	107.8	98.7	116.8
广东	Guangdong	1038.4	604.6	91.8	342.0	108.2	108.1	91.4	114.1
广西	Guangxi	216.7	172.5	14.6	29.5	108.4	108.0	96.9	118.1
海南	Hainan	57.5	46.7	2.5	8.2	104.0	104.3	98.5	104.1
重庆	Chongqing	173.2	129.0	17.7	26.5	107.8	106.9	95.6	123.6
四川	Sichuan	436.9	338.7	40.5	57.7	109.6	110.1	101.6	112.9
贵州	Guizhou	144.6	116.4	10.2	18.0	111.4	111.1	98.9	122.8
云南	Yunnan	254.5	209.5	16.8	28.2	107.9	106.9	95.5	125.8
西藏	Tibet	23.2	22.2	0.5	0.5	114.7	115.5	86.3	111.8
陕西	Shaanxi	257.3	214.3	14.4	28.5	111.0	110.5	105.7	118.0
甘肃	Gansu	173.0	147.8	17.6	7.6	112.7	113.7	116.8	89.7
青海	Qinghai	49.8	46.4	2.3	1.1	102.4	102.4	90.8	139.2
宁夏	Ningxia	54.8	44.8	3.5	6.5	113.9	114.3	109.7	113.9
新疆	Xinjiang	234.5	200.8	12.6	21.1	110.7	108.1	91.4	171.0

注：1998年及以后工资总额为在岗职工工资总额，1998年及以后指数按可比口径计算（以下各表同）。

a)Data on total wages since 1998 refer to wages of fully employed staff and workers, and the indices since 1998 was calculated on the basis of comparable coverage. (Similarly in the following tables).

5-20 职工平均工资及指数

Average Wage of Staff and Workers and Related Indices

年份 Year 地区 Region	平均货币工资（元） Average Money Wage (yuan)				指数（上年=100） Indices (preceding year=100) 货币工资 Average Money Wage				实际工资 Average Real Wage			
	合计 Total	国有单位 State-owned Units	城镇集体单位 Urban Collective-owned Units	其他单位 Units of Other Types of Ownership	合计 Total	国有单位 State-owned Units	城镇集体单位 Urban Collective-owned Units	其他单位 Units of Other Types of Ownership	合计 Total	国有单位 State-owned Units	城镇集体单位 Urban Collective-owned Units	其他单位 Units of Other Types of Ownership
1978	615	644	506		100.0	100.0	100.0		106.0	106.2	105.1	
1979	668	705	542		108.6	109.5	107.1		106.6	107.5	105.1	
1980	762	803	623		114.1	113.9	114.9		106.1	106.0	106.9	
1981	772	812	642		101.3	101.1	103.0		98.8	98.6	100.5	
1982	798	836	671		103.4	103.0	104.5		101.3	101.0	102.5	
1983	826	865	698		103.5	103.5	104.0		101.5	101.5	102.0	
1984	974	1034	811	1048	117.9	119.5	116.2		114.8	116.4	113.1	
1985	1148	1213	967	1436	117.9	117.3	119.2	137.0	105.3	104.8	106.6	122.5
1986	1329	1414	1092	1629	115.8	116.6	112.9	113.4	108.2	108.9	105.5	106.0
1987	1459	1546	1207	1879	109.8	109.3	110.5	115.3	100.9	100.5	101.6	106.0
1988	1747	1853	1426	2382	119.7	119.9	118.1	126.8	99.2	99.3	97.9	105.0
1989	1935	2055	1557	2707	110.8	110.9	109.2	113.6	95.2	95.4	93.9	97.7
1990	2140	2284	1681	2987	110.6	111.1	108.0	110.3	109.2	109.7	106.6	108.9
1991	2340	2477	1866	3468	109.3	108.5	111.0	116.1	104.0	103.2	105.6	110.5
1992	2711	2878	2109	3966	115.9	116.2	113.0	114.4	106.7	107.0	104.1	105.3
1993	3371	3532	2592	4966	124.3	122.7	122.9	125.2	107.1	105.7	105.9	107.9
1994	4538	4797	3245	6303	134.6	135.8	125.2	126.9	107.7	108.7	100.2	101.5
1995	5500	5625	3931	7463	121.2	117.3	121.1	118.4	103.8	100.4	103.7	101.4
1996	6210	6280	4302	8261	112.9	111.6	109.4	110.7	103.8	102.6	100.6	101.7
1997	6470	6747	4512	8789	104.2	107.4	104.9	106.4	101.1	104.2	101.7	103.2
1998	7479	7668	5331	8972	106.6	106.1	102.5	97.7	107.2	106.7	103.1	98.3
1999	8346	8543	5774	9829	111.6	111.4	108.3	109.6	113.1	112.9	109.7	111.0
2000	9371	9552	6262	10984	112.3	111.8	108.5	111.8	111.4	110.9	107.6	110.9
北京 Beijing	16350	16431	10005	18926	116.3	116.0	113.2	114.3	115.4	115.1	112.3	113.4
天津 Tianjin	12480	12721	7646	13887	112.9	114.8	110.5	106.8	112.0	113.9	109.6	106.0
河北 Hebei	7781	8146	5187	7846	110.8	110.8	107.3	110.4	109.9	109.9	106.4	109.5
山西 Shanxi	6918	7249	4193	7783	114.1	114.9	112.4	108.8	113.2	114.0	111.5	107.9
内蒙古 Inner Mongolia	6974	7261	4826	6947	109.9	110.3	106.1	106.5	109.0	109.4	105.3	105.7
辽宁 Liaoning	8811	9221	5721	10196	111.6	110.2	110.9	111.8	110.7	109.3	110.0	110.9
吉林 Jilin	7924	8121	5501	9244	110.7	110.2	110.0	109.7	109.8	109.3	109.1	108.8
黑龙江 Heilongjiang	7835	7792	4708	11499	110.4	104.8	105.3	134.0	109.5	104.0	104.5	132.9
上海 Shanghai	18531	18865	12020	19752	111.4	111.9	108.0	108.4	110.5	111.0	107.1	107.5
江苏 Jiangsu	10299	11109	6962	10698	112.3	112.7	107.9	109.6	111.4	111.8	107.0	108.7
浙江 Zhejiang	13076	14465	10403	11975	116.7	118.3	115.5	113.5	115.8	117.4	114.6	112.6
安徽 Anhui	6989	7471	4762	7310	107.3	105.3	108.0	114.3	106.4	104.5	107.1	113.4
福建 Fujian	10584	11170	8140	10422	111.5	113.2	111.2	108.7	110.6	112.3	110.3	107.8
江西 Jiangxi	7014	7249	4676	7798	103.9	104.6	99.7	98.5	103.1	103.8	98.9	97.7
山东 Shandong	8772	9656	5586	7770	114.6	115.1	112.0	112.9	113.7	114.2	111.1	112.0
河南 Henan	6930	7453	4913	7212	111.9	113.0	105.9	113.0	111.0	112.1	105.1	112.1
湖北 Hubei	7565	7989	5090	7327	108.2	108.2	101.8	109.7	107.3	107.3	101.0	108.8
湖南 Hunan	8128	8401	5995	8705	111.8	111.7	109.3	113.3	110.9	110.8	108.4	112.4
广东 Guangdong	13823	14387	8615	15240	112.9	114.0	105.6	110.5	112.0	113.1	104.8	109.6
广西 Guangxi	7651	7663	5583	9264	112.9	112.6	109.3	113.5	112.0	111.7	108.4	112.6
海南 Hainan	7408	7146	5919	10346	107.9	108.5	104.4	104.4	107.0	107.6	103.6	103.6
重庆 Chongqing	8020	8390	5816	8334	111.7	111.3	111.8	109.1	110.8	110.4	110.9	108.2
四川 Sichuan	8323	8909	5749	7763	114.8	114.6	116.7	111.0	113.9	113.7	115.8	110.1
贵州 Guizhou	7468	7594	5444	8325	113.2	113.4	108.7	111.7	112.3	112.5	107.8	110.8
云南 Yunnan	9231	9422	7033	9566	111.5	111.5	108.1	111.7	110.6	110.6	107.2	110.8
西藏 Tibet	14976	15566	5835	12135	115.5	114.7	108.8	113.5	114.6	113.8	107.9	112.6
陕西 Shaanxi	7804	8043	4920	8417	112.6	112.3	113.9	111.4	111.7	111.4	113.0	110.5
甘肃 Gansu	8560	8916	6806	7251	115.3	114.2	120.7	115.5	114.4	113.3	119.7	114.6
青海 Qinghai	10050	10744	4785	6989	110.7	111.2	104.7	102.0	109.8	110.3	103.9	101.2
宁夏 Ningxia	8590	8913	6538	7943	116.2	116.4	117.4	113.2	115.3	115.5	116.5	112.3
新疆 Xinjiang	8717	8731	7489	9498	114.5	114.7	109.9	109.4	113.6	113.8	109.0	108.5

5-21 分行业职工工资总额

单位：亿元

年份 Year 地区 Region	合计 Total	农、林、牧、渔业 Farming, Forestry, Animal Husbandry and Fishery	采掘业 Mining and Quarrying	制造业 Manufacturing	电力、煤气及水的生产和供应业 Production and Supply of Electricity Gas and Water	建筑业 Construction	地质勘查业水利管理业 Geological Prospecting and Water Conservancy
1978	568.9	39.0	44.1	214.8	9.1	43.6	12.6
1979	646.7	43.0	49.9	244.0	10.3	50.9	14.2
1980	772.4	48.9	58.4	289.7	11.9	59.7	16.7
1981	820.0	50.5	60.9	306.3	12.7	62.5	17.4
1982	882.0	52.7	64.1	323.7	13.5	68.6	18.1
1983	934.6	55.2	66.2	337.7	14.3	74.8	19.5
1984	1133.4	61.1	81.3	418.0	17.5	96.6	23.0
1985	1383.0	68.7	103.4	504.0	17.1	120.0	27.7
1986	1659.7	81.8	125.8	601.9	22.0	139.0	31.6
1987	1881.1	90.1	135.4	695.4	26.5	156.3	35.1
1988	2316.2	101.1	162.1	866.8	33.6	184.3	40.9
1989	2618.5	109.1	199.0	983.8	40.0	196.2	44.3
1990	2951.1	120.3	234.3	1089.3	49.4	211.5	48.8
1991	3323.9	128.0	262.9	1230.2	57.7	244.5	53.6
1992	3939.2	139.6	289.3	1443.0	70.9	300.2	64.6
1993	4916.2	143.0	337.7	1796.3	96.5	433.4	53.5
1994	6656.1	191.5	417.0	2292.3	146.5	527.1	75.9
1995	8100.0	230.1	516.2	2760.4	197.0	609.8	79.8
1996	9080.0	246.4	565.2	2939.5	234.8	647.5	83.9
1997	9405.3	262.8	574.3	2993.4	268.8	673.3	91.7
1998	9296.5	249.9	513.9	2724.3	293.4	635.0	92.2
1999	9875.5	252.9	494.9	2758.9	324.1	633.4	97.5
2000	10656.2	260.1	496.0	2882.6	361.2	669.6	107.5
北京 Beijing	663.9	3.4	2.9	135.0	8.9	65.6	2.5
天津 Tianjin	244.5	1.1	11.2	91.1	7.6	15.7	2.9
河北 Hebei	427.2	4.1	30.1	111.9	17.3	25.0	9.7
山西 Shanxi	256.1	2.1	39.0	59.1	10.1	13.3	2.1
内蒙古 Inner Mongolia	186.0	12.7	16.3	33.4	10.2	9.8	2.2
辽宁 Liaoning	525.1	13.3	28.1	169.1	21.2	35.0	5.4
吉林 Jilin	265.0	6.7	22.8	72.7	8.8	14.2	1.8
黑龙江 Heilongjiang	421.5	21.2	50.5	89.4	16.4	29.7	6.9
上海 Shanghai	587.7	2.9	0.1	215.9	13.5	24.7	1.7
江苏 Jiangsu	705.4	13.8	18.4	236.7	20.9	28.6	5.2
浙江 Zhejiang	490.6	5.2	2.4	124.4	18.0	49.0	2.1
安徽 Anhui	275.5	6.9	23.9	69.8	8.1	14.3	3.4
福建 Fujian	334.6	5.2	4.1	122.2	10.3	22.5	1.2
江西 Jiangxi	204.7	8.1	8.6	49.1	7.6	9.6	2.3
山东 Shandong	695.1	7.4	78.6	200.7	25.1	24.9	4.2
河南 Henan	495.7	4.5	36.0	120.0	20.8	32.5	10.1
湖北 Hubei	405.3	17.6	10.7	110.5	12.4	22.2	5.7
湖南 Hunan	358.1	14.5	10.2	80.0	11.9	17.2	3.7
广东 Guangdong	1038.4	11.3	5.1	317.2	33.8	62.8	4.7
广西 Guangxi	216.7	8.0	3.8	52.3	9.4	9.5	1.8
海南 Hainan	57.5	8.8	1.1	6.4	2.5	2.0	0.4
重庆 Chongqing	173.2	2.1	7.8	51.6	5.5	12.8	1.4
四川 Sichuan	436.9	7.3	21.4	110.8	15.6	36.0	4.7
贵州 Guizhou	144.6	2.7	7.1	36.4	6.3	13.3	1.0
云南 Yunnan	254.5	12.2	8.1	54.1	9.0	15.3	2.5
西藏 Tibet	23.2	0.7	0.3	0.6	0.6	0.9	0.4
陕西 Shaanxi	257.3	3.8	15.5	70.2	8.5	14.8	5.8
甘肃 Gansu	173.0	5.3	9.0	45.9	8.8	11.9	3.7
青海 Qinghai	49.8	1.9	2.1	7.1	2.5	3.3	4.4
宁夏 Ningxia	54.8	2.5	5.6	11.5	3.0	4.1	0.9
新疆 Xinjiang	234.5	43.1	15.2	27.5	6.8	29.1	3.1

Total Wages of Staff and Workers by Sector

(100 million yuan)

交通运输仓储和邮电通信业 Transport, Storage, Post & Telecommunication Services	批发零售贸易和餐饮业 Wholesale and Retail Trade & Catering Services	金融、保险业 Finance and Insurance	房地产业 Real Estate	社会服务业 Social Services	卫生体育和社会福利业 Health Care, Sports & Social Welfare	教育、文化艺术和广播电影电视业 Education, Culture and Arts, Radio, Film and Television	科学研究和综合技术服务业 Scientific Research and Polytechnic Services	国家机关、政党机关和社会团体 Government Agencies, Party Agencies and Social Organizations	其他 Others
46.4	59.4	3.6	1.8	9.2	13.7	38.6	5.9	27.0	
52.0	68.3	4.3	2.2	11.1	15.5	43.6	6.9	30.5	
58.8	83.0	5.9	2.8	14.5	19.9	55.6	8.7	37.9	
61.2	90.7	6.9	2.7	16.5	21.9	59.7	9.3	40.9	
65.8	96.7	7.6	2.9	18.2	25.4	69.1	9.9	45.8	
68.5	101.8	8.1	3.2	20.4	27.4	72.2	11.8	53.6	
84.6	123.6	10.7	3.8	24.2	31.3	82.0	13.2	62.6	
103.0	149.7	13.8	4.1	29.3	37.7	109.3	16.3	78.7	
123.1	175.7	17.9	5.0	36.9	46.6	130.8	20.1	101.5	
138.3	198.3	21.2	5.7	42.9	51.9	145.4	22.6	116.0	
168.3	250.6	28.4	7.0	53.5	64.5	187.2	27.4	140.4	
192.0	275.3	33.3	8.3	62.0	73.8	207.3	30.8	163.3	
214.6	308.2	39.7	9.7	72.7	85.1	238.6	36.0	192.9	
243.3	346.8	45.5	11.7	86.8	95.3	260.7	39.5	217.5	
286.0	400.0	60.6	15.8	107.5	116.5	323.9	49.1	272.3	
346.4	468.7	85.1	26.9	147.1	139.5	389.7	63.4	357.7	18.3
470.9	637.0	170.1	44.1	220.2	216.8	607.4	106.8	500.2	32.3
565.6	758.1	197.9	54.9	264.3	253.8	690.8	121.4	559.5	40.4
645.7	823.0	240.4	66.3	305.5	303.2	812.2	141.9	672.1	67.6
702.8	848.5	288.0	75.1	357.4	348.1	931.1	161.9	744.0	84.1
693.5	746.6	319.6	89.7	374.3	395.3	1070.5	172.6	835.4	90.3
753.0	722.3	359.3	103.0	418.8	453.5	1244.9	192.4	971.0	95.5
820.4	718.9	399.7	116.5	472.8	517.0	1410.3	224.5	1090.4	108.7
32.7	63.3	16.9	18.8	92.7	28.8	72.3	56.5	43.9	19.7
21.5	17.1	5.8	3.1	10.4	9.8	22.9	5.9	15.7	2.6
28.9	24.7	15.7	1.9	13.8	18.4	63.6	4.9	54.8	2.2
24.2	13.8	8.6	0.8	6.5	9.4	31.3	3.5	29.9	2.3
19.4	7.2	7.1	1.4	4.7	8.5	25.6	2.4	22.8	2.3
46.4	26.1	21.9	7.1	23.7	21.8	52.0	9.6	40.5	3.9
21.9	14.2	10.1	3.1	11.8	12.1	34.8	4.9	22.5	2.8
38.9	25.7	14.2	4.1	17.2	16.5	45.9	4.5	37.0	3.3
53.3	50.7	24.3	12.6	42.9	29.4	58.2	17.4	29.8	10.2
52.4	57.6	22.2	7.7	26.5	35.3	98.2	12.2	62.9	6.8
33.9	37.4	23.8	5.8	21.7	34.1	68.9	7.0	52.5	4.3
16.1	20.3	8.1	1.9	8.5	13.0	42.6	3.5	33.5	1.6
21.5	17.2	13.6	3.7	10.7	12.7	49.0	3.9	33.3	3.6
18.1	13.3	8.0	1.2	4.3	11.2	32.7	2.7	27.0	1.1
39.8	38.6	24.8	4.4	19.9	36.4	100.9	7.3	76.4	5.7
41.8	35.3	18.4	2.7	14.2	23.2	66.3	6.9	58.9	4.1
32.8	28.7	12.8	3.1	13.8	21.2	56.7	7.2	47.4	2.6
29.1	24.2	14.9	2.1	10.4	22.8	62.8	5.6	45.4	3.3
91.8	82.7	54.0	18.8	59.8	50.6	118.2	13.6	103.9	9.9
17.8	13.6	8.3	1.5	8.5	13.1	36.3	3.3	27.5	1.9
5.0	3.2	2.8	0.9	3.4	3.3	8.1	1.1	8.2	0.3
13.5	9.8	5.9	1.5	4.5	8.1	25.4	5.3	17.8	0.4
27.4	24.7	18.4	2.8	11.5	25.0	63.9	10.9	54.6	1.9
9.0	8.3	5.4	1.0	3.3	6.3	22.0	2.0	19.0	1.5
19.4	22.7	7.9	1.3	8.0	12.8	43.2	4.0	33.0	1.2
1.8	0.7	1.2		0.6	1.7	4.4	0.3	9.0	
24.4	13.5	8.0	0.9	7.0	10.7	35.0	10.2	27.9	1.3
13.5	9.0	5.0	0.8	4.4	6.5	24.0	3.1	19.8	2.3
5.0	2.0	2.2	0.3	1.1	2.6	7.1	0.9	6.7	0.6
4.0	2.7	2.6	0.3	1.4	2.3	7.1	0.7	5.3	0.7
14.9	10.6	7.0	1.0	5.7	9.2	30.9	3.0	23.6	3.7

5-22 分行业职工平均工资

单位：元

年份 地区	Year Region	合计 Total	农、林、牧、渔业 Farming, Forestry, Animal Husbandry and Fishery	采掘业 Mining and Quarrying	制造业 Manufacturing	电力、煤气及水的生产和供应业 Production and Supply of Electricity Gas and Water	建筑业 Construction	地质勘查业水利管理业 Geological Prospecting and Water Conservancy
	1978	615	470	676	597	850	714	708
	1979	668	528	755	664	941	769	782
	1980	762	616	854	752	1035	855	895
	1981	772	637	855	758	1045	869	926
	1982	798	661	869	773	1067	912	955
	1983	826	691	880	789	1104	954	1016
	1984	974	770	1066	955	1321	1154	1179
	1985	1148	878	1324	1112	1239	1362	1406
	1986	1329	1048	1569	1275	1497	1536	1604
	1987	1459	1143	1663	1418	1677	1684	1768
	1988	1747	1280	1964	1710	1971	1959	2025
	1989	1935	1389	2378	1900	2241	2166	2199
	1990	2140	1541	2718	2073	2656	2384	2465
	1991	2340	1652	2942	2289	2922	2649	2707
	1992	2711	1828	3209	2635	3392	3066	3222
	1993	3371	2042	3711	3348	4319	3779	3717
	1994	4538	2819	4679	4283	6155	4894	5450
	1995	5500	3522	5757	5169	7843	5785	5962
	1996	6210	4050	6482	5642	8816	6249	6581
	1997	6470	4311	6833	5933	9649	6655	7160
	1998	7479	4528	7242	7064	10478	7456	7951
	1999	8346	4832	7521	7794	11513	7982	8821
	2000	9371	5184	8340	8750	12830	8735	9622
北京	Beijing	16350	11303	10821	14423	19807	12899	16607
天津	Tianjin	12480	9408	16532	11444	16863	12579	16166
河北	Hebei	7781	3886	9225	7056	12048	6887	11073
山西	Shanxi	6918	5100	7357	6228	9308	6890	6836
内蒙古	Inner Mongolia	6974	4729	6067	6135	11777	6022	6990
辽宁	Liaoning	8811	4441	8509	8373	12011	7716	9708
吉林	Jilin	7924	4070	6868	8103	11366	6878	6300
黑龙江	Heilongjiang	7835	4536	6553	7244	11479	6983	11843
上海	Shanghai	18531	13341	15980	17185	24266	16441	18648
江苏	Jiangsu	10299	6317	10101	9182	16480	9582	9864
浙江	Zhejiang	13076	10535	10018	10767	20074	12090	12541
安徽	Anhui	6989	5018	8111	6620	9976	6146	7030
福建	Fujian	10584	6065	7437	9666	14518	10632	9667
江西	Jiangxi	7014	4152	6118	6457	8303	6856	7425
山东	Shandong	8772	7574	12067	7101	13058	7530	8821
河南	Henan	6930	4689	7557	6114	9842	6423	11014
湖北	Hubei	7565	4294	8954	6992	10512	8213	7762
湖南	Hunan	8128	4520	6119	7535	11350	7643	7485
广东	Guangdong	13823	6597	8428	12519	17473	11590	10511
广西	Guangxi	7651	4876	6497	7887	11609	7368	6671
海南	Hainan	7408	3477	7030	8466	11978	6538	7238
重庆	Chongqing	8020	5884	7027	7709	10687	7239	10964
四川	Sichuan	8323	6140	8083	7774	10764	7693	9167
贵州	Guizhou	7468	5431	7366	7796	12538	7556	6818
云南	Yunnan	9231	6031	7892	9712	13293	8305	8677
西藏	Tibet	14976	11801	10161	7831	10848	9131	18589
陕西	Shaanxi	7804	5693	8325	7353	10824	7128	8886
甘肃	Gansu	8560	6572	9594	8261	12530	8349	8346
青海	Qinghai	10050	7348	10724	7569	17277	6122	19585
宁夏	Ningxia	8590	4605	9361	7946	15519	7823	8514
新疆	Xinjiang	8717	5573	13524	8209	13223	10220	8999

Average Wage of Staff and Workers by Sector

(yuan)

交通运输仓储和邮电通信业 Transport, Storage, Post & Telecommunication Services	批发零售贸易和餐饮业 Wholesale and Retail Trade & Catering Services	金融、保险业 Finance and Insurance	房地产业 Real Estate	社会服务业 Social Services	卫生体育和社会福利业 Health Care, Sports & Social Welfare	教育、文化艺术和广播电影电视业 Education, Culture and Arts, Radio, Film and Television	科学研究和综合技术服务业 Scientific Research and Polytechnic Services	国家机关、政党机关和社会团体 Government Agencies, Party Agencies and Social Organizations	其他 Others
694	551	610	548	392	573	545	669	655	
760	610	652	606	421	598	584	717	684	
832	692	720	694	475	718	700	851	800	
842	704	750	632	478	750	716	850	815	
877	709	768	684	484	833	811	857	821	
895	724	779	737	508	867	836	990	923	
1082	859	973	919	588	948	920	1072	989	
1275	1007	1154	1028	777	1124	1166	1272	1127	
1476	1148	1353	1216	980	1343	1330	1492	1356	
1621	1270	1458	1327	1085	1446	1409	1620	1468	
1941	1556	1739	1715	1719	1752	1747	1931	1707	
2197	1660	1867	1925	1926	1959	1883	2118	1874	
2426	1818	2097	2243	2170	2209	2117	2403	2113	
2686	1981	2255	2507	2431	2370	2243	2573	2275	
3114	2204	2829	3106	2844	2812	2715	3115	2768	
4273	2679	3740	4320	3588	3413	3278	3904	3505	3371
5690	3537	6712	6288	5026	5126	4923	6162	4962	5213
6948	4248	7376	7330	5982	5860	5435	6846	5526	6295
7870	4661	8406	8337	6778	6790	6144	8048	6340	7184
8600	4845	9734	9190	7553	7599	6759	9049	6981	6838
9808	5865	10633	10302	8333	8493	7474	10241	7773	8481
10991	6417	12046	11505	9263	9664	8510	11601	8978	10068
12319	7190	13478	12616	10339	10930	9482	13620	10043	11098
18558	14396	23789	18836	16549	21717	18265	20186	18106	19409
16820	10256	15822	13618	10708	14366	12219	13098	13575	9379
9899	4988	10339	8471	8006	8807	7787	10229	8587	7313
10306	4141	9553	7229	5510	7109	7156	8770	7209	6249
10239	4824	9519	8012	6126	8146	7426	8538	7780	8609
11721	6645	13281	9782	8080	9561	9404	11958	10223	8151
9167	5410	11419	9102	8484	8516	8558	10650	9014	8426
10979	6364	13176	8961	7650	9138	9319	10351	9592	8033
23679	15374	28511	21183	15451	20705	19906	20517	22295	21547
12000	7382	14323	13298	11275	12172	11576	15571	13898	11516
15513	11222	16850	16058	12209	17136	13979	16964	15520	13296
7397	4660	8879	7635	6377	8103	7403	9731	8388	8363
14335	8682	15465	13138	10380	12043	10893	14603	11652	13555
10111	5066	10163	7417	6580	8486	7375	8561	7940	7725
11781	5397	12612	10477	8733	11129	9784	12219	9896	8261
11333	4602	9531	7391	6468	7838	6584	9373	7415	7797
9363	5390	9616	9040	7337	8270	8474	10447	9042	8426
10377	6647	12599	9123	7842	10176	8708	10580	8647	9198
19864	11620	20239	18170	15967	15607	13255	20628	15005	13563
10582	5478	10365	8332	7806	9255	6643	9772	8111	7730
13342	6355	13782	10301	8244	11421	9419	8673	9506	8503
8456	6011	11804	8520	7476	9407	8159	9377	9061	9019
10352	5745	13274	9104	8170	9788	7923	11409	9236	8425
9795	5062	10633	8506	7274	7462	6631	10225	7159	8426
11247	9164	10818	9908	8404	10258	9019	11350	9077	9761
17054	9666	19408		10045	16752	15727	20579	17545	15348
11417	5351	10062	7297	7208	8081	7442	11350	7441	7232
11371	5606	9892	9278	7279	8953	8548	9614	8778	9643
13847	6036	14134	11675	6979	11303	10945	12749	10992	10387
12258	6507	13594	8627	7528	9318	8620	10470	8691	10306
12790	8243	13714	11044	8340	10114	9398	11505	9494	12388

5-23 分细行业职工平均工资 （2000年）

Average Wage of Staff and Workers by Sector in Detail (2000)

单位：元

(yuan)

项 目	Item	合 计 Total	国有单位 State-owned Units	城镇集体单位 Urban Collective-owned Units	其他单位 Units of Other Types of Ownership
全国总计	**National Total**	**9371**	**9552**	**6262**	**10984**
按企、事业和机关分组	**Grouped by Enterprises, Institutions and Agencies**				
企业	Enterprises	9189	9324	6144	10985
事业	Institutions	9634	9749	7388	10560
机关	Agencies & Organizations	10020	10025	8718	
按国民经济行业分组	**Grouped by Sector**				
农、林、牧、渔业	**Farming, Forestry, Animal Husbandry and Fishery**	**5184**	**5132**	**5536**	**8519**
农业	Farming	4665	4648	5752	5343
林业	Forestry	4771	4763	3773	9664
畜牧业	Animal Husbandry	5093	4673	6093	11395
渔业	Fishery	7131	6846	6718	9588
农、林、牧、渔服务业	Services	6673	6780	5445	8388
采掘业	**Mining and Quarrying**	**8340**	**8283**	**4857**	**9842**
制造业	**Manufacturing**	**8750**	**8554**	**5722**	**10192**
电力、煤气及水的生产和供应业	**Production and Supply of Electricity, Gas and Water**	**12830**	**12458**	**10707**	**15486**
建筑业	**Construction**	**8735**	**9512**	**6873**	**10391**
土木工程建筑业	Civil Engineering	8271	9058	6472	9862
线路管道和设备安装业	Circuit, Pipelines and Equipment Installation	12011	12538	10261	13645
装修装饰业	Buildings Fitting up and Decoration	9499	9072	7216	11885
地质勘查业水利管理业	**Geological Prospecting and Water Conservancy**	**9622**	**9651**	**7509**	**13064**
地质勘查业	Geological Prospecting	11534	11536	9556	17818
水利管理业	Water Conservancy	7836	7861	6847	7758
交通运输、仓储及邮电通信业	**Transport, Storage, Post and Telecommunication Services**	**12319**	**12613**	**5816**	**16173**
铁路运输业	Railway Transport	13920	13920	4494	19503
公路运输业	Highway Transport	6832	6946	5558	7927
管道运输业	Pipeline Transport	15672	15671	9651	22093
水上运输业	Water Way Transport	12347	16203	5210	12882
航空运输业	Air Transport	23454	21342	8163	31645
交通运输辅助业	Transport Supporting and Auxiliary Services	11657	11546	6266	20097
其他交通运输业	Other Transport	10006	11478	6540	11631
仓储业	Storage	8685	8140	7736	16739
邮电通信业	Post and Telecommunication Services	16359	15714	9895	25730
批发和零售贸易餐饮业	**Wholesale and Retail Trade & Catering Services**	**7190**	**7414**	**5089**	**10250**
食品、饮料、烟草和家庭日用品批发业	Wholesale Trade of Food, Beverages, Tobacco and Household Goods	7333	7322	5500	10613
能源、材料和机械电子设备批发业	Wholesale Trade of Energy, Materials and Electronic Equipment	9096	9152	6827	11433
其他批发业	Other Wholesale Trade	7082	9172	4633	12155
零售业	Retail Trade	6326	6332	4705	9573
商业经纪与代理业	Commercial Brokerage and Agencies	16087	15107	5473	22149
餐饮业	Catering Services	7791	6996	6046	9751
金融、保险业	**Finance and Insurance**	**13478**	**13729**	**9754**	**21538**
金融业	Finance	13446	13816	9753	22536
保险业	Insurance	13884	12745	11095	17609

5-23 续表 1 continued

单位：元 (yuan)

项目	Item	合计 Total	国有单位 State-owned Units	城镇集体单位 Urban Collective-owned Units	其他单位 Units of Other Types of Ownership
房地产业	**Real Estate Trade**	**12616**	**11626**	**10371**	**15485**
房地产开发与经营业	Real Estate Development and Operation	13342	12445	9990	15437
房地产管理业	Real Estate Management	11995	11163	11371	15468
房地产代理与经纪业	Real Estate Brokerages and Agencies	11989	11105	9116	18376
社会服务业	**Social Services**	**10339**	**9847**	**7269**	**14544**
公共设施服务业	Public Facilities Services	10156	10143	8041	12368
居民服务业	Resident Services	8453	10123	6163	9939
旅馆业	Hotels	9201	8382	6595	11798
租赁服务业	Leasing Services	9810	10228	7573	10351
旅游业	Tourism	10736	10450	7922	12094
娱乐服务业	Recreational Services	10109	9606	7480	10898
信息、咨询服务业	Information and Consultative Services	15409	12386	11670	22118
计算机应用服务业	Computer Application Services	28333	15750	13072	33126
其他社会服务业	Other Social Services	9614	9831	7057	14364
卫生体育和社会福利业	**Health Care, Sports and Social Welfare**	**10930**	**11234**	**8521**	**17883**
卫生	Health Care	10910	11230	8528	19443
体育	Sports	13380	13246	7319	16612
社会福利保障业	Social Welfare	10343	10457	8150	9157
教育、文化艺术及广播电影电视业	**Education, Culture and Arts, Radio, Film and Television**	**9482**	**9599**	**5854**	**12027**
教育	Education	9336	9455	5760	10846
#普通高等学校	Regular Institution of Higher Education	14198	14200	9799	15223
普通中学	Regular Secondary Schools	9239	9239	7921	12869
小学校	Primary Schools	8085	8273	5277	8525
文化艺术业	Culture and Arts	12159	12349	6673	14090
广播电影电视业	Radio, Film and Television	10388	10388	8422	13539
科学研究和综合技术服务业	**Scientific Research and Polytechnic Services**	**13620**	**13221**	**10434**	**20299**
科学研究业	Scientific Research	13602	13600	13377	14503
自然科学研究	Natural Science Research	13232	13224	14404	14685
社会科学研究	Social Science Research	13006	13014	11800	6850
其他科学研究	Other Science Research	15413	15435	9215	14000
综合技术服务业	Polytechnic Services	13634	12877	10312	20408
#气象	Meteorology	11084	11087	9706	10235
地震	Seismology	10944	10943		13000
测绘	Survey and Mapping	12738	12714	11276	22510
技术监督	Technological Supervision	11770	11610	10765	19589
海洋环境	Oceanic Environment	14141	14138		16286
环境保护	Environmental Protection	10051	10047	7563	13985
技术推广和科技交流服务业	Technology Application & Dissemination Science and Technology Exchange Services	12123	10466	9501	22973
工程设计业	Engineering Design	14899	14816	12061	19753
其他综合技术服务业	Other Polytechnic Services	16186	14145	10765	20143
国家机关、政党机关和社会团体	**Government Agencies, Party Agencies and Social Organizations**	**10043**	**10048**	**8899**	
#国家机关	Government Agencies	10024	10028	8980	
政党机关	Party Agencies	10125	10126	5389	
其他	**Others**	**11098**	**10198**	**9044**	**26677**
#企业管理机构	Enterprise Management Organizations	10577	10943	8109	16726

5-24 国有单位分行业职工平均工资

单位：元

年份 地区	Year Region	合计 Total	农、林、牧、渔业 Farming, Forestry, Animal Husbandry and Fishery	采掘业 Mining and Quarrying	制造业 Manufacturing	电力、煤气及水的生产和供应业 Production and Supply of Electricity Gas and Water	建筑业 Construction	地质勘查业水利管理业 Geological Prospecting and Water Conservancy
	1978	644	482	704	663	873	760	712
	1979	705	536	786	726	971	819	787
	1980	803	628	891	821	1073	924	895
	1981	812	645	890	820	1074	941	925
	1982	836	670	905	835	1095	979	955
	1983	865	701	915	847	1134	1018	1016
	1984	1034	785	1112	1028	1357	1275	1180
	1985	1213	892	1384	1190	1272	1532	1408
	1986	1414	1062	1638	1382	1518	1731	1607
	1987	1546	1154	1734	1543	1692	1882	1773
	1988	1853	1291	2038	1872	1994	2192	2025
	1989	2055	1401	2449	2081	2248	2419	2199
	1990	2284	1559	2763	2289	2648	2667	2463
	1991	2477	1665	2982	2505	2883	2924	2718
	1992	2878	1845	3239	2889	3354	3406	3235
	1993	3532	2043	3856	3562	4317	4182	3729
	1994	4797	2821	4863	4508	6124	5498	5476
	1995	5625	3527	5944	5352	7734	6512	5987
	1996	6280	4038	6709	5798	8701	6992	6610
	1997	6747	4304	7091	6008	9541	7388	7180
	1998	7668	4522	7499	6981	10324	8171	7968
	1999	8543	4813	7732	7611	11239	8734	8843
	2000	9552	5132	8283	8554	12458	9512	9651
北京	Beijing	16431	11583	10869	13901	19622	13480	16827
天津	Tianjin	12721	8379	17768	10137	17105	13099	16178
河北	Hebei	8146	3861	8784	7439	11661	7997	11124
山西	Shanxi	7249	5148	7545	6017	9370	7241	6855
内蒙古	Inner Mongolia	7261	4781	6114	5597	11306	6570	6997
辽宁	Liaoning	9221	4307	9025	8995	11283	8850	9797
吉林	Jilin	8121	4077	6915	8268	11298	7583	6344
黑龙江	Heilongjiang	7792	4599	4199	7096	10976	8090	11956
上海	Shanghai	18865	13255	23191	16461	22542	17246	18606
江苏	Jiangsu	11109	6293	10725	9264	16296	10957	9947
浙江	Zhejiang	14465	10384	10230	10843	18521	14484	12568
安徽	Anhui	7471	5028	9261	6699	10087	7167	7040
福建	Fujian	11170	5961	6917	9148	14132	11925	9765
江西	Jiangxi	7249	4155	6177	6349	7934	8297	7426
山东	Shandong	9656	7223	12698	7422	12946	8373	8824
河南	Henan	7453	4733	7190	6011	9647	7342	11072
湖北	Hubei	7989	4279	9562	7712	10454	9369	7780
湖南	Hunan	8401	4509	6161	7936	10973	8466	7545
广东	Guangdong	14387	6022	8293	12715	16923	14237	10550
广西	Guangxi	7663	4917	6505	7372	11293	8282	6679
海南	Hainan	7146	3430	7051	8311	10617	7212	7243
重庆	Chongqing	8390	6078	7287	7780	10798	8715	11019
四川	Sichuan	8909	6353	8705	8323	11508	8907	9277
贵州	Guizhou	7594	5427	7792	7904	12482	8340	6829
云南	Yunnan	9422	6046	7890	10530	13202	8284	8697
西藏	Tibet	15566	12226	10745	10686	10848	9586	18589
陕西	Shaanxi	8043	5779	8305	7333	10847	8107	8905
甘肃	Gansu	8916	6607	9544	8916	12966	8585	8446
青海	Qinghai	10744	7344	11151	8389	17903	6896	19585
宁夏	Ningxia	8913	4604	9784	8596	15541	7876	8514
新疆	Xinjiang	8731	5570	14576	8095	12608	11037	8618

Average Wage of Staff and Workers in State-owned Units by Sector

(yuan)

交通运输仓储和邮电通信业 Transport, Storage, Post & Telecommunication Services	批发零售贸易和餐饮业 Wholesale and Retail Trade & Catering Services	金融、保险业 Finance and Insurance	房地产业 Real Estate	社会服务业 Social Services	卫生体育和社会福利业 Health Care, Sports & Social Welfare	教育、文化艺术和广播电影电视业 Education, Culture and Arts, Radio, Film and Television	科学研究和综合技术服务业 Scientific Research` and Polytechnic Services	国家机关、政党机关和社会团体 Government Agencies, Party Agencies and Social Organizations	其他 Others
720	569	650	630	607	605	566	670	661	
808	632	689	690	676	625	606	719	691	
902	716	754	758	795	751	722	853	807	
905	730	788	727	801	781	738	852	820	
927	739	806	788	815	861	827	860	826	
949	756	813	848	863	895	851	992	928	
1164	776	1038	1063	988	981	934	1074	993	
1383	1087	1234	1170	1208	1164	1184	1268	1133	
1610	1268	1427	1364	1417	1376	1344	1494	1361	
1773	1398	1540	1500	1545	1481	1422	1624	1472	
2140	1737	1842	1750	1842	1793	1764	1935	1709	
2423	1851	1960	1992	2028	1999	1899	2123	1875	
2697	2028	2200	2247	2307	2263	2134	2411	2115	
2967	2201	2355	2476	2547	2417	2257	2580	2277	
3452	2478	2967	3082	3008	2883	2732	3130	2774	
4604	2933	3885	4278	3661	3494	3292	3898	3512	3793
6212	3856	7017	5997	5098	5267	4944	6212	4967	5744
7572	4568	7595	6884	5949	6009	5457	6835	5528	6854
8546	4940	8679	7897	6695	6967	6161	7984	6344	7643
9303	5134	10012	8570	7425	7794	6810	8974	6985	6891
10302	6150	10898	9441	8136	8704	7537	10146	7776	8258
11345	6678	12249	10475	9054	9899	8590	11543	8982	9762
12613	7414	13729	11626	9847	11234	9599	13221	10048	10198
18037	16301	21969	17815	14479	22244	18394	19567	18113	14096
16952	11611	14703	12988	10574	14548	12317	13736	13576	9239
10217	5343	10788	8489	8230	9004	7793	10225	8591	7525
10995	4469	10513	7343	5906	7554	7187	8818	7211	6730
10646	5091	10198	8238	6291	8580	7427	8570	7781	9247
11947	6897	13637	9341	8184	9871	9415	12075	10198	8095
9567	5708	12576	8843	8770	8733	8556	10708	9014	8328
11398	6383	13813	8800	8131	9244	9309	10547	9601	8782
24038	16318	23159	20996	15412	20873	19953	20547	22322	17477
12944	7695	14845	13439	11498	13029	11640	15560	13932	11180
16119	12935	16962	16274	12710	18095	13998	17098	15523	13148
8604	4961	9235	8230	7134	9178	7418	9765	8404	8515
14492	9726	15953	12681	10961	12253	10892	14536	11674	12152
10684	5669	10501	7369	6860	8582	7376	8553	7947	8060
12277	5877	13806	10488	8690	11647	9797	12226	9900	9102
12343	4871	9937	7057	6662	7907	7438	9413	7419	7974
10071	5473	9856	8302	7120	8337	8480	10486	9053	8519
11484	7048	12911	9216	7843	10844	8710	10607	8656	9628
19247	11921	20555	16900	16115	15697	13247	20264	15007	11724
10714	5956	11072	8307	7826	9268	6657	9788	8115	8051
13043	6574	14681	9975	7953	11778	9400	8566	9529	8507
9289	6690	12119	8006	7408	10315	8164	9255	9065	9977
11410	6443	14403	9344	8415	10721	7928	11398	9246	8801
9935	5411	10685	9375	7234	7483	6629	10244	7160	9441
11468	10974	11157	9983	8244	10271	9020	11374	9075	9256
16993	9721	19803		10275	16752	15737	20579	17545	16322
11789	5397	10389	7495	7409	8415	7458	11361	7442	7657
11720	5858	10655	9364	7475	9087	8549	9724	8781	9768
13995	6415	14839	12861	7393	11309	10945	12749	11138	10486
12281	7159	13690	8545	7567	9368	8624	10590	8691	10743
12935	8594	14626	11635	8508	10126	9397	11547	9502	12492

5-25 城镇集体单位分行业职工平均工资

单位：元

年份 地区	Year Region	合计 Total	农、林、牧、渔业 Farming, Forestry, Animal Husbandry and Fishery	采掘业 Mining and Quarrying	制造业 Manufacturing	电力、煤气及水的生产和供应业 Production and Supply of Electricity Gas and Water	建筑业 Construction	地质勘查业水利管理业 Geological Prospecting and Water Conservancy
	1978	506	304	443	503	333	594	600
	1979	542	423	478	535	364	652	571
	1980	623	458	548	619	333	716	700
	1981	642	500	568	641	500	737	700
	1982	671	527	575	654	500	794	800
	1983	698	532	594	679	500	847	800
	1984	811	618	702	805	615	959	900
	1985	967	725	852	963	667	1101	900
	1986	1092	875	945	1075	875	1232	1286
	1987	1207	979	1016	1180	1250	1380	1333
	1988	1426	1111	1208	1388	1294	1597	1500
	1989	1557	1178	1433	1523	1625	1763	1000
	1990	1681	1238	1844	1622	2133	1935	1212
	1991	1866	1366	1960	1798	2588	2216	1765
	1992	2109	1487	2000	2017	2737	2554	2188
	1993	2592	1887	2327	2469	3539	3182	2843
	1994	3245	2510	2793	3076	5734	3936	3692
	1995	3931	2927	3680	3717	7461	4677	4294
	1996	4302	3814	3968	4007	8324	5092	4784
	1997	4512	3945	4164	4120	9064	5466	6342
	1998	5331	4358	4567	5016	9470	5941	7017
	1999	5774	4878	4545	5327	9834	6296	7636
	2000	6262	5536	4857	5722	10707	6873	7509
北京	Beijing	10005	9578	6608	9105	14346	10486	9337
天津	Tianjin	7646	9868	7640	7012	10279	9508	8357
河北	Hebei	5187	4935	6816	4890	7314	5505	6381
山西	Shanxi	4193	4219	4557	3705	8327	4812	5497
内蒙古	Inner Mongolia	4826	3405	3652	4065	6995	5597	3640
辽宁	Liaoning	5721	5576	4129	5246	10508	6317	5033
吉林	Jilin	5501	4244	4651	5485	8513	5759	4764
黑龙江	Heilongjiang	4708	3133	4804	3985	13606	4987	10097
上海	Shanghai	12020	14926	3000	9547	25540	16257	
江苏	Jiangsu	6962	6849	5376	6475	12439	7737	7858
浙江	Zhejiang	10403	12392	8111	8943	13089	10978	12084
安徽	Anhui	4762	4529	3909	4872	3959	4844	6162
福建	Fujian	8140	9093	8159	7312	13659	9076	5717
江西	Jiangxi	4676	3905	4926	4170	6496	5409	5200
山东	Shandong	5586	10193	4911	5256	7354	6272	7691
河南	Henan	4913	4134	5202	4474	7823	4929	4343
湖北	Hubei	5090	4890	5943	5056	7550	5855	5590
湖南	Hunan	5995	4717	4854	5342	10760	6328	6012
广东	Guangdong	8615	8273	7263	7744	11738	7919	9640
广西	Guangxi	5583	4313	6910	5862	13821	5847	
海南	Hainan	5919	3003	3997	5890	6582	5091	6831
重庆	Chongqing	5816	5242	3507	5751	5293	6018	4705
四川	Sichuan	5749	5173	4645	5549	7074	6124	5877
贵州	Guizhou	5444	5670	5527	5405	4978	6097	5316
云南	Yunnan	7033	4162	6443	7056	10910	7357	5952
西藏	Tibet	5835		9003	4406		5839	
陕西	Shaanxi	4920	3703	5910	4789	4750	4683	5397
甘肃	Gansu	6806	4415	6104	6431	10272	8170	2821
青海	Qinghai	4785	7634	4771	4254	11225	4445	
宁夏	Ningxia	6538	5113	6474	5779	18436	7463	
新疆	Xinjiang	7489	6255	7388	7225	8709	7914	12446

Average Wage of Staff and Workers in Urban Collective-owned Units by Sector

(yuan)

交通运输仓储和邮电通信业 Transport, Storage, Post & Telecommunication Services	批发零售贸易和餐饮业 Wholesale and Retail Trade & Catering Services	金融、保险业 Finance and Insurance	房地产业 Real Estate	社会服务业 Social Services	卫生体育和社会福利业 Health Care, Sports & Social Welfare	教育、文化艺术和广播电影电视业 Education, Culture and Arts, Radio, Film and Television	科学研究和综合技术服务业 Scientific Research and Polytechnic Services	国家机关、政党机关和社会团体 Government Agencies, Party Agencies and Social Organizations	其他 Others
632	453	526	467	451	484	317	500	455	
652	499	571	475	531	522	339	500	467	
676	584	640	638	584	618	433	571	538	
694	598	654	590	603	647	433	667	615	
757	597	667	660	621	735	523	600	615	
762	607	690	760	675	768	535	750	714	
878	1017	800	860	736	831	634	900	885	
1009	912	945	1050	806	975	779	1052	1046	
1139	1008	1150	1238	1057	1212	945	1286	1227	
1236	1118	1235	1130	1167	1296	1033	1319	1368	
1409	1335	1450	1602	1333	1570	1202	1636	1648	
1575	1417	1597	1967	1521	1774	1352	1710	1860	
1661	1548	1806	1969	1638	1956	1533	1997	2042	
1854	1691	1965	2432	1905	2135	1689	2120	2206	
2070	1827	2428	2763	2082	2416	1987	2392	2565	
2711	2213	3182	4006	2727	2935	2539	3474	3071	2547
3110	2823	5625	5290	3754	4238	3548	4719	4411	4067
3584	3449	6407	6706	4707	4890	4291	6046	5314	4935
3961	3818	6857	6820	5032	5603	4949	7206	5686	5675
4057	3873	7634	7687	5663	6294	4955	7749	6244	5780
5163	4517	8144	9144	5990	6883	5192	8116	7033	7048
5707	4802	9088	10516	6621	7826	5750	8771	7985	8135
5816	5089	9754	10371	7269	8521	5854	10434	8899	9044
9012	9708	10685	12999	8518	15438	12612	12802	12436	12850
7323	6696	15904	10039	8533	8893	5817	10609	12900	8796
4767	4061	8225	8571	6640	5925	6525	10671	7178	6590
4424	3475	7226	5748	4264	4759	4831	7690	6448	4797
4759	4189	7568	4293	4569	5424	6236	4952	7536	6608
5735	4651	10150	7869	6072	5778	6769	7632	8811	8327
4421	3803	8384	6921	5993	6105	8436	8438	9228	7754
5189	3694	9794	10423	4891	6990	8513	7786	7831	6349
10008	9358	20186	16133	12292	19826	14509	13882	17055	21689
6236	5426	10692	11311	9361	10207	8442	13462	10738	12160
9912	8345	15578	14272	10545	12791	12428	13831	13919	13483
4269	4027	7611	5320	4731	5848	5414	6714	6803	7390
7676	5478	12799	11787	7934	10454	10185	11706	7078	9476
4338	3652	8814	7622	4626	6743	3925	4774	6840	6961
5425	4050	8935	7599	6676	8472	8530	10626	7695	5874
4665	3938	8130	6078	5304	6174	5265	6917	6081	6875
4916	3973	7557	6770	7036	6097	7086	6636	7125	7855
4800	5443	11354	7360	6177	6440	7494	8028	7089	6642
8949	7674	12678	13660	11296	13120	12464	15911	14780	12153
5450	4319	7891	7045	6282	7309	7220	6631	6885	5564
6427	4134	9674	8766	6382	8313	9995	13188	6328	7736
4823	4080	9958	6183	5766	6425	5497	9549	8412	7737
4651	4408	9743	7766	6029	6383	6475	9254	7435	5686
5598	3970	7958	7018	5691	5692	7929	7631	5924	5548
8287	5990	9259	8362	7279	8029	7930	9691	9600	9354
6818	6731			8162		3273			11000
3793	4416	7648	5211	5214	5266	4897	6429	7239	6324
6179	5236	6756	7291	6350	6513	5339	7795	7396	8701
7696	4566	9800	7205	4060	10983	8111		3574	8669
8870	5008	8688	4967	6941	5936	7767	5984		7218
8664	6732	9315	9505	6120	9394	8984	5061	6738	11447

5-26 其他单位分行业职工平均工资

单位：元

年 份 地 区	Year Region	合 计 Total	农、林、牧、渔业 Farming, Forestry, Animal Husbandry and Fishery	采掘业 Mining and Quarrying	制造业 Manufacturing	电力、煤气及水的生产和供应业 Production and Supply of Electricity Gas and Water	建筑业 Construction	地质勘查业水利管理业 Geological Prospecting and Water Conservancy
	1984	1048	543		1007		1513	
	1985	1436	1519	1270	1328	1270	1000	
	1986	1629	1806		1528		2299	
	1987	1879	2106		1789		2503	
	1988	2382	2560	2239	2462	2104	4000	
	1989	2707	2938	2427	2889	3232	5000	
	1990	2987	3778	2270	3055	3088	3571	5714
	1991	3468	3760	3855	3626	3333	4641	4615
	1992	3966	4069	3579	4154	4238	5061	5263
	1993	4966	3905	3423	4874	6309	4464	7441
	1994	6303	5394	4233	6096	8005	5766	4362
	1995	7463	6992	5174	7245	10746	6798	5408
	1996	8261	7389	5217	7945	12030	6937	6464
	1997	8789	7061	5385	8367	12127	7517	5770
	1998	8972	5685	6749	8556	12158	8983	6909
	1999	9829	6740	7651	9316	13856	9540	8439
	2000	10984	8519	9842	10192	15486	10391	13064
北 京	Beijing	18926	10271	9430	16572	21046	15274	20976
天 津	Tianjin	13887	17819	16225	13255	15719	14123	
河 北	Hebei	7846	3128	12160	7503	15632	4378	4565
山 西	Shanxi	7783	4384	7589	8215	9111	9215	4347
内蒙古	Inner Mongolia	6947	3377	7085	7002	14838	5621	13000
辽 宁	Liaoning	10196	13669	10258	9571	15795	7910	
吉 林	Jilin	9244	2494	7482	9783	12902	6421	
黑龙江	Heilongjiang	11499	3855	15709	9920	16718	9617	9140
上 海	Shanghai	19752	13322	12263	18935	33666	15135	21185
江 苏	Jiangsu	10698	6727	8208	10279	18131	9583	8251
浙 江	Zhejiang	11975	10843	8833	11127	26402	12132	12117
安 徽	Anhui	7310	5426	8087	7592	9933	5700	3680
福 建	Fujian	10422	7360	9691	10016	16463	11087	10239
江 西	Jiangxi	7798	4182	6214	7727	11856	7387	
山 东	Shandong	7770	7052	8166	7482	15227	8094	8985
河 南	Henan	7212	5135	8045	6964	11430	6279	5357
湖 北	Hubei	7327	5843	4496	6717	11032	7481	3606
湖 南	Hunan	8705	8219	5002	8230	16458	9696	6846
广 东	Guangdong	15240	15232	11905	13600	22340	15353	11965
广 西	Guangxi	9264	2938	5812	9715	14288	7783	5727
海 南	Hainan	10346	8708	11728	9200	15436	7571	
重 庆	Chongqing	8334	7766	6039	8620	10976	6995	
四 川	Sichuan	7763	7408	5883	7913	8932	6820	8520
贵 州	Guizhou	8325	7034	6639	8502	16015	7328	
云 南	Yunnan	9566	6769	8609	9301	13820	9467	8417
西 藏	Tibet	12135	6083	7346	15240		10892	
陕 西	Shaanxi	8417	6349	8953	8614	10753	5505	
甘 肃	Gansu	7251	2778	13395	6706	16161	4502	
青 海	Qinghai	6989		7091	6142	5546	5456	
宁 夏	Ningxia	7943		6507	7789	10926	8201	
新 疆	Xinjiang	9498	7162	9740	8751	14887	8822	47166

Average Wage of Staff and Workers in Other Ownership Units by Sector

(yuan)

交通运输仓储和邮电通信业 Transport, Storage, Post & Telecommunication Services	批发零售贸易和餐饮业 Wholesale and Retail Trade & Catering Services	金融、保险业 Finance and Insurance	房地产业 Real Estate	社会服务业 Social Services	卫生体育和社会福利业 Health Care, Sports & Social Welfare	教育、文化艺术和广播电影电视业 Education, Culture and Arts, Radio, Film and Television	科学研究和综合技术服务业 Scientific Research and Polytechnic Services	其他 Others
1696	1428	2500		1741				
2429	1955	2107		1904		3184	1728	
2543	1971	2457		2126	1583	2245	2533	
2760	2142	2745		2310	2793	2451	1967	
3368	2512	3902	1296	2856	2903	2498	2544	
3846	2882	4376	1776	3202	2945	3604	3241	
3667	3284	5565	2517	3463	5430	4022	3425	
5500	3585	6041	4923	4004	4817	4560	3906	
5955	4368	9761	5561	4545	5461	5107	5033	
6450	4975	6073	4940	5934	3665	5289	5645	4953
8713	6460	10400	9610	8013	7051	8360	7882	9691
10492	7190	12949	10746	9274	8668	8968	9678	10502
11931	7862	15818	11801	10820	11014	10172	13358	13508
13734	8051	17970	13249	11812	11863	10017	14370	16423
11858	8320	16255	13636	12027	15124	11687	14847	20393
14241	9001	18648	14693	12785	16618	12871	15671	20548
16173	10250	21538	15485	14544	17883	12027	20299	26677
28350	14403	36532	20106	22365	17966	15306	22643	50582
22278	12610	20048	15303	13741	16727	10221	11688	20615
8630	5359	16225	8221	6274		9275	10592	8860
5521	4671	10082	7407	4111	4690	5100	9080	4059
4847	4477	13853	6098	6811	5467	8319	6366	4525
14737	8678	17477	12035	10539	14885	13805	12744	10135
11500	6230	12773	9930	9154	15222	11957	9474	16701
9961	10931	14706	8690	11265	8308	14926	6873	13007
26052	18780	44076	22086	16328	20858	21535	21481	26539
14566	10650	18760	14496	12906	16278	14370	18806	15008
15755	11645	18751	15991	12100	14936	13574	17873	13781
6014	5074	10218	6071	6485	8723	6852	6980	7343
18905	10459	17657	13680	10158	30465	11837	18136	23943
5826	7017	11625	7830	6941	5333		26214	4129
11869	6739	14798	11605	10066	15205	9663	13211	12272
6907	5206	13151	8191	7117	6289	9332	8906	8423
7733	8138	13360	12543	8731	19129	6377	10229	6096
7999	8407	14919	9000	8943		11696	11558	5466
26537	15920	32231	21430	17947	19055	19713	29935	28313
14884	6461	11609	8785	8358	9157	4296	8667	10603
15705	9565	15018	10887	8908	7714	10291	12313	16567
6211	7252	12158	9412	8219	15538	10614	9813	17015
8323	6050	21394	8797	8283	7150	6769	14122	8292
10107	6188	18975	8080	10427	8191	6146	14393	9250
9889	8503	13030	10015	9481	11767	9462	12334	13746
27924		14924		13605				18200
6439	6805	14656	8038	7536	9784	11183	11589	6757
4541	5372		9194	6999			11452	
6982	6758	14258	6522	10220				
7994	6162	30495	8901	7458		6441	8097	
9661	10087	13226	8549	8501	17750	11240	10135	9279

5-27 其他单位分登记注册类型职工平均工资

Average Wage of Staff and Workers in Units of Other Types of Ownership by Registration Status

单位：元 (yuan)

年份 地区	Year Region	合计 Total	股份合作单位 Cooperative Units	联营单位 Joint Ownership Units	有限责任公司 Limited Liability Corporations	股份有限公司 Share-Holding Corporations Ltd.	其他 Others	港、澳、台商投资单位 Units with Funds from Hong Kong, Macao & Taiwan	外商投资单位 Foreign Funded Units
	1993	4966		3741		5171	3279	5147	5315
	1994	6303		4982		6383	4954	6376	6533
	1995	7463		6056		7277	6494	7484	8058
	1996	8261		6856		7623	7131	8334	9383
	1997	8789		7310		7693	7063	9329	10361
	1998	8972	6054	8431	7750	8833	6133	10027	11767
	1999	9829	6709	9501	8632	9720	8425	10991	12951
	2000	10984	7473	10663	9766	11131	10223	11914	14372
北京	Beijing	18926	11126	13086	17122	17762	11579	21082	29621
天津	Tianjin	13887	10826	10516	13636	14922	12322	12337	15018
河北	Hebei	7846	5709	7057	7735	8112	8161	9028	8620
山西	Shanxi	7783	4955	5295	8669	6345	5257	7588	8984
内蒙古	Inner Mongolia	6947	4548	8453	7284	6888	3301	6015	6831
辽宁	Liaoning	10196	6422	6460	9816	10051	5104	10539	12109
吉林	Jilin	9244	8408	5248	7837	9587	4979	9055	12309
黑龙江	Heilongjiang	11499	9177	8366	6628	16282	4392	9946	7565
上海	Shanghai	19752	13825	15402	16468	21757	6998	17232	23525
江苏	Jiangsu	10698	7254	9470	10286	11011	11710	11074	13167
浙江	Zhejiang	11975	9485	11830	11362	14581	13099	12006	12974
安徽	Anhui	7310	5134	6057	6672	9082	6199	7062	8341
福建	Fujian	10422	8248	11915	10613	12674	9321	10084	10397
江西	Jiangxi	7798	5250	4392	7993	9571	4317	7149	7131
山东	Shandong	7770	5510	7189	7765	7723	6382	7201	8792
河南	Henan	7212	5637	5063	6925	7547	5573	9227	7794
湖北	Hubei	7327	5726	7545	7364	7067	8755	7797	10180
湖南	Hunan	8705	6712	6937	9017	8867	6424	7972	10396
广东	Guangdong	15240	10079	16402	19006	18126	11499	13124	16454
广西	Guangxi	9264	5999	7007	9759	10008	6399	6048	9447
海南	Hainan	10346	10468	8420	9454	11794	7904	9474	10859
重庆	Chongqing	8334	6463	5780	7046	9715	5636	9007	13085
四川	Sichuan	7763	6183	6099	7256	8346	6266	9482	9466
贵州	Guizhou	8325	5657	5832	8512	8856	5086	9395	8414
云南	Yunnan	9566	6779	9544	9268	10780	7482	9908	12301
西藏	Tibet	12135	27924	9579	13600	11669		9000	
陕西	Shaanxi	8417	5011	7417	8246	9201	6049	8642	12501
甘肃	Gansu	7251	6112	6405	5625	10626	5660	10884	12672
青海	Qinghai	6989	5967	5963	6287	6726	10512	9000	7643
宁夏	Ningxia	7943	7531	6791	7785	8183		6330	9444
新疆	Xinjiang	9498	6987	6615	8989	11187	6000	9544	10792

5-28 分地区国有及国有控股企业年底从业人员数和劳动报酬（2000年）

Employed Persons at the Year-end and Earnings in State-owned and State-controlling Enterprises by Region (2000)

地 区	Region	从业人员（万人）Number of Employed Persons (10 000 persons)	#女性 Female	职工（万人）Staff and Workers (10 000 persons)	#专业技术人员 Technical Personnel	从业人员劳动报酬（万元）Earnings of Employed Persons (10 000 yuan)	职工工资总额（万元）Wages of Staff and Workers (10 000 yuan)	职工平均工资（元）Average Wage of Staff and Workers (yuan)
全 国	**National Total**	**5732.0**	**2068.7**	**5564.2**	**1180.4**	**56070133.5**	**54754994.5**	**9632**
北 京	Beijing	204.5	69.5	192.2	47.7	3406397.4	3262056.3	16118
天 津	Tianjin	90.4	30.9	87.5	22.7	1203389.3	1177324.8	13066
河 北	Hebei	255.4	90.9	252.8	47.5	2182080.5	2158667.7	8279
山 西	Shanxi	221.3	71.0	215.3	43.2	1698706.9	1656658.1	7657
内蒙古	Inner Mongolia	134.8	48.1	132.6	24.8	991119.8	979600.4	7301
辽 宁	Liaoning	465.9	168.1	454.9	130.7	4401808.9	4330110.6	9375
吉 林	Jilin	181.0	62.1	178.2	38.2	1536583.8	1514600.4	8313
黑龙江	Heilongjiang	354.5	120.3	334.6	65.5	2866277.4	2765323.4	8101
上 海	Shanghai	188.3	63.0	168.0	35.0	3528056.8	3294560.0	18698
江 苏	Jiangsu	309.6	115	300.5	57.4	3336596.1	3260797.3	10554
浙 江	Zhejiang	112.2	43.2	108.0	26.7	1630816.1	1581139.5	14049
安 徽	Anhui	173.0	62.6	169.3	29.7	1264161.9	1245323.5	7286
福 建	Fujian	96.1	34.4	93.2	19.1	1110892.7	1081813.9	11358
江 西	Jiangxi	153.4	57.0	149.4	31.1	1062996.8	1042394.7	6909
山 东	Shandong	358.3	130.5	353.2	69.5	3345440.8	3309011.9	9275
河 南	Henan	340.6	124.4	333.7	56.0	2580234.2	2544121.7	7590
湖 北	Hubei	275.1	108.9	269.6	43.8	2104989.1	2077325.0	7568
湖 南	Hunan	224.5	81.6	213.6	40.1	1778157.6	1713545.1	7982
广 东	Guangdong	260.3	95.8	256.2	58.2	4221702.2	4159041.5	15973
广 西	Guangxi	124.0	47.1	120.3	24.1	1012626.0	997165.0	8245
海 南	Hainan	51.2	21.7	50.2	8.8	335023.1	328161.9	6524
重 庆	Chongqing	158.4	55.2	155.9	51.4	1391106.7	1375532.6	8430
四 川	Sichuan	245.1	89.0	237.7	50.9	2258262.5	2190483.3	8858
贵 州	Guizhou	106.9	37.9	103.3	24.6	896899.7	870013.5	8375
云 南	Yunnan	120.0	44.1	118.2	26.7	1172857.9	1162662.3	9692
西 藏	Tibet	5.2	1.7	4.8	1.0	62701.7	60600.6	13288
陕 西	Shaanxi	172.4	60.5	168.5	35.7	1453370.0	1428795.8	8356
甘 肃	Gansu	122.0	44.6	119.8	25.8	1111032.4	1093922.7	9008
青 海	Qinghai	21.9	7.8	21.5	4.9	244113.0	241137.7	10165
宁 夏	Ningxia	34.2	12.3	33.3	7.0	313672.3	305682.6	9045
新 疆	Xinjiang	171.4	69.7	167.9	32.6	1568059.9	1547420.7	8646

5-29 分地区职业介绍工作情况（2000年底）

单位：人

地区	Region	本年末职业介绍机构个数(个) Number of Careers Service	本年末职业介绍机构人数 Staff and Workers in Careers Service	本年登记招聘人数 Total Registered Job Vacancies This Year	本年登记求职人数 Total Registered Job-seekers This Year	#女性 Female	#下岗职工 Laid-off Workers
全国	**National Total**	**29024**	**86742**	**15094189**	**19916690**	**8128199**	**3623737**
北京	Beijing	380	3920	825000	800000	380000	172000
天津	Tianjin	207	3144	346121	1415442		758998
河北	Hebei	1425	4201	493272	666295	285626	74638
山西	Shanxi	1969	5130	174306	212838	68713	49366
内蒙古	Inner Mongolia	719	1713	193785	257706	97833	65389
辽宁	Liaoning	1339	2939	750228	1173113	554750	434369
吉林	Jilin	827	2057	151562	206498	105507	84742
黑龙江	Heilongjiang	1139	2443	243181	466460	137178	201338
上海	Shanghai	465	2807	231425	202386	92030	41660
江苏	Jiangsu	1810	5332	726092	851301	472879	131010
浙江	Zhejiang	1801	4149	2060979	2366130	1035779	103784
安徽	Anhui	1886	5039	239267	551212	155611	83496
福建	Fujian	932	2404	613770	767551	396455	57968
江西	Jiangxi	889	2821	327477	468305	205227	101953
山东	Shandong	1295	3823	813454	1039103	474050	103147
河南	Henan	1351	4671	569874	1161360	540150	232490
湖北	Hubei	831	2894	705375	813776	309504	164254
湖南	Hunan	788	2232	627267	811768	407733	180425
广东	Guangdong	1446	5302	2151196	2249179	884351	63675
广西	Guangxi	422	1279	282800	410337	199545	40494
海南	Hainan	103	610	104871	212400	84960	5700
重庆	Chongqing	277	997	224561	275267	127203	54966
四川	Sichuan	1409	4834	630136	711456	354928	175305
贵州	Guizhou	1151	1911	118896	137762	63720	21889
云南	Yunnan	1311	2552	244913	248416	128376	24753
西藏	Tibet	8	47	70	508		27
陕西	Shaanxi	1323	3612	404956	466056	228584	57851
甘肃	Gansu	641	1643	232334	281505	115501	79524
青海	Qinghai	266	543	243067	256130	35885	23051
宁夏	Ningxia	226	558	53674	105102	30877	5698
新疆	Xinjiang	388	1135	310280	331328	155244	29777

Situations of Careers Service by Region (End of 2000)

(person)

#失业人员 Unemployment	#获得职业资格人员 person with Certificates	本年职业指导人数 Person-times of Vocational Guidance	本年介绍成功人数 Placed Job-seekers	#女性 Female	#下岗职工 Laid-off Workers	#失业人员 Unemployment	#获得职业资格人员 Person with Certificates
5881234	**3752214**	**10048334**	**9752428**	**4555588**	**1550220**	**2962448**	**1494794**
241000	286000	720000	280000	136000	92400	186000	168000
181171	925685	587371	189327	127418	72294	60813	100378
93406	76662	483371	434860	205446	62578	44304	60419
70230	11953	98646	142717	48457	29026	42775	10978
143777	10477	92021	159113	64481	44282	85922	8405
509348	208280	808139	622434	307023	184557	226092	39458
81982	27833	109286	96392	43040	29936	45051	19908
144093	43714	221753	239828	103999	98173	90471	28107
122686	15897	213612	71102	34031	17520	42098	5342
472637	230574	480841	515608	223797	73729	210824	119416
433364	131049	346107	1278159	558233	57281	237369	119922
127023	28576	180754	246585	95746	50489	63691	18438
198946	45339	302832	370689	221303	32360	119085	28652
165674	81414	210109	260478	124769	48328	112982	21709
340157	92163	388244	541124	266981	51537	165561	74659
361788	319175	724828	558776	305740	100561	85020	82680
290427	134609	500371	477833	217361	90967	191360	78985
265641	111412	503678	397935	211040	94796	134337	56092
356625	542880	976511	762860	377993	28395	146744	199462
174933	70693	197132	219090	107710	17128	88198	35646
167600	21240	61	40457	16292	1026	30168	3823
118918	34962	126991	147518	72635	20940	60402	18224
259734	137079	587427	426981	220563	102204	159109	66938
69707	9999	110513	88971	42813	10055	47655	5491
87716	28163	197634	180981	83046	15076	42822	16219
481	130	132	278	67	27	251	130
99630	69132	280708	237194	82415	50705	48864	61331
123881	32803	239377	210812	107012	42556	73283	27170
23794	4851	127662	228312	24604	11885	12235	3272
22327	3243	94703	69446	23519	4699	12757	3036
132538	16227	137520	256568	102054	14710	96205	12504

主 要 统 计 指 标 解 释

经济活动人口 指在16岁以上，有劳动能力，参加或要求参加社会经济活动的人口；包括从业人员和失业人员。

从业人员 指从事一定社会劳动并取得劳动报酬或经营收入的人员，包括全部职工、再就业的离退休人员、私营业主、个体户主、私营和个体从业人员、乡镇企业从业人员、农村从业人员、其他从业人员(包括民办教师、宗教职业者、现役军人等)。这一指标反映了一定时期内全部劳动力资源的实际利用情况，是研究我国基本国情国力的重要指标。

各单位的从业人员 指在各级国家机关、政党机关、社会团体及企业、事业单位中工作，取得工资或其他形式的劳动报酬的全部人员。包括在岗职工、再就业的离退休人员、民办教师以及在各单位中工作的外方人员和港澳台方人员、兼职人员、借用的外单位人员和第二职业者。不包括离开本单位仍保留劳动关系的职工。各单位的从业人员反映了各单位实际参加生产或工作的全部劳动力。

城镇私营和个体从业人员 城镇私营从业人员指在工商管理部门注册登记，其经营地址设在县城关镇(含城关镇)以上的私营企业从业人员；包括私营企业投资者和雇工。城镇个体从业人员指在工商管理部门注册登记，并持有城镇户口或在城镇长期居住，经批准从事个体工商经营的从业人员；包括个体经营者和在个体工商户劳动的家庭帮工和雇工。

城镇登记失业人员 指有非农业户口，在一定的劳动年龄内，有劳动能力，无业而要求就业，并在当地就业服务机构进行求职登记的人员。

城镇登记失业率 指城镇登记失业人数同城镇从业人数与城镇登记失业人数之和的比。计算公式为：

城镇登记失业率＝城镇登记失业人数／（城镇从业人数＋城镇登记失业人数）×100%

职工 指在国有经济、城镇集体经济、联营经济、股份制经济、外商和港、澳、台投资经济、其他经济单位及其附属机构工作，并由其支付工资的各类人员，不包括返聘的离退休人员、民办教师、在国有经济单位工作的外方人员和港、澳、台人员（1998年以后的数据均为在岗职工数据，其他相关指标如职工工资总额，职工平均工资等指标也从1998年按此口径进行了相应调整）。

国有单位职工 指在国有经济单位及其附属机构工作，并由其支付工资的各类人员。

城镇集体单位职工 指在城镇集体经济单位及其管理部门工作，并由其支付工资的各类人员。

其他单位职工 指在联营经济、股份制经济、外商投资经济、港、澳、台投资经济单位工作，并由其支付工资的各类人员。

在岗职工 指在本单位工作并由单位支付工资的人员，以及有工作岗位，但由于学习、病伤产假等原因暂未工作，仍由单位支付工资的人员。

职工工资总额 指各单位在一定时期内直接支付给本单位全部职工的劳动报酬总额。工资总额的计算原则应以直接支付给职工的全部劳动报酬为根据。各单位支付给职工的劳动报酬以及其他根据有关规定支付的工资，不论是计入成本的还是不计入成本的，不论是按国家规定列入计征奖金税项目的，还是未列入计征奖金税项目的，不论是以货币形式支付的还是以实物形式支付的，均包括在工资总额内。

职工平均工资 指企业、事业、机关单位的职工在一定时期内平均每人所得的货币工资额。它表明一定时期职工工资收入的高低程度，是反映职工工资水平的主要指标。计算公式为：

职工平均工资＝报告期实际支付的全部职工工资总额／报告期全部职工平均人数

职工平均工资指数 指报告期职工平均工资与基期职工平均工资的比率，是反映不同时期职工货币工资水平变动情况的相对数。计算公式为：

职工平均工资指数＝报告期职工平均工资／基期职工平均工资×100%

职工平均实际工资指数 职工平均实际工资指扣除物价变动因素后的职工平均工资。职工平均实际工资指数是反映实际工资变动情况的相对数，表明职工实际工资水平提高或降低的程度。计算公式为：

职工平均实际工资指数＝报告期职工平均工资指数／报告期城镇居民消费价格指数×100%

专业技术人员 指从事专业技术工作的人员以及从事专业技术管理工作且已在1983年以前评定了专业技术职称或在1984年以后聘任了专业技术职务的人员。

专业技术人员具体指工程技术人员、农业技术人员、科研人员（自然科学研究、社会科学研究及实验技术人员）、卫生技术人员、教学人员（含高等院校、中等专业学校、技工学校、中学、小学）、民用航空飞行技术人员、船舶技术人员、经济人员、会计人员、统计人员、翻译人员、图书资料、档案、文博人员、新闻、出版人员、律师、公证人员、广播电视播音人员、工艺美术人员、体育人员、艺术人员及政工人员。

专业技术管理人员具体指企业、事业单位的领导；企业、事业单位下设的职能机构、企业的生产车间和辅助车间（或附属辅助生产单位）中从事生产、技术、经济管理和政治工作人员。

按照公务员管理或参照公务员管理的人员不统计为专业技术人员。

Explanatory Notes on Main Statistical Indicators

Economically Active Population refers to the population aged 16 and over who are capable to work, are participating in or willing to participate in economic activities, including employed persons and unemployed persons.

Employed Persons refer to the persons who are engaged in social working and receive remuneration payment or earn business income, including total staff and workers, re-employed retirees, employers of private enterprises, self-employed workers, employees in private enterprises and individual economy, employees in township enterprises, employed persons in the rural areas, and other employed persons (including teachers in the schools run by the local people, people engaged in religious profession and the servicemen, etc.). This indicator reflects the actual utilization of total labour force during a certain period of time and is often used for the research on China's economic situation and national power.

Persons Employed in Various Units refer to all the persons working in government agencies of various levels, political and party organizations, social organizations, enterprises and institutions, and receiving wages or other forms of payment. They include fully-employed staff and workers, re-employed retirees, teachers in schools run by the local people, foreigners and Chinese compatriots from Hong Kong, Macao, and Taiwan working in various units, part-time employees, employees of other units working temporarily at current posts, and employees holding the second job, but exclude staff and workers who have left their working units while keeping their labour contract (employment relation) unchanged. This indicator reflects the total number of laborers actually engaged in production or other operations in various units.

Persons Employed in Private Enterprises and Self-Employed Individuals in Urban Areas Persons employed in private enterprises refer to the persons employed in the private enterprises which have been registered at the departments of industrial and commercial administration and are situated at a county town (i.e. a town where the county government is located) for business operation or at urban areas with the level higher than a county town. The self-employed individuals in urban areas refer to persons who hold the certificates of residence in urban areas or have resided in the urban areas for a long time and have been registered at the departments of industrial and commercial administration and approved to be engaged in individual industrial or commercial business, including self-employed persons as well as helpers and hired labourers who work in the individual households engaged in industrial or commercial business.

Registered Urban Unemployed Persons The registered unemployed persons in urban areas refer to the persons who are registered as permanent residents in the urban areas engaged in non-agricultural activities, aged within the range of working age, capable to labour, unemployed but desirous to be employed and have been registered at the local employment service agencies to apply for a job.

Registered Urban Unemployment Rate Registered unemployment rate in urban areas refers to the ratio of the number of the registered unemployed persons to the sum of the number of employed persons and the registered unemployed persons. The formula is as follows:

Registered urban unemployment rate = number of registered urban unemployed persons ÷ (number of urban employed persons + number of registered urban unemployed persons) × 100%.

Staff and Workers refer to the persons who work in (and receive payment therefrom) enterprises and institutions of state ownership, collective ownership, joint ownership, share holding, foreign ownership, and ownership by entrepreneurs from Hong Kong, Macao, and Taiwan, and other types of ownership and their affiliated units, excluding the retired persons invited to work in the units again, teachers in the schools run by the local people and foreigners and persons coming from Hong Kong, Macao and Taiwan and working in the state-owned economic units. (Number of staff and workers in this yearbook include only fully employed staff and workers, excluding those who have left their working units while keeping their labour contract/employment relation unchanged).

Staff and Workers in State-owned Economic Units refer to the persons who work in the state-owned economic units or their attached units and are listed in their payrolls.

Staff and Workers of Collective Owned Units in Urban Areas refer to the persons who work in collective owned units in urban areas and their administration departments and receive payment therefrom

Staff and Workers in Units of Other types of Ownership refer to those who work in (and receive payment therefrom) enterprises and institutions of joint ownership, share holding, foreign ownership, and ownership by entrepreneurs from Hong Kong, Macao, and Taiwan.

Fully Employed Staff and Workers refer to persons who work in, and receive wages from their working units, as well as persons who have their work posts, but are temporarily absent from work for reasons of study or on sick, injury or maternal leave and still receive wages from their working units.

Total Wages of Staff and Workers refer to the total remuneration payment to staff and workers in various units during a certain period of time. The calculation of total wages is based on the total remuneration payment to the staff and workers. Therefore, all the wages and salaries and other payments to staff and workers are included in the total wages regardless of their sources, category, and forms (in kind or cash). (Total wages of staff and workers in this yearbook include only total wages of fully employed staff and workers, excluding the living allowances distributed to those who have left their working units while keeping their labour contract/employment relation unchanged).

Average Wage of Staff and Workers refers to the average wage in money terms per person during a certain period of time for staff and workers in enterprises, institutions, and government agencies, which reflects the general level of wage income during a certain period of time and is calculated as follows:

Average Wage of Staff and Workers = Total Wages of Staff and Workers in Reference Period/Average Number of Staff and Workers in Reference Period.

Average Real Wage of Staff and Workers refers to average wage of staff and workers after removing the effects of price changes, which is calculated as follows:

Average Real Wage of Staff and Workers =Average Wage of Staff and Workers in Reference Period.

Professional Personnel refers to the persons who are engaged in special professional work or in professional management who got the titles of a professional post before 1983 or who were appointed to professional positions since 1984.

Professional personnel specifically refers to engineering professionals, agricultural professionals, scientific research professionals (natural science researchers, social science researchers and laboratory technicians), health professionals, teaching professionals (including institutions of higher education, specialized secondary schools, technical schools, regular secondary schools, and primary schools), civil aviation professionals, nautical professionals, economic professionals, accounting professionals, statistical professionals, interpretation professionals, library professionals, archives professionals, professionals of culture, arts and cultural relics, newsman and publishing professionals, lawyers, notary professionals, radio and television announcers, industrial arts professionals, sports professionals, artists and political professionals.

Professional management personnel specifically refers to the managers of enterprises and institutions, the personnel engaged in the management of production, techniques, economic and political aspects in the functional departments under the enterprise and institution, production workshops and accessorial workshops (or accessorial production units) under the enterprises.

Professional personnel excluded the personnel managed by or according to the system of civil servants.

六、固定资产投资

Investment in Fixed Assets

简要说明

一、固定资产投资统计的范围包括：基本建设投资，更新改造投资，房地产开发投资，国有其他固定资产投资，城镇集体固定资产投资，农村集体固定资产投资，城镇和工矿区私人建房投资，农村个人固定资产投资。从1999年起，城镇私营和个体投资纳入固定资产投资统计范围。

二、固定资产投资统计资料来源为：跨省、区项目资料来自国务院各部门；农村集体和农村个人固定资产投资资料由国家统计局农村经济调查总队根据乡村社会经济调查资料整理提供；除此以外固定资产投资统计资料均由国家统计局固定资产投资统计司整理提供。

三、固定资产投资统计的调查方法，除农村集体和农村个人固定资产投资统计采用抽样调查方法外，其他均为全面统计报表。

四、自1997年起，除房地产开发投资、农村集体投资、个人投资及城镇和工矿区私人建房投资外，基本建设、更新改造和其他固定资产投资的统计起点由5万元提高到50万元。为便于比较，对1996年的相应数据作了全面调整，括号内的数为原口径数。

Brief Introduction

I. The statistics of the investment in fixed assets cover the investment in capital construction, the investment in innovation, the investment in real estate development, the investment in other state-owned fixed assets, the investment in fixed assets by urban collective units, the investment in fixed assets by rural collective units, the housing investment by urban individuals and the investment in fixed assets by rural individuals. Starting from 1999, investment statistics also include investment in fixed assets by urban private units and individuals.

II. The data sources for the statistics of investment in fixed assets are as follows: The data on the trans-regional projects are provided by the various departments under the State Council. The data on the investment in fixed assets in collective units and by individuals in rural areas are prepared and provided by the Rural Socio-economic Survey Organization, NBS on the basis of the data collected by the survey on the rural social and economic development. The other statistical data on the investment in fixed assets are prepared and provided by the Department of Statistics of Investment in Fixed Assets, NBS.

III. Method of data collection: All the data on the investment in fixed assets are collected by the statistical reporting scheme with the coverage of complete enumeration, with the only exception that the data on the investment in fixed assets in collective units and by individuals in rural areas are collected by sample surveys.

IV. Since 1997, the cut-off point of projects to be covered in the investment statistics are modified from an investment of 50,000 yuan to 500,000 yuan in the statistics of investment in capital construction, investment in innovation and other investments, while the cut-off point of projects in the statistics of investment in real estate development, rural collective investment and individual investment remain unchanged. For the convenience of comparison, relevant data of 1996 are adjusted accordingly, and figures in brackets are compiled on the basis of the old coverage.

6-1 全社会固定资产投资

Total Investment in Fixed Assets

指　　标	Item	1999	2000	2000年比上年增长(%) Increase Rate in 2000 over 1999(%)
投资总额（亿元）	**Total Investment (100 million yuan)**	**29854.71**	**32917.73**	**10.3**
按经济类型分	Grouped by Ownership			
国有经济	State-owned Units	15947.76	16504.44	3.5
集体经济	Collective-owned Units	4338.55	4801.45	10.7
#农　村	Rural	3343.13	3791.62	13.4
个体经济	Individuals Economy	4195.70	4709.36	12.2
#农　村	Rural	2779.59	2904.26	4.5
联营经济	Joint Ownership Economic Units	97.90	94.73	-3.2
股份制经济	Share Holding Economic Units	2478.88	4061.88	63.9
外商投资经济	Foreign Funded Economic Units	1433.40	1313.21	-8.4
港澳台投资经济	Economic Units with Funds from Hong Kong, Macao and Taiwan	1218.07	1293.05	6.2
其他经济	Others	144.44	139.61	-3.3
按管理渠道分	Grouped by Channel of Management			
基本建设	Capital Construction	12455.28	13427.27	7.8
更新改造	Innovation	4485.08	5107.60	13.9
房地产开发	Real Estate Development	4103.20	4984.05	21.5
其他投资	Others	8811.15	9398.81	6.7
按资金来源分	Grouped by Source of Funds			
国家预算内资金	State Budgetary Appropriation	1852.14	2109.45	13.9
国内贷款	Domestic Loans	5725.93	6727.27	17.5
利用外资	Foreign Investment	2006.78	1696.24	-15.5
自筹资金	Fundraising	15885.26	17270.28	8.7
其他资金	Others	4284.54	5306.86	23.9
按构成分	Grouped by Use of Funds			
建筑安装工程	Construction and Installation	18795.93	20536.26	9.3
设备工具器具购置	Purchase of Equipment and Instruments	7053.04	7785.62	10.4
其他费用	Others	4005.74	4595.85	14.7
房屋建筑面积(万平方米)	**Floor Space of Buildings (10 000 sq.m)**			
施工面积	Floor Space under Construction	263294.25	265293.53	0.8
竣工面积	Floor Space Completed	187357.07	181974.44	-2.9
#住宅	Residential Buildings	139305.93	134528.83	-3.4

注：1.按资金来源分组为财务拨款数，各项相加不等于投资总额。以下各表同。
　　2.增长速度未扣除价格因素，以下各表同。

a)Total investment grouped by source of funds refers to financial appropriation, and the subentry figures do not add up to the total. The same as in the following tables.

b)The growth rates are calculated without removing the factor of price. The same as in the following tables.

6-2 全社会固定资产投资(按经济类型分)

Total Investment in Fixed Assets by Ownership

指 标 Item	总 计 Total	国有经济 State-owned Units	集体经济 Collective-owned Units	个体经济 Individuals Economy	其他经济 Other Types of Ownership
投资额（亿元） Investment (100 million yuan)					
1980	910.9	745.9	46.0	119.0	
1981	961.0	667.5	115.2	178.3	
1982	1230.4	845.3	174.3	210.8	
1983	1430.1	952.0	156.3	321.8	
1984	1832.9	1185.2	238.7	409.0	
1985	2543.2	1680.5	327.5	535.2	
1986	3120.6	2079.4	391.8	649.4	
1987	3791.7	2448.8	547.0	795.9	
1988	4753.8	3020.0	711.7	1022.1	
1989	4410.4	2808.2	570.0	1032.2	
1990	4517.0	2986.3	529.5	1001.2	
1991	5594.5	3713.8	697.8	1182.9	
1992	8080.1	5498.7	1359.4	1222.0	
1993	13072.3	7925.9	2317.3	1476.2	1352.9
1994	17042.1	9615.0	2758.9	1970.6	2697.6
1995	20019.3	10898.2	3289.4	2560.2	3271.5
1996	(22974.0)	(12056.2)	(3660.6)	(3211.2)	(4046.0)
	22913.5	12006.2	3651.5	3211.2	4044.6
1997	24941.1	13091.7	3850.9	3429.4	4569.1
1998	28406.2	15369.3	4192.2	3744.4	5100.3
1999	29854.7	15947.8	4338.6	4195.7	5372.7
2000	32917.7	16504.4	4801.5	4709.4	6902.5
增长速度（上年=100） Growth Rate (previous year=100)					
1981	5.5	-10.5	150.4	49.8	
1982	28.0	26.6	51.3	18.2	
1983	16.2	12.6	-10.3	52.7	
1984	28.2	24.5	52.7	27.1	
1985	38.8	41.8	37.2	30.9	
1986	22.7	23.7	19.6	21.3	
1987	21.5	17.8	39.6	22.6	
1988	25.4	23.3	30.1	28.4	
1989	-7.2	-7.0	-19.9	1.0	
1990	2.4	6.3	-7.1	-3.0	
1991	23.9	24.4	31.7	18.1	
1992	44.4	48.1	94.8	3.3	
1993	61.8	44.1	70.5	20.8	
1994	30.4	21.3	19.1	33.5	99.4
1995	17.5	13.3	19.2	29.9	21.3
1996	14.8	10.6	11.3	25.4	23.7
1997	8.8	9.0	5.5	6.8	13.0
1998	13.9	17.4	8.9	9.2	11.6
1999	5.1	3.8	3.5	7.9	5.3
2000	10.3	3.5	10.7	12.2	28.5

注：1.其他经济类型包括联营经济、股份制经济、外商投资经济、港澳台投资经济等国有、集体和个体经济以外的经济成份。

2.根据1994年房地产快速调查结果，对1990年至1994年的全社会固定资产投资数据进行了调整。

a)Other types of ownership refer to the types of ownership other than state-owned units, collective-owned units and individuals economy, including joint owner economic units, share holding economic units, foreign funded economic units, and economic units with funds from Hong Kong, Macao and Taiwan, etc.

b)The data of the total investment in fixed assets from 1990 to 1994 have been adjusted in accordance with the data obtained from the fast survey on the real estates in 1994.

6-3 全社会固定资产投资(按资金来源和构成分)

Total Investment in Fixed Assets by Source of Funds and Use of Funds

年份 Year	按资金来源分 Grouped by Source of Funds				按构成分 Grouped by Use of Funds		
	国家预算内资金 State Budgetary Appropriation	国内贷款 Domestic Loans	利用外资 Foreign Investment	自筹和其他资金 Fundraising and Others	建筑安装工程 Construction and Installation	设备工具器具购置 Purchase of Equipment and Instruments	其他费用 Others
投资额（亿元） Investment (100 million yuan)							
1981	269.76	122.00	36.36	532.89	689.83	223.64	47.54
1982	279.26	176.12	60.51	714.51	871.12	291.41	67.87
1983	339.71	175.50	66.55	848.30	993.32	358.31	78.43
1984	421.00	258.47	70.66	1082.74	1217.58	509.23	106.06
1985	407.80	510.27	91.48	1533.64	1655.46	718.08	169.65
1986	455.62	658.46	137.31	1869.19	2059.66	851.95	208.99
1987	496.64	871.98	181.97	2241.11	2475.65	1038.78	277.26
1988	431.96	977.84	275.31	2968.69	3099.66	1305.37	348.77
1989	366.05	762.98	291.08	2990.28	2994.59	1115.81	300.00
1990	393.03	885.45	284.61	2954.41	3008.72	1165.54	342.74
1991	380.43	1314.73	318.89	3580.44	3647.68	1460.19	486.63
1992	347.46	2214.03	468.66	5049.95	5163.37	2125.14	791.58
1993	483.67	3071.99	954.28	8562.36	8201.21	3315.92	1555.18
1994	529.57	3997.64	1768.95	11530.96	10786.52	4328.26	1928.08
1995	621.05	4198.73	2295.89	13409.19	13173.33	4262.46	2583.48
1996	(629.72)	(4576.53)	(2747.41)	(15465.35)	(15153.41)	(4940.79)	(2879.83)
	625.88	4573.69	2746.60	15412.40	15109.29	4925.98	2878.28
1997	696.74	4782.55	2683.89	17096.49	15614.03	6044.84	3282.25
1998	1197.39	5542.89	2617.03	19359.61	17874.53	6528.53	4003.10
1999	1852.14	5725.93	2006.78	20169.80	18795.93	7053.04	4005.74
2000	2109.45	6727.27	1696.24	22577.14	20536.26	7785.62	4595.85
构成(%) Percentage							
1981	28.1	12.7	3.8	55.4	71.8	23.3	4.9
1982	22.7	14.3	4.9	58.1	70.8	23.7	5.5
1983	23.8	12.3	4.7	59.2	69.5	25.1	5.4
1984	23.0	14.1	3.9	59.0	66.4	27.8	5.8
1985	16.0	20.1	3.6	60.3	65.1	28.2	6.7
1986	14.6	21.1	4.4	59.9	66.0	27.3	6.7
1987	13.1	23.0	4.8	59.1	65.3	27.4	7.3
1988	9.3	21.0	5.9	63.8	65.2	27.5	7.3
1989	8.3	17.3	6.6	67.8	67.9	25.3	6.8
1990	8.7	19.6	6.3	65.4	66.6	25.8	7.6
1991	6.8	23.5	5.7	64.0	65.2	26.1	8.7
1992	4.3	27.4	5.8	62.5	63.9	26.3	9.8
1993	3.7	23.5	7.3	65.5	62.7	25.4	11.9
1994	3.0	22.4	9.9	64.7	63.3	25.4	11.3
1995	3.0	20.5	11.2	65.3	65.8	21.3	12.9
1996	2.7	19.6	11.8	66.0	66.0	21.5	12.5
1997	2.8	18.9	10.6	67.7	62.6	24.2	13.2
1998	4.2	19.3	9.1	67.4	62.9	23.0	14.1
1999	6.2	19.2	6.7	67.8	63.0	23.6	13.4
2000	6.4	20.3	5.1	68.2	62.4	23.7	13.9

6-4 按经济类型分的全社会固定资产投资（2000年）

指　　标	Item	总　计 Total	国有经济 State-owned Units	集体经济 Collective-owned Units	#农　村 Rural
投资总额（亿元）	**Total Investment (100 million yuan)**	**32917.73**	**16504.44**	**4801.45**	**3791.62**
按资金来源分	Grouped by Source of Funds				
国家预算内资金	State Budgetary Appropriations	2109.45	1719.10	318.69	314.43
国内贷款	Domestic Loans	6727.27	4160.24	592.25	412.36
利用外资	Foreign Investment	1696.24	398.69	190.82	170.10
自筹资金	Fundraising	17270.28	7478.66	3200.50	2667.65
其他资金	Others	5306.86	2177.55	574.12	227.08
按构成分	Grouped by Use of Funds				
建筑安装工程	Construction and Installation	20536.26	10413.97	2708.97	2015.79
设备、工具、器具购置	Purchase of Equipment and Instruments	7785.62	3720.27	1655.82	1488.84
其他费用	Others	4595.85	2370.20	436.66	286.99
房屋建筑面积（万平方米）	**Floor Space of Buildings (10 000 sq.m)**				
施工面积	Floor Space under Construction	265293.53	67585.51	36889.63	25370.38
竣工面积	Floor Space Completed	181974.43	33953.87	26106.89	20196.32
#住宅	Residential Buildings	134528.83	20281.60	8000.32	4153.67
按地区分投资总额（亿元）	**Total Investment by Region (100 million yuan)**				
北　京	Beijing	1280.46	758.06	76.65	53.58
天　津	Tianjin	610.94	255.52	75.36	56.47
河　北	Hebei	1816.79	827.66	504.59	440.67
山　西	Shanxi	548.16	347.21	48.36	31.70
内蒙古	Inner Mongolia	423.64	263.04	27.14	19.13
辽　宁	Liaoning	1267.68	649.42	154.13	118.53
吉　林	Jilin	603.51	318.52	47.59	39.74
黑龙江	Heilongjiang	832.64	452.45	31.91	16.35
上　海	Shanghai	1869.38	826.83	265.75	161.32
江　苏	Jiangsu	2569.97	1137.93	624.44	482.85
浙　江	Zhejiang	2349.95	875.69	569.00	492.82
安　徽	Anhui	803.97	428.76	75.35	57.14
福　建	Fujian	1112.20	407.19	161.78	132.17
江　西	Jiangxi	516.08	279.78	60.33	49.87
山　东	Shandong	2531.10	1167.85	680.61	570.85
河　南	Henan	1377.74	728.56	204.44	179.68
湖　北	Hubei	1339.20	762.24	175.09	145.73
湖　南	Hunan	1012.24	520.08	118.79	100.02
广　东	Guangdong	3145.13	1260.84	356.55	214.28
广　西	Guangxi	583.34	314.77	38.09	27.92
海　南	Hainan	198.87	83.14	11.36	9.09
重　庆	Chongqing	572.59	268.79	68.52	47.59
四　川	Sichuan	1418.04	667.30	223.52	191.34
贵　州	Guizhou	396.98	247.73	28.32	20.37
云　南	Yunnan	683.96	437.27	61.99	51.61
西　藏	Tibet	64.05	61.42	0.17	0.00
陕　西	Shaanxi	653.67	428.82	44.78	31.14
甘　肃	Gansu	395.40	277.82	25.98	20.39
青　海	Qinghai	151.14	96.07	6.69	5.25
宁　夏	Ningxia	157.52	97.88	9.23	6.83
新　疆	Xinjiang	610.39	329.42	24.91	17.19
不分地区	Not Classified by Region	1021.01	926.38		

Total Investment in Fixed Assets by Ownership (2000)

个体经济 Individuals Economy	#农 村 Rural	联营经济 Joint Ownership Economic Units	股份制经济 Share Holding Economic Units	外商投资经济 Foreign Funded Economic Units	港澳台投资经济 Economic Units with Funds From Hong Kong, Macao and Taiwan	其他经济 Others Ownership
4709.36	**2904.26**	**94.73**	**4061.88**	**1313.21**	**1293.05**	**139.61**
0.68		1.19	60.37	3.83	2.33	3.26
234.92	69.11	16.86	1137.21	239.25	326.02	20.52
2.08		1.09	186.73	578.58	336.88	1.37
3765.50	2422.11	49.98	1914.79	340.79	445.90	74.16
798.02	413.03	32.37	1087.26	180.09	415.11	42.34
3666.57	2174.47	52.95	2313.19	574.11	723.85	82.65
550.07	450.06	25.52	924.89	552.51	323.14	33.40
492.72	279.73	16.26	823.80	186.59	246.06	23.56
119752.62	88231.83	719.47	24366.71	4849.16	10135.63	994.80
107128.46	81270.20	316.32	9500.84	1618.59	2904.26	445.20
97174.80	75515.31	145.83	6462.14	663.94	1601.03	199.16
69.35	30.58	1.24	186.01	64.86	124.19	0.10
43.97	13.10	1.64	121.51	81.04	15.02	16.88
283.24	182.34	9.34	104.15	54.03	27.88	5.90
56.03	34.44	5.75	47.03	32.05	11.16	0.57
74.21	45.88	0.05	53.17	2.74	1.35	1.94
149.10	82.05	2.43	182.15	53.65	72.99	3.81
87.21	32.75	1.84	108.64	18.04	17.74	3.93
82.52	41.99	1.58	250.39	5.84	7.56	0.39
56.03	10.36	15.03	394.78	220.32	86.36	4.28
374.00	273.59	1.85	142.85	199.17	88.16	1.57
368.09	225.89	2.66	430.99	49.05	45.14	9.33
178.77	120.64	6.48	62.51	35.30	11.67	5.13
175.88	87.09	7.25	96.52	125.50	130.63	7.45
137.13	90.01	0.45	19.59	9.74	8.64	0.42
353.93	254.11	5.36	218.23	63.70	38.62	2.80
319.56	254.95	1.77	74.76	13.39	26.32	8.94
187.08	84.88	3.94	139.61	23.70	36.77	10.77
281.89	202.40	1.36	49.80	24.72	13.69	1.91
460.05	250.58	10.30	479.75	140.71	416.34	20.59
162.15	85.59	0.69	35.17	14.75	13.49	4.23
34.68	19.18	1.09	42.44	12.23	12.14	1.79
116.29	43.10	3.16	80.36	12.86	19.11	3.50
231.57	147.37	3.14	229.98	27.42	23.66	11.45
84.09	49.90	0.55	29.62	3.25	2.90	0.52
110.42	72.61	0.53	48.98	8.52	13.25	3.00
1.27	0.00	0.03	0.92	0.02	0.18	0.04
85.44	70.32	1.52	75.93	7.71	6.70	2.77
42.95	32.76	2.69	33.22	4.06	3.53	5.15
14.34	7.72	0.22	31.47	1.62	0.63	0.10
25.44	21.72	0.77	22.07	1.71	0.28	0.14
62.69	36.35	0.01	174.66	1.53	16.97	0.20
			94.63			

6-5 国有经济按各种分组的固定资产投资

Investment in Fixed Assets of State-owned Units

指　　标	Item	1990	1995	1998	1999	2000
投资总额（亿元）	**Total Investment (100 million yuan)**	**2986.30**	**10898.24**	**15369.30**	**15947.76**	**16504.44**
按资金来源分	Grouped by Source of Funds					
国家预算内资金	State Budgetary Appropriation	394.27	544.98	1080.62	1555.89	1719.10
国内贷款	Domestic Loans	704.91	2578.19	3578.07	3737.61	4160.24
利用资金	Foreign Investment	271.80	859.38	665.89	612.24	398.69
自筹资金	Fundraising	1289.58	5307.15	7664.69	7441.67	7478.66
其他资金	Others	325.74	1731.82	2247.46	2240.08	2177.55
按构成分	Grouped by Use of Funds					
建筑安装工程	Construction and Installation	1789.44	6604.61	9594.45	10477.19	10413.97
设备、工具、器具购置	Purchase of Equipment and Instruments	892.09	2750.51	3315.78	3336.31	3720.27
其他费用	Others	304.77	1543.12	2459.07	2134.26	2370.20
按建设性质分	Grouped by Type of Construction					
#新建	New Construction	911.60	3362.17	5507.37	5639.07	6133.01
扩建	Expansion	1161.72	3722.60	4984.90	4748.68	4732.19
改建	Reconstruction	581.25	1986.23	3058.98	3434.81	3052.76
按产业分	Grouped by Type of Industry					
第一产业	Primary Industry	28.65	73.64	201.32	251.58	303.80
第二产业	Secondary Industry	1765.69	4692.72	4874.79	4805.91	4820.51
第三产业	Tertiary Industry	1191.96	6131.88	10293.19	10890.27	11380.13
按国民经济主要行业分	Grouped by Main Sector					
#农业	Agriculture	34.09	93.40	237.08	304.03	357.42
工业	Industry	1747.58	4526.20	4703.30	4591.06	4578.68
#能源工业	Energy	823.88	2025.28	2862.10	2963.21	2839.58
运输邮电业	Transport, Postal and Telecommunication Services	333.67	2306.54	4695.28	4642.61	4902.23
新增固定资产(亿元)	**Newly Increased Fixed Assets (100 million yuan)**	**2408.45**	**7390.14**	**11471.31**	**12252.69**	**12924.63**
房屋建筑面积(万平方米)	**Floor Space of Buildings (10000 sq.m)**					
施工面积	Floor Space under Construction	41695	70420	73606	72981	67586
竣工面积	Floor Space Completed	20481	31829	33907	38059	33954
#住宅	Residential Buildings	10189	17714	20288	24519	20282

注：1.改建投资中含单纯建造生活设施投资。

2.按国民经济行业分、按建设性质分不含房地产投资，其他统计分组均含。以下各表同。

3.根据新国民经济核算标准，对第一产业投资进行了调整。

a)The investment in reconstruction includes the investment in construction of facilities simply for the improvement of residents' life.

b)The total investment grouped by main sector and by type of construction exclude the investment in the real estate development, and total investment grouped by others include that.The same as in the following tables.

c)Data on the investment in primary industry has been adjusted according to the new classification standards of national economic accounting.

6-6 基本建设和更新改造投资

Investment in Capital Construction and Innovation

单位：亿元 (100 million yuan)

年 份 Year	基本建设投资 Investment in Capital Construction	#国家预算内投资 State Budgetary Appropriation	更新改造投资 Investment in Innovation	#国家预算内投资 State Budgetary Appropriation
1953	90.44	75.49	1.15	
1957	143.32	131.48	7.91	
1958	269.00	216.44	10.06	
1959	349.72	272.07	18.30	
1960	388.69	301.75	27.89	
1961	127.42	93.87	28.64	
1962	71.26	60.25	16.02	
1963	98.16	84.69	18.50	
1964	144.12	123.96	21.77	
1965	179.61	163.09	37.29	
1966	209.42	188.30	45.38	
1967	140.17	124.86	47.55	
1968	113.06	103.79	38.51	
1969	200.83	181.60	46.09	
1970	312.55	272.73	55.53	
1971	340.84	282.77	76.47	
1972	327.98	264.41	84.83	
1973	338.10	282.20	100.02	
1974	347.71	289.76	115.48	
1975	409.32	335.58	135.62	
1976	376.44	310.93	147.50	
1977	382.37	299.23	165.93	
1978	500.99	389.21	167.73	
1979	523.48	396.92	175.88	
1980	558.89	300.11	187.01	
1981	442.91	222.62	195.30	34.88
1982	555.53	232.48	250.37	32.95
1983	594.13	295.97	291.13	36.55
1984	743.15	359.85	309.28	45.57
1985	1074.37	381.18	449.14	19.69
1986	1176.11	417.39	619.21	20.58
1987	1343.10	438.52	758.59	32.35
1988	1574.31	381.66	980.55	27.02
1989	1551.74	323.33	788.78	14.15
1990	1703.81	363.59	830.19	17.56
1991	2115.80	348.45	1023.23	17.36
1992	3012.65	307.87	1461.10	20.11
1993	4615.50	431.76	2195.85	31.31
1994	6436.74	434.57	2918.61	30.60
1995	7403.62	491.67	3299.35	38.32
1996	(8610.84)	(524.38)	(3622.74)	(29.58)
	8570.79	521.11	3615.00	29.31
1997	9917.02	574.51	3921.94	36.48
1998	11916.42	1021.32	4516.75	60.96
1999	12455.28	1478.88	4485.08	107.48
2000	13427.27	1594.07	5107.60	155.31

注：1980年及以前年份更新改造投资中含国有经济其他固定资产投资。

a)Before 1981,the data on the investment in innovation included other investments in fixed assets of state-owned units.

6-7 按资金来源和隶属关系分的基本建设投资
Investment in Capital Construction by Source of Funds and Administrative Relationship

单位：亿元 (100 million yuan)

年份 Year 地区 Region	按资金来源分 By Source of Funds					按隶属关系分 By Administrative Relationship	
	国家预算内资金 State Budgetary Appropriations	国内贷款 Domestic Loans	利用外资 Foreign Investment	自筹资金 Fund-Raising	其他资金 Others	中央项目 Central Government Projects	地方项目 Local Projects
1978	389.21		28.16	83.62		266.43	234.56
1979	396.92	5.31	16.34	104.91		273.20	250.28
1980	300.11	41.22	53.65	163.90		292.61	266.28
1981	222.62	44.60	34.82	140.87		241.03	201.88
1982	232.48	72.87	57.41	170.16	22.61	296.57	258.96
1983	295.97	53.74	63.25	152.96	28.21	355.03	239.10
1984	359.85	78.59	67.04	193.05	44.62	441.17	301.98
1985	381.18	187.92	73.52	339.99	91.76	575.24	499.13
1986	417.39	200.13	109.54	344.65	104.40	632.52	543.59
1987	438.52	255.46	139.01	382.78	127.33	761.66	581.44
1988	381.66	284.66	218.31	488.75	200.92	873.71	700.60
1989	323.33	293.00	221.45	495.03	218.91	837.71	714.03
1990	363.59	378.62	224.05	529.92	207.62	919.15	784.67
1991	348.45	527.07	239.96	746.73	253.59	1060.44	1055.37
1992	307.87	831.48	334.15	1242.92	296.24	1341.69	1670.96
1993	431.76	1117.55	456.15	1991.25	608.57	1834.90	2780.60
1994	434.57	1583.45	912.03	2820.48	584.48	2430.75	4005.99
1995	491.67	1646.24	1055.42	3121.86	899.98	2970.67	4432.95
1996	(524.38)	(1938.86)	(1235.43)	(3778.83)	(965.00)	(3379.33)	(5231.50)
	521.11	1937.76	1234.84	3752.32	956.86	3376.28	5194.50
1997	574.51	2239.88	1351.92	4432.24	1036.13	3858.22	6058.80
1998	1021.32	2814.36	1445.78	4870.26	1461.22	4122.92	7793.51
1999	1478.88	2972.04	1064.15	4857.15	1467.25	4046.79	8408.49
2000	1594.07	3586.35	852.18	5233.10	1396.78	4290.92	9136.35
北京 Beijing	92.56	87.11	14.23	214.76	24.95	182.22	264.76
天津 Tianjin	16.47	49.70	67.89	122.90	18.05	127.68	152.68
河北 Hebei	32.66	145.23	25.84	268.36	89.11	157.13	467.35
山西 Shanxi	28.18	65.65	27.86	76.10	44.56	107.70	170.80
内蒙古 Inner Mongolia	35.79	48.21	12.89	80.90	38.45	27.58	201.83
辽宁 Liaoning	58.01	124.70	39.28	172.18	43.60	132.90	318.46
吉林 Jilin	26.67	66.37	14.44	105.19	40.61	69.06	207.59
黑龙江 Heilongjiang	30.95	77.75	13.42	148.70	80.64	110.79	269.04
上海 Shanghai	33.30	141.26	71.42	309.24	40.23	145.21	558.29
江苏 Jiangsu	52.43	193.09	42.44	355.07	44.12	147.82	603.48
浙江 Zhejiang	49.07	213.67	79.54	382.99	66.94	190.41	630.57
安徽 Anhui	39.60	67.29	12.48	120.27	36.58	45.14	272.87
福建 Fujian	37.48	80.60	31.87	113.13	32.25	38.66	295.93
江西 Jiangxi	40.14	65.09	4.84	64.19	24.05	68.89	129.72
山东 Shandong	46.71	231.34	31.21	373.65	68.60	193.34	568.89
河南 Henan	72.42	150.51	26.71	238.43	82.14	208.80	377.36
湖北 Hubei	102.98	156.52	16.50	191.32	91.57	280.31	320.13
湖南 Hunan	45.66	95.14	7.98	135.33	44.92	114.93	252.49
广东 Guangdong	33.61	249.06	154.70	580.17	67.68	128.79	1004.54
广西 Guangxi	36.97	73.86	12.67	102.96	36.95	71.48	196.06
海南 Hainan	13.22	25.52	29.28	64.39	17.37	18.33	113.68
重庆 Chongqing	50.00	53.27	2.21	71.25	30.77	28.70	186.88
四川 Sichuan	40.31	180.60	35.58	261.39	84.73	133.53	503.40
贵州 Guizhou	26.82	56.38	6.96	48.71	15.42	35.86	112.13
云南 Yunnan	33.80	83.92	2.39	148.51	36.32	103.13	238.78
西藏 Tibet	37.17	2.12	0.02	13.23	6.01	9.91	44.77
陕西 Shaanxi	43.48	71.92	12.43	103.75	55.83	70.23	233.33
甘肃 Gansu	29.89	72.11	4.85	57.98	38.15	65.73	142.55
青海 Qinghai	21.14	26.31	1.50	23.10	21.39	42.95	56.04
宁夏 Ningxia	15.17	35.52	1.97	22.79	8.39	19.65	66.56
新疆 Xinjiang	42.78	94.84	8.52	185.76	42.81	234.37	158.37
不分地区 Not Classified by Region	328.66	501.68	38.28	76.45	23.59	979.67	17.02

注：1993年以后的资金来源为财务拨款数。以下各表同。
a)Since 1993, the source of funds refers to financial appropriation.The same as in the following tables.

6-8 按构成和建设性质分的基本建设投资
Investment in Capital Construction by Use of Funds and Type of Construction

单位：亿元 (100 million yuan)

年份 地区	Year Region	投资额 Total	按构成分 By Use of Funds 建筑安装工程 Construction and Installation	设备、工器具购置 Purchase of Equipment and Instruments	其他费用 Others	按建设性质分 By Type of Construction #新建 New Construction	#扩建 Expansion	#改建 Reconstruction
	1978	500.99	300.85	165.78	34.36	286.62	187.58	
	1979	523.48	343.80	143.64	36.04	279.67	210.38	
	1980	558.89	381.07	136.53	41.29	290.24	237.49	
	1981	442.91	317.32	84.22	41.37	218.27	142.17	67.32
	1982	555.53	397.35	101.67	56.51	269.90	168.17	96.78
	1983	594.13	414.99	117.13	62.01	272.47	177.04	94.35
	1984	743.15	507.71	151.88	83.56	349.81	237.25	117.70
	1985	1074.37	726.71	217.39	130.27	481.42	350.29	171.60
	1986	1176.11	770.60	260.34	145.17	549.89	415.01	154.64
	1987	1343.10	856.76	325.19	161.15	610.16	507.87	140.52
	1988	1574.31	1010.15	372.61	191.55	726.65	566.59	179.30
	1989	1551.74	998.73	380.94	172.07	708.49	569.54	159.49
	1990	1703.81	1045.37	453.76	204.69	822.96	610.99	175.28
	1991	2115.80	1308.83	521.22	285.76	983.06	778.86	230.39
	1992	3012.65	1889.39	667.34	455.92	1484.57	1003.45	351.45
	1993	4615.50	3018.74	899.55	697.22	2400.13	1472.47	296.78
	1994	6436.74	4123.89	1402.84	910.01	3523.90	1898.03	383.41
	1995	7403.62	4641.13	1635.04	1127.44	3971.94	2348.01	443.32
	1996	(8610.84)	(5345.27)	(1861.15)	(1404.42)	(4600.81)	(2797.68)	(521.42)
		8570.79	5310.07	1857.29	1403.43	4590.02	2782.24	516.56
	1997	9917.02	6215.22	2060.60	1641.20	5513.98	3030.69	611.36
	1998	11916.42	7695.75	2101.83	2118.84	6765.24	3204.87	1032.42
	1999	12455.28	8543.60	2132.30	1779.39	6775.46	3241.87	1250.68
	2000	13427.27	8936.81	2457.88	2032.59	7324.86	3368.07	1685.57
北京	Beijing	446.98	284.90	47.09	114.99	135.91	247.75	28.37
天津	Tianjin	280.36	190.19	65.70	24.47	189.14	49.14	28.10
河北	Hebei	624.48	444.21	106.52	73.74	390.03	131.64	58.56
山西	Shanxi	278.50	189.16	55.46	33.88	150.70	51.86	44.02
内蒙古	Inner Mongolia	229.40	170.26	33.62	25.53	61.77	100.92	47.52
辽宁	Liaoning	451.37	309.51	77.69	64.17	221.97	120.35	78.21
吉林	Jilin	276.65	228.84	26.58	21.23	122.94	80.82	51.69
黑龙江	Heilongjiang	379.82	286.46	52.96	40.40	203.16	119.73	26.24
上海	Shanghai	703.50	282.82	193.68	226.99	515.16	119.08	25.35
江苏	Jiangsu	751.30	565.03	100.43	85.84	337.15	264.80	137.44
浙江	Zhejiang	820.98	527.79	135.09	158.11	521.58	178.91	93.00
安徽	Anhui	318.01	221.91	52.35	43.74	189.69	83.55	28.82
福建	Fujian	334.59	229.74	59.66	45.20	225.46	61.97	37.99
江西	Jiangxi	198.61	140.59	36.28	21.74	84.16	56.84	53.28
山东	Shandong	762.23	522.59	173.25	66.39	270.17	358.93	76.75
河南	Henan	586.16	354.42	153.32	78.42	344.27	128.10	81.11
湖北	Hubei	600.44	365.07	95.33	140.04	362.80	128.11	74.32
湖南	Hunan	367.42	275.02	48.27	44.13	186.01	97.45	55.11
广东	Guangdong	1133.32	748.01	200.88	184.44	825.03	214.88	60.48
广西	Guangxi	267.54	192.54	38.54	36.46	130.13	56.97	68.80
海南	Hainan	132.02	75.31	38.53	18.18	79.99	27.26	2.47
重庆	Chongqing	215.58	165.54	24.36	25.68	111.00	49.51	31.07
四川	Sichuan	636.92	440.59	118.70	77.64	315.99	164.27	90.81
贵州	Guizhou	147.99	111.12	16.25	20.62	74.78	42.04	20.18
云南	Yunnan	341.91	255.55	44.14	42.22	200.87	77.02	39.06
西藏	Tibet	54.67	51.39	1.92	1.36	37.23	2.38	13.28
陕西	Shaanxi	303.56	235.07	32.47	36.02	177.92	61.13	32.58
甘肃	Gansu	208.28	157.29	26.72	24.26	106.31	50.07	26.55
青海	Qinghai	98.99	84.63	9.34	5.01	62.68	11.48	17.82
宁夏	Ningxia	86.21	66.08	12.21	7.92	46.69	19.49	16.91
新疆	Xinjiang	392.75	296.58	62.70	33.47	124.28	114.59	112.14
不分地区	Not Classified by Region	996.69	468.58	317.82	210.30	519.90	97.05	127.54

注：1980年以前按建设性质分的的扩建中含改建。

a)Before 1980, investment in expansion by type of construction include investment in reconstruction.

6-9 国民经济各行业按建设性质分的基本建设投资（2000年）

Investment in Capital Construction by Type of Construction and by Sector (2000)

单位：亿元 (100 million yuan)

行业	Sector	投资额 Investment	#新建 New Construction	#扩建 Expansion	#改建 Reconstruction
全国总计	**National Total**	**13427.27**	**7324.86**	**3368.07**	**1685.57**
农、林、牧、渔业	**Farming, Forestry, Animal Husbandry and Fishery**	**360.93**	**247.80**	**63.95**	**31.57**
农业	Farming	105.59	53.82	19.50	19.29
林业	Forestry	174.22	146.16	22.12	4.71
畜牧业	Animal Husbandry	17.32	11.57	4.19	0.94
渔业	Fishery	8.86	6.08	2.29	0.07
农林牧渔服务业	Agricultural Services	54.94	30.17	15.84	6.55
采掘业	**Mining and Quarrying**	**589.36**	**271.37**	**162.39**	**143.12**
煤炭采选业	Coal Mining and Dressing	116.34	86.30	23.53	0.38
石油和天然气开采业	Extraction of Petroleum and Natural Gas	420.66	167.98	112.02	139.06
黑色金属矿采选业	Mining and Dressing of Ferrous Metals	12.81	1.39	8.76	0.01
有色金属矿采选业	Mining and Dressing of Nonferrous Metals	12.10	3.92	7.20	0.09
非金属矿采选业	Mining and Dressing of Nonmetal Minerals	5.73	2.30	2.63	0.35
其他矿采选业	Mining and Dressing of Other Minerals	0.15	0.15	0.00	0.00
木材及竹材采运业	Logging and Transport of Wood and Bamboo	21.57	9.34	8.25	3.22
制造业	**Manufacturing**	**1175.11**	**657.80**	**343.13**	**39.91**
食品加工业	Food Processing	32.43	20.64	8.09	0.84
食品制造业	Food Production	37.57	30.96	4.09	0.67
饮料制造业	Beverages	26.27	17.22	6.73	0.46
烟草加工业	Tobacco	18.23	2.33	12.07	2.12
纺织业	Textiles	29.57	13.70	6.77	0.94
服装及纤维制品制造业	Garments and Other Fiber Products	17.67	11.71	4.67	0.45
皮革毛皮羽绒及其制品业	Leather, Furs, Down and Related Products	12.18	9.68	1.52	0.46
木材加工及竹藤棕草制品业	Timber Processing, Bamboo, Cane, Palm Fiber and Straw Products	8.22	6.33	1.13	0.10
家具制造业	Furniture Manufacturing	7.15	5.84	0.65	0.01
造纸及纸制品业	Papermaking and Paper Products	39.54	31.82	6.04	0.35
印刷业、记录媒介的复制	Printing and Record Medium Reproduction	13.05	4.09	5.28	1.23
文教体育用品制造业	Cultural, Educational and Sports Goods	2.66	1.57	0.68	0.01
石油加工及炼焦业	Petroleum Processing and Coking	32.79	11.12	15.49	1.89
化学原料及化学制品制造业	Raw Chemical Materials and Chemical Products	172.18	114.79	46.69	1.72
医药制造业	Medical and Pharmaceutical Products	42.42	26.39	11.43	0.49
化学纤维制造业	Chemical Fiber	11.79	2.87	6.52	0.22
橡胶制品业	Rubber Products	8.40	3.22	4.77	0.05
塑料制品业	Plastic Products	27.70	20.53	5.07	0.32
非金属矿物制品业	Nonmetal Mineral Products	61.42	38.84	11.23	2.52
黑色金属冶炼及压延加工业	Smelting and Pressing of Ferrous Metals	50.85	17.90	26.30	2.73
有色金属冶炼及压延加工业	Smelting and Pressing of Nonferrous Metals	39.76	11.96	23.14	0.94
金属制品业	Metal Products	17.28	11.97	3.40	0.44
普通机械制造业	Ordinary Machinery	31.18	12.74	5.63	1.54
专用设备制造业	Equipment for Special Purposes	29.93	10.66	10.51	1.82
交通运输设备制造业	Transport Equipment	107.56	45.80	31.22	11.29
电气机械及器材制造业	Electric Equipment and Machinery	29.19	16.77	5.53	3.01
电子及通信设备制造业	Electronic and Telecommunications Equipment	214.80	137.52	62.15	1.98
仪器仪表及文化办公用机械制造业	Instruments, Meters, Cultural and Office Machinery	9.21	5.88	1.36	0.21
其他制造业	Other Manufacturing	44.11	12.95	14.96	1.13
电力、煤气及水的生产和供应业	**Production and Supply of Electric Power, Gas and Water**	**2479.80**	**1315.18**	**655.40**	**482.57**
电力、蒸汽、热水生产和供应业	Production and Supply of Electric Power, Steam and Hot Water	2267.08	1191.65	588.00	466.54
煤气的生产和供应业	Production and Supply of Gas	55.74	33.68	12.78	8.03
自来水的生产和供应业	Production and Supply of Tap Water	156.97	89.85	54.62	8.01
建筑业	**Construction**	**197.47**	**86.23**	**38.95**	**38.79**
土木工程建筑业	Civil Engineering Construction	186.27	82.29	34.38	37.93

6-9 续表 1 continued

单位：亿元 (100 million yuan)

行业	Sector	投资额 Investment	#新建 New Construction	#扩建 Expansion	#改建 Reconstruction
线路、管道和设备安装业	Installation of lines, Pipelines and Equipment	8.50	1.53	4.35	0.84
装修装饰业	Fitting and Decoration	2.70	2.41	0.23	0.02
地质勘查、水利管理业	**Geological Prospecting and Water Conservancy**	**596.64**	**300.31**	**132.17**	**148.49**
地质勘查业	Geological Prospecting	16.56	3.14	8.75	1.35
水利管理业	Water Conservancy	580.08	297.17	123.42	147.14
交通运输、仓储及邮电通信业	**Transport, Storage, Postal and Telecommunication Services**	**3641.94**	**2080.39**	**694.96**	**493.38**
铁路运输业	Railway Transport	672.25	282.64	143.68	84.66
公路运输业	Highway Transport	1317.61	1003.10	90.34	214.23
管道运输业	Pipeline Transport	23.59	20.79	0.33	2.24
水上运输业	Waterway Transport	46.94	16.43	24.78	5.21
航空运输业	Air Transport	209.00	22.86	21.91	0.80
交通运输辅助业	Transport Subsidiary Services	578.14	302.12	109.37	158.28
其他交通运输业	Other Transport	31.41	19.66	3.96	7.02
仓储业	Storage	83.96	41.83	37.95	1.83
邮电通信业	Postal and Telecommunications Services	679.04	370.95	262.63	19.11
批发和零售贸易餐饮业	**Wholesale & Retail Trade and Catering Services**	**292.59**	**168.50**	**74.79**	**21.79**
食品饮料烟草和家庭用品批发业	Wholesale Trade of Food, Beverage, Tobacco and Household Articles	91.03	51.85	26.05	4.64
能源材料和机械电子设备批发业	Wholesale Trade of Energy, Materials and Electronic Equipment	41.91	17.15	11.71	2.77
其他批发业	Other Wholesale Trade	22.99	13.87	5.14	1.18
零售业	Retail Trade	118.65	74.73	28.11	10.50
商业经纪与代理业	Commercial Brokerage and Agencies	3.13	1.70	0.78	0.51
餐饮业	Catering Trade	14.88	9.20	3.00	2.19
金融、保险业	**Finance and Insurance**	**90.26**	**38.33**	**28.48**	**4.37**
金融业	Finance	79.05	32.06	25.82	4.16
保险业	Insurance	11.22	6.27	2.66	0.21
房地产业	**Real Estate**	**151.71**	**96.34**	**9.74**	**13.61**
房地产开发与经营业	Real Estate Development and Operation	102.60	70.63	5.79	10.14
房地产管理业	Real Estate Management	47.80	24.58	3.88	3.46
房地产代理与经纪业	Real Estate Brokerage and Agencies	1.31	1.13	0.07	0.00
社会服务业	**Social Services**	**1611.52**	**1071.64**	**360.65**	**143.37**
公共设施服务业	Public Services	1402.70	930.27	314.60	129.51
居民服务业	Resident Services	10.28	4.91	2.60	1.60
旅馆业	Hotels	82.92	50.71	22.82	7.58
租赁服务业	Leasing Services	2.99	2.92	0.06	0.01
旅游业	Tourism	29.01	16.88	9.92	1.14
娱乐服务业	Recreational Services	32.73	27.15	3.20	1.63
信息、咨询服务业	Information and Consultative Services	3.36	2.07	0.59	0.31
计算机应用服务业	Computer Application Services	25.44	23.45	1.28	0.01
其他社会服务业	Other Social Services	22.08	13.25	5.58	1.59
卫生体育和社会福利业	**Health Care, Sports and Social Welfare**	**218.36**	**89.09**	**87.58**	**12.40**
卫生	Health Care	152.89	39.80	79.32	9.68
体育	Sports	48.67	40.53	5.90	1.09
社会福利保障业	Social Welfare and Social Security	16.80	8.76	2.35	1.63
教育、文化艺术和广播电影电视业	**Education, Culture and Arts, Radio, Film and Television**	**823.37**	**308.19**	**379.31**	**38.74**
教育	Education	661.67	210.56	333.58	31.05
文化艺术业	Culture and Arts	99.66	65.35	24.43	4.69
广播、电影、电视业	Radio, Film and Television	62.04	32.29	21.31	3.00
科学研究和综合技术服务业	**Scientific Research and Polytechnic Services**	**103.10**	**39.64**	**43.11**	**5.25**
科学研究业	Scientific Research	61.52	17.03	31.62	3.20
综合技术服务业	Polytechnic Services	41.57	22.61	11.49	2.05
国家机关、政党机关和社会团体	**Governments Agencies, Party agencies and Social Organizations**	**878.18**	**393.04**	**266.13**	**63.32**
#国家机关	Governments	835.91	378.03	247.17	60.54
政党机关	Party	25.57	5.75	14.29	1.53
其他行业	**Others**	**216.94**	**161.02**	**27.33**	**4.90**

注：改建不含单纯建造生活设施投资。

a) Investment in reconstruction excludes that only for human services.

6-10 按国民经济行业分的基本建设投资

单位：亿元

年份 地区	Year Region	合计 Total	农、林、牧、渔业 Farming, Forestry, Animal Husbandry and Fishery	采掘业 Mining and Quarrying	制造业 Manufacturing	电力、煤气及水的生产和供应业 Production and Supply of Electric Power, Gas and Water	建筑业 Construction	地质勘查业水利管理业 Geological Prospecting and Water Conservancy
	1978	500.99	17.95		273.16		8.84	46.33
	1979	523.48	22.44		256.85		11.47	42.36
	1980	558.89	24.96		275.61		11.22	29.56
	1981	442.91	15.72		216.01		9.09	15.63
	1982	555.53	15.99		260.61		10.52	20.33
	1983	594.13	13.84		282.28		10.52	24.45
	1984	743.15	16.68		341.59		11.24	23.54
	1985	1074.37	16.71	101.56	223.33	121.60	22.00	26.45
	1986	1176.11	15.81	109.11	243.90	178.63	18.53	26.36
	1987	1343.10	19.61	129.68	322.80	230.31	15.43	29.82
	1988	1574.31	23.10	153.17	385.57	273.84	15.26	29.01
	1989	1551.74	20.20	170.68	361.14	290.40	13.84	35.62
	1990	1703.81	25.78	204.64	382.03	365.93	10.41	46.21
	1991	2115.80	33.46	243.31	477.96	425.94	12.60	59.03
	1992	3012.65	43.51	303.22	599.31	555.78	23.25	81.80
	1993	4615.50	46.22	351.32	884.52	768.61	115.02	98.38
	1994	6436.74	56.77	394.55	1216.33	1150.79	138.35	120.61
	1995	7403.62	76.59	437.77	1540.08	1258.49	145.55	165.83
	1996	(8610.84)	(111.30)	(498.75)	(1681.22)	(1546.83)	(183.70)	(228.46)
		8570.79	109.40	498.56	1679.71	1545.97	183.36	227.90
	1997	9917.02	153.88	648.57	1532.05	1938.89	150.95	277.42
	1998	11916.42	225.38	540.52	1484.08	2144.55	158.28	433.16
	1999	12455.28	299.01	474.19	1182.72	2193.18	223.65	556.56
	2000	13427.27	360.93	589.36	1175.11	2479.80	197.47	596.64
北京	Beijing	446.98	3.62	0.32	39.48	50.85	6.27	3.82
天津	Tianjin	280.36	0.88	59.85	70.13	34.80	7.11	10.34
河北	Hebei	624.48	18.06	15.23	60.51	138.96	5.02	28.28
山西	Shanxi	278.50	4.58	20.65	16.74	108.85	3.27	5.80
内蒙古	Inner Mongolia	229.40	15.20	6.97	21.27	33.12	1.43	17.45
辽宁	Liaoning	451.37	7.20	35.90	49.09	83.72	8.69	12.31
吉林	Jilin	276.65	3.21	17.62	31.05	47.64	5.40	4.92
黑龙江	Heilongjiang	379.82	10.43	32.42	24.39	61.87	14.55	11.50
上海	Shanghai	703.50	4.09	7.68	139.62	81.51	0.03	9.98
江苏	Jiangsu	751.30	6.89	7.33	75.12	148.70	20.99	47.64
浙江	Zhejiang	820.98	2.59	0.04	45.32	175.14	4.00	46.45
安徽	Anhui	318.01	3.99	10.45	32.44	40.04	9.88	28.85
福建	Fujian	334.59	8.30	1.19	37.52	86.98	2.81	12.86
江西	Jiangxi	198.61	2.32	1.32	11.59	56.22	1.71	26.01
山东	Shandong	762.23	7.74	66.40	73.61	163.34	15.96	20.01
河南	Henan	586.16	11.68	25.26	57.30	123.05	3.25	59.38
湖北	Hubei	600.44	12.72	7.23	40.07	203.61	17.06	28.90
湖南	Hunan	367.42	3.96	0.65	12.41	84.18	1.09	28.81
广东	Guangdong	1133.32	9.04	4.75	170.61	146.70	33.89	34.38
广西	Guangxi	267.54	7.43	1.05	13.33	77.79	1.69	16.07
海南	Hainan	132.02	16.15	5.43	11.70	11.43	1.01	2.87
重庆	Chongqing	215.58	6.08	0.38	10.84	39.21	2.20	6.78
四川	Sichuan	636.92	12.77	4.27	39.04	124.04	7.28	19.43
贵州	Guizhou	147.99	3.38	1.98	7.37	39.14	1.68	3.90
云南	Yunnan	341.91	9.46	2.59	13.97	59.63	1.61	12.77
西藏	Tibet	54.67	2.44	0.06	0.56	7.83	4.05	1.80
陕西	Shaanxi	303.56	9.86	8.83	26.20	56.11	3.12	10.54
甘肃	Gansu	208.28	9.61	7.69	15.49	45.01	2.20	7.93
青海	Qinghai	98.99	5.65	11.07	3.19	13.56	2.28	3.87
宁夏	Ningxia	86.21	1.68	0.02	12.33	16.24	0.40	8.57
新疆	Xinjiang	392.75	26.71	130.80	12.82	42.28	7.54	20.92
不分地区	Not Classified by Region	996.69	113.19	93.93	0.00	78.25	0.00	43.52

Investment in Capital Construction by Sector

(100 million yuan)

交通运输仓储和邮电通信业 Transport, Storage, Post & Telecommunication Services	批发零售贸易和餐饮业 Wholesale and Retail Trade & Catering Services	金融、保险业 Finance and Insurance	房地产业 Real Estate	社会服务业 Social Services	卫生体育和社会福利业 Health Care, Sports & Social Welfare	教育、文化艺术和广播电影电视业 Education, Culture and Arts, Radio, Film and Television	科学研究和综合技术服务业 Scientific Research and Polytechnic Services	国家机关、政党机关和社会团体 Government Agencies, Party Agencies and Social Organizations	其他 Others
68.04	15.29			15.39		22.49		33.50	
64.09	20.57			29.91		33.99		41.80	
62.34	28.57			33.81		44.83		47.99	
40.47	28.01	3.08		31.85		34.29	9.70	39.06	
57.21	35.97	5.88	22.31	19.90		40.85	10.50	55.46	
78.04	28.93	3.36	18.69	19.33		48.85	11.11	54.73	
108.46	35.17	3.09	33.34	24.02		65.74	13.66	66.61	
178.10	39.85	7.13	62.32	55.60	23.10	78.12	20.83	49.63	48.08
188.11	34.62	8.20	54.74	55.26	24.85	91.64	25.39	50.27	50.67
195.39	42.10	13.18	35.86	56.71	28.56	96.99	26.44	59.99	40.21
216.29	50.14	18.90	42.88	90.98	31.84	100.32	23.39	74.02	45.61
170.23	41.62	15.59	39.55	72.45	28.30	100.33	21.98	58.33	111.43
211.01	38.92	15.09	15.04	66.64	35.28	102.52	21.03	62.10	101.18
340.18	63.78	18.80	27.89	93.90	32.83	119.39	23.13	87.75	55.85
457.58	136.50	29.55	56.40	154.01	45.56	151.34	31.56	141.65	201.24
901.24	203.45	66.67	140.90	301.73	66.23	204.45	48.65	301.44	116.66
1372.94	254.73	96.06	316.34	417.45	93.66	261.53	52.76	376.58	117.29
1587.53	249.37	125.50	183.19	490.01	105.05	352.69	68.28	474.08	143.60
(1847.12)	(254.61)	(136.24)	(139.82)	(609.10)	(125.02)	(430.29)	(65.78)	(591.64)	(160.98)
1844.62	251.05	135.14	139.64	607.79	122.50	418.31	65.29	580.89	160.70
2197.45	265.00	142.79	146.47	820.36	148.51	529.21	68.17	715.99	181.33
3252.19	295.37	148.28	186.18	1123.87	184.54	615.56	75.82	888.00	160.63
3429.28	279.23	126.63	184.85	1355.52	198.70	711.65	88.56	1006.19	145.35
3641.94	292.59	90.26	151.71	1611.52	218.36	823.37	103.10	878.18	216.94
27.60	6.06	8.03	0.90	138.78	7.82	60.85	26.43	50.48	15.69
44.07	1.71	0.04	2.86	24.30	2.90	13.00	2.94	5.37	0.07
154.03	30.47	4.62	12.37	65.71	9.39	47.09	3.09	24.51	7.14
61.20	6.19	2.77	2.71	10.74	3.64	11.07	1.82	14.43	4.04
70.50	6.05	2.30	2.32	15.93	2.20	11.06	0.71	20.03	2.89
94.31	19.89	3.14	13.70	51.07	5.95	28.17	6.23	28.61	3.38
55.81	16.72	2.97	1.12	32.25	2.31	18.17	1.31	33.73	2.43
93.35	10.50	3.92	1.83	41.39	4.13	22.69	1.41	41.61	3.83
76.44	14.18	1.78	37.50	214.03	14.97	57.79	8.91	17.80	17.17
189.18	12.87	4.00	1.71	86.58	16.41	73.66	4.03	42.71	13.47
235.40	13.64	2.97	1.60	166.81	20.33	63.78	2.12	33.46	7.31
84.02	7.64	3.54	4.41	26.97	5.94	20.15	1.46	33.79	4.44
86.08	7.56	1.78	2.15	33.48	6.55	22.83	1.46	21.84	1.22
50.69	4.25	1.76	0.81	12.51	3.12	10.06	1.58	14.41	0.26
191.90	17.96	5.13	3.95	60.97	15.51	51.06	2.63	63.55	2.52
163.34	9.85	5.98	1.49	33.95	9.75	26.38	4.51	44.58	6.41
123.25	8.64	7.01	3.11	41.25	9.69	34.70	4.92	55.08	3.18
116.18	13.10	2.54	1.11	44.39	6.27	28.67	2.34	19.42	2.31
265.56	17.84	1.49	16.30	230.88	27.55	65.59	4.59	87.90	16.25
77.47	3.89	2.25	0.71	30.58	4.19	13.89	1.13	15.28	0.77
37.46	3.16	1.44	1.25	21.24	2.19	7.10	0.89	8.35	0.34
37.64	5.60	1.83	7.88	40.87	3.16	16.54	0.66	30.70	5.21
206.12	12.56	5.46	14.62	77.90	9.00	40.97	4.58	49.84	9.03
46.71	3.51	0.95	1.50	18.56	2.35	7.95	0.39	8.27	0.34
138.97	7.64	4.23	3.08	27.13	9.72	16.48	3.18	30.97	0.49
21.68	0.68	0.56	0.07	3.59	1.21	2.53	0.48	6.95	0.18
89.79	14.10	2.34	2.33	16.08	3.70	22.01	5.07	20.51	12.96
62.36	6.00	2.10	3.59	7.49	2.01	7.71	1.46	22.87	4.77
36.96	1.69	0.61	0.08	8.91	0.98	3.18	0.11	6.76	0.08
30.20	1.82	0.36	0.19	5.74	0.85	2.90	0.68	3.93	0.31
73.13	6.86	2.37	4.44	21.43	4.58	15.32	1.16	20.44	1.95
600.53	0.00	0.00	0.00	0.00	0.00	0.00	0.83	0.00	66.46

6-11 按项目规模分的基本建设投资及项目个数

Number of Capital Construction Projects by Project Size

年份 地区	Year Region	项目投资 (亿元) Investment in Projects (100 million yuan)		施工项目(个) Number of Projects under Construction	#大中型 Large and Medium Sized	全部建成投产项目(个) Number of Projects Completed and Put into Use	#大中型 Large and Medium Sized
		大中型 Large and Medium Sized	小型 Small Sized				
	1978	243.94	233.92	45261	1723	11762	99
	1979	216.16	291.49	53519	1610	17036	128
	1980	215.98	330.67	67618	1106	24823	82
	1981	169.18	267.57	59616	893	23532	79
	1982	219.89	327.08	70819	819	29143	116
	1983	262.46	318.99	76804	814	40861	91
	1984	313.25	404.20	69380	821	37524	113
	1985	394.24	627.60	87766	961	44477	121
	1986	482.82	640.52	79667	930	45107	102
	1987	619.61	666.42	76964	932	40520	119
	1988	746.85	714.66	77475	952	41289	121
	1989	729.70	686.59	66382	969	35370	95
	1990	896.31	702.56	67842	1059	36502	152
	1991	1058.23	935.54	77704	1053	41783	148
	1992	1322.43	1528.32	90609	1153	50633	158
	1993	1946.31	2543.70	90954	1340	51886	186
	1994	2738.13	3562.00	88841	1412	49021	224
	1995	3196.29	4053.07	88685	1408	50512	238
	1996	(3615.88)	(4751.59)	(93997)	(1266)	(55436)	(200)
		3615.88	4714.14	77954	1266	42008	200
	1997	4042.57	5634.40	84480	1240	48102	184
	1998	4539.21	7192.94	99665	1308	54950	175
	1999	3743.71	8332.93	97084	1135	57090	174
	2000	3771.38	9251.13	91252	1245	52645	241
北京	Beijing	85.98	360.81	1210	37	486	10
天津	Tianjin	160.14	117.23	545	50	313	13
河北	Hebei	186.62	424.77	4965	59	3029	14
山西	Shanxi	60.11	218.17	2274	11	1170	1
内蒙古	Inner	41.99	186.67	2630	33	1871	2
辽宁	Liaoning	119.79	327.80	2113	42	1239	7
吉林	Jilin	50.87	225.76	1516	16	1051	2
黑龙江	Heilongjiang	62.66	314.67	2603	21	1880	2
上海	Shanghai	270.74	404.48	1245	56	373	7
江苏	Jiangsu	107.07	643.93	3658	30	2482	5
浙江	Zhejiang	183.77	635.39	4967	48	2607	7
安徽	Anhui	79.58	233.15	2951	37	1599	7
福建	Fujian	124.67	209.09	2788	55	1336	9
江西	Jiangxi	63.00	134.37	2367	20	1360	5
山东	Shandong	117.68	627.70	5051	32	2780	7
河南	Henan	173.54	406.76	4573	49	2615	4
湖北	Hubei	179.20	419.07	4887	27	3301	7
湖南	Hunan	32.61	333.73	4225	32	2467	9
广东	Guangdong	357.31	765.65	4845	100	2508	21
广西	Guangxi	29.78	236.23	3432	25	2010	9
海南	Hainan	30.53	85.31	1182	35	699	4
重庆	Chongqing	25.10	190.14	2088	62	945	16
四川	Sichuan	104.63	503.68	5978	67	3412	11
贵州	Guizhou	54.87	91.70	2554	25	1527	5
云南	Yunnan	44.97	293.59	4364	27	2488	5
西藏	Tibet	17.79	36.74	997	43	741	16
陕西	Shaanxi	72.60	230.78	2896	33	1522	4
甘肃	Gansu	60.01	148.00	2519	64	1334	16
青海	Qinghai	32.97	64.07	1282	11	769	2
宁夏	Ningxia	17.37	68.83	756	5	507	1
新疆	Xinjiang	157.49	234.28	3060	24	2219	8
不分地区	Not Classified by Region	665.91	78.58	731	69	5	5

6-12 基本建设房屋建筑面积

Floor Space of Buildings Through Capital Construction

单位：万平方米 (10 000 sq.m)

年份 地区	Year Region	施工面积 Floor Space of under Construction	#住宅 Residential Buildings	竣工面积 Floor Space of Completed	#住宅 Residential Buildings
	1978	18484.90	7314.33	9010.92	3752.47
	1979	23829.70	11998.30	11999.70	6255.80
	1980	27537.60	14817.40	14499.90	8230.30
	1981	25177.00	14774.00	12941.00	7904.00
	1982	28450.40	16761.80	14356.60	9019.60
	1983	25277.60	14018.10	13211.50	8124.50
	1984	27928.80	14198.20	13809.10	7703.00
	1985	37029.20	18893.90	17161.20	9565.10
	1986	33086.20	15940.40	16650.50	8915.50
	1987	29435.70	11990.10	14359.00	6452.80
	1988	28413.79	11334.02	13307.84	6008.99
	1989	24744.18	9749.94	11611.55	5064.20
	1990	23236.54	9259.90	11245.93	4824.78
	1991	27262.61	11309.23	12604.48	5687.92
	1992	32709.19	13399.25	15133.72	6919.15
	1993	39535.76	15016.40	17070.05	7993.44
	1994	42749.88	16981.97	18644.05	8955.12
	1995	41948.29	16739.06	19929.32	9249.25
	1996	(43661.23)	(17269.40)	(21256.63)	(9824.79)
		42786.07	16974.08	20544.83	9589.36
	1997	44206.26	18065.42	21439.12	10091.49
	1998	52023.11	24529.90	24685.04	12552.44
	1999	52833.80	25642.02	28620.79	16033.23
	2000	50968.27	21559.64	26292.93	13145.97
北京	Beijing	2131.47	936.54	839.77	402.94
天津	Tianjin	428.90	90.34	200.04	52.36
河北	Hebei	2619.63	1108.78	1487.04	727.62
山西	Shanxi	1396.87	883.98	733.80	512.29
内蒙古	Inner Mongolia	1006.28	494.78	655.04	367.84
辽宁	Liaoning	1710.99	734.72	907.97	490.80
吉林	Jilin	1082.97	461.59	754.86	393.75
黑龙江	Heilongjiang	1807.65	1034.85	1209.74	757.11
上海	Shanghai	1316.10	235.35	513.26	69.33
江苏	Jiangsu	2274.01	534.44	1365.52	396.77
浙江	Zhejiang	2300.74	382.04	1020.93	194.44
安徽	Anhui	1229.14	518.57	768.95	374.69
福建	Fujian	1259.18	264.28	503.88	151.05
江西	Jiangxi	1066.30	401.61	552.09	244.90
山东	Shandong	3859.86	1189.46	1485.85	717.08
河南	Henan	2562.13	1266.45	1172.41	613.77
湖北	Hubei	2219.47	1122.73	1290.13	701.92
湖南	Hunan	2032.06	920.61	1071.75	553.70
广东	Guangdong	3814.74	1142.84	1753.48	547.66
广西	Guangxi	1032.40	417.85	541.94	286.75
海南	Hainan	516.57	206.01	247.50	136.37
重庆	Chongqing	1692.50	943.65	854.34	522.04
四川	Sichuan	3171.02	1765.57	1733.91	1075.20
贵州	Guizhou	968.89	411.83	460.10	268.25
云南	Yunnan	1608.22	827.38	867.84	491.50
西藏	Tibet	179.69	23.78	109.10	21.93
陕西	Shaanxi	1848.36	1014.09	829.16	542.80
甘肃	Gansu	1338.63	703.02	632.37	394.52
青海	Qinghai	262.01	147.62	141.86	83.76
宁夏	Ningxia	234.12	90.33	143.11	65.65
新疆	Xinjiang	1541.06	957.90	1100.06	760.85
不分地区	Not Classified by Region	456.31	326.66	345.12	226.31

6-13 国民经济各行业基本建设新增固定资产

单位：亿元

年份 地区 Year Region	合计 Total	农、林、牧、渔业 Farming, Forestry, Animal Husbandry and Fishery	采掘业 Mining and Quarrying	制造业 Manufacturing	电力、煤气及水的生产和供应业 Production and Supply of Electric Power, Gas and Water	建筑业 Construction	地质勘查业 水利管理业 Geological Prospecting and Water Conservancy
1985	733.16	11.91	68.04	133.16	86.13	14.01	23.69
1986	929.88	11.52	81.58	243.28	102.49	15.63	23.52
1987	959.09	13.55	98.01	221.50	159.70	12.05	23.45
1988	1112.13	16.64	111.15	260.96	179.71	10.91	17.57
1989	1179.03	15.20	169.49	240.59	194.25	12.41	26.48
1990	1362.61	18.09	203.36	295.31	238.78	9.54	30.92
1991	1498.73	22.41	163.33	343.67	317.10	10.01	34.96
1992	1975.00	27.30	195.59	381.85	398.90	20.86	47.91
1993	2758.93	34.83	193.82	588.30	452.20	62.17	54.01
1994	3729.78	34.85	212.79	757.62	667.43	65.50	76.55
1995	4712.67	46.90	285.53	878.89	816.90	67.80	110.14
1996	(6168.14)	(63.08)	(281.64)	(1361.73)	(1029.85)	(100.12)	(109.91)
	6129.65	61.30	281.46	1360.26	1029.04	99.81	109.38
1997	7443.15	82.53	480.14	1407.61	1207.22	125.87	146.28
1998	8499.82	109.64	348.18	1272.65	1774.65	115.17	200.50
1999	9519.30	208.99	451.96	1327.96	1719.39	131.55	308.71
2000	10431.66	212.98	510.91	1028.28	2092.12	111.82	378.08
北 京 Beijing	495.96	2.79	0.01	41.10	129.16	7.67	0.15
天 津 Tianjin	174.07	0.55	13.61	52.06	15.38	1.38	11.21
河 北 Hebei	505.29	14.50	10.46	43.39	109.14	4.30	33.26
山 西 Shanxi	210.47	2.79	12.78	15.96	80.23	3.50	2.88
内蒙古 Inner Mongolia	141.87	12.61	1.28	4.35	9.99	1.23	10.42
辽 宁 Liaoning	365.70	3.71	44.49	48.72	33.48	5.88	7.30
吉 林 Jilin	215.17	2.61	15.35	21.85	46.47	4.22	1.44
黑龙江 Heilongjiang	290.19	9.05	24.32	16.73	37.78	8.69	7.34
上 海 Shanghai	587.43	3.46	11.22	91.74	171.68	0.02	4.95
江 苏 Jiangsu	714.47	8.52	10.55	85.01	142.60	3.59	33.81
浙 江 Zhejiang	585.14	1.39	0.06	27.43	113.44	6.00	20.85
安 徽 Anhui	295.13	2.83	17.34	38.05	60.11	3.95	15.24
福 建 Fujian	202.10	1.73	0.75	62.94	35.48	1.79	8.46
江 西 Jiangxi	149.05	1.42	1.49	21.88	26.83	1.36	9.88
山 东 Shandong	688.82	5.80	93.21	57.11	159.71	7.31	16.29
河 南 Henan	294.19	9.29	11.30	26.14	69.00	2.47	18.04
湖 北 Hubei	362.22	11.27	8.03	21.45	77.21	6.15	26.59
湖 南 Hunan	230.52	4.23	0.69	20.60	59.80	1.07	13.75
广 东 Guangdong	856.00	7.26	1.68	162.53	163.55	11.94	22.28
广 西 Guangxi	308.79	2.78	0.65	31.52	90.85	2.03	10.91
海 南 Hainan	95.27	15.72	5.38	6.01	9.95	0.95	2.55
重 庆 Chongqing	130.69	3.83	0.26	5.21	19.03	0.87	3.41
四 川 Sichuan	491.60	7.65	2.63	27.27	98.76	5.72	27.30
贵 州 Guizhou	142.96	2.77	2.21	11.02	51.60	1.75	2.45
云 南 Yunnan	220.15	7.88	2.78	24.76	33.10	0.82	9.24
西 藏 Tibet	57.66	2.07	0.06	0.14	8.56	2.01	1.64
陕 西 Shaanxi	281.50	5.72	5.56	18.10	38.58	4.06	8.63
甘 肃 Gansu	132.99	3.64	10.64	11.88	39.19	1.41	4.28
青 海 Qinghai	45.69	3.61	9.40	1.39	5.03	1.73	2.65
宁 夏 Ningxia	75.05	0.92	0.02	19.10	9.39	0.51	2.76
新 疆 Xinjiang	481.37	50.57	144.43	12.84	42.17	7.45	9.39
不分地区 Not Classified by Region	604.13		48.26		104.91		28.74

Newly Increased Fixed Assets through Capital Construction by Sector

(100 million yuan)

交通运输仓储和邮电通信业 Transport Storage, Postal and Telecom-munication Services	批发零售贸易和餐饮业 Wholesale & Retail Trade and Catering Services	金融、保险业 Finance and Insurance	房地产业 Real Estate	社会服务业 Social Services	卫生体育和社会福利业 Health Care, Sports and Social Welfare	教育、文化艺术和广播电影电视业 Education, Culture, Arts, Radio, Film and Television	科学研究和综合技术服务业 Scientific Research and Polytechnic Services	国家机关、政党机关和社会团体 Governments Agencies, Party Agencies and Social Organizations	其他行业 Others
132.73	24.77	4.54	43.01	36.12	15.49	57.60	13.70	34.40	33.85
140.90	26.76	5.76	50.23	35.54	17.72	73.12	16.80	44.54	40.48
130.74	28.52	9.55	28.34	33.48	21.78	80.56	19.18	46.92	31.78
181.20	38.78	12.97	35.17	40.77	22.03	81.59	17.05	56.00	29.63
129.60	37.41	14.61	38.08	34.97	22.65	81.96	17.46	54.18	89.70
160.23	32.43	12.59	13.28	46.66	40.08	98.25	21.61	57.55	83.93
203.15	48.44	15.61	13.53	77.73	30.11	102.14	19.75	68.16	28.63
261.00	79.18	24.15	30.12	100.33	35.02	120.40	18.79	102.34	131.27
491.22	124.63	42.93	65.41	172.16	42.14	148.84	27.19	195.29	63.81
710.00	162.96	63.86	122.38	228.69	64.90	191.57	35.25	264.38	71.06
1099.05	162.44	76.75	84.06	272.23	69.16	275.97	49.75	355.78	61.33
(1414.87)	(190.09)	(100.10)	(100.65)	(356.06)	(98.65)	(356.06)	(43.86)	(449.13)	(112.34)
1412.52	186.58	99.02	100.47	354.84	96.22	344.37	43.42	438.86	112.10
1809.58	219.70	114.17	100.77	479.43	111.95	418.11	50.00	543.39	146.40
1784.80	256.88	152.56	135.68	826.72	132.22	501.52	57.22	717.21	114.22
2090.66	231.85	118.82	124.07	1006.28	168.03	619.58	73.95	833.86	103.65
2897.78	262.26	86.98	84.04	986.56	163.72	685.47	64.38	755.48	110.81
80.52	14.98	5.62	0.71	55.08	8.38	60.16	18.90	59.94	10.78
46.41	2.19	0.04	1.04	12.29	1.36	11.74	1.08	3.67	0.07
144.78	19.09	2.59	10.43	43.45	6.85	36.93	1.56	21.25	3.31
48.48	5.32	2.33	1.23	4.43	3.26	9.06	1.40	14.23	2.60
47.48	5.11	3.44	1.77	12.25	2.23	10.60	0.36	18.22	0.52
118.78	15.00	1.68	4.26	28.52	4.50	22.76	3.26	19.72	3.64
32.41	10.40	2.35	1.10	26.87	1.42	16.41	1.19	30.12	0.97
61.82	12.09	4.85	1.82	39.10	3.54	21.50	0.88	33.32	7.36
121.69	19.43	0.00	15.13	53.69	14.63	50.15	2.52	12.39	14.74
172.44	12.22	2.97	1.00	100.61	12.15	63.69	1.96	48.33	15.00
180.87	17.80	2.93	1.46	115.06	16.48	49.35	2.45	24.37	5.20
78.62	6.43	4.41	2.46	16.64	5.36	15.63	0.68	23.49	3.90
30.58	4.28	1.62	1.02	19.25	3.27	10.86	0.43	18.98	0.67
50.32	3.74	1.75	0.77	5.00	2.72	9.67	0.36	11.66	0.21
178.22	13.40	5.03	3.26	40.63	9.68	42.27	2.77	52.75	1.39
53.10	8.62	5.49	0.90	26.81	5.41	17.47	2.23	34.52	3.40
79.50	8.31	7.61	1.81	23.87	7.73	27.81	3.44	47.85	3.58
38.93	12.56	2.86	0.37	25.75	5.29	24.00	1.98	17.45	1.19
143.17	19.02	1.91	7.39	162.07	17.61	54.22	2.76	71.53	7.08
114.96	2.74	1.47	0.77	22.94	2.60	9.21	0.57	14.01	0.79
24.13	1.94	1.36	1.26	10.87	0.78	5.38	0.28	7.41	1.29
23.62	4.46	1.64	3.99	21.54	2.49	14.38	0.31	23.06	2.60
158.53	8.79	4.08	8.41	45.11	6.70	32.61	4.49	44.71	8.83
38.64	5.22	1.68	0.53	9.00	1.75	6.15	0.56	7.29	0.32
59.91	5.88	4.35	2.13	21.39	4.99	14.56	2.66	25.15	0.55
28.43	0.60	0.65	0.07	2.37	0.76	2.37	0.50	7.21	0.23
130.98	6.38	2.02	2.46	15.88	3.61	21.07	2.33	12.69	3.41
15.73	5.62	1.43	1.87	5.37	1.60	6.09	0.95	20.94	2.35
8.46	1.44	1.31	0.07	1.73	0.74	1.92	0.06	6.12	0.04
28.85	1.40	0.26	0.42	4.17	0.90	2.56	0.58	3.12	0.11
139.41	7.80	7.24	4.11	14.80	4.94	14.89	0.79	19.99	0.56
418.02									4.12

6-14 各地区基本建设施工、投产项目个数和新增固定资产

Number of Capital Construction Projects under Construction and Put into Use and Newly Increased Fixed Assets by Region

年份 地区	Year Region	施工项目(个) Number of Projects under Construction (unit)	全部建成投产项目(个) Number of Projects Completed and Put into Use (unit)	项目建成投产率(%) Rate of Projects Completed and Put into Use (%)	新增固定资产(亿元) Newly Increased Fixed Assets (100 million yuan)	固定资产交付使用率(%) Rate of Fixed Assets Put into Use (%)
	1978	45261	11762	26.0	372.30	74.3
	1979	53519	17036	31.8	438.02	83.7
	1980	67618	24823	36.7	442.06	79.1
	1981	59616	23532	39.5	383.40	86.6
	1982	70819	29143	41.2	413.10	74.4
	1983	76804	40861	53.2	453.10	76.3
	1984	69380	37524	54.1	533.28	71.8
	1985	87766	44477	50.7	733.16	68.2
	1986	79667	45107	56.6	929.88	79.1
	1987	76964	40520	52.6	959.08	71.4
	1988	77475	41289	53.3	1112.13	70.6
	1989	66382	35370	53.3	1179.03	76.0
	1990	67842	36502	53.8	1362.61	80.0
	1991	77704	41783	53.8	1498.73	70.8
	1992	90609	50633	55.9	1975.00	65.6
	1993	90954	51886	57.0	2758.93	59.8
	1994	88841	49021	55.2	3729.78	57.9
	1995	88685	50512	57.0	4712.67	63.7
	1996	(93997)	(55436)	(59.0)	(6168.14)	(71.6)
		77954	42008	53.9	6129.65	71.5
	1997	84480	48102	56.9	7443.15	75.1
	1998	99665	54950	55.1	8499.82	71.3
	1999	97084	57090	58.8	9519.30	76.4
	2000	91252	52645	57.7	10431.66	77.7
北京	Beijing	1210	486	40.2	495.96	111.0
天津	Tianjin	545	313	57.4	174.07	62.1
河北	Hebei	4965	3029	61.0	505.29	80.9
山西	Shanxi	2274	1170	51.5	210.47	75.6
内蒙古	Inner Mongolia	2630	1871	71.1	141.87	61.8
辽宁	Liaoning	2113	1239	58.6	365.70	81.0
吉林	Jilin	1516	1051	69.3	215.17	77.8
黑龙江	Heilongjiang	2603	1880	72.2	290.19	76.4
上海	Shanghai	1245	373	30.0	587.43	83.5
江苏	Jiangsu	3658	2482	67.9	714.47	95.1
浙江	Zhejiang	4967	2607	52.5	585.14	71.3
安徽	Anhui	2951	1599	54.2	295.13	92.8
福建	Fujian	2788	1336	47.9	202.10	60.4
江西	Jiangxi	2367	1360	57.5	149.05	75.0
山东	Shandong	5051	2780	55.0	688.82	90.4
河南	Henan	4573	2615	57.2	294.19	50.2
湖北	Hubei	4887	3301	67.5	362.22	60.3
湖南	Hunan	4225	2467	58.4	230.52	62.7
广东	Guangdong	4845	2508	51.8	856.00	75.5
广西	Guangxi	3432	2010	58.6	308.79	115.4
海南	Hainan	1182	699	59.1	95.27	72.2
重庆	Chongqing	2088	945	45.3	130.69	60.6
四川	Sichuan	5978	3412	57.1	491.60	77.2
贵州	Guizhou	2554	1527	59.8	142.96	96.6
云南	Yunnan	4364	2488	57.0	220.15	64.4
西藏	Tibet	997	741	74.3	57.66	105.5
陕西	Shaanxi	2896	1522	52.6	281.50	92.7
甘肃	Gansu	2519	1334	53.0	132.99	63.9
青海	Qinghai	1282	769	60.0	45.69	46.2
宁夏	Ningxia	756	507	67.1	75.05	87.1
新疆	Xinjiang	3060	2219	72.5	481.37	122.6
不分地区	Not Classified by Region	731	5	0.7	604.13	60.6

6-15 国民经济各行业基本建设施工、投产项目个数（2000年）

Number of Capital Construction Projects under Construction and Put into Use by Sector (2000)

单位：亿元

(100 million yuan)

行业	Sector	施工项目（个）Number of Projects under Construction (unit)	# 新开工 Started This Year	全部建成投产项目（个）Number of Projects Completed and Put into Use (unit)	项目建成投产率（%）Rate of Projects Completed & Put into Use (%)
全国总计	**National Total**	**91252**	**55702**	**52645**	**57.7**
农、林、牧、渔业	**Farming, Forestry, Animal Husbandry and Fishery**	**3866**	**2777**	**2481**	**64.2**
农业	Farming	1355	1041	910	67.2
林业	Forestry	989	719	634	64.1
畜牧业	Animal Husbandry	309	212	179	57.9
渔业	Fishery	98	64	59	60.2
农林牧渔服务业	Agricultural Services	1115	741	699	62.7
采掘业	**Mining and Quarrying**	**775**	**411**	**397**	**51.2**
煤炭采选业	Coal Mining and Dressing	294	114	114	38.8
石油和天然气开采业	Extraction of Petroleum and Natural Gas	76	41	36	47.4
黑色金属矿采选业	Mining and Dressing of Ferrous Metals	42	25	20	47.6
有色金属矿采选业	Mining and Dressing of Nonferrous Metals	142	94	88	62.0
非金属矿采选业	Mining and Dressing of Nonmetal Minerals	93	61	58	62.4
其他矿采选业	Mining and Dressing of Other Minerals	5	3	2	40.0
木材及竹材采运业	Logging and Transport of Wood and Bamboo	123	73	79	64.2
制造业	**Manufacturing**	**7063**	**4372**	**3917**	**55.5**
食品加工业	Food Processing	505	354	327	64.8
食品制造业	Food Production	287	198	151	52.6
饮料制造业	Beverages	279	196	171	61.3
烟草加工业	Tobacco	118	55	85	72.0
纺织业	Textiles	380	251	238	62.6
服装及纤维制品制造业	Garments and Other Fiber Products	157	113	89	56.7
皮革毛皮羽绒及其制品业	Leather, Furs, Down and Related Products	88	63	51	58.0
木材加工及竹藤棕草制品业	Timber Processing, Bamboo, Cane, Palm Fiber and Straw Products	120	86	86	71.7
家具制造业	Furniture Manufacturing	59	39	37	62.7
造纸及纸制品业	Papermaking and Paper Products	135	84	78	57.8
印刷业、记录媒介的复制	Printing and Record Medium Reproduction	161	103	93	57.8
文教体育用品制造业	Cultural, Educational and Sports Goods	40	25	26	65.0
石油加工及炼焦业	Petroleum Processing and Coking	82	37	39	47.6
化学原料及化学制品制造业	Raw Chemical Materials and Chemical Products	633	374	328	51.8
医药制造业	Medical and Pharmaceutical Products	284	169	128	45.1
化学纤维制造业	Chemical Fiber	36	18	15	41.7
橡胶制品业	Rubber Products	65	41	36	55.4
塑料制品业	Plastic Products	210	146	124	59.0
非金属矿物制品业	Nonmetal Mineral Products	539	335	325	60.3
黑色金属冶炼及压延加工业	Smelting and Pressing of Ferrous Metals	157	80	76	48.4
有色金属冶炼及压延加工业	Smelting and Pressing of Nonferrous Metals	147	83	71	48.3
金属制品业	Metal Products	217	159	114	52.5
普通机械制造业	Ordinary Machinery	458	258	254	55.5
专用设备制造业	Equipment for Special Purposes	381	239	212	55.6
交通运输设备制造业	Transport Equipment	542	289	269	49.6
电气机械及器材制造业	Electric Equipment and Machinery	270	159	146	54.1
电子及通信设备制造业	Electronic and Telecommunications Equipment	398	230	175	44.0
仪器仪表及文化办公用机械制造业	Instruments, Meters, Cultural and Office Machinery	107	69	50	46.7
其他制造业	Other Manufacturing	208	119	123	59.1
电力、煤气及水的生产和供应业	**Production and Supply of Electric Power, Gas and Water**	**5670**	**2778**	**2583**	**45.6**
电力、蒸汽、热水生产和供应业	Production and Supply of Electric Power, Steam and Hot Water	4159	2040	1937	46.6
煤气的生产和供应业	Production and Supply of Gas	330	156	128	38.8
自来水的生产和供应业	Production and Supply of Tap Water	1181	582	518	43.9
建筑业	**Construction**	**1738**	**1111**	**1025**	**59.0**
土木工程建筑业	Civil Engineering Construction	1593	1031	941	59.1

6-15 续表 1 continued

单位：亿元 (100 million yuan)

行业	Sector	施工项目（个）Number of Projects under Construction (unit)	# 新开工 Started This Year	全部建成投产项目（个）Number of Projects Completed and Put into Use (unit)	项目建成投产率(%) Rate of Projects Completed & Put into Use (%)
线路、管道和设备安装业	Installation of lines, Pipelines and Equipment	119	63	69	58.0
装修装饰业	Fitting and Decoration	26	17	15	57.7
地质勘查、水利管理业	**Geological Prospecting and Water Conservancy**	**3714**	**2163**	**2035**	**54.8**
地质勘查业	Geological Prospecting	268	128	154	57.5
水利管理业	Water Conservancy	3446	2035	1881	54.6
交通运输、仓储及邮电通信业	**Transport, Storage, Postal and Telecommunication Services**	**10752**	**6458**	**5903**	**54.9**
铁路运输业	Railway Transport	227	88	88	38.8
公路运输业	Highway Transport	3453	2020	1847	53.5
管道运输业	Pipeline Transport	20	9	7	35.0
水上运输业	Waterway Transport	205	76	72	35.1
航空运输业	Air Transport	110	42	44	40.0
交通运输辅助业	Transport Subsidiary Services	2289	1437	1354	59.2
其他交通运输业	Other Transport	127	76	69	54.3
仓储业	Storage	943	516	459	48.7
邮电通信业	Postal and Telecommunications Services	3378	2194	1963	58.1
批发和零售贸易餐饮业	**Wholesale & Retail Trade and Catering Services**	**5171**	**3332**	**3280**	**63.4**
食品饮料烟草和家庭用品批发业	Wholesale Trade of Food, Beverage, Tobacco and Household Articles	1672	1026	1017	60.8
能源材料和机械电子设备批发业	Wholesale Trade of Energy, Materials and Electronic Equipment	734	492	475	64.7
其他批发业	Other Wholesale Trade	440	265	276	62.7
零售业	Retail Trade	2045	1379	1353	66.2
商业经纪与代理业	Commercial Brokerage and Agencies	49	25	24	49.0
餐饮业	Catering Trade	231	145	135	58.4
金融、保险业	**Finance and Insurance**	**1920**	**1083**	**1237**	**64.4**
金融业	Finance	1603	904	1024	63.9
保险业	Insurance	317	179	213	67.2
房地产业	**Real Estate**	**1154**	**667**	**578**	**50.1**
房地产开发与经营业	Real Estate Development and Operation	554	313	225	40.6
房地产管理业	Real Estate Management	567	331	328	57.8
房地产代理与经纪业	Real Estate Brokerage and Agencies	33	23	25	75.8
社会服务业	**Social Services**	**8304**	**5270**	**4258**	**51.3**
公共设施服务业	Public Services	6261	4069	3237	51.7
居民服务业	Resident Services	286	170	135	47.2
旅馆业	Hotels	849	466	436	51.4
租赁服务业	Leasing Services	32	29	23	71.9
旅游业	Tourism	331	214	145	43.8
娱乐服务业	Recreational Services	167	95	74	44.3
信息、咨询服务业	Information and Consultative Services	50	31	27	54.0
计算机应用服务业	Computer Application Services	42	19	12	28.6
其他社会服务业	Other Social Services	286	177	169	59.1
卫生体育和社会福利业	**Health Care, Sports and Social Welfare**	**4327**	**2444**	**2522**	**58.3**
卫生	Health Care	3487	2002	2096	60.1
体育	Sports	350	168	142	40.6
社会福利保障业	Social Welfare and Social Security	490	274	284	58.0
教育、文化艺术和广播电影电视业	**Education, Culture and Arts, Radio, Film and Television**	**15413**	**9707**	**9838**	**63.8**
教育	Education	13543	8795	8876	65.5
文化艺术业	Culture and Arts	963	431	464	48.2
广播、电影、电视业	Radio, Film and Television	907	481	498	54.9
科学研究和综合技术服务业	**Scientific Research and Polytechnic Services**	**1209**	**608**	**537**	**44.4**
科学研究业	Scientific Research	583	276	219	37.6
综合技术服务业	Polytechnic Services	626	332	318	50.8
国家机关、政党机关和社会团体	**Governments Agencies, Party agencies and Social Organizations**	**18570**	**11714**	**11558**	**62.2**
#国家机关	Governments	17602	11123	10982	62.4
政党机关	Party	568	368	342	60.2
其他行业	**Others**	**1606**	**807**	**496**	**30.9**

6-16 国民经济各行业基本建设投资和新增固定资产（2000年）

Investment in Capital Construction and Newly Increased Fixed Assets by Sector (2000)

行业	Sector	投资额（亿元）Investment (100 million yuan)	新增固定资产（亿元）Newly Increased Fixed Assets (100 million yuan)	固定资产交付使用率(%) Rate of Fixed Assets Put into Use (%)
全国总计	**National Total**	**13427.27**	**10431.66**	**77.7**
农、林、牧、渔业	**Farming, Forestry, Animal Husbandry and Fishery**	**360.93**	**212.98**	**59.0**
农业	Farming	105.59	110.55	104.7
林业	Forestry	174.22	43.60	25.0
畜牧业	Animal Husbandry	17.32	12.56	72.5
渔业	Fishery	8.86	7.55	85.2
农林牧渔服务业	Agricultural Services	54.94	38.71	70.5
采掘业	**Mining and Quarrying**	**589.36**	**510.91**	**86.7**
煤炭采选业	Coal Mining and Dressing	116.34	134.47	115.6
石油和天然气开采业	Extraction of Petroleum and Natural Gas	420.66	336.92	80.1
黑色金属矿采选业	Mining and Dressing of Ferrous Metals	12.81	12.70	99.1
有色金属矿采选业	Mining and Dressing of Nonferrous Metals	12.10	12.47	103.0
非金属矿采选业	Mining and Dressing of Nonmetal Minerals	5.73	6.27	109.3
其他矿采选业	Mining and Dressing of Other Minerals	0.15	0.12	81.3
木材及竹材采运业	Logging and Transport of Wood and Bamboo	21.57	7.96	36.9
制造业	**Manufacturing**	**1175.11**	**1028.28**	**87.5**
食品加工业	Food Processing	32.43	28.73	88.6
食品制造业	Food Production	37.57	38.19	101.7
饮料制造业	Beverages	26.27	19.98	76.1
烟草加工业	Tobacco	18.23	23.48	128.8
纺织业	Textiles	29.57	23.60	79.8
服装及纤维制品制造业	Garments and Other Fiber Products	17.67	16.67	94.3
皮革毛皮羽绒及其制品业	Leather, Furs, Down and Related Products	12.18	5.89	48.4
木材加工及竹藤棕草制品业	Timber Processing, Bamboo, Cane, Palm Fiber and Straw Products	8.22	8.30	101.0
家具制造业	Furniture Manufacturing	7.15	6.20	86.6
造纸及纸制品业	Papermaking and Paper Products	39.54	65.86	166.6
印刷业、记录媒介的复制	Printing and Record Medium Reproduction	13.05	10.37	79.4
文教体育用品制造业	Cultural, Educational and Sports Goods	2.66	1.69	63.6
石油加工及炼焦业	Petroleum Processing and Coking	32.79	31.09	94.8
化学原料及化学制品制造业	Raw Chemical Materials and Chemical Products	172.18	223.70	129.9
医药制造业	Medical and Pharmaceutical Products	42.42	33.01	77.8
化学纤维制造业	Chemical Fiber	11.79	14.89	126.3
橡胶制品业	Rubber Products	8.40	4.01	47.8
塑料制品业	Plastic Products	27.70	20.93	75.6
非金属矿物制品业	Nonmetal Mineral Products	61.42	56.50	92.0
黑色金属冶炼及压延加工业	Smelting and Pressing of Ferrous Metals	50.85	24.38	47.9
有色金属冶炼及压延加工业	Smelting and Pressing of Nonferrous Metals	39.76	21.56	54.2
金属制品业	Metal Products	17.28	11.73	67.9
普通机械制造业	Ordinary Machinery	31.18	22.65	72.6
专用设备制造业	Equipment for Special Purposes	29.93	27.14	90.7
交通运输设备制造业	Transport Equipment	107.56	75.60	70.3
电气机械及器材制造业	Electric Equipment and Machinery	29.19	22.64	77.6
电子及通信设备制造业	Electronic and Telecommunications Equipment	214.80	145.96	68.0
仪器仪表及文化办公用机械制造业	Instruments, Meters, Cultural and Office Machinery	9.21	7.07	76.7
其他制造业	Other Manufacturing	44.11	36.43	82.6
电力、煤气及水的生产和供应业	**Production and Supply of Electric Power, Gas and Water**	**2479.80**	**2092.12**	**84.4**
电力、蒸汽、热水生产和供应业	Production and Supply of Electric Power, Steam and Hot Water	2267.08	1945.51	85.8
煤气的生产和供应业	Production and Supply of Gas	55.74	30.87	55.4
自来水的生产和供应业	Production and Supply of Tap Water	156.97	115.74	73.7
建筑业	**Construction**	**197.47**	**111.82**	**56.6**
土木工程建筑业	Civil Engineering Construction	186.27	103.28	55.4

6-16 续表 1 continued

行业	Sector	投资额(亿元) Investment (100 million yuan)	新增固定资产(亿元) Newly Increased Fixed Assets (100 million yuan)	固定资产交付使用率(%) Rate of Fixed Assets Put into Use (%)
线路、管道和设备安装业	Installation of lines, Pipelines and Equipment	8.50	7.43	87.5
装修装饰业	Fitting and Decoration	2.70	1.11	41.1
地质勘查、水利管理业	**Geological Prospecting and Water Conservancy**	**596.64**	**378.08**	**63.4**
地质勘查业	Geological Prospecting	16.56	18.17	109.7
水利管理业	Water Conservancy	580.08	359.91	62.0
交通运输、仓储及邮电通信业	**Transport, Storage, Postal and Telecommunication Services**	**3641.94**	**2897.78**	**79.6**
铁路运输业	Railway Transport	672.25	544.13	80.9
公路运输业	Highway Transport	1317.61	974.57	74.0
管道运输业	Pipeline Transport	23.59	5.65	24.0
水上运输业	Waterway Transport	46.94	33.97	72.4
航空运输业	Air Transport	209.00	209.94	100.5
交通运输辅助业	Transport Subsidiary Services	578.14	538.78	93.2
其他交通运输业	Other Transport	31.41	32.17	102.4
仓储业	Storage	83.96	82.54	98.3
邮电通信业	Postal and Telecommunications Services	679.04	476.02	70.1
批发和零售贸易餐饮业	**Wholesale & Retail Trade and Catering Services**	**292.59**	**262.26**	**89.6**
食品饮料烟草和家庭用品批发业	Wholesale Trade of Food, Beverage, Tobacco and Household Articles	91.03	75.61	83.1
能源材料和机械电子设备批发业	Wholesale Trade of Energy, Materials and Electronic Equipment	41.91	31.84	76.0
其他批发业	Other Wholesale Trade	22.99	24.82	107.9
零售业	Retail Trade	118.65	104.18	87.8
商业经纪与代理业	Commercial Brokerage and Agencies	3.13	7.29	233.2
餐饮业	Catering Trade	14.88	18.52	124.5
金融、保险业	**Finance and Insurance**	**90.26**	**86.98**	**96.4**
金融业	Finance	79.05	75.21	95.1
保险业	Insurance	11.22	11.78	105.0
房地产业	**Real Estate**	**151.71**	**84.04**	**55.4**
房地产开发与经营业	Real Estate Development and Operation	102.60	44.91	43.8
房地产管理业	Real Estate Management	47.80	38.37	80.3
房地产代理与经纪业	Real Estate Brokerage and Agencies	1.31	0.77	58.6
社会服务业	**Social Services**	**1611.52**	**986.56**	**61.2**
公共设施服务业	Public Services	1402.70	832.10	59.3
居民服务业	Resident Services	10.28	7.93	77.1
旅馆业	Hotels	82.92	75.86	91.5
租赁服务业	Leasing Services	2.99	4.30	143.6
旅游业	Tourism	29.01	22.33	77.0
娱乐服务业	Recreational Services	32.73	22.40	68.4
信息、咨询服务业	Information and Consultative Services	3.36	1.96	58.3
计算机应用服务业	Computer Application Services	25.44	5.63	22.2
其他社会服务业	Other Social Services	22.08	14.05	63.6
卫生体育和社会福利业	**Health Care, Sports and Social Welfare**	**218.36**	**163.72**	**75.0**
卫生	Health Care	152.89	126.13	82.5
体育	Sports	48.67	23.22	47.7
社会福利保障业	Social Welfare and Social Security	16.80	14.37	85.6
教育、文化艺术和广播电影电视业	**Education, Culture and Arts, Radio, Film and Television**	**823.37**	**685.47**	**83.3**
教育	Education	661.67	556.70	84.1
文化艺术业	Culture and Arts	99.66	87.22	87.5
广播、电影、电视业	Radio, Film and Television	62.04	41.54	67.0
科学研究和综合技术服务业	**Scientific Research and Polytechnic Services**	**103.10**	**64.38**	**62.4**
科学研究业	Scientific Research	61.52	40.17	65.3
综合技术服务业	Polytechnic Services	41.57	24.21	58.2
国家机关、政党机关和社会团体	**Governments Agencies, Party agencies and Social Organizations**	**878.18**	**755.48**	**86.0**
#国家机关	Governments	835.91	715.91	85.6
政党机关	Party	25.57	20.74	81.1
其他行业	**Others**	**216.94**	**110.81**	**51.1**

6-17 基本建设新增主要产品生产能力

Newly Increased Production Capacity Through Capital Construction

能力名称	Item	1996	1997	1998	1999	2000
铁矿开采（原矿）（万吨/年）	Iron-Ore Mining (10 000 tons/year)	16	274	402	913	12
烧结铁矿 （万吨/年）	Sintering of Iron-Ore (10 000 tons/year)			20	498	
生铁 （万吨/年）	Iron Smelting (10 000 tons/year)	35	33	12	180	5
炼钢 （万吨/年）	Steel-making (10 000 tons/year)	72	65	40	456	
初轧 （万吨/年）	Rough Rolling (10 000 tons/year)	5				
铁合金 （万吨/年）	Iron Alloy, Electric Furnace (10 000 tons/year)	2	1	2		1
铜选矿	Copper Ore Dressing					
处理原矿 （万吨/年）	Crude Ore Dressing (10 000 tons/year)	31	77	1	38	25
铜含量 （吨/年）	Copper Content in Concentrate Ore (ton/year)	200	8314			
原煤开采 （万吨/年）	Coal Mining (10 000 tons/year)	1694	3002	969	2347	2255
天然原油开采 （万吨/年）	Petroleum Extraction (10 000 tons/year)	903	1246	835	950	920
硫酸 （万吨/年）	Sulfuric Acid (10 000 tons/year)	90	75	1		10
纯碱 （万吨/年）	Soda Ash (10 000 tons/year)		2		20	20
烧碱 （万吨/年）	Caustic Soda (10 000 tons/year)	2				8
合成氨 （万吨/年）	Synthetic Ammonia (10 000 tons/year)	40	111	52	68	90
化肥 （万吨/年）	Chemical Fertilizer (10 000 tons/year)	77	195	59	136	62
乙烯 （吨/年）	Ethylene (ton/year)	260960		350000	80000	
塑料 （吨/年）	Plastics (ton/year)	24900	124855	540953	325400	16700
轮胎 （万条/年）	Tires (10 000 /year)					
内胎	Inner Tube			494	416	
外胎	Tire (Cover)	300	15	215	179	
发电机组容量 （万千瓦）	Capacity of Power Generating Sets (10 000 kw/year)	1741	1398	2194	2201	1907
#火电	Thermal Power	1360	1026	1544	1275	1337
水电	Hydropower	373	369	622	908	452
汽车制造 （辆/年）	Motor Vehicles (unit/year)	122349	150200	151510	30000	119000
#载重汽车制造	Trucks	11649		210		
拖拉机制造 （混合台/年）	Tractors (unit/year)					
#手扶拖拉机制造 （混合台/年）	Walking Tractors (unit/year)					
蒸汽锅炉制造 （台/年）	Steam Boilers (unit/year)					
蒸汽锅炉蒸发量(小时吨/年)	Evaporative Capacity of Steam Boilers (hr.tons/year)					
交流电动机制造(万千瓦/年)	Electric Motors (10 000 kw/year)					2000
金属切削机床制造（台/年）	Metal-Cutting Machine Tools (unit/year)	50	2000		50	
民用钢质船舶制造（综合吨/年）	Civilian Ships (ton/year)					
胶合板 （万立方米/年）	Plywood (10 000 cu.m/year)	8	1	19	2	12

6-17 续表 1 continued

能力名称	Item	1996	1997	1998	1999	2000
水泥 (万吨/年)	Cement (10 000 tons/year)	794	1038	601	231	490
化学纤维 (吨/年)	Chemical Fiber (ton/year)	112780	183330	159873	117524	97080
棉纺锭 (万锭)	Cotton Spindles (10 000 units)	6	10	2	1	2
棉布织机 (台)	Cotton Loom (unit)	362	1254	216		
棉印染布 (万米/年)	Printed and Dyed Cloth (10 000 m/year)			420	5409	3000
毛纺锭 (锭)	Wool Spindles		12800	3000		
机制糖	Machine-processed Sugar					
年生产 (万吨)	Annual Production Capacity(10000 tons)	9	3	9	3	0.3
日处理原料 (吨)	Raw Materials Processing (ton/day)	7830	2800	7000	1776	42000
卷烟 (万箱/年)	Cigarettes (10 000 cases/year)					
酒 (万吨/年)	Liquors (10 000 tons/year)	49		5	14	16
糖果 (吨/年)	Candy (ton/year)	11221	8100	42300		4700
奶粉 (吨/年)	Milk Powder (ton/year)		2350	5200		
原盐 (万吨/年)	Raw Salt (10 000 tons/year)	19	20	2	2	2
机制纸及纸板 (万吨/年)	Machine-made Paper and Paperboards (10 000 tons/year)	19	31	78	87	8
肥皂 (万箱/年)	Soap (10 000 cases/year)					1
合成洗涤剂 (万吨/年)	Synthetic Detergent (10 000 tons/year)			5	3	
鞣制皮革 (万张/年)	Tanning (10 000 pcs/year)	200		6	1	
皮鞋 (万双/年)	Leather Shoes (10 000 pairs/year)	53	218	300	906	85
日用搪瓷制品 (万件/年)	Daily-use Enamelware (10 000 pcs/year)					
日用陶瓷器 (万件/年)	Daily-use Ceramics (10 000 pcs/year)	1207	690	800	300	400
保温瓶 (万个/年)	Thermos Bottles (10 000 units/year)					
灯泡 (万只/年)	Bulbs (10 000 units/year)		2411			
自行车 (万辆/年)	Bicycles (10 000 units/year)		50			
家用电冰箱 (万台/年)	Refrigerators (10 000 units/year)			60		
电视机 (万台/年)	Television Sets (10 000 set/year)			60	6	46
录放音机 (万部/年)	Tape Recorders (10 000/year)					
家用洗衣机 (万台/年)	Washing Machines (10 000/year)					
新建铁路主线正线交付营业里程 (公里)	Length of Newly Built Railways Put into Operation (km)	2171	970	1408	1438	514
新(扩)建港口码头	Newly Built or Expanded Ports					
年吞吐量 (万吨)	Annual Handling Capacity (10 000 tons)	2537	8374	2398	6393	4491
泊位 (个)	Number of Berths (unit)	89	114	95	98	96
新建公路 (公里)	Length of New Highways (km)	10179	12203	16205	18068	15432
改建公路 (公里)	Length of Reconstructed Highways (km)	17090	20600	26361	28009	29561
商业石油库 (万立方米)	Commercial Petroleum Depot (10 000cu.m)	10	76	14	44	8
物资储备石油库(万立方米)	Petroleum Tanks in Materials Warehouse System (10 000 cu.m)	19	9	5	2	5
商业冷藏库 (万吨)	Commercial Freezers (10 000 tons)	53	61	3	25	2413
粮食仓库 (万平方米)	Grain Storehouses (10 000 sq.m)	47	104	94	249	237
粮食仓库 (万公斤)	Grain Storehouses (10 000 kg)	135718	311683	243331	1001811	1018885
高等院校：学生席位 (个)	Students Capacity of Universities and Colleges	100606	117445	127717	180886	406072
医院病床床位 (张)	Number of Hospital Beds	66737	58835	60937	64670	61490
城市自来水供水能力(万吨/日)	Tap Water Supply Capacity (10 000tons/day)	842	886	870	758	555

6-18 按资金来源和隶属关系分的更新改造投资

Investment on Innovation by Source of Funds and Administrative Relationship

单位：亿元 (100 million yuan)

年份 地区	Year Region	按资金来源分 By Source of Funds					按隶属关系分 By Administrative Relationship	
		国家预算内资金 State Budgetary Appropriations	国内贷款 Domestic Loans	利用外资 Foreign Investment	自筹资金 Fundraising	其他资金 Others	中央项目 Central Government Projects	地方项目 Local Projects
	1978	26.48	11.28		129.97			
	1979	43.64	19.86		112.38			
	1980	32.98	45.83		108.20		23.80	113.58
	1981	34.88	40.01	1.27	113.00	6.14	60.88	134.42
	1982	32.95	64.03	2.71	142.89	7.79	65.40	184.97
	1983	36.55	74.52	2.58	172.05	5.43	74.93	216.20
	1984	45.57	91.95	2.78	163.96	5.02	75.76	233.52
	1985	19.69	186.75	5.55	226.08	11.07	104.82	344.32
	1986	20.58	249.18	8.34	317.61	23.50	148.67	470.54
	1987	32.35	306.23	17.46	366.37	36.17	177.01	581.58
	1988	27.02	378.72	26.01	501.18	47.61	211.65	768.90
	1989	14.15	233.21	26.73	440.69	74.01	205.99	582.79
	1990	17.56	269.55	33.85	455.37	53.87	228.46	601.73
	1991	17.36	411.22	36.49	508.62	49.53	279.37	743.86
	1992	20.11	604.56	53.15	722.56	60.73	370.46	1090.65
	1993	31.31	800.71	84.97	1227.57	106.60	633.31	1562.54
	1994	30.60	830.11	212.85	1675.08	151.10	909.26	2009.35
	1995	38.32	803.55	321.11	1929.77	157.89	1081.46	2217.89
	1996	(29.58)	(831.26)	(353.97)	(2191.19)	(166.72)	(1250.29)	(2372.45)
		29.31	830.45	353.90	2185.05	166.24	1249.49	2365.51
	1997	36.48	796.09	272.35	2522.36	185.72	1407.73	2514.20
	1998	60.96	845.29	219.29	3019.81	226.19	1739.79	2776.96
	1999	107.48	933.06	237.11	2883.76	214.55	1581.91	2903.18
	2000	155.31	1041.22	217.65	3449.94	220.10	1861.89	3245.71
北京	Beijing	13.72	31.09	0.18	148.81	1.58	96.00	89.95
天津	Tianjin	0.41	20.56	18.48	67.50	6.36	15.26	96.67
河北	Hebei	9.50	64.53	4.84	216.81	11.64	51.19	254.73
山西	Shanxi	4.15	25.32	1.81	82.48	7.11	34.95	75.89
内蒙古	Inner Mongolia	1.41	8.72	1.84	41.31	4.21	22.72	35.86
辽宁	Liaoning	4.97	49.72	19.83	191.00	14.76	105.16	178.29
吉林	Jilin	10.23	30.14	3.73	70.67	7.31	36.22	78.32
黑龙江	Heilongjiang	2.43	25.68	2.04	206.24	5.14	188.43	51.22
上海	Shanghai	9.36	60.51	34.94	250.99	3.51	105.48	290.78
江苏	Jiangsu	8.14	66.14	24.18	222.71	19.20	96.97	241.02
浙江	Zhejiang	12.20	52.50	3.14	156.09	4.13	100.61	141.95
安徽	Anhui	4.07	51.01	2.35	89.61	4.44	49.07	103.76
福建	Fujian	2.14	40.05	6.57	114.97	5.77	23.23	152.19
江西	Jiangxi	1.20	16.16	1.38	50.01	6.64	13.28	62.10
山东	Shandong	11.34	103.00	9.69	256.16	13.53	145.08	253.52
河南	Henan	2.53	26.27	1.64	117.35	15.24	60.53	102.83
湖北	Hubei	5.71	45.60	5.34	169.28	16.54	85.39	159.77
湖南	Hunan	5.17	62.20	5.78	91.03	7.13	104.92	70.29
广东	Guangdong	5.82	50.65	48.53	323.45	23.35	105.24	330.20
广西	Guangxi	0.39	17.25	0.71	57.91	2.84	38.51	41.65
海南	Hainan	0.19	0.33	4.98	3.53	0.75	5.11	4.73
重庆	Chongqing	8.18	30.74	1.92	50.18	4.14	59.01	30.90
四川	Sichuan	3.52	33.99	9.10	120.13	7.35	57.51	116.41
贵州	Guizhou	5.10	37.76	0.97	45.33	2.47	29.06	64.25
云南	Yunnan	2.00	12.60	0.43	58.98	3.12	30.61	50.51
西藏	Tibet	2.93	0.67		1.58	0.19	0.67	3.78
陕西	Shaanxi	8.80	27.33	0.46	95.67	6.65	61.89	73.29
甘肃	Gansu	5.94	22.94	1.79	54.72	5.95	47.26	41.74
青海	Qinghai	0.33	3.20	0.04	10.54	2.94	9.65	7.44
宁夏	Ningxia	0.88	6.74	0.20	14.13	1.24	6.11	16.62
新疆	Xinjiang	2.56	17.81	0.77	46.45	4.86	52.47	25.07
不分地区	Not Classified by Region				24.32		24.32	

6-19 按构成和建设性质分的更新改造投资

Investment in Innovation by Use of Funds and Type of Construction

单位：亿元 (100 million yuan)

年份 地区	Year Region	投资额 Total	按构成分 By Use of Funds 建筑安装工程 Construction and Installation	设备、工器具购置 Purchase of Equipment and Instruments	其他费用 Others	按建设性质分 By Type of Construction #新建 New Construction	#扩建 Expansion	#改建 Reconstruction
	1978	167.73						
	1979	175.88						
	1980	187.01	74.21	59.65	3.52			
	1981	195.30	113.77	76.15	5.38	19.75	75.01	89.02
	1982	250.37	143.81	99.51	7.05	18.21	80.06	136.68
	1983	291.13	160.66	118.10	12.37	17.58	86.11	164.99
	1984	309.28	152.22	141.36	15.70	14.59	85.55	178.76
	1985	449.14	196.23	224.94	27.97	23.06	194.45	191.16
	1986	619.21	267.80	308.58	42.83	36.26	274.59	261.84
	1987	758.59	349.18	353.29	56.11	41.22	350.33	313.18
	1988	980.55	477.76	430.87	71.92	58.08	462.78	402.41
	1989	788.78	377.25	355.89	55.64	38.87	345.54	363.49
	1990	830.19	372.91	397.36	59.92	45.62	370.35	364.57
	1991	1023.23	426.33	513.35	83.54	42.82	460.91	448.46
	1992	1461.10	620.64	715.34	125.12	71.63	659.72	642.35
	1993	2195.85	945.27	1070.93	179.65	140.31	1069.26	888.40
	1994	2918.61	1258.72	1419.79	240.09	189.95	1486.20	1076.44
	1995	3299.35	1343.62	1682.20	273.53	288.19	1640.28	1179.86
	1996	(3622.74)	(1396.77)	(1900.50)	(325.47)	(349.02)	(1818.44)	(1190.99)
		3615.00	1394.07	1895.69	325.24	347.03	1816.62	1188.12
	1997	3921.94	1540.77	2033.74	347.43	381.82	1947.48	1298.31
	1998	4516.75	1681.38	2445.24	390.13	452.61	2324.42	1407.51
	1999	4485.08	1667.61	2465.70	351.77	364.83	2206.87	1531.27
	2000	5107.60	1943.25	2776.41	387.93	455.86	2506.31	1746.58
北京	Beijing	185.94	70.69	95.86	19.39	1.23	93.45	64.51
天津	Tianjin	111.93	47.31	58.15	6.47	16.95	53.17	29.58
河北	Hebei	305.91	129.65	153.24	23.02	40.35	91.02	152.15
山西	Shanxi	110.84	44.60	55.44	10.80	17.84	44.00	44.95
内蒙古	Inner Mongolia	58.58	23.02	33.59	1.97	1.58	36.98	16.91
辽宁	Liaoning	283.44	118.48	150.08	14.88	11.80	99.10	162.10
吉林	Jilin	114.54	48.63	56.99	8.92	7.57	60.75	44.04
黑龙江	Heilongjiang	239.65	126.99	101.35	11.31	30.34	151.47	31.32
上海	Shanghai	396.26	142.99	212.04	41.23	89.73	86.74	167.50
江苏	Jiangsu	337.99	134.79	181.97	21.22	17.44	172.06	121.46
浙江	Zhejiang	242.55	65.13	159.39	18.03	7.08	148.02	74.18
安徽	Anhui	152.83	46.72	96.96	9.15	15.48	86.37	46.35
福建	Fujian	175.42	49.27	119.66	6.49	23.96	102.49	33.32
江西	Jiangxi	75.38	27.95	43.48	3.95	1.72	36.58	34.37
山东	Shandong	398.60	141.65	232.88	24.06	13.74	251.29	117.75
河南	Henan	163.36	69.52	80.79	13.05	8.04	87.22	59.31
湖北	Hubei	245.16	81.59	142.62	20.94	15.45	109.57	98.28
湖南	Hunan	175.20	75.62	89.09	10.49	2.59	114.86	49.57
广东	Guangdong	435.44	164.50	219.29	51.65	36.47	239.94	84.32
广西	Guangxi	80.16	22.11	53.80	4.25	8.85	46.11	18.10
海南	Hainan	9.84	2.89	5.11	1.84	5.71	2.29	0.73
重庆	Chongqing	89.91	32.83	50.00	7.09	16.89	49.35	17.38
四川	Sichuan	173.92	59.31	102.45	12.16	22.00	99.00	47.79
贵州	Guizhou	93.30	35.01	50.41	7.88	13.38	34.90	41.20
云南	Yunnan	81.12	32.29	42.12	6.71	5.74	38.67	31.06
西藏	Tibet	4.45	2.83	1.39	0.23	1.08	1.11	2.11
陕西	Shaanxi	135.19	52.09	74.37	8.73	3.55	81.32	45.20
甘肃	Gansu	88.99	35.36	47.42	6.21	6.39	46.61	32.73
青海	Qinghai	17.09	7.68	9.18	0.23	0.48	10.05	4.82
宁夏	Ningxia	22.73	8.06	12.26	2.41	2.36	11.54	8.42
新疆	Xinjiang	77.54	34.07	42.18	1.28	10.09	19.41	41.61
不分地区	Not Classified by Region	24.32	9.61	2.82	11.88		0.86	23.46

6-20 国民经济各行业按建设性质分的更新改造投资（2000年）

Investment in Innovation by Type of Construction and Sector (2000)

单位：亿元 (100 million yuan)

行业	Sector	投资额 Investment	#新建 New Construction	#扩建 Expansion	#改建 Reconstruction
全国总计	**National Total**	**5107.60**	**455.86**	**2506.31**	**1746.58**
农、林、牧、渔业	**Farming, Forestry, Animal Husbandry and Fishery**	**26.35**	**5.10**	**7.31**	**11.07**
农业	Farming	12.95	3.40	1.68	6.65
林业	Forestry	3.91	0.47	3.14	0.28
畜牧业	Animal Husbandry	1.82	0.35	1.22	0.22
渔业	Fishery	3.13	0.73	0.26	1.49
农林牧渔服务业	Agricultural Services	4.54	0.14	1.01	2.43
采掘业	**Mining and Quarrying**	**373.86**	**6.05**	**207.47**	**137.74**
煤炭采选业	Coal Mining and Dressing	76.16	2.10	15.17	56.27
石油和天然气开采业	Extraction of Petroleum and Natural Gas	256.45	0.09	172.89	64.04
黑色金属矿采选业	Mining and Dressing of Ferrous Metals	7.59	0.38	1.58	5.38
有色金属矿采选业	Mining and Dressing of Nonferrous Metals	21.77	0.97	12.41	8.30
非金属矿采选业	Mining and Dressing of Nonmetal Minerals	8.55	0.88	4.54	2.91
其他矿采选业	Mining and Dressing of Other Minerals	0.02	0.00	0.01	0.01
木材及竹材采运业	Logging and Transport of Wood and Bamboo	3.34	1.62	0.87	0.84
制造业	**Manufacturing**	**2104.15**	**158.96**	**1031.22**	**782.01**
食品加工业	Food Processing	43.95	5.84	24.22	12.36
食品制造业	Food Production	47.75	6.41	25.87	12.01
饮料制造业	Beverages	82.52	7.21	58.70	14.22
烟草加工业	Tobacco	45.24	1.23	13.07	23.61
纺织业	Textiles	107.86	4.39	40.21	51.86
服装及纤维制品制造业	Garments and Other Fiber Products	17.28	2.18	9.46	3.19
皮革毛皮羽绒及其制品业	Leather, Furs, Down and Related Products	4.54	0.34	2.95	0.59
木材加工及竹藤棕草制品业	Timber Processing, Bamboo, Cane, Palm Fiber and Straw Products	15.15	3.74	7.50	3.19
家具制造业	Furniture Manufacturing	5.55	1.25	2.56	0.72
造纸及纸制品业	Papermaking and Paper Products	79.91	6.33	53.86	16.49
印刷业、记录媒介的复制	Printing and Record Medium Reproduction	22.85	2.42	10.85	4.92
文教体育用品制造业	Cultural, Educational and Sports Goods	3.66	0.45	1.40	0.70
石油加工及炼焦业	Petroleum Processing and Coking	129.91	3.91	43.67	82.06
化学原料及化学制品制造业	Raw Chemical Materials and Chemical Products	274.67	17.82	171.19	76.25
医药制造业	Medical and Pharmaceutical Products	91.20	9.26	44.28	30.94
化学纤维制造业	Chemical Fiber	34.94	3.84	19.69	10.44
橡胶制品业	Rubber Products	20.86	2.96	11.96	4.11
塑料制品业	Plastic Products	38.96	5.76	24.23	6.53
非金属矿物制品业	Nonmetal Mineral Products	112.18	9.99	53.61	42.65
黑色金属冶炼及压延加工业	Smelting and Pressing of Ferrous Metals	269.11	9.55	81.00	175.56
有色金属冶炼及压延加工业	Smelting and Pressing of Nonferrous Metals	82.00	2.93	39.39	37.43
金属制品业	Metal Products	29.20	2.73	15.10	7.74
普通机械制造业	Ordinary Machinery	61.08	4.63	27.88	19.02
专用设备制造业	Equipment for Special Purposes	43.10	4.55	19.39	12.97
交通运输设备制造业	Transport Equipment	178.90	6.56	98.91	64.26
电气机械及器材制造业	Electric Equipment and Machinery	79.09	8.18	36.58	25.27
电子及通信设备制造业	Electronic and Telecommunications Equipment	147.52	21.38	78.25	35.97
仪器仪表及文化办公用机械制造业	Instruments, Meters, Cultural and Office Machinery	10.55	0.80	5.44	1.89
其他制造业	Other Manufacturing	24.60	2.37	10.03	5.05
电力、煤气及水的生产和供应业	**Production and Supply of Electric Power, Gas and Water**	**481.67**	**49.31**	**162.91**	**264.93**
电力、蒸汽、热水生产和供应业	Production and Supply of Electric Power, Steam and Hot Water	438.19	40.72	139.75	253.42
煤气的生产和供应业	Production and Supply of Gas	12.99	3.07	6.55	3.27
自来水的生产和供应业	Production and Supply of Tap Water	30.50	5.51	16.61	8.23
建筑业	**Construction**	**65.82**	**5.18**	**3.74**	**42.91**
土木工程建筑业	Civil Engineering Construction	62.59	4.60	2.88	41.91

6-20 续表 1 continued

单位：亿元　　　　(100 million yuan)

行　　业	Sector	投资额 Investment	#新　建 New Construction	#扩　建 Expansion	#改　建 Reconstruction
线路、管道和设备安装业	Installation of lines, Pipelines and Equipment	2.51	0.58	0.64	0.68
装修装饰业	Fitting and Decoration	0.72	0.00	0.22	0.32
地质勘查、水利管理业	**Geological Prospecting and Water Conservancy**	**24.89**	**1.79**	**5.00**	**17.14**
地质勘查业	Geological Prospecting	1.62	0.03	1.03	0.22
水利管理业	Water Conservancy	23.28	1.76	3.97	16.92
交通运输、仓储及邮电通信业	**Transport, Storage, Postal and Telecommunication Services**	**1553.60**	**170.70**	**964.68**	**299.85**
铁路运输业	Railway Transport	98.44	0.01	19.73	69.11
公路运输业	Highway Transport	83.52	2.77	11.45	41.08
管道运输业	Pipeline Transport	1.46	0.72	0.05	0.52
水上运输业	Waterway Transport	23.37	0.25	3.33	5.81
航空运输业	Air Transport	49.29	0.36	4.92	0.59
交通运输辅助业	Transport Subsidiary Services	58.27	5.86	15.48	34.08
其他交通运输业	Other Transport	1.32	0.04	0.13	0.85
仓储业	Storage	11.29	0.08	0.83	10.32
邮电通信业	Postal and Telecommunications Services	1226.63	160.63	908.76	137.49
批发和零售贸易餐饮业	**Wholesale & Retail Trade and Catering Services**	**57.74**	**5.70**	**16.30**	**33.06**
食品饮料烟草和家庭用品批发业	Wholesale Trade of Food, Beverage, Tobacco and Household Articles	9.85	1.34	2.22	5.83
能源材料和机械电子设备批发业	Wholesale Trade of Energy, Materials and Electronic Equipment	24.11	0.90	5.70	16.13
其他批发业	Other Wholesale Trade	1.29	0.15	0.22	0.71
零售业	Retail Trade	19.46	2.66	7.37	9.09
商业经纪与代理业	Commercial Brokerage and Agencies	0.19	0.02	0.01	0.08
餐饮业	Catering Trade	2.83	0.63	0.79	1.21
金融、保险业	**Finance and Insurance**	**6.22**	**0.07**	**0.76**	**0.89**
金融业	Finance	6.11	0.05	0.75	0.84
保险业	Insurance	0.11	0.02	0.02	0.05
房地产业	**Real Estate**	**32.25**	**18.74**	**0.51**	**7.44**
房地产开发与经营业	Real Estate Development and Operation	5.68	1.05	0.36	4.19
房地产管理业	Real Estate Management	26.52	17.69	0.13	3.22
房地产代理与经纪业	Real Estate Brokerage and Agencies	0.05	0.00	0.02	0.03
社会服务业	**Social Services**	**225.13**	**19.71**	**65.24**	**80.55**
公共设施服务业	Public Services	202.76	17.46	60.88	65.65
居民服务业	Resident Services	1.17	0.07	0.07	0.68
旅馆业	Hotels	13.97	0.80	1.92	10.96
租赁服务业	Leasing Services	1.05	0.03	0.00	1.00
旅游业	Tourism	1.08	0.22	0.56	0.23
娱乐服务业	Recreational Services	0.60	0.05	0.23	0.32
信息、咨询服务业	Information and Consultative Services	0.21		0.20	
计算机应用服务业	Computer Application Services	2.92	1.00	1.11	0.78
其他社会服务业	Other Social Services	1.37	0.09	0.27	0.91
卫生体育和社会福利业	**Health Care, Sports and Social Welfare**	**19.67**	**1.41**	**4.79**	**4.78**
卫生	Health Care	17.96	1.19	4.58	3.94
体育	Sports	0.91	0.22	0.20	0.04
社会福利保障业	Social Welfare and Social Security	0.80			0.80
教育、文化艺术和广播电影电视业	**Education, Culture and Arts, Radio, Film and Television**	**33.67**	**3.35**	**8.95**	**12.51**
教育	Education	13.75	1.01	3.89	3.94
文化艺术业	Culture and Arts	5.36	0.79	0.86	2.40
广播、电影、电视业	Radio, Film and Television	14.56	1.56	4.19	6.17
科学研究和综合技术服务业	**Scientific Research and Polytechnic Services**	**34.35**	**0.69**	**3.55**	**26.10**
科学研究业	Scientific Research	7.88	0.44	2.86	2.06
综合技术服务业	Polytechnic Services	26.47	0.24	0.69	24.04
国家机关、政党机关和社会团体	**Governments Agencies, Party agencies and Social Organizations**	**50.19**	**7.71**	**16.69**	**18.68**
#国家机关	Governments	49.21	7.64	16.30	18.26
政党机关	Party	0.29		0.26	0.01
其他行业	**Others**	**18.05**	**1.41**	**7.19**	**6.92**

6-21 各地区更新改造施工、投产项目个数和新增固定资产

Number of Innovation Projects Under Construction and Put into Use and Newly Increased Fixed Assets by Region

年份 地区	Year Region	施工项目（个）Number of Projects under Construction (unit)	全部建成投产项目（个）Number of Projects Completed and Put into Use (unit)	项目建成投产率（%）Rate of Projects Completed and Put into Use (%)	新增固定资产（亿元）Newly Increased Fixed Assets (100 million yuan)	固定资产交付使用率（%）Rate of Fixed Assets Put into Use (%)
	1980	46152	23105	50.1	92.58	67.4
	1981	66339	34832	52.5	143.24	73.3
	1982	89926	47686	53.0	187.95	75.1
	1983	83091	45631	54.9	222.61	76.5
	1984	68051	36780	54.0	242.46	78.4
	1985	77604	43149	55.6	316.79	70.5
	1986	82618	46623	56.4	468.58	75.7
	1987	87775	47952	54.6	582.62	76.8
	1988	88964	46760	52.6	690.53	70.4
	1989	60146	31805	52.6	636.88	80.7
	1990	56825	31537	55.5	722.94	87.1
	1991	64574	36770	56.9	858.30	83.9
	1992	69781	40574	58.1	1105.05	75.6
	1993	64670	35932	55.6	1531.93	69.8
	1994	59089	33091	56.0	2192.57	75.1
	1995	55242	35267	63.8	2524.87	76.5
	1996	(57501)	(36534)	(63.5)	(3002.69)	(82.9)
		55235	34580	62.6	2995.31	82.9
	1997	51576	33590	65.1	3250.55	82.9
	1998	51054	33407	65.4	3690.36	81.7
	1999	52484	34319	65.4	3644.67	81.3
	2000	53641	33093	61.7	4111.51	80.5
北京	Beijing	1240	780	62.9	138.87	74.7
天津	Tianjin	823	581	70.6	93.57	83.6
河北	Hebei	3648	2640	72.4	231.79	75.8
山西	Shanxi	1507	1056	70.1	83.87	75.7
内蒙古	Inner Mongolia	1249	1032	82.6	47.26	80.7
辽宁	Liaoning	3592	1884	52.5	243.80	86.0
吉林	Jilin	1052	641	60.9	78.31	68.4
黑龙江	Heilongjiang	1285	1032	80.3	194.34	81.1
上海	Shanghai	2475	104	4.2	270.68	68.3
江苏	Jiangsu	3595	2718	75.6	274.84	81.3
浙江	Zhejiang	3519	2601	73.9	186.20	76.8
安徽	Anhui	1023	639	62.5	109.63	71.7
福建	Fujian	1965	1340	68.2	159.96	91.2
江西	Jiangxi	1192	597	50.1	48.95	64.9
山东	Shandong	2408	1695	70.4	300.99	75.5
河南	Henan	1675	1089	65.0	135.38	82.9
湖北	Hubei	2756	2067	75.0	220.91	90.1
湖南	Hunan	2140	1418	66.3	143.53	81.9
广东	Guangdong	5303	2192	41.3	423.41	97.2
广西	Guangxi	1785	1122	62.9	81.67	101.9
海南	Hainan	146	125	85.6	8.00	81.3
重庆	Chongqing	890	563	63.3	62.76	69.8
四川	Sichuan	1675	1061	63.3	145.73	83.8
贵州	Guizhou	1509	874	57.9	75.01	80.4
云南	Yunnan	1142	649	56.8	66.37	81.8
西藏	Tibet	82	59	72.0	4.79	107.5
陕西	Shaanxi	1108	670	60.5	89.35	66.1
甘肃	Gansu	1069	552	51.6	74.44	83.6
青海	Qinghai	268	146	54.5	11.84	69.3
宁夏	Ningxia	229	128	55.9	13.95	61.4
新疆	Xinjiang	1273	1031	81.0	73.77	95.1
不分地区	Not Classified by Region	18	7	38.9	17.50	72.0

6–22 按国民经济行业分的更新改造投资(2000)

单位：亿元

年份 地区	Year Region	合计 Total	农、林、牧、渔业 Farming, Forestry, Animal Husbandry and Fishery	采掘业 Mining and Quarrying	制造业 Manufacturing	电力、煤气及水的生产和供应业 Production and Supply of Electricity Gas and Water	建筑业 Construction	地质勘查业水利管理业 Geological Prospecting and Water Conservancy
	1980	137.38	1.21	34.55	73.72	5.62	1.07	0.14
	1981	195.30	5.04	43.17	92.20	7.60	2.22	0.28
	1982	250.37	8.40	36.51	125.11	9.22	4.35	0.23
	1983	291.13	6.13	47.62	148.02	11.82	4.29	0.17
	1984	309.28	5.24	32.87	181.14	11.42	4.88	0.32
	1985	449.14	5.56	44.09	289.71	17.25	6.97	0.79
	1986	619.21	6.08	50.91	402.78	25.47	8.29	1.79
	1987	758.59	7.75	59.71	495.70	29.15	8.92	2.12
	1988	980.55	10.67	87.49	646.24	41.24	11.21	1.96
	1989	788.78	8.40	87.83	500.12	35.23	7.66	3.34
	1990	830.19	7.32	85.49	518.20	43.79	7.69	3.15
	1991	1023.23	13.16	92.96	646.29	43.98	8.51	3.53
	1992	1461.10	14.77	90.13	920.59	65.96	14.20	5.23
	1993	2195.85	17.83	141.69	1298.33	99.31	32.98	7.04
	1994	2918.61	19.64	171.02	1606.03	150.99	31.47	5.50
	1995	3299.35	18.83	206.67	1775.84	217.64	45.80	8.26
	1996	(3622.74)	(23.22)	(228.29)	(1843.01)	(259.21)	(34.17)	(10.35)
		3615.00	22.91	228.09	1839.23	258.93	33.98	10.31
	1997	3921.94	27.21	244.37	1866.24	275.43	47.91	25.10
	1998	4516.75	27.11	308.78	1797.30	344.52	30.04	33.48
	1999	4485.08	26.33	251.66	1796.07	463.86	31.28	30.52
	2000	5107.60	26.35	373.86	2104.15	481.67	65.82	24.89
北　京	Beijing	185.94		0.53	47.13	8.16	1.13	7.59
天　津	Tianjin	111.93	0.10	0.54	65.41	3.55	3.86	0.30
河　北	Hebei	305.91	3.56	12.35	139.78	33.79	0.75	2.14
山　西	Shanxi	110.84	0.09	15.08	56.67	3.77	2.04	0.06
内蒙古	Inner Mongolia	58.58	0.01	3.67	25.14	5.81		
辽　宁	Liaoning	283.44	0.86	38.79	150.73	16.34	0.94	0.05
吉　林	Jilin	114.54	2.35	4.78	76.36	17.19	0.11	
黑龙江	Heilongjiang	239.65	0.12	126.86	49.70	9.05	0.11	0.25
上　海	Shanghai	396.26	1.13	0.03	220.79	19.83	2.93	1.27
江　苏	Jiangsu	337.99	1.74	9.79	152.10	45.68	6.39	0.20
浙　江	Zhejiang	242.55	1.09	0.71	93.61	35.04	0.46	0.57
安　徽	Anhui	152.83	0.18	7.23	58.75	29.92	0.97	0.41
福　建	Fujian	175.42	0.40	1.71	63.45	20.09	0.32	0.15
江　西	Jiangxi	75.38		5.24	30.02	6.59	0.23	
山　东	Shandong	398.60	0.37	36.59	190.28	44.71	0.20	1.08
河　南	Henan	163.36	0.42	24.55	75.70	5.93	1.16	0.65
湖　北	Hubei	245.16	2.32	7.69	115.42	19.11	4.26	0.61
湖　南	Hunan	175.20	0.01	3.12	75.02	3.51	0.22	0.03
广　东	Guangdong	435.44	1.22	1.32	91.90	36.27	22.43	7.64
广　西	Guangxi	80.16	0.40	1.00	23.83	13.59	0.10	0.13
海　南	Hainan	9.84	1.46		1.77	0.28		
重　庆	Chongqing	89.91	0.01	1.22	24.69	10.98	0.08	0.01
四　川	Sichuan	173.92	0.03	11.03	91.74	12.19	1.31	0.14
贵　州	Guizhou	93.30	0.02	3.05	28.57	33.12	0.15	0.15
云　南	Yunnan	81.12	0.51	2.06	34.08	2.43	0.26	0.39
西　藏	Tibet	4.45	0.01	0.15	0.54	1.97	0.18	0.01
陕　西	Shaanxi	135.19	0.09	18.31	43.62	26.15	1.28	0.28
甘　肃	Gansu	88.99	1.30	5.34	30.07	10.09	0.68	0.24
青　海	Qinghai	17.09	0.01	2.98	5.41	0.50	0.26	
宁　夏	Ningxia	22.73		2.51	14.27	0.89	0.05	0.01
新　疆	Xinjiang	77.54	6.55	2.49	27.58	5.15	12.96	0.53
不分地区	Not Classified by Region	24.32		23.15				

Investment in Innovation by Sector (2000)

(100 million yuan)

交通运输仓储和邮电通信业 Transport, Storage, Post & Telecommunication Services	批发零售贸易和餐饮业 Wholesale and Retail Trade & Catering Services	金融、保险业 Finance and Insurance	房地产业 Real Estate	社会服务业 Social Services	卫生体育和社会福利业 Health Care, Sports & Social Welfare	教育、文化艺术和广播电影电视业 Education, Culture and Arts, Radio, Film and Television	科学研究和综合技术服务业 Scientific Research and Polytechnic Services	国家机关、政党机关和社会团体 Government Agencies, Party Agencies and Social Organizations	其他 Others
12.17	4.02	0.06	2.28		0.23	0.50	0.43	0.99	0.39
21.88	7.46	0.65	6.63		0.73	1.85	1.13	2.60	1.86
30.42	12.95	1.37	9.29		1.38	3.26	1.17	3.84	2.87
32.58	14.08	2.07	9.97		1.72	3.60	1.34	4.28	3.44
34.93	11.31	1.37	12.79		1.90	3.89	1.69	3.14	2.39
41.49	10.37	0.97	3.05	17.41	1.78	2.91	2.35	3.24	1.49
55.95	15.93	1.53	5.64	29.11	2.44	4.07	2.33	4.72	2.17
65.63	24.48	1.94	10.45	30.19	2.77	4.20	2.41	9.17	3.94
74.03	32.00	2.66	12.52	35.07	3.33	4.57	2.35	9.16	6.13
65.28	22.46	2.07	8.95	27.49	2.13	4.31	2.35	6.19	4.26
81.32	22.10	1.72	8.54	27.68	3.16	4.65	2.18	7.05	6.14
113.67	27.83	2.11	8.90	34.74	3.22	5.62	2.29	9.22	7.20
192.77	48.12	2.42	13.02	52.93	4.22	6.08	3.16	12.81	14.69
361.47	65.47	3.73	33.80	78.68	6.04	9.37	3.18	21.22	15.73
576.95	101.04	3.63	59.79	120.03	4.47	10.07	5.02	27.38	25.58
680.73	97.30	2.85	56.57	108.50	5.93	15.27	6.29	29.94	22.93
-875.97	-70.93	-8.11	-41.76	-131.30	-10.38	-13.38	-5.77	-37.47	-29.42
875.19	70.38	8.07	41.75	131.01	10.17	12.98	5.64	36.93	29.42
1050.13	61.06	11.77	56.92	151.47	10.77	17.95	4.85	37.55	33.21
1542.25	52.64	12.86	25.54	189.48	11.64	20.41	5.83	49.86	64.99
1420.67	46.03	6.89	35.51	228.33	15.31	26.77	18.89	54.87	32.09
1553.60	57.74	6.22	32.25	225.13	19.67	33.67	34.35	50.19	18.05
65.84	0.54			24.59	0.84	2.33	20.72	2.82	3.73
18.80	9.63	0.12	1.55	2.90	0.03	1.29	0.30	1.95	1.58
90.10	3.58	0.17	0.29	14.18	1.24	3.10	0.02	0.51	0.37
27.19				5.57	0.05	0.16	0.05	0.11	0.00
20.45	0.26			1.42	0.25	0.03	0.60		0.95
69.92	0.86	0.22	0.03	3.88	0.03	0.28	0.25	0.26	
8.05	0.05		0.04	1.43	0.03	0.12	0.05	3.98	
52.48	0.19			0.43		0.02		0.32	0.11
43.54	8.31	0.10	27.44	50.70	5.51	5.42	3.09	4.52	1.66
88.00	3.97	0.18	0.01	18.88	1.47	2.33	0.28	1.02	5.95
99.52	0.28	0.63	0.10	6.42	1.84	1.60	0.38	0.22	0.08
50.52	0.51	0.02	0.04	0.87	0.13	0.80		2.24	0.23
85.24	0.46			1.24	0.20	0.64	0.22	1.13	0.18
31.15	0.02			0.65	0.13	1.19		0.16	0.00
100.24	4.21	0.01	0.56	13.91	0.37	0.26	0.03	4.94	0.85
40.47	0.34	0.03	0.55	7.53	0.36	0.83	0.35	4.44	0.06
57.92	10.68	2.69		13.60	1.09	2.35	2.04	4.27	1.11
87.34	0.69	0.14		2.59	0.58	0.88	0.68	0.31	0.08
224.78	0.81	1.23	0.50	27.55	4.11	6.13	1.00	8.25	0.31
36.91	1.93		0.01	1.42	0.23	0.15	0.17	0.28	
5.50	0.01	0.01		0.08		0.22		0.21	0.30
48.39	0.76	0.01	0.51	1.77	0.04	0.46	0.12	0.84	
50.07	0.15		0.30	4.29	0.25	1.38	0.38	0.65	
23.33	3.01	0.01		1.15	0.10	0.07	0.08	0.45	0.04
22.44	1.36	0.59	0.32	8.44	0.31	0.75	3.39	3.76	0.03
1.08	0.01			0.08		0.20	0.01	0.22	
39.40	0.45	0.01		5.09	0.05	0.01	0.08	0.38	
34.64	4.19			0.35	0.01	0.09		1.65	0.33
6.67	0.05			0.97	0.06	0.02	0.02	0.07	0.06
4.75	0.02			0.18	0.02	0.00	0.02		
17.71	0.39	0.07	0.01	2.97	0.36	0.54	0.02	0.19	0.04
1.17									

6-23 国民经济各行业更新改造施工、投产项目个数（2000年）

Number of Innovation Projects under Construction and Put into Use by Sector (2000)

行业	Sector	施工项目（个）Number of Projects under Construction (unit)	#新开工 Started This Year	全部建成投产项目（个）Number of Projects Completed and Put into Use (unit)	项目建成投产率（%）Rate of Projects Completed & Put into Use (%)
全国总计	**National Total**	**53641**	**38051**	**33093**	**61.7**
农、林、牧、渔业	**Farming, Forestry, Animal Husbandry and Fishery**	**660**	**579**	**537**	**81.4**
农业	Farming	411	376	364	88.6
林业	Forestry	77	61	59	76.6
畜牧业	Animal Husbandry	49	42	40	81.6
渔业	Fishery	41	36	30	73.2
农林牧渔服务业	Agricultural Services	82	64	44	53.7
采掘业	**Mining and Quarrying**	**2150**	**1477**	**1260**	**58.6**
煤炭采选业	Coal Mining and Dressing	1055	724	612	58.0
石油和天然气开采业	Extraction of Petroleum and Natural Gas	83	45	52	62.7
黑色金属矿采选业	Mining and Dressing of Ferrous Metals	175	128	132	75.4
有色金属矿采选业	Mining and Dressing of Nonferrous Metals	561	390	293	52.2
非金属矿采选业	Mining and Dressing of Nonmetal Minerals	215	165	143	66.5
其他矿采选业	Mining and Dressing of Other Minerals	4	4	1	25.0
木材及竹材采运业	Logging and Transport of Wood and Bamboo	57	21	27	47.4
制造业	**Manufacturing**	**21400**	**15194**	**12886**	**60.2**
食品加工业	Food Processing	921	760	698	75.8
食品制造业	Food Production	550	421	353	64.2
饮料制造业	Beverages	816	588	535	65.6
烟草加工业	Tobacco	413	207	132	32.0
纺织业	Textiles	1144	937	756	66.1
服装及纤维制品制造业	Garments and Other Fiber Products	192	148	132	68.8
皮革毛皮羽绒及其制品业	Leather, Furs, Down and Related Products	69	55	44	63.8
木材加工及竹藤棕草制品业	Timber Processing, Bamboo, Cane, Palm Fiber and Straw Products	217	170	148	68.2
家具制造业	Furniture Manufacturing	77	56	48	62.3
造纸及纸制品业	Papermaking and Paper Products	603	464	403	66.8
印刷业、记录媒介的复制	Printing and Record Medium Reproduction	189	136	112	59.3
文教体育用品制造业	Cultural, Educational and Sports Goods	53	37	26	49.1
石油加工及炼焦业	Petroleum Processing and Coking	1264	1003	842	66.6
化学原料及化学制品制造业	Raw Chemical Materials and Chemical Products	2928	2121	1928	65.8
医药制造业	Medical and Pharmaceutical Products	977	605	474	48.5
化学纤维制造业	Chemical Fiber	172	131	106	61.6
橡胶制品业	Rubber Products	145	95	79	54.5
塑料制品业	Plastic Products	345	266	191	55.4
非金属矿物制品业	Nonmetal Mineral Products	2015	1590	1404	69.7
黑色金属冶炼及压延加工业	Smelting and Pressing of Ferrous Metals	2099	1418	1275	60.7
有色金属冶炼及压延加工业	Smelting and Pressing of Nonferrous Metals	1233	851	675	54.7
金属制品业	Metal Products	421	335	243	57.7
普通机械制造业	Ordinary Machinery	851	494	414	48.6
专用设备制造业	Equipment for Special Purposes	663	357	308	46.5
交通运输设备制造业	Transport Equipment	1466	937	760	51.8
电气机械及器材制造业	Electric Equipment and Machinery	666	427	340	51.1
电子及通信设备制造业	Electronic and Telecommunications Equipment	503	289	230	45.7
仪器仪表及文化办公用机械制造业	Instruments, Meters, Cultural and Office Machinery	116	71	58	50.0
其他制造业	Other Manufacturing	292	225	172	58.9
电力、煤气及水的生产和供应业	**Production and Supply of Electric Power, Gas and Water**	**9043**	**4914**	**3816**	**42.2**
电力、蒸汽、热水生产和供应业	Production and Supply of Electric Power, Steam and Hot Water	8367	4537	3446	41.2
煤气的生产和供应业	Production and Supply of Gas	126	75	61	48.4
自来水的生产和供应业	Production and Supply of Tap Water	550	302	309	56.2
建筑业	**Construction**	**474**	**324**	**322**	**67.9**
土木工程建筑业	Civil Engineering Construction	418	288	297	71.1

6–23 续表 1 continued

行业	Sector	施工项目 (个) Number of Projects under Construction (unit)	# 新开工 Started This Year	全部建成投产项目 (个) Number of Projects Completed and Put into Use (unit)	项目建成投产率 (%) Rate of Projects Completed & Put into Use (%)
线路、管道和设备安装业	Installation of lines, Pipelines and Equipment	34	29	20	58.8
装修装饰业	Fitting and Decoration	22	7	5	22.7
地质勘查、水利管理业	**Geological Prospecting and Water Conservancy**	**334**	**233**	**210**	**62.9**
地质勘查业	Geological Prospecting	22	21	21	95.5
水利管理业	Water Conservancy	312	212	189	60.6
交通运输、仓储及邮电通信业	**Transport, Storage, Postal and Telecommunication Services**	**14679**	**11765**	**11010**	**75.0**
铁路运输业	Railway Transport	2228	1642	1695	76.1
公路运输业	Highway Transport	592	429	387	65.4
管道运输业	Pipeline Transport	59	58	59	100.0
水上运输业	Waterway Transport	247	151	175	70.9
航空运输业	Air Transport	53	31	16	30.2
交通运输辅助业	Transport Subsidiary Services	601	443	394	65.6
其他交通运输业	Other Transport	12	5	5	41.7
仓储业	Storage	671	645	486	72.4
邮电通信业	Postal and Telecommunications Services	10216	8361	7793	76.3
批发和零售贸易餐饮业	**Wholesale & Retail Trade and Catering Services**	**1098**	**838**	**715**	**65.1**
食品饮料烟草和家庭用品批发业	Wholesale Trade of Food, Beverage, Tobacco and Household Articles	214	144	105	49.1
能源材料和机械电子设备批发业	Wholesale Trade of Energy, Materials and Electronic Equipment	439	378	316	72.0
其他批发业	Other Wholesale Trade	35	23	18	51.4
零售业	Retail Trade	358	257	246	68.7
商业经纪与代理业	Commercial Brokerage and Agencies	6	3	4	66.7
餐饮业	Catering Trade	46	33	26	56.5
金融、保险业	**Finance and Insurance**	**40**	**25**	**31**	**77.5**
金融业	Finance	34	20	28	82.4
保险业	Insurance	6	5	3	50.0
房地产业	**Real Estate**	**90**	**37**	**32**	**35.6**
房地产开发与经营业	Real Estate Development and Operation	60	26	22	36.7
房地产管理业	Real Estate Management	28	9	9	32.1
房地产代理与经纪业	Real Estate Brokerage and Agencies	2	2	1	50.0
社会服务业	**Social Services**	**1755**	**1240**	**1085**	**61.8**
公共设施服务业	Public Services	1497	1073	935	62.5
居民服务业	Resident Services	18	12	9	50.0
旅馆业	Hotels	157	98	99	63.1
租赁服务业	Leasing Services	8	8	5	62.5
旅游业	Tourism	20	14	10	50.0
娱乐服务业	Recreational Services	15	12	10	66.7
信息、咨询服务业	Information and Consultative Services	4	4	1	25.0
计算机应用服务业	Computer Application Services	19	9	5	26.3
其他社会服务业	Other Social Services	17	10	11	64.7
卫生体育和社会福利业	**Health Care, Sports and Social Welfare**	**246**	**170**	**147**	**59.8**
卫生	Health Care	227	161	140	61.7
体育	Sports	9	3	3	33.3
社会福利保障业	Social Welfare and Social Security	10	6	4	40.0
教育、文化艺术和广播电影电视业	**Education, Culture and Arts, Radio, Film and Television**	**493**	**354**	**260**	**52.7**
教育	Education	275	209	144	52.4
文化艺术业	Culture and Arts	38	20	21	55.3
广播、电影、电视业	Radio, Film and Television	180	125	95	52.8
科学研究和综合技术服务业	**Scientific Research and Polytechnic Services**	**269**	**216**	**192**	**71.4**
科学研究业	Scientific Research	92	61	35	38.0
综合技术服务业	Polytechnic Services	177	155	157	88.7
国家机关、政党机关和社会团体	**Governments Agencies, Party agencies and Social Organizations**	**721**	**551**	**468**	**64.9**
#国家机关	Governments	694	528	455	65.6
政党机关	Party	11	9	8	72.7
其他行业	**Others**	**189**	**134**	**122**	**64.6**

6-24 按国民经济行业分的更新改造新增固定资产

单位：亿元

年份 地区	Year Region	合计 Total	农、林、牧、渔业 Farming, Forestry, Animal Husbandry and Fishery	采掘业 Mining and Quarrying	制造业 Manufacturing	电力、煤气及水的生产和供应业 Production and Supply of Electric Power, Gas and Water	建筑业 Construction	地质勘查业水利管理业 Geological Prospecting and Water Conservancy
	1980	92.58	0.90	21.91	49.59	3.53	0.94	0.09
	1981	143.24	3.70	27.96	68.17	5.40	1.82	0.12
	1982	187.95	6.63	24.18	95.36	5.86	3.71	0.21
	1983	222.61	5.09	32.72	114.60	7.81	3.96	0.16
	1984	242.46	4.18	23.96	140.35	8.00	3.87	0.29
	1985	316.79	4.30	32.13	196.46	11.95	6.40	0.67
	1986	468.58	5.20	38.72	300.45	16.85	7.68	1.54
	1987	582.62	6.60	45.23	372.71	24.82	8.20	1.63
	1988	690.53	7.73	61.72	453.01	26.72	9.19	1.80
	1989	636.88	7.15	67.58	399.22	27.48	7.07	2.50
	1990	722.94	7.14	67.81	460.33	33.12	6.69	2.41
	1991	858.30	11.43	75.91	542.84	38.30	8.05	3.93
	1992	1105.05	12.71	70.87	685.35	49.34	12.82	2.46
	1993	1531.93	15.23	110.63	876.43	68.59	27.27	4.28
	1994	2192.57	17.12	145.08	1210.46	103.14	18.72	5.00
	1995	2524.87	17.37	164.06	1381.19	146.54	29.86	6.38
	1996	(3002.69)	(21.10)	(187.10)	(1512.97)	(218.13)	(30.27)	(7.39)
		2995.31	20.87	186.92	1509.36	217.86	30.10	7.34
	1997	3250.55	23.36	219.23	1504.22	230.45	41.85	12.83
	1998	3690.36	22.51	242.82	1518.86	284.26	24.82	15.42
	1999	3644.67	20.24	217.48	1527.02	324.89	25.82	16.37
	2000	4111.51	20.44	284.27	1660.99	351.38	61.12	16.22
北京	Beijing	138.87		0.41	20.61	9.80	1.38	1.67
天津	Tianjin	93.57	0.09	0.51	45.36	3.27	3.61	0.31
河北	Hebei	231.79	4.08	9.22	111.12	20.34	0.62	2.13
山西	Shanxi	83.87	0.08	11.65	47.08	4.28	1.97	0.04
内蒙古	Inner Mongolia	47.26	0.01	2.64	15.73	5.21		
辽宁	Liaoning	243.80	0.34	28.08	133.43	7.02	0.95	0.06
吉林	Jilin	78.31	1.40	2.67	56.34	9.36	0.02	
黑龙江	Heilongjiang	194.34	0.10	88.21	48.80	5.66	0.08	
上海	Shanghai	270.68	0.81		143.74	14.74	1.98	2.05
江苏	Jiangsu	274.84	0.65	9.60	125.74	37.20	6.11	0.20
浙江	Zhejiang	186.20	0.99	0.74	72.87	15.30	0.45	0.44
安徽	Anhui	109.63	0.04	5.51	37.92	21.03	0.94	0.30
福建	Fujian	159.96	0.04	1.13	58.74	16.29	0.32	0.04
江西	Jiangxi	48.95		5.16	24.06	2.26	0.18	
山东	Shandong	300.99	0.37	32.10	128.04	34.48	0.19	1.08
河南	Henan	135.38	0.42	19.36	64.51	2.47	1.09	0.75
湖北	Hubei	220.91	1.79	6.18	108.68	14.41	3.47	0.51
湖南	Hunan	143.53	0.01	2.55	55.28	2.38	0.28	0.04
广东	Guangdong	423.41	1.07	1.04	83.66	47.71	21.87	5.35
广西	Guangxi	81.67	0.37	0.73	22.45	19.13	0.08	0.09
海南	Hainan	8.00	1.29		1.61	0.28		
重庆	Chongqing	62.76	0.01	1.14	19.91	8.09	0.08	0.01
四川	Sichuan	145.73	0.03	10.12	76.32	6.72	1.05	0.23
贵州	Guizhou	75.01	0.02	2.27	28.91	18.06	0.13	0.06
云南	Yunnan	66.37	0.43	1.99	21.96	1.49	0.25	0.18
西藏	Tibet	4.79		0.23	0.91	2.28	0.12	0.01
陕西	Shaanxi	89.35	0.07	14.48	28.11	12.25	1.16	0.19
甘肃	Gansu	74.44		4.15	35.08	4.35	0.38	0.06
青海	Qinghai	11.84	0.01	2.28	5.57	0.22	0.29	
宁夏	Ningxia	13.95		2.57	6.60	1.14	0.05	
新疆	Xinjiang	73.77	5.94	2.06	31.85	4.15	12.04	0.41
不分地区	Not Classified by Region	17.50		15.49				

Newly Increased Fixed Assets through Investment in Innovation by Sector

(100 million yuan)

交通运输仓储和邮电通信业 Transport, Storage, Post & Telecommunication Services	批发零售贸易和餐饮业 Wholesale and Retail Trade & Catering Services	金融、保险业 Finance and Insurance	房地产业 Real Estate	社会服务业 Social Services	卫生体育和社会福利业 Health Care, Sports & Social Welfare	教育、文化艺术和广播电影电视业 Education, Culture and Arts, Radio, Film and Television	科学研究和综合技术服务业 Scientific Research and Polytechnic Services	国家机关、政党机关和社会团体 Government Agencies, Party Agencies and Social Organizations	其他 Others
9.15	3.00	0.03	1.53		0.16	0.38	0.27	0.76	0.34
18.10	6.18	0.46	4.86		0.62	1.52	0.69	2.08	1.56
24.24	10.58	1.12	6.99		1.03	2.80	0.98	2.56	1.70
25.35	11.68	1.96	7.12		1.40	3.12	1.05	3.69	2.90
30.83	9.16	1.39	9.28		1.61	3.12	1.14	2.87	2.41
33.24	7.91	0.77	2.54	11.13	1.67	2.47	1.93	2.33	0.90
45.10	13.03	1.22	4.87	20.11	2.30	3.66	1.76	4.24	1.84
54.77	18.28	1.60	9.29	21.03	2.30	3.02	1.80	8.99	2.37
50.26	23.58	2.09	9.36	25.65	2.49	3.26	1.59	7.63	4.43
49.23	21.34	2.23	8.29	26.31	2.72	3.82	2.12	5.46	4.39
68.48	23.05	1.45	8.16	25.26	3.05	3.53	1.58	5.48	5.41
98.28	21.32	1.85	7.97	26.03	2.86	4.96	1.50	7.12	5.95
154.62	34.44	2.03	9.14	39.88	3.49	5.36	2.81	10.05	9.68
285.30	36.62	2.82	18.31	51.72	4.21	5.40	1.89	14.63	8.58
473.56	50.30	2.47	31.24	91.29	3.95	5.90	3.09	20.09	11.16
563.74	49.92	2.32	38.80	69.34	4.60	11.23	3.00	21.19	15.33
(739.95)	(65.07)	(6.28)	(36.99)	(100.87)	(7.79)	(10.23)	(5.76)	(28.51)	(24.28)
739.21	64.53	6.24	36.98	100.60	7.60	9.82	5.63	27.99	24.26
884.03	36.10	9.15	57.87	137.14	10.31	13.46	5.98	33.81	30.76
1210.86	64.86	12.86	26.41	157.94	10.39	16.39	4.91	42.91	34.15
1109.86	54.22	6.16	32.32	189.42	13.02	20.95	16.20	43.18	27.51
1317.75	48.69	6.17	30.00	186.59	17.37	27.68	30.51	37.56	14.75
59.81	0.33			17.43	0.43	0.78	20.29	2.90	3.03
24.12	7.61	0.02	2.94	1.39	0.07	0.62	0.29	1.63	1.76
67.05	1.60	0.17	0.25	11.13	1.08	2.20	0.02	0.51	0.27
15.81	0.26			2.46	0.00	0.16	0.05	0.04	0.00
21.12	0.25			0.89	0.25	0.03	0.19		0.95
69.51	0.58	0.34		2.78	0.03	0.28	0.28	0.13	
6.82	0.05		0.10	1.26	0.03	0.12	0.01	0.13	
50.85	0.01			0.05		0.02		0.45	0.11
23.51	7.47	0.03	23.79	37.86	4.49	5.06	0.37	3.72	1.08
65.21	2.18	0.22	0.01	18.06	1.55	2.37	0.28	0.99	4.48
84.06	0.22	0.63	0.10	5.75	1.56	1.51	1.26	0.21	0.11
40.15	0.32	0.02	0.04	0.77	0.13	0.70	0.00	1.54	0.23
80.48	0.22			1.01	0.20	0.24	0.20	0.86	0.18
15.19	0.02			0.78	0.13	1.12		0.06	
84.09	2.91	0.01	0.56	11.33	0.21	0.17	0.03	4.58	0.84
35.36	0.22	0.03	0.05	7.08	0.36	0.37	0.31	2.98	0.04
47.09	12.81	2.90		13.10	1.01	2.05	2.04	3.90	1.00
78.22	0.28	0.14		2.63	0.58	0.70	0.02	0.31	0.12
217.23	0.73	0.99	0.50	27.72	3.89	5.92	0.83	4.67	0.24
33.31	3.36		0.01	1.45	0.20	0.17	0.04	0.28	
4.36	0.01			0.08		0.22		0.06	0.08
28.95	0.89	0.01	1.15	1.88	0.04	0.25	0.05	0.31	
45.97	0.17		0.30	2.57	0.25	0.93	0.35	0.73	
21.30	2.39	0.01		1.11	0.10	0.11	0.07	0.43	0.04
22.17	2.33	0.59	0.21	6.73	0.28	0.64	3.38	3.70	0.03
0.80	0.01			0.08		0.20	0.01	0.15	
27.03	0.50	0.01		5.01	0.05	0.01	0.08	0.41	
27.67	0.54			0.35	0.01	0.10		1.63	0.12
2.54	0.04			0.70	0.07	0.03	0.03	0.05	
3.33	0.02			0.18	0.02		0.04		
12.66	0.39	0.06	0.01	2.98	0.38	0.60	0.02	0.19	0.04
2.01									

6-25 国民经济各行业更新改造投资和新增固定资产（2000年）

Investment in Innovation and Newly Increased Fixed Assets by Sector (2000)

行业	Sector	投资额（亿元）Investment (100 million yuan)	新增固定资产（亿元）Newly Increased Fixed Assets (100 million yuan)	固定资产交付使用率（%）Rate of Fixed Assets Put into Use (%)
全国总计	**National Total**	**5107.60**	**4111.51**	**80.5**
农、林、牧、渔业	**Farming, Forestry, Animal Husbandry and Fishery**	**26.35**	**20.44**	**77.6**
农业	Farming	12.95	10.33	79.7
林业	Forestry	3.91	2.51	64.2
畜牧业	Animal Husbandry	1.82	1.58	87.0
渔业	Fishery	3.13	2.40	76.5
农林牧渔服务业	Agricultural Services	4.54	3.62	79.8
采掘业	**Mining and Quarrying**	**373.86**	**284.27**	**76.0**
煤炭采选业	Coal Mining and Dressing	76.16	65.27	85.7
石油和天然气开采业	Extraction of Petroleum and Natural Gas	256.45	186.76	72.8
黑色金属矿采选业	Mining and Dressing of Ferrous Metals	7.59	6.50	85.7
有色金属矿采选业	Mining and Dressing of Nonferrous Metals	21.77	17.16	78.8
非金属矿采选业	Mining and Dressing of Nonmetal Minerals	8.55	7.76	90.7
其他矿采选业	Mining and Dressing of Other Minerals	0.02	0.01	46.8
木材及竹材采运业	Logging and Transport of Wood and Bamboo	3.34	0.81	24.3
制造业	**Manufacturing**	**2104.15**	**1660.99**	**78.9**
食品加工业	Food Processing	43.95	37.74	85.9
食品制造业	Food Production	47.75	43.93	92.0
饮料制造业	Beverages	82.52	72.80	88.2
烟草加工业	Tobacco	45.24	34.67	76.6
纺织业	Textiles	107.86	87.54	81.2
服装及纤维制品制造业	Garments and Other Fiber Products	17.28	17.78	102.9
皮革毛皮羽绒及其制品业	Leather, Furs, Down and Related Products	4.54	3.72	81.9
木材加工及竹藤棕草制品业	Timber Processing, Bamboo, Cane, Palm Fiber and Straw Products	15.15	10.45	68.9
家具制造业	Furniture Manufacturing	5.55	4.73	85.2
造纸及纸制品业	Papermaking and Paper Products	79.91	60.62	75.9
印刷业、记录媒介的复制	Printing and Record Medium Reproduction	22.85	20.15	88.2
文教体育用品制造业	Cultural, Educational and Sports Goods	3.66	2.37	64.8
石油加工及炼焦业	Petroleum Processing and Coking	129.91	85.68	66.0
化学原料及化学制品制造业	Raw Chemical Materials and Chemical Products	274.67	207.31	75.5
医药制造业	Medical and Pharmaceutical Products	91.20	72.04	79.0
化学纤维制造业	Chemical Fiber	34.94	23.46	67.2
橡胶制品业	Rubber Products	20.86	20.08	96.3
塑料制品业	Plastic Products	38.96	32.88	84.4
非金属矿物制品业	Nonmetal Mineral Products	112.18	100.84	89.9
黑色金属冶炼及压延加工业	Smelting and Pressing of Ferrous Metals	269.11	241.22	89.6
有色金属冶炼及压延加工业	Smelting and Pressing of Nonferrous Metals	82.00	58.40	71.2
金属制品业	Metal Products	29.20	24.59	84.2
普通机械制造业	Ordinary Machinery	61.08	51.78	84.8
专用设备制造业	Equipment for Special Purposes	43.10	36.15	83.9
交通运输设备制造业	Transport Equipment	178.90	105.43	58.9
电气机械及器材制造业	Electric Equipment and Machinery	79.09	59.20	74.8
电子及通信设备制造业	Electronic and Telecommunications Equipment	147.52	116.55	79.0
仪器仪表及文化办公用机械制造业	Instruments, Meters, Cultural and Office Machinery	10.55	8.55	81.1
其他制造业	Other Manufacturing	24.60	20.32	82.6
电力、煤气及水的生产和供应业	**Production and Supply of Electric Power, Gas and Water**	**481.67**	**351.38**	**73.0**
电力、蒸汽、热水生产和供应业	Production and Supply of Electric Power, Steam and Hot Water	438.19	314.97	71.9
煤气的生产和供应业	Production and Supply of Gas	12.99	8.34	64.2
自来水的生产和供应业	Production and Supply of Tap Water	30.50	28.07	92.0
建筑业	**Construction**	**65.82**	**61.12**	**92.9**
土木工程建筑业	Civil Engineering Construction	62.59	57.87	92.5

6-25 续表 1 continued

行业	Sector	投资额（亿元）Investment (100 million yuan)	新增固定资产（亿元）Newly Increased Fixed Assets (100 million yuan)	固定资产交付使用率（%）Rate of Fixed Assets Put into Use (%)
线路、管道和设备安装业	Installation of lines, Pipelines and Equipment	2.51	2.28	90.6
装修装饰业	Fitting and Decoration	0.72	0.98	136.2
地质勘查、水利管理业	**Geological Prospecting and Water Conservancy**	**24.89**	**16.22**	**65.2**
地质勘查业	Geological Prospecting	1.62	1.58	97.9
水利管理业	Water Conservancy	23.28	14.64	62.9
交通运输、仓储及邮电通信业	**Transport, Storage, Postal and Telecommunication Services**	**1553.60**	**1317.75**	**84.8**
铁路运输业	Railway Transport	98.44	82.99	84.3
公路运输业	Highway Transport	83.52	70.41	84.3
管道运输业	Pipeline Transport	1.46	1.46	100.0
水上运输业	Waterway Transport	23.37	18.05	77.2
航空运输业	Air Transport	49.29	49.08	99.6
交通运输辅助业	Transport Subsidiary Services	58.27	54.68	93.8
其他交通运输业	Other Transport	1.32	1.03	77.8
仓储业	Storage	11.29	5.07	44.9
邮电通信业	Postal and Telecommunications Services	1226.63	1034.99	84.4
批发和零售贸易餐饮业	**Wholesale & Retail Trade and Catering Services**	**57.74**	**48.69**	**84.3**
食品饮料烟草和家庭用品批发业	Wholesale Trade of Food, Beverage, Tobacco and Household Articles	9.85	7.44	75.5
能源材料和机械电子设备批发业	Wholesale Trade of Energy, Materials and Electronic Equipment	24.11	17.59	73.0
其他批发业	Other Wholesale Trade	1.29	0.72	55.4
零售业	Retail Trade	19.46	20.36	104.6
商业经纪与代理业	Commercial Brokerage and Agencies	0.19	0.20	108.6
餐饮业	Catering Trade	2.83	2.39	84.2
金融、保险业	**Finance and Insurance**	**6.22**	**6.17**	**99.2**
金融业	Finance	6.11	6.08	99.5
保险业	Insurance	0.11	0.09	83.4
房地产业	**Real Estate**	**32.25**	**30.00**	**93.0**
房地产开发与经营业	Real Estate Development and Operation	5.68	6.10	107.4
房地产管理业	Real Estate Management	26.52	23.88	90.0
房地产代理与经纪业	Real Estate Brokerage and Agencies	0.05	0.03	66.7
社会服务业	**Social Services**	**225.13**	**186.59**	**82.9**
公共设施服务业	Public Services	202.76	169.47	83.6
居民服务业	Resident Services	1.17	0.61	52.7
旅馆业	Hotels	13.97	10.54	75.5
租赁服务业	Leasing Services	1.05	0.86	81.3
旅游业	Tourism	1.08	0.88	81.7
娱乐服务业	Recreational Services	0.60	0.66	109.7
信息、咨询服务业	Information and Consultative Services	0.21	0.15	70.3
计算机应用服务业	Computer Application Services	2.92	1.78	60.9
其他社会服务业	Other Social Services	1.37	1.63	119.7
卫生体育和社会福利业	**Health Care, Sports and Social Welfare**	**19.67**	**17.37**	**88.3**
卫生	Health Care	17.96	16.39	91.3
体育	Sports	0.91	0.77	84.5
社会福利保障业	Social Welfare and Social Security	0.80	0.21	25.9
教育、文化艺术和广播电影电视业	**Education, Culture and Arts, Radio, Film and Television**	**33.67**	**27.68**	**82.2**
教育	Education	13.75	12.01	87.4
文化艺术业	Culture and Arts	5.36	4.11	76.7
广播、电影、电视业	Radio, Film and Television	14.56	11.55	79.4
科学研究和综合技术服务业	**Scientific Research and Polytechnic Services**	**34.35**	**30.51**	**88.8**
科学研究业	Scientific Research	7.88	3.83	48.6
综合技术服务业	Polytechnic Services	26.47	26.68	100.8
国家机关、政党机关和社会团体	**Governments Agencies, Party agencies and Social Organizations**	**50.19**	**37.56**	**74.8**
#国家机关	Governments	49.21	36.80	74.8
政党机关	Party	0.29	0.28	97.3
其他行业	**Others**	**18.05**	**14.75**	**81.7**

6-26 各地区限额以上更新改造项目个数、投资和新增固定资产（2000年）

Number of Innovation Projects, Investment and Newly Increased Fixed Assets above Designated Size by Region (2000)

地区	Region	施工项目（个）Number of Projects under Construction	全部建成投产项目（个）Number of Projects Completed and Put into Use	项目建成投产率（%）Rate of Projects Completed and Put into Use	投资完成额 Investment 绝对数（亿元）Value (100 million yuan)	比重（%）Percentage	新增固定资产（亿元）Newly Increased Fixed Assets (100 million yuan)	固定资产交付使用率（%）Rate of Fixed Assets Put into Use
全国	**National Total**	**1886**	**520**	**27.6**	**1496.31**	**100.0**	**1147.26**	**76.7**
北京	Beijing	156	40	25.6	86.25	5.8	45.45	52.7
天津	Tianjin	44	11	25.0	33.23	2.2	26.58	80.0
河北	Hebei	112	30	26.8	71.31	4.8	47.82	67.1
山西	Shanxi	15	2	13.3	16.98	1.1	18.43	108.5
内蒙古	Inner Mongolia	35	10	28.6	15.10	1.0	9.25	61.3
辽宁	Liaoning	123	39	31.7	148.90	10.0	123.29	82.8
吉林	Jilin	55	11	20.0	25.30	1.7	21.34	84.3
黑龙江	Heilongjiang	49	16	32.7	146.63	9.8	109.75	74.8
上海	Shanghai	373	104	27.9	220.50	14.7	138.20	62.7
江苏	Jiangsu	61	18	29.5	46.99	3.1	17.52	37.3
浙江	Zhejiang	74	23	31.1	61.06	4.1	43.96	72.0
安徽	Anhui	71	13	18.3	46.08	3.1	24.48	53.1
福建	Fujian	50	10	20.0	26.66	1.8	31.28	117.4
江西	Jiangxi	9	2	22.2	5.86	0.4	5.95	101.7
山东	Shandong	57	17	29.8	62.78	4.2	25.96	41.4
河南	Henan	20	5	25.0	15.14	1.0	16.10	106.4
湖北	Hubei	28	12	42.9	12.46	0.8	22.29	178.9
湖南	Hunan	38	8	21.1	46.77	3.1	37.96	81.1
广东	Guangdong	186	52	28.0	168.41	11.3	186.09	110.5
广西	Guangxi	30	9	30.0	14.30	1.0	22.89	160.1
海南	Hainan							
重庆	Chongqing	21	5	23.8	7.18	0.5	6.81	94.9
四川	Sichuan	74	17	23.0	67.71	4.5	57.83	85.4
贵州	Guizhou	45	12	26.7	36.77	2.5	24.35	66.2
云南	Yunnan	34	7	20.6	16.90	1.1	7.87	46.5
西藏	Tibet	4	1	25.0	1.74	0.1	2.55	146.7
陕西	Shaanxi	52	16	30.8	42.20	2.8	27.68	65.6
甘肃	Gansu	17	6	35.3	8.20	0.5	7.46	91.0
青海	Qinghai	9	4	44.4	4.86	0.3	4.65	95.7
宁夏	Ningxia	6	1	16.7	5.04	0.3	0.46	9.0
新疆	Xinjiang	20	12	60.0	10.72	0.7	15.52	144.8
不分地区	Not Classified by Region	18	7	38.9	24.32	1.6	17.50	72.0

6-27 国民经济各行业更新改造限额以上施工、投产项目个数(2000年)

Number of Innovation Projects above Designated Size under Construction or Completed and Put into Use by Sector (2000)

行业	Sector	施工项目(个) Number of Projects under Construction (unit)	#新开工 Started This Year	全部建成投产项目(个) Number of Projects Completed and Put into Use (unit)	项目建成投产率(%) Rate of Projects Completed & Put into Use (%)
全国总计	**National Total**	**1886**	**733**	**520**	**27.6**
农、林、牧、渔业	**Farming, Forestry, Animal Husbandry and Fishery**	**1**	**1**	**1**	**100.0**
农业	Farming	1	1	1	100.0
林业	Forestry				
畜牧业	Animal Husbandry				
渔业	Fishery				
农林牧渔服务业	Agricultural Services				
采掘业	**Mining and Quarrying**	**49**	**12**	**16**	**32.7**
煤炭采选业	Coal Mining and Dressing	7	1	1	14.3
石油和天然气开采业	Extraction of Petroleum and Natural Gas	28	7	13	46.4
黑色金属矿采选业	Mining and Dressing of Ferrous Metals	4	1	1	25.0
有色金属矿采选业	Mining and Dressing of Nonferrous Metals	6	3	1	16.7
非金属矿采选业	Mining and Dressing of Nonmetal Minerals	4			
其他矿采选业	Mining and Dressing of Other Minerals				
木材及竹材采运业	Logging and Transport of Wood and Bamboo				
制造业	**Manufacturing**	**1293**	**491**	**337**	**26.1**
食品加工业	Food Processing	10	1	4	40.0
食品制造业	Food Production	18	11	11	61.1
饮料制造业	Beverages	53	21	21	39.6
烟草加工业	Tobacco	27	8	10	37.0
纺织业	Textiles	45	27	14	31.1
服装及纤维制品制造业	Garments and Other Fiber Products	5	1	3	60.0
皮革毛皮羽绒及其制品业	Leather, Furs, Down and Related Products	2			
木材加工及竹藤棕草制品业	Timber Processing, Bamboo, Cane, Palm Fiber and Straw Products	7	3	1	14.3
家具制造业	Furniture Manufacturing				
造纸及纸制品业	Papermaking and Paper Products	39	14	11	28.2
印刷业、记录媒介的复制	Printing and Record Medium Reproduction	13	4		
文教体育用品制造业	Cultural, Educational and Sports Goods	5		2	40.0
石油加工及炼焦业	Petroleum Processing and Coking	45	23	16	35.6
化学原料及化学制品制造业	Raw Chemical Materials and Chemical Products	171	69	52	30.4
医药制造业	Medical and Pharmaceutical Products	63	20	13	20.6
化学纤维制造业	Chemical Fiber	25	12	10	40.0
橡胶制品业	Rubber Products	20	3	4	20.0
塑料制品业	Plastic Products	27	13	8	29.6
非金属矿物制品业	Nonmetal Mineral Products	74	29	20	27.0
黑色金属冶炼及压延加工业	Smelting and Pressing of Ferrous Metals	169	60	50	29.6
有色金属冶炼及压延加工业	Smelting and Pressing of Nonferrous Metals	51	17	9	17.6
金属制品业	Metal Products	13	4	5	38.5
普通机械制造业	Ordinary Machinery	55	17	13	23.6
专用设备制造业	Equipment for Special Purposes	45	15	12	26.7
交通运输设备制造业	Transport Equipment	154	39	20	13.0
电气机械及器材制造业	Electric Equipment and Machinery	58	25	12	20.7
电子及通信设备制造业	Electronic and Telecommunications Equipment	78	46	14	17.9
仪器仪表及文化办公用机械制造业	Instruments, Meters, Cultural and Office Machinery	7	5	2	28.6
其他制造业	Other Manufacturing	14	4		
电力、煤气及水的生产和供应业	**Production and Supply of Electric Power, Gas and Water**	**134**	**52**	**33**	**24.6**
电力、蒸汽、热水生产和供应业	Production and Supply of Electric Power, Steam and Hot Water	104	37	23	22.1
煤气的生产和供应业	Production and Supply of Gas	8	4	5	62.5
自来水的生产和供应业	Production and Supply of Tap Water	22	11	5	22.7
建筑业	**Construction**	**8**	**4**	**2**	**25.0**
土木工程建筑业	Civil Engineering Construction	7	3	2	28.6

6-27 续表 1 continued

行　　业	Sector	施工项目（个）Number of Projects under Construction (unit)	# 新开工 Started This Year	全部建成投产项目（个）Number of Projects Completed and Put into Use (unit)	项目建成投产率（%）Rate of Projects Completed & Put into Use (%)
线路、管道和设备安装业	Installation of lines, Pipelines and Equipment	1	1		
装修装饰业	Fitting and Decoration				
地质勘查、水利管理业	**Geological Prospecting and Water Conservancy**	**25**	**9**	**6**	**24.0**
地质勘查业	Geological Prospecting				
水利管理业	Water Conservancy	25	9	6	24.0
交通运输、仓储及邮电通信业	**Transport, Storage, Postal and Telecommunication Services**	**168**	**76**	**74**	**44.0**
铁路运输业	Railway Transport	12	2	4	33.3
公路运输业	Highway Transport	21	7	7	33.3
管道运输业	Pipeline Transport				
水上运输业	Waterway Transport	2			
航空运输业	Air Transport	5		1	20.0
交通运输辅助业	Transport Subsidiary Services	24	4	5	20.8
其他交通运输业	Other Transport				
仓储业	Storage				
邮电通信业	Postal and Telecommunications Services	104	63	57	54.8
批发和零售贸易餐饮业	**Wholesale & Retail Trade and Catering Services**	**21**	**4**	**1**	**4.8**
食品饮料烟草和家庭用品批发业	Wholesale Trade of Food, Beverage, Tobacco and Household Articles	4	2		
能源材料和机械电子设备批发业	Wholesale Trade of Energy, Materials and Electronic Equipment	3			
其他批发业	Other Wholesale Trade	1			
零售业	Retail Trade	12	1		
商业经纪与代理业	Commercial Brokerage and Agencies				
餐饮业	Catering Trade	1	1	1	100.0
金融、保险业	**Finance and Insurance**	**1**			
金融业	Finance	1			
保险业	Insurance				
房地产业	**Real Estate**	**9**	**2**	**1**	**11.1**
房地产开发与经营业	Real Estate Development and Operation	6	1	1	16.7
房地产管理业	Real Estate Management	3	1		
房地产代理与经纪业	Real Estate Brokerage and Agencies				
社会服务业	**Social Services**	**119**	**53**	**29**	**24.4**
公共设施服务业	Public Services	106	49	26	24.5
居民服务业	Resident Services	1			
旅馆业	Hotels	9	4	2	22.2
租赁服务业	Leasing Services				
旅游业	Tourism				
娱乐服务业	Recreational Services				
信息、咨询服务业	Information and Consultative Services				
计算机应用服务业	Computer Application Services	3		1	33.3
其他社会服务业	Other Social Services				
卫生体育和社会福利业	**Health Care, Sports and Social Welfare**	**8**	**5**	**1**	**12.5**
卫生	Health Care	5	4	1	20.0
体育	Sports	2			
社会福利保障业	Social Welfare and Social Security	1	1		
教育、文化艺术和广播电影电视业	**Education, Culture and Arts, Radio, Film and Television**	**11**	**5**	**5**	**45.5**
教育	Education	3	2	2	66.7
文化艺术业	Culture and Arts	6	2	2	33.3
广播、电影、电视业	Radio, Film and Television	2	1	1	50.0
科学研究和综合技术服务业	**Scientific Research and Polytechnic Services**	**21**	**11**	**4**	**19.0**
科学研究业	Scientific Research	12	8		
综合技术服务业	Polytechnic Services	9	3	4	44.4
国家机关、政党机关和社会团体	**Governments Agencies, Party agencies and Social Organizations**	**7**	**4**	**4**	**57.1**
#国家机关	Governments	7	4	4	57.1
政党机关	Party				
其他行业	**Others**	**11**	**4**	**6**	**54.5**

6-28 更新改造新增主要产品生产能力

Newly Increased Production Capacity Through Investment in Innovation

能力名称	Item	1996	1997	1998	1999	2000
铁矿开采（原矿）(万吨/年)	Iron-Ore Mining (10 000 tons/year)	88	88	173	47	185
烧结铁矿 (万吨/年)	Sintering of Iron-Ore (10 000 tons/year)	164	220	509	1176	284
生铁 (万吨/年)	Iron Smelting (10 000 tons/year)	175	172	429	189	333
炼钢 (万吨/年)	Steel-making (10 000 tons/year)	231	454	154	376	338
初轧 (万吨/年)	Rough Rolling (10 000 tons/year)	15	41	23		120
铁合金 (万吨/年)	Iron Alloy, Electric Furnace (10 000 tons/year)	9	5	3	3	55
铜选矿:	Copper Ore Dressing					
处理原矿 (万吨/年)	Crude Ore Dressing (10 000 tons/year)	20			8	42
铜含量 (吨/年)	Copper Content in Concentrate Ore (ton/year)		4747		4700	1790
原煤开采 (万吨/年)	Coal Mining (10 000 tons/year)	456	530	680	901	614
天然原油开采 (万吨/年)	Petroleum Extraction (10 000 tons/year)	14	39	76	35	340
硫酸 (万吨/年)	Sulfuric Acid (10 000 tons/year)	155	98	65	109	83
纯碱 (万吨/年)	Soda Ash (10 000 tons/year)	32	47	28	26	4
烧碱 (万吨/年)	Caustic Soda (10 000 tons/year)	52	27	25	15	58
合成氨 (万吨/年)	Synthetic Ammonia (10 000 tons/year)	229	204	180	141	142
化肥 (万吨/年)	Chemical Fertilizer (10 000 tons/year)	280	240	290	232	216
乙烯 (吨/年)	Ethylene (ton/year)	216446	98000	280740	137500	42500
塑料 (吨/年)	Plastics (ton/year)	196100	279765	263180	512603	440801
轮胎: (万条/年)	Tires (10 000 /year)					
内胎	Inner Tube	651	448	245	120	304
外胎	Tire (Cover)	770	826	334	792	406
发电机组容量 (万千瓦)	Capacity of Power Generating Sets (10 000 kw/year)	231	194	323	217	341
#火电	Thermal Power	209	181	142	159	157
水电	Hydropower	19	9	105	53	28
汽车制造 (辆/年)	Motor Vehicles (unit/year)	339174	187092	253460	143000	144120
#载重汽车制造	Trucks	198617	151232	152000	9500	800
拖拉机制造 (混合台/年)	Tractors (unit/year)	253159	225100	302953	90499	64400
#手扶拖拉机制造 (混合台/年)	Walking Tractors (unit/year)	71659	200000	220000	3000	50000
蒸汽锅炉制造 (台/年)	Steam Boilers (unit/year)	18795	530	20	231	2
蒸汽锅炉蒸发量(小时吨/年)	Evaporative Capacity of Steam Boilers (hr.tons/year)	5757	4074			
交流电动机制造(万千瓦/年)	Electric Motors (10 000 kw/year)	211	92	85	34	256
金属切削机床制造 (台/年)	Metal-Cutting Machine Tools (unit/year)	6100	57761	2580	2803	4042
民用钢质船舶制造 (综合吨/年)	Civilian Ships (ton/year)	380000	560000	140000	65011	330000
胶合板 (万立方米/年)	Plywood (10 000 cu.m/year)	5	60	19	12	28
水泥 (万吨/年)	Cement (10 000 tons/year)	2152	1529	1191	1834	1616

6-28 续表 1 continued

能 力 名 称	Item	1996	1997	1998	1999	2000
化学纤维 (吨/年)	Chemical Fiber (ton/year)	51170	109156	200175	112000	191393
棉纺锭 (万锭)	Cotton Spindles (10 000 units)	50	47	32	15	31
棉布织机 (台)	Cotton Loom (unit)	3757	4718	19063	2747	3370
棉印染布 (万米/年)	Printed and Dyed Cloth (10 000 m/year)	20953	13146	12815	11952	23271
毛纺锭 (锭)	Wool Spindles	31974	22580	12392	15200	5442
机制糖	Machine-processed Sugar					
年生产 (万吨)	Annual Production Capacity(10000 tons)	34	31	38	21	6
日处理原料 (吨)	Raw Materials Processing (ton/day)	25689	22000	29786	18250	14260
卷烟 (万箱/年)	Cigarettes (10 000 cases/year)	168	259	288	95	51
酒 (万吨/年)	Liquors (10 000 tons/year)	239	337	233	5730	300
糖果 (吨/年)	Candy (ton/year)	81020	18240	5800	7010	11724
奶粉 (吨/年)	Milk Powder (ton/year)	29080	25515	8620	36910	2000
原盐 (万吨/年)	Raw Salt (10 000 tons/year)	10	99	33	25	80
机制纸及纸板 (万吨/年)	Machine-made Paper and Paperboards (10 000 tons/year)	142	96	86	159	174
肥皂 (万箱/年)	Soap (10 000 cases/year)	3	10	2	2	1
合成洗涤剂 (万吨/年)	Synthetic Detergent (10 000 tons/year)	11	25	49	20	7
鞣制皮革 (万张/年)	Tanning (10 000 pcs/year)	262	210	490	157	9
皮鞋 (万双/年)	Leather Shoes (10 000 pairs/year)	411	180	463	370	826
日用搪瓷制品 (万件/年)	Daily-use Enamelware (10 000 pcs/year)	1		50	1	
日用陶瓷器 (万件/年)	Daily-use Ceramics (10 000 pcs/year)	11405	3014	14202	14647	11382
保温瓶 (万个/年)	Thermos Bottles (10 000 units/year)	200	1340	950	1000	84
灯泡 (万只/年)	Bulbs (10 000 units/year)	18698	22990	5853	17083	24660
自行车 (万辆/年)	Bicycles (10 000 units/year)		80		70	20
家用电冰箱 (万台/年)	Refrigerators (10 000 units/year)	122	220	222	275	45
电视机 (万台/年)	Television Sets (10 000 set/year)	150	340	80	336	80
录放音机 (万部/年)	Tape Recorders (10 000/year)		8	50		248
家用洗衣机 (万台/年)	Washing Machines (10 000/year)	92	94	117	60	156
新建铁路主线正线交付营业里程 (公里)	Length of Newly Built Railways Put into Operation (km)				4	46
新(扩)建港口码头	Newly Built or Expanded Ports					
年吞吐量 (万吨)	Annual Handling Capacity (10 000 tons)	337	1876	344	138	261
泊位 (个)	Number of Berths (unit)	20	41	14	8	7
新建公路 (公里)	Length of New Highways (km)	307	572	822	978	437
改建公路 (公里)	Length of Reconstructed Highways (km)	4053	6790	6413	6991	4760
商业石油库 (万立方米)	Commercial Petroleum Depot (10 000cu.m)	13		3	19	6
物资储备石油库(万立方米)	Petroleum Tanks in Materials Warehouse System (10 000 cu.m)	7	1			2
商业冷藏库 (万吨)	Commercial Freezers (10 000 tons)	3		57	1	123
粮食仓库 (万平方米)	Grain Storehouses (10 000 sq.m)	5	9	18	17	11
粮食仓库 (万公斤)	Grain Storehouses (10 000 kg)	18110	56079	56048	48591	30461
高等院校：学生席位 (个)	Students Capacity of Universities and Colleges	810		176		
医院病床床位 (张)	Number of Hospital Beds	4779	1765	4555	3360	2641
城市自来水供水能力(万吨/日)	Tap Water Supply Capacity (10 000tons/day)	187	253	197	162	183

6−29 按用途分的更新改造投资和房屋建筑面积

Investment on Innovation by Purpose and Floor Space of Buildings

年份 Year	按用途分的更新改造投资（亿元） Investment on Innovation by Purpose (100 million yuan)							房屋建筑面积 （万平方米） Floor Space of Buildings (10 000 sq.m)			
	增产 Increasing Production	节约能源 Energy Saving	其他节约 Other Saving Measures	增加品种 Increasing Product Variety	提高产品质量 Improving Product Quality	三废治理 Environ-mental Protection	其他 Others	施工面积 Under Construc-tion	# 住宅 Residential Buildings	竣工面积 Completed	# 住宅 Residential Buildings
1980	77.87	4.71	2.44		6.57	3.42	42.37	4019.90	1206.10	2133.00	683.80
1981	93.20	7.79	1.61		7.08	2.65	82.97	6305.80	2429.20	3603.60	1439.50
1982	87.01	11.98	2.15	15.70	11.46	4.12	117.95	8963.50	3531.40	5047.40	2108.50
1983	106.46	13.27	2.62	17.66	15.22	4.37	131.53	9363.60	3701.70	5358.70	2271.90
1984	106.83	17.35	2.09	23.80	17.50	6.11	135.60	8105.90	2652.32	4454.66	1554.78
1985	160.35	17.37	1.50	61.30	26.58	9.08	172.96	8784.45	2447.56	4596.04	1434.01
1986	211.20	22.75	2.10	97.88	39.16	11.78	234.34	10515.85	3591.34	5741.57	2070.70
1987	273.25	25.90	1.93	108.61	42.82	14.33	291.75	12318.43	4398.89	6330.23	2328.10
1988	394.78	30.55	2.93	140.12	48.38	16.79	347.00	13963.02	4820.65	6930.15	2467.93
1989	303.08	25.25	2.32	119.00	39.38	14.99	284.76	10616.70	3825.33	5403.15	1995.63
1990	291.95	27.28	2.65	130.10	52.00	14.76	311.45	9179.22	3386.48	4738.65	1771.70
1991	359.48	33.49	4.43	165.75	73.48	19.56	367.04	9270.12	3306.25	4793.31	1694.35
1992	496.47	41.38	5.16	225.97	107.66	23.33	561.13	10815.77	3530.70	5208.79	1750.73
1993	797.79	49.57	9.19	334.88	142.04	32.13	830.25	11337.62	3663.37	5282.45	1748.54
1994	1026.45	79.93	14.94	381.76	177.04	45.67	1192.81	11998.32	4373.66	5638.70	2031.18
1995	1222.17	92.86	10.53	409.58	196.93	47.47	1319.82	10691.39	3886.85	5360.98	1991.92
1996	(1301.97)	(80.84)	(14.95)	(434.35)	(201.79)	(61.35)	(1527.49)	(9619.27)	(3449.37)	(4799.24)	(1847.04)
	1299.96	80.66	14.90	433.54	201.20	61.24	1523.49	9580.36	3441.55	4764.94	1840.50
1997	1389.54	102.19	20.34	417.93	214.77	64.63	1712.54	8470.86	3263.66	4409.81	1771.22
1998	1426.53	103.11	32.46	422.79	245.17	71.17	2215.51	7467.81	2990.87	3861.51	1570.83
1999	1422.22	148.83	35.05	407.54	280.35	89.08	2102.02	6099.82	2270.36	3587.06	1516.71
2000	1707.78	163.66	55.15	440.37	392.33	120.41	2227.91	5595.94	1284.61	2913.96	802.06

6-30 城镇集体单位各行业固定资产投资和新增固定资产（2000年）

Investment in Fixed Assets of Urban Collective-owned Units by Sector (2000)

单位：亿元 (100 million yuan)

行业	Sector	投资额 Investment	新增固定资产 Newly Increased Fixed Assets	固定资产交付使用率(%) Rate of Fixed Assets Put into Use(%)
全国总计	**National Total**	**1009.82**	**839.96**	**83.2**
农、林、牧、渔业	Farming, Forestry, Animal Husbandry and Fishery	8.98	7.27	80.9
采掘业	Mining and Quarrying	7.79	6.31	81.0
制造业	Manufacturing	244.60	204.20	83.5
电力、煤气及水的生产和供应业	Production and Supply of Electric Power, Gas and Water	13.99	8.60	61.5
建筑业	Construction	24.47	18.85	77.0
地质勘查、水利管理业	Geological Prospecting and Water Conservancy	3.05	2.46	80.4
交通运输、仓储及邮电通信业	Transport, Storage, Postal and Telecommunication Services	23.40	43.66	186.6
批发和零售贸易餐饮业	Wholesale, Retail Trade and Catering Services	75.61	62.00	82.0
金融、保险业	Finance and Insurance	20.34	20.03	98.5
房地产业	Real Estate	482.04	372.77	77.3
社会服务业	Social Services	30.18	29.61	98.1
卫生体育和社会福利业	Health Care, Sports and Social Welfare	8.31	7.61	91.5
教育、文化艺术和广播电影电视业	Education, Culture and Arts, Radio, Film and Television	12.99	12.90	99.3
科学研究和综合技术服务业	Scientific Research and Polytechnic Services	1.61	0.57	35.5
国家机关、政党机关和社会团体	Governments Agencies, Parties Agencies and Social Organizations	27.22	25.48	93.6
其他行业	Other Sectors	25.24	17.63	69.9

6-31 各地区城镇集体单位按构成分的固定资产投资和房屋建筑面积

Investment in Fixed Assets of Urban Collective-owned Units by Use of Funds and Floor Space of Buildings by Region

年 份 地 区	Year Region	合 计 (亿元) Total Investment (100 million yuan)	建筑安装工程 Construction and Installation	设备工具器具购置 Purchase of Equipment and Instruments	其他费用 Others	房屋建筑面积（万平方米）Floor Space of Buildings(10 000 sq.m) 施工面积 Under Construction	#住宅 Residential Buildings	竣工面积 Completed	#住宅 Residential Buildings
	1985	128.23	71.28	51.20	5.75	5087.10	1606.90	2746.30	896.60
	1986	146.39	77.06	61.90	7.43	4963.50	1671.60	2869.40	973.70
	1987	181.30	96.25	71.77	13.28	5311.69	1516.91	2959.38	883.56
	1988	254.97	131.76	104.57	18.65	5853.96	1528.39	3303.85	900.88
	1989	185.63	98.94	72.27	14.41	4323.40	1256.99	2477.70	701.80
	1990	163.38	84.81	69.18	9.39	3357.93	1085.76	1970.45	636.17
	1991	203.83	106.51	84.84	12.48	3828.53	1110.36	2112.81	639.00
	1992	364.49	182.52	159.91	22.05	5412.32	1418.52	2766.74	752.62
	1993	686.12	381.97	253.44	50.71	6318.01	2176.48	3342.14	1129.77
	1994	770.27	455.89	270.06	44.32	5060.25	1842.81	3086.87	1128.89
	1995	921.74	616.06	167.08	138.61	12229.83	7677.71	5459.69	3286.38
	1996	(858.31)	(565.92)	(176.52)	(115.87)	(10999.99)	(6650.62)	(5059.03)	(2966.39)
		849.24	560.71	172.91	115.62	10879.67	6615.88	4958.59	2939.13
	1997	795.24	543.82	141.18	110.23	10094.11	6277.70	4927.40	3012.26
	1998	958.93	654.10	165.31	139.52	11205.85	7085.82	5542.54	3492.10
	1999	995.42	680.17	174.97	140.28	11466.58	7487.48	5856.91	3739.26
	2000	1009.83	693.18	166.99	149.67	11519.24	7766.26	5910.57	3846.65
北 京	Beijing	23.07	17.78	1.42	3.88	267.72	186.35	104.42	74.72
天 津	Tianjin	18.89	12.59	1.43	4.87	219.62	173.85	66.95	52.49
河 北	Hebei	63.92	42.07	16.06	5.79	537.12	281.39	335.80	143.25
山 西	Shanxi	16.66	11.55	3.67	1.43	132.84	93.56	65.80	44.31
内蒙古	Inner Mongolia	8.01	6.55	0.61	0.86	94.37	61.38	55.57	36.93
辽 宁	Liaoning	35.60	27.02	3.79	4.79	408.68	270.41	263.30	178.73
吉 林	Jilin	7.85	5.42	1.57	0.86	72.20	53.66	48.02	36.10
黑龙江	Heilongjiang	15.56	11.15	2.42	1.99	200.28	125.65	119.57	74.64
上 海	Shanghai	104.43	68.89	13.04	22.51	918.82	710.31	388.53	304.03
江 苏	Jiangsu	141.59	89.17	34.24	18.18	1144.31	737.93	741.89	467.08
浙 江	Zhejiang	76.18	44.03	14.98	17.17	767.48	479.59	359.01	212.70
安 徽	Anhui	18.21	13.79	2.23	2.19	253.32	179.08	136.79	90.28
福 建	Fujian	29.61	21.58	4.30	3.73	373.51	239.02	153.83	96.30
江 西	Jiangxi	10.46	6.89	2.35	1.23	150.50	113.04	89.91	68.90
山 东	Shandong	109.76	74.39	25.45	9.93	1288.01	841.60	628.33	365.91
河 南	Henan	24.76	16.85	5.79	2.12	324.40	199.32	178.68	100.13
湖 北	Hubei	29.36	19.01	7.06	3.30	337.94	240.84	211.86	156.12
湖 南	Hunan	18.77	13.84	1.24	3.70	310.81	211.47	150.02	108.35
广 东	Guangdong	142.27	104.79	13.58	23.90	1918.21	1378.20	938.01	647.78
广 西	Guangxi	10.17	5.81	2.65	1.71	123.74	62.32	57.42	27.41
海 南	Hainan	2.27	1.97	0.12	0.18	15.81	11.98	7.57	5.18
重 庆	Chongqing	20.93	15.66	1.23	4.04	395.17	286.51	163.33	124.98
四 川	Sichuan	32.18	25.24	1.34	5.59	603.72	433.80	294.57	211.44
贵 州	Guizhou	7.95	4.87	1.39	1.69	131.22	87.63	54.43	35.66
云 南	Yunnan	10.38	7.81	1.54	1.03	109.81	54.07	68.22	33.08
西 藏	Tibet	0.17	0.17			1.09	0.35	0.49	0.35
陕 西	Shaanxi	13.64	10.76	1.04	1.84	181.76	95.47	104.72	54.28
甘 肃	Gansu	5.59	4.68	0.51	0.40	111.72	71.65	49.80	40.01
青 海	Qinghai	1.44	0.97	0.35	0.12	16.29	11.12	8.33	6.18
宁 夏	Ningxia	2.40	2.04	0.12	0.24	34.59	26.65	20.18	13.77
新 疆	Xinjiang	7.72	5.82	1.49	0.40	74.19	48.07	45.24	35.58

6-32 各地区城镇集体单位按国民经济行业分的固定资产投资（2000年）

单位：亿元

地区	Region	合计 Total	农、林、牧、渔业 Farming, Forestry, Animal Husbandry and Fishery	采掘业 Mining and Quarrying	制造业 Manufacturing	电力、煤气及水的生产和供应业 Production and Supply of Electric Power, Gas and Water	建筑业 Construction	地质勘查业水利管理业 Geological Prospecting and Water Conservancy
全国	**National Total**	**1009.83**	**8.98**	**7.79**	**244.60**	**13.99**	**24.47**	**3.05**
北京	Beijing	23.07			1.74	0.16	1.78	
天津	Tianjin	18.89		0.04	1.59	0.18	0.12	0.18
河北	Hebei	63.92	2.11	1.04	22.03	0.52	3.68	0.02
山西	Shanxi	16.66	0.92	1.02	5.96	1.77	0.03	
内蒙古	Inner Mongolia	8.01		0.24	1.48	0.19	0.18	
辽宁	Liaoning	35.60	0.51	0.11	5.73	0.24	1.01	0.01
吉林	Jilin	7.85	0.07	0.09	2.61		0.46	
黑龙江	Heilongjiang	15.56	0.16	0.10	4.23	0.09	2.72	
上海	Shanghai	104.43		0.14	18.69	0.71		
江苏	Jiangsu	141.59	0.98	0.23	45.99	2.28	2.02	0.52
浙江	Zhejiang	76.18			20.68	2.74	0.69	0.03
安徽	Anhui	18.21	0.11	0.31	3.18	0.01	0.53	0.06
福建	Fujian	29.61	0.60	0.25	4.97	1.04	1.86	
江西	Jiangxi	10.46	0.04	0.04	2.82	0.07	0.38	
山东	Shandong	109.76	0.36	2.20	40.86	0.13	2.04	1.80
河南	Henan	24.76	0.21	0.13	9.01	0.10	0.70	
湖北	Hubei	29.36	0.69	0.58	9.76	0.45	0.29	0.05
湖南	Hunan	18.77	0.14	0.03	3.11	0.24	0.66	0.06
广东	Guangdong	142.27	0.46	0.07	20.54	1.86	0.88	0.23
广西	Guangxi	10.17	0.09	0.29	3.17	0.10	0.05	
海南	Hainan	2.27	0.23	0.04	0.35	0.08	0.02	
重庆	Chongqing	20.93	0.10	0.01	1.71	0.32	0.66	0.02
四川	Sichuan	32.18	0.09	0.14	2.82	0.09	1.79	0.07
贵州	Guizhou	7.95	0.02	0.19	1.58	0.20	0.07	
云南	Yunnan	10.38	0.33	0.10	3.88	0.16	0.31	
西藏	Tibet	0.17					0.03	
陕西	Shaanxi	13.64	0.46	0.17	3.17	0.11	0.21	
甘肃	Gansu	5.59	0.11	0.07	0.77	0.13	0.28	
青海	Qinghai	1.44	0.07		0.60	0.01	0.15	
宁夏	Ningxia	2.40			0.22		0.01	
新疆	Xinjiang	7.72	0.13	0.17	1.33	0.02	0.84	

Investment in Fixed Assets of Urban Collective-owned Units by Sector and Region (2000)

(100 million yuan)

交通运输仓储和邮电通信业 Transport, Storage, Post & Telecommunication Services	批发零售贸易和餐饮业 Wholesale and Retail Trade & Catering Services	金融、保险业 Finance and Insurance	房地产业 Real Estate	社会服务业 Social Services	卫生体育和社会福利业 Health Care, Sports & Social Welfare	教育、文化艺术和广播电影电视业 Education, Culture and Arts, Radio, Film and Television	科学研究和综合技术服务业 Scientific Research and Polytechnic Services	国家机关、政党机关和社会团体 Government Agencies, Party Agencies and Social Organizations	其他 Others
23.40	**75.61**	**20.34**	**482.04**	**30.18**	**8.31**	**12.99**	**1.61**	**27.22**	**25.24**
0.03	1.79		15.13	0.40		0.09	0.92	0.35	0.68
0.20	0.19	0.02	13.32	0.26	0.64	0.16		0.28	1.71
1.45	15.28	0.86	8.68	2.60	1.00	0.57	0.12	1.46	2.50
0.07	1.14	0.53	3.95	0.72	0.02	0.18	0.02	0.24	0.08
	0.78	0.32	4.55	0.20	0.02			0.04	0.02
0.11	2.84	0.59	22.67	0.31		0.02	0.07	0.10	1.29
0.32	0.46	0.37	3.12		0.01	0.09		0.01	0.27
0.18	1.81	0.62	4.68	0.11	0.02	0.20		0.20	0.45
0.15	2.10		78.69	1.64	0.40	0.35	0.14	1.40	0.03
7.04	8.81	0.49	56.72	3.18	1.41	2.43	0.04	4.22	5.23
1.40	3.26	2.44	37.69	2.69	1.13	1.71		0.47	1.25
0.31	1.20	0.14	9.30	1.60	0.05	0.37		0.81	0.23
0.92	2.12	0.14	13.95	2.23	0.64	0.25	0.04	0.58	0.03
0.17	0.62	0.31	5.60	0.12			0.02	0.24	0.03
2.73	10.18	1.33	36.11	1.12	0.60	1.30	0.17	7.47	1.35
0.13	3.63	1.26	5.09	1.62	0.36	0.55		1.56	0.41
0.32	2.31	0.29	8.52	0.69	0.19	0.13		2.47	2.62
0.30	2.86	0.56	9.77	0.09	0.13	0.29	0.02	0.29	0.21
5.13	1.37	5.16	87.24	5.99	0.59	3.61		3.27	5.87
0.58	1.39	0.11	3.25	0.30		0.01		0.67	0.15
0.08	0.26	0.07	0.75	0.31	0.07				
0.89	1.18	0.58	14.60	0.40	0.21	0.10		0.09	0.06
0.34	1.99	1.83	21.37	0.37	0.50	0.18	0.02	0.36	0.21
0.03	0.43	0.33	4.51	0.54		0.01			0.05
0.07	1.47	0.52	2.18	1.04	0.04	0.08		0.14	0.06
	0.02			0.10			0.02		
0.32	2.70	0.91	4.13	0.48	0.15	0.30		0.32	0.20
0.04	0.59	0.21	2.80	0.30	0.01	0.01		0.12	0.14
0.02	0.06	0.06	0.36	0.06				0.05	
	0.31		1.73	0.12					
0.08	2.47	0.29	1.59	0.59	0.10				0.11

6-33 城镇和工矿区个人建房

Building Construction by Individuals in Cities and Towns and in Industrial and Mining Areas

年份 地区	Year Region	城镇工矿区个数(个) Number of Cities, Towns, Industrial and Mining Areas	建房户数(户) Number of Households with Building Construction	竣工房屋建筑面积(万平方米) Floor Space of Buildings Completed (10 000 sq.m)	#住宅 Residential Buildings	竣工房屋价值(万元) Value of Buildings Completed (10 000 yuan)	#住宅 Residential Buildings
	1985	5941	910362	7081.36	6306.80	567917	493872
	1986	7182	1005549	8115.37	7234.80	745623	654192
	1987	7110	1061119	9120.19	8294.36	1005133	899614
	1988	7845	1108554	10526.83	9433.15	1568475	1401141
	1989	8590	945178	8565.38	7822.55	1402278	1260234
	1990	8304	775011	7180.55	6492.93	1247034	1103317
	1991	8637	773083	7554.40	6808.24	1403230	1250861
	1992	9367	919069	9673.43	8586.22	2164663	1897651
	1993	10170	1052853	11463.44	9812.95	3385002	2804212
	1994	11728	1234606	14098.18	12268.36	4513203	3870038
	1995	12189	1279426	15194.84	13333.90	5523894	4770290
	1996	13214	1294859	16556.86	14518.78	6552198	5629097
	1997	21218	1338976	17570.24	15165.03	7041112	5938633
	1998	14943	1552136	20781.49	18227.39	8485630	7272165
	1999	15262	1490469	21830.37	19246.43	9175357	7818281
	2000	13910	1440145	21763.53	18929.01	9529931	8120255
北京	Beijing	15	12280	33.89	29.74	22503	18378
天津	Tianjin	79	10268	96.77	93.68	63163	61306
河北	Hebei	680	93368	1465.70	1142.93	758373	607076
山西	Shanxi	469	30601	347.08	309.39	125763	109271
内蒙古	Inner Mongolia	370	30906	280.40	238.81	109790	93030
辽宁	Liaoning	226	27926	265.81	225.95	177778	140746
吉林	Jilin	495	65531	655.32	524.25	360425	288340
黑龙江	Heilongjiang	420	50418	510.00	441.47	231192	189665
上海	Shanghai		2992	37.92	37.28	15017	14762
江苏	Jiangsu	779	96504	1285.11	1187.27	648033	595316
浙江	Zhejiang	822	90846	2060.87	1829.14	974618	853895
安徽	Anhui	862	85101	983.66	814.40	394678	317762
福建	Fujian	510	44842	1002.65	944.62	556848	521233
江西	Jiangxi	625	54894	1075.65	974.88	359544	276386
山东	Shandong	515	79763	928.55	675.83	455016	322103
河南	Henan	181	68689	1114.46	951.01	490666	411239
湖北	Hubei	836	85582	1326.15	1144.11	499147	430284
湖南	Hunan	1022	80301	1663.82	1507.28	660908	595977
广东	Guangdong	350	46274	1168.84	1050.21	654437	581448
广西	Guangxi	793	108443	1884.70	1776.31	644685	608949
海南	Hainan	150	11736	220.27	168.90	137566	105052
重庆	Chongqing	567	33090	510.11	437.93	179913	144775
四川	Sichuan	1607	108539	1271.17	1067.12	442422	361686
贵州	Guizhou	646	42791	555.24	485.08	151417	128668
云南	Yunnan	246	22976	393.07	345.22	182909	156105
西藏	Tibet	132	2160	51.74	48.18	12216	11154
陕西	Shaanxi	119	10637	128.39	102.42	46561	34180
甘肃	Gansu	178	18994	156.55	133.58	54470	45627
青海	Qinghai	45	7077	62.56	52.62	22381	19182
宁夏	Ningxia	23	1750	18.46	14.34	9008	6739
新疆	Xinjiang	148	14866	208.64	175.09	88484	69921

6-34 农村个人固定资产投资和建房
Individual Investment in Fixed Assets and Building Construction in Rural Areas

年份 地区	Year Region	投资总额（亿元） Total Investment (100 million yuan)	#竣工房屋投资 Investment in Buildings Completed 小计 Subtotal	 #住宅 Residential Buildings	施工房屋建筑面积（万平方米） Floor Space of Buildings under Construction (10 000 sq.m)	竣工房屋建筑面积（万平方米） Floor Space of Buildings Completed (10 000 sq.m) 总计 Total	 #住宅 Residential Buildings	竣工房屋造价（元/平方米） Cost of Buildings Completed (yuan/sq.m) 总计 Total	 #住宅 Residential Buildings
	1985	478.43	350.13	313.15		78973	69542	44	45
	1986	574.82	503.00	388.56	109622	103225	94468	49	41
	1987	695.35	603.17	487.21	100923	96477	85524	63	57
	1988	865.23	741.22	580.97	92781	89092	80799	83	72
	1989	892.03	794.15	641.68	74906	71026	66134	112	97
	1990	876.47	777.14	649.78	76819	71136	67812	109	96
	1991	1042.56	912.48	759.25	85405	79501	74193	115	102
	1992	1005.52	937.51	678.52	83392	65338	60442	143	112
	1993	1137.73	1015.37	760.26	57432	56012	46129	181	165
	1994	1519.24	1315.92	1002.73	72283	65390	57646	201	174
	1995	2007.85	1709.41	1349.85	78192	73522	66230	233	204
	1996	2544.03	2250.87	1766.40	96115	87277	79531	258	222
	1997	2691.16	2405.80	1890.65	89309	85888	77287	280	245
	1998	2681.52	2402.24	1907.23	89099	83864	77031	286	248
	1999	2779.59	1908.20	1799.10	89050	83244	76758	229	234
	2000	2904.26	1969.32	1846.85	88232	81270	75515	242	245
北京	Beijing	30.58	20.14	18.31	471	450	374	447	490
天津	Tianjin	13.10	7.14	5.85	197	172	133	415	441
河北	Hebei	182.34	118.56	106.05	4562	4157	3847	285	276
山西	Shanxi	34.44	23.61	22.73	973	793	765	298	297
内蒙古	Inner Mongolia	45.88	22.09	20.02	1092	985	860	224	233
辽宁	Liaoning	82.05	58.16	50.79	1811	1750	1711	332	297
吉林	Jilin	32.75	14.33	14.02	461	446	425	321	330
黑龙江	Heilongjiang	41.99	17.96	17.09	623	523	483	343	354
上海	Shanghai	10.36	10.21	9.11	194	187	168	547	541
江苏	Jiangsu	273.59	222.58	209.60	6322	6184	5981	360	350
浙江	Zhejiang	225.89	186.27	178.35	5291	4742	4452	393	401
安徽	Anhui	120.64	83.22	82.25	4859	4771	4712	174	175
福建	Fujian	87.09	56.97	53.26	2849	2067	1930	276	276
江西	Jiangxi	90.01	58.71	57.53	5204	4781	4704	123	122
山东	Shandong	254.11	172.17	157.50	7731	6960	6351	247	248
河南	Henan	254.95	162.51	154.75	7596	7333	6950	222	223
湖北	Hubei	84.88	57.11	53.95	3855	3654	3319	156	163
湖南	Hunan	202.40	145.80	137.12	6826	6701	6241	218	220
广东	Guangdong	250.58	170.08	163.98	5552	4992	4788	341	342
广西	Guangxi	85.59	59.87	58.81	2864	2625	2553	228	230
海南	Hainan	19.18	6.56	6.25	181	171	168	384	372
重庆	Chongqing	43.10	33.68	32.30	2163	2049	1726	164	187
四川	Sichuan	147.37	99.87	86.17	6750	6224	5128	160	168
贵州	Guizhou	49.90	17.95	16.95	1306	1079	1013	166	167
云南	Yunnan	72.61	37.94	33.41	2469	2122	1723	179	194
西藏	Tibet								
陕西	Shaanxi	70.32	58.58	56.09	3450	3418	3247	171	173
甘肃	Gansu	32.76	15.95	15.35	781	769	725	207	212
青海	Qinghai	7.72	3.13	2.88	197	197	175	159	164
宁夏	Ningxia	21.72	16.49	15.63	367	357	342	462	458
新疆	Xinjiang	36.35	11.66	10.76	1234	611	523	191	206

6-35 房地产开发主要指标
Main Indicators of Real Estate Development

指 标	Item	1997	1998	1999	2000
一、企业个数（个）	**Number of Enterprises**	**21286**	**24378**	**25762**	**27303**
内资	Domestic Funded	17202	19960	21422	23277
#国有	State-owned Enterprises		7958	7370	6641
集体	Collective-owned Enterprises		4538	4127	3492
港、澳、台投资	Enterprises with Funds from Hong Kong, Macao and Taiwan	1989	3214	3167	2899
外商投资	Foreign Funded	2095	1204	1173	1127
二、平均从业人数（万人）	**Average Number of Employed Persons (10 000 persons)**	**68.32**	**82.59**	**88.03**	**97.19**
内资	Domestic Funded	57.89	70.87	76.72	86.22
#国有	State-owned Enterprises		33.28	31.22	29.23
集体	Collective-owned Enterprises		13.49	12.74	11.64
港、澳、台投资	Enterprises with Funds from Hong Kong, Macao and Taiwan	5.00	8.38	8.02	7.91
外商投资	Foreign Funded	5.43	3.34	3.29	3.06
三、土地开发及购置（万平方米）	**Land Development and Purchase (10 000 sq.m)**				
本年土地开发面积	Land Space Developed This Year	7371.3	7730.1	9319.6	11666.1
本年土地购置面积	Land Space Purchased This Year	6641.7	10109.3	11958.9	16905.2
四、本年完成投资额（亿元）	**Investment Completed This Year (100 million yuan)**	**3178.37**	**3614.23**	**4103.20**	**4984.05**
#住宅	Residential Buildings	1539.38	2081.56	2638.48	3311.98
#经济适用房屋	Economical Houses	185.50	270.85	437.02	542.44
五、资金来源小计（亿元）	**Source of Funds (100 million yuan)**	**3817.06**	**4414.94**	**4795.90**	**5997.63**
#国内贷款	Domestic Loans	911.19	1053.17	1111.57	1385.08
利用外资	Foreign Investment	460.86	361.76	256.60	168.70
自筹资金	Fundraising	972.88	1166.98	1344.62	1614.21
六、房屋建筑面积（万平方米）	**Floor Space of Buildings (10 000 sq.m)**				
施工面积	Floor Space under Construction	44985.5	50770.1	56857.6	65896.9
竣工面积	Floor Space Completed	15819.7	17566.6	21410.8	25104.9
本年新开工面积	Floor Space Started This Year	14027.0	20387.9	22579.4	29582.6
#住宅	Residential Buildings	10996.6	16637.5	18797.9	24401.2
#经济适用房屋	Economical Houses	1720.6	3466.4	3970.4	5313.3
七、商品房屋销售面积（万平方米）	**Floor Space of Selling House (10 000 sq.m)**	**9010.2**	**12185.3**	**14556.5**	**18637.1**
#住宅	Residential Buildings	7864.3	10827.1	12997.9	16570.3
#经济适用房屋	Economical Houses	1211.9	1666.5	2701.3	3760.1
商品房屋销售价格（元/平方米）	Selling Price of House	1997	2063	2053	2112
#住宅	Residential Buildings	1790	1854	1857	1948
#经济适用房屋	Economical Houses	1097	1035	1093	1202
八、实收资本合计（亿元）	**Total Capital Hold (100 million yuan)**	**3812.07**	**5778.73**	**4520.88**	**5302.91**
#国家资本金	State Capital	244.30	841.90	302.45	215.57
资产负债率（%）	Ratio of Liabilities to Assets	76.2	76.1	76.1	75.6
九、经营总收入（亿元）	**Total Revenue (100 million yuan)**	**2218.46**	**2951.21**	**3026.01**	**4515.71**
#土地转让收入	Land Transferred	103.28	132.25	103.25	129.61

6-36 房地产开发企业（单位）个数

Number of Enterprises for Real Estate Development

单位：个 (unit)

年份 地区	Year Region	企业个数 Number of Enterprises	内资企业 Domestic Funded Enterprises	#国有 State-owned Enterprises	#集体 Collective-owned Enterprises	港、澳、台投资企业 Enterprises with Funds from Hong Kong Macao and Taiwan	外商投资企业 Foreign Funded Enterprises
	1997	21286	17202			1989	2095
	1998	24378	19960	7958	4538	3214	1204
	1999	25762	21422	7370	4127	3167	1173
	2000	27303	23277	6641	3492	2899	1127
北　京	Beijing	618	403	126	20	148	67
天　津	Tianjin	695	634	189	59	38	23
河　北	Hebei	460	416	181	31	22	22
山　西	Shanxi	262	246	119	30	13	3
内蒙古	Inner Mongolia	364	360	69	31	1	3
辽　宁	Liaoning	1417	1235	282	120	109	73
吉　林	Jilin	271	250	82	10	9	12
黑龙江	Heilongjiang	439	405	170	32	25	9
上　海	Shanghai	2549	2264	571	298	201	84
江　苏	Jiangsu	1930	1636	563	411	197	97
浙　江	Zhejiang	1750	1637	354	258	69	44
安　徽	Anhui	988	901	291	118	65	22
福　建	Fujian	1777	1093	337	163	474	210
江　西	Jiangxi	539	446	186	61	61	32
山　东	Shandong	1297	1138	399	249	115	44
河　南	Henan	1020	902	247	117	85	33
湖　北	Hubei	1052	848	370	87	149	55
湖　南	Hunan	703	620	217	61	63	20
广　东	Guangdong	3792	3029	789	836	685	78
广　西	Guangxi	528	407	156	71	92	29
海　南	Hainan	97	68	22	8	15	14
重　庆	Chongqing	1339	1189	149	80	102	48
四　川	Sichuan	1273	1190	220	152	56	27
贵　州	Guizhou	541	483	87	55	31	27
云　南	Yunnan	329	301	128	12	21	7
西　藏	Tibet	2	2	1			
陕　西	Shaanxi	359	334	133	34	13	12
甘　肃	Gansu	387	343	110	57	21	23
青　海	Qinghai	177	170	18	7	4	3
宁　夏	Ningxia	139	132	25	13	4	3
新　疆	Xinjiang	209	195	50	11	11	3

6-37 房地产开发企业（单位）从业人数

Number of Employed Persons in Enterprises for Real Estate Development

单位：人 (person)

年份 地区	Year Region	平均从业人数 Number of Employed Persons	内资企业 Domestic Funded Enterprises	#国有 State-owned Enterprises	#集体 Collective-owned Enterprises	港、澳、台投资企业 Enterprises with Funds from Hong Kong Macao and Taiwan	外商投资企业 Foreign Funded Enterprises
	1997	683217	578927			50000	54290
	1998	825888	708738	332834	134939	83784	33366
	1999	880257	767187	312240	127370	80216	32854
	2000	971942	862245	292252	116416	79066	30631
北京	Beijing	35320	23505	11002	1572	8098	3717
天津	Tianjin	21223	19457	7119	1856	1148	618
河北	Hebei	22263	20848	10656	1091	783	632
山西	Shanxi	14590	14234	8575	1490	306	50
内蒙古	Inner Mongolia	18427	18177	2972	800	35	215
辽宁	Liaoning	45268	41084	12069	4433	2327	1857
吉林	Jilin	15063	14230	6338	388	306	527
黑龙江	Heilongjiang	27841	27093	12830	1503	509	239
上海	Shanghai	78155	68413	21256	7228	7118	2624
江苏	Jiangsu	57405	51702	24878	9995	3689	2014
浙江	Zhejiang	40463	38100	10209	4760	1285	1078
安徽	Anhui	27948	26155	9269	3211	1342	451
福建	Fujian	40873	28073	9087	3182	9109	3691
江西	Jiangxi	17737	15250	9102	1678	1440	1047
山东	Shandong	58349	52803	21808	13032	3427	2119
河南	Henan	32775	27924	9643	3151	3769	1082
湖北	Hubei	46142	41523	20146	3591	3168	1451
湖南	Hunan	23044	21021	8344	1914	1438	585
广东	Guangdong	127812	109910	29575	27419	16335	1567
广西	Guangxi	14063	11521	4936	1346	1974	568
海南	Hainan	3013	2233	615	166	574	206
重庆	Chongqing	63764	57004	7555	7478	5152	1608
四川	Sichuan	65451	62834	13425	9376	1705	912
贵州	Guizhou	14042	12917	2548	1488	520	605
云南	Yunnan	11850	11207	4048	257	489	154
西藏	Tibet	58	58	38			
陕西	Shaanxi	13658	12947	5497	1556	486	225
甘肃	Gansu	8225	7658	3541	1009	302	265
青海	Qinghai	8110	7744	1506	460	96	270
宁夏	Ningxia	6109	5847	1305	574	101	161
新疆	Xinjiang	12901	10773	2360	412	2035	93

6−38 各地区房地产开发企业（单位）的土地开发及其购置

Land Development and Purchase of Enterprises Real Estate Development by Region

单位：万平方米 (10 000 sq.m)

年份 地区	Year Region	本年完成开发土地面积 Land Space Developed This Year	正在开发的土地面积 Land Space under Development	待开发的土地面积 Land Space Needed to Development	本年购置土地面积 Land Space Purchased This Year
	1997	7371.3	8384.6	17670.1	6641.7
	1998	7730.1	9242.8	13530.7	10109.3
	1999	9319.6	8016.4	13505.2	11958.9
	2000	11666.1	8587.6	14754.8	16905.2
北京	Beijing	460.1	250.5	482.8	539.0
天津	Tianjin	492.2	332.0	483.3	330.8
河北	Hebei	334.9	164.2	123.0	415.1
山西	Shanxi	114.9	103.7	76.7	117.8
内蒙古	Inner Mongolia	51.1	5.0	14.1	167.9
辽宁	Liaoning	770.0	343.0	298.1	1019.3
吉林	Jilin	220.7	56.4	44.1	125.6
黑龙江	Heilongjiang	238.4	8.3	8.2	256.5
上海	Shanghai	165.6	241.5	875.3	592.7
江苏	Jiangsu	886.6	543.5	928.3	1396.0
浙江	Zhejiang	826.5	426.9	1056.5	1777.1
安徽	Anhui	428.0	297.7	343.8	641.3
福建	Fujian	585.7	462.9	666.9	901.1
江西	Jiangxi	258.7	127.4	108.8	287.8
山东	Shandong	1089.5	512.3	941.6	1165.9
河南	Henan	239.1	318.0	305.5	503.9
湖北	Hubei	469.3	393.3	1076.6	838.1
湖南	Hunan	371.6	183.2	371.3	297.3
广东	Guangdong	1754.5	2321.8	4071.9	1942.3
广西	Guangxi	176.5	179.3	254.9	195.3
海南	Hainan	20.0	29.0	16.8	29.6
重庆	Chongqing	384.7	425.7	922.3	619.2
四川	Sichuan	235.8	319.5	427.9	943.1
贵州	Guizhou	202.5	175.5	120.4	288.7
云南	Yunnan	380.0	93.1	258.5	473.7
西藏	Tibet	3.7			11.1
陕西	Shaanxi	125.0	114.4	149.8	304.7
甘肃	Gansu	87.1	33.7	44.7	117.4
青海	Qinghai	36.6	14.8	21.0	39.3
宁夏	Ningxia	8.4	11.1	6.5	71.7
新疆	Xinjiang	248.2	99.9	255.2	496.0

6-39 各地区房地产开发建设投资总规模及完成投资

General Scale of and Actually Completed Investment in Real Estate Development by Region

单位：亿元 (100 million yuan)

年份 地区	Year Region	实际需要总投资 Total Investment Actually Needed	自开始建设至本年底累计完成投资 Accumulative Investment Actually Made Since Starting of Construction up to the End of This Year	#本年完成投资 Investment Made This Year	全部建成尚需投资 Further Investment Required for the Completion of Construction
	1997	17685.72	9109.72	3178.37	8576.00
	1998	19623.04	10515.44	3614.23	9107.60
	1999	20207.68	11509.43	4103.20	8698.25
	2000	22664.18	12816.37	4984.05	9847.82
北京	Beijing	4111.09	2043.88	522.07	2067.21
天津	Tianjin	472.84	317.87	133.93	154.97
河北	Hebei	321.72	190.64	108.39	131.09
山西	Shanxi	144.99	80.45	39.46	64.53
内蒙古	Inner Mongolia	86.44	61.53	45.22	24.91
辽宁	Liaoning	771.21	495.18	264.91	276.03
吉林	Jilin	139.58	90.00	63.52	49.57
黑龙江	Heilongjiang	220.20	157.59	104.10	62.61
上海	Shanghai	2754.75	1916.68	566.17	838.07
江苏	Jiangsu	998.81	644.03	358.72	354.77
浙江	Zhejiang	1196.95	733.09	362.18	463.86
安徽	Anhui	309.12	153.14	87.93	155.98
福建	Fujian	1222.61	587.47	207.37	635.15
江西	Jiangxi	122.79	70.65	42.37	52.13
山东	Shandong	820.26	471.27	223.29	348.99
河南	Henan	317.75	178.86	77.88	138.89
湖北	Hubei	708.95	375.36	134.63	333.59
湖南	Hunan	293.38	141.67	74.83	151.71
广东	Guangdong	5035.25	2628.10	858.61	2407.15
广西	Guangxi	234.80	132.82	38.67	101.98
海南	Hainan	67.71	37.79	10.34	29.92
重庆	Chongqing	636.64	333.37	139.63	303.27
四川	Sichuan	543.15	327.89	195.97	215.26
贵州	Guizhou	168.59	93.85	46.58	74.74
云南	Yunnan	300.18	177.50	83.23	122.68
西藏	Tibet	0.98	0.98	0.98	
陕西	Shaanxi	341.67	166.72	78.89	174.96
甘肃	Gansu	130.66	89.18	27.71	41.49
青海	Qinghai	45.55	23.98	13.50	21.57
宁夏	Ningxia	26.52	19.45	15.57	7.07
新疆	Xinjiang	119.02	75.38	57.43	43.65

6-40 各地区按用途分的房地产开发企业（单位）投资完成额

Actually Completed Investment of Enterprises for Real Estate Development by Region and by Use

单位：万元 (10 000 yuan)

年份 地区	Year Region	本年完成投资额 Investment Made This Year	住宅 Residential Buildings	#别墅、高档公寓 Villas and Good Apartments	#经济适用房屋 Economical Houses	办公楼 Office Buildings	商业营业用房 Houses for Business Use	其他 Other
	1997	31783702	15393805	1562955	1854959	3889819	4258452	8241626
	1998	36142292	20815647	1818526	2708523	4337956	4758297	6230392
	1999	41032024	26384794	1786233	4370211	3385973	4843349	6417908
	2000	49840529	33119839	2700142	5424365	2978511	5799927	7942252
北　京	Beijing	5220737	2882583	636550	341873	452191	306195	1579768
天　津	Tianjin	1339294	900198	82704	259413	31251	71834	336011
河　北	Hebei	1083938	711174	35393	220962	26187	132174	214403
山　西	Shanxi	394556	272280	2210	170266	19201	48178	54897
内蒙古	Inner Mongolia	452181	289025	15290	186380	16257	107678	39221
辽　宁	Liaoning	2649062	1812920	127834	250726	155384	445326	235432
吉　林	Jilin	635194	399799	32238	207725	19680	124702	91013
黑龙江	Heilongjiang	1040979	712644	36598	351905	35691	162186	130458
上　海	Shanghai	5661700	4088159	407160		574661	515052	483828
江　苏	Jiangsu	3587177	2607891	141193	367680	215891	484781	278614
浙　江	Zhejiang	3621771	2553026	96093	173659	231193	397485	440067
安　徽	Anhui	879261	575174	13362	169288	48313	160520	95254
福　建	Fujian	2073691	1250655	140028	154671	152004	299123	371909
江　西	Jiangxi	423705	264555	14316	83853	14324	67984	76842
山　东	Shandong	2232870	1462130	83972	341542	112497	274111	384132
河　南	Henan	778754	503744	43139	166053	44129	53817	177064
湖　北	Hubei	1346280	931505	42832	235263	92844	107348	214583
湖　南	Hunan	748269	401941	31136	151990	24176	88463	233689
广　东	Guangdong	8586126	5937459	419876	195289	368029	927409	1353229
广　西	Guangxi	386747	207861	12331	32545	11944	36306	130636
海　南	Hainan	103372	67330	31853	5205	3517	11934	20591
重　庆	Chongqing	1396327	728125	69366	89333	86377	311708	270117
四　川	Sichuan	1959674	1283368	86892	282243	69134	276928	330244
贵　州	Guizhou	465815	271393	8553	87121	29140	74296	90986
云　南	Yunnan	832253	566317	59972	159968	34544	118938	112454
西　藏	Tibet	9771	9672		9672			99
陕　西	Shaanxi	788862	581607	24265	390727	53356	65653	88246
甘　肃	Gansu	277135	173772	1011	57124	24331	36622	42410
青　海	Qinghai	134990	81416		21979	8369	24031	21174
宁　夏	Ningxia	155691	91735	1585	22987	10725	26544	26687
新　疆	Xinjiang	574347	500381	2390	236923	13171	42601	18194

6-41 各地区房地产开发企业（单位）的资金来源

Source of Funds of Enterprises for Real Estate Development

单位：万元 (10 000 yuan)

年份 地区	Year Region	本年资金来源小计 Total Funds This Year	国家预算内资金 State Budgetary Appropriation	国内贷款 Domestic Loans	债券 Bonds	利用外资 Foreign Investment	#外商直接投资 Direct Foreign Investment	自筹资金 Fundraising	其他资金来源 Others
	1997	38170650	124789	9111902	48691	4608565	3279010	9728831	14547872
	1998	44149422	149480	10531712	62319	3617581	2588698	11669821	18118509
	1999	47959012	100457	11115664	98703	2566022	1804807	13446210	20631956
	2000	59976309	68720	13850756	34760	1687046	1348026	16142122	28192905
北京	Beijing	7811518	3000	2388175	5900	370593	292080	1306631	3737219
天津	Tianjin	1597319		403967		21772	19258	489096	682484
河北	Hebei	1161315	6131	201174		7737	7737	379971	566302
山西	Shanxi	429243	165	100228	915	3924	3754	102060	221951
内蒙古	Inner Mongolia	438525	2000	87469		1872	1872	183052	164132
辽宁	Liaoning	2837089	5380	645522	3458	55167	45198	971842	1155720
吉林	Jilin	663896	3127	112150		5716	4966	307407	235496
黑龙江	Heilongjiang	919019	1000	182528		10543	10543	362915	362033
上海	Shanghai	6646769	17911	1553671	1089	281100	162464	2118601	2674397
江苏	Jiangsu	3911941	360	880054	5151	58195	41393	1013385	1954796
浙江	Zhejiang	5260118	1917	1514388	400	16267	15767	837603	2889543
安徽	Anhui	977459	407	185685	195	19163	17303	325053	446956
福建	Fujian	2768523	3643	447781	1250	249419	229891	542060	1524370
江西	Jiangxi	444086	620	71414	700	33925	32997	134697	202730
山东	Shandong	2465145	9003	477047		40400	28646	664099	1274596
河南	Henan	851700	253	189573		7617	7186	282919	371338
湖北	Hubei	1222817	2216	180817	6150	11542	8502	515185	506907
湖南	Hunan	808181	3110	156630	34	9513	6933	302928	335966
广东	Guangdong	10645133	1829	2285310	3963	391615	335597	2877111	5085305
广西	Guangxi	502039	2260	92998		12916	11052	131654	262211
海南	Hainan	104859	360	10932	500	648	161	47635	44784
重庆	Chongqing	1546651		435492		13998	13657	554272	542889
四川	Sichuan	2308142	410	455696	3020	19996	13996	747134	1081886
贵州	Guizhou	609149	110	138960	1250	4355	3437	165154	299320
云南	Yunnan	968424	950	259084		26742	26555	152588	529060
西藏	Tibet	9780		1200				3481	5099
陕西	Shaanxi	793235	2167	158692	785	6192	1362	164386	461013
甘肃	Gansu	285545	51	62245		2414	2414	98297	122538
青海	Qinghai	128862		21719		3105	3105	85719	18319
宁夏	Ningxia	158495	340	36332				42419	79404
新疆	Xinjiang	701332		113823		600	200	232768	354141

6-42 各地区房地产开发建设房屋建筑面积和造价

Floor Space of Buildings and their Cost in Real Estate Development by Region

年 份 地 区	Year Region	施工房屋面积 (万平方米) Floor Space of Buildings under Construction (10 000 sq.m)	竣工房屋面积 (万平方米) Floor Space of Buildings Completed (10 000 sq.m)	房屋建筑面积竣工率 (%) Rate of Floor Space of Buildings Completed (%)	竣工房屋价值 (万 元) Value of Buildings Completed (10 000 yuan)	竣工房屋造价 (元/平方米) Cost of Buildings Completed (yuan/sq.m)
	1997	44985.5	15819.7	35.2	18592458	1175
	1998	50770.1	17566.6	34.6	21391927	1218
	1999	56857.6	21410.8	37.7	24675822	1152
	2000	65896.9	25104.9	38.1	28593463	1139
北 京	Beijing	4455.0	1365.6	30.7	2662474	1950
天 津	Tianjin	1783.0	583.5	32.7	565469	969
河 北	Hebei	1670.0	771.3	46.2	693774	899
山 西	Shanxi	789.5	306.4	38.8	245472	801
内蒙古	Inner Mongolia	704.4	412.9	58.6	329269	797
辽 宁	Liaoning	3301.8	1619.0	49.0	1507495	931
吉 林	Jilin	781.1	464.8	59.5	450250	969
黑龙江	Heilongjiang	1451.4	827.9	57.0	749084	905
上 海	Shanghai	5523.2	1643.6	29.8	3557851	2165
江 苏	Jiangsu	4268.5	2143.2	50.2	1974602	921
浙 江	Zhejiang	4612.5	1676.9	36.4	2059460	1228
安 徽	Anhui	1687.2	759.3	45.0	531122	699
福 建	Fujian	3422.9	1009.4	29.5	1177552	1167
江 西	Jiangxi	896.6	402.8	44.9	263455	654
山 东	Shandong	3551.1	1426.5	40.2	1275288	894
河 南	Henan	1657.5	597.5	36.0	405910	679
湖 北	Hubei	2102.9	843.5	40.1	692336	821
湖 南	Hunan	1318.4	577.6	43.8	414185	717
广 东	Guangdong	9911.8	3161.6	31.9	5114726	1618
广 西	Guangxi	766.2	226.7	29.6	164650	726
海 南	Hainan	138.7	36.0	26.0	54601	1516
重 庆	Chongqing	2833.4	849.4	30.0	767601	904
四 川	Sichuan	3224.1	1285.3	39.9	955033	743
贵 州	Guizhou	1014.9	349.2	34.4	251406	720
云 南	Yunnan	959.0	426.0	44.4	556914	1307
西 藏	Tibet	7.3	6.7	91.1	4453	669
陕 西	Shaanxi	1337.1	585.3	43.8	468544	801
甘 肃	Gansu	478.5	187.1	39.1	189552	1013
青 海	Qinghai	218.6	74.3	34.0	74089	998
宁 夏	Ningxia	258.6	155.5	60.1	107651	692
新 疆	Xinjiang	771.9	330.1	42.8	329195	997

6-43 各地区按用途分的房地产开发企业（单位）新开工房屋面积

Floor Space Started in Real Estate Development by Region and by Use

单位：万平方米 (10 000 sq.m)

年份 地区	Year Region	本年新开工房屋面积 Floor Space Started This Year	住宅 Residential Buildings	#别墅、高档公寓 Villas and Good Apartments	#经济适用房屋 Economical Houses	办公楼 Office Buildings	商业营业用房 Houses for Business Use	其他 Other
	1997	14027.00	10996.60	469.70	1720.60	872.40	1462.50	695.40
	1998	20387.90	16637.50	638.60	3466.40	871.50	1938.60	940.20
	1999	22579.41	18797.94	594.06	3970.36	690.29	2198.56	892.62
	2000	29582.64	24401.15	1169.09	5313.32	898.81	3034.77	1247.91
北京	Beijing	1676.86	1322.06	152.83	148.32	57.05	50.57	247.18
天津	Tianjin	617.86	567.84	16.55	210.67	16.54	26.15	7.33
河北	Hebei	859.72	748.85	33.91	197.79	13.01	80.78	17.08
山西	Shanxi	242.78	222.97	0.69	143.66	3.75	13.37	2.69
内蒙古	Inner Mongolia	480.37	353.56	13.65	219.52	11.83	109.75	5.23
辽宁	Liaoning	1966.96	1589.50	42.25	225.57	63.14	264.48	49.84
吉林	Jilin	616.39	477.01	21.56	250.08	21.96	101.88	15.55
黑龙江	Heilongjiang	847.31	691.85	19.32	355.79	21.06	117.28	17.13
上海	Shanghai	1992.31	1781.64	120.54		18.89	91.21	100.58
江苏	Jiangsu	2167.92	1772.85	87.43	277.70	62.23	230.80	102.05
浙江	Zhejiang	2376.09	1922.96	88.62	108.25	126.31	218.08	108.74
安徽	Anhui	896.08	708.67	9.72	240.92	31.26	135.67	20.49
福建	Fujian	1102.85	891.87	25.97	134.42	35.00	125.55	50.44
江西	Jiangxi	490.92	398.50	19.58	155.75	11.67	69.57	11.18
山东	Shandong	2110.73	1801.83	39.23	437.65	41.29	227.56	40.05
河南	Henan	786.94	705.61	68.86	245.73	19.90	45.45	15.98
湖北	Hubei	954.36	832.00	16.61	222.30	45.38	47.55	29.42
湖南	Hunan	678.37	551.95	34.58	243.58	18.94	75.68	31.80
广东	Guangdong	3245.03	2599.92	182.06	111.31	107.39	324.37	213.35
广西	Guangxi	300.00	261.52	15.32	43.32	4.44	25.51	8.54
海南	Hainan	30.47	26.84	7.15	4.85	0.42	2.51	0.69
重庆	Chongqing	1290.05	969.26	49.28	134.57	34.63	234.20	51.95
四川	Sichuan	1627.48	1365.51	47.79	303.07	37.24	187.06	37.67
贵州	Guizhou	412.67	320.46	7.05	78.27	15.87	57.17	19.18
云南	Yunnan	351.37	278.19	17.84	90.37	18.53	38.05	16.60
西藏	Tibet	7.31	7.31		7.31			
陕西	Shaanxi	517.80	466.15	25.61	308.57	20.27	15.07	16.32
甘肃	Gansu	182.14	144.22	0.11	57.09	10.17	24.64	3.10
青海	Qinghai	127.88	96.45		25.52	7.51	21.40	2.53
宁夏	Ningxia	171.98	126.03	1.76	35.14	12.99	30.41	2.55
新疆	Xinjiang	453.63	397.77	3.21	296.25	10.17	43.00	2.69

6-44 商品房屋销售情况

Selling of Commercial Houses

年份 地区	Year Region	房屋销售面积（万平方米）Floor Space Sold (10 000 sq.m)	# 住宅 Residential Buildings	个人购买商品住宅（万平方米）Commercial Houses Purchased by Individuals (10 000 sq.m)	商品房销售额（万元）Total Sales of Commercial Houses (10 000 yuan)	# 住宅 Residential Buildings
	1991	3025.46	2745.17	926.55	2378597	2075979
	1992	4288.86	3812.21	1456.01	4265938	3798493
	1993	6687.91	6035.19	2943.39	8637141	7291913
	1994	7230.35	6118.03	3344.53	10184950	7305208
	1995	7905.94	6787.03	3344.81	12577269	10240705
	1996	7900.41	6898.46	3666.82	14271292	11069006
	1997	9010.17	7864.30	5233.72	17994763	14075553
	1998	12185.33	10827.08	7792.62	25133027	20068676
	1999	14556.53	12997.87	10408.53	29878734	24137347
	2000	18637.13	16570.28	14464.38	39354423	32286046
北京	Beijing	956.90	898.22	772.71	4707247	4093363
天津	Tianjin	391.76	378.34	354.62	912027	860428
河北	Hebei	489.44	443.52	295.64	708819	598658
山西	Shanxi	190.64	177.39	117.61	213052	174809
内蒙古	Inner Mongolia	293.84	239.46	223.48	333670	235743
辽宁	Liaoning	948.67	804.39	700.35	1969468	1514151
吉林	Jilin	309.34	267.49	256.09	435515	347385
黑龙江	Heilongjiang	499.85	424.43	383.54	869447	669929
上海	Shanghai	1557.87	1445.87	1242.68	5554492	4809654
江苏	Jiangsu	1740.93	1555.97	1397.09	2859863	2375442
浙江	Zhejiang	1502.23	1308.98	1205.13	2925114	2301115
安徽	Anhui	535.86	462.91	420.20	628613	472366
福建	Fujian	810.65	675.73	594.01	1689647	1193865
江西	Jiangxi	286.69	242.29	221.97	272008	206842
山东	Shandong	1078.38	934.20	765.23	1538824	1254872
河南	Henan	509.21	438.41	345.44	641788	505119
湖北	Hubei	612.05	571.04	494.14	837368	731015
湖南	Hunan	377.76	343.28	329.41	407772	338900
广东	Guangdong	2259.95	2009.34	1838.43	7295026	5973630
广西	Guangxi	191.36	177.80	167.60	277384	245721
海南	Hainan	42.15	39.72	39.19	83450	77705
重庆	Chongqing	579.96	491.09	473.60	783709	528698
四川	Sichuan	945.64	837.54	715.02	1267444	950444
贵州	Guizhou	251.71	228.83	208.38	319315	250815
云南	Yunnan	343.16	311.03	179.54	596712	512009
西藏	Tibet	4.80	4.80	4.80	5160	5160
陕西	Shaanxi	396.40	370.69	324.36	496868	448659
甘肃	Gansu	123.01	109.12	76.08	160101	130790
青海	Qinghai	39.91	36.84	15.88	49413	41847
宁夏	Ningxia	104.49	90.61	79.82	141306	103746
新疆	Xinjiang	262.52	250.95	222.35	373801	333166

6-45 各地区按用途分的商品房屋实际销售面积

Floor Space of Commercial Houses Actually Sold by Region and by Use

单位：万平方米 (10 000 sq.m)

年份 地区	Year Region	房屋销售面积 Floor Space Sold	住宅 Residential Buildings	#别墅、高档公寓 Villas and Good Apartments	#经济适用房屋 Economical Houses	办公楼 Office Buildings	商业营业用房 Houses for Business Use	其他 Other
	1997	9010.20	7864.30	254.20	1211.90	341.40	634.10	170.40
	1998	12185.30	10827.10	345.30	1666.50	400.60	810.80	146.80
	1999	14556.53	12997.87	435.74	2701.31	403.43	1003.17	152.06
	2000	18637.13	16570.28	640.72	3760.07	436.98	1399.31	230.56
北　京	Beijing	956.90	898.22	107.58	166.18	41.23	6.14	11.31
天　津	Tianjin	391.76	378.34	16.93	155.34	3.44	9.01	0.98
河　北	Hebei	489.44	443.52	13.98	164.34	1.81	41.30	2.81
山　西	Shanxi	190.64	177.39	0.08	103.76	3.18	9.76	0.31
内蒙古	Inner Mongolia	293.84	239.46	2.77	114.56	5.35	47.98	1.04
辽　宁	Liaoning	948.67	804.39	35.04	146.87	20.29	114.27	9.71
吉　林	Jilin	309.34	267.49	2.25	141.88	4.45	34.49	2.92
黑龙江	Heilongjiang	499.85	424.43	15.69	205.63	10.68	58.60	6.14
上　海	Shanghai	1557.87	1445.87	53.45		47.76	54.54	9.70
江　苏	Jiangsu	1740.93	1555.97	54.24	313.98	35.58	124.27	25.11
浙　江	Zhejiang	1502.23	1308.98	26.29	95.54	48.93	113.82	30.50
安　徽	Anhui	535.86	462.91	6.16	142.97	12.82	58.41	1.72
福　建	Fujian	810.65	675.73	45.57	61.65	41.74	77.89	15.30
江　西	Jiangxi	286.69	242.29	1.69	85.97	3.57	37.31	3.52
山　东	Shandong	1078.38	934.20	19.27	235.85	21.40	103.78	18.99
河　南	Henan	509.21	438.41	23.44	173.77	5.52	59.02	6.26
湖　北	Hubei	612.05	571.04	11.17	172.99	13.98	24.07	2.97
湖　南	Hunan	377.76	343.28	5.84	151.34	2.64	28.77	3.06
广　东	Guangdong	2259.95	2009.34	112.37	106.74	40.46	163.71	46.44
广　西	Guangxi	191.36	177.80	13.81	43.32	1.38	9.44	2.73
海　南	Hainan	42.15	39.72	7.50	4.27	1.29	1.01	0.12
重　庆	Chongqing	579.96	491.09	18.46	71.07	20.08	61.09	7.70
四　川	Sichuan	945.64	837.54	13.88	195.82	20.39	82.69	5.01
贵　州	Guizhou	251.71	228.83	1.71	75.25	3.11	18.69	1.08
云　南	Yunnan	343.16	311.03	21.32	131.76	5.69	18.70	7.74
西　藏	Tibet	4.80	4.80		4.80			
陕　西	Shaanxi	396.40	370.69	6.74	247.69	11.70	8.55	5.46
甘　肃	Gansu	123.01	109.12	1.96	41.60	4.43	8.54	0.92
青　海	Qinghai	39.91	36.84		8.66	0.37	2.50	0.20
宁　夏	Ningxia	104.49	90.61	0.78	20.72	2.23	11.12	0.54
新　疆	Xinjiang	262.52	250.95	0.73	175.73	1.46	9.82	0.28

6-46 各地区按用途分的商品房屋平均销售价格

Average Selling Price of Commercial Houses by Region and by Use

单位：元/平方米 (yuan/sq.m)

年份 地区	Year Region	房屋平均销售价格 Average Selling Price of Houses	住宅 Residential Buildings	#别墅、高档公寓 Villas and Good Apartments	#经济适用房屋 Economical Houses	办公楼 Office Buildings	商业营业用房 Houses for Business Use	其他 Other
	1997	1997	1790	5382	1097	4677	3090	2129
	1998	2063	1854	4596	1035	5552	3170	1837
	1999	2053	1857	4503	1093	5265	3333	1804
	2000	2112	1948	4288	1202	4751	3260	1864
北京	Beijing	4919	4557	8315	2644	12563	6915	4722
天津	Tianjin	2328	2274	4540	2138	4389	3790	2423
河北	Hebei	1448	1350	2538	1141	1834	2428	2331
山西	Shanxi	1118	985	1694	903	3064	2805	3645
内蒙古	Inner Mongolia	1136	984	1701	969	1790	1804	1729
辽宁	Liaoning	2076	1882	3651	1453	4007	3070	2384
吉林	Jilin	1408	1299	2291	1278	2125	2080	2384
黑龙江	Heilongjiang	1739	1578	4495	1296	2947	2639	2187
上海	Shanghai	3565	3326	6108		9223	5111	2644
江苏	Jiangsu	1643	1527	2282	1109	2988	2846	974
浙江	Zhejiang	1947	1758	2337	1652	2643	3960	1444
安徽	Anhui	1173	1020	2581	878	1692	2273	1032
福建	Fujian	2084	1767	3110	1245	2617	4561	2049
江西	Jiangxi	949	854	2026	804	850	1577	941
山东	Shandong	1427	1343	3533	1081	2704	2019	870
河南	Henan	1260	1152	2107	950	1996	1952	1668
湖北	Hubei	1368	1280	2755	952	2295	2956	1054
湖南	Hunan	1079	987	1960	835	1258	2193	801
广东	Guangdong	3228	2973	4018	1389	8108	5411	2316
广西	Guangxi	1450	1382	2562	919	2521	2587	1375
海南	Hainan	1980	1956	4299	1260	3080	1592	1194
重庆	Chongqing	1351	1077	2455	907	2227	3275	1328
四川	Sichuan	1340	1135	3837	845	2286	3164	1740
贵州	Guizhou	1269	1096	3426	888	2353	3191	1418
云南	Yunnan	1739	1646	2444	1317	2135	3143	1781
西藏	Tibet	1075	1075		1075			
陕西	Shaanxi	1253	1210	2594	999	1525	2455	1718
甘肃	Gansu	1302	1199	1565	1065	2069	2226	1246
青海	Qinghai	1238	1136		811	3770	2257	2662
宁夏	Ningxia	1352	1145	3213	925	1958	2934	1074
新疆	Xinjiang	1424	1328	1338	1259	3306	3578	2262

6-47 各地区房地产开发企业（单位）的资产负债

Asset Balance of Enterprises for Real Estate Development by Region

单位：万元 (10 000 yuan)

年份 地区	Year Region	实收资本 合计 Total Capital Hold	#国家资本金 State Capital	资产总计 Total Assets	累计折旧 Total Depreciation	#本年折旧 Depreciation This Year	负债总计 Total Liabilities	所有者权益 Creditors Equity	资产负债率 (%) Ratio of Liabilities to Assets
	1997	38120741	2443003	164169597	1756884	410656	125154596	39015001	76.2
	1998	57787310	8418989	195261772	1910386	390176	148572535	46689237	76.1
	1999	45208800	3024487	187448042	2087894	398180	142638782	44809260	76.1
	2000	53029071	2155664	251859857	2992816	577153	190321015	61538842	75.6
北京	Beijing	5628449	113545	33426958	205486	46921	27262814	6164144	81.6
天津	Tianjin	1638557	50972	5955607	46201	8893	4610036	1345571	77.4
河北	Hebei	345948	11276	2149814	23016	5829	1776614	373200	82.6
山西	Shanxi	155705	4579	1034418	24481	5188	859306	175112	83.1
内蒙古	Inner Mongolia	198722	1750	637145	8534	1703	444938	192207	69.8
辽宁	Liaoning	1866983	136231	10049579	158829	29226	7982621	2066958	79.4
吉林	Jilin	294925	18532	1474387	17788	6621	1184910	289477	80.4
黑龙江	Heilongjiang	724032	11829	6832979	58784	13822	5918124	914855	86.6
上海	Shanghai	13641534	808828	57926046	413774	94938	39406062	18519984	68.0
江苏	Jiangsu	2102800	147760	12018229	132472	27534	9584655	2433574	79.8
浙江	Zhejiang	2102178	80222	12165290	101944	22442	9931814	2233476	81.6
安徽	Anhui	801091	28926	2471288	51914	11650	1685674	785614	68.2
福建	Fujian	2724571	47464	9404295	135815	24045	6563088	2841207	69.8
江西	Jiangxi	349564	13547	1070575	33802	4586	757204	313371	70.7
山东	Shandong	1664110	66592	7072211	106924	20671	5623072	1449139	79.5
河南	Henan	817805	22529	3018825	56674	12183	2338003	680822	77.4
湖北	Hubei	1552130	113518	5203333	98578	18113	3730780	1472553	71.7
湖南	Hunan	643969	37277	2131887	45064	11551	1498638	633249	70.3
广东	Guangdong	9570743	222123	52127709	807326	127040	39903491	12224218	76.5
广西	Guangxi	543513	14606	2358698	28188	4485	1923579	435119	81.6
海南	Hainan	422898	29724	1436433	24403	3089	898460	537973	62.5
重庆	Chongqing	1722040	50409	6814885	120715	26134	4952547	1862338	72.7
四川	Sichuan	1379307	40537	6368674	153601	22033	4697329	1671345	73.8
贵州	Guizhou	577011	27511	1513452	21901	3460	1121227	392225	74.1
云南	Yunnan	358815	22130	2459081	36287	6331	2072247	386834	84.3
西藏	Tibet	11053		24472	135		11452	13020	46.8
陕西	Shaanxi	475963	10745	1798703	24601	9028	1359745	438958	75.6
甘肃	Gansu	235301	2303	871685	18131	2707	666188	205497	76.4
青海	Qinghai	189125	273	262676	14540	423	129894	132782	49.5
宁夏	Ningxia	89467	8932	448079	7881	2057	344569	103510	76.9
新疆	Xinjiang	200762	10994	1332444	15027	4450	1081934	250510	81.2

6-48 房地产开发经营情况

Real Estate Development and Management

单位：万元 (10 000 yuan)

年份 地区 Year Region	经营总收入 Total Revenue	土地转让收入 Land Transferred	商品房屋销售收入 Commercial Houses Sold	房屋出租收入 Houses Leased	其他收入 Others	经营税金及附加 Business Tax and Extra Charges	营业利润 Operating Surplus
1991	2840325	153810	2378597	39221	268697	205551	275239
1992	5285565	427420	4265938	59617	532590	414435	635196
1993	11359074	839281	8637141	106348	1776304	965917	1559223
1994	12881866	959357	10184950	172817	1564742	951029	1674350
1995	17316624	1943981	12582817	257927	2531899	903047	1434087
1996	19687850	1203378	15337647	299899	2846926	927779	179805
1997	22184557	1032847	17552061	387878	3211770	1042143	-103462
1998	29512078	1322454	24084097	493192	3612325	1388134	-106565
1999	30260108	1032492	25550245	627408	3049963	1453611	-350926
2000	45157119	1296054	38968215	953237	3939613	2145704	732836
北京 Beijing	3568022	98589	3105123	194363	169947	183527	-186159
天津 Tianjin	1098566	13887	890540	8072	186067	50642	35545
河北 Hebei	836577	25093	719271	3164	89049	33487	9301
山西 Shanxi	244503	8754	211181	750	23818	10335	-4825
内蒙古 Inner Mongolia	331787	1948	326780	1022	2037	14094	9704
辽宁 Liaoning	2339911	33981	2156412	10251	139267	129169	-4952
吉林 Jilin	414847	3057	401650	1753	8387	21351	-4140
黑龙江 Heilongjiang	2222492	1247	2211716	4792	4737	61820	15917
上海 Shanghai	7836931	229857	5566293	296825	1743956	326932	131283
江苏 Jiangsu	2939961	31916	2748391	34975	124679	131079	77748
浙江 Zhejiang	3035439	46988	2925589	12565	50297	165083	116411
安徽 Anhui	701896	12293	651668	1781	36154	38186	-14439
福建 Fujian	1717929	80073	1472091	23029	142736	96971	22045
江西 Jiangxi	302608	8797	281019	1481	11311	13066	6721
山东 Shandong	1721014	14081	1524013	9183	173737	81635	54809
河南 Henan	590082	5061	540250	2006	42765	25251	33386
湖北 Hubei	726012	23689	635023	11459	55841	35137	-27695
湖南 Hunan	464019	48753	398573	3515	13178	23149	-4986
广东 Guangdong	9155672	413278	7884333	281392	576669	477037	435483
广西 Guangxi	338043	44056	275710	4073	14204	17404	-16017
海南 Hainan	109286	14120	58179	1100	35887	6704	-4370
重庆 Chongqing	936822	33104	763810	16518	123390	45803	-20402
四川 Sichuan	1490581	58998	1370937	11052	49594	64530	37021
贵州 Guizhou	331670	3229	310162	3603	14676	16138	-16284
云南 Yunnan	525512	24885	478540	4282	17805	28944	5794
西藏 Tibet	70528		70528			122	-914
陕西 Shaanxi	339462	12254	309938	1743	15527	12961	2186
甘肃 Gansu	225381	3816	175245	5155	41165	8644	28342
青海 Qinghai	55580		47182	28	8370	1538	-1636
宁夏 Ningxia	143586	250	138608	747	3981	7268	8399
新疆 Xinjiang	342400		319460	2558	20382	17697	9560

主 要 统 计 指 标 解 释

全社会固定资产投资　固定资产投资是社会固定资产再生产的主要手段。通过建造和购置固定资产的活动，国民经济不断采用先进技术装备，建立新兴部门，进一步调整经济结构和生产力的地区分布，增强经济实力，为改善人民物质文化生活创造物质条件。这对我国的社会主义现代化建设具有重要意义。

固定资产投资额是以货币表现的建造和购置固定资产活动的工作量，它是反映固定资产投资规模、速度、比例关系和使用方向的综合性指标。全社会固定资产投资按登记注册类型可分为国有、集体、个体、联营、股份制、外商、港澳台商、其他等。按照管理渠道，全社会固定资产投资总额分为基本建设、更新改造、房地产开发投资和其他固定资产投资四个部分。

基本建设投资　基本建设指企业、事业、行政单位以扩大生产能力或工程效益为主要目的的新建、扩建工程及有关工作。其综合范围为总投资50万元以上(含50万元，下同)的基本建设项目。具体包括：(1)列入中央和各级地方本年基本建设计划的建设项目，以及虽未列入本年基本建设计划，但使用以前年度基建计划内结转投资(包括利用基建库存设备材料)在本年继续施工的建设项目；(2)本年基本建设计划内投资与更新改造计划内投资结合安排的新建项目和新增生产能力(或工程效益)达到大中型项目标准的扩建项目，以及为改变生产力布局而进行的全厂性迁建项目；(3)国有单位既未列入基建计划，也未列入更新改造计划的总投资在50万元以上的新建、扩建、恢复项目和为改变生产力布局而进行的全厂性迁建项目，以及行政、事业单位增建业务用房和行政单位增建生活福利设施的项目。

更新改造投资　更新改造指企业、事业单位对原有设施进行固定资产更新和技术改造，以及相应配套的工程和有关工作(不包括大修理和维护工程)。其综合范围为总投资50万元以上的更新改造项目。具体包括：(1)列入中央和各级地方本年更新改造计划的投资单位（项目）和虽未列入本年更新改造计划，但使用上年更新改造计划内结转的投资在本年继续施工的项目；(2)本年更新改造计划内投资与基本建设计划内投资结合安排的对企、事业单位原有设施进行技术改造或更新的项目和增建主要生产车间、分厂等其新增生产能力(或工程效益)未达到大中型项目标准的项目，以及由于城市环境保护和安全生产的需要而进行的迁建工程；(3)国有企、事业单位既未列入基建计划也未列入更新改造计划，总投资在50万元以上的属于改建或更新改造性质的项目，以及由于城市环境保护和安全生产的需要而进行的迁建工程。

房地产开发投资　指房地产开发公司、商品房建设公司及其他房地产开发法人单位和附属于其他法人单位实际从事房地产开发或经营的活动单位统一开发的包括统代建、拆迁还建的住宅、厂房、仓库、饭店、宾馆、度假村、写字楼、办公楼等房屋建筑物和配套的服务设施，土地开发工程（如道路、给水、排水、供电、供热、通讯、平整场地等基础设施工程）的投资；不包括单纯的土地交易活动。

其他固定资产投资　指全社会固定资产投资中未列入基本建设、更新改造和房地产开发投资的建造和购置固定资产的活动。具体包括：

⑴国有单位按规定不纳入基本建设计划和更新改造计划管理，计划总投资（或实际需要总投资）在50万元以上的以下工程：①用油田维护费和石油开发基金进行的油田维护和开发工程；②煤炭、铁矿、森工等采掘采伐业用维简费进行的开拓延伸工程；③交通部门用公路养路费对原有公路、桥梁进行改建的工程；④商业部门用简易建筑费建造的仓库工程。

⑵城镇集体固定资产投资：指所有隶属城市、县城(城关镇)领导的集体单位（乡镇企业局管理的除外）建造和购置固定资产计划总投资（或实际需要总投资）在50万元以上的项目。

⑶除上述以外的其他各种企、事业单位、个体建造和购置固定资产总投资在50万元以上的、未列入基本建设计划和更新改造计划的项目。

城镇和工矿区私人建房投资和农村个人投资　城镇和工矿区私人建房包括市、县城、城关镇、工矿区所辖范围内的全部私人建房，不论其房主是否系本地的常住户口均应包括。农村个人投资包括农村个人建房及购置生产性固定资产的投资。

固定资产投资的资金来源　根据固定资产投资的资金来源不同，分为国家预算内资金、国内贷款、利用外资、自筹资金和其他资金来源。

⑴国家预算内资金：指中央财政和地方财政中由国家统筹安排的基本建设拨款和更新改造拨款，以及中央财政安排的专项拨款中用于基本建设的资金和基本建设拨款改贷款的资金等。

⑵国内贷款：指报告期内企、事业单位向银行及非银行金融机构借入的用于固定资产投资的各种国内借款。包括银行利用自有资金及吸收的存款发放的贷款、上级主管部门拨入的国内贷款、国家专项贷款(包括煤代油贷款、劳改煤矿专项贷款等)、地方财政专项资金安排的贷款、国内储备贷款、周转贷款等。

⑶利用外资：指报告期内收到的用于固定资产投资的国外资金，包括统借统还、自借自还的国外贷款，中外合资项目中的外资，以及对外发行债券和股票等。国家统借统还的外资指由我国政府出面同外国政府、团体或金融组织签订贷款协议、并负责偿还本息的国外贷款。

⑷自筹资金：指建设单位报告期内收到的，用于进行固定资产投资的上级主管部门、地方和企、事业单位自筹资金。

⑸其他资金来源：指报告期内收到的除以上各种拨款、借款、自筹资金以外其他用于固定资产投资的资金。

固定资产投资按国民经济行业分 建设项目归哪个行业，按其建成投产后的主要产品或主要用途及社会经济活动性质来确定。基本建设按建设项目划分国民经济行业，更新改造、国有单位其他固定资产投资及城镇集体投资根据整个企业、事业单位所属的行业来划分。一般情况下，一个建设项目或一个企业、事业单位只能属于一种国民经济行业。为了更准确地反映国民经济各行业之间的比例关系，联合企业(总厂)所属分厂属于不同行业的，原则上按分厂划分行业。

固定资产投资按建设性质分 建设项目的性质一般分为新建、扩建、改建、迁建、恢复。基本建设按建设项目划分建设性质，更新改造、国有单位其他固定资产投资及城镇集体投资等按整个企业、事业单位的建设情况确定建设性质，房地产开发单位、农村投资、城镇工矿区私人建房等投资不划分建设性质。 ⑴新建：一般是指从无到有、“平地起家”新开始建设的单位。有的单位原有的基础很小，经过建设后其新增加的固定资产价值超过原有固定资产价值(原值)三倍以上的也算新建。

⑵扩建：一般是指为扩大原有产品的生产能力，在厂内或其他地点增建主要生产车间(或主要工程)、独立的生产线或分厂的企业；事业单位和行政单位在原单位增建业务用房(如学校增建教学用房、医院增建门诊部或病床用房、行政机关增建办公楼等)也作为扩建。

⑶改建：一般是指现有企业、事业单位为了技术进步，提高产品质量，增加花色品种，促进产品升级换代，降低消耗和成本，加强资源综合利用和三废治理、劳保安全等，采用新技术、新工艺、新设备、新材料等对现有设施、工艺条件进行技术改造或更新(包括相应配套的辅助性生产、生活福利设施)。有的企业为充分发挥现有生产能力，进行填平补齐而增建不增加本单位主要产品生产能力的车间等，也属于改建。

固定资产投资按构成分 固定资产投资活动按其工作内容和实现方式分为建筑安装工程，设备、工具、器具购置，其他费用三个部分。

⑴建筑安装工程(建筑安装工作量)：指各种房屋、建筑物的建造工程和各种设备、装置的安装工程。包括各种房屋建造工程，各种用途设备基础和各种工业窑炉的砌筑工程；为施工而进行的各种准备工作和临时工程以及完工后的清理工作等；铁路、道路的铺设，矿井的开凿及石油管道的架设等；水利工程；防空地下建筑等特殊工程；以及各种机械设备的安装工程；为测定安装工程质量，对设备进行的试运工作。在安装工程中，不包括被安装设备本身的价值 。

⑵设备、工具、器具购置：指购置或自制达到固定资产标准的设备、工具、器具的价值，固定资产的标准按财务部门规定。新建单位、扩建单位的新建车间按照设计和计划要求购置或自制的全部设备、工具、器具，不论是否达到固定资产标准均计入“设备、工具、器具购置”中。

⑶其他费用：指在固定资产建造和购置过程中发生的，除建筑安装工程和设备、工具、器具购置以外的各种应摊入固定资产的费用。

基本建设项目按大中小型划分 基本建设划分大中小型项目原则上应按照上级批准的设计任务书或初步设计所确定的总规模或总投资划分，没有正式批准设计任务书或初步设计的，按国家或省、自治区、直辖市年度基本建设投资计划中所列的总规模或总投资划分。上述两条均不具备的，按本年计划施工工程的建设总规模或总投资划分。生产单一产品的工业项目，按产品的设计能力划分；生产多种产品的工业项目，按其主要产品的设计能力划分。品种繁多，难以按生产能力划分的，按全部计划投资额划分。划分标准以国家颁发的《大中小型建设项目划分标准》为依据。国家曾在1953年、1962年、1972年、1977年和1979年先后五次修订《大中小型建设项目划分标准》，因此各历史时期的大中型项目数不完全可比。

施工项目 指报告期内曾进行建筑或安装工程施工活动的建设项目，包括报告期内新开工项目、报告期以前开工跨入报告期继续施工的项目以及报告期施过工并在报告期内全部建成投产或停缓建的项目。

全部建成投产项目 工业项目是指设计文件规定形成生产能力的主体工程及其相应配套的辅助设施全部建成，经负荷试运转，证明具备生产设计规定合格产品的条件，并经过验收鉴定合格或达到竣工验收标准，与生产性工程配套的生活福利设施可以满足近期正常生产的需要，正式移交生产的建设项目。非工业项目是指设计文件规定的主体工程和相应的配套工程全部建成，能够发挥设计规定的全部效益，经验收鉴定合格或达到竣工验收标准，正式移交使用的建设项目。

新增生产能力 指通过固定资产投资活动而增加的设计能力或工程效益，它是用实物形态表示的固定资产投资的成果。新增生产能力的计算，是以能独立发挥生产能力或工程效益的单项工程(或项目)为对象。当单项工程(或项目)建成，经有关部门鉴定合格，正式移交投入生产，即可计算新增生产能力。

新增生产能力或工程效益有以下几种表现形式：

⑴以建设项目或单项工程建成后的年产能力表示，如煤炭开采、石油开采等。

⑵以建设项目或单项工程建成后处理原料的能力表示，如选矿工程的年处理矿石能力、洗煤厂年洗原煤能力等。

⑶以新增的主要设备数量或容量表示，如棉纺锭锭数、发电机组容量等。

⑷以建筑物容积、容量、面积或长度表示，如水库容量、铁路公路里程等。

新增生产能力的数量一般按设计能力计算。设计能力是指设计文件中规定的在正常情况下能够达到的生产能力，而不论投产后的实际产量如何。以设备数量、建筑物容积、面积、长度等表示的新增生产能力或工程效益，则按建成的实际数量计算。

房屋建筑面积　指从房屋外墙线算起的各层平面面积的总和，包括可供使用的有效面积和房屋结构(如柱、墙)占用的面积。多层建筑按各层（包括地下室）面积总和计算 。

住宅建筑面积　指施工和竣工房屋建筑面积中供居住用的施工和竣工房屋建筑面积。

施工面积　指报告期内施工的全部房屋建筑面积。包括本期新开工的面积、上期跨入本期继续施工的房屋面积、上期停缓建在本期恢复施工的房屋面积、本期竣工的房屋面积及本期施工后又停缓建的房屋面积。

竣工面积　指在报告期内房屋建筑按照设计要求已全部完工，达到住人和使用条件，经验收鉴定合格，正式移交使用单位的建筑面积。

房屋建筑面积竣工率　指一定时期内房屋竣工面积占同期房屋施工面积的比率。它是从房屋建筑施工速度的角度反映投资效果和建筑业经济效益的指标。

新增固定资产　指通过投资活动所形成的新的固定资产价值，包括已经建成投入生产或交付使用的工程价值和达到固定资产标准的设备、工具、器具的价值及有关应摊入的费用。它是以价值形式表示的固定资产投资成果的综合性指标，可以综合反映不同时期、不同部门、不同地区的固定资产投资成果。

建设项目投产率　指一定时期内全部建成投入生产项目个数与同期正式施工项目个数的比率。它是从项目建设速度的角度反映投资效果的指标。

固定资产交付使用率　指一定时期新增固定资产与同期完成投资额的比率。它是反映各个时期固定资产动用速度，衡量建设过程中投资效果的一个综合性指标。

Explanatory Notes on Main Statistical Indicators

Total Investment in Fixed Assets in the Whole Country Investment in fixed assets is the essential means for social reproduction of fixed assets. By means of construction and purchase of fixed assets, more advanced technologies and equipment are adopted in the national economy, and new sectors are established, which promote the adjustment of economic structure and the regional distribution of productive forces and enhance the economic strengths so as to provide the material conditions for improving people's livelihood. This is significant for speeding up the drive of socialist modernization in China.

Amount of investment in fixed assets refers to the volume of activities in construction and purchases of fixed assets in monetary terms. It is a comprehensive indicator which shows the size, pace, proportional relations and use orientation of the investment in fixed assets. Total investment in fixed assets in the whole country includes, by registration type of ownership, the investment by the state-owned units, collective units, individuals, joint ownership units, share-holding units, as well as investment by businessmen from foreign countries and from Hong Kong, Macau and Taiwan, and by other units. According to China's current management system, the investment in fixed assets in the whole country is classified into the following four parts: investment in capital construction, investment in innovation, investment in real estates development and other investment in fixed assets.

Investment in Capital Construction Capital construction refers to the new construction projects or extension projects and the related work of the enterprises, institutions or administrative units mainly for the purpose of expanding production capacity or improving project efficiency covering only projects each with a total investment of 500,000 RMB yuan and over. It includes: (1) projects listed in the capital construction plan of the current year of the central government and the local governments at various levels as well as the projects, though not listed in the capital construction plan of the current year, but continued to be constructed in this year, using the investment listed in the plan of capital construction of previous years and carried forward to this year (also using the equipment and materials kept in stock of the capital construction); (2) new construction projects arranged both in the plan of capital construction and the plan of innovation; extension projects with the newly increased production capacity (or project efficiency) up to the standard of a large and medium-sized project; and the projects of moving the whole factory to a new site so as to improve the distribution of productive forces; (3) new construction projects, extension projects or restoration projects with the total investment of 500,000 RMB yuan and over by the state-owned units, though listed neither in the plan of capital construction nor in the plan of innovation; the projects in the state-owned units of moving the whole factory to a new site so as to improve the distribution of productive forces; and the projects of building additional business houses by the administrative units and institutions and building welfare facilities by the administrative units.

Investment in Innovation Innovation refers to the renewal of fixed assets and technological innovation of the original facilities by the enterprises and institutions as well as the corresponding supplementary projects and the related work (excluding major overhaul and maintenance projects) covering only projects each with a total investment of 500,000 RMB yuan and over. It includes: (1) projects listed in the innovation plan of the current year of the central government and the local governments at various levels as well as the projects, though not listed in the innovation plan of the current year, but continued to be constructed in this year, using the investment listed in the plan of innovation of previous years and carried forward to this year; (2) projects of technological innovation or renewal of the original facilities, arranged both in the plan of innovation and in the plan of capital construction; extension projects (main workshops or a branch of the factory) with the newly increased production capacity (or project efficiency) not up to the standard of a large and medium-sized project; and the projects of moving the whole factory to a new site so as to meet the requirements of urban environmental protection or safe production; (3) projects of reconstruction or technological innovation with the total investment of 500,000 RMB yuan and over by the state-owned units, though listed neither in the plan of capital construction nor in the plan of innovation; the projects in the state-owned units of moving the whole factory to a new site so as to meet the requirements of urban environmental protection or safe production.

Investment in Real Estate Development It includes the investment by the real estate development companies, commercial buildings construction companies and other real estate development units of various types of ownership in the construction of house buildings, such as residential buildings, factory buildings, warehouses, hotels, guesthouses, holiday villages, office buildings, and the complementary service facilities and land development projects, such as roads, water supply, water drainage, power supply, heating, telecommunications, land leveling and other projects of infrastructure. It excludes the activities in simple land transactions.

Other Investment in Fixed Assets refers to the construction and purchases of fixed assets not listed in the investment in capital construction, investment in innovation and investment in real estate development. It includes:

A) The following projects of the state-owned units with the total planned (or actually needed) investment of 500,000 yuan and over, which are not included in the plan of capital construction and the plan of innovation: (1) projects of oil fields maintenance and exploitation with the oil fields maintenance funds and petroleum development funds; (2) opening and extending projects with the maintenance funds in coal, ore and other mining enterprises and logging enterprises; (3) project of reconstruction of the original highways and bridges with the highway maintenance funds in the department of communication; (4) projects of construction of warehouses with the funds of simple construction in the commercial department.

B) The investment in fixed assets by urban collective units: refer to projects of construction and purchases of fixed assets with the planned total investment of 500,000 yuan and over by all collective units in cities and county towns and in townships which are approved by the State Council or provincial governments, excluding investment by collective units under township enterprise administration offices.

C) The projects of construction and purchases of fixed assets by the enterprises, institutions or individuals other than those mentioned above with total investment of 500,000 yuan and over, which are not included in the plan of capital construction and the plan of innovation.

Private Investment in House Construction in Urban Areas, Industrial and Mining Areas and Individual Investment in Rural Areas The private house construction in the urban areas and industrial and mining areas includes all the private house construction under the jurisdiction of cities, counties, towns and industrial and mining areas, no matter whether the owner of the house is registered as the permanent resident in the locality or not. The individual investment in the rural areas includes the investment in house construction and purchase of productive fixed assets by the individuals in the rural areas.

Sources of Funds for Investment in Fixed Assets state budgetary appropriation, domestic loans, foreign investment, self-raised funds, and others.

(1)State budgetary appropriation refers to appropriation in the budget of the central and local governments earmarked for capital construction and for innovation projects, and the special appropriation from the budget of the central government for capital construction and for the transfer fund to banks to be issued as loans for capital construction projects.

(2)Domestic loans refer to various funds borrowed by enterprises and institutions from banks and non-bank financial institutions during the reference period for the purpose of investment in fixed assets, including loans issued by banks from their self-owned funds and deposit, loans appropriated by higher responsible authorities, special loans by government (including loan for replacing petroleum with coal, special loan for reform-through-labour coal mines), loans arranged by local government from special funds, domestic reserve loan, and working loan, etc..

(3) Foreign Investment refers to foreign funds received during the reference period for the purpose of investment in fixed assets, including foreign funds borrowed and managed by the government, by individual units, foreign fund in joint venture program, and issue of bonds and stocks at the international financial markets. The foreign funds borrowed and managed by the government refer to foreign loans borrowed by the government from foreign governments, organizations, or financial institutions under official agreements signed by both parties, under which government is responsible for the repayment of both the principal and interests of the foreign loans.

(4)Self-raised funds refer to funds received by construction enterprises from their higher responsible authorities, local governments, or raised by enterprises or institutions themselves for the purpose of investment in fixed assets during the reference period.

(5) Others refer to funds received during the reference period which are not included in the above-mentioned sources.

Investment in Fixed Assets by Sector The classification of construction projects by sector is determined by the major products or the purpose of the projects when they are put into production or use, and by the nature of their social economic activities. The investment in capital construction is classified by construction projects, while investment in innovation, other investment by state-owned units and urban collective units are classified according to the sector which the whole enterprise or institution belongs to. In general, one project or one enterprise or institution can only belong to one sector. In order to reflect more accurately the proportions among various sectors, the branch factories of integrated complex are classified into different sectors according to their economic activities.

Investment in Fixed Assets by Type of Construction The construction projects in general can be classified by the type of construction into new construction, expansion, reconstruction and moving away. In capital construction, the type of construction is determined by the condition of the project. In investment in innovation, in other investment by state-owned units and investment by collective-owned units, the type of construction is determined by the condition of the whole enterprise or institutions. Investment by type of construction is not applied to investment by real-estate development units, investment in rural areas and investment in housing by urban individuals.

(1)New construction in general refers to newly constructed

units. In the case in which the value of the original fixed assets is quite small, and the value of newly added fixed assets exceeds the original ones by three times, the expansion construction is considered as new construction.

(2)Expansion refers to construction of new major production workshop or independent production line within a factory or in other locations, or construction of a branch factory so as to increase the production capacity of the original products. Newly constructed business houses in institutions and administrative organizations (such as the newly constructed teaching buildings in schools, clinics or bed building in hospitals, and office buildings in administrative agencies, etc.) are also classified as expansion.

(3) Reconstruction refers to technical innovation and transformation of the existing equipment and technical conditions undertaken by enterprises and institutions for the purposes of technological advancement, improvement in product quality, enlarging variety of products, promoting new generation of products, reducing production consumption and cost, promoting comprehensive utilization of resources, strengthening treatment of waste gas, waste water and solid wastes, and safety in production, etc. through application of new technologies and techniques, use of new equipment and new materials (including accessory facilities for production or for living and welfare purposes). Construction of new workshops for improving existing production capacity rather than increasing production capacity is also considered as reconstruction.

Investment in Fixed Assets by Structure refers to the three major parts of investment activities, i.e. construction and installation, purchase of equipment and instrument, and other expenses.

(1) Construction and installation (work volume of construction and installation) refers to the construction of various houses and buildings and installation of various kinds of equipment and instruments, including construction of various houses, equipment foundations and industrial kilns and stoves, preparation works for project construction, and clearing up works post project construction, pavement of railways and roads, drilling of mines and putting up of oil pipes, construction of projects of water conservancy, construction of underground air-raid shelters and construction of other special projects, installation of various machinery equipment, testing operation for pre-testing the quality of installation projects. The value of equipment installed is not included in the value of installation projects.

(2)Purchase of equipment and instruments refers to the total value of equipment, tools, and vessels purchased or self-produced which come up to standards for fixed assets. Equipment, tools and vessels purchased or self-produced for new workshops by newly established or expanded units are categorized as "purchase of equipment and instruments" no matter whether they come up to the standards for fixed assets or not.

(3)Other expenses refer to expenses occurring during the construction or purchase of fixed assets other than construction, installation or purchase of equipment and instruments.

Capital Construction Projects by Size The classification of size of capital construction projects should be determined according to the total scale or total investment set in the approved construction plan by higher responsible authorities or in the tentative design, otherwise according to the total scale or total investment set in the current capital construction plan of the state, provinces, autonomous regions, and municipalities directly under central government. Industrial projects which produce unitary products are classified according to its design capacity of products; projects which produce multi-products are classified by the design capacity of the major product or by the total planned investment. Standards for the Classification of Construction Projects into large, medium-sized and small ones issued by the government are the base for size division of construction projects, which was revised five times in 1958, 1962, 1972,1977, and 1979 respectively and therefore, data on projects by size are not entirely comparable from year to year.

Projects under Construction refer to projects having construction and installation activities undertaken in the reference period, including projects started in the reference period, or continued from the previous period, or completed and put into production or suspended in the reference period.

Projects Completed and Put into Use Industrial projects refer to the major projects and accessory facilities completed which result in forming production capacity and have been checked and accepted while the living and welfare facilities have been completed and can ensure normal production and formally put into production. Non-industrial projects refer to the major projects and accessory facilities completed which possess the designed capacity and have been checked, accepted and formally put into production.

Newly Increased Production Capacity refers to the increase of designed capacity and project efficiency through investment in fixed assets, which reflects the accomplishment of investment in fixed assets in kind. The calculation of newly increased production capacity is based on individual project which operates independently and efficiently. When an individual project is completed and checked and accepted and put into production, it is counted as newly increased production capacity.

The newly increased production capacity and project efficiency are usually expressed in one of the following forms:

(1)annual production capacity, such as extraction of coal and petroleum;

(2)raw material processing capacity, such as ore dressing

capacity of ore dressing projects, the dressing capacity of a coal washery;

(3)number or capacity of major equipment increased, such as the number of cotton spindles increased and the capacity of generating sets increased;

(4)physical measures of construction, such as volume, capacity, area, and length, for instance, the capacity of reservoirs, the length of railways or highways.

Newly increased production capacity in terms of quantity is calculated in designed capacity in general, which refers to the production capacity of a project under normal conditions designed in construction documents regardless of the actual output.

Floor Space of Buildings under Construction and Completed refers to total floor space in each story of buildings calculated from the outside line of building walls, including both usable space and the space occupied by constructions like pillars or walls. The floor space of multi-story buildings includes the total floor space of each story (including basement).

Floor Space of Residential Buildings refers to the floor space of the residential buildings under construction and completed among the total space of buildings under construction and completed.

Floor Space under Construction refers to total floor space of all buildings under construction during the reference period, including floor space of newly started buildings during the reference period, floor space of construction extended from the previous period to the current period, floor space of construction suspended during the previous period and resumed in the current period, floor space of construction completed in the current period, and floor space of construction started and then suspended in the current period.

Floor Space of Buildings Completed refers to the floor space of buildings completed in the reference period, which have come up to the designed standards and have been put into use.

Completion Rate of Floor Space of Buildings refers to the ratio of the floor space of buildings completed in certain period of time to the floor space of buildings under construction in the same period, which reflects the investment result and economic efficiency of the construction industry from the angle of the speed of project construction.

Newly Increased Fixed Assets refer to the newly increased value of fixed assets through investment, including the value of projects completed and put into production, the value of equipment, tools, and vessels considered as fixed assets, as well as the relevant expenses as investment in fixed assets. This is a comprehensive indicator of investment in fixed assets, reflecting the achievements of investment in fixed assets in different periods, different sectors, and different regions.

Rate of Construction Projects Completed and Put into Use refers to the ratio of the number of construction projects completed and put into use in certain period of time to the number of projects under construction in the same period. This reflects the investment efficiency from the angle of the speed of projects construction.

Rate of Projects of Fixed Assets Completed and Put into Operation refers to the ratio of the newly increased fixed assets to the total investment made in the same period. This is a comprehensive indicator, reflecting the speed of the employment of fixed assets and the investment efficiency.

七、能源生产和消费

Production and Consumption of Energy

简要说明

一、本篇包括的主要内容有：能源生产、消费及品种构成，能源生产和消费弹性系数，综合能源平衡表和主要能源品种的单项平衡表，分行业分主要能源品种的消费量，能源加工转换效率及生活用能源消费量等。

二、本篇全国能源平衡表的资料是国家统计局工业交通司根据有关资料和调查结果编制的。

三、关于数据口径与计算的说明

1.一次能源生产量与工业统计数字一致。

2.能源生产与消费弹性系数分别以能源生产、消费增长速度与国内生产总值增长速度相比求得。

3.能源平衡表中，进口量和出口量采用海关统计数据。进口量中包括我国轮船、飞机在国外加油量，出口量中包括外国轮船、飞机在我国加油量。电力折算标准煤系数按平均发电煤耗计算。

4.能源加工转换效率表中，电力折算标准煤系数采用当量值计算，每千瓦小时折0.1229千克标准煤。

Brief Introduction

I. The data in this chapter cover mainly the energy production and consumption and their composition, the elasticity ratio of energy production and consumption, the overall balance of energy and the balance by the variety of energy, the consumption of energy by sector and by main variety, efficiency of energy conversion and the consumption of energy for residential use.

II. The national energy balance in this chapter is compiled by the Department of Industry and Transport Statistics, NBS on the basis of data from surveys and from input-output tables.

III. Coverage and calculation of data:

(1) The data on the production of primary energy are the same as the concerned data of the industrial statistics.

(2) The elasticity ratio of energy production is calculated as the quotient of the growth rate of energy production divided by the growth rate of GDP; and the elasticity ratio of energy consumption is calculated as the quotient of the growth rate of energy consumption divided by the growth rate of GDP.

(3) In the energy balance, the data on the imports and exports are data from the customs statistics. The refueling by Chinese ships and airplanes abroad is included in the imports. The refueling by foreign ships and airplanes in China is included in the exports. The coefficient for conversion of electric power into the standard coal equivalent is calculated according to the average consumption of coal for generating electricity.

(4) In the table on the efficiency of energy conversion, the coefficient for conversion of electric power into the standard coal equivalent is calculated on the basis of heat value equivalent. One kwh is equal to 0.1229 kg SCE.

7-1 能源生产总量及构成

Total Production of Energy and Its Composition

年 份 Year	能源生产总量 (万吨标准煤) Total Energy Production (10 000 tons of SCE)	占能源生产总量的比重(%) As Percentage of Total Energy Production			
		原 煤 Coal	原 油 Crude Oil	天然气 Natural Gas	水 电 Hydro-power
1978	62770	70.3	23.7	2.9	3.1
1979	64562	70.2	23.5	3.0	3.3
1980	63735	69.4	23.8	3.0	3.8
1981	63227	70.2	22.9	2.7	4.2
1982	66778	71.3	21.8	2.4	4.5
1983	71270	71.6	21.3	2.3	4.8
1984	77855	72.4	21.0	2.1	4.5
1985	85546	72.8	20.9	2.0	4.3
1986	88124	72.4	21.2	2.1	4.3
1987	91266	72.6	21.0	2.0	4.4
1988	95801	73.1	20.4	2.0	4.5
1989	101639	74.1	19.3	2.0	4.6
1990	103922	74.2	19.0	2.0	4.8
1991	104844	74.1	19.2	2.0	4.7
1992	107256	74.3	18.9	2.0	4.8
1993	111059	74.0	18.7	2.0	5.3
1994	118729	74.6	17.6	1.9	5.9
1995	129034	75.3	16.6	1.9	6.2
1996	132616	75.2	17.0	2.0	5.8
1997	132410	74.1	17.3	2.1	6.5
1998	124250	71.9	18.5	2.5	7.1
1999	109126	68.3	21.0	3.1	7.6
2000	109000	67.2	21.4	3.4	8.0

注：电力折算标准煤的系数根据当年平均发电煤耗计算，下表同。

a)The coefficient for conversion of electric power into SCE (standard coal equivalent) is calculated on the basic of the data on the average coal consumption in generating electric power in the same year. The same as in the following tables.

7-2 能源消费总量及构成

Total Consumption of Energy and Its Composition

年 份 Year	能源消费总量 (万吨标准煤) Total Energy Consumption (10 000 tons of SCE)	占能源消费总量的比重(%) As Percentage of Total Energy Consumption			
		煤 炭 Coal	石 油 Crude Oil	天然气 Natural Gas	水 电 Hydro-power
1978	57144	70.7	22.7	3.2	3.4
1979	58588	71.3	21.8	3.3	3.6
1980	60275	72.2	20.7	3.1	4.0
1981	59447	72.7	20.0	2.8	4.5
1982	62067	73.7	18.9	2.5	4.9
1983	66040	74.2	18.1	2.4	5.3
1984	70904	75.3	17.4	2.4	4.9
1985	76682	75.8	17.1	2.2	4.9
1986	80850	75.8	17.2	2.3	4.7
1987	86632	76.2	17.0	2.1	4.7
1988	92997	76.2	17.0	2.1	4.7
1989	96934	76.0	17.1	2.0	4.9
1990	98703	76.2	16.6	2.1	5.1
1991	103783	76.1	17.1	2.0	4.8
1992	109170	75.7	17.5	1.9	4.9
1993	115993	74.7	18.2	1.9	5.2
1994	122737	75.0	17.4	1.9	5.7
1995	131176	74.6	17.5	1.8	6.1
1996	138948	74.7	18.0	1.8	5.5
1997	137798	71.5	20.4	1.7	6.2
1998	132214	69.6	21.5	2.2	6.7
1999	130119	68.0	23.2	2.2	6.6
2000	128000	67.0	23.6	2.5	6.9

注:2000年能源消费量为估算数。

a)Data on energy consumption in 2000 were estimated figures.

7-3 综合能源平衡表

Overall Energy Balance Sheet

单位：万吨标准煤 (10 000 tons of SCE)

项　　目	Item	1985	1990	1995	1998	1999
可供消费的能源总量	**Total Energy Available for Consumption**	**77603**	**96138**	**129535**	**128368**	**115829**
一次能源生产量	Primary Energy Output	85546	103922	129034	124250	109126
回收能	Recovery of Energy			2312	1920	1694
进口量	Imports	340	1310	5456	8474	9513
出口量(–)	Exports (-)	5774	5875	6776	7153	6477
年初年末库存差额	Stock Changes in the Year	-2509	-3219	-491	878	1974
能源消费总量	**Total Energy Consumption**	**76682**	**98703**	**131176**	**132214**	**130119**
在总量中：	Consumption by Sector					
1.农、林、牧、渔、水利业	1.Farming,Forestry,Animal Husbandry, Fishery and Water Conservancy	4045	4852	5505	5790	5832
2.工　业	2.Industry	51068	67578	96191	94409	90797
3.建筑业	3.Construction	1302	1213	1335	1612	1381
4.交通运输、仓储及邮电通讯业	4.Transport, Storage, Post and Telecommunication Services	3713	4541	5863	8245	9243
5.批发和零售贸易餐饮业	5.Wholesale and Retail Trade and Catering Services	766	1247	2018	2552	2812
6.其他	6.Others	2470	3473	4519	5213	5502
7.生活消费	7.Residential Consumption	13318	15799	15745	14393	14552
在总量中：	Consumption by Usage					
(一) 终端消费	(I)Final Consumption	73586	94289	124252	126039	124096
#工业	Industry	48021	63239	89473	88522	85095
(二) 加工转换损失量	(II)Losses in Processing and Transformation	1491	2264	3634	2629	2336
#炼焦	Coking	572	905		684	544
炼油	Petroleum Refining	110	326		616	648
(三) 损失量	(III)Other Losses	1605	2150	3289	3546	3688
平衡差额	**Balance**	**921**	**-2565**	**-1641**	**-3846**	**-14290**

注：1.村办工业包括在工业中(下同)。

2.电力、热力按等价热值折算，因此加工转换损失量中不包括发电、供热损失量。

3.进口量包括我国飞机、轮船在国外加油量；出口量包括外国飞机、轮船在我国加油量。

a)Data on industry include the data of village-run industry. (The sane as in the following tables).

b)Electric power and heat are converted on the basic of equal caloric value. Therefore, losses in processing and transformation exclude losses in power generation and heating.

c)Data on imports include the petroleum consumed by the Chinese airplanes and ships in refueling abroad. Data on exports include the petroleum consumed by the foreign airplanes and ships in refueling in China.

7-4 石油平衡表

Petroleum Balance Sheet

单位：万吨 (10 000 tons)

项　　目	Item	1985	1990	1995	1998	1999
可供量	**Total Energy Available for Consumption**	**9193.7**	**11435.0**	**16072.7**	**19686.1**	**20964.4**
生产量	Output	12489.5	13830.6	15005.0	16100.0	16000.0
进口量	Imports	90.0	755.6	3673.2	5738.7	6483.3
出口量(-)	Exports (-)	3630.4	3110.4	2454.5	2326.5	1643.5
年初年末库存差额	Stock Changes in the Year	244.6	-40.8	-151.0	174.0	124.6
消费量	**Total Energy Consumption**	**9168.8**	**11485.6**	**16064.9**	**19817.8**	**21072.9**
在消费量中：	Consumption by Sector					
1.农、林、牧、渔、水利业	1.Farming,Forestry,Animal Husbandry, Fishery and Water Conservancy	758.7	1033.6	1203.2	1294.7	1422.1
2.工　业	2.Industry	6171.4	7321.6	9349.3	10870.8	10852.8
3.建筑业	3.Construction	292.2	327.3	242.8	293.9	323.0
4.交通运输、仓储及邮电通讯业	4.Transport, Storage, Post and Telecommunication Services	1176.4	1683.2	2863.6	4245.3	5004.3
5.批发和零售贸易餐饮业	5.Wholesale and Retail Trade and Catering Services	38.1	77.6	333.9	426.0	537.2
6.其他	6.Others	506.1	757.8	1390.3	1704.8	1800.3
7.生活消费	7.Residential Consumption	225.9	284.5	682.0	983.3	1133.1
在消费量中：	Consumption by Usage					
(一) 终端消费	(I)Final Consumption	7063.3	9304.7	13676.3	17514.3	18664.7
#工　业	Industry	4462.0	5180.4	7095.5	8717.3	8596.4
(二) 中间消费	(II)Intermediate Consumption					
(用于加工转换)	(Consumed in Transformation)	1745.6	1630.4	2230.0	2106.1	2222.2
发　电	Power Generation	1425.5	1234.4	1358.5	1304.8	1228.6
供　热	Heating	285.6	356.3	399.9	455.5	394.6
炼　焦	Coking	34.5	39.7	51.6	35.4	32.5
制　气	Gas Production	112.9	295.8	420.1	310.4	566.6
(三) 洗选损耗	(III) Losses in Coal Washing and Dressing	247.0	254.7	158.6	197.3	186.0
平衡差额	**Balance**	**24.9**	**-50.6**	**7.8**	**-131.5**	**-108.5**

注：1.生产量为原油产量。

2.进口量包括我国飞机、轮船在国外加油量；出口量包括外国飞机、轮船在我国加油量。

a)Data on output refer to the output of crude oil.

b)Data on imports include the petroleum consumed by the Chinese airplanes and ships in refueling abroad. Data on exports include the petroleum consumed by the foreign airplanes and ships in refueling in China.

7-5 煤炭平衡表

Coal Balance Sheet

单位：万吨 (10 000 tons)

项　目	Item	1985	1990	1995	1998	1999
可供量	**Total Energy Available for Consumption**	**82776.6**	**102221.0**	**133461.7**	**122810.6**	**103576.1**
生产量	Output	87228.4	107988.3	136073.1	125000.0	104500.0
进口量	Imports	230.7	200.3	163.5	158.6	167.3
出口量(-)	Exports (-)	777.0	1729.0	2861.7	3229.7	3743.9
年初年末库存差额	Stock Changes in the Year	-3905.5	-4238.5	86.8	881.7	2652.7
消费量	**Total Energy Consumption**	**81603.0**	**105523.0**	**137676.5**	**129492.2**	**126365.3**
在消费量中：	Consumption by Sector					
1.农、林、牧、渔、水利业	1.Farming,Forestry,Animal Husbandry, Fishery and Water Conservancy	2208.6	2095.2	1856.7	1923.3	1735.6
2.工　业	2.Industry	58613.3	81090.9	117570.7	114952.4	112757.3
3.建筑业	3.Construction	531.9	437.6	439.8	611.6	522.5
4.交通运输、仓储及邮电通讯业	4.Transport, Storage, Post and Telecommunication Services	2307.1	2160.9	1315.1	1390.6	1294.3
5.批发和零售贸易餐饮业	5.Wholesale and Retail Trade and Catering Services	738.2	1058.3	977.4	947.6	896.2
6.其他	6.Others	1579.5	1980.4	1986.7	782.7	751.1
7.生活消费	7.Residential Consumption	15624.4	16699.7	13530.1	8884.0	8408.4
在消费量中：	Consumption by Usage					
(一) 终端消费	(I)Final Consumption	52704.4	60205.9	66156.1	56347.1	51572.2
#工　业	Industry	29715.0	35773.8	46050.3	41807.3	37964.2
(二) 中间消费	(II)Intermediate Consumption					
(用于加工转换)	(Consumed in Transformation)	25397.4	41257.8	69487.6	73145.1	74793.1
发　电	Power Generation	16440.7	27204.3	44440.2	49489.3	51163.5
供　热	Heating	1462.3	2995.5	5887.3	6319.9	6473.0
炼　焦	Coking	7303.8	10697.6	18396.4	15628.1	14941.7
制　气	Gas Production	190.6	360.4	763.7	685.1	847.6
(三) 洗选损耗	(III) Losses in Coal Washing and Dressing	3501.2	4059.3	2032.8	1159.3	1491.5
平衡差额	**Balance**	**1173.6**	**-3302.0**	**-4214.8**	**-6681.6**	**-22789.2**

注：生产量为原煤产量。

a)Data on output refer to the output of raw coal.

7-6 电力平衡表

Electricity Balance Sheet

单位：亿千瓦小时 (100 million kwh)

项　目	Item	1985	1990	1995	1998	1999
可供量	**Total Energy Available for Consumption**	**4117.6**	**6230.4**	**10023.4**	**11590.4**	**12305.2**
生产量	Output	4106.9	6212.0	10077.3	11662.0	12393.0
水　电	Hydropower	923.7	1267.2	1905.8	2080.0	2038.1
火　电	Thermal Power	3183.2	4944.8	8043.2	9441.0	10205.4
核　电	Nuclear Power			128.3	141.0	149.5
进口量	Imports	11.1	19.3	6.4	0.2	3.7
出口量(-)	Exports (-)	0.4	0.9	60.3	71.7	91.5
消费量	**Total Energy Consumption**	**4117.6**	**6230.4**	**10023.4**	**11598.4**	**12305.2**
在消费量中：	Consumption by Sector					
1.农、林、牧、渔、水利业	1.Farming,Forestry,Animal Husbandry, Fishery and Water Conservancy	317.4	426.8	582.4	623.5	660.4
2.工　业	2.Industry	3283.4	4873.3	7659.8	8406.0	8832.7
3.建筑业	3.Construction	71.2	65.0	159.6	188.8	142.3
4.交通运输、仓储及邮电通讯业	4.Transport, Storage, Post and Telecommunication Services	63.4	105.9	182.3	255.6	254.8
5.批发和零售贸易餐饮业	5.Wholesale and Retail Trade and Catering Services	38.0	76.2	199.5	293.4	342.8
6.其他	6.Others	121.7	202.4	234.2	506.7	591.4
7.生活消费	7.Residential Consumption	222.5	480.8	1005.6	1324.5	1480.8
在消费量中：	Consumption by Usage					
(一) 终端消费	(I)Final Consumption	3813.3	5795.8	9278.9	10807.5	11443.3
#工　业	Industry	2979.1	4438.7	6915.3	7615.0	7970.8
(二) 输配电损失量	(II)Losses in Transmission	304.3	434.6	744.5	790.9	861.9

7-7 能源生产弹性系数

Elasticity Ratio of Energy Production

年 份 Year	能源生产比上年增长% Growth Rate of Energy Production over Preceding Year (%)	电力生产比上年增长% Growth Rate of Electricity Production over Preceding Year (%)	国内生产总值比上年增长% Growth Rate of Gross Domestic Product(GDP) over Preceding Year (%)	能源生产弹性系数 Elasticity Ratio of Energy Production	电力生产弹性系数 Elasticity Ratio of Electricity Production
1984	9.2	7.3	15.2	0.61	0.48
1985	9.9	8.9	13.5	0.73	0.66
1986	3.0	9.5	8.8	0.34	1.08
1987	3.6	10.6	11.6	0.31	0.91
1988	5.0	9.6	11.3	0.44	0.85
1989	6.1	7.3	4.1	1.49	1.78
1990	2.2	6.2	3.8	0.58	1.63
1991	0.9	9.1	9.2	0.10	1.00
1992	2.3	11.3	14.2	0.16	0.80
1993	3.6	15.3	13.5	0.31	1.13
1994	6.9	10.7	12.6	0.55	0.85
1995	8.7	8.6	10.5	0.83	0.82
1996	2.8	7.2	9.6	0.29	0.75
1997	-0.2	5.0	8.8	-	0.57
1998	-6.2	2.9	7.8	-	0.37
1999	-12.2	6.3	7.1	-	0.89
2000	-0.1	9.4	8.0	-	1.18

注：国内生产总值增长速度按可比价格计算，下表同。

a)The growth rates of GDP are calculated at comparable prices. The same as in the following tables.

7-8 能源消费弹性系数

Elasticity Ratio of Energy Consumption

年 份 Year	能源消费比上年增长% Growth Rate of Energy Consumption over Preceding Year (%)	电力消费比上年增长% Growth Rate of Electricity Consumption over Preceding Year (%)	国内生产总值比上年增长% Growth Rate of Gross Domestic Product(GDP),over Preceding Year (%)	能源消费弹性系数 Elasticity Ratio of Energy Consumption	电力消费弹性系数 Elasticity Ratio of Electricity Consumption
1984	7.4	7.4	15.2	0.49	0.49
1985	8.1	9.0	13.5	0.60	0.67
1986	5.4	9.5	8.8	0.61	1.08
1987	7.2	10.6	11.6	0.62	0.91
1988	7.3	9.7	11.3	0.65	0.86
1989	4.2	7.3	4.1	1.02	1.78
1990	1.8	6.2	3.8	0.47	1.63
1991	5.1	9.2	9.2	0.55	1.00
1992	5.2	11.5	14.2	0.37	0.81
1993	6.3	11.0	13.5	0.21	0.70
1994	5.8	9.9	12.6	0.46	0.79
1995	6.9	8.2	10.5	0.66	0.78
1996	5.9	7.4	9.6	0.62	0.77
1997	-0.8	4.8	8.8	-	0.55
1998	-4.1	2.8	7.8	-	0.36
1999	-1.6	6.1	7.1	-	0.86
2000	-1.6	9.4	8.0	-	1.17

注:2000年为估算数。

a)The data in 2000 were estimated figures.

7-9 分行业能源消费总量和主要能源品种消费量（1999年）

行业	Sector	能源消费总量（万吨标准煤）Total Energy Consumption (10000 tons of SCE)	煤炭消费量（万吨）Coal Consumption (10000 tons)
消费总量	**Total Consumption**	**130119.09**	**126365.35**
农、林、牧、渔业	**Farming,Forestry,Animal Husbandry,Fishery and Water Conservancy**	**5831.75**	**1735.61**
工业	**Industry**	**90797.48**	**112757.32**
采掘业	**Mining and Quarrying**	**9287.51**	**8641.15**
煤炭采选业	Coal Mining and Dressing	4324.25	7084.91
石油和天然气开采业	Petroleum and Natural Gas Extraction	3535.11	783.78
黑色金属矿采选业	Ferrous Metals Mining and Dressing	327.74	73.00
有色金属矿采选业	Nonferrous Metals Mining and Dressing	358.53	98.13
非金属矿采选业	Nonmetal Minerals Mining and Dressing	543.12	447.45
其他矿采选业	Other Minerals Mining and Dressing	30.73	7.76
木材及竹材采运业	Logging and Transport of Wood and Bamboo	168.03	146.12
制造业	**Manufacturing**	**70720.09**	**50926.85**
食品加工业	Food Processing	1611.22	1609.15
食品制造业	Food Production	982.81	733.16
饮料制造业	Beverage Production	695.5	699.48
烟草加工业	Tobacco Processing	297.24	175.90
纺织业	Textile Industry	2502.79	1446.14
服装及其他纤维制品制造	Garments and Other Fiber Products	311.73	143.27
皮革毛皮羽绒及其制品业	Leather, Furs, Down and Related Products	187.96	85.76
木材加工及竹藤棕草制品业	Timber Processing,Bamboo,Cane,Palm Fiber & Straw Products	306.17	236.01
家具制造业	Furniture Manufacturing	91.57	51.82
造纸及纸制品业	Papermaking and Paper Products	1741.12	1628.48
印刷业记录媒介的复制	Printing and Record Medium Reproduction	175.74	54.10
文教体育用品制造业	Cultural, Educational and Sports Articles	103.72	20.14
石油加工及炼焦业	Petroleum Processing and Coking	7085.07	7730.35
化学原料及制品制造业	Raw Chemical Materials and Chemical Products	12884.61	8004.76
医药制造业	Medical and Pharmaceutical Products	796.81	572.84
化学纤维制造业	Chemical Fiber	1538.2	799.30
橡胶制品业	Rubber Products	586.36	342.48
塑料制品业	Plastic Products	564.62	177.05
非金属矿物制品业	Nonmetal Mineral Products	10962.31	11005.85
黑色金属冶炼及压延加工业	Smelting and Pressing of Ferrous Metals	16960.67	11432.85
有色金属冶炼及压延加工业	Smelting and Pressing of Nonferrous Metals	3540.27	1360.42
金属制品业	Metal Products	1036.67	300.48
普通机械制造业	Ordinary Machinery	1156.09	477.69
专用设备制造业	Equipment for Special Purposes	788.32	397.28
交通运输设备制造业	Transportation Equipment	1299.2	770.71
电气机械及器材制造业	Electric Equipment and Machinery	573.4	241.47
电子及通信设备制造业	Electronic and Telecommunications Equipment	590.99	82.38
仪器仪表文化办公用机械	Instruments,Meters,Cultural and Office Machinery	140.08	42.38
其他制造业	Other Manufacturing Industry	1208.85	305.15
电力煤气及水生产供应业	**Electric Power,Gas and Water Production and Supply**	**10789.88**	**53189.32**
电力蒸汽热水生产供应业	Production and Supply of Electric Power, Steam and Hot Water	9536.65	51966.90
煤气的生产和供应业	Production and Supply of Gas	671.95	1170.82
自来水的生产和供应业	Production and Supply of Tap Water	581.28	51.60
建筑业	**Construction**	**1381.44**	**522.46**
交通运输、仓储及邮电通信业	**Transportation, Storage, Postal & Telecommunications Services**	**9242.62**	**1294.26**
批发和零售贸易餐饮业	**Wholesale, Retail Trade and Catering Services**	**2811.77**	**896.20**
其他行业	**Others**	**5501.85**	**751.08**
生活消费	**Residential Consumption**	**14552.18**	**8408.42**

注：1.工业能源消费量中包括村办工业。

2.工业分行业数字中不包括其他石油制品和其他焦化产品，但工业合计中包括。

Consumption of Total Energy and Its Main Varieties by Sector (1999)

焦炭消费量 (万吨) Coke Consumption (10 000 tons)	原油消费量 (万吨) Crude Oil Consumption (10 000 tons)	汽油消费量 (万吨) Gasoline Consumption (10 000 tons)	煤油消费量 (万吨) Kerosene Consumption (10 000tons)	柴油消费量 (万吨) Diesel Oil Consumption (10 000tons)	燃料油消费量 (万吨) Fuel Oil Consumption (10 000 tons)	天然气消费量 (亿立方米) Natural Gas Consumption (100 million cu.m)	电力消费量 (亿千瓦小时) Electricity Consumption (100 million kwh)
10456.94	**18949.38**	**3380.73**	**824.21**	**6231.63**	**3934.11**	**214.94**	**12305.23**
145.81		**178.14**	**1.43**	**1241.84**	**0.35**		**660.35**
10091.31	**18775.16**	**646.50**	**78.35**	**1506.84**	**3047.68**	**180.17**	**8832.74**
131.11	**2822.98**	**117.63**	**6.97**	**247.23**	**213.68**	**62.29**	**912.67**
45.64	1.88	36.88	5.01	45.41	5.51	0.11	395.24
5.24	2821.10	43.14	0.41	143.80	206.77	62.14	299.86
38.10		6.90	0.04	10.76			58.86
19.11		5.08	1.19	11.34	0.21		68.94
22.72		8.46	0.31	25.43	1.19	0.04	69.48
0.15		0.27		1.16			6.20
0.15		16.90	0.01	9.33			14.11
9893.09	**15877.31**	**498.94**	**70.98**	**1004.00**	**1926.89**	**110.28**	**5875.12**
14.41	0.38	33.59	0.26	31.33	8.36	0.14	150.90
15.95	0.44	13.06	0.08	16.33	8.58	0.06	96.31
3.24	0.48	11.82	0.09	9.66	7.63	0.02	55.42
1.15		34.34	0.09	3.91	2.78	0.07	29.72
3.83	0.04	40.76	3.52	42.93	79.47	0.93	305.94
1.56	0.12	8.75	0.38	13.46	11.93		43.68
1.58		4.63	0.17	19.76	4.18		24.07
1.37		2.95	0.10	5.97	2.72		27.90
1.05		3.29	0.04	2.69	0.67		10.86
1.48	0.53	11.08	3.39	19.98	18.90	0.26	192.88
0.27		6.43	5.34	6.69	2.86	0.07	26.89
1.57	0.09	2.55	1.21	13.32	1.03		17.28
60.99	13670.78	14.29	16.79	61.52	509.57	11.56	207.46
1001.89	1613.17	44.89	8.12	101.73	380.62	83.91	1058.15
0.67		10.34	0.13	6.19	5.81	0.57	76.88
25.14	531.85	3.73	0.41	9.10	89.91	0.04	158.75
2.48	0.04	9.14	0.06	6.63	11.15		76.76
6.26	0.33	12.78	0.43	38.38	9.86	0.09	93.90
286.92	47.84	48.65	2.24	271.60	312.28	2.21	660.71
7763.80	9.10	29.21	5.03	62.93	326.05	1.14	1004.72
212.12	0.67	11.51	0.57	38.29	54.72	0.45	608.07
130.31	0.03	17.68	1.54	33.66	10.04	0.57	160.61
205.41	0.10	22.61	3.04	32.80	8.05	0.19	137.27
68.56	0.25	32.11	1.24	15.17	12.02	1.22	80.67
37.81	0.05	23.48	5.84	47.42	14.00	1.35	170.74
11.42	0.45	17.55	0.25	26.34	12.38	0.78	78.10
0.33		9.90	0.17	37.48	12.13	2.91	105.66
4.83		3.14	0.13	10.38	0.14	0.02	21.30
26.69	0.57	14.68	10.32	18.35	9.05	1.72	193.44
67.11	**74.87**	**29.93**	**0.40**	**255.61**	**907.11**	**7.60**	**2044.95**
9.15	74.87	25.06	0.36	247.16	877.11	6.12	1874.58
51.25		1.82	0.01	5.94	29.99	1.46	28.03
6.71		3.05	0.03	2.51	0.01	0.02	142.34
17.10	**3.19**	**113.77**	**3.87**	**178.06**	**16.18**	**0.68**	**142.34**
10.14	**169.49**	**1265.52**	**505.62**	**2221.65**	**840.00**	**4.80**	**254.78**
36.52	**0.17**	**206.32**	**11.45**	**260.91**	**10.54**	**2.94**	**342.82**
12.98	**1.37**	**849.35**	**152.68**	**759.67**	**19.36**	**0.63**	**591.42**
143.08		**121.13**	**70.81**	**62.66**		**25.72**	**1480.78**

a)The energy consumption by the industrial sector includes the consumption by village-run industry.

b)The consumption of other petroleum products and other coking products(such as benzene etc.) is included in the total consumption of the industrial sector, but not included in consumption of the various industrial branches.

7-10 能源加工转换效率

Efficiency of Energy Conversion

单位：%　　　　　　　　　　　　　　　　　　　　(%)

年份 Year	总效率 Total Efficiency	发电及电站供热 Electricity Generation and Heating by Power Stations	炼焦 Coking	炼油 Petroleum Refining
1983	69.93	36.94	91.18	99.16
1984	69.16	36.95	90.08	99.17
1985	68.29	36.85	90.79	99.10
1986	68.32	36.69	90.63	99.04
1987	67.48	36.75	90.46	98.81
1988	66.54	36.34	90.77	98.76
1989	66.51	36.74	90.30	98.57
1990	67.20	37.34	91.28	97.90
1991	65.90	37.60	89.90	98.10
1992	66.00	37.80	92.70	96.80
1993	67.32	39.90	98.05	98.49
1994	65.20	39.35	89.62	97.48
1995	71.05	37.31	91.99	97.67
1996	71.50	38.30	94.07	97.46
1997	69.23	35.89	92.08	97.37
1998	69.44	37.06	94.97	97.42
1999	70.45	38.84	95.80	97.51

7-11 平均每天各种能源消费量

Average Daily Energy Consumption by Variety

能源品种	Item	1985	1990	1995	1998	1999
合计 （万吨标准煤）	**Total (10 000 tons of SCE)**	**210.1**	**270.4**	**359.4**	**362.2**	**365.7**
煤炭 （万吨）	Coal (10 000 tons of SCE)	223.6	289.1	377.2	354.8	346.2
焦炭 （万吨）	Coke (10 000 tons of SCE)	12.8	18.9	29.4	30.4	28.6
原油 （万吨）	Crude Oil (10 000 tons of SCE)	26.1	32.2	40.8	47.7	51.9
燃料油 （万吨）	Fuel Oil (10 000 tons of SCE)	7.8	9.2	10.2	10.5	10.8
汽油 （万吨）	Gasoline (10 000 tons of SCE)	3.8	5.2	8.0	9.1	9.3
煤油 （万吨）	Kerosene (10 000 tons of SCE)	1.1	1.0	1.4	1.8	2.3
柴油 （万吨）	Diesel Oil(10 000 tons of SCE)	5.3	7.4	11.8	14.5	17.1
天然气 （亿立方米）	Natural Gas (100 million cu.m)	0.4	0.4	0.5	0.6	0.6
电力 （亿千瓦小时）	Electricity (100 million kwh)	11.3	17.1	27.5	31.8	33.7

7-12 分品种生活能源年消费总量

Average Annual Energy Consumption for Non-Production Purposes by Variety

能源品种	Item	1985	1990	1995	1998	1999
合计 (万吨标准煤)	**Total (10 000 tons of SCE)**	**13318**	**15800**	**15745**	**14393**	**14552**
煤炭 (万吨)	Coal (10 000 tons)	15624	16700	13530	8884	8408
煤油 (万吨)	Kerosene (10 000 tons)	122	105	64	63	71
液化石油气 (万吨)	Liquefied Petroleum Gas (10 000 tons)	91	159	534	769	878
天然气 (亿立方米)	Natural Gas (100 million cu.m)	4	19	19	24	26
煤气 (亿立方米)	Gas (100 million cu.m)	13	29	57	74	81
热力 (万百万千焦)	Heat (10 billion kilo-joule)	5651	8972	12637	18711	20127
电力 (亿千瓦小时)	Electricity (100 million kwh)	223	481	1006	1325	1481

7-13 每人年平均生活用能源

Annual Average Per Capita Energy Consumption for Non-Production Purpose

年份 Year	平均每人生活消费能源 Annual Average Non-productive Consumption per Capita (千克标准煤) (Kg of SCE)	煤炭 (千克) Coal (kg)	电力 (千瓦小时) Electricity (kwh)	煤油 (千克) Kerosene (kg)	液化石油气 (千克) Liquefied Petroleum Gas (kg)	天然气 (立方米) Natural Gas (cu.m)	煤气 (立方米) Gas (cu.m)
1983	106.6	127.7	13.4	1.2	0.6	0.1	1.5
1984	113.5	134.9	15.3	1.4	0.6	0.5	1.5
1985	126.7	148.7	21.2	1.2	0.9	0.4	1.2
1986	127.3	148.3	23.2	1.3	1.1	0.7	1.3
1987	132.1	152.1	26.4	1.2	1.1	0.7	1.6
1988	141.0	159.1	31.2	1.1	1.2	1.4	1.5
1989	139.3	152.4	35.3	1.1	1.4	1.5	2.4
1990	139.2	147.1	42.4	0.9	1.4	1.6	2.5
1991	138.1	142.0	46.9	0.8	1.7	1.6	3.1
1992	133.4	126.1	54.6	0.7	2.0	1.8	4.4
1993	130.6	120.5	61.2	0.6	2.5	1.4	4.5
1994	129.3	109.5	72.7	0.6	3.2	1.7	6.3
1995	130.8	112.3	83.5	0.5	4.4	1.6	4.7
1996	145.5	118.3	93.1	0.5	5.8	1.6	3.9
1997	133.1	99.5	101.8	0.5	6.0	1.7	4.9
1998	115.9	71.5	106.6	0.5	6.2	1.9	6.0
1999	115.3	66.6	159.4	0.6	7.0	2.0	6.5

注：按年平均人口数计算。

a)Data in the table are calculated with the data on the annual average population in each year.

主 要 统 计 指 标 解 释

能源生产总量 指一定时期内全国一次能源生产量的总和，是观察全国能源生产水平、规模、构成和发展速度的总量指标。一次能源生产量包括原煤，原油，天然气，水电、核能及其他动力能(如风能、地热能等)发电量，不包括低热值燃料生产量、生物质能、太阳能等的利用和由一次能源加工转换而成的二次能源产量。

能源消费总量 指一定时期内全国物质生产部门、非物质生产部门和生活消费的各种能源的总和，是观察能源消费水平、构成和增长速度的总量指标。能源消费总量包括原煤和原油及其制品、天然气、电力，不包括低热值燃料、生物质能和太阳能等的利用。能源消费总量分为终端能源消费量、能源加工转换损失量和损失量三部分。

⑴终端能源消费量：指一定时期内全国生产和生活消费的各种能源在扣除了用于加工转换二次能源消费量和损失量以后的数量。

⑵能源加工转换损失量：指一定时期内全国投入加工转换的各种能源数量之和与产出各种能源产品之和的差额，是观察能源在加工转换过程中损失量变化的指标。

⑶能源损失量：指一定时期内能源在输送、分配、储存过程中发生的损失和由客观原因造成的各种损失量，不包括各种气体能源放空、放散量。

能源生产弹性系数 是研究能源生产增长速度与国民经济增长速度之间关系的指标。计算公式为：

能源生产弹性系数＝能源生产总量年平均增长速度／国民经济年平均增长速度

国民经济年平均增长速度，可根据不同的目的或需要，用国民生产总值、国内生产总值等指标来计算，本年鉴是采用国内生产总值指标计算的。

电力生产弹性系数 是研究电力生产增长速度与国民经济增长速度之间关系的指标。一般来说，电力的发展应当快于国民经济的发展，也就是说电力应超前发展。计算公式为：

电力生产弹性系数＝电力生产量年平均增长速度／国民经济年平均增长速度

能源消费弹性系数 是反映能源消费增长速度与国民经济增长速度之间比例关系的指标。计算公式为：

能源消费弹性系数＝能源消费量年平均增长速度／国民经济年平均增长速度

电力消费弹性系数 反映电力消费增长速度与国民经济增长速度之间比例关系的指标。计算公式为：

电力消费弹性系数＝电力消费量年平均增长速度／国民经济年平均增长速度

能源加工转换效率 指一定时期内能源经过加工、转换后，产出的各种能源产品的数量与同期内投入加工转换的各种能源数量的比率。它是观察能源加工转换装置和生产工艺先进与落后、管理水平高低等的重要指标。计算公式为：

能源加工转换效率＝能源加工、转换产出量／能源加工、转换投入量×100%

Explanatory Notes on Main Statistical Indicators

Total Energy Production refers to the total production of primary energy by all energy producing enterprises in the country in a given period of time. It is a comprehensive indicator to show the capacity, scale, composition and development of energy production of the country. The production of primary energy includes that of coal, crude oil, natural gas, hydro-power and electricity generated by nuclear energy and other means such as wind power and geothermal power. However, it excludes the production of fuels of low calorific value, bio-energy, solar energy and the secondary energy converted from the primary energy.

Total Domestic Energy Consumption refers to the total consumption of energy of various kinds by material production sectors, non material production sectors and households in the country in a given period of time. It is a comprehensive indicator to show the scale, composition and development of energy consumption. The total energy consumption includes that of coal, crude oil and their products, natural gas and electricity, However, it excludes the consumption of fuel of low calorific value, bio-energy and solar energy. Total domestic energy consumption can be divided into three parts:

(1)Final Energy Consumption: It refers to the total energy consumption by material production sectors, non material production sectors and households in the country (region) in a given period of time, but excludes the consumption in conversion of the primary energy into the secondary energy and the loss in the process of energy conversion.

(2)Loss During the Process of Energy Conversion: It refers to the total input of various kinds of energy for conversion, minus the total output of various kinds of energy in the country in a given period of time. It is an indicator to show the loss that occurs during the process of energy conversion.

(3)Loss: It refers to the total of the loss of energy during the course of energy transport, distribution and storage and the loss caused by any objective reason in a given period of time. The loss of various kinds of gas due to gas discharges and stocktaking is excluded.

Elasticity Ratio of Energy Production is an indicator to show the relationship between the growth rate of energy production and the growth rate of the national economy. The formula is:

Elasticity Ratio of Energy Production = Average Annual Growth Rate of Energy Production Average Annual Growth Rate of National Economy

The average annual growth rate of the national economy can be shown by the gross national product, gross domestic product and other indicators, depending upon the purposes or needs. The gross domestic product is used in calculation of the ratio in this chapter.

Elasticity Ratio of Electricity Production is an indicator to show the relationship between the growth rate of electricity production and the growth rate of the national economy. Generally speaking, the growth rate of electricity production should be higher than that of the national economy.

Its formula is:

Elasticity Ratio of Electricity Production = Average Annual Growth Rate of Electricity Production Average Annual Growth Rate of National Economy

Elasticity Ratio of Energy Consumption is an indicator to show the relationship between the growth rate of energy consumption and the growth rate of the national economy. The formula is:

Elasticity Ratio of Energy Consumption = Average Annual Growth Rate of Energy Consumption Average Annual Growth Rate of National Economy

Elasticity Ratio of Electricity Consumption is an indicator to show the relationship between the growth rate of electricity consumption and the growth rate of the national economy. The formula is:

Elasticity Ratio of Electricity Consumption = Average Annual Growth Rate of Electricity Average Annual Growth Rate of National Economy

Efficiency of Energy Processing and Conversion refers to the ratio of the total output of energy products of various kinds after processing and conversion and the total input of energy of various kinds for processing and conversion in the same reference period. It is an important indicator to show the current conditions of energy processing and conversion equipment, production technique and management. The formula is:

Efficiency of Energy Processing & Conversion = Output of Energy After Processing & Conversion / Input of Energy for Processing & Conversion × 100%

八、财政

Government Finance

简要说明

一、本篇反映国家财政收支状况，资料来源于财政部门，资料基础为国家财政决算、预算外资金收支决算和有关财务报表。

国家财政决算由中央级决算和地方总决算组成。省(自治区、直辖市)级决算及其所属州、县(市)总决算汇总组成省(自治区、直辖市)总决算；各省(自治区、直辖市)总决算汇总成地方总决算。

中央级决算、省(自治区、直辖市)级决算和县(市)总决算，由同级主管部门汇总的行政事业单位决算、企业财务决算、基本建设财务决算和金库年报、税收年报等组成。

为了保证决算数据的准确和完整，年度终了以前，各级财政总预算之间，财政总预算和部门单位预算之间，部门单位预算和所属单位预算之间，都对上下级之间的全年预算数据进行核对。年终后各级财政部门、国家金库会同预算缴款单位将决算收入数据进行核对一致，填制对帐单办理签证后，分别按系统上报。

为保持决算口径的一致，财政部每年要制定和颁发各省(自治区、直辖市)总决算表格和中央单位决算表格。各级财政部门和中央主管部门也要结合本部门的具体情况下达有关决算表格。决算表格按国家决算的组成，分为各级财政部门适用的总决算表格和各级主管部门、单位预算机关适用的单位决算表格，决算表数据根据总预算或单位预算会计帐簿填报。

有关财政收支方面的资料，主要来源于决算收支总表、决算收入明细表、决算支出明细表和根据这些表的数据进行的加工整理。

预算外资金收支决算和有关财务报表的编报与国家决算的编报基本相同。

二、针对历年财政收入、财政支出以及各项财政收支之间由于财政体制、预算编列方法的改变，而存在口径不统一的情况，本年鉴对有关数据进行了调整，使各年之间基本可比。主要调整的项目有：

1.财政收入：将1993年及以前各年的国内外债务收入从财政收入中剔除，不再作为财政收入。将1978—1985年财政价格补贴由冲减财政收入改列财政支出。相应地，“国家财政分项目收入”中取消债务收入一项，“国家财政分部门收入”和“国家财政分经济类型收入”有关项目也进行了调整。

2.财政支出：将1993年及以前各年的国内外债务还本付息支出和利用国外借款安排的基本建设支出从财政支出中剔除，不再作为财政支出。将1978—1985年财政价格补贴由冲减财政收入改列财政支出。相应地，“国家财政分项目支出”、“国家财政分费用类别支出”取消债务支出一项，“国家财政分项目支出”中的基本建设支出不再包括利用国外借款安排的基本建设支出，“国家财政分费用类别支出”中的有关项目也进行了调整。从2000年起，财政支出中包括国内外债务付息支出。

3.中央财政和地方财政收支：根据上述财政收入和财政支出的调整，中央财政收支也相应进行了调整，地方支出个别年份有所调整。“中央财政和地方财政收支总额”表，反映的是按当年的财政体制划分的中央、地方财政组织的收入和负责安排的支出状况，由于财政体制的变化和企业隶属关系的变化对中央、地方财政收支的影响未作调整。此外，中央与地方财政之间还存在着上解、补助和税收返还的关系。因此，“中央财政和地方财政收支总额”表不反映各级财力情况。

预算外资金从1982年开始建立统计制度，预算外收入和预算外支出项目几经变化。1993年由于实施新的财务通则和会计准则，预算外收支范围又一次作了较大调整，国营企业更新改造资金、大修理基金等不再作为预算外资金，因此1992年以前年度与1993年以后年度的预算外资金收支不可比。

Brief Introduction

I. The data in this chapter show the government revenue and expenditure. The data come from the departments of finance. The data are based on the final state financial accounts, the final accounts of extra-budgetary revenue and expenditure and the concerned financial reports.

The final state financial accounts are composed of the final accounts at the level of central government and the total final accounts at the level of local governments. The total final accounts at the level of local governments are composed of the total final accounts of the governments of provinces, autonomous regions and municipalities directly under the central government. The total final accounts at the provincial (autonomous region, municipality directly under the central government) level are composed of the final accounts at the provincial level and the total final accounts at the level of governments of prefectures and counties (cities).

The final accounts at the central level, at the provincial level and at the county (city) level are respectively composed of the final accounts of the administrative and institutional units, the final financial accounts of enterprises, final financial accounts of capital construction, annual reports on treasury and annual reports on tax revenue, pooled together by the responsible departments at the same level.

In order to ensure the accuracy and completeness of the data of final accounts, the financial departments at different levels should check the budgetary data of the higher and lower levels of the whole year before the end of the year, including the related figures of the total government budgets between different levels, the related figures between the government total budget and the budgets of the departments and the related figures between the budget of the departments and the budgets of the subordinate units. After the end of the year, the financial departments of different levels and the state treasury should check the data of the revenue in the final accounts together with the units which hand over the budget, filled out the accounts checking sheet, made signatures and reported to the higher authorities respectively.

In order to ensure the consistency in the coverage of the final accounts, the Ministry of Finance works out and issues the final accounts forms for the provinces, autonomous regions and municipalities directly under the central government and the final accounts forms for the departments at the central level. The financial departments at various levels and the central government departments should also work out and issue the final accounts forms in the light of the specific conditions of the department to the departments or units at the lower level. The final account forms are designed in accordance with the composition of the state final account and are composed of the total final accounts forms suitable for the financial departments of different levels and the unit final accounts forms suitable for the budgetary agencies of the responsible departments or units. The data for the final accounts are filled out in accordance with the data in the account books of the total budget or unit budget.

The data on the government revenue and expenditure come mainly from the total final accounts table of the revenue and expenditure and the subsidiary table of the final accounts of the revenue and the subsidiary table of the final accounts of the expenditure as well as the data calculated from the above data.

The procedures for the compilation of the extra-budgetary revenue and expenditure and the related financial tables are basically the same as those for the compilation of the state final accounts.

II. Owing to the changes in financial system and in the methods of compiling and listing the items of the budget, the coverage of the government revenue and expenditure and their breakdowns are not consistent over the years. In view of the above situation, the concerned data in this yearbook have been adjusted so as to make them basically comparable over the years. The main adjusted items are as follows:

(1) Government revenue. The revenues from the domestic and foreign debts in 1993 and the previous years are deducted from the government revenue and no longer listed as the component of the government revenue. The financial subsidies for the price adjustment in 1978-1985 were listed formerly as an item to eat up part of the government revenue and are now listed as an item of government expenditure. Correspondingly, the original item " revenue from debts" under the "government revenue by item" is cancelled; and the concerned items in "government revenue by sector" and "government revenue by ownership" have also been adjusted.

(2) Government expenditure. The expenditures for repayment of the principal and interest of the domestic and foreign debts in 1993 and the previous years are deducted from the government expenditure and no longer listed as the component of the government expenditure. The financial subsidies on the price adjustment in 1978-1985 were listed formerly as an item to eat up part of the government revenue and are now listed as an item of government expenditure. Correspondingly, the original item " expenditure for debts" under the "government expenditure by account item" and the "government expenditure by general categories" is canceled; the expenditure for capital construction under the "government expenditure by account item "no longer includes the expenditure for capital construction as a result of the utilization of the foreign loans; the related items under the "government expenditure by general catego-

ries" have also been adjusted. Total government expenditures include the payment for capital and its' interest of domestic and foreign debts since 2000.

(3) Revenue and expenditure of the central government and local governments. According to the above-mentioned adjustments in the government revenue and expenditure, adjustments are also made in the revenue and expenditure of the central government correspondingly and in the revenue and expenditure of the local governments in a few years. The table on "Total Revenue and Total Expenditure of the Central Government and Local Governments" show the revenues and expenditures of the central government and local governments at the current years. The changes in the financial structure and in the subordinate relationship of the enterprises have the impact on the revenues and expenditures of the central government and local governments. However, no adjustments have been made in the data of the past years. In addition, there are also appropriate adaptations made in the specific conditions in the relationship between the central government and local governments: Sometimes some local governments hand certain amount of their funds over to the central government; Sometimes the central government pays subsidies to the difficult provinces and autonomous regions or send back parts of the tax revenue to the local government. Therefore the table on "Total Revenue and Total Expenditure of the Central Government and Local Governments" does not show the real financial strengths of the governments at different levels.

Data on the extra-budgetary funds have been collected in accordance with the statistical reporting scheme since 1982. Changes have been made in the items in the extra-budgetary revenue and the extra-budgetary expenditure several times. In 1993, new financial general rules and accounting standards were implemented. As a result, significant changes have been made again in the scope of extra-budgetary revenue and extra-budgetary expenditure. The innovation fund and the major repair fund in the state-owned enterprises were no longer listed as the extra-budgetary funds. Therefore the extra-budgetary revenues and the extra-budgetary expenditures in the years before 1993 and since 1993 are incomparable.

8-1 国家财政收支总额及增长速度

Total Government Revenue and Expenditures and Their Increase Rate

年份 Year	财政收入 (亿元) Total Revenue (100 million yuan)	财政支出 (亿元) Total Expenditures (100 million yuan)	收支差额 (亿元) Balance (100 million yuan)	增长速度 (%) Increase Rate(%) 财政收入 Total Revenue	财政支出 Total Expenditures
1950	62.17	68.05	-5.88		
1951	124.96	122.07	2.89	101.0	79.4
1952	173.94	172.07	1.87	39.2	41.0
1953	213.24	219.21	-5.97	22.6	27.4
1954	245.17	244.11	1.06	15.0	11.4
1955	249.27	262.73	-13.46	1.7	7.6
1956	280.19	298.52	-18.33	12.4	13.6
1957	303.20	295.95	7.25	8.2	-0.9
1958	379.62	400.36	-20.74	25.2	35.3
1959	487.12	543.17	-56.05	28.3	35.7
1960	572.29	643.68	-71.39	17.5	18.5
1961	356.06	356.09	-0.03	-37.8	-44.7
1962	313.55	294.88	18.67	-11.9	-17.2
1963	342.25	332.05	10.20	9.2	12.6
1964	399.54	393.79	5.75	16.7	18.6
1965	473.32	459.97	13.35	18.5	16.8
1966	558.71	537.65	21.06	18.0	16.9
1967	419.36	439.84	-20.48	-24.9	-18.2
1968	361.25	357.84	3.41	-13.9	-18.6
1969	526.76	525.86	0.90	45.8	47.0
1970	662.90	649.41	13.49	25.8	23.5
1971	744.73	732.17	12.56	12.3	12.7
1972	766.56	765.86	0.70	2.9	4.6
1973	809.67	808.78	0.89	5.6	5.6
1974	783.14	790.25	-7.11	-3.3	-2.3
1975	815.61	820.88	-5.27	4.1	3.8
1976	776.58	806.20	-29.62	-4.8	-1.8
1977	874.46	843.53	30.93	12.6	4.6
1978	1132.26	1122.09	10.17	29.5	33.0
1979	1146.38	1281.79	-135.41	1.2	14.2
1980	1159.93	1228.83	-68.90	1.2	-4.1
1981	1175.79	1138.41	37.38	1.4	-7.5
1982	1212.33	1229.98	-17.65	3.1	8.0
1983	1366.95	1409.52	-42.57	12.8	14.6
1984	1642.86	1701.02	-58.16	20.2	20.7
1985	2004.82	2004.25	0.57	22.0	17.8
1986	2122.01	2204.91	-82.90	5.8	10.0
1987	2199.35	2262.18	-62.83	3.6	2.6
1988	2357.24	2491.21	-133.97	7.2	10.1
1989	2664.90	2823.78	-158.88	13.1	13.3
1990	2937.10	3083.59	-146.49	10.2	9.2
1991	3149.48	3386.62	-237.14	7.2	9.8
1992	3483.37	3742.20	-258.83	10.6	10.5
1993	4348.95	4642.30	-293.35	24.8	24.1
1994	5218.10	5792.62	-574.52	20.0	24.8
1995	6242.20	6823.72	-581.52	19.6	17.8
1996	7407.99	7937.55	-529.56	18.7	16.3
1997	8651.14	9233.56	-582.42	16.8	16.3
1998	9875.95	10798.18	-922.23	14.2	16.9
1999	11444.08	13187.67	-1743.59	15.9	22.1
2000	13395.23	15886.50	-2491.27	17.0	20.5

注：1.在国家财政收支中，价格补贴1985年以前冲减财政收入，1986年以后列为财政支出。为了可比，本表将1985年以前冲减财政收入的价格补贴改列在财政支出中。

2.从2000年起，财政支出中包括国内外债务付息支出。

a)Government price subsidies were listed as negative revenue items prior to 1986, but they have been listed as expenditure items in government accounts since 1986. For comparison purpose, government price subsidies before 1985 were adjusted, and listed as expenditure items.

b)Total government expenditures include the payment for interest of domestic and foreign debts from 2000.

8-2 国家财政收入占国内生产总值的比重
Government Revenue as Percentage to Gross Domestic Product

年份 Year	财政收入（亿元） Total Revenue (100 million yuan)	国内生产总值（亿元） Gross Domestic Products (100 million yuan)	财政收入占国内生产总值的比重（%） Percentage of Government Revenue to GDP(%)
1950	62.17		
1951	124.96		
1952	173.94	679.0	25.6
1953	213.24	824.0	25.9
1954	245.17	859.0	28.5
1955	249.27	910.0	27.4
1956	280.19	1028.0	27.3
1957	303.20	1068.0	28.4
1958	379.62	1307.0	29.0
1959	487.12	1439.0	33.9
1960	572.29	1457.0	39.3
1961	356.06	1220.0	29.2
1962	313.55	1149.3	27.3
1963	342.25	1233.3	27.8
1964	399.54	1454.0	27.5
1965	473.32	1716.1	27.6
1966	558.71	1868.0	29.9
1967	419.36	1773.9	23.6
1968	361.25	1723.1	21.0
1969	526.76	1937.9	27.2
1970	662.90	2252.7	29.4
1971	744.73	2426.4	30.7
1972	766.56	2518.1	30.4
1973	809.67	2720.9	29.8
1974	783.14	2789.9	28.1
1975	815.61	2997.3	27.2
1976	776.58	2943.7	26.4
1977	874.46	3201.9	27.3
1978	1132.26	3624.1	31.2
1979	1146.38	4038.2	28.4
1980	1159.93	4517.8	25.7
1981	1175.79	4862.4	24.2
1982	1212.33	5294.7	22.9
1983	1366.95	5934.5	23.0
1984	1642.86	7171.0	22.9
1985	2004.82	8964.4	22.4
1986	2122.01	10202.2	20.8
1987	2199.35	11962.5	18.4
1988	2357.24	14928.3	15.8
1989	2664.90	16909.2	15.8
1990	2937.10	18547.9	15.8
1991	3149.48	21617.8	14.6
1992	3483.37	26638.1	13.1
1993	4348.95	34634.4	12.6
1994	5218.10	46759.4	11.2
1995	6242.20	58478.1	10.7
1996	7407.99	67884.6	10.9
1997	8651.14	74462.6	11.6
1998	9875.95	78345.2	12.6
1999	11444.08	82067.5	13.9
2000	13395.23	89403.6	15.0

注：国家财政收入中不包括国内外债务收入。

a) Both domestic and foreign debts are excluded in this table.

8-3 国家财政分项目收入

Government Revenue by Source

单位：亿元 (100 million yuan)

年份 Year	收入合计 Total Revenue	各项税收 Taxes	企业收入 Revenue from Enterprises	企业亏损补贴 Subsidies to Loss-making Enterprises	能源交通重点建设基金收入 Revenue Raised from Funds for Key Construction Projects in Energy Industry and Transportation	预算调节基金收入 Revenue Raised from Budget Adjustment Fund	教育费附加收入 Revenue from Extra-charges for Education	其他收入 Other Revenue
1950	62.17	48.98	8.69					4.50
1951	124.96	81.13	30.54					13.29
1952	173.94	97.69	57.27					18.98
1953	213.24	119.67	76.69					16.88
1954	245.17	132.18	99.61					13.38
1955	249.27	127.45	111.94					9.88
1956	280.19	140.88	134.26					5.05
1957	303.20	154.89	144.18					4.13
1958	379.62	187.36	189.19					3.07
1959	487.12	204.71	279.10					3.31
1960	572.29	203.65	365.84					2.80
1961	356.06	158.76	191.31					5.99
1962	313.55	162.07	146.22					5.26
1963	342.25	164.31	172.68					5.26
1964	399.54	182.00	212.93					4.61
1965	473.32	204.30	264.27					4.75
1966	558.71	221.96	333.32					3.43
1967	419.36	196.63	218.47					4.26
1968	361.25	191.56	166.73					2.96
1969	526.76	235.44	286.74					4.58
1970	662.90	281.20	378.97					2.73
1971	744.73	312.56	428.40					3.77
1972	766.56	317.02	445.69					3.85
1973	809.67	348.95	457.02					3.70
1974	783.14	360.40	407.26					15.48
1975	815.61	402.77	400.20					12.64
1976	776.58	407.96	338.06					30.56
1977	874.46	468.27	402.35					3.84
1978	1132.26	519.28	571.99					40.99
1979	1146.38	537.82	495.03					113.53
1980	1159.93	571.70	435.24					152.99
1981	1175.79	629.89	353.68					192.22
1982	1212.33	700.02	296.47					215.84
1983	1366.95	775.59	240.52		93.00			257.84
1984	1642.86	947.35	276.77		122.45			296.29
1985	2004.82	2040.79	43.75	-507.02	146.79			280.51
1986	2122.01	2090.73	42.04	-324.78	157.07			156.95
1987	2199.35	2140.36	42.86	-376.43	180.18			212.38
1988	2357.24	2390.47	51.12	-446.46	185.93			176.18
1989	2664.90	2727.40	63.60	-598.88	202.18	91.19		179.41
1990	2937.10	2821.86	78.30	-578.88	185.08	131.21		299.53
1991	3149.48	2990.17	74.69	-510.24	188.22	138.53	28.01	240.10
1992	3483.37	3296.91	59.97	-444.96	157.11	117.47	31.72	265.15
1993	4348.95	4255.30	49.49	-411.29	117.72	102.46	44.23	191.04
1994	5218.10	5126.88		-366.22	53.96	59.10	64.20	280.18
1995	6242.20	6038.04		-327.77	17.42	34.92	83.40	396.19
1996	7407.99	6909.82		-337.40	3.78	11.09	96.04	724.66
1997	8651.14	8234.04		-368.49			103.29	682.30
1998	9875.95	9262.80		-333.49			113.34	833.30
1999	11444.08	10682.58		-290.03			126.10	925.43
2000	13395.23	12581.51		-278.78			147.52	944.98

注：国家财政收入中不包括国内外债务收入。

a) Revenue from both domestic and foreign borrowings are excluded in this table.

8-4 各 项 税 收 收 入

Government Tax Revenue

单位：亿元 (100 million yuan)

年 份 Year	合 计 Total	#工商税收 Industrial and Commercial Tax	#关 税 Tariffs	#农业各税 Agricultural and Related	#国有企业所得税 Income Tax of State-owned Enterprises	#集体企业所得税 Income Tax of Collective-owned Enterprises
1950	48.98	26.32	3.56	19.10		
1951	81.13	50.84	6.94	23.35		
1952	97.69	65.53	4.81	27.35		
1953	119.67	87.11	5.05	27.51		
1954	132.18	94.93	4.12	33.13		
1955	127.45	92.07	4.66	30.72		
1956	140.88	105.81	5.42	29.65		
1957	154.89	119.43	5.79	29.67		
1958	187.36	148.37	6.40	32.59		
1959	204.71	164.67	7.03	33.01		
1960	203.65	169.61	6.00	28.04		
1961	158.76	130.87	6.23	21.66		
1962	162.07	134.42	4.82	22.83		
1963	164.31	136.16	4.15	24.00		
1964	182.00	151.73	4.38	25.89		
1965	204.30	172.82	5.70	25.78		
1966	221.96	185.91	6.50	29.55		
1967	196.63	163.76	3.92	28.95		
1968	191.56	155.21	6.33	30.02		
1969	235.44	199.52	6.36	29.56		
1970	281.20	242.22	7.00	31.98		
1971	312.56	276.70	5.00	30.86		
1972	317.02	283.65	5.00	28.37		
1973	348.95	309.43	9.00	30.52		
1974	360.40	316.34	14.00	30.06		
1975	402.77	358.32	15.00	29.45		
1976	407.96	363.82	15.00	29.14		
1977	468.27	412.71	26.23	29.33		
1978	519.28	462.12	28.76	28.40		
1979	537.82	482.31	26.00	29.51		
1980	571.70	510.50	33.53	27.67		
1981	629.89	547.50	54.04	28.35		
1982	700.02	623.18	47.46	29.38		
1983	775.59	688.75	53.88	32.96		
1984	947.35	809.44	103.07	34.84		
1985	2040.79	1097.47	205.21	42.05	595.84	100.22
1986	2090.73	1202.19	151.62	44.52	595.40	97.00
1987	2140.36	1282.47	142.37	50.81	563.20	101.51
1988	2390.47	1485.72	155.02	73.69	570.93	105.11
1989	2727.40	1760.49	181.54	84.94	583.59	116.84
1990	2821.86	1858.99	159.01	87.86	604.12	111.88
1991	2990.17	1981.11	187.28	90.65	627.59	103.54
1992	3296.91	2244.21	212.75	119.17	624.77	96.01
1993	4255.30	3194.49	256.47	125.74	582.91	95.69
1994	5126.88	3914.22	272.68	231.49	609.75	98.74
1995	6038.04	4589.68	291.83	278.09	759.38	119.06
1996	6909.82	5270.04	301.84	369.46	822.33	146.15
1997	8234.04	6553.89	319.49	397.48	794.43	168.75
1998	9262.80	7625.42	313.04	398.80	743.93	181.61
1999	10682.58	8885.44	562.23	423.50	639.00	172.41
2000	12581.51	10366.09	750.48	465.31	827.41	172.22

注：1. 农业各税包括农业税、牧业税、耕地占用税、农业特产税和契税。
　　2. 国有企业所得税中1985—1993年包括国有企业调节税，1994年以后包括地方金融企业所得税。

a) The agricultural and retail taxes include the agricultural tax, the animal husbandry tax, the tax on the use of cultivated land, the tax on special agricultural products and the contract tax.

b) During the years 1985 to 1993, the income tax levied on state-owned enterprises included the tax for adjusting income. Since 1994, it has also included the income tax levied on finance institutions.

8-5 产品税、增值税、营业税和消费税收入

Product Tax, Value-added Tax, Operation Tax and Consumption Tax Revenue

单位：亿元　　　　(100 million yuan)

年份 Year	产品税 Product Tax	增值税 Value-added Tax	营业税 Operation Tax	消费税 Consumption Tax
1985	594.60	147.70	211.07	
1986	546.59	232.19	261.07	
1987	533.26	254.20	302.00	
1988	480.93	384.37	397.92	
1989	530.28	430.83	487.30	
1990	580.93	400.00	515.75	
1991	629.41	406.36	564.00	
1992	693.25	705.93	658.67	
1993	821.42	1081.48	966.09	
1994		2308.34	670.02	487.40
1995		2602.33	865.56	541.48
1996		2962.81	1052.57	620.23
1997		3283.92	1324.27	678.70
1998		3628.46	1575.08	814.93
1999		3881.87	1668.56	820.66
2000		4553.17	1868.78	858.29

注：1994年税制改革后，流转税由增值税、消费税和营业税组成，取消产品税。

a) Since the reform of tax system in 1994, turnover tax was composed of value-added tax, consumption tax and operation tax, and excluded product tax.

8-6 国家财政债务发行情况

Government Debts Issuance

单位:亿元　　　　(100 million yuan)

年 份 Year	合 计 Total	国内债务 Domestic Debts	国外借款 Foreign Borrowing	国内其他债务 Other Domestic Debts
1950	3.02	3.02		
1951	8.18	0.01	5.49	2.68
1952	9.78		9.78	
1953	9.62		9.62	
1954	17.20	8.36	8.84	
1955	22.76	6.19	16.57	
1956	7.24	6.07	1.17	
1957	6.99	6.84	0.15	
1958	7.98	7.98		
1979	35.31		35.31	
1980	43.01		43.01	
1981	121.74	48.66	73.08	
1982	83.86	43.83	40.03	
1983	79.41	41.58	37.83	
1984	77.34	42.53	34.81	
1985	89.85	60.61	29.24	
1986	138.25	62.51	75.74	
1987	223.55	63.07	106.48	54.00
1988	270.78	92.17	138.61	40.00
1989	407.97	56.07	144.06	207.84
1990	375.45	93.46	178.21	103.78
1991	461.40	199.30	180.13	81.97
1992	669.68	395.64	208.91	65.13
1993	739.22	314.78	357.90	66.54
1994	1175.25	1028.57	146.68	
1995	1549.76	1510.86	38.90	
1996	1967.28	1847.77	119.51	
1997	2476.82	2412.03	64.79	
1998	3310.93	3228.77	82.16	
1999	3715.03	3702.13		12.90
2000	4180.10	4153.59	23.10	3.41

注：从1999年开始，国内其他债务项目为债务收入大于支出部分增列的偿债基金。

a)Since 1999, other domestic debts were the sinking fund which come from the excessive part of the revenue from borrowings minus the expenditure for debts.

8-7 国家财政主要支出项目

Government Expenditures by Accounting Item

单位：亿元 (100 million yuan)

年份 Year	基本建设支出 Expenditure for Capital Construction	增拨企业流动资金 Additional Appropriation for Circulating Capital of Enterprises	挖潜改造资金和科技三项费用 Innovation Funds and Science and Technology Promotion Funds	地质勘探费 Geological Prospecting Expenses	工、交、商业部门事业费 Operating Expenses of Industrial, Transportation and Commercial Departments	支援农村生产支出和各项农业事业费 Expenditure for Supporting Agricultural Production and Agricultural Operating Expenses
1950	12.50					
1951	27.03					
1952	46.68	18.56				
1953	70.34	13.78		0.68	6.39	2.99
1954	84.28	26.30	1.82	0.75	6.91	3.98
1955	88.53	30.81	3.09	3.66	10.08	5.82
1956	139.58	10.79	2.48	5.17	10.80	7.70
1957	123.71	20.82	2.29	6.27	12.36	7.99
1958	229.38	25.66	0.83	6.90	16.25	9.34
1959	302.34	54.28	2.20	8.96	14.98	22.05
1960	354.45	67.47	2.55	10.25	19.58	33.73
1961	110.18	29.39	2.67	6.47	13.54	31.01
1962	55.65	47.78	14.65	4.79	10.29	19.29
1963	80.21	36.65	18.28	4.68	7.89	22.19
1964	123.83	23.35	20.86	6.43	12.71	20.92
1965	158.49	27.55	25.23	7.71	15.91	17.29
1966	191.04	40.28	27.54	7.95	16.40	19.11
1967	161.25	29.10	10.32	7.71	12.01	16.12
1968	117.85	12.03	5.66	6.35	6.80	12.89
1969	206.22	26.61	10.74	8.07	6.37	14.87
1970	298.36	31.23	14.78	8.76	6.58	15.91
1971	309.56	35.30	26.40	10.30	6.49	19.65
1972	309.09	42.95	25.46	11.29	7.55	25.10
1973	317.17	53.82	25.49	12.20	8.90	35.49
1974	312.83	44.76	27.20	13.09	10.09	38.23
1975	326.96	41.84	31.47	14.16	12.76	42.53
1976	311.25	45.36	34.34	15.96	13.12	46.01
1977	300.88	65.68	39.45	17.26	14.43	50.68
1978	451.92	66.60	63.24	20.15	17.79	76.95
1979	443.68	52.05	71.79	21.67	20.90	89.97
1980	346.36	36.71	80.45	22.57	22.85	82.12
1981	257.55	22.84	65.30	21.85	23.68	73.68
1982	269.12	23.63	69.02	23.05	23.83	79.88
1983	344.98	12.89	78.71	23.60	27.88	86.66
1984	454.12	9.96	111.77	26.22	30.66	95.93
1985	554.56	14.30	103.42	29.58	35.16	101.04
1986	596.08	9.94	129.85	30.60	36.56	124.30
1987	521.64	12.06	124.93	30.29	33.13	134.16
1988	494.76	9.59	151.01	32.51	38.95	158.74
1989	481.70	12.09	146.30	33.16	45.01	197.12
1990	547.39	10.90	153.91	36.19	46.93	221.76
1991	559.62	13.08	180.81	38.34	52.41	243.55
1992	555.90	10.63	223.62	44.07	64.58	269.04
1993	591.93	18.48	421.38	49.06	76.22	323.42
1994	639.72	17.33	415.13	64.13	100.77	399.70
1995	789.22	34.80	494.45	66.32	102.76	430.22
1996	907.44	42.93	523.02	68.56	120.41	510.07
1997	1019.50	52.20	643.20	73.37	136.41	560.77
1998	1387.74	42.36	641.18	83.13	121.56	626.02
1999	2116.57	56.41	766.05	83.69	128.07	677.46
2000	2094.89	71.06	865.24	88.12	150.07	766.89

注：行政管理费中包括公检法司支出和外交外事支出。

a) Expenditure for Government Administration includes the expenditure for public security, procuratorial work and the court of justice and for foreign affairs.

8-7 续表 1 continued

单位：亿元 (100 million yuan)

年份 Year	文教、科学、卫生事业费 Operating Expenses for Culture, Education Science & Health Care	抚恤和社会福利救济费 Pensions, Social and Relief Funds	国防费 Expenditure for National Defense	行政管理费 Expenditure for Government Administration	政策性补贴支出 Price Subsidies
1950	5.02		28.01		
1951	10.56		52.64		
1952	13.47	2.95	57.84	14.54	
1953	19.03	3.62	75.38	17.53	
1954	19.70	6.04	58.13	18.26	
1955	19.82	4.94	65.00	18.73	
1956	23.90	5.67	61.17	24.16	
1957	27.76	5.29	55.11	21.68	
1958	28.64	3.22	50.00	21.56	
1959	36.47	4.41	58.00	26.62	
1960	50.46	7.94	58.00	27.98	
1961	41.23	10.09	50.00	26.76	
1962	36.74	8.14	56.94	21.72	
1963	37.96	10.15	66.42	23.50	
1964	43.34	17.04	72.86	25.17	
1965	45.59	10.94	86.76	25.34	
1966	51.68	9.21	101.01	25.90	
1967	48.56	8.16	83.02	22.80	
1968	40.96	5.61	94.09	22.91	
1969	40.97	6.67	126.18	24.78	
1970	43.65	6.53	145.26	25.27	
1971	52.31	6.83	169.47	30.89	
1972	62.01	8.15	159.39	34.63	
1973	69.88	9.97	145.39	35.58	
1974	76.49	9.16	133.39	36.92	
1975	81.29	12.88	142.46	38.83	
1976	85.49	24.07	134.45	41.01	
1977	90.20	18.76	149.04	43.32	
1978	112.66	18.91	167.84	49.09	11.14
1979	132.07	22.11	222.64	57.24	79.20
1980	156.26	20.31	193.84	66.79	117.71
1981	171.36	21.72	167.97	70.88	159.41
1982	196.96	21.43	176.35	81.60	172.22
1983	223.54	24.04	177.13	102.20	197.37
1984	263.17	25.16	180.76	125.23	218.34
1985	316.70	31.15	191.53	130.58	261.79
1986	379.93	35.58	200.75	168.03	257.48
1987	402.75	37.40	209.62	179.33	294.60
1988	486.10	41.77	218.00	220.89	316.82
1989	553.33	49.60	251.47	261.86	373.55
1990	617.29	55.04	290.31	303.10	380.80
1991	708.00	67.32	330.31	343.60	373.77
1992	792.96	66.45	377.86	424.58	321.64
1993	957.77	75.27	425.80	535.77	299.30
1994	1278.18	95.14	550.71	729.43	314.47
1995	1467.06	115.46	636.72	872.68	364.89
1996	1704.25	128.03	720.06	1040.80	453.91
1997	1903.59	142.14	812.57	1137.16	551.96
1998	2154.38	171.26	934.70	1326.77	712.12
1999	2408.06	179.88	1076.40	1525.68	697.64
2000	2736.88	213.03	1207.54	1787.58	1042.28

8-8 国家财政按功能性质分类的支出

Government Expenditure by Category of Expenses

单位：亿元 (100 million yuan)

年份 Year	支出合计 Total Expenditures	经济建设费 Economic Construction	社会文教费 Social, Cultural and Educational Development	国防费 National Defense	行政管理费 Government Administration	其他支出 Others
1950	68.05	17.36	7.55	28.01	13.13	2.00
1951	122.07	35.11	13.44	52.64	17.45	3.43
1952	172.07	73.23	21.11	57.84	15.49	4.40
1953	219.21	87.43	32.44	75.38	19.72	4.24
1954	244.11	123.58	34.61	58.13	21.62	6.17
1955	262.73	137.62	31.89	65.00	21.54	6.68
1956	298.52	159.14	45.96	61.17	26.60	5.65
1957	295.95	163.04	46.42	55.11	22.70	8.68
1958	400.36	278.86	43.54	50.00	22.72	5.24
1959	543.17	389.33	58.60	58.00	30.00	7.24
1960	643.68	460.71	86.95	58.00	31.39	6.63
1961	356.09	210.01	61.25	50.00	27.14	7.69
1962	294.88	152.64	51.73	56.94	21.91	11.66
1963	332.05	174.12	51.45	66.42	23.86	16.20
1964	393.79	209.99	66.09	72.86	26.22	18.63
1965	459.97	254.11	62.70	86.76	26.34	30.06
1966	537.65	309.43	67.06	101.01	26.59	33.56
1967	439.84	244.03	60.83	83.02	22.95	29.01
1968	357.84	166.03	47.88	94.09	22.91	26.93
1969	525.86	295.52	49.77	126.18	29.82	24.57
1970	649.41	392.61	52.22	145.26	32.00	27.32
1971	732.17	418.30	63.80	169.47	37.62	42.98
1972	765.86	431.96	75.31	159.39	38.93	60.27
1973	808.78	468.27	88.57	145.39	38.59	67.96
1974	790.25	460.93	95.02	133.39	39.76	61.15
1975	820.88	481.66	103.55	142.46	41.81	51.40
1976	806.20	466.22	120.06	134.45	43.38	42.09
1977	843.53	493.73	119.43	149.04	45.18	36.15
1978	1122.09	718.98	146.96	167.84	52.90	35.41
1979	1281.79	769.89	175.18	222.64	63.07	51.01
1980	1228.83	715.46	199.01	193.84	75.53	44.99
1981	1138.41	630.76	211.46	167.97	82.63	45.59
1982	1229.98	675.37	242.98	176.35	90.84	44.44
1983	1409.52	794.75	282.51	177.13	103.08	52.05
1984	1701.02	968.18	332.06	180.76	139.80	80.22
1985	2004.25	1127.55	408.43	191.53	171.06	105.68
1986	2204.91	1158.97	485.09	200.75	220.04	140.06
1987	2262.18	1153.47	505.83	209.62	228.20	165.06
1988	2491.21	1258.39	581.18	218.00	271.60	162.04
1989	2823.78	1291.19	668.44	251.47	386.26	226.42
1990	3083.59	1368.01	737.61	290.31	414.56	273.10
1991	3386.62	1428.47	849.65	330.31	414.01	364.18
1992	3742.20	1612.81	970.12	377.86	463.41	318.00
1993	4642.30	1834.79	1178.27	425.80	634.26	569.18
1994	5792.62	2393.69	1501.53	550.71	847.68	499.01
1995	6823.72	2855.78	1756.72	636.72	996.54	577.96
1996	7937.55	3233.78	2080.56	720.06	1185.28	717.87
1997	9233.56	3647.33	2469.38	812.57	1358.85	945.43
1998	10798.18	4179.51	2930.78	934.70	1600.27	1152.92
1999	13187.67	5061.46	3638.74	1076.40	2020.60	1390.47
2000	15886.50	5748.36	4384.51	1207.54	2768.22	1777.87

注：本表数字不包括国内外债务还本付息支出和用国外借款收入安排的基本建设支出。

a) Figures in the table do not include the payment for the principal and interest of the domestic and foreign debts, and the investment in capital construction using foreign loans.

8-9 国家财政用于农业的支出

Government Expenditure For Agriculture

单位：亿元

(100 million yuan)

年份 Year	合计 Total	支援农村生产支出和农林水利气象等部门的事业费 Expenditure for Supporting Agricultural Production and Agricultural Operating Expenses	农业基本建设支出 Expenditure for Capital Construction	农业科技三项费用 Science & Technology Promotion Funds	农村救济费 Rural Relief Funds	其他 Others	用于农业支出占财政支出的比重(%) Percentage to Total Government Expenditure
1950	2.74	1.99			0.75		4.03
1951	4.19	3.67			0.52		3.43
1952	9.04	2.69	3.84		1.25	1.26	5.25
1953	13.07	4.22	5.77		1.43	1.65	5.96
1954	15.79	6.26	4.87		3.74	0.92	6.47
1955	17.01	7.84	5.71		2.27	1.19	6.47
1956	29.14	9.85	13.63		3.10	2.56	9.76
1957	24.57	9.06	10.93		3.07	1.51	8.30
1958	43.28	8.76	30.26		1.50	2.76	10.81
1959	58.24	22.06	29.91		2.70	3.57	10.72
1960	90.52	33.73	45.43		5.47	5.89	14.06
1961	54.79	30.92	12.35		7.35	4.17	15.39
1962	36.82	17.88	8.67		5.22	5.05	12.49
1963	54.98	21.57	18.48	0.81	6.96	7.16	16.56
1964	66.98	20.74	26.17	1.00	13.55	5.52	17.01
1965	55.02	17.33	23.51	1.05	7.37	5.76	11.96
1966	54.14	18.86	23.70	1.28	5.20	5.10	10.07
1967	45.64	15.94	22.08	0.30	4.14	3.18	10.38
1968	33.24	12.66	12.23		2.79	5.56	9.29
1969	48.03	14.87	17.92		3.58	11.66	9.13
1970	49.40	15.91	22.52		3.14	7.83	7.61
1971	60.75	19.65	33.27	0.05	3.14	4.64	8.30
1972	65.13	25.10	31.47	0.07	4.10	4.39	8.50
1973	85.17	35.49	37.48	0.08	5.08	7.04	10.53
1974	91.21	38.23	36.97	0.13	4.01	11.87	11.54
1975	98.96	42.53	35.56	0.10	7.42	13.35	12.06
1976	110.49	46.01	39.91	0.78	10.48	13.31	13.71
1977	108.12	50.68	35.98	0.93	8.40	12.13	12.82
1978	150.66	76.95	51.14	1.06	6.88	14.63	13.43
1979	174.33	90.11	62.41	1.52	9.80	10.49	13.60
1980	149.95	82.12	48.59	1.31	7.26	10.67	12.20
1981	110.21	73.68	24.15	1.18	9.08	2.12	9.68
1982	120.49	79.88	28.81	1.13	8.60	2.07	9.80
1983	132.87	86.66	34.25	1.81	9.38	0.77	9.43
1984	141.29	95.93	33.63	2.18	9.55		8.31
1985	153.62	101.04	37.73	1.95	12.90		7.66
1986	184.20	124.30	43.87	2.70	13.33		8.35
1987	195.72	134.16	46.81	2.28	12.47		8.65
1988	214.07	158.74	39.67	2.39	13.27		8.59
1989	265.94	197.12	50.64	2.48	15.70		9.42
1990	307.84	221.76	66.71	3.11	16.26		9.98
1991	347.57	243.55	75.49	2.93	25.60		10.26
1992	376.02	269.04	85.00	3.00	18.98		10.05
1993	440.45	323.42	95.00	3.00	19.03		9.49
1994	532.98	399.70	107.00	3.00	23.28		9.20
1995	574.93	430.22	110.00	3.00	31.71		8.43
1996	700.43	510.07	141.51	4.94	43.91		8.82
1997	766.39	560.77	159.78	5.48	40.36		8.30
1998	1154.76	626.02	460.70	9.14	58.90		10.69
1999	1085.76	677.46	357.00	9.13	42.17		8.23
2000		766.89					

注：从1998年开始，"农业基本建设支出"包括增发国债安排的支出。

a) Expenditure for agricultural capital construction since 1998 included the expenditure funded from additional issuing national debt.

8-10 科学研究支出

Government Expenditure on Scientific Research

单位：亿元 (100 million yuan)

年 份 Year	合 计 Total	科技三项费用 Expense on S&T Promotion	科学事业费 Operating Expenses for Sciences	科研基建费 Expenses for Capital Construction of S&T Institutes	其他科研事业费 Other S&T Operating Expenses
1953	0.56	0.27		0.29	
1954	1.22	1.10		0.12	
1955	2.13	1.92		0.21	
1956	5.23	3.53		1.70	
1957	5.23	2.98		2.25	
1958	11.24	7.25		3.99	
1959	19.15	12.33		6.82	
1960	33.81	22.68		11.13	
1961	19.49	15.54		3.95	
1962	13.73	10.62		3.11	
1963	18.61	13.85		4.76	
1964	24.27	17.62		6.65	
1965	27.17	20.27		6.90	
1966	25.06	19.26		5.80	
1967	15.35	13.56		1.79	
1968	14.80	11.29		3.51	
1969	24.15	10.74	0.07	4.56	8.78
1970	29.96	14.78	1.68	4.05	9.45
1971	37.68	19.95	2.50	4.27	10.96
1972	36.10	18.71	3.44	4.49	9.46
1973	34.59	19.41	5.09	3.07	7.02
1974	34.65	20.59	7.13	3.05	3.88
1975	40.31	24.59	9.49	2.67	3.56
1976	39.25	21.65	10.34	4.17	3.09
1977	41.48	22.35	11.64	3.90	3.59
1978	52.89	25.47	15.46	6.66	5.30
1979	62.29	28.41	18.60	9.40	5.88
1980	64.59	27.57	19.63	11.27	6.12
1981	61.58	24.12	21.45	10.46	5.55
1982	65.29	26.38	22.37	11.17	5.37
1983	79.10	35.51	25.13	11.90	6.56
1984	94.72	42.32	30.09	14.74	7.57
1985	102.59	44.35	32.00	18.83	7.41
1986	112.57	49.63	34.56	20.30	8.08
1987	113.79	50.60	29.50	22.87	10.82
1988	121.12	54.05	35.65	19.70	11.72
1989	127.87	59.13	38.45	17.91	12.38
1990	139.12	63.48	44.44	17.47	13.73
1991	160.69	73.32	54.15	18.40	14.82
1992	189.26	89.41	57.16	24.55	18.14
1993	225.61	106.56	65.59	33.95	19.51
1994	268.25	114.22	87.90	36.06	30.07
1995	302.36	136.02	96.86	38.00	31.48
1996	348.63	155.01	109.66	48.55	35.41
1997	408.86	189.97	127.12	42.74	49.03
1998	438.60	189.90	151.92	47.28	49.50
1999	543.85	272.80	168.06	52.89	50.10
2000		277.22	189.03		

注：1953—1968年"科技三项费用"包括"科学事业费"。

a) Expense on S&T Promotion from 1953 to 1968 include the operating expenses for science.

8-11 国家财政用于抚恤和社会福利支出
Government Expenditure for Pensions and Social Welfare

单位：亿元 (100 million yuan)

年 份 Year	合 计 Total	抚恤支出 Pension for Handicapped and Bereaved Families	离退休费 Pension for Retires	社会救济福利费 Social Welfare and Relief Funds	救灾支出 Expenses on Disaster Relief	其 他 Others
1952	2.95	1.23		0.66	1.06	
1953	3.62	1.55		0.77	1.30	
1954	6.04	1.76		1.08	3.20	
1955	4.94	2.03		1.25	1.66	
1956	5.67	1.75		1.61	2.31	
1957	5.29	1.52		1.36	2.41	
1958	3.22	1.20		1.15	0.87	
1959	4.41	1.11		1.17	2.13	
1960	7.94	1.46		2.15	4.33	
1961	10.09	1.45		2.44	6.20	
1962	8.14	1.73		2.39	4.02	
1963	10.15	1.93		2.80	5.42	
1964	17.04	2.06		2.87	12.11	
1965	10.94	2.31		2.92	5.71	
1966	9.21	2.27		3.19	3.75	
1967	8.16	2.44		2.91	2.81	
1968	5.61	1.97				
1969	6.67	2.39				
1970	6.53	2.67		3.86		
1971	6.83	2.61		2.69	1.53	
1972	8.15	2.88		2.95	2.32	
1973	9.97	3.32		3.29	3.36	
1974	9.16	3.49		3.40	2.27	
1975	12.88	3.75		3.47	5.66	
1976	24.07	4.15		3.86	16.06	
1977	18.76	4.64		3.98	10.14	
1978	18.91	2.93	2.34	4.62	9.02	
1979	22.11	3.57	2.89	5.41	10.24	
1980	20.31	4.51	3.41	5.36	7.03	
1981	21.72	4.54	3.44	5.08	8.66	
1982	21.43	4.86	3.48	5.45	7.64	
1983	24.04	5.39	3.62	6.58	8.45	
1984	25.16	6.20	3.64	7.92	7.40	
1985	31.15	7.13	4.88	7.71	10.25	1.18
1986	35.58	8.77	5.77	8.69	10.64	1.71
1987	37.40	9.87	6.68	9.04	9.91	1.90
1988	41.77	11.32	7.59	9.73	10.64	2.49
1989	49.60	14.43	8.56	10.80	12.88	2.93
1990	55.04	16.61	9.60	12.07	13.33	3.43
1991	67.32	17.21	10.32	13.18	22.51	4.10
1992	66.45	18.45	12.40	14.36	15.89	5.35
1993	75.27	20.78	14.09	17.01	15.40	7.99
1994	95.14	24.78	20.12	20.55	19.42	10.27
1995	115.46	29.11	22.78	24.19	27.27	12.11
1996	128.03	32.78	10.67	28.98	39.06	16.54
1997	142.14	37.62	13.51	36.57	34.51	19.93
1998	171.26	40.38	16.24	35.29	52.32	27.03
1999	179.88	54.57	19.68	48.52	34.05	23.06
2000	213.03	59.72	23.72	59.71	28.73	41.15

注：1.1977年及以前各年退休费包括在抚恤支出中。从1996年起离退休费不包括已划入行政事业离退休经费支出类中的由民政部门管理的地方离退休费。

2.从1976年起救灾支出中包括抗震救灾费。

a) Prior to 1978, the pension for retires was included in the pension for handicapped and bereaved families. Since 1996, the pension for retires had excluded the local pension for retires which had been transferred to the pension of administration operation and run by the department of civil affairs.

b) Since 1976, expense on disaster relief include the expense on earthquake relief.

8-12 国家财政债务还本付息支出

Government Payment for the Principal and Interest of Debts

单位:亿元　　(100 million yuan)

年份 Year	合计 Total	国内债务还本付息 Payment for the Principal and Interest of Domestic Debts	国外债务还本付息 Payment for the Principal and Interest of Foreign Debts	归还向人民银行借款的利息 Payment of the Interest of Loans from People's Bank	债务收入大于支出部分增列偿债基金 Sinking Fund from the Excessive Part of the Revenue from Borrowings minus the Expenditure for Debts.
1950	0.03	0.03			
1951	0.42	0.40	0.01	0.01	
1952	3.92	0.58	0.23	3.11	
1953	0.91	0.65	0.26		
1954	2.21	0.89	1.32		
1955	6.56	1.58	4.98		
1956	7.22	1.25	5.97		
1957	8.26	2.18	6.08		
1958	9.04	1.81	7.23		
1959	9.69	2.58	7.11		
1960	10.46	3.73	6.73		
1961	10.93	4.35	6.58		
1962	10.37	3.95	6.42		
1963	7.58	4.72	2.86		
1964	5.23	4.27	0.96		
1965	6.36	5.66	0.70		
1966	3.91	3.91			
1967	2.01	2.01			
1968	2.00	2.00			
1972	0.50	0.50			
1973	0.50	0.50			
1974	0.50	0.50			
1980	28.58		24.40	4.18	
1981	62.89		57.89	5.00	
1982	55.52		49.62	5.90	
1983	42.47		36.56	5.91	
1984	28.90		22.73	6.17	
1985	39.56		32.59	6.97	
1986	50.17	7.98	34.50	7.69	
1987	79.83	23.18	51.96	4.69	
1988	76.76	28.44	42.59	5.73	
1989	72.37	19.30	45.84	7.23	
1990	190.07	113.42	68.21	8.44	
1991	246.80	156.69	80.22	9.89	
1992	438.57	342.42	80.26	15.89	
1993	336.22	224.30	89.22	22.70	
1994	499.36	364.96	107.17	27.23	
1995	882.96	784.06	71.69	27.21	
1996	1355.03	1266.29	60.76	27.98	
1997	1918.37	1820.40	70.76	27.21	
1998	2352.92	2245.79	76.60	30.53	
1999	1910.53	1792.33	90.99	27.21	12.90
2000	1579.82	1552.21	27.61		

注：从2000年开始，表中数据均为债务还本支出。

a) Since 2000, expenditure in this table refers to payment for the principal of debts.

8-13 中央和地方财政收入及比重

Total Revenue and Ratio of Central and Local Governments

年份 Year	绝对数(亿元) Total Revenue (100 million yuan)			比重(%) Ratio (%)	
	全国 Total	中央 Central Government	地方 Local Governments	中央 Central Government	地方 Local Governments
1953	213.24	177.02	36.22	83.0	17.0
1954	245.17	187.72	57.45	76.6	23.4
1955	249.27	193.44	55.83	77.6	22.4
1956	280.19	222.10	58.09	79.3	20.7
1957	303.20	222.94	80.26	73.5	26.5
1958	379.62	305.26	74.36	80.4	19.6
1959	487.12	118.78	368.34	24.4	75.6
1960	572.29	142.80	429.49	25.0	75.0
1961	356.06	76.65	279.41	21.5	78.5
1962	313.55	93.07	220.48	29.7	70.3
1963	342.25	78.92	263.33	23.1	76.9
1964	399.54	100.81	298.73	25.2	74.8
1965	473.32	156.07	317.25	33.0	67.0
1966	558.71	196.49	362.22	35.2	64.8
1967	419.36	132.44	286.92	31.6	68.4
1968	361.25	107.11	254.14	29.6	70.4
1969	526.76	171.10	355.66	32.5	67.5
1970	662.90	182.95	479.95	27.6	72.4
1971	744.73	119.36	625.37	16.0	84.0
1972	766.56	105.81	660.75	13.8	86.2
1973	809.67	119.86	689.81	14.8	85.2
1974	783.14	134.77	648.37	17.2	82.8
1975	815.61	96.63	718.98	11.8	88.2
1976	776.58	98.91	677.67	12.7	87.3
1977	874.46	113.85	760.61	13.0	87.0
1978	1132.26	175.77	956.49	15.5	84.5
1979	1146.38	231.34	915.04	20.2	79.8
1980	1159.93	284.45	875.48	24.5	75.5
1981	1175.79	311.07	864.72	26.5	73.5
1982	1212.33	346.84	865.49	28.6	71.4
1983	1366.95	490.01	876.94	35.8	64.2
1984	1642.86	665.47	977.39	40.5	59.5
1985	2004.82	769.63	1235.19	38.4	61.6
1986	2122.01	778.42	1343.59	36.7	63.3
1987	2199.35	736.29	1463.06	33.5	66.5
1988	2357.24	774.76	1582.48	32.9	67.1
1989	2664.90	822.52	1842.38	30.9	69.1
1990	2937.10	992.42	1944.68	33.8	66.2
1991	3149.48	938.25	2211.23	29.8	70.2
1992	3483.37	979.51	2503.86	28.1	71.9
1993	4348.95	957.51	3391.44	22.0	78.0
1994	5218.10	2906.50	2311.60	55.7	44.3
1995	6242.20	3256.62	2985.58	52.2	47.8
1996	7407.99	3661.07	3746.92	49.4	50.6
1997	8651.14	4226.92	4424.22	48.9	51.1
1998	9875.95	4892.00	4983.95	49.5	50.5
1999	11444.08	5849.21	5594.87	51.1	48.9
2000	13395.23	6989.17	6406.06	52.2	47.8

注:1.中央、地方财政收入均为本级收入。
2.本表数字不包括国内外债务收入。

a) The revenue of the central and local governments refers to revenue actually collected by the central and local governments.
b) Revenue in this table does not include revenue from domestic and foreign borrowings.

8-14 中央和地方财政支出及比重

Total Expenditures and Ratio of Central and Local Governments

年份 Year	绝对数(亿元) Total Expenditure (100 million yuan) 全国 Total	中央 Central Government	地方 Local Governments	比重(%) Ratio (%) 中央 Central Government	地方 Local Governments
1953	219.21	162.05	57.16	73.9	26.1
1954	244.11	183.70	60.41	75.3	24.7
1955	262.73	201.05	61.68	76.5	23.5
1956	298.52	210.02	88.50	70.4	29.6
1957	295.95	210.03	85.92	71.0	29.0
1958	400.36	177.22	223.14	44.3	55.7
1959	543.17	249.34	293.83	45.9	54.1
1960	643.68	278.63	365.05	43.3	56.7
1961	356.09	160.32	195.77	45.0	55.0
1962	294.88	181.64	113.24	61.6	38.4
1963	332.05	192.31	139.74	57.9	42.1
1964	393.79	224.86	168.93	57.1	42.9
1965	459.97	284.17	175.80	61.8	38.2
1966	537.65	339.11	198.54	63.1	36.9
1967	439.84	269.94	169.90	61.4	38.6
1968	357.84	219.49	138.35	61.3	38.7
1969	525.86	319.16	206.70	60.7	39.3
1970	649.41	382.37	267.04	58.9	41.1
1971	732.17	435.67	296.50	59.5	40.5
1972	765.86	431.40	334.46	56.3	43.7
1973	808.78	449.33	359.45	55.6	44.4
1974	790.25	397.84	392.41	50.3	49.7
1975	820.88	409.40	411.48	49.9	50.1
1976	806.20	377.63	428.57	46.8	53.2
1977	843.53	393.70	449.83	46.7	53.3
1978	1122.09	532.12	589.97	47.4	52.6
1979	1281.79	655.08	626.71	51.1	48.9
1980	1228.83	666.81	562.02	54.3	45.7
1981	1138.41	625.65	512.76	55.0	45.0
1982	1229.98	651.81	578.17	53.0	47.0
1983	1409.52	759.60	649.92	53.9	46.1
1984	1701.02	893.33	807.69	52.5	47.5
1985	2004.25	795.25	1209.00	39.7	60.3
1986	2204.91	836.36	1368.55	37.9	62.1
1987	2262.18	845.63	1416.55	37.4	62.6
1988	2491.21	845.04	1646.17	33.9	66.1
1989	2823.78	888.77	1935.01	31.5	68.5
1990	3083.59	1004.47	2079.12	32.6	67.4
1991	3386.62	1090.81	2295.81	32.2	67.8
1992	3742.20	1170.44	2571.76	31.3	68.7
1993	4642.30	1312.06	3330.24	28.3	71.7
1994	5792.62	1754.43	4038.19	30.3	69.7
1995	6823.72	1995.39	4828.33	29.2	70.8
1996	7937.55	2151.27	5786.28	27.1	72.9
1997	9233.56	2532.50	6701.06	27.4	72.6
1998	10798.18	3125.60	7672.58	28.9	71.1
1999	13187.67	4152.33	9035.34	31.5	68.5
2000	15886.50	5519.85	10366.65	34.7	65.3

注：1. 中央、地方财政支出均为本级支出。
2. 本表数字2000年以前不包括国内外债务还本付息支出和利用国外借款收入安排的基本建设支出。从2000年起，全国财政支出和中央财政支出中包括国内外债务付息支出。

a) The expenditure of the central and local governments refers to expenditure actually collected by the central and local governments.

b) Expenditure in this table does not include the payment of the principal and interest of domestic and foreign debts and the expenditure for capital construction using foreign loans.

8-15 预算外资金分项目收入

Extra-budgetary Revenue by Item

单位：亿元　　　　(100 million yuan)

年　份 Year	合　计 Total	# 行政事业性收费 Revenue of Administrative and Institutional Units	# 乡镇自筹、统筹资金 Revenue form Fund-raising Programs of Township Governments	# 地方财政收入 Revenue of Local Governments	# 国有企业和主管部门收入 State-owned Enterprises and Its Governing Department
1952	13.62			12.53	1.09
1953	8.91	2.07		1.40	5.44
1954	14.23	3.34		2.07	8.82
1955	17.02	3.68		3.27	10.07
1956	21.42	3.85		5.00	12.57
1957	26.33	3.80		5.66	16.87
1958	55.99	9.29		17.59	29.11
1959	96.55	11.78		35.39	49.38
1960	117.78	23.13		23.39	71.26
1961	57.40	15.61		13.29	28.50
1962	63.63	15.21		20.50	27.92
1963	51.85	11.99		7.19	32.67
1964	65.86	16.07		8.87	40.92
1965	75.56	18.74		9.47	47.35
1966	81.13	20.00		10.36	50.77
1967	83.61	22.00		9.72	51.89
1968	77.44	24.00		9.96	43.48
1969	87.42	26.00		12.19	49.23
1970	100.94	28.00		13.45	59.49
1971	118.56	30.00		14.72	73.84
1972	134.24	31.66		23.28	79.30
1973	191.29	32.57		24.14	134.58
1974	219.72	34.60		22.65	162.47
1975	251.48	42.30		27.86	181.32
1976	275.32	48.81		28.35	198.16
1977	311.31	56.84		30.76	223.71
1978	347.11	63.41		31.09	252.61
1979	452.85	68.66		39.94	344.25
1980	557.40	74.44		40.85	442.11
1981	601.07	84.90		41.30	474.87
1982	802.74	101.15		45.27	656.32
1983	967.68	113.88		49.79	804.01
1984	1188.48	142.52		55.23	990.73
1985	1530.03	233.22		44.08	1252.73
1986	1737.31	294.22		43.20	1399.89
1987	2028.80	358.41		44.61	1625.78
1988	2360.77	438.94		48.94	1872.89
1989	2658.83	500.66		54.36	2103.81
1990	2708.64	576.95		60.59	2071.10
1991	3243.30	697.00		68.77	2477.53
1992	3854.92	885.45		90.88	2878.59
1993	1432.54	1317.83		114.71	
1994	1862.53	1722.50		140.03	
1995	2406.50	2234.85		171.65	
1996	3893.34	3395.75	272.90	224.69	
1997	2826.00	2414.32	295.78	115.90	
1998	3082.29	1981.92	337.31		54.67
1999	3385.17	2354.28	358.86		50.11

注：1993—1995年和1996年的预算外资金收入范围分别有所调整，与以前各年不可比。从1997年起，预算外资金收入不包括纳入预算内管理的政府性基金（收费），与以前各年也不可比。

a) Since adjustment on the coverage of extra-budgetary revenues from 1993 to 1995 and in 1998 has made, the figures are not comparable with the previous years. Since 1997, the extra-budgetary revenues do not include the intra-budgetary government fund (fee), the figures are not comparable with the previous years.

8-16 预算外资金分项目支出

Extra-budgetary Expenditures by Item

单位:亿元　　(100 million yuan)

年份 Year	合计 Total	# 基本建设支出 Capital Construction	# 专项支出 Special Expenditure	# 事业行政经费 Operating and Administrative Expenses	# 乡镇统筹支出 Expenditure by Township Governments	# 其他支出 Other Expenses
1996	3838.32	1490.23	307.27	1254.36	136.39	650.07
1997	2685.54	502.03	311.59	1280.19	288.69	303.04
1998	2918.31	393.98	423.60	1588.28	335.26	177.19
1999	3139.14	539.82		1816.13	350.34	305.40

注：1996年预算外资金支出范围有所调整，与以前各年不可比。从1997年起，预算外资金支出不包括纳入预算内管理的政府性基金(收费)，与以前各年也不可比。

a) Because adjustment on the coverage of extra-budgetary expenditures in 1998 has made, the figures are not comparable with the previous years. Since 1997, the extra-budgetary expenditures do not include the intra-budgetary government fund (fee), the figures are not comparable with the previous years.

8-17 政策性补贴支出

Government Expenditure for Price Subsidies

单位：亿元　　(100 million yuan)

年份 Year	合计 Total	粮棉油价格补贴 Subsidies on Price Increases in Grain, Cotton and Edible Oil	平抑物价等补贴 Subsidies on Curbing Price Increase	肉食品价格补贴 Subsidies on Increase in Meat Price	其他价格补贴 Other Price Subsidies
1978	11.14	11.14			
1979	79.20	54.85			24.35
1980	117.71	102.80			14.91
1981	159.41	142.22			17.19
1982	172.22	156.19			16.03
1983	197.37	182.13			15.24
1984	218.34	201.67			16.67
1985	261.79	198.66		33.52	29.61
1986	257.48	169.37		42.24	45.87
1987	294.60	195.43		42.74	56.43
1988	316.82	204.03		40.40	72.39
1989	373.55	262.52		41.29	69.74
1990	380.80	267.61		41.78	71.41
1991	373.77	267.03		42.46	64.28
1992	321.64	224.35		38.54	58.75
1993	299.30	224.75		29.86	44.69
1994	314.47	202.03	41.25	25.41	45.78
1995	364.89	228.91	50.17	24.17	61.64
1996	453.91	311.39	53.38	27.46	61.68
1997	551.96	413.67	43.20	28.25	66.84
1998	712.12	565.04	28.10	26.09	92.89
1999	697.64	492.29	14.25	20.55	170.55
2000	1042.28	758.74	17.71	19.39	246.44

注：政策性补贴支出，1985年以前冲减财政收入，1986年以后作为支出项目列在财政支出中。

a) The government expenditure for price subsidies were listed as a negative revenue item prior to 1986, but they have been listed as a government expenditure item since 1986.

8-18 中央和地方预算外资金收支及比重

Total Extra-budgetary Revenues and Expenditures and Ratio of Central and Local Governments

项 目 Item	绝对数(亿元) Total (100 million yuan)			比重(%) Ratio (%)	
	全国 Total	中央 Central Government	地方 Local Governments	中央 Central Government	地方 Local Governments
一、收 入 Revenue					
1982	802.74	270.70	532.04	33.7	66.3
1983	967.68	359.90	607.78	37.2	62.8
1984	1188.48	470.54	717.94	39.6	60.4
1985	1530.03	636.10	893.93	41.6	58.4
1986	1737.31	716.63	1020.68	41.2	58.8
1987	2028.80	828.03	1200.77	40.8	59.2
1988	2360.77	907.15	1453.62	38.4	61.6
1989	2658.83	1072.28	1586.55	40.3	59.7
1990	2708.64	1073.28	1635.36	39.6	60.4
1991	3243.30	1381.10	1862.20	42.6	57.4
1992	3854.92	1707.73	2147.19	44.3	55.7
1993	1432.54	245.90	1186.64	17.2	82.8
1994	1862.53	283.32	1579.21	15.2	84.8
1995	2406.50	317.57	2088.93	13.2	86.8
1996	3893.34	947.66	2945.68	24.3	75.7
1997	2826.00	145.08	2680.92	5.1	94.9
1998	3082.29	164.15	2918.14	5.3	94.7
1999	3385.17	230.45	3154.72	6.8	93.2
二、支 出 Expenditure					
1982	734.53	227.05	507.48	30.9	69.1
1983	875.81	300.38	575.43	34.3	65.7
1984	1114.74	420.24	694.50	37.7	62.3
1985	1375.03	562.05	812.98	40.9	59.1
1986	1578.37	640.94	937.43	40.6	59.4
1987	1840.75	741.61	1099.14	40.3	59.7
1988	2145.27	842.86	1302.41	39.3	60.7
1989	2503.10	975.87	1527.23	39.0	61.0
1990	2707.06	1037.69	1669.37	38.3	61.7
1991	3092.26	1263.27	1828.99	40.9	59.1
1992	3649.90	1592.81	2057.09	43.6	56.4
1993	1314.30	198.87	1115.43	15.1	84.9
1994	1710.39	225.02	1485.37	13.2	86.8
1995	2331.26	351.38	1979.88	15.1	84.9
1996	3838.32	1034.92	2803.40	27.0	73.0
1997	2685.54	143.91	2541.63	5.4	94.6
1998	2918.31	139.74	2778.57	4.8	95.2
1999	3139.14	164.82	2974.32	5.3	94.7

注：1993—1995年和1996年的预算外资金收支范围分别有所调整，与以前各年不可比。从1997年起，预算外资金收支不包括纳入预算内管理的政府性基金（收费），与以前各年也不可比。

a) Because adjustment on the coverage of extra-budgetary revenues and expenditures from 1993 to 1995 and in 1998 has made, the figures are not comparable with the previous years. Since 1997, the extra-budgetary revenues and expenditures do not include the intra-budgetary government fund (fee), the figures are not comparable with the previous years.

8-19 分地区财政收入（2000年）

Final Statement of Government Revenue by Region (2000)

单位：万元 (10 000 yuan)

地区	Region	收入合计 Total Revenue	增值税 Value-added Tax	营业税 Operation tax	企业所得税 Enterprises' Income Tax	企业所得税退税 Return for Enterprises' Income Tax	个人所得税 Individual Income Tax	资源税 Resources Tax
地方合计	**Total**	**64060557**	**11399679**	**16256742**	**10054992**	**-138525**	**5101814**	**636158**
北京	Beijing	3449968	459557	1490539	616582	-36314	563847	2213
天津	Tianjin	1336069	261214	381590	292561	-85	113352	3722
河北	Hebei	2487621	436945	461942	354946	-208	169936	47591
山西	Shanxi	1144762	255173	240567	111532	-6689	105842	50713
内蒙古	Inner Mongolia	950320	133854	186796	105983	-1403	50865	20415
辽宁	Liaoning	2956274	566997	800239	390181	-1034	220472	81230
吉林	Jilin	1038267	204117	255547	142840	-1502	69547	9024
黑龙江	Heilongjiang	1853379	461244	338898	133158	-2	97314	123510
上海	Shanghai	4853777	935468	1538082	1031183	-928	602434	
江苏	Jiangsu	4483097	1086395	960024	886525		332823	9514
浙江	Zhejiang	3427745	900353	972052	879077	-32023	292230	1998
安徽	Anhui	1787187	262559	319719	233524	-4865	94675	18343
福建	Fujian	2341061	353461	582053	321959	-3243	247517	7007
江西	Jiangxi	1115536	150826	263986	95048		57271	7415
山东	Shandong	4636788	896895	876638	818659	-408	247492	62164
河南	Henan	2464694	422382	481846	396014	-90	128764	24356
湖北	Hubei	2143450	337775	441120	254244	-4300	105913	15295
湖南	Hunan	1770403	260989	343357	135892	-16040	114397	6002
广东	Guangdong	9105560	1321309	2724229	1674188	-13	847976	9702
广西	Guangxi	1470539	206622	284979	147960	-322	101497	7795
海南	Hainan	391995	28575	115710	24774		42949	5359
四川	Sichuan	2338630	338425	566747	347832	-297	126431	37619
重庆	Chongqing	872442	147717	242542	89999	-6185	72999	10477
贵州	Guizhou	852324	121820	203388	67843	-231	47324	7365
云南	Yunnan	1807450	313725	359978	201689	-8829	78343	9235
西藏	Tibet	53848	7892	19390	16123	-8	3127	1654
陕西	Shaanxi	1149711	189980	317014	116123	-2293	44466	13046
甘肃	Gansu	612849	119471	158995	60957	-857	25921	8486
青海	Qinghai	165843	29822	41495	22246	-6387	7141	3706
宁夏	Ningxia	208244	35449	65682	26147	-2464	12531	605
新疆	Xinjiang	790724	152668	221598	59203	-1505	76418	30597

8-19 续表 1 continued

单位：万元 (10 000 yuan)

地　区	Region	固定资产投资方向调节税 Tax on the Adjustment of the Investment in the Fixed Assets	城市维护建设税 Tax on Town Maintenance and Construction	房产税 Tax on Real Estates	印花税 Stamp Tax	城镇土地使用税 Tax on the Use of Urban Land	土地增值税 Land Value Added Tax	车船使用和牌照税 Tax on the Use of Vehicles and Ships
地方合计	**Total**	**462837**	**3489588**	**2093819**	**989006**	**647648**	**83936**	**234177**
北　京	Beijing	21388	173539	190116	47729	28860	5284	14553
天　津	Tianjin	8629	70994	46716	11616	6852		4354
河　北	Hebei	18415	118616	73719	12083	29610	2583	8284
山　西	Shanxi	23044	64317	41342	7894	21138	184	3674
内蒙古	Inner Mongolia	6935	46060	43785	6825	28918	1581	4873
辽　宁	Liaoning	28165	176239	142784	27242	60668	5534	9726
吉　林	Jilin	10903	66332	44842	6700	7520	1664	3181
黑龙江	Heilongjiang	20873	156717	60581	7731	31649	996	5566
上　海	Shanghai	10251	220122	132416	331773	20098	6180	10941
江　苏	Jiangsu	15274	266210	118332	32734	15133	1478	17393
浙　江	Zhejiang	10604	235683	93244	22900	9949	3993	8138
安　徽	Anhui	3274	88339	46044	9275	33532	3529	7683
福　建	Fujian	8784	97646	95496	18309	15746	4326	6055
江　西	Jiangxi	11452	55555	26620	4517	12833	1211	2323
山　东	Shandong	107162	276205	155591	22440	88204	7423	31852
河　南	Henan	18853	136424	67201	10749	18045	530	6212
湖　北	Hubei	16039	118426	55886	14048	39993	559	6984
湖　南	Hunan	9413	113841	44018	12686	21589	863	4290
广　东	Guangdong	21122	299973	248071	329418	43320	26728	47176
广　西	Guangxi	9600	57294	40889	3668	17190	1137	3184
海　南	Hainan		14831	23232	1998	2747	471	2346
四　川	Sichuan	10209	132280	69798	10765	14827	3175	4819
重　庆	Chongqing	6703	47456	25366	5668	6464	932	1342
贵　州	Guizhou	9579	59654	27256	3210	12804	1545	1746
云　南	Yunnan	32297	205483	57041	11475	28601	659	9667
西　藏	Tibet		2117		168		144	
陕　西	Shaanxi	10467	71585	50331	6364	17556	609	4697
甘　肃	Gansu	4055	41067	25834	2693	5409	46	1340
青　海	Qinghai	1952	10483	6242	874	897	40	395
宁　夏	Ningxia	1119	12124	8874	1425	2965	275	431
新　疆	Xinjiang	6276	53976	32152	4029	4531	257	952

8-19 续表 2 continued

单位：万元 (10 000 yuan)

地　区	Region	屠宰税 Slaughter Tax	筵席税 Banquet Tax	农业税 Agricultural Tax	农业特产税 Tax on Special Agricultural Products	牧业税 Tax on the Animal Husbandry	耕地占用税 Tax on The Occupancy of Cultivated Land	契税 Contract Tax
地方合计	**Total**	**317660**	**4362**	**1654453**	**1307434**	**27245**	**353160**	**1310811**
北　京	Beijing	524		6074	2651		6972	133750
天　津	Tianjin	210		3348	760		2086	29892
河　北	Hebei	6587		70928	28042		18220	25510
山　西	Shanxi	1974		34899	8254		6156	4349
内蒙古	Inner Mongolia	11723	3805	66947	34290	14126	4382	6699
辽　宁	Liaoning	5826	106	36821	33425		10099	69416
吉　林	Jilin	2061		30939	21627		9907	17644
黑龙江	Heilongjiang	2854		102767	34638		5999	32224
上　海	Shanghai	696		19088	1826		10727	143760
江　苏	Jiangsu	19710		104674	35324		30340	159564
浙　江	Zhejiang	7874		50455	24468		34747	117501
安　徽	Anhui	5186		260827	30003		10621	23493
福　建	Fujian	5051		18220	81425		13474	55799
江　西	Jiangxi	35022		55788	58859		2163	15592
山　东	Shandong	15091		76084	176148		31222	40160
河　南	Henan	21348		81285	97672		12244	26601
湖　北	Hubei	30747		94921	83895	28	15329	22321
湖　南	Hunan	25219		84512	45314		12656	16591
广　东	Guangdong	20617		72941	32677		36638	230025
广　西	Guangxi	9494		42808	64394		13406	14129
海　南	Hainan	1830		5357	29744		7126	8107
四　川	Sichuan	52642		111741	53582	105	14887	50732
重　庆	Chongqing	11967		41483	15519		5860	13140
贵　州	Guizhou	6014		37333	47991		8453	6837
云　南	Yunnan	8163		38893	152967	106	12693	18955
西　藏	Tibet						45	
陕　西	Shaanxi	1077	451	39320	73438	14	9330	9268
甘　肃	Gansu	3432		25470	22467	3795	3494	4549
青　海	Qinghai	1366		4230	2113	4635	380	1163
宁　夏	Ningxia	176		7454	607	178	1079	3235
新　疆	Xinjiang	3179		28846	13314	4258	2425	9805

8-19 续表 3 continued

单位：万元 (10 000 yuan)

地　区	Region	国有资产经营收益 State-downed Assets Profit	国有企业计划亏损补贴 Planning Subsidies to Loss-suffering Stated-owned Enterprises	行政性收费收入 Income from Administrative Fees	罚没收入 Penalty and confiscatory income	土地和海域有偿使用收入 Income on the Use of Land and Sea Area	专项收入 Expert Project Income	其他收入 Other Income
地方合计	**Total**	**601691**	**-2301464**	**2857709**	**3022454**	**37808**	**2259787**	**1295576**
北　京	Beijing	1135	-541807	71791	73001	8592	101923	7469
天　津	Tianjin		-50000	56812	42987	1691	37624	9144
河　北	Hebei	42192	-38442	245937	179019	4008	118147	53011
山　西	Shanxi	17165	-31298	43742	69410	63	50817	20500
内蒙古	Inner Mongolia	19615	-6800	70349	36595	147	36734	16221
辽　宁	Liaoning	37002	-96570	86441	114121	4659	127109	19376
吉　林	Jilin	4304	-63860	66226	64454	169	44389	19692
黑龙江	Heilongjiang	15565	-29919	50048	66969	296	108947	24756
上　海	Shanghai		-372325	3079	96811		111301	794
江　苏	Jiangsu	5230	-75362	48458	219647	1103	162162	30412
浙　江	Zhejiang	3021	-547970	53205	122881	2255	153498	7612
安　徽	Anhui	13026	-26703	179404	69858	222	48925	56694
福　建	Fujian	46372	-3553	74946	101764	695	64036	127716
江　西	Jiangxi	14667	-2645	89973	88753	2	34159	34146
山　东	Shandong	33382	-63177	305651	152440	6679	195281	77510
河　南	Henan	38386	-20593	144797	190951	526	95030	65161
湖　北	Hubei	5184	-50036	185416	165092	573	59955	128043
湖　南	Hunan	15266	-49152	185640	188953	258	68341	125508
广　东	Guangdong	76485	-59686	410541	407084	43	210140	74856
广　西	Guangxi	51579	-9420	125257	113996	134	62290	100979
海　南	Hainan	9035	-5136	38475	19969	3554	8132	2810
四　川	Sichuan	66579	-31376	111452	131130	41	67373	47112
重　庆	Chongqing	17408	-25379	46241	57610	300	28658	8155
贵　州	Guizhou	23758	-6302	43044	41360		32141	48392
云　南	Yunnan	9014	-27211	15036	76332	1	75593	127544
西　藏	Tibet	837	-10156	834	2029	402	1607	7643
陕　西	Shaanxi	14469	-26890	45401	59881	319	65399	18289
甘　肃	Gansu	6354	-13259	25057	20944	31	35065	22033
青　海	Qinghai	6852	-374	4847	4183	370	7307	9865
宁　夏	Ningxia	4534	-967	9535	8238		7662	1350
新　疆	Xinjiang	3275	-15096	20074	35992	675	40042	2783

8-20 分地区财政支出（2000年）

Final Statement of Government Expenditure by Region (2000)

单位：万元　　(10 000 yuan)

地　区	Region	支出合计 Total Expenditure	基本建设 Expenditure for Capital Construction	挖潜改造支出 Expenditure for Innovation Enterprises	地质勘探费 Expenditure for Geological Prospecting	科技三项费用 Expenditure for Science and Technology Promotion	流动资金 Expenditure for Circulating Funds	支援农村生产支出 Expenditure for Supporting Agriculture Production	农业综合开发支出 Expenditure for Comprehensive Development of Agriculture
地方合计	**Total**	**104542771**	**11679727**	**4980676**	**441429**	**1206701**	**215600**	**2293766**	**929886**
北　京	Beijing	4429969	574884	327083	4349	38441	6627	98712	24164
天　津	Tianjin	1870521	297084	161112	2534	36933		22066	7930
河　北	Hebei	4155374	305316	165326	18554	47416		70714	36847
山　西	Shanxi	2250554	161358	43291	18577	22579	19058	57393	23782
内蒙古	Inner Mongolia	2472681	343664	92525	25346	18456	77	55171	27614
辽　宁	Liaoning	5180841	529498	263831	17538	96968		137441	43126
吉　林	Jilin	2606694	212105	97099	17266	26234	3310	26416	23233
黑龙江	Heilongjiang	3818736	271794	135381	15719	42156	2000	66112	41407
上　海	Shanghai	6085621	1326644	753121	1194	13515	150000	81937	28396
江　苏	Jiangsu	5912810	457956	523863	10526	79241	1935	167076	65470
浙　江	Zhejiang	4312958	280042	263372	9425	91987		106999	52368
安　徽	Anhui	3234728	410893	137764	20709	21049		65691	40684
福　建	Fujian	3241839	291301	110869	9268	51227	952	90951	28217
江　西	Jiangxi	2234722	277294	71371	24985	10025		46747	30841
山　东	Shandong	6130774	295068	395370	11872	92459	683	127960	72394
河　南	Henan	4455295	327994	163141	20310	39708	3814	76312	45373
湖　北	Hubei	3687701	282037	73745	14817	39921	11388	74360	31535
湖　南	Hunan	3478324	380819	86561	23230	37969		67576	32433
广　东	Guangdong	10803189	1533503	292549	12874	214706	3398	268853	40043
广　西	Guangxi	2584866	252679	71491	11910	15229		83874	27562
海　南	Hainan	641193	78697	3224	2106	1615		17061	7549
四　川	Sichuan	4520041	482355	241783	27539	35980	9822	77607	56969
重　庆	Chongqing	1876433	258184	74243	6146	21341		24481	21094
贵　州	Guizhou	2015698	248180	64123	18772	13425	580	47462	16442
云　南	Yunnan	4141074	604507	158680	13783	32685	1329	163951	28987
西　藏	Tibet	599693	145768	3465	9974	2261		13397	8877
陕　西	Shaanxi	2717597	414083	67498	22967	25926	571	67413	21312
甘　肃	Gansu	1882322	204571	71981	17088	13614	36	38128	10115
青　海	Qinghai	682614	109123	12296	5341	5516		12663	7428
宁　夏	Ningxia	608380	93938	32790	5577	6495	20	14928	8558
新　疆	Xinjiang	1909529	228388	21728	21133	11624		24314	19136

8-20 续表 1 continued

单位：万元 (10 000 yuan)

地区	Region	农林水利气象等部门事业费 Expenditure for Operating Expenses of Agriculture, Forestry, Water Conservancy and Meteorology	工业交通部门事业费 Expenditure for Operating Expenses of Departments of Industry & Transportation	流通部门事业费 Expenditure for Operating Expenses of Department of Commerce	文体广播事业费 Expenditure for Operating Expenses of Departments of Culture, Sport & Broadcasting	教育事业费 Expenditure for Operating Expenses of Education	科学事业费 Expenditure for Operating Expenses of Department of Science	卫生经费 Expenditure for Public Health
地方合计	**Total**	**3671046**	**900214**	**178517**	**2665966**	**16241384**	**777783**	**4823944**
北京	Beijing	39582	20127	2187	92628	600709	62070	285305
天津	Tianjin	16478	6975	251	46354	308729	13301	86869
河北	Hebei	106508	62908	7212	107250	736530	20793	174629
山西	Shanxi	73472	18930	3005	64985	381627	10807	104507
内蒙古	Inner Mongolia	152357	14557	4941	66084	297521	12018	91072
辽宁	Liaoning	102491	40697	9494	101047	659091	32621	171323
吉林	Jilin	139530	27089	11094	60911	358104	17547	93788
黑龙江	Heilongjiang	280119	40174	13640	85710	489795	27297	136114
上海	Shanghai	42525	32763	1113	116716	841031	73169	325811
江苏	Jiangsu	146388	37825	4636	170500	1174225	46259	325667
浙江	Zhejiang	159929	63785	4050	136936	781943	39404	272422
安徽	Anhui	99562	22626	3549	79151	539913	13907	117124
福建	Fujian	99551	35932	8090	100475	619670	31231	161411
江西	Jiangxi	70232	21970	6501	54808	381436	11859	103154
山东	Shandong	211560	45107	7305	175745	1181042	38543	282598
河南	Henan	140367	35940	5190	114886	773334	23362	172990
湖北	Hubei	112524	39536	10357	98803	576580	15419	190881
湖南	Hunan	121524	30763	9375	90316	508830	17541	118790
广东	Guangdong	333980	47350	12219	263304	1447466	109580	477313
广西	Guangxi	86498	16167	2502	81826	447127	21344	116401
海南	Hainan	22809	4044	822	16514	96278	3826	28021
四川	Sichuan	307943	35401	10614	106266	648048	32961	218952
重庆	Chongqing	49799	6567	1565	33740	254532	7293	80400
贵州	Guizhou	96471	18838	5337	57826	317809	15448	110566
云南	Yunnan	199080	73411	19139	106336	623109	33796	223789
西藏	Tibet	27320	19172	619	20080	69788	1868	32365
陕西	Shaanxi	162059	43863	9090	76041	384560	14902	82890
甘肃	Gansu	122342	11970	1322	57512	275477	12703	80568
青海	Qinghai	30192	8532	597	13867	72712	1918	28220
宁夏	Ningxia	33106	3945	1763	18094	80830	4583	23519
新疆	Xinjiang	84748	13250	938	51255	313538	10413	106485

8-20 续表 2 continued

单位：万元 (10 000 yuan)

地 区	Region	税务等部门的事业费 Expenditure for Operating Expenses of Department of Tax, etc.	抚恤和社会福利救济费 Expenditure for Pensions and Relief Funds for Social Welfare	行政事业单位离退休经费 Expenditure for Retired Persons in Administrative Department	社会保障补助支出 Expenditure on Subsidies to Social Security Programs	国防支出 Expenditure for National Defense	行政管理费 Expenditure for Government Administration	外交外事支出 Expenditure for Foreign Affairs	武装警察部队支出 Expenditure for Armed Police Troops
地方合计	**Total**	**4775360**	**2108210**	**4352977**	**5529445**	**90447**	**9366543**	**88249**	**132513**
北 京	Beijing	175772	111436	181622	44755	780	209237	1141	
天 津	Tianjin	45880	28386	7425	174027	785	89182	1886	751
河 北	Hebei	314599	106812	204414	225350	3239	373495	4783	3188
山 西	Shanxi	102755	51541	140649	182633	2310	271913	753	1784
内蒙古	Inner Mongolia	144599	40656	152047	146199	1809	242583	838	2713
辽 宁	Liaoning	295883	145394	226971	735991	8515	309706	15102	2564
吉 林	Jilin	130120	49705	177174	192626	2602	180167	3205	6863
黑龙江	Heilongjiang	217637	58615	47216	484787	3891	259248	2098	6855
上 海	Shanghai	155832	72495	59543	64537	2111	226210	7414	
江 苏	Jiangsu	203468	135494	205180	116273	3702	557050	6225	7371
浙 江	Zhejiang	263612	80094	35101	57559	3015	439777	3070	7465
安 徽	Anhui	116467	79268	181575	192444	3704	347527	3498	2632
福 建	Fujian	148725	59513	158782	69452	6656	270645	1973	9364
江 西	Jiangxi	100364	45784	83767	162072	1332	210217	622	2546
山 东	Shandong	288353	155043	248829	160953	3840	622058	3900	3908
河 南	Henan	208574	101567	259003	270557	1485	478380	820	
湖 北	Hubei	138291	88514	132295	285541	1820	369245	1131	2434
湖 南	Hunan	158395	73506	200466	281159	3367	327797	1084	3791
广 东	Guangdong	550512	143037	429525	197211	8122	1009542	6656	27060
广 西	Guangxi	174081	39947	95354	77596	4027	282021	5627	5409
海 南	Hainan	52246	14433	32042	32649	828	64798	1182	1314
四 川	Sichuan	137757	100685	200030	277924	7933	513038	3265	7233
重 庆	Chongqing	42969	54157	123270	205691	1685	185102	650	7452
贵 州	Guizhou	70756	31922	12892	118670	1659	243089	1320	1248
云 南	Yunnan	191333	88609	263218	158853	6215	372394	3134	10317
西 藏	Tibet	9178	9279	11320	10758	541	106392	511	1651
陕 西	Shaanxi	154185	56709	104432	250022	900	276547	3107	2324
甘 肃	Gansu	69573	34235	95170	135710	1024	195859	1394	973
青 海	Qinghai	24213	14014	78829	82051	512	67060	489	783
宁 夏	Ningxia	21483	8843	25108	53824	417	45521	957	532
新 疆	Xinjiang	67748	28517	179728	81571	1621	220743	414	1988

8-20 续表 3 continued

单位：万元 (10 000 yuan)

地 区	Region	公检法司支出 Expenditure for Public Security Agency, Procuratorial Agency and Court of Justice	城市维护费 Expenditure for City Maintenance	政策性补贴支出 Expenditure for Price Subsidies	支援不发达地区支出 Expenditure for Supporting Underdeveloped Areas	海域开发建设和场地使用费支出 Expenditure for Developing Land and Sea Area	专项支出 Expenditure for Special Items	其他支出 Other Expenditure
地方合计	**Total**	**7139953**	**4677936**	**3958598**	**1229521**	**10201**	**2078419**	**7997760**
北 京	Beijing	335916	237058	91891	257		102053	761183
天 津	Tianjin	122307	158954	52219	164	1841	36937	143161
河 北	Hebei	331025	135634	214895	48091	915	107607	221324
山 西	Shanxi	153021	70142	92108	34267	21	49096	94190
内蒙古	Inner Mongolia	145405	73168	186028	43733		30755	60745
辽 宁	Liaoning	322457	310144	247882	16533	384	107105	231044
吉 林	Jilin	158410	81416	393940	18896	51	35483	62310
黑龙江	Heilongjiang	219457	162005	444204	31884		108624	124797
上 海	Shanghai	343093	231487	86070			111958	936936
江 苏	Jiangsu	403569	470433	122953	5619	735	153417	309754
浙 江	Zhejiang	350119	335422	60205	16322	93	145878	252564
安 徽	Anhui	189001	105081	155154	53346	43	44881	187485
福 建	Fujian	213027	102382	122127	35268	117	56138	348525
江 西	Jiangxi	153539	74438	119808	29692	66	29393	109859
山 东	Shandong	379550	388802	188804	11686	3213	181155	552974
河 南	Henan	315271	159194	310106	63486	774	89136	254221
湖 北	Hubei	233733	125192	135968	41868	378	60217	499171
湖 南	Hunan	256110	149062	127822	46802	246	63254	259736
广 东	Guangdong	944016	534781	181131	25363	280	202870	1485945
广 西	Guangxi	215983	81372	70576	72148	113	59205	166797
海 南	Hainan	46157	23056	14418	12291	30	7312	55871
四 川	Sichuan	316066	138246	147212	100517	72	61481	216342
重 庆	Chongqing	134334	90341	66756	33336	77	26840	64388
贵 州	Guizhou	145316	64898	38447	88819	66	26882	138435
云 南	Yunnan	234401	146200	57764	138795	224	49855	137180
西 藏	Tibet	34407	3848	11834	20395	308	1223	23094
陕 西	Shaanxi	152539	73820	53876	51091	68	54188	90614
甘 肃	Gansu	95226	51109	70926	81494	36	33258	98908
青 海	Qinghai	37208	6067	16791	29913	50	4708	11521
宁 夏	Ningxia	31562	17710	17031	19783		6288	31175
新 疆	Xinjiang	127728	76474	59652	57662		31222	67511

8-21 国家外债余额

Balance of Foreign Debts

债务类型	Type of Debts	1995	1996	1997	1998	1999	2000
总计(亿美元)	**Total (USD 100 million)**	**1065.90**	**1162.75**	**1309.60**	**1460.43**	**1518.30**	**1457.30**
按债务类型分	**By Type of Debt**						
外国政府贷款	Loans from Foreign Governments	220.58	221.64	207.82	224.06	265.60	246.10
国际金融组织贷款	Loans from International Financial Institutions	147.99	167.39	192.12	229.54	251.39	263.50
国际商业贷款	International Commercial Loans	526.27	569.44	647.68	682.22	653.80	947.70
其他	Others	171.06	204.28	261.98	324.61	347.51	
按偿还期限分	**By Repayment Terms**						
长期债务余额	Balance of Long-term Debts	946.74	1021.67	1128.20	1287.00	1366.50	1326.50
短期债务余额	Balance of Short-term Debts	119.16	141.08	181.40	173.40	151.80	130.80
构成(%)	**Percentage (%)**	**100.0**	**100.0**	**100.0**	**100.0**	**100.0**	**100.0**
按债务类型分	**By Type of Debt**						
外国政府贷款	Loans from Foreign Governments	20.7	19.1	15.9	15.4	17.5	16.9
国际金融组织贷款	Loans from International Financial Institutions	13.9	14.4	14.7	15.7	16.5	18.1
国际商业贷款	International Commercial Loans	49.4	49.0	49.4	46.7	43.1	65.0
其他	Others	16.0	17.5	20.0	22.2	22.9	
按偿还期限分	**By Repayment Terms**						
长期债务余额	Balance of Long-term Debts	88.8	87.9	86.1	88.1	90.0	91.0
短期债务余额	Balance of Short Term of Debts	11.2	12.1	13.9	11.9	10.0	9.0

8-22 外 债 风 险 指 标

Risk Indicators on Foreign Debts

单位：% (%)

年份 Year	偿债率 Debt Service Ratio	负债率 Liability Ratio	债务率 Foreign Debt Ratio
1985	2.7	5.2	56.0
1986	15.4	7.3	72.1
1987	9.0	9.4	77.1
1988	6.5	10.0	87.1
1989	8.3	9.2	86.4
1990	8.7	13.5	91.6
1991	8.5	14.9	91.9
1992	7.1	14.4	87.9
1993	10.2	13.9	96.5
1994	9.1	17.1	78.0
1995	7.6	15.2	72.4
1996	6.0	14.2	67.7
1997	7.3	14.5	63.2
1998	10.9	15.2	70.4
1999	11.3	15.3	69.5
2000	9.2	13.5	52.1

注：1.偿债率指偿还外债本息与当年贸易和非贸易外汇收入(国际收支口径)之比。
2.负债率指外债余额与当年国民生产总值之比。
3.债务率指外债余额与当年贸易和非贸易外汇收入(国际收支口径)之比。

a)Debt service ratio refers to the ratio of the payment of principal and interest of foreign debts to the foreign exchange receipts from foreign trade and non-trade services of the current year.

b)Liability ratio refers to the ratio of the balance of foreign debts to the gross national product of the current year.

c)Foreign debt ratio refers to the ratio of the balance of foreign debts to the foreign exchange receipts from foreign trade and non-trade services of the current year.

主 要 统 计 指 标 解 释

财政收入 指国家财政参与社会产品分配所取得的收入，是实现国家职能的财力保证。财政收入所包括的内容几经变化，目前主要包括：

(1)各项税收：包括增值税、营业税、消费税、土地增值税、城市维护建设税、资源税、城市土地使用税、印花税、个人所得税、企业所得税、关税、农牧业税和耕地占用税等。

(2)专项收入：包括征收排污费收入、征收城市水资源费收入、教育费附加收入等。

(3)其他收入：包括基本建设贷款归还收入、基本建设收入、捐赠收入等。

(4)国有企业亏损补贴：这项为负收入，冲减财政收入。

财政支出 国家财政将筹集起来的资金进行分配使用，以满足经济建设和各项事业的需要，主要包括：

(1)基本建设支出：指按国家有关规定，属于基本建设范围内的基本建设有偿使用、拨款、资本金支出以及经国家批准对专项和政策性基建投资贷款，在部门的基建投资额中统筹支付的贴息支出。

(2)企业挖潜改造资金：指国家预算内拨给的用于企业挖潜、革新和改造方面的资金。包括各部门企业挖潜改造资金和企业挖潜改造贷款资金，为农业服务的县办"五小"企业技术改造补助，挖潜改造贷款利息支出。

(3)地质勘探费用：指国家预算用于地质勘探单位的勘探工作费用，包括地质勘探管理机构及其事业单位经费、地质勘探经费。

(4)科技三项费用：指国家预算用于科技支出的费用，包括新产品试制费、中间试验费、重要科学研究补助费。

(5)支援农村生产支出：指国家财政支援农村集体(户)各项生产的支出。包括对农村举办的小型农田水利和打井、喷灌等的补助费，对农村水土保持措施的补助费，对农村举办的小水电站的补助费，特大抗旱的补助费，农村开荒补助费，扶持乡镇企业资金，农村农技推广和植保补助费，农村草场和畜禽保护补助费，农村造林和林木保护补助费，农村水产补助费，发展粮食生产专项资金。

(6)农林水利气象等部门的事业费用：指国家财政用于农垦、农场、农业、畜牧、农机、林业、森工、水利、水产、气象、乡镇企业的技术推广、良种推广(示范)、动植物(畜禽、森林)保护、水质监测、勘探设计、资源调查、干部训练等项费用，园艺特产场补助费，中等专业学校经费，飞播牧草试验补助费，营林机构、气象机构经费，渔政费以及农业管理事业费等。

(7)工业交通商业等部门的事业费：指国家预算支付给工交商各部门用于事业发展的经费，包括勘探设计费、中等专业学校经费、技术学校经费、干部训练费。

(8)文教科学卫生事业费：指国家预算用于文化、出版、文物、教育、卫生、中医、公费医疗、体育、档案、地震、海洋、通讯、电影电视、计划生育、党政群干部训练、自然科学、社会科学、科协等项事业的经费支出和高技术研究专项经费。主要包括工资、补助工资、福利费、离退休费、助学金、公务费、设备购置费、修缮费、业务费、差额补助费。

(9)抚恤和社会福利救济费：指国家预算用于抚恤和社会福利救济事业的经费。包括由民政部门开支的烈士家属和牺牲病残人员家属的一次性、定期抚恤金，革命伤残人员的抚恤金，各种伤残补助费，烈军属、复员退伍军人生活补助费，退伍军人安置费，优抚事业单位经费，烈士纪念建筑物管理、维修费，自然灾害救济事业费和特大自然灾害灾后重建补助费等。

(10)国防支出：指国家预算用于国防建设和保卫国家安全的支出，包括国防费、国防科研事业费、民兵建设以及专项工程支出等。

(11)行政管理费：包括行政管理支出，党派团体补助支出，外交支出，公安安全支出，司法支出，法院支出，检察院支出和公检法办案费用补助。

(12)价格补贴支出：指经国家批准，由国家财政拨给的政策性补贴支出。主要包括粮食加价款，粮、棉、油差价补贴，棉花收购价外奖励款，副食品风险基金，市镇居民的肉食价格补贴，平抑市价肉食、蔬菜价差补贴等以及经国家批准的教材课本、报刊新闻纸等价格补贴。

中央财政收入和地方财政收入 指按财政体制划分的中央本级收入和地方本级收入。1994年分税制财政体制以后，属于中央财政的收入包括关税、海关代征消费税和增值税，消费税，中央企业所得税，地方银行和外资银行及非银行金融企业所得税，铁道、银行总行、保险总公司等集中缴纳的营业税、所得税、利润和城市维护建设税，增值税的75%部分，证券交易税(印花税)50%部分和海洋石油资源税。属于地方财政的收入包括营业税，地方企业所得税，个人所得税，城镇土地使用税，固定资产投资方向调节税，城镇维护建设税，房产税，车船使用税，印花税，屠宰税，农牧业税，农业特产税，耕地占用税，契税，增值税25%部分，证券交易税(印花税)50%部分和除海洋石油资源税以外的其他资源税。

中央财政支出和地方财政支出 指根据政府在经济和社会活动中的不同职责，划分中央和地方政府的责权，按照政府的责权划分确定的支出。中央财政支出包括国防支出，武装警察部队支出，中央级行政管理费和各项事业费，重点建设支出以及中央政府调整国民经济结构、协调地区发展、实施宏观调控的支出。地方财政支出主要包括地方行政管理和各项事业费，地方统筹的基本建设、技术改造支出，支援农村生产支出，城市维护和建设经费，价格补贴支出等。

预算外资金收支 预算外资金指国家机关、事业单位和社会团体为履行或代行政府职能，依据国家法律、法规和具有法律效力的规章而收取、提取和安排使用的未纳入国家预算管理的各种财政性资金。其范围主要包括：法律、法规规定的行政事业性收费、基金和附加收入等；国务院或省级人民政府及其财政、计划（物价）部门审批的行政事业性收费；国务院及财政部审批建立的基金、附加收入等；主管部门所属单位集中上缴资金；用于乡镇政府开支的乡自筹和乡统筹资金；其他未纳入预算管理的财政性资金。社会保障基金在国家财政尚未建立社会保障预算制度以前，先按预算外资金管理制度进行管理，专款专用。财政部门在银行开设统一的专户，用于预算外资金收入和支出管理。部门和单位的预算外收入必须上缴同级财政专户，支出由同级财政按预算外资金收支计划和单位财务收支计划统筹安排，从财政专户中拨付，实行收支两条线管理。

Explanatory Notes on Main Statistical Indicators

Government Revenue refers to the revenue of the government finance by means of participating in the distribution of the social products, which is the financial resources for ensuring the government to function. The contents of government revenue have been changed several times. Now it includes the following main items:

(1) Various tax revenues, including value added tax, business tax, consumption tax, land value added tax, tax on city maintenance and construction, resources tax, tax on use of urban land, stamp tax, personal income tax, enterprise income tax, tariff, tax on agriculture and animal husbandry and tax on occupancy of cultivated land, etc.

(2) Special revenues, including revenue collected from imposing fee on sewage treatment, revenue collected from imposing fee on urban water resources, and extra-charges for education, etc.

(3) Other revenues, including revenue from the repayment of capital construction loan, revenue from capital construction projects, and donations and grants.

(4) Planned subsidies for the losses of the state-owned enterprises. This is an item of negative revenue, used to eat up part of the government revenue.

Government Expenditure refers to the distribution and use of the funds the government finance has raised, so as to meet the needs of economic construction and various causes. It includes the following main items:

(1) Expenditure for capital construction: It refers to the non-gratuitous use and appropriation of funds for capital construction in the range of capital construction, outlay of capital as well as the loans on capital construction approved by the government for special purpose or policy purpose and the expenditure with discount paid in an overall way within the amount of the funds appropriated to the departments for capital construction.

(2) Innovation funds of the enterprises: They refer to the funds appropriated from the government budget for the enterprises to tap the latent power, upgrade the technology and carry out innovation, including the innovation fund of the departments, loan of the enterprises for innovation, subsidies on the innovation of the small fertilizer plant, small cement plant, small coal mines, small machinery plant and small steel plant, the expenditure of interest for the loan for innovation.

(3) Geological prospecting expenses: They refer to the expenses appropriated from the government budget to the geological prospecting units for the expenditure of the prospecting work, including the expenditures of the administrative agencies for geological prospecting and their institutional units as well as the geological prospecting expenditure.

(4) expenditures for science and technology promotion: They refer to the expenses appropriated from the government budget for the scientific and technological expenditure, including new products development expenditure, expenditure for intermediate trial and subsidies on important scientific researches.

(5) Expenditure for supporting rural production: It refers to the expenditures appropriated from the government budget for supporting the various expenditures of the rural collective units or households for production, including the subsidies to the small water conservancy projects and well drilling, sprinkling irrigation projects run by the villages; subsidies on the rural water and soil conserving measures; subsidies to the small power stations run by the villages; subsidies to the expenditure for fighting against particularly severe draughts; subsidies on the rural waste land exclamation; fund for supporting the township enterprises; subsidies to the expenditure for popularization of the agricultural technologies and plant protection in the rural areas; subsidies to the expenditure for the protection of grasslands and cattle and fowls; subsidies on afforestation and forest protection in rural areas; subsidies on the rural aquatic products industry; special fund for developing grain production.

(6) Operating expenses of the departments of farming, forestry, water conservancy and meteorology etc.: They refer to the expenses appropriated from the government budget for the expenditures of agricultural exclamation, farms, agriculture, animal husbandry, agricultural machinery, forestry, timber industry, water conservancy, aquatic products industry, meteorology, technology popularization in township enterprises, popularization (demonstration) of improved varieties, plant (cattle and fowls, forest) protection, water quality monitoring, prospecting and designing, resources investigation, cadres training, subsidies to horticulture gardens, expenditure of specialized secondary schools, subsidies on the experiments of sowing herbage seeds by flights, expenditures of afforestation agencies and meteorology agencies, expenses for fishery administration and operating expenses for agricultural administration, etc.

(7) Operating expenses of the departments of industry, transport and commerce: They refer to the expenses appropriated from the government budget to the departments of industry, transport and commerce for the expenditure of business development, including expenses for prospecting and designing, expenditures of specialized secondary schools, expenditures of the tech-

nical training schools and expenditures for cadres training, etc.

(8) Operating expenses of the departments of culture, education, science and public health: They refer to the expenses appropriated from the government budget for the expenditures of the causes of culture, publication, cultural relics, education, public health, traditional Chinese medical science, free medical services, sports, archives, earthquake, ocean, communications, broadcasting, film and television, family planning; expenditure for training of cadres of government, party and mass organization; expenditures for natural sciences, social sciences, associations for science and technology and the special expenditure for the high-tech researches. They include mainly wages, extra wages, welfare funds, pension for the retirees, stipend, expenses for official business, expenses for equipment purchases, expenses for repairs, business expenses and subsidies to the units which are unable to support their expenditures by their own earnings.

(9) Pension for the disabled or for the families of the bereaved and relief funds for social welfare: They refer to the funds appropriated from the government budget for the expenditures of pension for the disabled or for the families of the bereaved and relief funds for social welfare, including the lump-sum or regular pension paid by the departments of civil affairs to the members of martyrs families and families of those who died for the public interest, pension to the revolutionary disabled, subsidies for permanent disability of various kinds, subsidies to the military martyrs dependents and the demobilized servicemen, expenditure for settling down the demobilized servicemen, operating expenses of the consoling institutions, expenses for management and repair of the commemorative buildings for the martyrs, the expenses managed by the departments of civil affairs for the retirees and those who have quitted their work, expenses for social relief in rural and urban areas, operating expenses for providing relief to the areas of natural calamity and subsidies on the reconstruction after the particularly severe natural calamities, etc.

(10) Expenditures for national defence: They refer to the funds appropriated from the government budget for the expenditures for building up national defence and safeguarding national security, including expenses of national defence, expenses of scientific researches on national defence, expenses for building up people's militia and expenditure for special projects, etc.

(11) Administrative expenses: They include expenditure for administration, subsidies to the parties and mass organizations, diplomatic expenditure, expenditure for public security, judicial expenditure, law court expenditure, procuratorial expenditure and subsidies to the expenses for treating the cases by the public security departments, procuratorial organs and law courts.

(12) Expenditure for price subsidies: It refers to the expenditure appropriated, with the approval of the government, from the government budget for the policy subsidies to price adjustment, including the fund for the increase of grain prices, the subsidies to the difference between the selling prices and purchasing prices of grains, cotton and edible oil, awards in addition to the purchasing prices of cotton, risk fund for non-staple food, subsidies on the prices of meat and meat products, subsidies on the price difference for curbing the high market prices of meat, meat products and vegetables and the subsidies approved by the government on the prices of textbooks and newsprint of newspapers and periodicals.

Revenue of the central government and revenue of the local governments: In accordance with the classification of the structure of the government finance in 1994 on the basis of the classification of channels for collection of tax revenues, the revenue of the central government and the revenue of the local governments have different coverage. The revenue of the central government includes tariff, consumption tax and value added tax levied by the customs, consumption tax, income tax of the enterprises subordinate to the central government, income taxes of the local banks, foreign-funded banks and non-bank financial institutions, business tax, income tax and profits of railways, head offices of banks, head office of insurance company , which are handed over to the government in a centralized way, tax on city maintenance and construction, 75% of the value added tax, tax on ocean petroleum resources, 50% of the tax on stock dealing (stamp tax). The revenue of the local governments includes business tax, income tax of the enterprises subordinate to the local government, personal income tax, tax on the use of urban land, tax on the adjustment of the investment in fixed assets, tax on town maintenance and construction, tax on real estates, tax on the use of vehicles and ships, stamp tax, slaughter tax, tax on agriculture and animal husbandry, tax on special agricultural products, tax on the occupancy of cultivated land, contract tax, 25% of the value added tax, 50% of the tax on stock dealing (stamp tax) and tax on resources other than the ocean petroleum resources.

Expenditure of the central government and expenditure of the local governments: according to the different functions of the central government and local governments in the economic and social activities, the rights of affairs administration are classified between the central government and local governments; and the classification of the expenditure between the central government and local governments are made on the basis of the classification of the rights of affairs administration between them. The expenditure of the central government includes the expenditure for national defence, expenditure for armed police forces, the administrative expenses and various operating expenses at the level of central government, expenditure for key projects and the expenditure of the central government for adjusting the national economic structure, coordinating the development among different regions and exercising the macro-economic regulation and control. The expenditure of the local governments includes mainly the administrative expenses and various operating expenses at the level of local governments, the expenditure for capital construction and technological innovation with the funds raised by the local government, expenditure for supporting rural production, expenditure for city maintenance and construction and expenditure for price subsidies, etc.

Extra-budgetary revenue and expenditure Extra-budgetary fund refers to financial fund of various types not covered by the regular government budgetary management, which is collected, allocated or arranged by government agencies, institutions and social organizations while performing duties delegated to them or on behalf of the government in accordance with laws, rules and regulations. It mainly covers following items: administrative and institutional fees, funds and extra charges that are stipulated by laws and regulations; administrative and institutional fees approved by the State Council and provincial governments and their financial and planning (price management) departments; funds and extra charges established by the State Council and the Ministry of Finance; funds turned over to competent departments by their subordinate institutions; self-raised and collected funds by township governments for their own expenditure; and other financial funds that are not covered in budgetary management. Social security funds are treated as extra-budget fund and managed for its exclusive use, given the circumstance that separate government budgetary system for social security is yet to be designed. Special accounts are opened by the financial departments in banks for the management of revenue and expenditure of extra-budgetary fund. Extra-budgetary revenue and expenditure is managed separately, namely, revenue of institutions and departments must enter into the special accounts of the financial departments at the same administrative level, and their extra-budgetary expenditure is arranged in line with the extra-budget plans and appropriated from these accounts.

九、物价指数

Price Indices

简要说明

一、本篇价格指数资料，反映生产、流通、消费与投资等环节的价格变动趋势和变动幅度。主要包括居民消费价格指数、商品零售价格指数、农业生产资料价格指数、农产品收购价格指数、工业品出厂价格指数(生产者价格指数)、固定资产投资价格指数。

二、价格指数统计由国家统计局城市社会经济调查总队组织实施，各省、自治区、直辖市城市社会经济调查队及抽选出的市、县城调队依据国家统计局统一制定的价格统计调查制度向基层采集原始数据汇总后上报。

三、编制居民消费、商品零售价格指数资料是采用分层抽样调查方法取得的，即在全国选择不同经济区域和分布合理的地区、以及有代表性的商品作为样本，对市场价格进行经常性的调查，以样本推断总体。目前，国家一级抽选出的调查市、县226个。编制过程按上列几个步骤进行：

1.调查地区和调查点的选择。调查地区按照经济区域和地区分布合理等原则，选出具有代表性的大、中、小城市和县作为国家的调查地区；在此基础上选定经营规模大、商品种类多的商场(包括集市)作为调查点。

2.代表商品和代表规格品的选择。代表商品是选择那些消费量大、价格变动有代表性的商品；代表规格品的确定是根据商品零售资料和3.6万户城市居民、6.7万户农村居民的消费支出记帐资料，按照有关规定筛选的。筛选原则：①与社会生产和人民生活关系密切；②销售数量(金额)大；③市场供应保持稳定；④价格变动趋势有代表性；⑤所选的代表规格品之间差异大。

3.价格调查方式。采用派员直接到调查点登记调查，同时全国聘请近万名辅助调查员协助登记调查。

4.权数的确定。商品零售价格指数的计算权数是根据社会商品零售额统计确定的，居民消费价格指数的计算权数是根据9万多户城乡居民家庭消费支出构成确定的。

四、工业品出厂价格是工业品第一次出售时的价格。该项调查采用重点调查与典型调查相结合的调查方法。重点调查对象为年销售收入500万元以上的工业企业，典型调查对象为年销售收入500万元以下的工业企业。

1.代表企业的确定原则：

(1)按工业行业选择调查企业，各中类行业原则上都要有调查企业；(2)大型企业应尽量都选上(或占相当大比重)；(3)选择生产稳定、正常的企业作为调查对象；(4)选择企业时要兼顾不同所有制形式。

2.代表产品的确定原则：

(1)按工业行业选择代表产品；(2)选择对国计民生影响大的产品；(3)选择生产较为稳定的产品；(4)选择有发展前景的产品；(5)选择具有地方特色的产品。

目前《工业品价格调查目录》包括1386种工业出厂产品(3000个规格)。上述代表产品所代表的行业销售额(购进额)超过当年全国工业品销售总额(购进额)的70%。

3.价格调查方式。采用企业报表形式，每月近两万家工业企业上报数据资料。

4.权数的确定。

编制工业品出厂价格指数所用的权数，用工业品销售额计算。权数一般五年更换一次。计算资料来源于工业普查数据。若近期没有工业普查数据时，可以用工业统计资料和部门统计资料来推算。

五、固定资产投资价格调查是一种非全面性调查，采用重点调查与典型调查相结合的方法。固定资产投资价格调查所涉及的价格是构成固定资产投资额实体的实际购进价格或结算价格。调查的内容包括建筑施工企业产值；构成当年建筑工程实体的钢材、木材、水泥、地方材料(如砖、瓦、灰、沙、石等)、化工材料(如油漆等)等主要建筑材料价格；作为活劳动投入的劳动力价格(单位工资)和各种费用的取费标准；设备工器具购置和其他费用投资价格。

固定资产投资价格调查样本的选择，应遵循以下原则：

1.选择建筑安装工程调查点的原则：

(1)样本单位应具有一定覆盖面；(2)投资经济活动代表性强；(3)兼顾不同经济类型；(4)选择重点工程；(5)兼顾国民经济各门类及不同工程类别。

2.选择其它费用调查点的原则：

在选择其它费用调查点时，所遵循的原则与建筑安装工程调查点的原则基本相同，特别是要注意选择那些投资额大的工程。但由于其它费用不易取得，所以在实际操作过程中，应同时在建设单位、施工单位开展重点调查，并辅以典型调查(从管理部门取得资料)。

3.价格调查方式。采用企业报表和调查员走访相结合的方式。

4.权数的确定。固定资产投资价格指数的计算权数是建筑安装工程、设备工器具购置和其它费用三者前三年的平均比重。

Brief Introduction

I. The data on the price indices in this chapter show the changing trend and the change rates in production, circulation, consumption and investment, etc., including mainly consumer price indices of residents, retail price indices, price indices of agricultural means of production, purchasing price indices of farm products, producers price indices of industrial products, and price indices of investment in fixed assets.

II. The statistics of price indices is organized by the Urban Socio-economic Survey Organization, NBS. The urban socio-economic survey organizations of the provinces, autonomous regions and municipalities directly under the central government as well as the urban socio-economic survey organizations of the selected cities and counties collect statistical data from the grassroots units in accordance with the scheme of price survey stipulated by the NBS, tabulate them and report them to the higher agencies.

III. The data for calculation of the consumer price indices of residents and the retail price indices in China are collected with the stratified sampling method. Areas distributed in different economic regions are selected as the sample areas and the representative commodities are selected as the sample commodities. Regular surveys are conducted to collect the data on the market prices. The data on the population are estimated on the basis of the sample. At present, 226 cities and counties have been selected for this purpose. Following are major steps in the process of calculation of the price indices:

(1) The selection of the areas and places for survey: Based on such principles as regional economic features and reasonable geographic distribution, representative sample areas for the national survey are selected which include large, medium and small cities and counties. When the sample areas are selected, large-scale shops and markets (including fairs) with great varieties of commodities are selected as the survey places.

(2) The selection of the representative commodities and their specifications or varieties: The representative commodities are the commodities consumed in large quantity and representative in price changes. The representative specifications or varieties are determined according to the data on the retail sales of commodities and the account data of the residents of 36 thousand urban households and 67 thousand rural households, following the related instructions for selection. In principle, only those specifications or varieties of the commodities can be selected: (a) They are closely related to the social production and people's livelihood; (b) They are sold in large quantities (or big values); (c) They are stable in the market supply; (d) The changes of their prices are representative in trend; (e) There is great difference among the specifications or varieties selected.

(3) Survey way: Enumerators are sent to the survey places to take the records of the prices. Nearly 10 thousand assistant enumerators are invited to assist the survey work.

(4) The determination of the weights: The weights for calculation of the retail price indices are determined according to the total retail sales of commodities. The weights for calculation of the consumer price indices are determined according to the composition of the consumption expenditures of more than 90 thousand urban and rural households.

IV. Producers price of industrial products refer to the first sale price of industrial products. The survey ways include the key units survey and typical units survey. The key units refer to the industrial enterprises with annual sale revenue above 5 million yuans. The typical units refer to the industrial enterprises with annual sale revenue below 5 million yuans.

(1)The principle to select the representative enterprises:

(a) The survey enterprises are selected by industrial sectors. In principle, every branch should have survey enterprises; (b) All (or a majority of) large-sized enterprises should be selected; (c) The normal enterprises with stable production are listed as survey object; (d) Different types of ownership should be considered in selecting enterprises.

(2) The principle to select the representative products:

(a) The survey products are selected by industrial sectors; (b) The products are relative with national economy and the people's livelihood; (c) The products are more stable in production; (d) The foreground of products is representative in trend; (e) The products are typical and with local color.

There are 1386 kinds (including 3000 specifications or varieties) of industrial products listed in Industrial Products Content on Price Survey at present. The industrial sale value (or purchasing value) of these branches represented by these products is more than 70 percent of nationwide industrial sale value (or purchasing value).

(3) Price survey way: Enterprises reporting way is adopted. Nearly 20 000 industrial enterprises report the above data every month.

(4) The determination of the weights: The weights for calculation of the producers' price indices of industrial products are determined according to the total sales value of industrial products. The weights will replace every five years. The data for calculation root from industrial census. If there are not industrial census data recently, industrial statistical data and department statistical data will be used to estimate the weights.

V. The price survey of investment in fixed assets is not a kind of comprehensive survey. Data are collected by the survey on key units and typical units. The prices of the survey of investment in fixed assets are the actual purchasing prices or balancing prices of entity of investment in fixed assets. The survey content includes the gross output value of construction, the prices of main construction materials that composing the architecture engineering entity in the year, such as steel, timber, cement, local construction materials (such as brick, tile, calcareousness, sand, stone, etc.), chemical materials (such as oil paint, etc.) , the price of labor force as live laboring input, the standard of various fees, the purchasing price of equipment, tools and instruments and the prices of others investments.

The following principle to select the sample of price survey of investment in fixed assets should be followed.

(1) The principle to select the prices survey point of construction and installation: (a) Sample units should be a certain coverage; (b) The economic activity of investment is great representative; (c) Different economic types of ownership should be considered; (d) The key projects need to be selected; (e) Give attention to both various branches and types of project.

(2) The principle to select the prices survey point of others investments: The principle to select the prices survey point of others fees is general the same as that of construction and installation, especially to select the projects with great investment value. Since it is not easy to obtain the other fees, it should do the key survey on the construction owner units and building units assisted with typical survey (gotten from the administration department), in the actual operation.

(3) Price survey way: Enterprises reporting system is used together with the enumerators visiting method.

(4) The determination of the weights: The weights for calculation of the price indices of investment in fixed assets are determined according to the average proportion of construction and installation, purchase of equipment, tools and instruments and others investment in the 3 previous years.

9-1 全国各种价格总指数

General Price Indices

(上年=100) (preceding year=100)

年份 Year	商品零售价格指数 General Retail Price Index	居民消费价格指数 General Consumer Price Index	城市居民消费价格指数 Urban Areas	农村居民消费价格指数 Rural Areas	农产品收购价格指数 General Purchasing Price Index of Farm Products	农村工业品零售价格指数 General Rural Retail Price Index of Industrial Products	工农业商品综合比价指数 General Price Parity Index of Industrial and Farm Products
1978	100.7		100.7		103.9	100.0	96.2
1979	102.0		101.9		122.1	100.1	82.0
1980	106.0		107.5		107.1	100.8	94.1
1981	102.4		102.5		105.9	101.0	95.4
1982	101.9		102.0		102.2	101.6	99.4
1983	101.5		102.0		104.4	101.0	96.7
1984	102.8		102.7		104.0	103.1	99.1
1985	108.8	109.3	111.9	107.6	108.6	103.2	95.0
1986	106.0	106.5	107.0	106.1	106.4	103.2	97.0
1987	107.3	107.3	108.8	106.2	112.0	104.8	93.6
1988	118.5	118.8	120.7	117.5	123.0	115.2	93.7
1989	117.8	118.0	116.3	119.3	115.0	118.7	103.2
1990	102.1	103.1	101.3	104.5	97.4	104.6	107.4
1991	102.9	103.4	105.1	102.3	98.0	103.0	105.1
1992	105.4	106.4	108.6	104.7	103.4	103.1	99.7
1993	113.2	114.7	116.1	113.7	113.4	111.8	98.6
1994	121.7	124.1	125.0	123.4	139.9	117.2	83.8
1995	114.8	117.1	116.8	117.5	119.9	114.7	95.7
1996	106.1	108.3	108.8	107.9	104.2	106.2	101.9
1997	100.8	102.8	103.1	102.5	95.5	101.1	105.9
1998	97.4	99.2	99.4	99.0	92.0	97.8	106.3
1999	97.0	98.6	98.7	98.5	87.8	97.3	110.8
2000	98.5	100.4	100.8	99.9	96.4	98.8	102.5

注：工农业商品综合比价指数是以农产品收购价格指数为100，下表同。

a)The general purchasing price index of farm products is taken as 100 in calculating the general price parity index of industrial and farm products. The same as in the following table.

9-2 全国各种价格总指数

General Price Indices

(1978年=100) (1978=100)

年 份 Year	商品零售价格指数 General Retail Price Index	居民消费价格指数 General Consumer Price Index (1985=100)	城市居民消费价格指数 Urban Areas	农村居民消费价格指数 Rural Areas (1985=100)	农产品收购价格指数 General Purchasing Price Index of Farm Products	农村工业品零售价格指数 General Rural Retail Price Index of Industrial Products	工农业商品综合比价指数 General Price Parity Index of Industrial and Farm Products
1978	100.0		100.0		100.0	100.0	100.0
1979	102.0		101.9		122.1	100.1	82.0
1980	108.1		109.5		130.8	100.9	77.1
1981	110.7		112.2		138.5	101.9	73.6
1982	112.8		114.4		141.5	103.5	73.1
1983	114.5		116.7		147.7	104.5	70.8
1984	117.7		119.9		153.6	107.7	70.1
1985	128.1	100.0	134.2	100.0	166.8	111.1	66.6
1986	135.8	106.5	143.6	106.1	177.5	114.7	64.6
1987	145.7	114.3	156.2	112.7	198.8	120.2	60.5
1988	172.7	135.8	188.5	132.4	244.5	138.5	56.6
1989	203.4	160.2	219.2	157.9	281.2	164.4	58.5
1990	207.7	165.2	222.0	165.1	273.9	172.0	62.8
1991	213.7	170.8	233.3	168.9	268.4	177.2	66.0
1992	225.2	181.7	253.4	176.8	277.5	182.7	65.8
1993	254.9	208.4	294.2	201.0	314.7	204.3	64.9
1994	310.2	258.6	367.8	248.0	440.3	239.4	54.4
1995	356.1	302.8	429.6	291.4	527.9	274.6	52.0
1996	377.8	327.9	467.4	314.4	550.1	291.6	53.0
1997	380.8	337.1	481.9	322.3	525.3	294.8	56.1
1998	370.9	334.4	479.0	319.1	483.3	288.3	59.7
1999	359.8	329.7	472.8	314.3	424.3	280.5	66.1
2000	354.4	331.0	476.6	314.0	409.0	277.1	67.8

9-3 全国居民消费价格分类指数（2000年）

Consumer Price Indices by Category (2000)

(上年=100) (preceding year=100)

项 目	Item	全国 National Indices	城市 Urban Indices	农村 Rural Indices
居民消费价格指数	**General Consumer Price Index**	**100.4**	**100.8**	**99.9**
食品	**Food**	**97.4**	**97.4**	**97.5**
粮食	Grain	88.6	88.8	88.4
细粮	Flour and Rice	88.3	88.6	88.0
粗粮	Coarse Food Grain	94.1	94.3	94.0
淀粉及薯类	Starches and Tubers	98.6	98.6	98.5
干豆类及豆制品	Bean and Its Products	102.0	102.5	101.5
油脂	Oil or Fat	86.8	85.7	87.9
肉禽及其制品	Meal, Poultry and Their Products	98.5	97.8	99.4
蛋	Eggs	84.5	84.2	84.9
水产品	Aquatic Products	101.7	102.3	100.8
菜	Vegetables	104.7	104.3	105.3
鲜菜	Fresh Vegetables	105.5	104.7	106.7
干菜	Dried Vegetables	98.9	100.1	98.2
菜制品	Vegetable Products	98.8	98.8	98.8
调味品	Flavoring	101.5	100.6	102.1
糖	Carbohydrate	103.7	102.0	104.9
食糖	Sugar	108.6	106.5	109.5
糖果	Candy	99.2	99.5	98.9
烟草	Tobacco	97.0	96.5	97.5
酒和饮料	Liquor and Beverages	98.6	98.2	98.9
干鲜瓜果	Dried and Fresh Melons and Fruits	96.6	95.9	97.9
鲜果	Fresh Fruits	96.0	95.3	97.4
干果	Dried Fruits	99.2	98.8	99.8
糕点	Cake	99.7	100.0	99.0
奶及奶制品	Milk and Its Products	100.0	100.2	99.3
其他食品	Other Food	98.5	98.2	99.0
饮食业	Catering Trade	99.7	99.6	99.8
主食	Staple Food	99.3	99.2	99.3
炒菜	Fried Dishes	99.5	99.3	100.1
地方小吃	Local Snack	101.1	101.5	100.1
衣着	**Clothing**	**99.1**	**99.5**	**98.6**
服装	Garments	99.1	99.3	98.7
衣着材料	Clothing Material	98.3	98.5	98.1
棉布	Cotton Cloth	98.7	98.8	98.7
棉花化纤混纺布	Blend Cloth	98.7	98.6	98.7
化纤布	Chemical Fiber Cloth	98.5	99.5	98.1
呢绒	Woolen Fabric	98.2	98.0	98.4
绸缎	Silk	98.5	98.7	98.3

9-3 续表 1 continued

(上年=100) (preceding year=100)

项 目	Item	全国 National Indices	城市 Urban Indices	农村 Rural Indices
毛线	Knitting Wool	97.3	97.6	97.2
鞋袜帽及其他衣着	Footwear, Hats & Other Clothing	99.8	100.4	99.1
鞋	Shoes	99.8	100.5	99.1
袜子	Socks and Stockings	99.5	99.8	99.2
帽子	Hats	99.3	100.7	98.6
其他衣着	Other Clothing	99.5	99.9	99.2
家庭设备及用品	**Household Facilities and Articles**	**97.7**	**97.7**	**97.8**
耐用消费品	Durable Consumer Goods	96.6	96.4	96.9
家具	Furniture	97.4	97.3	97.6
家庭设备	Household Facilities	96.2	95.9	96.5
室内装饰品	Interior Decorations	98.6	98.9	98.1
床上用品	Bed Articles	98.7	99.7	98.0
家庭日用杂品	Daily Use Household Articles	98.2	98.3	98.1
其他日用品	Other Articles for Daily Use	99.4	99.3	99.5
医疗保健用品	**Medicine and Medical Articles**	**100.3**	**100.1**	**100.6**
医疗器具及保健用品	Medical Appliances and Articles	99.5	99.6	99.5
中药材及中成药	Traditional Chinese Medicine	105.2	105.3	105.0
西药	Western Medicine	97.0	96.7	97.5
交通和通讯工具	**Means of Transportation and Communication**	**93.8**	**94.1**	**93.6**
交通工具	Means of Transportation	95.9	97.2	95.0
通讯工具	Means of Communication	89.9	90.1	89.7
娱乐教育文化用品	**Recreation, Education and Culture Articles**	**97.4**	**96.9**	**98.1**
文娱用耐用消费品	Durable Consumer Goods for Recreational Use	92.0	91.5	92.5
教材及参考书	Teaching Materials and Reference Books	107.5	106.6	108.1
文化娱乐用品	Cultural and Recreational Articles	101.7	102.1	101.1
文娱用品	Cultural and Recreational Articles	99.5	99.9	99.0
书报杂志	Newspapers and Magazines	104.6	104.9	104.1
居住	**Residence**	**104.8**	**106.7**	**102.8**
住房	Housing	101.9	104.4	99.8
建筑材料	Building Materials	98.5	98.0	98.8
房租	Rent	109.2	111.3	104.4
水电燃料	Water, Electricity and Fuels	107.7	108.3	106.7
服务项目	**Services**	**114.1**	**115.1**	**112.6**
电讯费	Telecommunication	100.9	101.3	99.6
邮费	Postage	107.8	107.4	108.1
交通费	Traffic	105.6	107.0	103.3
洗理美容费	Bathing and Haircut	101.7	101.4	102.2
文娱费	Recreation	108.2	110.1	103.1
学杂保育费	Tuition and Child Care	128.8	131.7	124.7
修理及其他服务费	Repair and Other Services	100.5	100.2	101.0
医疗保健服务费	Medical and Health Care Services	111.1	112.7	109.9

9-4 全国商品零售价格分类指数（2000年）

Retail Price Indices by Category of Commodities (2000)

(上年=100) (preceding year=100)

项　目	Item	全国 National Indices	城市 Urban Indices	农村 Rural Indices
商品零售价格指数	**General Retail Price Index**	**98.5**	**98.5**	**98.5**
食品	**Food**	**97.5**	**97.6**	**97.4**
粮食	Grain	90.1	91.2	88.9
细粮	Flour and Rice	88.8	89.8	87.6
粗粮	Coarse Food Grain	102.0	105.7	98.9
油脂	Oil or Fat	86.2	84.7	88.4
肉禽蛋	Meal, Poultry and Eggs	96.1	95.5	97.1
水产品	Aquatic Products	102.7	103.4	101.0
鲜菜	Fresh Vegetables	105.3	104.8	106.3
干菜	Dried Vegetables	99.2	100.3	98.0
鲜果	Fresh Fruits	95.7	94.9	97.1
干果	Dried Fruits	99.1	98.8	99.6
其他食品	Other Food	100.9	100.4	101.6
调味品	Condiments	101.2	100.6	101.8
食糖	Sugar	108.6	106.7	110.1
糖果	Candy	99.2	99.6	98.7
糕点	Cake	99.5	99.6	99.2
奶及奶制品	Milk and Its Products	100.0	100.2	99.4
罐头	Canned Food	98.0	97.6	98.9
饮食业	Catering Trade	99.8	99.8	100.0
主食	Staple Food	99.0	99.0	99.0
炒菜	Fried Dishes	99.7	99.5	100.3
地方小吃	Local Snack	101.3	101.7	100.3
饮料烟酒	**Beverages, Tobacco and Liquor**	**98.0**	**97.7**	**98.4**
饮料	Beverages	98.5	97.9	99.5
烟酒	Tobacco and Liquor	97.8	97.6	98.2
服装鞋帽	**Garments, Shoes and Hats**	**99.2**	**99.4**	**98.8**
服装	Garments	98.7	98.8	98.5
鞋	Shoes	99.8	100.3	99.0
其他衣着	Other Clothing	99.9	100.4	99.1
纺织品	**Textiles**	**98.6**	**99.0**	**98.1**
棉布	Cotton Cloth	98.9	99.1	98.7
棉花化纤混纺布	Blend Cloth	98.5	98.4	98.5
化纤布	Chemical Fiber Cloth	99.0	99.8	98.3
呢绒	Woolen Fabric	98.4	98.6	98.1
绸缎	Silk	98.8	98.9	98.5
其他纺织品	Other Textiles	98.1	98.9	97.0
中西药品	**Traditional Chinese and Western Medicines**	**100.2**	**100.1**	**100.4**
中药	Traditional Chinese Medicine	104.6	104.7	104.5
西药	Western Medicine	97.3	97.0	97.7
医疗用品	Medical Articles	99.6	99.7	99.5
化妆品	**Cosmetics**	**98.9**	**98.5**	**99.8**
书报杂志	**Newspapers and Magazines**	**105.4**	**105.1**	**105.7**
文化体育用品	**Cultural and Sports Goods**	**98.9**	**98.8**	**99.2**
文化用品	Cultural Goods	98.7	98.5	99.3
体育用品	Sports Goods	99.5	99.8	99.1
日用品	**Articles for Daily Use**	**98.1**	**98.3**	**97.8**
一般日用品	Ordinary Articles for Daily Use	97.9	98.1	97.6
家具	Furniture	97.8	97.8	97.8
日用杂品	Sundries for Daily Use	99.4	100.0	98.4
家用电器	**Household Appliances**	**93.6**	**93.4**	**94.0**
首饰	**Jewelry**	**97.6**	**97.1**	**98.8**
燃料	**Fuels**	**117.7**	**118.9**	**115.8**
建筑装潢材料	**Building Decoration Materials**	**98.4**	**98.6**	**98.1**
机电产品	**Mechanical and Electrical Products**	**95.6**	**96.0**	**94.2**

9-5 各地区居民消费价格指数和商品零售价格指数

Consumer Price Indices and Retail Price Indices of Commodities by Region

(上年=100) (preceding year=100)

年份 地区	Year Region	居民消费价格指数 Consumer Price Index			商品零售价格指数 Retail Price Index of commodities		
		全省（区、市） Province	城市 Urban Areas	农村 Rural Areas	全省（区、市） Province	城市 Urban Areas	农村 Rural Areas
	1994	124.1	125.0	123.4	121.7	120.9	122.9
	1995	117.1	116.8	117.5	114.8	113.5	116.4
	1996	108.3	108.8	107.9	106.1	105.8	106.4
	1997	102.8	103.1	102.5	100.8	100.8	100.7
	1998	99.2	99.4	99.0	97.4	97.4	97.6
	1999	98.6	98.7	98.5	97.0	97.0	97.1
	2000	100.4	100.8	99.9	98.5	98.5	98.5
北京	Beijing	103.5			98.9		
天津	Tianjin	99.6			98.6		
河北	Hebei	99.7	100.5	99.1	99.1	99.2	98.9
山西	Shanxi	103.9	104.7	103.0	97.1	96.8	97.5
内蒙古	Inner Mongolia	101.3	101.3	101.2	98.8	98.7	98.9
辽宁	Liaoning	99.9	100.0	99.7	98.4	98.4	98.6
吉林	Jilin	98.6	98.3	99.6	98.0	97.6	99.2
黑龙江	Heilongjiang	98.3	98.7	97.2	97.8	97.9	97.6
上海	Shanghai	102.5			96.4		
江苏	Jiangsu	100.1	100.0	100.1	98.6	98.5	98.8
浙江	Zhejiang	101.0	100.9	101.1	99.0	98.8	99.1
安徽	Anhui	100.7	100.9	100.5	98.0	97.9	98.0
福建	Fujian	102.1	103.2	101.3	98.9	99.0	98.9
江西	Jiangxi	100.3	102.1	99.1	98.5	98.6	98.5
山东	Shandong	100.2	101.2	99.3	98.6	98.8	98.3
河南	Henan	99.2	99.1	99.2	98.5	98.8	98.3
湖北	Hubei	99.0	100.0	98.2	97.8	98.1	97.1
湖南	Hunan	101.4	101.3	101.4	99.3	99.8	98.4
广东	Guangdong	101.4	102.2	100.0	99.9	100.0	99.6
广西	Guangxi	99.7	100.0	99.5	98.6	98.4	98.8
海南	Hainan	101.1	101.5	100.2	99.9	101.0	99.0
重庆	Chongqing	96.7			95.5		
四川	Sichuan	100.1	99.7	100.6	97.7	97.5	97.8
贵州	Guizhou	99.5	99.2	100.2	97.3	96.9	97.8
云南	Yunnan	97.9	97.6	98.4	97.6	97.0	98.4
西藏	Tibet	99.9	100.4	99.8	99.2	99.1	99.5
陕西	Shaanxi	99.5	100.3	99.0	98.3	98.8	97.7
甘肃	Gansu	99.5	99.2	100.1	99.1	98.9	99.6
青海	Qinghai	99.5	99.6	99.4	99.0	99.3	98.9
宁夏	Ningxia	99.6	99.7	99.5	97.6	97.8	97.4
新疆	Xinjiang	99.4	100.1	97.6	98.3	98.9	97.4

9-6 各地区居民消费价格分类指数

Consumer Price Indices by Category and by Region

(上年=100) (preceding year=100)

年份 地区	Year Region	总指数 General Index	食品 Food	# 粮食 Grain	# 油脂 Oil or Fat	# 肉禽及其制品 Meat and Poultry	# 蛋 Eggs	# 水产品 Aquatic Products	# 菜 Vegetables	# 酒和饮料 Liquor and Beverages
	1994	124.1	131.8	150.7	161.3	141.6	115.0	120.3	133.3	114.1
	1995	117.1	122.9	136.8	116.0	126.4	114.6	114.4	127.3	112.3
	1996	108.3	107.6	106.5	92.1	104.5	116.5	106.0	119.1	106.1
	1997	102.8	99.9	91.1	101.5	105.5	79.3	100.2	100.0	102.3
	1998	99.2	96.8	96.9	100.0	90.9	100.9	93.9	99.6	98.9
	1999	98.6	95.8	96.9	94.5	90.7	91.6	93.3	101.0	98.0
	2000	100.4	97.4	88.6	86.8	98.5	84.5	101.7	104.7	98.6
北京	Beijing	103.5	97.9	91.4	85.8	98.4	84.2	107.3	98.7	100.0
天津	Tianjin	99.6	98.0	90.3	89.4	99.9	83.8	104.0	100.9	99.1
河北	Hebei	99.7	97.5	90.1	91.7	102.8	83.6	104.1	102.2	99.2
山西	Shanxi	103.9	95.4	90.5	90.7	101.8	82.9	106.8	98.0	96.9
内蒙古	Inner Mongolia	101.3	97.2	93.0	88.0	100.7	83.1	104.8	100.1	98.6
辽宁	Liaoning	99.9	97.7	88.9	81.4	100.3	83.8	107.4	106.7	100.2
吉林	Jilin	98.6	95.9	89.1	82.5	96.6	80.5	103.4	103.8	98.2
黑龙江	Heilongjiang	98.3	96.0	92.3	80.9	97.1	82.5	104.9	101.3	98.6
上海	Shanghai	102.5	98.1	92.1	77.1	95.7	84.6	100.9	107.4	99.1
江苏	Jiangsu	100.1	97.8	87.7	84.2	99.6	85.5	98.0	108.7	98.3
浙江	Zhejiang	101.0	99.5	87.5	84.2	97.8	83.9	103.5	112.1	98.4
安徽	Anhui	100.7	97.2	85.0	83.8	101.9	84.7	102.6	108.0	98.4
福建	Fujian	102.1	98.6	88.8	95.5	97.0	83.6	101.5	109.8	100.1
江西	Jiangxi	100.3	97.2	85.9	84.2	99.1	85.9	98.6	111.3	97.4
山东	Shandong	100.2	97.7	88.3	87.9	100.6	82.9	106.6	104.0	98.6
河南	Henan	99.2	97.5	84.8	88.3	100.8	82.4	104.1	106.9	97.0
湖北	Hubei	99.0	97.6	83.3	81.0	100.6	88.2	100.2	107.5	98.9
湖南	Hunan	101.4	98.4	87.2	91.9	100.8	90.8	95.1	105.8	96.4
广东	Guangdong	101.4	98.5	94.3	94.7	96.4	87.5	101.0	102.9	99.0
广西	Guangxi	99.7	96.6	91.6	96.0	95.5	84.8	96.3	98.9	100.8
海南	Hainan	101.1	98.3	91.4	93.2	96.7	90.1	103.3	108.0	97.9
重庆	Chongqing	96.7	93.1	85.3	79.1	93.3	93.6	92.8	92.4	99.7
四川	Sichuan	100.1	95.5	88.4	84.1	96.5	86.4	92.7	96.8	98.5
贵州	Guizhou	99.5	95.3	92.7	82.1	94.8	91.7	94.2	100.1	97.8
云南	Yunnan	97.9	94.6	90.6	86.1	91.5	85.9	91.8	98.2	98.2
西藏	Tibet	99.9	98.9	101.1	98.8	94.0	98.0	97.6	105.0	98.7
陕西	Shaanxi	99.5	96.8	89.8	79.7	99.9	84.4	100.9	103.5	99.7
甘肃	Gansu	99.5	97.6	94.1	86.1	98.3	84.5	103.3	104.2	95.7
青海	Qinghai	99.5	97.8	94.4	81.6	99.4	84.1	106.4	103.5	97.9
宁夏	Ningxia	99.6	97.2	91.1	94.1	99.1	84.6	108.0	101.0	98.0
新疆	Xinjiang	99.4	95.9	88.5	84.4	96.1	78.6	93.4	107.1	97.8

9-6 续表 1 continued

(上年=100) (preceding year=100)

年 份 地 区	Year Region	#干鲜瓜果 Melons and Fruits	#饮食业 Catering Trade	衣着 Clothing	家庭设备及用品 Household Appliances	医疗保健用品 Health Care	交通和通讯工具 Means of Transportation & Communication	娱乐教育文化用品 Recreational, Educational & Cultural Goods	居住 Housing	服务项目 Services
	1994	120.6	129.8	117.1	112.0	111.7	107.8	112.5	121.3	125.7
	1995	121.2	124.6	114.5	107.0	111.3	99.9	106.4	110.6	120.2
	1996	104.5	109.4	107.4	103.8	109.3	98.8	110.4	111.4	116.0
	1997	94.4	104.7	103.0	100.7	104.7	97.4	100.9	108.3	116.5
	1998	96.2	101.1	99.2	98.4	102.8	95.8	96.6	101.7	110.1
	1999	97.8	99.9	97.3	97.7	100.9	94.5	96.8	101.7	110.6
	2000	96.6	99.7	99.1	97.7	100.3	93.8	97.4	104.8	114.1
北 京	Beijing	89.8	100.8	102.6	96.3	113.5	92.3	97.8	117.9	116.2
天 津	Tianjin	95.1	100.2	100.1	95.3	99.7	95.7	84.6	104.3	111.6
河 北	Hebei	94.8	100.2	100.0	98.6	100.9	96.0	96.9	105.3	110.2
山 西	Shanxi	94.0	97.4	99.2	97.6	100.6	93.7	96.8	107.3	163.8
内蒙古	Inner Mongolia	92.1	99.5	98.6	98.9	99.9	96.2	97.8	103.0	120.8
辽 宁	Liaoning	92.8	99.9	99.7	97.3	97.4	95.6	98.6	105.8	106.9
吉 林	Jilin	92.4	99.8	99.0	97.6	99.1	91.6	97.6	105.4	107.7
黑龙江	Heilongjiang	94.9	99.8	99.6	97.7	96.9	93.9	95.4	105.7	105.3
上 海	Shanghai	94.8	99.8	94.9	96.6	99.9	93.3	92.1	103.3	130.4
江 苏	Jiangsu	95.4	99.0	99.1	98.4	100.5	95.6	97.5	103.6	109.0
浙 江	Zhejiang	102.9	99.9	97.7	97.7	102.2	93.2	96.8	104.1	114.0
安 徽	Anhui	94.5	98.1	98.0	98.6	101.8	93.8	96.6	104.4	117.5
福 建	Fujian	102.7	99.5	98.4	97.7	101.1	91.7	94.4	106.7	129.9
江 西	Jiangxi	103.2	101.9	97.1	97.4	102.8	92.0	97.8	104.6	116.2
山 东	Shandong	95.7	99.7	99.7	97.1	99.6	93.2	96.9	104.5	114.6
河 南	Henan	96.6	98.6	98.8	97.8	97.2	95.6	97.4	101.6	108.8
湖 北	Hubei	96.8	98.5	98.3	96.0	98.0	87.8	93.5	105.0	105.4
湖 南	Hunan	102.7	99.6	99.8	97.6	102.0	89.5	103.2	102.9	113.6
广 东	Guangdong	98.5	100.3	99.2	98.5	98.9	95.4	99.1	106.6	113.0
广 西	Guangxi	98.4	99.3	99.6	98.5	97.5	91.3	98.6	105.9	113.6
海 南	Hainan	94.5	97.3	102.4	99.1	107.1	92.8	95.8	108.8	113.4
重 庆	Chongqing	89.9	101.7	90.4	94.1	100.5	88.8	99.3	101.2	112.3
四 川	Sichuan	94.0	100.6	98.7	97.6	101.5	94.1	99.2	101.7	119.4
贵 州	Guizhou	91.4	98.2	99.6	95.9	98.5	94.4	97.2	104.8	117.2
云 南	Yunnan	93.3	101.0	101.3	99.8	100.6	95.5	99.3	101.9	103.8
西 藏	Tibet	97.8	99.9	99.7	101.5	100.3	98.4	97.4	103.5	106.4
陕 西	Shaanxi	95.2	99.5	99.0	96.8	100.2	90.5	99.1	103.5	110.9
甘 肃	Gansu	100.5	97.9	100.9	97.1	99.1	93.2	97.0	104.2	105.6
青 海	Qinghai	101.1	100.6	99.5	98.5	101.6	96.3	99.4	107.3	103.8
宁 夏	Ningxia	95.1	99.5	96.6	97.3	99.7	90.8	94.6	105.8	110.1
新 疆	Xinjiang	96.9	99.6	99.7	98.9	102.9	94.2	97.1	103.9	113.9

9-7 各地区商品零售价格分类指数

Retail Price Indices by Category of Commodities by Region

(上年=100) (preceding year=100)

年份 地区	Year Region	总指数 General Index	食品 Food	#粮食 Grain	#油脂 Oil or Fat	#肉禽蛋 Meat, Poultry & Eggs	#水产品 Aquatic Products	#鲜菜 Vegetables	#鲜果 Fresh Fruits	#干果 Dried Fruits
	1994	121.7	135.2	148.7	161.4	137.2	120.7	138.2	119.4	125.5
	1995	114.8	124.7	134.4	116.3	124.2	114.2	129.3	120.4	124.4
	1996	106.1	107.7	107.5	92.1	106.4	105.6	118.4	102.8	110.3
	1997	100.8	99.8	92.1	101.6	101.3	101.2	99.5	92.1	106.6
	1998	97.4	96.8	96.9	100.7	92.6	94.2	100.3	95.7	94.8
	1999	97.0	95.8	96.4	94.4	91.1	93.6	100.4	99.4	91.5
	2000	98.5	97.5	90.1	86.2	96.1	102.7	105.3	95.7	99.1
北京	Beijing	98.9	97.5	92.0	85.8	96.6	107.3	98.5	88.4	94.9
天津	Tianjin	98.6	98.0	100.4	88.1	95.0	102.1	101.2	94.1	99.9
河北	Hebei	99.1	97.8	91.5	91.7	98.5	105.2	102.6	93.7	99.6
山西	Shanxi	97.1	95.9	91.0	90.8	96.2	104.2	98.9	92.7	102.0
内蒙古	Inner Mongolia	98.8	97.0	93.4	88.5	98.2	103.6	100.5	91.3	93.9
辽宁	Liaoning	98.4	98.3	90.2	81.0	97.1	108.4	107.0	91.2	99.4
吉林	Jilin	98.0	95.9	90.7	83.6	92.5	103.1	103.6	91.5	97.0
黑龙江	Heilongjiang	97.8	96.2	92.7	81.0	94.7	104.9	101.1	94.6	96.7
上海	Shanghai	96.4	97.5	97.1	77.3	93.4	101.0	108.4	93.4	99.4
江苏	Jiangsu	98.6	97.0	88.5	83.5	97.3	98.6	109.4	93.6	98.6
浙江	Zhejiang	99.0	98.9	87.8	82.8	95.7	102.9	111.5	102.8	100.7
安徽	Anhui	98.0	96.8	86.5	84.0	98.9	102.7	108.1	92.9	98.5
福建	Fujian	98.9	98.4	90.2	96.2	94.3	101.9	110.1	101.7	98.9
江西	Jiangxi	98.5	97.9	87.2	83.4	96.7	99.1	112.9	106.1	99.6
山东	Shandong	98.6	98.0	90.8	90.4	96.2	105.4	105.4	95.0	101.1
河南	Henan	98.5	96.9	85.3	88.5	96.5	103.7	107.4	95.6	99.1
湖北	Hubei	97.8	97.3	83.4	80.8	98.8	101.1	109.7	96.4	97.7
湖南	Hunan	99.3	98.2	87.7	91.6	99.4	96.1	107.5	101.9	99.7
广东	Guangdong	99.9	98.8	95.1	94.5	95.6	101.8	104.0	98.1	98.7
广西	Guangxi	98.6	96.4	91.7	95.8	94.5	94.9	99.8	100.6	96.6
海南	Hainan	99.9	98.8	90.9	92.5	96.3	102.1	109.2	93.5	96.5
重庆	Chongqing	95.5	92.8	87.2	79.8	93.7	94.0	92.1	88.8	98.9
四川	Sichuan	97.7	95.2	88.7	84.2	95.3	92.9	97.4	92.2	99.7
贵州	Guizhou	97.3	94.4	93.2	81.6	94.6	95.2	99.4	89.3	99.3
云南	Yunnan	97.6	94.3	90.8	86.8	91.1	92.0	97.8	93.9	94.0
西藏	Tibet	99.2	98.5	100.3	102.6	94.0	95.4	103.7	94.0	99.5
陕西	Shaanxi	98.3	97.0	91.1	80.0	97.3	102.9	104.7	94.1	100.5
甘肃	Gansu	99.1	97.6	94.9	85.8	96.7	102.8	104.4	101.0	94.8
青海	Qinghai	99.0	97.9	95.8	82.1	96.3	106.3	102.8	101.3	97.9
宁夏	Ningxia	97.6	97.6	92.1	94.6	97.4	107.9	101.1	94.4	98.3
新疆	Xinjiang	98.3	96.4	88.9	83.6	94.5	95.3	107.4	94.6	101.9

9-7 续表 1 continued

(上年=100) (preceding year=100)

年份 地区	Year Region	饮食业 Catering Trade	饮料烟酒 Beverages, Tobacco and Liquor	服装鞋帽 Clothing, Shoes and Hats	纺织品 Textiles	中西药品 Traditional Chinese & Western Medicines	化妆品 Cosmetics	书报杂志 Newspapers and Magazines
	1994	128.2	111.3	119.6	114.7	111.8	116.4	133.5
	1995	123.5	107.8	116.8	115.4	111.5	109.9	115.2
	1996	108.6	105.1	108.5	106.4	108.8	105.0	136.9
	1997	104.7	101.2	103.5	101.9	104.4	102.3	112.8
	1998	101.1	98.8	99.3	99.1	102.8	100.5	105.1
	1999	99.6	97.3	97.3	98.0	101.0	99.6	104.9
	2000	99.8	98.0	99.2	98.6	100.2	98.9	105.4
北京	Beijing	101.2	101.9	102.9	98.3	113.6	95.3	107.9
天津	Tianjin	99.9	98.1	103.9	96.7	100.1	97.9	98.5
河北	Hebei	100.5	98.6	100.5	99.2	100.8	99.4	101.9
山西	Shanxi	97.2	94.2	100.3	94.5	100.8	99.1	101.7
内蒙古	Inner Mongolia	99.6	97.4	99.2	97.3	99.9	100.2	100.3
辽宁	Liaoning	99.9	96.8	99.0	99.4	96.9	98.6	109.6
吉林	Jilin	100.0	97.3	99.6	98.4	99.6	100.1	101.9
黑龙江	Heilongjiang	99.9	98.5	99.5	97.9	97.1	101.7	102.2
上海	Shanghai	99.8	96.9	93.8	99.6	99.6	98.6	100.2
江苏	Jiangsu	98.8	96.3	99.3	100.0	100.2	99.1	105.4
浙江	Zhejiang	100.1	98.8	98.2	99.3	102.0	99.4	103.3
安徽	Anhui	98.1	97.8	98.4	97.7	101.9	99.1	101.4
福建	Fujian	99.0	99.8	98.3	98.9	100.9	99.9	103.8
江西	Jiangxi	101.9	96.4	96.9	97.9	102.0	97.4	101.0
山东	Shandong	99.8	98.7	100.0	98.5	99.6	97.0	102.5
河南	Henan	100.2	97.7	98.7	99.3	97.2	98.9	105.5
湖北	Hubei	98.5	97.3	99.1	98.1	98.0	98.3	102.4
湖南	Hunan	99.2	97.6	99.8	97.7	100.9	99.9	111.0
广东	Guangdong	100.3	100.9	98.7	98.7	98.4	99.9	109.7
广西	Guangxi	99.4	99.7	100.0	98.8	96.6	98.1	105.6
海南	Hainan	98.0	97.5	103.7	98.8	107.3	99.1	105.1
重庆	Chongqing	101.7	98.1	91.9	96.7	100.6	92.6	110.0
四川	Sichuan	100.7	96.6	98.6	98.7	101.5	101.3	110.1
贵州	Guizhou	98.3	96.2	100.6	98.4	98.6	97.6	103.4
云南	Yunnan	101.1	95.3	102.0	96.3	99.9	103.2	109.1
西藏	Tibet	100.2	98.6	100.7	96.6	99.9	104.7	100.8
陕西	Shaanxi	99.5	98.4	99.6	97.9	100.8	101.0	107.3
甘肃	Gansu	97.0	95.6	101.8	98.0	99.2	99.8	110.3
青海	Qinghai	100.5	97.9	99.9	99.2	99.9	98.4	104.4
宁夏	Ningxia	99.4	96.3	97.7	95.2	98.1	99.8	102.6
新疆	Xinjiang	99.5	96.9	99.8	97.1	102.6	97.3	101.3

9-7 续表 2 continued

(上年=100) (preceding year=100)

年份 地区	Year Region	文化体育用品 Cultural and Sports Goods	日用品 Articles for Daily Use	家用电器 Household Appliances	首饰 Jewelry	燃料 Fuels	建筑装璜材料 Building Decoration Materials	机电产品 Mechanical and Electrical Products
	1994	109.8	113.9	106.7	110.1	115.1	112.9	100.4
	1995	108.9	109.7	100.7	99.4	107.4	105.7	96.6
	1996	106.7	105.3	98.7	99.4	105.0	101.2	95.8
	1997	101.7	102.3	95.6	97.8	107.3	99.0	95.5
	1998	99.0	99.0	93.9	90.9	96.1	97.1	92.3
	1999	99.5	97.9	94.0	94.5	100.4	98.3	95.1
	2000	98.9	98.1	93.6	97.6	117.7	98.4	95.6
北京	Beijing	99.9	98.3	92.1	89.6	109.4	97.7	97.1
天津	Tianjin	98.3	99.0	92.3	99.7	115.2	98.0	97.5
河北	Hebei	99.5	98.6	95.5	95.4	113.4	100.5	97.1
山西	Shanxi	99.2	98.0	93.9	96.2	113.5	98.5	94.0
内蒙古	Inner Mongolia	100.4	99.0	96.2	97.8	116.5	99.8	97.0
辽宁	Liaoning	98.4	97.2	92.5	94.0	118.2	98.2	97.1
吉林	Jilin	99.5	98.3	96.0	91.5	114.4	100.5	95.1
黑龙江	Heilongjiang	98.6	100.0	92.1	95.3	111.5	100.2	95.2
上海	Shanghai	98.0	95.6	90.6	98.7	119.7	95.3	98.7
江苏	Jiangsu	99.6	99.3	94.6	101.2	118.4	97.7	96.3
浙江	Zhejiang	99.7	97.8	93.7	100.4	121.0	100.6	95.1
安徽	Anhui	99.6	98.8	94.9	99.4	111.6	97.2	94.7
福建	Fujian	98.6	98.4	94.1	97.4	117.7	99.8	95.3
江西	Jiangxi	100.1	97.4	95.6	96.2	118.9	97.7	94.2
山东	Shandong	98.3	97.3	94.0	94.9	115.7	99.2	96.4
河南	Henan	99.4	98.2	94.2	95.4	115.7	97.5	96.2
湖北	Hubei	96.4	97.1	90.8	97.1	122.6	95.8	88.4
湖南	Hunan	98.8	98.6	94.2	98.1	120.1	97.0	93.4
广东	Guangdong	99.1	99.2	95.3	101.4	122.5	99.2	94.4
广西	Guangxi	100.1	99.1	94.7	98.0	126.1	98.2	91.1
海南	Hainan	98.8	98.3	96.2	94.6	116.0	99.4	96.0
重庆	Chongqing	96.3	95.8	91.6	99.7	121.7	93.3	91.5
四川	Sichuan	99.2	97.9	92.8	99.9	117.9	99.6	95.9
贵州	Guizhou	98.5	97.2	93.8	95.1	113.4	95.8	95.2
云南	Yunnan	98.0	97.5	95.5	104.6	123.1	96.0	94.3
西藏	Tibet	102.0	99.9	98.0	92.6	106.2	99.3	94.1
陕西	Shaanxi	98.9	98.2	92.0	94.6	112.8	99.5	95.5
甘肃	Gansu	97.4	98.5	94.5	95.4	115.8	100.4	96.3
青海	Qinghai	99.7	98.0	94.0	96.7	108.3	98.4	95.4
宁夏	Ningxia	97.7	98.7	90.5	97.6	122.9	96.3	91.8
新疆	Xinjiang	99.3	98.5	95.0	97.5	109.3	97.2	96.1

9-8 各地区服务项目价格分类指数

Retail Price Indices by Category of Commodities by Region

(上年=100) (preceding year=100)

年份 地区	Year Region	总指数 General Index	电讯费 Telecommunication	邮费 Postage	交通费 Transport	洗理美容费 Bathing and Haircut	文娱费 Recreation	学杂保育费 Tuition and Children Care	修理及其他服务费 Repair and Other Services	医疗保健服务费 Medical & Health Care Services
	1994	125.7	114.5	102.7	112.2	130.1	136.1	135.2	117.6	120.2
	1995	120.2	106.0	101.5	111.9	122.3	125.5	129.6	117.2	111.1
	1996	116.0	103.5	109.6	117.0	115.6	122.8	120.0	109.7	112.4
	1997	116.5	118.8	203.5	106.5	110.6	113.8	119.0	108.1	122.9
	1998	110.1	100.8	100.8	102.9	106.5	110.5	116.4	103.8	117.2
	1999	110.6	99.0	135.7	104.1	103.4	108.0	119.2	102.2	111.7
	2000	114.1	100.9	107.8	105.6	101.7	108.2	128.8	100.5	111.1
北京	Beijing	116.2	100.0	107.2	137.6	106.4	118.7	122.5	94.5	128.6
天津	Tianjin	111.6	100.0	105.7	112.8	100.0	101.9	124.4	98.4	100.0
河北	Hebei	110.2	98.9	105.5	105.3	102.2	106.3	123.0	100.6	101.4
山西	Shanxi	163.8	99.7	107.6	107.0	98.4	101.6	241.5	98.8	100.4
内蒙古	Inner Mongolia	120.8	98.6	106.4	102.9	101.6	100.8	151.6	100.6	103.4
辽宁	Liaoning	106.9	99.7	105.9	102.6	101.4	105.5	108.0	100.6	137.1
吉林	Jilin	107.7	100.2	107.5	107.7	100.4	111.1	114.2	100.1	100.7
黑龙江	Heilongjiang	105.3	100.2	106.6	104.7	101.9	107.0	104.4	104.6	114.3
上海	Shanghai	130.4	124.4	106.6	108.6	101.3	124.7	170.9	100.1	100.0
江苏	Jiangsu	109.0	100.6	107.7	101.6	102.2	108.3	119.0	101.0	105.0
浙江	Zhejiang	114.0	99.6	108.8	103.6	101.2	113.2	134.2	98.9	102.0
安徽	Anhui	117.5	98.7	106.7	103.9	101.4	102.8	135.8	100.7	104.1
福建	Fujian	129.9	98.4	110.1	103.8	102.6	101.6	179.3	100.3	153.9
江西	Jiangxi	116.2	99.6	109.4	106.4	104.7	109.1	133.7	103.3	105.1
山东	Shandong	114.6	97.8	106.0	103.5	101.9	106.3	125.9	101.5	126.2
河南	Henan	108.8	100.1	110.4	104.1	101.4	104.5	118.2	100.6	101.6
湖北	Hubei	105.4	95.6	107.2	109.0	102.0	103.0	107.7	101.5	110.0
湖南	Hunan	113.6	99.7	107.6	104.4	100.7	100.5	124.5	100.3	100.8
广东	Guangdong	113.0	101.0	110.1	101.6	99.5	104.9	129.5	101.3	117.5
广西	Guangxi	113.6	100.2	107.1	101.0	104.7	103.5	125.4	99.8	103.5
海南	Hainan	113.4	100.1	105.8	99.9	99.2	91.0	137.2	98.8	107.1
重庆	Chongqing	112.3	100.0	109.6	100.6	97.4	137.5	126.1	97.6	112.3
四川	Sichuan	119.4	102.9	109.0	106.8	103.3	102.0	139.7	101.2	108.3
贵州	Guizhou	117.2	100.1	107.3	104.8	103.1	121.3	141.7	101.5	121.0
云南	Yunnan	103.8	100.1	108.4	103.4	106.5	101.9	104.5	106.5	102.1
西藏	Tibet	106.4	96.3	98.6	101.8	112.9	102.0	107.4	106.1	111.8
陕西	Shaanxi	110.9	99.0	107.9	107.5	103.4	106.6	122.8	101.9	103.1
甘肃	Gansu	105.6	100.2	106.2	102.7	101.0	103.3	107.9	100.7	114.5
青海	Qinghai	103.8	100.4	110.1	106.6	104.8	102.8	103.4	99.0	107.2
宁夏	Ningxia	110.1	99.5	107.8	112.0	108.5	107.9	125.8	99.7	100.1
新疆	Xinjiang	113.9	99.4	107.3	108.3	102.4	103.3	135.6	100.4	103.1

9–9 各地区农业生产资料价格分类指数

Price Indices of Agricultural Means of Production by Category and by Region

(上年=100) (preceding year=100)

年份 地区	Year Region	总指数 General Index	小农具 Small Farm Tools	饲料 Forage	幼禽家畜 Young Livestock & Fowls	半机械化农具 Semi-mechanized Farm Tools	机械化农具 Mechanized Farm Machinery	化学肥料 Chemical Ferti-lizer	农药及农药械 Pesticide & Its Appli-ances	农机用油 Oil for Farm Machi-nery
	1994	121.6	124.4	127.0	138.7	117.8	115.9	124.9	105.9	119.8
	1995	127.4	120.0	150.3	130.4	111.0	116.4	135.4	117.4	103.0
	1996	108.4	113.2	109.6	102.7	105.5	103.6	110.8	109.5	103.9
	1997	99.5	106.9	94.8	132.9	101.4	99.0	92.2	98.6	109.0
	1998	94.5	100.1	102.6	86.4	99.6	97.6	91.4	96.4	94.9
	1999	95.8	98.8	97.0	82.9	98.3	96.4	94.9	95.3	103.9
	2000	99.1	99.3	93.4	119.0	98.2	96.5	92.9	95.3	123.9
北京	Beijing									
天津	Tianjin									
河北	Hebei	101.5	98.8	96.2	113.5	99.1	97.7	95.0	97.7	120.3
山西	Shanxi	102.5	100.4	91.5	149.0	98.4	95.9	91.3	96.0	123.9
内蒙古	Inner Mongolia	106.1	100.1	97.7	144.3	99.3	95.3	94.6	96.9	123.5
辽宁	Liaoning	97.5	102.1	97.4	120.7	101.4	97.2	91.5	96.8	117.8
吉林	Jilin	98.9	98.8	91.5	100.9	96.5	97.6	97.0	98.2	117.8
黑龙江	Heilongjiang	98.6	97.8	93.4	106.2	95.5	94.7	89.1	94.3	125.4
上海	Shanghai									
江苏	Jiangsu	98.9	102.0	91.5	128.8	97.5	95.2	93.3	94.8	120.9
浙江	Zhejiang	100.4	98.2	95.1	116.3	99.3	97.8	93.0	95.0	123.2
安徽	Anhui	98.2	100.5	94.0	111.8	97.6	96.0	92.2	97.1	122.0
福建	Fujian	97.4	102.0	94.3	112.3	98.9	98.4	92.1	95.1	126.2
江西	Jiangxi	95.9	96.5	99.2	111.2	97.0	92.4	88.6	93.2	120.1
山东	Shandong	98.7	100.2	92.6	113.5	99.2	96.5	92.6	94.6	123.4
河南	Henan	99.6	99.2	88.0	125.0	96.2	94.2	93.3	97.7	126.2
湖北	Hubei	97.6	98.8	91.1	151.0	92.8	95.6	91.7	96.3	118.4
湖南	Hunan	99.3	96.1	91.8	147.4	99.6	95.9	89.6	92.6	138.2
广东	Guangdong	98.1	97.6	92.2	106.8	95.7	99.0	94.0	94.5	120.6
广西	Guangxi	99.9	97.1	94.5	117.1	98.0	97.3	91.8	94.6	128.7
海南	Hainan	98.0	95.4	94.9	101.6	98.1	99.6	92.6	98.6	115.4
重庆	Chongqing									
四川	Sichuan	96.2	96.5	93.3	106.0	94.8	92.3	93.4	93.1	133.7
贵州	Guizhou	100.6	94.6	106.7	102.5	99.9	96.3	104.7	98.0	116.2
云南	Yunnan	98.9	103.6	93.4	97.2	101.0	98.1	97.3	97.9	122.7
西藏	Tibet	96.0	100.0	94.4	99.8	110.7	91.4	98.7	95.5	100.8
陕西	Shaanxi	102.2	102.6	92.3	132.9	99.2	97.9	92.4	99.4	127.1
甘肃	Gansu	103.9	96.8	95.7	131.3	98.8	96.0	95.5	95.6	131.5
青海	Qinghai	100.7	99.8	98.1	121.1	99.0	95.9	95.5	98.1	115.8
宁夏	Ningxia	96.0	96.3	86.0	127.6	95.1	92.0	91.5	95.8	130.6
新疆	Xinjiang	97.9	99.1	93.5	94.4	97.8	97.7	92.8	98.5	110.3

9-10 全国农产品收购价格分类指数

Purchasing Price Indices of Farm Products by Category of Commodities

(上年=100) (preceding year=100)

年 份 Year	总指数 General Index	粮 食 Grain	小 麦 Wheat	稻 谷 Rice	玉 米 Corn	高 粱 Sorghum	黄 豆 Soybeans	经济作物 Industrial Crops	食用植物油及油料 Edible Vegetable Oil and Oil Bearing Crops	棉 花 Cotton
1978	103.9	100.7	100.0	100.0	100.0	100.0	124.7	107.4	104.3	112.0
1979	122.1	130.5	131.1	130.2	130.0	127.9	124.0	123.4	132.7	125.3
1980	107.1	107.9	107.8	107.8	107.8	107.8	110.5	110.9	105.5	116.2
1981	105.9	109.7	105.2	105.2	105.2	105.2	157.8	106.9	104.9	104.8
1982	102.2	103.8	103.8	100.8	103.8	103.8	103.9	101.6	101.5	101.5
1983	104.4	110.3	110.2	110.2	110.2	110.2	110.2	100.3	100.6	100.2
1984	104.0	112.0	100.6	100.0	100.0	100.0	100.0	101.3	101.2	101.1
1985	108.6	101.8	100.1	102.0	101.9	104.8	102.8	101.5	104.3	97.7
1986	106.4	109.9	104.3	106.3	115.5	128.6	120.2	103.6	104.6	99.5
1987	112.0	108.0	103.4	113.2	104.1	123.4	103.4	103.3	106.0	104.7
1988	123.0	114.6	115.2	119.8	104.7	100.4	109.1	111.3	119.7	108.6
1989	115.0	126.9	121.9	130.7	131.8	120.7	122.8	116.7	119.8	122.7
1990	97.4	93.2	92.0	92.6	97.6	97.6	98.4	111.9	101.1	129.1
1991	98.0	93.8	94.2	95.9	88.2	94.1	99.8	101.6	97.9	102.1
1992	103.4	105.3	110.1	97.4	108.2	106.9	119.5	96.5	95.8	95.0
1993	113.4	116.7	105.4	124.6	119.2	119.1	122.7	112.6	120.7	111.5
1994	139.9	146.6	152.2	154.0	151.3	133.8	114.6	144.4	157.6	160.4
1995	119.9	129.0	133.1	120.8	140.9	143.2	113.1	122.5	103.1	131.5
1996	104.2	105.8	109.2	104.2	95.4	104.9	128.2	105.7	96.6	103.2
1997	95.5	90.2	89.0	88.2	94.2	79.0	100.1	98.0	104.8	99.8
1998	92.0	96.7	95.8	96.7	101.9	108.2	85.2	91.2	97.7	88.8
1999	87.8	87.1	88.9	87.7	86.3	87.2	81.8	83.7	84.8	69.8
2000	96.4	90.2	81.8	90.2	89.9	102.7	105.8	101.8	93.6	121.2

9-10 续表 1 continued

(上年=100) (preceding year=100)

年 份 Year	麻 Jute and Ambary Hemp	烟 叶 Tobacco	糖 料 Sugarcane and Beetroots	茶 叶 Tea	竹木材 Bamboo and Timber	工业用油漆 Oil and Lacquer for Industrial Use	禽畜产品 Livestock Products, Poultry and Eggs	肉 畜 Livestock for Slaughtering	#肥 猪 Fattened Hogs	禽 蛋 Poultry Eggs
1978	104.4	102.6	102.4	104.6	101.0	110.1	100.5	100.3	100.3	101.7
1979	112.3	107.4	130.8	118.3	115.0	105.6	122.6	124.2	124.4	120.3
1980	112.1	109.9	108.0	105.4	115.8	112.1	103.4	102.7	102.4	100.4
1981	104.5	122.5	109.1	106.6	127.0	99.6	101.1	100.3	100.2	106.7
1982	101.0	101.3	102.6	101.9	105.9	100.7	100.3	100.3	100.1	101.6
1983	98.4	100.5	100.2	99.7	100.2	100.1	100.5	99.9	99.7	107.3
1984	103.5	100.2	103.6	100.1	103.3	101.0	104.1	103.0	102.1	103.7
1985	109.5	102.4	102.1	113.5	155.5	101.6	124.1	122.6	121.1	115.1
1986	117.8	100.2	104.8	114.3	114.9	99.8	103.0	104.5	104.4	112.1
1987	74.1	105.9	110.3	112.6	120.3	103.9	117.9	119.0	118.6	123.7
1988	77.3	107.1	116.1	130.7	136.7	126.9	140.2	149.1	150.6	118.7
1989	115.1	95.5	135.1	92.6	105.2	107.0	110.2	109.6	110.5	115.6
1990	100.2	114.9	107.2	96.1	84.5	91.1	92.3	93.1	92.9	99.9
1991	101.7	100.7	104.5	112.7	102.4	109.5	97.4	97.4	96.6	93.6
1992	110.5	101.6	90.8	111.2	107.3	112.6	106.3	107.3	106.3	100.1
1993	101.9	109.8	100.0	117.3	111.1	83.9	114.2	114.7	114.5	113.3
1994	133.8	113.8	124.6	97.5	111.8	110.5	144.6	152.4	154.6	125.4
1995	131.6	144.3	142.6	120.4	105.1	109.0	115.8	116.2	116.0	113.5
1996	105.5	120.5	118.6	102.2	104.4	103.7	103.3	102.0	102.2	113.2
1997	86.4	89.3	97.6	90.9	98.9	107.0	101.8	107.7	110.1	86.3
1998	54.1	93.9	89.5	100.0	101.1	80.9	86.9	84.9	82.9	94.2
1999	106.0	107.4	80.4	97.0	101.4	99.0	88.5	87.2	85.2	91.7
2000	100.9	103.4	88.8	100.3	90.0	93.2	99.0	100.4	100.2	90.6

9-10 续表 2 continued

(上年=100) (preceding year=100)

年 份 Year	#鸡 蛋 Chicken Eggs	皮 张 Hides and Skins	鬃 毛 Bristles	蚕茧蚕丝 Silkworm Cocoons and Silk	干鲜果 Dried and Fresh Fruits	干鲜菜及调味品 Dried and Fresh Vegetables and Condiments	#鲜 菜 Fresh Vegetables	药 材 Crude Drugs	土副产品 Local Products	水产品 Aquatic Products
1978	100.8	101.5	102.0	100.1	110.4	103.0	100.3	102.7	105.4	102.5
1979	123.2	111.7	108.5	122.0	102.8	109.8	112.2	102.1	103.9	118.2
1980	101.0	112.7	104.7	101.8	106.5	108.5	107.3	102.7	105.2	101.8
1981	106.9	104.5	102.7	100.0	101.7	104.8	107.2	101.2	101.0	100.6
1982	100.5	99.6	99.8	100.6	102.7	100.0	99.3	102.1	101.3	101.0
1983	99.8	97.1	97.6	101.2	108.9	106.8	103.6	106.6	103.2	103.2
1984	101.6	108.0	116.4	100.0	121.0	99.9	98.7	106.3	101.7	109.8
1985	115.8	139.4	169.0	105.5	124.7	122.2	150.4	122.7	108.1	151.3
1986	110.7	117.0	82.1	107.4	108.0	104.8	101.2	77.9	112.9	110.4
1987	126.6	112.6	113.4	124.0	109.2	119.5	126.2	111.8	115.5	122.8
1988	116.5	122.5	134.6	187.8	139.6	122.2	130.9	162.1	119.1	134.3
1989	112.4	101.9	109.9	106.7	90.2	101.3	117.3	70.7	142.5	99.8
1990	102.9	80.9	74.9	96.7	97.5	94.1	96.3	95.5	92.4	98.8
1991	94.2	108.7	97.4	99.7	106.8	112.4	107.8	115.9	105.5	104.7
1992	98.8	117.6	102.8	95.7	92.8	117.3	111.4	114.8	109.9	108.1
1993	110.4	119.1	112.0	104.7	100.5	113.7	122.9	96.8	112.1	122.1
1994	116.6	133.1	132.1	155.5	119.9	124.6	135.1	99.6	120.0	122.0
1995	112.1	114.3	111.6	80.4	113.2	117.8	122.7	118.7	121.6	112.4
1996	114.5	96.5	92.7	86.5	99.5	103.6	102.0	111.6	102.2	103.4
1997	77.6	90.0	94.7	129.1	88.6	92.8	91.6	99.9	101.0	91.7
1998	99.9	87.6	81.5	94.9	94.5	92.5	91.7	106.0	88.4	93.9
1999	86.9	82.1	94.8	88.0	88.1	94.3	94.9	96.1	101.1	92.5
2000	85.7	106.2	128.7	137.7	98.6	99.5	99.9	100.8	101.3	100.5

9-11 全国农产品收购价格分类指数

Purchasing Price Indices of Farm Products by Category of Commodities

(1978年=100) (1978=100)

年 份 Year	总指数 General Index	粮 食 Grain	小 麦 Wheat	稻 谷 Rice	玉 米 Corn	高 粱 Sorghum	黄 豆 Soybeans	经济作物 Industrial Crops	食用植物油及油料 Edible Vegetable Oil and Oil Bearing Crops	棉 花 Cotton
1978	100.0	100.0	100.0	100.0	100.0	100.0	100.0	100.0	100.0	100.0
1979	122.1	130.5	131.1	130.2	130.0	127.9	124.0	123.4	132.7	125.3
1980	130.8	140.8	141.3	140.4	140.1	137.9	137.0	136.9	140.0	145.6
1981	138.5	154.5	148.7	147.7	147.4	145.0	216.2	146.3	146.9	152.6
1982	141.5	160.3	154.3	148.8	153.0	150.6	224.7	148.6	149.1	154.9
1983	147.7	176.9	170.1	164.0	168.6	165.9	247.6	149.1	150.0	155.2
1984	153.6	198.1	171.1	164.0	168.6	165.9	247.6	151.0	151.8	156.9
1985	166.8	201.6	171.3	167.3	171.8	173.9	254.5	153.3	158.3	153.3
1986	177.5	221.6	178.6	177.8	198.5	223.6	305.9	158.8	165.6	152.5
1987	198.8	239.3	184.7	201.3	206.6	275.9	316.3	164.0	175.5	159.7
1988	244.5	274.3	212.8	241.2	216.3	277.0	345.1	182.6	210.1	173.4
1989	281.2	348.1	259.4	315.2	285.1	334.4	423.8	213.1	251.7	212.8
1990	273.9	324.4	238.6	291.9	278.3	326.4	417.0	238.4	254.4	274.7
1991	268.4	304.3	224.8	279.9	245.4	307.1	416.2	242.2	249.1	280.5
1992	277.5	320.4	247.5	272.6	265.6	328.3	497.3	233.8	238.6	266.5
1993	314.7	373.9	260.8	339.7	316.6	391.0	610.2	263.2	288.0	297.1
1994	440.3	548.1	396.9	523.1	479.0	523.2	699.3	380.1	453.9	476.5
1995	527.9	707.0	528.3	631.9	674.9	749.2	790.9	465.6	468.0	626.6
1996	550.1	748.0	576.9	658.4	643.9	786.2	1013.9	492.1	452.1	646.7
1997	525.3	674.7	513.4	580.7	606.6	621.1	1014.9	482.3	473.8	645.4
1998	483.3	652.4	491.8	561.5	618.1	672.0	864.7	439.9	462.9	573.1
1999	424.3	568.2	437.2	492.4	533.4	586.0	707.3	368.2	392.5	400.0
2000	409.0	512.5	357.6	444.1	479.5	601.8	748.3	374.8	367.4	484.8

9–11 续表 1 continued

(1978年=100) (1978=100)

年份 Year	麻 Jute and Ambary Hemp	烟叶 Tobacco	糖料 Sugarcane and Beetroots	茶叶 Tea	竹木材 Bamboo and Timber	工业用油漆 Oil and Lacquer for Industrial Use	禽畜产品 Livestock Products, Poultry and Eggs	肉畜 Livestock for Slaughtering	#肥猪 Fattened Hogs	禽蛋 Poultry Eggs
1978	100.0	100.0	100.0	100.0	100.0	100.0	100.0	100.0	100.0	100.0
1979	112.3	107.4	130.8	118.3	115.0	105.6	122.6	124.2	124.4	120.3
1980	125.9	118.0	141.3	124.7	133.2	118.4	126.8	127.6	127.4	120.8
1981	131.6	144.6	154.1	132.9	169.1	117.9	128.2	127.9	127.6	128.9
1982	132.9	146.5	158.1	135.4	179.1	118.7	128.5	128.3	127.8	130.9
1983	130.7	147.2	158.4	135.0	179.5	118.8	129.2	128.2	127.4	140.5
1984	135.3	147.5	164.1	135.2	185.2	120.0	134.5	132.0	130.1	145.7
1985	148.2	151.0	167.6	153.4	288.0	122.0	166.9	161.9	157.5	167.7
1986	174.5	151.3	175.6	175.4	330.9	121.7	171.9	169.2	164.4	188.0
1987	129.3	160.3	193.7	197.5	398.1	126.5	202.7	201.3	195.0	232.5
1988	100.0	171.6	224.9	258.1	544.2	160.5	284.2	300.1	293.7	276.0
1989	115.1	163.9	303.9	239.0	572.5	171.7	313.1	329.0	324.5	319.1
1990	115.3	188.3	325.7	229.7	483.7	156.4	289.0	306.3	301.5	318.8
1991	117.3	189.7	340.4	258.8	495.3	171.3	281.5	298.3	291.2	298.4
1992	129.6	192.7	309.1	287.8	531.5	192.9	299.2	320.1	309.6	298.7
1993	132.0	211.6	309.1	337.6	590.5	161.8	341.7	367.1	354.5	338.4
1994	176.6	240.8	385.1	329.2	660.2	178.8	494.1	559.5	548.1	424.4
1995	232.4	347.5	549.2	396.4	693.9	194.9	572.2	650.1	635.8	481.7
1996	245.2	418.7	651.4	405.1	724.4	202.1	591.1	663.1	649.8	545.3
1997	211.9	373.9	635.8	368.2	716.4	216.2	601.7	714.2	715.4	470.6
1998	114.6	351.1	569.0	368.2	724.3	174.9	522.9	606.4	593.1	443.3
1999	121.5	377.1	457.5	357.2	734.4	173.2	462.8	528.8	505.3	406.5
2000	122.6	389.9	406.3	358.3	661.0	161.4	458.2	530.9	506.3	368.3

9–11 续表 2 continued

(1978年=100) (1978=100)

年份 Year	#鸡蛋 Chicken Eggs	皮张 Hides and Skins	鬃毛 Bristles	蚕茧蚕丝 Silkworm Cocoons and Silk	干鲜果 Dried and Fresh Fruits	干鲜菜及调味品 Dried and Fresh Vegetables and Condiments	#鲜菜 Fresh Vegetables	药材 Crude Drugs	土副产品 Local Products	水产品 Aquatic Products
1978	100.0	100.0	100.0	100.0	100.0	100.0	100.0	100.0	100.0	100.0
1979	123.2	111.7	108.5	122.0	102.8	109.8	112.2	102.1	103.9	118.2
1980	124.4	125.9	113.6	124.2	109.5	119.1	120.4	104.9	109.3	120.3
1981	133.0	131.6	116.7	124.2	111.3	124.9	129.1	106.1	110.4	121.0
1982	133.7	131.0	116.4	124.9	114.3	124.9	128.2	108.3	111.8	122.3
1983	133.4	127.2	113.6	126.4	124.5	133.3	132.8	115.5	115.4	126.2
1984	135.6	137.4	132.3	126.4	150.7	133.2	131.0	122.8	117.4	138.5
1985	157.0	191.5	223.5	133.4	187.9	162.8	197.1	150.6	126.9	209.6
1986	173.8	224.1	183.5	143.3	202.9	170.6	199.5	117.3	143.2	231.4
1987	220.0	252.3	208.1	177.6	221.6	203.9	251.7	131.2	165.4	284.2
1988	256.3	309.1	280.1	333.6	309.3	249.1	329.5	212.7	197.0	381.6
1989	288.1	315.0	307.9	356.0	279.0	252.4	386.5	150.4	280.8	380.9
1990	296.4	254.8	230.6	344.2	272.1	237.5	372.2	143.6	259.5	376.3
1991	279.2	277.0	224.6	343.2	290.6	266.9	401.2	166.4	273.7	394.0
1992	275.9	325.7	230.9	328.4	269.6	313.1	447.0	191.1	300.8	425.9
1993	304.6	388.0	258.6	343.9	271.0	356.0	549.3	184.9	337.2	520.0
1994	355.2	516.4	341.6	534.8	324.9	443.6	742.1	184.2	404.6	634.4
1995	398.2	590.2	381.2	430.0	367.8	522.6	910.6	218.6	492.0	713.1
1996	455.9	569.5	353.4	372.0	366.0	541.4	928.8	244.0	502.8	737.3
1997	353.8	512.6	334.7	480.3	324.3	502.4	850.8	243.8	507.8	676.1
1998	353.4	449.0	272.8	455.8	306.5	464.7	780.2	258.4	448.9	634.9
1999	307.1	368.6	258.6	401.1	270.0	438.2	740.4	248.3	453.8	587.3
2000	263.2	391.5	332.8	552.3	266.2	436.0	739.7	250.3	459.7	590.2

9-12 分行业工业品出厂价格指数
Ex-Factory Price Indices of Industrial Products by Sector

(上年=100) (preceding year=100)

年 份 Year	总指数 General Index	冶金工业 Metallurgical Industry	电力工业 Power Industry	煤炭工业 Coal Industry	石油工业 Petroleum Industry	化学工业 Chemical Industry	机械工业 Machine Building Industry	建筑材料工业 Building Materials Industry
1980	100.5	106.2	98.4	106.4	102.1	98.2	97.5	102.5
1981	100.2	101.8	101.6	102.6	99.3	97.2	98.6	101.6
1982	99.8	101.0	98.9	101.9	100.5	99.6	99.3	102.2
1983	99.9	101.3	105.6	101.5	106.3	101.0	99.3	102.7
1984	101.4	103.8	102.1	102.6	112.0	102.4	101.1	102.0
1985	108.7	114.3	103.4	117.6	107.2	102.9	111.8	115.4
1986	103.8	107.4	102.4	96.8	104.6	102.9	102.8	113.7
1987	107.9	107.0	103.1	102.8	104.0	112.2	104.9	105.6
1988	115.0	115.4	101.7	110.6	106.8	120.4	111.8	113.4
1989	118.6	121.0	105.9	112.2	108.4	119.4	121.2	123.6
1990	104.1	110.3	107.4	106.2	107.1	101.6	102.8	99.6
1991	106.2	114.2	116.9	113.1	118.8	102.4	102.8	106.1
1992	106.8	114.2	108.8	116.1	115.3	102.7	106.6	111.1
1993	124.0	157.7	135.9	139.7	171.3	108.3	119.7	142.8
1994	119.5	106.8	139.5	122.2	148.7	115.4	109.5	107.6
1995	114.9	105.5	109.5	111.3	121.2	126.2	106.3	106.4
1996	102.9	97.7	113.1	113.7	104.6	103.4	101.6	104.3
1997	99.7	97.3	114.0	108.0	107.4	95.5	98.1	99.6
1998	95.9	93.1	105.5	96.6	93.0	92.9	97.0	96.6
1999	97.6	95.8	100.9	94.8	109.6	96.5	97.0	97.7
2000	102.8	103.3	102.4	98.1	144.3	101.0	97.4	99.6

9-12 续表 1 continued

(上年=100) (preceding year=100)

年 份 Year	森林工业 Timber Industry	食品工业 Food Industry	纺织工业 Textile Industry	缝纫工业 Tailoring Industry	皮革工业 Leather Industry	造纸工业 Paper Industry	文教艺术用品工业 Cultural, Educational & Handicrafts Articles
1980	104.5	101.2	101.6	100.8	102.4	100.5	101.6
1981	111.3	102.3	99.1	99.9	101.7	100.6	99.0
1982	105.8	103.1	96.5	96.1	99.5	100.3	100.0
1983	100.3	100.8	94.8	95.7	100.9	101.1	99.9
1984	103.2	101.7	96.6	100.4	100.6	99.7	100.4
1985	114.9	105.5	104.3	105.1	112.1	113.7	103.2
1986	107.1	102.5	102.6	100.0	101.7	105.7	99.6
1987	144.9	109.4	108.3	109.6	102.9	112.1	120.0
1988	119.6	116.3	122.3	116.2	114.4	120.7	112.1
1989	115.7	114.3	122.4	118.9	118.3	123.0	111.0
1990	94.6	101.0	107.2	109.1	106.3	102.3	107.3
1991	100.4	103.3	104.1	109.0	109.0	102.9	105.8
1992	105.9	106.2	99.3	100.8	112.8	102.7	102.3
1993	131.8	113.5	103.8	117.9	111.8	108.9	110.6
1994	106.9	123.4	136.8	116.1	121.9	106.6	109.1
1995	99.5	123.2	117.3	116.5	121.7	144.5	111.4
1996	98.2	104.2	96.0	108.2	111.3	116.1	101.5
1997	99.3	99.6	98.0	103.9	98.3	94.5	100.0
1998	95.4	98.6	94.1	97.7	98.3	94.1	94.4
1999	100.1	96.7	96.0	98.0	96.8	95.9	93.6
2000	99.2	95.8	104.7	99.4	100.2	99.9	99.2

9-13 工业品出厂价格分类指数
Ex-Factory Price Indices of Industrial Products

(上年=100) (preceding year=100)

类 别	Item	1994	1995	1996	1997	1998	1999	2000
全部工业品	**Total Industry Products**	**119.5**	**114.9**	**102.9**	**99.7**	**95.9**	**97.6**	**102.8**
生产资料	**Means of Production**	**116.7**	**113.6**	**103.5**	**99.7**	**95.4**	**98.3**	**105.1**
采掘工业	Mining & Quarrying Industry	133.1	119.7	108.9	105.5	98.4	104.5	124.9
原材料工业	Raw Materials Industry	117.9	113.6	101.7	100.0	93.4	98.2	108.4
加工工业	Manufacturing Industry	111.1	112.0	104.1	98.1	96.8	97.1	98.6
生活资料	**Consumer Goods**	**123.8**	**116.9**	**102.1**	**99.6**	**96.9**	**96.4**	**97.8**
食品类	Food	123.4	123.2	104.7	100.8	98.9	97.4	96.0
衣着类	Clothing	136.4	115.6	100.5	101.1	96.2	96.1	100.6
一般日用品	Articles for Daily Use	112.3	115.1	102.9	98.3	96.7	96.0	98.0
耐用消费品	Durable Consumer Goods	108.4	105.2	97.7	94.9	94.0	95.6	96.4

9-14 各地区固定资产投资价格指数

Price Indices of Investment in Fixed Assets by Region

(上年=100) (preceding year=100)

地区	Region	1999				2000			
		固定资产投资 Investment in Fixed Assets	建筑安装工程 Construction and Installation	设备工、器具 Purchase of Equipment, Tools and Instruments	其他费用 Others	固定资产投资 Investment in Fixed Assets	建筑安装工程 Construction and Installation	设备工、器具 Purchase of Equipment, Tools and Instruments	其他费用 Others
全国	**National Total**	**99.6**	**100.3**	**97.5**	**99.9**	**101.1**	**102.4**	**97.4**	**101.0**
北京	Beijing	99.9	100.4	98.8	99.0	101.0	101.3	100.5	100.6
天津	Tianjin	99.2	100.2	96.5	99.8	99.9	100.7	97.8	100.1
河北	Hebei	99.4	100.0	96.4	104.3	101.1	102.3	98.4	100.9
山西	Shanxi	99.7	100.1	99.3	98.4	101.8	103.5	98.5	98.0
内蒙古	Inner Mongolia	101.9	102.8	98.0	102.1	101.9	103.9	98.0	98.7
辽宁	Liaoning	100.0	100.9	97.9	99.3	101.1	101.9	98.5	99.8
吉林	Jilin	102.2	106.1	100.1	98.6	102.0	103.2	99.4	100.1
黑龙江	Heilongjiang	99.7	99.7	99.8	99.4	101.5	103.1	97.3	100.7
上海	Shanghai	98.1	97.8	96.9	99.8	100.0	101.5	97.0	99.9
江苏	Jiangsu	98.3	99.3	95.5	100.5	101.1	102.3	97.8	102.6
浙江	Zhejiang	98.2	98.8	96.8	97.8	100.3	101.5	96.4	101.7
安徽	Anhui	99.3	100.8	96.1	100.1	101.6	102.8	100.1	98.2
福建	Fujian	98.5	99.3	94.8	101.2	100.2	102.4	94.9	98.8
江西	Jiangxi	98.6	99.5	96.6	98.2	101.4	103.7	96.2	101.2
山东	Shandong	99.6	101.3	96.2	98.3	102.4	105.1	97.2	100.4
河南	Henan	98.0	98.1	97.5	98.9	102.9	105.0	99.0	100.4
湖北	Hubei	99.5	99.2	99.0	101.0	101.7	103.0	98.9	101.4
湖南	Hunan	100.5	100.6	98.6	103.1	102.3	103.3	99.0	101.4
广东	Guangdong								
广西	Guangxi	96.1	96.6	94.5	95.9	101.4	102.4	95.7	104.5
海南	Hainan					101.8	104.0	97.4	100.0
重庆	Chongqing	100.5	100.7	97.7	104.4	102.5	103.1	97.0	108.7
四川	Sichuan	100.5	101.8	96.5	101.9	100.9	103.4	93.6	100.3
贵州	Guizhou	99.4	100.2	97.5	100.3	102.2	102.5	102.7	100.0
云南	Yunnan	100.7	102.0	96.5	101.4	101.6	102.4	98.3	103.6
西藏	Tibet								
陕西	Shaanxi	101.2	102.4	97.2	99.6	103.6	105.5	97.8	100.0
甘肃	Gansu	101.0	101.4	100.0	101.5	103.3	105.4	98.9	102.9
青海	Qinghai	100.1	101.0	96.2	100.0	101.6	102.7	97.9	100.3
宁夏	Ningxia	99.7	101.0	97.0	98.4	104.5	106.3	99.5	103.9
新疆	Xinjiang	99.0	99.9	97.6	96.6	103.6	105.5	97.4	103.2

主要统计指标解释

商品零售价格指数　是反映城乡商品零售价格变动趋势的一种经济指数。零售物价的调整变动直接影响到城乡居民的生活支出和国家的财政收入，影响居民购买力和市场供需平衡，影响消费与积累的比例。因此，计算零售价格指数，可以从一个侧面对上述经济活动进行观察和分析。

居民消费价格指数　是反映一定时期内城乡居民所购买的生活消费品价格和服务项目价格变动趋势和程度的相对数，是对城市居民消费价格指数和农村居民消费价格指数进行综合汇总计算的结果。利用居民消费价格指数，可以观察和分析消费品的零售价格和服务价格变动对城乡居民实际生活费支出的影响程度。

城市居民消费价格指数　是反映城市居民家庭所购买的生活消费品价格和服务项目价格变动趋势和程度的相对数。城市居民消费价格指数可以观察和分析消费品的零售价格和服务项目价格变动对职工货币工资的影响，作为研究职工生活和确定工资政策的依据。

农村居民消费价格指数　是反映农村居民家庭所购买的生活消费品价格和服务项目价格变动趋势和程度的相对数。农村居民消费价格指数可以观察农村消费品的零售价格和服务项目价格变动对农村居民生活消费支出的影响，直接反映农民生活水平的实际变化情况，为分析和研究农村居民生活问题提供依据。

农产品收购价格指数　是反映国有商业、集体商业、个体商业、外贸部门、国家机关、社会团体等各种经济类型的商业企业和有关部门收购农产品价格的变动趋势和程度的相对数。农产品收购价格指数可以观察和研究农产品收购价格总水平的变化情况，以及对农民货币收入的影响，作为制订和检查农产品价格政策的依据。

农村工业品零售价格指数　是反映农村市场工业品零售价格水平变动趋势和程度的相对数。通过农村工业品零售价格指数，可以观察工业品零售价格变动对农民货币支出的影响。

工业品出厂价格指数　是反映全部工业产品出厂价格总水平的变动趋势和程度的相对数，包括工业企业售给本企业以外所有单位的各种产品和直接售给居民用于生活消费的产品。通过工业品出厂价格指数能观察出厂价格变动对工业总产值的影响。

固定资产投资价格指数　是反映固定资产投资价格变动趋势和程度的相对数。固定资产投资额是由建筑安装工程投资完成额、设备、工器具购置投资完成额和其他费用投资完成额三部分组成的。编制固定资产投资价格指数应首先分别编制上述三部分投资的价格指数，然后采用加权算术平均法求出固定资产投资价格总指数。

编制固定资产投资价格指数可以准确地反映固定资产投资中涉及的各类商品和取费项目价格变动趋势和变动幅度，消除按现价计算的固定资产投资指标中的价格变动因素，真实地反映固定资产投资的规模、速度、结构和效益，为国家科学地制定、检查固定资产投资计划并提高宏观调控水平，为完善国民经济核算体系提供科学的、可靠的依据。

Explanatory Notes on Main Statistical Indicators

Retail Price Index reflects the general change in retail prices of commodities. The change and adjustment in retail prices directly affect the living expenditure of urban and rural residents, government revenue, purchasing power of residents and the equilibrium of market supply and demand, and the ratio of consumption to accumulation. Therefore, the calculation of retail price index is useful to analyze the changes of the above economic activities.

Consumer Price Index reflects the trend and degree of changes in prices of consumer goods and services purchased by urban and rural residents, and is a composite index derived from the urban consumer price index and the rural consumer price index. Consumer price index can be used to analyze the impact of consumer price change on actual expenditure for living cost of urban and rural residents.

Urban Consumer Price Index reflects the trend and degree of changes in prices of consumer goods and services purchased by urban households. It can be used to observe and analyze the impact of price changes in consumer goods and services on money wages of staff and workers, and provide basis for policy making concerning the living cost and wages of staff and workers.

Rural Consumer Price Index reflects the trend and degree of changes in prices of consumer goods and services purchased by rural households. It can be used to observe the impact of change in retail prices of consumer goods and service prices in rural areas on living expenditure of rural households, and to show the changes in the living standard of peasants. It provides basis for analysis and research on condition of life in rural areas.

Index of Purchasing Prices of Farm Products reflects the trend and degree of changes in purchasing prices of farm products purchased by state-owned, collective-owned, and individual commercial enterprises, foreign trade sectors, government agencies, social organizations and other units of various types of ownership. It is used to observe the impact of change in purchasing prices of farm products on the cash income of peasants, and serves as basis for the formulation and supervision of pricing policies for farm products.

Retail Price Index of Rural Industrial Products reflects the trend and degree of changes in prices of industrial products in rural market and can be used to observe the impact of the price change on farmers money expenditure.

Ex-factory Price Index of Industrial Products reflects the trend and degree of changes in general ex-factory prices of all industrial products, including sales of industrial products by an industrial enterprise to all units outside the enterprise, as well as sales of consumer goods to residents. It can be used to analyze the impact of ex-factory prices on gross industrial output value.

Price Index of Investment in Fixed Assets reflects the trend and degree of changes in prices of investment in fixed assets. The investment in fixed assets consists of three components, namely the investment in construction and installation, the investment in purchases of equipment and instrument, and the investment in other items. Price index of investment in fixed assets is calculated as the weighted arithmetic mean of the price indices of the three components of investment in fixed assets. Removing the factor of price change in the aggregates of investment at current prices, this indicator shows the changes in the prices of commodities and fees involved in the investment of fixed assets, and can be used to observe the actual size, growth, structure, and efficiency of investment in fixed assets and provides reliable and scientific data for government planning, management, decision making, and further improving the current national accounting system.

十、人民生活

People's Livelihood

简要说明

一、本篇资料反映我国人民生活状况，包括就业、居民收支、消费住房及主要耐用品拥有量、文化、教育、卫生、家庭设施等。

二、本篇中有关城市居民生活状况的数据来源于城市住户调查资料，是对城市居民家庭抽样调查汇总的结果。主要内容包括家庭人口及其构成、家庭现金收支、主要商品购买数量及支出金额、劳动就业状况、居住状况和耐用消费品的拥有量等。

城市住户调查是由国家统计局城市社会经济调查总队组织实施，各省、自治区、直辖市城调队及抽中城市的城调队依据国家统计局统一制定的城市住户调查方案，收集资料并逐级汇总上报。

城市住户调查采用固定样本户进行连续记帐的调查方式，每一调查期为3年，每年轮换三分之一。调查户是按"二阶段"、"划类选点"、"等距抽样"随机抽选的。

第一阶段，在全国范围内划类选点直接抽选调查城市。把全国市县按人口规模划分为特大、大、中、小城市和县城五种类型，然后在此基础上按六大行政区分组。每一行政区内又按城市职工平均工资水平高低排列，再把各城市的职工人数累计起来进行等距抽样，每隔100万职工抽取一个样本城市，作为调查城市。

第二阶段，在抽中的城市内采用多阶段和二相抽样相结合的方法抽取调查户。特大、大城市采用三阶段抽选一相调查样本，即先抽选调查街道，从抽中街道再抽调查居委会、最后从抽中居委会抽选调查户；中小城市及县城采用二阶段抽选一相调查样本，即直接抽选居委会，再从中抽选调查户。第二相样本是在一相样本基础上，采取分层抽选经常性调查户。

按上述办法国家统计局共抽选出调查市、县226个，调查户25000户。加上各地根据同一方案抽选的地方点调查户，共有40000户左右。

三、有关农村居民生活的统计资料主要来源于国家统计局农村经济调查总队的农村居民住户调查。主要内容包括农村居民家庭基本情况、人均总收入和纯收入、生活消费支出、主要消费品消费量、耐用消费品拥有量等。

农村居民住户调查是以各省（区、直辖市）为总体，直接抽选调查村，在抽中村中抽选调查户。采取综合运用多阶段、多重、分层、系统随机抽样等多种方法确定住户调查网点。农村住户调查网点分布在全国7100多个村、68000多个农户中。

农村居民住户调查在95%的概率把握程度下要求抽样误差不得超过±3%。为保证农村居民住户调查资料的准确性，国家统计局农村经济调查总队为调查户设置了现金和实物两本帐，并聘请了近万名辅助调查员帮助做好记帐工作，及时核实、汇总住户调查资料。

为解决调查户的厌烦情绪及样本老化问题，增强抽样调查网点的代表性，更加准确、及时地反映农村社会经济情况，国家统计局农村经济调查总队对农村住户调查网点实行样本轮换制度，每五年为一个周期。

Brief Introduction

I. The data in this chapter show the conditions of China's people's livelihood, including employment, income and expenditure of the residents, housing , possession of durable consumer goods, culture, education, health care and household facilities.

II. The data on the livelihood of the urban residents in this chapter come from the data collected by the sample survey on the urban households. The main content of the survey includes the population in the household and its composition, the cash income and expenditure of the household, the quantity of major commodities purchased and the expenditure for them, the employment of the household members, the housing condition and the ownership of the durable consumer goods.

The survey on the urban households is organized by the Urban Socio-economic Survey Organization, NBS. The urban socio-economic survey organizations of the provinces, autonomous regions and municipalities directly under the central government as well as the urban socio-economic survey organizations of the selected cities and counties collect the data in accordance with the survey scheme stipulated by NBS and report them to the higher organization.

The survey on the urban households is conducted in such a way that the selected households by sampling method should keep accounts for successive three years and be interviewed by the enumerators. By a rotation sampling scheme, one third of the old sample households should be replaced by the new sample households every year. The respondent households are selected by the two-stage stratified systematic random sampling scheme.

At the first stage, the cities and counties are firstly classified into 5 categories by their population size, namely the particularly large cities, large cities, medium-sized cities, small cities and counties. Secondly, they are grouped into the 6 administrative regions (northeastern region, north region, eastern region, central region, northwestern region and southwestern region). In each administrative region, the cities and counties are arranged in the order of the average wages of their staff and workers in the urban areas. Thirdly, the number of the staff and workers of the cities are accumulated and the sample cities or counties are selected by a systematic sampling scheme; the sampling interval is one million staff and workers.

At the second stage, the sample households are selected by the multi-stage and two-phase sampling scheme. In the particularly large and large cities, the first phase sample is selected by three-stage sampling method: Firstly, the sample sub-districts are selected; Secondly, the sample residents committees are selected from the sample sub-districts; Thirdly, the sample households are selected from the sample residents committees. In the medium-sized and small cities and counties, the first phase sample is selected by two-stage sampling method: Firstly, the sample residents committees are directly selected; Secondly, the sample households are selected from the sample residents committees. The second phase sample is composed of the sample households which are surveyed in a regular way and these households are selected with stratified sampling method from the households in the first phase sample.

In total, 25,000 households in 226 cities and countries are selected by the National Bureau of Statistics in the above-mentioned way. Additional samples are selected by local statistical offices by the same sample design, making the total sample size to reach 40,000 households.

III. The data on the livelihood of the rural residents come mainly from the data collected by the sample survey on the rural households, which is organized by the Rural Socio-economic Survey Organization, NBS. The main content of the survey includes the basic condition of the rural households, the per capita total income and net income, the expenditure for the residential consumption, the consumption of major consumer goods and the quantity of durable consumer goods owned.

The sample survey on the rural households is conducted by first selecting sample villages and then selecting households in the selected villages in each province, will all rural households in the province as the population. A combination of multi-stage, stratified, systematic sampling approaches is used to identify a total of 68,000 households are selected from 7,100 villages throughout the whole country.

It is required that the sampling error should not exceed to $\pm 0.3\%$, with confidence of probability as 95%. In order to ensure the accuracy of the data of the survey on the rural households, two accounts are designed for the respondent households by the Rural Socio-economic Survey Organization, NBS, the cash account and the account on goods in kind. Nearly 10 thousand assistant enumerators have been invited to help the households to keep good accounts and check and tabulate the data of the survey.

In order to overcome the boring feeling of the respondent households and solve the problem of aging samples to make the sample more representative of the population and able to reflect the rural social and economic situation more accurately and timely, a rotation sampling scheme is implemented by the Rural Socio-economic Survey Organization, NBS in selecting the rural sample households, with the cycle of complete rotation being 5 years.

10−1 人民物质文化生活情况

People's Material and Cultural Life

项　　目	Item	1985	1990	1995	2000
就业	**Employment**				
每一农村劳动力负担人数（人）	Number of Dependents per Rural Laborer (persons)	1.74	1.64	1.56	1.52
每一城镇就业者负担人数（人）	Number of Dependents per Urban Employee (persons)	1.81	1.77	1.73	1.86
城镇登记失业率(%)	Urban Registered Unemployment Rate (%)	1.8	2.5	2.9	3.1
收入	**Income of Rural and Urban Residents**				
农村居民家庭人均纯收入（元）	Annual Per Capita Net Income of Rural Residents (yuan)	398	686	1578	2253
农村居民家庭人均纯收入指数 (1978=100)	Index of Annual Per Capita Net Income of Rural Residents (1978=100)	268.9	311.2	383.7	483.5
城镇居民家庭人均可支配收入（元）	Annual Per Capita Disposable Income of Urban Residents (yuan)	739	1510	4283	6280
城镇居民家庭人均可支配收入指数（1978=100)	Index of Annual Per Capita Disposable Income Urban Residents (1978=100)	160.4	198.1	290.3	383.7
职工年平均工资（元）	Annual Average Wages of Staff and Workers (yuan)	1148	2140	5500	9371
消费水平　（元）	**Annual Per Capita Consumption (yuan)**				
全国居民	All Residents	437	803	2236	3397
农村居民	Rural Residents	347	571	1434	
城镇居民	Urban Residents	802	1686	4874	
储蓄	**Savings**				
城乡居民年底储蓄存款余额（亿元）	Balance of Savings Deposit of Rural and Urban Residents (year-end) (100 million yuan)	1622.6	7034.2	29662.3	64332.4
平均每人储蓄存款余额（元）	Per Capita Balance of Saving Deposit (yuan)	153	615	2449	5077
住房面积　（平方米）	**Per Capita Floor Space of Residential Buildings (sq.m)**				
农村平均每人居住	Rural Areas (Net)	14.7	17.8	21.0	24.8
城市平均每人使用	Urban Areas (Gross)		9.9	11.8	14.9
城市平均每人居住	Urban Areas (Net)	5.2	6.7	8.1	10.3
交通	**Traffic**				
城镇每百户拥有摩托车（辆）	Number of Motor Cycles per 100 Households in Urban Areas			6.3	18.8
城市每万人拥有公共车辆（辆）	Number of Buses per 10 000 Persons in Cities	3.9	4.8	7.3	10.8
城市公用事业	**Public Utilities in Urban Areas**				
自来水普及率　(%)	Rate of Access to Tap Water (%)	81.0	89.2	93.0	96.7
用气普及率 (%)	Rate of Access to Gas (%)	22.4	42.2	70.0	84.2
每万人拥有绿地（公顷）	Green Area per 10 000 Persons (hectare)	13.7	32.2	36.7	41.3
文化	**Culture**				
城镇每百户有彩色电视机（台）	Number of Color TV Sets per 100 Households in Urban Areas	17.2	59.0	89.8	116.6
农村每百户有电视机　（台）	Number of TV Sets per 100 Households in Rural Areas	11.7	44.4	80.7	101.7
广播综合人口覆盖率　(%)	Broadcast Covering Rate of Population (%)	68.3	74.7	78.8	92.5
电视综合人口覆盖率　(%)	TV Covering Rate of Population (%)	68.4	79.4	84.5	93.7
教育	**Education**				
学龄儿童入学率(%)	Enrollment Ratio of School-Age Children (%)	96.0	97.8	98.5	99.1
每万人口中在校大学生数（人）	Number of University Students per 10 000 Persons (person)	16.1	18.0	24.0	43.9
卫生	**Public Health**				
每万人有医院、卫生院病床（张）	Number of Hospital Beds per 10 000 Persons	21.1	23.0	23.4	23.8
每万人有医生数（人）	Number of Doctors per 10 000 Persons (person)	13.3	15.4	15.8	16.8

注：城市平均每人使用面积和居住面积为建设部统计数字。

a)Data on the per capital floor space of residential buildings in urban areas are obtained from the Ministry of Construction.

10−2 全国城乡居民储蓄存款年底余额和年增加额
Savings Deposit in Urban and Rural Areas (Year-end)

单位：亿元 (100 million yuan)

年 份 Year	年底余额 Outstanding Amount			年增加额 Increased Amount		
	总计 Total	定期 Fixed Deposits	活期 Current Deposits	总计 Total	定期 Fixed Deposits	活期 Current Deposits
1978	210.6	128.9	81.7	29.0	17.2	11.8
1979	281.0	166.4	114.6	70.4	37.5	32.9
1980	399.5	304.9	94.6	118.5	138.5	-20.0
1981	523.7	396.4	127.3	124.2	91.5	32.7
1982	675.4	519.3	156.1	151.7	122.9	28.8
1983	892.5	682.3	210.2	217.1	163.0	54.1
1984	1214.7	900.9	313.8	322.2	218.6	103.6
1985	1622.6	1225.2	397.4	407.9	324.3	83.6
1986	2238.5	1729.7	508.8	615.9	504.5	111.4
1987	3081.4	2361.3	720.1	842.9	631.6	211.3
1988	3822.2	2848.5	973.7	740.8	487.2	253.6
1989	5196.4	4215.4	981.0	1374.2	1366.9	7.3
1990	7119.8	5911.2	1208.6	1923.4	1695.8	227.6
1991	9241.6	7691.7	1549.9	2121.8	1780.5	341.3
1992	11759.4	9425.2	2334.2	2517.8	1733.5	784.3
1993	15203.5	11971.0	3232.5	3444.1	2545.8	898.3
1994	21518.8	16838.7	4680.1	6315.3	4867.7	1447.6
1995	29662.3	23778.2	5884.1	8143.5	6939.5	1204.0
1996	38520.8	30873.4	7647.4	8858.5	7095.2	1763.3
1997	46279.8	36226.7	10053.1	7759.0	5353.3	2405.7
1998	53407.5	41791.6	11615.9	7615.4	5473.7	2141.7
1999	59621.8	44955.1	14666.7	6253.0	3198.5	3054.5
2000	64332.4	46141.7	18190.7	4976.7	1310.3	3666.4

10−3 城乡居民家庭人均收入及恩格尔系数
Per Capita Annual Income and Engle Coefficient of Urban and Rural Households

年 份 Year	农村居民家庭人均纯收入（元） Per Capital Annual Net Income of Rural Households (yuan)		城镇居民家庭人均可支配收入（元） Per Capital Annual Disposable Income of Urban Households (yuan)		农村居民家庭恩格尔系数（%） Engle Coefficient of Rural Households (%)	城镇居民家庭恩格尔系数（%） Engle Coefficient of Urban Households (%)
	绝对数（元） Value (yuan)	指数（1978=100） Index	绝对数（元） Value (yuan)	指数（1978=100） Index		
1978	133.6	100.0	343.4	100.0	67.7	57.5
1979	160.2	119.2	387.0	112.7	64.0	57.2
1980	191.3	139.0	477.6	127.0	61.8	56.9
1981	223.4	160.4	491.9	127.6	59.9	56.7
1982	270.1	192.3	526.6	133.9	60.7	58.7
1983	309.8	219.6	564.0	140.6	59.4	59.2
1984	355.3	249.5	651.2	158.1	59.2	58.0
1985	397.6	268.9	739.1	160.4	57.8	53.3
1986	423.8	277.6	899.6	182.5	56.4	52.4
1987	462.6	292.0	1002.2	186.9	55.8	53.5
1988	544.9	310.7	1181.4	182.5	54.0	51.4
1989	601.5	305.7	1375.7	182.8	54.8	54.4
1990	686.3	311.2	1510.2	198.1	58.8	54.2
1991	708.6	317.4	1700.6	212.4	57.6	53.8
1992	784.0	336.2	2026.6	232.9	57.6	52.9
1993	921.6	346.9	2577.4	255.1	58.1	50.1
1994	1221.0	364.4	3496.2	276.8	58.9	49.9
1995	1577.7	383.7	4283.0	290.3	58.6	49.9
1996	1926.1	418.2	4838.9	301.6	56.3	48.6
1997	2090.1	437.4	5160.3	311.9	55.1	46.4
1998	2162.0	456.2	5425.1	329.9	53.4	44.5
1999	2210.3	473.5	5854.0	360.6	52.6	41.9
2000	2253.4	483.5	6280.0	383.7	49.1	39.2

10-4 城镇居民家庭基本情况

Basic Conditions of Urban Households

项目	Item	1985	1990	1995	1999	2000
调查户数 （户）	**Number of Households Surveyed (household)**	**24338**	**35660**	**35520**	**40044**	**42220**
平均每户家庭人口 （人）	**Average Household Size (person)**	**3.89**	**3.50**	**3.23**	**3.14**	**3.13**
平均每户就业人口（人）	**Average Number of Employed Persons per Household (persons)**	**2.15**	**1.98**	**1.87**	**1.77**	**1.68**
平均每户就业面 （%）	**Percentage of Employment per Household (%)**	**55.27**	**56.57**	**57.89**	**56.43**	**53.67**
平均每一就业者负担人数（包括就业者本人）（人）	**Number of Persons Supported by Each Employee (including the employee himself or herself) (person)**	**1.81**	**1.77**	**1.73**	**1.77**	**1.86**
平均每人全部年收入（元）	**Per Capita Annual Income (yuan)**	**748.92**	**1522.79**	**4288.09**	**5888.77**	**6316.81**
#可支配收入	Disposable Income	739.08	1510.16	4283.00	5854.02	6279.98
国有单位职工工资	Wages of Staff and Workers in State-owned Units	455.88	857.59	2590.03	3448.40	3500.63
集体及其它经济类型单位职工工资	Wages of Staff and Workers in Collective-owned Units and Units of Other Type of Ownership	113.52	170.39	400.40	560.00	582.15
职工从工作单位得到的其他收入	Other Income of Staff and Workers from Their Working Units	44.88	99.11	228.67		
个体经营劳动者收入	Income of Individual Laborers	10.20	18.71	90.60	221.92	348.20
被聘用或留用的离退休人员收入	Income of Re-employed Retirees	4.56	15.51	42.86	60.39	60.74
其他就业者收入	Income of Other Employees	1.95	3.79	8.44	15.58	30.96
其他劳动收入	Part-time Income	12.36	22.61	96.91	190.87	197.74
财产性收入	Property Income	3.74	15.60	90.43	128.65	128.38
转移性收入	Transfer Income	65.88	250.01	734.83	1257.17	1211.86
其他收入	Other Income	35.95	69.46	4.92	5.79	256.16
平均每人消费性支出（元）	**Per Capita Annual Living Expenditures for Consumption (yuan)**	**673.20**	**1278.89**	**3537.57**	**4615.91**	**4998.00**
食　品	Food	351.72	693.77	1766.02	1932.10	1958.31
衣　着	Clothing	98.04	170.90	479.20	482.37	500.46
家庭设备用品及服务	Household Facilities, Articles and Service	57.87	108.45	296.94	395.48	439.29
医疗保健	Medicine and Medical Service	16.71	25.67	110.11	245.59	318.07
交通通讯	Transport, Post and Communication Services	14.39	40.51	171.01	310.55	395.01
娱乐教育文化服务	Recreation, Education and Cultural Services	55.01	112.26	312.71	567.05	627.82
居住	Residence	32.23	60.86	250.18	453.99	500.49
杂项商品与服务	Miscellaneous Commodities and Services	47.23	66.57	151.39	228.79	258.54
平均每人消费性支出构成（人均消费性支出=100）	**Composition of Per Capita Annual Living Expenditures for Consumption (%)**					
食　品	Food	52.25	54.25	49.92	41.86	39.18
衣　着	Clothing	14.56	13.36	13.55	10.45	10.01
家庭设备用品及服务	Household Facilities, Articles and Service	8.60	10.14	8.39	8.57	8.79
医疗保健	Medicine and Medical Service	2.48	2.01	3.11	5.32	6.36
交通通讯	Transport, Post and Communication Services	2.14	1.20	4.83	6.73	7.90
娱乐教育文化服务	Recreation, Education and Cultural Services	8.17	11.12	8.84	12.28	12.56
居住	Residence	4.79	6.98	7.07	9.84	10.01
杂项商品与服务	Miscellaneous Commodities and Services	7.01	0.94	4.28	4.96	5.17

注：1.本表至10-14表为城镇居民家庭收支抽样调查材料。

2.自1997年起，取消职工从工作单位得到的其他收入项，其值被计入相应的国有、集体单位职工收入中。

3.自1992年起，取消特别收入项，其中主要内容计入转移性收入项中，另外少部分内容计入其他收入项中。

a)Data in Tables 10-4 to 10-14 are obtained from the sample survey on income and expenditures of urban households.

b)Since 1997, other income of staff and workers from their working units had canceled and its value had been divided in the wages of staff and workers in state-owned units or in collective owned units.

c)Since 1992, special income had canceled. Its main value had been divided in the transfer income and other minor value had in other income.

10-5 城镇居民家庭基本情况（2000年）

项　　目	Item	全　国 All Cities and County Towns	按城市规模分 (Grouped by Size) #特大城市 Especially Large Cities	#大 城 市 Large Cities	#中等城市 Medium-sized Cities
调查户数　（户）	Number of Households Surveyed (household)	42220	8700	5750	7460
比重　（%）	Proportion (%)	100.00	20.60	13.60	17.70
平均每户家庭人口　（人）	Average Household Size (person)	3.13	3.06	3.05	3.11
平均每户就业人口　（人）	Average Number of Employees per Household (person)	1.68	1.68	1.58	1.69
平均每户就业面　（%）	Percentage of Employed Persons per Household(%)	53.6	54.88	51.76	54.43
平均每一就业者负担人数（包括就业者本人）（人）	Number of Persons Supported by Each Employee (including the employee himself or herself) (person)	1.87	1.82	1.93	1.84
平均每人全部年收入（元）	Per Capita Annual Income (yuan)	6316.81	8427.48	6346.57	5894.52
平均每人可支配收入（元）	Per Capita Disposable Income (yuan)	6279.98	8371.66	6309.57	5860.92
平均每人消费性支出（元）	Per Capita Annual Living Expenditure (yuan)	4998.00	6870.18	5014.89	4626.04

10-6 城镇居民家庭平均每人全年消费性支出（2000年）

单位：元

项　　目	Item	总平均 Average	最低收入户 Lowest Income Households (first decile)	#困难户 Poor Households (first five percent)
消费性支出	**Total Living Expenditures**	**4998.00**	**2540.13**	**2320.36**
食品	Food	1958.31	1256.62	1172.77
#粮食	Grain	188.66	171.34	167.95
肉禽及其制品	Meat, Poultry and Related Products	411.31	283.41	261.07
蛋类	Eggs	56.59	44.60	42.19
水产品	Aquatic Products	143.54	88.35	80.01
奶及奶制品	Milk and Dairy Products	68.57	32.37	28.37
衣着	Clothing	500.46	190.07	166.66
#服装	Garments	337.24	115.75	101.14
家庭设备用品及服务	Household Facilities, Articles and Services	439.29	118.49	106.15
#耐用消费品	Durable Consumer Goods	259.10	48.97	41.10
医疗保健	Medicine and Medical Services	318.07	162.71	140.69
交通通讯	Transport, Post and Communication Services	395.01	142.73	124.55
娱乐教育文化服务	Recreation, Education and Cultural Services	627.82	286.83	258.18
#文娱用耐用消费品	Durable Consumer Goods for Recreational Use	146.92	29.34	20.51
居住	Residence	500.49	301.40	280.56
#住房	Housing	201.59	90.61	79.23
杂项商品与服务	Miscellaneous Commodities and Services	258.54	81.28	70.79

10-7 城镇居民家庭平均每人全年消费性支出构成（2000年）

单位：%

项　　目	Item	总平均 Average	最低收入户 Lowest Income Households (first decile)	#困难户 Poor Households (first five percent)
消费性支出	**Total Living Expenditures**	**100.00**	**100.00**	**100.00**
食品	Food	39.18	49.47	50.54
衣着	Clothing	10.01	7.48	7.18
家庭设备用品及服务	Household Facilities, Articles and Services	8.79	4.66	4.57
医疗保健	Medicine and Medical Services	6.36	6.41	6.06
交通通讯	Transport, Post and Communication Services	7.90	5.62	5.37
娱乐教育文化服务	Recreation, Education and Cultural Services	12.56	11.29	11.13
居住	Residence	10.01	11.87	12.09
杂项商品与服务	Miscellaneous Commodities and Services	5.17	3.20	3.05

Basic Conditions of Urban Households (2000)

of Cities)		按收入等级分 (Grouped by Percentile of Households)							
#小城市 Small Cities	#县 城 County Towns	最低收入户 Lowest Income Households (first decile)	# 困难户 Poor Households (first five percent)	低收入户 Low Income Households (second decile)	中等偏下户 Lower Middle Income Households (second quintile)	中等收入户 Middle Income Households (third quintile)	中等偏上户 Upper Middle Income Households (fourth quintile)	高收入户 High Income Households (ninth decile)	最高收入户 Highest Income Households (tenth decile)
3150	8480	4222	2111	4222	8444	8444	8444	4222	4222
7.46	20.08	10.00	5.00	10.00	20.00	20.00	20.00	10.00	10.00
3.11	3.20	3.56	3.60	3.40	3.28	3.14	2.97	2.87	2.66
1.69	1.71	1.59	1.54	1.66	1.69	1.72	1.71	1.69	1.60
54.42	53.35	44.60	42.81	48.61	51.55	54.77	57.42	58.97	60.04
1.84	1.87	2.24	2.34	2.06	1.94	1.83	1.74	1.70	1.67
6699.72	5190.18	2678.32	2350.75	3658.53	4651.72	5930.82	7524.98	9484.67	13390.49
6655.91	5162.17	2653.02	2325.05	3633.51	4623.54	5897.92	7487.37	9434.21	13311.02
5515.02	3970.87	2540.13	2320.36	3274.93	3947.91	4794.56	5894.92	7102.33	9250.63

Per Capita Annual Living Expenditure of Urban Households (2000)

(yuan)

低收入户 Low Income Households (second decile)	中等偏下户 Lower Middle Income Households (second quintile)	中等收入户 Middle Income Households (third quintile)	中等偏上户 Upper Middle Income Households (fourth quintile)	高收入户 High Income Households (ninth decile)	最高收入户 Highest Income Households (tenth decile)
3274.93	**3947.91**	**4794.56**	**5894.92**	**7102.33**	**9250.63**
1524.48	1748.90	1960.82	2215.56	2458.60	2847.03
178.29	186.53	188.18	192.24	201.71	210.87
340.08	388.58	422.22	453.29	485.99	534.10
50.68	54.39	57.53	61.02	63.11	67.36
107.32	128.08	144.42	167.68	178.59	205.34
43.24	56.69	69.34	82.13	95.54	117.29
279.10	375.07	504.70	627.81	760.39	933.52
175.51	242.54	338.28	428.23	531.01	658.57
184.27	256.85	376.25	526.42	780.47	1219.75
88.03	132.12	210.19	317.59	487.83	801.84
198.92	247.84	300.29	373.83	442.70	638.30
212.52	281.32	353.19	487.11	628.15	876.61
390.21	469.16	597.55	758.84	925.35	1223.97
51.23	78.47	130.04	188.72	270.22	401.49
368.20	407.82	470.95	578.89	681.61	864.71
122.64	139.90	176.93	249.45	310.16	435.79
117.22	160.95	230.82	326.46	425.06	646.73

Composition of Per Capita Annual Living Expenditure of Urban Households (2000)

%

低收入户 Low Income Households (second decile)	中等偏下户 Lower Middle Income Households (second quintile)	中等收入户 Middle Income Households (third quintile)	中等偏上户 Upper Middle Income Households (fourth quintile)	高收入户 High Income Households (ninth decile)	最高收入户 Highest Income Households (tenth decile)
100.00	**100.00**	**100.00**	**100.00**	**100.00**	**100.00**
46.55	44.30	40.90	37.58	34.62	30.78
8.52	9.50	10.53	10.65	10.71	10.09
5.63	6.51	7.85	8.93	10.99	13.19
6.07	6.28	6.26	6.34	6.23	6.90
6.49	7.13	7.37	8.26	8.84	9.48
11.92	11.88	12.46	12.87	13.03	13.23
11.24	10.33	9.82	9.82	9.60	9.35
3.58	4.08	4.81	5.54	5.98	6.99

10-8 城镇居民家庭平均每人全年购买的主要商品数量

Per Capita Annual Purchases of Major Commodities in Urban Households

项目	Item	1985	1990	1995	1998	1999	2000
粮食（千克）	Grain (kg)	134.76	130.72	97.00	86.72	84.91	82.31
鲜菜（千克）	Fresh Vegetables (kg)	144.36	138.70	116.47	113.76	114.94	114.74
食用植物油（千克）	Edible Vegetable Oil (kg)	5.76	6.40	7.11	7.55	7.78	8.16
猪肉（千克）	Pork (kg)	16.68	18.46	17.24	15.88	16.91	16.73
牛羊肉（千克）	Beef and Mutton (kg)	2.04	3.28	2.44	3.34	3.09	3.33
家禽（千克）	Poultry (kg)	3.24	3.42	3.97	4.65	4.92	5.44
鲜蛋（千克）	Fresh Eggs (kg)	6.84	7.25	9.74	10.76	10.92	11.21
水产品（千克）	Aquatic Products (kg)	7.08	7.69	9.20	9.84	10.34	9.87
食糖（千克）	Sugar (kg)	2.52	2.14	1.68	1.76	1.81	1.7
卷烟（盒）	Cigarettes (pack)	36.12	35.12	28.58	27.25	26.81	27.5
酒（千克）	Liquor (kg)	7.80	9.25	9.93	9.68	9.61	10.01
棉布（米）	Cotton Cloth (m)	2.61	1.33	0.47	0.36	0.34	0.32
化纤布（米）	Chemical Fiber Cloth (m)	1.47	1.46	1.04	0.73	0.55	0.37
呢绒（米）	Woolen Fabric (m)	0.36	0.26	0.19	0.08	0.07	0.05
绸缎（米）	Silk and Satin (m)	0.50	0.41	0.18	0.07	0.04	0.03
皮鞋（双）	Leather Shoes (pair)	0.55	0.61	0.82	0.74	0.79	0.78
煤炭（千克）	Coal (kg)	270.57	206.04	129.52	116.93	115.46	128.07

10-9 城镇居民家庭平均每百户年底耐用消费品拥有量

Number of Major Durable Consumer Goods Owned Per 100 Urban Households at Year-end

项目	Item	1985	1990	1995	1998	1999	2000
呢大衣（件）	Woolen Coat	116.2	169.98	204.15	191.12	195.23	169.63
毛毯（条）	Woolen Blanket	86.79	123.82	139.75	142.07	145.72	143.27
大衣柜（个）	Wardrobe	102.08	99.85	88.3	84.02	85.06	83.45
沙发（个）	Sofa	131.49	157.3	210.12	207.62	210.11	198.82
写字台（张）	Writing Desk	80.06	87.23	88.14	86.28	86.63	83.44
组合家具（套）	Composite Furniture	4.29	19.29	46.23	55.13	57.36	57.82
沙发床（个）	Sofa Bed	5.53	16.45	36.46	44.43	47.91	52.22
自行车（辆）	Bicycle	152.27	188.59	194.26	182.05	183.03	162.72
缝纫机（台）	Sewing Machine	70.82	70.14	63.67	56	55.43	51.46
电风扇（台）	Electric Fan	73.91	135.5	167.35	168.37	171.73	167.91
洗衣机（台）	Washing Machine	48.29	78.41	88.97	90.57	91.44	90.52
电冰箱（台）	Refrigerator	6.58	42.33	66.22	76.08	77.74	80.13
彩色电视机（台）	Color Television Set	17.21	59.04	89.79	105.43	111.57	116.56
影碟机（台）	Video Disc Player				16.02	24.71	37.53
录音机（台）	Tape Recorder	41.16	69.75	72.83	57.63	57.18	47.93
照相机（架）	Camera	8.52	19.22	30.56	36.26	38.11	38.44

10-10 按收入等级分的城镇居民家庭平均每人全年购买商品数量（2000年）

Per Capita Annual Purchases of Major Commodities of Urban Households by Level of Income (2000)

项目	Item	总平均 Average	最低收入户 Lowest Income Households	#困难户 Poor Households	低收入户 Low Income Households	中等偏下户 Lower Middle Income Households	中等收入户 Middle Income Households	中等偏上户 Upper Middle Income Households	高收入户 High Income Households	最高收入户 Highest Income Households
淀粉及薯类（千克）	Starches and Tubers (kg)	13.43	12.42	12.42	12.90	13.43	13.30	13.73	13.89	14.81
大豆（千克）	Soybeans (kg)	0.33	0.29	0.26	0.32	0.30	0.35	0.33	0.38	0.43
豆腐（千克）	Bean Curd (kg)	5.19	4.57	4.48	4.75	4.99	5.16	5.36	5.67	6.32
食用植物油（千克）	Edible Vegetable Oil (kg)	8.16	7.80	7.69	8.31	8.40	8.19	8.13	7.89	8.16
食用动物油（千克）	Edible Animal Oil (kg)	0.45	0.49	0.46	0.49	0.52	0.45	0.40	0.41	0.39
猪肉（千克）	Pork (kg)	16.73	13.28	12.63	15.07	16.40	17.01	17.60	18.71	19.78
牛肉（千克）	Beef (kg)	1.98	1.45	1.26	1.67	1.94	2.08	2.14	2.21	2.39
羊肉（千克）	Mutton (kg)	1.35	0.81	0.73	1.05	1.23	1.35	1.59	1.59	1.98
家禽（千克）	Poultry (kg)	5.44	3.74	3.45	4.60	5.21	5.62	5.95	6.31	6.88
鲜蛋（千克）	Fresh Eggs (kg)	11.21	9.26	8.81	10.30	10.95	11.38	11.92	12.08	12.89
鱼（千克）	Fish (kg)	4.30	3.19	2.95	3.72	4.07	4.40	4.71	4.84	5.41
虾（千克）	Shrimp (kg)	0.96	0.57	0.52	0.70	0.84	0.99	1.13	1.23	1.35
鲜菜（千克）	Fresh Vegetables(kg)	114.74	98.43	96.42	105.04	112.39	114.58	118.78	124.95	136.72
食糖（千克）	Sugar (kg)	1.70	1.50	1.45	1.69	1.76	1.71	1.69	1.67	1.90
糖果（千克）	Candy (kg)	0.62	0.34	0.32	0.45	0.53	0.62	0.74	0.85	0.99
卷烟（盒）	Cigarettes (pack)	27.50	22.32	20.60	25.85	28.14	27.68	28.79	28.42	30.88
白酒（千克）	Liquor (kg)	2.66	2.18	2.00	2.54	2.82	2.77	2.66	2.77	2.73
果酒（千克）	Fruit Wine (kg)	0.18	0.07	0.07	0.12	0.15	0.16	0.23	0.27	0.34
啤酒（千克）	Beer (kg)	6.51	3.68	3.39	5.23	6.50	7.23	7.05	7.51	7.99
其他酒（千克）	Other Liquor (kg)	0.66	0.60	0.61	0.67	0.65	0.69	0.64	0.71	0.68
鲜瓜果（千克）	Fresh Melons & Fruits (kg)	49.13	31.55	29.03	39.07	44.92	50.38	55.84	59.47	67.18
糕点（千克）	Cake (kg)	3.25	1.87	1.71	2.47	2.89	3.42	3.69	4.18	4.60
鲜乳品（千克）	Fresh Dairy Products (kg)	9.94	4.59	3.95	6.04	8.27	9.83	11.95	14.07	17.52
奶粉（千克）	Milk Powder (kg)	0.49	0.26	0.24	0.36	0.43	0.52	0.56	0.67	0.70
酸奶（千克）	Sour Milk (kg)	1.12	0.51	0.41	0.62	0.88	1.09	1.42	1.52	2.06
男士服装（件）	Men's Clothing (piece)	2.16	1.09	0.96	1.48	1.84	2.27	2.57	2.90	3.28
女士服装（件）	Women's Clothing (piece)	3.05	1.50	1.33	2.01	2.56	3.18	3.68	4.12	4.82
儿童服装（件）	Children's Clothing (piece)	1.03	0.61	0.58	0.87	0.91	1.05	1.19	1.26	1.44
棉布（米）	Cotton Cloth (m)	0.32	0.16	0.14	0.19	0.26	0.31	0.36	0.44	0.59
棉花化纤混纺布（米）	Cotton/Chemical Fiber Blend Cloth(m)	0.09	0.05	0.04	0.05	0.08	0.09	0.11	0.12	0.16
化纤布（米）	Chemical Fiber Cloth (m)	0.37	0.18	0.16	0.23	0.33	0.37	0.47	0.50	0.56
呢绒（米）	Woolen Fabric (m)	0.05	0.01	0.01	0.02	0.04	0.05	0.06	0.08	0.09
绸缎（米）	Silk and Satin (m)	0.03	0.02	0.01	0.01	0.03	0.04	0.04	0.05	0.07
毛线（千克）	Knitting Wool (kg)	0.18	0.11	0.09	0.15	0.17	0.20	0.20	0.21	0.22
皮鞋（双）	Leather Shoes (pair)	0.78	0.42	0.37	0.58	0.69	0.82	0.91	1.00	1.11
布鞋（双）	Cloth Shoes (pair)	0.21	0.21	0.21	0.20	0.21	0.21	0.21	0.20	0.23
其他鞋（双）	Other Shoes (pair)	1.52	1.07	1.00	1.28	1.41	1.59	1.65	1.76	1.92

10-11 按收入等级分的城镇居民家庭平均每百户年底耐用消费品拥有量（2000年）

Number of Durable Consumer Goods Owned Per 100 Urban Households at Year-end by Level of Income (2000)

项目	Item	总平均 Average	最低收入户 Lowest Income Households	#困难户 Poor Households	低收入户 Low Income Households	中等偏下户 Lower Middle Income Households	中等收入户 Middle Income Households	中等偏上户 Upper Middle Income Households	高收入户 High Income Households	最高收入户 Highest Income Households
毛皮大衣 （件）	Fur Coat	61.88	35.06	32.58	40.42	51.22	63.51	70.90	81.45	90.60
呢大衣 （件）	Woolen Coat	169.63	124.01	116.77	137.97	152.40	174.44	186.62	198.54	208.89
毛毯 （条）	Woolen Blanket	143.27	101.20	93.44	116.68	130.25	146.58	157.83	167.70	177.75
地毯（平方米）	Carpet (sq.m)	92.79	53.41	52.86	63.86	75.97	86.61	110.93	122.12	141.51
组合家具 （套）	Composite Furniture (set)	57.82	46.16	45.02	51.57	55.54	59.59	62.03	61.80	64.32
沙发床 （个）	Sofa Bed	52.22	34.91	32.68	38.95	45.08	53.09	58.66	63.56	71.17
沙发 （个）	Sofa	198.82	143.75	147.69	169.64	174.13	202.63	215.67	234.14	255.81
大衣柜 （个）	Wardrobe	83.45	75.16	73.84	77.17	79.41	83.05	85.55	90.16	95.98
写字台 （张）	Desk	83.44	69.59	68.60	73.77	77.55	83.14	88.84	93.52	98.44
摩托车 （辆）	Motorcycle	18.83	12.34	11.16	15.14	15.74	19.37	22.05	24.18	22.27
自行车 （辆）	Bicycle	162.72	155.80	150.80	161.86	165.06	166.33	163.41	162.13	157.78
家用汽车 （辆）	Automobile	0.51	0.24	0.29	0.34	0.36	0.36	0.61	0.75	1.13
缝纫机 （台）	Sewing Machine	51.46	49.73	49.59	51.56	51.85	49.67	51.50	52.72	54.50
洗衣机 （台）	Washing Machine	90.52	77.14	74.37	84.33	87.66	90.90	95.26	97.76	98.35
电风扇 （台）	Electric Fan	167.91	146.47	141.07	156.02	164.32	169.91	175.85	176.11	180.34
电冰箱 （台）	Refrigerator	80.13	61.95	58.68	68.52	75.43	82.45	86.26	89.71	92.80
冰柜 （台）	Freezer	6.52	5.87	6.33	5.55	6.02	6.13	6.20	8.16	8.96
彩色电视机（台）	Color TV Set	116.56	98.79	95.97	105.55	112.29	116.59	121.11	127.38	133.91
影碟机 （台）	Video Disc Player	37.53	21.30	19.04	26.72	32.73	38.71	42.54	48.72	50.65
录放像机 （台）	Video-recorder	20.13	13.68	13.27	15.02	16.86	20.17	21.93	26.17	28.51
家用电脑 （台）	Computer	9.72	2.99	2.88	4.17	6.01	9.01	12.12	15.25	20.50
组合音响 （套）	Hi-Fi Stereo Component System	22.20	11.76	11.60	14.50	18.50	22.49	25.96	29.64	32.18
录音机 （台）	Tape Recorder	47.93	37.85	36.24	45.05	46.04	48.90	50.37	52.81	52.97
摄相机 （架）	Pickup Camera	1.34	0.60	0.63	0.63	0.67	1.13	1.45	2.02	3.66
照相机 （架）	Camera	38.44	19.04	16.28	25.19	31.03	38.30	44.41	52.61	60.11
钢琴 （架）	Piano	1.26	0.21	0.21	0.67	0.85	0.88	1.68	2.41	2.52
中高档乐器（件）	Other Medium and High Grade Musical Instrument	5.34	1.51	1.24	2.75	3.81	5.22	6.71	8.06	9.65
微波炉 （台）	Oven	17.61	6.70	5.99	9.81	12.36	16.85	21.52	26.42	31.69
空调器 （台）	Air Conditioner	30.76	12.23	11.33	17.59	22.44	29.18	36.53	45.62	55.92
电炊具 （台）	Electric Cooking Appliances	101.94	75.69	72.44	81.10	92.35	103.49	111.07	119.53	129.25
淋浴热水器（台）	Shower	49.11	29.00	26.34	35.75	42.17	50.25	55.96	62.05	67.58
排油烟机 （台）	Smoke Absorber	54.07	32.37	30.10	38.65	52.13	54.32	60.37	65.86	70.16
吸尘器 （台）	Dust Catcher	11.17	4.74	4.28	5.87	7.50	10.49	13.81	16.81	20.71
健身器材 （件）	Healthy Equipment	3.48	0.87	0.78	1.42	2.03	2.80	4.34	6.21	7.98
移动电话 （台）	Hand Telephone	19.49	6.26	5.69	8.56	11.40	17.79	24.60	32.83	39.68

10-12 各地区城镇居民平均每人全年家庭收入来源（2000年）

Per Capita Annual Income in Urban Residents by Source and by Region (2000)

单位：元 (yuan)

地 区	Region	可支配收入 Disposable Income	实际收入 Real Income	国有单位职工收入 Income of Staff & Workers in State-owned Units	集体单位职工收入 Income of Staff & Workers in Collective-owned Units	其他经济类型单位职工收入 Income of Staff & Workers in Other Types of Ownership	财产性收入 Income from Property	转移性收入 Transfer Income
全 国	**National Total**	**6279.98**	**6316.81**	**3500.63**	**312.33**	**269.82**	**128.38**	**1461.68**
北 京	Beijing	10349.69	10416.39	5678.55	295.29	842.50	112.25	2862.24
天 津	Tianjin	8140.50	8165.12	3920.84	145.70	502.27	112.04	2568.71
河 北	Hebei	5661.16	5686.24	3378.50	245.36	71.42	146.13	1292.32
山 西	Shanxi	4724.11	4745.27	2728.86	148.96	191.19	50.94	1285.18
内蒙古	Inner Mongolia	5129.05	5150.84	2989.50	132.77	60.74	58.82	1110.14
辽 宁	Liaoning	5357.79	5389.03	2541.51	417.26	160.45	49.99	1512.60
吉 林	Jilin	4810.00	4829.17	2755.48	207.53	24.74	28.38	1167.12
黑龙江	Heilongjiang	4912.88	4945.45	2540.50	184.41	56.20	32.90	1388.87
上 海	Shanghai	11718.01	11802.40	5119.50	313.67	1284.44	64.68	3740.27
江 苏	Jiangsu	6800.23	6841.45	3307.85	726.89	209.80	87.45	1844.14
浙 江	Zhejiang	9279.16	9334.18	4010.90	599.80	1126.37	156.44	2253.26
安 徽	Anhui	5293.55	5331.58	2672.86	399.90	285.03	73.21	1284.06
福 建	Fujian	7432.26	7486.39	4225.45	325.24	304.31	155.55	1393.42
江 西	Jiangxi	5103.58	5129.51	3362.29	176.17	28.94	134.50	1027.32
山 东	Shandong	6489.97	6521.60	4631.85	526.31	240.85	112.52	774.00
河 南	Henan	4766.26	4784.04	2641.47	182.86	45.85	299.93	1216.13
湖 北	Hubei	5524.54	5542.60	3620.05	227.86	100.03	136.26	1062.36
湖 南	Hunan	6218.73	6261.15	4379.49	218.27	123.80	158.79	1008.11
广 东	Guangdong	9761.57	9853.65	5045.97	755.68	999.32	429.94	1459.81
广 西	Guangxi	5834.43	5881.65	3813.90	132.75	26.36	305.85	1027.72
海 南	Hainan	5358.32	5416.17	3314.25	103.87	52.05	100.81	1031.83
重 庆	Chongqing	6275.98	6296.74	3897.32	433.54	132.85	122.47	1263.18
四 川	Sichuan	5894.27	5925.59	3298.69	236.45	144.19	183.38	1462.27
贵 州	Guizhou	5122.21	5137.19	3243.42	183.18	25.32	40.04	1192.66
云 南	Yunnan	6324.64	6369.58	4181.53	447.71	63.71	178.46	1012.51
西 藏	Tibet	7426.32	7477.49	6667.54	309.71	45.65	4.69	355.95
陕 西	Shaanxi	5124.24	5149.30	2944.74	133.68	34.97	152.62	1495.59
甘 肃	Gansu	4916.25	4944.32	3427.04	162.63	33.66	17.46	877.80
青 海	Qinghai	5169.96	5196.69	3099.13	97.98	6.18	29.29	1394.00
宁 夏	Ningxia	4912.40	4948.04	2925.15	134.38	119.52	41.20	1143.00
新 疆	Xinjiang	5644.86	5686.52	3846.07	94.82	36.57	38.03	1285.16

10-13 各地区城镇居民家庭平均每人全年消费性支出 （2000年）

Per Capita Annual Living Expenditure of Urban Residents by Region (2000)

单位：元 (yuan)

地 区	Region	消费性支出 Living Expenditure	食品 Food	粮食 Grain	淀粉及薯类 Starches and Tubers	干豆类及豆制品 Beans and Bean Products	油脂类 Oil and Fats	肉禽及制品 Meat, Poultry and Related Products	蛋类 Eggs
全 国	**National Total**	**4998.00**	**1958.31**	**188.66**	**19.07**	**29.86**	**66.48**	**411.31**	**56.59**
北 京	Beijing	8493.49	3083.37	224.38	23.65	44.20	70.35	553.55	66.69
天 津	Tianjin	6121.04	2454.79	215.86	26.92	45.19	67.39	438.56	89.50
河 北	Hebei	4348.47	1517.94	199.05	19.38	24.74	84.83	287.98	72.55
山 西	Shanxi	3941.87	1375.97	239.85	30.02	26.96	65.04	223.94	58.42
内蒙古	Inner Mongolia	3927.75	1353.45	179.82	21.94	16.03	42.53	270.61	41.32
辽 宁	Liaoning	4356.06	1772.14	196.85	25.37	29.57	56.98	358.65	65.42
吉 林	Jilin	4020.87	1582.70	194.77	29.27	31.90	62.58	311.53	55.65
黑龙江	Heilongjiang	3824.44	1469.52	194.42	25.41	26.60	66.19	287.83	56.50
上 海	Shanghai	8868.19	3915.59	234.23	23.26	58.85	80.14	653.95	65.86
江 苏	Jiangsu	5323.18	2189.80	156.87	18.27	41.01	65.75	486.98	61.00
浙 江	Zhejiang	7020.22	2752.25	183.80	14.52	48.08	55.91	448.15	47.90
安 徽	Anhui	4232.98	1934.83	168.26	13.22	43.03	83.62	420.55	73.13
福 建	Fujian	5638.74	2518.02	235.12	12.84	26.18	92.60	547.62	58.52
江 西	Jiangxi	3623.56	1559.45	168.17	11.33	33.85	85.91	392.54	46.19
山 东	Shandong	5022.00	1744.09	152.05	17.60	21.94	43.91	326.32	72.16
河 南	Henan	3830.71	1386.76	219.78	23.45	26.43	55.61	264.88	67.48
湖 北	Hubei	4644.50	1779.39	147.21	15.46	30.57	70.03	343.41	50.68
湖 南	Hunan	5218.79	1943.68	173.10	11.17	31.38	81.31	442.12	45.37
广 东	Guangdong	8016.91	3096.33	225.84	11.65	26.20	79.32	836.39	42.73
广 西	Guangxi	4852.31	1936.07	159.31	10.55	27.16	72.94	656.57	39.45
海 南	Hainan	4082.56	2013.22	158.63	7.70	10.99	64.72	603.67	25.02
重 庆	Chongqing	5569.84	2308.70	180.46	22.64	31.46	87.76	526.39	72.05
四 川	Sichuan	4855.78	2014.30	168.91	15.27	22.77	83.33	505.94	55.73
贵 州	Guizhou	4278.28	1837.49	185.68	13.46	26.94	59.61	424.62	54.96
云 南	Yunnan	5185.31	2091.70	195.34	17.34	26.53	51.62	448.29	51.25
西 藏	Tibet	5554.42	2570.04	279.89	34.54	11.01	71.87	531.66	49.63
陕 西	Shaanxi	4276.67	1532.09	188.85	21.50	28.52	61.21	245.58	44.63
甘 肃	Gansu	4126.47	1552.77	185.62	20.40	18.61	63.59	250.18	44.52
青 海	Qinghai	4185.73	1711.03	241.08	25.78	9.89	63.84	354.45	41.46
宁 夏	Ningxia	4200.50	1500.85	186.86	21.83	19.40	66.24	282.42	37.45
新 疆	Xinjiang	4422.93	1609.17	196.02	14.50	14.81	65.50	394.03	37.22

10-13 续表 1 continued

单位：元 (yuan)

地 区	Region	水产品类 Aquatic Products	菜 类 Vegetables	调 味 品 Condiments	糖 类 Sugar	烟 草 类 Tobacco	酒和饮料 Liquor and Beverages	干鲜瓜果类 Dried and Fresh Melons and Fruits	坚果及果仁 Nuts and Kernels
全 国	**National Total**	**143.54**	**192.32**	**29.73**	**24.31**	**100.85**	**103.18**	**127.51**	**23.84**
北 京	Beijing	132.00	235.72	54.85	40.76	97.51	214.92	216.47	56.01
天 津	Tianjin	224.83	197.82	46.76	23.66	102.16	131.51	164.77	42.95
河 北	Hebei	75.27	176.09	22.63	29.21	74.37	114.23	110.65	27.54
山 西	Shanxi	30.22	146.53	26.24	16.90	111.71	78.53	87.95	15.19
内蒙古	Inner Mongolia	36.63	117.51	21.73	17.80	77.75	84.43	94.78	17.92
辽 宁	Liaoning	130.94	241.85	31.44	26.45	96.93	107.44	151.38	29.32
吉 林	Jilin	84.17	198.78	30.09	23.03	58.57	87.69	141.43	21.79
黑龙江	Heilongjiang	75.24	159.12	24.06	21.16	64.56	85.81	127.50	19.47
上 海	Shanghai	604.07	305.43	47.49	49.55	192.38	189.63	245.10	47.53
江 苏	Jiangsu	220.60	197.49	35.22	23.73	126.64	108.61	111.15	25.16
浙 江	Zhejiang	403.76	236.88	32.48	28.15	196.04	138.10	187.25	36.55
安 徽	Anhui	115.57	190.97	31.45	16.97	164.95	145.89	96.23	16.97
福 建	Fujian	415.73	250.70	30.97	18.20	128.18	142.89	183.11	17.80
江 西	Jiangxi	95.31	180.53	23.12	16.94	61.27	55.46	88.98	19.50
山 东	Shandong	121.93	143.26	22.05	20.12	56.27	120.87	120.26	24.24
河 南	Henan	34.76	138.55	26.50	16.42	87.18	110.75	74.92	23.12
湖 北	Hubei	90.71	198.35	27.27	20.56	108.42	85.81	80.68	16.40
湖 南	Hunan	98.73	190.65	20.38	22.69	96.77	75.62	146.36	18.27
广 东	Guangdong	326.90	269.52	31.80	32.81	72.64	76.07	168.82	21.48
广 西	Guangxi	119.39	168.13	20.25	25.63	57.74	63.00	122.90	18.29
海 南	Hainan	267.27	204.79	32.84	14.74	63.28	35.97	86.75	4.72
重 庆	Chongqing	85.29	225.41	49.19	35.16	132.91	101.31	141.14	19.01
四 川	Sichuan	53.58	205.55	39.46	31.76	136.40	103.99	99.60	19.51
贵 州	Guizhou	38.58	198.18	31.63	35.28	159.93	105.46	110.43	26.26
云 南	Yunnan	71.05	220.96	26.88	27.55	215.65	74.27	141.42	17.56
西 藏	Tibet	96.58	307.47	20.34	69.28	274.91	157.02	174.63	21.48
陕 西	Shaanxi	33.09	146.02	27.35	16.28	91.06	76.96	92.23	21.64
甘 肃	Gansu	35.06	155.01	27.78	20.89	128.95	122.79	112.38	19.86
青 海	Qinghai	40.17	156.45	24.29	23.35	108.37	123.32	94.17	18.73
宁 夏	Ningxia	41.00	158.59	23.50	20.05	94.97	69.13	112.80	22.49
新 疆	Xinjiang	46.04	157.92	20.14	27.27	50.75	69.81	120.10	28.03

10-13 续表 2 continued

单位：元 (yuan)

地区	Region	糕点类 Cake	奶及奶制品 Milk and Dairy Products	其他食品 Other Food	在外用餐 Dining Out	食品加工服务费 Food Processing Service Fees	衣着 Clothing	服装 Garments	衣着材料 Clothing Materials
全国	**National Total**	**41.81**	**68.57**	**41.99**	**287.80**	**0.87**	**500.46**	**337.24**	**23.46**
北京	Beijing	107.27	178.33	99.69	666.75	0.27	755.03	497.23	36.60
天津	Tianjin	67.88	98.59	58.51	410.36	1.58	544.35	369.84	31.38
河北	Hebei	30.09	63.33	19.64	85.00	1.35	534.35	339.69	36.45
山西	Shanxi	32.16	63.02	29.98	92.70	0.61	511.19	335.18	36.43
内蒙古	Inner Mongolia	24.12	54.87	37.89	194.65	1.12	560.57	361.73	33.71
辽宁	Liaoning	33.36	64.42	19.31	105.71	0.75	568.25	377.11	21.60
吉林	Jilin	25.02	47.16	37.69	140.70	0.88	506.85	335.67	25.00
黑龙江	Heilongjiang	24.27	57.61	19.22	133.76	0.78	508.85	339.97	15.60
上海	Shanghai	113.93	200.90	124.68	678.61	0.00	567.37	387.20	24.07
江苏	Jiangsu	45.12	79.74	58.41	326.04	2.01	492.10	329.79	23.15
浙江	Zhejiang	56.42	81.86	51.89	503.94	0.57	569.95	388.62	27.53
安徽	Anhui	41.13	51.99	20.20	240.22	0.48	437.55	294.40	22.20
福建	Fujian	36.35	104.48	16.72	199.86	0.16	491.75	365.05	12.86
江西	Jiangxi	27.84	43.43	33.34	175.34	0.39	321.69	206.20	17.62
山东	Shandong	55.04	84.25	47.58	292.87	1.35	665.62	434.02	46.23
河南	Henan	31.07	43.28	14.04	127.27	1.29	460.99	314.99	28.10
湖北	Hubei	36.17	43.35	30.42	383.00	0.88	530.28	368.37	19.19
湖南	Hunan	31.84	40.32	41.57	375.74	0.29	495.16	337.68	18.95
广东	Guangdong	63.23	65.18	86.68	658.52	0.55	369.99	271.62	4.05
广西	Guangxi	31.27	46.11	24.59	272.32	0.46	313.42	219.26	14.13
海南	Hainan	32.28	27.87	21.79	349.97	0.22	187.25	133.44	3.19
重庆	Chongqing	44.68	111.42	31.62	409.97	0.82	551.14	394.90	8.58
四川	Sichuan	32.56	70.66	20.77	346.74	1.78	463.81	330.61	12.95
贵州	Guizhou	41.72	47.79	23.77	251.92	1.24	453.10	297.93	18.43
云南	Yunnan	44.99	45.76	45.02	370.03	0.18	521.92	383.41	14.73
西藏	Tibet	35.12	282.74	36.08	102.83	12.96	876.01	656.99	22.13
陕西	Shaanxi	41.76	50.91	59.20	284.05	1.25	403.24	257.38	26.11
甘肃	Gansu	24.45	58.60	61.09	202.01	0.97	517.16	329.23	35.59
青海	Qinghai	22.79	56.73	60.63	244.95	0.58	458.57	317.22	20.09
宁夏	Ningxia	29.32	58.53	33.67	222.12	0.49	561.93	377.03	34.02
新疆	Xinjiang	36.73	59.95	28.98	240.63	0.76	577.40	369.73	37.64

10-13 续表 3 continued

单位：元 (yuan)

地　区	Region	鞋帽袜及其他衣着 Foot,Wear,Hats and Other Clothing	衣着加工服务费 Tailoring and Laundering Service Fees	家庭设备用品及服务 Household Facilities, Articles and Services	耐用消费品 Durable Consumer Goods	室内装饰品 Room Decorations	床上用品 Bed Articles	家庭日用杂品 Household Articles for Daily Use	家具材料 Furniture Materials
全　国	**National Total**	**130.75**	**9.02**	**439.29**	**259.10**	**15.66**	**20.47**	**91.61**	**6.60**
北　京	Beijing	202.73	18.48	1097.82	725.95	27.20	29.65	190.45	14.48
天　津	Tianjin	131.74	11.39	722.24	513.37	18.02	20.97	91.80	5.11
河　北	Hebei	147.06	11.16	444.60	326.68	13.72	15.29	67.54	1.34
山　西	Shanxi	133.04	6.54	356.05	204.95	17.19	21.14	65.19	20.52
内蒙古	Inner Mongolia	151.28	13.84	288.77	156.86	15.71	15.84	67.34	7.27
辽　宁	Liaoning	160.13	9.41	298.66	177.93	9.67	18.37	63.55	13.37
吉　林	Jilin	137.73	8.44	232.07	113.61	5.21	14.76	74.78	1.36
黑龙江	Heilongjiang	146.39	6.88	227.52	109.09	6.29	14.00	55.14	1.97
上　海	Shanghai	147.36	8.74	735.75	393.25	21.54	33.38	145.89	1.98
江　苏	Jiangsu	125.97	13.18	570.37	346.88	11.55	22.97	112.16	7.32
浙　江	Zhejiang	140.53	13.27	662.31	413.68	16.99	30.44	103.49	7.43
安　徽	Anhui	112.90	8.06	301.43	173.05	10.55	10.72	63.24	2.64
福　建	Fujian	103.23	10.61	484.67	261.74	13.68	33.35	93.23	9.90
江　西	Jiangxi	90.27	7.60	264.29	144.44	8.98	16.40	77.34	3.82
山　东	Shandong	168.59	16.78	561.15	379.73	29.76	18.16	100.53	3.55
河　南	Henan	108.48	9.42	312.97	187.41	11.15	20.37	59.40	3.75
湖　北	Hubei	136.34	6.38	377.27	198.65	19.83	13.35	111.78	9.28
湖　南	Hunan	131.48	7.06	544.53	335.59	17.79	25.02	114.60	18.02
广　东	Guangdong	91.67	2.65	603.19	324.01	15.69	29.72	144.49	7.80
广　西	Guangxi	74.79	5.25	436.88	259.50	18.35	21.01	95.82	5.44
海　南	Hainan	49.48	1.14	201.76	67.01	6.93	22.32	93.15	1.47
重　庆	Chongqing	145.16	2.50	476.45	299.63	12.51	22.53	91.19	0.13
四　川	Sichuan	117.87	2.38	418.81	213.58	20.42	19.28	96.15	11.51
贵　州	Guizhou	130.88	5.87	408.93	239.24	13.69	22.78	97.03	2.67
云　南	Yunnan	122.29	1.49	384.15	221.11	29.80	33.56	61.55	3.17
西　藏	Tibet	195.34	1.56	274.84	150.89	16.53	28.45	73.03	0.20
陕　西	Shaanxi	110.83	8.93	472.63	282.71	25.36	19.43	94.06	2.10
甘　肃	Gansu	137.18	15.16	402.03	227.10	24.44	20.05	104.00	6.89
青　海	Qinghai	112.37	8.89	334.91	204.85	19.27	18.07	67.84	10.02
宁　夏	Ningxia	138.68	12.20	389.45	228.34	20.92	19.29	74.21	6.55
新　疆	Xinjiang	152.84	17.19	410.88	229.10	20.54	12.46	88.67	6.77

10-13 续表 4 continued

单位：元 (yuan)

地 区	Region	家务服务 Household Services	医疗保健 Medicine and Medical Services	交通和通讯 Transport and Communication Services	交 通 Transport	通 讯 Communication Services	娱乐教育文化服务 Recreation Education and Cultural Services	文娱用耐用消费品 Recreational Durable Consumer Goods	教 育 Education
全 国	**National Total**	**45.85**	**318.07**	**395.01**	**162.22**	**232.79**	**627.82**	**146.92**	**363.75**
北 京	Beijing	110.08	588.80	604.69	230.39	374.31	1283.85	367.05	616.27
天 津	Tianjin	72.96	407.75	348.92	133.75	215.17	787.65	227.49	393.82
河 北	Hebei	20.03	376.71	337.15	134.05	203.10	529.35	143.89	319.15
山 西	Shanxi	27.06	300.81	285.25	108.80	176.45	501.78	113.50	309.53
内蒙古	Inner Mongolia	25.75	287.03	358.51	172.41	186.10	488.61	86.15	302.16
辽 宁	Liaoning	15.77	352.20	307.21	97.29	209.92	490.83	96.50	321.29
吉 林	Jilin	22.35	336.00	294.99	118.22	176.77	458.92	76.23	295.30
黑龙江	Heilongjiang	41.03	341.85	288.88	94.94	193.94	457.55	60.23	314.39
上 海	Shanghai	139.71	500.86	691.61	307.47	384.14	1227.70	407.99	585.45
江 苏	Jiangsu	69.50	294.39	392.38	154.67	237.71	670.56	161.53	378.43
浙 江	Zhejiang	90.27	541.06	623.05	274.38	348.67	917.23	263.87	489.63
安 徽	Anhui	41.22	181.23	307.87	113.52	194.35	508.62	103.34	316.58
福 建	Fujian	72.76	266.00	487.04	155.87	331.17	584.76	153.32	324.58
江 西	Jiangxi	13.32	148.80	255.26	77.51	177.75	411.72	73.75	265.30
山 东	Shandong	29.42	322.60	353.61	157.53	196.07	712.42	172.76	405.76
河 南	Henan	30.88	280.78	246.24	94.36	151.89	407.26	100.19	234.20
湖 北	Hubei	24.38	208.96	280.74	129.35	151.40	607.00	86.27	417.24
湖 南	Hunan	33.53	270.24	395.65	151.73	243.92	753.83	151.40	473.47
广 东	Guangdong	81.49	346.56	1076.80	524.22	552.58	921.44	203.24	525.44
广 西	Guangxi	36.77	228.01	372.78	195.56	177.22	585.67	133.43	348.93
海 南	Hainan	10.88	247.31	350.38	176.71	173.67	472.95	64.84	328.01
重 庆	Chongqing	50.44	293.23	406.44	157.91	248.53	785.74	136.36	496.94
四 川	Sichuan	57.86	266.07	304.52	115.48	189.04	627.18	134.18	367.92
贵 州	Guizhou	33.52	233.28	335.28	135.62	199.66	460.44	110.57	252.51
云 南	Yunnan	34.96	291.76	421.76	170.04	251.72	649.33	208.53	332.13
西 藏	Tibet	5.75	264.80	442.69	134.08	308.61	418.92	105.01	256.36
陕 西	Shaanxi	48.97	336.24	297.66	117.87	179.79	549.25	128.20	317.97
甘 肃	Gansu	19.56	272.44	265.29	102.05	163.24	563.10	182.79	264.44
青 海	Qinghai	14.86	307.24	297.72	124.05	173.67	495.34	92.44	313.71
宁 夏	Ningxia	40.15	327.05	371.83	143.47	228.36	536.29	168.17	255.99
新 疆	Xinjiang	53.34	330.54	331.03	133.70	197.33	600.34	138.14	332.21

10-13 续表 5 continued

单位：元 (yuan)

地 区	Region	文化娱乐 Recreation	居住 Residence	住房 Housing	水电燃料及其他 Water, Electricity, Fuels and Others	杂项商品和服务 Miscellaneous Commodities and Services	个人消费 Personal Consumption	其他商品 Other Commodities	其他服务 Other Services
全 国	**National Total**	**117.15**	**500.49**	**201.59**	**298.89**	**258.54**	**210.49**	**20.65**	**27.40**
北 京	Beijing	300.53	587.42	265.38	322.04	492.51	433.76	14.30	44.45
天 津	Tianjin	166.34	560.74	217.95	342.80	294.59	226.45	17.28	50.86
河 北	Hebei	66.32	416.66	101.58	315.08	191.71	155.70	12.69	23.31
山 西	Shanxi	78.75	343.03	120.63	222.40	267.79	234.30	19.35	14.15
内蒙古	Inner Mongolia	100.30	338.53	109.96	228.57	252.28	208.49	15.09	28.70
辽 宁	Liaoning	73.05	364.28	97.58	266.69	202.50	174.13	15.70	12.68
吉 林	Jilin	87.39	419.31	108.36	310.95	190.04	157.27	19.79	12.99
黑龙江	Heilongjiang	82.93	360.58	74.87	285.71	169.70	139.10	8.15	22.45
上 海	Shanghai	234.26	741.19	234.41	506.79	488.11	386.15	57.55	44.41
江 苏	Jiangsu	130.59	436.26	123.51	312.75	277.32	213.27	25.42	38.63
浙 江	Zhejiang	163.73	599.98	274.03	325.94	354.39	283.51	25.71	45.17
安 徽	Anhui	88.69	370.90	109.01	261.89	190.55	156.54	8.10	25.91
福 建	Fujian	106.87	530.19	164.82	365.37	276.30	234.04	20.18	22.09
江 西	Jiangxi	72.67	459.00	228.09	230.90	203.35	150.84	33.52	18.99
山 东	Shandong	133.90	395.26	146.44	248.82	267.24	213.05	26.04	28.16
河 南	Henan	72.87	547.19	341.08	206.11	188.52	144.07	11.65	32.80
湖 北	Hubei	103.50	654.10	358.03	296.07	206.75	162.44	21.91	22.40
湖 南	Hunan	128.96	576.65	331.80	244.84	239.05	180.59	18.34	40.12
广 东	Guangdong	192.76	1099.99	485.86	614.13	502.60	411.57	45.14	45.89
广 西	Guangxi	103.31	752.52	419.07	333.45	226.96	169.63	19.82	37.51
海 南	Hainan	80.10	355.76	96.01	259.75	253.93	135.98	94.81	23.13
重 庆	Chongqing	152.45	494.04	180.93	313.11	254.10	216.76	26.91	10.43
四 川	Sichuan	125.08	531.80	249.13	282.66	229.30	182.81	15.57	30.91
贵 州	Guizhou	97.36	331.41	110.83	220.58	218.35	178.38	20.98	18.99
云 南	Yunnan	108.67	480.04	240.78	239.26	344.65	295.12	14.03	35.50
西 藏	Tibet	57.55	340.27	99.98	240.29	366.84	333.79	26.98	6.07
陕 西	Shaanxi	103.08	469.51	245.76	223.76	216.05	183.46	11.75	20.84
甘 肃	Gansu	115.87	302.27	100.14	202.14	251.41	216.13	19.08	16.20
青 海	Qinghai	89.18	274.48	97.66	176.81	306.45	257.67	28.67	20.11
宁 夏	Ningxia	112.14	282.42	72.66	209.76	230.67	191.12	17.54	22.00
新 疆	Xinjiang	129.98	343.25	113.71	229.54	220.31	195.81	8.80	15.70

10-14 各地区城镇居民家庭平均每百户年底耐用消费品拥有量 （2000年）

Number of Major Durable Consumer Goods Owned Per 100 Urban Households at the Year-end by Region (2000)

地　区	Region	毛皮大衣 (件) Fur Coat	呢大衣 (件) Woolen Coat	毛　毯 (条) Woolen Blanket	地　毯 (平方米) Carpet (sq.m)	组合家具 (套) Composite Furniture (sets)	沙发床 (个) Sofa Bed	沙　发 (个) Sofa	大衣柜 (个) Wardrobe	写字台 (张) Desk
全　国	**National Total**	**61.88**	**169.63**	**143.27**	**92.79**	**57.82**	**52.22**	**198.82**	**83.45**	**83.44**
北　京	Beijing	120.00	212.60	143.00	94.70	78.00	83.60	154.10	86.00	97.40
天　津	Tianjin	83.40	260.20	149.00	69.80	76.00	48.40	111.20	68.40	78.20
河　北	Hebei	69.54	147.67	133.21	80.39	67.86	54.99	243.93	88.41	89.46
山　西	Shanxi	73.35	140.10	159.61	70.83	63.64	29.13	207.21	75.75	84.09
内蒙古	Inner Mongolia	112.00	152.05	168.71	192.21	55.78	31.84	291.78	67.98	63.71
辽　宁	Liaoning	61.29	177.14	106.68	173.83	42.98	47.37	98.60	55.53	57.48
吉　林	Jilin	67.26	160.26	97.84	86.55	37.03	33.06	135.93	54.41	49.23
黑龙江	Heilongjiang	56.53	151.88	100.42	88.53	43.44	43.95	136.68	49.53	46.22
上　海	Shanghai	23.00	305.00	180.40	133.88	31.80	44.20	114.60	94.00	76.00
江　苏	Jiangsu	51.40	235.05	146.75	81.81	51.82	40.82	139.71	87.35	97.57
浙　江	Zhejiang	50.44	214.93	163.32	105.83	55.39	34.68	162.00	84.07	96.66
安　徽	Anhui	65.74	173.66	130.47	39.45	49.66	26.86	139.67	80.83	97.48
福　建	Fujian	57.07	114.33	135.20	36.93	55.80	45.13	175.67	81.60	82.60
江　西	Jiangxi	32.99	147.95	141.72	18.86	44.91	49.32	228.21	89.68	104.54
山　东	Shandong	74.73	190.00	164.17	156.05	74.14	78.98	311.31	83.67	92.39
河　南	Henan	61.89	131.20	105.35	50.63	60.34	47.67	241.71	93.53	85.61
湖　北	Hubei	69.84	245.73	152.08	95.69	72.83	49.92	200.83	84.68	100.39
湖　南	Hunan	53.77	151.32	137.41	40.53	69.62	46.94	184.56	99.26	101.90
广　东	Guangdong	44.63	79.99	186.28	30.76	61.63	81.16	136.46	170.50	119.23
广　西	Guangxi	24.23	81.60	119.38	19.94	69.27	55.25	202.95	93.02	86.32
海　南	Hainan	31.33	40.33	120.67	7.17	45.00	53.50	93.83	106.00	108.50
重　庆	Chongqing	71.67	228.33	164.00	8.00	78.67	34.33	121.33	94.67	80.00
四　川	Sichuan	63.80	180.45	159.21	20.30	88.92	57.78	269.41	89.00	96.02
贵　州	Guizhou	59.05	167.11	162.61	71.07	52.94	39.27	256.54	93.56	93.32
云　南	Yunnan	56.52	112.79	182.18	102.70	52.98	53.71	342.55	91.47	96.81
西　藏	Tibet	109.00	160.00	313.00	877.00	107.00	38.00	290.00	64.00	72.00
陕　西	Shaanxi	35.89	141.36	140.65	60.47	58.37	75.95	197.21	69.54	79.90
甘　肃	Gansu	92.50	164.98	210.30	100.90	72.00	92.47	337.79	88.80	94.24
青　海	Qinghai	79.09	187.27	221.45	164.55	50.55	59.09	350.91	77.45	88.00
宁　夏	Ningxia	64.92	129.95	151.51	130.28	30.12	65.54	340.74	77.14	81.25
新　疆	Xinjiang	67.19	217.13	194.62	680.38	48.52	91.79	471.67	80.66	79.20

10-14 续表 1 continued

地 区	Region	摩托车 (辆) Motorcycle	自行车 (辆) Bicycle	家用汽车 (辆) Automobile	缝纫机 (架) Sewing Machine	洗衣机 (台) Washing Machine	电风扇 (台) Electric Fan	电冰箱 (台) Refrigerator	冰柜 (台) Freezer	彩色电视机 (台) Color TV Set
全 国	**National Total**	**18.83**	**162.72**	**0.51**	**51.46**	**90.52**	**167.91**	**80.13**	**6.52**	**116.56**
北 京	Beijing	5.70	230.70	2.50	50.60	102.80	153.40	107.40	16.30	145.50
天 津	Tianjin	9.40	230.00	0.20	71.60	97.60	127.20	99.80	19.40	132.00
河 北	Hebei	37.12	220.98	0.94	65.93	92.97	166.16	83.97	14.48	112.09
山 西	Shanxi	21.34	181.94	0.66	59.51	93.44	80.49	75.95	8.09	107.17
内蒙古	Inner Mongolia	26.21	206.31	1.30	38.01	91.23	52.81	70.48	11.33	106.66
辽 宁	Liaoning	7.37	156.06	0.40	44.30	87.10	72.98	80.97	7.54	114.30
吉 林	Jilin	7.84	149.70	0.45	42.06	89.63	64.50	69.37	6.67	107.34
黑龙江	Heilongjiang	6.02	120.92	0.31	41.09	83.40	47.43	66.26	10.11	102.48
上 海	Shanghai	1.20	125.60	0.00	67.60	93.40	227.00	102.20	1.60	147.00
江 苏	Jiangsu	27.28	206.08	0.00	57.27	96.15	239.33	85.64	4.42	124.45
浙 江	Zhejiang	16.32	198.65	0.48	67.64	90.03	263.56	96.32	3.21	139.17
安 徽	Anhui	16.56	142.61	0.65	42.23	87.17	244.60	83.50	5.81	111.47
福 建	Fujian	36.60	158.07	0.40	50.40	93.20	235.13	87.80	2.53	128.07
江 西	Jiangxi	12.96	146.41	0.39	57.10	80.15	245.09	75.82	4.29	106.01
山 东	Shandong	33.14	217.05	0.19	56.22	88.50	184.37	86.54	14.70	115.32
河 南	Henan	19.47	195.49	0.10	57.09	87.87	209.52	71.78	6.97	108.02
湖 北	Hubei	13.27	143.48	0.20	53.95	92.73	228.81	88.11	5.10	109.34
湖 南	Hunan	13.17	108.12	0.10	49.44	91.63	242.03	83.37	6.30	109.35
广 东	Guangdong	58.84	180.97	1.70	67.95	97.50	312.83	81.87	1.49	135.58
广 西	Guangxi	38.32	183.98	0.21	65.30	88.33	309.18	80.17	2.44	114.76
海 南	Hainan	45.83	108.00	0.83	48.17	68.50	166.67	49.50	2.00	108.83
重 庆	Chongqing	1.00	9.67	0.33	46.00	94.67	209.33	99.67	2.67	132.00
四 川	Sichuan	7.92	92.70	0.47	29.75	91.31	194.93	80.72	2.99	118.61
贵 州	Guizhou	8.92	24.82	0.19	39.18	96.08	98.17	82.82	2.98	113.78
云 南	Yunnan	16.77	138.56	1.37	47.29	91.71	42.19	69.75	2.93	116.27
西 藏	Tibet	5.00	200.00	0.00	15.00	100.00	4.00	74.00	0.00	120.00
陕 西	Shaanxi	10.24	159.85	0.11	51.03	92.82	147.85	72.36	2.53	113.77
甘 肃	Gansu	5.89	179.22	0.25	47.60	96.97	49.20	73.11	2.82	121.08
青 海	Qinghai	8.91	103.64	0.18	33.09	100.73	6.00	80.18	5.82	111.64
宁 夏	Ningxia	15.48	181.27	0.28	33.23	87.10	63.13	71.68	2.89	109.33
新 疆	Xinjiang	8.53	137.63	0.82	38.35	95.48	51.30	81.76	3.20	102.41

10-14 续表 2 continued

地　区	Region	影碟机 (台) Video Disc Player	录放像机 (台) Video Recorder	家用电脑 (台) Computer	组合音响 (套) Hi-Fi Stereo Component System	录音机 (台) Tape Recorder	摄相机 (台) Pickup Camera	照相机 (架) Camera	钢琴 (架) Piano
全　国	**National Total**	**37.53**	**20.13**	**9.72**	**22.20**	**47.93**	**1.34**	**38.44**	**1.26**
北　京	Beijing	46.10	56.90	32.10	30.10	72.70	5.40	95.70	2.20
天　津	Tianjin	31.20	33.80	16.40	19.00	64.40	3.00	64.60	0.60
河　北	Hebei	32.42	14.39	7.43	17.55	49.31	1.99	37.71	0.82
山　西	Shanxi	25.03	12.36	6.23	17.26	50.50	0.92	33.63	0.95
内蒙古	Inner Mongolia	23.32	9.26	3.47	12.14	47.29	1.08	25.21	0.51
辽　宁	Liaoning	24.61	21.30	5.79	18.48	51.54	1.45	40.31	1.15
吉　林	Jilin	24.24	19.38	4.62	15.41	54.15	1.18	30.02	0.77
黑龙江	Heilongjiang	25.86	14.62	4.79	16.42	41.52	1.09	25.36	1.22
上　海	Shanghai	49.80	52.20	25.60	31.80	77.20	2.60	70.60	3.40
江　苏	Jiangsu	39.10	22.56	10.65	20.05	49.12	1.26	36.75	0.91
浙　江	Zhejiang	44.29	27.43	14.02	23.17	58.67	2.18	45.92	0.78
安　徽	Anhui	33.57	16.96	6.72	19.04	26.75	1.12	27.82	0.82
福　建	Fujian	58.33	19.20	11.47	24.87	33.67	1.47	33.20	1.60
江　西	Jiangxi	33.10	10.07	4.56	16.00	41.87	0.60	25.48	0.71
山　东	Shandong	33.75	25.13	9.53	20.60	63.71	1.97	50.23	2.52
河　南	Henan	30.82	9.54	5.72	13.28	37.96	0.68	27.24	0.92
湖　北	Hubei	41.97	15.89	8.36	24.79	43.98	0.90	36.20	1.35
湖　南	Hunan	43.14	18.82	10.73	28.18	37.79	1.08	31.16	1.41
广　东	Guangdong	65.19	30.14	25.78	48.55	57.10	1.97	51.38	2.68
广　西	Guangxi	57.31	14.90	9.36	28.91	40.25	0.38	33.55	0.76
海　南	Hainan	29.50	14.17	4.33	17.67	51.00	0.00	16.83	0.83
重　庆	Chongqing	55.33	25.00	13.67	33.67	32.67	2.00	58.00	0.67
四　川	Sichuan	47.71	18.24	7.69	24.86	38.26	0.84	39.01	1.83
贵　州	Guizhou	50.44	16.22	5.74	31.29	29.06	0.28	30.19	0.66
云　南	Yunnan	59.71	22.79	7.89	31.65	50.86	1.17	47.87	2.08
西　藏	Tibet	52.00	38.00	1.00	24.00	69.00	2.00	54.00	0.00
陕　西	Shaanxi	33.27	15.43	7.03	17.27	45.18	0.66	33.27	0.59
甘　肃	Gansu	32.11	10.16	5.39	25.27	48.34	0.58	32.65	1.74
青　海	Qinghai	36.36	12.73	2.36	22.00	52.73	0.36	42.73	0.55
宁　夏	Ningxia	33.86	9.70	3.78	19.40	36.52	0.52	27.62	0.68
新　疆	Xinjiang	33.56	18.71	5.68	17.53	53.69	1.02	33.71	1.38

10-14 续表 3 continued

地区	Region	其他高中档乐器(件) Other Medium and High Grade Musical Instrument	微波炉(台) Oven	空调器(台) Air Conditioner	电炊具(台) Electric Cooking Appliances	淋浴热水器(个) Shower	排油烟机(台) Smoke Absorber	吸尘器(台) Dust Catcher	健身器材(件) Health Equipment	移动电话(台) Mobile Telephone
全国	**National Total**	**5.34**	**17.61**	**30.76**	**101.94**	**49.11**	**54.07**	**11.17**	**3.48**	**19.49**
北京	Beijing	13.70	58.40	69.60	104.00	74.40	112.40	24.90	9.30	27.60
天津	Tianjin	2.80	30.80	65.60	78.80	70.20	70.80	20.60	3.40	8.80
河北	Hebei	6.51	10.40	32.98	49.86	43.05	55.13	9.63	5.51	14.14
山西	Shanxi	5.56	5.32	4.34	30.15	23.06	52.41	6.85	2.83	8.09
内蒙古	Inner Mongolia	5.47	4.97	1.38	142.77	20.12	40.18	9.34	2.87	15.12
辽宁	Liaoning	5.61	12.23	4.35	85.18	43.83	60.91	22.84	3.30	17.61
吉林	Jilin	4.65	6.87	1.54	128.04	30.96	61.58	13.42	1.54	12.16
黑龙江	Heilongjiang	3.32	6.23	1.78	152.09	19.75	62.38	13.52	1.06	13.41
上海	Shanghai	4.80	78.00	96.40	148.60	63.60	57.00	46.20	5.60	28.80
江苏	Jiangsu	3.57	37.09	45.90	128.69	58.81	62.58	14.92	5.09	25.47
浙江	Zhejiang	6.90	23.00	57.72	105.84	68.39	74.43	14.55	4.67	31.73
安徽	Anhui	5.40	11.28	30.77	88.28	44.36	46.62	7.23	2.81	17.69
福建	Fujian	5.20	27.53	43.53	113.87	82.60	50.67	3.33	4.60	50.40
江西	Jiangxi	5.13	6.94	17.07	74.41	58.02	32.27	2.39	1.91	14.37
山东	Shandong	7.96	15.66	25.83	79.95	53.11	71.71	15.62	5.20	19.52
河南	Henan	3.30	6.27	34.46	48.47	24.27	31.94	3.16	1.88	12.18
湖北	Hubei	5.39	10.26	38.16	98.60	51.24	42.86	4.80	3.22	11.44
湖南	Hunan	8.47	15.15	33.41	62.22	55.10	33.30	3.79	4.59	21.37
广东	Guangdong	5.94	29.86	98.04	100.23	99.20	70.83	6.84	6.69	57.94
广西	Guangxi	3.06	14.66	24.33	112.14	83.63	53.52	3.23	3.34	16.81
海南	Hainan	1.67	6.83	12.83	137.00	58.00	34.33	1.50	2.50	17.00
重庆	Chongqing	8.00	36.33	81.33	94.33	83.33	33.67	7.00	7.00	18.33
四川	Sichuan	5.89	14.67	17.74	120.22	67.21	35.55	5.08	2.72	17.10
贵州	Guizhou	4.30	13.16	3.30	112.92	34.84	41.74	4.25	2.04	6.26
云南	Yunnan	5.25	17.26	0.11	169.49	39.10	61.20	8.20	3.58	21.67
西藏	Tibet	2.00	3.00	3.00	9.00	12.00	11.00	7.00	0.00	30.00
陕西	Shaanxi	3.31	8.26	25.49	80.31	37.14	51.15	4.74	1.84	7.80
甘肃	Gansu	8.42	6.60	1.08	52.03	40.34	62.49	4.98	2.49	9.46
青海	Qinghai	3.64	7.27	0.00	22.91	17.64	65.82	4.73	0.73	10.00
宁夏	Ningxia	3.68	7.38	1.47	136.60	39.83	44.40	8.23	0.55	13.56
新疆	Xinjiang	9.09	5.39	2.78	82.07	47.91	64.75	17.43	2.35	4.81

10-15 农村居民家庭基本情况

Basic Conditions of Rural Households

项　目	Item	1990	1995	1999	2000
调查户数　（户）	**Number of Households Surveyed**	**66960**	**67340**	**67430**	**68116**
调查户人口　（人）	**Number of Residents Surveyed (person)**				
常住人口	Number of Permanent Residents in the Households Surveyed	321429	301878	286348	286162
平均每户常住人口	Average Number of Permanent Residents per Household	4.80	4.48	4.25	4.20
平均每户整半劳力	Average Number of Able-bodied and Semi-able-bodied Laborers per Household	2.92	2.88	2.77	2.76
平均每个劳动力负担人口(含本人)	Average Number of Persons Supported by a Laborer (including the laborer himself or herself)	1.64	1.56	1.53	1.52
平均每人年收入(元)	**Per Capita Annual Income (yuan)**				
总收入	Total Revenue	990.38	2337.87	2987.44	3087.80
工资性收入	Wages Income	138.80	353.70	630.25	702.30
家庭经营收入	Household Business Income	815.79	1877.42	2211.57	2251.28
财产性收入	Property Income		40.98	31.54	45.04
转移性收入	Transfer Income	35.79	65.77	114.08	89.18
现金收入	Cash Income	676.67	1595.56	2206.69	2398.28
工资性收入	Wages Income	136.43	352.88	628.43	700.41
家庭经营收入	Household Business Income	481.19	1116.73	1380.23	1498.81
财产性收入	Property Income		38.19	43.46	54.26
转移性收入	Transfer Income	59.05	87.76	154.57	144.79
平均每人年支出(元)	**Per Capita Annual Expenditures (yuan)**				
总支出	Total Expenditure	903.47	2138.33	2390.37	2535.01
家庭经营费用支出	Expenditure for Household Business	241.09	621.71	599.72	654.27
购置生产性固定资产	Purchasing Productive Fixed Assets	20.29	62.33	57.63	63.91
税费支出	Expenditure for Tax	38.66	88.65	99.98	95.52
生活消费支出	Expenditure for Consumption	584.63	1310.36	1577.42	1670.13
转移性和财产性支出	Expenditure for Transfer and Property	18.80	55.28	55.62	51.18
现金支出	Cash Expenditure	639.06	1545.81	1917.23	2140.37
家庭经营费用支出	Expenditure for Household Business	162.90	454.74	470.73	544.49
购买生产性固定资产	Purchasing Productive Fixed Assets	20.46	62.32	57.63	63.91
税费支出	Expenditure for Tax	33.37	76.96	93.06	89.81
生活消费支出	Expenditure for Consumption	374.74	859.43	1144.61	1284.74
转移性和财产性支出	Expenditure for Transfer and Property	47.59	92.36	151.20	157.42
平均每人年纯收入	**Per Capita Annual Net Income**	**686.31**	**1577.74**	**2210.34**	**2253.42**
工资性收入	Wages Income	138.80	353.70	630.26	702.30
家庭经营纯收入	Household Business Income	518.55	1125.79	1448.36	1427.27
财产性收入	Property Income		40.98	31.55	45.04
转移性收入	Transfer Income	28.96	57.27	100.17	78.81

注:1.本表至10—29表为农村住户抽样调查资料。

Data from Tables 10-15 to 10-29 are obtained from the sample surveys on rural households.

10-16 农村居民按纯收入分组的户数占调查户比重

Percentage of Rural Households Grouped by Per Capita Annual Net Income

项　　目	Item	1985	1990	1995	1999	2000
按纯收入分组户数占调查户比重(%)	**Percentage of Households Grouped by Per Capita Annual Net Income (%)**					
100元以下	100 Yuan and below	0.95	0.30	0.21	0.17	0.31
100—200 (元)	100-200 Yuan	11.20	1.78	0.36	0.13	0.20
200—300 (元)	200-300 Yuan	25.64	6.56	0.78	0.24	0.43
300—400 (元)	300-400 Yuan	24.10	12.04	1.47	0.48	0.69
400—500 (元)	400-500 Yuan	15.94	14.37	2.30	0.86	1.01
500—600 (元)	500-600 Yuan	9.13	13.94	3.37	1.35	1.37
600—800 (元)	600-800 Yuan	7.99	20.80	9.54	3.99	4.44
800—1000 (元)	800-1000 Yuan	2.85	12.49	11.63	5.77	5.72
1000—1200 (元)	1000-1200 Yuan			11.83	7.04	6.75
1200—1300 (元)	1200-1300 Yuan	1.76	12.25	5.38	3.80	3.75
1300—1500 (元)	1300-1500 Yuan			9.74	8.08	7.42
1500—1700 (元)	1500-1700 Yuan	0.29	3.48	7.92	8.05	7.48
1700—2000 (元)	1700-2000 Yuan			9.39	11.15	10.45
2000—2500 (元)	2000-2500 Yuan			10.29	15.18	14.54
2500—3000 (元)	2500-3000 Yuan			5.89	10.33	10.29
3000—3500 (元)	3000-3500 Yuan			3.49	7.05	7.11
3500—4000 (元)	3500-4000 Yuan	0.15	1.99	1.95	4.67	4.76
4000—4500 (元)	4000-4500 Yuan			1.34	3.18	3.44
4500—5000 (元)	4500-5000 Yuan			0.86	2.13	2.40
5000元以上	5000 Yuan and over			2.26	6.35	7.45

10-17 农村居民家庭平均每人纯收入

Per Capita Annual Net Income of Rural Households

单位：元　　(yuan)

项　　目	Item	1985	1990	1995	1999	2000
纯收入	**Net Income**	**397.60**	**686.31**	**1577.74**	**2210.34**	**2253.42**
按收入来源分	**By Source**					
工资性收入	Wages Income	72.15	138.80	353.70	630.26	702.30
家庭经营纯收入	Net Income from Household Business	295.98	518.55	1125.79	1448.36	1427.27
农业收入	Farming	202.10	344.59	799.44	918.27	833.93
#种植业收入	Planting	191.46	330.11	775.12	882.09	783.64
林业收入	Forestry	6.16	7.53	13.52	21.58	22.44
牧业收入	Animal Husbandry	51.96	96.81	127.81	174.30	207.35
渔业收入	Fishery	3.59	7.11	15.69	24.80	26.95
工业收入	Industry	2.18	9.15	13.63	29.95	52.67
建筑业收入	Construction	7.41	12.18	34.53	61.18	46.73
交通、运输、邮电业收入	Transport, Post and Telecommunication Services	8.47	13.45	27.76	56.73	63.63
批发.零售贸易及餐饮业	Wholesale and Retail Trade and Catering Services	6.13	12.69	34.26	74.82	78.54
社会服务业收入	Social Services	3.27	6.55	17.18	34.01	28.09
文教卫生业收入	Culture, Education and Health Care					6.86
其他收入	Others	4.73	8.49	41.97	52.71	60.08
转移性和财产性收入	Transfer Income and Property Income	29.47	28.96	98.25	131.72	123.85
按收入性质分	**Grouped by Type of Income**					
生产性纯收入	Productive Income	367.69	657.35	1479.49	2078.62	2129.58
第一产业收入	Primary Industry	298.28	510.86	996.51	1180.02	1136.09
第二产业收入	Secondary Industry	29.47	70.68	287.24	564.30	598.28
第三产业收入	Tertiary Industry	39.95	75.81	195.74	334.30	395.21
非生产性纯收入	Non-productive Income	29.91	28.96	98.25	131.72	123.84

10-18 各地区农村居民家庭平均每人纯收入

Per Capita Net Income of Rural Households by Region

单位：元 (yuan)

地　区	Region	1985	1990	1995	1999	2000
全　国	**National Total**	**397.60**	**686.31**	**1577.74**	**2210.34**	**2253.42**
北　京	Beijing	775.08	1297.05	3223.65	4226.59	4604.55
天　津	Tianjin	564.55	1069.04	2406.38	3411.11	3622.39
河　北	Hebei	385.23	621.67	1668.73	2441.50	2478.86
山　西	Shanxi	358.32	603.51	1208.30	1772.62	1905.61
内蒙古	Inner Mongolia	360.41	607.15	1208.38	2002.93	2038.21
辽　宁	Liaoning	467.84	836.17	1756.50	2501.04	2355.58
吉　林	Jilin	413.74	803.52	1609.60	2260.59	2022.50
黑龙江	Heilongjiang	397.84	759.86	1766.27	2165.93	2148.22
上　海	Shanghai	805.92	1907.32	4245.61	5409.11	5596.37
江　苏	Jiangsu	492.60	959.06	2456.86	3495.20	3595.09
浙　江	Zhejiang	548.60	1099.04	2966.19	3948.39	4253.67
安　徽	Anhui	369.41	539.16	1302.82	1900.29	1934.57
福　建	Fujian	396.45	764.41	2048.59	3091.39	3230.49
江　西	Jiangxi	377.31	669.90	1537.36	2129.45	2135.30
山　东	Shandong	408.12	680.18	1715.09	2549.58	2659.20
河　南	Henan	329.37	526.95	1231.97	1948.36	1985.82
湖　北	Hubei	421.24	670.80	1511.22	2217.08	2268.59
湖　南	Hunan	395.26	664.24	1425.16	2127.46	2197.16
广　东	Guangdong	495.31	1043.03	2699.24	3628.95	3654.48
广　西	Guangxi	302.96	639.45	1446.14	2048.33	1864.51
海　南	Hainan		696.22	1519.71	2087.46	2182.26
重　庆	Chongqing				1736.63	1892.44
四　川	Sichuan	315.07	557.76	1158.29	1843.47	1903.60
贵　州	Guizhou	287.83	435.14	1086.62	1363.07	1374.16
云　南	Yunnan	338.34	540.86	1010.97	1437.63	1478.60
西　藏	Tibet	352.97	649.71	1200.31	1309.46	1330.81
陕　西	Shaanxi	295.26	530.80	962.89	1455.86	1443.86
甘　肃	Gansu	255.22	430.98	880.34	1357.28	1428.68
青　海	Qinghai	342.95	559.78	1029.77	1466.67	1490.49
宁　夏	Ningxia	321.17	578.13	998.75	1754.15	1724.30
新　疆	Xinjiang	394.30	683.47	1136.45	1473.17	1618.08

10-19 各地区农村居民家庭按来源分的纯收入(2000年)

Per Capita Net Income of Rural Households by Source and by Region (2000)

单位：元 (yuan)

地　区	Region	纯收入 Net Income	工资性收入 Wage Income	家庭经营纯收入 Family Business Income	财产性收入 Property Income	转移性收入 Transfer Income
全　国	**National Total**	**2253.42**	**702.30**	**1427.27**	**45.04**	**78.81**
北　京	Beijing	4604.55	2819.06	1437.63	158.28	189.58
天　津	Tianjin	3622.39	1638.28	1857.36	42.88	83.88
河　北	Hebei	2478.86	949.25	1417.99	62.66	48.96
山　西	Shanxi	1905.61	726.05	1113.56	19.70	46.29
内蒙古	Inner Mongolia	2038.21	287.63	1690.81	35.18	24.58
辽　宁	Liaoning	2355.58	882.96	1353.39	58.19	61.05
吉　林	Jilin	2022.50	343.86	1611.20	31.26	36.18
黑龙江	Heilongjiang	2148.22	337.97	1699.37	60.62	50.26
上　海	Shanghai	5596.37	4309.89	933.74	142.83	209.92
江　苏	Jiangsu	3595.09	1663.11	1770.87	48.09	113.02
浙　江	Zhejiang	4253.67	2000.51	1917.92	181.01	154.23
安　徽	Anhui	1934.57	547.83	1298.40	24.70	63.64
福　建	Fujian	3230.49	1069.01	1844.27	76.97	240.23
江　西	Jiangxi	2135.30	744.47	1319.94	18.80	52.09
山　东	Shandong	2659.20	850.56	1676.90	57.80	73.94
河　南	Henan	1985.82	473.68	1427.24	29.15	55.75
湖　北	Hubei	2268.59	547.69	1617.81	19.55	83.54
湖　南	Hunan	2197.16	789.74	1329.10	20.74	57.58
广　东	Guangdong	3654.48	1362.16	2002.92	73.67	215.73
广　西	Guangxi	1864.51	483.75	1297.16	7.47	76.13
海　南	Hainan	2182.26	151.38	1897.73	38.15	95.00
重　庆	Chongqing	1892.44	623.32	1155.63	8.54	104.96
四　川	Sichuan	1903.60	606.93	1194.19	29.96	72.52
贵　州	Guizhou	1374.16	274.90	1029.45	6.97	62.84
云　南	Yunnan	1478.60	263.58	1115.68	47.94	51.40
西　藏	Tibet	1330.81	227.63	934.48	106.54	62.16
陕　西	Shaanxi	1443.86	445.97	901.15	47.03	49.71
甘　肃	Gansu	1428.68	355.03	1011.78	16.13	45.73
青　海	Qinghai	1490.49	312.30	1119.77	24.70	33.72
宁　夏	Ningxia	1724.30	484.02	1121.38	80.77	38.13
新　疆	Xinjiang	1618.08	104.58	1451.33	40.43	21.74

10-20 农村居民家庭平均每人生活消费支出构成

Composition of Per Capita Living Expenditure of Rural Households

单位：%　　　　(%)

指　　标	Item	1985	1990	1995	1999	2000
生活消费总支出	**Living Expenditure**	**100.00**	**100.00**	**100.00**	**100.00**	**100.00**
食品	Food	57.79	58.80	58.62	52.56	49.13
衣着	Clothing	9.69	7.77	6.85	5.83	5.75
居住	Residence	18.23	17.34	13.91	14.75	15.47
家庭设备用品及服务	Household Facilities, Articles and Services	5.10	5.29	5.23	5.22	4.52
医疗保健	Medicines and Medical Services	2.42	3.25	3.24	4.44	5.24
交通通讯	Transport, Post and Communication Services	1.76	1.44	2.58	4.36	5.58
文教娱乐用品及服务	Cultural, Educational and Recreational Articles and Services	3.89	5.37	7.81	10.67	11.18
其他商品及服务	Other Commodities and Services	1.12	0.74	1.76	2.18	3.14
生活消费现金支出	**Consumption Paid in Cash**	**100.00**	**100.00**	**100.00**	**100.00**	**100.00**
食品	Food	39.33	41.59	41.10	37.22	36.14
衣着	Clothing	15.48	11.75	10.32	7.99	7.41
居住	Residence	22.00	21.66	17.20	17.79	17.98
家庭设备用品及服务	Household Facilities, Articles and Services	8.25	8.20	7.92	7.18	5.79
医疗保健	Medicines and Medical Services	3.93	5.06	4.94	6.12	6.82
交通通讯	Transport, Post and Communication Services	2.87	2.24	3.92	6.00	7.25
文教娱乐用品及服务	Cultural, Educational and Recreational Articles and Services	6.34	8.36	11.91	14.71	14.53
其他商品及服务	Other Commodities and Services	1.81	1.13	2.68	3.00	4.08

10-21 各地区农村居民家庭平均每人生活消费支出（2000年）

Per Capita Living Expenditure of Rural Households by Region (2000)

单位：元 (yuan)

地区	Region	生活消费支出合计 Living Expenditure	食品 Food	衣着 Clothing	居住 Residence	家庭设备及服务 Household Facilities, Articles and Services	医疗保健 Medicines and Medical Services	交通和通讯 Transport, Post and Communication Services	文教、娱乐用品及服务 Cultural, Educational and Recreational Articles and Services	其他商品及服务 Other Commodities and Services
全国	**National Total**	**1670.13**	**820.52**	**95.95**	**258.34**	**75.45**	**87.57**	**93.13**	**186.72**	**52.46**
北京	Beijing	3425.71	1304.72	245.93	539.57	235.28	249.00	236.00	484.86	130.34
天津	Tianjin	1995.61	800.02	162.12	282.52	94.95	270.90	87.43	235.22	62.46
河北	Hebei	1365.23	539.33	104.84	322.04	65.41	78.28	84.55	130.71	40.06
山西	Shanxi	1149.01	558.86	113.37	143.90	48.77	60.35	48.82	135.39	39.55
内蒙古	Inner Mongolia	1614.91	723.36	110.88	249.38	60.96	104.46	93.44	232.58	39.87
辽宁	Liaoning	1753.54	815.70	152.73	243.07	70.50	109.51	112.77	195.38	53.89
吉林	Jilin	1553.35	705.39	103.22	273.40	63.61	102.65	85.05	171.77	48.25
黑龙江	Heilongjiang	1540.35	682.82	105.26	304.20	50.85	117.20	84.17	150.67	45.17
上海	Shanghai	4137.61	1822.55	201.24	723.65	225.22	208.92	278.63	559.12	118.29
江苏	Jiangsu	2337.46	1017.57	126.66	441.57	114.97	129.52	155.47	268.99	82.72
浙江	Zhejiang	3230.88	1406.37	167.40	580.53	145.89	200.06	275.46	327.99	127.18
安徽	Anhui	1321.50	693.15	71.16	196.85	57.58	58.05	58.44	145.46	40.81
福建	Fujian	2409.69	1172.35	116.99	350.72	110.24	87.38	206.08	254.30	111.63
江西	Jiangxi	1642.66	894.50	84.42	223.94	55.46	63.48	95.60	184.24	41.04
山东	Shandong	1770.75	781.88	117.51	299.76	114.94	118.69	101.64	207.87	28.45
河南	Henan	1315.83	654.13	86.88	206.12	69.41	63.55	56.38	133.08	46.29
湖北	Hubei	1555.61	827.25	75.19	179.42	69.40	69.67	72.67	209.89	52.11
湖南	Hunan	1942.94	1053.37	89.78	251.92	78.05	82.23	99.38	222.50	65.72
广东	Guangdong	2646.02	1317.48	104.21	378.86	125.65	100.31	205.52	313.46	100.53
广西	Guangxi	1487.96	824.97	51.58	201.12	62.95	52.38	64.83	186.76	43.37
海南	Hainan	1483.90	844.29	59.05	180.31	63.59	44.15	61.28	174.39	56.84
重庆	Chongqing	1395.53	747.55	61.96	199.07	66.76	68.87	61.31	154.52	35.48
四川	Sichuan	1484.59	810.82	72.31	212.85	62.63	72.84	54.38	159.55	39.21
贵州	Guizhou	1096.64	687.36	53.03	138.90	38.23	27.68	26.92	97.26	27.25
云南	Yunnan	1270.83	749.22	55.35	177.14	47.53	64.31	31.96	106.14	39.18
西藏	Tibet	1116.59	885.60	87.06	47.21	39.77	16.07	15.42	11.11	14.36
陕西	Shaanxi	1251.21	543.84	82.32	199.92	57.82	91.40	58.49	181.81	35.61
甘肃	Gansu	1084.00	525.17	60.54	171.12	42.21	70.60	43.76	143.87	26.74
青海	Qinghai	1218.23	705.24	93.35	126.19	44.81	78.20	53.15	79.38	37.92
宁夏	Ningxia	1417.13	691.31	96.70	227.35	62.10	88.53	79.79	144.98	26.38
新疆	Xinjiang	1236.45	618.17	114.26	170.89	45.74	73.67	61.04	105.98	46.69

10—22 各地区农村居民家庭平均每人生活消费现金支出（2000年）

Per Capita Living Expenditure in Cash of Rural Households by Region (2000)

单位：元 (yuan)

地区	Region	生活消费现金支出合计 Living Expenditure in Cash	食品 Food	衣着 Clothing	居住 Residence	家庭设备及服务 Household Facilities, Articles and Services	医疗保健 Medicines and Medical Services	交通和通讯 Transport, Post and Communication Services	文教、娱乐用品及服务 Cultural, Educational and Recreational Articles and Services	其他商品及服务 Other Commodities and Services
全国	**National Total**	**1284.74**	**464.26**	**95.18**	**231.06**	**74.37**	**87.57**	**93.13**	**186.72**	**52.46**
北京	Beijing	3336.52	1216.66	245.77	538.62	235.25	249.00	236.00	484.86	130.34
天津	Tianjin	1833.60	650.29	162.12	270.23	94.95	270.90	87.43	235.22	62.46
河北	Hebei	1156.25	330.95	104.25	322.04	65.41	78.28	84.55	130.71	40.06
山西	Shanxi	901.59	313.60	113.34	141.82	48.72	60.35	48.82	135.39	39.55
内蒙古	Inner Mongolia	1170.97	337.86	110.86	190.95	60.96	104.46	93.44	232.58	39.87
辽宁	Liaoning	1386.04	483.76	152.69	208.21	69.84	109.51	112.77	195.38	53.89
吉林	Jilin	1204.51	446.31	103.22	183.64	63.61	102.65	85.05	171.77	48.25
黑龙江	Heilongjiang	1187.60	454.83	105.26	179.45	50.85	117.20	84.17	150.67	45.17
上海	Shanghai	3763.47	1451.21	201.20	720.89	225.22	208.92	278.63	559.12	118.29
江苏	Jiangsu	1922.13	635.98	123.30	412.08	114.07	129.52	155.47	268.99	82.72
浙江	Zhejiang	2911.84	1098.30	167.39	569.83	145.63	200.06	275.46	327.99	127.18
安徽	Anhui	954.93	362.25	70.76	161.58	57.57	58.05	58.44	145.46	40.81
福建	Fujian	2074.58	854.48	116.99	336.94	106.78	87.38	206.08	254.30	111.63
江西	Jiangxi	1170.68	466.22	83.39	181.28	55.43	63.48	95.60	184.24	41.04
山东	Shandong	1482.43	506.71	116.18	288.05	114.83	118.69	101.64	207.87	28.45
河南	Henan	889.66	286.52	85.55	161.44	56.84	63.55	56.38	133.08	46.29
湖北	Hubei	1058.31	358.34	72.21	154.92	68.49	69.67	72.67	209.89	52.11
湖南	Hunan	1467.92	590.19	89.61	240.26	78.04	82.23	99.38	222.50	65.72
广东	Guangdong	2197.64	908.45	101.76	343.87	123.73	100.31	205.52	313.46	100.53
广西	Guangxi	1087.20	437.01	51.56	188.35	62.95	52.38	64.83	186.76	43.37
海南	Hainan	1083.21	495.62	59.05	128.29	63.59	44.15	61.28	174.39	56.84
重庆	Chongqing	927.23	299.85	61.96	178.49	66.75	68.87	61.31	154.52	35.48
四川	Sichuan	1021.27	376.13	72.22	184.57	62.38	72.84	54.38	159.55	39.21
贵州	Guizhou	622.51	224.92	53.00	127.24	38.23	27.68	26.92	97.26	27.25
云南	Yunnan	808.34	305.83	55.31	158.09	47.53	64.31	31.96	106.14	39.18
西藏	Tibet	476.59	256.57	87.05	36.25	39.77	16.07	15.42	11.11	14.36
陕西	Shaanxi	1007.55	327.74	81.99	172.69	57.82	91.40	58.49	181.81	35.61
甘肃	Gansu	747.61	213.82	60.53	146.11	42.18	70.60	43.76	143.87	26.74
青海	Qinghai	765.53	262.68	93.31	116.16	44.74	78.20	53.15	79.38	37.92
宁夏	Ningxia	1017.35	302.72	96.70	216.17	62.10	88.53	79.79	144.98	26.38
新疆	Xinjiang	871.37	270.54	110.85	156.86	45.74	73.67	61.04	105.98	46.69

10-23 各地区农村居民家庭平均每人主要食品消费量（2000年）

Per Capita Consumption of Major Food in Rural Households by Region (2000)

单位：公斤 (kg)

地 区	Region	粮 食 Grain	蔬 菜 Vegetables	食 油 Edible Oil	猪牛羊肉 Pork, Beef and Mutton	家 禽 Poultry	蛋类及其制品 Eggs and Related Products	水产品 Aquatic Products	食 糖 Sugar	酒 Liquor
全 国	**National Total**	**249.49**	**111.98**	**7.06**	**14.63**	**2.85**	**4.97**	**3.92**	**1.28**	**7.02**
北 京	Beijing	137.06	110.10	9.40	15.01	2.03	8.73	3.86	1.16	16.90
天 津	Tianjin	214.53	73.60	9.54	10.81	0.85	9.80	6.17	0.74	10.44
河 北	Hebei	213.76	61.45	5.91	7.16	0.37	5.09	1.79	0.59	6.50
山 西	Shanxi	241.55	70.58	6.01	5.22	0.30	5.63	0.46	1.30	2.29
内蒙古	Inner Mongolia	252.09	83.13	4.79	20.16	0.88	3.34	1.22	1.15	10.08
辽 宁	Liaoning	222.18	199.54	7.14	15.17	1.84	9.51	4.74	0.79	10.89
吉 林	Jilin	220.28	92.25	6.48	9.54	1.53	8.09	3.09	0.56	11.56
黑龙江	Heilongjiang	252.30	110.52	7.46	8.60	2.10	7.04	2.93	0.85	14.69
上 海	Shanghai	222.28	92.41	7.99	18.40	7.96	10.71	14.51	2.47	9.14
江 苏	Jiangsu	288.09	115.69	9.56	12.38	4.44	8.22	7.74	1.48	7.40
浙 江	Zhejiang	227.26	85.94	5.59	17.38	5.92	5.52	12.84	2.46	13.78
安 徽	Anhui	270.24	80.28	7.66	9.50	3.57	5.56	3.67	1.59	9.99
福 建	Fujian	260.70	131.33	5.25	18.49	6.64	4.43	12.23	2.47	13.82
江 西	Jiangxi	303.62	148.72	10.31	12.64	2.49	3.26	3.73	1.36	5.86
山 东	Shandong	235.39	120.53	8.58	9.33	2.96	12.66	4.32	1.38	13.39
河 南	Henan	255.82	146.54	5.09	6.55	1.72	9.73	0.96	1.19	4.62
湖 北	Hubei	300.59	155.06	10.34	16.94	2.19	3.94	6.42	1.27	6.98
湖 南	Hunan	287.46	156.18	9.68	18.74	3.70	3.56	4.76	1.31	4.95
广 东	Guangdong	252.79	116.39	5.93	22.39	9.23	2.78	11.72	1.34	3.56
广 西	Guangxi	231.81	118.64	6.20	14.08	6.29	1.28	3.08	1.27	4.96
海 南	Hainan	236.07	67.46	6.01	13.83	7.09	1.25	11.96	1.38	3.14
重 庆	Chongqing	210.00	175.60	5.59	26.54	2.01	4.58	1.61	2.26	7.25
四 川	Sichuan	249.11	143.36	6.57	24.54	2.81	3.69	1.53	1.44	6.13
贵 州	Guizhou	227.15	139.14	4.97	24.35	1.00	1.25	0.34	0.91	5.77
云 南	Yunnan	238.25	104.07	4.63	22.96	2.11	1.78	1.05	1.18	5.27
西 藏	Tibet	280.17	23.58	6.17	11.73	0.01	0.64	0.01	2.62	0.89
陕 西	Shaanxi	221.39	61.36	6.27	7.17	0.29	2.22	0.24	0.89	2.08
甘 肃	Gansu	256.53	44.62	5.95	10.01	0.73	1.88	0.14	0.76	2.30
青 海	Qinghai	270.79	42.60	9.09	19.63	0.37	0.69	0.83	1.06	2.39
宁 夏	Ningxia	248.64	91.19	7.11	11.56	1.85	2.37	0.51	1.57	1.64
新 疆	Xinjiang	244.83	89.24	9.64	10.93	1.36	1.20	0.47	0.42	1.12

10-24 农村居民家庭平均每人主要消费品消费量

Per Capita Consumption of Major Consumer Goods in Rural Households

品　名	Item	1985	1990	1995	1999	2000
粮食(原粮)(公斤)	Grain (Unprocessed) (kg)	257.45	262.08	258.92	247.45	249.49
#小麦 (公斤)	Wheat (kg)	73.75	80.03	81.11	79.23	80.27
稻谷 (公斤)	Rice (kg)	135.30	134.99	129.19	121.61	126.82
豆类及豆制品	Soybeans and Related Products (kg)			5.16	5.40	5.49
#大豆 (公斤)	Soybean			2.28	2.67	2.53
蔬　菜 (公斤)	Fresh Vegetable (kg)	131.13	134.00	104.62	108.89	111.98
食　油 (公斤)	Edible Oil (kg)	4.04	5.17	5.80	6.17	7.06
#植物油 (公斤)	Vegetable Oil (kg)	2.60	3.54	4.25	4.58	5.45
肉禽及制品 (公斤)	Meats,Poultry and Related Products (kg)			13.56	17.07	18.30
#猪肉 (公斤)	Pork (kg)	10.32	10.54	10.58	12.70	13.44
牛肉 (公斤)	Beef (kg)			0.36	0.54	0.55
羊肉 (公斤)	Mutton (kg)	0.65	0.80	0.35	0.63	0.64
家禽 (公斤)	Poultry (kg)	1.03	1.25	1.83	2.48	2.85
蛋及制品 (公斤)	Eggs and Related Products (kg)	2.05	2.41	3.22	4.28	4.97
水产品 (公斤)	Aquatic Product (kg)	1.64	2.13	3.36	3.82	3.92
#鱼类 (公斤)	Fish (kg)			2.92	3.32	3.25
虾贝蟹类 (公斤)	Shrimp, Shellfish and Crab (kg)			0.25	0.24	0.29
食　糖 (公斤)	Sugar (kg)	1.46	1.50	1.28	1.46	1.28
酒 (公斤)	Liquor (kg)	4.37	6.14	6.53	6.98	7.02
糖　果 (公斤)	Candy (kg)	0.34	0.32	0.30	0.31	0.35
糕　点 (公斤)	Cake (kg)	0.88	1.01	1.31	1.11	0.96
水果及制品(公斤)	Fruits and Related Products (kg)	3.40	5.89	13.01	18.35	18.31
坚果及制品(公斤)	Nuts and Related Product (kg)			0.13	1.82	0.74

10-25 农村居民家庭平均每百户年底耐用消费品拥有量

Number of Durable Consumer Goods Owned Per 100 Rural Households at the Year-end

品　名	Item	1985	1990	1995	1999	2000
洗衣机 (台)	Washing Machine	1.90	9.12	16.90	24.32	28.58
电风扇 (台)	Electric Fan	9.66	41.36	88.96	116.07	122.62
电冰箱 (台)	Refrigerator	0.06	1.22	5.15	10.64	12.31
空调机 (台)	Air Conditioner			0.18	0.74	1.32
抽油烟机 (台)	Exhaust Fan			0.61	2.33	2.75
自行车 (辆)	Bicycle	80.64	118.33	147.02	136.85	120.48
摩托车 (辆)	Motorcycle		0.89	4.91	16.49	21.94
电话机 (部)	Telephone Set					26.38
移动电话 (部)	Mobile Telephone					4.32
组合音响 (台)	Hi-Fi Stereo Component System					7.76
寻呼机 (台)	Beep-pager					7.74
黑白电视机 (台)	Black and White TV Set	10.94	39.72	63.81	62.35	52.97
彩色电视机 (台)	Color TV Set	0.80	4.72	16.92	38.24	48.74
录放像机 (台)	Video-recorder					3.30
收录机 (台)	Radio Cassette Player	4.33	17.83	28.25	31.99	21.58
照相机 (架)	Camera		0.70	1.42	2.69	3.12

10-26 各地区农村居民家庭平均每百户主要耐用消费品拥有量（2000年底）

Number of Durable Consumer Goods Owned Per 100 Rural Households by Region at the Year-end (2000)

地 区	Region	大型家具（件）Large Furniture	洗衣机（台）Washing Machine	电风扇（台）Electric Fan	电冰箱（台）Refrigerator	空调机（台）Air Conditioner	抽油烟机（台）Exhaust Fan	自行车（辆）Bicycle
全 国	**National Total**	**278.67**	**28.58**	**122.62**	**12.31**	**1.32**	**2.75**	**120.48**
北 京	Beijing	286.93	86.00	147.73	87.73	15.33	17.87	219.20
天 津	Tianjin	189.17	83.67	125.50	42.33	9.50	6.17	186.00
河 北	Hebei	186.00	58.86	150.36	21.74	1.93	1.86	185.69
山 西	Shanxi	253.62	51.71	47.43	10.33	0.29	1.90	128.24
内蒙古	Inner Mongolia	157.47	25.64	8.45	5.94		0.74	79.08
辽 宁	Liaoning	123.49	54.97	48.84	14.97	0.21	2.59	127.99
吉 林	Jilin	114.38	55.06	17.88	5.44	0.06	0.31	98.31
黑龙江	Heilongjiang	71.88	48.26	13.79	7.19	0.04	1.70	91.83
上 海	Shanghai	316.67	69.17	326.00	74.00	13.83	35.33	218.83
江 苏	Jiangsu	295.29	45.97	201.26	19.94	5.35	5.06	175.12
浙 江	Zhejiang	364.63	34.70	270.52	42.04	5.85	18.81	180.19
安 徽	Anhui	281.61	14.74	162.16	8.16	0.03	0.35	127.42
福 建	Fujian	212.25	35.55	173.46	19.40	1.65	3.96	101.15
江 西	Jiangxi	326.08	3.55	138.53	3.63	0.04	0.41	116.12
山 东	Shandong	264.10	18.33	145.12	15.71	1.07	2.40	176.93
河 南	Henan	225.31	24.52	138.29	6.90	0.60	0.43	151.95
湖 北	Hubei	267.55	16.33	150.55	6.91	0.24	0.67	110.58
湖 南	Hunan	540.19	15.95	171.11	6.84	0.11	0.51	80.59
广 东	Guangdong	365.00	25.00	271.48	15.12	3.05	8.91	162.46
广 西	Guangxi	140.43	3.25	180.82	2.90	0.17	0.30	124.98
海 南	Hainan	272.22	2.50	98.61	3.47		0.56	56.81
重 庆	Chongqing	421.22	8.94	121.50	5.67	0.06	0.50	16.11
四 川	Sichuan	429.63	16.40	122.13	4.83	0.18	0.25	49.30
贵 州	Guizhou	392.63	12.05	21.96	2.37			8.17
云 南	Yunnan	140.67	19.67	9.21	3.67		1.00	49.00
西 藏	Tibet	466.88	2.29		0.42			79.38
陕 西	Shaanxi	239.46	34.14	69.86	5.23	0.23	0.68	127.43
甘 肃	Gansu	304.06	27.72	15.94	4.39	0.17	0.78	125.94
青 海	Qinghai	337.00	17.33	1.67	1.83			58.83
宁 夏	Ningxia	401.67	37.50	21.33	6.00		0.33	162.83
新 疆	Xinjiang	247.60	20.87	11.60	9.93		1.13	136.60

10-26 续表 1 continued

地区	Region	摩托车 (辆) Motorcycle	电话机 (部) Telephone Set	黑白电视机 (台) Black and White TV Set	彩色电视机 (台) Color TV Set	录放像机 (台) Video-recorder	收录机 (台) Radio Cassette Player	照相机 (架) Camera
全国	**National Total**	**21.94**	**26.38**	**52.97**	**48.74**	**3.30**	**21.58**	**3.12**
北京	Beijing	36.67	80.13	20.13	103.20	14.40	31.60	26.67
天津	Tianjin	34.00	41.00	21.33	89.33	6.33	20.83	4.17
河北	Hebei	34.33	31.17	51.17	64.76	3.24	19.74	4.17
山西	Shanxi	25.00	16.10	41.05	63.48	2.19	24.67	2.57
内蒙古	Inner Mongolia	25.69	5.94	50.88	45.19	1.42	35.85	2.60
辽宁	Liaoning	23.81	39.37	37.99	72.65	4.55	20.26	4.92
吉林	Jilin	19.69	25.81	43.94	61.13	2.50	26.13	2.63
黑龙江	Heilongjiang	15.76	24.11	47.59	58.93	2.54	20.31	3.35
上海	Shanghai	72.67	96.17	61.33	97.33	12.67	38.00	13.67
江苏	Jiangsu	28.47	51.32	61.76	53.91	5.47	20.44	4.00
浙江	Zhejiang	29.78	61.26	50.78	83.15	9.04	28.15	6.44
安徽	Anhui	8.65	20.87	68.65	39.29	3.16	19.65	2.03
福建	Fujian	49.67	62.09	42.09	73.02	7.36	15.55	6.15
江西	Jiangxi	17.47	21.63	74.65	30.16	2.04	14.65	2.08
山东	Shandong	37.14	40.14	56.31	51.62	3.81	19.26	4.40
河南	Henan	14.57	25.40	61.21	38.43	1.24	16.57	1.29
湖北	Hubei	15.94	15.24	70.33	31.70	2.21	12.64	1.42
湖南	Hunan	10.51	23.14	66.78	30.32	2.43	13.11	1.59
广东	Guangdong	54.18	40.82	29.22	73.20	5.55	27.19	3.98
广西	Guangxi	18.01	8.14	60.78	30.04	1.69	14.24	0.87
海南	Hainan	53.33	7.92	10.42	48.06	3.61	23.06	0.83
重庆	Chongqing	3.67	16.44	63.78	31.33	1.28	11.44	1.00
四川	Sichuan	9.85	9.28	67.78	34.23	2.25	14.68	1.10
贵州	Guizhou	6.25	3.44	40.27	21.16	1.03	12.19	0.80
云南	Yunnan	5.04	9.63	32.92	38.04	3.96	24.83	2.79
西藏	Tibet	0.21	0.21	4.79	8.96	1.88	45.00	0.83
陕西	Shaanxi	14.64	18.02	47.84	48.83	1.31	22.79	1.49
甘肃	Gansu	12.56	13.00	42.39	49.94	1.50	40.83	3.61
青海	Qinghai	11.50	4.00	40.83	34.33	0.83	52.33	2.17
宁夏	Ningxia	25.83	18.50	34.50	67.00	2.33	35.50	3.33
新疆	Xinjiang	18.33	15.07	59.33	31.87	1.40	54.87	2.20

10–27 城乡新建住宅面积和居民住房情况

Floor Space Completed and Housing Conditions of Urban and Rural Residents

年份 Year	城镇新建住宅面积 (亿平方米) Floor Space of New Residential Buildings in Urban Areas (100 million sq.m)	# 城镇个人 Constructed by Urban Individuals	农村新建房屋面积 (亿平方米) Floor Space of Newly-Built Houses in Rural Areas (100 million sq.m)	城市人均使用面积 (平方米) Per Capita Gross Living Space in Urban Areas (sq.m)	城市人均居住面积 (平方米) Per Capita Net Living Space in Urban Areas (sq.m)	农村人均居住面积 (平方米) Per Capita Net Living Space in Rural Areas (sq.m)
1978	0.38		1.00		3.6	8.1
1979						8.4
1980	0.92		5.00		3.9	9.4
1981						10.2
1982						10.7
1983						11.6
1984						13.6
1985	1.88	0.63	7.22		5.2	14.7
1986	1.93	0.72	9.84	8.8	6.0	15.3
1987	1.93	0.83	8.84	9.0	6.1	16.0
1988	2.03	0.94	8.45	9.3	6.3	16.6
1989	1.56	0.78	6.76	9.7	6.6	17.2
1990	1.73	0.65	6.91	9.9	6.7	17.8
1991	1.93	0.68	7.54	10.3	6.9	18.5
1992	2.40	0.86	6.19	10.7	7.1	18.9
1993	3.07	0.98	4.81	11.0	7.5	20.7
1994	3.57	1.23	6.18	11.4	7.8	20.2
1995	3.75	1.33	6.99	11.8	8.1	21.0
1996	3.94	1.46	8.28	12.3	8.5	21.7
1997	4.05	1.53	8.06	13.0	8.8	22.5
1998	4.77	1.82	7.99	13.6	9.3	23.3
1999	5.59	2.08	8.34	14.2	9.8	24.2
2000	5.48	2.17	7.97	14.9	10.3	24.8

注:城市平均每人使用面积和居住面积为建设部统计数字。

a) Data on per capita gross and net living space in urban areas are statistics from the Ministry of Construction.

10–28 农村居民家庭住房情况

Housing Conditions of Rural Households

本表为农村住户抽样调查资料。

Data in this table are obtained from the sample surveys on rural households.

项　目	Item	1985	1990	1995	1999	2000
本年新建房屋	**Rooms Newly Built within the Year**					
面积（平方米/人）	Per Capita Floor Space of Houses (sq.m)	1.08	0.82	0.78	0.83	0.87
价值（元/平方米）	Value of Houses (yuan/sq.m)	40.17	92.32	200.30	226.92	260.23
住房结构	Structure of House (sq.m/person)					
#钢筋混凝土结构	Reinforced Concrete Structure	0.09	0.23	0.33	0.48	0.47
砖木结构	Brick and Wood Structure	0.70	0.47	0.37	0.29	0.36
年末住房情况	**House at the End of Year**					
住房面积（平方米/人）	Per Capita Floor Space of Houses (sq.m)	14.70	17.83	21.01	24.23	24.82
住房价值（元/平方米）	Value of Houses (yuan/sq.m)	26.27	44.60	101.64	157.57	187.41
住房结构	Structure of House (sq.m/person)					
#钢筋混凝土结构	Reinforced Concrete Structure	0.31	1.22	3.10	6.35	6.15
砖木结构	Brick and Wood Structure	7.47	9.84	11.91	12.28	13.61

10−29 各地区农村居民家庭年末住房情况（2000年）

Housing Conditions of Rural Households at the Year-end by Region (2000)

地区	Region	住房面积（平方米/人）Per Capita Floor Space of Houses (sq.m)	住房价值（元/平方米）Value of Houses (yuan/sq.m)	住房结构（平方米/人）House Structures (sq.m/person)	
				钢筋混凝土结构 Reinforced Concrete Structure	砖木结构 Brick and Wood Structure
全国	**National Total**	**24.82**	**187.41**	**6.15**	**13.61**
北京	Beijing	28.37	432.16	3.63	24.23
天津	Tianjin	21.14	372.77	1.03	19.95
河北	Hebei	22.87	231.40	2.98	18.35
山西	Shanxi	21.57	198.97	3.52	14.84
内蒙古	Inner Mongolia	16.84	128.97	0.04	8.37
辽宁	Liaoning	22.02	258.15	2.46	18.83
吉林	Jilin	17.72	235.39	0.42	13.27
黑龙江	Heilongjiang	18.26	203.65	0.53	10.98
上海	Shanghai	53.58	329.78	28.30	24.84
江苏	Jiangsu	33.70	278.87	8.41	24.80
浙江	Zhejiang	46.42	268.97	21.53	22.50
安徽	Anhui	22.16	166.29	7.11	12.93
福建	Fujian	32.14	256.49	13.25	10.34
江西	Jiangxi	27.79	134.65	10.89	12.92
山东	Shandong	23.61	193.56	2.69	18.35
河南	Henan	23.14	153.38	6.02	16.08
湖北	Hubei	30.11	110.88	10.07	16.09
湖南	Hunan	30.92	162.88	9.05	19.76
广东	Guangdong	22.42	288.25	13.03	7.52
广西	Guangxi	23.40	129.41	9.40	8.71
海南	Hainan	19.22	164.77	3.32	14.96
重庆	Chongqing	29.58	136.68	4.90	15.51
四川	Sichuan	28.03	114.80	5.01	12.45
贵州	Guizhou	19.75	95.15	2.71	11.37
云南	Yunnan	22.18	168.40	2.92	3.80
西藏	Tibet	15.12	79.77	0.06	4.89
陕西	Shaanxi	22.87	155.07	6.60	9.67
甘肃	Gansu	16.04	130.33	0.40	4.18
青海	Qinghai	15.32	79.82	0.19	1.75
宁夏	Ningxia	17.98	123.97	0.65	7.20
新疆	Xinjiang	17.25	120.83	0.53	2.75

主 要 统 计 指 标 解 释

城市居民家庭全部收入 指被调查城市居民家庭全部的实际收入，包括经常或固定得到的收入和一次性收入。不包括周转性收入，如提取银行存款、向亲友借款、收回借出款以及其他各种暂收款。

城市居民家庭可支配收入 指被调查的城市居民家庭在支付个人所得税、记帐补贴、家庭副业生产支出后所余下的实际收入。

城市居民家庭消费性支出 指被调查的城市居民家庭用于日常生活的全部支出，包括购买商品支出和文化生活、服务等非商品性支出。不包括罚没、丢失款和缴纳的各种税款(如个人所得税、牌照税、房产税等)，也不包括个体劳动者生产经营过程中发生的各项费用。

城市居民家庭购买商品支出 指被调查的城市居民家庭购买商品的全部支出，包括从商店、工厂、饮食业、工作单位食堂、集市以及直接从农民手中购买各种商品的开支。商品支出分为以下八类：食品；衣着；家庭设备用品及服务；医疗保健；交通与通信；娱乐、教育、文化服务；居住；杂项商品和服务。

农村居民家庭纯收入 指农村常住居民家庭总收入中，扣除从事生产和非生产经营费用支出、缴纳税款和上交承包集体任务金额以后剩余的，可直接用于进行生产性、非生产性建设投资、生活消费和积蓄的那一部分收入。农村居民家庭纯收入包括从事生产性和非生产性的经营收入，取自在外人口寄回带回和国家财政救济、各种补贴等非经营性收入；既包括货币收入，又包括自产自用的实物收入。但不包括向银行、信用社和向亲友借款等属于借贷性的收入。

农村居民家庭生活消费支出 指农村常住居民家庭用于日常生活的全部开支，是反映和研究农民家庭实际生活消费水平高低的重要指标。

全国城乡居民储蓄存款余额 指某一时点城乡居民存入银行及农村信用社的储蓄金额，包括城镇居民储蓄存款和农民个人储蓄存款，不包括居民的手存现金和工矿企业、部队、机关、团体等单位存款。

Explanatory Notes on Main Statistical Indicators

Total Income of Urban Households refers to the total actual income of the sample households, including regular or fixed income and occasional income. The income of a circulating nature such as withdrawal from bank deposits, loans borrowed from relatives or friends, repayment of loans received and various temporary collection of money is excluded.

Disposable Income of Urban Households refers to the actual income of the sample households which can be used for daily expenses, i.e., total income minus personal income tax, sample household subsidy and expenditure on household sideline production.

Expenditure for Consumption of Urban Households refers to total expenditure of the sample households for consumption in daily life, including expenditure for various commodities and expenses for non-commodity items such as culture and service, etc. ,but excluding fines and confiscation, loss, tax payments (such as income tax, license tax, real estates tax, etc.) and various expenses by individual laborers for business purposes.

Expenditure for Purchases of Commodities of Urban Households refers to total expenses of the sample households for the purchases of commodities from shops, factories, catering trade, canteens, markets and from the peasants. Such expenditure is classified into eight categories: food, clothing, household appliances and services, health care and medical services, transport and communications, recreation, education and cultural services, housing, miscellaneous goods and services.

Net Income of Rural Households refers to the total income of the permanent residents of the rural households during a year after the deduction of the expenses for productive and non-productive business operation, the payment for taxes and the payment for collective units for their contracted tasks, which can then be spent for investments in productive and non-productive construction, for consumption in daily life and for savings deposit. It is a comprehensive indicator to show the actual level of the income of the peasants' household. The net income of the rural households includes not only the income from the productive and non-productive business operation, but also the income from the non-business operation, such as the money remitted or brought back by the members of the household who are in other places, the government relief payment and various subsidies. It includes not only the money income, but also the income in kind. But the income from borrowing from banks, friends and relatives is excluded.

Expenditure of Rural Households for Consumption refers to total expenses of rural households on daily life, including expenses on food, clothing, housing, fuel, articles for daily use, and expenses on cultural life and services. This indicator is used to show the actual consumption level of peasants.

The Savings Deposits of Urban and Rural Residents refers to the total value of savings deposits of urban and rural households in banks and rural credit cooperatives at a given point of time, including the savings deposit of urban residents and the savings deposit of rural residents. The cash in hand by residents and the deposits of organizations such as enterprises, military units, government agencies, institutions, etc. are not included.

十一、城市概况

General Survey of Cities

简要说明

本篇资料反映我国城市社会、经济发展和城市建设的规模、速度、效益及综合水平等基本情况，主要内容有四部分：

1.全国城市分布情况；

2.沿海开放城市和经济特区城市社会经济主要指标；

3.省会城市和计划单列市主要经济指标；

4.城市房屋及公用设施指标。

前三部分资料由各省、自治区、直辖市统计局依据国家统计局制定的《市、县社会经济基本情况统计报表制度》收集整理提供。

“城市概况”中的有关城市面积、房屋及公用设施方面的资料均由建设部提供。该资料的收集通过两个渠道：

一是建设部系统统计调查资料，根据建设部制订的《城市建设统计报表制度》收集整理，统计范围是各城市建设系统企事业单位。

二是非建设系统统计调查资料，根据建设部和国家统计局联合制发的《建设系统以外市政公用设施统计报表制度》收集整理，统计范围是全社会非建设部门企事业单位经营和自管的市政公用设施。

Brief Introduction

Data in this chapter show the social and economic development as well as the scale, growth rate, economic efficiency, overall level and other basic conditions of China's cities. The main content is composed of the following four parts:

(1) The distribution of the cities in China;

(2) The main indicators on the social and economic development of the open coastal cities and the cities in special economic zones.

(3) The main indicators on the social and economic development of the provincial capitals and the important cities separately listed in the national plan;

(4) The indicators on the urban residential buildings and public facilities.

The data of the first three parts are prepared and provided by the statistical bureaus of the provinces, autonomous regions and municipalities directly under the central government in accordance with the statistical reporting scheme on the basic social and economical situations of the cities and counties, which is stipulated by the NBS.

Data on the areas, buildings and public facilities of the cities in the "General Survey of Cities" are provided by the Ministry of Construction. The data are collected through two channels:

(1) The data from statistical surveys on units under the system of the Ministry of Construction are collected in accordance with the *Statistical Reporting System of Urban Construction*, which covers the enterprises and institutions in the system of urban construction.

(2) The data from statistical surveys on units outside the system of construction are collected in accordance with the *Statistical Reporting System on Urban Public Facilities Outside the System of Ministry of Construction*, which was jointly stipulated and issued by the Ministry of Construction and the National Bureau of Statistics in 1991. The statistical coverage includes the urban public facilities run and managed by the enterprises and institutions outside the system of urban construction.

11-1 全国城市数（2000年）
Number of Cities (2000)

单位：个 (number)

地区	Region	合计 Total	按城区非农业人口分组 Grouped by Non-agricultural Population in Urban Districts				
			200 万以上 2 million and over	100–200万 1 million- 2 million	50–100万 0.5 million- 1 million	20–50万 0.2 million- 0.5 million	20 万以下 under 0.2 million
全 国	**National Total**	**663**	**13**	**27**	**53**	**218**	**352**
北 京	Beijing	1	1				
天 津	Tianjin	1	1				
河 北	Hebei	34		3	3	5	23
山 西	Shanxi	22		1	1	4	16
内蒙古	Inner Mongolia	20		1	1	7	11
辽 宁	Liaoning	31	2	2	6	7	14
吉 林	Jilin	28	1	1		11	15
黑龙江	Heilongjiang	31	1	1	6	10	13
上 海	Shanghai	1	1				
江 苏	Jiangsu	41	1	3	3	23	11
浙 江	Zhejiang	35		1	2	7	25
安 徽	Anhui	22		1	4	10	7
福 建	Fujian	23		1	1	4	17
江 西	Jiangxi	21		1		8	12
山 东	Shandong	48		3	6	23	16
河 南	Henan	38		2	7	8	21
湖 北	Hubei	36	1		4	12	19
湖 南	Hunan	29		1	3	8	17
广 东	Guangdong	52	1	1	2	29	19
广 西	Guangxi	19			2	4	13
海 南	Hainan	9				2	7
重 庆	Chongqing	5	1			3	1
四 川	Sichuan	32	1		1	12	18
贵 州	Guizhou	13		1		3	9
云 南	Yunnan	15		1		2	12
西 藏	Tibet	2					2
陕 西	Shaanxi	13	1			5	7
甘 肃	Gansu	14		1		2	11
青 海	Qinghai	3			1		2
宁 夏	Ningxia	5				2	3
新 疆	Xinjiang	19		1		7	11

11-2 沿海开放城市和经济特区城市社会经济指标（2000年）

Main Social and Economic Indicators of Open Coastal Cities and Cities in Special Economic Zones (2000)

指标	Item	沿海开放城市合计 Total of Open Coastal Cities		经济特区城市合计 Total of Cities in Special Economic Zones	
		包括市辖县 Counties Included	不包括市辖县 Counties Excluded	包括市辖县 Counties Included	不包括市辖县 Counties Excluded
年底人口数（万人）	**Population (year-end) (10 000 persons)**	**9296.0**	**3881.0**	**788.9**	**418.5**
#非农业人口	Non-agricultural Population	3887.6	2831.7	369.9	296.0
单位从业者人数（万人）	**Number of Employed Persons(10 000 persons)**	**2130.4**	**1419.1**	**378.7**	**223.5**
#职工人数	Staff and Workers	1351.5	1022.5	200.7	187.7
按产业分	Grouped by industry				
第一产业	Primary Industry	351.3	88.2	76.5	9.6
第二产业	Secondary Industry	852.7	629.6	169.3	119.5
第三产业	Tertiary Industry	926.5	701.3	132.9	94.4
土地面积（万平方公里）	**Total Area (10 000 sq.km)**	**14.1**	**2.8**	**0.7**	**0.5**
国内生产总值（亿元）	**Gross Domestic Product (100 million yuan)**	**17109.5**	**11422.9**	**2974.3**	**2674.3**
第一产业	Primary Industry	1380.2	313.3	100.1	49.2
第二产业	Secondary Industry	8215.9	5406.8	1552.2	1394.3
第三产业	Tertiary Industry	7513.3	5700.9	1322.0	1230.8
年末实有耕地面积(万公顷)	**Area of Cultivated Land (year-end 10 000 hectares)**	**419.2**		**10.2**	
主要农产品产量（万吨）	**Output of Major Agricultural Products (10 000 tons)**				
蔬菜	Vegetable	3734.6		232.1	
水果	Fruit	732.5		21.7	
肉类	Meat	373.7		26.7	
水产品	Aquatic Products	1374.9		66.9	
限额以上工业企业主要指标	**Main Indicators of Industrial Enterprises above Designated Size**				
工业企业单位数（个）	**Number of Industrial Enterprises above Designated Size (unit)**	**33316.0**	**20966.0**	**4260.0**	**3776.0**
#内资企业	Domestic Funded Enterprises	23400.0	13479.0	1408.0	1100.0
工业总产值(当年价格，亿元)	**Gross Industrial Output Value (at current prices, 100 million yuan)**	**20067.5**	**14922.6**	**4241.1**	**3991.1**
#内资企业	Domestic Funded Enterprises	11381.7	7673.8	1056.5	932.3
产品销售收入（亿元）	Product Sales (100 million yuan)	19625.3	15003.7	4128.1	3889.6
利税总额（亿元）	Pre-tax Profits (100 million yuan)	2074.1	1651.9	422.6	412.6
资产总额（亿元）	Total Assets (100 million yuan)	20881.4	17291.3	3830.8	3652.8
每百元资产提供利税(元)	Pre-tax Profits per 100 Yuan Assets (yuan)	9.9	9.6	11.0	11.3
运输邮电	**Transport, Post and Telecommunication Services**				
客运量(发送)（亿人）	Passenger Traffic (sent) (100 million persons)	14.9		1.9	
货运量(发送)（亿吨）	Freight Traffic (sent) (100 million tons)	19.7		1.2	

注：限额以上工业企业的统计范围为全部国有及年销售收入500万元以上非国有工业企业。

a) Statistical coverage of industrial enterprises above designated size is all state-owned industrial enterprises and non-state-owned industrial enterprises of annual sale above 5 million yuan.

11-2 续表 1 continued

指标	Item	沿海开放城市合计 Total of Open Coastal Cities		经济特区城市合计 Total of Cities in Special Economic Zones	
		包括市辖县 Counties Included	不包括市辖县 Counties Excluded	包括市辖县 Counties Included	不包括市辖县 Counties Excluded
年底邮电局所数 (个)	Number of Post and Telecommunications Offices (year-end)	6517	3045	1018	878
邮电业务总量 (1990年不变价.亿元)	Revenue of Post and Telecommunication Services (at 1990 constant prices) (100 million yuan)	848.7	647.9	229.9	210.6
本地电话用户 (万户)	Number of Telephone Sets (year-end) (10 000 households)	2168.4	1469.2	346.8	289.5
用电量 (亿千瓦小时)	**Annual Electricity Consumption (100 million kwh)**	**1776.9**	**1369.8**	**308.2**	**284.8**
固定资产投资额(亿元)	**Total Investment in Fixed Assets (100 million yuan)**	**4364.7**	**3667.1**	**813.8**	**781.2**
房地产开发投资额 (亿元)	**Total Investment in Real Estate Development (100 million yuan)**	**1511.3**	**1401.5**	**378.3**	**373.2**
#住宅	Residential Buildings	1056.5	977.7	258.4	254.8
批发零售贸易业商品销售总额 (亿元)	**Total Retail Sales of Consumer Goods (100 million yuan)**	**13662.9**	**10958.3**	**1988.4**	**1811.4**
实际利用外资金额 (亿美元)	**Amount of Foreign Capital Actually Utilized (USD 100 million)**	**139.9**	**117.3**	**39.7**	**38.3**
在校学生数 (万人)	**Student Enrollment (10 000 persons)**				
普通高等学校	Number of Regular Institutes of Higher Education (unit)	90.4	88.5	4.7	4.7
中等专业学校	Number of Specialized Secondary Schools (unit)	59.8	54.6	3.0	2.8
普通中学	Number of Regular Secondary Schools (unit)	561.3	235.2	53.0	29.8
小学	Number of Primary Schools (unit)	819.7	299.1	119.7	68.2
成人高等学校	Number of Schools of Higher Education for Adults (unit)	47.3	45.9	3.6	3.4
医院、卫生院数(个)	**Number of Hospitals (unit)**	**4019**	**1616**	**246**	**183**
医院、卫生院床位数(万张)	**Number of Beds in Hospitals (10 000 beds)**	**30.3**	**20.5**	**2.5**	**2.2**
医生数 (万人)	**Number of Doctors (10 000 persons)**	**20.0**	**13.8**	**1.8**	**1.5**
在岗职工工资总额 (亿元)	**Total Wages of Staff and Workers (100 million yuan)**	**1874.9**	**1570.8**	**364.4**	**350.4**
年底全国城乡储蓄存款余额 (亿元)	**Outstanding Amount of Savings Deposit in Urban and Rural Areas (year-end) (100 million yuan)**	**10889.1**	**8069.2**	**1868.6**	**1693.3**

注:沿海开放城市系指上海、天津、大连、秦皇岛、青岛、烟台、威海、连云港、南通、宁波、温州、福州、广州、湛江、北海共15个城市;经济特区城市系指深圳、珠海、汕头和厦门4个城市。

a) Open coastal cities refer to following 15 cities: Shanghai, Tianjin, Dalian, Qinhuangdao, Qingdao, Yantai, Weihai, Lianyungang, Nantong, Ningbo, Wenzhou, Fuzhou, Guangzhou, Zhanjiang and Beihai. Cities in special economic zones refer to following 4 cities: Shenzhen, Zhuhai, Shantou and Xiamen.

11-3 省会城市和计划单列市主要经济指标（2000年）

Main Social and Economic Indicators of Provincial Capitals and Separate Planning Cities (2000)

包括市辖县。

Counties under the jurisdiction of city governments are included.

城市名称 City		年底总人口（万人） Total Population (year-end) (10 000)	#非农业人口 Non-agricultural Population	工业总产值（万元） Gross Industrial Output Value (10 000 yuan)	客运总量（万人） Total Passenger Traffic (10 000 persons)	货运总量（万吨） Total Freight Traffic (10 000 tons)
北京	Beijing	1107.53	760.70	25653086	18396	30657
天津	Tianjin	912.00	532.51	26063753	3474	26013
石家庄	Shijiazhuang	889.80	213.52	7814259	9410	11384
太原	Taiyuan	308.75	203.92	3105185	2518	14207
呼和浩特	Hohhot	209.17	92.21	998038	2591	2361
沈阳	Shenyang	685.10	433.32	7142822	6865	15220
大连	Dalian	551.47	275.35	10991552	11035	19935
长春	Changchun	699.64	287.84	7497110	6612	10268
哈尔滨	Harbin	934.64	435.02	5054153	10017	15246
上海	Shanghai	1321.63	986.16	62045227	6893	47954
南京	Nanjing	544.89	309.52	16027881	15294	12699
杭州	Hangzhou	621.58	226.99	15435682	18608	11459
宁波	Ningbo	540.94	142.03	14276977	22740	10731
合肥	Hefei	438.18	143.04	2968552	5114	1635
福州	Fuzhou	589.23	165.20	7501107	9132	7320
厦门	Xiamen	131.27	66.22	6996757	4194	2465
南昌	Nanchang	432.55	175.89	2519913	3983	3171
济南	Jinan	562.65	233.10	6800393	6286	12193
青岛	Qingdao	706.65	292.35	14005038	13501	21791
郑州	Zhengzhou	628.02	220.70	5659152	11386	7108
武汉	Wuhan	749.19	441.14	9080045	11438	16228
长沙	Changsha	586.00	186.42	3301641	9052	5909
广州	Guangzhou	700.69	436.11	25685694	23430	24156
深圳	Shenzhen	124.92	100.15	25669281	9346	4712
南宁	Nanning	291.41	119.08	1268047	5149	3291
海口	Haikou	57.34	48.40	858508	6061	2100
重庆	Chongqing	3091.09	660.89	9623226	56567	26654
成都	Chengdu	1013.35	345.90	6326268	46217	21496
贵阳	Guiyang	331.57	152.40	2496275	16459	4650
昆明	Kunming	480.94	189.15	3833943	6275	12655
西安	Xi'an	688.01	285.79	5381269	10756	10191
兰州	Lanzhou	290.67	159.75	3685709	2002	5167
西宁	Xining	197.92	76.61	827813	2362	1813
银川	Yinchuan	100.94	56.44	789124	2465	1474
乌鲁木齐	Urumqi	164.38	133.76	2237258	2205	10134

注：工业总产值的统计范围为全部国有及年销售收入500万元以上的非国有工业企业。

a) The gross industrial output value is covered all state-owned industrial enterprises and non-state-owned industrial enterprises of annual sale above 5 million yuan。

11-3 续表 1 continued

城市名称	City	地方财政预算内收入(万元) Budgetary Revenue of Local Governments (10 000 yuan)	固定资产投资总额(万元) Total Investment in Fixed Assets (10 000 yuan)	城乡居民年底储蓄余额(万元) Outstanding Amount of Savings Deposit of Urban and Rural Residents (year-end) (10 000 yuan)	在岗职工人数(万人) Number of Fully-employed Staff and Workers (10 000 persons)	在岗职工工资总额(万元) Total Wages of Fully-employed Staff and Workers (10 000 yuan)
北京	Beijing	3449968	6705682	29232063	406.08	6639343
天津	Tianjin	1336069	5350412	11723997	195.89	2444866
石家庄	Shijiazhuang	377137	2303645	7514860	93.19	836114
太原	Taiyuan	214828	1047702	4196300	86.30	724376
呼和浩特	Hohhot	127755	687898	1525042	32.35	244190
沈阳	Shenyang	611225	2622376	9580898	123.50	1171301
大连	Dalian	776055	1242495	7776033	90.25	1074069
长春	Changchun	303609	1602510	5336997	97.88	954511
哈尔滨	Harbin	536444	2536952	7140508	170.29	1433861
上海	Shanghai	4979600	18696749	25240500	317.12	5876557
南京	Nanjing	925667	2328417	5966974	105.65	1469875
杭州	Hangzhou	691891	3766473	7885600	88.56	1267524
宁波	Ningbo	643513	2452652	5860592	59.81	927748
合肥	Hefei	243797	927775	1839468	43.42	385633
福州	Fuzhou	492577	1087540	4844713	68.42	759607
厦门	Xiamen	518511	1063127	2184618	49.17	751290
南昌	Nanchang	191351	433460	2768864	58.45	511784
济南	Jinan	490485	1861968	4630411	82.26	857337
青岛	Qingdao	749888	2426820	5353197	118.30	1204000
郑州	Zhengzhou	460092	1477513	5657835	87.07	785160
武汉	Wuhan	697711	4619265	6594360	138.68	1348970
长沙	Changsha	360639	2023194	3732175	66.11	670168
广州	Guangzhou	2005460	5680860	22398602	174.44	3432069
深圳	Shenzhen	2250212	5945958	10826400	91.73	2113366
南宁	Nanning	173434	643205	2410407	45.23	394832
海口	Haikou	136170	648515	1641936	17.83	207800
重庆	Chongqing	1044570	3737576	10853600	216.00	1732318
成都	Chengdu	587936	4759020	8310016	128.48	1332340
贵阳	Guiyang	241483	1068008	1976579	53.92	473641
昆明	Kunming	545299	2391121	4438300	84.19	882931
西安	Xi'an	469638	1511662	6758327	110.77	1016778
兰州	Lanzhou	166061	1536000	2979869	59.69	559653
西宁	Xining	63393	538189	1025512	26.15	234412
银川	Yinchuan	88569	485979	884821	23.26	208322
乌鲁木齐	Urumqi	261569	1207759	2548648	54.43	576819

注：本表价值量指标按当年价格计算。

a)Data in value terms in this table are calculated at current prices.

11-4 城市公用事业基本情况

Basic Statistics on Urban Public Utilities

本表1990年以后各项指标按全社会范围计算，1985年按城建部门管理的范围计算。

Data since 1990 have covered the public utilities of all urban units, whereas data in the preceding years only covered the urban units under the city construction department.

项　目	Item	1985	1990	1995	1999	2000
城市及建筑物面积	**Cities Areas and Floor Space of Buildings**					
建成区面积 (平方公里)	Developed Areas (sq.m)	**9386**	**12856**	**19264**	**21525**	**22439**
城市人口密度 (人/平方公里)	Population Density of Urban Districts (persons/sq.km)	262	279	322	462	441
年末实有房屋建筑面积 (亿平方米)	Total Floor Space of Buildings (year-end) (10 000 sq.m)	23.2	39.8	57.3	73.5	76.6
年末实有住宅建筑面积 (亿平方米)	Total Floor Space of Residential Buildings (year-end) (10 000 sq.m)	11.3	19.6	31.0	41.7	44.1
年末实有住宅居住面积 (亿平方米)	Total Living Space of Buildings (year-end) (10 000 sq.m)	5.8	9.8	15.5	21.0	22.3
供水、供气及供热	**Water Supply, Gas Supply and Heating**					
自来水年供水量 (亿吨)	Annual Supply of Tap Water (100 million tons)	128.0	382.3	496.6	467.5	469.0
#生活用水量	Water Consumption for Residential use	51.9	100.1	158.1	189.6	200.0
平均每人生活用水 (吨)	Per Capita Water Consumption for Residential Use (ton)	55.1	67.9	71.3	94.1	95.5
用水普及率 (%)	Percentage of Population with Access to Tap Water (%)	81.0	89.2	93.0	96.3	96.7
煤气供气量 (万立方米)	Coal Gas Supply (10 000 cu.m)	249754	1747065	1266894	1320925	1523615
#家庭用量	Consumption of Coal Gas for Residential Use	107060	274127	456585	494001	630937
天然气供气量 (万立方米)	Natural Gas Supply (10 000 cu.m)	162099	642289	673354	800556	821476
#家庭用量	Consumption of Coal Gas for Residential Use		115662	163788	215006	247580
液化石油气供气量 (万吨)	Liquefied Petroleum Gas (10 000 ton)	·	203.0	488.7	761.2	1053.7
#家庭用量 (万吨)	Consumption of Liquefied Gas for Residential Use (10 000 ton)	54.7	142.8	370.2	499.0	532.3
煤气管道长度 (公里)	Length of Gas Pipelines (km)	10567	16312	33890	45847	48376
用气普及率 (%)	Percentage of Population with Access to Gas (%)	22.40	42.20	70.00	81.74	84.15
集中供热面积 (万平方米)	Heated Area (10 000 sq.m)	.	21263	64645	96775	110766
市政工程	**Municipal Engineering**					
铺装道路长度 (公里)	Length of Paved Roads (km)	38282	94820	130308	152385	159617
平均每万人拥有 (公里)	Length of Paved Roads per 10 000 Population (km)	3.3	6.4	7.0	7.6	7.6
铺装道路面积 (万平方米)	Area of Paved Roads (10 000 sq.m)	35872	89160	135810	177337	190357
每万人拥有 (万平方米)	Area of Paved Roads per 10 000 Population	3.1	6.0	7.3	8.8	9.1
下水道长度 (公里)	Length of Sewer Pipelines (km)	31556	57787	110293	134486	141758
平均每万人拥有 (公里)	Length of Sewer Pipelines per 10 000 Population (km)	2.7	3.9	6.0	6.7	6.8
公共交通	**Public Traffic**					
公共汽(电)车数量 (辆)	Number of Public Transportation Vehicles (Buses and Trolley Buses etc.) (unit)	45155	62215	136821	209884	225993
平均每万人拥有 (辆)	Number of Public Transportation Vehicles per 10 000 Population (unit)	3.9	4.8	7.3	9.4	10.8
出租汽车数量 (万辆)	Taxi (10 000 units)		11.1	50.4	79.1	82.6
城市绿化	**Afforestation in Cities**					
绿地面积 (公顷)	Public Green Areas (hectare)	159291	474613	678310	778161	865295
每万人绿地面积 (公顷)	Public Green Areas per 10 000 Population (hectare)	13.7	32.2	36.7	38.6	41.3
公园动物园个数 (个)	Number of Parks and Zoos	1026	1970	3619	4219	4455
公园动物园面积 (公顷)	Area of Parks and Zoos (hectare)	21896	40081	72857	77137	82090
环境卫生	**Environmental Sanitation**					
清运垃圾 (万吨)	Volume of Garbage Disposal (10 000 tons)	4477	6767	10748	11415	11819
清运粪便 (万吨)	Volume of Disposal of Excrement and Urine (10 000 tons)	1731	2385	3071	2844	2829
每万人有公厕 (座)	Number of Public Lavatories per 10 000 Population	5.8	6.6	6.1	5.3	5.1

注：人均拥有指标按城市人口中非农业人口计算。

a)Data on the public utilities per 10 000 population are based on the non-agricultural population in urban areas.

11-5 各地区城市房屋建筑及住房情况（2000年）

Basic Statistics on Building Construction and Housing Condition in Cities by Region (2000)

地区	Region	建成区面积 (平方公里) Developed Areas (sq.km)	征用土地面积 (平方公里) Land Put in Requisition for State Construction Projects (sq.km)	市区人口密度(人/平方公里) Population Density of Urban Districts (persons/sq.km)	年末全市实有房屋建筑面积 (万平方米) Total Floor Space of Buildings (year-end) (10 000sq.m)	年末全市实有住宅建筑面积 (万平方米) Total Floor Space of Residential Buildings (year-end) (10 000sq.m)	年末全市住房居住面积 (万平方米) Total Living Space of Residential Buildings (year-end) (10 000sq.m)	解决缺房户 (户) Number of Households with Housing Problems to be Solved
全国	**National Total**	**22439.28**	**447.25**	**441**	**765891**	**440989**	**223213.09**	**860932**
北京	Beijing	490.11	1.83	2557	29109	15196	7075.30	166058
天津	Tianjin	385.86	0.58	1383	15789	8404	4303.70	119200
河北	Hebei	962.87	15.41	1815	31328	16958	9253.75	20433
山西	Shanxi	616.98	3.23	761	20818	11695	6297.55	12488
内蒙古	Inner Mongolia	593.00	6.23	289	14990	8578	4555.02	33590
辽宁	Liaoning	1558.62	22.63	1172	52481	30841	15605.57	
吉林	Jilin	787.16	12.17	836	23643	14362	7412.01	8791
黑龙江	Heilongjiang	1310.15	7.68	233	35683	21588	11091.23	57025
上海	Shanghai	549.58		1757	34205	20864	10932.90	
江苏	Jiangsu	1382.27	37.59	2260	51629	27731	13829.06	9252
浙江	Zhejiang	964.03	51.28	1244	37592	23512	11994.57	6634
安徽	Anhui	885.95	18.92	1542	20759	11554	5593.79	31794
福建	Fujian	449.06	14.20	1281	18956	11757	5784.45	19356
江西	Jiangxi	542.97	5.97	440	15623	9232	4684.19	12696
山东	Shandong	1540.79	36.61	625	57264	31607	16037.96	30253
河南	Henan	1073.81	26.91	1390	35234	19504	9661.20	15894
湖北	Hubei	1354.71	14.14	436	44533	26580	15174.95	14226
湖南	Hunan	799.27	61.45	939	25884	15749	8753.51	45919
广东	Guangdong	1763.98	10.62	1344	58669	34895	14116.00	23065
广西	Guangxi	585.93	7.56	470	18380	10590	4758.82	11319
海南	Hainan	256.44	0.23	2110	5096	3359	1857.52	10965
重庆	Chongqing	324.26	16.21	556	15434	8966	4650.48	1309
四川	Sichuan	991.71	26.91	544	33768	19640	9706.18	30379
贵州	Guizhou	291.65	7.84	330	8537	4845	2765.67	696
云南	Yunnan	338.12	11.74	243	14540	7082	3819.20	5411
西藏	Tibet	68.99		593	880	559	297.74	424
陕西	Shaanxi	476.13	16.65	1419	15580	8785	4717.58	20799
甘肃	Gansu	402.92	4.05	87	10791	6151	3072.15	4342
青海	Qinghai	91.78	3.00	2070	2334	1207	694.90	
宁夏	Ningxia	126.77	3.19	472	3585	1844	1010.29	10443
新疆	Xinjiang	473.41	2.42	26	12777	7354	3705.85	55366

11-6 各地区城市自来水情况（2000年）

Basic Statistics on Tap Water Supply in Cities by Region (2000)

地 区	Region	年末自来水生产能力（万吨/日）Production Capacity of Tap Water (year-end) (10 000 tons/day)	年末供水管道长度（公里）Length of Water Supply Pipelines (year-end) (km)	全年供水总量（万吨）Total Annual Volume of Water Supply (10 000tons)	#生活用水 For Residential Use	#生产用水 For Productive Use	用水人口（万人）Number of Residents with Access to Tap Water (10 000)	人均日生活用水量（升）Per Capita Daily Consumption of Tap Water for Residential Use (liter)
全 国	**National Total**	**21841.99**	**254561**	**4689838**	**1999960**	**2279239**	**24879.52**	**220.24**
北 京	Beijing	590.17	8387	109335	69420	24037	764.45	248.80
天 津	Tianjin	347.10	5049	61142	25714	26645	534.50	131.80
河 北	Hebei	930.41	9664	170733	72852	88653	1084.55	184.03
山 西	Shanxi	326.97	4801	89836	36231	48330	698.10	142.19
内蒙古	Inner Mongolia	268.63	4499	61757	22548	33439	435.18	141.95
辽 宁	Liaoning	1393.20	20627	308500	103812	163667	1748.15	162.70
吉 林	Jilin	683.99	5815	150924	39926	95155	727.79	150.30
黑龙江	Heilongjiang	664.56	8219	154208	56985	85361	1042.91	149.70
上 海	Shanghai	1333.00	15053	291109	141109	119523	1136.82	340.07
江 苏	Jiangsu	1641.57	20427	353366	145707	172552	1503.09	265.58
浙 江	Zhejiang	982.73	14236	196199	80205	93834	1031.63	213.00
安 徽	Anhui	958.81	6181	200115	60988	123426	778.47	214.64
福 建	Fujian	598.16	5116	128161	52303	64700	570.91	251.00
江 西	Jiangxi	647.31	3968	131816	50548	68954	593.39	233.38
山 东	Shandong	1165.00	18949	231941	93394	125719	1722.76	148.53
河 南	Henan	958.79	9211	191706	76801	100156	1227.35	171.44
湖 北	Hubei	1309.08	13731	298256	131757	153678	1546.25	233.45
湖 南	Hunan	1162.21	7650	282357	95233	162733	839.29	310.87
广 东	Guangdong	2326.08	27761	525615	309008	173544	2231.04	379.46
广 西	Guangxi	618.59	4985	135826	55896	65934	536.02	285.70
海 南	Hainan	147.46	1397	23765	11929	5004	160.39	203.77
重 庆	Chongqing	355.82	4948	60946	36178	24132	576.25	172.00
四 川	Sichuan	884.06	11573	198400	80009	106119	1056.23	207.53
贵 州	Guizhou	216.39	2904	45931	18652	19162	367.80	138.94
云 南	Yunnan	216.85	4889	52323	29174	16739	400.40	199.62
西 藏	Tibet	16.00	334	4824	3995	829	23.64	463.00
陕 西	Shaanxi	311.55	3932	67062	38177	25943	554.62	188.59
甘 肃	Gansu	319.20	3811	74326	21442	51779	368.55	159.40
青 海	Qinghai	60.09	765	14239	6364	7137	88.04	198.04
宁 夏	Ningxia	116.27	1231	25471	8400	12398	112.59	204.40
新 疆	Xinjiang	291.94	4448	49649	25203	19957	418.36	165.05

11-7 各地区城市煤气、液化石油气、天然气情况（2000年）

Basic Statistics on Supply of Gas, Liquefied Petroleum Gas and Natural Gas in Cities by Region (2000)

地区	Region	人工煤气生产能力（万立方米/日）Production Capacity of Coal Gas(10 000 cu.m/day)	管道长度（公里）Length of Gas Pipelines (km)		全年供气总量 Total Gas Supply			用气人口(万人) Population with Access to Gas (10 000 persons)		
			人工煤气 Coal Gas	天然气 Natural Gas	人工煤气（万立方米）Coal Gas (10 000 cu.m)	液化石油气（吨）Liquefied Petroleum Gas (ton)	天然气（万立方米）Natural Gas (10 000 cu.m)	人工煤气 Coal Gas	液化石油气 Liquefied Petroleum Gas	天然气 Natural Gas
全国	**National Total**	**2651.36**	**48376**	**33653**	**1523615**	**10537147**	**821476**	**3944.45**	**11106.62**	**2580.98**
北京	Beijing	240.00	544	4231	47310	176460	95740	82.94	252.69	295.30
天津	Tianjin	90.00	1270	4268	9882	44203	23474	72.62	89.40	304.12
河北	Hebei	112.80	2710	566	45918	189612	4647	278.73	475.66	31.08
山西	Shanxi	109.53	2700	290	241869	34152	5611	295.07	102.28	35.68
内蒙古	Inner Mongolia	16.40	755		7485	59425		77.93	191.86	
辽宁	Liaoning	163.10	4470	2951	81957	379194	24923	422.10	568.82	409.88
吉林	Jilin	64.50	1889	1017	15508	169062	13162	149.88	350.34	76.50
黑龙江	Heilongjiang	184.00	1949	476	30347	601427	4185	211.03	546.44	55.71
上海	Shanghai	630.00	6606	1742	213147	490561	25974	449.95	421.15	66.99
江苏	Jiangsu	220.27	4277		362606	705010		324.65	882.85	
浙江	Zhejiang	36.74	1084		27796	630895		47.77	555.11	
安徽	Anhui	36.80	1918	16	22996	458621	600	168.76	378.80	5.29
福建	Fujian		567		12727	737609		21.21	340.72	
江西	Jiangxi	37.00	1548		39463	164698		125.38	220.08	
山东	Shandong	145.00	4676	1279	43041	276543	84065	335.43	886.80	61.88
河南	Henan	32.80	1816	2339	81775	162199	55018	136.31	429.88	185.89
湖北	Hubei	142.80	2874		14588	296179	1	180.08	908.34	0.20
湖南	Hunan	104.50	1116		60375	199873		81.29	460.65	
广东	Guangdong	95.00	1730	127	12097	3108612	339	150.07	1485.28	4.00
广西	Guangxi		158	20	2817	204904		14.51	373.57	0.12
海南	Hainan					77856			116.53	
重庆	Chongqing		30	4195	100	38769	68049	0.50	35.05	328.63
四川	Sichuan		364	8595	111677	66154	388394	30.08	80.54	556.00
贵州	Guizhou	45.00	1121	17	8727	28973	450	73.35	89.71	1.89
云南	Yunnan	65.92	1298	3	15407	82954	1533	99.60	137.50	2.00
西藏	Tibet					16680			13.80	
陕西	Shaanxi	23.40	328	843	4447	79038	17770	32.67	205.97	125.95
甘肃	Gansu	55.80	358	36	6691	783739	78	70.24	101.73	1.60
青海	Qinghai		17	176	24	11496	2022	2.50	29.50	3.93
宁夏	Ningxia		203	81	2838	18231	56	9.80	69.87	1.35
新疆	Xinjiang			385		244018	5385		305.70	26.99

11-8 各地区城市集中供热情况（2000年）

Basic Statistics on Heating in Cities by Region (2000)

地 区	Region	供应能力 Heating Capacity		供热总量 Volume Supplied		管道长度(公里) Length of Pipelines(km)		供热面积（万平方米） Heated Area (10 000 sq.m)
		蒸汽（吨/小时） Steam (ton/hour)	热水（兆瓦） Hot Water (1 billion kw)	蒸汽（吨） Steam (ton)	热水（万百万千焦） Hot Water (10 billion joule)	蒸汽 Steam	热水 Hot Water	
全 国	**National Total**	**74148**	**97417**	**23828**	**83321**	**7963**	**35819**	**110766.45**
北 京	Beijing	3408	4755	1722	8634	345	1855	7843.00
天 津	Tianjin	9106	5608	160	4869	310	2950	6184.80
河 北	Hebei	6427	8388	6299	5224	706	3232	10200.47
山 西	Shanxi	3316	5347	796	5320	512	1619	5062.16
内蒙古	Inner Mongolia	1200	5687	107	4857	60	1456	5215.51
辽 宁	Liaoning	11569	19154	2201	11388	1303	7211	20030.43
吉 林	Jilin	3425	10564	510	8814	276	3566	9305.51
黑龙江	Heilongjiang	4513	13750	1422	12653	364	5510	14321.04
上 海	Shanghai							
江 苏	Jiangsu	2554	8	676		342		1338.39
浙 江	Zhejiang	1516		494		179		356.80
安 徽	Anhui	1915	214	493	10	110	5	208.29
福 建	Fujian		43		68		49	800.00
江 西	Jiangxi							
山 东	Shandong	12498	9206	2900	8934	2084	3144	12378.12
河 南	Henan	3261	1334	904	974	489	888	3302.55
湖 北	Hubei	775		236		61		581.00
湖 南	Hunan	493		568		39		562.00
广 东	Guangdong							
广 西	Guangxi							
海 南	Hainan							
重 庆	Chongqing							
四 川	Sichuan							
贵 州	Guizhou							
云 南	Yunnan							
西 藏	Tibet							
陕 西	Shaanxi	1923	551	1046	273	283	235	1697.39
甘 肃	Gansu	3949	3611	2493	3203	111	1390	4260.49
青 海	Qinghai		89		34		47	54.00
宁 夏	Ningxia	662	2963	247	2862	139	598	1894.90
新 疆	Xinjiang	1638	6145	554	5204	250	2064	5169.60

11-9 各地区城市市政工程情况（2000年）

Basic Statistics on Municipal Engineering in Cities by Region (2000)

地　区	Region	年末实有铺装道路长度（公里）Length of Paved Roads (year-end) (km)	年末实有铺装道路面积（万平方米）Area of Paved Roads (year-end) (10 000 sq.m)	城市桥梁（座）Number of Bridges (unit)	城市下水道总长度（公里）Length of Sewer Pipelines (km)	城市污水日处理能力（万吨）Daily Disposal Capacity of Sewage (10 000 tons)	城市路灯（盏）Number of Street Lights (unit)
全　国	**National Total**	**159617**	**190356.52**	**34739**	**141758.44**	**4740.98**	**4727297**
北　京	Beijing	3624	4198.84	687	4146.09	165.00	156733
天　津	Tianjin	3608	4168.07	469	7032.00	161.80	107608
河　北	Hebei	6730	8405.09	1172	7201.15	196.24	186543
山　西	Shanxi	4360	5153.50	746	2469.17	82.44	103524
内蒙古	Inner Mongolia	2771	3168.53	244	2692.50	42.96	65605
辽　宁	Liaoning	9249	10151.93	1253	8354.03	177.70	297666
吉　林	Jilin	4112	4899.48	449	3935.35	63.97	113172
黑龙江	Heilongjiang	8286	7725.27	618	4877.34	274.50	142043
上　海	Shanghai	6641	8147.06	4432	3736.00	481.11	181935
江　苏	Jiangsu	11011	13357.47	4343	11096.81	711.58	437423
浙　江	Zhejiang	7253	9049.50	4232	7795.26	242.84	259446
安　徽	Anhui	6107	6864.59	933	4199.79	180.95	124614
福　建	Fujian	3648	4401.27	998	3466.53	119.76	127439
江　西	Jiangxi	3033	3293.03	601	2073.64	20.27	66484
山　东	Shandong	15856	21755.42	2841	12131.94	253.10	322004
河　南	Henan	4920	6937.70	822	6069.63	140.53	197206
湖　北	Hubei	13096	14287.03	1957	7518.80	335.69	209546
湖　南	Hunan	4739	4815.93	637	3754.31	127.65	115147
广　东	Guangdong	14181	18891.83	2535	16780.90	327.34	613262
广　西	Guangxi	3810	4362.23	431	2885.46	159.38	128551
海　南	Hainan	1445	2314.35	144	1572.99	34.11	57587
重　庆	Chongqing	2693	2533.65	692	2223.11	60.61	98189
四　川	Sichuan	5433	6458.52	1631	5370.37	73.35	249507
贵　州	Guizhou	1682	1584.05	310	1665.18	5.20	43863
云　南	Yunnan	2168	2445.05	480	2006.71	110.40	80225
西　藏	Tibet	253	311.62	24	229.92		9531
陕　西	Shaanxi	2537	2970.36	385	1856.00	32.61	63716
甘　肃	Gansu	2334	2541.27	285	1866.71	71.15	46477
青　海	Qinghai	438	599.30	59	262.80		19595
宁　夏	Ningxia	790	910.96	76	479.60	11.86	29775
新　疆	Xinjiang	2809	3653.62	253	2008.35	76.88	72881

11-10 各地区城市公共汽(电)车、出租汽车情况（2000年）

Basic Statistics on Buses, Trolley Buses and Taxis in Cities by Region (2000)

地区	Region	年末实有公共汽(电)车 (辆) Number of Public Transportation Vehicles(year-end)				运客总数 (万人次) Number of Passengers Carried (10 000 person-times)				出租汽车 (辆) Number of Taxis
		合计 Total	公共汽车 Buses	电车 Trolley	地铁 Subways	合计 Total	公共汽车 Buses	电车 Trolley	地铁 Subways	
全国	**National Total**	**225993**	**221672**	**3380**	**941**	**3410451**	**3211940**	**137792**	**60719**	**825746**
北京	Beijing	12741	11545	609	587	396121	331596	21047	43478	65127
天津	Tianjin	5382	5358		24	53381	53046		335	31939
河北	Hebei	7413	7413			65390	65390			41324
山西	Shanxi	2958	2836	122		39288	35905	3383		27638
内蒙古	Inner Mongolia	2128	2128			19313	19313			28856
辽宁	Liaoning	13136	12919	217		297305	278836	18469		75389
吉林	Jilin	7158	7084	74		79621	77886	1735		44000
黑龙江	Heilongjiang	9314	9094	220		100995	93101	7894		49581
上海	Shanghai	18155	17358	581	216	278465	248107	16802	13556	42943
江苏	Jiangsu	14838	14838			246314	246314			36603
浙江	Zhejiang	10015	9792	223		167846	146548	21298		23911
安徽	Anhui	6359	6359			94277	94277			31726
福建	Fujian	5508	5479	29		88597	87514	1083		11311
江西	Jiangxi	4031	3959	72		54780	48476	6304		7818
山东	Shandong	12195	11945	250		163546	159408	4138		45994
河南	Henan	8519	8333	186		78204	73311	4893		44369
湖北	Hubei	17621	17337	284		178773	170365	8408		23733
湖南	Hunan	9083	9083			106067	106067			19534
广东	Guangdong	18352	18049	189	114	291063	280036	7677	3350	40197
广西	Guangxi	2718	2718			51821	51821			9135
海南	Hainan	1610	1610			8426	8426			4184
重庆	Chongqing	4379	4218	161		78015	69358	8657		15511
四川	Sichuan	7229	7229			117893	117893			20591
贵州	Guizhou	5646	5646			68629	68629			7352
云南	Yunnan	4258	4258			45808	45808			11575
西藏	Tibet	687	687			109	109			1145
陕西	Shaanxi	4305	4220	85		67694	65064	2630		16377
甘肃	Gansu	2733	2655	78		45063	41689	3374		14413
青海	Qinghai	1125	1125			25085	25085			5785
宁夏	Ningxia	719	719			7559	7559			5492
新疆	Xinjiang	5678	5678			95003	95003			22193

11-11 各地区城市园林绿化情况（2000年）

Basic Statistics on Parks, Gardens and Green Areas in Cities by Region(2000)

地 区	Region	城市园林绿地面积（公顷）Total Area of Parks, Gardens and Green Areas in Cities (hectare)	# 公共绿地 Public Green Areas	公园（个）Number of Parks	公园面积（公顷）Area of Parks (hectare)	年游人量（万人次）Number of Visitors to Parks and Zoos in the Year (10 000 person-times)	全年植树（万株）Number of Trees Planted in the Year (10 000 trees)
全 国	**National Total**	**865295**	**143114.83**	**4455**	**82090.33**	**123564**	**15759.75**
北 京	Beijing	20600	5513.00	96	4192.00	7849	344.00
天 津	Tianjin	7550	2600.89	168	1016.47	3975	82.62
河 北	Hebei	24564	5397.45	220	3157.25	4564	1190.49
山 西	Shanxi	9270	2684.03	104	1840.63	1743	322.55
内蒙古	Inner Mongolia	15392	2781.22	73	2052.46	1051	99.39
辽 宁	Liaoning	57589	8945.79	197	4751.17	5800	753.74
吉 林	Jilin	21197	4818.62	65	2166.60	1222	225.14
黑龙江	Heilongjiang	33768	7607.61	118	4009.89	4855	561.56
上 海	Shanghai	10886	4071.40	104	846.52	8184	728.25
江 苏	Jiangsu	60064	10247.99	313	5159.25	5731	788.92
浙 江	Zhejiang	26394	4723.48	360	2343.45	7586	978.95
安 徽	Anhui	32852	4973.20	105	3471.91	3856	407.11
福 建	Fujian	18039	3023.30	200	2264.76	4159	524.82
江 西	Jiangxi	16706	2921.97	109	1820.15	2019	66.53
山 东	Shandong	56301	11493.74	346	5570.60	6038	825.91
河 南	Henan	25792	6328.67	228	3341.93	6119	839.85
湖 北	Hubei	67959	11958.25	187	4895.11	4176	502.53
湖 南	Hunan	44672	3525.18	116	2646.41	2361	269.86
广 东	Guangdong	152248	17161.73	582	11041.24	19756	3113.71
广 西	Guangxi	44149	3407.31	86	2765.77	2972	570.32
海 南	Hainan	6059	1692.24	30	1051.50	788	309.88
重 庆	Chongqing	9327	1187.67	52	865.16	701	56.25
四 川	Sichuan	46854	4239.97	208	2938.35	7257	620.77
贵 州	Guizhou	9939	2505.75	41	1621.30	2892	655.17
云 南	Yunnan	10113	2746.61	86	2063.16	2983	166.77
西 藏	Tibet	1466	171.32	3	67.00	51	40.00
陕 西	Shaanxi	9079	2065.09	84	1254.27	2720	147.40
甘 肃	Gansu	4496	1302.81	64	834.40	832	272.59
青 海	Qinghai	1388	275.00	11	221.00	292	17.28
宁 夏	Ningxia	3316	462.99	15	253.00	346	50.54
新 疆	Xinjiang	17266	2280.55	84	1567.62	686	226.85

11-12 各地区城市公共卫生情况（2000年）

Basic Statistics on Urban Sanitation in Cities by Region (2000)

地 区	Region	清扫面积 (万平方米) Area under Cleaning Program (10 000 sq.m)	生活垃圾清运量 (万吨) Volume of Garbage Disposal (10 000 tons)	粪便清运量 (万吨) Volume of Excrement and Urine Disposal (10 000 tons)	环卫机械总数 (台) Environmental Sanitation Equipment (unit)	公共厕所 (座) Number of Public Lavatories (unit)	#水冲式 Water-Closet
全 国	**National Total**	**166155.36**	**11818.88**	**2828.85**	**44846**	**106471**	**47965**
北 京	Beijing	5098.40	244.39	249.24	2592	5096	1879
天 津	Tianjin	4825.10	224.60	18.50	659	2656	1606
河 北	Hebei	7739.16	563.11	122.88	1813	6352	1577
山 西	Shanxi	4309.14	575.72	152.83	1296	3386	885
内蒙古	Inner Mongolia	3983.93	310.69	91.90	1186	4007	529
辽 宁	Liaoning	16588.01	837.96	160.32	3009	10523	1062
吉 林	Jilin	6471.71	640.68	136.46	1826	6772	607
黑龙江	Heilongjiang	7140.11	917.56	245.00	3064	10335	923
上 海	Shanghai	4517.00	523.89	219.20	3775	1200	1200
江 苏	Jiangsu	8773.33	515.15	308.81	2569	7393	5573
浙 江	Zhejiang	7039.89	436.42	112.74	2022	2984	2463
安 徽	Anhui	4405.35	327.47	54.63	1175	4755	2330
福 建	Fujian	4129.06	216.97	25.79	1052	1364	1338
江 西	Jiangxi	2128.09	197.37	16.43	568	1892	1045
山 东	Shandong	14851.65	767.54	136.40	3131	4777	3188
河 南	Henan	7939.22	551.74	65.49	1777	4322	2693
湖 北	Hubei	8226.22	650.57	79.92	1805	5180	3304
湖 南	Hunan	3236.22	358.46	24.25	1213	3001	1771
广 东	Guangdong	18861.57	879.06	129.33	3546	4191	3881
广 西	Guangxi	3549.85	175.11	21.17	739	1422	1330
海 南	Hainan	2080.05	70.66	9.48	297	384	364
重 庆	Chongqing	2382.14	173.30	203.82	515	2854	1515
四 川	Sichuan	5455.38	373.44	81.54	1565	3362	2441
贵 州	Guizhou	953.09	248.35	14.62	592	1697	822
云 南	Yunnan	2154.58	162.28	59.09	791	1198	780
西 藏	Tibet	357.30	33.26	2.80	60	99	81
陕 西	Shaanxi	2407.92	224.15	16.23	626	1386	680
甘 肃	Gansu	2000.71	187.96	37.26	456	953	437
青 海	Qinghai	395.88	95.70	7.84	114	307	232
宁 夏	Ningxia	930.90	76.08	9.12	246	939	298
新 疆	Xinjiang	3224.40	259.24	15.76	767	1684	1131

11-13 各地区城市设施水平（2000年）

Level of Public Facilities in Cities by Region(2000)

地 区	Region	人均房屋使用面积(平方米) Per Capita Gross Living Space (sq.m)	人均居住面积(平方米) Per Capita Net Living Space (sq.m)	城市人口用水普及率(%) Percentage of Population with Access to Tap Water	城市煤气普及率(%) Percentage of Population with Access to Gas	每万人拥有公共汽(电)车辆(标台) Number of Public Buses and Trolley Buses per 10 000 Persons	人均拥有铺装道路面积(平方米) Per Capita Area of Paved Roads (sq.m)	人均公共绿地面积(平方米) Per Capita Public Green Areas (sq.m)	每万人拥有公共厕所(座) Number of Public Lavatories per 10 000 Population
全 国	**National Total**	**14.87**	**10.25**	**96.70**	**84.15**	**9.81**	**9.09**	**6.83**	**5.08**
北 京	Beijing	16.52	10.91	100.00	99.30	25.27	6.61	8.68	8.02
天 津	Tianjin	13.88	8.90	100.00	96.80	10.85	8.66	5.40	5.52
河 北	Hebei	14.31	10.39	99.94	94.01	7.97	10.06	6.46	7.60
山 西	Shanxi	13.42	10.03	96.82	74.89	4.69	8.91	4.64	5.86
内蒙古	Inner Mongolia	13.16	9.29	89.10	58.60	3.92	6.88	6.04	8.70
辽 宁	Liaoning	12.84	8.84	98.20	89.31	8.46	6.47	5.70	6.71
吉 林	Jilin	13.11	9.16	87.49	73.29	7.82	6.23	6.12	8.61
黑龙江	Heilongjiang	12.69	8.91	86.49	71.91	7.03	6.83	6.73	9.14
上 海	Shanghai	15.19	11.03	100.00	99.99	20.17	8.68	4.34	1.28
江 苏	Jiangsu	15.60	10.60	99.18	95.79	10.58	10.60	8.13	5.87
浙 江	Zhejiang	20.63	14.42	99.93	98.01	13.82	14.71	7.68	4.85
安 徽	Anhui	12.13	8.15	93.76	77.51	7.60	9.62	6.97.	6.67
福 建	Fujian	19.87	12.42	98.69	86.81	11.07	10.56	7.25	3.27
江 西	Jiangxi	14.23	9.61	93.28	69.23	6.53	6.60	5.86	3.79
山 东	Shandong	15.82	11.03	97.91	90.01	8.32	15.25	8.06	3.35
河 南	Henan	12.95	8.94	96.80	72.09	6.93	6.65	6.07	4.14
湖 北	Hubei	15.53	11.17	98.86	86.80	11.95	11.39	9.54	4.13
湖 南	Hunan	15.63	11.75	97.50	78.35	10.43	6.96	5.10	4.34
广 东	Guangdong	18.71	10.54	98.12	94.23	8.37	10.86	9.86	2.41
广 西	Guangxi	15.94	10.08	98.38	90.75	6.06	10.20	7.97	3.32
海 南	Hainan	16.29	11.66	97.61	94.24	10.34	18.72	13.69	3.11
重 庆	Chongqing	14.52	10.23	96.86	79.04	8.88	5.50	2.58	6.19
四 川	Sichuan	15.20	10.42	97.19	74.63	7.52	7.23	4.75	3.76
贵 州	Guizhou	12.13	9.15	92.96	54.21	13.62	5.21	8.24	5.58
云 南	Yunnan	15.58	11.88	98.36	79.18	12.70	8.10	9.10	3.97
西 藏	Tibet	23.13	15.01	83.75	82.73	27.28	18.68	10.27	5.94
陕 西	Shaanxi	12.50	9.34	96.48	74.53	7.82	6.07	4.22	2.83
甘 肃	Gansu	12.22	9.03	94.61	53.27	7.02	7.80	4.00	2.92
青 海	Qinghai	12.06	9.17	97.29	48.88	13.90	8.15	3.74	4.18
宁 夏	Ningxia	12.31	9.36	97.69	80.00	5.82	9.00	4.57	9.27
新 疆	Xinjiang	13.61	9.71	98.81	92.84	13.79	10.20	6.36	4.70

主 要 统 计 指 标 解 释

年末自来水生产能力 指年底城建部门管理的自来水厂和自备水源的社会单位取水、净化、送水、出厂输水干管等环节的实际生产能力。

年末供水管道长度 指从送水泵到用户水表之间所有管道的长度。

全年供水总量 指公用自来水厂和自备水源的社会单位全年的供水总量，包括有效供水量及损失水量。

生活用水量 指居民日常生活与公共福利设施的用水量，包括居民、饮食店、旅馆、医院、理发店、浴池、洗衣店、游泳池、商店、学校、机关、部队等单位的用水量。

城市人口用水普及率 指城市用水的非农业人口数(不包括临时人口和流动人口)与城市非农业人口总数之比。计算公式为:

用水普及率=城市用水的非农业人口数/城市非农业人口数×100%

人工煤气生产能力 指城市煤气厂制气、净化、输送等环节的综合实际生产能力。

输气管道长度 指由压缩机、鼓风机、储气罐的出口到用户煤气表之间的全部管道长度。

全年供气总量 指全年售给各类用户的全部煤气量，包括工业用量、家庭用量和其他用量。

城市用气普及率 指使用煤气(包括人工煤气、液化石油气、天然气)的城市非农业人口数(不包括临时人口和流动人口)与城市非农业人口总数之比。计算公式为:

城市煤气普及率=城市用气的非农业人口数/城市非农业人口总数×100%

城市供热能力 指热电厂、热力公司和达到标准的集中采暖锅炉房向城市输送的供热源的设计能力，即每小时向城市输送蒸汽、热水的能力。

城市供热总量 指热电厂、热力公司和达到标准的集中采暖锅炉房向城市输送的全部蒸汽、热水量。

城市供热管道长度 指热电厂、热力公司和达到标准的集中采暖锅炉房管理的集中供热热源到用户之间的全部供气、供热水的管道长度。

年底实有铺装道路长度 指除土路外，路面经过铺装宽度在3.5米以上的道路，包括高级、次高级道路和普通道路。

城市桥梁 指城市范围内，修建在河道上的桥梁和道路与道路立交、道路跨越铁路的立交桥及人行天桥。包括永久性桥和半永久性桥，不包括临时性桥、铁路桥、涵洞。

城市下水道总长度 指所有排水总管、干管、支管及暗渠、检查井、连接井进出水口等长度之和。

城市污水日处理能力 指污水处理厂每昼夜处理污水量的设计能力。

年末实有公共汽(电)车 指年底可参加营运的全部车辆数，包括营运车辆数和库存查封未参加营运的车辆。不包括非营运车辆，如架线车、油罐车、工程车、货车及其他专用车辆和借入的客运车辆。

城市园林绿地面积 指城市公共绿地、专用绿地、生产绿地、防护绿地、郊区风景名胜区的全部面积。

公共绿地 指供游览休息的各种公园、动物园、植物园、陵园以及花园、游园和供游览休息用的林荫道绿地、广场绿地，不包括一般栽植的行道树及林荫道的面积。

Explanatory Notes on Main Statistical Indicators

Production Capacity of Tap Water at the Year-end refers to the actual comprehensive production capacity of the waterworks administered by the urban construction department and those owned by enterprises or institutions, taking the capacity of the main links, such as water inflow, purification, conveyance and outflow of the trunk pipelines into account.

Length of Water Supply Pipelines at the Year-end refers to the total length of all the pipelines between the water pumps and the users water meters.

Annual Volume of Water Supply refers to the total volume of water supplied by the public water-works and those owned by individual enterprises and institutions during the whole year, including both the effective water supply and loss during the water supply.

Consumption of Water for Residential Use refers to the water consumption of households for daily life and the water consumption of public welfare facilities, including the consumption of restaurants, hotels, hospitals, barber shops, public bathhouses, laundries, swimming pools, shops, schools, institutions, army units and other units.

Percentage of Urban Population with Access to Tap Water refers to the ratio of the urban non-agricultural population (excluding temporary and mobile population) with access to tap water to the total urban non-agricultural population. The formula is:

Percentage of Population with Access to Tap Water=(Urban Non-agricultural Population with Access to Tap Water) / (Urban Non-agricultural Population)

Production Capacity of Gaswork Gas refers to the actual comprehensive production capacity of the urban gasworks in gas generation, purification and delivery.

Length of Gas Pipelines refers to the total length of pipelines between the outlet of the compressor, blower or gas tank and the gas meters of users.

Volume of Gas Supply refers to the total volume of gas sold to users in a year, including the volume for industrial use, residential use and other uses.

Percentage of Urban Population with Access to Gas refers to the ratio of the urban non-agricultural population with access to gas (including gas, liquefied petroleum gas and natural gas) to the urban non-agricultural population (excluding temporary and mobile population). The formula is:

Percentage of Population with Access to Gas =(Urban Non-agricultural Population with Access to Gas × 100%) / Urban Non-agricultural Population)

Heating Capacity in Urban Area refers to the capacity of hourly supply of steam and hot water to cities by thermal power plants, heating corporations and centralized heating boiler rooms which meet certain standard.

Heating Volume in Urban Area refers to the total volume of steam and hot water supplied to cities every year by thermal power plants, heating corporations and centralized heating boiler rooms which meet certain standard.

Length of Heating Pipelines refers to the total length of pipelines for centralized supply of steam and hot water from the thermal power plants, heating corporations and centralized heating boiler rooms which meet certain standard to the users.

Length of Paved Roads at the Year-end refers to the length of roads with a paved surface, and with a width of more than 3-5 meters, including high quality, medium quality and ordinary roads.

Urban Bridges refer to bridges over river courses, great separated junctions and overpasses in urban areas. Permanent bridges and semi-permanent bridges are included. Temporary bridges, railway bridges and culverts are excluded.

Length of Urban Sewage Pipes refers to the total length of general drainage, trunks. branch and blind drainage, inspection wells, connection wells, inlets and outlets, etc.

Daily Disposal Capacity of Urban Sewage refers to the designed 24 hour capacity of sewage disposal at the sewage treatment works.

Number of Public Vehicles (Buses and Trolley buses) at the Year-end refers to the total number of operational buses available at the year-end, including the year-end operational vehicles and vehicles in stock. Non-operational vehicles such as stringing cars, tank cars, machine shop cars, trucks and other special vehicles and the borrowed passenger vehicles are excluded.

Area of Urban Gardens and Green Areas refers to the total area of urban public green land, special green land, production green land, protection green land and suburban scenic spots.

Public Green Area refers to green areas of various parks, zoos, botanical gardens, cemeteries, amusement parks, tree-flanked boulevards greenland squares for tourism and relaxing. Areas with trees planted along-side the streets and boulevards are excluded.

十二、农业

Agriculture

简要说明

一、本篇资料反映我国农业生产和农村经济的基本情况，内容主要包括农村劳动力、耕地、农业机械拥有量、农林牧渔业产值、主要农产品产量、水利设施与除涝治碱、农村居民家庭拥有生产性固定资产、国营农场基本情况等方面的统计资料。

农业统计范围包括全社会除军马生产及农业科研机构进行的农业生产以外的所有农业生产活动内容。如各种专业性农、林、牧、渔场的农业生产活动；国家各级机关、团体、学校、部队进行的农业生产活动；集体所有制的乡、镇、村办农场的农业生产活动；工矿企业经营的农、林、牧、渔业生产活动；以及农村各种经济组织和农户经营的农林牧渔业生产活动和农民家庭兼营的商品性工业生产活动等。

1．农业：包括种植业和其他农业。种植业是指谷物、豆类、薯类、棉、油料、糖料、麻类、烟叶、蔬菜、药材、瓜类和其他农作物的种植，以及茶园、桑园、果园的生产经营。其他农业是指采集野生植物的果实、纤维、树胶、树脂、油料以及柴草、野生药材、菌类等及农民家庭兼营的商品性工业。

2．林业：包括林木的栽培(不包括茶园、桑园和果园的栽培、管理和收获等活动)、林产品的采集和村及村以下合作经济组织、农户的竹木采伐。

3．牧业：包括牲畜饲养和放牧、家禽饲养以及野生动物的捕猎和饲养。

4．渔业：包括水生动物和海藻类植物的养殖和捕捞。

农村社会经济统计范围包括除县城关镇以外所有乡镇的社会经济活动。

二、本篇资料来源及调查方法

1．农村基层组织、乡村劳动力和农业生产基本情况等(12−1至12−8表、12−14至12−21表、12−27表)，由国家统计局农村社会经济调查总队根据《农林牧渔业综合统计报表制度》、《乡村社会经济调查方案》和《农产量抽样调查制度》的有关资料整理提供。

《农林牧渔业综合统计报表制度》是各省、自治区、直辖市统计局上报国家统计局的全面报表，由各级统计部门根据当地实际情况，采取抽样调查、重点调查或全面调查的办法搜集资料；或利用同级业务部门统计资料、国家农产量抽样调查和农村住户抽样调查资料进行加工推算。如农业生产条件中的部分指标及林业生产情况、渔业生产情况等指标取自同级业务部门的统计资料，粮食产量等部分指标来源于《农产量抽样调查制度》。

《农产量抽样调查制度》是国家统计局为取得高质量的粮食产量等相关指标数据，在全国范围内统一抽选样本调查、推算，并由直属调查队伍实施的抽样调查制度。主要以农业普查资料作为有关标识编制抽样框，采取综合运用多阶段、多重、分层、系统随机抽样等多种方法确定调查网点选取样本，利用了多目标与规模成比例的概率抽样确定样本容量，开展多主题调查，全国共抽选了1.48万个村，12.82万个样本地块进行实割实测调查，并运用这些样本科学地推算全国粮食产量数据。在95%的概率把握程度下，误差系数不超过±2%，农产量抽样调查实行样本轮换制度，五年为一个周期。

《乡村社会经济调查方案》是国家统计局为了解乡镇社会经济基本情况、农村劳动力总量规模和转移情况、以及农村固定资产投资情况等内容而专门设置的统计调查制度。制度规定对乡镇和村基本情况每三年进行一次全面调查；其他内容采用抽样调查方法，调查网点包括乡镇级调查网点、村级调查网点和住户调查网点，前两套网点分别是以全省乡镇一级单位编制抽样框和以全省村一级单位编制抽样框，抽选样本进行直接调查，住户调查网点与农村住户调查网点相同。

2．农村家庭固定资产、经营耕地及农产品出售情况(12−11至12−13表、12−22至12−24表)，由国家统计局农村社会经济调查总队根据《农村住户调查方案》的有关资料整理提供。《农村住户调查方案》的说明见本年鉴“十、人民生活”部分。

3．国营农场基本情况资料主要取材于农业部农垦局汇总的统计报表。其调查范围涉及全国除西藏外的30个省、自治区、直辖市。统计方法为逐级上报、全面汇总。指标设置及统计口径均与国家统计局一致。

4．灌溉、水库和除涝、治水、治碱情况及各地区水利设施和除涝、治碱面积资料，主要来源于水利部汇总的统计报表。其统计范围包括各省、自治区、直辖市。资料收集以县为基本统计单位，采取逐级汇总上报的方式。有些特殊指标如灌区数、大型水库、跨县的中小型水库，由地区直接统计，上报省水利厅。

5．受灾面积和成灾面积资料来源于民政部门的灾情统计。

Brief Introduction

I. The data in this chapter show the basic conditions of agricultural production and rural economy, including mainly rural labour force, cultivated land, quantity of agricultural machinery, output of farming, forestry, animal husbandry and fishery, output of major products, facilities of water conservancy and efforts to eliminate water-logging and combat alkalinity, productive fixed assets owned by the rural households, and basic conditions of the state-owned farms.

Statistics on agriculture cover all agricultural production activities except horse raising for military purpose and activities undertaken by agriculture research institutions. Included in agriculture statistics are production activities of farms specializing in crop cultivation, forestry, animal husbandry and fishery; production activities undertaken by government agencies, institutions, schools and military units; production of collective farms run by townships and villages; production activities in crop cultivation, forestry, animal husbandry and fishery undertaken by rural economic units of various types and by rural households, and commercial industrial activities undertaken by rural households as sideline production.

(1) Agriculture: includes crop cultivation and other agricultural activities. Crop cultivation refers to the cultivation of cereals, beans, tuber crops, cotton, oil-bearing crops, sugar crops, hemp, tobacco leaves, vegetables, medicinal herbs, gourds and other farm crops, as well as the operation on tea plantations, mulberry fields and orchards. Other agriculture refers to collection of the seeds, fiber, resin, oil of wild plants; gathering of firewood, wild herbs, mushrooms and fungus; and commercial industrial activities undertaken by rural households as sideline production.

(2) Forestry: includes the planting of trees (excluding the operation on tea plantations, mulberry fields and orchards), collection of forest products and the felling of bamboo and trees by village cooperative units and rural households.

(3) Animal husbandry: includes the raising and grazing of domestic animals and poultry, and the hunting and raising of wild animals.

(4) Fishery: includes cultivation and catching of aquatic animals and seaweed.

The rural social and economic statistics cover all social and economic activities in all townships except that taking place in county towns.

II. Source of data and survey methodology

(1) Data on rural grassroots units, labour force and agricultural production (tables 12-1 to 12-8, tables 12-14 to 12-21, and tables 12-27) are provided by the Rural Socio-economic Survey Organization, NBS using data from the Comprehensive Statistical Reporting on Farming, Forestry, Animal Husbandry and Fishery, the Rural Social and Economic Survey, and the Sample Survey of Farm Crops.

Comprehensive Statistical Reporting on Farming, Forestry, Animal Husbandry and Fishery is a comprehensive reporting program reported by provincial statistical bureaus to the National Bureau of Statistics. Data required in this reporting program are collected by statistical offices at all levels by means of sample surveys, surveys of key units or full enumeration depending on the local circumstances, or estimated by using information from other government agencies at the same level or from the sample survey of farm crops and rural household survey conducted by NBS. For instance, some data on condition of agriculture production and on forestry and fishery are obtained from statistics collected by other government agencies at the same level, while data on crop production are collected from the sample survey of farm crops.

Sample Survey of Farm Crops is a nation-wide survey designed by NBS and implemented by sample survey teams throughout China with unified sample selection and estimation procedure, in order to obtain high quality data on grain production and related statistics. Using data from the agriculture census as sampling frame, a total of 128,000 sample plots are selected from 714,800 villages in the country through multi-stage, stratified, systematic sampling approaches is used to estimate the crop output for China. The survey is characterized by a multi-purpose probability proportional to size sample design that keeps sampling error to $\pm 2\%$ with the confidence probability as 95%. Like the sample survey on rural households, a rotation scheme is used in the sample survey on farm crops with the cycle of a complete rotation being 5 years.

Rural Social and Economic Survey is a special survey designed by the NBS to understand the basic condition of social and economic activities at township level, the size and transfer of total rural labour force and investment in fixed assets in rural areas. Under this survey program, a complete enumeration is conducted every 3 years to collect information on basic condition of social and economic activities at township and village levels, while sample survey is used to collect information on other items with the same sampling units as in the Rural Household Survey.

(2) Data on the fixed assets, cultivated land and sales of farm products of rural households (tables 12-11 to 12-13, tables 12-22 to12-24) are collected and provided by the Rural Socio-economic Survey Organization, NBS through the Rural Household Survey. A summary of this survey is given in Chapter 10 of this yearbook.

(3) Data on the basic conditions of the state-owned farms come from the statistical reports tabulated by the Bureau of Reclamation, Ministry of Agriculture. The statistical coverage includes 30 prov-

inces, autonomous regions and municipalities directly under the central government; only Tibet is not included.

The data are collected from the grassroots units in accordance with the statistical reporting scheme and tabulated and reported level by level. The content of indicators and calculation methods are the same as those stipulated by the National Bureau of Statistics.

(4) Data on irrigation and reservoirs, the data on the efforts to eliminate water-logging, prevent floods by water control and combat alkalinity as well as the data on the facilities of water conservancy and the area of water-logging eliminated and the improved area of saline-alkaline land come mainly from statistical reports of the Ministry of Water Conservancy. The statistical coverage includes provinces, autonomous regions and municipalities directly under the central government. County is the basic statistical unit. The data are collected from the counties in accordance with the statistical reporting scheme and tabulated and reported level by level. Data on some special indicators such as the number of irrigated areas, large reservoirs and the medium-sized and small reservoirs that cut across counties are collected directly by the prefectures and reported to the water conservancy departments of the provinces.

(5) Data covered and affected by natural disaster are collected from the statistics of natural disater.

12-1 农村基层组织和农业基本情况

Basic Conditions of Rural Grassroots Units and Agriculture

指标	Item	1996	1997	1998	1999	2000
乡镇数 (个)	Number of Township and Town Governments	45484	44689	45462	44741	43735
#镇数	Number of Town Governments	17998	18402	19060	19184	19692
村民委员会 (个)	Number of Villagers' Committees	740128	739447	739980	737429	734715
乡村户数 (万户)	Number of Rural Households (10 000 units)	23437.6	23406.2	23678.0	23810.5	24148.7
乡村劳动力 (万人)	Number of Rural Laborers (10 000 persons)	45288.0	45961.7	46432.3	46896.5	47962.1
男	Male	24154.9	24500.6	24733.1	24995.7	25517.8
女	Female	21133.1	21462.1	21699.2	21900.8	22444.3
按行业分乡村劳动力(万人)	Number of Rural Laborers by Sector (10 000 persons)	45288.0	45961.7	46432.3	46896.5	47962.1
农林牧渔业	Farming, Forestry, Animal Husbandry & Fishery	32260.4	32434.9	32626.4	32911.8	32797.5
工业	Industry	4018.5	4031.3	3928.6	3953.0	4108.6
建筑业	Construction	2304.3	2372.7	2453.5	2531.9	2691.7
交通运输业、仓储及邮电通信业	Transport, Storage, Post and Telecommunication Services	1027.6	1057.8	1087.9	1115.8	1170.6
批发零售贸易业餐饮业	Wholesale, Retail Trade and Catering Services	1261.5	1381.5	1461.9	1584.6	1751.8
其他非农行业	Other Non-agricultural Trades	4415.7	4683.9	4874.0	4799.3	5441.9
年末实有耕地面积(千公顷)	Cultivated Areas(Year-end) (1 000 hectares)	130039.2				
农业机械总动力 (万千瓦)	Total Agricultural Machinery Power (10 000kw)	38546.9	42015.6	45207.7	48996.1	52573.6
农用大中型拖拉机 (台)	Number of Large and Medium Agricultural Tractors (unit)	670848	689051	725215	784216	827003
农用大中型拖拉机(万千瓦)	Capacity of Large and Medium Agricultural Tractors (10 000 kw)	2415.1	2486.5	2587.9	2772.8	2873.4
小型拖拉机 (万台)	Number of Mini-tractors (10 000 unit)	918.9	1048.5	1122.1	1200.3	1264.4
小型拖拉机 (万千瓦)	Capacity of Mini-tractors (10 000 kw)	8385.2	9337.2	10031.5	11008.9	11663.9
大中型拖拉机机引农具 (万部)	Number of Large and Medium Tractor Towing Farm Machinery (10 000 unit)	105.0	115.7	120.4	132.0	140.0
小型拖拉机机引农具(万部)	Mini-Tractor Towing Farm Machinery (10000unit)	1091.2	1253.0	1437.8	1621.0	1788.8
农用排灌柴油机 (万台)	Number of Diesel Engines (10 000 unit)	509.3	546.1	581.6	645.0	688.1
农用排灌柴油机 (万千瓦)	Capacity of Diesel Engines (10000 kw)	3984.9	4292.4	4499.0	4934.6	5232.6
农用载重汽车 (辆)	Number of Trucks for Agricultural Use (unit)	836899	875571	901105	933809	927072
农用载重汽车 (万千瓦)	Capacity of Trucks for Agricultural Use(10000 kw)	6422.7	6575.0	6781.3	6881.8	6763.4
渔用机动船 (艘)	Number of Motorized Fishing Boats (unit)	358869	400010	411322	417379	455544
渔用机动船 (万吨)	Loading Capacity of Motorized Fishing Boats (10 000 tons)	469.5	586.5	653.0		
渔用机动船 (万千瓦)	Capacity of Motorized Fishing Boats (10 000 kw)	864.0	1084.0	1174.4	1253.1	1338.1
有效灌溉面积 (千公顷)	Irrigated Area (1 000 hectares)	50381	51239	52296	53158	53820
化肥施用量 (万吨)	Consumption of Chemical Fertilizers (10 000tons)	3827.9	3980.7	4083.7	4124.3	4146.4
乡村办水电站个数 (个)	Number of Hydropower Stations in Rural Areas	37743	36117	33185	31678	29962
乡村办水电站发电能力 (万千瓦)	Generating Capacity of Hydropower Station in Rural Areas (10 000 kw)	533.7	562.4	634.8	664.1	698.5
农村用电量 (亿千瓦小时)	Electricity Consumed in Rural Areas(100 million kwh)	1812.7	1980.1	2042.1	2173.4	2421.3
农作物总播种面积(千公顷)	Total Sown Area (1 000 hectares)	152381	153969	155706	156373	156300
粮食	Grain Crops	112548	112912	113787	113161	108463
谷物	Cereal	92208	91964	92117	91617	85264
#稻谷	Rice	31407	31765	31214	31284	29962
小麦	Wheat	29611	30057	29774	28855	26653
玉米	Corn	24498	23775	25239	25904	23056
豆类	Beans	10543	11164	11671	11190	12660
薯类	Tubers	9798	9785	10000	10355	10538
油料	Oil-bearing Crops	12555	12381	12919	13906	15400
棉花	Cotton	4722	4491	4459	3726	4041
麻类	Fiber Crops	350	327	224	205	262
糖料	Sugar Crops	1846	1923	1984	1644	1514
烟叶	Tobacco	1853	2353	1361	1374	1437
蔬菜	Vegetables	10491	11288	12293	13347	15237
茶园面积 (千公顷)	Area of Tea Plantations (1 000 hectares)	1103	1076	1057	1130	1089
果园面积 (千公顷)	Area of Orchards (1 000 hectares)	8553	8648	8535	8667	8932

12-2 主要农牧渔业生产情况

Output of Farming, Animal Husbandry and Fishery

指　标	Item	1996	1997	1998	1999	2000
农产品产量 （万吨）	Yield of Farm Crops (10 000 tons)					
粮食	Grain	50453.5	49417.1	51229.5	50838.6	46217.5
谷物	Cereal	45127.1	44349.3	45624.7	45304.1	40522.4
＃稻谷	Rice	19510.3	20073.5	19871.3	19848.7	18790.8
小麦	Wheat	11056.9	12328.9	10972.6	11388.0	9963.6
玉米	Corn	12747.1	10430.9	13295.4	12808.6	10600.0
豆类	Beans	1790.3	1875.5	2000.6	1894.0	2010.0
薯类	Tubers	3536.0	3192.3	3604.2	3640.6	3685.2
油料	Oil-bearing Crops	2210.6	2157.4	2313.9	2601.2	2954.8
＃花生	Peanuts	1013.8	964.8	1188.6	1263.9	1443.7
油菜籽	Rapeseeds	920.1	957.8	830.1	1013.2	1138.1
芝麻	Sesame	57.5	56.6	65.6	74.3	81.1
棉花	Cotton	420.3	460.3	450.1	382.9	441.7
麻类	Fiber Crops	79.5	74.9	49.5	47.2	52.9
＃黄红麻	Jute and Ambary Hemp	36.5	43.0	24.8	16.4	12.6
甘蔗	Sugarcane	6687.6	7889.7	8343.8	7470.3	6828.0
甜菜	Beetroots	1672.6	1496.8	1446.6	863.9	807.3
烟叶	Tobacco	323.4	425.1	236.4	246.9	255.2
＃烤烟	Flue-Cured Tobacco	294.6	390.8	208.8	218.5	223.8
蚕茧	Silkworm Cocoons	50.8	46.9	53.5	48.5	54.8
＃桑蚕茧	Mulberry Silkworm Cocoons	47.1	42.3	48.2	44.7	50.1
茶叶	Tea	59.3	61.3	66.5	67.6	68.3
水果	Fruits	4652.8	5089.3	5452.9	6237.6	6225.1
农产品单位面积产量(公斤/公顷)	Yield of Farm Crops per Hectare (kg/hectare)					
谷物	Cereal	4894	4823	4953	4945	4753
棉花	Cotton	890	1025	1009	1028	1093
花生	Peanuts	2804	2592	2943	2961	2973
油菜籽	Rapeseeds	1367	1479	1272	1469	1519
芝麻	Sesames	969	919	1042	1066	1034
黄红麻	Jute and Ambary Hemp	2491	2649	2677	2540	2516
甘蔗	Sugarcane	56225	60158	59550	57338	57626
甜菜	Beetroots	25483	24475	24806	25335	24518
烤烟	Flue-Cured Tobacco	1750	1809	1737	1797	1763
大牲畜年底头数(万头)	Number of Large Animals (year-end,10 000 heads)	13360.6	14541.8	14803.2	15024.8	15151.5
＃牛	Cattle and Buffaloes	11031.8	12182.2	12441.9	12698.3	12866.3
马	Horses	871.5	891.2	898.1	891.4	876.6
驴	Donkeys	944.4	952.8	955.8	934.8	922.7
骡	Mules	478.0	480.6	473.9	467.3	453.0
骆驼	Camels	34.5	35.0	33.5	33.0	32.6
肉猪出栏头数(万头)	Number of Slaughtered Fattened Hogs (10000 heads)	41225.1	46483.7	50215.1	50749.0	52673.3
猪年底头数（万头）	Number of Hogs (year-end,10 000 heads)	36283.6	40034.8	42256.3	43144.2	44681.5
羊年底只数（万只）	Number of Sheep and Goats (year-end,10 000 heads)	23728.3	25575.7	26903.5	27925.8	29031.9
山羊	Goats	12315.8	13480.1	14168.3	14816.3	15715.9
绵羊	Sheep	11412.5	12095.6	12735.2	13109.5	13316.0
肉类产量 （万吨）	Output of Meat (10 000 tons)	4584.0	5268.8	5723.8	5820.7	6125.4
＃猪牛羊肉	Pork Beef and Mutton	3694.7	4249.9	4598.2	4647.4	4838.2
猪肉	Pork	3158.0	3596.3	3883.7	3890.7	4031.4
牛肉	Beef	355.7	440.9	479.9	505.4	532.8
羊肉	Mutton	181.0	212.8	234.6	251.3	274.0
奶类 （万吨）	Milk (10 000 tons)	735.8	681.1	745.4	806.9	919.1
＃牛奶	Cow Milk	629.4	601.1	662.9	717.6	827.4
绵羊毛 （吨）	Sheep Wool (ton)	298102	255059	277545	283152	292502
山羊毛 （吨）	Goat Wool (ton)	35255	25865	31417	31849	33266
羊绒 （吨）	Cashmere (ton)	9585	8626	9799	10180	11057
禽蛋 （万吨）	Poultry Eggs (10 000 tons)	1965.2	1897.1	2021.3	2134.7	2243.3
水产品总产量(万吨)	Total Aquatic Products (10 000 tons)	3288.1	3601.8	3906.5	4122.4	4278.5
海水产品	Seawater Aquatic Products	2012.9	2176.4	2356.7	2471.9	2538.7
淡水产品	Freshwater Aquatic Products	1275.2	1425.4	1549.8	1650.5	1739.7

12-3 农村基层组织情况

Basic Conditions of Rural Grassroots Units

年份 地区	Year Region	乡镇数（个） Number of Township and Town Governments	#镇数 Town Governments	村民委员会（个） Number of Villagers' Committees	乡村户数（万户） Number of Households (10 000 households)	乡村人口数（万人） Rural Population (10 000 persons)	乡村劳动力（万人） Number of Rural Laborers (10 000 persons)	男 Male	女 Female
	1978	52781		690000	17347.0	80320.0	30638.0	16548.4	14089.6
	1979	53348		698613	17491.0	80738.7	31024.5		
	1980	54183		709820	17673.0	81096.0	31835.7	17379.7	14456.2
	1981	54371		718022	18016.0	81880.7	32672.3	17839.5	14832.8
	1982	54352		719438	18279.0	82798.8	33866.5	18517.4	15349.1
	1983	56331		750141	18523.0	83536.0	34689.8	18946.5	15743.3
	1984	91420		933485	18793.0	84300.5	35967.6	19663.3	16304.3
	1985	91138	7956	940617	19077.0	84419.7	37065.1	20153.2	16911.9
	1986	71521	9755	847894	19575.0	85007.2	37989.8	20692.4	17297.4
	1987	68296	10280	830302	20168.0	85713.1	39000.4	21212.5	17787.9
	1988	56002	10609	740375	20859.0	83725.4	40066.7	21727.7	18339.0
	1989	55764	11060	746432	21504.0	87831.0	40938.8	22218.3	18720.5
	1990	55838	11392	743278	22237.0	89590.3	42009.5	22551.8	19457.7
	1991	55542	11882	804153	22566.0	90525.1	43092.5	23121.9	19970.6
	1992	48250	14135	806032	22849.0	91154.4	43801.6	23449.9	20351.7
	1993	48179	15223	802352	22984.0	91333.5	44255.7	23653.1	20602.6
	1994	48075	16433	802052	23165.0	91526.2	44654.1	23854.1	20800.1
	1995	47136	17282	740150	23282.0	91674.6	45041.8	24037.4	21004.4
	1996	45484	17998	740128	23437.6	91941.0	45288.0	24154.9	21133.1
	1997	44689	18402	739447	23406.2	91524.7	45961.7	24500.6	21462.1
	1998	45462	19060	739980	23678.0	91960.1	46432.3	24733.1	21699.2
	1999	44741	19184	737429	23810.5	92216.3	46896.5	24995.7	21900.8
	2000	43735	19692	734715	24148.7	92819.7	47962.1	25517.8	22444.3
北京	Beijing	215	144	4043	126.8	363.7	165.8	85.3	80.5
天津	Tianjin	220	104	3870	112.1	386.1	168.1	92.2	75.8
河北	Hebei	1973	900	49951	1422.6	5382.4	2707.1	1447.7	1259.4
山西	Shanxi	1834	446	32338	620.8	2322.6	988.6	547.6	441.0
内蒙古	Inner Mongolia	1448	341	13648	349.0	1376.8	631.5	355.6	275.9
辽宁	Liaoning	1587	653	16192	680.1	2311.5	966.0	538.9	427.0
吉林	Jilin	856	455	10107	370.0	1440.5	641.0	368.8	272.2
黑龙江	Heilongjiang	1161	437	14206	458.3	1864.2	913.2	524.4	388.9
上海	Shanghai	153	150	2784	115.6	366.3	255.6	127.7	127.9
江苏	Jiangsu	1482	1202	33259	1496.3	5150.6	2688.0	1382.5	1305.5
浙江	Zhejiang	1723	971	42226	1076.0	3545.5	2108.4	1135.8	972.6
安徽	Anhui	1841	941	30658	1294.6	5089.1	2797.8	1487.9	1309.9
福建	Fujian	943	578	14988	660.0	2689.4	1244.1	669.3	574.8
江西	Jiangxi	1817	746	20738	741.5	3203.2	1547.2	809.6	737.6
山东	Shandong	2207	1426	87817	2026.5	7035.9	3639.6	1934.0	1705.7
河南	Henan	2031	742	48437	1972.3	7826.7	4712.4	2492.8	2219.6
湖北	Hubei	1329	853	32400	983.9	3947.3	1781.7	937.7	844.0
湖南	Hunan	2353	1039	50068	1444.0	5386.2	2856.1	1549.8	1306.3
广东	Guangdong	1612	1577	22962	1412.0	6017.3	2785.1	1448.1	1337.0
广西	Guangxi	1360	745	14849	914.0	4026.4	2145.4	1129.9	1015.5
海南	Hainan	309	205	2647	105.0	499.1	224.0	116.1	107.9
重庆	Chongqing	1472	650	20589	710.3	2420.3	1352.6	723.2	629.4
四川	Sichuan	5062	1788	55020	1959.9	6941.2	3789.0	1997.8	1791.2
贵州	Guizhou	1463	692	25692	734.7	3123.5	1802.6	948.0	854.7
云南	Yunnan	1564	462	13433	829.8	3449.6	1948.9	1008.5	940.4
西藏	Tibet	720	154	6449	37.8	216.8	100.8	50.8	50.0
陕西	Shaanxi	1933	844	31329	689.8	2768.4	1343.2	730.7	612.6
甘肃	Gansu	1534	219	17825	449.0	2031.3	934.5	490.5	444.0
青海	Qinghai	430	40	4120	69.9	336.6	172.0	88.7	83.3
宁夏	Ningxia	309	64	2692	85.6	388.4	197.9	103.1	94.9
新疆	Xinjiang	794	124	9378	200.9	913.2	354.1	195.1	159.0

注：本表乡村人口数是指户口在乡村的常住人口，具体范围按1964年建镇标准划分，包括后来的新建制镇人口，口径大于人口篇的乡村总人口。

a)Total rural population refers to persons residing and registered in rural areas. This indicator is calculated on the basis of the town classification standards of 1964 which includes rural population in what are now established towns. Therefore, the statistical coverage in the table are larger than the rural population shown in Chapter 4.

12-4 乡村劳动力(年底数)

Rural Labor Force by Sector (Year-end)

本表分行业劳动力是按从事的主行业划分的，如以农业为主、兼营商业的，仍作为农林牧渔业劳动力。

The number of laborers by sector in this table is classified by main activity. For example, those engaged primarily in agriculture and secondarily in commerce are classified under farming, forestry, animal husbandry and fishery.

单位：万人 (10 000 persons)

年份 Year / 地区 Region	农林牧渔业 Farming, Forestry, Animal Husbandry and Fishery	工业 Industry	建筑业 Construction	交通运输业、仓储及邮电通信业 Transport Storage, Post and Communication Services	批发零售贸易业餐饮业 Wholesale, Retail Trade and Catering Services	其他非农行业 Other Nonagricultural Trades
1978	28455.6					
1979	29071.6	897.6				
1980	29808.4	916.3				
1981	30677.6	882.7				
1982	31152.7	878.7	378.9	114.7		
1983	31645.1	873.0	482.5	160.9		
1984	31685.0	3228.2	811.4	316.4		
1985	30351.5	2741.0	1130.1	434.1	462.6	1945.8
1986	30467.9	3139.3	1308.6	506.1	531.8	2036.1
1987	30870.0	3297.2	1431.3	562.5	606.9	2232.5
1988	31455.7	3412.8	1525.5	607.3	657.1	2408.3
1989	32440.5	3255.6	1501.8	614.2	652.4	2474.3
1990	33336.4	3228.7	1522.8	635.3	693.2	2593.1
1991	34186.3	3267.9	1533.8	655.0	722.8	2726.7
1992	34037.0	3468.2	1658.8	706.3	813.7	3117.6
1993	33258.2	3659.0	1886.8	799.9	948.8	3703.1
1994	32690.3	3849.5	2057.3	908.3	1084.3	4064.5
1995	32334.5	3970.7	2203.6	983.0	1170.4	4379.7
1996	32260.4	4018.5	2304.3	1027.6	1261.5	4415.7
1997	32434.9	4031.3	2372.7	1057.8	1381.5	4683.9
1998	32626.4	3928.6	2453.5	1087.9	1461.9	4874.0
1999	32911.8	3953.0	2531.9	1115.8	1584.6	4799.3
2000	32797.5	4108.6	2691.7	1170.6	1751.8	5441.9
北京 Beijing	69.7	33.5	13.9	13.3	12.1	23.3
天津 Tianjin	79.7	42.9	11.0	10.5	10.7	13.4
河北 Hebei	1665.5	388.4	202.5	92.1	135.3	223.4
山西 Shanxi	658.3	114.7	51.0	53.8	46.0	64.9
内蒙古 Inner Mongolia	524.3	17.9	22.9	11.3	14.9	40.3
辽宁 Liaoning	651.2	77.6	56.3	37.5	49.8	93.7
吉林 Jilin	516.8	21.2	21.6	13.7	19.4	48.3
黑龙江 Heilongjiang	744.1	36.2	26.4	18.1	26.8	61.6
上海 Shanghai	84.6	104.1	13.1	6.8	13.0	34.0
江苏 Jiangsu	1480.2	436.8	252.0	89.1	104.8	325.1
浙江 Zhejiang	1014.9	474.3	110.7	69.0	141.3	298.3
安徽 Anhui	2001.8	161.5	172.2	61.3	103.9	297.1
福建 Fujian	768.7	141.1	79.4	36.4	60.8	157.6
江西 Jiangxi	983.4	84.9	60.7	22.5	33.5	362.2
山东 Shandong	2462.6	352.9	285.6	112.7	153.2	272.6
河南 Henan	3558.6	354.4	279.9	107.5	170.6	241.5
湖北 Hubei	1159.1	116.1	104.1	44.6	72.1	285.7
湖南 Hunan	2071.4	191.6	126.3	51.7	85.1	330.0
广东 Guangdong	1570.1	419.8	195.1	76.3	129.6	394.2
广西 Guangxi	1556.8	65.0	83.6	33.2	51.2	355.6
海南 Hainan	177.2	6.4	7.6	6.0	9.1	17.7
重庆 Chongqing	921.5	59.3	75.6	18.5	33.5	244.3
四川 Sichuan	2631.1	175.5	212.5	54.1	113.6	602.3
贵州 Guizhou	1372.1	64.7	34.4	18.5	32.8	280.1
云南 Yunnan	1674.3	52.1	53.2	35.8	36.9	96.7
西藏 Tibet	90.1	1.6	2.3	1.9	2.0	2.9
陕西 Shaanxi	1002.2	61.9	74.3	36.1	47.6	121.2
甘肃 Gansu	697.5	29.8	41.7	19.4	20.5	125.5
青海 Qinghai	142.3	6.1	5.0	3.9	3.6	11.0
宁夏 Ningxia	153.1	8.1	12.1	7.6	7.3	9.8
新疆 Xinjiang	314.5	8.5	4.9	7.7	10.9	7.7

注：工业劳动力中包括村及村以下办的工业的劳动力。

a)The number of industrial laborers includes those working in enterprises at village and lower levels.

12-5 1996年农业普查分地区耕地面积及占全国比重

Cultivated Area and Percentage to Total Area by Regions (1996)

地 区	Region	耕地面积(千公顷) Cultivated Area (10 000 hectares)	比重(%) Percentage (%)
全国总计	**Total**	**130039.2**	**100.00**
北 京	Beijing	343.9	0.26
天 津	Tianjin	485.6	0.37
河 北	Hebei	6883.3	5.29
山 西	Shanxi	4588.6	3.53
内蒙古	Inner Mongolia	8201.0	6.31
辽 宁	Liaoning	4174.8	3.21
吉 林	Jilin	5578.4	4.29
黑龙江	Heilongjiang	11773.0	9.05
上 海	Shanghai	315.1	0.24
江 苏	Jiangsu	5061.7	3.89
浙 江	Zhejiang	2125.3	1.63
安 徽	Anhui	5971.7	4.59
福 建	Fujian	1434.7	1.10
江 西	Jiangxi	2993.4	2.30
山 东	Shandong	7689.3	5.91
河 南	Henan	8110.3	6.24
湖 北	Hubei	4949.5	3.81
湖 南	Hunan	3953.0	3.04
广 东	Guangdong	3272.2	2.52
广 西	Guangxi	4407.9	3.39
海 南	Hainan	762.1	0.59
四 川	Sichuan	9169.1	7.05
贵 州	Guizhou	4903.5	3.77
云 南	Yunnan	6421.6	4.94
西 藏	Tibet	362.6	0.28
陕 西	Shaanxi	5140.5	3.95
甘 肃	Gansu	5024.7	3.86
青 海	Qinghai	688.0	0.53
宁 夏	Ningxia	1268.8	0.98
新 疆	Xinjiang	3985.7	3.07

注：数据来源于国土资源部、国家统计局、全国农业普查办公室"关于土地利用现状调查数据成果的公报"，耕地数据为1996年10月31日时点数。

a) Data come from the "Communique of Main Data on Land Use Survey" issued by the Ministry of Land and Resources, National Bureau of Statistics, and National Agricultural Census Office of China. The cultivated areas is the data at Oct. 31, 1996.

12-6 农、林、牧、渔业总产值及指数

Gross Output Value of Farming, Forestry, Animal Husbandry and Fishery and Related Indices

本表绝对数按当年价格计算，指数按可比价格计算。

Data in value terms in this table are calculated at current prices, while the indices are calculated at comparable prices.

年份 地区 Year Region	绝对数（亿元） Gross Output Value of Farming, Forestry, Animal Husbandry and Fishery (100 million yuan)					指数（上年=100） Indices of Gross Output of Farming, Forestry, Animal Husbandry and Fishery (preceding year=100)				
	农林牧渔业总产值 Total	农业 Farming	林业 Forestry	牧业 Animal Husbandry	渔业 Fishery	农林牧渔业总产值 Total	农业 Farming	林业 Forestry	牧业 Animal Husbandry	渔业 Fishery
1978	1397.0	1117.5	48.1	209.3	22.1					
1979	1697.6	1325.3	60.7	285.6	26.0	107.6	106.7	101.3	114.6	96.6
1980	1922.6	1454.1	81.4	354.2	32.9	101.4	99.7	112.2	107.0	107.7
1981	2180.6	1635.9	98.9	402.2	43.7	106.5	106.8	104.1	105.9	104.4
1982	2483.3	1865.3	110.0	456.7	51.2	111.3	110.9	108.5	113.4	112.3
1983	2750.0	2074.5	127.2	485.1	63.2	107.8	108.5	110.2	103.9	108.6
1984	3214.1	2380.2	161.6	587.3	85.1	112.3	111.5	119.0	113.4	117.6
1985	3619.5	2506.4	188.7	798.3	126.1	103.4	99.8	104.5	117.2	118.9
1986	4013.0	2771.8	201.2	875.7	164.4	103.4	102.7	96.4	105.6	120.6
1987	4675.7	3160.5	222.0	1068.4	224.9	105.8	106.4	99.7	103.2	118.1
1988	5865.3	3666.9	275.3	1600.6	322.5	103.9	101.3	102.3	112.6	111.6
1989	6534.7	4100.6	284.9	1800.4	348.9	103.1	102.5	100.4	105.5	107.2
1990	7662.1	4954.3	330.3	1967.0	410.6	107.6	108.0	103.1	107.0	110.0
1991	8157.0	5146.4	367.9	2159.2	483.5	103.7	100.9	108.0	108.8	107.6
1992	9084.7	5588.0	422.6	2460.5	613.5	106.4	104.2	107.7	108.8	115.3
1993	10995.5	6605.1	494.0	3014.4	882.0	107.8	105.2	108.0	110.8	118.4
1994	15750.5	9169.2	611.1	4672.0	1298.2	108.6	103.2	108.9	116.7	120.0
1995	20340.9	11884.6	709.9	6045.0	1701.3	110.9	107.9	105.0	114.8	119.4
1996	22353.7	13539.8	778.0	6015.5	2020.4	109.4	107.8	105.7	111.4	114.0
1997	23788.4	13852.5	817.8	6835.4	2282.7	106.7	104.5	103.3	110.1	111.5
1998	24541.9	14241.9	851.3	7025.8	2422.9	106.0	104.9	102.9	107.4	108.8
1999	24519.1	14106.2	886.3	6997.6	2529.0	104.7	104.3	103.2	104.6	107.2
2000	24915.8	13873.6	936.5	7393.1	2712.6	103.6	101.4	105.4	106.3	106.5
北京 Beijing	195.2	91.1	5.4	90.6	8.1	113.1	110.3	122.7	116.0	111.6
天津 Tianjin	156.3	83.4	1.4	51.8	19.8	104.2	95.6	93.8	119.6	106.1
河北 Hebei	1544.7	846.7	25.4	613.7	58.9	105.7	105.4	98.4	106.2	108.7
山西 Shanxi	322.4	218.3	12.7	89.7	1.6	109.3	111.6	105.4	105.4	102.9
内蒙古 Inner Mongolia	543.2	308.4	23.6	205.5	5.7	102.5	100.3	115.0	104.1	104.9
辽宁 Liaoning	967.4	463.5	19.7	304.2	180.0	99.2	91.7	102.3	105.9	104.0
吉林 Jilin	609.4	320.3	11.4	268.7	9.0	94.4	86.2	102.1	105.8	97.4
黑龙江 Heilongjiang	625.1	414.4	18.3	175.7	16.8	99.3	95.3	100.1	108.1	103.0
上海 Shanghai	216.5	89.8	1.4	87.4	37.9	103.9	106.0	160.7	99.2	111.3
江苏 Jiangsu	1869.7	1096.0	30.2	430.5	313.0	105.0	103.1	119.9	107.5	107.4
浙江 Zhejiang	1062.9	520.4	67.8	177.3	297.4	104.6	98.6	111.1	108.6	110.9
安徽 Anhui	1220.0	675.3	64.0	349.4	131.3	101.7	98.6	107.6	105.5	105.0
福建 Fujian	1037.3	421.0	82.3	208.2	325.8	103.1	98.3	105.9	105.5	107.3
江西 Jiangxi	760.3	387.3	51.1	221.8	100.1	102.8	101.7	108.0	99.8	109.0
山东 Shandong	2294.3	1300.4	47.6	599.2	347.1	103.9	104.0	106.2	105.4	100.5
河南 Henan	1981.5	1264.3	56.2	641.6	19.5	105.4	104.2	105.6	107.2	112.1
湖北 Hubei	1125.6	615.7	40.2	338.8	130.9	102.8	102.8	98.5	103.6	102.4
湖南 Hunan	1221.7	633.8	51.0	455.9	80.9	104.2	103.3	104.3	103.6	111.4
广东 Guangdong	1640.7	807.9	59.6	389.7	383.4	104.0	100.6	103.5	109.8	107.5
广西 Guangxi	829.0	418.8	38.8	275.3	96.1	100.2	94.7	101.9	109.4	105.3
海南 Hainan	311.9	145.0	48.1	50.3	68.6	111.5	110.4	101.6	117.0	120.9
重庆 Chongqing	412.6	244.7	10.8	142.0	15.1	100.9	100.3	86.6	102.7	103.8
四川 Sichuan	1413.3	785.4	49.1	541.5	37.3	104.9	102.9	103.1	107.4	112.6
贵州 Guizhou	413.0	279.6	18.0	110.7	4.6	103.8	103.1	110.9	103.7	113.4
云南 Yunnan	680.9	416.4	49.7	201.5	13.3	106.5	106.1	104.1	108.5	102.7
西藏 Tibet	51.2	26.4	1.3	23.5		101.9	102.2	103.5	101.6	
陕西 Shaanxi	464.9	327.8	27.2	106.4	3.5	104.6	103.8	105.4	106.8	99.8
甘肃 Gansu	323.0	239.0	11.2	71.7	1.2	104.9	103.4	122.4	107.1	109.6
青海 Qinghai	57.0	24.9	1.5	30.5	0.1	97.5	90.7	103.7	104.3	128.0
宁夏 Ningxia	77.8	47.0	3.1	25.7	1.9	103.8	97.7	128.5	112.5	114.8
新疆 Xinjiang	487.2	360.5	8.3	114.5	3.8	105.2	104.2	110.3	108.0	116.2

12-7 主要农业机械和农产品加工机械年底拥有量
Agricultural Machinery and Machinery For Processing Farm Products at Year-end

年份 地区 Year Region		农业机械总动力(万千瓦) Total Power of Agricultural Machinery (10 000 kw)	农用大中型拖拉机 Large and Medium Agricultural Tractors		小型拖拉机 Mini-Tractors		大中型拖拉机机引农具(部) Number of Large and Medium Tractor Towing Farm Machinery (unit)	小型拖拉机机引农具(部) Number of Mini-Tractor Towing Farm Machinery (unit)
			数量 Number (台) (unit)	动力 Capacity (万千瓦) (10 000 kw)	数量 Number (台) (unit)	动力 Capacity (万千瓦) (10 000 kw)		
1978		11749.9	557358	1756.2	1373000	1172.0	1192000	1454000
1979		13379.2	666823	2104.0	1671000	1433.5	1313000	1934000
1980		14745.7	744865	2369.3	1874000	1615.5	1369000	2191000
1981		15679.8	792032	2522.7	2037000	1759.8	1390000	2215000
1982		16614.2	812447	2613.2	2287000	1988.9	1374000	2305000
1983		18022.1	840776	2708.1	2623000	2391.7	1308000	2623000
1984		19497.2	853914	2719.7	3298000	2887.3	1170000	2918200
1985		20912.5	852357	2743.6	3824000	3367.0	1128000	3202000
1986		22950.0	866463	2807.0	4526000	4003.0	1006000	3830000
1987		24836.0	880952	2876.0	5300000	4713.0	1035000	4134000
1988		26575.0	870187	2896.0	5958000	5319.0	971000	5201000
1989		28067.0	848220	2814.0	6543000	5848.0	991000	6043000
1990		28707.7	813512	2745.5	6981000	6231.4	974000	6488000
1991		29388.6	784466	2682.4	7304000	6528.6	991000	7327000
1992		30308.4	758904	2630.2	7507000	6720.0	1044000	8308000
1993		31816.6	721216	2532.5	7883000	7042.7	1001000	8657000
1994		33802.5	693154	2463.5	8237000	7399.7	980000	8662000
1995		36118.1	671846	2404.0	8646266	7848.0	991220	9579774
1996		38546.9	670848	2415.1	9189200	8385.2	1049900	10911500
1997		42015.6	689051	2486.5	10484813	9337.2	1157316	12530020
1998		45207.7	725215	2587.9	11220551	10031.5	1203687	14378324
1999		48996.1	784216	2772.8	12002509	11008.9	1320429	16210408
2000		52573.6	827003	2873.4	12643696	11663.9	1399886	17887868
北　京	Beijing	399.2	11781	54.4	25004	26.6	21822	12416
天　津	Tianjin	593.4	9500	40.8	37800	36.2	12600	42800
河　北	Hebei	7000.4	63624	233.3	1298453	1266.0	108349	1566911
山　西	Shanxi	1701.3	23160	87.1	198058	193.7	43449	209028
内蒙古	Inner Mongolia	1350.3	32900	141.0	435933	468.5	48786	505568
辽　宁	Liaoning	1339.8	35101	138.3	158238	154.2	47676	180065
吉　林	Jilin	1015.4	32548	110.6	389256	372.1	74659	827250
黑龙江	Heilongjiang	1613.8	75553	322.8	651685	624.6	192166	628076
上　海	Shanghai	142.5	7844	29.3	9253	8.3	20253	8895
江　苏	Jiangsu	2925.3	53000	178.7	888900	667.3	86200	1524500
浙　江	Zhejiang	1990.1	6758	18.1	251967	215.8	4175	242950
安　徽	Anhui	2975.9	14500	51.0	1657766	1297.7	27993	3519187
福　建	Fujian	873.3	1897	6.5	153250	158.7	435	58986
江　西	Jiangxi	902.3	8144	17.1	78634	65.3	3037	105813
山　东	Shandong	7025.2	140529	451.2	1442665	1164.1	276967	2148446
河　南	Henan	5780.6	66200	216.8	2246700	2317.7	118700	3573200
湖　北	Hubei	1414.0	68163	143.8	236342	174.2	48135	374763
湖　南	Hunan	2209.7	4954	19.4	209271	191.6	6428	63865
广　东	Guangdong	1763.9	6746	24.4	335452	261.7	3541	266809
广　西	Guangxi	1467.9	11320	40.8	261001	266.0	9091	391992
海　南	Hainan	200.9	2573	9.7	29931	25.1	1744	3991
重　庆	Chongqing	586.5	493	1.1	14900	16.6	500	6000
四　川	Sichuan	1679.7	9545	23.5	132898	149.2	7866	94905
贵　州	Guizhou	618.6	16800	45.7	55000	55.3	1600	7500
云　南	Yunnan	1301.3	13000	45.1	300694	299.4	8138	150317
西　藏	Tibet	114.5	2025	12.7	30999	33.2	1033	11450
陕　西	Shaanxi	1042.9	26700	79.3	199300	220.5	36200	266000
甘　肃	Gansu	1056.9	12260	48.0	328559	331.8	18118	528065
青　海	Qinghai	256.2	2409	10.5	167830	150.7	8249	113482
宁　夏	Ningxia	380.6	4774	16.9	157061	155.4	5608	131549
新　疆	Xinjiang	851.2	62202	255.7	260896	296.5	156368	323089

12-7 续表 1 continued

年份 地区	Year Region	柴油机 Diesel Engines 数量 Number (台) (unit)	柴油机 Diesel Engines 动力 Capacity (万千瓦) (10 000kw)	农用载重汽车 Trucks for Agricultural Use 数量 Number (台) (unit)	农用载重汽车 Trucks for Agricultural Use 动力 Capacity (万千瓦) (10 000kw)	渔用机动船 Motorized Fishing Boats 数量 Number (台) (unit)	渔用机动船 Motorized Fishing Boats 动力 Capacity (万千瓦) (10 000kw)
	1978	2657000	2521.6	74070	467.9	47176	213.7
	1979	2813000	2665.7	97105	613.9	52225	230.1
	1980	2899000	2717.7	134745	879.5	61022	258.5
	1981	2855000	2673.3	175126	1158.3	73586	293.2
	1982	2842000	2653.3	206383	1389.0	95692	322.3
	1983	2947000	2701.3	274751	1884.8	120167	326.8
	1984	2890000	2616.0	349261	2462.7	143430	335.2
	1985	2865000	2567.8	429554	3075.6	172582	367.2
	1986	3043000	2690.0	499164	3581.0	205923	424.0
	1987	3202000	2818.0	550192	3966.0	238628	486.0
	1988	3490000	2998.0	591406	4325.0	265126	545.0
	1989	3867000	3207.0	625116	4634.0	289205	609.0
	1990	4111000	3348.5	624384	4621.0	320927	696.0
	1991	4330000	3447.1	616637	4690.5	329843	733.4
	1992	4377000	3441.6	642356	4851.9	335875	786.1
	1993	4554275	3613.1	690469	5245.8	334656	804.4
	1994	4711516	3731.0	747981	5719.4	351327	831.0
	1995	4912068	3839.0	793520	6090.9	376813	965.6
	1996	5092934	3984.9	836899	6422.7	358869	864.1
	1997	5461235	4292.4	875571	6575.0	398788	1080.4
	1998	5816118	4499.0	901105	6781.3	411322	1174.4
	1999	6449528	4934.6	933809	6881.8	417379	1253.1
	2000	6881174	5232.6	927072	6763.4	455544	1338.1
北京	Beijing	1257	1.1	16282	116.4	2	2.0
天津	Tianjin	35800	25.7	9135	71.2	10400	6.6
河北	Hebei	1382338	1194.6	88727	678.6	13502	38.9
山西	Shanxi	16397	19.2	57448	479.4		
内蒙古	Inner Mongolia	123280	104.0	14113	108.2	41	0.1
辽宁	Liaoning	86854	78.3	32705	232.5	37572	103.5
吉林	Jilin	241020	155.2	11360	81.3	155	0.3
黑龙江	Heilongjiang	166961	149.1	10668	78.3	4771	3.6
上海	Shanghai	20		953	5.9	2905	20.5
江苏	Jiangsu	155000	152.9	34455	196.6	59444	108.6
浙江	Zhejiang	78393	39.7	32710	209.4	58168	416.7
安徽	Anhui	314121	227.4	38716	274.8	14605	13.7
福建	Fujian	59150	41.4	18161	165.3	67632	151.5
江西	Jiangxi	144926	111.7	26306	194.2	14023	9.0
山东	Shandong	1726906	1408.2	102144	543.8	42736	117.9
河南	Henan	475200	458.7	60757	423.1	966	1.2
湖北	Hubei	185708	148.6	19719	131.9	12557	6.2
湖南	Hunan	742261	350.9	69479	550.4	12216	5.8
广东	Guangdong	162550	101.4	66754	442.8	68272	237.3
广西	Guangxi	211931	108.9	27501	257.8	13294	44.6
海南	Hainan	61504	26.4	5792	45.2	17421	46.3
重庆	Chongqing	58782	38.8	22798	198.1	1739	1.0
四川	Sichuan	272194	158.2	49950	387.0	1556	1.0
贵州	Guizhou	67400	43.2	13568	102.3	700	1.1
云南	Yunnan	51300	28.1	38819	337.1	327	0.4
西藏	Tibet	2608	2.5	5256	45.4		
陕西	Shaanxi	31300	26.3	17117	130.2	256	0.2
甘肃	Gansu	15264	15.7	14296	117.6	20	
青海	Qinghai	732	1.0	4914	42.6	37	0.1
宁夏	Ningxia	1653	1.6	5457	47.9	4	
新疆	Xinjiang	8364	14.2	11012	68.0	223	0.3

12-8 有效灌溉面积、农用化肥施用量、农村水电及用电情况

Irrigated Area, Consumption of Chemical Fertilizers, Number of Hydropower Stations and Electricity Consumption in Rural Areas

年 份 Year	地 区 Region	有效灌溉面积（千公顷） Irrigated Area (1 000 hectares)	化肥施用量（万 吨） Consumption of Chemical Fertilizer (10 000 tons)	氮 肥 Nitrogenous Fertilizer	磷 肥 Phosphate Fertilizer	钾 肥 Potash Fertilizer	复合肥 Compound Fertilizer	乡村办水电站 Hydropower Station in Rural Areas: 个数 Number	发电能力（万千瓦） Generating Capacity (10 000 kw)	农村用电量（亿千瓦时） Electricity Consumed in Rural Area (100 million kwh)
1978		44965.0	884.0					82387	228.4	253.1
1979		45003.1	1086.3	825.9	223.5	31.6		83224	276.3	282.7
1980		44888.1	1269.4	934.2	273.3	34.6	27.2	80319	304.1	320.8
1981		44573.8	1406.9	942.0	295.6	40.7	56.6	74017	336.0	369.8
1982		44176.9	1513.4	1043.3	344.8	56.8	68.5	66256	353.0	396.9
1983		44644.1	1659.8	1163.8	351.4	58.4	86.2	62328	346.3	435.2
1984		44453.0	1739.8	1215.3	328.6	69.4	126.5	60062	361.5	464.0
1985		44035.9	1775.8	1204.9	310.9	80.4	179.6	55754	380.2	508.9
1986		44225.8	1930.6	1312.6	359.8	77.4	180.8	54136	387.9	586.7
1987		44403.0	1999.3	1326.8	371.9	91.9	208.7	51978	394.1	658.8
1988		44375.9	2141.5	1417.1	382.1	101.2	241.2	51558	428.9	712.0
1989		44917.2	2357.1	1536.8	418.9	120.5	280.9	50862	416.8	790.5
1990		47403.1	2590.3	1638.4	462.4	147.9	341.6	52387	428.8	844.5
1991		47822.1	2805.1	1726.1	499.6	173.9	405.5	49644	456.9	963.2
1992		48590.1	2930.2	1756.1	515.7	196.0	462.4	48082	478.6	1106.9
1993		48727.9	3151.9	1835.1	575.1	212.3	529.4	45153	481.7	1244.8
1994		48759.1	3317.9	1882.0	600.7	234.8	600.6	48722	503.7	1473.9
1995		49281.2	3593.7	2021.9	632.4	268.5	670.8	40699	520.2	1655.7
1996		50381.4	3827.9	2145.3	658.4	289.6	734.7	37743	533.7	1812.7
1997		51238.5	3980.7	2171.7	689.1	322.0	798.1	36117	562.4	1980.1
1998		52295.6	4083.7	2233.3	682.5	345.7	822.0	33185	634.8	2042.1
1999		53158.4	4124.3	2180.9	697.8	365.6	880.0	31678	664.1	2173.4
2000		53820.3	4146.4	2161.6	690.5	376.5	917.9	29962	698.5	2421.3
北 京	Beijing	328.2	17.9	10.4	1.0	0.4	6.1	40	2.0	31.0
天 津	Tianjin	353.2	16.6	9.2	2.0	0.7	4.7			35.5
河 北	Hebei	4482.3	270.6	148.0	43.9	16.8	62.0	105	1.9	180.4
山 西	Shanxi	1105.0	87.0	42.2	19.8	5.2	19.9	106	2.5	53.1
内蒙古	Inner Mongolia	2371.7	74.8	42.8	14.4	3.1	14.4	4		21.3
辽 宁	Liaoning	1440.7	109.8	66.7	11.1	8.3	23.7	119	12.8	103.5
吉 林	Jilin	1315.1	112.1	64.7	5.5	8.5	33.4	63	3.7	23.8
黑龙江	Heilongjiang	2032.0	121.6	52.4	28.7	10.5	29.9	15	1.0	27.5
上 海	Shanghai	285.9	19.3	14.9	1.6	0.5	2.3			73.2
江 苏	Jiangsu	3900.9	335.5	189.3	51.2	16.2	78.7	4	40.0	314.6
浙 江	Zhejiang	1403.2	89.7	59.7	12.2	5.8	12.1	2319	104.0	255.3
安 徽	Anhui	3197.2	253.2	118.4	42.6	24.9	67.3	550	9.5	45.8
福 建	Fujian	940.2	123.3	55.7	16.8	23.8	27.1	3507	92.8	72.4
江 西	Jiangxi	1903.4	106.9	47.5	19.6	17.2	22.7	1298	19.6	35.3
山 东	Shandong	4824.9	423.2	198.6	57.8	36.8	130.1	17	0.4	200.3
河 南	Henan	4725.3	419.5	205.7	97.2	36.7	79.9	475	6.8	125.8
湖 北	Hubei	2072.5	247.1	132.7	52.5	16.2	45.7	893	34.8	60.9
湖 南	Hunan	2677.5	182.2	98.1	24.3	29.9	29.9	4509	42.0	44.5
广 东	Guangdong	1478.5	176.2	95.9	18.4	35.8	26.1	5478	142.6	405.4
广 西	Guangxi	1501.6	157.8	56.9	22.5	36.1	42.3	1120	14.9	29.6
海 南	Hainan	179.8	26.3	10.7	1.8	2.8	11.0	83	2.8	1.5
重 庆	Chongqing	624.6	72.0	46.0	16.3	2.5	7.2	814	22.7	27.9
四 川	Sichuan	2469.0	212.6	123.0	42.1	10.0	37.5	3070	78.4	82.8
贵 州	Guizhou	653.4	71.3	42.2	10.9	5.0	13.1	798	15.0	14.2
云 南	Yunnan	1403.4	112.1	66.1	18.3	9.1	18.5	1776	26.6	31.7
西 藏	Tibet	157.0	2.5	1.2	0.5	0.2	0.6	231	1.6	0.3
陕 西	Shaanxi	1308.0	131.2	73.0	16.9	8.2	33.3	2087	9.2	59.5
甘 肃	Gansu	981.5	64.5	30.0	18.6	2.4	13.5	229	2.9	29.4
青 海	Qinghai	211.4	7.2	3.3	1.4	0.3	2.2	57	1.6	2.3
宁 夏	Ningxia	398.8	23.6	13.6	3.1	0.3	6.6			7.9
新 疆	Xinjiang	3094.3	79.2	42.8	17.7	2.4	16.3	195	6.5	24.5

12-9 灌溉、水库和除涝、治水、治碱情况

Irrigation, Reservoirs, Flood Prevention, Water and Soil Conservation and Improvement of Saline-Alkaline Land

项　目	Item	1985	1990	1995	1998	2000
年底灌区数　(处)	Number of Irrigation Areas (year-end)	5281	5363	5562	5611	5683
3.3万公顷以上	33 000 Hectares and Over	71	72	74	79	101
2.0-3.3万公顷	20 000-33 000 Hectares	66	76	99	114	141
灌区有效灌溉面积(万公顷)	Effective Irrigated Areas (10 000 hectares)	2077.7	2123.1	2249.9	2274.6	2449.3
3.3万公顷以上	33 000 Hectares and Over	599.6	604.7	631.4	669.1	788.3
2.0-3.3万公顷	20 000-33 000 Hectares	167	189.6	244.4	276.9	344
水库　(座)	Number of Reservoirs	83219	83387	84775	84994	85120
大型水库	Large	340	366	387	403	420
中型水库	Medium-sized	2401	2499	2593	2653	2704
小型水库	Small	80478	80522	81795	81938	81996
水库库容量　(亿立方米)	Capacity of Reservoirs (100 million cu.m)	4301	4660	4797	4924	5184
大型水库	Large	3076	3397	3493	3597	3842
中型水库	Medium-sized	661	690	719	736	746
小型水库	Small	564	573	585	591	594
节水灌溉面积　(万公顷)	Water-saving Irrigated Areas (10 000 hectares)				1523.5	1638.9
除涝面积　(万公顷)	Flooded or Waterlogged Area	1858.4	1933.7	2006.5	2068.1	2098.9
水土流失治理面积(万公顷)	Area of Soil Erosion under Control (10 000 hectares)	4640	5300	6690	7502	8096
治碱面积　(万公顷)	Improved Area of Saline-Alkaline Land (10 000 hectares)	456.9	499.5	543.4	565.3	584.1
堤防长度　(万公里)	Total Length of Dikes (10 000 km)	17.7	22.0	24.7	25.8	27.0
堤防保护面积　(万公顷)	Area of Land Protected by Dikes (10 000 hectares)	3106	3200	3060.9	3629.0	3960

注：大型水库库容：1亿立方米以上；中型水库库容：1千万至1亿立方米；小型水库库容：10万至1千万立方米。

a)The capacity of the large reservoirs is over 100 million cubic meters, while that of the medium ones is from 10 million to 100 million cubic meters, and that of the small ones is from 100 000 to 10 million cubic meters.

12-10 各地区水利设施和除涝、治碱面积（2000年）

Water Conservancy Facilities and Area with Flood Prevention Measures and Improved Area of Saline-Alkaline Land by Region (2000)

地区	Region	水库数（座）Number of Reservoirs	水库总库容量（亿立方米）Capacity of Reservoirs (100 million cu.m)	除涝面积（万公顷）Area with Flood Prevention Measures (10 000 hectares)	治碱面积（万公顷）Improved Area of Saline-alkaline Land (10 000 hectares)	水土流失治理面积（万公顷）Area of Soil Erosion under Control (10 000 hectares)
全国	**National Total**	**85120**	**5183.5**	**2098.9**	**584.1**	**8096.1**
北京	Beijing	86	93.5	16.1	4.3	55.5
天津	Tianjin	109	27.2	40.3	21.2	2.4
河北	Hebei	1110	158.4	163.8	81.9	540.7
山西	Shanxi	746	53.2	8.9	21.1	596.9
内蒙古	Inner Mongolia	457	74.8	27.2	29.7	673.9
辽宁	Liaoning	921	303.4	99.9	32.4	471.4
吉林	Jilin	1313	306.8	100.9	12.3	300.8
黑龙江	Heilongjiang	609	84.2	313.8	19.7	322.5
上海	Shanghai			6.5	2.8	
江苏	Jiangsu	912	189.0	279.3	68.4	74.3
浙江	Zhejiang	3828	352.7	47.7	0.5	211.8
安徽	Anhui	4815	185.1	214.8	10.3	176.3
福建	Fujian	2889	83.2	11.6	3.8	92.1
江西	Jiangxi	9602	275.5	33.8		275.9
山东	Shandong	5578	190.4	256.4	91.3	339.2
河南	Henan	2392	396.0	184.8	68.2	381.0
湖北	Hubei	5835	501.9	119.9	4.3	386.9
湖南	Hunan	13299	365.3	45.5		212.1
广东	Guangdong	6547	405.2	50.0		121.5
广西	Guangxi	4375	225.5	20.1	11.7	115.3
海南	Hainan	1003	93.7	1.0		2.3
重庆	Chongqing	2730	36.9	1.4		146.4
四川	Sichuan	6657	87.6	8.6		391.8
贵州	Guizhou	1927	74.4	4.5		193.6
云南	Yunnan	5178	83.1	21.7	0.5	309.1
西藏	Tibet	47	10.2	1.9		10.8
陕西	Shaanxi	1043	36.4	13.2	6.3	850.3
甘肃	Gansu	289	86.6	1.2	6.8	656.4
青海	Qinghai	147	297.9		1.0	63.8
宁夏	Ningxia	196	18.3		6.9	114.1
新疆	Xinjiang	478	68.1	3.9	78.7	6.8

12-11 农村居民家庭年末生产性固定资产原值

Original Value of Productive Fixed Assets of Rural Household at the End of Year

本表为农村住户抽样调查资料。

Data in this table are obtained from the sample surveys on rural households.

单位:元/人 (yuan/person)

年 份 Year	地 区 Region	固定资产原值合计 Total	农 业 Agriculture	工 业 Industry	建筑业 Construction	交通运输及邮电业 Transport, Post and Telecommunication Services	批发零售贸易及餐饮业 Wholesale and Retail Trade and Catering Services	社会服务业 Social Services	文教卫生事业 Education, Culture, and Health Care	其 他 Others
1985		792.53	603.34	42.28		112.84				34.07
1990		1258.06	898.93	82.56		215.82				60.45
1995		2774.27	2088.23	182.73		444.73				58.57
1999		4045.48	2915.49	274.45		638.02				217.53
2000		4676.98	3321.66	334.79	29.02	621.04	149.24	60.16	12.86	144.30
北 京	Beijing	6973.86	1611.20	600.00	173.87	2514.80	1060.87	1097.47	6.67	15.67
天 津	Tianjin	5860.90	3587.40	70.00	161.50	1575.50	310.00	126.00	15.00	15.50
河 北	Hebei	6328.32	4132.77	586.06	31.57	1101.14	309.91	104.06	10.00	52.80
山 西	Shanxi	4289.95	2517.52	247.48	47.81	1113.21	135.38	89.90	8.43	130.22
内蒙古	Inner Mongolia	7912.81	6982.26	161.91	5.89	350.69	158.15	4.67	11.98	237.25
辽 宁	Liaoning	4434.57	3227.56	268.76	7.94	609.38	181.06	14.60	21.80	103.47
吉 林	Jilin	5576.72	5245.98	80.68		126.88	16.44	9.06	4.38	93.32
黑龙江	Heilongjiang	5969.04	5408.97	71.31	4.24	266.79	97.10	36.65	6.70	75.57
上 海	Shanghai	3506.97	1986.05	159.25	27.67	911.67	193.83	19.67		208.83
江 苏	Jiangsu	4710.13	2890.40	625.19	88.89	800.38	117.65	106.58	0.74	69.00
浙 江	Zhejiang	7070.87	3711.85	1503.00	68.36	1133.76	387.64	135.49	23.96	99.57
安 徽	Anhui	4160.98	3382.72	214.79	30.43	292.19	136.91	31.39	7.42	65.13
福 建	Fujian	4427.79	2095.53	900.31	51.87	616.90	150.58	138.41	56.81	417.38
江 西	Jiangxi	2695.23	1902.78	118.90	6.93	459.85	114.78	48.37	9.71	33.92
山 东	Shandong	5252.78	3792.59	330.58	20.34	651.87	230.15	19.52	14.50	132.81
河 南	Henan	4311.30	3677.39	174.65	30.05	286.00	81.68	23.95	20.12	17.46
湖 北	Hubei	2482.02	1858.18	137.57	17.10	313.52	92.08	9.17	2.91	51.49
湖 南	Hunan	3006.28	1969.43	250.46	16.85	601.13	98.89	20.09	1.49	47.95
广 东	Guangdong	4504.29	2172.85	434.11	51.69	826.67	198.91	130.70	28.95	660.43
广 西	Guangxi	3006.05	2077.97	314.21	13.16	463.53	103.98	14.50	7.79	10.91
海 南	Hainan	4596.92	3410.81	156.94	1.39	646.10	53.47	11.11	11.11	305.99
重 庆	Chongqing	2012.80	1572.18	115.75	1.25	224.72	40.67	15.17	1.94	41.12
四 川	Sichuan	3551.77	2744.14	115.24	8.15	409.66	107.65	10.10	9.96	146.87
贵 州	Guizhou	2971.43	2247.91	202.98	41.16	319.71	63.27	5.43	25.34	65.62
云 南	Yunnan	4641.36	3233.78	373.21	4.79	457.74	48.46	3.80	2.50	517.08
西 藏	Tibet	16070.54	14036.14	133.43		1525.15	19.79			356.45
陕 西	Shaanxi	3695.07	2174.05	379.26	42.18	799.84	165.19	65.57	20.59	48.38
甘 肃	Gansu	4359.79	3491.28	197.36	18.61	428.10	74.52	42.03	34.39	73.51
青 海	Qinghai	6559.23	5475.13	173.80	13.33	725.02	27.17	5.00	36.67	50.40
宁 夏	Ningxia	10168.09	6051.06	480.93	4.50	1658.58	118.96	42.60	1.17	1810.29
新 疆	Xinjiang	7994.76	6964.28	135.65		627.57	13.33	153.33		100.59

注：2000年交通、运输、邮电业数据与2000年前数据口径不一致。

a)Data coverage on transport, post and telecommunication service in 2000 is different from that before 2000.

12-12 农村居民家庭平均每百户年底拥有主要生产性固定资产数量

Number of Major Productive Fixed Assets Per 100 Rural Households at the End of Year

本表为农村住户抽样调查资料。

Data in this table are obtained from the sample surveys on rural households.

年 份 Year	地 区 Region	汽 车 (辆) Motor Vehicles	大中型拖拉机 (台) Large and Medium Tractors	小型和手扶拖拉机 (台) Mini and Walking Tractors	机动脱粒机 (台) Motorized Threshing Machines	胶轮大车 (辆) Carts with Rubber Tyres	农用水泵 (台) Pumps	役畜 (头) Draught Animals	产品畜 (头) Commodity Animals
	1985	0.25	0.35	2.71	1.91	5.49	1.69	57.15	32.12
	1990	0.28	0.45	5.30	3.55	7.89	3.86	57.27	30.91
	1991	0.24	0.51	6.61	3.85	8.24	4.73	53.93	28.73
	1992	0.28	0.55	7.25	4.16	8.67	5.48	52.95	30.07
	1993	0.33	0.64	8.40	5.30	9.60	8.54	59.98	53.15
	1994	0.40	0.79	8.77	5.15	9.32	7.90	58.79	56.70
	1995	0.51	0.77	9.93	6.33	9.29	9.07	55.99	50.72
	1996	0.78	0.99	12.46	6.87	8.78	10.97	54.99	56.26
	1997	0.82	1.39	14.26	7.41	8.83	12.12	55.58	52.72
	1998	1.01	1.22	14.34	8.58	8.52	13.73	48.39	52.20
	1999	1.09	1.44	16.26	8.36	7.87	14.02	45.02	54.08
	2000	1.32	1.41	16.72	9.59	13.26	17.73	41.75	41.56
北 京	Beijing	4.80	0.93	16.00	0.80	1.20	1.07	2.40	39.20
天 津	Tianjin	4.83	2.13	19.00	2.50	13.17	21.17	23.33	14.67
河 北	Hebei	2.33	2.03	34.49	6.30	12.34	25.91	25.04	19.88
山 西	Shanxi	2.52	1.95	16.79	1.20	8.21	5.33	33.47	33.90
内蒙古	Inner Mongolia	0.85	1.91	36.84	3.39	37.89	25.98	101.47	63.16
辽 宁	Liaoning	1.43	1.75	10.11	2.96	30.33	27.67	49.66	31.16
吉 林	Jilin	0.19	1.81	25.00	6.56	37.22	28.34	68.88	27.00
黑龙江	Heilongjiang	0.63	3.79	38.54	6.63	10.65	18.38	35.94	37.99
上 海	Shanghai	2.67		1.33	4.80	0.67	3.67	2.17	9.27
江 苏	Jiangsu	1.03	0.49	18.11	24.20	19.66	13.23	6.60	26.85
浙 江	Zhejiang	1.52	0.44	6.15	33.05	15.34	22.49	5.27	29.77
安 徽	Anhui	0.47	1.40	29.02	19.18	12.19	39.55	23.22	28.06
福 建	Fujian	0.91	0.93	3.54	7.23	5.82	7.42	17.80	32.35
江 西	Jiangxi	0.82	0.49	2.12	18.07	14.39	8.15	49.67	23.68
山 东	Shandong	4.02	3.49	24.53	5.07	25.17	37.90	26.94	28.45
河 南	Henan	0.55	3.29	35.66	12.40	18.95	35.48	25.36	25.83
湖 北	Hubei	0.56	0.85	7.69	1.93	10.18	12.64	42.38	27.55
湖 南	Hunan	1.03	0.26	3.31	16.24	3.86	15.58	23.34	23.47
广 东	Guangdong	1.35	0.20	9.06	12.41	5.86	13.36	39.73	27.93
广 西	Guangxi	0.30	0.26	7.98	10.01	3.49	10.35	63.74	40.33
海 南	Hainan	0.56	0.83	6.81	9.31	2.36	22.92	81.96	58.47
重 庆	Chongqing	0.72		0.28	8.81	0.61	6.17	22.36	31.49
四 川	Sichuan	1.01	0.58	1.23	10.82	1.00	17.27	33.56	50.01
贵 州	Guizhou	0.58	0.54	0.94	0.80	2.99	3.62	78.10	28.84
云 南	Yunnan	0.83	0.46	7.31	5.15	5.96	2.24	73.33	56.54
西 藏	Tibet	2.29	2.29	20.00	3.33	15.00		326.25	605.42
陕 西	Shaanxi	1.24	1.89	13.54	3.90	16.53	10.71	23.49	32.07
甘 肃	Gansu	0.56	1.72	25.39	1.33	17.09	5.61	80.81	58.39
青 海	Qinghai	2.75	1.08	41.67	3.25	24.00	1.00	123.67	135.67
宁 夏	Ningxia	3.50	1.00	45.08	2.18	7.17	9.00	67.25	33.50
新 疆	Xinjiang	1.00	3.07	23.10	1.53	25.00	2.07	99.73	202.27

12-13 各地区农村居民家庭土地经营情况（2000年）

Area of Land Managed by Rural Households by Region (2000)

本表为农村住户抽样调查资料。

Data in this table are obtained from the sample surveys on rural households.

单位：亩/人 (mu/person)

地区	Region	经营耕地面积 Area of Cultivated Land under Management	#自留地 Family Plots	经营山地面积 Hilly Area under Management	园地面积 Area of Garden Plot	牧草地面积 Area of Grassland	养殖水面面积 Water Area for Breeding Aquatics
全　国	**National Total**	**1.98**	**0.09**	**0.28**	**0.06**	**3.28**	**0.03**
北　京	Beijing	0.66	0.03	0.03	0.31	0.01	0.02
天　津	Tianjin	1.43	0.01	0.01	0.04		
河　北	Hebei	1.75	0.04	0.19	0.06		
山　西	Shanxi	2.37	0.09	0.18	0.17	0.01	
内蒙古	Inner Mongolia	7.37	0.13	0.48	0.01	100.42	0.01
辽　宁	Liaoning	3.04	0.14	0.16	0.08		0.08
吉　林	Jilin	5.52	0.22	0.32	0.01	0.06	0.01
黑龙江	Heilongjiang	8.56	0.20	0.05	0.02		
上　海	Shanghai	0.92	0.08				0.02
江　苏	Jiangsu	1.21	0.08	0.03	0.02		0.10
浙　江	Zhejiang	0.84	0.05	0.40	0.11		0.05
安　徽	Anhui	1.43	0.03	0.19	0.03		0.02
福　建	Fujian	0.80	0.05	0.45	0.18		0.07
江　西	Jiangxi	1.17	0.07	0.72	0.03		0.04
山　东	Shandong	1.45	0.03	0.04	0.05		
河　南	Henan	1.50	0.04	0.01	0.03		0.03
湖　北	Hubei	1.44	0.08	0.37	0.03	0.01	0.06
湖　南	Hunan	1.09	0.09	0.39	0.04	0.04	0.05
广　东	Guangdong	0.75	0.07	0.36	0.10		0.10
广　西	Guangxi	1.25	0.09	0.51	0.07		0.03
海　南	Hainan	1.01	0.16	0.32	0.13		0.06
重　庆	Chongqing	1.02	0.07	0.22	0.03	0.02	0.02
四　川	Sichuan	1.03	0.09	0.24	0.03		0.02
贵　州	Guizhou	1.06	0.11	0.36	0.01	0.01	
云　南	Yunnan	1.39	0.13	0.66	0.04	0.01	
西　藏	Tibet	2.18	0.05			0.18	
陕　西	Shaanxi	1.66	0.09	0.36	0.24	0.01	
甘　肃	Gansu	2.43	0.19	0.69	0.06	0.05	0.02
青　海	Qinghai	2.21	0.40	0.17	0.01	30.26	
宁　夏	Ningxia	3.88	0.20	0.59	0.07	0.07	0.06
新　疆	Xinjiang	4.20	0.14	0.01	0.08	0.04	

12-14 农作物总播种面积

Total Sown Areas of Farm Crops

单位：千公顷 (1 000 hectares)

年份 Year	地区 Region	农作物总播种面积 Total Sown Area	粮食作物播种面积 Sown Area of Grain Crops	谷物 Cereal	#稻谷 Rice	#小麦 Wheat	#玉米 Corn	豆类 Soybeans
1978		150105	120587		34421	29183	19961	
1979		148476	119263		33873	29357	20133	
1980		146381	117234		33879	28844	20087	
1981		145159	114958		33295	28307	19425	
1982		144757	113462		33071	27955	18543	
1983		143993	114047		33136	29050	18824	
1984		144221	112884		33179	29576	18537	
1985		143626	108845		32070	29218	17694	
1986		144204	110933		32266	29616	19124	
1987		144957	111268		32193	28798	20212	
1988		144866	110123		31987	28785	19692	
1989		146552	112205		32700	29841	20353	
1990		148363	113466		33064	30753	21401	
1991		149586	112314	94073	32590	30948	21574	9163
1992		149008	110560	92520	32090	30496	21044	8983
1993		147741	110509	88912	30355	30235	20694	12377
1994		148241	108544	87537	30171	28981	21152	12736
1995		149879	110060	89310	30744	28860	22776	11232
1996		152381	112548	92208	31406	29611	24498	10543
1997		153969	112912	91964	31765	30057	23775	11164
1998		155706	113787	92117	31214	29774	25239	11671
1999		156373	113161	91617	31284	28855	25904	11190
2000		156300	108463	85264	29962	26653	23056	12660
北京	Beijing	457.3	308.3	277.6	14.1	121.7	135.8	24.6
天津	Tianjin	533.1	345.9	303.0	35.4	121.7	131.2	40.8
河北	Hebei	9024.4	6918.7	5879.2	143.9	2678.8	2478.6	592.2
山西	Shanxi	4042.4	3186.5	2326.7	4.5	893.2	793.7	484.1
内蒙古	Inner Mongolia	5914.4	4435.9	2648.2	118.4	617.1	1298.2	1137.4
辽宁	Liaoning	3622.0	2858.6	2365.3	489.7	117.6	1422.5	326.2
吉林	Jilin	4542.2	3833.7	3043.8	584.8	77.3	2197.3	666.5
黑龙江	Heilongjiang	9329.5	7852.5	4279.5	1605.9	590.2	1801.3	3178.3
上海	Shanghai	520.7	258.8	249.5	176.1	57.1	5.2	8.3
江苏	Jiangsu	7944.9	5304.3	4754.6	2203.5	1954.6	423.2	391.4
浙江	Zhejiang	3554.3	2300.3	1907.6	1598.0	177.6	52.2	215.7
安徽	Anhui	9005.8	6183.8	4942.0	2236.7	2126.4	485.9	773.7
福建	Fujian	2793.3	1828.5	1320.5	1222.3	38.7	36.8	138.7
江西	Jiangxi	5650.8	3322.0	2920.8	2832.0	51.4	25.3	239.1
山东	Shandong	11147.3	7363.2	6436.5	176.8	3748.2	2413.9	480.5
河南	Henan	13136.9	9029.6	7743.7	459.6	4922.3	2201.3	683.4
湖北	Hubei	7584.1	4156.2	3329.8	1995.3	845.1	424.1	358.8
湖南	Hunan	8002.1	5029.9	4340.4	3896.1	118.6	278.5	294.6
广东	Guangdong	5156.9	3311.1	2696.5	2467.4	13.7	189.3	128.4
广西	Guangxi	6260.7	3655.9	2955.6	2301.6	19.5	610.7	359.2
海南	Hainan	906.0	542.0	391.1	367.5		18.0	17.2
重庆	Chongqing	3590.8	2773.4	1793.5	776.6	466.2	500.6	219.1
四川	Sichuan	9609.1	6854.5	5202.2	2123.8	1605.0	1235.5	445.0
贵州	Guizhou	4696.7	3151.3	2126.6	750.5	567.4	727.3	322.2
云南	Yunnan	5786.0	4238.7	3473.6	1073.6	645.6	1129.7	245.0
西藏	Tibet	231.1	201.4	190.7	1.0	51.9	3.2	10.5
陕西	Shaanxi	4555.4	3821.5	3015.7	144.8	1537.2	1057.0	395.3
甘肃	Gansu	3740.2	2798.2	2119.4	7.2	1192.2	464.4	261.7
青海	Qinghai	553.7	322.7	226.0		165.6	2.1	50.5
宁夏	Ningxia	1016.5	807.1	650.7	76.7	292.6	131.1	80.0
新疆	Xinjiang	3391.6	1468.2	1353.9	78.1	838.8	382.4	91.8

12-14 续表 1 continued

单位：千公顷 (1 000 hectares)

年份 Year	地区 Region	薯类 Tubers	油料 Oil-bearing Crops	# 花生 Peanuts	# 油菜籽 Rapeseeds	棉花 Cotton	麻类 Fiber Crops	# 黄红麻 Jute and Ambary Hemp	糖料 Sugar Crops
1978		11796	6222	1768	2599	4867	751	412	879
1979		10952	7051	2074	2761	4512	698	362	837
1980		10153	7929	2339	2844	4920	667	314	922
1981		9620	9134	2472	3801	5185	591	306	987
1982		9370	9343	2416	4122	5828	459	246	115
1983		9402	8390	2201	3669	6077	389	227	1198
1984		8988	8678	2422	3413	6923	486	320	1230
1985		8572	11800	3319	4494	5141	1230	991	1524
1986		8685	11414	3253	4916	4306	762	345	1470
1987		8867	11180	3022	5267	4844	967	272	1357
1988		9054	10619	2977	4937	5535	735	277	1669
1989		9097	10504	2946	4993	5203	563	286	1529
1990		9121	10900	2907	5503	5588	495	300	1679
1991		9078	11530	2880	6133	6538	453	270	1947
1992		9057	11489	2976	5976	6835	434	277	1906
1993		9220	11142	3379	5300	4985	420	274	1687
1994		9270	12081	3776	5783	5528	372	176	1755
1995		9519	13101	3809	6907	5422	376	147	1820
1996		9798	12556	3616	6734	4722	350	147	1846
1997		9785	12381	3722	6475	4491	327	162	1923
1998		10000	12919	4039	6527	4459	224	93	1984
1999		10355	13906	4268	6899	3726	205	65	1644
2000		10538	15400	4855	7494	4041	262	50	1514
北京	Beijing	6.0	15.4	12.8		1.6			
天津	Tianjin	2.1	26.3	3.9		15.1	0.1	0.1	
河北	Hebei	447.4	686.4	463.3	28.4	307.4	3.0	2.5	9.9
山西	Shanxi	375.6	417.1	21.1	8.6	43.0	0.6		7.6
内蒙古	Inner Mongolia	650.3	879.3	5.2	295.0	0.6	1.5		58.9
辽宁	Liaoning	167.1	199.5	142.8	1.3	7.3	0.7	0.5	16.5
吉林	Jilin	123.4	271.9	54.2			0.7		22.7
黑龙江	Heilongjiang	394.7	362.7	18.6	79.9		95.2		145.7
上海	Shanghai	1.0	71.5	1.4	70.1	1.0			1.1
江苏	Jiangsu	158.3	897.2	227.9	650.5	295.3	0.9	0.2	5.2
浙江	Zhejiang	177.0	315.6	14.3	297.2	26.6	0.8	0.6	16.3
安徽	Anhui	468.1	1457.4	334.0	964.7	308.4	15.0	8.5	8.4
福建	Fujian	369.3	125.0	106.1	17.4	0.1	0.3	0.2	14.4
江西	Jiangxi	162.1	858.1	179.9	629.2	69.0	10.7	1.7	28.4
山东	Shandong	446.3	956.9	923.5	24.5	568.7	2.3	2.0	0.2
河南	Henan	602.5	1492.5	984.8	248.3	779.3	16.5	15.3	5.2
湖北	Hubei	467.6	1503.4	193.4	1158.9	318.1	22.8	3.1	22.2
湖南	Hunan	394.9	935.0	141.7	784.4	146.0	35.1	1.0	25.2
广东	Guangdong	486.2	343.8	331.1	10.0		1.1	1.0	178.1
广西	Guangxi	341.1	341.4	240.6	89.2	1.8	6.7	5.8	508.7
海南	Hainan	133.7	54.1	48.9			0.7	0.7	61.8
重庆	Chongqing	760.8	226.4	42.2	173.2	1.2	6.1	0.7	2.3
四川	Sichuan	1207.3	1026.1	239.6	776.7	70.1	25.6	5.8	30.7
贵州	Guizhou	702.5	512.7	44.3	461.3	2.3	3.0	0.3	17.1
云南	Yunnan	520.1	212.6	41.2	126.0	1.2	2.1		260.3
西藏	Tibet	0.2	16.1	0.0	16.1				
陕西	Shaanxi	410.5	303.6	33.4	163.7	30.1	0.9		1.4
甘肃	Gansu	417.1	312.1	0.8	137.6	34.7	2.1		10.1
青海	Qinghai	46.2	191.6		185.5				
宁夏	Ningxia	76.4	78.5		0.5		0.1		0.1
新疆	Xinjiang	22.5	310.0	4.7	96.2	1012.3	7.1		55.7

12-14 续表 2 continued

单位：千公顷 (1 000 hectares)

年 份 Year	地 区 Region	# 甘蔗 Sugarcane	# 甜菜 Beetroots	烟叶 Tobacco	# 烤烟 Flue-cured Tobacco	蔬 菜 Vegetables	茶园面积 Area of Tea Plantations at Year-end	果园面积 Area of Orchards at Year-end
1978		549	331	784	613	3331	1048	1657
1979		512	325	633	509	3230	1051	1756
1980		479	443	512	397	3163	1041	1783
1981		551	443	757	586	3448	1041	1797
1982		653	436	1124	888	3887	1061	1952
1983		654	462	768	572	4102	1097	2015
1984		728	534	897	715	4320	1105	2219
1985		965	502	1313	1077	4753	1077	2736
1986		950	521	1125	895	5304	1024	3672
1987		859	498	1128	913	5572	1044	4508
1988		924	745	1555	1304	6032	1056	5066
1989		959	569	1798	1503	6290	1065	5372
1990		1009	670	1593	1342	6338	1061	5179
1991		1164	783	1804	1562	6546	1060	5318
1992		1246	660	2093	1849	7031	1084	5818
1993		1088	599	2089	1835	8084	1171	6432
1994		1057	698	1490	1302	8921	1135	7264
1995		1125	695	1470	1309	9515	1115	8098
1996		1208	638	1853	1683	10491	1103	8553
1997		1312	612	2353	2161	11288	1076	8648
1998		1401	583	1361	1200	12293	1057	8535
1999		1303	341	1374	1216	13347	1130	8667
2000		1185	329	1437	1269	15237	1089	8932
北 京	Beijing					107.8		85.3
天 津	Tianjin					128.3		37.7
河 北	Hebei		9.9	5.5	3.7	866.1		1041.8
山 西	Shanxi		7.6	8.0	7.7	242.1		288.9
内蒙古	Inner		58.9	7.9	7.0	209.4		70.5
辽 宁	Liaoning		16.5	18.4	16.7	413.2		392.8
吉 林	Jilin		22.7	26.6	14.7	264.9		115.4
黑龙江	Heilongjiang		145.7	49.4	44.7	446.5		48.4
上 海	Shanghai	1.1				140.0		12.1
江 苏	Jiangsu	5.2	0.1	0.5		1056.0	19.9	153.3
浙 江	Zhejiang	16.3		1.4		498.9	128.9	249.0
安 徽	Anhui	8.4		19.7	18.9	539.7	108.4	90.9
福 建	Fujian	14.4		55.3	53.7	538.1	129.2	559.1
江 西	Jiangxi	28.4		14.1	11.5	560.1	50.1	283.7
山 东	Shandong		0.2	62.9	61.2	1788.4	8.8	764.3
河 南	Henan	5.2		166.4	163.3	1189.2	20.7	355.8
湖 北	Hubei	22.2		74.6	48.1	968.6	121.0	233.9
湖 南	Hunan	25.2		88.9	79.7	720.3	74.1	330.3
广 东	Guangdong	178.1		31.1	25.8	1010.1	43.2	1001.6
广 西	Guangxi	508.7		23.9	11.5	899.5	26.1	785.0
海 南	Hainan	61.8		0.2		148.9	3.3	141.9
重 庆	Chongqing	2.3		70.8	55.2	317.6	23.8	97.6
四 川	Sichuan	30.6	0.1	82.2	54.6	858.6	82.8	306.1
贵 州	Guizhou	17.0	0.1	213.7	193.4	355.4	44.8	75.5
云 南	Yunnan	260.1	0.2	339.5	330.1	353.3	167.4	229.3
西 藏	Tibet					7.1		1.2
陕 西	Shaanxi	0.1	1.3	52.0	47.1	228.7	35.3	664.8
甘 肃	Gansu		10.1	21.0	19.7	185.1	1.3	273.4
青 海	Qinghai		0.0	0.1		15.8		5.2
宁 夏	Ningxia		0.1	0.7	0.7	49.2		43.9
新 疆	Xinjiang		55.7	2.7	0.5	130.5		193.1

12-15 主要农作物种植结构

Planting Structure of Major Farm Crops

单位：% (%)

项目	Item	1990	1995	1999	2000
农作物总播种面积	**Total Sown Areas of Farm Crops**	**100.00**	**100.00**	**100.00**	**100.00**
粮食作物	**Grain Crops**	**76.50**	**73.43**	**72.37**	**69.39**
谷物	Cereal		59.59	58.59	54.55
稻谷	Rice	22.30	20.51	20.01	19.17
小麦	Wheat	6.30	19.26	18.45	17.05
玉米	Corn	20.70	15.20	16.57	14.75
谷子	Millet	14.40	1.02	0.85	0.80
高粱	Jowar	1.50	0.81	0.63	0.57
其它谷物	Other Cereal	1.00	2.80	2.09	2.21
豆类	Soybeans		7.49	7.16	**8.10**
#大豆	Soja	5.10	5.42	5.09	5.95
杂豆	Miscellaneous Beans		2.07	2.06	2.15
薯类	Tubers	6.10	6.35	6.62	6.74
#马铃薯	Potato	1.90	2.29	2.83	3.02
油料作物	**Oil-bearing Crops**	**7.30**	**8.74**	**8.89**	**9.85**
#花生	Peanuts	2.00	2.54	2.73	3.11
油菜籽	Rapeseeds	3.70	4.61	4.41	4.79
芝麻	Sesame	0.50	0.43	0.45	0.50
胡麻籽	Benne	0.50	0.41	0.35	0.32
向日葵	Helianthus	0.50	0.54	0.72	0.79
棉花	**Cotton**	**14.40**	**3.62**	**2.38**	**2.59**
麻类	**Fiber Crops**	**0.30**	**0.25**	**0.13**	**0.17**
#黄红麻	Jute and Ambary Hemp	0.20	0.10	0.04	0.03
苎　麻	Ramee		0.06	0.05	0.06
大　麻	Hemp				0.01
亚　麻	Flax	0.10	0.08		0.06
糖料	**Sugar Crops**	**1.10**	**1.21**	**1.05**	**0.97**
甘蔗	Sugarcane	0.70	0.75	0.83	0.76
甜菜	Beetsroots	0.50	0.46	0.22	0.21
烟叶	**Tobacco**	**1.10**	**0.98**	**0.88**	**0.92**
#烤烟	Flue-cured Tobacco	0.90	0.87	0.78	0.81
药材	**Medicinal Materials**	**0.10**	**0.19**	**0.31**	**0.43**
蔬菜、瓜类	**Vegetables and Melon**	**4.80**	**7.08**	**9.66**	**11.06**
#蔬菜	Vegetables	4.30	6.35	8.54	9.75
其他农作物	**Other Farm Crops**	**4.20**	**4.49**	**4.33**	**4.70**
#青饲料	Succulence	1.30	1.22	1.18	1.37

12-16 主要农产品单位面积产量
Yield of Major Farm Crops Per Hectare

单位：公斤/公顷 (kg/hectare)

年份 地区	Year Region	谷物 Cereals	棉花 Cotton	花生 Peanuts	油菜籽 Rapeseeds	芝麻 Sesame	黄红麻 Jute and Ambary Hemp	甘蔗 Sugar-cane	甜菜 Beet-roots	烤烟 Flue-cured Tobacco
	1978		450	1354	720	503	2641	38505	8175	1725
	1979		489	1360	870	495	3008	42008	9557	1583
	1980		555	1545	840	330	3497	47565	14250	1815
	1981		572	1547	1451	623	4118	53844	14587	2183
	1982		617	1621	1372	353	4309	56481	14528	2079
	1983		763	1795	1168	443	4489	47616	16879	2012
	1984		904	1989	1232	555	4663	54284	16502	2158
	1985		810	2010	1245	660	4165	53430	15915	1920
	1986		825	1815	1200	615	4116	52860	15960	1530
	1987		870	2040	1260	600	4180	55140	16350	1785
	1988		750	1905	1020	570	3884	53115	17190	1800
	1989		735	1815	1095	465	2310	50850	16245	1605
	1990		810	2190	1260	705	2415	57120	21660	1680
	1991	4206	870	2189	1215	645	1905	58350	20790	1710
	1992	4342	660	2000	1281	692	2233	58605	22832	1687
	1993	4557	750	2492	1309	747	2449	59012	20124	1654
	1994	4500	785	2564	1296	794	2020	57671	17936	1491
	1995	4659	879	2687	1416	908	2534	58136	20132	1584
	1996	4894	890	2804	1367	969	2491	56225	25483	1750
	1997	4823	1025	2592	1479	919	2649	60158	24475	1809
	1998	4953	1009	2943	1272	1042	2677	59549	24806	1740
	1999	4945	1028	2961	1469	1066	2540	57338	25335	1797
	2000	4753	1093	2973	1519	1034	2516	57626	24518	1763
北京	Beijing	4903	982	2622		1044				
天津	Tianjin	3930	1165	2117		619	1840			
河北	Hebei	4007	976	2862	828	784	2974		11696	1978.5
山西	Shanxi	3021	1041	1967	1004	952			27819	2025.4
内蒙古	Inner Mongolia	3579		1691	1033	559			23998	1725.5
辽宁	Liaoning	4351	763	1794	1663	596			17357	1716.1
吉林	Jilin	4758		2418		1366			19555	2058.7
黑龙江	Heilongjiang	4613		1135	850	567			17482	1810.1
上海	Shanghai	6834	1162	4694	2241			62077		
江苏	Jiangsu	6114	1065	3499	2198	1497	3220	54374	29557	
浙江	Zhejiang	5735	1100	2523	1472	1289	3213	60293		
安徽	Anhui	4400	888	3328	1625	1049	2621	38219		1638.1
福建	Fujian	5007	764	2246	1058	794	2718	57437		1700.7
江西	Jiangxi	5172	986	2245	842	682	2580	48241		1316.9
山东	Shandong	5387	1037	3792	1962	1809	2747		4305	1843.2
河南	Henan	4739	903	3411	1360	863	2155	62641		1664.3
湖北	Hubei	5894	957	3397	1713	1498	5821	45854		1708.4
湖南	Hunan	5880	1082	2052	1394	1073	2289	46065		1951.7
广东	Guangdong	5601		2346	818	1025	2593	70373		1921.9
广西	Guangxi	4791	475	2059	915	783	1980	57755		1475.1
海南	Hainan	4010		1949		1074	4213	54858		
重庆	Chongqing	4703	421	1792	1305	736	934	38866		1393.2
四川	Sichuan	5443	840	2266	1770	1101	1800	54434	11092	1715.9
贵州	Guizhou	4399	496	1682	1435	670	2070	39210	1950	1607.8
云南	Yunnan	3691	440	1301	1517	519	1733	54614	15805	1957.5
西藏	Tibet	4887		1528	2458					
陕西	Shaanxi	3190	911	2192	1368	1011	1300	39143	11062	1563.8
甘肃	Gansu	2693	1656	1704	1603				37491	1694.8
青海	Qinghai	2708			1029				30133	
宁夏	Ningxia	3539			829				38711	2249.2
新疆	Xinjiang	5515	1438	4246	1560	946			47559	2238.3

12-17 主要农产品产量

Yield of Major Farm Crops

单位：万吨 (10 000 tons)

年份 Year	地区 Region	粮食 Grain	谷物 Cereal	#稻谷 Rice	#小麦 Wheat	#玉米 Corn	豆类 Beans	薯类 Tubers	油料 Oil-bearing Crops
1978		30476.5		13693.0	5384.0	5594.5		3174.0	521.8
1979		33211.5		14375.0	6273.0	6003.5		2846.0	643.5
1980		32055.5		13990.5	5520.5	6260.0		2872.5	769.1
1981		32502.0		14395.5	5964.0	5920.5		2597.0	1020.5
1982		35450.0		16159.5	6847.0	6056.0		2704.5	1181.7
1983		38727.5		16886.5	8139.0	6820.5		2924.5	1055.0
1984		40730.5		17825.5	8781.5	7341.0		2847.5	1191.0
1985		37910.8		16856.9	8580.5	6382.6		2603.6	1578.4
1986		39151.2		17222.4	9004.0	7085.6		2533.7	1473.8
1987		40473.3		17441.6	8776.8	7982.2		2820.0	1527.8
1988		39408.0		16910.8	8543.2	7735.1		2696.5	1320.3
1989		40755.0		18013.0	9080.7	7892.8		2730.0	1295.2
1990		44624.0		18933.1	9822.9	9681.9		2743.2	1613.2
1991		43529.0	39566.3	18381.3	9595.3	9877.3	1247.1	2715.9	1638.3
1992		44265.8	40169.6	18622.2	10158.7	9538.3	1252.0	2844.2	1641.2
1993		45648.8	40517.4	17751.4	10639.0	10270.4	1950.4	3181.1	1803.9
1994		44510.1	39389.1	17593.3	9929.7	9927.5	2095.6	3025.4	1989.6
1995		46661.8	41611.6	18522.6	10220.7	11198.6	1787.5	3262.6	2250.3
1996		50453.5	45127.1	19510.3	11056.9	12747.1	1790.3	3536.0	2210.6
1997		49417.1	44349.3	20073.5	12328.9	10430.9	1875.5	3192.3	2157.4
1998		51229.5	45624.7	19871.3	10972.6	13295.4	2000.6	3604.2	2313.9
1999		50838.6	45304.1	19848.7	11388.0	12808.6	1894.0	3640.6	2601.2
2000		46217.5	40522.4	18790.8	9963.6	10600.0	2010.0	3685.2	2954.8
北京	Beijing	144.2	136.1	9.4	66.9	58.7	5.0	3.0	3.8
天津	Tianjin	124.1	119.1	14.5	59.5	41.0	4.3	0.7	3.3
河北	Hebei	2551.1	2355.6	65.8	1208.0	994.5	74.5	121.0	147.0
山西	Shanxi	853.4	703.0	3.3	215.2	354.8	57.8	92.6	44.8
内蒙古	Inner Mongolia	1241.9	947.9	72.2	181.8	629.2	109.7	184.3	116.4
辽宁	Liaoning	1140.0	1029.1	377.1	35.8	551.1	50.2	60.7	29.6
吉林	Jilin	1638.0	1448.3	374.8	16.3	993.2	140.6	49.1	39.0
黑龙江	Heilongjiang	2545.5	1974.1	1042.2	95.8	790.8	489.6	81.8	43.8
上海	Shanghai	174.0	170.5	137.2	24.7	3.7	2.7	0.8	16.4
江苏	Jiangsu	3106.6	2907.1	1801.3	796.4	236.8	105.3	94.2	225.6
浙江	Zhejiang	1217.7	1093.9	990.2	55.1	20.3	45.4	78.4	57.9
安徽	Anhui	2472.1	2174.5	1221.6	707.1	219.0	103.6	194.0	285.1
福建	Fujian	854.7	661.2	632.8	11.0	11.1	27.6	165.9	25.8
江西	Jiangxi	1614.6	1510.6	1491.9	7.9	8.5	35.5	68.5	96.7
山东	Shandong	3837.7	3467.3	110.8	1860.0	1467.5	108.2	262.2	356.9
河南	Henan	4101.5	3669.7	318.8	2236.0	1075.0	140.1	291.6	392.6
湖北	Hubei	2218.5	1962.6	1497.2	233.7	216.7	71.1	184.8	287.2
湖南	Hunan	2767.9	2552.3	2392.5	23.3	125.1	59.4	156.2	139.3
广东	Guangdong	1760.1	1510.2	1423.4	3.9	76.1	26.1	223.8	78.8
广西	Guangxi	1528.5	1415.9	1226.5	2.7	184.2	45.0	67.6	58.6
海南	Hainan	199.6	156.9	150.2		5.2	2.9	39.8	10.1
重庆	Chongqing	1106.9	843.4	532.9	101.3	197.5	24.2	239.3	31.1
四川	Sichuan	3372.0	2831.5	1634.3	532.1	547.4	92.7	447.8	193.0
贵州	Guizhou	1161.3	935.4	477.4	103.5	342.2	39.5	186.4	74.3
云南	Yunnan	1467.8	1282.1	568.2	152.4	473.3	40.2	145.5	27.0
西藏	Tibet	96.2	93.2	0.6	30.7	1.4	3.0	0.1	4.0
陕西	Shaanxi	1089.1	962.0	94.7	418.6	413.7	31.0	96.1	38.8
甘肃	Gansu	713.5	570.8	6.2	266.1	210.5	37.7	105.0	41.7
青海	Qinghai	82.7	61.2		43.9	1.2	6.6	14.9	19.4
宁夏	Ningxia	252.7	230.3	62.4	74.5	82.0	4.8	17.6	7.0
新疆	Xinjiang	783.7	746.6	60.4	399.5	268.5	25.7	11.4	60.1

12-17 续表 1 continued

单位：万吨

年份 Year	地区 Region				棉花	麻类		甘蔗	甜菜
		# 花生 Peanuts	# 油菜籽 Rapeseeds	# 芝麻 Sesame	Cotton	Fiber Crops	# 黄红麻 Jute and Ambary Hemp	Sugarcane	Beetroots
1978		237.7	186.8	32.2	216.7	135.1	108.8	2111.6	270.2
1979		282.2	240.2	41.7	220.7	136.1	108.9	2150.8	310.6
1980		360.0	238.4	25.9	270.7	143.6	109.8	2280.7	630.5
1981		382.6	406.5	51.0	296.8	143.6	126.0	2966.8	636.0
1982		391.6	565.6	34.2	359.8	157.6	106.0	3688.2	671.2
1983		395.1	428.7	34.9	463.7	123.9	101.9	3114.1	918.2
1984		481.5	420.5	47.6	625.8	124.8	149.2	3951.9	828.4
1985		666.4	560.7	69.1	414.7	444.8	411.9	5154.9	891.9
1986		588.2	588.1	61.8	354.0	192.7	142.0	5021.9	830.6
1987		617.1	660.5	52.6	424.5	208.4	113.7	4736.3	814.0
1988		569.3	504.4	40.4	414.9	127.0	107.8	4906.4	1281.0
1989		536.3	543.6	33.8	378.8	112.4	66.0	4879.5	924.3
1990		636.8	695.8	46.9	450.8	109.7	72.6	5762.0	1452.5
1991		630.3	743.6	43.5	567.5	88.4	51.3	6789.8	1628.9
1992		595.3	765.3	51.6	450.8	93.8	61.9	7301.1	1506.9
1993		842.1	693.9	56.3	373.9	96.0	67.2	6419.4	1204.8
1994		968.2	749.2	54.8	434.1	74.7	35.5	6092.7	1252.5
1995		1023.5	977.7	58.3	476.8	89.7	37.1	6542.0	1398.4
1996		1013.8	920.1	57.5	420.3	79.5	36.5	6687.6	1541.5
1997		964.8	957.8	56.6	460.3	74.9	43.0	7889.7	1496.8
1998		1188.6	830.1	65.6	450.1	49.5	24.8	8343.8	1446.6
1999		1263.9	1013.2	74.3	382.9	47.2	16.4	7470.3	863.9
2000		1443.7	1138.1	81.1	441.7	52.9	12.6	6828.0	807.3
北京	Beijing	3.4		0.0	0.2				
天津	Tianjin	0.8		0.1	1.8				
河北	Hebei	132.6	2.3	2.0	30.0	0.8	0.7		11.5
山西	Shanxi	4.1	0.9	1.9	4.5	0.1			21.0
内蒙古	Inner Mongolia	0.9	30.5	0.5	0.2	0.1			141.3
辽宁	Liaoning	25.6	0.2	0.8	0.6	0.1	0.1		28.7
吉林	Jilin	13.1	0.0	1.1		0.1			44.4
黑龙江	Heilongjiang	2.1	6.8	0.1		18.7			254.8
上海	Shanghai	0.7	15.7		0.1			6.8	
江苏	Jiangsu	79.7	143.0	2.7	31.4	0.3	0.1	28.1	0.2
浙江	Zhejiang	3.6	43.7	0.5	2.9	0.2	0.2	98.5	
安徽	Anhui	111.2	156.8	16.6	27.4	3.5	2.2	32.0	
福建	Fujian	23.8	1.8	0.1		0.1		82.7	
江西	Jiangxi	40.4	53.0	3.3	6.8	1.6	0.4	136.8	
山东	Shandong	350.1	4.8	1.0	59.0	0.6	0.6		0.1
河南	Henan	335.9	33.8	22.0	70.4	3.6	3.3	32.6	
湖北	Hubei	65.7	198.5	21.5	30.4	5.1	1.8	101.7	
湖南	Hunan	29.1	109.4	0.8	15.8	7.0	0.2	115.9	
广东	Guangdong	77.7	0.8	0.3		0.3	0.3	1253.2	
广西	Guangxi	49.6	8.2	0.6	0.1	1.3	1.2	2937.9	
海南	Hainan	9.5		0.6		0.3	0.3	338.9	
重庆	Chongqing	7.6	22.6	0.5		0.8	0.1	9.1	
四川	Sichuan	54.3	137.5	0.4	5.9	4.0	1.0	166.7	0.1
贵州	Guizhou	7.5	66.2		0.1	0.3	0.1	66.7	
云南	Yunnan	5.4	19.1		0.1	0.2	0.0	1420.3	0.3
西藏	Tibet	0.0	4.0						
陕西	Shaanxi	7.3	22.4	3.3	2.7	0.1		0.3	1.5
甘肃	Gansu	0.1	22.1		5.7	0.2			37.9
青海	Qinghai	0.0	19.1						0.1
宁夏	Ningxia								0.3
新疆	Xinjiang	2.0	15.0	0.1	145.6	3.5			265.0

12-17 续表 2 continued

单位：万吨 (10 000 tons)

年 份 Year	地 区 Region	烟 叶 Tobacco	# 烤 烟 Flue-cured Tobacco	蚕 茧 (吨) Silkworm Cocoons (ton)	# 桑蚕茧 Mulberry Silkworm Cocoons	茶 叶 (吨) Tea (ton)	水 果 (吨) Fruits (ton)	# 苹 果 Apples	# 柑 桔 Citrus	# 梨 Pears	# 葡 萄 Grapes	# 香 蕉 Bananas
1978		124.2	105.2	228150	173300	268000	6569700	2275150	382700	1516950	103850	85350
1979		94.2	80.6	326000		277150	7014550	2868800	581650	1437950	125650	74450
1980		84.5	71.7	325750	249800	303700	6792550	2363100	712600	1466300	110000	61300
1981		149.7	127.9	311050	251650	342600	7800850	3005750	797550	1593400	147500	126250
1982		217.9	184.8	314050	270850	397300	7712950	2429550	938900	1755250	185950	201200
1983		138.1	115.1	339950	267850	400550	9487050	3541050	1296400	1795100	247100	206650
1984		178.9	154.3	356550	306400	414150	9845300	2941200	1498750	2099900	293850	299900
1985		242.5	207.5	371354	335760	432337	11639456	3614111	1808347	2136766	361409	631017
1986		170.7	137.4	369069	336214	460468	1347471	3336783	2547983	2347600	441590	1251094
1987		194.3	163.6	403152	353537	507972	16679158	4263836	3223848	2489040	640878	2029498
1988		273.4	233.7	440804	394397	545417	16661004	4344394	2560013	2721242	792247	1829672
1989		283.0	240.5	488098	434758	534876	18319316	4498920	4561104	2564959	874245	1403736
1990		262.7	225.9	534421	480179	540070	18744222	4319315	4854935	2352753	858525	1455927
1991		303.1	267.0	583656	550541	541581	21761256	4540445	6332543	2497760	915882	1981170
1992		349.9	311.9	692205	659522	559827	24400930	6555836	5160081	2846121	1125102	2450988
1993		345.1	303.6	756667	711622	599941	30112154	9069557	6560974	3217130	1354770	2700680
1994		223.8	194.0	813078	776941	588468	34998152	11129017	6805445	4042932	1522083	2897832
1995		231.4	207.2	800218	759835	588553	42146267	14007662	8224984	4942445	1741707	3125003
1996		323.4	294.6	508312	470942	593386	46528224	17047250	8456587	5806627	1883142	2535591
1997		425.1	390.8	469432	422976	613366	50893223	17218571	10102200	6414831	2032805	2892268
1998		236.4	208.8	525669	475453	665034	54528533	19480719	8590360	7275464	2358219	3518175
1999		206.9	218.5	484702	447261	675871	62376432	20801641	10787059	7742331	2708127	4194244
2000		255.2	223.8	547613	500640	683324	62251470	20431230	8783129	8412413	3281698	4941454
北 京	Beijing						585907	157654		102693	33961	
天 津	Tianjin						282801	79466		30172	102201	
河 北	Hebei	1.2	0.7	791	790		6773066	1806155		2551647	523601	
山 西	Shanxi	1.6	1.6	3754	3754		2044859	1629575		128577	50564	
内蒙古	Inner Mongolia	1.4	1.2	635	1		214463	46853		109605	15853	
辽 宁	Liaoning	3.2	2.9	39051	92		2499660	1231479		455404	430282	
吉 林	Jilin	6.0	3.0	1767			485585	100543		140779	65716	
黑龙江	Heilongjiang	9.6	8.1	1382			192079	112086		26250	9611	
上 海	Shanghai			79	79		225413	21	101765	17369	23124	
江 苏	Jiangsu	0.1		90127	90127	12029	1764369	695294	42747	390137	87697	
浙 江	Zhejiang	0.3		95123	95123	116352	1703691	845	971896	147563	114569	
安 徽	Anhui	3.2	3.1	24563	24563	45376	1106071	302040	5282	616192	56156	
福 建	Fujian	9.4	9.1	3	3	125969	3564358	380	1306027	96394	38702	746454
江 西	Jiangxi	1.8	1.5	3266	3266	15703	423403		282976	42109	2681	
山 东	Shandong	11.7	11.3	54700	53300	2254	9666284	6476586		911298	475325	
河 南	Henan	27.6	27.2	15190	12560	9163	3647279	2388997	21201	333000	208280	
湖 北	Hubei	13.7	8.2	12195	12122	63703	2156788	30224	946236	633197	74788	
湖 南	Hunan	16.8	15.5	453	450	57294	1505029		1259154	35558	18764	
广 东	Guangdong	6.2	5.0	30909	30909	42124	6435174		810595	42144		2353047
广 西	Guangxi	3.9	1.7	29542	29515	17923	3601420		879914	60863	39427	1111565
海 南	Hainan					2239	1055207		13741			600274
重 庆	Chongqing	10.4	7.7	29098	29098	14526	816841	7020	583944	76251	9917	1984
四 川	Sichuan	15.6	9.4	87341	87341	54513	2525654	202283	1327534	344472	116037	8464
贵 州	Guizhou	33.8	31.1	1196	1196	18376	310986	7675	101340	47677	10241	9938
云 南	Yunnan	65.6	64.6	7496	7436	79396	769537	101105	91640	158112	17746	109728
西 藏	Tibet					1	7418	5299		803		
陕 西	Shaanxi	7.7	7.4	15431	15394	6126	4937906	3885700	35155	458306	41550	
甘 肃	Gansu	3.8	3.3	349	349	257	1215921	690671	1982	245941	22194	
青 海	Qinghai						22415	14144		5963	107	
宁 夏	Ningxia	0.1	0.1	290	290		193155	159462		9058	8959	
新 疆	Xinjiang	0.5	0.1	2882	2882		1518732	299673		194879	683645	

12-18 主要林产品产量

Output of Major Forest Products

单位：吨 (ton)

年份 地区	Year Region	橡胶 Rubber	松脂 Pine Resin	生漆 Lacquer	油桐籽 Tung-oil Seeds	油茶籽 Tea-oil Seeds	核桃 Walnuts
	1978	101600	337600	2200	391150	478900	118650
	1979		403500	2700	324500	617300	90310
	1980	112945	420750	2450	303350	490350	118900
	1981	127700	562300	2950	359850	653800	106550
	1982	152605	469800	2900	338500	493900	103250
	1983	172393	303600	2750	368200	434500	119250
	1984	188778	369300	2300	361600	535550	128150
	1985	187901	343946	2168	378770	619229	121917
	1986	209709	416287	2874	346227	437746	136335
	1987	237578	522917	3296	341742	518398	147243
	1988	239810	461370	3334	358697	462622	177098
	1989	242766	486837	2951	334757	667245	160053
	1990	264243	435244	2683	350770	523313	149560
	1991	296353	440431	2945	327544	620727	151644
	1992	309348	469331	3350	437154	629112	163862
	1993	326062	580780	3376	421027	487942	192159
	1994	374002	569270	3219	434539	630737	209997
	1995	424025	548133	2976	404929	623128	230867
	1996	402450	580819	3740	407744	696633	237989
	1997	451970	701183	4416	453535	856868	249834
	1998	462344	543156	4577	438680	722846	265121
	1999	489991	571477	5314	448323	792690	274246
	2000	480248	551057	5279	453461	823224	309875
北京	Beijing						8816
天津	Tianjin						371
河北	Hebei						30102
山西	Shanxi						46988
内蒙古	Inner Mongolia						
辽宁	Liaoning						5603
吉林	Jilin						4489
黑龙江	Heilongjiang						
上海	Shanghai						
江苏	Jiangsu				38	38	
浙江	Zhejiang		5352	137	501	32547	
安徽	Anhui		8851	280	3109	10419	182
福建	Fujian	147	72949	71	18121	62983	17
江西	Jiangxi		41638		13973	194763	176
山东	Shandong						10866
河南	Henan		2371	569	57054	3270	17143
湖北	Hubei		5377	358	16030	17343	2628
湖南	Hunan		18713	78	42064	337956	2663
广东	Guangdong	26168	113118		3817	26268	
广西	Guangxi	1403	216015	13	63002	118620	262
海南	Hainan	280880	4328				
重庆	Chongqing		126	449	39478	1171	2958
四川	Sichuan		2717	826	46534	4372	32095
贵州	Guizhou		4392	1006	116593	8195	7492
云南	Yunnan	171650	54360	445	19698	4886	68788
西藏	Tibet						1829
陕西	Shaanxi		750	990	12935	393	34498
甘肃	Gansu			57	514		20095
青海	Qinghai						154
宁夏	Ningxia						137
新疆	Xinjiang						11523

12-19 牲畜饲养情况

Number of Livestock

单位：万头(只) (10 000 heads)

年份 地区	Year Region	大牲畜年底头数 Large Animals (year-end)	牛 Cattle and Buffaloes	马 Horses	驴 Donkeys	骡 Mules	骆驼 Camels
	1996	13360.6	11031.8	871.5	944.4	478.0	34.5
	1997	14541.8	12182.2	891.2	952.8	480.6	35.0
	1998	14803.2	12441.9	898.1	955.8	473.9	33.5
	1999	15024.8	12698.3	891.4	934.8	467.3	33.0
	2000	15151.5	12866.3	876.6	922.7	453.0	32.6
北京	Beijing	23.6	18.9	0.6	2.7	1.5	
天津	Tianjin	31.6	21.5	1.0	6.9	2.3	
河北	Hebei	955.4	697.9	45.0	149.1	63.3	
山西	Shanxi	309.3	225.0	5.8	37.2	41.3	
内蒙古	Inner Mongolia	622.1	351.6	111.8	85.9	60.8	12.0
辽宁	Liaoning	420.7	254.0	37.0	95.3	34.4	
吉林	Jilin	539.8	431.9	72.2	16.8	18.9	
黑龙江	Heilongjiang	547.7	461.4	72.8	7.9	5.6	
上海	Shanghai	6.3	6.1				
江苏	Jiangsu	74.5	59.1	1.4	12.6	1.4	
浙江	Zhejiang	39.0	39.0				
安徽	Anhui	559.4	553.0	1.6	3.7	1.1	
福建	Fujian	111.6	111.4	0.1			
江西	Jiangxi	369.4	369.4				
山东	Shandong	1140.3	1008.6	19.8	94.3	17.5	
河南	Henan	1445.7	1340.2	29.3	49.5	26.8	
湖北	Hubei	431.5	428.4	1.8	1.0	0.3	
湖南	Hunan	509.8	504.8	4.5	0.2	0.3	
广东	Guangdong	420.7	420.6	0.1			
广西	Guangxi	814.5	775.3	36.8	0.1	2.4	
海南	Hainan	144.9	144.9				
重庆	Chongqing	167.5	164.1	2.2	0.2	1.0	
四川	Sichuan	1089.0	1002.8	71.3	7.5	7.5	
贵州	Guizhou	731.5	658.1	71.3	0.2	2.0	
云南	Yunnan	1036.3	854.8	86.3	32.1	63.1	
西藏	Tibet	578.6	526.2	38.5	12.5	1.3	
陕西	Shaanxi	301.9	257.7	1.8	30.0	12.5	
甘肃	Gansu	562.8	343.4	26.4	125.3	65.6	2.2
青海	Qinghai	441.4	391.0	33.8	6.0	9.0	1.7
宁夏	Ningxia	92.1	60.5	1.0	19.9	10.6	0.1
新疆	Xinjiang	632.9	385.0	102.6	125.9	2.7	16.7

12-19 续表 1 continued

单位：万头(只) (10 000 heads)

年份 Year	地区 Region	肉猪出栏头数 Slaughtered Fattened Hogs	猪年底头数 Hogs (year-end)	羊年底只数 Sheep and Goats (year-end)	山羊 Goats	绵羊 Sheep
1996		41225.1	36283.6	23728.3	12315.8	11412.5
1997		46483.7	40034.8	25575.7	13480.1	12095.6
1998		50215.1	42256.3	26903.5	14168.3	12735.2
1999		50749.0	43144.2	27925.8	14816.3	13109.5
2000		52673.3	44681.5	29031.9	15715.9	13316.0
北京	Beijing	415.6	250.1	120.1	51.3	68.9
天津	Tianjin	235.8	164.8	65.2	15.9	49.3
河北	Hebei	3239.1	2415.8	2090.0	999.3	1090.7
山西	Shanxi	567.5	468.4	1058.4	474.9	583.6
内蒙古	Inner Mongolia	851.3	801.3	3551.6	1304.3	2247.3
辽宁	Liaoning	1320.1	1300.2	386.1	187.3	198.8
吉林	Jilin	1153.9	646.0	353.0	54.1	298.8
黑龙江	Heilongjiang	1101.8	992.6	507.4	123.8	383.6
上海	Shanghai	473.0	230.0	55.4	46.0	9.5
江苏	Jiangsu	2780.0	2015.0	1023.0	994.4	28.6
浙江	Zhejiang	1359.8	1043.0	233.5	113.4	120.1
安徽	Anhui	2226.8	1858.4	794.9	792.5	2.4
福建	Fujian	1347.7	1108.6	96.2	96.2	
江西	Jiangxi	1863.0	1755.0	81.1	75.1	6.0
山东	Shandong	3426.8	2660.3	2784.7	2160.2	624.6
河南	Henan	3930.0	3587.7	2961.4	2730.1	231.2
湖北	Hubei	2418.6	1900.4	224.8	223.6	1.3
湖南	Hunan	5491.3	3583.8	375.2	374.9	0.3
广东	Guangdong	2955.0	2034.8	29.3	29.3	
广西	Guangxi	2749.9	3171.8	241.8	241.8	
海南	Hainan	256.5	344.0	92.5	92.5	
重庆	Chongqing	1821.0	1610.0	160.6	160.5	0.2
四川	Sichuan	5774.9	4781.1	1321.6	902.2	419.4
贵州	Guizhou	1164.5	1802.7	341.8	321.4	20.4
云南	Yunnan	2033.3	2587.1	892.9	770.8	122.1
西藏	Tibet	13.6	23.5	1664.3	589.4	1074.8
陕西	Shaanxi	752.4	639.9	635.3	499.9	135.5
甘肃	Gansu	562.6	548.2	1163.3	301.2	862.0
青海	Qinghai	112.0	104.0	1642.0	272.6	1369.5
宁夏	Ningxia	133.5	120.3	394.3	130.4	263.8
新疆	Xinjiang	142.0	133.0	3690.2	586.7	3103.5

12-20 畜产品产量

Output of Livestock Products

年份 地区	Year Region	肉类产量（万吨） Output of Meat (10000 tons)	# 猪牛羊肉 Output of Pork, Beef and Mutton	猪肉 Pork	牛肉 Beef	羊肉 Mutton	奶类（万吨） Milk (10 000 tons)	# 牛奶 Cow Milk
	1996	4584.0	3694.7	3158.0	355.7	181.0	735.8	629.4
	1997	5268.8	4249.9	3596.3	440.9	212.8	681.1	601.1
	1998	5723.8	4598.2	3883.7	479.9	234.6	745.4	662.9
	1999	5820.7	4647.4	3890.7	505.4	251.3	806.9	717.6
	2000	6125.4	4838.2	4031.4	532.8	274.0	919.1	827.4
北京	Beijing	55.9	33.9	29.1	3.3	1.6	30.4	30.3
天津	Tianjin	28.9	22.1	17.3	2.8	2.0	16.5	16.5
河北	Hebei	419.4	332.7	242.8	65.3	24.6	96.2	84.2
山西	Shanxi	63.7	57.9	43.5	7.3	7.0	35.9	33.5
内蒙古	Inner Mongolia	143.4	130.3	76.6	21.8	31.8	83.0	79.8
辽宁	Liaoning	225.7	146.2	117.0	25.8	3.4	21.9	18.9
吉林	Jilin	216.3	132.2	95.5	33.5	3.2	15.0	14.3
黑龙江	Heilongjiang	151.6	117.6	87.1	27.1	3.5	156.5	154.3
上海	Shanghai	55.0	26.7	25.9		0.7	25.9	25.9
江苏	Jiangsu	328.0	226.6	205.7	5.1	15.8	25.7	25.5
浙江	Zhejiang	117.6	93.3	89.8	0.9	2.6	11.2	11.2
安徽	Anhui	297.8	227.9	184.8	31.9	11.2	4.1	4.1
福建	Fujian	137.6	109.9	106.5	2.1	1.3	9.9	9.6
江西	Jiangxi	184.4	149.6	143.5	5.2	0.9	5.8	5.6
山东	Shandong	560.2	379.9	285.9	69.2	24.8	70.5	45.7
河南	Henan	502.0	437.9	322.9	83.0	32.0	20.2	16.1
湖北	Hubei	248.8	210.3	193.5	13.8	3.0	5.9	5.6
湖南	Hunan	434.7	391.3	371.8	13.5	6.1	1.1	1.1
广东	Guangdong	322.2	212.4	206.8	5.2	0.4	9.5	9.2
广西	Guangxi	276.2	219.1	206.8	9.8	2.5	1.7	1.7
海南	Hainan	38.0	25.7	22.7	2.1	1.0	0.0	0.0
重庆	Chongqing	153.6	138.4	132.1	4.4	1.9	5.6	5.6
四川	Sichuan	555.5	459.2	419.1	23.8	16.2	28.9	28.5
贵州	Guizhou	123.8	116.0	104.8	7.0	4.2	1.7	1.7
云南	Yunnan	204.9	191.2	172.6	12.8	5.8	14.7	13.0
西藏	Tibet	14.9	14.9	0.8	8.5	5.7	20.4	16.2
陕西	Shaanxi	83.2	74.2	60.9	7.9	5.4	63.9	39.2
甘肃	Gansu	58.9	54.3	38.9	7.9	7.5	13.7	13.3
青海	Qinghai	20.8	20.3	7.0	6.4	7.0	21.3	20.6
宁夏	Ningxia	18.5	15.5	8.8	3.3	3.3	23.6	23.6
新疆	Xinjiang	83.6	70.5	10.8	22.2	37.5	78.2	72.5

12-20 续表 1 continued

年份 地区	Year Region	绵羊毛 (吨) Sheep Wool (ton)	#细羊毛 Fine Wool	#半细羊毛 Semi-Fine Wool	山羊毛 (吨) Goat Wool (ton)	羊绒 (吨) Cashmere (ton)	禽蛋 (万吨) Poultry Eggs (10 000 tons)	蜂蜜 (万吨) Honey (10 000 tons)
	1996	298102	121020	74099	35284	9585	1965.2	18.3
	1997	255059	116054	55683	25865	8626	1897.1	21.1
	1998	277545	115752	68775	31417	9799	2021.3	20.7
	1999	283152	114103	73700	31849	10180	2134.7	23.0
	2000	292502	117386	84921	33266	11057	2243.3	24.6
北京	Beijing	762	53	50	199	68	16.0	0.3
天津	Tianjin	1418	307	4603	49	506	25.6	0.1
河北	Hebei	27789	5432	11104	5567	981	357.0	0.9
山西	Shanxi	7287	1498	745	1659	632	40.3	0.3
内蒙古	Inner Mongolia	65051	36959	13601	3442	3815	24.4	0.2
辽宁	Liaoning	7567	3721	3411	748	356	140.3	0.6
吉林	Jilin	21228	19045	2183	365	34	80.0	0.5
黑龙江	Heilongjiang	13550	4365	9185	62	22	75.3	0.4
上海	Shanghai	127		127	214		16.6	0.1
江苏	Jiangsu	1104	863	54	17		181.4	0.7
浙江	Zhejiang	2132	2132				37.2	7.1
安徽	Anhui	174	9	165	82	1	107.4	1.1
福建	Fujian				9		40.7	0.5
江西	Jiangxi				2		33.5	0.7
山东	Shandong	17808	3917	9629	8618	1042	366.2	1.0
河南	Henan	7736	1585	4875	2641	277	270.0	2.3
湖北	Hubei	35	24	10	52		102.6	0.9
湖南	Hunan	3	3		18		52.3	0.5
广东	Guangdong				10		33.1	1.6
广西	Guangxi						14.5	0.6
海南	Hainan						2.9	
重庆	Chongqing	6	6				27.9	0.4
四川	Sichuan	4108	291	1624	398	25	99.7	2.3
贵州	Guizhou	273	39	220	26		6.5	0.2
云南	Yunnan	1690	365	1085	118		10.6	0.7
西藏	Tibet	7947	103	5418	1834	682	0.2	
陕西	Shaanxi	3593	2080	390	1007	546	42.5	0.3
甘肃	Gansu	14145	5274	3044	1559	503	11.2	0.2
青海	Qinghai	15588	308	4447	745	310	1.3	
宁夏	Ningxia	4703	154	590	715	364	7.6	0.1
新疆	Xinjiang	66678	28853	8361	3110	893	18.5	0.3

12-21 水 产 品 产 量

Output of Aquatic Products

单位：千吨 (1 000 tons)

年份 地区	Year Region	水产品总产量 Total Aquatic Products	海水产品 Seawater Aquatic Products	天然生产 Naturally Grown	人工养殖 Artificially Cultured	鱼类 Fish	虾蟹类 Shrimps, Prawns and Crabs	贝类 Shell-fish	藻类 Algae	其他 Others
	1978	4653.5	3594.8	3145.2	449.5	2560.7	505.9	268.4	259.8	
	1979	4304.7	3188.8	2772.9	415.9	2312.6	408.3	217.6	250.4	
	1980	4497.0	3257.0	2812.7	444.3	2341.2	420.5	233.8	261.6	
	1981	4605.7	3232.3	2774.1	458.1	2317.4	418.0	269.2	227.7	
	1982	5155.1	3593.1	3098.4	494.7	2578.5	469.4	316.9	228.4	
	1983	5458.1	3617.4	3072.3	545.1	2514.2	490.9	367.4	244.9	
	1984	6193.4	3943.7	3305.2	638.5	2670.4	593.8	412.9	266.6	
	1985	7051.5	4197.5	3485.2	712.3	2745.3	706.2	473.0	273.0	
	1986	8235.6	4753.7	3896.1	857.6	3093.5	768.7	658.4	233.1	
	1987	9953.5	5481.6	4380.8	1100.8	3516.3	839.7	889.0	236.6	
	1988	10609.2	6057.0	4632.8	1424.1	3628.6	1033.0	1144.3	251.1	
	1989	11516.9	6612.1	5036.5	1575.6	3829.4	1057.2	1375.3	300.1	50.2
	1990	12370.2	7132.9	5508.9	1624.1	4231.5	1070.5	1473.3	275.2	82.5
	1991	13507.8	8001.0	6096.4	1904.6	4662.4	1193.6	1585.8	400.3	159.0
	1992	15571.2	9336.5	6912.3	2424.2	5176.2	1273.9	2043.6	568.2	274.6
	1993	18230.0	10760.4	7673.4	3087.0	5573.9	1386.6	2885.9	693.9	220.1
	1994	21432.3	12415.0	8958.3	3456.7	6473.7	1708.9	3236.4	745.2	250.8
	1995	25171.8	14391.3	10268.4	4122.9	7581.4	1848.3	3922.8	749.1	289.6
	1996	32880.9	20128.8	12489.8	7639.0	8235.2	2046.5	8526.8	929.1	391.3
	1997	36017.8	21764.2	13853.8	7910.4	9641.5	2257.1	8241.8	979.8	644.0
	1998	39065.1	23567.2	14966.8	8600.4	10559.7	2585.8	8700.7	1041.2	679.7
	1999	41224.1	24719.2	14976.2	9743.0	10579.1	2770.7	9592.8	1194.4	582.2
	2000	42784.8	25387.4	14774.5	10612.9	10329.9	2970.9	10386.7	1222.0	477.9
北 京	Beijing	75.0								
天 津	Tianjin	242.2	39.8	35.1	4.7	11.3	12.2	16.1		0.2
河 北	Hebei	809.5	482.0	327.4	154.7	187.9	80.7	184.6		28.8
山 西	Shanxi	26.0								
内蒙古	Inner Mongolia	72.1								
辽 宁	Liaoning	3384.6	3023.1	1501.9	1521.2	766.9	379.4	1383.4	350.2	143.2
吉 林	Jilin	140.1								
黑龙江	Heilongjiang	382.2								
上 海	Shanghai	288.7	122.3	120.2	2.1	67.3	21.5	31.5		2.1
江 苏	Jiangsu	3087.9	908.7	660.0	248.7	434.3	129.2	297.8	8.4	38.9
浙 江	Zhejiang	4695.1	4104.6	3395.7	708.8	2251.5	913.5	905.6	27.2	6.7
安 徽	Anhui	1598.0								
福 建	Fujian	5278.9	4705.1	2078.0	2627.1	1668.8	357.8	2318.4	317.8	42.2
江 西	Jiangxi	1271.2								
山 东	Shandong	6982.3	5951.1	3078.4	2872.7	2078.9	538.0	2777.9	458.8	97.4
河 南	Henan	321.7								
湖 北	Hubei	2343.4								
湖 南	Hunan	1332.1								
广 东	Guangdong	5931.9	3604.5	1914.8	1689.7	1685.7	307.6	1525.8	24.1	61.3
广 西	Guangxi	2398.6	1594.5	888.4	706.1	586.3	171.0	790.4		46.8
海 南	Hainan	830.6	675.9	598.9	77.0	513.3	57.8	59.1	35.4	10.4
重 庆	Chongqing	200.3								
四 川	Sichuan	513.1								
贵 州	Guizhou	62.4								
云 南	Yunnan	166.2								
西 藏	Tibet	1.8								
陕 西	Shaanxi	60.8								
甘 肃	Gansu	14.1								
青 海	Qinghai	1.2								
宁 夏	Ningxia	37.0								
新 疆	Xinjiang	60.1								
中国水产总公司	China Aquatic Company	175.8	175.8	175.8		77.6	2.2	96.0		

12−21 续表1 continued

单位：千吨 (1 000 tons)

年份 地区	Year Region	淡水产品 Freshwater Aquatic Products	天然生产 Naturally Grown	人工养殖 Artificially Cultured	鱼类 Fish	虾蟹类 Shrimps, Prawns and Crabs	贝类 Shell-fish	其他 Others
	1978	1058.7	296.4	762.3	997.0	38.1	23.5	
	1979	1115.9	302.6	813.3	1052.8	43.5	19.6	
	1980	1239.9	338.5	901.5	1163.3	51.6	25.0	
	1981	1373.5	359.4	1014.1	1289.8	51.3	32.4	
	1982	1562.0	354.8	1207.2	1479.0	56.5	26.5	
	1983	1840.8	412.6	1428.2	1758.3	56.2	26.3	
	1984	2249.7	438.6	1811.1	2167.9	51.9	29.8	
	1985	2854.1	476.3	2377.7	2764.8	55.4	33.9	
	1986	3481.9	537.9	2944.0	3363.8	62.1	56.1	
	1987	4071.9	599.5	3472.4	3938.0	80.5	53.3	
	1988	4552.2	654.4	3897.8	4408.5	84.7	59.0	
	1989	4904.8	734.5	4170.3	4727.6	95.4	72.9	9.0
	1990	5237.3	783.0	4454.2	5049.3	94.6	75.8	17.6
	1991	5506.8	914.9	4591.9	5303.8	107.3	85.3	10.4
	1992	6234.7	901.0	5333.7	5984.2	124.0	105.0	21.5
	1993	7469.6	1028.5	6441.1	7105.9	133.3	162.9	67.5
	1994	9017.3	1166.9	7850.4	8593.4	202.9	152.7	68.2
	1995	10780.5	1372.9	9407.6	10186.1	273.0	205.1	116.2
	1996	12752.2	1762.7	10989.5	11778.0	362.8	484.0	127.3
	1997	14253.5	1886.4	12367.1	13248.8	477.9	363.8	163.0
	1998	15497.9	2283.6	13214.3	14252.2	604.4	458.2	183.1
	1999	16504.9	2277.7	14227.1	15170.9	707.0	429.6	197.4
	2000	17397.5	2263.7	15133.8	15730.6	883.0	463.1	320.7
北京	Beijing	75.0		75.0	74.9	0.2		
天津	Tianjin	202.4	13.8	188.6	194.6	5.7	2.0	
河北	Hebei	327.5	70.6	256.9	306.5	15.1	3.8	2.0
山西	Shanxi	26.0	0.2	25.8	26.0			
内蒙古	Inner Mongolia	72.1	26.8	45.4	68.3	3.3		0.5
辽宁	Liaoning	361.5	31.5	330.0	332.4	22.0		7.0
吉林	Jilin	140.1	43.9	96.2	139.5	0.2	0.5	
黑龙江	Heilongjiang	382.2	57.6	324.5	380.5	1.6		
上海	Shanghai	166.4	7.4	159.0	141.2	22.2	1.0	1.9
江苏	Jiangsu	2179.2	296.9	1882.4	1775.2	315.0	33.6	55.4
浙江	Zhejiang	590.5	76.3	514.2	469.4	45.2	45.0	30.9
安徽	Anhui	1598.0	316.9	1281.1	1313.6	149.1	88.8	46.5
福建	Fujian	573.9	76.6	497.3	501.1	11.4	44.6	16.8
江西	Jiangxi	1271.2	232.5	1038.7	1164.2	36.7	53.0	17.3
山东	Shandong	1031.2	89.9	941.3	943.0	63.6	11.4	13.1
河南	Henan	321.7	19.4	302.3	310.8	6.6	1.1	3.2
湖北	Hubei	2343.4	412.2	1931.2	2206.6	74.9	47.1	14.7
湖南	Hunan	1332.1	150.4	1181.7	1273.4	20.9	23.6	14.3
广东	Guangdong	2327.3	135.2	2192.1	2120.4	64.9	74.8	67.3
广西	Guangxi	804.1	91.5	712.5	772.1	9.4	19.5	3.1
海南	Hainan	154.8	20.1	134.7	133.6	1.4	2.2	17.6
重庆	Chongqing	200.3	12.8	187.5	197.4	0.4	1.3	1.4
四川	Sichuan	513.1	38.1	475.0	505.8	1.3	1.2	4.8
贵州	Guizhou	62.4	8.0	54.4	61.7	0.5	0.1	0.1
云南	Yunnan	166.2	21.2	144.9	144.6	11.3	8.3	2.0
西藏	Tibet	1.8	0.1	1.7	1.8			
陕西	Shaanxi	60.8	3.2	57.6	60.5	0.2		0.1
甘肃	Gansu	14.1	0.6	13.4	14.1			
青海	Qinghai	1.2	0.1	1.1	1.2			
宁夏	Ningxia	37.0	0.6	36.4	36.9			
新疆	Xinjiang	60.1	9.2	50.9	59.4			0.6
中国水产总公司	China Aquatic Company							

12-22 农村居民家庭平均每人出售主要农产品

Per Capita Main Farm Produce Sold by Rural Households by Region

本表为农村住户抽样调查资料。

Data in this table are obtained from the sample surveys on rural households.

单位：公斤 (kg)

年 份 Year	地 区 Region	出售粮食 Sales of Grain	出售棉花 Sales of Cotton	出售油料 Sales of Oil-bearing Corps	出售麻类 Sales of Fiber Corps	出售烟叶 Sales of Tobacco	出售蔬菜 Sales of Vegetables	出售水果 Sales of Fruits
	1985	123.49	4.13	14.37	2.80	2.25	53.76	6.78
	1990	180.24	4.31	12.87	1.56	2.67	65.07	13.17
	1991	179.44	5.54	13.22	1.32	3.17	68.70	15.74
	1992	165.89	4.16	11.27	1.18	3.58	75.58	16.92
	1993	159.35	3.26	10.48	0.86	3.19	77.73	19.60
	1994	188.53	4.01	10.68	0.50	2.02	72.68	22.64
	1995	179.20	4.31	12.02	0.73	2.21	79.96	24.28
	1996	203.47	3.90	11.64	0.83	3.07	97.00	29.78
	1997	228.01	5.12	11.13	0.57	4.45	106.22	36.21
	1998	227.53	5.10	12.39	0.41	2.33	108.72	38.51
	1999	243.34	4.43	15.59	0.28	2.42	111.66	43.17
	2000	264.74	5.59	18.43	0.47	2.73	132.07	46.43
北 京	Beijing	160.89		1.17		0.06	146.30	208.06
天 津	Tianjin	192.50	12.20	1.77			501.48	37.96
河 北	Hebei	232.05	7.30	12.33	0.24	0.18	135.28	96.33
山 西	Shanxi	121.95	1.95	6.28	0.06	0.38	144.68	115.40
内蒙古	Inner Mongolia	626.69		87.99	0.32	0.52	106.70	4.15
辽 宁	Liaoning	689.87	0.11	12.11		1.70	199.72	72.25
吉 林	Jilin	1345.30		6.10	0.04	1.01	125.34	6.06
黑龙江	Heilongjiang	1373.84		8.59	4.02	4.71	202.44	2.44
上 海	Shanghai	140.67	0.03	29.47			161.68	37.40
江 苏	Jiangsu	311.57	6.95	23.16	0.04		59.63	12.84
浙 江	Zhejiang	102.63	0.94	8.30			195.30	86.67
安 徽	Anhui	319.00	5.50	42.19	0.09	0.41	68.54	2.18
福 建	Fujian	64.19		2.20		5.68	127.14	78.26
江 西	Jiangxi	216.60	2.38	8.66	0.06	1.43	61.18	8.66
山 东	Shandong	315.19	7.45	24.40	0.12	1.37	306.16	89.57
河 南	Henan	272.67	7.28	35.60	1.81	2.11	95.93	34.60
湖 北	Hubei	299.21	10.75	50.11	1.38	2.98	118.99	55.43
湖 南	Hunan	111.59	2.92	9.26	0.52	5.01	72.03	33.37
广 东	Guangdong	86.36		4.42		2.03	255.31	24.20
广 西	Guangxi	72.24		3.84	0.86	0.95	90.54	35.07
海 南	Hainan	74.67		11.04	0.35		255.82	60.38
重 庆	Chongqing	58.33	0.04	4.43	0.33	1.94	65.96	17.40
四 川	Sichuan	76.50	0.27	14.05	0.15	1.89	113.27	20.23
贵 州	Guizhou	77.12		15.07		14.19	52.58	3.15
云 南	Yunnan	93.23		5.97		21.11	95.95	21.44
西 藏	Tibet	47.34		3.21			6.47	0.86
陕 西	Shaanxi	144.56	1.26	7.43	0.05	1.15	99.45	172.63
甘 肃	Gansu	96.96	8.29	3.44		1.01	81.56	20.87
青 海	Qinghai	44.43		38.21			34.50	9.36
宁 夏	Ningxia	381.95		4.99			164.20	18.22
新 疆	Xinjiang	316.30	89.09	36.52	1.69		208.37	85.98

12-23 农村居民家庭平均每人出售主要牧业产品及水产品

Sales of Livestock, Poultry, Small Animals and Fishery Per Capita Rural Household

本表为农村住户抽样调查资料。

Data in this table are obtained from the sample surveys on rural households.

年份 Year	地区 Region	猪肉 (公斤) Pork (kg)	牛肉 (公斤) Beef (kg)	羊肉 (公斤) Mutton (kg)	家禽 (公斤) Poultry (kg)	蛋类 (公斤) Poultry Eggs (kg)	羊毛 (公斤) Wool (kg)	牛羊奶 (公斤) Milk (kg)	蚕茧 (公斤) Silkworm Cocoons (kg)	蜂蜜 (公斤) Honey (kg)	水产品 (公斤) Aquatic Products (kg)
	1985	16.27	0.52	0.57	1.00	2.21	0.18	1.02	0.36	0.05	1.74
	1990	17.84	0.55	0.71	1.45	1.89	0.20	1.68	0.58	0.04	2.05
	1991	20.07	0.76	0.90	2.18	2.65	0.16	1.91	0.65	0.04	2.92
	1992	21.17	0.72	0.86	2.23	2.90	0.15	1.85	0.70	0.03	3.21
	1993	23.80			2.41	2.89	0.15	1.76	0.74	0.03	3.10
	1994				2.30	3.35	0.15	1.81	0.83	0.02	2.97
	1995				2.42	3.54	0.17	1.90	0.79	0.03	2.94
	1996				2.45	2.58	0.23	2.55	0.50	0.02	3.27
	1997	26.08	2.33	1.76	2.99	3.76	0.23	2.76	0.54	0.02	4.50
	1998	23.04	1.04	1.67	2.42	3.57	0.18	2.60	0.65	0.02	4.31
	1999	28.41	1.86	1.85	3.41	4.07	0.17	3.00	0.62	0.03	6.20
	2000	30.19	2.40	2.06	4.60	6.32	0.25	2.67	0.64	0.04	5.82
北京	Beijing	14.93	0.47	2.21	17.38	4.64	0.04				13.95
天津	Tianjin	61.66	1.18	0.14	5.08	25.91					8.12
河北	Hebei	20.27	2.32	1.09	4.35	18.05	0.04	2.96		0.09	2.43
山西	Shanxi	14.42	1.88	2.17	1.06	9.38	0.10	3.31	0.21	0.06	
内蒙古	Inner Mongolia	20.74	11.63	19.45	0.47	0.57	5.28	9.74			
辽宁	Liaoning	54.91	3.40	1.33	8.56	14.09	0.07	1.93	1.85	0.08	19.27
吉林	Jilin	29.20	5.95	0.59	4.01	3.44	0.25	0.16		0.34	0.17
黑龙江	Heilongjiang	29.74	2.79	0.52	5.99	8.60	0.26	7.11		0.07	1.08
上海	Shanghai	12.93		0.67	2.40	4.51					7.71
江苏	Jiangsu	33.85	0.33	1.03	9.17	10.35		1.04	1.66		11.21
浙江	Zhejiang	25.42	0.14	0.62	4.51	8.00	0.01	3.41	5.37	0.30	7.99
安徽	Anhui	27.18	3.93	0.78	3.49	3.40			0.98	0.04	1.61
福建	Fujian	32.18	0.59	0.15	10.62	13.38		0.48	0.00	0.01	10.70
江西	Jiangxi	40.57	0.31	0.02	1.77	1.57		0.10	0.23	0.01	6.59
山东	Shandong	36.85	5.81	2.15	13.04	12.55	0.01	3.89	0.81		1.58
河南	Henan	29.92	3.14	1.78	3.13	7.42	0.01		0.03	0.01	3.23
湖北	Hubei	28.40	0.90	0.15	1.87	5.54			0.22	0.01	12.24
湖南	Hunan	50.26	0.33	0.33	3.17	1.84					6.34
广东	Guangdong	31.57	0.44	0.01	10.53	0.36		0.02	0.73	0.09	34.14
广西	Guangxi	51.62	1.46	0.53	4.96	0.25			0.81	0.04	4.90
海南	Hainan	26.43	4.48	0.79	4.33	0.13				0.02	17.25
重庆	Chongqing	41.78	0.98	0.18	4.80	2.10		0.01	2.15	0.03	4.38
四川	Sichuan	45.76	0.61	0.78	4.42	5.88			1.32	0.02	1.91
贵州	Guizhou	27.70	1.69	0.82	1.98	1.04	0.01		0.03		0.11
云南	Yunnan	28.33	2.16	0.87	1.33	0.52		3.34	0.46		0.25
西藏	Tibet	1.07	3.00	1.11	0.07	0.10	0.30	0.28		0.01	0.02
陕西	Shaanxi	17.35	0.34	1.37	0.93	9.30	0.05	7.83	0.35		0.23
甘肃	Gansu	9.35	1.92	1.45	0.63	3.71	0.31	0.42		0.07	
青海	Qinghai	4.31	5.21	18.54	0.15	0.26	4.00	3.85		0.01	6.65
宁夏	Ningxia	16.70	2.63	6.70	5.12	14.74	0.49	87.71			6.36
新疆	Xinjiang	1.85	8.35	14.17	1.40	3.99	0.34	4.00	0.17	0.01	

注：1992年以前蛋类不包括蛋制品；1992年以前水产品出售量是指鱼虾出售量。

a)Sales of poultry eggs before 1992 exclude egg product. Sales of aquatic products before 1992 refereed to the sales of fish and shrimp.

12-24 农村居民家庭平均每人出售主要农产品

Per Capita Main Farm Produce Sold by Rural Households by Region

本表为农村住户抽样调查资料。

Data in this table are obtained from the sample surveys on rural households.

单位：公斤 (kg)

年份 Year	地区 Region	出售粮食 Sales of Grain	出售棉花 Sales of Cotton	出售油料 Sales of Oil-bearing Corps	出售麻类 Sales of Fiber Corps	出售烟叶 Sales of Tobacco	出售蔬菜 Sales of Vegetables	出售水果 Sales of Fruits
1985		123.49	4.13	14.37	2.80	2.25	53.76	6.78
1990		180.24	4.31	12.87	1.56	2.67	65.07	13.17
1991		179.44	5.54	13.22	1.32	3.17	68.70	15.74
1992		165.89	4.16	11.27	1.18	3.58	75.58	16.92
1993		159.35	3.26	10.48	0.86	3.19	77.73	19.60
1994		188.53	4.01	10.68	0.50	2.02	72.68	22.64
1995		179.20	4.31	12.02	0.73	2.21	79.96	24.28
1996		203.47	3.90	11.64	0.83	3.07	97.00	29.78
1997		228.01	5.12	11.13	0.57	4.45	106.22	36.21
1998		227.53	5.10	12.39	0.41	2.33	108.72	38.51
1999		243.34	4.43	15.59	0.28	2.42	111.66	43.17
2000		264.74	5.59	18.43	0.47	2.73	132.07	46.43
北京	Beijing	160.89		1.17		0.06	146.30	208.06
天津	Tianjin	192.50	12.20	1.77			501.48	37.96
河北	Hebei	232.05	7.30	12.33	0.24	0.18	135.28	96.33
山西	Shanxi	121.95	1.95	6.28	0.06	0.38	144.68	115.40
内蒙古	Inner Mongolia	626.69		87.99	0.32	0.52	106.70	4.15
辽宁	Liaoning	689.87	0.11	12.11		1.70	199.72	72.25
吉林	Jilin	1345.30		6.10	0.04	1.01	125.34	6.06
黑龙江	Heilongjiang	1373.84		8.59	4.02	4.71	202.44	2.44
上海	Shanghai	140.67	0.03	29.47			161.68	37.40
江苏	Jiangsu	311.57	6.95	23.16	0.04		59.63	12.84
浙江	Zhejiang	102.63	0.94	8.30			195.30	86.67
安徽	Anhui	319.00	5.50	42.19	0.09	0.41	68.54	2.18
福建	Fujian	64.19		2.20		5.68	127.14	78.26
江西	Jiangxi	216.60	2.38	8.66	0.06	1.43	61.18	8.66
山东	Shandong	315.19	7.45	24.40	0.12	1.37	306.16	89.57
河南	Henan	272.67	7.28	35.60	1.81	2.11	95.93	34.60
湖北	Hubei	299.21	10.75	50.11	1.38	2.98	118.99	55.43
湖南	Hunan	111.59	2.92	9.26	0.52	5.01	72.03	33.37
广东	Guangdong	86.36		4.42		2.03	255.31	24.20
广西	Guangxi	72.24		3.84	0.86	0.95	90.54	35.07
海南	Hainan	74.67		11.04	0.35		255.82	60.38
重庆	Chongqing	58.33	0.04	4.43	0.33	1.94	65.96	17.40
四川	Sichuan	76.50	0.27	14.05	0.15	1.89	113.27	20.23
贵州	Guizhou	77.12		15.07		14.19	52.58	3.15
云南	Yunnan	93.23		5.97		21.11	95.95	21.44
西藏	Tibet	47.34		3.21			6.47	0.86
陕西	Shaanxi	144.56	1.26	7.43	0.05	1.15	99.45	172.63
甘肃	Gansu	96.96	8.29	3.44		1.01	81.56	20.87
青海	Qinghai	44.43		38.21			34.50	9.36
宁夏	Ningxia	381.95		4.99			164.20	18.22
新疆	Xinjiang	316.30	89.09	36.52	1.69		208.37	85.98

12-25 主要农产品产量与解放前最高年产量比较
Output of Major Agricultural Products in Comparison with Peak Year Prior to 1949

产品名称	Item	解放前最高年 Peak Year prior to 1949		指数（以解放前最高年为100） Indices(peak year prior to 1949=100)		
		年份 Year	产量 Output	1949	1952	2000
种植业　（万吨）	**Planting　(10 000 tons)**					
粮　食	Grain	1936	15000	75.45	109.28	308.12
#稻　谷	Rice	1936	5735	84.83	119.32	327.65
小　麦	Wheat	1936	2330	59.27	77.81	427.62
玉　米	Corn	1936	1010		166.83	1049.50
大　豆	Soybeans	1936	1130	45.04	84.25	136.36
薯　类	Tubers	1936	635	155.12	257.17	580.35
棉　花	Cotton	1936	84.9	52.3	153.59	520.26
花　生	Peanuts	1933	317.1	39.99	73.04	455.28
油菜籽	Rapeseeds	1934	190.7	38.49	48.87	596.80
芝　麻	Sesame	1933	99.1	32.9	48.54	81.84
黄红麻	Jute and Ambary Hemp	1945	5.5	34.55	278.18	229.09
桑蚕茧	Mulberry Silkworm Cocoons	1931	22.1	14.03	28.05	226.24
茶　叶	Tea	1932	22.5	18.22	36.44	303.56
甘　蔗	Sugarcane	1940	565.2	46.74	125.9	677.28
甜　菜	Beetroots	1939	32.9	58.05	145.59	2452.89
烤　烟	Flue-cured Tobacco	1948	17.9	24.02	124.02	1250.28
苹　果	Apples	1926	12.1		97.52	16885.12
柑　桔	Citrus	1926	40.1		51.62	2190.27
香　蕉	Bananas	1927	10.3		106.8	4797.09
畜牧业（万头.只）	**Animal Husbandry (10 000 head)**					
大牲畜年底头数	Large Animals (year-end)	1935	7151	83.93	106.92	211.88
牛	Cattle and Buffaloes	1935	4827	91.02	117.26	266.55
马	Horses	1935	649	75.12	94.45	135.07
驴	Donkeys	1935	1215	78.14	97.17	75.94
骡	Mules	1935	460	31.98	35.59	98.48
猪年底头数	Hogs (year-end)	1934	7853	73.54	114.31	568.97
羊年底只数	Sheep and Goats (year-end)	1937	6252	67.74	98.82	464.36
渔　业						
水产品　（万吨）	Aquatic Products (10 000 tons)	1936	150	30	111.33	2852.33

12−26 受灾面积和成灾面积

Areas Covered and Affected by Natural Disaster

单位：千公顷 (1 000 hectares)

年份 Year	地区 Region	受灾面积 Areas Covered	成灾面积 Areas Affected	成灾面积占受灾面积% Percentage of Disaster Areas Affected to Areas Covered	水灾 Flood 受灾面积 Areas Covered	水灾 Flood 成灾面积 Areas Affected	旱灾 Drought 受灾面积 Areas Covered	旱灾 Drought 成灾面积 Areas Affected
1978		50790	24457	48.2	2850	2012	40170	17970
1979		39370	15120	38.4	6760	2870	24650	9320
1980		44526	29777	66.9	9146	6070	26111	14174
1981		39786	18743	47.1	8625	3973	25693	12134
1982		33133	15985	48.2	8361	4397	20697	9972
1983		34713	16209	46.7	12162	5747	16089	7586
1984		31887	15607	48.9	10632	5395	15819	7015
1985		44365	22705	51.2	14197	8949	22989	10063
1986		47135	23656	50.2	9155	5601	31042	14765
1987		42086	20393	48.5	8686	4104	24920	13033
1988		50874	23945	47.1	11949	6128	32904	15303
1989		46991	22449	52.0	11328	5917	29358	15262
1990		38474	17819	46.3	11804	5605	18175	7805
1991		55472	27814	50.1	24596	14614	29414	10559
1992		51333	25859	50.4	9423	4464	32980	17049
1993		48829	23133	47.4	16387	8611	21098	8657
1994		55043	31383	57.0	17329	10744	30425	17049
1995		45821	22267	48.6	12731	7630	23455	10401
1996		46989	21233	45.2	18146	10855	20151	6247
1997		53429	30309	56.7	11414	5840	33514	20250
1998		50145	25181	50.2	22292	13785	14236	5060
1999		49981	26731	53.5	9020	5071	30156	16614
2000		54688	34374	62.9	7323	4321	40541	26784
北京	Beijing	204	89	43.6	14	1	170	78
天津	Tianjin	310	185	59.7	0		300	180
河北	Hebei	2710	1855	68.5	220	135	2390	1640
山西	Shanxi	2455	1616	65.8	45	32	2320	1546
内蒙古	Inner Mongolia	3397	2345	69.0	77	63	3160	2200
辽宁	Liaoning	2831	1885	66.6	5	2	2786	1860
吉林	Jilin	3245	2584	79.6	53	37	3102	2490
黑龙江	Heilongjiang	3483	2299	66.0	30	20	3393	2239
上海	Shanghai	18	13	72.2				
江苏	Jiangsu	3177	2062	64.9	80	36	1901	1360
浙江	Zhejiang	787	416	52.9	41	30	98	66
安徽	Anhui	3502	2499	71.4	373	190	2990	2250
福建	Fujian	502	328	65.3	215	125	72	40
江西	Jiangxi	1416	1008	71.2	290	172	820	627
山东	Shandong	3697	2271	61.4	120	73	3336	2106
河南	Henan	4608	2646	57.4	1940	1257	2398	1320
湖北	Hubei	3190	1996	62.6	582	365	2210	1470
湖南	Hunan	1551	687	44.3	334	161	930	400
广东	Guangdong	688	313	45.5	175	61	100	80
广西	Guangxi	1523	836	54.9	234	150	1004	541
海南	Hainan	541	264	48.8	297	132		
重庆	Chongqing	708	434	61.3	361	202	270	190
四川	Sichuan	2315	1127	48.7	513	293	1637	763
贵州	Guizhou	1020	504	49.4	505	290	216	160
云南	Yunnan	941	470	49.9	375	204	206	113
西藏	Tibet	32	15	46.9	28	13		
陕西	Shaanxi	1908	1242	65.1	198	116	1654	1110
甘肃	Gansu	2319	1311	56.5	144	106	1855	1105
青海	Qinghai	444	345	77.7	25	19	404	313
宁夏	Ningxia	526	370	70.3	27	22	450	320
新疆	Xinjiang	640	359	56.1	22	14	369	217

12-27 国营农场基本情况

Basic Statistics on State Farms

本表为农垦系统数据。

Data in this table cover those of the land reclamation department.

指标	Item	1998	1999	2000
农场数 (个)	**Number of Farms**	**2101**	**2051**	**2026**
职工人数 (万人)	**Number of Staff and Workers (10 000 persons)**	**437.5**	**417.7**	**391.9**
耕地面积 (万公顷)	**Cultivated Area (10 000 hectares)**	**4816.7**	**4835.8**	**4801.0**
农业机械总动力 (亿瓦)	**Total Power of Agricultural Machinery (100 million watts)**	**112.7**	**114.0**	**115.9**
农业机械拥有量 (台.辆)	**Ownership of Agricultural Machinery (unit)**			
大中型农用拖拉机	Large and Medium Agricultural Tractors	63044	65566	66562
小型及手扶拖拉机	Mini and Walking Agricultural Tractors	194616	208000	214000
农用排灌动力机械	Machinery for Agricultural Drainage and Irrigation	126009	132000	139000
联合收割机	Combine Harvesters	14544	14000	15000
农用载重汽车	Trucks for Agricultural Use	16226	14177	12524
农用化肥施用量 (万吨)	**Consumption of Chemical Fertilizers(10 000 tons)**	**131.1**	**125.5**	**131.7**
农业总产值 (亿元)	**Gross Agricultural Output Value (100 million yuan)**	**680.7**	**633.2**	**644.0**
农作物总播种面积 (千公顷)	**Sown Area of Farm Crops (1 000 hectares)**	**4885.6**	**4858.1**	**4755.8**
粮食作物	Grain	3439.9	3376.1	3163.9
棉花	Cotton	510.0	490.5	527.3
油料	Oil-bearing Crops	304.2	415.5	461.2
糖料	Sugar Crops	195.1	146.1	103.6
麻类	Fiber Crops	1.3	2.2	9.4
年底实有茶园面积	Area of Tea Plantations (year-end)	36.9	34.9	34.1
年底实有桑园面积	Area of Mulberry Plantations (year-end)	1.8	1.2	3.9
年底实有果园面积	Area of Orchards (year-end)	175.4	182.6	193.6
年底实有橡胶园面积	Area of Rubber Plantations (year-end)	380.9	384.4	382.3
主要农产品产量	**Yield of Major Farm Crops**			
粮食作物 (万吨)	Grain (10 000 tons)	1645.9	1697.2	1465.2
棉花 (万吨)	Cotton (10 000 tons)	72.1	73.4	97.1
油料 (万吨)	Oil-bearing Crops (10 000 tons)	46.5	64.1	45.7
糖料 (万吨)	Sugar Crops (10 000 tons)	995.7	808.7	589.5
麻类 (万吨)	Fiber Crops (10 000 tons)	0.6	0.7	2.9
茶叶 (万吨)	Tea (10 000 tons)	4.4	4.1	3.9
桑蚕茧 (吨)	Mulberry Silkworm Cocoons (ton)			
水果 (万吨)	Fruits (10 000 tons)	100.4	122.3	118.6
干胶 (万吨)	Rubber (10 000 tons)	34.7	36.3	34.7
畜牧业、渔业生产	**Production of Animal Husbandry and Fishery**			
大牲畜年底头数 (万头)	Number of Large Animals(year-end) (10 000 heads)	240.6	223.8	214.6
猪年底头数 (万头)	Number of Hogs (10 000 heads)	482.8	478.9	478.1
羊年底只数 (万只)	Number of Sheep and Goats (10 000 heads)	1069.2	1094.5	1104.7
#绵羊	Sheep	865.7	887.9	888.4
畜产品产量 (万吨)	**Output of Livestock Products (10 000 tons)**			
猪牛羊肉产量	Pork, Beef and Mutton	65.6	66.3	68.3
#猪肉	Pork	50.0	49.1	51.4
牛奶	Milk	113.1	108.8	116.5
禽蛋	Poultry Eggs	23.2	21.4	20.4
羊毛	Sheep Wool	2.1	3.0	2.1
水产品总产量 (万吨)	**Total output of Aquatic Products (10 000 tons)**	**47.8**	**49.7**	**49.1**

主要统计指标解释

农林牧渔业总产值 指以货币表现的农、林、牧、渔业全部产品的总量，它反映一定时期内农业生产总规模和总成果。农业总产值的计算方法通常是按农林牧渔业产品及其副产品的产量分别乘以各自单位产品价格求得；少数生产周期较长，当年没有产品或产品产量不易统计的，则采用间接方法匡算其产值；然后将四业产品产值相加即为农业总产值。1957年以前的农业总产值中包括了厩肥和农民自给性手工业（如农民自制衣服、鞋、袜，自己从事粮食初步加工等）。1958年及以后的农业总产值，林业中增加了村及村以下竹木采伐产值；牧业中取消了厩肥产值；副业中取消了农民自给性手工业产值，增加了村及村以下办的工业产值；渔业中增加了海洋捕捞水产品产值。1980年及以后的农业总产值，在副业中增加了农民家庭兼营工业商品部分的产值。从1984年起村及村以下工业产值划归工业。从1993年起取消副业，将野生动物的捕猎划入牧业、野生植物采集和农民家庭兼营商品性工业划归农业。1996年第一次农业普查以后；由于畜牧业产品年报数据与普查数据之间存在一定的差距，国家统计局农调总队对畜牧业年报数据与普查数据进行衔接，相应的畜牧业产值进行调整。

粮食产量 指全社会的产量。包括国有经济经营的、集体统一经营的和农民家庭经营的粮食产量，还包括工矿企业办的农场和其他生产单位的产量。粮食除包括稻谷、小麦、玉米、高粱、谷子及其他杂粮外，还包括薯类和豆类。其产量计算方法，豆类按去豆荚后的干豆计算；薯类(包括甘薯和马铃薯，不包括芋头和木薯)1963年以前按每4公斤鲜薯折1公斤粮食计算，从1964年开始改为按5公斤鲜薯折1公斤粮食计算。城市郊区作为蔬菜的薯类(如马铃薯等)按鲜品计算，并且不作粮食统计。其他粮食一律按脱粒后的原粮计算。

油料产量 指全部油料作物的生产量。包括花生、油菜籽、芝麻、向日葵籽、胡麻籽（亚麻籽）和其他油料。不包括大豆、木本油料和野生油料。花生以带壳干花生计算。

水产品产量 指人工养殖的水产品和天然生长的水产品的捕捞量。包括海水的鱼类、虾蟹类、贝类和藻类以及内陆水域的鱼类、虾蟹类和贝类，不包括淡水生植物。

猪、牛、羊肉产量 指当年出栏并已屠宰、除去头蹄下水后带骨肉(即胴体重)的重量。

期初(末)畜禽存栏头(只)数 指报告期初(末)农村各种合作经济组织和国营农场、农民个人、机关、团体、学校、工矿企业、部队等单位以及城镇居民饲养的大牲畜、猪、羊、家禽等畜禽的存栏数。

耕地面积 指可以用来种植农作物、经常进行耕锄的田地，包括熟地、当年新开荒地、连续撂荒未满三年的耕地和当年的休闲地(轮歇地)，还包括以种植农作物为主并附带种植桑树、茶树、果树和其他林木的土地，以及沿海、沿湖地区已围垦利用的“海涂”、“湖田”等面积。不包括属于专业性的桑园、茶园、果园、果木苗圃、林地、芦苇地、天然或人工草地面积。南方小于一米、北方小于两米宽的渠、路、田埂，包括在耕地中。

农作物播种面积 指实际播种或移植有农作物的面积。凡是实际种植有农作物的面积，不论种植在耕地上还是种植在非耕地上，均包括在农作物播种面积中。在播种季节基本结束后，因遭灾而重新改种和补种的农作物面积，也包括在内。

有效灌溉面积 指具有一定的水源，地块比较平整，灌溉工程或设备已经配套，在一般年景下当年能够进行正常灌溉的耕地面积。在一般情况下，有效灌溉面积应等于灌溉工程或设备已经配备，能够进行正常灌溉的水田和水浇地面积之和。

农用化肥施用量 指本年内实际用于农业生产的化肥数量，包括氮肥、磷肥、钾肥和复合肥。化肥施用量要求按折纯量计算数量。折纯量是指把氮肥、磷肥、钾肥分别按含氮、含五氧化二磷、含氧化钾的百分之一百成份进行折算后的数量。复合肥按其所含主要成分折算。

农业机械总动力 指主要用于农、林、牧、渔业的各种动力机械的动力总和。包括耕作机械、排灌机械、收获机械、农用运输机械、植物保护机械、牧业机械、林业机械、渔业机械和其他农业机械〔内燃机按引擎马力折成瓦(特)计算、电动机按功率折成瓦(特)计算〕。不包括专门用于乡、镇、村、组办工业、基本建设、非农业运输、科学试验和教学等非农业生产方面用的动力机械与作业机械。

农林牧渔业劳动力 指全社会直接参加农林牧渔业生产活动的劳动力。

Explanatory Notes on Main Statistical Indicators

Gross Output Value of Farming, Forestry, Animal Husbandry and Fishery refers to the total value of products of farming, forestry, animal husbandry and fishery, which reflects the total scale and result of agricultural production during a given period. Gross output value of agriculture is obtained by first multiplying the output of each product or by product by its price, resulting in the output value of each single item. For a small number of products, annual output of which is not available or difficult to get due to the long production growing process involved, the output value is estimated through an indirect approach. The sum of output value of all products of farming, forestry, animal husbandry, and fishery is then equal to the gross output value of agriculture. Prior to 1957, Chinas gross agricultural output value included barnyard manure and handicraft products for self consumption (clothes, shoes, stockings, and initial grain processing undertaken by peasants). Since 1958, cutting and felling of bamboo and trees by villages and other cooperative organizations under villages have been included in forestry; value of barnyard manure has been excluded from animal husbandry; self consumed handicrafts has been excluded from sideline occupations, while the output value of industries run by villages and cooperative organizations under village had been included in sideline occupations and the output value of fish catches by motor fishing boats has been added to fishery. Since 1980, the value of handicraft products made for sale by individuals in households had been added to sideline occupations. Since 1984, industries run by villages and under villages have been included in the sector of industry. Since 1993, the subdivision of sideline occupations has been canceled, and the hunting of wild animals has been classified into animal husbandry, and the gathering of wild plants and commodity industry run by rural household have been included in farming. The first agriculture census of China in 1996 revealed some discrepancy between the production of animal products from the annual reports and that from the census. Efforts were made by the Rural Socio-economic Survey Organization of NBS to adjust the output value of animal husbandry to make the figures from the annual reports consistent with the census data.

Grain Yield refers to the yield in the whole country including grains produced by state farms, collective units, industrial enterprises and mines. Grain includes rice, wheat, corn, sorghum, millet and other miscellaneous grains as well as tubers and beans. Output of beans refers to dry beans without pods. The output of tubers (sweet potatoes and potatoes, not including taros and cassava) was converted into that of grain at the ratio 4:1, i.e. 4 kilograms of fresh tubers was equivalent to 1 kilogram of grain up to 1963. Since 1964 the ratio for conversion has been 5:1. Tubers supplied as vegetables (such as potatoes) in cities and suburbs are calculated as fresh vegetables and their output is not included in the output of grain. Output of all other grains refers to husked grain.

Yield of Oil-bearing Crops refers to the total yield of oil bearing crops of various kinds, including peanuts, (dry, in shell) rapeseeds, sesame, sunflower seeds, flax seeds, and other oil bearing crops. Soybeans, oil-bearing woody plants, and wild oil-bearing crops are not included.

Output of Aquatic Products refers to catches of both artificially cultured and naturally grown aquatic products, including fish, shrimps, crabs and shellfish in sea and inland water as well as seaweed. Freshwater plants are not included.

Output of Pork, Beef, and Mutton refers to the meat of slaughtered hogs, cattle, sheep and goats with head, feet, and offal taken away.

Number of Livestock or Poultry in Stock at Beginning (or End) refers to the total number of large animals, pigs, sheep, fowls, etc. raised by rural cooperative organizations, state farms, rural individuals, government agencies, schools, industrial and mining enterprises, army, and urban residents at the beginning (or end) of the reference period.

Cultivated Area (Area under cultivation) refers to farmland which is plowed constantly for growing crops, including cultivated land, newly cultivated land in the current year, farmland left without cultivation for less than three years and fallow land in the current year, rotation land, rotation land of grass and crops, farmland with some fruit trees, mulberry trees and other trees and cultivated seashore land, lake land, and etc. The land of mulberry fields, tea plantations, orchards, nurseries of young plants, forest land, reed land, natural and man-made grassland and other land are not included in cultivated land. Ditches, roads and ridges between cultivated fields that are less than 1 meter in width in the south or less than 2 meters in width in the north are included in the cultivated land.

Sown Area of Crops refers to area of land sown or transplanted with crops regardless of being in cultivated area or non cultivated area. Area of land re-sown due to natural disasters is also included.

Irrigated Area refers to areas that are effectively irrigated, i.e. level land which has water source and complete sets of irrigation facilities to lift and move adequate water for irrigation purpose under normal conditions. Under normal conditions, irrigated area is the sum of watered fields and irrigated fields where irrigation systems or equipment have been installed for regular irrigation purpose.

Consumption of Chemical Fertilizers in Agriculture refers to the quantity of chemical fertilizers applied in agriculture in the year, including nitrogenous fertilizer, phosphate fertilizer, potash fertilizer, and compound fertilizer. The consumption of chemical fertilizers is required in calculation to convert the gross weight into weight containing 100% effective component (e.g. 100% nitrogen content in nitrogenous fertilizer, 100% phosphorous pentoxide contents in phosphate fertilizer, 100% potassium oxide contents in potash fertilizer). Compound fertilizer is converted with its major component.

Total Power of Farm Machinery refers to total mechanical power of machinery used in farming, forestry, animal husbandry, and fishery, including ploughing, irrigation and drainage, harvesting, transport, plant protection, stock breeding, forestry and fishery. The power of internal combustion engines is required to convert horsepower into watts and the power of electric motors is required to be converted into watts. Machinery employed for non agricultural purposes, such as the machines used in township run and village-run industry, construction, non agricultural transport, scientific experiments and teaching, is excluded.

Labour Force Engaged in Farming, Forestry, Animal Husbandry and Fishery refers to the total laborers who are directly engaged in production of farming, forestry, animal husbandry and fishery.

十三、工业

Industry

简要说明

一、本篇主要包括以下几部分汇总资料：

1.全部国有及规模以上非国有工业企业单位数和工业总产值；

2.全部国有及规模以上非国有(规模以上非国有指年产品销售收入在500万元以上的非国有企业)工业企业按地区和行业分组的主要经济指标和经济效益指标，主要包括工业总产值、工业增加值、实收资本、资产合计、负债合计、流动资产、固定资产、流动负债、长期负债、所有者权益、产品销售收入、销售成本、销售税金及附加、销售利润、利润总额、应交增值税、工业增加值率、总资产贡献率、资产负债率、成本费用利润率、流动资产周转次数、全员劳动生产率、产品销售率；

3.国有及国有控股工业企业按地区和行业分组的主要经济指标和经济效益指标；

4."三资"工业企业按地区和行业分组的主要经济指标和经济效益指标；

5.大中型工业企业按地区和行业分组的主要经济指标和经济效益指标；

6.主要工业产品产量；

7.重点工业企业主要产品生产能力；

8.各行业主要经济指标占全国比重(1998-2000年)。

二、资料来源：资料由国家统计局工业交通司整理提供。

三、1991-1994年全部工业按各种经济类型分的总产值及指数，根据1995年第三次工业普查数据作了相应调整，与以往年鉴数据有所不同。

四、1998年工业统计范围改为全部国有企业及年产品销售收入500万元以上企业，因此，工业产品产量数据不能按全社会口径范围进行统计。考虑到与历年统计公报、统计年鉴数据相衔接，主要产品产量全国总计是参照上年全社会产量数据和按新统计范围统计的产量情况，并通过与有关部门数据核实，将这些产品调整到全社会口径范围，从而形成分地区数据之和小于全国总计的情况。另外，个别产品由于企业兼并、重组，出现了许多跨地区企业集团，造成重复上报。全国总计中将重复因素进行了扣除，造成分地区数据之和大于总计的情况。

Brief Introduction

I. Data in this chapter cover the following data:

(1) The number of industrial enterprises, the gross industrial output value and its indexes of all state-owned industrial enterprises and the non-state enterprises that are above designated size;

(2) Main economic indicators and efficiency indicators of all state-owned industrial enterprises, and of non-state enterprises above designated size (referring to enterprises each with an annual sales of over 5 million yuan), classified by region and by industrial division, including gross industrial output value, industrial value-added, total capital hold, total assets, total liabilities, working capital (circulating assets), fixed assets, liquid liabilities, long-term liabilities, creditors' equity, sales income, sales cost, sales tax and extra-charges, sales profit, total profits, value-added tax payable, ratio of value-added to gross industrial output value, ratio of profits, taxes and interests to average assets, ratio of debts to assets, ratio of profits to cost and charges, turnover of working capital and overall labour productivity, proportion of products sold;

(3) Main economic indicators and efficiency indicators of the state-owned industrial enterprises and enterprises where the state holds the majority of shares, classified by region and by industrial division ;

(4) Major indicators of foreign-funded industrial enterprises by region and by branch of industry;

(5) Major indicators of large and medium scale industrial enterprises by region and by branch of industry;

(6) Output of key industrial products;

(7) Production capacity of main products by key industrial enterprises;

(8) Proportion of economic indicators by branch of industry in national total (1998-2000).

II. Data sources: All data are prepared and provided by the Department of Industrial and Transport Statistics, NBS.

III. Data on the gross output value of all industrial enterprises and the indices by ownership in 1991-1994 have been adjusted in accordance with data from the Third National Industrial Census undertaken in 1995. Such data are therefore somewhat different from those published in the yearbooks of the previous years.

IV. As the coverage of industrial statistics was adjusted in 1998 to cover all state-owned industrial enterprises and enterprises with an annual sales of over 5 million yuan, it is impossible to collect statistics on the output of industrial products of all enterprises. In order to make such statistics comparable with data published in previous statistical communiqués and statistical yearbooks, efforts were made to estimate the national total of output of key industrial products by analyzing national totals of the previous years (with the old coverage) and data collected by new coverage and by verification of figures by relevant departments. As this process was done only at the national level, the result is that the sum of output data by province is smaller than the national totals. On the other hand, a large number of trans-regional enterprise groups were established through the merge and re-organization of enterprises, resulting in duplicated reports of the output of selected products. For such products, there are cases where the sum of output by province is larger than the national total.

13-1 全部国有及规模以上非国有工业企业单位数和总产值

Number of All State-owned and Non-state-owned above Designated Size Industrial Enterprises and Their Gross Output Value

指　标	Item	1999		2000	
		企业单位数(个) Number of Enterprises (unit)	工业总产值(亿元) Gross Industrial Output Value (100 million yuan)	企业单位数(个) Number of Enterprises (unit)	工业总产值(亿元) Gross Industrial Output Value (100 million yuan)
全国总计	**National Total**	**162033**	**72707.04**	**162885**	**85673.66**
按注册登记类型分	**Grouped by Status of Registration**				
内资企业	Domestic Funded Enterprises	135196	53752.81	134440	62209.11
国有企业	State-owned Industry	50651	22215.89	42426	20156.29
集体企业	Collective-owned Industry	42585	12414.11	37841	11907.92
股份合作企业	Cooperative Enterprises	10149	2594.62	10852	2897.26
联营企业	Joint Ownership Enterprises	2771	903.65	2510	900.55
#国有联营	State Joint Ownership Enterprises	462	223.34	419	230.33
集体联营	Collective Joint Ownership Enterprises	827	246.74	736	245.23
国有与集体联营	Joint State-collective Ownership Enterprises	1091	316.98	954	293.91
有限责任公司	Limited Liability Corporations	9714	7027.24	13215	10926.38
#国有独资公司	Sole State-funded Corporations	1026	3173.48	1226	4510.74
股份有限公司	Share Holding Enterprises	4480	5247.08	5086	10090.29
私营企业	Private Enterprises	14601	3244.56	22128	5220.36
其他企业	Other Enterprises	245	105.67	382	110.06
港澳台商投资企业	Enterprises with Funds from Hong Kong, Macao and Taiwan	15783	8994.00	16490	10574.30
外商投资企业	Foreign Funded Enterprises	11054	9960.23	11955	12890.25
#国有及国有控股	**State-owned and State-holding Enterprises**	**61301**	**35571.18**	**53489**	**40554.37**
按轻重工业分	**Grouped by Light & Heavy Industry**				
轻工业	Light Industry	81820	30514.98	81902	34094.51
以农产品为原料	Using Farm Produces as Raw Materials	54286	18931.06	53777	21069.85
以非农产品为原料	Using Non-Farm Produces as Raw Materials	27534	11583.91	28125	13024.66
重工业	Heavy Industry	80213	42192.06	80983	51579.15
采掘工业	Mining and Quarrying	7079	4239.03	6937	5398.75
原料工业	Raw Materials Industry	23469	16640.11	23724	20889.10
加工工业	Manufacturing Industry	49665	21312.92	50322	25291.30
按大中小型分	**Grouped by Size of Enterprises**				
特大型工业企业	Supers-scale Industrial Enterprises	322	10592.19	336	14114.28
大一型工业企业	Large-scale #1 Industrial Enterprises	2247	11726.04	2308	13987.63
大二型工业企业	Large-scale #2 Industrial Enterprises	5295	9263.98	5339	10201.30
中一型工业企业	Medium-scale #1 Industrial Enterprises	4720	4227.76	4687	4791.84
中二型工业企业	Medium-scale #2 Industrial Enterprises	9651	5629.45	9054	5897.97
小型工业企业	Small-scale Industrial Enterprises	139798	31267.62	141161	36680.64

注:1.规模以上非国有工业企业是指产品销售收入在500万元以上的非国有的工业企业（下表同）。
2.工业总产值按当年价格计算。

a)Non-state-owned industrial enterprises above designated size refer to the non-state-owned industrial enterprises with an annual sales income of over 5 million yuan. Similarly in following tables.

b)The gross industrial output value is calculated at current prices.

13-2 工业分行业职工人数

Number of Industrial Staff and Workers by Industrial Branch

单位：万人 (10 000 persons)

项　　目	Item	1996	1997	1998	1999	2000
全国总计	**National Total**	**6450**	**6215**	**4753**	**4428**	**4102**
按登记注册类型分	**Grouped by Status of Registration**					
国有	State-owned	4278	4040	2721	2412	2096
集体	Collective-owned	1429	1327	802	673	563
其他	Others	743	847	1230	1343	1443
按行业分	**Grouped by Sector**					
采掘业	**Mining and Quarrying**	**886**	**851**	**702**	**650**	**581**
煤炭采选业	Coal Mining and Processing	505	493	405	372	343
石油和天然气开采业	Petroleum and Natural Gas Extraction	125	116	109	100	80
黑色金属矿采选业	Ferrous Metals Mining and Dressing	21	20	16	16	15
有色金属矿采选业	Nonferrous Metals Mining and Dressing	60	54	40	37	35
非金属矿采选业	Nonmetal Minerals Mining and Dressing	58	54	43	38	33
其他矿采选业	Other Minerals Mining and Dressing	2	1	2	1	1
木材及竹材采运业	Logging and Transport of Timber and Bamboo	114	111	88	85	73
制造业	**Manufacturing**	**5293**	**5082**	**3769**	**3496**	**3240**
食品加工业	Food Processing	198	190	141	128	113
食品制造业	Food Production	119	114	77	72	67
饮料制造业	Beverage Production	121	123	94	89	84
烟草加工业	Tobacco Processing	33	33	30	29	27
纺织业	Textile Industry	634	596	393	353	327
服装及其他纤维制品制造	Garments and Other Fiber Products	168	162	127	122	120
皮革毛皮羽绒及其制品业	Leather, Furs, Down and Related Products	91	85	62	57	58
木材加工及竹藤棕草制品业	Timber Processing, Bamboo, Cane, Palm Fiber and Straw Products	72	67	39	35	31
家具制造业	Furniture Manufacturing	31	30	19	18	16
造纸及纸制品业	Papermaking and Paper Products	128	124	84	75	66
印刷业记录媒介的复制	Printing and Record Medium Reproduction	96	90	69	64	58
文教体育用品制造业	Cultural, Educational and Sports Goods	37	35	30	29	28
石油加工及炼焦业	Petroleum Refining and Coking	76	74	67	63	61
化学原料及化学制品制造业	Raw Chemical Materials and Chemical Products	407	392	304	282	254
医药制造业	Medical and Pharmaceutical Products	102	101	86	83	83
化学纤维制造业	Chemical Fiber	49	50	40	34	33
橡胶制品业	Rubber Products	75	69	52	48	43
塑料制品业	Plastic Products	105	101	73	67	61
非金属矿物制品业	Nonmetal Mineral Products	407	387	284	263	240
黑色金属冶炼及压延加工业	Smelting and Pressing of Ferrous Metals	337	321	256	242	222
有色金属冶炼及压延加工业	Smelting and Pressing of Nonferrous Metals	101	98	84	83	80
金属制品业	Metal Products	181	174	119	106	96
普通机械制造业	Ordinary Machinery	422	403	275	249	222
专用设备制造业	Special Purposes Equipment	280	274	197	179	163
交通运输设备制造业	Transport Equipment	354	346	279	269	244
电气机械及器材制造业	Electric Equipment and Machinery	236	227	170	158	145
电子及通信设备制造业	Electronic and Telecommunications	163	165	134	133	138
仪器仪表及文化办公用机械	Instruments, Meters, Cultural and Clerical Machinery	82	79	53	48	46
其他制造业	Other Manufacturing	129	115	86	77	76
电力煤气及水生产供应业	**Production & Supply of Power, Gas & Water**	**272**	**282**	**281**	**283**	**282**
电力蒸汽热水生产供应业	Production and Supply of Power, Steam and Hot Water	212	220	218	219	218
煤气的生产和供应业	Production and Supply of Gas	18	19	19	19	19
自来水的生产和供应业	Production and Supply of Tap Water	42	43	44	45	45

13-3 各地区全部国有及规模以上非国有工业企业单位数和工业总产值（2000年）

Number of All State-owned and Non-state-owned above Designated Size Industrial Enterprises and Their Gross Output Value by Region (2000)

单位：个、亿元 (unit) (100 million yuan)

地区	Region	全部国有及规模以上非国有 All States-owned and Non-state-owned above Designated Size			# 国有及国有控股企业 State-owned and State-holding Enterprises		
		企业单位数 Number of Enterprise	总产值 Gross Output Value		企业单位数 Number of Enterprise	总产值 Gross Output Value	
			1990年不变价格 At 1990 Constant Prices	当年价格 At Current Prices		1990年不变价格 At 1990 Constant Prices	当年价格 At Current Prices
全国	**National Total**	**162885**	**75710.69**	**85673.66**	**53489**	**31958.43**	**40554.37**
北京	Beijing	4572	2583.02	2565.38	2430	1761.40	1742.66
天津	Tianjin	5430	2469.81	2606.38	1843	615.37	856.86
河北	Hebei	7261	2757.48	3426.05	2707	1305.85	1797.35
山西	Shanxi	3275	944.90	1216.86	1791	614.81	837.80
内蒙古	Inner Mongolia	1373	529.71	748.97	757	401.92	598.08
辽宁	Liaoning	6017	3291.01	4249.46	2454	1900.63	2827.94
吉林	Jilin	2728	1426.29	1679.91	1667	1136.66	1377.42
黑龙江	Heilongjiang	2666	1267.37	2460.88	1588	914.33	2071.08
上海	Shanghai	8574	6035.45	6204.52	2473	3030.92	3205.11
江苏	Jiangsu	18309	9599.09	10452.87	2554	2887.60	3067.86
浙江	Zhejiang	14575	6902.33	6603.65	1418	1041.84	1292.72
安徽	Anhui	3680	1442.30	1661.44	1128	792.44	1044.54
福建	Fujian	6011	2469.65	2616.12	1367	718.38	854.95
江西	Jiangxi	3549	764.98	932.21	2509	587.73	737.36
山东	Shandong	11679	7132.15	8311.53	2774	2605.33	3486.54
河南	Henan	9930	2578.48	3494.96	3069	1370.47	1880.99
湖北	Hubei	6282	2664.61	3064.43	2965	1601.06	1929.02
湖南	Hunan	4808	1221.75	1627.94	2339	795.57	1077.47
广东	Guangdong	19695	12289.24	12480.93	3320	2881.17	3126.12
广西	Guangxi	3155	879.74	1003.24	2027	567.62	664.36
海南	Hainan	596	165.53	202.87	401	113.78	136.89
重庆	Chongqing	2040	957.43	962.32	931	624.31	653.58
四川	Sichuan	4394	1912.66	2076.96	1699	1108.23	1249.62
贵州	Guizhou	2087	531.89	631.64	1397	410.16	500.76
云南	Yunnan	2124	712.73	1063.36	1388	531.94	854.89
西藏	Tibet	362	8.34	16.43	232	6.23	12.62
陕西	Shaanxi	2553	952.79	1184.58	1633	739.05	927.07
甘肃	Gansu	2851	555.05	840.58	960	378.69	642.22
青海	Qinghai	445	105.76	196.08	362	88.86	174.72
宁夏	Ningxia	409	162.93	239.11	209	105.59	174.58
新疆	Xinjiang	1455	396.24	852.01	1097	320.52	751.19

注：全部国有及规模以上非国有工业系指全部国有工业企业及年销售收入500万元以上非国有工业企业。

a)All state-owned and non-state-owned industrial enterprises above designated size refer to all state-owned industrial enterprises plus the non-state-owned industrial enterprises with an annual sales income of over 5 million yuan.

13-3 续表 1 continued

单位：个、亿元 (unit) (100 million yuan)

地区	Region	# 集体企业 Collective-owned Enterprises			# 股份有限公司 Share-holding Corporation Ltd.			# 外商投资企业 Foreign Funded Enterprises		
		企业单位数 Number of Enterprise	总产值 Gross Output Value		企业单位数 Number of Enterprise	总产值 Gross Output Value		企业单位数 Number of Enterprise	总产值 Gross Output Value	
			1990年不变价格 At 1990 Constant Prices	当年价格 At Current Prices		1990年不变价格 At 1990 Constant Prices	当年价格 At Current Prices		1990年不变价格 At 1990 Constant Prices	当年价格 At Current Prices
全　国	**National Total**	**37841**	**11007.85**	**11907.92**	**5086**	**7606.76**	**10090.29**	**11955**	**13662.07**	**12890.25**
北　京	Beijing	899	160.28	175.34	83	148.73	163.97	643	969.26	810.82
天　津	Tianjin	1593	345.23	373.8	85	76.48	194.17	811	1174.39	1009.1
河　北	Hebei	2110	649.85	732.08	349	196.56	283.47	379	158.86	172.37
山　西	Shanxi	766	150.68	171.19	107	69.88	86.3	46	19.19	22.14
内蒙古	Inner Mongolia	122	16.1	20.32	106	115.85	149.24	48	16.97	19.05
辽　宁	Liaoning	1275	286.28	315.12	190	502.87	855.37	766	594.63	672.03
吉　林	Jilin	450	90.37	99.72	169	270.65	364	163	268.63	257.37
黑龙江	Heilongjiang	396	88.29	105.97	112	371.56	1357	84	78.48	84.41
上　海	Shanghai	1686	308.73	394.78	68	428.9	464.83	1842	2819.6	2387.96
江　苏	Jiangsu	4091	1806.54	1987.83	495	782.34	860.85	1644	1766.08	1943.31
浙　江	Zhejiang	2183	1219.95	1078.65	283	599.28	706.75	936	677.92	603.79
安　徽	Anhui	979	168.06	177.65	192	219.91	248.6	133	154.6	152.4
福　建	Fujian	870	140.55	157.72	119	169	153.59	615	460.65	477.52
江　西	Jiangxi	476	65.86	72.16	38	21.6	30.07	68	66.74	70.06
山　东	Shandong	3942	2305.02	2393.99	491	565.22	687.98	1148	813.8	865.71
河　南	Henan	4206	680.57	910.92	413	257.73	320.33	174	83.91	102.94
湖　北	Hubei	1960	511.6	564.47	424	448.54	545.8	142	235.56	206.96
湖　南	Hunan	1364	181.52	241.69	155	161.88	238.31	79	37.56	48.75
广　东	Guangdong	4158	1168.41	1202.49	265	1066.82	809.62	1682	2833.26	2527.06
广　西	Guangxi	548	119.24	132.62	88	115.98	115.91	104	72.67	84.18
海　南	Hainan	24	3.34	3.85	27	36.18	38.75	40	16.84	22.18
重　庆	Chongqing	370	60.9	57.59	127	206.87	183.52	81	88.39	88.05
四　川	Sichuan	660	141.77	153.97	342	268.52	319.43	128	119.68	111.14
贵　州	Guizhou	305	44.93	50.54	49	60.93	43.29	31	13.05	13.8
云　南	Yunnan	333	73.81	85.63	85	89.65	96.55	54	26.84	33.05
西　藏	Tibet	92	1.73	3.35	7	0.76	1.9	5	0.05	0.06
陕　西	Shaanxi	429	69.15	75.86	124	138.5	217.23	64	68.91	76.37
甘　肃	Gansu	1336	117.61	128.42	20	73.64	97.29	9	4.78	6.03
青　海	Qinghai	35	4.89	5.46	32	7.1	11.24			
宁　夏	Ningxia	47	6.33	7.63	18	11.9	15.49	17	15.82	15.18
新　疆	Xinjiang	136	20.24	27.08	23	122.94	429.4	19	4.94	6.46

13-3 续表 2 continued

单位：个、亿元 (unit) (100 million yuan)

地区	Region	# 港澳台商投资企业 Enterprises with Funds from Hong Kong, Macao & Taiwan			轻工业 Enterprises of Light Industry			重工业 Enterprises of Heavy Industry		
		企业单位数 Number of Enterprises	总产值 Gross Output Value		企业单位数 Number of Enterprises	总产值 Gross Output Value		企业单位数 Number of Enterprises	总产值 Gross Output Value	
			1990年不变价格 At 1990 Constant Prices	当年价格 At Current Prices		1990年不变价格 At 1990 Constant Prices	当年价格 At Current Prices		1990年不变价格 At 1990 Constant Prices	当年价格 At Current Prices
全 国	**National Total**	**16490**	**10323.03**	**10574.30**	**81902**	**33090.19**	**34094.51**	**80983**	**42620.51**	**51579.15**
北 京	Beijing	364	511.62	339.50	2248	578.63	615.86	2324	2004.39	1949.52
天 津	Tianjin	398	183.59	186.61	2766	985.57	895.24	2664	1484.24	1711.14
河 北	Hebei	307	166.66	200.30	3251	1129.73	1175.02	4010	1627.74	2251.03
山 西	Shanxi	56	37.34	38.63	944	159.11	175.20	2331	785.78	1041.66
内蒙古	Inner Mongolia	42	33.83	35.51	608	189.97	221.07	765	339.74	527.90
辽 宁	Liaoning	294	144.16	173.68	2285	771.08	796.58	3732	2519.93	3452.88
吉 林	Jilin	76	55.93	54.78	1247	395.86	368.62	1481	1030.43	1311.29
黑龙江	Heilongjiang	65	51.70	44.76	1268	413.35	442.47	1398	854.02	2018.41
上 海	Shanghai	1465	978.66	1043.24	4592	2257.68	2345.82	3982	3777.76	3858.71
江 苏	Jiangsu	1516	866.66	953.64	8918	4114.82	4518.12	9391	5484.28	5934.75
浙 江	Zhejiang	1181	689.12	628.62	8609	3976.27	3573.00	5966	2926.05	3030.65
安 徽	Anhui	118	78.38	60.84	1903	661.59	690.89	1777	780.71	970.55
福 建	Fujian	2076	1174.14	1127.70	3656	1365.28	1364.97	2355	1104.37	1251.15
江 西	Jiangxi	92	24.33	26.80	1705	284.96	321.37	1844	480.01	610.84
山 东	Shandong	592	277.78	307.64	6063	3607.14	3748.88	5616	3525.00	4562.65
河 南	Henan	232	123.43	154.77	4687	1081.89	1283.08	5243	1496.60	2211.87
湖 北	Hubei	220	130.92	129.35	3026	1096.38	1177.24	3256	1568.22	1887.18
湖 南	Hunan	118	37.08	48.30	1986	411.77	565.49	2822	809.98	1062.45
广 东	Guangdong	6731	4475.03	4747.30	12255	6727.50	6607.84	7440	5561.73	5873.09
广 西	Guangxi	103	30.44	30.35	1426	367.80	399.51	1729	511.94	603.73
海 南	Hainan	58	14.55	17.78	319	115.69	127.88	277	49.84	74.99
重 庆	Chongqing	57	60.79	40.97	965	357.23	329.72	1075	600.20	632.60
四 川	Sichuan	121	55.81	55.94	1883	923.17	873.98	2511	989.49	1202.98
贵 州	Guizhou	30	4.82	4.75	810	185.06	206.33	1277	346.83	425.31
云 南	Yunnan	63	25.40	27.20	896	319.57	556.63	1228	393.16	506.73
西 藏	Tibet				162	2.96	5.86	200	5.38	10.58
陕 西	Shaanxi	62	62.33	56.55	1164	326.05	350.23	1389	626.74	834.35
甘 肃	Gansu	23	19.14	23.88	1192	114.28	135.61	1659	440.77	704.97
青 海	Qinghai	6	3.14	4.83	168	15.04	17.96	277	90.71	178.12
宁 夏	Ningxia	10	1.69	2.87	149	31.66	38.06	260	131.27	201.04
新 疆	Xinjiang	14	4.55	7.23	751	123.08	165.99	704	273.17	686.02

13-3 续表 3 continued

单位：个、亿元

(unit) (100 million yuan)

地区	Region	大型企业 Large Enterprises 企业单位数 Number of Enterprises	总产值 Gross Output Value 1990年不变价格 At 1990 Constant Prices	当年价格 At Current Prices	中型企业 Medium-sized Enterprises 企业单位数 Number of Enterprises	总产值 Gross Output Value 1990年不变价格 At 1990 Constant Prices	当年价格 At Current Prices	小型企业 Small Enterprises 企业单位数 Number of Enterprises	总产值 Gross Output Value 1990年不变价格 At 1990 Constant Prices	当年价格 At Current Prices
全国	**National Total**	**7983**	**31838.39**	**38303.21**	**13741**	**9989.02**	**10689.81**	**141161**	**33883.28**	**36680.64**
北京	Beijing	242	878.96	1080.64	234	101.84	127.06	4096	1602.22	1357.67
天津	Tianjin	316	1430.07	1486.91	378	180.89	179.87	4736	858.84	939.59
河北	Hebei	358	999.40	1392.04	769	383.60	464.47	6134	1374.47	1569.54
山西	Shanxi	138	429.71	600.35	228	87.55	100.98	2909	427.63	515.53
内蒙古	Inner Mongolia	87	215.27	322.23	198	156.63	227.59	1088	157.80	199.16
辽宁	Liaoning	403	1940.82	2771.90	454	252.83	270.25	5160	1097.36	1207.30
吉林	Jilin	212	993.04	1190.74	354	167.17	196.41	2162	266.07	292.76
黑龙江	Heilongjiang	276	850.15	1942.06	325	137.10	158.05	2065	280.12	360.76
上海	Shanghai	664	3689.14	3602.59	703	680.28	688.61	7207	1666.04	1913.32
江苏	Jiangsu	582	3020.68	3255.60	1500	1397.80	1491.82	16227	5180.61	5705.44
浙江	Zhejiang	318	1523.54	1649.88	932	1247.10	1086.26	13325	4131.69	3867.50
安徽	Anhui	193	613.06	819.68	436	240.52	246.87	3051	588.72	594.89
福建	Fujian	92	461.46	497.53	209	325.66	318.69	5710	1682.53	1799.90
江西	Jiangxi	108	354.66	457.93	330	138.58	156.35	3111	271.74	317.94
山东	Shandong	1087	3537.49	4176.23	1653	1001.86	1123.91	8939	2592.80	3011.38
河南	Henan	319	974.46	1289.90	684	316.97	432.53	8927	1287.06	1772.52
湖北	Hubei	306	1092.56	1362.75	542	439.05	462.26	5434	1133.00	1239.42
湖南	Hunan	222	586.40	809.47	375	123.19	146.97	4211	512.16	671.49
广东	Guangdong	823	4497.84	4523.91	1228	1386.70	1427.64	17644	6404.69	6529.37
广西	Guangxi	198	414.71	467.93	400	185.87	202.50	2557	279.18	332.81
海南	Hainan	32	46.08	60.03	86	68.45	75.17	478	50.99	67.67
重庆	Chongqing	136	487.90	499.13	235	180.79	168.85	1669	288.74	294.34
四川	Sichuan	293	990.84	1056.75	490	305.65	344.92	3611	616.16	675.30
贵州	Guizhou	103	255.14	322.56	119	59.41	67.63	1865	217.35	241.44
云南	Yunnan	92	362.64	601.76	295	126.58	151.48	1737	223.51	310.11
西藏	Tibet				4	1.29	4.32	358	7.05	12.12
陕西	Shaanxi	194	535.00	706.60	245	140.56	151.79	2114	277.24	326.19
甘肃	Gansu	85	301.48	520.27	110	38.89	50.99	2656	214.69	269.33
青海	Qinghai	21	62.85	137.85	24	7.56	10.16	400	35.34	48.07
宁夏	Ningxia	32	88.64	127.46	75	37.93	48.39	302	36.36	63.26
新疆	Xinjiang	51	204.41	570.50	126	70.72	106.98	1278	121.12	174.54

13-4 各行业主要经济指标占全国比重(1998-2000年)

Proportion to Total Industry of Main Indicators by Sectors (1998-2000)

单位:% (%)

行业	Sector	企业单位数 Number of Industrial Enterprises	工业总产值 Gross Industrial Output Value	工业增加值 Value-added of Industry	资产总计 Total Assets	产品销售收入 Sales Revenue
煤炭采选业	Coal Mining and Dressing					
1998年	1998	1.94	1.92	3.10	3.22	1.86
1999年	1999	1.72	1.70	2.62	3.31	1.62
2000年	2000	1.64	1.49	2.30	3.07	1.44
石油和天然气开采业	Petroleum and Natural Gas Extraction					
1998年	1998	0.05	2.65	6.11	3.08	2.58
1999年	1999	0.05	2.87	6.67	3.49	2.72
2000年	2000	0.05	3.65	8.70	3.24	3.46
黑色金属矿采选业	Ferrous Metals Mining and Dressing					
1998年	1998	0.35	0.22	0.28	0.32	0.21
1999年	1999	0.36	0.20	0.25	0.28	0.19
2000年	2000	0.37	0.19	0.25	0.26	0.18
有色金属矿采选业	Nonferrous Metals Mining and Dressing					
1998年	1998	0.86	0.50	0.57	0.46	0.48
1999年	1999	0.88	0.50	0.58	0.44	0.47
2000年	2000	0.88	0.47	0.55	0.43	0.45
非金属矿采选业	Nonmetal Minerals Mining and Dressing					
1998年	1998	1.12	0.48	0.57	0.49	0.45
1999年	1999	1.12	0.47	0.55	0.49	0.47
2000年	2000	1.09	0.42	0.48	0.53	0.38
木材及竹材采运业	Logging and Transport of Timber and Bamboo					
1998年	1998	0.38	0.24	0.42	0.39	0.22
1999年	1999	0.35	0.19	0.31	0.35	0.17
2000年	2000	0.31	0.14	0.24	0.32	0.13
食品加工业	Food Processing					
1998年	1998	7.21	5.19	3.51	2.95	4.96
1999年	1999	6.93	4.84	3.53	2.67	4.60
2000年	2000	6.55	4.35	3.29	2.44	4.13
食品制造业	Food Manufacturing					
1998年	1998	3.25	1.79	1.67	1.44	1.75
1999年	1999	3.06	1.74	1.60	1.38	1.69
2000年	2000	2.88	1.68	1.64	1.33	1.61
饮料制造业	Beverage Manufacturing					
1998年	1998	2.31	2.33	2.80	2.29	2.32
1999年	1999	2.21	2.28	2.72	2.28	2.24
2000年	2000	2.09	2.05	2.44	2.17	1.96
烟草加工业	Tobacco Processing					
1998年	1998	0.21	2.03	4.56	1.58	2.07
1999年	1999	0.22	1.91	4.14	1.58	1.96
2000年	2000	0.21	1.69	3.69	1.56	1.70
纺织业	Textile Industry					
1998年	1998	6.83	6.46	5.24	5.41	6.02
1999年	1999	6.78	6.23	5.18	5.02	5.94
2000年	2000	6.73	6.01	5.01	4.69	5.72
服装及其他纤维制品制造	Garments and Other Fiber Products					
1998年	1998	4.10	2.98	2.48	1.45	2.77
1999年	1999	4.08	2.80	2.35	1.40	2.64
2000年	2000	4.34	2.67	2.33	1.39	2.53
皮革毛皮羽绒及其制品业	Leather, Furs, Down and Related Products					
1998年	1998	2.01	1.76	1.41	0.85	1.69
1999年	1999	1.97	1.65	1.32	0.79	1.57
2000年	2000	1.94	1.57	1.27	0.74	1.47

注：工业总产值按当年价格计算(下表同)。

a)The gross industrial output value is calculated at current prices.Similarly in following tables.

13-4 续表 1 continued

单位:%　　(%)

行　业	Sector	企业单位数 Number of Industrial Enterprises	工业总产值 Gross Industrial Output Value	工业增加值 Value-added of Industry	资产总计 Total Assets	产品销售收入 Sales Revenue
木材加工及竹藤棕草制品业	Timber Processing, Bamboo, Cane, Palm Fiber and Straw Products					
1998年	1998	1.51	0.73	0.58	0.57	0.69
1999年	1999	1.49	0.77	0.62	0.55	0.73
2000年	2000	1.57	0.77	0.62	0.55	0.74
家具制造业	Furniture Manufacturing					
1998年	1998	0.89	0.44	0.39	0.27	0.42
1999年	1999	0.91	0.44	0.36	0.27	0.42
2000年	2000	0.92	0.43	0.37	0.29	0.41
造纸及纸制品业	Papermaking and Paper Products					
1998年	1998	2.89	1.84	1.64	1.81	1.75
1999年	1999	2.87	1.83	1.65	1.80	1.75
2000年	2000	2.87	1.86	1.62	1.99	1.79
印刷业记录媒介的复制	Printing and Record Medium Reproduction					
1998年	1998	2.34	0.80	0.94	0.76	0.78
1999年	1999	2.36	0.80	0.92	0.78	0.78
2000年	2000	2.27	0.72	0.79	0.77	0.70
文教体育用品制造业	Cultural, Educational and Sports Goods					
1998年	1998	1.08	0.82	0.73	0.46	0.79
1999年	1999	1.12	0.80	0.65	0.42	0.74
2000年	2000	1.15	0.72	0.61	0.41	0.70
石油加工及炼焦业	Petroleum Processing and Coking					
1998年	1998	0.64	3.44	2.72	3.06	3.68
1999年	1999	0.61	3.72	2.74	3.06	3.92
2000年	2000	0.61	5.17	3.10	3.00	5.43
化学原料及制品制造业	Raw Chemical Materials and Chemical Products					
1998年	1998	6.85	6.83	5.68	7.15	6.54
1999年	1999	7.00	6.77	5.64	6.99	6.51
2000年	2000	7.02	6.71	5.58	6.88	6.44
医药制造业	Medical and Pharmaceutical Products					
1998年	1998	1.99	2.03	2.23	2.00	1.97
1999年	1999	2.02	2.06	2.39	2.08	1.97
2000年	2000	2.03	2.08	2.50	2.22	1.93
化学纤维制造业	Chemical Fiber					
1998年	1998	0.49	1.22	0.95	1.62	1.22
1999年	1999	0.50	1.34	1.17	1.60	1.35
2000年	2000	0.51	1.45	1.16	1.43	1.42
橡胶制品业	Rubber Products					
1998年	1998	1.08	1.13	1.05	1.00	1.08
1999年	1999	1.11	1.07	0.94	0.97	0.99
2000年	2000	1.09	0.95	0.86	0.89	0.87
塑料制品业	Plastic Products					
1998年	1998	3.64	2.21	1.82	1.58	2.10
1999年	1999	3.73	2.23	1.80	1.59	2.18
2000年	2000	3.82	2.22	1.83	1.63	2.14
非金属矿物制品业	Nonmetal Mineral Products					
1998年	1998	8.78	4.73	4.68	5.41	4.47
1999年	1999	8.87	4.67	4.66	5.15	4.36
2000年	2000	8.93	4.31	4.44	4.84	4.00

13-4 续表 2 continued

单位:% (%)

行业	Sector	企业单位数 Number of Industrial Enterprises	工业总产值 Gross Industrial Output Value	工业增加值 Value-added of Industry	资产总计 Total Assets	产品销售收入 Sales Revenue
黑色金属冶炼及压延加工业	Smelting and Pressing of Ferrous Metals					
1998年	1998	1.97	5.73	5.06	7.56	6.03
1999年	1999	1.88	5.64	5.01	7.32	5.75
2000年	2000	1.84	5.52	5.12	7.31	5.81
有色金属冶炼及压延加工业	Smelting and Pressing of Nonferrous Metals					
1998年	1998	1.46	2.40	1.71	2.33	2.39
1999年	1999	1.50	2.47	1.88	2.32	2.49
2000年	2000	1.56	2.54	2.02	2.27	2.48
金属制品业	Metal Products					
1998年	1998	4.93	3.18	2.60	2.16	3.04
1999年	1999	5.05	3.05	2.51	2.07	2.90
2000年	2000	5.14	2.96	2.40	2.02	2.82
普通机械制造业	Ordinary Machinery					
1998年	1998	5.62	3.81	3.59	4.08	3.67
1999年	1999	5.65	3.71	3.45	3.89	3.53
2000年	2000	5.73	3.56	3.31	3.79	3.37
专用设备制造业	Special Purpose Equipment					
1998年	1998	4.02	2.83	2.50	2.83	2.67
1999年	1999	3.99	2.72	2.39	2.66	2.57
2000年	2000	3.93	2.56	2.29	2.58	2.38
交通运输设备制造业	Transport Equipment					
1998年	1998	4.02	2.83	2.50	2.83	2.67
1999年	1999	4.14	6.41	5.53	6.38	6.44
2000年	2000	4.21	6.26	5.21	6.44	6.21
电气机械及器材制造业	Electric Equipment and Machinery					
1998年	1998	4.57	5.36	4.53	4.25	5.12
1999年	1999	4.71	5.53	4.65	4.21	5.28
2000年	2000	4.82	5.64	4.85	4.17	5.38
电子及通信设备制造业	Electronic and Telecommunications Equipment					
1998年	1998	2.52	7.22	5.77	4.86	7.01
1999年	1999	2.65	8.02	6.25	5.28	7.98
2000年	2000	2.74	8.81	7.18	5.96	8.75
仪器仪表文化办公用机械	Instruments, Meters, Cultural and Office Machinery					
1998年	1998	1.10	1.02	0.87	0.81	1.03
1999年	1999	1.12	0.97	0.84	0.80	0.99
2000年	2000	1.14	1.01	0.84	0.78	1.01
电力蒸汽热水生产供应业	Production and Supply of Electric Power, Steam and Hot Water					
1998年	1998	3.03	5.34	9.66	12.31	7.79
1999年	1999	3.05	5.50	10.02	13.39	7.93
2000年	2000	2.96	5.38	9.17	14.76	8.10
煤气的生产和供应业	Production and Supply of Gas					
1998年	1998	0.18	0.15	0.07	0.46	0.23
1999年	1999	0.18	0.18	0.17	0.48	0.26
2000年	2000	0.18	0.20	0.14	0.48	0.28
自来水的生产和供应业	Production and Supply of Tap Water					
1998年	1998	1.43	0.40	0.64	1.08	0.40
1999年	1999	1.48	0.43	0.68	1.20	0.43
2000年	2000	1.48	0.38	0.59	1.21	0.37

13-5 全部国有及规模以上非国有工业企业主要指标（2000年）

单位：亿元

行　　业	Item	企业单位数（个）Number of Enterprises (unit)	工业总产值 Gross Industrial Output Value	工业增加值 Value-added of Industry
全 国 总 计	**National Total**	**162885**	**85673.66**	**25394.80**
按注册登记类型分	**Grouped by Status of Registration**			
在总计中：	Of the Total:			
国有及国有控股企业	State-owned and State-holding Enterprises	53489	40554.37	13777.68
在总计中：	Of the Total:			
集体企业	Collective-owned Enterprises	37841	11907.92	3071.58
股份有限公司	Share-holding Corporations Ltd.	5086	10090.29	3584.25
外商投资企业	Foreign Funded Enterprises	11955	12890.25	3202.55
港澳台商投资企业	Enterprises with Funds from Hong Kong, Macao and Taiwan	16490	10574.30	2887.80
按轻重工业分	**Grouped by Light & Heavy Industry**			
轻工业	Light Industry	81902	34094.51	9513.81
以农产品为原料	Using Farm Products as Raw Materials	53777	21069.85	6166.14
以非农产品为原料	Using Non-Farm Products as Raw Materials	28125	13024.66	3347.67
重工业	Heavy Industry	80983	51579.15	15880.99
采掘工业	Mining and Quarrying	6937	5398.75	3148.07
原料工业	Raw Materials Industry	23724	20889.10	6212.59
加工工业	Manufacturing Industry	50322	25291.30	6520.33
按企业规模分：大型企业	**Grouped by Size of Enterprises:** Large	7983	38303.21	12605.52
中型企业	Medium-sized	13741	10689.81	3141.80
小型企业	Small	141161	36680.64	9647.48
按行业分	**Grouped by Sector**			
#煤炭采选业	Coal Mining and Dressing	2666	1276.81	583.09
石油和天然气开采业	Petroleum and Natural Gas Extraction	82	3130.11	2209.02
黑色金属矿采选业	Ferrous Metals Mining and Dressing	598	164.86	62.31
有色金属矿采选业	Nonferrous Metals Mining and Dressing	1439	405.36	139.77
非金属矿采选业	Nonmetal Minerals Mining and Dressing	1770	356.94	122.64
木材及竹材采运业	Logging and Transport of Timber and Bamboo	498	121.09	61.49
食品加工业	Food Processing	10676	3722.70	835.29
食品制造业	Food Manufacturing	4691	1442.52	415.81
饮料制造业	Beverage Manufacturing	3409	1752.37	618.90
烟草加工业	Tobacco Processing	343	1451.29	935.80
纺织业	Textile Industry	10968	5149.30	1272.84
服装及其他纤维制品制造	Garments and Other Fiber Products	7064	2291.16	592.02
皮革毛皮羽绒及其制品业	Leather, Furs, Down and Related Products	3164	1345.17	323.62
木材加工及竹藤棕草制品业	Timber Processing, Bamboo, Cane, Palm Fiber and Straw Products	2552	656.77	157.53
家具制造业	Furniture Manufacturing	1498	370.18	94.86
造纸及纸制品业	Papermaking and Paper Products	4672	1590.36	412.62
印刷业记录媒介的复制	Printing and Record Medium Reproduction	3703	616.71	201.39
文教体育用品制造业	Cultural, Educational and Sports Goods	1879	617.94	155.30
石油加工及炼焦业	Petroleum Processing and Coking	993	4429.19	787.99
化学原料及制品制造业	Raw Chemical Materials and Chemical Products	11430	5749.02	1415.81
医药制造业	Medical and Pharmaceutical Products	3301	1781.37	633.88
化学纤维制造业	Chemical Fiber	834	1243.07	295.78
橡胶制品业	Rubber Products	1783	812.70	218.98
塑料制品业	Plastic Products	6230	1899.70	464.43
非金属矿物制品业	Nonmetal Mineral Products	14540	3692.85	1126.72
黑色金属冶炼及压延加工业	Smelting and Pressing of Ferrous Metals	2997	4732.90	1299.29
有色金属冶炼及压延加工业	Smelting and Pressing of Nonferrous Metals	2538	2180.23	512.69
金属制品业	Metal Products	8376	2539.76	609.46
普通机械制造业	Ordinary Machinery	9338	3046.95	840.75
专用设备制造业	Special Purpose Equipment	6406	2192.63	580.97
交通运输设备制造业	Transport Equipment	6850	5364.83	1323.61
电气机械及器材制造业	Electric Equipment and Machinery	7845	4834.68	1231.50
电子及通信设备制造业	Electronic and Telecommunications Equipment	4459	7549.58	1824.31
仪器仪表文化办公用机械	Instruments, Meters, Cultural and Office	1860	867.91	214.36
电力蒸汽热水生产供应业	Production and Supply of Electric Power, Steam and Hot Water	4825	4611.39	2328.62
煤气的生产和供应业	Production and Supply of Gas	300	170.30	34.74
自来水的生产和供应业	Production and Supply of Tap Water	2408	325.53	150.88

Main Indicators of All State-owned and Non-state-owned Above Designed Size Industrial Enterprises (2000)

(100 million yuan)

实收资本 Total Capital Hold	资产合计 Total Assets	流动资产合计 Circulating Funds	流动资产年平均余额 Annual Average Balance of Circulating Funds	固定资产原价 Original Value of Fixed Assets	固定资产净值年平均余额 Annual Average Balance of Net Value of Fixed Assets
32940.45	**126211.24**	**54338.15**	**51910.37**	**78646.30**	**51792.33**
20156.14	84014.94	32628.81	31485.38	57294.96	36886.64
2310.98	9631.40	5182.30	5039.17	4743.96	3262.95
3756.60	14930.13	6146.36	5650.69	10535.89	6452.65
5225.57	13849.30	6957.45	6352.75	7510.19	5252.30
3854.54	11864.76	5892.09	5573.92	6808.12	4556.44
10565.47	39433.35	19324.46	18557.91	20328.98	14066.11
6127.59	23741.54	11567.76	11070.74	12393.47	8696.66
4437.88	15691.81	7756.70	7487.17	7935.52	5369.45
22374.98	86777.89	35013.69	33352.46	58317.31	37726.22
3270.11	9738.91	2951.78	2899.54	9268.68	5472.93
10386.75	42112.70	13314.06	12924.20	32620.30	21470.86
8718.13	34926.28	18747.85	17528.72	16428.33	10782.43
17611.67	71069.97	27915.16	26684.12	48776.39	30911.02
3797.86	16239.87	7367.71	7078.98	9571.76	6382.77
11530.92	38901.41	19055.28	18147.27	20298.15	14498.54
1033.56	3868.51	1407.08	1366.15	2969.14	1978.99
1706.96	4088.12	889.97	888.33	5190.99	2706.01
128.92	326.00	112.44	112.93	164.18	106.04
144.38	548.93	201.54	194.28	370.72	247.55
191.83	669.14	246.75	237.10	435.63	326.31
99.49	401.53	162.23	162.16	249.74	181.11
769.63	3078.22	1451.28	1404.83	1673.09	1232.67
544.14	1684.43	765.17	717.45	937.86	648.35
727.29	2742.77	1252.28	1193.90	1462.36	1057.87
330.46	1973.82	971.66	953.29	912.03	608.89
1460.83	5917.01	2825.60	2708.18	3446.19	2319.03
533.66	1758.77	1057.49	1011.57	717.44	494.23
262.33	939.10	577.21	559.06	381.11	274.16
205.57	694.94	302.81	293.03	404.25	306.36
119.66	363.48	192.82	182.60	163.80	118.75
634.64	2511.99	1058.78	1010.96	1426.23	1073.99
299.09	973.73	446.41	422.62	599.66	384.30
174.86	516.01	298.56	289.59	221.87	152.44
805.04	3785.91	1311.34	1279.74	3284.17	1990.02
2064.06	8688.03	3487.78	3400.07	5560.53	3733.17
682.33	2798.90	1480.84	1405.32	1062.82	749.56
498.47	1808.44	601.62	593.09	1359.05	900.42
295.38	1118.81	541.27	534.75	565.38	386.57
647.94	2052.16	1005.24	961.22	1109.94	763.01
1703.65	6113.11	2423.00	2341.68	3948.43	2759.58
2473.13	9228.25	3303.83	3107.31	6457.44	3985.88
797.42	2866.65	1239.00	1179.15	1797.13	1202.58
765.81	2545.63	1418.43	1366.84	1210.28	835.72
1214.68	4787.90	2688.69	2594.27	2217.06	1425.22
771.98	3255.29	1881.51	1768.85	1498.17	944.83
2013.67	8129.68	4248.41	4048.39	3592.73	2386.16
1382.21	5260.20	3138.58	3006.14	2086.11	1409.22
1715.73	7518.79	4832.46	4208.03	2561.78	1564.49
277.57	984.52	595.23	568.06	401.68	258.40
4251.23	18626.94	4650.04	4626.66	15752.50	10570.73
270.06	610.91	179.40	169.49	441.60	312.64
550.39	1523.19	357.06	329.69	1272.93	879.40

13-5 续表 1

单位：亿元

行业	Item	流动负债合计 Liquid Liabilities	长期负债合计 Long-term Liabilities	所有者权益 Creditors' Equity
全国总计	**National Total**	**53052.64**	**22825.72**	**49406.88**
按注册登记类型分	**Grouped by Status of Registration**			
在总计中：	Of the Total:			
国有及国有控股企业	State-owned and State-holding Enterprises	32237.41	18456.43	32714.81
在总计中：	Of the Total:			
集体企业	Collective-owned Enterprises	5184.26	1048.31	3314.27
股份有限公司	Share-holding Corporations Ltd.	5103.97	2185.34	7552.06
外商投资企业	Foreign Funded Enterprises	6171.55	1520.51	6051.29
港澳台商投资企业	Enterprises with Funds from Hong Kong, Macao and Taiwan	5445.12	1341.42	5003.07
按轻重工业分	**Grouped by Light & Heavy Industry**			
轻工业	Light Industry	19186.03	4646.09	15348.09
以农产品为原料	Using Farm Products as Raw Materials	12025.96	2821.18	8709.61
以非农产品为原料	Using Non-Farm Products as Raw Materials	7160.07	1824.91	6638.48
重工业	Heavy Industry	33866.61	18179.63	34058.79
采掘工业	Mining and Quarrying	2975.91	2093.35	4490.24
原料工业	Raw Materials Industry	13492.88	11568.02	16767.18
加工工业	Manufacturing Industry	17397.81	4518.27	12801.37
按企业规模分：大型企业	**Grouped by Size of Enterprises:** Large	25929.08	14639.14	29991.21
中型企业	Medium-sized	8006.89	2944.93	5174.37
小型企业	Small	19116.67	5241.65	14241.30
按行业分	**Grouped by Sector**			
#煤炭采选业	Coal Mining and Dressing	1439.87	1072.39	1341.35
石油和天然气开采业	Petroleum and Natural Gas Extraction	805.04	691.01	2451.23
黑色金属矿采选业	Ferrous Metals Mining and Dressing	112.16	20.18	174.80
有色金属矿采选业	Nonferrous Metals Mining and Dressing	228.04	119.02	199.03
非金属矿采选业	Nonmetal Minerals Mining and Dressing	259.34	149.57	258.86
木材及竹材采运业	Logging and Transport of Timber and Bamboo	214.36	57.14	129.18
食品加工业	Food Processing	1828.04	355.36	851.61
食品制造业	Food Manufacturing	845.45	186.23	638.59
饮料制造业	Beverage Manufacturing	1328.57	303.85	1089.01
烟草加工业	Tobacco Processing	787.25	123.16	1062.12
纺织业	Textile Industry	3253.11	861.24	1758.77
服装及其他纤维制品制造	Garments and Other Fiber Products	923.44	89.44	735.31
皮革毛皮羽绒及其制品业	Leather, Furs, Down and Related Products	560.29	58.94	313.55
木材加工及竹藤棕草制品业	Timber Processing, Bamboo, Cane, Palm Fiber and Straw Products	332.68	120.36	238.69
家具制造业	Furniture Manufacturing	173.44	26.14	158.89
造纸及纸制品业	Papermaking and Paper Products	1115.57	521.65	852.44
印刷业记录媒介的复制	Printing and Record Medium Reproduction	428.14	107.75	434.47
文教体育用品制造业	Cultural, Educational and Sports Goods	261.58	26.30	226.12
石油加工及炼焦业	Petroleum Processing and Coking	1410.85	788.14	1529.51
化学原料及制品制造业	Raw Chemical Materials and Chemical Products	3670.81	1829.21	3144.06
医药制造业	Medical and Pharmaceutical Products	1269.41	298.51	1204.31
化学纤维制造业	Chemical Fiber	632.89	397.11	773.74
橡胶制品业	Rubber Products	545.62	184.30	379.78
塑料制品业	Plastic Products	955.06	244.21	838.94
非金属矿物制品业	Nonmetal Mineral Products	2819.18	1122.86	2124.44
黑色金属冶炼及压延加工业	Smelting and Pressing of Ferrous Metals	3473.52	1519.05	4203.06
有色金属冶炼及压延加工业	Smelting and Pressing of Nonferrous Metals	1285.04	552.41	1003.30
金属制品业	Metal Products	1378.88	238.54	911.63
普通机械制造业	Ordinary Machinery	2505.94	524.81	1736.57
专用设备制造业	Special Purpose Equipment	1772.17	330.05	1137.10
交通运输设备制造业	Transport Equipment	4047.62	1019.33	3022.90
电气机械及器材制造业	Electric Equipment and Machinery	2821.75	436.54	1979.48
电子及通信设备制造业	Electronic and Telecommunications Equipment	3836.59	607.01	3026.30
仪器仪表文化办公用机械	Instruments, Meters, Cultural and Office	510.70	101.76	364.94
电力蒸汽热水生产供应业	Production and Supply of Electric Power, Steam and Hot Water	3958.24	7189.66	7363.60
煤气的生产和供应业	Production and Supply of Gas	179.84	98.18	331.91
自来水的生产和供应业	Production and Supply of Tap Water	316.48	278.27	926.31

continued

(100 million yuan)

产　　品 销售收入 Sales Revenue	产　　品 销售成本 Cost of Sales	产品销售 税金及附加 Sales Tax and Extra Charges	产　　品 销售利润 Sales Profit	利润总额 Total Profits	本年应交 增 值 税 Value Added Tax Payable
84151.75	**68653.95**	**1434.17**	**10732.30**	**4393.48**	**3685.20**
42203.12	33473.62	1150.28	6263.42	2408.33	2320.36
10803.15	9195.11	97.73	1066.73	451.22	341.22
9815.56	7313.09	173.63	1954.81	1250.10	524.05
12503.78	10127.45	81.42	1574.33	748.46	435.15
10041.96	8455.82	48.34	1104.26	534.02	303.73
32343.29	26392.15	846.31	3358.33	1313.20	1235.35
19744.16	15946.19	757.15	2049.89	839.53	806.92
12599.13	10445.96	89.16	1308.44	473.67	428.43
51808.46	42261.80	587.86	7373.97	3080.28	2449.85
5040.75	2945.44	111.31	1833.83	1195.96	429.06
22775.53	19547.39	303.04	2452.01	782.82	1187.28
23992.19	19768.97	173.50	3088.14	1101.50	833.52
39755.15	31261.95	1016.94	6047.29	2832.59	2093.91
10365.15	8506.94	156.51	1260.76	350.68	472.25
34031.45	28885.06	260.72	3424.25	1210.21	1119.05
1213.77	894.44	17.89	210.57	0.50	98.11
2914.99	1363.76	75.09	1465.36	1148.42	297.41
152.84	117.00	4.23	21.29	6.54	7.09
375.18	284.04	3.90	74.74	30.84	12.90
323.20	243.65	7.51	47.08	10.69	16.43
108.50	66.13	6.13	28.40	1.13	2.61
3477.52	3097.72	14.03	232.59	68.74	70.25
1353.07	1056.25	6.51	156.74	54.79	64.34
1647.47	1096.30	109.10	225.82	97.51	108.06
1430.76	673.20	567.16	172.50	142.58	143.95
4810.45	4240.35	23.53	447.31	136.88	158.41
2133.01	1828.48	9.63	199.31	86.44	55.11
1238.19	1103.42	4.62	95.85	34.86	26.40
621.00	537.96	4.09	51.51	17.75	20.83
344.59	287.45	2.29	36.87	15.96	9.89
1503.09	1267.60	7.90	169.46	59.52	62.91
588.00	461.35	3.31	105.13	47.31	31.02
588.09	503.62	2.07	57.90	22.79	13.05
4571.03	4140.98	180.91	197.44	2.38	118.37
5422.06	4466.20	46.05	642.65	170.95	213.78
1627.48	1026.76	10.62	323.30	136.58	115.43
1192.80	1019.98	9.42	146.57	63.53	42.16
731.78	613.36	20.24	66.31	10.35	26.97
1799.73	1552.20	7.75	176.70	70.82	50.46
3364.17	2730.58	33.64	417.97	97.50	172.58
4887.05	4193.62	32.18	563.61	158.09	247.76
2087.59	1787.50	10.26	254.67	63.52	82.31
2369.79	2030.21	11.95	232.21	71.65	68.50
2839.72	2298.08	16.06	397.54	96.76	122.96
2003.48	1644.55	10.78	261.76	60.89	73.57
5229.58	4298.47	89.54	681.84	194.76	202.50
4527.29	3685.67	17.36	515.83	195.40	156.39
7363.27	6210.20	12.54	840.50	497.13	179.69
849.59	702.02	2.71	107.69	38.21	23.89
6819.67	5733.81	39.91	944.69	457.16	532.19
234.65	227.83	0.85	-5.38	-3.69	6.82
308.07	231.94	3.77	59.26	9.27	18.44

13-6 按行业分全部国有及规模以上非国有工业企业主要经济效益指标（2000年）

行业	Branch	工业增加值率 (%) Ratio of Value Added to Gross Industrial Output Value (%)	总资产贡献率 (%) Ratio of Total Assets to Industrial Output Value (%)
全国总计	**National Total**	**29.64**	**9.00**
按轻重工业分	**Grouped by Light & Heavy Industry**		
轻工业	Light Industry	27.90	9.99
重工业	Heavy Industry	30.79	8.54
按行业分	**Grouped by Sector**		
煤炭采选业	Coal Mining and Dressing	45.67	3.99
石油和天然气开采业	Petroleum and Natural Gas Extraction	70.57	38.20
黑色金属矿采选业	Ferrous Metals Mining and Dressing	37.79	6.55
有色金属矿采选业	Nonferrous Metals Mining and Dressing	34.48	10.46
非金属矿采选业	Nonmetal Minerals Mining and Dressing	34.36	6.21
木材及竹材采运业	Logging and Transport of Timber and Bamboo	50.78	3.49
食品加工业	Food Processing	22.44	6.82
食品制造业	Food Production	28.83	8.90
饮料制造业	Beverage Production	35.32	12.68
烟草加工业	Tobacco Processing	64.48	44.24
纺织业	Textile Industry	24.72	7.20
服装及其他纤维制品制造	Garments and Other Fiber Products	25.84	9.77
皮革毛皮羽绒及其制品业	Leather, Furs, Down and Related Products	24.06	8.47
木材加工及竹藤棕草制品业	Timber Processing, Bamboo, Cane, Palm Fiber and Straw Products	23.99	7.95
家具制造业	Furniture Manufacturing	25.63	9.17
造纸及纸制品业	Papermaking and Paper Products	25.95	6.92
印刷业记录媒介的复制	Printing and Record Medium Reproduction	32.66	9.52
文教体育用品制造业	Cultural, Educational and Sports Goods	25.13	8.19
石油加工及炼焦业	Petroleum Processing and Coking	17.79	9.66
化学原料及制品制造业	Raw Chemical Materials and Chemical Products	24.63	6.55
医药制造业	Medical and Pharmaceutical Products	35.58	10.76
化学纤维制造业	Chemical Fiber	23.79	8.14
橡胶制品业	Rubber Products	26.94	6.85
塑料制品业	Plastic Products	24.45	7.65
非金属矿物制品业	Nonmetal Mineral Products	30.51	6.66
黑色金属冶炼及压延加工业	Smelting and Pressing of Ferrous Metals	27.45	6.18
有色金属冶炼及压延加工业	Smelting and Pressing of Nonferrous Metals	23.52	7.77
金属制品业	Metal Products	24.00	7.51
普通机械制造业	Ordinary Machinery Manufacturing	27.59	6.38
专用设备制造业	For Special Purposes Equipment Manufacturing	26.50	5.85
交通运输设备制造业	Transport Equipment Manufacturing	24.67	7.30
电气机械及器材制造业	Electric Equipment and Machinery	25.47	8.46
电子及通信设备制造业	Electronic and Telecommunications Equipment	24.16	10.15
仪器仪表文化办公用机械	Instruments,Meters,Cultural and Office Machinery	24.70	7.71
电力蒸汽热水生产供应业	Production and Supply of Electric Power, Steam and Hot Water	50.50	7.18
煤气的生产和供应业	Production and Supply of Gas	20.40	1.16
自来水的生产和供应业	Production and Supply of Tap Water	46.35	2.71

Main Indicators on Economic Benefit of All State-owned and Non-state-owned Industrial Enterprises by Industrial Branch (2000)

资产负债率 (%) Assets-Liability Ratio (%)	流动资产周转次数（次/年） Number of Times of Annual of Turnover Circulating Funds (times/year)	工业成本费用利润率 (%) Ratio of Profits to Industrial Cost (%)	全员劳动生产率（元/人.年） Overall Labor Productivity (yuan/person-year)	产品销售率 (%) Proportion of Products Sold (%)
60.81	**1.62**	**5.56**	**45679**	**97.67**
61.07	1.74	4.31	42119	97.06
60.68	1.55	6.35	48116	98.07
65.33	0.89	0.04	14604	99.05
40.04	3.28	72.54	382513	99.22
46.38	1.35	4.61	25568	95.67
63.64	1.93	8.83	28776	97.48
61.31	1.36	3.49	22232	94.76
67.83	0.67	1.17	8313	99.47
72.33	2.48	2.01	49749	97.33
62.09	1.89	4.22	45309	96.02
60.30	1.38	6.68	60544	97.37
46.19	1.50	18.11	361452	99.98
70.28	1.78	2.92	26359	97.21
58.19	2.11	4.24	27455	96.62
66.61	2.21	2.90	28704	96.65
65.65	2.12	2.95	31481	96.05
56.29	1.89	4.83	35080	96.30
65.98	1.49	4.09	36384	96.67
55.37	1.39	8.62	36078	96.78
56.18	2.03	4.04	23796	96.91
59.48	3.57	0.05	123716	99.33
63.81	1.59	3.24	40848	97.13
56.97	1.16	9.12	63666	93.93
57.21	2.01	5.64	68884	97.40
66.06	1.37	1.46	32894	96.03
59.12	1.87	4.10	41675	96.68
65.14	1.44	2.98	27436	96.37
54.24	1.57	3.34	49649	99.49
65.00	1.77	3.15	48500	97.50
64.19	1.73	3.12	37518	96.78
63.73	1.09	3.50	29498	96.64
64.92	1.13	3.10	28095	96.61
62.58	1.29	3.87	43233	99.33
62.36	1.51	4.49	53741	96.88
59.75	1.75	7.16	92932	97.82
62.93	1.50	4.69	38116	98.15
60.45	1.47	7.24	99845	99.62
45.67	1.38	-1.40	21779	101.51
39.19	0.93	3.01	33656	97.49

13-7 各地区全部国有及规模以上非国有工业企业主要指标（2000年）

Main Indicators of All State-owned and Non-state-owned above Designated Size Industrial Enterprises by Region (2000)

单位：亿元 (100 million yuan)

地 区	Region	企业单位数（个） Number of Enterprises	工业总产值 Gross Industrial Output Value	工业增加值 Value-added of Industry	实收资本 Total Capital Hold	资产合计 Total Assets	流动资产合计 Total Circulating Funds
全 国	**National Total**	**162885**	**85673.66**	**25394.80**	**32940.45**	**126211.24**	**54338.15**
北 京	Beijing	4572	2565.38	722.65	1174.24	4322.55	2005.63
天 津	Tianjin	5430	2606.38	630.09	1089.28	4001.01	1787.41
河 北	Hebei	7261	3426.05	1132.66	1304.96	5199.74	2000.19
山 西	Shanxi	3275	1216.86	428.71	766.51	3159.85	1221.05
内蒙古	Inner Mongolia	1373	748.97	279.54	537.11	1821.16	603.70
辽 宁	Liaoning	6017	4249.46	1194.03	2056.58	7771.29	3155.90
吉 林	Jilin	2728	1679.91	496.19	712.87	3184.67	1291.93
黑龙江	Heilongjiang	2666	2460.88	1213.05	1197.13	4080.37	1567.07
上 海	Shanghai	8574	6204.52	1687.18	3123.97	9437.09	4370.38
江 苏	Jiangsu	18309	10452.87	2604.37	2941.09	11089.33	5499.34
浙 江	Zhejiang	14575	6603.65	1560.11	1756.31	7008.09	3377.81
安 徽	Anhui	3680	1661.44	507.38	795.54	2977.85	1212.57
福 建	Fujian	6011	2616.12	797.12	1038.74	3368.64	1401.27
江 西	Jiangxi	3549	932.21	269.73	403.60	1835.97	730.33
山 东	Shandong	11679	8311.53	2549.35	2295.46	9701.96	4076.79
河 南	Henan	9930	3494.96	1116.39	1174.90	5234.70	2216.51
湖 北	Hubei	6282	3064.43	1011.77	1135.46	4776.01	1941.97
湖 南	Hunan	4808	1627.94	528.06	599.96	2768.85	1107.19
广 东	Guangdong	19695	12480.93	3423.86	3984.31	14370.57	6891.49
广 西	Guangxi	3155	1003.24	323.88	440.76	1890.92	684.22
海 南	Hainan	596	202.87	63.25	127.80	422.41	156.70
重 庆	Chongqing	2040	962.32	283.73	559.91	1945.11	865.97
四 川	Sichuan	4394	2076.96	662.44	1025.58	4586.11	1845.51
贵 州	Guizhou	2087	631.64	216.99	332.03	1517.13	676.07
云 南	Yunnan	2124	1063.36	531.47	510.45	2310.22	812.81
西 藏	Tibet	362	16.43	9.25	47.25	83.72	25.62
陕 西	Shaanxi	2553	1184.58	411.17	679.47	2683.07	1084.49
甘 肃	Gansu	2851	840.58	244.73	438.03	1758.37	713.65
青 海	Qinghai	445	196.08	65.34	131.52	684.54	223.06
宁 夏	Ningxia	409	239.11	73.68	124.54	511.12	212.73
新 疆	Xinjiang	1455	852.01	356.62	435.07	1708.81	578.79

13-7 续表 1 continued

单位：亿元 (100 million yuan)

地　区	Region	流动资产年平均余额 Annual Average Balance of Circulating Funds	固定资产原价合计 Original Value of Fixed Assets	固定资产净值年平均余额 Annual Average Balance of Net Value of Fixed Assets	流动负债合　计 Total Liquid Liabilities	长期负债合　计 Long-term Liabilities	所有者权益合　计 Creditors' Equity
全　国	**National Total**	**51910.37**	**78646.30**	**51792.33**	**53052.64**	**22825.72**	**49406.88**
北　京	Beijing	1888.05	2402.79	1517.20	1813.75	666.05	1830.51
天　津	Tianjin	1488.27	2488.60	1561.39	1727.00	680.14	1567.19
河　北	Hebei	1962.28	3532.84	2285.01	2132.30	1001.40	1989.95
山　西	Shanxi	1175.88	2170.68	1473.69	1164.12	855.54	1115.49
内蒙古	Inner Mongolia	597.80	1385.74	946.87	626.73	439.83	742.17
辽　宁	Liaoning	2958.51	5372.79	3449.08	3220.90	1454.41	3066.26
吉　林	Jilin	1238.36	1833.04	1253.02	1408.48	681.04	1088.56
黑龙江	Heilongjiang	1538.85	3233.51	1961.25	1654.24	708.74	1708.81
上　海	Shanghai	4123.09	5373.06	3383.13	3698.81	981.82	4733.66
江　苏	Jiangsu	5223.40	6181.57	4183.89	5305.70	1510.55	4236.60
浙　江	Zhejiang	3207.75	3753.68	2624.63	3073.84	926.66	3005.97
安　徽	Anhui	1177.06	1880.95	1226.15	1198.87	656.24	1096.28
福　建	Fujian	1307.81	2032.18	1464.57	1293.67	635.86	1430.52
江　西	Jiangxi	708.39	1154.45	763.58	803.21	430.47	575.00
山　东	Shandong	3895.40	6297.37	3983.70	4121.17	1765.13	3634.25
河　南	Henan	2168.87	3447.01	2207.10	2295.92	1155.40	1757.36
湖　北	Hubei	1914.07	2989.31	1943.85	1831.87	1081.86	1743.45
湖　南	Hunan	1081.10	1947.23	1268.61	1154.88	672.00	897.07
广　东	Guangdong	6626.81	8005.77	5420.33	6438.74	1687.96	6098.21
广　西	Guangxi	663.84	1296.41	920.13	832.18	447.45	597.63
海　南	Hainan	150.19	264.43	187.48	156.25	121.54	141.61
重　庆	Chongqing	815.76	1151.58	754.33	926.20	316.98	684.68
四　川	Sichuan	1749.95	2917.04	1943.99	1773.71	1166.33	1630.26
贵　州	Guizhou	650.77	913.15	608.02	690.00	356.58	460.98
云　南	Yunnan	811.01	1409.92	969.90	806.72	475.02	1028.47
西　藏	Tibet	21.34	59.58	35.14	17.21	5.15	61.14
陕　西	Shaanxi	1015.04	1730.35	1170.09	1142.37	673.97	843.12
甘　肃	Gansu	713.08	1165.68	799.99	663.82	480.01	614.55
青　海	Qinghai	310.81	505.81	361.62	232.08	266.69	185.53
宁　夏	Ningxia	198.31	362.21	233.31	199.38	104.18	204.40
新　疆	Xinjiang	528.51	1387.56	891.27	648.51	420.71	637.17

13-7 续表 2 continued

单位：亿元 (100 million yuan)

地　区	Region	产品销售收入 Sales Revenue	产品销售成本 Cost of Sales	产品销售税金及附加 Sales Tax and Extra Charges	产品销售利润 Sales Profit	利润总额 Total Profits	本年应交增值税 Value Added Tax Payable
全　国	**National Total**	**84151.75**	**68653.95**	**1434.17**	**10732.30**	**4393.48**	**3685.20**
北　京	Beijing	2691.05	2230.70	25.54	324.70	130.51	99.91
天　津	Tianjin	2656.98	2198.27	23.51	332.50	164.86	85.89
河　北	Hebei	3425.08	2812.34	43.94	451.38	184.94	151.95
山　西	Shanxi	1154.40	897.49	18.73	178.13	21.84	75.36
内蒙古	Inner Mongolia	739.54	601.78	11.68	94.32	16.10	49.06
辽　宁	Liaoning	4311.86	3623.54	65.38	501.15	176.25	191.21
吉　林	Jilin	1569.75	1262.98	33.90	225.01	85.58	86.00
黑龙江	Heilongjiang	2464.15	1524.35	57.96	810.26	564.95	212.64
上　海	Shanghai	6429.68	5217.56	89.05	858.93	391.51	253.25
江　苏	Jiangsu	9971.01	8533.46	85.63	994.86	370.03	377.99
浙　江	Zhejiang	6488.67	5495.26	84.83	706.41	353.44	248.80
安　徽	Anhui	1688.08	1369.24	42.32	167.88	38.22	88.65
福　建	Fujian	2468.69	2052.32	44.40	266.63	110.80	91.40
江　西	Jiangxi	896.87	729.56	22.35	106.75	12.42	45.83
山　东	Shandong	8061.39	6582.35	97.91	1081.39	544.00	360.68
河　南	Henan	3297.78	2708.84	57.13	414.40	139.97	140.02
湖　北	Hubei	2870.36	2294.40	55.85	358.45	106.47	131.53
湖　南	Hunan	1563.26	1222.39	84.19	194.45	34.48	87.25
广　东	Guangdong	12380.65	10381.40	117.19	1328.68	564.75	362.08
广　西	Guangxi	987.51	777.32	18.75	136.26	35.94	62.39
海　南	Hainan	174.75	135.65	3.42	17.98	4.67	8.53
重　庆	Chongqing	959.36	778.68	19.69	114.84	15.64	50.78
四　川	Sichuan	2073.17	1613.98	50.15	293.23	71.32	112.69
贵　州	Guizhou	593.80	434.80	31.42	95.45	12.56	43.73
云　南	Yunnan	1058.91	685.26	174.86	172.14	69.75	88.52
西　藏	Tibet	15.24	8.63	0.44	3.00	2.67	1.14
陕　西	Shaanxi	1133.82	861.23	28.75	193.72	63.80	63.20
甘　肃	Gansu	770.85	665.42	18.04	68.76	10.35	38.88
青　海	Qinghai	195.74	157.94	2.86	28.80	0.79	13.36
宁　夏	Ningxia	238.10	198.96	3.22	28.82	4.39	11.72
新　疆	Xinjiang	821.26	597.83	21.08	183.03	90.49	50.75

13-8 各地区全部国有及规模以上非国有工业企业主要经济效益指标(2000年)

Main Indicators on Economic Benefit of All State-owned and Non-state-owned above Designated Size Industrial Enterprises by Region (2000)

地 区	Region	工业增加值率(%) Ratio of Value Added to Gross Industrial Output Value (%)	总资产贡献率(%) Ratio of Total Assets to Industrial Output Value (%)	资产负债率(%) Assets-Liability Ratio (%)	流动资产周转次数(次/年) Number of Times of Turnover of Circulating Fund (times/year)	工业成本费用利润率(%) Ratio of Profits to Industrial Cost (%)	全员劳动生产率(元/人.年) Overall Labor Productivity (yuan-person-year)	产品销售率(%) Proportion of Products Sold (%)
全 国	**National Total**	**29.64**	**9.00**	**60.81**	**1.62**	**5.56**	**45679**	**97.67**
北 京	Beijing	28.17	6.94	57.65	1.43	5.02	63878	95.95
天 津	Tianjin	24.18	8.50	60.83	1.79	6.48	52425	98.39
河 北	Hebei	33.06	9.00	61.73	1.75	5.75	41990	97.64
山 西	Shanxi	35.23	5.52	63.92	0.98	1.94	23356	96.88
内蒙古	Inner Mongolia	37.32	6.19	59.25	1.24	2.23	32756	98.45
辽 宁	Liaoning	28.10	6.91	60.46	1.46	4.27	40451	97.79
吉 林	Jilin	29.54	7.91	65.82	1.27	5.70	36796	98.09
黑龙江	Heilongjiang	49.29	21.60	58.07	1.60	31.39	62152	98.12
上 海	Shanghai	27.19	8.87	49.80	1.56	6.43	82327	99.02
江 苏	Jiangsu	24.92	8.92	61.80	1.91	3.87	50259	97.15
浙 江	Zhejiang	23.62	11.26	57.11	2.02	5.77	48268	96.87
安 徽	Anhui	30.54	7.09	63.19	1.43	2.40	31203	98.48
福 建	Fujian	30.47	8.60	57.52	1.89	4.76	51244	96.95
江 西	Jiangxi	28.93	6.20	68.30	1.27	1.43	24780	97.27
山 东	Shandong	30.67	11.86	62.54	2.07	7.31	48804	97.86
河 南	Henan	31.94	8.28	66.43	1.52	4.47	32340	98.00
湖 北	Hubei	33.02	7.86	63.50	1.50	3.95	43921	99.14
湖 南	Hunan	32.44	8.86	67.60	1.45	2.38	31675	98.61
广 东	Guangdong	27.43	8.55	57.56	1.87	4.82	59775	97.40
广 西	Guangxi	32.28	7.82	68.39	1.49	3.86	35494	97.85
海 南	Hainan	31.18	5.54	66.48	1.16	2.73	52707	94.41
重 庆	Chongqing	29.48	6.09	64.80	1.18	1.67	31252	99.09
四 川	Sichuan	31.89	6.85	64.45	1.18	3.60	31848	98.21
贵 州	Guizhou	34.35	7.17	69.29	0.91	2.31	31751	96.61
云 南	Yunnan	49.98	15.80	55.48	1.31	8.39	68960	98.79
西 藏	Tibet	56.29	5.31	26.97	0.71	21.97	31634	92.11
陕 西	Shaanxi	34.71	7.60	68.17	1.12	6.06	32899	96.70
甘 肃	Gansu	29.11	5.10	65.05	1.08	1.34	26819	95.15
青 海	Qinghai	33.32	4.77	72.90	0.63	0.41	41175	97.22
宁 夏	Ningxia	30.81	5.50	60.01	1.20	1.87	32874	96.26
新 疆	Xinjiang	41.86	11.01	62.71	1.55	12.83	76656	97.62

13-9 按行业分国有及国有控股工业企业主要指标（2000年）

单位：亿元

行业	Item	企业单位数（个）Number of Enterprises (unit)	工业总产值 Gross Industrial Output Value	工业增加值 Value-added of Industry
全国总计	**National Total**	**53489**	**40554.37**	**13777.68**
煤炭采选业	Coal Mining and Dressing	1321	1045.89	498.14
石油和天然气开采业	Petroleum and Natural Gas Extraction	67	2959.50	2047.61
黑色金属矿采选业	Ferrous Metals Mining and Dressing	179	64.96	28.87
有色金属矿采选业	Nonferrous Metals Mining and Dressing	662	186.64	75.65
非金属矿采选业	Nonmetal Minerals Mining and Dressing	621	124.96	54.52
木材及竹材采运业	Logging and Transport of Timber and Bamboo	486	120.30	61.24
食品加工业	Food Processing	5082	1302.83	291.72
食品制造业	Food Manufacturing	2071	428.64	126.33
饮料制造业	Beverage Manufacturing	1663	863.93	336.89
烟草加工业	Tobacco Processing	299	1426.66	927.62
纺织业	Textile Industry	2631	1659.60	446.05
服装及其他纤维制品制造	Garments and Other Fiber Products	638	135.81	40.75
皮革毛皮羽绒及其制品业	Leather, Furs, Down and Related Products	331	56.58	14.05
木材加工及竹藤棕草制品业	Timber Processing, Bamboo, Cane, Palm Fiber and Straw Products	638	101.46	27.61
家具制造业	Furniture Manufacturing	239	23.54	7.44
造纸及纸制品业	Papermaking and Paper Products	1028	432.13	121.92
印刷业记录媒介的复制	Printing and Record Medium Reproduction	2148	234.02	91.19
文教体育用品制造业	Cultural, Educational and Sports Goods	268	35.61	12.04
石油加工及炼焦业	Petroleum Processing and Coking	281	4029.58	694.20
化学原料及制品制造业	Raw Chemical Materials and Chemical Products	3692	2900.22	705.15
医药制造业	Medical and Pharmaceutical Products	1496	883.93	321.05
化学纤维制造业	Chemical Fiber	233	684.11	170.50
橡胶制品业	Rubber Products	374	279.14	72.30
塑料制品业	Plastic Products	967	217.85	55.09
非金属矿物制品业	Nonmetal Mineral Products	4279	1125.45	363.42
黑色金属冶炼及压延加工业	Smelting and Pressing of Ferrous Metals	702	3490.92	1031.39
有色金属冶炼及压延加工业	Smelting and Pressing of Nonferrous Metals	608	1153.62	295.27
金属制品业	Metal Products	1426	307.97	80.50
普通机械制造业	Ordinary Machinery	2761	1168.83	334.95
专用设备制造业	Special Purpose Equipment	2622	903.43	238.34
交通运输设备制造业	Transport Equipment	2747	3593.62	889.12
电气机械及器材制造业	Electric Equipment and Machinery	1684	935.54	262.64
电子及通信设备制造业	Electronic and Telecommunications Equipment	1330	2847.71	741.11
仪器仪表文化办公用机械	Instruments, Meters, Cultural and Office Machinery	710	198.31	58.39
电力蒸汽热水生产供应业	Production and Supply of Electric Power, Steam and Hot Water	4128	3939.61	2026.52
煤气的生产和供应业	Production and Supply of Gas	252	121.99	27.07
自来水的生产和供应业	Production and Supply of Tap Water	2231	285.97	136.14

Main Indicators of State-owned and State-holding Industrial Enterprises by Industrial Branch (2000)

(100 million yuan)

实收资本 Total Capital Hold	资产合计 Total Assets	流动资产合计 Circulating Funds	流动资产年平均余额 Annual Average Balance of Circulating Funds	固定资产原价 Original Value of Fixed Assets	固定资产净值年平均余额 Annual Average Balance of Net Value of Fixed Assets
20156.14	**84014.94**	**32628.81**	**31485.38**	**57294.96**	**36886.64**
959.98	3587.53	1258.17	1221.49	2821.89	1874.96
1681.82	4041.55	885.01	884.42	5182.77	2700.91
109.05	254.46	77.58	77.91	126.12	77.42
105.70	407.54	139.64	134.94	290.30	190.05
145.07	514.99	166.59	160.16	357.44	271.47
99.20	400.16	161.58	161.47	249.22	180.75
326.23	1564.53	704.25	692.83	913.67	654.24
160.70	692.28	309.47	299.92	361.46	257.27
309.92	1608.13	773.88	727.65	768.73	549.05
322.91	1937.53	956.39	935.18	887.30	591.17
581.74	2734.83	1258.39	1210.60	1604.32	1038.50
55.95	219.57	127.30	124.78	91.29	64.39
24.65	112.78	61.72	63.32	54.40	43.29
66.93	266.78	91.40	90.58	174.60	130.27
16.87	54.15	23.15	22.75	24.21	17.37
224.97	1125.72	429.63	405.56	633.97	461.17
151.02	498.72	202.75	190.32	332.16	207.43
20.82	89.99	46.92	48.53	31.00	21.58
709.38	3418.05	1124.26	1094.08	3097.81	1851.45
1242.24	6034.00	2129.55	2060.12	4224.03	2778.57
365.10	1702.68	899.95	856.86	638.47	442.41
314.47	1259.01	417.41	410.13	955.51	613.60
109.64	567.79	262.28	264.39	276.38	187.02
112.61	462.85	204.99	193.21	250.24	176.18
708.73	2976.44	1158.94	1118.69	1912.30	1324.03
2181.74	7970.32	2755.22	2608.78	5952.87	3613.36
572.98	2057.49	822.79	782.13	1394.56	915.98
146.65	611.87	331.41	320.82	295.15	197.93
632.82	2906.69	1606.05	1554.78	1344.27	844.32
440.80	2061.48	1157.22	1085.98	1020.21	628.87
1502.20	6358.66	3273.01	3140.16	2851.12	1876.17
414.62	1871.52	1058.02	1046.27	756.95	496.33
706.38	3832.99	2441.65	2238.58	1191.11	723.45
110.12	480.50	267.21	262.05	211.94	135.03
3566.94	16588.56	4226.23	4222.39	13943.35	9304.30
255.57	572.43	161.13	154.05	424.78	299.19
521.85	1375.47	321.87	295.08	1173.83	814.87

13-9 续表 1

单位：亿元

行业	Item	流动负债合计 Liquid Liabilities	长期负债合计 Long-term Liabilities	所有者权益 Creditors' Equity
全国总计	**National Total**	**32237.41**	**18456.43**	**32714.81**
煤炭采选业	Coal Mining and Dressing	1284.72	1039.44	1251.25
石油和天然气开采业	Petroleum and Natural Gas Extraction	796.72	690.35	2413.65
黑色金属矿采选业	Ferrous Metals Mining and Dressing	75.00	13.00	148.14
有色金属矿采选业	Nonferrous Metals Mining and Dressing	169.05	96.86	139.52
非金属矿采选业	Nonmetal Minerals Mining and Dressing	186.33	135.34	192.73
木材及竹材采运业	Logging and Transport of Timber and Bamboo	213.62	56.99	128.71
食品加工业	Food Processing	1031.60	219.04	293.11
食品制造业	Food Manufacturing	359.23	99.19	228.96
饮料制造业	Beverage Manufacturing	778.90	178.60	646.16
烟草加工业	Tobacco Processing	762.72	122.22	1051.60
纺织业	Textile Industry	1501.09	534.17	681.92
服装及其他纤维制品制造	Garments and Other Fiber Products	124.54	15.65	78.43
皮革毛皮羽绒及其制品业	Leather, Furs, Down and Related Products	82.86	14.35	15.21
木材加工及竹藤棕草制品业	Timber Processing, Bamboo, Cane, Palm Fiber and Straw Products	121.41	72.86	71.20
家具制造业	Furniture Manufacturing	27.50	7.65	18.82
造纸及纸制品业	Papermaking and Paper Products	481.28	278.85	360.16
印刷业记录媒介的复制	Printing and Record Medium Reproduction	202.48	76.02	218.67
文教体育用品制造业	Cultural, Educational and Sports Goods	44.10	8.57	37.31
石油加工及炼焦业	Petroleum Processing and Coking	1225.13	749.11	1387.70
化学原料及制品制造业	Raw Chemical Materials and Chemical Products	2374.99	1559.04	2070.73
医药制造业	Medical and Pharmaceutical Products	792.67	198.17	697.43
化学纤维制造业	Chemical Fiber	408.05	303.63	547.39
橡胶制品业	Rubber Products	282.49	114.62	167.22
塑料制品业	Plastic Products	207.26	90.29	163.89
非金属矿物制品业	Nonmetal Mineral Products	1326.72	627.66	1001.02
黑色金属冶炼及压延加工业	Smelting and Pressing of Ferrous Metals	2909.23	1433.41	3603.81
有色金属冶炼及压延加工业	Smelting and Pressing of Nonferrous Metals	868.00	466.99	706.71
金属制品业	Metal Products	349.15	93.34	166.76
普通机械制造业	Ordinary Machinery	1548.00	391.67	960.46
专用设备制造业	Special Purpose Equipment	1153.94	249.74	647.53
交通运输设备制造业	Transport Equipment	3133.63	878.87	2318.64
电气机械及器材制造业	Electric Equipment and Machinery	977.58	233.28	657.18
电子及通信设备制造业	Electronic and Telecommunications Equipment	1855.02	418.84	1526.79
仪器仪表文化办公用机械	Instruments, Meters, Cultural and Office Machinery	266.04	68.37	140.51
电力蒸汽热水生产供应业	Production and Supply of Electric Power, Steam and Hot Water	3460.89	6430.92	6589.46
煤气的生产和供应业	Production and Supply of Gas	160.42	95.92	315.16
自来水的生产和供应业	Production and Supply of Tap Water	267.54	252.35	854.13

continued

(100 million yuan)

产　品 销售收入 Sales Revenue	产　品 销售成本 Cost of Sales	产品销售 税金及附加 Sales Tax and Extra Charges	产　品 销售利润 Sales Profit	利润总额 Total Profits	本年应交 增 值 税 Value-added Tax Payable
42203.12	**33473.62**	**1150.28**	**6263.42**	**2408.33**	**2320.36**
1003.31	724.33	13.83	186.42	-7.33	86.20
2835.63	1335.39	68.68	1420.92	1106.57	292.43
60.74	42.85	2.40	11.26	0.47	4.00
173.15	123.26	1.37	43.88	11.25	8.58
117.04	79.17	3.97	21.85	-0.02	9.08
107.79	65.70	6.07	28.31	1.14	2.58
1247.48	1110.07	5.33	81.86	0.87	33.48
401.04	315.27	1.95	48.31	15.38	20.52
827.55	521.23	70.43	138.03	70.80	61.19
1406.72	654.64	565.12	170.07	142.44	142.29
1606.23	1388.24	6.22	180.79	31.94	69.93
135.04	115.88	0.51	13.73	2.27	3.40
44.44	38.60	0.18	3.50	-2.47	1.29
93.67	79.17	0.93	9.21	-1.39	5.03
22.02	18.18	0.12	2.49	0.46	0.94
425.06	352.35	2.24	57.07	14.95	23.48
228.30	172.23	1.52	49.11	17.15	15.00
37.36	29.58	0.18	6.09	1.33	1.93
4181.96	3810.38	175.27	164.21	-10.44	106.48
2753.30	2321.30	26.19	324.79	49.53	111.41
853.83	548.48	5.60	175.88	67.83	60.66
662.20	554.65	7.33	91.25	33.10	27.15
244.96	205.94	10.69	18.19	-6.68	10.62
223.07	186.47	0.81	27.97	7.61	7.60
1056.00	825.20	8.61	157.15	8.27	67.73
3677.84	3104.08	25.02	472.89	117.44	217.97
1118.73	912.77	5.85	184.12	35.30	59.19
299.38	249.29	1.19	37.34	2.23	11.98
1119.38	888.40	5.17	176.85	8.96	55.74
857.25	703.25	4.16	114.29	-3.47	33.07
3573.03	2894.98	70.30	502.54	125.87	149.54
907.31	720.46	3.61	126.88	24.60	40.03
2774.97	2323.33	5.88	316.25	173.32	70.02
200.81	152.45	1.27	35.61	2.80	8.62
6202.47	5289.95	36.70	792.31	378.69	471.82
184.23	180.82	0.78	-7.53	-5.21	6.47
269.98	208.23	3.30	46.48	4.93	16.79

13-10 按行业分国有及国有控股工业企业主要经济效益指标（2000年）

行　业	Branch	工业增加值率 (%) Ratio of Value Added to Gross Industrial Output Value (%)	总资产贡献率 (%) Ratio of Total Assets to Industrial Output Value (%)
全国总计	**National Total**	**33.97**	**8.43**
煤炭采选业	Coal Mining and Dressing	47.63	3.52
石油和天然气开采业	Petroleum and Natural Gas Extraction	69.19	37.32
黑色金属矿采选业	Ferrous Metals Mining and Dressing	44.45	3.45
有色金属矿采选业	Nonferrous Metals Mining and Dressing	40.53	7.00
非金属矿采选业	Nonmetal Minerals Mining and Dressing	43.63	3.38
木材及竹材采运业	Logging and Transport of Timber and Bamboo	50.91	3.48
食品加工业	Food Processing	22.39	4.42
食品制造业	Food Production	29.47	6.92
饮料制造业	Beverage Production	38.99	13.64
烟草加工业	Tobacco Processing	65.02	44.84
纺织业	Textile Industry	26.88	5.76
服装及其他纤维制品制造	Garments and Other Fiber Products	30.00	4.10
皮革毛皮羽绒及其制品业	Leather, Furs, Down and Related Products	24.84	0.73
木材加工及竹藤棕草制品业	Timber Processing, Bamboo, Cane, Palm Fiber and Straw Products	27.21	3.49
家具制造业	Furniture Manufacturing	31.59	4.25
造纸及纸制品业	Papermaking and Paper Products	28.21	5.18
印刷业记录媒介的复制	Printing and Record Medium Reproduction	38.97	7.79
文教体育用品制造业	Cultural, Educational and Sports Goods	33.82	4.99
石油加工及炼焦业	Petroleum Processing and Coking	17.23	9.65
化学原料及制品制造业	Raw Chemical Materials and Chemical Products	24.31	4.70
医药制造业	Medical and Pharmaceutical Products	36.32	9.25
化学纤维制造业	Chemical Fiber	24.92	7.02
橡胶制品业	Rubber Products	25.90	4.19
塑料制品业	Plastic Products	25.29	4.97
非金属矿物制品业	Nonmetal Mineral Products	32.29	4.38
黑色金属冶炼及压延加工业	Smelting and Pressing of Ferrous Metals	29.54	5.97
有色金属冶炼及压延加工业	Smelting and Pressing of Nonferrous Metals	25.60	7.40
金属制品业	Metal Products	26.14	3.90
普通机械制造业	Ordinary Machinery Manufacturing	28.66	3.86
专用设备制造业	For Special Purposes Equipment Manufacturing	26.38	3.05
交通运输设备制造业	Transport Equipment Manufacturing	24.74	6.76
电气机械及器材制造业	Electric Equipment and Machinery	28.07	5.22
电子及通信设备制造业	Electronic and Telecommunications Equipment	26.02	7.65
仪器仪表文化办公用机械	Instruments,Meters,Cultural and Office Machinery	29.45	4.29
电力蒸汽热水生产供应业	Production and Supply of Electric Power, Steam and Hot Water	51.44	6.90
煤气的生产和供应业	Production and Supply of Gas	22.19	0.84
自来水的生产和供应业	Production and Supply of Tap Water	47.61	2.36

Main Indicators on Economic Benefit of State-owned and State-holding Industrial Enterprises by Industrial Branch (2000)

资产负债率 (%) Assets-Liability Ratio (%)	流动资产周转次数（次/年） Number of Times of Annual of Turnover Circulating Funds (times/year)	工业成本费用利润率 (%) Ratio of Profits to Industrial Cost (%)	全员劳动生产率（元/人.年） Overall Labor Productivity (yuan/person-year)	产品销售率 (%) Proportion of Products Sold (%)
60.99	**1.34**	**6.15**	**45998**	**98.88**
65.12	0.82	-0.71	14423	99.47
40.28	3.21	71.30	356616	99.30
41.78	0.78	0.82	20521	94.99
65.63	1.28	6.64	22784	97.68
62.58	0.73	-0.02	16262	93.09
67.83	0.67	1.18	8311	99.52
81.27	1.80	0.07	35211	98.80
66.93	1.34	3.91	33681	95.42
59.82	1.14	10.10	54759	97.87
45.72	1.50	18.60	379933	99.99
75.07	1.33	2.01	19387	98.07
64.28	1.08	1.68	20352	97.92
86.52	0.70	-5.14	17775	92.85
73.31	1.03	-1.41	20360	96.58
65.25	0.97	2.03	23926	96.14
67.83	1.05	3.56	28230	98.11
56.14	1.20	7.84	28772	97.62
58.54	0.77	3.56	25418	99.87
59.27	3.82	-0.26	146065	99.48
65.68	1.34	1.81	31743	98.31
59.04	1.00	8.51	52798	94.69
56.52	1.61	5.28	63390	98.33
70.55	0.93	-2.73	26088	97.49
64.59	1.15	3.47	32818	97.61
66.16	0.94	0.78	22095	97.35
54.54	1.41	3.29	50432	100.40
65.65	1.43	3.27	42028	97.99
72.75	0.93	0.74	24643	98.98
66.96	0.72	0.79	21933	98.00
68.35	0.79	-0.39	18501	97.52
63.23	1.14	3.65	41980	100.56
64.86	0.87	2.73	33104	98.28
60.16	1.24	6.53	98855	98.35
70.76	0.77	1.37	21341	97.27
60.26	1.47	6.56	93804	99.70
44.94	1.20	-2.44	17364	100.42
37.90	0.91	1.79	31622	97.11

13-11 各地区国有及国有控股工业企业主要指标（2000年）

Main Indicators of State-owned and State-holding Industrial Enterprises by Region (2000)

单位：亿元 (100 million yuan)

地　区	Region	企业单位数（个）Number of Enterprises	工业总产值 Gross Industrial Output Value	工业增加值 Value Added of Industry	实收资本 Total Capital Hold	资产合计 Total Assets	流动资产合计 Total Circulating Funds
全　国	**National Total**	**53489**	**40554.37**	**13777.68**	**20156.14**	**84014.94**	**32628.81**
北　京	Beijing	2430	1742.66	483.56	855.42	3345.36	1400.83
天　津	Tianjin	1843	856.86	274.66	602.13	2396.17	884.92
河　北	Hebei	2707	1797.35	668.34	950.10	3914.98	1362.08
山　西	Shanxi	1791	837.80	306.70	648.53	2709.96	984.63
内蒙古	Inner Mongolia	757	598.08	225.35	485.00	1621.40	495.67
辽　宁	Liaoning	2454	2827.94	817.92	1477.57	6082.61	2332.24
吉　林	Jilin	1667	1377.42	392.29	593.03	2781.01	1092.27
黑龙江	Heilongjiang	1588	2071.08	1102.49	1061.64	3559.55	1283.95
上　海	Shanghai	2473	3205.11	1002.09	1962.06	6283.64	2563.52
江　苏	Jiangsu	2554	3067.86	841.12	1125.70	4978.57	2251.65
浙　江	Zhejiang	1418	1292.72	407.28	526.34	2413.15	954.34
安　徽	Anhui	1128	1044.54	340.42	591.98	2291.10	865.63
福　建	Fujian	1367	854.95	292.29	342.51	1477.70	537.31
江　西	Jiangxi	2509	737.36	214.77	330.00	1633.21	643.11
山　东	Shandong	2774	3486.54	1262.56	1337.95	6117.20	2250.29
河　南	Henan	3069	1880.99	594.30	791.95	3817.19	1544.56
湖　北	Hubei	2965	1929.02	655.92	909.98	3983.45	1571.02
湖　南	Hunan	2339	1077.47	374.88	449.59	2262.67	874.67
广　东	Guangdong	3320	3126.12	1035.47	1194.57	5593.75	2411.27
广　西	Guangxi	2027	664.36	226.14	312.66	1459.14	511.20
海　南	Hainan	401	136.89	41.08	88.63	326.96	110.91
重　庆	Chongqing	931	653.58	199.31	468.49	1599.16	684.39
四　川	Sichuan	1699	1249.62	405.36	743.78	3522.23	1347.30
贵　州	Guizhou	1397	500.76	175.83	283.77	1354.71	595.18
云　南	Yunnan	1388	854.89	468.54	411.85	1955.93	661.24
西　藏	Tibet	232	12.62	7.29	43.66	76.26	22.05
陕　西	Shaanxi	1633	927.07	326.88	576.68	2322.12	932.62
甘　肃	Gansu	960	642.22	194.00	379.91	1527.41	592.14
青　海	Qinghai	362	174.72	58.36	120.96	650.92	209.22
宁　夏	Ningxia	209	174.58	53.43	99.38	423.81	168.78
新　疆	Xinjiang	1097	751.19	329.04	390.34	1533.60	489.81

13-11 续表 1 continued

单位：亿元 (100 million yuan)

地 区	Region	流动资产年平均余额 Annual Average Balance of Circulating Funds	固定资产原价合计 Original Value of Fixed Assets	固定资产净值年平均余额 Annual Average Balance of Net Value of Fixed Assets	流动负债合计 Total Liquid Liabilities	长期负债合计 Long-term Liabilities	所有者权益合计 Creditors' Equity
全 国	**National Total**	**31485.38**	**57294.96**	**36886.64**	**32237.41**	**18456.43**	**32714.81**
北 京	Beijing	1375.64	2039.13	1274.28	1264.94	591.36	1480.00
天 津	Tianjin	844.82	1716.58	1124.65	937.43	593.08	855.61
河 北	Hebei	1351.15	2856.31	1783.09	1510.53	857.27	1505.41
山 西	Shanxi	944.04	1933.23	1292.41	926.54	797.46	961.27
内蒙古	Inner Mongolia	494.04	1288.30	878.35	524.52	416.15	669.66
辽 宁	Liaoning	2183.51	4462.71	2813.37	2421.65	1273.43	2374.92
吉 林	Jilin	1049.20	1623.21	1099.85	1204.03	639.07	935.16
黑龙江	Heilongjiang	1268.89	2998.51	1778.46	1370.42	642.75	1538.95
上 海	Shanghai	2424.58	3910.97	2377.87	2113.19	806.68	3353.68
江 苏	Jiangsu	2135.42	3037.48	1961.52	2118.89	880.30	1964.10
浙 江	Zhejiang	929.09	1558.17	1063.42	786.61	520.42	1105.33
安 徽	Anhui	847.38	1528.38	970.57	818.13	556.69	894.16
福 建	Fujian	500.91	1038.93	720.61	501.23	391.66	582.82
江 西	Jiangxi	625.65	1050.08	684.89	710.51	400.84	498.20
山 东	Shandong	2155.99	4434.62	2686.55	2282.14	1378.78	2310.41
河 南	Henan	1510.68	2653.09	1626.28	1606.95	917.50	1276.05
湖 北	Hubei	1550.89	2595.52	1659.55	1493.81	989.15	1416.86
湖 南	Hunan	854.05	1639.02	1059.85	916.68	597.11	706.14
广 东	Guangdong	2270.87	3513.50	2420.20	2211.90	888.95	2435.24
广 西	Guangxi	501.68	1042.00	730.85	637.12	365.20	447.17
海 南	Hainan	107.61	210.02	149.63	113.38	106.04	105.63
重 庆	Chongqing	652.77	988.61	643.79	742.90	279.34	561.39
四 川	Sichuan	1275.26	2383.24	1561.46	1260.77	1031.02	1222.86
贵 州	Guizhou	574.61	839.57	554.77	605.21	337.46	405.04
云 南	Yunnan	667.33	1204.84	825.69	633.11	415.08	907.74
西 藏	Tibet	17.83	56.29	32.39	15.75	4.68	55.60
陕 西	Shaanxi	872.31	1534.74	1017.70	1013.59	587.03	701.28
甘 肃	Gansu	592.07	1053.72	718.53	554.07	445.81	527.53
青 海	Qinghai	297.52	488.47	347.11	218.76	258.94	172.98
宁 夏	Ningxia	156.52	313.05	197.38	156.50	90.95	173.29
新 疆	Xinjiang	453.07	1302.67	831.57	566.13	396.23	570.34

13-11 续表 2 continued

单位：亿元 (100 million yuan)

地区	Region	产品销售收入 Sales Revenue	产品销售成本 Cost of Sales	产品销售税金及附加 Sales Tax and Extra Charges	产品销售利润 Sales Profit	利润总额 Total Profits	本年应交增值税 Value-added Tax Payable
全国	**National Total**	**42203.12**	**33473.62**	**1150.28**	**6263.42**	**2408.33**	**2320.36**
北京	Beijing	1871.36	1581.80	22.17	209.62	81.82	70.21
天津	Tianjin	984.16	816.65	16.37	128.98	33.63	41.20
河北	Hebei	1951.62	1580.21	31.84	287.93	93.01	109.10
山西	Shanxi	829.07	637.41	11.99	143.27	12.64	58.61
内蒙古	Inner Mongolia	605.04	490.67	9.49	78.84	11.42	41.58
辽宁	Liaoning	2983.17	2519.54	55.36	348.25	114.26	143.90
吉林	Jilin	1309.15	1055.06	30.87	191.53	73.01	74.78
黑龙江	Heilongjiang	2113.49	1235.58	54.77	772.02	554.33	197.90
上海	Shanghai	3352.40	2711.52	81.41	475.33	220.56	160.59
江苏	Jiangsu	3233.09	2733.65	49.95	363.59	110.46	141.60
浙江	Zhejiang	1481.20	1247.07	46.55	146.85	73.86	70.64
安徽	Anhui	1127.43	903.33	36.30	113.54	24.34	66.58
福建	Fujian	826.74	656.30	33.95	109.14	42.28	44.40
江西	Jiangxi	722.16	586.83	20.03	90.80	8.33	38.96
山东	Shandong	3797.07	2976.67	70.19	616.87	303.87	220.55
河南	Henan	1823.92	1481.09	41.95	248.83	60.93	95.28
湖北	Hubei	1856.43	1469.28	43.48	257.80	63.93	98.61
湖南	Hunan	1071.23	823.21	78.52	137.12	13.10	67.48
广东	Guangdong	3583.55	2924.01	69.13	480.92	226.08	138.20
广西	Guangxi	665.04	521.02	14.38	103.58	24.83	47.50
海南	Hainan	121.39	97.38	3.09	12.22	3.62	5.94
重庆	Chongqing	666.10	534.78	16.12	82.66	5.41	39.29
四川	Sichuan	1284.50	984.68	42.47	196.02	37.79	78.87
贵州	Guizhou	482.42	346.78	30.36	84.83	12.03	38.36
云南	Yunnan	849.46	514.39	171.88	145.81	63.26	77.03
西藏	Tibet	12.58	7.53	0.36	2.23	1.86	0.92
陕西	Shaanxi	899.12	688.25	26.30	161.05	44.94	50.03
甘肃	Gansu	615.13	533.39	15.61	54.02	6.52	33.37
青海	Qinghai	176.68	141.25	2.74	27.43	0.98	12.68
宁夏	Ningxia	179.15	150.08	2.44	22.64	2.35	9.25
新疆	Xinjiang	729.28	524.22	20.21	169.69	82.88	46.95

13-12 各地区国有及国有控股工业企业主要经济效益指标（2000年）

Main Indicators on Economic Benefit of State-owned and State-holding Industrial Enterprises by Region (2000)

地区	Region	工业增加值率(%) Ratio of Value-added to Gross Industrial Output Value (%)	总资产贡献率(%) Ratio of Total Assets to Industrial Output Value (%)	资产负债率(%) Assets-Liability Ratio (%)	流动资产周转次数(次/年) Number of Times of Turnover of Circulating Fund (times/year)	工业成本费用利润率(%) Ratio of Profits to Industrial Cost (%)	全员劳动生产率(元/人.年) Overall Labor Productivity (yuan-person-year)	产品销售率(%) Proportion of Products Sold (%)
全国	**National Total**	**33.97**	**8.43**	**60.99**	**1.34**	**6.15**	**45998**	**98.88**
北京	Beijing	27.75	6.27	55.76	1.36	4.47	62496	97.05
天津	Tianjin	32.05	5.49	64.29	1.16	3.49	47922	99.67
河北	Hebei	37.18	7.56	61.55	1.44	5.03	40257	98.70
山西	Shanxi	36.61	4.96	63.62	0.88	1.56	22881	97.83
内蒙古	Inner Mongolia	37.68	5.86	58.70	1.22	1.93	33587	99.39
辽宁	Liaoning	28.92	6.48	60.85	1.37	3.98	41669	98.95
吉林	Jilin	28.48	7.88	66.37	1.25	5.82	36512	98.60
黑龙江	Heilongjiang	53.23	23.77	56.71	1.67	37.86	66967	98.98
上海	Shanghai	31.27	8.45	46.57	1.38	6.99	98330	99.74
江苏	Jiangsu	27.42	7.28	60.55	1.51	3.56	48072	98.99
浙江	Zhejiang	31.51	8.74	54.20	1.59	5.28	70552	98.76
安徽	Anhui	32.59	6.84	60.97	1.33	2.32	33569	99.26
福建	Fujian	34.19	9.67	60.52	1.65	5.56	66704	98.68
江西	Jiangxi	29.13	5.95	69.07	1.15	1.19	24120	97.67
山东	Shandong	36.21	11.16	62.23	1.76	8.85	51593	99.19
河南	Henan	31.59	6.78	66.57	1.21	3.48	28663	98.42
湖北	Hubei	34.00	6.85	64.43	1.20	3.65	42655	100.95
湖南	Hunan	34.79	8.34	68.79	1.25	1.33	32014	99.32
广东	Guangdong	33.12	9.25	56.47	1.58	6.81	99191	98.95
广西	Guangxi	34.04	7.60	69.35	1.33	3.92	34631	98.68
海南	Hainan	30.01	5.51	67.69	1.13	3.04	44309	95.29
重庆	Chongqing	30.49	5.45	64.89	1.02	0.83	31523	99.44
四川	Sichuan	32.44	6.19	65.28	1.01	3.07	30689	99.24
贵州	Guizhou	35.11	7.35	69.73	0.84	2.76	30910	98.30
云南	Yunnan	54.81	17.26	53.59	1.27	10.07	79310	99.12
西藏	Tibet	57.79	4.35	27.09	0.71	18.26	32759	93.35
陕西	Shaanxi	35.26	6.97	69.33	1.03	5.36	31144	97.24
甘肃	Gansu	30.21	4.91	65.46	1.04	1.05	29409	96.89
青海	Qinghai	33.40	4.80	73.42	0.59	0.57	41065	97.12
宁夏	Ningxia	30.60	4.97	59.11	1.14	1.33	32315	97.71
新疆	Xinjiang	43.80	11.31	62.81	1.61	13.39	84154	98.39

13-13 按行业分"三资"工业企业主要指标(2000年)

单位：亿元

行业	Item	企业单位数(个) Number of Enterprises (unit)	工业总产值 Gross Industrial Output Value	工业增加值 Value-added of Industry
全国总计	**National Total**	**28445**	**23464.55**	**6090.35**
煤炭采选业	Coal Mining and Dressing	11	6.81	0.88
石油和天然气开采业	Petroleum and Natural Gas Extraction			
黑色金属矿采选业	Ferrous Metals Mining and Dressing	9	1.26	0.34
有色金属矿采选业	Nonferrous Metals Mining and Dressing	14	3.27	1.23
非金属矿采选业	Nonmetal Minerals Mining and Dressing	74	18.00	5.06
木材及竹材采运业	Logging and Transport of Timber and Bamboo			
食品加工业	Food Processing	1154	859.81	172.76
食品制造业	Food Manufacturing	867	564.06	174.43
饮料制造业	Beverage Manufacturing	432	514.68	172.41
烟草加工业	Tobacco Processing	5	7.28	4.55
纺织业	Textile Industry	2063	1094.13	263.80
服装及其他纤维制品制造	Garments and Other Fiber Products	3061	1112.06	289.07
皮革毛皮羽绒及其制品业	Leather, Furs, Down and Related Products	1276	759.40	176.77
木材加工及竹藤棕草制品业	Timber Processing, Bamboo, Cane, Palm Fiber and Straw Products	545	207.76	44.10
家具制造业	Furniture Manufacturing	421	166.17	41.62
造纸及纸制品业	Papermaking and Paper Products	671	502.23	118.71
印刷业记录媒介的复制	Printing and Record Medium Reproduction	460	198.21	59.13
文教体育用品制造业	Cultural, Educational and Sports Goods	884	368.73	92.34
石油加工及炼焦业	Petroleum Processing and Coking	94	239.81	44.94
化学原料及制品制造业	Raw Chemical Materials and Chemical Products	1477	1183.87	305.00
医药制造业	Medical and Pharmaceutical Products	542	403.73	155.71
化学纤维制造业	Chemical Fiber	212	436.46	116.17
橡胶制品业	Rubber Products	328	286.75	77.92
塑料制品业	Plastic Products	1888	828.86	205.84
非金属矿物制品业	Nonmetal Mineral Products	1420	647.92	194.88
黑色金属冶炼及压延加工业	Smelting and Pressing of Ferrous Metals	189	339.32	61.25
有色金属冶炼及压延加工业	Smelting and Pressing of Nonferrous Metals	289	293.15	57.18
金属制品业	Metal Products	1637	964.98	212.24
普通机械制造业	Ordinary Machinery	1043	652.68	186.46
专用设备制造业	Special Purpose Equipment	658	334.59	86.70
交通运输设备制造业	Transport Equipment	886	1624.85	408.25
电气机械及器材制造业	Electric Equipment and Machinery	1666	1603.06	421.69
电子及通信设备制造业	Electronic and Telecommunications Equipment	2114	5403.41	1192.97
仪器仪表文化办公用机械	Instruments, Meters, Cultural and Office Machinery	504	492.51	105.88
电力蒸汽热水生产供应业	Production and Supply of Electric Power, Steam and Hot Water	276	714.13	359.88
煤气的生产和供应业	Production and Supply of Gas	36	47.82	7.32
自来水的生产和供应业	Production and Supply of Tap Water	12	6.46	3.13

Main Indicators of Foreign Funded Enterprises by Industrial Branch (2000)

(100 million yuan)

实收资本 Total Capital Hold	资产合计 Total Assets	流动资产合计 Circulating Funds	流动资产年平均余额 Annual Average Balance of Circulating Funds	固定资产原价 Original Value of Fixed Assets	固定资产净值年平均余额 Annual Average Balance of Net Value of Fixed Assets
9080.11	**25714.06**	**12849.54**	**11926.66**	**14318.30**	**9808.74**
0.92	7.72	5.70	4.46	1.74	1.40
0.49	1.04	0.45	0.46	0.38	0.24
0.85	4.00	2.10	2.10	0.96	0.69
9.77	20.24	9.98	10.06	10.10	6.85
251.90	711.12	360.07	340.00	386.76	278.43
300.23	635.04	296.54	262.67	392.80	253.90
345.85	762.51	296.49	296.96	515.88	378.51
6.29	12.91	6.40	6.53	9.47	6.15
481.99	1228.46	610.22	582.77	749.29	507.82
277.82	797.56	493.78	473.12	351.89	233.83
155.11	500.39	319.43	312.55	204.35	137.39
94.77	256.33	121.17	116.71	150.31	112.13
54.93	166.55	97.25	91.68	72.17	50.98
294.23	910.20	383.22	366.93	538.59	435.01
110.83	286.44	148.52	139.03	173.23	109.15
125.53	307.39	178.98	172.22	143.70	95.42
45.00	172.06	61.40	58.13	120.42	98.15
535.35	1398.57	649.42	636.30	778.62	573.12
174.43	529.81	289.86	278.00	219.55	154.53
208.40	527.50	159.58	164.25	440.75	282.74
146.12	409.92	187.21	183.12	231.26	157.71
372.89	925.55	453.64	433.30	544.32	377.54
538.15	1270.12	461.67	431.12	852.00	617.02
153.57	443.24	187.43	177.10	276.71	215.35
132.43	341.47	151.04	145.51	193.78	143.73
389.55	999.16	547.88	523.12	512.69	357.27
384.60	919.11	509.63	483.39	445.03	308.04
149.84	411.65	255.35	237.36	163.82	110.30
663.86	1980.78	995.29	913.47	1000.81	682.32
591.01	1598.64	917.43	885.00	740.41	499.96
1093.14	4202.18	2814.99	2359.85	1570.46	940.09
127.82	355.82	237.10	221.57	144.01	92.20
687.00	2182.70	421.58	405.66	2205.74	1468.92
15.39	42.95	18.74	14.63	21.33	13.98
8.77	31.34	5.36	4.77	12.29	8.57

13-13 续表 1

单位：亿元

行业	Item	流动负债合计 Liquid Liabilities	长期负债合计 Long-term Liabilities	所有者权益 Creditors' Equity
全国总计	**National Total**	**11616.67**	**2861.93**	**11054.36**
煤炭采选业	Coal Mining and Dressing	6.19	0.10	1.44
石油和天然气开采业	Petroleum and Natural Gas Extraction			
黑色金属矿采选业	Ferrous Metals Mining and Dressing	0.39	0.15	0.46
有色金属矿采选业	Nonferrous Metals Mining and Dressing	2.24	0.85	0.89
非金属矿采选业	Nonmetal Minerals Mining and Dressing	8.42	2.04	9.78
木材及竹材采运业	Logging and Transport of Timber and Bamboo			
食品加工业	Food Processing	389.81	60.26	253.18
食品制造业	Food Manufacturing	300.22	43.96	285.51
饮料制造业	Beverage Manufacturing	339.49	82.74	329.30
烟草加工业	Tobacco Processing	5.04	0.20	7.68
纺织业	Textile Industry	608.54	111.13	496.78
服装及其他纤维制品制造	Garments and Other Fiber Products	404.82	31.34	355.37
皮革毛皮羽绒及其制品业	Leather, Furs, Down and Related Products	298.85	19.77	178.24
木材加工及竹藤棕草制品业	Timber Processing, Bamboo, Cane, Palm Fiber and Straw Products	120.98	41.37	93.45
家具制造业	Furniture Manufacturing	88.05	7.34	67.91
造纸及纸制品业	Papermaking and Paper Products	365.64	207.18	332.54
印刷业记录媒介的复制	Printing and Record Medium Reproduction	123.31	16.64	146.25
文教体育用品制造业	Cultural, Educational and Sports Goods	151.44	10.17	144.09
石油加工及炼焦业	Petroleum Processing and Coking	74.39	40.36	57.31
化学原料及制品制造业	Raw Chemical Materials and Chemical Products	596.88	151.20	645.43
医药制造业	Medical and Pharmaceutical Products	227.43	43.82	255.33
化学纤维制造业	Chemical Fiber	161.48	80.28	282.10
橡胶制品业	Rubber Products	188.52	63.29	156.12
塑料制品业	Plastic Products	416.66	80.58	419.69
非金属矿物制品业	Nonmetal Mineral Products	499.90	209.47	556.88
黑色金属冶炼及压延加工业	Smelting and Pressing of Ferrous Metals	220.76	58.17	160.83
有色金属冶炼及压延加工业	Smelting and Pressing of Nonferrous Metals	159.77	31.90	132.54
金属制品业	Metal Products	505.91	73.74	415.38
普通机械制造业	Ordinary Machinery	399.62	53.41	464.06
专用设备制造业	Special Purpose Equipment	206.27	19.51	185.07
交通运输设备制造业	Transport Equipment	786.54	248.61	941.78
电气机械及器材制造业	Electric Equipment and Machinery	838.93	81.11	667.58
电子及通信设备制造业	Electronic and Telecommunications Equipment	2283.74	192.66	1693.26
仪器仪表文化办公用机械	Instruments, Meters, Cultural and Office Machinery	171.78	21.08	161.71
电力蒸汽热水生产供应业	Production and Supply of Electric Power, Steam and Hot Water	476.73	751.01	940.65
煤气的生产和供应业	Production and Supply of Gas	19.51	6.04	17.40
自来水的生产和供应业	Production and Supply of Tap Water	8.81	10.73	11.79

continued

(100 million yuan)

产　品 销售收入 Sales Revenue	产　品 销售成本 Cost of Sales	产品销售 税金及附加 Tax and Sales Extra Charges	产　品 销售利润 Sales Profit	利润总额 Total Profits	本年应交 增 值 税 Value-added Tax Payable
22545.74	**18583.27**	**129.76**	**2678.60**	**1282.48**	**738.88**
7.29	6.32	0.06	0.41	0.21	0.24
1.10	0.96	0.01	0.08	0.03	0.04
3.12	2.39	0.01	0.50	0.15	0.10
16.43	11.73	0.13	2.60	1.03	0.44
846.38	756.85	0.92	52.64	13.28	14.52
552.17	402.33	0.80	71.32	24.04	32.24
489.88	316.20	18.93	58.59	19.61	33.93
7.40	4.16	1.92	1.11	0.44	0.72
1017.86	902.25	2.25	86.05	33.70	25.85
1046.25	899.48	2.79	99.61	43.54	22.53
708.98	641.70	1.27	48.59	16.17	11.98
203.47	177.35	0.55	15.46	2.92	7.41
158.38	132.95	0.44	16.68	6.86	4.55
473.74	389.74	0.63	58.55	22.96	18.51
191.21	150.18	0.27	34.45	20.33	9.23
355.58	309.10	0.52	31.97	12.85	4.60
249.70	219.23	4.60	17.46	7.22	6.13
1143.62	853.20	7.71	162.89	56.62	54.02
365.83	204.27	1.54	73.86	32.86	30.13
423.39	354.02	5.56	57.37	29.15	17.67
261.77	219.05	9.05	20.96	2.18	9.08
791.66	682.09	1.22	77.88	34.32	20.15
594.42	474.65	1.99	81.64	26.82	28.66
329.70	295.93	0.39	27.85	12.57	10.03
282.31	253.27	0.30	21.32	6.29	5.27
930.72	799.55	1.46	88.64	29.63	21.48
621.85	494.23	1.10	96.10	42.05	26.07
321.61	258.79	0.41	45.07	22.18	10.88
1613.32	1237.99	48.25	271.86	127.85	78.45
1532.97	1261.98	1.71	172.80	80.74	45.73
5317.06	4580.07	4.35	551.72	350.23	103.30
488.35	420.55	0.45	49.71	25.67	9.02
676.79	461.29	1.15	199.19	120.32	61.99
49.60	46.36	0.04	2.09	1.34	0.52
7.11	2.89	0.03	4.15	2.06	0.34

13-14 按行业分“三资”工业企业主要经济效益指标（2000年）

行　业	Branch	工业增加值率 (%) Ratio of Value Added to Gross Industrial Output Value (%)	总资产贡献率 (%) Ratio of Total Assets to Industrial Output Value (%)
全国总计	**National Total**	**25.96**	**9.76**
煤炭采选业	Coal Mining and Dressing	12.93	6.77
石油和天然气开采业	Petroleum and Natural Gas Extraction		
黑色金属矿采选业	Ferrous Metals Mining and Dressing	26.96	8.50
有色金属矿采选业	Nonferrous Metals Mining and Dressing	37.72	8.62
非金属矿采选业	Nonmetal Minerals Mining and Dressing	28.11	9.14
木材及竹材采运业	Logging and Transport of Timber and Bamboo		
食品加工业	Food Processing	20.09	5.68
食品制造业	Food Production	30.92	10.01
饮料制造业	Beverage Production	33.50	10.68
烟草加工业	Tobacco Processing	62.45	24.73
纺织业	Textile Industry	24.11	6.65
服装及其他纤维制品制造	Garments and Other Fiber Products	25.99	9.63
皮革毛皮羽绒及其制品业	Leather, Furs, Down and Related Products	23.28	6.98
木材加工及竹藤棕草制品业	Timber Processing, Bamboo, Cane, Palm Fiber and Straw Products	21.23	6.05
家具制造业	Furniture Manufacturing	25.05	8.48
造纸及纸制品业	Papermaking and Paper Products	23.64	6.46
印刷业记录媒介的复制	Printing and Record Medium Reproduction	29.83	11.46
文教体育用品制造业	Cultural, Educational and Sports Goods	25.04	6.52
石油加工及炼焦业	Petroleum Processing and Coking	18.74	13.54
化学原料及制品制造业	Raw Chemical Materials and Chemical Products	25.76	9.89
医药制造业	Medical and Pharmaceutical Products	38.57	13.40
化学纤维制造业	Chemical Fiber	26.62	11.70
橡胶制品业	Rubber Products	27.17	6.96
塑料制品业	Plastic Products	24.83	7.16
非金属矿物制品业	Nonmetal Mineral Products	30.08	6.12
黑色金属冶炼及压延加工业	Smelting and Pressing of Ferrous Metals	18.05	6.55
有色金属冶炼及压延加工业	Smelting and Pressing of Nonferrous Metals	19.51	5.31
金属制品业	Metal Products	21.99	6.66
普通机械制造业	Ordinary Machinery Manufacturing	28.57	8.57
专用设备制造业	For Special Purposes Equipment Manufacturing	25.91	9.12
交通运输设备制造业	Transport Equipment Manufacturing	25.13	14.14
电气机械及器材制造业	Electric Equipment and Machinery	26.31	9.30
电子及通信设备制造业	Electronic and Telecommunications Equipment	22.08	11.75
仪器仪表文化办公用机械	Instruments,Meters,Cultural and Office Machinery	21.50	10.22
电力蒸汽热水生产供应业	Production and Supply of Electric Power, Steam and Hot Water	50.39	11.27
煤气的生产和供应业	Production and Supply of Gas	15.31	5.62
自来水的生产和供应业	Production and Supply of Tap Water	48.50	8.93

Main Indicators on Economic Benefit of Foreign Funded Industrial Enterprises by Industrial Branch (2000)

资产负债率 (%) Assets-Liability Ratio (%)	流动资产周转次数（次/年） Number of Times of Annual of Turnover Circulating Funds (times/year)	工业成本费用利润率 (%) Ratio of Profits to Industrial Cost (%)	全员劳动生产率（元/人.年） Overall Labor Productivity (yuan/person-year)	产品销售率 (%) Proportion of Products Sold (%)
57.01	**1.89**	**49.68**	**71403**	**97.74**
81.41	1.63	2.92	58040	105.51
55.33	2.41	2.48	50651	98.98
77.74	1.49	5.03	110682	94.89
51.69	1.63	6.91	53396	94.91
64.40	2.49	1.59	78713	97.72
55.04	2.10	4.58	84792	96.58
56.81	1.65	4.30	102583	97.40
40.53	1.13	8.58	204118	99.80
59.56	1.75	3.40	43450	96.77
55.44	2.21	4.34	28097	97.53
64.38	2.27	2.34	25933	97.69
63.54	1.74	1.45	41174	96.79
59.23	1.73	4.46	39447	97.00
63.47	1.29	5.05	70020	95.15
48.94	1.38	11.89	68992	96.86
53.13	2.06	3.75	23160	97.36
66.69	4.30	3.01	351841	101.81
53.85	1.80	5.25	129899	96.35
51.81	1.32	9.93	134188	92.92
46.52	2.58	7.49	148470	98.28
61.91	1.43	0.85	46174	95.15
54.65	1.83	4.52	52022	97.20
56.16	1.38	4.68	55406	96.72
63.72	1.86	3.95	92170	98.54
61.18	1.94	2.28	85430	97.68
58.43	1.78	3.29	58372	98.03
49.51	1.29	7.12	73662	98.08
55.04	1.35	7.29	69640	97.47
52.42	1.77	8.84	128823	99.43
58.24	1.73	5.53	74092	96.94
59.71	2.25	7.02	120219	98.38
54.55	2.20	5.56	66968	99.13
56.90	1.67	21.09	403414	99.51
59.49	3.39	2.74	248932	104.37
62.39	1.49	45.72	156854	111.04

13-15 各地区“三资”工业企业主要指标（2000年）

Main Indicators of Foreign Funded Industrial Enterprises by Region (2000)

单位：亿元 (100 million yuan)

地区	Region	企业单位数（个） Number of Enterprises	工业总产值 Gross Industrial Output Value	工业增加值 Value Added of Industry	实收资本 Total Capital Hold	资产合计 Total Assets	流动资产合计 Total Circulating Funds
全 国	**National Total**	**28445**	**23464.55**	**6090.35**	**9080.11**	**25714.06**	**12849.54**
北 京	Beijing	1007	1150.32	285.77	374.95	1121.75	716.78
天 津	Tianjin	1209	1195.71	265.49	427.03	1289.68	715.05
河 北	Hebei	686	372.67	101.05	178.60	474.41	207.47
山 西	Shanxi	102	60.77	18.68	32.01	82.01	40.25
内蒙古	Inner Mongolia	90	54.56	15.16	24.76	99.73	70.50
辽 宁	Liaoning	1060	845.71	239.87	373.12	1030.54	428.98
吉 林	Jilin	239	312.15	83.88	109.11	325.85	149.93
黑龙江	Heilongjiang	149	129.17	41.33	61.35	237.76	110.40
上 海	Shanghai	3307	3431.20	838.88	1524.73	4101.57	2198.11
江 苏	Jiangsu	3160	2896.95	709.80	1095.97	2904.26	1411.67
浙 江	Zhejiang	2117	1232.40	279.78	429.13	1219.28	634.26
安 徽	Anhui	251	213.23	55.81	127.81	302.93	130.97
福 建	Fujian	2691	1605.23	462.12	634.82	1810.54	800.84
江 西	Jiangxi	160	96.86	22.79	47.12	153.50	69.89
山 东	Shandong	1740	1173.34	324.89	445.73	1145.04	546.42
河 南	Henan	406	257.71	113.73	112.62	412.35	189.32
湖 北	Hubei	362	336.31	105.50	151.06	497.66	186.02
湖 南	Hunan	197	97.05	30.55	40.93	115.70	52.50
广 东	Guangdong	8413	7274.35	1866.98	2403.65	7142.18	3658.68
广 西	Guangxi	207	114.53	33.37	83.01	235.36	78.02
海 南	Hainan	98	39.96	10.05	35.96	77.95	36.67
重 庆	Chongqing	138	129.02	39.23	106.76	213.96	90.45
四 川	Sichuan	249	167.09	55.03	101.38	262.28	115.34
贵 州	Guizhou	61	18.55	5.01	15.81	37.70	18.34
云 南	Yunnan	117	60.25	20.01	52.18	119.66	49.01
西 藏	Tibet	5	0.06	0.03	0.36	0.78	0.20
陕 西	Shaanxi	126	132.92	46.25	58.04	194.97	89.92
甘 肃	Gansu	32	29.91	6.33	10.24	45.24	24.61
青 海	Qinghai	6	4.83	2.60	2.31	6.69	1.97
宁 夏	Ningxia	27	18.05	6.83	10.36	27.07	14.49
新 疆	Xinjiang	33	13.69	3.54	9.22	25.68	12.50

13-15 续表 1 continued

单位：亿元 (100 million yuan)

地　区	Region	流动资产年平均余额 Annual Average Balance of Circulating Funds	固定资产原价合计 Original Value of Fixed Assets	固定资产净值年平均余额 Annual Average Balance of Net Value of Fixed Assets	流动负债合　计 Total Liquid Liabilities	长期负债合　计 Long-term Liabilities	所有者权益合　计 Creditors' Equity
全　国	**National Total**	**11926.66**	**14318.30**	**9808.74**	**11616.67**	**2861.93**	**11054.36**
北　京	Beijing	622.65	452.80	287.19	631.61	65.27	417.88
天　津	Tianjin	449.72	633.38	350.98	600.49	70.19	602.74
河　北	Hebei	198.53	291.72	222.47	187.81	78.52	179.39
山　西	Shanxi	38.06	41.50	32.94	42.98	8.62	30.40
内蒙古	Inner Mongolia	66.27	32.24	21.64	41.48	12.84	45.24
辽　宁	Liaoning	408.92	714.50	496.97	400.84	137.22	488.71
吉　林	Jilin	139.24	208.21	148.36	138.51	43.66	143.67
黑龙江	Heilongjiang	104.90	120.89	96.28	120.49	54.36	62.89
上　海	Shanghai	2068.96	2087.47	1348.53	1788.47	254.53	2045.50
江　苏	Jiangsu	1333.31	1645.27	1206.85	1367.01	366.73	1163.52
浙　江	Zhejiang	596.48	651.19	474.75	582.18	111.95	525.14
安　徽	Anhui	127.25	190.93	128.80	121.79	50.13	130.78
福　建	Fujian	753.48	1013.20	753.77	744.41	260.28	801.05
江　西	Jiangxi	65.93	79.24	59.55	65.21	31.04	56.41
山　东	Shandong	514.97	673.83	476.34	541.61	149.11	447.62
河　南	Henan	177.10	294.02	186.38	183.96	45.35	181.51
湖　北	Hubei	174.08	282.19	219.95	161.83	123.69	194.17
湖　南	Hunan	52.65	80.99	44.92	50.39	8.49	56.29
广　东	Guangdong	3523.87	4081.62	2698.28	3368.17	789.78	2919.22
广　西	Guangxi	73.39	153.98	121.19	76.61	55.89	100.83
海　南	Hainan	35.42	46.29	32.38	36.71	13.25	27.70
重　庆	Chongqing	86.48	159.53	107.06	76.10	23.32	114.52
四　川	Sichuan	108.86	137.47	104.33	109.52	38.24	113.28
贵　州	Guizhou	17.79	14.93	10.02	20.16	2.18	14.92
云　南	Yunnan	46.92	72.26	56.07	40.47	19.27	59.91
西　藏	Tibet	0.17	0.27	0.24	0.07	0.05	0.65
陕　西	Shaanxi	86.49	99.68	82.28	71.66	33.57	86.37
甘　肃	Gansu	26.26	24.15	17.18	20.51	5.97	18.76
青　海	Qinghai	1.87	3.31	2.95	2.02	1.90	2.78
宁　夏	Ningxia	15.01	14.59	8.90	12.98	1.76	12.33
新　疆	Xinjiang	11.64	16.67	11.16	10.60	4.74	10.14

13-15 续表 2 continued

单位：亿元 (100 million yuan)

地区	Region	产品销售收入 Sales Revenue	产品销售成本 Cost of Sales	产品销售税金及附加 Sales Tax and Extra Charges	产品销售利润 Sales Profit	利润总额 Total Profits	本年应交增值税 Value-added Tax Payable
全国	**National Total**	**22545.74**	**18583.27**	**129.76**	**2678.60**	**1282.48**	**738.88**
北京	Beijing	1137.59	924.57	2.84	148.10	70.83	34.21
天津	Tianjin	1184.48	954.99	4.31	148.35	97.03	33.86
河北	Hebei	342.30	279.10	2.22	45.32	20.31	14.16
山西	Shanxi	53.28	41.62	1.05	6.03	2.11	2.73
内蒙古	Inner Mongolia	51.59	41.10	0.02	8.34	4.06	2.03
辽宁	Liaoning	812.64	673.26	5.15	97.60	46.62	29.39
吉林	Jilin	302.77	227.15	9.63	53.89	31.63	18.30
黑龙江	Heilongjiang	115.71	88.19	1.94	14.75	0.70	5.58
上海	Shanghai	3514.32	2765.41	32.29	512.60	246.19	122.77
江苏	Jiangsu	2756.07	2343.79	6.40	286.14	141.41	106.36
浙江	Zhejiang	1175.26	981.66	4.56	144.15	70.58	40.53
安徽	Anhui	199.27	163.18	1.96	20.70	9.40	8.92
福建	Fujian	1491.14	1264.11	8.21	147.61	62.55	42.64
江西	Jiangxi	90.08	71.16	1.08	12.73	3.54	3.50
山东	Shandong	1060.83	890.19	4.52	123.30	60.74	41.63
河南	Henan	235.80	177.86	1.46	40.15	23.06	12.63
湖北	Hubei	303.16	227.16	5.54	46.30	15.31	19.37
湖南	Hunan	87.08	66.22	0.60	15.62	8.97	4.79
广东	Guangdong	6953.62	5888.49	31.36	714.79	326.37	159.49
广西	Guangxi	109.24	86.66	0.39	12.57	4.63	6.29
海南	Hainan	37.86	27.05	0.26	3.27	-0.20	1.53
重庆	Chongqing	119.80	94.78	1.83	16.70	5.77	6.99
四川	Sichuan	157.74	118.69	0.74	21.60	8.09	7.11
贵州	Guizhou	19.24	14.23	0.03	2.05	-0.96	0.97
云南	Yunnan	58.58	44.18	0.12	11.65	6.43	3.41
西藏	Tibet	0.08	0.05	0.00	0.02	0.01	0.00
陕西	Shaanxi	116.19	78.27	0.49	17.89	15.08	7.72
甘肃	Gansu	26.53	22.44	0.21	2.75	0.69	0.94
青海	Qinghai	5.17	4.73	0.02	0.38	0.06	0.05
宁夏	Ningxia	15.77	13.04	0.46	1.40	0.60	0.70
新疆	Xinjiang	12.54	9.94	0.06	1.85	0.88	0.29

13-16 各地区"三资"工业企业主要经济效益指标（2000年）

Main Indicators on Economics Benefit of Foreign Funded Industrial Enterprises by Region (2000)

地区	Region	工业增加值率 (%) Ratio of Value-added to Gross Industrial Output Value (%)	总资产贡献率 (%) Ratio of Total Assets to Industrial Output Value (%)	资产负债率 (%) Assets-Liability Ratio (%)	流动资产周转次数（次/年） Number of Times of Annual of Turnover Circulating Funds (times/year)	成本费用利润率 (%) Ratio of Profits to Industrial Cost (%)	全员劳动生产率（元/人.年） Overall Labor Productivity (yuan/person-year)	产品销售率 (%) Proportion of Products Sold (%)
全国	**National Total**	**25.96**	**9.76**	**57.01**	**1.89**	**49.68**	**71403**	**97.74**
北京	Beijing	24.84	10.52	62.75	1.83	102.00	131280	95.07
天津	Tianjin	22.20	12.41	53.26	2.63	141.31	88832	98.47
河北	Hebei	27.12	9.91	62.19	1.72	52.25	61685	97.76
山西	Shanxi	30.73	8.47	62.93	1.40	38.33	57570	92.94
内蒙古	Inner Mongolia	27.78	8.50	54.64	0.78	14.03	42911	103.49
辽宁	Liaoning	28.36	9.63	52.58	1.99	89.28	80705	97.93
吉林	Jilin	26.87	20.08	55.91	2.17	69.46	125277	97.62
黑龙江	Heilongjiang	32.00	5.32	73.55	1.10	40.92	67970	95.29
上海	Shanghai	24.45	10.80	50.13	1.70	17.79	105689	99.06
江苏	Jiangsu	24.50	10.25	59.94	2.07	132.38	83803	97.85
浙江	Zhejiang	22.70	11.18	56.93	1.97	58.69	54164	96.60
安徽	Anhui	26.17	8.33	56.83	1.57	38.08	61293	99.62
福建	Fujian	28.79	7.55	55.75	1.98	63.16	56856	96.47
江西	Jiangxi	23.53	7.28	62.83	1.37	22.49	39419	96.60
山东	Shandong	27.69	10.86	60.91	2.06	58.85	56904	97.23
河南	Henan	44.13	11.18	55.98	1.33	26.54	109875	97.61
湖北	Hubei	31.37	10.63	60.98	1.74	85.50	102969	97.68
湖南	Hunan	31.48	13.86	51.34	1.65	49.86	68368	97.36
广东	Guangdong	25.67	8.43	59.13	1.97	82.52	59588	98.01
广西	Guangxi	29.14	6.03	57.16	1.49	31.03	55695	95.78
海南	Hainan	25.15	3.38	64.46	1.07	18.81	59104	96.70
重庆	Chongqing	30.41	9.22	46.47	1.39	37.76	101008	99.30
四川	Sichuan	32.94	7.84	56.81	1.45	17.59	82458	95.64
贵州	Guizhou	27.03	1.66	60.40	1.08	12.22	34029	93.46
云南	Yunnan	33.22	9.51	49.93	1.25	42.04	89273	98.68
西藏	Tibet	44.72	1.27	15.98	0.48	17.23	4428	100.00
陕西	Shaanxi	34.80	13.18	55.70	1.34	20.65	151173	97.55
甘肃	Gansu	21.16	5.44	58.54	1.01	22.30	43974	96.88
青海	Qinghai	53.81	4.49	58.47	2.77	39.14	288542	100.73
宁夏	Ningxia	37.84	7.98	54.45	1.05	26.99	62344	88.67
新疆	Xinjiang	25.88	6.79	60.50	1.08	35.93	62202	95.31

13-17 按行业分大中型工业企业主要指标（2000年）

单位：亿元

行　　业	Branch	企业单位数（个）Number of Enterprises (unit)	工业总产值 Gross Industrial Output Value	工业增加值 Value-added of Industry
全国总计	**National Total**	**21724**	**48993.02**	**15747.32**
煤炭采选业	Coal Mining and Dressing	283	952.32	458.05
石油和天然气开采业	Petroleum and Natural Gas Extraction	39	3090.45	2193.64
黑色金属矿采选业	Ferrous Metals Mining and Dressing	45	59.22	26.42
有色金属矿采选业	Nonferrous Metals Mining and Dressing	170	153.77	61.81
非金属矿采选业	Nonmetal Minerals Mining and Dressing	178	108.92	45.21
木材及竹材采运业	Logging and Transport of Timber and Bamboo	99	94.23	50.95
食品加工业	Food Processing	1108	1399.59	303.65
食品制造业	Food Manufacturing	534	647.09	194.80
饮料制造业	Beverage Manufacturing	757	1218.59	456.07
烟草加工业	Tobacco Processing	140	1311.31	874.95
纺织业	Textile Industry	1889	2437.50	621.36
服装及其他纤维制品制造	Garments and Other Fiber Products	392	507.69	138.42
皮革毛皮羽绒及其制品业	Leather, Furs, Down and Related Products	216	309.89	71.30
木材加工及竹藤棕草制品业	Timber Processing, Bamboo, Cane, Palm Fiber and Straw Products	162	175.02	38.96
家具制造业	Furniture Manufacturing	73	55.23	14.82
造纸及纸制品业	Papermaking and Paper Products	575	660.64	183.31
印刷业记录媒介的复制	Printing and Record Medium Reproduction	379	229.64	82.40
文教体育用品制造业	Cultural, Educational and Sports Goods	112	135.33	34.77
石油加工及炼焦业	Petroleum Processing and Coking	119	3793.81	621.56
化学原料及制品制造业	Raw Chemical Materials and Chemical Products	1764	3429.64	851.27
医药制造业	Medical and Pharmaceutical Products	712	1096.96	388.91
化学纤维制造业	Chemical Fiber	240	938.80	228.23
橡胶制品业	Rubber Products	260	440.79	117.80
塑料制品业	Plastic Products	615	545.72	136.10
非金属矿物制品业	Nonmetal Mineral Products	1654	1326.72	418.34
黑色金属冶炼及压延加工业	Smelting and Pressing of Ferrous Metals	369	3689.57	1076.50
有色金属冶炼及压延加工业	Smelting and Pressing of Nonferrous Metals	370	1342.84	334.65
金属制品业	Metal Products	616	647.36	152.66
普通机械制造业	Ordinary Machinery	1470	1556.15	439.98
专用设备制造业	Special Purpose Equipment	1109	1200.21	309.70
交通运输设备制造业	Transport Equipment	1286	3934.03	968.59
电气机械及器材制造业	Electric Equipment and Machinery	1129	2539.61	664.06
电子及通信设备制造业	Electronic and Telecommunications Equipment	856	4400.09	1075.33
仪器仪表文化办公用机械	Instruments, Meters, Cultural and Office Machinery	321	393.95	95.25
电力蒸汽热水生产供应业	Production and Supply of Electric Power, Steam and Hot Water	1059	3463.08	1795.84
煤气的生产和供应业	Production and Supply of Gas	97	124.16	33.88
自来水的生产和供应业	Production and Supply of Tap Water	221	200.99	98.05

Main Indicators of Large-scale and Medium-scale Industrial Enterprises by Industrial Branch (2000)

(100 million yuan)

实收资本 Total Capital Hold	资产合计 Total Assets	流动资产合计 Circulating Funds	流动资产年平均余额 Annual Average Balance of Circulating Funds	固定资产原价 Original Value of Fixed Assets	固定资产净值年平均余额 Annual Average Balance of Net Value of Fixed Assets
21409.53	**87309.83**	**35282.86**	**33763.10**	**58348.15**	**37293.79**
878.22	3254.90	1145.27	1110.65	2579.98	1707.19
1694.76	4018.09	875.19	876.40	5122.79	2658.69
101.44	223.39	64.69	66.28	106.83	64.41
84.85	319.79	110.05	107.71	234.51	151.30
129.46	448.90	151.50	144.27	309.40	236.27
79.94	321.20	132.29	132.20	215.02	156.54
340.15	1470.61	664.81	636.27	853.45	600.53
284.55	854.09	380.59	349.33	491.75	320.25
492.99	1967.98	906.66	862.15	1053.99	749.13
287.63	1746.52	828.88	819.54	823.65	545.39
738.13	3408.09	1561.36	1489.53	2067.47	1335.76
142.01	569.84	328.01	306.11	229.09	153.70
66.31	300.61	182.78	178.41	126.02	92.12
78.21	287.61	104.71	103.58	188.09	138.70
30.42	95.96	43.80	42.82	47.58	33.24
312.57	1389.36	558.84	524.16	786.17	565.03
145.06	457.51	192.02	178.03	301.41	185.80
45.01	161.87	87.71	86.64	61.88	40.93
611.88	3142.98	1011.82	981.17	2877.16	1726.85
1333.31	6137.48	2270.65	2211.64	4229.83	2759.94
418.07	1871.26	984.20	939.59	726.69	503.87
380.91	1465.28	481.18	480.87	1129.12	732.43
163.17	722.92	339.13	341.85	362.20	245.72
215.19	818.69	370.62	352.56	464.24	314.19
825.36	3121.56	1201.02	1170.37	2041.29	1382.58
2189.86	8004.90	2783.08	2632.68	5961.24	3617.37
590.77	2160.36	882.38	841.49	1457.93	943.33
243.18	898.39	487.94	478.54	441.23	291.62
758.14	3262.52	1807.10	1749.41	1512.74	956.26
470.23	2160.30	1229.92	1155.26	1025.61	632.38
1557.71	6573.02	3415.72	3263.02	2911.52	1914.48
759.90	3174.50	1843.18	1772.91	1303.84	861.87
1007.96	5054.94	3151.29	2718.25	1797.92	1060.88
141.14	541.24	310.90	302.10	238.82	149.09
3013.27	14534.80	3630.64	3632.57	12511.54	8268.75
221.77	481.67	142.96	133.98	352.20	240.42
369.31	1009.09	232.81	215.20	890.60	599.98

13-17 续表 1

单位：亿元

行 业	Branch	流动负债合计 Liquid Liabilities	长期负债合计 Long-term Liabilities	所有者权益 Creditors' Equity
全国总计	**National Total**	**33935.97**	**17584.07**	**35165.58**
煤炭采选业	Coal Mining and Dressing	1131.57	956.26	1155.29
石油和天然气开采业	Petroleum and Natural Gas Extraction	786.24	682.45	2410.45
黑色金属矿采选业	Ferrous Metals Mining and Dressing	57.19	9.45	138.82
有色金属矿采选业	Nonferrous Metals Mining and Dressing	126.87	68.52	123.26
非金属矿采选业	Nonmetal Minerals Mining and Dressing	162.40	114.49	171.97
木材及竹材采运业	Logging and Transport of Timber and Bamboo	180.67	45.31	94.76
食品加工业	Food Processing	858.01	173.46	429.84
食品制造业	Food Manufacturing	402.24	104.78	341.55
饮料制造业	Beverage Manufacturing	895.49	210.60	848.83
烟草加工业	Tobacco Processing	635.08	104.99	1005.48
纺织业	Textile Industry	1776.20	573.78	1033.79
服装及其他纤维制品制造	Garments and Other Fiber Products	289.05	35.66	242.37
皮革毛皮羽绒及其制品业	Leather, Furs, Down and Related Products	194.70	21.19	83.37
木材加工及竹藤棕草制品业	Timber Processing, Bamboo, Cane, Palm Fiber and Straw Products	129.29	64.30	93.79
家具制造业	Furniture Manufacturing	43.26	9.90	42.65
造纸及纸制品业	Papermaking and Paper Products	584.34	298.64	492.01
印刷业记录媒介的复制	Printing and Record Medium Reproduction	172.79	61.02	223.28
文教体育用品制造业	Cultural, Educational and Sports Goods	75.13	11.80	74.86
石油加工及炼焦业	Petroleum Processing and Coking	1135.81	672.57	1279.76
化学原料及制品制造业	Raw Chemical Materials and Chemical Products	2411.08	1472.49	2225.30
医药制造业	Medical and Pharmaceutical Products	827.52	209.80	814.76
化学纤维制造业	Chemical Fiber	487.59	342.86	632.60
橡胶制品业	Rubber Products	356.97	130.96	229.26
塑料制品业	Plastic Products	363.66	132.14	316.50
非金属矿物制品业	Nonmetal Mineral Products	1349.37	631.88	1124.00
黑色金属冶炼及压延加工业	Smelting and Pressing of Ferrous Metals	2909.35	1424.13	3646.79
有色金属冶炼及压延加工业	Smelting and Pressing of Nonferrous Metals	918.89	467.70	757.54
金属制品业	Metal Products	490.77	102.43	302.41
普通机械制造业	Ordinary Machinery	1670.66	403.25	1181.11
专用设备制造业	Special Purpose Equipment	1167.99	247.16	736.45
交通运输设备制造业	Transport Equipment	3216.77	869.10	2454.97
电气机械及器材制造业	Electric Equipment and Machinery	1664.20	305.73	1194.99
电子及通信设备制造业	Electronic and Telecommunications Equipment	2480.99	485.48	2054.37
仪器仪表文化办公用机械	Instruments, Meters, Cultural and Office Machinery	276.76	63.95	195.06
电力蒸汽热水生产供应业	Production and Supply of Electric Power, Steam and Hot Water	2921.48	5704.30	5814.14
煤气的生产和供应业	Production and Supply of Gas	133.53	65.91	281.54
自来水的生产和供应业	Production and Supply of Tap Water	185.27	157.78	665.15

continued

(100 million yuan)

产　　品 销售收入 Sales Revenue	产　　品 销售成本 Cost of Sales	产品销售 税金及附加 Sales Tax and Extra Charges	产　　品 销售利润 Sales Profit	利润总额 Total Profits	本年应交 增 值 税 Value-added Tax Payable
50120.30	**39768.89**	**1173.45**	**7308.05**	**3183.28**	**2566.15**
917.05	658.33	12.09	175.13	-3.58	78.81
2885.90	1343.55	73.86	1458.15	1145.54	295.40
60.46	43.59	2.43	9.47	1.25	3.28
144.50	103.33	1.12	36.20	10.97	6.81
103.98	70.57	3.67	19.54	1.50	7.64
87.86	52.65	4.30	24.72	1.84	1.90
1375.38	1218.10	4.00	102.15	29.05	33.50
623.82	471.41	2.58	79.29	26.39	35.66
1178.60	743.88	87.35	179.73	91.96	83.76
1306.38	582.52	554.82	157.06	139.10	134.36
2358.99	2057.17	9.95	247.13	68.81	90.05
469.64	391.51	1.72	53.97	27.11	13.18
289.13	260.17	0.47	21.85	7.42	6.99
169.39	146.81	0.67	14.95	3.75	7.27
55.38	43.91	0.25	8.05	3.10	2.16
642.84	524.71	2.67	89.72	32.05	33.51
232.22	171.68	1.25	53.25	26.47	15.05
136.44	114.01	0.59	16.45	7.36	3.64
3921.73	3580.42	165.14	147.24	-9.91	98.47
3278.20	2676.81	32.10	408.42	101.19	139.02
1069.00	661.22	6.79	220.10	90.82	79.19
907.11	770.13	8.15	117.31	49.04	33.47
398.82	334.79	15.16	31.01	-0.95	15.21
538.68	456.02	1.73	64.37	24.81	17.35
1260.37	978.03	11.54	192.20	41.57	78.20
3862.36	3263.75	25.67	496.43	137.68	222.86
1309.68	1082.62	6.02	201.49	45.34	62.98
628.55	523.84	1.75	73.20	19.79	21.29
1493.42	1184.08	6.51	233.90	42.42	71.33
1120.30	924.85	4.59	145.33	22.93	41.52
3900.77	3178.29	74.43	537.33	145.45	159.02
2407.83	1916.74	7.26	286.78	98.66	89.90
4351.15	3627.28	7.06	539.97	327.55	112.31
397.07	320.74	1.25	58.22	17.89	11.64
5523.12	4677.15	29.85	739.89	413.90	432.06
170.08	166.42	0.59	-4.79	-2.42	5.09
191.59	150.04	1.94	31.17	4.88	12.57

13-18 按行业分大中型工业企业主要经济效益指标（2000年）

行　　业	Branch	工业增加值率 (%) Ratio of Value-added to Gross Industrial Output Value (%)	总资产贡献率 (%) Ratio of Total Assets to Industrial Output Value (%)
全国总计	**National Total**	**32.14**	**9.40**
煤炭采选业	Coal Mining and Dressing	48.10	3.62
石油和天然气开采业	Petroleum and Natural Gas Extraction	70.98	38.70
黑色金属矿采选业	Ferrous Metals Mining and Dressing	44.61	3.82
有色金属矿采选业	Nonferrous Metals Mining and Dressing	40.20	7.67
非金属矿采选业	Nonmetal Minerals Mining and Dressing	41.51	3.71
木材及竹材采运业	Logging and Transport of Timber and Bamboo	54.07	3.63
食品加工业	Food Processing	21.70	6.47
食品制造业	Food Production	30.10	9.09
饮料制造业	Beverage Production	37.43	14.45
烟草加工业	Tobacco Processing	66.72	48.26
纺织业	Textile Industry	25.49	6.89
服装及其他纤维制品制造	Garments and Other Fiber Products	27.26	8.62
皮革毛皮羽绒及其制品业	Leather, Furs, Down and Related Products	23.01	6.39
木材加工及竹藤棕草制品业	Timber Processing, Bamboo, Cane, Palm Fiber and Straw Products	22.26	6.14
家具制造业	Furniture Manufacturing	26.83	7.19
造纸及纸制品业	Papermaking and Paper Products	27.75	6.63
印刷业记录媒介的复制	Printing and Record Medium Reproduction	35.88	10.42
文教体育用品制造业	Cultural, Educational and Sports Goods	25.69	8.05
石油加工及炼焦业	Petroleum Processing and Coking	16.38	9.82
化学原料及制品制造业	Raw Chemical Materials and Chemical Products	24.82	6.05
医药制造业	Medical and Pharmaceutical Products	35.45	10.86
化学纤维制造业	Chemical Fiber	24.31	7.98
橡胶制品业	Rubber Products	26.72	5.79
塑料制品业	Plastic Products	24.94	6.89
非金属矿物制品业	Nonmetal Mineral Products	31.53	5.85
黑色金属冶炼及压延加工业	Smelting and Pressing of Ferrous Metals	29.18	6.29
有色金属冶炼及压延加工业	Smelting and Pressing of Nonferrous Metals	24.92	7.84
金属制品业	Metal Products	23.58	6.46
普通机械制造业	Ordinary Machinery Manufacturing	28.27	5.16
专用设备制造业	For Special Purposes Equipment Manufacturing	25.80	4.66
交通运输设备制造业	Transport Equipment Manufacturing	24.62	7.08
电气机械及器材制造业	Electric Equipment and Machinery	26.15	7.72
电子及通信设备制造业	Electronic and Telecommunications Equipment	24.44	9.92
仪器仪表文化办公用机械	Instruments,Meters,Cultural and Office Machinery	24.18	7.14
电力蒸汽热水生产供应业	Production and Supply of Electric Power, Steam and Hot Water	51.86	7.63
煤气的生产和供应业	Production and Supply of Gas	27.28	1.09
自来水的生产和供应业	Production and Supply of Tap Water	48.79	2.36

Main Indicators on Economic Benefit of Large-scale and Medium-scale Industrial Enterprises by Industrial Branch (2000)

资产负债率 (%) Assets-Liability Ratio (%)	流动资产周转次数（次/年） Number of Times of Annual of Turnover Circulating Funds (times/year)	工业成本费用利润率 (%) Ratio of Profits to Industrial Cost (%)	全员劳动生产率（元/人.年） Overall Labor Productivity (yuan/person-year)	产品销售率 (%) Proportion of Products Sold (%)
59.65	**1.48**	**6.88**	**54667**	**98.64**
64.51	0.83	-0.38	15213	99.44
40.01	3.29	73.47	388585	99.22
37.86	0.91	2.19	20285	95.92
61.28	1.34	7.84	25110	98.61
61.69	0.72	1.49	18216	92.93
70.50	0.66	2.40	7802	100.09
70.77	2.16	2.14	48641	97.69
60.01	1.79	4.41	58461	96.20
56.87	1.37	9.04	72856	98.34
42.43	1.59	20.54	449238	100.15
69.67	1.58	2.98	24300	97.96
57.47	1.53	6.06	35140	95.94
72.27	1.62	2.61	29811	97.67
67.39	1.64	2.22	36017	96.46
55.55	1.29	5.82	32525	96.65
64.44	1.23	5.16	37692	98.34
51.18	1.30	12.47	44686	98.41
53.75	1.57	5.69	30143	97.81
59.14	4.00	-0.26	148251	99.28
63.74	1.48	3.17	40710	97.90
56.46	1.14	9.24	67062	96.10
56.83	1.89	5.74	73962	97.74
68.29	1.17	-0.24	35201	96.84
61.34	1.53	4.79	52284	97.13
63.79	1.08	3.37	28342	97.40
54.20	1.47	3.69	52584	100.34
64.93	1.56	3.60	45593	97.95
66.34	1.31	3.24	37827	98.00
63.80	0.85	2.88	28917	97.83
65.69	0.97	2.05	25842	97.37
62.36	1.20	3.87	46011	100.35
62.34	1.36	4.23	62991	97.72
59.35	1.60	8.01	110048	98.56
63.96	1.31	4.67	34494	97.89
59.98	1.52	8.17	132785	99.86
41.55	1.27	-1.26	28917	102.02
34.08	0.89	2.52	47778	98.44

13-19 各地区大中型工业企业主要指标（2000年）

Main Indicators of Large-scale and Medium-scale Industrial Enterprises by Region (2000)

单位：亿元 (100 million yuan)

地 区	Region	企业单位数(个) Number of Enterprises	工业总产值 Gross Industrial Output Value	工业增加值 Value-added of Industry	实收资本 Total Capital Hold	资产合计 Total Assets	流动资产合计 Total Circulating Funds
全 国	**National Total**	**21724**	**48993.02**	**15747.32**	**21409.53**	**87309.83**	**35282.86**
北 京	Beijing	476	1207.71	337.01	761.05	2776.82	1026.18
天 津	Tianjin	694	1666.78	454.66	795.69	2932.83	1219.34
河 北	Hebei	1127	1856.51	676.89	893.22	3760.85	1347.34
山 西	Shanxi	366	701.33	258.08	493.15	2184.13	837.93
内蒙古	Inner Mongolia	285	549.81	209.42	437.24	1456.72	448.08
辽 宁	Liaoning	857	3042.16	856.32	1458.65	5908.55	2312.97
吉 林	Jilin	566	1387.15	390.97	587.39	2701.78	1068.12
黑龙江	Heilongjiang	601	2100.12	1108.80	1066.59	3526.51	1285.74
上 海	Shanghai	1367	4291.20	1256.98	2411.13	7383.27	3150.78
江 苏	Jiangsu	2082	4747.42	1256.98	1434.33	6303.61	2981.74
浙 江	Zhejiang	1250	2736.15	724.49	834.22	3692.72	1598.84
安 徽	Anhui	629	1066.55	348.42	571.88	2218.89	849.83
福 建	Fujian	301	816.22	279.30	271.35	1195.76	467.10
江 西	Jiangxi	438	614.27	175.15	271.74	1358.76	532.82
山 东	Shandong	2740	5300.14	1727.70	1723.62	7527.39	2974.41
河 南	Henan	1003	1722.44	530.00	704.37	3407.61	1414.48
湖 北	Hubei	848	1825.01	615.98	875.09	3742.05	1496.97
湖 南	Hunan	597	956.45	329.82	374.28	1875.49	754.97
广 东	Guangdong	2051	5951.57	1858.46	2005.07	8275.56	3680.14
广 西	Guangxi	598	670.43	225.94	297.92	1361.29	485.33
海 南	Hainan	118	135.20	35.05	91.38	301.72	104.88
重 庆	Chongqing	371	667.98	202.07	442.42	1529.49	674.35
四 川	Sichuan	783	1401.66	443.17	751.59	3607.02	1421.73
贵 州	Guizhou	222	390.20	132.89	231.23	1100.37	479.56
云 南	Yunnan	387	753.25	416.67	286.89	1532.84	544.06
西 藏	Tibet	4	4.32	2.49	5.54	15.98	8.88
陕 西	Shaanxi	439	858.40	317.98	504.39	2055.67	844.53
甘 肃	Gansu	195	571.26	171.27	299.75	1278.17	506.09
青 海	Qinghai	45	148.01	45.57	99.52	579.76	188.00
宁 夏	Ningxia	107	175.84	53.84	98.19	395.78	173.77
新 疆	Xinjiang	177	677.47	304.97	330.64	1322.47	403.88

13-19 续表 1 continued

单位：亿元 (100 million yuan)

地 区	Region	流动资产年平均余额 Annual Average Balance of Circulating Funds	固定资产原价合计 Original Value of Fixed Assets	固定资产净值年平均余额 Annual Average Balance of Net Value of Fixed Assets	流动负债合计 Total Liquid Liabilities	长期负债合计 Long-term Liabilities	所有者权益合计 Creditors' Equity
全 国	**National Total**	**33763.10**	**58348.15**	**37293.79**	**33935.97**	**17584.07**	**35165.58**
北 京	Beijing	1062.89	1897.25	1186.37	1021.09	562.57	1187.63
天 津	Tianjin	954.32	1995.70	1241.57	1154.59	551.04	1207.08
河 北	Hebei	1335.30	2726.64	1693.54	1453.32	760.73	1493.83
山 西	Shanxi	802.22	1551.64	990.08	730.91	636.09	792.44
内蒙古	Inner Mongolia	448.40	1167.03	779.58	473.09	352.08	621.01
辽 宁	Liaoning	2162.03	4351.57	2733.46	2338.83	1171.62	2386.85
吉 林	Jilin	1032.16	1575.41	1061.92	1141.90	605.37	953.14
黑龙江	Heilongjiang	1276.58	2965.66	1761.14	1347.29	617.68	1556.33
上 海	Shanghai	2964.90	4506.33	2803.08	2631.34	864.32	3873.69
江 苏	Jiangsu	2827.42	3734.58	2402.21	2738.75	1005.24	2538.40
浙 江	Zhejiang	1523.06	2170.31	1467.18	1383.87	647.95	1660.09
安 徽	Anhui	833.63	1454.20	930.94	797.37	534.32	866.22
福 建	Fujian	424.22	821.88	550.21	422.94	275.14	495.63
江 西	Jiangxi	516.10	895.17	577.36	564.13	341.21	434.20
山 东	Shandong	2825.18	5141.73	3184.77	2995.10	1481.43	2895.29
河 南	Henan	1384.25	2355.98	1400.28	1405.82	796.89	1191.83
湖 北	Hubei	1474.32	2429.09	1535.79	1360.24	894.42	1400.30
湖 南	Hunan	740.26	1347.25	837.85	773.01	432.18	630.08
广 东	Guangdong	3478.49	5062.90	3425.18	3416.28	1225.17	3567.76
广 西	Guangxi	472.88	967.82	682.11	587.84	355.37	412.74
海 南	Hainan	103.49	197.65	142.44	103.82	94.53	102.33
重 庆	Chongqing	637.40	919.25	591.33	709.37	256.52	553.33
四 川	Sichuan	1352.85	2374.75	1555.69	1285.79	1010.12	1301.09
贵 州	Guizhou	469.67	694.42	450.86	468.65	281.96	343.97
云 南	Yunnan	551.35	920.25	597.96	511.84	255.22	765.77
西 藏	Tibet	7.97	5.62	3.84	3.14	0.92	11.91
陕 西	Shaanxi	788.56	1384.76	917.40	855.98	527.73	654.59
甘 肃	Gansu	502.31	871.55	582.43	467.38	374.54	436.25
青 海	Qinghai	277.35	431.01	308.55	190.40	229.59	159.58
宁 夏	Ningxia	161.96	269.82	168.91	154.14	86.10	154.44
新 疆	Xinjiang	371.60	1160.95	729.76	447.72	356.02	517.77

13-19 续表 2 continued

单位：亿元 (100 million yuan)

地 区	Region	产品销售收入 Sales Revenue	产品销售成本 Cost of Sales	产品销售税金及附加 Sales Tax and Extra Charges	产品销售利润 Sales Profit	利润总额 Total Profits	本年应交增值税 Value-added Tax Payable
全 国	**National Total**	**50120.30**	**39768.89**	**1173.45**	**7308.05**	**3183.28**	**2566.15**
北 京	Beijing	1387.70	1186.98	21.40	143.89	36.26	54.53
天 津	Tianjin	1762.68	1442.23	18.24	228.76	112.77	61.55
河 北	Hebei	1993.84	1612.42	31.34	294.74	103.34	109.72
山 西	Shanxi	706.61	537.34	9.91	128.60	17.06	49.06
内蒙古	Inner Mongolia	554.32	448.22	9.29	73.81	12.43	38.41
辽 宁	Liaoning	3196.35	2681.87	56.32	383.29	142.54	151.11
吉 林	Jilin	1322.27	1061.09	30.90	195.00	78.09	74.58
黑龙江	Heilongjiang	2135.14	1246.87	54.67	777.50	556.78	197.75
上 海	Shanghai	4477.30	3569.54	83.81	632.50	302.77	194.08
江 苏	Jiangsu	4760.32	4018.76	58.17	524.47	203.04	196.45
浙 江	Zhejiang	2824.60	2355.55	56.98	317.82	176.39	120.69
安 徽	Anhui	1132.07	900.04	36.80	117.20	28.01	67.83
福 建	Fujian	786.49	632.16	29.51	97.53	48.67	36.06
江 西	Jiangxi	614.54	496.40	17.32	77.78	9.22	34.73
山 东	Shandong	5420.94	4316.31	72.44	812.04	416.80	279.30
河 南	Henan	1696.76	1368.97	42.51	235.46	65.68	88.81
湖 北	Hubei	1810.97	1425.13	41.26	258.61	77.81	96.96
湖 南	Hunan	956.92	732.83	77.31	120.03	19.10	59.91
广 东	Guangdong	6136.75	4919.66	85.65	847.89	429.89	234.77
广 西	Guangxi	655.96	505.89	13.71	105.52	33.94	46.63
海 南	Hainan	122.25	95.50	2.94	13.73	5.24	6.19
重 庆	Chongqing	680.58	542.95	15.38	86.95	14.48	38.60
四 川	Sichuan	1440.83	1100.51	43.47	217.74	57.64	84.30
贵 州	Guizhou	389.43	271.29	28.04	74.92	12.67	32.73
云 南	Yunnan	755.93	443.58	172.46	127.26	61.60	68.67
西 藏	Tibet	4.67	2.75	0.05	1.30	1.15	0.41
陕 西	Shaanxi	842.79	629.73	24.18	158.58	58.92	49.69
甘 肃	Gansu	542.45	471.77	14.97	45.89	6.39	28.20
青 海	Qinghai	160.72	127.61	2.54	25.82	2.57	11.57
宁 夏	Ningxia	187.42	157.48	2.26	22.63	5.63	9.93
新 疆	Xinjiang	660.70	467.45	19.61	160.80	86.39	42.93

13-20 各地区大中型工业企业主要经济效益指标（2000年）

Main Indicators on Economics Benefit of Large-scale and Medium-scale Industrial Enterprises by Region (2000)

地 区	Region	工业增加值率 (%) Ratio of Value-added to Gross Industrial Output Value (%)	总资产贡献率 (%) Ratio of Total Assets to Industrial Output Value (%)	资产负债率 (%) Assets-Liability Ratio (%)	流动资产周转次数（次/年） Number of Times of Annual of Turnover Circulating Funds (times/year)	成本费用利润率 (%) Ratio of Profits to Industrial Cost (%)	全员劳动生产率 (元/人.年) Overall Labor Productivity (yuan/person-year)	产品销售率 (%) Proportion of Products Sold (%)
全 国	**National Total**	**32.14**	**9.40**	**59.65**	**1.48**	**6.88**	**54667**	**98.64**
北 京	Beijing	27.90	5.22	57.23	1.31	2.63	53988	98.10
天 津	Tianjin	27.28	8.12	58.84	1.85	6.80	78191	99.35
河 北	Hebei	36.46	8.12	60.28	1.49	5.49	42630	98.90
山 西	Shanxi	36.80	5.41	62.59	0.88	2.49	24414	97.97
内蒙古	Inner Mongolia	38.09	6.09	57.37	1.24	2.31	35130	99.02
辽 宁	Liaoning	28.15	7.36	59.49	1.48	4.67	47956	98.37
吉 林	Jilin	28.18	8.28	64.72	1.28	6.20	40141	98.89
黑龙江	Heilongjiang	52.80	24.07	55.81	1.67	37.64	73120	99.07
上 海	Shanghai	29.29	9.01	47.48	1.51	7.21	118816	99.46
江 苏	Jiangsu	26.48	8.58	59.73	1.68	4.48	56045	98.26
浙 江	Zhejiang	26.48	10.84	55.04	1.85	6.67	66785	98.22
安 徽	Anhui	32.67	7.35	60.96	1.36	2.67	35674	99.11
福 建	Fujian	34.22	10.89	58.52	1.85	6.79	91264	97.84
江 西	Jiangxi	28.51	6.40	67.53	1.19	1.55	29123	98.11
山 东	Shandong	32.60	11.70	61.54	1.92	8.42	52621	98.32
河 南	Henan	30.77	7.39	65.02	1.23	4.07	29297	98.31
湖 北	Hubei	33.75	7.46	62.58	1.23	4.58	49375	101.23
湖 南	Hunan	34.48	9.67	66.40	1.29	2.20	38180	99.61
广 东	Guangdong	31.23	10.56	56.89	1.76	7.59	120863	97.99
广 西	Guangxi	33.70	8.63	69.68	1.39	5.54	44141	98.16
海 南	Hainan	25.93	6.44	66.08	1.18	4.46	58522	94.96
重 庆	Chongqing	30.25	6.11	63.82	1.07	2.19	36638	99.54
四 川	Sichuan	31.62	6.84	63.93	1.07	4.22	35014	98.98
贵 州	Guizhou	34.06	7.99	68.29	0.83	3.71	32317	99.71
云 南	Yunnan	55.32	20.93	50.04	1.37	11.59	96703	99.09
西 藏	Tibet	57.56	10.67	25.43	0.59	29.89	103001	95.78
陕 西	Shaanxi	37.04	8.28	67.63	1.07	7.67	38103	98.00
甘 肃	Gansu	29.98	5.14	65.87	1.08	1.18	34353	97.47
青 海	Qinghai	30.79	5.21	72.47	0.58	1.67	51600	97.38
宁 夏	Ningxia	30.62	6.32	60.98	1.16	3.07	33621	96.65
新 疆	Xinjiang	45.02	12.81	60.85	1.78	15.81	118600	98.73

13-21 重点工业企业主要工业产品生产能力(1999年)

Production Capacity of Major Industrial Products of Key Industry Enterprises (1999)

指标	Item	年末能力 Capacity in Year-end
原煤(核定能力) (万吨)	Coal (10 000 tons)	76194
原油 (万吨)	Crude Oil (10 000 tons)	14179
天然气 (亿立方米)	Natural Gas (100 000 000 cu.m)	177
发电设备容量总计(万千瓦)	Power Generating Equipment (10 000 kw)	29877
机制糖(年产糖量) (万吨)	Sugar (10 000 tons)	749
白酒 (万吨)	Liquor (10 000 tons)	513
啤酒 (万吨)	Beer (10 000 tons)	2618
卷烟综合生产能力(二班) (万箱)	Cigarettes (10 000 cases)	3789
化学纤维 (万吨)	Chemical Fiber (10 000 tons)	657
胶合板 (万立方米)	Plywood (10 000 cu.m)	105
纤维板 (万立方米)	Fiberboard (10 000 cu.m)	143
机制纸 (万吨)	Machine-made Paper (10 000 tons)	1038
机制纸板 (万吨)	Machine-made Paperboard (10 000 tons)	709
石油加工蒸馏设备能力 (处理万吨)	Petroleum Processing and Distillation Equipment (10 000 tons)	24645
硫酸(折100%) (万吨)	Sulfuric Acid (10 000 tons)	2759
氢氧化钠(烧碱) (折100%) (万吨)	Caustic Soda (10 000 tons)	700
碳酸钠(纯碱) (万吨)	Soda Ash (10 000 tons)	743
合成氨 (万吨)	Synthetic Ammonia (10 000 tons)	4017
农用氮、磷、钾化学肥料总计(折纯) (万吨)	Chemical Fertilizer (10 000 tons)	3845
化学农药原药(折100%) (万吨)	Chemical Pesticide (10 000 tons)	88
乙烯 (万吨)	Ethene (10 000 tons)	431
塑料树脂及共聚物 (万吨)	Plastics (10 000 tons)	910
合成洗涤剂 (万吨)	Synthetic Detergents (10 000 tons)	445
水泥 (万吨)	Cement (10 000 tons)	70175
平板玻璃 (万重量箱)	Plate Glass (10 000 weight cases)	19961
生铁 (万吨)	Pig Iron (10 000 tons)	12586
钢 (万吨)	Steel (10 000 tons)	14549
钢材轧制能力(轧制量)(万吨)	Steel-rolling Capacity (10 000 tons)	15179
铁合金 (万吨)	Iron Alloy (10 000 tons)	451
金属切削机床 (万台)	Metal-cutting Machine Tools (10 000)	20
大中型拖拉机 (万台)	Large and Medium Tractors (10 000)	15
汽车 (万辆)	Motor Vehicles (10 000)	289
摩托车 (万辆)	Motorcycles (10 000)	597
自行车(按两班生产)(万辆)	Bicycles (10 000)	3474
家用洗衣机 (万台)	Household Washing Machines (10 000)	2297
家用电冰箱 (万台)	Household Refrigerators (10 000)	1501
电风扇 (万台)	Electric Fans (10 000)	2534
微波炉 (万台)	Microwave Ovens (10 000)	302
微型电子计算机 (万部)	Microcomputers (10 000)	830
彩色电视机 (万部)	Color Television Sets (10 000)	7028
影碟机 (VCD) (万台)	Video-CD Players (10 000)	3021

13-22 主要工业产品产量
Output of Major Industrial Products

年 份 地 区	Year Region	化学纤维（万吨） Chemical Fiber (10 000 tons)	纱（万吨） Yarn (10 000 tons)	布（亿米） Cloth (100 million m)	丝（万吨） Silk (10 000 tons)	机制纸及纸板（万吨） Machine-made Paper and Paperboards (10 000 tons)	原盐（万吨） Salt (10 000 tons)	糖（万吨） Sugar (10 000 tons)
	1952		65.60	38.30	0.56	37.00	495.00	45.00
	1957	0.02	84.40	50.50	0.99	91.00	828.00	86.00
	1962	1.36	54.80	25.30	0.47	112.00	994.00	34.00
	1965	5.01	130.00	62.80	0.91	173.00	1147.00	146.00
	1970	10.09	205.20	91.50	1.67	241.00	1109.00	135.00
	1975	15.48	210.80	94.00	2.31	341.00	1481.00	174.00
	1978	28.46	238.20	110.30	2.97	439.00	1953.00	227.00
	1979	32.63	263.50	121.50	2.97	493.00	1477.00	250.00
	1980	45.03	292.60	134.70	3.54	535.00	1728.00	257.00
	1981	52.73	317.00	142.70	3.74	540.00	1832.00	317.00
	1982	51.70	335.40	153.50	3.71	589.00	1638.00	338.00
	1983	54.07	327.00	148.80	3.69	661.00	1613.00	377.00
	1984	73.49	321.90	137.00	3.76	756.00	1642.00	380.00
	1985	94.78	353.50	146.70	4.22	911.00	1479.00	451.00
	1986	101.73	397.80	164.70	4.72	998.00	1766.00	525.00
	1987	117.50	436.80	173.00	5.19	1141.00	1764.00	506.00
	1988	130.12	465.70	187.90	5.10	1270.00	2264.00	461.00
	1989	148.09	476.70	189.20	5.23	1333.00	2829.00	501.00
	1990	165.42	462.60	188.80	5.66	1372.00	2023.00	582.00
	1991	191.03	460.80	181.70	6.07	1479.00	2410.00	640.00
	1992	213.04	501.70	190.70	7.42	1725.00	2838.00	829.00
	1993	237.37	501.50	203.00	9.40	1914.00	2943.00	771.00
	1994	280.33	489.50	211.30	10.64	2138.00	2996.00	592.00
	1995	341.17	542.20	260.18	11.34	2812.30	2977.72	558.64
	1996	375.45	512.21	209.10	9.49	2638.20	2903.57	640.20
	1997	471.62	559.83	248.79	8.25	2733.20	3082.66	702.58
	1998	510.00	542.00	241.00	6.77	2125.63	2242.52	826.00
	1999	600.00	567.00	250.00	7.02	2159.30	2812.36	861.00
	2000	694.00	657.00	277.00	7.33	2486.94	3128.00	700.00
北 京	Beijing	1.63	4.09	1.22		10.60		
天 津	Tianjin	11.19	8.80	2.92		25.18	241.50	
河 北	Hebei	10.24	43.70	15.60		216.34	432.62	1.28
山 西	Shanxi	2.90	9.14	3.26	0.04	10.08		0.77
内蒙古	Inner Mongolia	0.37	1.57	0.33		12.19	126.68	12.04
辽 宁	Liaoning	34.18	18.29	4.99	0.24	55.16	275.91	2.12
吉 林	Jilin	14.89	6.39	1.26		40.75		2.49
黑龙江	Heilongjiang	18.13	5.75	1.22		43.03		16.41
上 海	Shanghai	47.15	14.95	3.34	0.02	43.54		
江 苏	Jiangsu	191.00	118.36	33.74	1.42	205.25	293.63	3.65
浙 江	Zhejiang	154.08	34.19	16.19	3.24	284.99	9.50	0.00
安 徽	Anhui	12.35	27.51	7.40	0.21	54.97	32.84	0.00
福 建	Fujian	41.22	14.36	5.59		85.07	28.37	6.11
江 西	Jiangxi	7.08	12.57	2.80	0.03	25.40	11.13	1.71
山 东	Shandong	39.62	94.43	27.60	0.54	436.67	829.90	0.80
河 南	Henan	18.63	61.06	11.09	0.11	290.06	59.38	0.12
湖 北	Hubei	9.82	64.73	17.15	0.13	54.42	240.57	0.82
湖 南	Hunan	7.79	16.63	3.41	0.00	70.07	72.93	4.44
广 东	Guangdong	45.00	16.99	10.84	0.05	260.30	17.87	91.30
广 西	Guangxi	2.62	9.22	0.87	0.09	82.55	15.62	325.76
海 南	Hainan	3.53		0.21		1.31	13.03	36.81
重 庆	Chongqing	2.17	5.20	2.26	0.24	10.70	44.98	0.19
四 川	Sichuan	9.05	15.37	6.03	0.75	71.52	215.48	7.79
贵 州	Guizhou	0.45	1.98	0.69	0.01	5.72		1.14
云 南	Yunnan	1.39	2.22	0.53	0.06	15.25	48.09	148.76
西 藏	Tibet							
陕 西	Shaanxi	2.04	15.68	7.18	0.12	23.89	7.50	
甘 肃	Gansu	2.22	1.50	0.15		8.49	3.06	2.44
青 海	Qinghai		0.55	0.26		0.37	67.65	
宁 夏	Ningxia	0.41				23.71		0.33
新 疆	Xinjiang	3.03	32.25	2.94	0.02	19.38	39.75	32.61

13-22 续表 1 continued

年份 Year 地区 Region	啤酒（万吨）Beer (10 000 tons)	卷烟（万箱）Cigarettes (10 000 cases)	家用电冰箱（万台）Household Refrigerators (10 000 units)	房间空调器（万台）Air-conditioners for Room (10 000 units)	家用洗衣机（万台）Household Washing Machines (10 000 units)	彩色电视机（万台）Color Television Sets (10 000 units)	原煤（亿吨）Coal (100 million tons)
1952		265.00					0.66
1957	5.00	446.00	0.16				1.31
1962	10.00	244.00	0.09				2.20
1965	9.00	478.00	0.30				2.32
1970	16.00	783.00	0.52			...	3.54
1975	27.00	992.00	1.80			0.29	4.82
1978	40.00	1182.00	2.80	0.02	0.04	0.38	6.18
1979	52.00	1303.00	3.18	0.86	1.81	0.95	6.35
1980	69.00	1520.00	4.90	1.32	24.53	3.21	6.20
1981	91.00	1704.00	5.56	1.40	128.08	15.21	6.22
1982	117.00	1885.00	9.99	2.44	253.26	28.81	6.66
1983	163.00	1938.00	18.85	3.45	365.86	53.11	7.15
1984	224.00	2132.00	54.74	6.12	578.06	133.95	7.89
1985	310.00	2370.00	144.81	12.35	887.20	435.28	8.72
1986	413.00	2596.00	225.02	9.65	893.40	414.60	8.94
1987	540.00	2881.00	401.34	13.22	990.20	672.72	9.28
1988	656.00	3096.00	757.63	25.91	1046.80	1037.66	9.80
1989	643.00	3195.00	670.79	37.47	825.43	940.02	10.54
1990	692.00	3298.00	463.06	24.07	662.68	1033.04	10.80
1991	838.00	3226.00	469.94	63.03	687.17	1205.06	10.87
1992	1021.00	3285.00	485.76	158.03	707.93	1333.08	11.16
1993	1192.00	3376.00	596.66	346.41	895.85	1435.76	11.50
1994	1415.00	3432.00	768.12	393.42	1094.24	1689.15	12.40
1995	1568.82	3485.02	918.54	682.56	948.41	2057.74	13.61
1996	1681.91	3401.92	979.65	786.21	1074.72	2537.60	13.97
1997	1888.94	3377.42	1044.43	974.01	1254.48	2711.33	13.73
1998	1987.67	3374.00	1060.00	1156.87	1207.31	3497.00	12.50
1999	2098.77	3340.00	1210.00	1337.64	1342.17	4262.00	10.45
2000	2231.32	3397.00	1279.00	1826.67	1442.98	3936.00	9.98
北京 Beijing	177.18	17.07	3.60	31.38	21.00	0.56	0.06
天津 Tianjin	8.27	17.00	8.42	104.15	37.18	72.28	
河北 Hebei	130.60	107.97		0.15			0.58
山西 Shanxi	12.36	30.34			19.47	10.15	1.96
内蒙古 Inner Mongolia	40.50	28.00					0.72
辽宁 Liaoning	149.66	23.00	23.11	25.33	13.73	374.39	0.45
吉林 Jilin	82.61	56.00		6.68	3.03	89.88	0.16
黑龙江 Heilongjiang	143.00	65.91	10.82	0.01		15.59	0.50
上海 Shanghai	33.07	122.42	43.12	186.08	62.11	147.97	
江苏 Jiangsu	76.75	103.20	127.66	165.90	241.60	285.18	0.25
浙江 Zhejiang	163.69	99.21	19.79	87.70	199.69	17.36	0.01
安徽 Anhui	115.29	157.66	169.94	115.80	131.70	156.13	0.47
福建 Fujian	110.40	98.62		0.01		204.19	0.04
江西 Jiangxi	45.56	50.99	32.88			19.56	0.18
山东 Shandong	296.48	230.06	280.30	283.96	312.38	254.77	0.80
河南 Henan	101.77	294.22	107.97	1.27		90.91	0.76
湖北 Hubei	81.70	207.25		55.51	78.19	3.47	0.04
湖南 Hunan	26.42	230.43	44.54	3.47			0.15
广东 Guangdong	158.89	177.30	320.70	697.91	244.18	1471.41	0.02
广西 Guangxi	31.99	72.33		0.07			0.07
海南 Hainan	5.40	11.45					
重庆 Chongqing	50.92	68.70			34.86	50.78	0.11
四川 Sichuan	74.52	128.65	19.13	61.18	5.90	558.61	0.21
贵州 Guizhou	9.32	187.35	25.96			22.04	0.37
云南 Yunnan	15.68	612.77					0.10
西藏 Tibet	2.50						
陕西 Shaanxi	36.55	104.63	37.56	0.11	3.94	80.31	0.20
甘肃 Gansu	23.85	29.51	3.00		34.01	0.02	0.16
青海 Qinghai	0.56						0.01
宁夏 Ningxia	4.67	3.12					0.16
新疆 Xinjiang	21.16	10.50					0.27

13-22 续表 2 continued

年份 地区	Year Region	原油（万吨） Crude Oil (10 000 tons)	天然气（亿立方米） Natural Gas (100 million cu.m)	发电量（亿千瓦小时） Electricity (100 million kwh)	# 水电 Hydropower	生铁（万吨） Pig Iron (10 000 tons)	钢（万吨） Steel (10 000 tons)	成品钢材（万吨） Steel Products (10 000 tons)	水泥（万吨） Cement (10000 tons)
	1952	44.00	0.08	73.00	13.00	193.00	135.00	106.00	286.00
	1957	146.00	0.70	193.00	48.00	594.00	535.00	415.00	686.00
	1962	575.00	12.10	458.00	90.00	805.00	667.00	455.00	600.00
	1965	1131.00	11.00	676.00	104.00	1077.00	1223.00	881.00	1634.00
	1970	3065.00	28.70	1159.00	205.00	1706.00	1779.00	1188.00	2575.00
	1975	7706.00	88.50	1958.00	476.00	2449.00	2390.00	1622.00	4626.00
	1978	10405.00	137.30	2566.00	446.00	3479.00	3178.00	2208.00	6524.00
	1979	10615.00	145.10	2820.00	501.00	3673.00	3448.00	2497.00	7390.00
	1980	10595.00	142.70	3006.00	582.00	3802.00	3712.00	2716.00	7986.00
	1981	10122.00	127.40	3093.00	655.00	3417.00	3560.00	2670.00	8290.00
	1982	10212.00	119.30	3277.00	744.00	3551.00	3716.00	2902.00	9520.00
	1983	10607.00	122.10	3514.00	864.00	3738.00	4002.00	3072.00	10825.00
	1984	11461.00	124.30	3770.00	868.00	4001.00	4347.00	3372.00	12302.00
	1985	12490.00	129.30	4107.00	924.00	4384.00	4679.00	3693.00	14595.00
	1986	13069.00	137.60	4495.00	945.00	5064.00	5220.00	4058.00	16606.00
	1987	13414.00	138.90	4973.00	1000.00	5503.00	5628.00	4386.00	18625.00
	1988	13705.00	142.60	5452.00	1092.00	5704.00	5943.00	4689.00	21014.00
	1989	13764.00	150.49	5848.00	1183.00	5820.00	6159.00	4859.00	21029.00
	1990	13831.00	152.98	6212.00	1267.00	6238.00	6635.00	5153.00	20971.00
	1991	14099.00	160.73	6775.00	1247.00	6765.00	7100.00	5638.00	25261.00
	1992	14210.00	157.88	7539.00	1307.00	7589.00	8094.00	6697.00	30822.00
	1993	14524.00	167.65	8395.00	1518.00	8739.00	8956.00	7716.00	36788.00
	1994	14608.00	175.59	9281.00	1674.00	9741.00	9261.00	8428.00	42118.00
	1995	15004.95	179.47	10070.30	1905.77	10529.27	9535.99	8979.80	47560.59
	1996	15733.39	201.14	10813.10	1879.66	10722.50	10124.06	9338.02	49118.90
	1997	16074.14	227.03	11355.53	1959.83	11511.41	10894.17	9978.93	51173.80
	1998	16100.00	232.79	11670.00	1988.90	11863.67	11559.00	10737.80	53600.00
	1999	16000.00	251.98	12393.00	1965.80	12539.24	12426.00	12109.78	57300.00
	2000	16300.00	272.00	13556.00	2224.14	13101.48	12850.00	13146.00	59700.00
北京	Beijing			145.26	8.64	773.24	803.42	696.69	827.00
天津	Tianjin	763.99	9.10	211.49	0.14	227.99	356.76	315.88	267.81
河北	Hebei	518.26	5.14	844.42	4.70	1709.23	1230.10	1306.52	4694.59
山西	Shanxi		1.14	620.31	13.04	1097.77	470.90	390.04	1193.65
内蒙古	Inner Mongolia		4.55	439.22	5.59	440.84	423.60	378.91	630.02
辽宁	Liaoning	1401.12	14.70	645.58	14.89	1555.40	1553.76	1443.25	1954.87
吉林	Jilin	348.46	2.05	313.50	47.84	162.24	159.31	141.70	758.86
黑龙江	Heilongjiang	5306.73	23.04	426.73	13.19	64.82	88.99	76.35	903.68
上海	Shanghai	52.73	2.60	553.09		1473.00	1778.70	1544.46	311.69
江苏	Jiangsu	155.02	0.24	909.70	0.13	322.83	617.16	1401.83	4599.52
浙江	Zhejiang		0.04	624.83	65.23	108.75	144.96	291.52	4256.61
安徽	Anhui			355.44	4.58	524.26	438.93	421.22	1905.57
福建	Fujian			403.73	195.22	149.37	124.94	283.79	1513.64
江西	Jiangxi			203.35	53.50	304.69	319.86	282.90	1463.04
山东	Shandong	2675.69	6.88	1005.26	0.03	729.70	635.42	681.93	6547.05
河南	Henan	562.18	14.95	694.93	15.52	508.88	404.84	405.62	3723.40
湖北	Hubei	75.11	0.91	559.12	281.40	778.84	895.92	811.10	2460.92
湖南	Hunan			354.42	191.15	332.72	304.13	299.05	2395.72
广东	Guangdong	1393.17	34.60	1292.69	106.11	201.57	286.99	406.28	5872.40
广西	Guangxi	3.29		289.09	168.87	125.32	104.73	102.63	2198.35
海南	Hainan			39.05	11.54	0.46	0.15	8.00	315.05
重庆	Chongqing		1.94	167.90	38.22	167.20	179.69	156.98	1402.78
四川	Sichuan	17.32	88.60	500.24	315.11	555.61	602.35	541.34	2766.42
贵州	Guizhou		0.70	404.70	183.44	150.22	166.90	150.93	783.88
云南	Yunnan		0.05	297.84	196.53	261.23	187.09	176.45	1512.00
西藏	Tibet			6.61	5.54				49.32
陕西	Shaanxi	746.44	21.10	272.28	34.80	62.53	53.65	57.70	989.44
甘肃	Gansu	55.25	0.20	253.52	102.54	201.57	227.22	197.99	723.50
青海	Qinghai	200.01	3.91	133.79	107.69		42.91	36.39	123.71
宁夏	Ningxia	139.01	0.15	136.61	8.18	6.08	0.79	5.59	280.25
新疆	Xinjiang	1848.24	35.38	182.12	30.83	105.16	112.19	126.23	894.55

13-22 续表 3 continued

年份 Year / 地区 Region	平板玻璃（万重量箱） Plate Glass (10 000 weight cases)	木材（万立方米） Timber (10 000 cu.m)	硫酸（万吨） Sulfuric Acid (10000 tons)	纯碱（万吨） Soda Ash (10000 tons)	烧碱（万吨） Caustic Soda (10000 tons)	农用氮、磷、钾化肥（万吨） Chemical Fertilizer (10000 tons)	化学农药（万吨） Chemical Pesticide (10 000 tons)
1952	198.00	1233.00	19.00	19.20	7.90	3.90	0.20
1957	430.00	2787.00	63.20	50.60	19.80	15.10	6.50
1962	367.00	2375.00	96.80	51.90	29.00	46.40	8.80
1965	599.00	3978.00	234.00	88.20	55.60	172.60	19.30
1970	928.00	3782.00	291.40	107.70	89.20	243.50	32.10
1975	1262.00	4703.00	484.70	124.30	128.90	524.70	42.20
1978	1784.00	5162.00	661.00	132.90	164.00	869.30	53.30
1979	2083.00	5439.00	699.80	148.60	182.60	1065.40	53.70
1980	2466.00	5359.00	764.30	161.30	192.30	1232.10	53.70
1981	2701.00	4942.00	780.70	165.20	192.30	1239.00	48.40
1982	3154.00	5041.00	817.50	173.50	207.30	1278.10	45.70
1983	3647.00	5232.00	869.60	179.30	212.30	1378.90	33.10
1984	4190.00	6385.00	817.20	188.00	222.20	1460.20	29.90
1985	4942.00	6323.00	676.40	201.10	235.30	1322.20	21.10
1986	5202.00	6502.00	763.10	214.60	251.80	1395.70	20.30
1987	5803.00	6408.00	983.30	236.30	273.90	1672.20	16.10
1988	7293.00	6218.00	1111.30	260.90	300.50	1740.20	17.90
1989	8442.00	5802.00	1153.30	304.20	321.10	1802.50	20.80
1990	8067.00	5571.00	1196.90	379.50	335.40	1879.70	22.80
1991	8712.00	5807.00	1332.90	393.60	354.10	1979.50	25.50
1992	9359.00	6174.00	1408.70	455.00	379.50	2047.90	28.10
1993	11086.00	6390.00	1336.50	534.90	395.40	1956.30	25.70
1994	11925.00	6615.00	1536.50	581.40	429.60	2272.80	29.00
1995	15731.71	6766.86	1811.00	597.71	531.82	2548.14	41.65
1996	16069.37	6710.27	1883.57	669.29	573.78	2809.04	44.75
1997	16630.70	6394.79	2036.87	725.76	574.40	2820.96	52.67
1998	17194.03	5966.20	2171.00	744.00	539.37	3010.00	55.90
1999	17419.79	5236.80	2356.00	766.00	580.14	3251.00	62.50
2000	18352.20	4723.97	2427.00	834.00	667.88	3186.00	60.70
北京 Beijing	432.10	6.74	7.97		15.14	6.79	
天津 Tianjin	417.05		11.17	69.85	49.28	12.09	1.54
河北 Hebei	2083.30	55.12	96.83	99.84	32.48	195.23	5.57
山西 Shanxi	356.72	13.49	47.16	2.11	16.16	160.67	0.40
内蒙古 Inner Mongolia	371.58	327.79	16.22	52.88	15.75	35.54	0.07
辽宁 Liaoning	1475.26	145.88	119.92	74.13	33.40	94.14	2.20
吉林 Jilin	330.96	456.82	10.80	0.11	7.66	14.68	0.32
黑龙江 Heilongjiang	528.09	819.99	5.71		15.55	39.24	0.28
上海 Shanghai	751.88		34.22	4.00	35.18	13.74	1.31
江苏 Jiangsu	1889.40	67.00	236.72	124.42	85.95	183.18	17.23
浙江 Zhejiang	736.98	212.19	50.24	8.70	36.92	59.22	8.01
安徽 Anhui	181.46	299.95	143.12	8.06	10.83	157.57	1.76
福建 Fujian	479.87	406.44	34.42	9.21	15.64	59.82	1.10
江西 Jiangxi	258.43	237.93	79.92		16.24	45.01	1.60
山东 Shandong	1559.65	174.30	246.31	154.75	105.27	398.24	4.22
河南 Henan	2425.41	176.97	75.01	33.65	37.62	258.56	2.10
湖北 Hubei	625.98	90.76	178.17	60.09	18.43	221.11	5.18
湖南 Hunan	735.34	368.19	128.17	13.03	20.96	141.74	4.58
广东 Guangdong	632.59	274.51	138.75	24.28	16.43	34.65	0.84
广西 Guangxi	192.73	315.17	86.04	1.90	14.07	53.30	1.84
海南 Hainan		30.32	1.13			25.53	0.07
重庆 Chongqing	125.39		50.65	8.87	7.36	72.26	1.04
四川 Sichuan	569.44	18.18	194.07	52.51	31.41	263.51	3.21
贵州 Guizhou	40.37	32.08	33.85		3.66	84.05	0.04
云南 Yunnan	287.71	127.15	199.13	7.73	3.05	174.44	0.24
西藏 Tibet		16.00					
陕西 Shaanxi	277.03	38.28	45.41	1.32	8.15	93.90	0.01
甘肃 Gansu	401.26		75.94	14.06	5.34	50.55	0.02
青海 Qinghai	99.81	2.37	1.79	1.44	1.29	67.06	
宁夏 Ningxia	67.08	0.80	9.17		3.49	59.52	
新疆 Xinjiang	19.35	9.55	7.04	7.35	5.13	71.79	

13-22 续表 4 continued

年份 Year / 地区 Region		塑料 (万吨) Plastics (10 000 tons)	金属切削机床 (万台) Metal-cutting Machine Tools (10 000 units)	汽车 (万辆) Motor Vehicles (10 000 units)	轿车 (万辆) Cars (10 000 units)	大中型拖拉机 (万台) Tractors (10 000 units)	微型电子计算机 (万部) Micro-Computers (10 000 units)	集成电路 (万块) Integrated Circuit (10 000 units)
	1952	0.20	1.37					
	1957	1.30	2.80	0.79				
	1962	4.00	2.25	0.97		0.71		
	1965	9.70	3.96	4.05		0.96		
	1970	17.60	13.89	8.72		3.19		423.00
	1975	33.00	17.49	13.98		7.84		579.00
	1978	67.90	18.32	14.91		11.35		3041.00
	1979	79.30	13.96	18.57		12.56		
	1980	89.80	13.36	22.23	0.54	9.77		1684.00
	1981	91.60	10.26	17.56	0.34	5.28		1279.00
	1982	100.30	9.98	19.63	0.51	4.03		1352.00
	1983	112.10	12.10	23.98	0.60	3.70		2604.00
	1984	118.00	13.35	31.64	0.65	3.97		4148.00
	1985	123.40	16.72	43.72	0.90	4.50		6385.00
	1986	132.10	16.37	36.98	1.17	2.86	4.21	5720.00
	1987	152.60	17.22	47.18	1.79	3.71	5.12	9544.00
	1988	190.40	19.17	64.47	2.96	4.72	11.61	13160.00
	1989	205.80	17.87	58.35	3.58	3.98	7.54	13156.00
	1990	227.00	13.45	51.40	3.50	3.94	8.21	10838.00
	1991	283.00	16.39	71.42	6.87	5.27	16.25	17049.00
	1992	330.80	22.87	106.67	16.17	5.70	12.62	16099.00
	1993	359.90	26.20	129.85	22.29	3.77	14.66	20101.00
	1994	401.40	20.65	136.69	26.87	4.67	24.57	48462.00
	1995	516.87	20.34	145.27	33.70	6.33	83.57	551686.00
	1996	576.86	17.74	147.52	38.29	8.37	138.83	388987.00
	1997	685.76	18.65	158.25	48.60	8.24	206.55	255455.00
	1998	692.58	11.91	163.00	50.71	6.78	291.40	262577.00
	1999	871.10	14.22	183.20	57.10	6.54	405.00	415000.00
	2000	1087.51	17.66	207.00	60.70	4.10	672.00	588000.00
北　京	Beijing	85.05	0.25	13.71	0.49		257.85	23684.00
天　津	Tianjin	66.96	0.06	10.18	8.20	0.32	1.00	23506.00
河　北	Hebei	31.25	0.06	0.94		0.02		
山　西	Shanxi	3.04	0.06	0.11			0.08	
内蒙古	Inner Mongolia	4.55		0.07			7.26	
辽　宁	Liaoning	94.15	1.56	8.37	0.00	0.03	83.72	240.10
吉　林	Jilin	37.24	0.04	32.26	12.54	0.01	0.43	
黑龙江	Heilongjiang	60.65	0.11	12.20			4.19	
上　海	Shanghai	95.47	2.23	25.27	25.15	1.10	42.04	239330.29
江　苏	Jiangsu	160.28	3.74	8.34		0.35	11.56	125006.93
浙　江	Zhejiang	29.59	2.63	1.08		0.29	2.08	29378.76
安　徽	Anhui	7.17	0.47	5.74		0.02	14.18	
福　建	Fujian	14.35	0.06	2.36			88.77	6888.00
江　西	Jiangxi	13.70	0.36	13.34		0.04	2.65	
山　东	Shandong	92.86	2.82	1.28		1.09	31.07	24.04
河　南	Henan	38.20	0.12	0.84		0.71	0.58	
湖　北	Hubei	23.04	0.17	18.62	5.45	0.09	2.56	
湖　南	Hunan	23.10	0.09	1.74	0.03			9.00
广　东	Guangdong	119.65	0.78	3.83	3.22		169.74	117618.43
广　西	Guangxi	3.90	0.31	12.78			1.55	
海　南	Hainan			0.31	0.17			
重　庆	Chongqing	0.03	0.20	25.28	4.82			
四　川	Sichuan	15.59	0.26	3.64		0.01	5.00	177.00
贵　州	Guizhou		0.03	0.14	0.09		2.99	1258.00
云　南	Yunnan	1.71	0.73	2.32				
西　藏	Tibet							
陕　西	Shaanxi	2.75	0.38	1.93	0.54		5.69	
甘　肃	Gansu	27.85	0.03					20384.70
青　海	Qinghai	1.16	0.02					
宁　夏	Ningxia	4.16	0.09					
新　疆	Xinjiang	30.05		0.14		0.03	0.02	

注：1998年以前包括土糖，1998年及以后糖为机制糖，。

c) Data on sugar before 1998 include home-made sugar, and data since 1998 refer to machine-made sugar.

13-23 工业产品产量

Output of Industrial Products

产品名称	Item	1999	2000
化学纤维 (万吨)	Chemical Fiber (10 000 tons)	600.00	694.00
纱 (万吨)	Yarn (10 000 tons)	567.00	657.00
布 (亿米)	Cloth (100 million m)	250.00	277.00
#纯棉布	Pure Cotton Cloth	118.46	139.22
针棉织品折用纱线量(万吨)	Cotton Knitwear (10 000 tons)	56.91	62.52
绒线（毛线） (万吨)	Knitting Wool (10 000 tons)	38.56	42.32
丝 (万吨)	Silk (10 000 tons)	7.02	7.33
呢绒 (万米)	Woolen Piece Goods (10 000 m)	27317.39	27832.37
机制纸及纸板 (万吨)	Machine-made Paper and Paperboard (10 000 tons)	2159.30	2486.94
家用电冰箱 (万台)	Household Refrigerators (10 000)	1210.00	1279.00
家用冷冻箱 (万台)	Household Freezers (10 000)	392.01	384.22
家用洗衣机 (万台)	Household Washing Machines (10 000)	1342.17	1442.98
吸尘器 (万台)	Vacuum Cleaners (10 000)	574.99	1010.30
电风扇 (万台)	Electric Fans (10 000)	6158.14	7661.61
房间空气调节器 (万台)	Air Conditioners (10 000)	1337.64	1826.67
排油烟机 (万台)	Smoke Absorbers (10 000)	351.41	366.15
日用陶瓷 (亿件)	Household Ceramics (100 million pcs)	71.38	67.59
合成洗涤剂 (万吨)	Synthetic Detergents (10 000 tons)	286.53	297.47
原盐 (万吨)	Salt (10 000 tons)	2812.36	3128.00
糖 (万吨)	Sugar (10 000 tons)	861.00	700.00
卷烟 (万箱)	Cigarettes (10 000 cases)	3340.00	3397.00
罐头 (万吨)	Canned Food (10 000 tons)	169.09	178.20
白酒 (万吨)	Liquor (10 000 tons)	502.26	476.11
啤酒 (万吨)	Beer (10 000 tons)	2098.77	2231.32
食用植物油 (万吨)	Edible Vegetable Oil (10 000 tons)	733.79	835.32
中成药 (万吨)	Traditional Chinese Medicine (10 000 tons)	34.25	38.80
化学原料药 (万吨)	Chemical Medicine (10 000 tons)	43.63	52.57
彩色电视机 (万台)	Color Television Sets (10 000)	4262.00	3936.00
录像机 (万部)	Video Recorders (10 000)	568.65	790.59
组合音响 (万部)	Hi-Fi Stereo Component Players (10 000)	2194.52	2917.28
照相机 (万架)	Cameras (10 000)	4832.29	5514.52
农用氮、磷、钾化学肥料总计（折纯） (万吨)	Chemical Fertilizers (10 000 tons)	3251.00	3186.00
#氮肥	Nitrogen Fertilizers	2471.96	2398.11
磷肥	Phosphate Fertilizers	636.07	663.03
化学农药 (万吨)	Chemical Pesticide (10 000 tons)	62.50	60.70
塑料树脂及共聚物 (万吨)	Plastics (10 000 tons)	871.10	1087.51
合成橡胶 (万吨)	Synthetic Rubber (10 000 tons)	73.28	86.52
轮胎外胎 (万条)	Tires (10 000)	10969.84	12157.87
矿山设备 (万吨)	Mining Equipment (10 000 tons)	30.14	30.50
化工设备 (万吨)	Equipment for Chemical Industry (10 000 tons)	17.63	17.52
发电设备 (万千瓦)	Power Generating Equipment (10 000 kw)	1369.00	1249.00
金属切削机床 (万台)	Metal-cutting Machine Tools (10 000)	14.22	17.66
#大型机床 (台)	Large Machine Tools	853.00	1538.00
#高精度机床 (台)	High-precision Machine Tools	491.00	662.00
数控机床 (台)	Numerically Controlled Machine Tools	9007.00	14053.00
汽车 (万辆)	Motor Vehicles (10 000)	183.20	207.00
#载货汽车	Trucks	83.96	86.29
客车	Buses	42.49	57.79
轿车	Cars	57.10	60.70
摩托车 (万辆)	Motorcycles (10 000)	978.20	960.19
自行车 (万辆)	Bicycles (10 000)	2397.57	2906.79
大中型拖拉机 (万台)	Large and Medium Tractors (10 000)	6.54	4.10
内燃机 (万千瓦)	Internal Combustion Engines (10 000 kw)	17801.62	18857.30
铁路客车 (辆)	Railway Passenger Coaches	1778.00	3244.00
铁路货车 (万辆)	Railway Freight Wagons (10 000)	1.86	2.73
载波通信设备 (万部)	Carrier Communication Equipment (10 000 units)	0.88	1.13
移动通信设备 (万部)	Mobile Communication Equipment (10 000 units)	726.61	1505.00

13-23 续表 1 continued

产品名称	Item	1999	2000
电话单机 (万部)	Telephone Sets (10 000)	7139.93	9597.99
传真机 (万部)	Fax Machines (10 000)	159.99	196.29
磁带（折6.30毫米）(亿米)	Tape(converted into 6.30mm) (100 000 000 m)	341.93	297.10
软磁盘 (亿片)	Floppy Disks (100 000 000 pcs)	4.60	4.73
电子计算机 (部)	Computers	8199.00	8625.00
微型电子计算机 (万部)	Micro-computers (10 000)	405.00	672.00
大规模半导体集成电路(亿块)	Large Semiconductor Integrated Circuit (100 000 000 pcs)	14.00	23.92
复印机械 (万台)	Copying Machines (10 000)	210.29	156.63
原煤 (亿吨)	Coal (100 000 000 tons)	10.45	9.98
原油 (万吨)	Crude Oil (10 000 tons)	16000.00	16300.00
汽油 (万吨)	Gasoline (10 000 tons)	3741.27	4134.67
柴油 (万吨)	Diesel Oil (10 000 tons)	6302.68	7079.62
天然气 (亿立方米)	Natural Gas (100 000 000 cu.m)	251.98	272.00
发电量 (亿千瓦小时)	Electricity (100 000 000 kwh)	12393.00	13556.00
#水电	Hydropower	1965.80	2224.14
生铁 (万吨)	Pig Iron (10 000 tons)	12539.24	13101.48
钢 (万吨)	Steel (10 000 tons)	12426.00	12850.00
成品钢材 (万吨)	Steel Products (10 000 tons)	12109.78	13146.00
#重轨	Heavy Rail	111.87	116.86
普通大型钢材	Ordinary Rolled-steel, Large	115.35	161.52
普通中型钢材	Ordinary Rolled-steel, Medium	513.03	518.09
普通小型钢材	Ordinary Rolled-steel, Small	3141.72	3336.49
优质型钢材	High Quality Section Steel	668.58	756.79
线材	Wire Rod	2594.85	2635.37
特厚钢板	Heavy Steel Plate	48.37	76.04
中厚钢板	Medium Steel Plate	1377.02	1636.81
薄钢板	Steel Sheet	1730.17	1903.81
硅钢片	Silicon Steel Sheet	88.84	130.00
无缝钢管	Seamless Steel Pipe	345.75	414.83
焦炭 (万吨)	Coke (10 000 tons)	12073.74	12184.02
水泥 (万吨)	Cement (10 000 tons)	57300.00	59700.00
平板玻璃 (万重量箱)	Plate Glass (10 000 weight cases)	17419.79	18352.20
木材 (万立方米)	Timber (10 000 cu.m)	5236.80	4723.97
硫酸 (万吨)	Sulfuric Acid (10 000 tons)	2356.00	2427.00
碳酸钠（纯碱） (万吨)	Soda Ash (10 000 tons)	766.00	834.00
氢氧化钠（烧碱） (万吨)	Caustic Soda (10 000 tons)	580.14	667.88
合成氨 (万吨)	Synthetic Ammonia (10 000 tons)	3431.72	3363.70

注：1.纱包括纯棉纱、棉混纺纱、纯化纤纱，不包括棉线、代用纤维纱和手工纺纱。
2.布包括纯棉布、棉混纺布、纯化纤布，不包括代用纤维布、手工织布。
3.针棉织品为折用棉纱量。
4.农用化肥按有效成分100%计算。
5.发电设备指500千瓦以上的，包括水轮发电机组、汽轮发电机和燃气轮发电机。
6.金属切削机床不包括台钻、 砂轮机、抛光机。
7.拖拉机是指14.7千瓦及以上的轮式和履带式拖拉机。用本厂自产的拖拉机装配的推土机，只计推土机产量，不计拖拉机产量。
8.原煤包括无烟煤、烟煤、褐煤，不包括石煤。
9.原油包括天然原油和人造原油。
10.成品钢材已剔除重复加工的钢材。
11.移动通信设备不含移动电话机，1999年数相应调整。

a)Yarn includes pure and blended cotton yarn, pure chemical-fiber yarn, but excludes cotton thread, substitute fiber yarn and hand-made yarn.
b)Cloth includes pure and blended cotton cloth, pure chemical-fiber cloth and canvas, but excludes substitute fiber cloth, hand-woven cloth and cord fabric.
c)Knitwear refers to cotton yarn substitutes.
d)The output of chemical fertilizers is calculated on the basis of 100 % effective content.
e)Power generating equipment refers to units with a generating capacity of 500 kw and over, including hydroturbine generating units, steam turbine generating units and gas turbine generating units.
f)Metal-cutting machine tools exclude bench drills, grinders and polishing machines.
g)Tractors refer to both wheel and crawler tractors with a haulage capacity of 14.7 kw and over. The tractors which are refitted into bulldozers by the same tractor factories are deducted.
h)Coal includes anthracite, bituminous coal and lignite, but excludes stone coal.
i)Crude oil includes natural and synthetic crue oil.
j)The output of rolled steel final products excludes the steel products reprocessed.
k)Mobile communication equipment excluded mibile telephone. Data in 1999 were adjusted accordingly.

主 要 统 计 指 标 解 释

工业 指从事自然资源的开采，对采掘品和农产品进行加工和再加工的物质生产部门。具体包括：(1)对自然资源的开采，如采矿、晒盐、森林采伐等(但不包括禽兽捕猎和水产捕捞)；(2)对农副产品的加工、再加工，如粮油加工、食品加工、轧花、缫丝、纺织、制革等；(3)对采掘品的加工、再加工，如炼铁、炼钢、化工生产、石油加工、机器制造、木材加工等，以及电力、自来水、煤气的生产和供应等；(4)对工业品的修理、翻新，如机器设备的修理、交通运输工具(包括小卧车)的修理等。

1984年以前农村的村及村以下办工业归属农业，1984年以后划归工业。

工业统计调查单位 工业统计调查单位分为两类：独立核算法人工业企业和工业活动单位。

(1)独立核算法人工业企业 是指从事工业生产经营活动的单位。独立核算法人工业企业应同时具备以下条件：①依法成立，有自己的名称、组织机构和场所，能够承担民事责任；②独立拥有和使用资产，承担负债，有权与其他单位签订合同；③独立核算盈亏，并能够编制资产负债表。

(2)工业活动单位 是指在一个场所从事一种或主要从事一种工业生产活动的经济单位。它包括独立核算工业企业按主营业务活动(即工业生产活动)划分的主营业务活动单位和非工业企业所属的工业生产活动单位(即原非独立核算工业生产单位)。工业活动单位，一般应同时具备以下三个条件：①具有一个场所，从事一种或主要从事一种工业活动；②单独组织工业生产、经营或业务活动；③单独核算收入和支出。

本年鉴中涉及的企业登记注册类型：

(1)国有及国有控股企业 指国有企业加上国有控股企业。国有企业（即过去的全民所有制工业或国营工业）是指企业全部资产归国家所有，并按《中华人民共和国企业法人登记管理条例》规定登记注册的非公司制的经济组织。包括国有企业、国有独资公司和国有联营企业。1957年以前的公私合营和私营工业，后均改造为国营工业，1992年改为国有工业，这部分工业的资料不单独分列时，均包括在国有企业内。国有控股企业是对混合所有制经济的企业进行的“国有控股”分类。它是指这些企业的全部资产中国有资产（股份）相对其他所有者中的任何一个所有者占资（股）最多的企业。该分组反映了国有经济控股情况。

(2)集体企业 指企业资产归集体所有，并按《中华人民共和国企业法人登记管理条例》规定登记注册的经济组织。是社会主义公有制经济的组成部分。包括城乡所有使用集体投资举办的企业，以及部分个人通过集资自愿放弃所有权并依法经工商行政管理机关认定为集体所有制的企业。

(3)股份有限公司 指根据《中华人民共和国企业法人登记管理条例》规定登记注册，其全部注册资本由等额股份构成并通过发行股票筹集资本，股东以其认购的股份对公司承担有限责任，公司以其全部资产对其债务承担责任的经济组织。

(4)港、澳、台商投资企业 指企业注册登记类型中的港、澳、台资合资、合作、独资经营企业和股份有限公司之和。

(5)外商投资企业 指企业注册登记类型中的中外合资、合作经营企业、外资企业和外商投资股份有限公司之和。

(6)本年鉴中涉及的名为“其他”的企业 均指除国有企业、集体企业、个体经营以外的其他类型工业企业(单位)。包括联营企业、私营企业、股份有限公司，有限责任公司；外商投资企业(中外合资经营、中外合作经营、外资企业)；港、澳、台投资企业(与大陆合资经营、与大陆合作经营、港、澳、台独资企业)及其他企业。

轻工业 指主要提供生活消费品和制作手工工具的工业。按其所使用的原料不同，可分为两大类：(1)以农产品为原料的轻工业，是指直接或间接以农产品为基本原料的轻工业。主要包括食品制造、饮料制造、烟草加工、纺织、缝纫、皮革和毛皮制作、造纸以及印刷等工业；(2)以非农产品为原料的轻工业，是指以工业品为原料的轻工业。主要包括文教体育用品、化学药品制造、合成纤维制造、日用化学制品、日用玻璃制品、日用金属制品、手工工具制造、医疗器械制造、文化和办公用机械制造等工业。

重工业 是指为国民经济各部门提供物质技术基础的主要生产资料的工业。按其生产性质和产品用途，可以分为下列三类：(1)采掘(伐)工业，是指对自然资源的开采，包括石油开采、煤炭开采、金属矿开采、非金属矿开采和木材采伐等工业；(2)原材料工业，指向国民经济各部门提供基本材料、动力和燃料的工业。包括金属冶炼及加工、炼焦及焦炭、化学、化工原料、水泥、人造板以及电力、石油和煤炭加工等工业；(3)加工工业，是指对工业原材料进行再加工制造的工业。包括装备国民经济各部门的机械设备制造工业、金属结构、水泥制品等工业，以及为农业提供的生产资料如化肥、农药等工业。

根据上述划分原则，修理业中以重工业产品为修理作业对象的划为重工业，反之划为轻工业。

工业总产值 是以货币表现的工业企业在一定时期内生产的已出售或可供出售工业产品总量，它反映一定时间内工业生产的总规模和总水平。它包括：在本企业内不再进行加工，经检验、包装入库(规定不需包装的产品除外)的成品价值，对外加工费收入，自制半成品、在产品期末初差额价值。工业总产值采用“工厂法”计算，即以工业企业作为一个整体，按企业工业生产活动的最终成果来计算，企业内部不允许重复计算，不能把企业内部各个车间(分厂)生产的成果相加。但在企业之间、行业之间、地区之间存在着重复计算。

轻重工业总产值的划分也是按“工厂法”计算的，即一个工业企业在正常情况下生产的主要产品的性质属于轻工业，产的主要产品的性质属于重工业，则该企业的全部总产值作为重工业总产值。

工业增加值　是指工业行业在报告期内以货币表现的工业生产活动的最终成果。

实收资本　指企业实际收到的投资人投入的资本。按投资主体可分为国家资本、集体资本、法人资本、个人资本、港澳台资本和外商资本等。

资产合计　指企业拥有或控制的能以货币计量的经济资源。包括各种财产、债权和其他权利。资产按其流动性划分为流动资产、长期投资、固定资产、无形及递延资产和其他资产。

(1)流动资产　指企业可以在一年内或者超过一年的一个生产周期内变现或耗用的资产合计。包括现金及各种存款、短期投资、应收及预付款项、存货等。

(2)固定资产　指企业固定资产净值、固定资产清理、在建工程、待处理固定资产损失所占用的资金合计。

(3)无形资产　指企业长期使用而没有实物形态的资产。包括专利权、非专利技术、商标权、著作权、土地使用权、商誉等。

负债合计　指企业承担的能以货币计量，将以资产或劳务偿付的债务。负债一般按偿还期长短分为流动负债和长期负债、递延税项等。

(1)流动负债　指企业在一年内或者超过一年的一个营业周期内需要偿还的债务合计，其中包括短期借款、应付及预收款项、应付工资、应交税金和应交利润等。

(2)长期负债　指企业在一年以上或者超过一年的一个营业周期以上需要偿还的债务合计，其中包括长期借款、应付债务、长期应付款项等。

所有者权益　指企业投资人对企业净资产的所有权。企业净资产等于企业全部资产减去全部负债后的余额，其中包括投资者对企业的最初投入，以及资本公积金、盈余公积金和未分配利润，对股份制企业即为股东权益。

固定资产原价　指企业在建造、购置、安装、改建、扩建、技术改造某项固定资产时所支出的全部货币总额。它一般包括买价、包装费、运杂费和安装费等。

固定资产净值　是指固定资产原价减去历年已提折旧额后的净额。

流动资产　是指可以在一年或者超过一年的一个营业周期内变现或者耗用的资产，包括现金及各种存款、短期投资、应收及预付货款、存货等。

产品销售收入　指企业销售产品和提供劳务等主要经营业务取得的业务总额。

产品销售成本　指企业销售产品和提供劳务等主要经营业务的实际成本。

产品销售税金及附加　指企业销售产品和提供工业性劳务等主要经营业务应负担的城市维护建设税、消费税、资源税和教育费附加。

产品销售利润　指企业销售产品和提供工业性劳务等主要经营业务收入扣除其成本、费用、税金后的利润。

利润总额　指企业实现的利润。

应交增值税　指企业在报告期内应交纳的增值税额。

总资产贡献率　反映企业全部资产的获利能力，是企业经营业绩和管理水平的集中体现，是评价和考核企业盈利能力的核心指标。计算公式为：

总资产贡献率(%)＝（利润总额＋税金总额＋利息支出）/平均资产总额×100 %

资产负债率　该指标既反映企业经营风险的大小，也反映企业利用债权人提供的资金从事经营活动的能力。计算公式为：

资产负债率(%)＝负债总额/资产总额×100 %

工业成本费用利润率　指在一定时期内实现的利润与成本费用之比，是反映工业生产成本及费用投入的经济效益指标，同时也是反映降低成本的经济效益的指标。计算公式为：

工业成本费用利润率(%)＝利润总额/成本费用总额×100%

工业增加值率　指在一定时期内工业增加值占同期工业总产值的比重，反映降低中间消耗的经济效益。计算公式为：

工业增加值率(%)＝工业增加值(现价)/工业总产值(现价)×100%

流动资产周转次数　指在一定时期内流动资产完成的周转次数，反映流动资产的周转速度。计算公式为：

流动资金周转次数＝产品销售收入/全部流动资产平均余额

产品销售率　指报告期工业销售产值与同期全部工业总产值之比，是反映工业产品已实现销售的程度，分析工业产销衔接情况，研究工业产品满足社会需求程度的指标。计算公式为：

产品销售率(%)＝工业销售产值/工业总产值（现价）×100%

全员劳动生产率　指根据产品的价值量指标计算的平均每一个从业人员在单位时间内的产品生产量。是考核企业经济活动的重要指标，是企业生产技术水平、经营管理水平、职工技术熟练程度和劳动积极性的综合表现。目前我国的全员劳动生产率是将工业企业的工业增加值除以同一时期全部从业人员的平均人数来计算的。计算公式为：

全员劳动生产率＝工业增加值/全部从业人员平均人数

为了使各年度的全员劳动生产率数字可以比较，1990年以前各年的全员劳动生产率均按指数换算成1990年不变价格 。

Explanatory Notes on Main Statistical Indicators

Industry refers to the material production sector which is engaged in extraction of natural resources and processing and reprocessing of minerals and agricultural products, including (1) extraction of natural resources, such as mining, salt production, logging (but not including hunting and fishing); (2) processing and reprocessing of farm and sideline produces, such as rice husking, flour milling, wine making, oil pressing, cotton ginning, silk reeling, spinning and weaving, and leather making; (3) manufacture of industrial products, such as steel making, iron smelting, chemicals manufacturing, petroleum processing, machine building, timber processing; water and gas production and electricity generation and supply; (4)repairing of industrial products such as the repairing of machinery and means of transport (including cars).

Prior to 1984, the rural industry run by villages and cooperative organizations under village was classified into agriculture. Since 1984, it has been grouped into industry.

Units of Industrial Statistics and Inquiry: They are classified into two categories (1) corporate industrial enterprises with independent accounting system (2) industrial establishments.

(1) **Corporate industrial enterprises with independent accounting system** refer to enterprises engaging in industrial production activities, which meet the following requirements: ① They are established legally, having their own names, organizations, location, able to take civil liability; ② They possess and use their assets independently, assume liabilities, and are entitled to sign contracts with other units; ③They are financially independent and compile their own balance sheets.

(2)**Industrial establishments** refer to economic units which located in one single place and engaged entirely or primarily in one kind of industrial activity, including financially independent industrial enterprises and units engaged in industrial activities under the non industrial enterprises (or financially dependent). Industrial establishments generally meet the following requirements: ① They have each one location and are engaged in one kind of industrial activity each; ② They operate and manage their industrial production activities separately;③ They have accounts of income and expenditures separately.

(1)State-owned Enterprises refers to industrial enterprises where the means of production or income are owned by the state. Joint state-private industries and private industries, which existed before 1957, have been transformed into state industries. Statistics on these enterprises has been included in the state-owned industries since 1957 when separation of data was no longer necessary.

(2)Collective-owned Enterprises refers to industrial enterprises where the means of production are owned collectively, including urban and rural enterprises invested by collectives and some enterprises which were formerly owned privately but have been registered in industrial and commercial administration agency as collective units through raising fund from the public.

(3) Share-holding Corporations Ltd. refer to economic units registered in accordance with *the regulation of the People's Republic of China on the Management of Registration of Corporate Enterprises*, with total registered capitals divided into equal shares and raised throught issuing stocks. Each investor bears limited liability to the corporation depending on the holding of shares, and the forporation bears liability to its debt to the maximum of its total assets.

(4) Enterprises with Funds form Hong Kong, Macao and Taiwan refers to all industrial enterprises registered as the joint-venture, cooperative, sole (exclsive) investment industrial enterprises and limited liability corporations with funds from Hong Kong, Macao and Taiwan.

(5) Foreign Funded Enterprises refers to all industrial enterprises registered as the joint-venture, cooperative, sole (exclsive) investment industrial enterprises and limited liability corporations with foreign funds.

(6)Industry of Other Types of Ownership in this yearbook refers to industrial enterprises (units) of the ownership other than the state-owned enterprises, collective enterprises and individual enterprises. They include private enterprises, joint-owned enterprises, share-holding economy (companies limited by shares and companies limited with liabilities.), foreign-funded enterprises (Sino-foreign joint ventures, Sino-foreign cooperative enterprises and foreign ventures exclusively with their own investment), enterprises funded by the entrepreneurs from Hong Kong, Macao and Taiwan (joint ventures and cooperative enterprises with the mainland as well as ventures exclusively with their own investment) and enterprises of other types of ownership.

Light Industry refers to the industry that produces consumer goods and hand tools. It consists of two categories, depending on the materials used:

(1)Industries using farm products as raw materials. These are branches of light industry which directly or indirectly use farm products as basic raw materials, including the manufacture of food and beverages, tobacco processing, textile, clothing, fur and leather manufacturing, paper making, printing, etc.

(2)Industries using non farm products as raw materials.

These are branches of light industry which use manufactured goods as raw materials, including the manufacture of cultural, educational articles and sports goods, chemicals, synthetic fiber, chemical products for daily use, glass products for daily use, metal products for daily use, hand tools, medical apparatus and instruments, and the manufacture of cultural and clerical machinery.

Heavy Industry refers to the industry which produces capital goods, and provides various sectors of the national economy with necessary material and technical basis. It consists of the following three branches according to the purpose of production or the use of products:

(1)Mining, quarrying and logging industry refers to the industry that extracts natural resources, including extraction of petroleum, coal, metal and non-metal ores and logging.

(2)Raw materials industry refers to the industry that provides various sectors of the national economy with raw materials, fuels and power. It includes smelting and processing of metals, coking and coke chemistry, chemical materials and building materials such as cement, plywood, and power, petroleum refining and coal dressing.

(3)Manufacturing industry refers to the industry that processes raw materials. It includes machine building industry which equips sectors of the national economy, industries of metal structure and cement products, industries producing means of agricultural production, such as chemical fertilizers and pesticides. According to the above principle of classification, the repairing trades which are engaged primarily in repairing products of heavy industry are classified into heavy industry while these engaged in repairing products of light industry are classified into light industry.

Gross Industrial Output Value is the total volume of industrial products sold or available for sale in value terms which reflects the total achievements and overall scale of industrial production during a given period. It includes the value of the finished products, which are not to be further processed in the enterprises and have been inspected, packed and put in storage, the value of industrial services rendered to other units, and the changes in the value of the semi-finished products and products in process between the beginning and closing of the period. The gross industrial output value is calculated with "factory method". No double calculations are to be made within the same enterprise. However, double counting does occur among different enterprises.

Output value of light and heavy industries is also classified with the "factory" method. Under normal conditions, if the major products of an industrial enterprise belong to light industry products, the gross output value of that enterprise is classified wholly into light industry; the same principle applies to heavy industry.

Value-added of Industry refers to the final results of industrial production of the industrial trade in money terms during the reference period.

Capital Obtained refers to capital actually received by the enterprise from investors. It can be further classified by investors as state capital, collective capital, corporate capital, individual capital, capital from Hong Kong, Macau and Taiwan and foreign capital.

Total Assets refer to all economic resources, owned or controlled by enterprises, that could be measured in monetary terms, including properties, creditors equity and other economic rights of all forms. Classified by the degree of equitability, total assets include circulating assets, long term investment, fixed assets, intangible assets and deferred assets, and other assets.

(1)Circulating assets (working capital) refer to assets which can be cashed in or spent or consumed in an operating cycle of one year or over one year, including cash, all kinds of deposits, short term investment, receivables, advance payment, stock, etc.

(2)Fixed assets refer to the net value of fixed assets, clearance of fixed assets, project under construction, fixed assets losses in suspense. These are corporations-¸ fund holdings.

(3)Intangible assets refer to the assets without material form used by enterprises over a long time, such as patents, non-patent technologies, trade marks, copyright, land use right, business reputation, etc.

Total Liabilities refer to the debts, measured in monetary terms, that enterprises are responsible for repayment in the form of cash, assets or labour. Classified by terms of repayment, liability include liquid liabilities and long-term liabilities.

(1)Liquid liabilities (also called quick liabilities or immediate liabilities) refer to enterprises' total debt payable within an operating cycle of one year or over one year, including short term loans, payable and advance payments, wages payable, taxes payable and profit payable, etc.

(2)Long term liabilities refers to total debt payable within an operating cycle of one year or over one year, including long-term loans, payable liabilities, long-term payable, etc.

Creditors' Equity refers to investors' ownership of net assets of the enterprise. It is equal to the total assets of the enterprise minus its total liabilities, including the primary input from investors, capital accumulation fund, surplus accumulation fund and undistributed profit. It is the shareholder's equity in share-holding companies.

Original Value of Fixed Assets refers to the original value of all fixed assets owned by industrial enterprises, calculated at the cost paid at the time of purchase, installation, reconstruction, expansion, and technical innovation and transformation of the said assets, which includes expenses on purchase, package, transportation, and installation, etc.

Net Value of Fixed Assets is obtained by deducting depreciation over years from the original value of fixed assets.

Working Capital (Circulating Assets) refers to assets which can be cashed in or spent or consumed in an operating cycle of one year or over one year, which includes cash, various deposits, short term investment, and receivable payments, and advance payments, stock, etc.

Sales Revenue of Industrial Products refers to the revenue from the sales of products by industrial enterprises and the revenue from services provided and etc.

Sales Cost of Industrial Products refers to the actual cost of products of industrial enterprises and industrial services provided, etc..

Tax and Extra Charges on Sales of Products refer to the tax on city maintenance and construction, consumption tax, resources tax and extra charges for education, which should be borne by the enterprises in selling products and providing industrial services.

Sales Profit of Products refers to the profit gained by the enterprises by deducting cost, charges and taxes from the business income of the enterprises obtained in selling products and providing industrial services.

Total Profits refer to the profits gained by the enterprises.

Value-added Tax Payable refers to the amount of the value added tax which should be paid by the enterprises in the reporting period.

Ratio of Profits, Taxes and Interests to Average Assets reflects the profit-making capability of all assets of the enterprise and is a key indicator manifesting the performance and management and evaluating the profit-making potential of the enterprise. It is calculated as follows:

Ratio of profits, taxes and interests to average assets (%) = [(Total profits+total Taxes+interest payment) / average assets] × 100%

Ratio of Debts to Assets reflect both the operation risk and the capability of the enterprise in making use of the capital from the creditors. It is calculated as follows:

Ratio of debts to assets (%) = (Total debts / total assets) × 100%

Ratio of Profits to Total Industrial Costs refers to the ratio of profits realized in a given period to the total costs in the same period, which reflects the economic efficiency of input cost and is calculated as follows:

Ratio of Profits to Total Industrial Cost(%)=(Total Profits/ Total Costs) × 100%

Value-added Rate of Industry refers to the ratio of value added of industry in a given period to the gross output value in the same period, which reflects the economic efficiency of cutting down the intermediate input and is calculated as follows:

Value-added Rate of Industry(%)=[Value-added of Industry (at current prices)] / [Gross Output Value (at Current Prices)] × 100%

Turnover of Working Capital refers to the number of times of turnover of working capital in a given period of time, which reflects the speed of the turnover of working capital and is calculated as follows:

Turnover of Working Capital(%)=(Sales Revenue of Products) / (Average Balance of Total Working Capital) × 100%

Ratio of Sales to Gross Output Value refers to the sales of industrial products to the gross industrial output value during the reference period, and is important in reflecting the linkage between production and sales and the extent of the needs of the society that has been met by the supply of industrial products. It is calculated as follows:

Ratio of Sales to Gross Output Value=[Industrial sales / Gross industrial output value (at current prices)] × 100%

Overall Labour Productivity of Industrial Enterprises refers to the average output per employed person in industrial enterprises in value terms. At present, the value added and the average number of staff and workers of an industrial enterprises in a given period are used to calculate the overall labour productivity. The formula used is:

Overall Labour Productivity=(Value Added of Industry) / (Average Number of Staff and Workers)

For the purpose of comparison of the overall labour productivity among different years, the data on the overall labour productivity of the years prior to 1990 have been adjusted on the basis of 1990 constant prices.

十四、建筑业

Construction

简要说明

一、本篇资料反映我国建筑业概况和发展情况。主要包括建筑业企业生产经营情况，指标有企业个数、从业人员数、建筑业总产值、建筑业增加值、房屋建筑面积、机械设备、资产负债、企业总收入、利润税金、劳动生产率、工程质量优良品率、技术装备率、建筑材料消耗等。此外，还包括勘察设计机构和人员情况，农村建筑队主要指标。

二、本篇中的建筑业企业资料由国家统计局固定资产投资司提供。根据建筑业发展的实际情况，建筑业统计范围从1996年年报起由原城镇及城镇以上各种经济类型的建筑业企业调整为凡具有建筑业资质等级四级及四级以上的独立核算的建筑业企业。为了尽可能全面反映全社会建筑业企业概况，从1996年开始，我们在14－1表中将“农村建筑队”一栏中的资料调整为建筑业资质等级四级以下的乡、村建筑队数据。勘察设计机构和人员表由建设部提供。资质等级四级以下乡、村建筑队资料由农业部提供。资料来源分别依据国家统计局制定的《建筑业统计报表制度》、建设部制定的《勘察设计报表制度》及农业部制定的《乡镇企业统计报表制度》规定收集的有关年报资料。

Brief Introduction

I. Data in this chapter show the general situation and the development of the construction in China. They cover mainly the situation of production and management of the enterprises of construction, including the number of employed persons, gross output value and value added of construction, floor space of the buildings, machinery and equipment, assets and liabilities, total revenue of enterprises, profits and taxes, labour productivity, percentage of high quality projects, per capita machinery, consumption of construction materials, etc. They also cover the situation of prospecting and designing institutions and the personnel as well as the main indicators of the rural construction teams.

II. Data on the enterprises of construction in this chapter are provided by the Department of Statistics of Investment in Fixed Assets, NBS. In line with the actual situation of the development of construction, the coverage of construction statistics has been enlarged since 1996 when the annual statistical reports were submitted. The original coverage includes all the construction enterprises of various types of ownership at and above town level. The new coverage includes all the construction enterprises of various types of ownership with qualification criteria at or above Class 8. In order to reflect the operation of construction enterprises of the whole society, 1996 and 1997 data of rural construction teams in table 14-1 are adjusted as township and village construction teams with qualification criteria below Class 4. The data on prospecting and designing institutions and the personnel are provided by the Department of Prospecting and Designing, Ministry of Construction. Data on township and village construction teams with qualification criteria below Class 4 are provided by the Bureau of Township Enterprises, Ministry of Agriculture. The annual data are collected in accordance with the " reporting scheme of construction statistics" stipulated by the National Bureau of Statistics, the "prospecting and designing statistical reporting scheme" stipulated by the Ministry of Construction and the " township enterprises statistical reporting scheme" stipulated by the Ministry of Agriculture.

14-1 建筑业企业概况

Main Indicators on Construction Enterprises

年份 Year	总计 Total	# 国有 State-owned	# 城镇集体 Urban Collective-owned	# 农村建筑队 Rural Construction Teams
企业单位数（个） Number of Enterprises				
1980	57404	1996	4608	50800
1981	55627	2586	4741	48300
1982	61684	2808	5076	53800
1983	66653	2885	6768	57000
1984	90141	3017	6724	80400
1985	93750	3385	7765	82600
1986	88771	3608	8977	76186
1987	87474	3788	9837	73849
1988	87224	3798	10336	73090
1989	80106	3927	9179	67000
1990	74145	4275	9052	60818
1991	73094	4638	9187	59269
1992	77857	4985	9551	63321
1993	94582	6363	14130	70486
1994	94942	7251	15196	69842
1995	96935	7531	15348	71017
1996	108555	9109	29044	67191
1997	95956	9650	29872	51939
1998	90926	9458	26970	45292
1999	96648	9394	25443	49414
2000	97263	9030	22905	49745
从业人员（万人） Number of Persons Employed (10 000 persons)				
1980	982.7	481.8	166.2	334.7
1981	1034.0	509.3	175.9	348.8
1982	1154.3	532.9	200.1	421.3
1983	1285.3	544.5	258.1	482.7
1984	1531.2	554.2	293.5	683.5
1985	1701.4	576.7	334.8	789.9
1986	1800.6	617.3	376.4	806.9
1987	1852.5	618.2	405.9	828.8
1988	1899.4	623.5	421.3	854.6
1989	1773.4	614.7	390.1	768.6
1990	1716.7	621.0	389.7	706.0
1991	1783.3	638.9	419.4	725.0
1992	1961.2	681.2	476.3	803.6
1993	2156.7	657.1	455.7	926.8
1994	2448.8	818.2	601.9	969.3
1995	2511.9	824.3	631.9	980.4
1996	2992.3	855.9	1171.4	870.4
1997	2804.6	828.6	1148.2	703.1
1998	2778.9	738.4	1008.5	748.9
1999	2765.7	690.6	934.6	739.9
2000	2740.9	635.6	823.2	746.6
建筑业总产值（亿元） Gross Output Value (100 million yuan)				
1980	346.98	220.90	66.03	60.05
1981	352.58	213.70	68.60	70.28
1982	445.71	258.03	87.30	100.38
1983	555.71	298.54	121.00	136.20
1984	733.69	371.56	145.59	216.54
1985	985.10	474.51	200.59	310.00
1986	1330.80	566.83	241.24	522.73
1987	1603.61	660.11	292.54	650.96
1988	1959.42	776.96	354.69	827.77
1989	2169.48	878.57	404.41	886.50
1990	1947.58	935.19	409.82	602.56
1991	2284.78	1062.48	501.85	720.45
1992	3298.70	1432.13	742.31	1124.26
1993	5498.35	2054.83	1163.85	2060.28
1994	7684.36	3033.66	1519.45	2952.34
1995	9505.00	3670.25	1899.47	3632.60
1996	11579.15	4160.21	3695.67	3296.90
1997	12462.57	4526.52	3925.81	3336.09
1998	13740.69	4571.44	3793.17	3678.70
1999	15151.46	4861.38	3786.35	3998.60
2000	16780.90	5053.79	3682.53	4283.30

注：1.1996年起国有、城镇集体栏内的建筑业企业的统计范围是资质等级四级及四级以上建筑业企业；农村建筑队是指资质等级四级以下的乡、村集体建筑队，因此数据存在着与以前年度不可比因素。

2.从业人员1993年以前是年末数，1993年起为年平均人数。

a)The statistical coverage of the state-owned and the urban collective-owned construction enterprises since 1996 included the fourth and higher grade construction enterprises. The statistical coverage of the rural construction teams in 1996 included the township and village construction teams lower than the fourth grade. Therefore the data were not entirely comparable with the data of the previous years.

b)The number of employed persons prior to 1993 refers to the year-end number. Since 1993,it refers to the annual average number.

14-2 建筑业企业主要经济指标（2000年）

指标	Item	合计 Total Enterprises
建筑业企业个数 （个）	Number of Construction Enterprises (unit)	47518
从业人员 （万人）	Number of Employed Persons (10 000 persons)	1994.30
自有固定资产原价 （亿元）	Fixed Assets Owned (original value) (100 million yuan)	4204.71
自有固定资产净价 （亿元）	Fixed Assets Owned (net value) (100 million yuan)	2831.25
自有机械设备台数 （万台）	Number of Machinery and Equipment Owned (10 000 set)	625.99
自有机械设备净值 （亿元）	Net Value of Machinery and Equipment Owned(100 million yuan)	1257.23
自有机械设备总功率 （万千瓦）	Total Power of Machinery and Equipment Owned (10 000 kw)	9228.11
建筑业总产值 （亿元）	Gross Output Value of Construction (100 million yuan)	12497.60
建筑业增加值 （亿元）	Value Added of Construction (100 million yuan)	3341.09
#固定资产折旧 （亿元）	Depreciation of Fixed Assets (100 million yuan)	211.54
应付工资 （亿元）	Wages Payable (100 million yuan)	1530.51
应付福利费 （亿元）	Welfare Expenses Payable (100 million yuan)	160.11
工程结算税金及附加 （亿元）	Taxes and Extra Charges on Project Settle Accounts (100 million yuan)	362.19
管理费用中的税金 （亿元）	Taxes in Management Expenses (100 million yuan)	24.96
工程结算利润 （亿元）	Profits of Project Settle Accounts (100 million yuan)	943.56
施工面积 （万平方米）	Floor Space of Buildings under Construction (10 000 sq.m)	160141.10
竣工面积 （万平方米）	Floor Space of Buildings Completed (10 000 sq.m)	80714.90
利润总额 （亿元）	Total Profits (100 million yuan)	192.06
税金总额 （亿元）	Total Tax (100 million yuan)	387.16
劳动生产率	Overall Labor Productivity	
按总产值计算 （元/人）	In Terms of Gross Output Value (yuan/person)	59585
按增加值计算 （元/人）	In Terms of Value-added (yuan/person)	15929
技术装备率 （元/人）	Value of Machines per Laborer (yuan/person)	6304
动力装备率 （千瓦/人）	Power of Machines per Laborer (kw/person)	4.6
房屋建筑面积竣工率 (%)	Rate of Floor Space of Buildings Completed (%)	50.4
工程质量优良品率 (%)	Rate of High Quality Projects (%)	29.0
产值利润率 (%)	Ratio of Profit to Gross Output Value (%)	1.5
产值利税率 (%)	Ratio of Pre-tax Profit to Gross Output Value (%)	4.6

Main Economic Indicators on Construction Enterprises (2000)

内资企业 Domestic Funded	#国有 State-owned	#集体 Collective-owned	港澳台商投资企业 Funded from Hong Kong, Macao and Taiwan	#独资 Solely Owned	外商投资企业 Foreign Funded	#独资 Solely Owned
46564	9030	22905	635	76	319	30
1981.68	635.55	823.23	8.22	0.58	4.40	0.28
4159.72	2211.39	1027.84	27.06	2.09	17.93	1.04
2802.35	1418.68	729.76	17.38	1.38	11.52	0.59
620.21	182.27	284.39	3.70	0.30	2.07	0.13
1244.62	548.54	369.08	7.32	0.74	5.29	0.24
9177.76	4150.75	2995.29	30.50	3.36	19.86	1.42
12330.93	5053.79	3682.53	99.18	7.08	67.49	2.31
3301.30	1390.76	992.14	24.46	1.87	15.33	0.74
208.42	112.86	46.95	1.80	0.14	1.31	0.06
1516.40	558.29	518.21	8.64	0.49	5.46	0.29
158.83	68.48	48.03	0.79	0.04	0.48	0.02
357.59	144.32	110.45	2.97	0.19	1.63	0.07
24.73	10.34	8.80	0.14	0.02	0.09	0.01
927.47	415.05	248.91	9.86	0.97	6.23	0.29
159332.24	46237.53	63082.34	379.48	61.43	429.38	22.27
80402.31	20144.98	35698.66	157.72	24.07	154.91	2.74
189.77	21.59	75.63	0.99	0.27	1.31	0.03
382.32	154.66	119.25	3.12	0.21	1.71	0.08
59280	73301	44142	93447	73394	100620	66245
15871	20172	11893	23042	19416	22853	21241
6280	8631	4483	8907	12773	12008	8587
4.6	6.5	3.6	3.7	5.8	4.5	5.1
50.5	43.6	56.6	41.6	39.2	36.1	12.3
29.1	28.3	27.5	24.9	59.4	23.6	15.0
1.5	0.4	2.1	1.0	3.8	1.9	1.5
4.6	3.5	5.3	4.1	6.7	4.5	4.7

14-3 各地区历年建筑业总产值

Total Output Value of Construction in Various Years by Region

单位：万元 (10 000 yuan)

地 区	Region	1996	1997	1998	1999	2000
全 国	**National Total**	**82822497**	**91264777**	**100619922**	**111528640**	**124975961**
北 京	Beijing	4680761	5192363	6230089	6814102	7274774
天 津	Tianjin	1685191	1909999	2111208	2227406	2380991
河 北	Hebei	3363064	3760962	3935044	4321432	4921005
山 西	Shanxi	1568405	1920095	2178150	2397739	2393974
内蒙古	Inner Mongolia	876393	963852	1017600	1168732	1367309
辽 宁	Liaoning	3976734	4291256	4189831	4893444	5980933
吉 林	Jilin	1358990	1369882	1460359	1713517	2391840
黑龙江	Heilongjiang	2229620	2435310	2739532	2996115	3340903
上 海	Shanghai	4406801	5524161	5859020	5683036	6223565
江 苏	Jiangsu	10140598	10716094	11962007	13299853	15388416
浙 江	Zhejiang	8362780	8773546	9425292	11282810	13837658
安 徽	Anhui	2399465	2359972	2356154	2773364	3028240
福 建	Fujian	2083515	2268855	2446658	2511292	2711420
江 西	Jiangxi	972574	856436	893804	1022296	1164115
山 东	Shandong	5780205	6479717	7001115	7672600	8170949
河 南	Henan	2715574	2946903	3049638	3169845	3573425
湖 北	Hubei	2844273	3059698	3436527	3990201	4541767
湖 南	Hunan	2783849	2965005	3273222	3338963	3544202
广 东	Guangdong	6240552	6747406	7886723	8719500	8919834
广 西	Guangxi	1233093	1275627	1344209	1491385	1509158
海 南	Hainan	151799	279923	308507	333933	302139
重 庆	Chongqing		2440552	2896198	3175927	3486579
四 川	Sichuan	6715859	5206436	5977644	6495237	7138102
贵 州	Guizhou	660970	767046	831976	966508	1090571
云 南	Yunnan	1733649	2189844	2517439	3114900	3092645
西 藏	Tibet	66122	79519	94455	134958	168178
陕 西	Shaanxi	1294163	1642493	1879804	2183009	2423046
甘 肃	Gansu	1037164	1056249	1133752	1187695	1251202
青 海	Qinghai	277727	309340	355576	396528	447162
宁 夏	Ningxia	253697	334919	393603	482827	562352
新 疆	Xinjiang	928911	1141318	1434787	1569486	2349506

14-4 各地区历年建筑业增加值

Value-added of Construction in Various Years by Region

单位：万元 (10 000 yuan)

地 区	Region	1996	1997	1998	1999	2000
全 国	**National Total**	**24056186**	**25405426**	**27837909**	**30222586**	**33410864**
北 京	Beijing	1348018	1424872	1787588	1809631	1861649
天 津	Tianjin	510525	508102	580644	599298	596889
河 北	Hebei	1004433	1058799	1026622	1176002	1255840
山 西	Shanxi	533155	571361	619820	623871	659211
内蒙古	Inner Mongolia	321049	309691	352602	387728	415530
辽 宁	Liaoning	1352915	1331824	1271822	1458714	1650483
吉 林	Jilin	451124	428432	410049	477403	648043
黑龙江	Heilongjiang	675666	720763	796891	838384	901381
上 海	Shanghai	995145	1209914	1311338	1224694	1381463
江 苏	Jiangsu	2540378	2620881	2915897	3212848	3700633
浙 江	Zhejiang	2099332	2212090	2431151	2861430	3521692
安 徽	Anhui	731606	680801	703797	783765	837832
福 建	Fujian	561023	618988	738348	662526	710129
江 西	Jiangxi	260372	256353	262760	303880	324209
山 东	Shandong	1770885	1894007	2020712	2162466	2269464
河 南	Henan	849905	795700	875188	915452	1006563
湖 北	Hubei	941654	951010	1063379	1208960	1346062
湖 南	Hunan	804491	836320	876333	909667	965511
广 东	Guangdong	1854934	1964243	2230076	2492533	2509568
广 西	Guangxi	365971	378210	436240	463926	495053
海 南	Hainan	35148	73788	67747	77185	68036
重 庆	Chongqing		677742	783224	870648	912266
四 川	Sichuan	1985461	1593421	1776678	1855648	2073881
贵 州	Guizhou	207235	230913	244071	276657	313945
云 南	Yunnan	496463	613405	678146	857556	819742
西 藏	Tibet	31016	33468	41089	40991	45811
陕 西	Shaanxi	440665	508819	509819	557333	591203
甘 肃	Gansu	382693	347624	380112	388427	402922
青 海	Qinghai	92589	97950	117884	137154	162241
宁 夏	Ningxia	89034	110707	120438	145697	173888
新 疆	Xinjiang	323300	345229	407445	442113	789737

14-5 各地区历年建筑业企业利税总额

Total Pre-Tax Profits of Construction Enterprises in Various Years by Region

单位：万元 (10 000 yuan)

地 区	Region	1996	1997	1998	1999	2000
全 国	**National Total**	**2479508**	**2716661**	**3019269**	**4944082**	**5792206**
北 京	Beijing	133026	149558	181706	341341	385714
天 津	Tianjin	44817	49575	53204	80172	96435
河 北	Hebei	106402	117092	124915	207616	224663
山 西	Shanxi	49022	55488	69685	72317	93678
内蒙古	Inner Mongolia	27891	35567	35960	51242	58719
辽 宁	Liaoning	122621	135564	132028	183582	255827
吉 林	Jilin	42521	43660	46878	54198	88242
黑龙江	Heilongjiang	65909	68615	79214	109410	134863
上 海	Shanghai	124981	138251	142681	278825	342818
江 苏	Jiangsu	256054	255623	278305	443934	585377
浙 江	Zhejiang	232144	254643	281932	571252	740235
安 徽	Anhui	74303	71736	79262	105523	126076
福 建	Fujian	73709	81560	103386	120981	141997
江 西	Jiangxi	28814	31303	33135	37586	44866
山 东	Shandong	187394	197489	217180	416839	419264
河 南	Henan	83210	86335	92265	132961	148742
湖 北	Hubei	89060	107238	113959	190966	216898
湖 南	Hunan	84155	92669	96355	121018	153028
广 东	Guangdong	209670	218956	270277	522531	543688
广 西	Guangxi	39107	45010	49408	63830	64151
海 南	Hainan	4507	11267	9391	17655	14801
重 庆	Chongqing		73410	84544	133598	152870
四 川	Sichuan	193794	158437	171098	268304	318422
贵 州	Guizhou	19910	24822	25871	32956	47008
云 南	Yunnan	57730	72166	84000	154874	160638
西 藏	Tibet	2257	1367	2353	8358	12805
陕 西	Shaanxi	38311	45563	54032	67403	84901
甘 肃	Gansu	41448	38004	40692	61307	67918
青 海	Qinghai	8847	9646	11387	8921	18312
宁 夏	Ningxia	8518	9729	10696	19804	29994
新 疆	Xinjiang	29377	36317	43472	64778	19257

14-6 各地区历年建筑业企业利润总额

Total Profits of Construction Enterprises in Various Years by Region

单位：万元 (10 000 yuan)

地区	Region	1996	1997	1998	1999	2000
全 国	**National Total**	**1093504**	**1099170**	**1173285**	**1547982**	**1920635**
北 京	Beijing	88896	104320	123744	135595	163561
天 津	Tianjin	13731	21445	29350	21991	27993
河 北	Hebei	40251	48968	40479	62006	67370
山 西	Shanxi	-2263	-828	-10161	-882	-514
内蒙古	Inner Mongolia	-2282	-5999	3241	13076	14561
辽 宁	Liaoning	28388	-8711	-42535	30962	66730
吉 林	Jilin	-12983	-15110	-16523	790	17339
黑龙江	Heilongjiang	4700	3122	10870	23741	31070
上 海	Shanghai	81808	126383	130723	141889	184252
江 苏	Jiangsu	142671	113507	138139	121082	206569
浙 江	Zhejiang	165803	170603	194607	235308	318850
安 徽	Anhui	29130	10221	774	15904	28127
福 建	Fujian	23532	28436	26052	25773	25831
江 西	Jiangxi	2569	-1710	-2548	3395	6157
山 东	Shandong	150203	161762	162328	176337	182235
河 南	Henan	40204	26029	21442	37901	31281
湖 北	Hubei	27263	16076	38036	51890	58425
湖 南	Hunan	35440	29655	19488	17230	43938
广 东	Guangdong	143255	131085	153969	199092	203926
广 西	Guangxi	11299	8418	16059	13227	9147
海 南	Hainan	841	4868	295	6439	3907
重 庆	Chongqing		27203	33093	41582	49310
四 川	Sichuan	60582	51222	58555	76014	100995
贵 州	Guizhou	-2880	-286	638	1775	9855
云 南	Yunnan	18013	34195	35929	53070	58350
西 藏	Tibet	1564	4858	4392	5033	7385
陕 西	Shaanxi	1528	3517	-3552	5799	14497
甘 肃	Gansu	12741	10906	14455	16917	19977
青 海	Qinghai	-658	-797	-1555	-3873	3812
宁 夏	Ningxia	-1217	157	-622	5559	13722
新 疆	Xinjiang	-8625	-4347	-5875	13359	-48022

14-7 各地区历年建筑业劳动生产率

Labor Productivity of Construction Enterprises in Various Years by Region

按建筑业增加值计算。

Calculated in terms of value-added of construction.

单位：元 (yuan)

地 区	Region	1996	1997	1998	1999	2000
全 国	**National Total**	**11337**	**12089**	**13350**	**14451**	**15929**
北 京	Beijing	16344	17736	21203	21900	22553
天 津	Tianjin	18077	17364	19791	20875	21765
河 北	Hebei	9816	10785	10807	12360	13070
山 西	Shanxi	12142	12101	14249	15071	16824
内蒙古	Inner Mongolia	9252	9529	11716	11753	11913
辽 宁	Liaoning	11661	11883	12163	13948	15062
吉 林	Jilin	11780	12059	11988	13355	16594
黑龙江	Heilongjiang	10365	11220	12917	13462	13991
上 海	Shanghai	18331	20666	23038	21488	24375
江 苏	Jiangsu	12045	12683	12904	14540	16793
浙 江	Zhejiang	14748	15863	17059	19013	21228
安 徽	Anhui	9875	10080	10902	11195	11738
福 建	Fujian	12754	12835	17159	16826	17061
江 西	Jiangxi	8049	7566	8749	10455	11240
山 东	Shandong	9725	10889	12026	12615	12517
河 南	Henan	8735	8501	10228	11656	12766
湖 北	Hubei	12308	12499	12869	14105	16268
湖 南	Hunan	10593	10297	10594	11787	12697
广 东	Guangdong	12868	14396	16332	17523	19829
广 西	Guangxi	9468	10578	12537	13273	15308
海 南	Hainan	7663	8198	9463	12660	11868
重 庆	Chongqing		9826	10245	11656	12859
四 川	Sichuan	8849	10331	11163	11589	13118
贵 州	Guizhou	9454	9780	11386	12296	14311
云 南	Yunnan	10842	11432	12717	14653	15531
西 藏	Tibet	19311	19937	23931	16375	17105
陕 西	Shaanxi	10531	10644	11827	13599	14559
甘 肃	Gansu	8202	8207	10728	11203	11701
青 海	Qinghai	6952	10241	12030	13505	15348
宁 夏	Ningxia	9354	10486	10448	11699	13895
新 疆	Xinjiang	11348	11739	13545	15660	25209

14-8 各地区按登记注册类型分的建筑业企业单位数（2000年）

Number of Construction Enterprises by Registration Status and Region (2000)

单位：个 (unit)

地区	Region	合计 Total	内资企业 Domestic Funded	#国有 State-owned	#集体 Collective-owned	港澳台商投资企业 Funded from Hong Kong, Macao and Taiwan	#港澳台商独资企业 Solely Owned	外商投资企业 Foreign Funded	#外商独资企业 Solely Owned
全　国	**National Total**	**47518**	**46564**	**9030**	**22905**	**635**	**76**	**319**	**30**
北　京	Beijing	1697	1566	353	634	78		53	
天　津	Tianjin	446	423	135	221	14		9	
河　北	Hebei	1730	1719	435	859	7	1	4	
山　西	Shanxi	792	783	205	426	8	2	1	
内蒙古	Inner Mongolia	916	912	133	192	3	1	1	
辽　宁	Liaoning	2381	2317	526	1214	34		30	2
吉　林	Jilin	752	748	331	267	3	1	1	1
黑龙江	Heilongjiang	1652	1639	473	652	7	2	6	1
上　海	Shanghai	1481	1319	230	368	106	2	56	1
江　苏	Jiangsu	3930	3842	540	2016	56		32	
浙　江	Zhejiang	3592	3545	297	981	28	4	19	4
安　徽	Anhui	1565	1554	257	911	9	1	2	
福　建	Fujian	1692	1610	266	761	59	26	23	5
江　西	Jiangxi	1005	1004	224	703			1	
山　东	Shandong	4190	4112	636	2300	55	14	23	10
河　南	Henan	1885	1861	440	1110	14	2	10	1
湖　北	Hubei	1959	1920	473	1094	32	3	7	
湖　南	Hunan	1754	1751	309	1200	3	1		
广　东	Guangdong	2773	2703	676	1309	58	2	12	
广　西	Guangxi	1078	1067	260	623	4	1	7	
海　南	Hainan	239	233	135	79	3	1	3	2
重　庆	Chongqing	1737	1716	171	819	12	1	9	1
四　川	Sichuan	3290	3268	380	1675	15	5	7	1
贵　州	Guizhou	620	618	155	362	2	1		
云　南	Yunnan	1402	1394	190	747	7		1	1
西　藏	Tibet	141	141	39	87				
陕　西	Shaanxi	848	844	161	490	4			
甘　肃	Gansu	504	500	100	283	3	2	1	
青　海	Qinghai	270	268	99	90	2	1		
宁　夏	Ningxia	508	505	161	140	2	1	1	
新　疆	Xinjiang	689	682	240	292	7	1		

14-9 各地区按登记注册类型分的建筑业企业从业人员（2000年）

Number of Staff and Workers in Construction Enterprises by Registration Status and Region (2000)

单位：万人 (10 000 persons)

地区	Region	合计 Total	内资企业 Domestic Funded	#国有 State-owned	#集体 Collective-owned	港澳台商投资企业 Funded from Hong Kong, Macao and Taiwan	#港澳台商独资企业 Solely Owned	外商投资企业 Foreign Funded	#外商独资企业 Solely Owned
全国	**National Total**	**1994.30**	**1981.68**	**635.55**	**823.23**	**8.22**	**0.58**	**4.40**	**0.28**
北京	Beijing	56.60	55.72	27.32	18.03	0.53		0.35	
天津	Tianjin	20.31	20.21	12.91	4.98	0.08		0.02	
河北	Hebei	87.60	87.39	32.62	36.14	0.08	0.01	0.12	
山西	Shanxi	37.33	37.29	23.97	9.66	0.04	0.01		
内蒙古	Inner Mongolia	25.71	25.63	7.87	5.20	0.05	0.03	0.03	
辽宁	Liaoning	95.26	94.33	37.77	40.05	0.42		0.51	0.01
吉林	Jilin	28.96	28.95	18.01	6.28				
黑龙江	Heilongjiang	45.41	45.13	22.74	12.86	0.25	0.01	0.03	
上海	Shanghai	35.10	34.10	10.65	7.16	0.57	0.03	0.43	0.01
江苏	Jiangsu	227.46	225.82	41.28	118.21	0.88		0.77	
浙江	Zhejiang	171.05	169.48	19.93	55.19	0.86	0.04	0.71	0.02
安徽	Anhui	71.20	70.90	20.87	36.14	0.07	0.01	0.24	
福建	Fujian	41.13	40.28	13.46	14.25	0.58	0.20	0.28	0.14
江西	Jiangxi	29.77	29.77	11.85	16.21	-			
山东	Shandong	170.72	169.70	32.57	84.83	0.76	0.06	0.26	0.08
河南	Henan	79.70	79.18	34.68	33.14	0.44		0.07	
湖北	Hubei	83.64	83.21	37.77	34.33	0.35	0.01	0.08	
湖南	Hunan	79.62	79.15	24.25	44.35	0.46			
广东	Guangdong	133.29	132.07	44.52	57.82	1.03	0.07	0.19	
广西	Guangxi	33.33	33.21	16.11	13.57	0.02		0.10	
海南	Hainan	5.54	5.53	3.33	1.76			0.01	0.01
重庆	Chongqing	73.16	72.77	12.81	31.19	0.27		0.13	
四川	Sichuan	163.45	163.13	41.73	71.61	0.26	0.08	0.06	
贵州	Guizhou	22.30	22.30	12.70	7.78				
云南	Yunnan	59.11	58.98	17.37	27.91	0.13			
西藏	Tibet	2.06	2.06	0.83	0.81	-			
陕西	Shaanxi	39.50	39.45	19.25	14.37	0.06			
甘肃	Gansu	32.64	32.63	9.98	11.15	0.01	0.01		
青海	Qinghai	8.82	8.82	4.56	2.36	0.01			
宁夏	Ningxia	8.37	8.36	3.84	1.64				
新疆	Xinjiang	26.16	26.14	17.99	4.25	0.02			

注：从业人员为年平均人数。

a)Number of staff and workers refers to the annual average number.

14-10 各地区建筑业企业技术装备情况

Number and Power of Machinery and Equipment Owned by Construction Enterprises by Region

年份 地区	Year Region	自有机械设备总台数（台） Number of Machinery and Equipment Owned	自有机械设备总功率（万千瓦） Total Power of Machinery and Equipment Owned (10 000 kw)	#施工机械功率 Power of Construction Machines	自有机械设备净值（万元） Net Value of Machinery and Equipment Owned (10 000yuan)	技术装备率（元/人） Value of Machines per Laborer (yuan/person)	动力装备率（千瓦/人） Power of Machines per Laborer (kw/person)
	1991	2528110	4250.2	2780.6	2722151	2572	4.0
	1992	2531578	4431.9	3006.6	3147398	2719	3.8
	1993	2608091	4948.9	3349.6	4671699	4105	4.3
	1994	2952629	5712.7	4012.5	4981982	3446	4.0
	1995	3482784	7056.5	4399.4	6386383	4264	4.7
	1996	5649612	9804.8	6448.9	8814352	4154	4.6
	1997	5604603	8668.5	6782.4	9938659	4729	4.1
	1998	5833748	8656.5	6641.1	10407189	5127	4.3
	1999	6110175	9077.8	6973.0	11628317	5756	4.5
	2000	6259885	9228.1	7100.1	12572317	6304	4.6
北京	Beijing	162403	337.9	248.9	440441	7781	6.0
天津	Tianjin	75479	157.2	121.0	217637	10715	7.7
河北	Hebei	380673	603.9	457.2	571565	6525	6.9
山西	Shanxi	94885	215.3	156.1	288115	7717	5.8
内蒙古	Inner Mongolia	81281	146.1	118.4	151299	5884	5.7
辽宁	Liaoning	270080	610.9	441.2	696543	7312	6.4
吉林	Jilin	79990	196.1	124.1	217253	7502	6.8
黑龙江	Heilongjiang	141843	329.2	252.7	481241	10598	7.3
上海	Shanghai	121659	204.9	159.1	373523	10641	5.8
江苏	Jiangsu	654644	754.2	644.3	1263097	5553	3.3
浙江	Zhejiang	526365	613.1	491.9	1192280	6971	3.6
安徽	Anhui	237663	250.4	197.4	326270	4582	3.5
福建	Fujian	138423	195.3	156.4	312640	7601	4.8
江西	Jiangxi	90371	105.4	80.0	115922	3894	3.5
山东	Shandong	436301	602.3	458.2	713993	4182	3.5
河南	Henan	265583	348.5	250.6	422476	5301	4.4
湖北	Hubei	311971	403.9	316.8	609725	7290	4.8
湖南	Hunan	279125	379.2	309.7	434056	5452	4.8
广东	Guangdong	572652	790.6	606.1	1021416	7663	5.9
广西	Guangxi	145627	200.7	145.1	226517	6797	6.0
海南	Hainan	13895	44.7	32.0	35961	6492	8.1
重庆	Chongqing	162218	221.8	183.5	370938	5070	3.0
四川	Sichuan	380174	490.8	406.1	743150	4547	3.0
贵州	Guizhou	54179	88.0	58.0	115612	5184	4.0
云南	Yunnan	197083	282.3	208.7	419312	7093	4.8
西藏	Tibet	5381	14.2	5.2	14509	7049	6.9
陕西	Shaanxi	122126	199.2	146.3	248027	6279	5.0
甘肃	Gansu	109448	144.5	107.1	152897	4684	4.4
青海	Qinghai	32291	49.9	36.1	80795	9157	5.7
宁夏	Ningxia	38138	66.3	54.0	90780	10845	7.9
新疆	Xinjiang	77934	181.6	127.9	224326	8576	6.9

14-11 各地区国有建筑业企业技术装备情况

Number and Power of Machinery and Equipment of State-owned Construction Enterprises by Region

年份 Year 地区 Region		自有机械设备总台数（台） Number of Machinery and Equipment Owned	自有机械设备总功率（万千瓦） Total Power of Machinery and Equipment Owned (10 000 kw)	#施工机械功率 Power of Construction Machinery	自有机械设备净值（万元） Net Value of Machinery and Equipment Owned (10 000yuan)	技术装备率（元/人） Value of Machinery per Laborer (yuan/person)	动力装备率（千瓦/人） Power of Machinery per Laborer (kw/person)
	1991	1519637	3248.9	2036.3	2213621	3465	5.1
	1992	1410064	3314.6	2137.4	2464943	3618	4.9
	1993	1309360	3323.8	2149.6	2848367	4335	5.1
	1994	1476295	3900.2	2555.7	3567576	4361	4.8
	1995	1637276	3984.6	2780.5	4161384	5048	4.8
	1996	1870826	4213.3	2995.3	4692164	5482	4.9
	1997	1865910	4419.9	3222.3	5211213	6289	5.3
	1998	1818321	4343.2	3157.3	5180338	7016	5.9
	1999	1876329	4405.0	3189.1	5548440	8035	6.4
	2000	1822716	4150.8	2996.3	5485356	8631	6.5
北　京	Beijing	68700	169.3	119.7	224451	8216	6.2
天　津	Tianjin	38115	102.1	75.9	122408	9480	7.9
河　北	Hebei	115405	304.1	204.4	311862	9559	9.3
山　西	Shanxi	52418	162.5	115.4	222870	9297	6.8
内蒙古	Inner Mongolia	20793	54.9	40.9	63576	8080	7.0
辽　宁	Liaoning	95953	313.3	208.4	321893	8522	8.3
吉　林	Jilin	50214	142.8	79.2	141932	7879	7.9
黑龙江	Heilongjiang	65098	192.0	141.0	269766	11864	8.4
上　海	Shanghai	42768	100.7	80.1	150822	14164	9.5
江　苏	Jiangsu	151229	229.3	182.5	380111	9208	5.6
浙　江	Zhejiang	53149	95.9	71.2	172572	8658	4.8
安　徽	Anhui	63023	127.9	94.1	160000	7667	6.1
福　建	Fujian	30292	73.3	57.3	124698	9268	5.5
江　西	Jiangxi	33881	59.9	41.9	67727	5714	5.1
山　东	Shandong	79056	169.4	117.8	245322	7533	5.2
河　南	Henan	115907	212.2	147.8	264912	7638	6.1
湖　北	Hubei	121962	233.2	183.3	399348	10572	6.2
湖　南	Hunan	75009	165.6	129.2	206825	8529	6.8
广　东	Guangdong	180648	338.7	257.7	458534	10300	7.6
广　西	Guangxi	42514	98.2	69.9	125314	7776	6.1
海　南	Hainan	7619	34.7	23.4	22494	6747	10.4
重　庆	Chongqing	24316	57.4	47.1	79778	6230	4.5
四　川	Sichuan	93199	181.9	136.3	238225	5709	4.4
贵　州	Guizhou	26361	55.3	34.7	86250	6791	4.4
云　南	Yunnan	35810	107.8	74.1	140842	8108	6.2
西　藏	Tibet	2180	5.6	2.9	6323	7641	6.8
陕　西	Shaanxi	42630	122.9	89.3	151422	7864	6.4
甘　肃	Gansu	27152	60.1	41.5	66871	6702	6.0
青　海	Qinghai	16180	36.0	25.0	66419	14569	7.9
宁　夏	Ningxia	14931	31.7	23.8	43558	11344	8.3
新　疆	Xinjiang	36204	112.0	80.3	148229	8238	6.2

14-12 各地区建筑业总产值（2000年）

Total Output Value of Construction by Region (2000)

单位：万元 (10 000 yuan)

地区	Region	建筑业总产值 Total Output Value	建筑工程产值 Output Value of Construction	安装工程产值 Output Value of Installation	房屋、构筑物修理产值 Output Value of Building Repair and Maintenance	非标准设备制造产值 Output Value of Non-Standard Equipment Manufactured
全　国	**National Total**	**124975961**	**108452657**	**13943775**	**1921038**	**658491**
北　京	Beijing	7274774	6467132	634278	166024	7340
天　津	Tianjin	2380991	1970207	359748	23935	27102
河　北	Hebei	4921005	4268471	593771	33915	24848
山　西	Shanxi	2393974	2114612	265088	10876	3399
内蒙古	Inner Mongolia	1367309	1209661	123376	31360	2913
辽　宁	Liaoning	5980933	4937818	870739	131194	41183
吉　林	Jilin	2391840	2013506	354839	19260	4235
黑龙江	Heilongjiang	3340903	2653232	573026	83453	31193
上　海	Shanghai	6223565	5132511	853402	210959	26693
江　苏	Jiangsu	15388416	13501045	1595124	205184	87062
浙　江	Zhejiang	13837658	12136694	1471271	172738	56954
安　徽	Anhui	3028240	2621894	331987	62315	12044
福　建	Fujian	2711420	2394110	291124	17972	8214
江　西	Jiangxi	1164115	1027595	117123	13842	5555
山　东	Shandong	8170949	6754439	1210484	132629	73397
河　南	Henan	3573425	2943504	546347	47882	35691
湖　北	Hubei	4541767	4028261	385424	96528	31554
湖　南	Hunan	3544202	3134891	295490	79485	34336
广　东	Guangdong	8919834	7879040	914646	108343	17806
广　西	Guangxi	1509158	1321161	157836	16574	13587
海　南	Hainan	302139	275743	25307	1070	19
重　庆	Chongqing	3486579	3221028	218062	36746	10743
四　川	Sichuan	7138102	6385595	636861	79720	35926
贵　州	Guizhou	1090571	973016	110819	4336	2400
云　南	Yunnan	3092645	2777488	254206	50415	10537
西　藏	Tibet	168178	153121	10099	3626	1332
陕　西	Shaanxi	2423046	2222068	174768	9957	16253
甘　肃	Gansu	1251202	1003973	220306	15579	11343
青　海	Qinghai	447162	374755	62524	2506	7379
宁　夏	Ningxia	562352	482922	71276	6755	1399
新　疆	Xinjiang	2349506	2073166	214425	45861	16055

14-13 各地区按登记注册类型分的建筑业总产值 （2000年）

Total Output Value of Construction by Registration Status and Region (2000)

单位：万元 (10 000 yuan)

地区	Region	合计 Total	内资企业 Domestic Funded	#国有 State-owned	#集体 Collective-owned	港澳台商投资企业 Funded from Hong Kong, Macao and Taiwan	#港澳台商独资企业 Solely Owned	外商投资企业 Foreign Funded	#外商独资企业 Solely Owned
全　国	**National Total**	**124975961**	**123309294**	**50537890**	**36825265**	**991805**	**70774**	**674862**	**23080**
北　京	Beijing	7274774	7025721	3404942	1579842	100970		148083	
天　津	Tianjin	2380991	2357721	1675670	342489	12213		11058	
河　北	Hebei	4921005	4908591	2636648	1381182	6379	1264	6035	
山　西	Shanxi	2393975	2387381	1966530	242968	6237	1900	357	
内蒙古	Inner Mongolia	1367309	1363118	486866	214549	2690	750	1501	
辽　宁	Liaoning	5980933	5849147	2653944	1762587	76951		54836	1797
吉　林	Jilin	2391840	2391293	1680214	332650	303	54	244	244
黑龙江	Heilongjiang	3340903	3320013	1806322	767439	18921	843	1970	130
上　海	Shanghai	6223565	5912418	2029338	729844	198171	8201	112976	5730
江　苏	Jiangsu	15388416	15187398	3781949	6970459	98683		102335	
浙　江	Zhejiang	13837658	13654417	1639080	3969177	112836	3892	70405	962
安　徽	Anhui	3028240	3016537	1349050	1130019	5587	600	6117	
福　建	Fujian	2711420	2630363	1318156	657786	59614	31152	21442	5954
江　西	Jiangxi	1164115	1163833	611052	449678			282	
山　东	Shandong	8170949	8107592	2581049	3089136	45455	10117	17902	6568
河　南	Henan	3573425	3534390	2111650	978300	31737	85	7298	21
湖　北	Hubei	4541767	4508679	2658933	1181484	26151	371	6937	
湖　南	Hunan	3544202	3530754	1595463	1515470	13448	66		
广　东	Guangdong	8919834	8719852	3830609	2752962	117310	1876	82672	
广　西	Guangxi	1509158	1502681	888224	466152	670	140	5807	
海　南	Hainan	302139	301081	233434	44890	517	12	540	60
重　庆	Chongqing	3486579	3459110	768029	1309602	18505	20	8964	67
四　川	Sichuan	7138102	7112161	2372949	2329642	20397	7540	5544	288
贵　州	Guizhou	1090571	1090052	769620	248931	519	483		
云　南	Yunnan	3092645	3084921	1329886	1065580	6465		1259	1259
西　藏	Tibet	168178	168178	104699	35099				
陕　西	Shaanxi	2423046	2415245	1601484	440189	7801			
甘　肃	Gansu	1251202	1250360	565040	338621	727	503	115	
青　海	Qinghai	447163	446937	329320	58952	225	50		
宁　夏	Ningxia	562352	561711	292191	76941	454	154	187	
新　疆	Xinjiang	2349506	2347637	1465550	362649	1869	699		

14-14 各地区按行业分的建筑业总产值（2000年）

Total Output Value of Construction by Branch and Region (2000)

单位：万元 (10 000 yuan)

地区	Region	建筑业总产值 Total	土木工程建筑业产值 Output Value of Civil Engineering	# 房屋建筑业 Building	# 矿山建筑业 Mines	# 铁路、隧道、公路、桥梁建筑业 Railways, Tunnels, Highways, and Bridges	线路、管道和设备安装业 Output Value of Pipes, Lines and Equipment Installation	# 设备安装业 Equipment Installation	建筑物装修装饰业 Output Value of Building Decoration
全 国	**National Total**	**124975961**	**109778964**	**83306321**	**1219854**	**17066506**	**10914629**	**5258808**	**4282368**
北 京	Beijing	7274774	5796962	4870682	7516	617903	1013877	405525	463935
天 津	Tianjin	2380991	1938002	1053112	5004	579612	394460	143710	48530
河 北	Hebei	4921005	4400043	3339067	206247	590224	411266	104307	109696
山 西	Shanxi	2393974	2268422	900712	29895	1118544	117556	37398	7996
内蒙古	Inner Mongolia	1367309	1230212	969433	22028	158149	128509	36574	8588
辽 宁	Liaoning	5980933	4932467	3579026	47453	887071	813580	443553	234886
吉 林	Jilin	2391840	2208339	1542708	1618	508966	171584	57636	11917
黑龙江	Heilongjiang	3340903	2633448	1763372	31858	668136	627634	470660	79821
上 海	Shanghai	6223565	5027898	3620718	9692	785994	542530	276902	653137
江 苏	Jiangsu	15388416	13801891	12230221	45668	786761	1126942	811838	459583
浙 江	Zhejiang	13837658	12380010	9705040	58988	1538372	910606	422502	547042
安 徽	Anhui	3028240	2780888	1982284	88394	526183	224136	29064	23216
福 建	Fujian	2711420	2394134	1791588	10415	380958	211040	113040	106246
江 西	Jiangxi	1164115	1136488	889791	2501	106885	20468	16782	7159
山 东	Shandong	8170949	7170890	5875068	111524	829654	829894	415216	170165
河 南	Henan	3573425	3062959	2188896	19796	684014	472947	209038	37518
湖 北	Hubei	4541767	4127739	2949950	13296	610893	292822	149495	121205
湖 南	Hunan	3544202	3240713	2513195	10768	507173	291745	143047	11745
广 东	Guangdong	8919834	7675022	6079376	6633	1040153	509530	247479	735282
广 西	Guangxi	1509158	1319983	869522	3441	296402	162663	59465	26512
海 南	Hainan	302139	289979	196435	1540	77163	6549	4387	5610
重 庆	Chongqing	3486579	3242061	2888155	28948	258448	180643	101053	63874
四 川	Sichuan	7138102	6443531	5061792	2217	1023554	510513	156841	184058
贵 州	Guizhou	1090571	915919	567447	17530	227820	163063	62859	11589
云 南	Yunnan	3092645	2863504	1994420	3073	643433	146724	63613	82418
西 藏	Tibet	168178	167666	129898		20211	512		
陕 西	Shaanxi	2423046	2247652	969411	19486	1054079	147765	81931	27629
甘 肃	Gansu	1251202	1065939	907777	19152	69114	179234	71128	6029
青 海	Qinghai	447162	382479	167267		84359	60140	24032	4543
宁 夏	Ningxia	562352	484490	300178	3190	111248	61410	15698	16452
新 疆	Xinjiang	2349506	2149233	1409780	391985	275032	184287	84033	15986

14-15 各地区建筑业增加值 （2000年）

Value-added of Construction by Region (2000)

单位：万元 (10 000 yuan)

地区	Region	建筑业增加值合计 Total Value-added of Construction	本年提取的固定资产折旧 Depreciation of Fixed Assets of the Year	主营业务应付工资 Wages Payable in Major Business	主营业务应付福利费 Welfare Expenses Payable in Major Business	管理费用中的劳动、待业保险费 Labor and Unemployment Insurance in Management Expenses	工程结算税金及附加 Taxes and Extra Charges on Project Settlement Accounts	工程结算利润 Profits of Project Settlement Accounts	管理费用中的税金 Taxes in Management Expenses
全　国	**National Total**	**33410864**	**2115372**	**15305078**	**1601086**	**1082167**	**3621939**	**9435591**	**249631**
北　京	Beijing	1861648	106035	655229	70724	71593	212745	735915	9408
天　津	Tianjin	596888	50044	207262	23523	43106	63567	204510	4875
河　北	Hebei	1255840	86576	534436	53857	45562	146970	378117	10323
山　西	Shanxi	659211	58103	220158	26084	36583	74423	224092	19768
内蒙古	Inner Mongolia	415530	26407	190639	18575	15378	39732	120373	4427
辽　宁	Liaoning	1650483	119917	728033	82335	57570	179924	473531	9173
吉　林	Jilin	648043	35175	300099	35920	23290	67769	182656	3133
黑龙江	Heilongjiang	901381	60530	406934	49490	21968	99106	258668	4686
上　海	Shanghai	1381463	89102	527494	48674	62998	152349	494629	6217
江　苏	Jiangsu	3700633	185686	2021994	209895	67307	360462	836943	18346
浙　江	Zhejiang	3521692	160285	1872010	178218	54090	405436	835703	15949
安　徽	Anhui	837832	55405	378617	41654	32862	89526	231345	8423
福　建	Fujian	710129	40054	332306	30291	19385	111754	171928	4411
江　西	Jiangxi	324209	20974	155313	12097	11874	35527	85242	3182
山　东	Shandong	2269464	130273	1058100	118806	56565	216534	668690	20496
河　南	Henan	1006563	69338	442596	41572	51026	109387	284569	8075
湖　北	Hubei	1346062	104970	503319	75082	56446	143592	447772	14881
湖　南	Hunan	965511	76829	460292	40304	28358	101064	250639	8026
广　东	Guangdong	2509568	153625	1118034	112809	67852	319280	717487	20481
广　西	Guangxi	495053	31954	229932	20832	21808	49198	135523	5806
海　南	Hainan	68036	5499	29284	1669	784	9892	19905	1003
重　庆	Chongqing	912266	51989	472329	45923	19285	97086	219181	6474
四　川	Sichuan	2073881	132150	1011213	108090	72639	203632	532362	13795
贵　州	Guizhou	313945	21783	143147	16080	11490	34593	84291	2560
云　南	Yunnan	819742	68374	341017	33176	33370	92418	241519	9870
西　藏	Tibet	45811	3985	17337	341	723	4536	18004	884
陕　西	Shaanxi	591203	52182	237832	25068	32356	64599	173361	5805
甘　肃	Gansu	402912	22648	192475	19039	16938	44034	103871	3908
青　海	Qinghai	162240	18088	58949	9183	9804	13311	51717	1189
宁　夏	Ningxia	173888	12008	78863	6726	4209	14879	55809	1393
新　疆	Xinjiang	789737	65383	379833	45052	34946	64614	197243	2665

14-16 各地区按登记注册类型分的建筑业增加值（2000年）

Value Added of Construction by Registration Status and Region (2000)

单位：万元 (10 000 yuan)

地 区	Region	合 计 Total	内资企业 Domestic Funded	#国 有 State-owned	#集 体 Collective-owned	港澳台商投资企业 Funded from Hong Kong, Macao and Taiwan	#港澳台商独资企业 Solely Owned	外商投资企业 Foreign Funded	#外商独资企业 Solely Owned
全 国	**National Total**	**33410864**	**33013036**	**13907626**	**9921357**	**244552**	**18723**	**153276**	**7400**
北 京	Beijing	1861648	1806160	974421	381696	24297		31192	
天 津	Tianjin	596888	591943	406130	87622	3704		1242	
河 北	Hebei	1255840	1252832	639736	398600	1274	256	1734	
山 西	Shanxi	659211	657231	523542	83636	1922	449	58	
内蒙古	Inner Mongolia	415530	414368	147345	76900	666	202	496	
辽 宁	Liaoning	1650483	1611580	725684	527036	23379		15524	394
吉 林	Jilin	648043	647876	442732	94514	99	22	68	68
黑龙江	Heilongjiang	901381	895528	484314	208895	4473	320	1380	141
上 海	Shanghai	1381463	1320421	529599	173454	37828	787	23214	1374
江 苏	Jiangsu	3700633	3656931	930395	1650823	24510		19192	
浙 江	Zhejiang	3521692	3478617	427097	1037288	25590	1148	17484	581
安 徽	Anhui	837832	834312	374640	311409	1426	230	2093	
福 建	Fujian	710129	689519	332144	173119	14482	6544	6128	2398
江 西	Jiangxi	324209	324155	180361	120953			54	
山 东	Shandong	2269464	2250277	701716	857642	13316	3411	5870	1548
河 南	Henan	1006563	992820	590709	275024	11234	42	2509	36
湖 北	Hubei	1346062	1335415	827145	342548	8730	146	1917	
湖 南	Hunan	965511	959698	432634	413529	5813	30		
广 东	Guangdong	2509568	2467865	1047761	789622	27154	2274	14549	
广 西	Guangxi	495053	492693	301790	144590	221	47	2139	
海 南	Hainan	68036	67316	46934	14014	178	15	542	432
重 庆	Chongqing	912266	906446	216456	324287	3787	9	2033	10
四 川	Sichuan	2073881	2065254	730543	668587	5244	2270	3384	83
贵 州	Guizhou	313945	313775	219916	70520	170	139		
云 南	Yunnan	819742	817476	332256	299740	1930		336	336
西 藏	Tibet	45811	45811	22486	15150				
陕 西	Shaanxi	591203	589224	371866	128212	1979			
甘 肃	Gansu	402912	402676	197653	99211	166	117	71	
青 海	Qinghai	162240	162124	122240	21770	116	55		
宁 夏	Ningxia	173888	173678	83264	25839	142	57	68	
新 疆	Xinjiang	789737	789016	544118	105127	721	153		

14-17 各地区按登记注册类型分的建筑业企业实收资本（2000年）

Capitals Hold of Construction Enterprises by Registration Status and Region (2000)

单位：万元 (10 000 yuan)

地区	Region	合计 Total	内资企业 Domestic Funded	#国有 State-owned	#集体 Collective-owned	港澳台商投资企业 Funded from Hong Kong, Macao and Taiwan	#港澳台商独资企业 Solely Owned	外商投资企业 Foreign Funded	#外商独资企业 Solely Owned
全国	**National Total**	**32198390**	**31473298**	**12592585**	**9446460**	**457444**	**44947**	**267649**	**13655**
北京	Beijing	1769608	1652044	789528	356333	66892		50672	
天津	Tianjin	613554	601774	374028	101952	6855		4925	
河北	Hebei	1329124	1324460	574805	438775	2116	153	2548	
山西	Shanxi	576789	569478	436449	80749	7180	633	130	
内蒙古	Inner Mongolia	398049	395439	137374	63469	1738	418	872	
辽宁	Liaoning	1734487	1690269	724266	519737	18111		26107	669
吉林	Jilin	539108	538647	370268	74185	361	51	101	101
黑龙江	Heilongjiang	1012418	1003183	482385	239876	5205	736	4031	500
上海	Shanghai	1800932	1646359	663492	223213	96121	2312	58452	986
江苏	Jiangsu	2967062	2904999	771185	1276408	43580		18482	
浙江	Zhejiang	2586413	2549539	289487	749433	15634	980	21240	977
安徽	Anhui	863365	857303	390254	288511	4494	678	1568	
福建	Fujian	1024266	972734	294997	288935	32837	13887	18696	3960
江西	Jiangxi	335582	335426	159872	144921			156	
山东	Shandong	1656050	1631106	476561	645310	16974	5489	7970	2465
河南	Henan	904498	894919	461044	280909	5617	154	3962	1170
湖北	Hubei	1231879	1198560	562593	403950	29075	2092	4245	
湖南	Hunan	1001654	994944	343240	487209	6710	100		
广东	Guangdong	2544258	2455386	1028495	807561	58868	8538	30005	
广西	Guangxi	1118279	1112708	809855	191358	2735	327	2835	
海南	Hainan	101285	96333	53838	21073	2728	517	2224	1224
重庆	Chongqing	952745	939692	188329	318498	11159	21	1894	52
四川	Sichuan	1888966	1870000	502972	631857	15021	6948	3944	345
贵州	Guizhou	244181	243976	141638	69873	204	194		
云南	Yunnan	921067	918256	291875	357157	1606		1206	1206
西藏	Tibet	67267	67267	25361	23571				
陕西	Shaanxi	474225	470679	239416	131704	3546			
甘肃	Gansu	288976	287300	119451	91350	408	216	1268	
青海	Qinghai	144094	143842	99314	20473	252	200		
宁夏	Ningxia	215464	215082	91132	34591	266	173	117	
新疆	Xinjiang	892746	891596	699080	83520	1150	130		

14-18 各地区建筑业企业资产（2000年）

Assets of Construction Enterprises by Region (2000)

单位：万元 (10 000 yuan)

地区	Region	资产合计 Total Assets	# 流动资产 Circulating Funds	# 固定资产 Fixed Assets	# 专项工程 Special Projects	# 无形及递延资产 Intangible and Deferred Assets
全国	**National Total**	**145783686**	**105875191**	**29697772**	**1627058**	**2281582**
北京	Beijing	10864580	8588493	1244720	191984	86965
天津	Tianjin	3097218	2295084	614399	34200	40089
河北	Hebei	5153809	3526259	1325602	58144	108141
山西	Shanxi	3221292	2286910	749035	55107	72811
内蒙古	Inner Mongolia	1525185	1049511	408576	8033	30403
辽宁	Liaoning	6984803	4996428	1625679	42831	158800
吉林	Jilin	2524158	1694338	689900	51980	31906
黑龙江	Heilongjiang	4192237	3066497	988901	18983	32696
上海	Shanghai	8891230	6572247	836065	98009	223216
江苏	Jiangsu	14802564	11765264	2413073	84980	138893
浙江	Zhejiang	10495810	7732475	2078445	98051	146254
安徽	Anhui	3284878	2340979	783277	40816	45972
福建	Fujian	4434975	3418347	718135	46371	52942
江西	Jiangxi	1643130	1188840	368647	16376	23575
山东	Shandong	8599834	6416062	1696440	78200	192249
河南	Henan	3545043	2332404	978805	42669	116978
湖北	Hubei	5351458	3371595	1530781	110516	108968
湖南	Hunan	3544822	2307984	1028691	34894	43736
广东	Guangdong	16980457	13521496	2211040	165463	254341
广西	Guangxi	3302364	2031262	858625	45500	29554
海南	Hainan	428187	298973	105708	5872	4593
重庆	Chongqing	2796456	1860896	780746	29461	52192
四川	Sichuan	6536346	4337135	1699109	94326	143065
贵州	Guizhou	1455461	1082253	297271	20469	8800
云南	Yunnan	3350287	2187775	975191	32048	37496
西藏	Tibet	194577	89937	88112	1434	1300
陕西	Shaanxi	2559749	1813274	617881	51344	23395
甘肃	Gansu	1409940	985832	362554	18403	21613
青海	Qinghai	616421	388568	179948	16890	6711
宁夏	Ningxia	740174	472911	227053	5211	8866
新疆	Xinjiang	3256241	1855164	1215366	28496	35063

14-19 各地区按登记注册类型分的建筑业企业资产（2000年）

Assets of Construction Enterprises by Registration Status and Region (2000)

单位：万元 (10 000 yuan)

地区	Region	合计 Total	内资企业 Domestic Funded	#国有 State-owned	#集体 Collective-owned	港澳台商投资企业 Funded from Hong Kong, Macao and Taiwan	#港澳台商独资企业 Solely Owned	外商投资企业 Foreign Funded	#外商独资企业 Solely Owned
全　国	**National Total**	**145783686**	**143558293**	**70341056**	**35040183**	**1426338**	**174697**	**799054**	**44783**
北　京	Beijing	10864580	10562641	6550600	1550169	170126		131814	
天　津	Tianjin	3097218	3062436	2169014	367139	25460		9322	
河　北	Hebei	5153808	5140368	3150110	1192732	6385	952	7056	
山　西	Shanxi	3221292	3201578	2605706	351245	19503	8114	211	
内蒙古	Inner Mongolia	1525185	1519877	610559	303447	3757	861	1551	
辽　宁	Liaoning	6984803	6833438	3339904	1866794	73473		77892	3718
吉　林	Jilin	2524158	2522881	1797267	316475	1037	118	240	240
黑龙江	Heilongjiang	4192237	4170244	2526932	811933	14710	1572	7283	915
上　海	Shanghai	8891230	8521683	3577056	949467	230912	3982	138635	4610
江　苏	Jiangsu	14802564	14553445	4983013	5563517	119478		129641	
浙　江	Zhejiang	10495810	10338732	1794834	3019630	90002	1573	67075	4304
安　徽	Anhui	3284878	3267231	1738378	979914	10300	1838	7347	
福　建	Fujian	4434975	4302512	1657948	1436150	87516	39201	44947	14053
江　西	Jiangxi	1643130	1642545	1023085	526028			585	
山　东	Shandong	8599834	8507318	2943819	2957969	59516	9872	33000	10073
河　南	Henan	3545043	3484327	2276951	783886	49192	1116	11525	1264
湖　北	Hubei	5351458	5267544	3529461	916687	72385	3984	11529	
湖　南	Hunan	3544822	3535535	1815455	1300132	9287	279		
广　东	Guangdong	16980457	16615962	7483427	4298278	289801	73449	74694	
广　西	Guangxi	3302364	3290373	2308180	562175	3483	394	8508	
海　南	Hainan	428187	421012	272798	60197	4200	517	2975	1908
重　庆	Chongqing	2796456	2763837	815427	867015	22652	26	9968	60
四　川	Sichuan	6536346	6477620	2554874	1761442	40297	22960	18429	592
贵　州	Guizhou	1455461	1455079	1097438	256073	382	297		
云　南	Yunnan	3350287	3340482	1604033	897103	6758		3047	3047
西　藏	Tibet	194577	194577	129896	33274				
陕　西	Shaanxi	2559749	2550812	1765990	373679	8937			
甘　肃	Gansu	1409940	1406945	803788	293016	1445	1208	1550	
青　海	Qinghai	616421	615563	492672	58843	858	212		
宁　夏	Ningxia	740174	739351	368712	97616	593	332	230	
新　疆	Xinjiang	3256241	3252348	2553727	288160	3894	1840		

14-20 各地区建筑业企业负债及所有者权益（2000年）

Liabilities and Creditors' Equity of Construction Enterprises by Region (2000)

单位：万元 (10 000 yuan)

地区	Region	负债合计 Total Liabilities	# 流动负债 Liquid Liabilities	# 长期负债 Long-term Liabilities	所有者权益 Creditors' Equity	# 实收资本 Capitals Hold
全国	**National Total**	**103452169**	**98021479**	**5430601**	**42331517**	**32198390**
北京	Beijing	8275634	7822187	453447	2588947	1769608
天津	Tianjin	2330873	2233007	97867	766344	613554
河北	Hebei	3476509	3292312	184197	1677299	1329124
山西	Shanxi	2308090	2197935	110155	913202	576789
内蒙古	Inner Mongolia	1024632	949278	75355	500553	398049
辽宁	Liaoning	4821262	4587496	233766	2163542	1734487
吉林	Jilin	1879194	1834014	45180	644964	539108
黑龙江	Heilongjiang	3057886	2911151	146735	1134351	1012418
上海	Shanghai	6149911	5904181	245730	2741319	1800932
江苏	Jiangsu	11043612	10745031	298581	3758952	2967062
浙江	Zhejiang	7021060	6747933	273127	3474750	2586413
安徽	Anhui	2350220	2117092	233127	934658	863365
福建	Fujian	3187347	3079742	107605	1247629	1024266
江西	Jiangxi	1218914	1134162	84752	424216	335582
山东	Shandong	6367070	5993606	373464	2232765	1656050
河南	Henan	2367022	2256184	110838	1178021	904498
湖北	Hubei	3700227	3321484	378743	1651232	1231879
湖南	Hunan	2283775	2061169	222606	1261047	1001654
广东	Guangdong	13059461	12435896	623565	3920996	2544258
广西	Guangxi	2005013	1858956	146056	1297351	1118279
海南	Hainan	263251	242078	21173	164936	101285
重庆	Chongqing	1679214	1534492	144722	1117243	952745
四川	Sichuan	4085484	3851394	234091	2450862	1888966
贵州	Guizhou	1117353	1064061	53292	338108	244181
云南	Yunnan	2241027	2082622	158405	1109260	921067
西藏	Tibet	73656	69002	4654	120921	67267
陕西	Shaanxi	1993902	1872506	121396	565847	474225
甘肃	Gansu	1033728	978318	55411	376212	288976
青海	Qinghai	449641	428525	21116	166780	144094
宁夏	Ningxia	518839	474475	44276	221336	215464
新疆	Xinjiang	2068364	1941193	127172	1187877	892746

14-21 各地区按登记注册类型分的建筑业企业所有者权益（2000年）

Creditors' Equity of Construction Enterprises by Registration Status and Region (2000)

单位：万元 (10 000 yuan)

地区	Region	合计 Total	内资企业 Domestic Funded	#国有 State-owned	#集体 Collective-owned	港澳台商投资企业 Funded from Hong Kong, Macao and Taiwan	#港澳台商独资企业 Solely Owned	外商投资企业 Foreign Funded	#外商独资企业 Solely Owned
全 国	**National Total**	**42331517**	**41543097**	**17287531**	**11871062**	**489075**	**52085**	**299345**	**14709**
北 京	Beijing	2588946	2465075	1311196	524292	67588		56283	
天 津	Tianjin	766344	755074	475067	136121	6842		4428	
河 北	Hebei	1677299	1670904	739504	556523	2457	181	3938	
山 西	Shanxi	913202	908344	746909	100328	4712	890	146	
内蒙古	Inner Mongolia	500553	498038	175244	89017	1672	345	843	
辽 宁	Liaoning	2163542	2099570	870965	611859	31967		32004	632
吉 林	Jilin	644964	644328	441459	89960	532	108	104	104
黑龙江	Heilongjiang	1134350	1125882	535494	271392	5747	670	2722	353
上 海	Shanghai	2741319	2594586	1122252	254388	87064	2382	59669	1414
江 苏	Jiangsu	3758952	3689385	1044880	1587265	49752		19816	
浙 江	Zhejiang	3474750	3428254	450976	962585	20575	1038	25922	1247
安 徽	Anhui	934658	927860	398904	328444	4716	678	2082	
福 建	Fujian	1247629	1187750	393153	369544	38113	17016	21766	4222
江 西	Jiangxi	424216	423980	221550	168268			236	
山 东	Shandong	2232765	2206729	596746	891244	19357	6775	6679	2157
河 南	Henan	1178021	1166746	628892	351297	8345	154	2930	-174
湖 北	Hubei	1651232	1624471	833035	507332	22897	1361	3863	
湖 南	Hunan	1261047	1254295	457186	603483	6752	142		
广 东	Guangdong	3920996	3813169	1685789	1092576	67576	10550	40250	
广 西	Guangxi	1297351	1291348	926814	245645	2805	327	3198	
海 南	Hainan	164936	160696	102854	25206	3005	517	1235	1654
重 庆	Chongqing	1117243	1102590	206256	366161	11905	21	2748	57
四 川	Sichuan	2450862	2429682	681612	778494	16390	7492	4789	378
贵 州	Guizhou	338108	337822	204160	89986	286	217		
云 南	Yunnan	1109260	1104871	354747	422543	1723		2666	2666
西 藏	Tibet	120921	120921	75063	24072				
陕 西	Shaanxi	565847	562627	305177	147068	3220			
甘 肃	Gansu	376212	374617	145366	111542	661	458	934	
青 海	Qinghai	166780	166112	118639	20969	668	197		
宁 夏	Ningxia	221336	221004	76720	40962	235	101	96	
新 疆	Xinjiang	1187877	1186366	960924	102492	1510	464		

14-22 各地区按登记注册类型分的建筑业企业负债（2000年）

Liabilities of Construction Enterprises by Registration Status and Region (2000)

单位：万元 (10 000 yuan)

地 区	Region	合 计 Total	内资企业 Domestic Funded	#国 有 State-owned	#集 体 Collective-owned	港澳台商投资企业 Funded from Hong Kong, Macao and Taiwan	#港澳台商独资企业 Solely Owned	外商投资企业 Foreign Funded	#外商独资企业 Solely Owned
全 国	**National Total**	**103452169**	**102015196**	**53053525**	**23169121**	**937263**	**122613**	**499710**	**30074**
北 京	Beijing	8275634	8097565	5239404	1025876	102538		75531	
天 津	Tianjin	2330873	2307362	1693947	231018	18618		4894	
河 北	Hebei	3476509	3469464	2410606	636209	3928	771	3118	
山 西	Shanxi	2308090	2293235	1858797	250916	14790	7224	65	
内蒙古	Inner Mongolia	1024632	1021839	435315	214430	2085	516	708	
辽 宁	Liaoning	4821262	4733868	2468940	1254935	41506		45888	3086
吉 林	Jilin	1879194	1878553	1355808	226515	504	10	136	136
黑龙江	Heilongjiang	3057886	3044362	1991438	540541	8963	902	4562	562
上 海	Shanghai	6149911	5927097	2454804	695079	143848	1600	78966	3196
江 苏	Jiangsu	11043612	10864059	3938133	3976252	69727		109826	
浙 江	Zhejiang	7021060	6910479	1343858	2057045	69427	535	41153	3057
安 徽	Anhui	2350220	2339371	1339474	651469	5584	1160	5265	
福 建	Fujian	3187347	3114762	1264796	1066606	49403	22185	23181	9832
江 西	Jiangxi	1218914	1218565	801536	357760			348	
山 东	Shandong	6367070	6300589	2347073	2066725	40159	3098	26322	7916
河 南	Henan	2367022	2317580	1648059	432588	40846	962	8595	1438
湖 北	Hubei	3700227	3643072	2696426	409354	49488	2622	7666	
湖 南	Hunan	2283775	2281240	1358268	696650	2535	137		
广 东	Guangdong	13059461	12802792	5797638	3205702	222225	62898	34444	
广 西	Guangxi	2005013	1999024	1381366	316529	678	67	5310	
海 南	Hainan	263251	260316	169944	34991	1195		1740	254
重 庆	Chongqing	1679214	1661247	609172	500854	10746	5	7220	4
四 川	Sichuan	4085484	4047938	1873262	982948	23906	15468	13640	213
贵 州	Guizhou	1117353	1117256	893279	166087	96	80		
云 南	Yunnan	2241027	2235611	1249286	474560	5035		381	381
西 藏	Tibet	73656	73656	54833	9202				
陕 西	Shaanxi	1993902	1988185	1460814	226610	5717			
甘 肃	Gansu	1033728	1032328	658422	181474	784	751	617	
青 海	Qinghai	449641	449451	374033	37874	190	15		
宁 夏	Ningxia	518839	518348	291992	56653	358	231	134	
新 疆	Xinjiang	2068364	2065981	1592803	185668	2383	1375		

14-23 各地区建筑业企业总收入（2000年）

Total Income of Construction Enterprises by Region (2000)

单位：万元 (10 000 yuan)

地区	Region	企业总收入 Total Income of Enterprises	工程结算收入 Revenue of Project Settlement Accounts	#工程结算成本 Costs of Project Settlement Accounts	#工程结算利润 Profits of Project Settlement Accounts	其他业务收入 Other Revenue from Business	#其他业务利润 Other Profit from Business
全国	**National Total**	**115068245**	**110030241**	**96972710**	**9435591**	**5038004**	**683235**
北京	Beijing	7639480	7068086	6119426	735915	571394	91008
天津	Tianjin	2398738	2299769	2031691	204510	98970	12094
河北	Hebei	4660847	4541030	4015944	378117	119817	16616
山西	Shanxi	2471030	2330894	2032379	224092	140136	11814
内蒙古	Inner Mongolia	1267976	1237682	1077578	120373	30294	5676
辽宁	Liaoning	5908924	5724446	5070991	473531	184478	36206
吉林	Jilin	3068530	2325394	2074969	182656	743136	16371
黑龙江	Heilongjiang	3380021	3262959	2905185	258668	117062	18826
上海	Shanghai	6068494	5818487	5171509	494629	250007	38519
江苏	Jiangsu	11026966	10590583	9393178	836943	436384	60452
浙江	Zhejiang	11511317	11172646	9931506	835703	338671	47454
安徽	Anhui	2789838	2653369	2332498	231345	136469	8197
福建	Fujian	2735619	2674632	2390950	171928	60987	12370
江西	Jiangxi	1019278	1001869	881100	85242	17408	2841
山东	Shandong	7149728	6845430	5960206	668690	304298	31456
河南	Henan	3280853	3198761	2804806	284569	82092	17254
湖北	Hubei	4378376	4167516	3576152	447772	210860	31429
湖南	Hunan	3162664	3050616	2698914	250639	112048	28626
广东	Guangdong	9330753	9010960	7974193	717487	319793	75060
广西	Guangxi	1487174	1409287	1224567	135523	77887	12661
海南	Hainan	265351	263784	233988	19905	1567	1016
重庆	Chongqing	2795294	2726719	2410452	219181	68575	8600
四川	Sichuan	6066069	5914320	5178325	532362	151749	22607
贵州	Guizhou	1057450	1018439	899555	84291	39011	5779
云南	Yunnan	2973728	2885006	2551070	241519	88721	12831
西藏	Tibet	110072	108808	86269	18004	1264	682
陕西	Shaanxi	2232572	2137636	1899675	173361	94936	13015
甘肃	Gansu	1193466	1141262	993357	103871	52204	6865
青海	Qinghai	436380	419853	354825	51717	16527	4658
宁夏	Ningxia	541560	515986	445298	55809	25573	2293
新疆	Xinjiang	2659696	2514010	2252154	197243	145686	29962

14-24 各地区按登记注册类型分的建筑业企业总收入（2000年）

Total Income of Construction by Registration Status and Region (2000)

单位：万元 (10 000 yuan)

地区	Region	合计 Total	内资企业 Domestic Funded	#国有 State-owned	#集体 Collective-owned	港澳台商投资企业 Funded from Hong Kong, Macao and Taiwan	#港澳台商独资企业 Solely Owned	外商投资企业 Foreign Funded	#外商独资企业 Solely Owned
全　国	**National Total**	**115068245**	**113523486**	**50964245**	**30403571**	**941052**	**62312**	**603707**	**21323**
北　京	Beijing	7639480	7338888	4136346	1262020	141213		159379	
天　津	Tianjin	2398738	2382047	1724557	304934	13117		3574	
河　北	Hebei	4660847	4650865	2583453	1294309	6025	1265	3958	
山　西	Shanxi	2471030	2464261	2032906	263459	6295	1900	475	
内蒙古	Inner Mongolia	1267976	1264579	446072	215789	1895	285	1503	
辽　宁	Liaoning	5908924	5783843	2636740	1759862	76964		48116	2448
吉　林	Jilin	3068530	3068083	1974412	327176	303	54	144	144
黑龙江	Heilongjiang	3380021	3365035	1924697	712904	12933	543	2053	130
上　海	Shanghai	6068494	5793812	1903491	702936	176831	8201	97851	5740
江　苏	Jiangsu	11026966	10876325	3336968	4402168	82091		68550	
浙　江	Zhejiang	11511317	11361991	1555233	3216346	87810	3004	61516	1044
安　徽	Anhui	2789838	2779454	1333352	960016	4267	634	6116	
福　建	Fujian	2735619	2658159	1335060	687978	54608	23161	22852	4815
江　西	Jiangxi	1019278	1019076	566187	373421			201	
山　东	Shandong	7149728	7094854	2458979	2472870	39002	9439	15872	4908
河　南	Henan	3280853	3245507	2048004	828029	29772	85	5574	56
湖　北	Hubei	4378376	4351520	2711139	1036163	20092	371	6764	
湖　南	Hunan	3162664	3149216	1491525	1287114	13448	66		
广　东	Guangdong	9330753	9131914	4101288	2590890	121190	2350	77649	
广　西	Guangxi	1487174	1482569	941452	400239	558	114	4047	
海　南	Hainan	265351	263745	205804	38431	720	22	886	406
重　庆	Chongqing	2795294	2773177	690874	988104	15416	20	6702	66
四　川	Sichuan	6066069	6039320	2171896	1883327	18404	8534	8346	288
贵　州	Guizhou	1057450	1056748	782460	208469	702	666		
云　南	Yunnan	2973728	2966265	1362808	996886	6185		1278	1278
西　藏	Tibet	110072	110072	53599	30658				
陕　西	Shaanxi	2232572	2224776	1491420	387008	7796			
甘　肃	Gansu	1193466	1192433	567024	299457	918	694	114	
青　海	Qinghai	436380	436155	327746	54197	225	50		
宁　夏	Ningxia	541560	540962	298190	67561	411	154	187	
新　疆	Xinjiang	2659696	2657836	1770562	350850	1860	699		

14-25 各地区建筑业企业利税总额（2000年）

Total Pre-Tax Profits of Construction Enterprises by Region (2000)

地 区	Region	利税总额合 计（万元）Total Pre-tax Profits (10 000 yuan)	利润总额 Total Profits	工程结算税金及附加 Taxes and Extra Charges on Project Settlement Accounts	管理费用中的税金 Taxes in Management Expenses	产值利税率 Ratio of Pre-tax Profits to Output Value (%)	资产利税率 Ratio of Pre-tax Profits to Assets (%)
全 国	**National Total**	**5792206**	**1920635**	**3621939**	**249631**	**4.6**	**4.0**
北 京	Beijing	385714	163561	212745	9408	5.3	3.6
天 津	Tianjin	96435	27993	63567	4875	4.1	3.1
河 北	Hebei	224663	67370	146970	10323	4.6	4.4
山 西	Shanxi	93678	-514	74423	19768	3.9	2.9
内蒙古	Inner Mongolia	58719	14561	39732	4427	4.3	3.8
辽 宁	Liaoning	255827	66730	179924	9173	4.3	3.7
吉 林	Jilin	88242	17339	67769	3133	3.7	3.5
黑龙江	Heilongjiang	134863	31070	99106	4686	4.0	3.2
上 海	Shanghai	342818	184252	152349	6217	5.5	3.9
江 苏	Jiangsu	585377	206569	360462	18346	3.8	4.0
浙 江	Zhejiang	740235	318850	405436	15949	5.3	7.1
安 徽	Anhui	126076	28127	89526	8423	4.2	3.8
福 建	Fujian	141997	25831	111754	4411	5.2	3.2
江 西	Jiangxi	44866	6157	35527	3182	3.9	2.7
山 东	Shandong	419264	182235	216534	20496	5.1	4.9
河 南	Henan	148742	31281	109387	8075	4.2	4.2
湖 北	Hubei	216898	58425	143592	14881	4.8	4.1
湖 南	Hunan	153028	43938	101064	8026	4.3	4.3
广 东	Guangdong	543688	203926	319280	20481	6.1	3.2
广 西	Guangxi	64151	9147	49198	5806	4.3	1.9
海 南	Hainan	14801	3907	9892	1003	4.9	3.5
重 庆	Chongqing	152870	49310	97086	6474	4.4	5.5
四 川	Sichuan	318422	100995	203632	13795	4.5	4.9
贵 州	Guizhou	47008	9855	34593	2560	4.3	3.2
云 南	Yunnan	160638	58350	92418	9870	5.2	4.8
西 藏	Tibet	12805	7385	4536	884	7.6	6.6
陕 西	Shaanxi	84901	14497	64599	5805	3.5	3.3
甘 肃	Gansu	67918	19977	44034	3908	5.4	4.8
青 海	Qinghai	18312	3812	13311	1189	4.1	3.0
宁 夏	Ningxia	29994	13722	14879	1393	5.3	4.1
新 疆	Xinjiang	19257	-48022	64614	2665	0.8	0.6

14-26 各地区按登记注册类型分的建筑业企业税金总额（2000年）

Tax of Construction Enterprises by Registration Status and by Region (2000)

单位：万元 (10 000 yuan)

地区	Region	合计 Total	内资企业 Domestic Funded	#国有 State-owned	#集体 Collective-owned	港澳台商投资企业 Funded from Hong Kong, Macao and Taiwan	#港澳台商独资企业 Solely Owned	外商投资企业 Foreign Funded	#外商独资企业 Solely Owned
全　国	**National Total**	**3871570**	**3823242**	**1546606**	**1192535**	**31184**	**2064**	**17145**	**751**
北　京	Beijing	222153	213839	114204	44131	4287		4028	
天　津	Tianjin	68442	67933	43539	13592	420		89	
河　北	Hebei	157293	156992	76174	52557	198	38	103	
山　西	Shanxi	94192	93947	74565	13204	230	58	14	
内蒙古	Inner Mongolia	44158	44050	14210	7592	65	9	44	
辽　宁	Liaoning	189097	184929	78580	61455	2380		1788	60
吉　林	Jilin	70903	70860	45965	12619	39	32	4	4
黑龙江	Heilongjiang	103792	103189	52807	25285	398	20	206	6
上　海	Shanghai	158566	150640	48523	21022	5259	217	2667	112
江　苏	Jiangsu	378808	374065	99762	166457	2860		1883	
浙　江	Zhejiang	421385	416039	47669	125261	3520	76	1827	69
安　徽	Anhui	97949	97480	42486	37054	154	18	316	
福　建	Fujian	116166	113329	61235	27343	2025	958	812	218
江　西	Jiangxi	38709	38698	18492	17202			12	
山　东	Shandong	237029	235011	71550	89714	1214	229	805	217
河　南	Henan	117461	116480	68360	34911	807	2	174	2
湖　北	Hubei	158473	157586	88863	46220	641	7	245	
湖　南	Hunan	109090	108558	40893	53717	531	2		
广　东	Guangdong	339762	333844	144448	107956	4440	95	1478	
广　西	Guangxi	55003	54875	30045	20031	14	3	114	
海　南	Hainan	10894	10837	7918	2225	25	1	33	14
重　庆	Chongqing	103559	102770	21817	39640	568	1	222	2
四　川	Sichuan	217427	216659	69830	76400	536	228	232	9
贵　州	Guizhou	37154	37133	24757	9385	21	20		
云　南	Yunnan	102288	102061	44484	37212	188		38	38
西　藏	Tibet	5420	5420	2018	2590				
陕　西	Shaanxi	70404	70138	42584	16184	267			
甘　肃	Gansu	47941	47907	16349	13372	31	21	3	
青　海	Qinghai	14500	14491	9982	2333	8	3		
宁　夏	Ningxia	16272	16260	8140	2200	6	6	6	
新　疆	Xinjiang	67279	67223	36356	13672	56	21		

14-27 各地区按登记注册类型分的建筑业企业利润总额（2000年）

Total Profits of Construction Enterprises by Registration Status and Region (2000)

单位：万元 (10 000 yuan)

地 区	Region	合 计 Total	内资企业 Domestic Funded	#国 有 State-owned	#集 体 Collective-owned	港澳台商投资企业 Funded from Hong Kong, Macao and Taiwan	#港澳台商独资企业 Solely Owned	外商投资企业 Foreign Funded	#外商独资企业 Solely Owned
全 国	**National Total**	**1920635**	**1897695**	**215894**	**756330**	**9856**	**2702**	**13084**	**341**
北 京	Beijing	163561	160389	48327	53077	-924		4096	
天 津	Tianjin	27993	27617	1354	9726	531		-155	
河 北	Hebei	67370	67312	9979	39009	150	47	-92	
山 西	Shanxi	-514	371	-5738	3481	-885	-6		
内蒙古	Inner Mongolia	14561	14558	3309	2416	1	4	1	
辽 宁	Liaoning	66730	62029	-5257	33157	3575		1126	-50
吉 林	Jilin	17339	17362	1697	4024	-19	-16	-4	-4
黑龙江	Heilongjiang	31070	31002	14121	7372	189	-268	-121	-71
上 海	Shanghai	184252	182845	41053	11777	166	-7	1241	298
江 苏	Jiangsu	206569	205070	29268	97324	1687		-188	
浙 江	Zhejiang	318850	315579	24627	89158	1533	44	1738	-55
安 徽	Anhui	28127	28099	-5159	24417	-2	15	30	
福 建	Fujian	25831	23064	2770	7378	2407	1022	360	18
江 西	Jiangxi	6157	6176	-351	5344			-19	
山 东	Shandong	182235	180488	26415	84341	2043	1625	-295	121
河 南	Henan	31281	30520	-5988	29048	230	-34	532	-9
湖 北	Hubei	58425	60014	6424	38245	-1363	-149	-226	
湖 南	Hunan	43938	43139	3329	29518	799	-13		
广 东	Guangdong	203926	199650	71415	53563	-199	1106	4475	
广 西	Guangxi	9147	9122	440	11263	-86	-2	111	
海 南	Hainan	3907	3904	3512	466	-48		51	82
重 庆	Chongqing	49310	49783	4137	17893	-491	-8	18	-2
四 川	Sichuan	100995	100764	-5168	42354	-252	-549	484	
贵 州	Guizhou	9855	9858	1924	2571	-3	3		
云 南	Yunnan	58350	58442	7606	33083	-104		13	13
西 藏	Tibet	7385	7385	2102	3061				
陕 西	Shaanxi	14497	13603	3342	8084	893			
甘 肃	Gansu	19977	20071	-5793	8252	-3	-4	-91	
青 海	Qinghai	3812	3815	3162	317	-3	-3		
宁 夏	Ningxia	13722	13724	2687	1590	-3	-14	1	
新 疆	Xinjiang	-48022	-48059	-63650	5018	37	-89		

14-28 各地区按登记注册类型分的建筑业企业工程结算利润（2000年）

Profits of Project Settlement Accounts of Construction Enterprises by Registration Status and Region (2000)

单位：万元 (10 000 yuan)

地区	Region	合计 Total	内资企业 Domestic Funded	#国有 State-owned	#集体 Collective-owned	港澳台商投资企业 Funded from Hong Kong, Macao and Taiwan	#港澳台商独资企业 Solely Owned	外商投资企业 Foreign Funded	#外商独资企业 Solely Owned
全　国	**National Total**	**9435591**	**9274695**	**4150534**	**2489144**	**98615**	**9750**	**62281**	**2891**
北　京	Beijing	735915	707754	348330	143230	10423		17738	
天　津	Tianjin	204510	201451	133277	29877	2285		773	
河　北	Hebei	378117	377031	199338	115277	672	160	414	
山　西	Shanxi	224092	223509	183525	23788	551	232	31	
内蒙古	Inner Mongolia	120373	120032	52794	19869	288	99	52	
辽　宁	Liaoning	473531	451548	214587	139578	15673		6310	152
吉　林	Jilin	182656	182604	123464	25537	12	-14	40	40
黑龙江	Heilongjiang	258668	257339	146031	55409	1129	96	200	45
上　海	Shanghai	494629	470572	174452	54225	15177	219	8880	962
江　苏	Jiangsu	836943	822874	249137	334093	8629		5440	
浙　江	Zhejiang	835703	824960	132539	223360	6145	329	4597	255
安　徽	Anhui	231345	230476	117387	76696	499	122	370	
福　建	Fujian	171928	163423	80728	38913	6553	3330	1952	441
江　西	Jiangxi	85242	85226	50306	27086			15	
山　东	Shandong	668690	660852	211183	246997	5769	2281	2069	463
河　南	Henan	284569	279069	164522	81177	4383	16	1118	11
湖　北	Hubei	447772	444102	274124	104822	3114	3	556	
湖　南	Hunan	250639	248186	119593	99203	2453	4		
广　东	Guangdong	717487	700536	294028	202042	9952	1699	7000	
广　西	Guangxi	135523	134589	86804	35313	36	20	899	
海　南	Hainan	19905	19493	14555	3126	98	3	314	272
重　庆	Chongqing	219181	217941	62076	69927	408		832	4
四　川	Sichuan	532362	527657	190043	140848	2248	1018	2458	49
贵　州	Guizhou	84291	84218	60532	14780	73	65		
云　南	Yunnan	241519	240858	95252	85152	463		198	198
西　藏	Tibet	18004	18004	6504	6524				
陕　西	Shaanxi	173361	172231	117065	31118	1130			
甘　肃	Gansu	103871	103821	52695	22872	45	27	5	
青　海	Qinghai	51717	51704	42580	5096	13	-2		
宁　夏	Ningxia	55809	55732	26736	6242	57	13	20	
新　疆	Xinjiang	197243	196904	126347	26967	339	30		

14-29 各地区建筑业劳动生产率（2000年）

Labor Productivity of Construction by Region (2000)

单位：元 (yuan)

地区	Region	按建筑业总产值计算的劳动生产率 Overall Labor Productivity in Terms of Total Output Value	# 国有 State-owned	# 集体 Collective-owned	按建筑业增加值计算的劳动生产率 Overall Labor Productivity in Terms of Added-Value	# 国有 State-owned	# 集体 Collective-owned
全国	**National Total**	**59585**	**73302**	**44142**	**15929**	**20172**	**11893**
北京	Beijing	88132	81575	75644	22553	23345	18276
天津	Tianjin	86819	92803	55509	21765	22492	14201
河北	Hebei	51217	71888	35283	13070	17442	10183
山西	Shanxi	61099	76676	26593	16824	20413	9154
内蒙古	Inner Mongolia	39198	53832	31965	11913	16292	11457
辽宁	Liaoning	54580	67199	40170	15062	18375	12011
吉林	Jilin	61248	69997	42241	16594	18444	12002
黑龙江	Heilongjiang	51855	60523	41932	13991	16228	11414
上海	Shanghai	109809	120116	78396	24375	31347	18632
江苏	Jiangsu	69831	85613	61105	16793	21062	14472
浙江	Zhejiang	83410	96567	74590	21228	25163	19493
安徽	Anhui	42424	62334	32253	11738	17310	8888
福建	Fujian	65143	96141	43227	17061	24225	11377
江西	Jiangxi	40358	52313	29002	11240	15441	7801
山东	Shandong	45066	65801	34714	12517	17889	9638
河南	Henan	45321	60829	30762	12766	17016	8648
湖北	Hubei	54889	72700	34510	16268	22616	10006
湖南	Hunan	46609	69798	36049	12697	18927	9837
广东	Guangdong	70478	85674	49291	19829	23434	14138
广西	Guangxi	46667	57079	35244	15308	19393	10932
海南	Hainan	52704	65331	25968	11868	13135	8107
重庆	Chongqing	49148	58360	43707	12859	16448	10823
四川	Sichuan	45152	57701	33898	13118	17764	9728
贵州	Guizhou	49713	60334	33117	14311	17240	9382
云南	Yunnan	58592	83840	43216	15531	20947	12156
西藏	Tibet	62795	81181	36032	17105	17435	15553
陕西	Shaanxi	59672	82156	29566	14559	19077	8611
甘肃	Gansu	36335	51251	27009	11701	17928	7913
青海	Qinghai	42300	55619	23968	15348	20645	8851
宁夏	Ningxia	44936	54485	27923	13895	15526	9377
新疆	Xinjiang	74999	88009	48780	25209	32675	14141

14-30 各地区建筑业企业工程质量

Construction Quality of Construction Enterprises by Region

年份 Year 地区 Region		单位工程竣工个数（个）Number of Projects Completed	# 优良品 High Quality	单位工程优良品率（%）Percentage of High Quality Projects	房屋建筑竣工面积（万平方米）Floor Space of Buildings Completed (10 000 sq.m)	# 优良品 High Quality	房屋建筑竣工面积优良品率(%) Percentage of Floor Space of High Quality Buildings
	1991	222304	70024	31.5	19791.7	6374.1	32.2
	1992	238909	77895	32.6	23476.9	7828.1	33.3
	1993	305041	118443	38.8	28684.8	9000.1	31.4
	1994	286884	89346	31.1	32383.3	10429.3	32.2
	1995	293698	94783	32.3	35666.3	11906.0	33.4
	1996	419246	124436	29.7	60047.9	19935.3	33.2
	1997	442604	131337	29.7	62244.0	22489.0	36.1
	1998	415501	126069	30.3	65682.6	24353.6	37.1
	1999	446236	142507	31.9	73924.9	29980.5	40.6
	2000	534319	155172	29.0	80714.9	35843.5	44.4
北　京	Beijing	15849	4055	25.6	2808.7	1553.9	55.3
天　津	Tianjin	9488	3501	36.9	1056.4	406.8	38.5
河　北	Hebei	18058	7755	42.9	3481.4	1806.8	51.9
山　西	Shanxi	9409	4919	52.3	946.7	425.1	44.9
内蒙古	Inner Mongolia	6392	3223	50.4	1119.5	543.3	48.5
辽　宁	Liaoning	24655	6915	28.0	3547.9	1563.5	44.1
吉　林	Jilin	8564	3062	35.8	1439.7	592.0	41.1
黑龙江	Heilongjiang	11408	4279	37.5	1886.9	799.1	42.4
上　海	Shanghai	14185	5516	38.9	1710.0	860.1	50.3
江　苏	Jiangsu	129179	19009	14.7	12237.6	6251.8	51.1
浙　江	Zhejiang	35930	10249	28.5	7145.3	3491.9	48.9
安　徽	Anhui	20435	5852	28.6	2595.3	868.0	33.5
福　建	Fujian	11867	3016	25.4	1729.0	465.9	27.0
江　西	Jiangxi	6968	2263	32.5	1359.8	464.5	34.2
山　东	Shandong	38424	13541	35.2	5924.2	2558.9	43.2
河　南	Henan	17223	7146	41.5	2629.3	1191.0	45.3
湖　北	Hubei	18973	6643	35.0	3149.1	1002.8	31.9
湖　南	Hunan	12847	4531	35.3	2603.3	1175.6	45.2
广　东	Guangdong	24180	7830	32.4	6029.7	2757.2	45.7
广　西	Guangxi	11219	2758	24.6	1188.7	415.8	35.0
海　南	Hainan	1399	265	18.9	167.5	67.5	40.3
重　庆	Chongqing	10566	2757	26.1	3083.7	1084.0	35.2
四　川	Sichuan	28908	10467	36.2	5839.3	2418.7	41.4
贵　州	Guizhou	5423	1214	22.4	824.0	253.2	30.7
云　南	Yunnan	14225	5035	35.4	2189.7	1025.0	46.8
西　藏	Tibet	686	284	41.4	81.1	29.6	36.6
陕　西	Shaanxi	7260	3153	43.4	1087.2	549.1	50.5
甘　肃	Gansu	5370	1631	30.4	1058.8	417.6	39.4
青　海	Qinghai	1923	844	43.9	192.9	102.3	53.0
宁　夏	Ningxia	4255	663	15.6	340.7	138.5	40.7
新　疆	Xinjiang	9051	2796	30.9	1261.4	564.1	44.7

14-31 各地区国有建筑业企业工程质量

Construction Quality of State-owned Construction Enterprises by Region

年份 Year / 地区 Region	单位工程竣工个数（个） Number of Projects Completed	# 优良品 High Quality	单位工程优良品率（%） Percentage of High Quality Projects	房屋建筑竣工面积（万平方米） Floor Space of Buildings Completed (10 000 sq.m)	# 优良品 High Quality	房屋建筑竣工面积优良品率(%) Percentage of Floor Space of High Quality Buildings
1991	114741	47602	41.5	9270.9	3427.7	37.0
1992	119590	51902	43.4	10660.2	4142.3	38.9
1993	128248	59163	46.1	12085.4	4671.4	38.7
1994	124918	52651	42.1	14143.0	5331.2	37.7
1995	132356	58273	44.0	15182.4	5937.9	39.1
1996	141350	61529	43.5	17491.3	7326.9	41.9
1997	153417	64685	42.2	18507.5	8274.1	44.7
1998	140169	59863	42.7	17577.4	8049.2	45.8
1999	147506	63033	42.7	19868.6	9680.1	48.7
2000	221288	62567	28.3	20145.0	10455.5	51.9
北京 Beijing	4174	1728	41.4	1278.7	794.5	62.1
天津 Tianjin	3284	1411	43.0	615.9	312.0	50.7
河北 Hebei	7939	3765	47.4	1097.4	600.2	54.7
山西 Shanxi	6204	4000	64.5	460.8	223.2	48.4
内蒙古 Inner Mongolia	1871	1206	64.5	175.2	81.6	46.6
辽宁 Liaoning	8262	3101	37.5	818.7	380.8	46.5
吉林 Jilin	5158	2130	41.3	768.6	321.7	41.9
黑龙江 Heilongjiang	4646	1958	42.1	641.2	274.3	42.8
上海 Shanghai	4182	2552	61.0	263.0	112.1	42.6
江苏 Jiangsu	86651	4115	4.7	1968.8	1202.5	61.1
浙江 Zhejiang	4330	1391	32.1	392.5	192.9	49.2
安徽 Anhui	6711	2802	41.8	566.5	285.2	50.3
福建 Fujian	4008	1160	28.9	546.4	189.7	34.7
江西 Jiangxi	2578	982	38.1	463.6	214.9	46.4
山东 Shandong	8379	4339	51.8	1030.0	628.7	61.0
河南 Henan	7169	3901	54.4	908.7	494.0	54.4
湖北 Hubei	8661	4266	49.3	1096.1	450.4	41.1
湖南 Hunan	4316	2082	48.2	582.2	357.6	61.4
广东 Guangdong	7941	3064	38.6	1792.6	1002.4	55.9
广西 Guangxi	4579	1434	31.3	464.9	223.0	48.0
海南 Hainan	887	127	14.3	100.0	45.5	45.5
重庆 Chongqing	2058	478	23.2	342.4	135.1	39.5
四川 Sichuan	8227	3451	41.9	1247.3	622.4	49.9
贵州 Guizhou	2240	530	23.7	404.5	157.0	38.8
云南 Yunnan	3841	1767	46.0	613.9	391.9	63.8
西藏 Tibet	252	120	47.6	31.7	11.8	37.2
陕西 Shaanxi	3306	1686	51.0	393.9	248.7	63.1
甘肃 Gansu	1485	617	41.5	253.6	121.5	47.9
青海 Qinghai	1085	530	48.8	82.0	44.3	54.1
宁夏 Ningxia	2268	328	14.5	128.7	63.8	49.6
新疆 Xinjiang	4596	1546	33.6	615.3	272.0	44.2

14-32 各地区房屋建筑面积

Floor Space of Building Construction by Region

单位：万平方米 (10 000 sq.m)

年份 Year / 地区 Region	房屋建筑面积 Floor Space of Building Construction		国有 State-owned		集体 Collective-owned	
	施工面积 Floor Space under Construction	竣工面积 Floor Space Completed	施工面积 Floor Space under Construction	竣工面积 Floor Space Completed	施工面积 Floor Space under Construction	竣工面积 Floor Space Completed
1985	35491.8	17072.7	19295.8	8563.1	16196.0	8509.6
1986	37773.9	18601.0	20266.3	8870.5	17507.6	9730.5
1987	39856.6	19437.9	21153.1	9209.0	18703.5	10228.9
1988	42735.2	19060.7	22297.0	8899.3	20438.2	10161.4
1989	40649.9	19723.4	21399.0	9143.3	19250.9	10580.1
1990	37923.0	19552.5	20303.2	9361.7	17619.7	10190.9
1991	41054.2	20256.3	21395.4	9566.2	19658.8	10690.1
1992	51885.4	24045.5	25896.1	10968.0	25989.3	13077.5
1993	65374.2	28684.8	32118.1	12085.4	32724.1	16379.0
1994	78032.2	32383.3	39445.8	14143.0	37004.4	17674.0
1995	89862.8	35666.3	44562.9	15182.4	41829.5	19262.0
1996	129087.0	60047.9	48372.8	17491.3	74668.4	39827.3
1997	128680.3	62244.0	48830.1	18507.5	70795.3	39859.3
1998	137593.6	65682.6	45866.9	17577.4	68199.9	37517.6
1999	147262.5	73924.9	47055.7	19868.6	65984.5	37399.9
2000	160141.1	80714.9	46237.5	20145.0	63082.3	35698.7
北京 Beijing	7246.8	2808.7	3287.5	1278.7	1875.5	840.1
天津 Tianjin	2254.0	1056.4	1504.7	615.9	499.6	338.7
河北 Hebei	6260.1	3481.4	2087.3	1097.4	2479.8	1469.7
山西 Shanxi	2008.4	946.7	1118.8	460.8	566.9	330.1
内蒙古 Inner Mongolia	1804.9	1119.5	379.8	175.2	288.6	201.6
辽宁 Liaoning	6334.9	3547.9	1721.4	818.7	2357.9	1574.6
吉林 Jilin	2209.5	1439.7	1282.4	768.6	402.2	320.2
黑龙江 Heilongjiang	2962.6	1886.9	1085.8	641.2	966.5	652.0
上海 Shanghai	4625.8	1710.0	929.1	263.0	838.4	390.0
江苏 Jiangsu	21190.2	12237.6	4110.6	1968.8	9932.8	6261.7
浙江 Zhejiang	16570.1	7145.3	930.5	392.5	5371.6	2365.0
安徽 Anhui	4631.3	2595.3	1166.5	566.5	2430.1	1447.0
福建 Fujian	4085.4	1729.0	1574.6	546.4	1294.4	618.7
江西 Jiangxi	2572.3	1359.8	1000.1	463.6	1457.4	830.4
山东 Shandong	11392.2	5924.2	2430.1	1030.0	5486.5	3091.6
河南 Henan	5308.3	2629.3	2156.6	908.7	2358.7	1320.5
湖北 Hubei	6255.5	3149.1	2888.9	1096.1	2388.9	1530.1
湖南 Hunan	5088.1	2603.3	1295.3	582.2	3032.6	1639.6
广东 Guangdong	15168.7	6029.7	4925.7	1792.6	6367.3	2759.8
广西 Guangxi	2327.5	1188.7	1050.1	464.9	1033.5	590.1
海南 Hainan	359.4	167.5	244.4	100.0	78.5	52.8
重庆 Chongqing	6088.5	3083.7	886.4	342.4	2462.0	1371.0
四川 Sichuan	10592.0	5839.3	2807.2	1247.3	4485.8	2803.7
贵州 Guizhou	1792.5	824.0	1015.9	404.5	628.7	346.4
云南 Yunnan	3479.2	2189.7	1192.6	613.9	1564.7	1097.4
西藏 Tibet	87.0	81.1	35.1	31.7	35.2	33.7
陕西 Shaanxi	2396.5	1087.2	1012.6	393.9	1031.8	522.8
甘肃 Gansu	1905.4	1058.8	642.8	253.6	652.2	428.4
青海 Qinghai	339.4	192.9	156.3	82.0	95.3	62.8
宁夏 Ningxia	563.1	340.7	238.4	128.7	127.8	87.2
新疆 Xinjiang	2241.5	1261.4	1080.3	615.3	491.3	321.0

14-33 各地区建筑业企业主要建筑材料消耗（2000年）

Consumption of Main Construction Materials of Construction Enterprises by Region (2000)

地 区	Region	材料费用合计（万元） Value of Material (10 000 yuan)	# 钢 材 Steel	# 木 材 Timber	# 水 泥 Cement	实物量 Consumption in Quantity 钢材(万吨) Steel (10 000 tons)	木材(万立方米) Timber (10 000 cu.m)	水泥(万吨) Cement (10 000 tons)
全 国	**National Total**	**57960826**	**16220274**	**3609926**	**9733449**	**6237.9**	**3681.0**	**33311.3**
北 京	Beijing	2513995	781907	106468	257068	284.5	98.9	839.8
天 津	Tianjin	707133	229496	22963	112788	82.2	19.4	350.3
河 北	Hebei	2092200	591113	118667	333023	235.0	119.6	1312.5
山 西	Shanxi	1112675	316676	54295	283598	109.5	55.2	1130.5
内蒙古	Inner Mongolia	741340	156964	39057	102322	61.6	42.4	334.9
辽 宁	Liaoning	2707881	753844	167912	384790	298.8	164.5	1263.2
吉 林	Jilin	1273246	271543	63079	170213	99.5	65.7	505.1
黑龙江	Heilongjiang	1692533	335394	78993	262480	118.5	93.9	679.8
上 海	Shanghai	1990629	574142	99759	250669	219.2	72.0	796.0
江 苏	Jiangsu	6258089	1846837	479887	1189743	721.5	385.8	4379.5
浙 江	Zhejiang	7832188	2119809	471320	1479589	816.2	439.2	4992.5
安 徽	Anhui	1419600	387279	107788	250637	152.3	98.5	884.8
福 建	Fujian	1216186	413936	108091	235337	163.1	135.6	679.7
江 西	Jiangxi	452858	158320	43983	112322	62.0	65.7	373.1
山 东	Shandong	3185426	927550	245954	475986	363.9	228.7	2006.6
河 南	Henan	1744558	521689	107256	285929	204.6	98.7	1126.4
湖 北	Hubei	2749893	609174	131595	341416	232.7	142.9	1196.3
湖 南	Hunan	1663194	456896	110588	277665	170.7	181.7	1032.3
广 东	Guangdong	4880439	1281720	376073	743462	525.3	426.4	2322.4
广 西	Guangxi	956495	300169	72259	172017	113.6	108.3	598.4
海 南	Hainan	91265	38360	11197	32564	17.3	16.2	108.2
重 庆	Chongqing	1625289	455648	99117	310993	178.1	101.7	1148.4
四 川	Sichuan	4065599	1237093	275321	770566	484.2	277.7	2362.4
贵 州	Guizhou	372273	135797	21680	83634	52.4	22.5	276.5
云 南	Yunnan	1492506	447408	61195	345454	168.4	78.8	1136.6
西 藏	Tibet	43146	10055	5277	17662	3.9	7.0	27.6
陕 西	Shaanxi	908317	259250	51898	165236	96.2	50.0	535.9
甘 肃	Gansu	532103	181416	29054	79844	73.4	30.5	271.8
青 海	Qinghai	175832	38090	9155	33528	17.2	7.6	90.9
宁 夏	Ningxia	260298	65602	10656	39353	22.3	9.6	139.3
新 疆	Xinjiang	1203639	317098	29391	133563	90.2	36.4	409.8

14-34 勘察设计机构和人员数（2000年）

Number of Prospecting and Designing Institutions and Their Staff and Workers (2000)

地区及部门	Region and Sector	单位数（个） Number of Institutions	年底职工人数（人） Number of Staff & Workers at Year-end	高级职称 Senior Title	中级职称 Middle Title	初级职称 Junior Title	非技术人员 Non-technicians
全　国	**National Total**	**10753**	**635198**	**124969**	**221204**	**154092**	**134933**
北　京	Beijing	407	42898	15325	13699	7734	6140
天　津	Tianjin	173	33792	8200	13159	8244	4189
河　北	Hebei	402	24340	4857	8479	5942	5062
山　西	Shanxi	204	10148	1866	4043	2662	1577
内蒙古	Inner Mongolia	228	15412	1826	4767	3186	5633
辽　宁	Liaoning	788	34791	8462	13496	8401	4432
吉　林	Jilin	211	14409	3095	4763	3399	3152
黑龙江	Heilongjiang	220	9062	1837	3300	1935	1990
上　海	Shanghai	328	23942	6091	8856	5020	3975
江　苏	Jiangsu	458	26525	4148	9239	6988	6150
浙　江	Zhejiang	315	14586	3830	4891	3620	2245
安　徽	Anhui	427	19636	3944	7163	5806	2723
福　建	Fujian	421	15822	2303	5180	4140	4199
江　西	Jiangxi	436	14625	2755	5132	4223	2515
山　东	Shandong	856	39243	6509	19034	8968	4732
河　南	Henan	479	30303	5591	10161	6944	7607
湖　北	Hubei	572	56188	7855	15168	11310	21855
湖　南	Hunan	393	23791	3828	8186	5070	6707
广　东	Guangdong	755	32280	4413	11076	9173	7618
广　西	Guangxi	315	14073	2779	5155	3814	2325
海　南	Hainan	66	2617	551	786	685	595
重　庆	Chongqing	174	10912	2872	3918	2594	1528
四　川	Sichuan	702	37427	7109	13047	9594	7677
贵　州	Guizhou	320	13170	1824	5215	3983	2148
云　南	Yunnan	234	11816	1850	3702	3800	2464
西　藏	Tibet	13	626	59	187	290	90
陕　西	Shaanxi	189	16512	3973	5070	3540	3929
甘　肃	Gansu	274	23977	2837	6777	7107	7256
青　海	Qinghai	68	3073	508	1035	863	667
宁　夏	Ningxia	84	3055	506	1075	971	503
新　疆	Xinjiang	202	12585	2272	4095	3451	2767

主要统计指标解释

建筑业统计单位　指从事房屋、构筑物建造和设备安装活动的法人企业。建筑业法人企业应同时具备的条件是：①依法成立，有自己的名称、组织机构和场所，能够承担民事责任；②独立拥有和使用资产，承担负债，有权与其他单位签订合同；③独立核算盈亏，能够编制资产负债表。

建筑业总产值(即自行完成施工产值)　是以货币表现的建筑安装企业在一定时期内生产的建筑业产品的总和。建筑业总产值包括：

⑴建筑工程产值：指列入建筑工程预算内的各种工程价值。

⑵设备安装工程产值：指设备安装工程价值，不包括被安装设备本身价值。

⑶房屋、构筑物修理产值：指房屋、构筑物修理所完成的价值，但不包括被修理房屋、构筑物本身的价值和生产设备的修理价值。

⑷非标准设备制造产值：指加工制造没有定型的、非标准的生产设备的加工费和原材料价值，以及附属加工厂为本企业承建工程制作的非标准设备的价值。

建筑业增加值　指建筑业企业在报告期内以货币表现的建筑业生产经营活动的最终成果。目前建筑业增加值采用分配法（收入法）计算，即从收入的角度出发，根据生产要素在生产过程中应得的收入份额计算。具体计算公式为：

建筑业增加值＝本年提取的固定资产折旧＋应付工资＋应付福利费＋管理费用中的劳动待业保险金、税金＋工程结算税金及附加＋工程结算利润

房屋建筑施工面积　指在报告期内施工的全部房屋建筑面积，包括本期新开工的房屋面积、上期施工跨入本期继续施工的房屋面积、上期停缓建在本期恢复施工的房屋面积、本期竣工的房屋面积及本期施工后又停缓建的房屋面积。

房屋建筑竣工面积　指在报告期内房屋建筑按照设计要求全部完工，达到了住人和使用条件，经验收鉴定合格，正式移交使用单位的房屋建筑面积。

自有机械设备年末总台数　指归本企业所有，属于本企业固定资产的生产性机械设备年末总台数。包括施工机械、生产设备、运输设备以及其他设备。

自有机械设备年末总功率　指本企业自有施工机械、生产设备、运输设备以及其他设备等列为在册固定资产的生产性机械设备年末总功率，按设定能力或查定能力计算。包括机械本身的动力和为该机械服务的单独动力设备，如电动机等。计算单位用千瓦，动力换算可按1马力＝0.735千瓦折合成千瓦数。电焊机、变压器、锅炉不计算动力。

工程结算收入　指企业承包工程实现的工程价款结算收入，以及向发包单位收取的除工程价款以外的按规定列作营业收入的各种款项，如临时设施费、劳动保险费、施工机械调迁费等以及向发包单位收取的各种索赔款。

工程结算利润　指已结算工程实现的利润，如亏损以“－”号表示。计算公式为：

工程结算利润＝工程结算收入－工程结算成本－工程结算税金及附加

企业总收入　指与企业生产经营直接有关的各项收入，包括工程结算收入和其他业务收入。计算公式为：

企业总收入＝工程结算收入＋其他业务收入

Explanatory Notes on Main Statistical Indicators

Statistical Unit in Construction refers to corporate enterprise engaged in the construction of buildings and structures and in the installation of equipment. A corporate construction enterprise should meet the following 3 requirements: ①being set up in line with relevant legal basis, having its full name, organization and location, and capable of taking civil liabilities; ② independently possessing and using its assets and assuming its liabilities, and entitled to sign contracts with other institutions; and ③ making independent accounts of its profits and losses, and capable of compiling its own balance sheet.

Gross Output Value of Construction (Output Value of Projects Under Construction) refers to total of construction products, expressed in money terms, completed by construction and installation enterprises during a given period of time. It includes:

(1)Output value of construction projects, that is the value of projects covered by the project budgets;

(2)Output value of installation projects, that is the value of the installation of equipment, (excluding the value of the equipment to be installed);

(3)Output value of repair of buildings and structures, that is the value created through the repairs of buildings or structures, but does not include the value of buildings or structures being repaired and the value of the repair of production equipment;

(4)Output value of manufactured non-standard equipment, that is the value of non-standard production equipment (including raw materials and manufacturing cost) made for the construction project, and the equipment manufactured by subsidiary workshops.

Value-added of Construction refers to the final result of the activities of production and management of construction in monetary terms in the reference period. At present, the value-added of construction is calculated with the income approach. In other words, it is the sum of income of various production factors in the production process. The formula is as follows:

Value-added of construction=depreciation of fixed assets in the year+wages payable+welfare expenses payable+insurance premium and tax for waiting for employment in the administrative expenses +taxes and surcharges on project settlement+profit gained from project settlement.

Floor Space of Buildings Under Construction refers to floor space of buildings under construction during the reference period, including newly started buildings, buildings started earlier and continued during the reference period, and buildings suspended earlier but restarted during the reference period, buildings completed during the reference period, and buildings under construction and then suspended during the reference period.

Floor Space of Buildings Completed refers to the floor space of buildings that are completed in the reference period in accordance with the requirements of the design, up to the standard for putting them into use, and have been checked and accepted by concerned departments as qualified ones.

Total Number of Machinery and Equipment Owned by the End of Year refers to the number of machines and equipment owned by the enterprises, and listed as the fixed assets of the enterprises by the end of the year, including machinery and equipment for construction, production and transportation.

Total Power of Machinery and Equipment Owned by the End of Year refers to the total power of machinery and equipment owned by the enterprises, and listed as the fixed assets of the enterprises by the end of the year, including machinery and equipment for construction, production and transportation. The power of the machinery is calculated on basis of the designed or verified capacity, covering the power of the machinery/equipment and the separate power equipment serving the machinery/equipment (such as electric motors), but excluding welders, transformers and boilers. The unit used for the calculation of power is kilowatt, with horsepower converted to kilowatt by 1 horsepower=0.735 kilowatt.

Income from Settlement of Projects refers to the income received by the construction enterprise from the contracted project through settlement procedures, and other charges to the contractoree as operational costs in addition to the value of the project, such as temporary facility fee, labour insurance premium, moving cost of construction equipment, as well as various types of claims to the contractee.

Profit from Settlement of Projects refers to profit realized through settled projects. It is calculated with the following formula:

Profit from Settlement of Projects=Income from Settlement of Projects−Settled Cost−Settled Taxes and Other Cost

Total Revenue of Enterprises refers to the sum of income from production and operation of enterprises, including income from settlement of projects and other operational income, namely:

Total Revenue of Enterprises=Income from Settlement of Projects+Other Operational Income

十五、运输和邮电

Transport, Post and Telecommunication Services

简要说明

一、本篇资料反映我国交通运输业和邮电通信业发展的基本状况。

交通运输业资料主要包括：五种运输方式的线路里程、运输设备拥有量、技术质量情况，各种运输方式完成的货物运输量和旅客运输量，铁路运输的固定资产构成及财务主要情况，主要港口码头长度及泊位情况，沿海主要港口货物吞吐量。

邮电通信业资料主要包括：全国邮电局(所)及邮路情况，邮电通信主要电路及设备拥有量，主要的邮电业务完成情况，邮电通信发展水平等资料。

二、本篇资料由国家统计局工业交通司负责整理、编辑。有关交通运输资料分别来源于铁道部、交通部、民航总局、公安部、中国石油天然气集团公司、中国石油化工集团公司和各省、自治区、直辖市统计局。邮电通信业资料来源于信息产业部。

三、各部分资料的调查范围及统计单位

1. 铁路资料：包括国家铁路、地方铁路和合资铁路运营情况，不含军用铁路及由厂矿企事业单位自建的铁路专用线和专用铁道。国家铁路和合资铁路运营资料来源于各铁路局下属分局及所属运输企业(公司)。地方铁路运营概况资料来源于各省地方铁路管理部门。

2. 公路、水运、港口资料：公路和水路线路里程为年末通车和通航里程数，不含在建和未正式投入使用的公路和航道里程。公路民用车辆拥有量是根据公安部交通管理局下属各省厅车管部门登记注册的车辆资料整理，不含军用车辆。民用运输船舶拥有量是根据交通部下属各省交通航运管理部门登记注册的船舶资料整理，不含渔船、水上施工作业船和军用船舶。公路、水路客货运输量资料，按照交通部和国家统计局1992年联合发布的《公路、水路运输全行业统计工作规定》的要求，由交通部和国家统计局分工负责收集整理。公路、水路运输全行业统计以全面调查和非全面调查两种方式进行，统计范围包括在我国注册从事公路、水路客、货运输的全部企事业单位和私人(包括个体联户)。沿海、内河主要港口的生产能力及吞吐量是根据各地港务管理部门注册的港口企业和从事港口生产活动单位的资料整理。

3. 管道运输资料：包括输原油、输成品油、输天然气、输其他气体的管线长度、输送能力及完成的运输量。具体包括：油气田企业直接通向炼油厂、化工厂、电站等用户及装车站、油码头的管道，炼油厂通向用户(包括商业石油公司油库)的成品油气管道，独立核算的管道运输企业通向用户及装车(站)栈桥、油码头的管道。管道运输统计数据主要来源于中国石油天然气集团公司和中国石油化工集团公司所属的管道运输企业，由两家集团公司分别负责收集审核本部门统计数据。

4. 民航运输资料：统计对象为在我国境内注册从事民用航空运输飞行和通用飞行的航空运输企业，包括民航总局直属企业和非民航总局直属企业，不包括外国航空公司在我国境内的运输飞行。统计范围为各航空公司从事国内运输、港澳台运输、国际运输的运输航线、运输量及飞机构成和运营情况、通用飞行完成情况等。

5. 邮电通信资料：包括全社会公众网邮政和电信业务，不含非邮电部门经营管理的专用通讯网业务资料。邮电业务量按业务种类分为邮政业务总量和电信业务总量；按业务范围分为国内业务量和国际及港澳业务量(对台业务量统计在港澳中)；按管理体制分为中央国有业务总量和地方国有业务总量。

Brief Introduction

I. Data in this chapter cover mainly the basic conditions of the development of transportation, post and telecommunications in China.

Data of transport cover mainly the length of the routes of five means of transportation, the ownership of the transport equipment, the technological quality, the freight traffic and passenger traffic accomplished by various means of transportation, the composition of the fixed assets and main financial conditions in the railway transport, the length of major ports and the situation of births, and cargo handled at principal sea ports.

Data of post and telecommunications cover mainly the situation of post and telecommunications offices and postal routes, the telephone lines, telegraph lines and the ownership of the telecommunication facilities, the principal postal and telecommunications services rendered, main financial indicators of postal and telecommunications enterprises, and the level of the development of the postal and telecommunications services, etc.

II. Data in this chapter are prepared and edited by the Department of Industrial and Transport Statistics, NBS. Data on transport come from the Ministry of Railways, Ministry of Communications, Civil Aviation Administration of China, Ministry of Public Security, China National Petroleum and Natural Gas Corporation Group, China Petrochemical Corporation Group and statistical bureaus of provinces, autonomous regions and municipalities directly under the central government. Data on posts and telecommunications come from the Ministry of Information Industry.

III. The statistical coverage and statistical units of the various data:

(1) Data on railways cover the operation and management of the national and local railways, not including the railways for military purpose, industrial lines and special railways. The data on the operation and management of the national railways come from the railway sub-bureaus and the transport enterprises subordinate to them . The data on the operation and management of local railways come from the provincial administrative departments of the local railways, and are collected by the China Association of Local Railways.

(2) Data on highways, waterways and ports: The length of highways and waterways refer to the length open to traffic or navigation at the end of the year, not including the highways and waterways under construction but not officially put into use. The data mentioned above are provided by the Ministry of Communications. The data on the ownership of the highway vehicles are provided by the divisions of vehicle management under the provincial departments of public security, subordinate to the Traffic Management Bureau, Ministry of Public Security, to the provincial statistical bureaus. The data on the ownership of ships are provided by the divisions of navigation or ports management under the provincial departments of communications, subordinate to the Ministry of Communications, to the provincial statistical bureaus. The provincial statistical bureaus examined, processed and tabulated the data. The data on the passenger traffic and freight traffic by highways and waterways are collected and prepared separately by the Ministry of Communications and the National Bureau of Statistics in accordance with the ¡°Provisions on the Statistical Work of the Whole Trades of Highway and Waterway Transport¡±, jointly issued by the Ministry of Communications and the National Bureau of Statistics in 1992. The statistical data of the whole trades of highway and waterway transport are collected by the method of complete enumeration and the method of sample survey. Statistical coverage: All the units and individuals (including joint-households) registered in the People's Republic of China and engaged in highway or waterway freight or passenger transport business or those engaged in non-business freight or passenger transport within the boundary of the People's Republic of China, whatever their subordinate relationships and ownership are, are included in the coverage of transport statistics. The Ministry of Communications is responsible for collecting the statistical data on the handling capacity of the seaports and inland river ports and the volume of freight handled.

(3) Data on the pipeline transport: The statistics of pipeline transport cover the length, transport capacity and the volume transported of the petroleum (crude oil) pipelines, petroleum products (refined oil) pipelines, natural gas pipelines and other gas pipelines. The coverage of statistics of pipeline transport includes the pipelines leading directly from the enterprises of oil fields or gas fields to the users such as refineries, chemical plants, power stations, etc. and to the loading stations and ports or piers, the petroleum products pipelines leading from the refineries to the users (including the oil depots of the commercial oil companies) and the pipelines leading from the enterprises engaged in pipeline transport with independent accounting system to the users and causeways and ports or piers. The data sources of the pipeline transport statistics are mainly the enterprises engaged in the pipeline transport subordinate to the China National Petroleum and Natural Gas Corporation Group and

China Petrochemical Corporation Group. The two corporations collect and examine the statistical data from the units subordinate to them respectively.

(4) Data on the civil aviation transport: The statistical units of the civil aviation transport include the enterprises engaged in the civil aviation transport flights and flights for general purpose, including the enterprises directly under the Civil Aviation Administration of China or not under the CAAC, but excluding the foreign companies. The statistical data cover the air lines and transport volume of the domestic transport, the transport between China mainland and Hong Kong, Macao and Taiwan, and the international transport engaged by the air companies as well as the composition of aircraft; the statistical data also cover the data on the operation and performance of the civil aviation. The data are collected from the domestic air companies and civil aviation airports by the Civil Aviation Administration of China.

(5) Data on post and telecommunications: The business volume of post and telecommunications is classified by business area into the domestic volume, the volume between China mainland and Hong Kong, Macao and Taiwan and the international volume. The business volume of post and telecommunications is also classified by administration into the volume accomplished by the enterprises subordinate to the central government and the volume accomplished by the enterprises subordinate to the local governments. All the data are the data of the public network administered by the department of post and telecommunications, excluding the data of the public network and the special network administered by the departments other than post and telecommunications. The data come from the post and telecommunications offices and enterprises of telecommunications subordinate to the provincial departments of posts and telecommunications. The Ministry of Information Industry is responsible for collecting such data.

15-1 各地区交通运输、邮电通信业职工人数（2000年底）

Number of Staff and Employed Workers in Transport, Post and Telecommunication Services by Region (End of 2000)

单位：万人 (10 000 persons)

地区	Region	铁路运输业 Railway Transport	公路运输业 Highway Transport	管道运输业 Pipeline Transport	水上运输业 Water way Transport	航空运输业 Air Transport	交通运输辅助业 Transport Supporting and Auxiliary Services	其他交通运输业 Other Transport	邮电通信业 Post and Telecommunication Services
全 国	**National Total**	**187.1**	**120**	**2.2**	**38.8**	**11.7**	**147.7**	**1.9**	**113.2**
北 京	Beijing	6.1	2.4			1	3.2		4
天 津	Tianjin	3.4	1.7		0.9	0.2	3.5		1.5
河 北	Hebei	9.7	5.8		0.2	0.1	7.1		4.7
山 西	Shanxi	11	3.5			0.2	4.6	0.1	3.3
内蒙古	Inner Mongolia	9.1	2			0.1	3.3		3
辽 宁	Liaoning	11.7	5.7	0.3	1.2	0.9	9.3	0.2	4.8
吉 林	Jilin	9.2	2.8	0.1	0.1	0.3	3.6		3.3
黑龙江	Heilongjiang	12.5	2.9		0.6	0.4	7.6		5.9
上 海	Shanghai	3.4	2.5	0.1	3.7	0.9	6.2	0.1	3.5
江 苏	Jiangsu	6	8.4	1.1	6.3	0.4	12	0.1	6.7
浙 江	Zhejiang	2.9	5.4		2	0.1	5		5.1
安 徽	Anhui	4.7	6.2		2.3	0.2	3.9	0.2	3.2
福 建	Fujian	2.7	3.1		1.5	0.6	2.6		3.7
江 西	Jiangxi	7.3	3.1		1	0.2	2.5	0.4	2.6
山 东	Shandong	7.9	8.7	0.1	1.6	0.3	8.1	0.1	5.4
河 南	Henan	12.9	8.7		0.4	0.1	7.8		5.7
湖 北	Hubei	9.1	6.1	0.1	3.7	0.4	9.1		5.1
湖 南	Hunan	9	6.5		1.5	0.1	5.3		4.8
广 东	Guangdong	5.9	6.3		5.4	1.2	13.4	0.1	12.5
广 西	Guangxi	5	3.1		1	0.2	4.2		2.8
海 南	Hainan	0.2	0.3		0.3	0.5	1.8		0.7
重 庆	Chongqing	3.7	2.3		3.1	0.3	3.6		1.9
四 川	Sichuan	4	7.1	0.1	1.7	0.9	6		5.1
贵 州	Guizhou	3.2	1.7		0.2	0.2	1.9		1.5
云 南	Yunnan	5.5	4.2		0.1	0.5	2.9	0.2	3.1
西 藏	Tibet		0.3			0.1	0.3		0.3
陕 西	Shaanxi	10.3	2.8			0.4	3.6		3.3
甘 肃	Gansu	5.4	1.9			0.3	2		1.7
青 海	Qinghai	1.4	0.9				0.5		0.7
宁 夏	Ningxia	1.3	0.5	0.1			0.5		0.8
新 疆	Xinjiang	2.6	3			0.6	2.4		2.5

15-2 交通运输业基本情况

Basic Conditions of Transport

指标	Item	1996	1997	1998	1999	2000
运输线路长度　（万公里）	**Length of Transport Routes　(10 000 km)**					
国家铁路营业里程	National Railways in Operation	5.67	5.76	5.76	5.79	5.87
#电气化里程	Electrified Railways	1.01	1.20	1.30	1.40	1.49
公路	Highways	118.58	122.64	127.85	135.17	140.27
内河	Navigable Inland Waterways	11.08	10.98	11.03	11.65	11.93
民航	Total Civil Aviation Routes	116.65	142.50	150.58	152.22	150.29
#国际航线	International Routes	38.63	50.44	50.44	52.33	50.84
管道	Petroleum and Gas Pipelines	1.93	2.04	2.31	2.49	2.47
客运量总计　（万人）	**Total Passenger Traffic　(10 000 persons)**	**1245356**	**1326094**	**1378717**	**1394413**	**1478573**
铁路	Railways	94796	93308	95085	100164	105073
国家	National Railways	93550	91919	92991	97725	101847
地方	Local Railways	612	659	629	528	519
合资	Joint-venture Railways	634	730	1465	1911	2707
公路	Highways	1122110	1204583	1257332	1269004	1347392
水运	Waterways	22895	22573	20545	19151	19386
民用航空	Civil Aviation	5555	5630	5755	6094	6722
旅客周转量总计（亿人公里）	**Total Passenger-Kilometers (100 million passenger-km)**	**9164.8**	**10055.5**	**10636.7**	**11299.7**	**12261.0**
铁路	Railways	3347.6	3584.9	3773.4	4135.9	4532.6
国家	National Railways	3322.0	3543.5	3691.0	4046.3	4414.7
地方	Local Railways	3.4	4.7	5.0	4.4	4.6
合资	Joint-venture Railways	22.2	36.6	77.4	85.3	113.3
公路	Highways	4908.8	5541.4	5942.8	6199.2	6657.4
水运	Waterways	160.6	155.7	120.3	107.3	100.5
民用航空	Civil Aviation	747.8	773.5	800.2	857.3	970.5
货运量总计　（万吨）	**Total Freight Traffic　(10 000 tons)**	**1298312**	**1278087**	**1267200**	**1292650**	**1358124**
铁路	Railways	170915	172019	164082	167196	178023
国家	National Railways	161678	161880	153208	156881	165498
地方	Local Railways	7125	7854	8035	7296	8369
合资	Joint-venture Railways	2112	2285	2839	3019	4156
公路	Highways	983860	976536	976004	990444	1038813
水运	Waterways	127430	113406	109555	114608	122391
民用航空	Civil Aviation	115.0	124.7	140.1	170.0	196.7
管道	Petroleum and Gas Pipelines	15992	16002	17419	20232	18700
货物周转量总计（亿吨公里）	**Total Freight Ton-kilometers (100 million ton-km)**	**36577**	**38368**	**38046**	**40496**	**44452**
铁路	Railways	13093	13253	12517	12838	13902
国家	National Railways	12922	13046	12261	12578	13336
地方	Local Railways	49	51	51	38	44
合资	Joint-venture Railways	122	156	205	223	522
公路	Highways	5011	5272	5483	5724	6129
水运	Waterways	17863	19235	19406	21263	23734
民用航空	Civil Aviation	24.9	29.1	33.5	42.3	50.3
管道	Petroleum and Gas Pipelines	585	579	606	628	636
民用汽车拥有量　（万辆）	**Number of Civil Motor Vehicles Owned (10 000 units)**	**1100.08**	**1219.09**	**1319.30**	**1452.94**	**1608.91**
#载客汽车	Number of Buses and Cars	488.02	580.56	654.83	740.23	853.73
载货汽车	Number of Trucks	575.03	601.23	627.89	676.95	716.32
#普通载货汽车	Ordinary Trucks	558.16	582.45	609.31	655.74	697.59
#公路部门营运汽车	Number of Working Motor Vehicles Owned by Highway Departments	28.81	29.89	31.88	501.77	702.82
#私人汽车	Number of Private-owned Motor Vehicles	289.67	358.36	423.65	533.88	625.33
其他机动车拥有量　（万辆）	**Number of Other Motor Vehicles　(10 000 units)**	**1773.13**	**2214.83**	**2770.72**	**3456.96**	**4168.06**
民用运输船舶拥有量　（艘）	**Number of Civil Transport Vessels　(unit)**					
机动船	Motor Vessels	269879	215814	212093	194590	185018
驳船	Barges	56128	49983	48115	47453	44658
帆船	Sailing Boats	4946	6059	3368		
#私人运输船舶拥有量　（艘）	Number of Private-owned Transport Vessels (unit)					
机动船	Motor Vessels	157370	147415	127130	113359	128654
驳船	Barges	6533	9944	7290	7262	13463
帆船	Sailing Boats	4556	3217	2934		
沿海主要港口货物吞吐量　（万吨）	**Volume of Freight Handled in Major Coastal Ports　(10 000 tons)**	**85152**	**90822**	**92237**	**105162**	**125603**

注：公路部门营运汽车1999年统计口径变为全社会营运汽车，2000年为全社会公路运输汽车(含营运和非营运汽车)。

a) The statistical coverage of number of working motor vehicles owned by highway departments extended to the working motor vehicles of all society in 1999, and the motor vehicle of all society (including working or non-working) in 2000.

15-3 各地区运输线路长度（2000年底）

Length of Transport Routes by Region (End of 2000)

单位：公里 (km)

地区	Region	国家铁路 National Railways: 营业里程 Length of Railways in Operation	国家铁路 National Railways: 正线延展里程 Extension Length of the Trunk Lines	内河航道里程 Length of Navigable Inland Waterways	公路里程 Total Length of Highways	等级路 Expressway and Class I to IV Highway	#高速 Express-way	一级 First Class	二级 Second Class	等外路 Highway Below Class IV
全　国	**National Total**	**58655.9**	**81736.3**	**119325**	**1402698**	**1216013**	**16314**	**20088**	**152672**	**186685**
北　京	Beijing	1140.9	1815.3		13597	13143	267	298	1444	454
天　津	Tianjin	531.2	962.4	443	8946	8869	305	370	1214	77
河　北	Hebei	3631.9	6069.3	75	59152	56776	1480	1458	8028	2376
山　西	Shanxi	2510.8	3860.7	170	55408	52767	518	614	8189	2641
内蒙古	Inner Mongolia	5011.1	6223.7	1164	67346	63622		140	3865	3724
辽　宁	Liaoning	3556.4	5041.8	813	45547	44969	1068	833	8347	578
吉　林	Jilin	3474.4	3843.6	1787	35216	33698	354	410	4150	1518
黑龙江	Heilongjiang	5013.2	6679.3	5057	50284	49622	285	387	4643	662
上　海	Shanghai	256.5	397.2	2100	4325	4325	98	390	982	
江　苏	Jiangsu	757.1	1442.6	23943	28198	26564	1090	2228	6999	1634
浙　江	Zhejiang	793.7	1263.4	10408	41605	37707	627	999	4212	3898
安　徽	Anhui	1842.9	2877.9	5611	44493	42579	470	264	6347	1914
福　建	Fujian	873.9	885.9	3701	51073	42512	345	406	4582	8561
江　西	Jiangxi	2152.6	3440.5	5537	37138	26448	414	248	4568	10690
山　东	Shandong	2401.6	3980.6	2486	70686	70579	2006	2599	18885	107
河　南	Henan	2353.1	4570.9	1104	64453	62192	505	38	9028	2261
湖　北	Hubei	2030.8	3070.9	7256	57850	48062	569	611	7911	9788
湖　南	Hunan	2312.7	3528	10041	60848	33380	449	239	3761	27468
广　东	Guangdong	693.8	1383.6	13696	102604	93693	1186	5391	13396	8911
广　西	Guangxi	2012.3	2431.6	5618	52910	45430	812	442	2628	7480
海　南	Hainan	219	222.2	414	17401	13405	601	121	636	3996
重　庆	Chongqing	598	597.4	2324	29252	21743	199	123	2951	7509
四　川	Sichuan	2333.3	2622.7	5980	90875	69723	1000	906	7451	21152
贵　州	Guizhou	1641.7	1711.6	2132	34643	17034	258	26	718	17609
云　南	Yunnan	1872.5	1931.1	1580	109560	102550	517	77	1722	7010
西　藏	Tibet				22503	10647			568	11856
陕　西	Shaanxi	2204.6	2638.1	998	44006	37459	349	175	3420	6547
甘　肃	Gansu	2318	3274.2	1306	39344	29393	13	75	3280	9951
青　海	Qinghai	1091.9	1097.3	372	18679	15178		31	1806	3501
宁　夏	Ningxia	716.1	806.7	402	10171	9649	83	127	1530	522
新　疆	Xinjiang	2309.9	3065.8		34585	32295	446	62	5411	2290
不分地区	Not Classified by Region			2807						

15-4 运输线路长度

Length of Transportation Routes

单位:万公里 (10 000 km)

年 份 Year	铁路营业里程 Length of Railways in Operation	# 电气化里程 Electrified Railways	公 路 Length of Highways	内 河 Length of Navigable Inland Waterways	民 航 Length of Civil Aviation Routes	# 国际航线 International Routes	管 道 Length of Petroleum and Gas Pipelines
1952	2.29		12.67	9.50	1.31	0.51	
1957	2.67		25.46	14.41	2.64	0.43	
1962	3.46	0.01	46.35	16.19	3.53	0.44	0.02
1965	3.64	0.01	51.45	15.77	3.94	0.45	0.04
1970	4.10	0.03	63.67	14.84	4.06	0.44	0.12
1975	4.60	0.07	78.36	13.56	8.42	3.71	0.53
1978	5.17	0.10	89.02	13.60	14.89	5.53	0.83
1979	5.30	0.10	87.58	10.78	16.00	5.13	0.91
1980	5.33	0.17	88.33	10.85	19.53	8.12	0.87
1981	5.39	0.17	89.75	10.87	21.83	8.28	0.97
1982	5.29	0.18	90.70	10.86	23.27	9.99	1.04
1983	5.41	0.23	91.51	10.89	22.91	9.99	1.08
1984	5.45	0.30	92.67	10.93	26.02	10.74	1.10
1985	5.50	0.42	94.24	10.91	27.72	10.60	1.17
1986	5.57	0.44	96.28	10.94	32.43	10.76	1.30
1987	5.58	0.46	98.22	10.98	38.91	14.89	1.38
1988	5.61	0.57	99.96	10.94	37.38	12.83	1.43
1989	5.69	0.64	101.43	10.90	47.19	16.64	1.51
1990	5.78	0.69	102.83	10.92	50.68	16.64	1.59
1991	5.78	0.78	104.11	10.97	55.91	17.74	1.62
1992	5.81	0.84	105.67	10.97	83.66	30.30	1.59
1993	5.86	0.89	108.35	11.02	96.08	27.87	1.64
1994	5.90	0.90	111.78	10.27	104.56	35.19	1.68
1995	5.97	0.97	115.70	11.06	112.90	34.82	1.72
1996	6.49	1.01	118.58	11.08	116.65	38.63	1.93
1997	6.60	1.20	122.64	10.98	142.50	50.44	2.04
1998	6.64	1.30	127.85	11.03	150.58	50.44	2.31
1999	6.74	1.40	135.17	11.65	152.22	52.33	2.49
2000	6.87	1.49	140.27	11.93	150.29	50.84	2.47

注:铁路营业里程包括国家铁路、地方铁路、合资铁路。其中,地方铁路1978-1981年为延展里程数。

a) Length of railways in operation include national railways' local railways and joint-venture railways, in which, local railways in 1978-1981 are are extention length of the trunk lines.

15-5 运输线路质量

Quality of Transport Routes

指 标	Item	1978	1990	1995	1999	2000
铁路营业里程 (公里)	**Length of Railways in Operation (km)**	**48618**	**53378**	**54616**	**57923**	**58656**
#复线里程 (公里)	Double-Tracking Length (km)	7630	13024	16909	20925	21408
复线里程比重 (%)	Proportion (%)	15.7	24.4	31	36.1	36.5
#自动闭塞里程 (公里)	Automatic Blocking Length (km)	5981	10370	12910	17969.4	18317.8
自动闭塞里程比重(%)	Proportion (%)	12.3	19.4	23.6	31.0	31.2
公路线路里程 (公里)	**Length of Highways (km)**	**890236**	**1028348**	**1157009**	**1351691**	**1402698**
#等级公路里程 (公里)	Expressway and Class I to IV Highway		741040	910754	1156736	1216013
等级公路里程比重 (%)	Proportion (%)		72.1	78.7	85.6	86.7
内河航道里程 (公里)	**Length of Navigable Inland Waterways (km)**	**135952**	**109192**	**110562**	**116504**	**119325**
#等级航道里程 (公里)	Standard Waterways (km)			56587	60156	61367
等级航道里程比重(%)	Proportion (%)			51.2	51.6	51.4

15-6 客　运　量

Passenger Traffic

单位：万人　　(10 000 persons)

年　份 Year	客运量总计 Total	铁　路 Railways	国　家 National Railways	地　方 Local Railways	合　资 Joint-venture Railways	公　路 Highways	水　运 Waterways	民用航空 Civil Aviation
1952	24518	16352	16352			4559	3605	2
1957	63821	31262	31262			23772	8780	7
1962	122154	75003	74067	936		30737	16397	17
1965	96334	41245	40708	537		43693	11369	27
1970	130056	52455	51646	809		61812	15767	22
1975	192969	70465	69648	817		101350	21015	139
1978	253993	81491	80729	762		149229	23042	231
1979	289665	86389	85611	778		178618	24360	298
1980	341785	92204	91246	958		222799	26439	343
1981	384763	95219	94239	980		261559	27584	401
1982	428964	99922	98888	1034		300610	27987	445
1983	470614	106044	104946	1098		336965	27214	391
1984	530217	113353	112265	1088		390336	25974	554
1985	620206	112110	110913	1197		476486	30863	747
1986	688212	108579	107358	1221		544259	34377	997
1987	746422	112479	111414	1065		593682	38951	1310
1988	809592	122645	121595	1050		650473	35032	1442
1989	791376	113807	112798	1009		644508	31778	1283
1990	772682	95712	94888	824		648085	27225	1660
1991	806048	95080	94208	872		682681	26109	2178
1992	860855	99693	98788	905		731774	26502	2886
1993	996634	105458	104580	878		860719	27074	3383
1994	1092883	108738	108009	729		953940	26165	4038
1995	1172596	102745	102081	664		1040810	23924	5117
1996	1245356	94796	93550	612	634	1122110	22895	5555
1997	1326094	93308	91919	659	730	1204583	22573	5630
1998	1378717	95085	92991	629	1465	1257332	20545	5755
1999	1394413	100164	97725	528	1911	1269004	19151	6094
2000	1478573	105073	101847	519	2707	1347392	19386	6722

15-7　旅　客　周　转　量

Passenger-Kilometers

单位：亿人公里　　(100 million passenger-km)

年　份 Year	旅客周转量总计 Total	铁　路 Railways	国　家 National Railways	地　方 Local Railways	合　资 Joint-venture Railways	公　路 Highways	水　运 Waterways	民用航空 Civil Aviation
1952	248.0	200.6	200.6			22.6	24.5	0.2
1957	496.6	361.3	361.3			88.1	46.4	0.8
1962	1085.6	859.0	857.3	1.8		141.5	83.9	1.2
1965	697.0	479.0	477.8	1.2		168.2	47.4	2.5
1970	1031.1	718.2	715.9	2.3		240.1	71.0	1.8
1975	1434.6	954.1	952.6	1.5		374.5	90.6	15.4
1978	1743.1	1093.2	1090.8	2.4		521.3	100.6	27.9
1979	1968.5	1216.2	1213.7	2.4		603.3	114.0	35.0
1980	2281.3	1383.2	1380.4	2.8		729.5	129.1	39.6
1981	2499.6	1472.6	1469.9	2.8		839.0	137.8	50.2
1982	2742.7	1574.8	1572.0	2.8		963.9	144.5	59.5
1983	3095.0	1776.5	1773.4	3.1		1105.6	153.9	59.0
1984	3620.3	2046.4	2043.2	3.2		1336.9	153.5	83.5
1985	4436.4	2416.1	2412.5	3.6		1724.9	178.7	116.7
1986	4896.8	2586.7	2583.1	3.6		1981.7	182.1	146.3
1987	5411.5	2843.1	2840.0	3.1		2190.4	195.9	182.1
1988	6209.4	3260.3	3257.3	3.0		2528.2	203.9	217.0
1989	6074.6	3037.4	3034.4	3.0		2662.1	188.3	186.8
1990	5628.3	2612.6	2610.1	2.5		2620.3	164.9	230.5
1991	6178.4	2828.1	2824.8	3.2		2871.7	177.2	301.3
1992	6949.4	3152.2	3148.3	4.0		3192.6	198.4	406.1
1993	7858.1	3483.3	3479.4	3.9		3700.7	196.5	477.6
1994	8591.4	3636.1	3632.8	3.2		4220.3	183.5	551.6
1995	9001.9	3545.7	3542.6	3.1		4603.1	171.8	681.3
1996	9164.8	3347.6	3322.0	3.4	22.2	4908.8	160.6	747.8
1997	10055.5	3584.9	3543.5	4.7	36.6	5541.4	155.7	773.5
1998	10636.7	3773.4	3691.0	5.0	77.4	5942.8	120.3	800.2
1999	11299.8	4136.0	4046.3	4.4	85.3	6199.2	107.3	857.3
2000	12261.0	4532.6	4414.7	4.6	113.3	6657.4	100.5	970.5

15-8 货 运 量
Freight Traffic

单位：万吨 (10 000 tons)

年 份 Year	货运量总计 Total	铁 路 Railways	国家 National Railways	地方 Local Railways	合资 Joint-venture Railways	公 路 Highways	水 运 Waterways	民用航空 Civil Aviation	管道输油(气)量 Petroleum and Gas Pipelines
1952	31516	13217	13217			13158	5141	0.2	
1957	80365	27421	27421			37505	15438	0.8	
1962	85521	35261	34598	663		32794	17464	1.8	
1965	121083	49100	48358	742		48987	22993	2.7	
1970	150359	68132	66552	1580		56779	25444	3.7	
1975	202478	88955	86746	2209		72499	34987	4.7	6032
1978	248946	110119	107492	2627		85182	43292	6.4	10347
1979	537508	111893	109495	2398		371036	43229	8.0	11342
1980	546537	111279	108584	2695		382048	42676	8.9	10525
1981	523764	107673	104836	2837		363663	41490	9.4	10929
1982	548205	113495	111048	2447		379205	44329	10.2	11166
1983	576887	118784	116070	2714		401413	45058	11.6	11620
1984	716907	124074	121215	2859		533382	46892	15.0	12544
1985	745763	130709	127516	3193		538062	63322	19.5	13650
1986	853557	135635	132219	3416		620113	82962	22.4	14825
1987	948229	140653	136949	3704		711424	80979	29.9	15143
1988	982195	144948	140553	4395		732315	89281	32.8	15618
1989	988435	151489	146804	4685		733781	87493	31.0	15641
1990	970602	150681	146209	4472		724040	80094	37.0	15750
1991	985793	152893	147898	4995		733907	83370	45.2	15578
1992	1045899	157627	152317	5310		780941	92490	57.5	14783
1993	1115771	162663	156660	6003		840256	97938	69.4	14845
1994	1180273	163093	157155	5938		894914	107091	82.9	15092
1995	1234810	165855	159346	6509		940387	113194	101.1	15274
1996	1298312	170915	161678	7125	2112	983860	127430	115.0	15992
1997	1278087	172019	161880	7854	2285	976536	113406	124.7	16002
1998	1267200	164082	153208	8035	2839	976004	109555	140.1	17419
1999	1292650	167196	156881	7296	3019	990444	114608	170.0	20232
2000	1358124	178023	165498	8369	4156	1038813	122391	196.7	18700

注：从1979年起，公路运输包括社会车辆完成数量，从1984年起，还包括私营运输完成的数量。

a)Since 1979, the freight traffic by highways has included the quantities transported by trucks of non-highway departments. Since 1984, it has also included the quantities transported by private trucks.

15-9 货 物 周 转 量
Freight Ton-Kilometers

单位：亿吨公里 (100 million ton-km)

年 份 Year	货物周转量总计 Total	铁 路 Railways	国家 National Railways	地方 Local Railways	合资 Joint-venture Railways	公 路 Highways	水 运 Waterways	民用航空 Civil Aviation	管道输油(气)量 Petroleum and Gas Pipelines
1952	762	601.6	601.6			14.5	145.8	0.02	
1957	1810	1345.9	1345.9			48.0	415.6	0.08	
1962	2236	1721.1	1719.1	2.0		62.1	452.6	0.15	
1965	3464	2698.7	2696.4	2.3		95.1	670.2	0.25	
1970	4566	3496.0	3491.4	4.6		138.1	931.3	0.35	
1975	7296	4255.7	4246.1	9.5		202.7	2574.7	0.60	262
1978	9829	5345.2	5333.5	11.7		274.1	3779.2	0.97	430
1979	11385	5598.7	5588.7	10.0		745.0	4564.2	1.23	476
1980	12026	5716.9	5707.3	9.6		764.0	5052.8	1.41	491
1981	12143	5712.0	5701.3	10.7		780.0	5149.9	1.70	499
1982	13049	6119.9	6109.0	10.8		949.0	5477.1	1.98	501
1983	14054	6646.5	6634.5	12.1		1084.0	5787.6	2.29	534
1984	15694	7247.6	7234.8	12.9		1536.0	6335.0	3.11	572
1985	18365	8125.7	8111.6	14.1		1903.2	7729.3	4.15	603
1986	20148	8764.8	8750.1	14.7		2118.0	8647.9	4.81	612
1987	22228	9471.5	9455.7	15.8		2660.4	9465.1	6.50	625
1988	23825	9877.6	9860.2	17.4		3220.4	10070.4	7.30	650
1989	25591	10394.2	10373.0	21.2		3374.8	11186.8	6.90	629
1990	26207	10622.4	10601.2	21.2		3358.1	11591.9	8.20	627
1991	27986	10972.0	10948.1	23.9		3428.0	12955.4	10.10	621
1992	29218	11575.6	11548.5	27.0		3755.4	13256.2	13.42	617
1993	30510	11954.6	11923.4	31.2		4070.5	13860.8	16.61	608
1994	33261	12457.5	12426.2	31.4		4486.3	15686.6	18.59	612
1995	35730	12870.3	12836.0	34.2		4694.9	17552.2	22.30	590
1996	36528	13044.4	12921.9	48.6	122.5	5011.2	17862.5	24.93	585
1997	38368	13253.3	13046.4	50.7	156.2	5271.5	19235.0	29.10	579
1998	38046	12517.1	12261.5	50.7	204.8	5483.4	19405.8	33.45	606
1999	40496	12838.4	12577.9	37.6	222.9	5724.3	21263.0	42.30	628
2000	44452	13902.1	13336.1	43.6	522.4	6129.4	23734.2	50.27	636

注：从1979年起，公路运输包括社会车辆完成数量，从1984年起，还包括私营运输完成的数量。

a)Since 1979, the freight traffic by highways has included the volume transported by trucks of non-highway departments. Since 1984, it has also included the volume transported by private trucks.

15-10 旅客运输平均运距

Average Transport Distance of Passengers

单位：公里 (km)

年份 Year	总计 Total	铁路 Railways	公路 Highways	水运 Waterways	民用航空 Civil Aviation
1952	101	123	50	68	1200
1957	78	116	37	53	1143
1962	89	115	46	51	688
1965	72	116	38	42	919
1970	79	137	39	45	814
1975	74	135	37	43	1107
1978	69	134	35	44	1208
1979	68	141	34	47	1174
1980	67	150	33	49	1153
1981	65	155	32	50	1252
1982	64	158	32	52	1337
1983	66	168	33	57	1509
1984	68	181	34	59	1507
1985	72	216	36	58	1563
1986	71	238	36	53	1468
1987	72	253	37	50	1390
1988	77	266	39	58	1505
1989	77	267	41	59	1456
1990	73	273	40	61	1388
1991	77	297	42	68	1383
1992	81	316	44	75	1407
1993	79	330	43	73	1412
1994	79	334	44	70	1366
1995	77	345	44	72	1331
1996	74	353	44	70	1346
1997	76	384	46	69	1374
1998	77	406	47	59	1391
1999	82	413	49	56	1407
2000	83	431	49	52	1444

15-11 货物运输平均运距

Average Transport Distance of Freight

单位：公里 (km)

年份 Year	总计 Total	铁路 Railways	公路 Highways	水运 Waterways	管道 Petroleum and Gas Pipelines	民用航空 Civil Aviation
1952	242	452	11	284		1188
1957	225	502	13	269		1034
1962	263	488	19	259		836
1965	286	549	19	291		924
1970	304	513	24	366		954
1975	360	478	28	736	434	1292
1978	395	485	32	873	416	1521
1979	212	500	20	1052	420	1538
1980	220	514	20	1184	467	1573
1981	231	530	21	1241	457	1809
1982	238	539	25	1236	449	1941
1983	244	560	27	1284	460	1974
1984	219	584	29	1351	456	2073
1985	243	636	31	1216	442	2128
1986	236	646	34	1042	413	2143
1987	234	673	37	1174	413	2183
1988	243	681	44	1128	416	2226
1989	258	686	46	1281	402	2226
1990	270	705	46	1447	398	2218
1991	284	718	46	1554	399	2234
1992	279	734	48	1433	417	2330
1993	274	735	48	1415	409	2393
1994	282	791	50	1465	406	2241
1995	289	807	50	1551	386	2206
1996	282	766	51	1402	366	2168
1997	300	770	54	1696	362	2334
1998	300	763	56	1771	348	2388
1999	313	768	58	1855	310	2482
2000	327	781	59	1939	340	2556

15-12 各地区全社会客运量（2000年）
Passenger Traffic by Region (2000)

单位：万人　　(10 000 persons)

地区	Region	合计 Total	国家铁路 National Railways	地方铁路 Local Railways	合资铁路 Joint-venture Railways	公路 Highways	水运 Waterways
全国	**National Total**	**1478573**	**101847**	**519**	**2707**	**1347392**	**19386**
北京	Beijing	17610	4600	1		13009	
天津	Tianjin	3532	1709	…		1820	3
河北	Hebei	65609	5268			60341	
山西	Shanxi	31809	2953			28821	35
内蒙古	Inner Mongolia	23330	3237		32	20061	
辽宁	Liaoning	51694	10681	12		40385	616
吉林	Jilin	24017	5785			18170	62
黑龙江	Heilongjiang	49806	9793	104		39864	45
上海	Shanghai	5175	2980			1282	913
江苏	Jiangsu	107180	4953			101713	514
浙江	Zhejiang	124457	3670		853	116996	2938
安徽	Anhui	61982	2975	3	180	58026	798
福建	Fujian	67324	1364		196	65038	726
江西	Jiangxi	35527	3133			31966	428
山东	Shandong	65936	3798	79		61237	822
河南	Henan	83946	4671	167		79017	91
湖北	Hubei	62829	2880		6	58896	1047
湖南	Hunan	87455	5247	17	92	81005	1094
广东	Guangdong	108529	6316	34	740	99417	2022
广西	Guangxi	42209	2012	89	21	39321	766
海南	Hainan	19974	14			19392	568
重庆	Chongqing	56667	1257			53170	2240
四川	Sichuan	123677	3660	10	376	117108	2523
贵州	Guizhou	53116	2251			50397	468
云南	Yunnan	33251	1422	2		31586	241
西藏	Tibet	95				95	
陕西	Shaanxi	28494	2605		56	25600	234
甘肃	Gansu	12904	1088			11624	192
青海	Qinghai	3587	337			3250	
宁夏	Ningxia	5497	245			5252	
新疆	Xinjiang	14631	943		155	13533	
不分地区	Not Classified by Region	6722					

注：不分地区合计为民航完成数。

a) The total passenger traffic not classified by region is that completed by civil aviation.

15-13 各地区全社会旅客周转量（2000年）

Passenger-kilometers by Region (2000)

单位：亿人公里 (100 million passenger-km)

地区	Region	合计 Total	国家铁路 National Railways	地方铁路 Local Railways	合资铁路 Joint-venture Railways	公路 Highways	水运 Waterways
全国	**National Total**	**12261.0**	**4414.7**	**4.6**	**113.3**	**6657.4**	**100.5**
北京	Beijing	118.2	65.4	...		52.8	
天津	Tianjin	91.6	73.0	...		18.6	...
河北	Hebei	795.8	390.2			405.6	
山西	Shanxi	219.3	83.4			135.9	...
内蒙古	Inner Mongolia	200.1	82.5		1.3	116.3	
辽宁	Liaoning	495.8	325.2	...		159.9	10.7
吉林	Jilin	206.7	129.8			76.8	0.1
黑龙江	Heilongjiang	377.4	161.0	1.8		214.5	0.1
上海	Shanghai	73.6	35.4			34.1	4.1
江苏	Jiangsu	762.7	166.8			594.5	1.4
浙江	Zhejiang	609.8	127.6		23.8	449.5	8.9
安徽	Anhui	519.0	195.9	...	7.2	314.1	1.7
福建	Fujian	403.9	69.8		2.7	330.0	1.4
江西	Jiangxi	418.9	246.4			171.3	1.2
山东	Shandong	549.1	221.3	1.0		323.5	3.3
河南	Henan	759.4	404.3	1.0		353.8	0.3
湖北	Hubei	512.6	202.0		0.7	297.5	12.4
湖南	Hunan	714.6	388.6	...	4.1	318.4	3.5
广东	Guangdong	937.0	187.9	0.1	54.5	685.4	9.2
广西	Guangxi	451.5	99.8	0.6	0.6	347.9	2.5
海南	Hainan	60.5	0.1			57.7	2.6
重庆	Chongqing	242.7	41.4			170.1	31.1
四川	Sichuan	496.8	123.5	...	11.2	358.7	3.4
贵州	Guizhou	238.4	120.8			116.5	1.0
云南	Yunnan	205.5	33.5	...		171.2	0.8
西藏	Tibet	4.1				4.1	
陕西	Shaanxi	331.1	177.8		1.9	151.0	0.4
甘肃	Gansu	226.0	155.2			70.6	0.2
青海	Qinghai	29.7	11.5			18.2	
宁夏	Ningxia	52.1	20.7			31.4	
新疆	Xinjiang	186.8	74.1		5.3	107.4	
不分地区	Not Classified by Region	970.5					

注：不分地区合计为民航完成数。

a) The total passenger-kilometers not classified by region is that completed by civil aviation.

15-14 各地区全社会货运量 （2000年）

Freight Traffic by Region(2000)

单位：万吨　　　　(10 000 tons)

地区	Region	合计 Total	国家铁路 National Railways	地方铁路 Local Railways	合资铁路 Joint-venture Railways	公路 Highways	水运 Waterways
全国	**National Total**	**1358124**	**165498**	**8369**	**4156**	**1038813**	**122391**
北京	Beijing	30714	2612	92		28010	
天津	Tianjin	26026	2007	1071		18764	4184
河北	Hebei	75604	11397	1314		62321	572
山西	Shanxi	86357	28469	44		57813	31
内蒙古	Inner Mongolia	44434	9174	87	194	34979	
辽宁	Liaoning	80663	12523	534		64515	3091
吉林	Jilin	29450	5629	135		23640	46
黑龙江	Heilongjiang	53550	12701	376		39685	788
上海	Shanghai	46789	1055			28369	17365
江苏	Jiangsu	86266	4077	428		59056	22705
浙江	Zhejiang	75282	1921	50	382	55008	17921
安徽	Anhui	43942	6087	384	87	32740	4644
福建	Fujian	36110	2475		681	28709	4245
江西	Jiangxi	23502	2954	91		19276	1181
山东	Shandong	92499	10589	680		76778	4452
河南	Henan	60894	9658	731		50133	372
湖北	Hubei	39009	3938	169	14	28618	6270
湖南	Hunan	50964	4668	22		42868	3406
广东	Guangdong	84626	4522	473	950	59288	19393
广西	Guangxi	29642	2815	979	424	23514	1910
海南	Hainan	6675	331			4438	1906
重庆	Chongqing	26716	1613	65		23646	1392
四川	Sichuan	51477	5516	328	62	43326	2245
贵州	Guizhou	15615	3577			11684	354
云南	Yunnan	52022	2891	138	70	48789	134
西藏	Tibet	131				131	
陕西	Shaanxi	29201	3279		649	25200	73
甘肃	Gansu	23070	3235			19799	36
青海	Qinghai	4697	647			4050	
宁夏	Ningxia	6493	1784	178		4531	
新疆	Xinjiang	23134	3355		644	19135	
不分地区	Not Classified by Region	22572					3675

注：不分地区合计中，包括民航、管道及中国远洋运输集团总公司海外公司完成数。

a)The freight traffic not classified by region includes that completed by enterprises directly under the departments of civil aviation, pipelines and abroad companies under China Ocean Shipping (Group) Company.

15-15 各地区全社会货物周转量（2000年）

Freight Ton-kilometers by region (2000)

单位：亿吨公里 (100 million ton-km)

地区	Region	合计 Total	国家铁路 National Railways	地方铁路 Local Railways	合资铁路 Joint-venture Railways	公路 Highways	水运 Waterways
全国	**National Total**	**44452.3**	**13336.1**	**43.6**	**522.4**	**6129.4**	**23734.2**
北京	Beijing	363.1	280.3	0.1		82.6	
天津	Tianjin	4621.9	247.3	5.4		62.7	4306.6
河北	Hebei	2323.9	1495.6	4.9		555.4	268.0
山西	Shanxi	866.0	595.8	0.1		270.0	...
内蒙古	Inner Mongolia	943.2	658.3	...	73.0	211.9	
辽宁	Liaoning	1745.5	962.4	1.3		209.4	572.4
吉林	Jilin	492.1	406.0	0.3		85.6	0.3
黑龙江	Heilongjiang	918.2	732.5	4.2		161.9	19.5
上海	Shanghai	6286.9	43.6			56.4	6187.0
江苏	Jiangsu	1459.3	371.3	0.9		340.7	746.4
浙江	Zhejiang	1199.8	167.7	0.1	19.4	280.0	732.6
安徽	Anhui	1050.9	606.8	1.3	8.8	274.7	159.3
福建	Fujian	929.2	128.8		23.7	195.0	581.7
江西	Jiangxi	645.0	459.0	0.3	2.7	147.2	35.8
山东	Shandong	4033.0	795.1	4.4		405.8	2827.8
河南	Henan	1553.5	1172.4	6.4		363.9	10.7
湖北	Hubei	1081.1	541.1	1.3	0.7	232.7	305.3
湖南	Hunan	1066.4	624.6	0.2		297.8	143.8
广东	Guangdong	3276.9	211.2	2.2	326.7	487.2	2249.6
广西	Guangxi	707.0	401.3	6.7	13.5	209.4	76.0
海南	Hainan	310.0	2.0			39.1	269.0
重庆	Chongqing	289.0	110.6	0.2		72.5	105.7
四川	Sichuan	622.9	407.2	1.2	15.0	187.7	11.8
贵州	Guizhou	404.1	334.1			65.9	4.1
云南	Yunnan	481.9	180.8	0.7	2.8	296.7	1.0
西藏	Tibet	13.5				13.5	
陕西	Shaanxi	573.0	418.5		10.6	143.6	0.3
甘肃	Gansu	639.5	530.1			109.4	0.1
青海	Qinghai	86.6	50.0			36.6	
宁夏	Ningxia	205.2	147.1	1.2		56.9	
新疆	Xinjiang	457.3	254.7		25.4	177.2	
不分地区	Not Classified by Region	4806.4					4120.0

注：不分地区合计中，包括民航、管道及中国远洋运输集团总公司海外公司完成数。

a)The freight ton-kilometers not classified by region includes that completed by enterprises directly under the departments of civil aviation, pipelines and abroad companies under China Ocean Shipping (Group) Company.

15-16 国家营业铁路基本情况

Basic Statistics on National Railways in Operation

项　目	Item	1978	1985	1990	1995	1999	2000
营业里程　（公里）	**Length of Railways in Operation (km)**	**48618**	**52119**	**53378**	**54616**	**57923**	**58656**
正式营业	In Formal Operation	45539	49433	50310	50866	51166	51262
临时营业	In Temporary Operation	3079	2686	3068	3750	6756	7394
正式营业里程比重　(%)	Proportion of the Length in Formal Operation	93.7	94.8	94.3	93.1	88.3	87.4
复线里程　（公里）	**Double-Tracking Length (km)**	**7630**	**9989**	**13024**	**16909**	**20925**	**21408**
占营业里程比重　(%)	As Percentage of the Length of Railways in Operation	15.7	19.2	24.4	31.0	36.1	36.5
电气化线路里程　（公里）	**Length of Electrified Railways (km)**	**1030**	**4151**	**6941**	**9703**	**14025**	**14864**
占营业里程比重　(%)	As Percentage of Railways in Operation	2.1	8.0	13.0	17.8	24.2	25.3
内燃机牵引线路里程（公里）	**Length of Diesel Engine Routes (km)**	**6550**	**10822**	**16097**	**24749**	**36859**	**39497**
占营业里程比重　(%)	As Percentage of Railways in Operation	13.5	20.8	30.2	45.3	63.6	67.3
调度集中里程　（公里）	**Length under Centralized Traffic Control**		**1307**	**1169**	**1226**	**1401**	**1200**
占营业里程比重　(%)	As Percentage of Railways in Operation		2.5	2.2	2.2	2.4	2.0
自动闭塞里程　（公里）	**Automatic Blocking Length (km)**	**5981**	**6921**	**10370**	**12910**	**17969**	**18318**
占营业里程比重　(%)	As Percentage of Railways in Operation	12.3	13.3	19.4	23.6	31.2	31.2
半自动闭塞里程　（公里）	**Semi-automatic Blocking Length (km)**	**34759**	**42625**	**38832**	**40859**	**40788**	**41695**
占营业里程比重　(%)	As Percentage of Railways in Operation	71.5	81.8	72.7	74.8	70.4	71.1
无缝线路里程　（公里）	**Length of Continuous Welded Rail (km)**	**6530**	**10439**	**14644**	**21854**	**27900**	**29975**
占正线里程比重　(%)	As Percentage of the Trunk Lines	12.2	16.7	21.7	40.0	34.7	51.1
有电气集中的车站　（个）	**Number of Stations with Electric Interlocking (unit)**	**1336**	**2320**	**3535**	**4587**	**5192**	**5232**
占营业车站比重　(%)	As Percentage of Railways Stations in Operation	27.7	46.9	62.9	73.9	90.1	90.4

15-17 铁路机车年末数

Number of Railway Locomotives at the Year-end

单位：台　　　　(unit)

项　目	Item	1978	1985	1990	1995	1999	2000
国家铁路	**Number of Locomotives Owned by National Railways**	**9854**	**11772**	**13592**	**15146**	**14480**	**14472**
蒸汽机车	Steam Locomotives	7828	7674	6279	4347	1015	601
#前进型	Qianjin Model	2772	4429	4188	2985	501	261
建设型	Jianshe Model	1092	1216	1644	1329	514	340
内燃机车	Diesel Locomotives	1805	3511	5680	8282	10121	10355
#东风 4 型	Dongfeng Model IV	326	955	2351	4362	6070	5623
电力机车	Electric Locomotives	221	587	1633	2517	3344	4413
#韶山 1 型	Shaoshan Model I	154	505	816	814	800	800
地方铁路	**Number of Locomotives Owned by Local Railways**	**325**	**368**	**378**	**398**	**355**	**327**
蒸汽机车	Steam Locomotives	211	239	253	260	199	159
内燃机车	Diesel Locomotives	114	129	125	129	156	168
合资铁路	**Number of Locomotives Owned by Joint-venture Railways**					**361**	**454**
蒸汽机车	Steam Locomotives					182	151
内燃机车	Diesel Locomotives					179	303

15-18 国家铁路客、货车拥有量

Number of Railway Passenger Coaches and Freight Cars Owned

项　目	Item	1978	1985	1990	1995	1999	2000
客　车　　（辆）	**Passenger Coaches　(coach)**	**14844**	**20872**	**27261**	**32404**	**34535**	**35989**
软卧车	Soft Berth Coaches	435	679	1061	1537	1975	2055
硬卧车	Hard Berth Coaches	2155	2633	4351	7607	9443	10139
软座车	Soft Seat Coaches	78	260	330	574	756	764
硬座车	Hard Seat Coaches	8888	13700	17503	18076	17156	17571
软硬座车	Soft and Hard Seat Coaches	131	114	63	35	25	25
餐　车	Dining Cars	820	1221	1520	1695	1774	1847
行李邮政车	Luggage and Post Cars	1149	1498	1686	1949	2107	2144
公务车	Business Cars	85	87	77	87	69	69
简易及代用客车	Simple and Substitute Cars	528	79	42	9		
其　他	Others	575	601	628	835	1230	1375
货　车　　（辆）	**Freight Cars　(coach)**	**250138**	**300886**	**364966**	**432731**	**436236**	**439943**
按车型分	Grouped by Type of Car						
棚　车	Covered Cars	40054	52667	66668	80437	89935	92569
敞　车	Open Cars	150745	185684	232999	268179	248243	252977
平　车	Flat Cars	20747	18753	18726	27461	28559	24685
毒品车	Hazardous Materials Cars			1229	1580	1578	1578
罐　车	Tank Cars	33045	31837	33646	37119	37486	37778
保温车	Refrigerator Cars	2439	3991	5150	7030	7988	7909
其　他	Others	3108	7944	6548	10925	22447	22447
按载重量分	Grouped by Capacity of Car						
20吨及以下	20 Tons and Under	1400	1476	949	1458		
25-40吨	25-40 Tons	44409	21520	8699	8786	8005①	7765
50吨	50 Tons	106792	104456	92442	48287	15857	15799
51-59吨	51-59 Tons	18068	16544	15500	27951		
60吨	60 Tons	72453	153198	238680	342086	315984	307521
65吨	65 Tons	3380	1571	6825	3546	90956②	103431
73吨及以上	73 Tons and Over	294	306	329	385	5434③	5427
其他	Others	3342	1815	1542	232		
货车总标记载重量（万吨）	**Total Loading Capacity of Freight Cars　(10 000 tons)**	**1230.2**	**1612.5**	**2055.3**	**2502.9**	**2595.8**	**2619.9**
平均每辆车标记载重量（吨）	**Average Marked Loading Capacity per Car　(ton)**	**49.8**	**53.9**	**56.6**	**57.9**	**59.5**	**59.6**

注：1997年起货车按标记载重量统计，分组与以前年份相比有所调整。带①号的数据含20吨及以下货车。带②号的数据是载重量61吨货车。带③号的数据是载重量70吨及以上货车（以后各年相同）。

a) Statistics on freight cars are based on marked loading capacity of cars since 1997, resulting in the adjustment of grouping of cars. Data marked ① refer to cars with a loading capacity of 20 tons and less, data marked ② refer to cars with a loading capacity of 61 tons, and ③ refer to cars with a loading capacity of 70 tons and over. The same as in the following years.

15-19 铁路运输固定资产情况

Fixed Assets of Railway Transport

单位：亿元　(100 million yuan)

项　目	Item	1985	1990	1995	1999	2000
固定资产原值	**Original Value of Fixed Assets**	**791.5**	**1253.9**	**3613.6**	**5414.8**	**5268.8**
#生产用	Fixed Assets for Productive Purpose	714.6	1116.1	3526.0	5349.8	5205.7
#机车车辆	Locomotives, Coaches and Freight Cars	172.1	312.1	776.9	1207.8	816.8
线　路	Lines	408.3	545.2	1850.7	2452.3	2854.4
通信线路	Communications Lines	12.4	19.5	43.2	66.3	0.2
通信信号设备	Communications & Signaling Equipment	18.6	35.4	80.8	166.5	153.6
房屋及建筑物	Buildings	56.9	107.4	489.9	826.2	683.1
机械动力设备	Machinery and Power Equipment	28.6	47.7	84.0	127.1	143.6
传导设备	Conduction Equipment	13.5	34.6	72.5	125.1	153.4
非生产用	Fixed Assets for Non-productive Purposes	59.7	106.8			
未使用	Unused Fixed Assets	12.7	24.5	73.2	57.3	56.3
不需用	Non-required Fixed Assets	0.7	1.0	2.1	1.8	1.4
封存及租出的	Sealed-up for Safekeeping and Leased	3.6	4.4	12.3	6.0	5.3
土　地	Land	0.3	0.3			
固定资产净值	**Net Value of Fixed Assets**	**589.5**	**889.3**	**2409.4**	**3817.7**	**3830.1**
固定资产折旧	**Depreciation of Fixed Assets**	**202.1**	**364.6**	**1204.1**	**1597.1**	**1438.7**

注：1995年起生产用固定资产统计口径变更为在用固定资产，原非生产用固定资产和土地包括其中。

a)Since 1995, the fixed assets for productive purposes have changed to be the fixed assets in use, and included land and the fixed assets for non-productive purpose.

15-20 铁路货物运输量（按货类分）

Railway Freight Traffic by Category of Cargo

本表统计范围为国家铁路。

The coverage of this table is national railways, excluding local railways.

项　目	Item	1999 货运量（万吨） Freight Traffic (10 000 tons)	1999 货物周转量（百万吨公里） Freight Ton-kilometers (million ton-kilometers)	1999 平均运距（公里） Average Transport Distance (km)	2000 货运量（万吨） Freight Traffic (10 000 tons)	2000 货物周转量（百万吨公里） Freight Ton-kilometers (million ton-kilometers)	2000 平均运距（公里） Average Transport Distance (km)
总　计	**Total**	**156881**	**1257789**	**802**	**165498**	**1333606**	**806**
煤	Coal	64917	357053	550	68545	380605	555
焦　炭	Coke	3890	32443	834	4725	40215	851
石　油	Petroleum	8703	77396	889	9391	81599	869
钢　铁	Steel and Iron	10453	110642	1058	11537	124445	1079
金属矿石	Metal Ores	12279	57907	472	13022	61646	473
非金属矿石	Nonmetal Ores	8158	45642	559	8138	47265	581
矿建材料	Mineral Building Materials	10344	53025	513	9671	49315	510
水　泥	Cement	3861	16229	420	3900	16739	429
木　材	Timber	3360	56971	1696	3436	58808	1712
化肥和农药	Chemical Fertilizers and Pesticides	5414	61933	1144	5189	61186	1179
粮　食	Grain	6464	91614	1417	7935	101257	1276
棉　花	Cotton	227	6892	3036	233	6472	2772
盐	Salt	1160	8535	736	1245	9383	753
其　他	Others	17651	281507	1595	18531	294671	1590

15-21 国家铁路平均每日装车数
Daily Average Number of Freight Car Loading

单位：车 (car)

年份 Year	合计 Total	# 煤 Coal	# 石油 Petroleum	# 钢铁 Steel and Iron	# 矿物性建筑材料 Mineral Building Materials	# 粮食 Grain
1952	12334	3911	116	450	1719	1251
1957	21259	6973	254	709	3740	1217
1962	23893	11145	615	792	1795	1136
1965	32784	11299	1013	1485	4537	1342
1970	42264	14685	2370	1912	5088	1249
1975	51789	17376	3685	2495	7595	1263
1978	62234	21595	3641	3425	9301	1335
1979	62789	21917	3521	3671	8946	1502
1980	61298	21627	3294	3399	8256	1590
1981	58620	21176	2965	3060	7167	1768
1982	61300	22262	3010	3230	8269	1773
1983	63149	23008	3214	3418	8106	1803
1984	64856	23965	3333	3653	7839	1796
1985	67228	25333	3448	3963	7765	2247
1986	68911	25744	3694	4446	7268	2285
1987	70004	25874	3863	4376	7056	2649
1988	70398	26513	3774	4035	7044	2580
1989	72919	28479	3785	4010	6936	2490
1990	72368	29323	3811	4165	5858	2530
1991	72911	29103	3823	4127	5628	2878
1992	74109	29523	3880	4146	5564	2919
1993	76306	30039	4059	4756	5959	3022
1994	75664	30183	3969	4636	5168	3430
1995	76416	30754	4230	4406	4818	2985
1996	76895	32720	4195	4426	4533	2670
1997	76948	31876	4419	4630	4570	3196
1998	72429	28757	4455	4700	4581	2529
1999	74038	28987	4893	4849	4666	2950
2000	77645	30582	5220	5352	4325	3591

15-22 国家铁路货车平均静载重
Average Static Load of Freight Cars

单位：吨/车 (ton/car)

年份 Year	合计 Total	# 煤 Coal	# 石油 Petroleum	# 钢铁 Steel and Iron	# 矿物性建筑材料 Mineral Building Materials	# 粮食 Grain
1952	28.9	32.5	27.3	27.8	32.5	32.0
1957	34.7	38.3	35.0	37.2	38.8	39.2
1962	39.0	42.3	39.5	41.4	43.0	40.5
1965	39.8	44.6	40.4	42.6	44.0	43.7
1970	42.5	46.9	42.8	43.5	47.2	45.5
1975	45.4	49.4	44.3	46.3	48.6	47.8
1978	46.9	50.6	46.3	47.5	49.9	50.3
1979	47.4	51.2	46.2	47.9	50.8	51.4
1980	48.0	52.5	46.3	49.0	52.6	54.2
1981	48.6	52.9	46.1	49.6	52.7	52.8
1982	49.2	53.6	46.1	50.2	53.2	53.3
1983	49.9	54.4	46.1	50.4	53.8	53.8
1984	50.6	55.1	46.1	51.0	54.5	54.2
1985	51.6	55.7	46.2	51.9	55.3	54.6
1986	52.2	56.2	46.3	52.8	56.0	55.3
1987	53.2	57.2	46.5	53.6	56.7	56.6
1988	54.1	57.9	46.7	54.2	57.4	57.3
1989	54.8	58.3	46.8	54.6	57.6	57.8
1990	55.0	58.5	47.0	55.0	57.9	58.3
1991	55.2	58.7	46.7	55.6	58.0	58.5
1992	55.8	59.1	47.1	56.4	58.3	58.9
1993	56.1	59.3	47.4	57.1	58.5	59.1
1994	56.6	59.6	47.6	57.8	59.0	59.3
1995	56.8	59.9	47.6	58.2	59.2	59.4
1996	57.1	60.0	47.5	58.5	59.4	59.6
1997	57.3	60.2	48.0	58.6	59.4	59.6
1998	57.6	60.8	48.6	58.9	59.7	59.7
1999	57.7	61.1	49.2	59.1	59.9	59.6
2000	57.9	61.1	49.8	58.9	59.7	59.7

15-23 铁路主要干线客货运输量（2000年）

Passenger and Freight Traffic of Principal Trunk Railways (2000)

线路名称	Name	客运量（万人）Passenger Traffic (10 000 persons)	旅客周转量（百万人公里）Passenger-kilometers (million passenger-km)	货运量（万吨）Freight Traffic (10 000 tons)	货物周转量（百万吨公里）Freight Ton-kilometers (million ton-km)
京　沈	Beijing-Shenyang	4554	21174	3462	83660
哈　大	Harbin-Dalian	7579	16117	3450	57566
津　沪	Tianjin-Shanghai	9043	47426	4627	101853
沪　杭	Shanghai-Hangzhou	2010	5517	167	6868
京　广	Beijing-Guangzhou	14222	80659	7385	124793
南北同蒲	Datong-Taiyuan-Fenglingdu	944	4382	9287	23782
太焦柳	Taiyuan-Jiaozuo-Liuzhou	1580	7807	7260	53569
京　九	Beijing-Kowloon	3858	19128	1404	54565
兰　新	Lanzhou-Urumqi	1482	14102	4063	56970
滨　洲	Harbin-Manzhouli	1786	3935	2772	19144
滨　绥	Harbin-Suifenhe	931	2135	1123	15236
京　包	Beijing-Baotou	1620	5471	5163	47122
石　太	Shijiazhuang-Taiyuan	1002	2004	3441	19061
石　德	Shijiazhuang-Dezhou	275	1400	382	11119
浙　赣	Hangzhou-Zhuzhou	3297	21982	2094	38174
陇　海	Lianyungang-Lanzhou	3822	32719	5400	86915
胶　济	Qingdao-Jinan	1330	5250	3311	20970
京　秦	Beijing-Qinhuangdao	122	3013	524	7127
新　石	Xinxiang-Rizhao	276	930	1708	13793
宝　成	Baoji-Chengdu	1639	8800	743	15582
成　昆	Chengdu-Kunming	1155	4443	3110	20998
大　秦	Datong-Qinhuangdao	41	231	443	44598
湘　黔	Zhuzhou-Guiying	1122	11440	1402	23958
贵　昆	Guiyang-Kunming	980	3971	1335	15890

15-24 铁路主要车站旅客发送量

Number of Passengers Dispatched from Principal Railway Stations

单位：万人 (10 000 persons)

车站名称	Name of Railway Station	1994	1995	1996	1997	1998	1999	2000
哈尔滨	Harbin	1379	1389	1286	1301	1346	1371	1252
沈　阳	Shenyang	1673	1503	1399	1280	1217	1168	1168
长　春	Changchun	991	1040	952	932	925	973	1062
鞍　山	Anshan	410	366	854	682	293	300	295
本　溪	Benxi	1074	977	854	682	599	569	574
锦　州	Jinzhou	556	518	438	401	416	436	421
吉　林	Jilin	513	482	405	400	396	438	397
北　京	Beijing	2529	2297	1541	1656	1691	1868	1997
北京南	Southern Beijing	708	648	566	443	403	366	382
天　津	Tianjin	960	937	876	876	925	1006	1004
石家庄	Shijiazhuang	745	680	657	722	732	817	864
太　原	Taiyuan	815	787	700	684	642	661	679
郑　州	Zhengzhou	893	962	992	1095	1170	1291	1333
武　昌	Wuchang	750	733	719	747	748	772	821
洛　阳	Luoyang	345	318	298	303	318	339	353
西　安	Xi'an	1075	1037	959	1023	1031	1096	1063
济　南	Jinan	370	373	549	597	645	658	702
徐　州	Xuzhou	385	281	371	619	653	674	632
南　京	Nanjing	818	768	766	776	787		897
蚌　埠	Bengbu	376	360	358	351	358	406	412
镇　江	Zhenjiang	377	342	313	310	309	333	327
常　州	Changzhou	639	604	439	460	465	516	4524
无　锡	Wuxi	820	813	743	662	633	702	704
苏　州	Suzhou	725	711	671	636	625	685	703
上　海	Shanghai	2502	2534	2492	2516	2430	2536	2595
杭　州	Hangzhou	889	893	815	395	1008	1074	726
南　昌	Nanchang	454	461	508	666	747	807	795
广　州	Guangzhou	1549	1560	1465	1469	1576	1728	1776
深　圳	Shenzhen	950	789	812	644	718	817	758
柳　州	Liuzhou	439	413	380	386	366	360	335
成　都	Chengdu	975	903	809	803	845	960	1042
重　庆	Chongqing	506	400	440	560	581	695	651
贵　阳	Guiyang	482	511	540	557	571	627	598
兰　州	Lanzhou	366	365	368	387	408	439	444
乌鲁木齐	Urumqi	293	297	312	352	403	411	399

15-25 铁路主要车站货物发送量

Volume of Freight Dispatched from Principal Railway Stations

单位：万吨 (10 000 tons)

车站名称	Name of Railway Station	1994	1995	1996	1997	1998	1999	2000
七台河	Qitaihe	1025	1046	1143	1289	1273	1317	1338
恒山	Hengshan	509	543	561	481	386	374	371
竣德	Junde	519	508	550	584	404	526	418
鹤岗	Hegang	779	746	649	821	656	725	822
双鸭山	Shuangyashan	735	643	560	669	621	722	751
大官屯	Daguantun	981	861	767	653	643	689	657
灵山	Lingshan	1234	1050	1008	910	909	957	999
甘井子	Ganjingzi	490	438	489	488	502	470	464
本溪	Benxi	436	419	410	384	377	356	405
阜新	Fuxin	532	557	640	686	602	503	531
白云鄂博	Baiyun'ebo	865	995	939	969	860	808	739
石景山南	Southern Shijingshan	415	474	419	517	564	522	602
古冶	Guye	974	822	896	970	837	847	866
唐山	Tangshan	461	431	406	429	418	394	404
沙河驿镇	Shaheyizhen	993	994	883	895	920	826	877
秦皇岛南	Southern Qinhuangdao	292	461	408	331	406	381	398
白羊墅	Baiyangshu	890	1017	1025	1029	856	959	986
云岗	Yungang	534	546	573	557	436	438	458
云岗西	Western Yungang	1073	1007	1051	1087	839	752	846
新高山	Xingaoshan	1057	1224	1198	1040	905	868	942
介休	Jiexiu	509	535	540	504	522	488	574
鹤壁北	Northern Hebi	300	269	292	289	261	316	331
晋城北	Northern Jincheng	1217	1272	1259	1100	1168	1265	1293
长治北	Northern Changzhi	674	637	684	947	939	947	952
蜜县	Mixian	628	654	645	452	370	342	345
平顶山东	Eastern Pindingshan	1990	2084	2174	2119	2013	1953	1984
武昌东	Eastern Wuchang	576	535	549	553	532	454	429
邹县	Zouxian	468	475	532	525	650	704	691
青龙山	Qinglongshan	480	486	470	386	380	455	502
茂名	Maoming	402	447	415	461	433	388	544

15-26 铁路运输主要财务指标

Financial Indicators of Railway Transport

单位：亿元 (100 million yuan)

指标	Item	1985	1990	1995	1999	2000
运输总收入	**Total Transport Revenue**	**213.9**	**411.1**	**632.1**	**998.9**	**1097.4**
客运收入	Revenue from Passenger Traffic	45.5	110.9	201.5	332.0	369.3
货运收入	Revenue from Freight Traffic	157.6	272.1	357.6	522.4	566.6
行李包裹收入	Revenue from Luggage	3.8	8.6	15.8	30.2	38.1
邮运收入	Revenue from Postal Delivery	0.6	1.0	1.9	2.6	3.5
其他收入	Other Revenue	6.5	18.4	55.2	66.0	119.9
运输总成本	**Total Transport Costs**	**111.5**	**253.9**	**640.6**	**902.9**	**951.1**
工资	Wages and Salaries	15.7	42.8	139.6	201.1	197.4
材料	Materials	13.6	32.6	85.5	90.4	769.3
燃料	Fuel	20.1	38.5	101.1	219.0	140.8
电力	Electricity	2.4	9.0	32.2	55.7	61.7
折旧	Depreciation	50.2	108.8	73.7	318.3	351.4
其他	Other Costs	9.4	22.3	208.5	127.3	122.9
营业外收支净额	**Non-operating Net Revenue or Expenditure**	**10.0**	**24.1**	**33.4**		**47.1**
应缴税金	**Taxes Payable**		**21.6**	**32.3**	**33.7**	**37.8**
实现利润	**Profits**	**64.0**	**113.1**	**-64.1**	**27.2**	**33.8**

15-27 铁路运输技术经济主要指标

Principal Economic and Technical Indicators of Railway Transport

指标	Item	1996	1997	1998	1999	2000
货运机车日产量（万吨公里）	Average Daily Ton-kilometers of Freight Locomotives (10 000 ton-km)	93.0	94.5	94.5	97.0	99.4
蒸汽机车	Steam Locomotives	53.9	50.5	44.3	42.0	42.3
内燃机车	Diesel Locomotives	101.7	101.5	98.6	98.8	101.1
电力机车	Electric Locomotives	100.3	99.3	99.0	99.5	99.6
货运机车平均牵引总重（吨）	Average Total Tonnage of Freight Locomotives (ton)	2603	2632	2633	2654	2676
蒸汽机车	Steam Locomotives	1984	1936	1804	1720	1712
内燃机车	Diesel Locomotives	2632	2642	2604	2596	2608
电力机车	Electric Locomotives	2865	2856	2861	2870	2869
货运机车日车公里（公里）	Daily Distance per Freight Locomotive (km)	422	428	430	438	443
客运机车日车公里（公里）	Daily Distance per Passenger Locomotive (km)	491	504	507	520	521
蒸汽机车每万吨公里耗煤（公斤）	Coal Consumption of Steam Locomotives (kg/10 000 ton-km)	141.9	155.6	175.8	206.6	207.8
内燃机车每万吨公里耗油（公斤）	Oil Consumption of Diesel Locomotives (kg/10 000 ton-km)	24.6	25.2	26.0	26.2	25.8
电力机车每万吨公里耗电（千瓦小时）	Electricity Consumption of Electric Locomotives (kwh/10 000 ton-km)	109.9	111.7	112.7	113.6	113.2
货物列车出发正点率（%）	Punctuality Rate of Freight Trains at Departure(%)	95.2	95.5	96.0	96.8	97.2
货物列车运行正点率（%）	Punctuality Rate of Freight Trains in Running (%)	94.6	94.6	96.0	96.6	96.8
旅客列车出发正点率（%）	Punctuality Rate of Passenger Trains at Departure (%)	99.4	99.3	99.6	99.8	99.8
旅客列车运行正点率（%）	Punctuality Rate of Passenger Trains in Running(%)	82.5	93.5	94.4	97.3	97.1
旅客列车技术速度(公里/小时)	Technical Speed of Passenger Trains (km/hr)	58.7	62.8	64.2	65.7	66.6
旅客列车旅行速度(公里/小时)	Travelling Speed of Passenger Trains (km/hr)	49.5	53.3	54.5	56.0	56.8
客运密度（万人公里/公里）	Density of Passenger Transport (10 000 passenger-km/km)	586.1	615.6	641.0	699.0	753.0
每百万旅客人公里拥有座	Number of Coaches per 1 Million Passengers (coach)					
货物列车技术速度(公里/小时)	Technical Speed of Freight Trains (km/hr)	44.1	45.3	45.8	46.5	46.4
货物列车旅行速度(公里/小时)	Running Speed of Freight Trains (km/hr)	30.4	31.4	31.8	31.6	31.8
货运密度（万吨公里/公里）	Density of Freight Transport(10 000 ton-km/km)	2279.9	2266.3	2129.4	2171.5	2273.6
每百万货物吨公里拥有货车数	Number of Freight Cars per million Ton-km					
货车周转时间（天）	Turning Around Time of Freight Cars (day)	4.48	4.57	5.48	5.50	5.39
一次货物作业时间（小时）	Handling Time of Freight (hour)	17.8	18.1	22.8	23.4	23.1
货车中转停留时间（小时）	Transfer Waiting Time per Car (hour)	4.6	4.6	5.2	4.9	4.7
货车静载重(准轨)（吨）	Static Load of Freight Cars (Standard Gauge) (ton)	57.2	57.3	57.6	57.7	57.9
货车载重力利用率（%）	Utilization Rate of Loading Capacity of Freight Cars (%)	98.3	96.5	96.6	96.8	97.1

15-28 民用车辆拥有量

Number of Civil Motor Vehicles Owned

年份 地区	Year Region	民用汽车总计(万辆) Total Number (10 000 units)	载客汽车 Passenger Vehicles 辆数(万辆) Number (10 000 units)	客位(万客位) Number of Seats (10 000 seats)	载货汽车 Trucks 辆数(万辆) Number (10 000 units)	#普通载货汽车 Ordinary Trucks	吨位(万吨) Capacity (10 000 tons)	#普通载货汽车 Ordinary Trucks
	1978	135.84	25.90		100.17			
	1979	155.49	39.68		114.39			
	1980	178.29	35.08		129.90			
	1981	199.14	40.57		144.09			
	1982	215.75	44.18		156.75			
	1983	232.63	47.78		169.44			
	1984	260.41	56.28		188.37			
	1985	321.12	79.45	1404.93	223.20		929.25	
	1986	361.95	96.61	1642.15	246.57		1038.60	
	1987	408.07	111.46	1800.41	281.21	272.60	1236.62	1176.69
	1988	464.39	130.38	2041.12	317.85	308.89	1349.87	1292.61
	1989	511.32	146.43	2186.37	346.37	336.43	1480.76	1429.46
	1990	551.36	162.19	2372.64	368.48	357.57	1519.40	1460.84
	1991	606.11	185.24	2631.56	398.62	386.67	1633.11	1572.67
	1992	691.74	226.16	3103.63	441.45	427.86	1834.60	1760.37
	1993	817.58	285.98	3940.08	501.00	483.27	2114.27	2006.34
	1994	941.95	349.74	4843.91	560.33	543.86	2396.33	2280.30
	1995	1040.00	417.90	5213.27	585.43	568.58	2370.93	2257.07
	1996	1100.08	488.02	6191.82	575.03	558.16	2280.62	2167.10
	1997	1219.09	580.56	7269.93	601.23	582.45	2287.50	2167.97
	1998	1319.30	654.83	7621.47	627.89	609.31	2408.94	2280.74
	1999	1452.94	740.23	9239.81	676.95	655.74	2730.42	2581.87
	2000	1608.91	853.73	10213.05	716.32	697.59	2920.26	2775.35
北京	Beijing	104.12	82.16	954.63	20.61	19.60	72.40	60.13
天津	Tianjin	47.89	25.39	231.42	21.31	20.61	72.03	66.92
河北	Hebei	104.13	50.20	1003.94	52.43	50.85	269.17	254.26
山西	Shanxi	55.01	25.35	249.17	27.82	27.47	160.35	157.74
内蒙古	Inner Mongolia	36.11	18.82	158.13	16.70	16.25	88.34	82.35
辽宁	Liaoning	78.61	43.79	645.43	33.23	31.74	247.68	234.25
吉林	Jilin	40.42	22.31	401.57	16.84	16.29	101.34	97.77
黑龙江	Heilongjiang	54.52	31.45	527.47	21.48	20.54	91.56	82.15
上海	Shanghai	49.19	32.69	282.45	14.38	13.86	44.46	40.41
江苏	Jiangsu	74.51	41.16	449.96	31.47	30.54	114.37	109.15
浙江	Zhejiang	68.06	32.32	272.28	34.46	33.78	88.99	82.95
安徽	Anhui	38.67	18.79	290.39	19.23	19.02	71.26	69.83
福建	Fujian	32.13	15.69	152.25	15.80	15.42	45.85	44.39
江西	Jiangxi	24.70	10.08	153.71	13.11	13.01	51.99	51.38
山东	Shandong	112.30	52.95	398.35	55.10	53.61	161.97	155.25
河南	Henan	84.73	45.61	785.63	37.55	36.37	165.42	158.79
湖北	Hubei	47.55	24.69	273.32	21.72	21.14	63.57	60.68
湖南	Hunan	46.10	22.06	263.53	23.50	23.20	82.11	80.64
广东	Guangdong	172.91	85.34	796.92	84.38	82.82	351.75	330.42
广西	Guangxi	29.13	15.23	192.57	13.42	13.16	59.52	58.20
海南	Hainan	9.01	5.22	47.36	3.65	3.55	10.86	10.33
重庆	Chongqing	21.13	10.93	121.42	9.80	9.63	30.47	29.68
四川	Sichuan	76.49	43.89	509.12	31.38	30.81	93.95	90.57
贵州	Guizhou	24.09	10.20	114.26	13.49	13.24	41.55	40.39
云南	Yunnan	60.02	28.28	245.53	30.85	30.39	98.32	96.68
西藏	Tibet	4.50	2.30	15.74	2.12	2.07	11.64	11.27
陕西	Shaanxi	36.47	19.42	122.94	14.02	13.52	67.30	64.91
甘肃	Gansu	22.20	11.17	208.11	10.62	10.40	37.60	36.28
青海	Qinghai	8.71	4.53	45.27	3.93	3.82	14.97	14.38
宁夏	Ningxia	8.54	3.76	21.68	4.46	4.35	23.51	22.89
新疆	Xinjiang	36.97	17.97	278.49	17.47	16.53	85.97	80.32

15-28 续表 1 continued

年份 地区	Year Region	其他专用汽车（万辆） Other Special Vehicles (10 000 units)	特种汽车（万辆） Special Motor Vehicles (10 000 units)	轮胎式拖拉机（万台） Tyre Tractors (10 000 units)	其他机动车（万辆） Number of Other Motor Vehicles (10 000 units)	#摩托车 Motors	机动车驾驶员（万人） Number of Motor Drivers (10 000 persons)	#汽车驾驶员 Automobile Drivers
	1978		9.77		23.03	12.60		192.45
	1979		11.44		27.22	14.65		224.84
	1980		13.31		30.55	18.02		245.23
	1981		14.48		35.59	24.47		227.25
	1982		14.82		44.02	32.00		303.10
	1983		15.41		51.25	40.56		326.82
	1984		15.76		79.93	59.89		348.11
	1985		18.47	178.35	156.18	94.60		462.44
	1986		18.77	223.53	228.29	148.32		517.03
	1987		15.40	374.74	278.22	247.76	1196.82	556.82
	1988	7.25	8.91	391.61	334.21	302.39	1396.86	654.49
	1989	7.60	10.91	410.41	396.80	359.33	1577.99	722.32
	1990	8.38	12.31	462.58	462.33	421.28	1635.85	790.96
	1991	9.21	13.05	494.53	557.02	505.15	1791.57	859.44
	1992	10.27	13.86	537.08	716.21	647.49	2017.83	969.55
	1993	13.55	17.06	564.68	949.38	858.79	2359.42	1112.97
	1994	14.65	17.49	584.76	1208.89	1093.82	2812.12	1269.23
	1995	17.27	19.41	591.91	1494.62	1371.93	3501.52	1673.39
	1996	15.90	21.12	693.34	1773.13	1610.05	4275.26	2100.74
	1997	16.75	20.55	732.81	2214.83	2022.22	5206.79	2619.25
	1998	16.52	20.06	772.00	2770.72	2520.44	5944.58	2974.06
	1999	14.76	20.99	764.47	3456.96	3161.94	6727.49	3361.12
	2000	17.25	21.60	820.92	4168.06	3771.79	7655.56	3746.51
北　京	Beijing	0.93	0.42	3.26	37.31	33.22	252.57	214.31
天　津	Tianjin	0.65	0.55	4.40	52.37	44.68	147.64	88.97
河　北	Hebei	0.53	0.97	135.18	252.63	251.23	476.83	254.32
山　西	Shanxi	0.44	1.41	21.91	96.52	81.15	159.86	100.92
内蒙古	Inner Mongolia	0.30	0.30	45.54	68.28	60.26	175.38	77.11
辽　宁	Liaoning	0.53	1.05	13.25	95.83	87.18	295.61	200.60
吉　林	Jilin	0.53	0.73	41.49	74.57	65.62	213.12	124.99
黑龙江	Heilongjiang	1.26	0.33	11.60	32.34	31.62	171.90	160.06
上　海	Shanghai	1.07	1.06	0.84	54.22	53.77	149.44	112.58
江　苏	Jiangsu	0.57	1.31	35.04	478.18	445.31	623.13	156.15
浙　江	Zhejiang	0.88	0.40	42.27	189.44	184.05	338.29	318.70
安　徽	Anhui	0.36	0.28	0.41	79.34	68.68	147.69	94.14
福　建	Fujian	0.50	0.14	6.99	162.21	155.36	300.43	86.84
江　西	Jiangxi	0.01	1.50	5.06	97.74	89.12	143.95	79.15
山　东	Shandong	1.00	3.25	53.13	613.16	493.67	725.90	246.25
河　南	Henan	0.62	0.96	172.06	239.49	177.90	411.98	191.53
湖　北	Hubei	0.43	0.70	1.76	134.08	124.10	233.49	12.60
湖　南	Hunan	0.24	0.31	15.79	101.08	95.51	207.55	108.19
广　东	Guangdong	2.24	0.95	15.62	681.63	679.92	1046.98	319.51
广　西	Guangxi	0.27	0.22	29.17	163.54	160.15	256.54	99.97
海　南	Hainan	0.02	0.11	3.37	38.35	37.39	65.54	34.24
重　庆	Chongqing	0.11	0.30	2.35	19.56	17.43	53.00	49.00
四　川	Sichuan	0.52	0.70	10.56	126.38	115.75	317.67	192.75
贵　州	Guizhou	0.05	0.35	7.18	18.76	18.25	79.60	54.54
云　南	Yunnan	0.60	0.28	34.84	61.84	61.72	216.81	111.49
西　藏	Tibet	0.04	0.05	1.39	1.28	1.21	6.67	6.59
陕　西	Shaanxi	1.32	1.71	22.00	77.72	67.52	150.68	86.33
甘　肃	Gansu	0.20	0.21	20.41	60.43	16.13	107.48	49.56
青　海	Qinghai	0.14	0.10	14.57	10.09	9.45	34.53	21.06
宁　夏	Ningxia	0.12	0.20	17.15	12.59	12.26	32.31	17.32
新　疆	Xinjiang	0.78	0.75	32.31	37.11	32.22	112.97	76.73

注：1.小轿车包括在载客汽车中。
2.1988年以前，特种汽车含其他专用汽车。1988年起，其他专用汽车和特种汽车互不包含。

a) Cars are included in passenger vehicles.

b) Before 1988, special motor vehicles include other special vehicles. Since 1988, special motor vehicles and other special vehicles have been separated.

15-29 私人汽车拥有量
Number of Private-owned Vehicles

年份 地区	Year Region	汽车总计 (万辆) Total Number (10 000 units)	载客汽车 Passenger Vehicles 辆数 (万辆) Number (10 000 units)	客位 (万客位) Number of Seats (10 000 seats)	载货汽车 Trucks 辆数 (万辆) Number (10 000 units)	#普通载货汽车 Ordinary Trucks	吨位 (万吨) Capacity (10 000 tons)	#普通载货汽车 Ordinary Trucks
	1985	28.49	1.93	42.89	26.48		110.41	
	1986	34.71	3.44	74.16	31.23		127.09	
	1987	42.29	7.34	119.60	34.91	34.43	153.72	151.89
	1988	60.42	15.29	200.69	45.06	44.80	195.59	194.51
	1989	73.12	20.28	250.05	52.79	52.50	225.46	224.32
	1990	81.62	24.07	277.47	57.48	57.30	251.30	250.85
	1991	96.04	30.36	351.66	65.61	65.42	282.30	281.45
	1992	118.20	41.78	498.98	76.15	75.82	321.74	320.16
	1993	155.77	59.85	740.59	94.00	93.18	418.76	414.64
	1994	205.42	78.62	1015.08	123.29	122.62	503.48	499.32
	1995	249.96	114.15	1322.63	131.83	131.01	543.57	537.79
	1996	289.67	143.04	1615.50	142.78	142.07	542.30	541.58
	1997	358.36	191.27	2253.34	163.19	161.94	585.90	578.45
	1998	423.65	230.65	2632.77	192.03	190.77	724.12	716.07
	1999	533.88	304.09	3603.93	228.68	226.91	843.80	833.05
	2000	625.33	365.09	4003.71	259.09	257.12	957.19	939.21
北　京	Beijing	49.41	43.48	472.95	5.93	5.93	18.25	18.25
天　津	Tianjin	20.84	13.76	145.80	7.08	6.96	22.70	21.54
河　北	Hebei	51.74	33.06	661.25	18.59	18.43	93.50	92.16
山　西	Shanxi	23.51	13.59	103.29	9.88	9.85	59.41	58.94
内蒙古	Inner Mongolia	20.47	11.39	134.58	8.99	8.90	43.52	40.51
辽　宁	Liaoning	23.55	16.34	191.24	7.18	7.09	34.69	33.92
吉　林	Jilin	13.98	9.35	154.26	4.58	4.48	25.25	24.64
黑龙江	Heilongjiang	17.11	11.91	201.08	5.15	5.04	21.40	20.15
上　海	Shanghai	5.07	4.75	16.93	0.31	0.31	0.49	0.48
江　苏	Jiangsu	18.94	12.29	103.78	6.59	6.56	18.92	18.75
浙　江	Zhejiang	21.18	9.91	98.84	11.25	11.20	27.99	27.49
安　徽	Anhui	15.66	7.92	103.90	7.69	7.67	26.78	26.66
福　建	Fujian	15.17	6.45	75.38	8.68	8.63	26.96	26.74
江　西	Jiangxi	5.45	2.05	30.73	3.39	3.37	15.59	15.50
山　东	Shandong	35.91	21.18	124.89	14.65	14.49	36.06	35.46
河　南	Henan	34.93	21.43	241.29	13.35	13.19	54.77	53.91
湖　北	Hubei	14.72	7.60	64.99	7.08	7.04	17.77	17.56
湖　南	Hunan	25.98	11.73	123.39	14.20	14.15	48.78	48.53
广　东	Guangdong	87.93	44.50	323.27	43.27	43.03	143.17	139.11
广　西	Guangxi	13.27	6.03	78.96	7.20	7.15	28.03	27.78
海　南	Hainan	2.85	0.97	11.71	1.87	1.86	6.91	6.87
重　庆	Chongqing	5.78	3.12	44.13	2.66	2.66	7.45	7.44
四　川	Sichuan	21.21	10.21	68.53	11.00	10.99	31.91	31.87
贵　州	Guizhou	9.65	4.19	48.41	5.45	5.42	16.68	16.59
云　南	Yunnan	26.53	11.41	80.35	15.11	15.05	49.71	49.47
西　藏	Tibet	1.79	0.67	4.40	1.11	1.10	6.29	6.22
陕　西	Shaanxi	14.12	8.95	56.00	5.16	5.12	24.76	24.57
甘　肃	Gansu	8.13	4.53	78.31	3.59	3.56	12.24	12.11
青　海	Qinghai	2.72	1.41	15.78	1.30	1.29	4.51	4.48
宁　夏	Ningxia	3.87	2.25	11.31	1.62	1.62	7.30	7.29
新　疆	Xinjiang	13.85	8.64	133.99	5.18	4.99	25.41	24.23

注：小轿车包括在载客汽车中。

a)Passenger Vehicles include cars.

15-30 全国公路运输汽车拥有量

Number of Vehicles for Business Transport

年份 地区	Year Region	汽车总计 (万辆) Total Number (10 000 units)	载客汽车 Passenger Vehicles 辆数 (万辆) Number (10 000 units)	客位 (万客位) Number of Seats (10 000 seats)	载货汽车 Trucks 辆数 (万辆) Number (10 000 units)	#普通载货汽车 Ordinary Trucks	吨位 (万吨) Capacity (10 000 tons)	#普通载货汽车 Ordinary Trucks
	1986	29.27	9.06	388.94	20.20		118.65	
	1987	30.32	9.63	418.13	20.54	20.25	122.73	119.87
	1988	30.69	10.16	441.84	20.26	19.93	127.26	124.11
	1989	30.85	10.49	457.23	20.09	19.73	128.62	124.74
	1990	31.30	10.76	468.92	20.22	19.82	131.61	127.06
	1991	31.67	11.53	497.35	19.83	19.36	132.02	126.54
	1992	30.87	12.70	528.87	18.17	17.59	125.91	118.42
	1993	28.96	12.85	509.56	16.15	15.53	116.20	108.37
	1994	27.97	13.05	493.94	14.87	14.22	109.80	101.21
	1995	27.49	13.73	480.61	13.75	13.12	103.13	94.56
	1996	28.81	15.41	499.58	13.40	12.74	102.08	91.83
	1997	29.89	17.01	519.10	12.88	12.22	95.31	85.09
	1998	31.88	19.40	536.43	12.48	11.81	90.02	79.51
	1999	501.77	92.14	1409.86	409.62	401.28	1481.02	1406.00
	2000	702.82	216.81	2524.45	486.02	475.24	1667.70	1573.73
北京	Beijing	7.94	0.33	12.14	7.61	7.05	32.34	27.28
天津	Tianjin	6.63	0.32	9.14	6.3	5.78	32.02	23.82
河北	Hebei	54.50	18.30	185.90	36.21	35.53	149.44	144.84
山西	Shanxi	21.72	6.31	57.44	15.41	15.21	67.28	65.98
内蒙古	Inner Mongolia	20.87	8.68	67.25	12.19	12.07	56.65	55.71
辽宁	Liaoning	25.69	1.73	46.44	23.96	23.03	89.98	79.85
吉林	Jilin	16.23	4.66	55.74	11.57	11.31	44.67	43.06
黑龙江	Heilongjiang	33.65	15.81	174.45	17.84	16.95	72.26	68.63
上海	Shanghai	15.59	3.08	30.98	12.51	11.93	48.36	39.20
江苏	Jiangsu	54.39	27.30	266.66	27.09	26.50	95.51	90.53
浙江	Zhejiang	53.79	25.95	210.55	27.83	27.33	66.91	62.47
安徽	Anhui	19.58	4.11	63.48	15.47	15.27	57.41	56.06
福建	Fujian	13.29	3.08	41.36	10.21	9.64	30.76	26.34
江西	Jiangxi	8.39	1.57	31.73	6.82	6.76	23.28	22.95
山东	Shandong	48.15	13.60	135.76	34.55	33.36	118.18	108.24
河南	Henan	22.62	4.28	77.00	18.34	18.00	70.06	67.95
湖北	Hubei	17.94	3.69	62.25	14.25	14.04	50.33	48.97
湖南	Hunan	20.58	5.90	88.25	14.69	14.49	51.74	50.71
广东	Guangdong	65.08	6.34	116.32	58.74	58.03	140.87	131.97
广西	Guangxi	13.48	2.74	57.28	10.74	10.64	36.63	36.04
海南	Hainan	2.71	0.81	13.41	1.9	1.89	7.12	7.04
重庆	Chongqing	20.55	10.93	121.42	9.63	9.47	26.35	25.60
四川	Sichuan	31.45	7.08	99.17	24.37	24.16	62.72	61.53
贵州	Guizhou	14.38	6.33	64.22	8.06	7.98	23.3	22.94
云南	Yunnan	43.24	20.21	264.87	23.03	22.88	64.83	63.64
西藏	Tibet	1.93	0.50	5.65	1.44	1.42	7.77	7.67
陕西	Shaanxi	11.97	3.03	43.25	8.94	8.66	32.14	30.49
甘肃	Gansu	10.27	2.97	35.88	7.3	7.19	27.31	26.50
青海	Qinghai	5.21	1.98	21.85	3.24	3.17	13.22	12.64
宁夏	Ningxia	5.89	2.04	20.94	3.85	3.80	12.1	11.62
新疆	Xinjiang	15.12	3.20	43.67	11.92	11.72	56.16	53.48

注：1.小轿车包括在载客汽车中。

2.1999年以前数据仅为公路部门营运汽车，1999年为全国营运汽车。2000年起为全国运输汽车(含营运和非营运汽车)。

a)Passenger vehicles include cars.

b)Before 1999, number of vehicles for business transportation only included those owned by the department of highway transportation. That referred to all working vehicles for business transportation in 1999, and all vehicles for business transportation, including working and non-working vehicles in 2000.

15−31 各地区民用运输船舶拥有量

Number of Civil Transport Vessels Owned by Region

年份 地区	Year Region	机动船 Motor Vessels				驳船 Barges		
		艘数（艘） Number (unit)	净载重量（吨） Dead Weight Tonnage (ton)	载客量（客位） Passenger Capacity (seat)	拖船功率（千瓦） Drawing Power (kw)	艘数（艘） Number (unit)	净载重量（吨） Dead Weight Tonnage (ton)	载客量（客位） Passenger Capacity (seat)
	1980	64307	12789410	545042	1514998	119464	5951401	100312
	1985	260296	20898230	877963	1665030	132682	8670224	99643
	1990	325858	29090082	1138937	1750351	82482	9066738	62926
	1991	307127	29959203	1169982	1845705	78410	9588216	61526
	1992	302313	31225749	1177035	1844101	71255	9437823	46337
	1993	307285	34682035	1124114	1734606	65196	8891435	43801
	1994	293472	39591864	1065140	1678066	59913	8898065	26335
	1995	299717	40940087	979985	1707115	57998	9449652	17722
	1996	269879	39774235	988046	1616585	56128	9315335	15148
	1997	215814	38749289	1022970	1468612	49983	9064891	13879
	1998	212093	38896576	983630	1584601	48115	9019417	14914
	1999	194590	38911462	929138	1494500	47453	8981998	10306
	2000	185018	42640605	1014013	1439743	44658	8640504	18258
北京	Beijing							
天津	Tianjin	190	3406655	3768	152582	31	34601	
河北	Hebei	41	614816		4065	7	6910	
山西	Shanxi	214	1282	1801		1	28	
内蒙古	Inner Mongolia							
辽宁	Liaoning	776	1463476	29999	17557	58	19841	
吉林	Jilin	574	6517	11717	3909	33	14840	
黑龙江	Heilongjiang	306	40716	10079	47285	414	247565	
上海	Shanghai	2236	7120655	93914	101701	949	322476	
江苏	Jiangsu	53941	4327641	31413	349564	18777	3023188	1748
浙江	Zhejiang	35631	3960271	67414	50218	3177	279347	1027
安徽	Anhui	21657	2887461	33325	53281	3732	557343	
福建	Fujian	2963	2087173	24269	8193	46	11800	
江西	Jiangxi	4511	356441	16172	12186	345	74504	
山东	Shandong	4053	2707883	14480	97740	7578	1152296	
河南	Henan	3314	444081	6237	5356	418	59852	
湖北	Hubei	4357	477665	86913	234716	2551	1637924	
湖南	Hunan	8987	483799	70519	22944	507	114917	
广东	Guangdong	17188	5520072	61490	66533	470	190910	78
广西	Guangxi	8472	849281	83676	7039	110	32725	
海南	Hainan	462	809310	16950	8287	15	14000	
重庆	Chongqing	3220	259838	156198	147568	1268	640818	
四川	Sichuan	7912	106726	131027	37355	3680	163038	11975
贵州	Guizhou	1696	17563	21372	7062	203	29033	
云南	Yunnan	869	18968	18008	3188	47	10884	
西藏	Tibet							
陕西	Shaanxi	938	6670	14187	243	185	1147	1712
甘肃	Gansu	231	1017	6691		43	127	908
青海	Qinghai							
宁夏	Ningxia	192		2394	1171	13	390	810
新疆	Xinjiang							
不分地区	Not Classified by Region	87	4664628					

注：不分地区数据为中国远洋运输集团总公司海外公司数。1999年起，民用运输船舶不再统计帆船（下表同）。

a) Number of civil transport vessels not classified by region is the number of abroad companies under China Ocean Shipping (Group) Company. Since 1999, the number of civil transport vessels is not included sailing boats. The same as in the following table.

15-32 各地区私人运输船舶拥有量

Number of Private-Owned Transport Vessels by Region

年份 Year / 地区 Region	机动船 Motor Vessels				驳船 Barges		
	艘数(艘) Number	净载重量(吨) Dead Weight Tonnage (ton)	载客量(客位) Passenger Capacity (seat)	拖船功率(千瓦) Drawing Power (kw)	艘数(艘) Number	净载重量(吨) Dead Weight Tonnage (ton)	载客量(客位) Passenger Capacity (seat)
1985	133165	2139297	140722	52736	12253	417664	2267
1986	169347	2871841	192835	53772	9971	299853	4706
1987	189581	3490660	222945	75304	12897	299854	12088
1988	217268	4397174	265022	61191	12953	392015	6706
1989	221024	4542693	283113	67449	12032	573692	12692
1990	206589	4257594	283248	70250	10927	586650	3352
1991	200357	4517888	312280	54028	11673	519506	9075
1992	190262	3976814	326587	60481	9192	503787	11622
1993	190820	5961873	302898	85806	9458	636200	3103
1994	198241	7112807	261908	59848	7379	506187	5116
1995	182060	6942745	276555	78867	7964	749329	180
1996	157370	4821091	289402	55129	6533	657652	1240
1997	147415	6714642	347405	115168	9944	879692	1948
1998	127130	6547095	328884	98537	7290	794618	1850
1999	113359	6070634	343208	85615	7262	775881	606
2000	128654	8244485	387405	168099	13463	1523260	13682
北京 Beijing							
天津 Tianjin	15	454	576	99	1	101	
河北 Hebei							
山西 Shanxi	164	1014	1347		1	28	
内蒙古 Inner Mongolia							
辽宁 Liaoning	330	25458					
吉林 Jilin	473	5741	5573	566	3	1800	
黑龙江 Heilongjiang	25	50	200	4780	20	8050	
上海 Shanghai	656	40901		331	4	400	
江苏 Jiangsu	40320	2403408	9857	47239	5668	857320	218
浙江 Zhejiang	33487	2056603	10582	5494	496	37411	
安徽 Anhui	12350	1820756	16282	10247	445	100306	
福建 Fujian	968	81341	14051				
江西 Jiangxi	2433	96397	8686		3	950	
山东 Shandong	3276	348431	175	71254	3213	392313	
河南 Henan							
湖北 Hubei	2566	202385	10834	19541			
湖南 Hunan	6855	206402	54095	1185	245	61556	
广东 Guangdong	7481	460879	10425	1891	81	622	
广西 Guangxi	3978	183964	50947		9	465	
海南 Hainan	279	20942	2580				
重庆 Chongqing	2391	173274	43626	315	94	14254	
四川 Sichuan	7204	84774	105167	5157	2889	44426	10099
贵州 Guizhou	1547	13704	18226		63	2841	
云南 Yunnan	641	10166	5093				
西藏 Tibet							
陕西 Shaanxi	919	6647	13512		178	52	1712
甘肃 Gansu	193	794	5099		42	125	893
青海 Qinghai							
宁夏 Ningxia	103		472		8	240	760
新疆 Xinjiang							

15-33 沿海主要港口分货类吞吐量

Volume of Freight Handled in Major Coastal Ports by Type of Freight

单位：万吨 (10 000 tons)

货物种类	Type of Freight	1999			2000		
		合 计 Total	出 港 Out-port	进 港 In-port	合 计 Total	出 港 Out-port	进 港 In-port
总 计	**Total**	**105162**	**51415**	**53747**	**125603**	**61590**	**64013**
煤 炭	Coal	26319	16730	9589	32536	20641	11895
石 油	Petroleum	18773	8347	10426	23397	9261	14136
金属矿石	Metal Ores	10410	2784	7626	11892	3158	8734
钢 铁	Steel and Iron	3960	1717	2243	4970	2397	2573
矿建材料	Mineral Building Materials	6273	2121	4152	7255	2844	4410
水 泥	Cement	957	525	432	983	472	511
木 材	Timber	902	372	530	1047	457	589
非金属矿石	Nonmetal Ores	2100	1393	707	2579	1721	859
化肥和农药	Chemical Fertilizers and Pesticides	1753	429	1324	1803	514	1289
盐	Salt	423	200	223	526	253	273
粮 食	Grain	4333	2332	2001	5616	2929	2688
其 他	Others	28960	14467	14493	32999	16943	16056

15-34 沿海主要港口货物吞吐量

Volume of Freight Handled in Major Coastal Ports

单位：万吨 (10 000 tons)

港 口	Seaport	1980	1985	1990	1995	1999	2000
总 计	**Total**	**21731**	**31154**	**48321**	**80166**	**105162**	**125603**
大 连	Dalian	3263	4381	4952	6417	8505	9084
营 口	Yingkou	24	98	237	1156	1945	2268
秦 皇 岛	Qinhuangdao	2641	4419	6945	8382	8261	9743
天 津	Tianjin	1192	1856	2063	5787	7298	9566
烟 台	Yantai	506	689	668	1361	1646	1774
青 岛	Qingdao	1708	2611	3034	5103	7257	8636
日 照	Rizhao			925	1452	2003	2674
连 云 港	Lianyungang	739	929	1137	1716	2017	2708
上 海	Shanghai	8483	11291	13959	16567	18641	20440
宁 波	Ningbo	326	1040	2554	6853	9660	11547
汕 头	Shantou	176	201	279	716	1191	1284
广 州	Guangzhou	1210	1772	4163	7299	10157	11128
湛 江	Zhanjiang	1075	1231	1557	1885	1751	2038
海 口	Haikou	72	170	288	468	674	808
八 所	Basuo	278	388	431	275	380	378
三 亚	Sanya	38	78	37	42	27	48
其他港口	Other Ports			5092	14687	23749	31479

15-35 沿海主要港口码头泊位数（2000年底）

Number of Berths in Major Coastal Ports (End of 2000)

名称	Name	总计 Total 码头长度（米）Length of Quay Line (m)	泊位个数（个）Number of Berths (unit)	#万吨级 10 000 Ton Class	生产用 For Productive Use 码头长度（米）Length of Quay Line (m)	泊位个数（个）Number of Berths (unit)	#万吨级 10 000 Ton Class	非生产用 For Nonproductive Use 码头长度（米）Length of Quay Line (m)	泊位个数（个）Number of Berths (unit)
总计	**Total**	**205042**	**1772**	**518**	**182856**	**1454**	**518**	**22186**	**318**
#大连	Dalian	18553	100	39	14547	73	39	4006	27
营口	Yingkou	5005	30	16	4924	27	16	81	3
秦皇岛	Qinhuangdao	7889	49	26	6694	29	26	1195	20
天津	Tianjin	12920	73	49	11896	64	49	1024	9
烟台	Yantai	5016	31	15	4816	29	15	200	2
青岛	Qingdao	10525	49	30	9522	46	30	1003	3
日照	Rizhao	3518	25	10	3198	18	10	320	7
连云港	Lianyungang	6252	34	25	5803	30	25	449	4
上海	Shanghai	23557	225	70	19382	134	70	4175	91
宁波	Ningbo	7489	69	20	6208	45	20	1281	24
汕头	Shantou	3152	28	6	2980	23	6	172	5
广州	Guangzhou	13496	141	32	11549	110	32	1947	31
湛江	Zhanjiang	6635	41	24	5587	31	24	1048	10
海口	Haikou	1719	15	2	1719	15	2		
八所	Basuo	1412	8	6	1412	8	6		
三亚	Sanya	802	5		802	5			

15-36 内河主要港口码头泊位数（2000年底）

Number of Berths in Major Ports of Inland Rivers (End of 2000)

名称	Name	总计 Total 码头长度（米）Length of Quay Line (m)	泊位个数（个）Number of Berths (unit)	#万吨级 10 000 Ton Class	生产用 For Productive Use 码头长度（米）Length of Quay Line (m)	泊位个数（个）Number of Berths (unit)	#万吨级 10 000 Ton Class	非生产用 For Nonproductive Use 码头长度（米）Length of Quay Line (m)	泊位个数（个）Number of Berths (unit)
总计	**Total**	**259116**	**6306**	**55**	**251540**	**6184**	**55**	**7576**	**122**
#重庆	Chongqing	3289	65		2748	55		541	10
涪陵	Fuling	1541	29		1206	21		335	8
万州	Wanzhou	9080	57		7050	44		2030	13
宜昌	Yichang	1314	27		1209	25		105	2
枝城	Zhicheng	1253	27		1037	22		216	5
城陵矶	Chenglingji	712	11		672	10		40	1
武汉	Wuhan	5407	82		4517	66		890	16
黄石	Huangshi	1326	24		1221	22		105	2
九江	Jiujiang	1020	13		890	11		130	2
安庆	Anqing	1148	23		1074	21		74	2
池州	Chizhou	895	16		895	16			
铜陵	Tongling	917	14		856	13		61	1
芜湖	Wuhu	1714	28		1494	23		220	5
马鞍山	Maanshan	878	15		878	15			
南京	Nanjing	5815	64	14	4888	48	14	927	16
镇江	Zhenjiang	3097	32	8	3033	30	8	64	2
泰州	Taizhou	1375	15	3	1351	14	3	24	1
扬州	Yangzhou	2176	44	3	2176	44	3		
江阴	Jiangyin	630	10	2	630	10	2		
常州	Changzhou	4143	132	1	4143	132	1		
太仓	Taicang	540	2	2	540	2	2		
张家港	Zhangjiagang	4358	41	13	4243	39	13	115	2
南通	Nantong	3959	47	9	3757	44	9	202	3

15-37 民用航空航线及飞机架数

Number of Civil Aviation Routes and Civil Aircrafts

指　标	Item	1985	1990	1995	1999	2000
民用航空航线条数（条）	**Number of Civil Aviation Routes**	**268**	**437**	**797**	**1115**	**1165**
国际航线	International Routes	27	44	85	128	133
国内航线	Domestic Routes	233	385	694	987	1032
地区航线	Regional Routes	8	8	18	22	42
民用航空航线里程（公里）	**Length of Civil Aviation Routes (km)**	**277217**	**506762**	**1128961**	**1522221**	**1502887**
国际航线	International Routes	105959	166350	348175	523300	508405
国内航线	Domestic Routes	160323	329493	750794	998921	994482
地区航线	Regional Routes	10935	10919	29992	30812	55759
民用航班飞行机场（个）	**Number of Civil Airports**	**82**	**94**	**139**	**142**	**139**
民用飞机架数　（架）	**Number of Civil Aircraft**	**472**	**499**	**852**	**949**	**982**
#运输飞机	Aerotransport				523	527
大型飞机	Air bus				445	462
#波音747	Boeing 747	6	11	16	17	19
波音737	Boeing 737	15	21	115	174	186
波音757	Boeing 757		9	44	48	48
波音767	Boeing 767	2	6	17	16	16
MD90	MD-90				20	22
MD82	MD-82	5	25	39	29	27
A310	Airbus A310	2	2	3	3	3
A320	Airbus A320				51	60
图154	Tupolov 154	2	20	33	13	10
Bae-146	BB-146		10	14	14	7
小型飞机	Puddle-jumper				65	65
#运7	Yun 7	13	45	67	33	22
通用飞机	General Aircraft				285	301

注：1.1985年和1990年民航机场和飞机数为民航总局直属企业数，1997年以后为民航全行业数字(下表同)。
2.1997年以前，地区航线含民航至香港、澳门航线，与国内航线、国际航线并列。1997年起，民航至香港航线统计在国内航线中，航线里程及运输量统计口径也做同样调整。1999年起，地区航线为国内航线的其中项，仍含民航至香港、澳门航线及运量(下表同)。
3.民用飞机合计中含教学校验用飞机。

a)The number of civil airports and aircrafts in 1985 and 1990 refers to those owned by enterprises directly under CAAC. Since then, it refers to those owned by all enterprises of civil aviation. The same as in the following table.

b)Before 1997, regional routes includes the routes to and from Hong Kong, Macao, and are taken as the parataxis item as the item of domestic routes and international routes. Since 1997, regional routes to and from Hong Kong are taken as domestic routes, and adjustment are also made on the length of aviation routes and traffic volume accordingly. Since 1999, regional routes are taken as a part of domestic routes, and include the aviation routes to and from Hong Kong, Macao. The same as in the following table.

c)Number of civil aircrafts include the teaching aircrafts and check aircrafts.

15-38 民用航空运输量及通用飞行时间
Civil Aviation Traffic and Flying Time of General Aviation

指　　标	Item	1985	1990	1995	1999	2000
客运量　（万人）	**Passenger Traffic (10 000 persons)**	**747**	**1660**	**5117**	**6094**	**6722**
国际航线	International Routes	75	114	368	631	690
国内航线	Domestic Routes	595	1346	4419	5463	6031
地区航线	Regional Routes	77	200	330	376	403
旅客周转量	**Passenger-tons**					
（万人公里）	**(10 000 person-km)**	**1167163**	**2304797**	**6813036**	**8572818**	**9705437**
国际航线	International Routes	381769	516910	1149710	2056091	2328154
国内航线	Domestic Routes	706092	1576554	5287232	6516727	7377283
地区航线	Regional Routes	79302	211333	376094	46076	502405
货(邮)运量　(吨)	**Freight Traffic (ton)**	**195059**	**369722**	**1011145**	**1704296**	**1967123**
国际航线	International Routes	37922	81102	229632	423745	492356
国内航线	Domestic Routes	134242	239467	702557	1280552	1474767
地区航线	Regional Routes	22895	49153	78956	3761794	135442
货邮周转量	**Freight Ton-kilometers**					
（万吨公里）	**(10 000 ton-km)**	**41513**	**81825**	**222981**	**423427**	**502683**
国际航线	International Routes	21990	43830	115894	241194	291550
国内航线	Domestic Routes	16405	31647	96604	182233	211133
地区航线	Regional Routes	3118	6348	10483	16958	19495
总周转量	**Total Air Traffic Ton-kilometers**					
（万吨公里）	**(10 000 ton-km)**	**127102**	**249950**	**714385**	**1061127**	**1225007**
国际航线	International Routes	50615	82595	201250	394489	465190
国内航线	Domestic Routes	67423	145156	474660	666638	759818
地区航线	Regional Routes	9064	22199	38475	51240	56878
通用飞行时间(小时)	**Flying Time of General Aviation (hr)**	**43022**	**34919**	**39485**	**40068**	**48707**
农林业航空作业	Flight for Agriculture and Forestry	14841	22540	16838	18555	22922
#航空护林	Forest Protection Service	3785	3573	2410	2929	3927
播种造林	Afforestation	6547	4605	1713	1383	4060
工业航空作业	Flight for Industry	28181	12379	22647	21513	25785

15-39 输油(气)管道长度和运输量（2000年底）

Length and Traffic of Petroleum and Gas Pipelines (End of 2000)

本表是中国石油天然气集团公司和中国石油化工集团公司数据。

Data in this table are provided by China National Petroleum Corporation and China Petro-chemical Corporation.

项　　目	Item	输油(气)管道里程(公里) Length of Pipelines (km)	输油(气)能　力(万吨) Capacity of Pipeline Traffic (10 000 tons)	输油(气)量(万吨或千万立方米) Pipeline Traffic (10 000 tons or 10 million cu.m)	输油(气)周转量(万吨公里或千万立方米公里) Ton-kilometer or Cubic Meter-kilometers (10 000 ton-km or 10 million cu.m-km)
总　　计	**Total**	**24659.24**	**33688.77**	**18700.33**	**6361503.11**
#输油管	Petroleum Pipelines	12397.21	31795.14	17292.43	6013242.76
输气管	Gas Pipelines	12262.03	1893.63	1407.90	348260.35
输原油管道	**Crude Oil Pipelines**	**11200.58**	**27382.00**	**15829.33**	**5915788.90**
管道分公司	Pipelines Subsidiary Company	3327.00	7100.00	4430.00	3588627.00
大庆油田有限责任公司	Daqing Oil Fields Limited Corporation	298.00	1547.00	1294.00	42612.00
新疆油田分公司	Xinjiang Oil Fields Subsidiary Company	1152.00	1730.00	884.00	180065.00
胜利油田有限公司	Shengli Oil Fields Limited Co.	268.70	1185.00	652.61	50477.34
吉林油田分公司	Jilin Oil Fields Subsidiary Company	35.00	369.00	353.00	4290.00
华北油田分公司	North China Oil Fields Subsidiary Company	636.00	1207.00	223.00	31119.00
大港油田分公司	Dagang Oil Fields Subsidiary Company	81.00	1200.00	352.00	4719.00
玉门油田分公司	Yumen Oil Fields Subsidiary Company	40.00	799.00	197.00	1064.00
辽河油田分公司	Liaohe Oil Fields Subsidiary Company	494.00	1425.00	1044.00	109009.00
青海油田分公司	Qinghai Oil Fields Subsidiary Company	435.00	200.00	193.00	
河南油田分公司	Henan Oil Fields Subsidiary Company	92.70	400.00	150.96	4492.60
茂名石油化工公司	Maoming Petrochemical Co.	178.97	2000.00	1077.96	76519.46
长庆油田分公司	Changqing Oil Fields Subsidiary Company	362.00	275.00	390.00	36171.00
塔里木油田分公司	Tarim Oil Fields Subsidiary Company	472.00	415.00	275.00	64490.00
鞍山炼油厂	Anshan Refinery	88.00	180.00	106.00	9328.00
锦州石化分公司	Jinzhou Petrochemical Subsidiary Company	58.00	600.00	443.00	
锦西石化分公司	Jinxi Petrochemical Subsidiary Company	30.00	300.00	79.00	2370.00
长岭炼化有限责任公司	Changling Refinery & Petrochemical Corporation	26.00	100.00	125.10	3252.67
吉林石化分公司	Jilin Petrochemical Subsidiary Company	150.00	400.00	397.00	58230.00
石化集团管道储运分公司	China Petrochemical Corporation Pipeline Transport Subsidiary Company	2372.21	4150.00	2629.16	1559530.00
哈尔滨石化分公司	Harbin Petrochemical Subsidiary Company	187.00	500.00	180.00	33757.00
石家庄炼油厂	Shijiazhuan Refinery	155.00	350.00	211.44	32773.20
荆门石化总厂	Jingmen Petrochemical Corporation	210.00	350.00	100.04	21008.40
广州石化总厂	Guangzhou Petrochemical Corporation	4.00	500.00	3.06	12.23
天津石化公司	Tianjin Petrochemical Co.	48.00	100.00	39.00	1872.00
输成品油管道	**Refined Oil Pipelines**	**1196.63**	**4413.14**	**1463.10**	**97453.86**
燕山石化有限公司	Yanshan Petrochemical Ltd.	25.80	469.00	50.67	380.93
天津石油化工公司	Tianjin Petrochemical Co.	19.88	357.00	44.00	124.20
沧州炼油厂	Cangzhou Refinery	8.40	32.94	19.27	80.94
抚顺石化分公司	Fushun Petrochemical Subsidiary Company	268.00	435.00	201.00	45578.00
锦州石化分公司	jinzhou Petrochemical Subsidiary Company	84.00	140.00	83.00	3486.00
锦西石化分公司	Jinxi Petrochemical Subsidiary Company	64.00	338.00	106.00	3094.00
鞍山炼油厂	Anshan Refinery	51.00	352.00	23.00	270.00
大连石化分公司	Dalian Petrochemical Subsidiary Company	11.00	80.00	11.00	77.00
中国石化长岭分公司	China Petrochemical Corporation Changling Subsidiary Company	24.50	34.00	0.33	4.00
大庆石化分公司	Daqing Petrochemical Subsidiary Company	51.00	188.00	22.00	21.00
镇海炼化股份有限公司	Zhenhai Refinery & Petrochemical Limited Co.	46.40	109.40	75.39	648.51
九江石油化工总厂	Jiujiang Petrochemical Corporation	18.73	259.50	7.01	32.23
荆门石油化工总厂	Jingmen Petrochemical Corporation	11.90	56.00	9.26	19.64
武汉石油化工厂	Wuhan Petrochemical Factory	15.20	349.00	29.15	105.86
安庆石油化工总厂	Anqing Petrochemical Corporation	2.10	10.50	23.57	19.74

15-39 续表 1 continued

项目	Item	输油(气)管道里程(公里) Length of Pipelines (km)	输油(气)能力(万吨) Capacity of Pipeline Traffic (10 000 tons)	输油(气)量(万吨或千万立方米) Pipeline Traffic (10 000 tons or 10 million cu.m)	输油(气)周转量(万吨公里或千万立方米公里) Ton-kilometer or Cubic Meter-kilometers (10 000 ton-km or 10 million cu.m-km)
中国石化广州分公司	China Petrochemical Corporation Guangzhou Subsidiary Company	47.51	331.80	420.65	1843.45
茂名炼化股份有限公司	Maoming Refinery & Petrochemical Limited Co.	25.21	213.00	43.76	135.24
齐鲁石油化工公司	Qilu Petrochemical Corporation	3.00	60.00	90.04	270.12
管道分公司	Pipelines Subsidiary Company	11.00	300.00		
大庆油田有限责任公司	Daqing Oil Fields Limited Corporation	36.00	98.00	53.00	857.00
新疆油田分公司	Xinjiang Oil Fields Subsidiary Company	291.00	130.00	138.00	40158.00
吉林油田分公司	Jilin Oil Fields Subsidiary Company	10.00	20.00		
哈尔滨石化分公司	Harbin Petrochemical Subsidiary Company	71.00	50.00	13.00	248.00
输天然气管道	**Natural Gas Pipelines**	**12041.13**	**1562.96**	**1347.21**	**347709.77**
管道分公司	Pipelines Subsidiary Company	857.00	120.00	84.00	26733.00
西南油气分公司	Southern North Oil & Gas Subsidiary Company	6199.00		765.00	165541.00
大庆油田有限责任公司	Daqing Oil Fields Limited Corporation	209.00	196.00	76.00	1827.00
胜利油田有限公司	Shengli Oil Fields Limited Corporation	152.00	40.00	22.01	3138.63
华北油田分公司	North China Oil Fields Subsidiary Company	87.00	29.00	28.00	2111.00
辽河油田分公司	Liaohe Oil Fields Subsidiary Company	788.00	248.00	50.00	688.00
大港油田分公司	Dagang Oil Fields Subsidiary Company	132.00	48.00	27.00	1869.00
中原石油勘探局	Zhongyuan Petroleum Prospecting Bureau	150.00	10.00	8.70	1305.00
滇黔桂石油勘探局	Yunna-Guizhou-Guangxi Petroleum Prospecting Bureau	6.63	72.31	6.63	3.40
江汉油田分公司	Jianghan Oil Fields Subsidiary Company	57.50	14.00	3.16	4.74
新疆油田分公司	Xinjiang Oil Fields Subsidiary Company	590.00	155.00	89.00	14977.00
青海油田分公司	Qinghai Oil Fields Subsidiary Company	639.00	127.00	30.00	
长庆油田分公司	Changqing Oil Fields Subsidiary Company	129.00	53.00	14.00	
塔里木油田分公司	Tarim Oil Fields Subsidiary Company	455.00	107.00	21.00	1910.00
吉林油田分公司	Jilin Oil Fields Subsidiary Company	239.00	36.00	4.00	112.00
石化集团管道储运分公司	China Petrochemical Corporation Pipeline Transport Subsidiary Company	261.00	7.65	1.71	445.00
北京天然气集输公司	Beijing Natural Gas Transport Corporation	1090.00	300.00	117.00	127045.00
输其他气体管道	**Other Gas pipelines**	**220.90**	**330.67**	**60.69**	**550.58**
燕山石化有限公司	Yanshan Petrochemical Co.	3.00	21.00	9.61	28.83
天津石油化工公司	Tianjin Petrochemical Co.	35.00	67.00	3.00	37.00
沧州炼油厂	Cangzhou Refinery	0.50	9.90	0.73	0.37
金陵石油化工公司	Jinling Petrochemical Co.	16.00	6.40	4.89	78.24
九江石油化工总厂	Jiujiang Petrochemical Corporation	4.00	50.00	0.28	1.12
镇海炼化股份有限公司	Zhenhai Refinery & Petrochemical Limited Co.	28.70	62.50	13.09	77.08
武汉石油化工厂	Wuhan Petrochemical Factory	22.60	16.00	12.68	182.57
兰州石化分公司	Lanzhou Petrochemical Subsidiary Company	9.00	1.00		
荆门石油化工总厂	Jingmen Petrochemical Corporation	3.00	1.20	0.28	0.84
石家庄炼油厂	Shijiazhuang Refinery	36.50	34.00	5.24	108.45
中国石化广州分公司	China Petrochemical Corporation Guangzhou Subsidiary Company	4.70	0.98	2.04	9.61
茂名炼化股份有限公司	Maoming Refinery & Petrochemical Limited Co.	8.90	29.69	4.85	11.47
大庆油田有限责任公司	Daqing Oil Fields Limited Corporation	9.00	1.00	2.00	14.00
锦西石化分公司	Jinxi Petrochemical Subsidiary Company	1.00	10.00	2.00	1.00
中国石化长岭分公司	China Petrochemical Corporation Changling Subsidiary Company	39.00	20.00		

注：管道输气量按一千立方米折一吨计算。

a) Gas transport though pipelines is converted from volume to tonnage using the conversion ratio of 100 cubic meters equal to one ton.

15-40 邮电业务基本情况

Basic Conditions of Post and Telecommunication Services

指　标	Item	1996	1997	1998	1999	2000
邮电业务总量　(亿元)	Business Volume of Post and Telecommunications Service (100 million yuan)	1342.04	1773.29	2431.21	3330.82	4792.70
函件　(亿件)	Number of Letters (100 million pcs)	78.68	68.55	65.51	60.52	77.71
包件　(万件)	Number of Parcels (10 000 pcs)	14920.0	9715.3	9726.5	9741.9	9600.3
特快专递　(万件)	Pieces of Express Mail Services (10 000 pcs)	7096.6	6878.9	7331.8	9091.3	11031.4
报刊期发数　(万份)	Number of Newspapers and Magazines Circulation (10 000 copies)	21157.4	21875.2	22989.3	25035.2	20089.7
长途电话　(亿次)	Number of Long-distance Calls (100 million times)	127.40	155.40	182.59	178.25	210.75
本地电话年末用户　(万户)	Local Telephone Subscribers of at Year-end (10 000 subscribers)	5494.7	7031.0	8742.1	10871.6	14482.9
年末市内电话用户　(万户)	Local (Urban) Telephone Subscribers at Year-end (10 000 subscribers)	4277.8	5244.4	6259.8	7463.3	9311.6
#住宅电话用户	Residential Telephone Subscribers	3224.6	4057.2	4911.1	5894.4	7219.4
年末无线寻呼电话用户(万户)	Number of Subscribers of Pageing Service at Year-end (10 000 subscribers)	2536.2	3254.6	3908.2	4674.5	4884.3
年末移动电话用户　(万户)	Number of Mobile Telephones Subscribers at Year-end (10 000 subscribers)	685.3	1323.3	2386.3	4329.6	8453.3
年末农村电话用户　(万户)	Number of Rural Telephones Subscribers at Year-end (10 000 subscribers)	1216.9	1786.6	2482.3	3408.4	5171.3
邮电局所　(处)	Number of Post & Telecommunications Offices	72496	79273	102225	66649	70968
邮路及农村投递路线总长度　(万公里)	Length of Postal Routes and Rural Delivery Routes (10 000 km)	547.70	576.61	621.54	632.71	643.00
长话业务电路　(路)	Number of Long-distance Telephone Lines (line)	998287	1146121	1576483	1869671	2201746
长途光缆线路长度　(公里)	Length of Long-distance Optical Cable Lines (km)	130159	150754	194100	239735	286642
局用交换机容量　(万门)	Capacity of Office Telephone Exchanges (10 000 lines)	9291.23	11269.17	13823.66	15346.13	17825.64
中央国有	Central State-owned	6923.67	8406.80	9951.35	11094.08	13306.16
地方国有	Local State-owned	2367.56	2862.37	3872.31	4252.05	4519.48
电话机(含移动电话)(万部)	Number of Telephone Sets (10 000 units)	7732.03	10111.12	13123.43	17567.44	25606.55
中央国有	Central State-owned	5537.78	6745.23	7963.28	9505.43	12634.36
地方国有	Local State-owned	1508.97	2042.61	2773.86	3732.41	4518.89

注:1.邮电业务总量按1990年不变价格计算。
2.从1997年起市内电话用户数为城市电话用户，农村电话用户数为乡村电话用户。1999年起，邮电局所为邮政局所(下表同)。

a)The business volume of post and telecommunications is calculated at 1990 constant prices.

b)Since 1997 figure of local telephone subscribers refers to telephone subscribers in urban areas, and rural telephone subscribers refers to subscribers of townships and village. Number of postal and telecommunications offices refers to number of postal offices since 1999. The same as the following table.

15-41 邮电业务量

Telecommunication Services

年份 Year	邮电业务总量（亿元） Business Volume of Post and Telecommunication Services (100 million yuan)	邮政业务总量 Business Volume of Post	电信业务总量 Business Volume of Telecommunication Services	函件（亿件） Number of Letters (100 million pcs)	特快专递（万件） Pieces of Express Mail Services (10 000 pcs)	报刊期发数（万份） Newspapers and Magazines Circulation (10 000 copies)
1978	34.09			28.35		11250
1979	36.73			30.80		12680
1980	39.03			33.13		16431
1981	41.02			33.88		18124
1982	42.89			33.94		19598
1983	46.79			35.21		22933
1984	52.60			39.48		28141
1985	62.21			46.78		30172
1986	69.06			49.59		28731
1987	81.63			54.79		31005
1988	102.88			59.77	153.0	27443
1989	123.46			57.28	247.3	17704
1990	155.54			54.87	343.3	20078
1991	204.39	52.75	151.63	52.11	566.7	23277
1992	290.94	64.36	226.57	57.18	959.2	25104
1993	462.71	80.26	382.45	68.70	2156.2	25511
1994	688.19	95.89	592.30	76.50	4019.5	24096
1995	988.85	113.34	875.51	79.55	5562.7	21689
1996	1342.04	133.29	1208.75	78.68	7096.6	21157
1997	1773.29	144.34	1628.95	68.55	6878.9	21875
1998	2431.21	166.28	2264.94	65.51	7331.8	22989
1999	3330.82	198.44	3132.38	60.52	9091.3	25035
2000	4792.70	232.80	4559.90	77.71	11031.4	20090

注：邮电业务总量按1990年不变价格计算。

a)The business volume of post and telecommunication services was calculated at 1990's constant prices.

15-41 续表 1 continued

年份 Year	集邮业务（万枚） Philately	长途电话（万次） Number of Long Distance Telephone Calls (10 000 times)	无线寻呼用户（万户） Number of Subscribers of Pageing Services (10 000 subscribers)	移动电话用户（万户） Number of Mobile Telephone Subscribers (10 000 subscribers)	电子信箱用户（户） Number of Subscribers of E-mail Services (subscriber)	国际互联网络用户（户） Number of Subscribers of Internet Services (subscriber)
1978		18574				
1979		20587				
1980		21404				
1981		22049				
1982		23574				
1983		26556				
1984		31553				
1985		38254				
1986		42303				
1987		51525	3.09			
1988		64617	9.72	0.32		
1989		78462	23.73	0.98		
1990	71233	116292	43.70	1.83		
1991	123523	172921	87.38	4.75		
1992	167303	287380	222.02	17.69		
1993	210885	506853	561.40	63.93		
1994	236849	757639	1033.00	156.78	2329	
1995	239250	1013966	1739.15	362.94	6068	7213
1996	303436	1273951	2536.20	685.28	10107	35652
1997	451729	1554026	3254.61	1323.29	15246	160157
1998	502850	1825941	3908.16	2386.29	20959	676755
1999	522475	1782529	4674.47	4329.60	19855	3014518
2000	453500	2107542	4884.30	8453.30		9021717

注：国际互联网络用户为拨号用户和专线用户合计数。

a) Number of subscribers of Internet service includes dial-up subscribers and ISDN subscribers.

15-41 续表 2 continued

年 份 Year	本地电话年末用户(万户) Number of Subscribers of Local Telephone at Year-end (subscribers)	城市电话用户 Number of Urban Telephone Subscribers	# 住宅电话 Residential Telephone Subscribers	乡村电话用户 Rural Telephone Subscribers	# 住宅电话 Residential Telephone Subscribers	公用电话(万户) Public Telephone (Subscribers)
1978	192.54	119.15		73.39		1.16
1979	203.30	127.02		76.28		1.27
1980	214.08	134.17		79.90		1.40
1981	222.09	142.64		79.45		1.54
1982	234.25	153.87		80.38		1.75
1983	250.76	168.86		81.90		2.03
1984	277.43	191.07		86.36		2.45
1985	312.03	218.96	4.08	93.07	2.05	2.75
1986	350.38	250.51	7.36	99.87	3.61	2.99
1987	390.72	293.04	17.17	97.68	6.91	3.27
1988	472.70	362.30	37.83	110.39	12.69	3.66
1989	568.04	439.62	89.56	128.42	21.34	3.99
1990	685.03	538.45	152.72	146.58	30.66	4.60
1991	845.06	670.83	239.00	174.23	49.55	5.38
1992	1146.91	920.57	415.41	226.34	79.01	8.41
1993	1733.16	1407.37	800.38	325.79	139.55	15.84
1994	2729.53	2246.78	1489.40	482.75	274.86	38.66
1995	4070.57	3263.56	2358.40	807.00	551.37	84.98
1996	5494.74	4277.82	3224.62	1216.92	907.27	138.04
1997	7031.04	5244.40	4057.16	1786.63	1406.56	193.94
1998	8742.09	6259.81	4911.08	2482.28	2070.75	259.49
1999	10871.60	7463.30	5894.40	3408.40	2949.20	297.40
2000	14482.90	9311.60	7219.40	5171.30	4597.80	352.00

15-42 邮电局所数及邮递线路(年底数)

Postal and Telecommunication Services Facilities (Year-end)

年 份 Region	邮电局所(处) Number of Post and Telecommunication Offices	信筒信箱(处) Number of Post Boxes	邮路总长度(公里) Length of Postal Routes (km)	# 汽车邮路 Highway Routes	# 铁路邮路 Railway Routes	农村投递线路(公里) Rural Delivery Routes (km)
1978	49623		4863282	572204	150249	
1979	49647	156398	4812271	574732	148876	
1980	49471	159009	4737124	582058	150819	
1981	49570	159153	4660172	599428	151956	
1982	49727	161431	1306340	612893	155951	3369931
1983	50162	164614	1308472	624558	164774	3412421
1984	51463	169269	1336324	638406	170513	3494266
1985	53107	174678	1416303	663016	182178	3565758
1986	52777	176843	1535898	703542	201919	3506131
1987	52882	179213	1535690	695384	199883	3497911
1988	52881	180085	1557762	681409	199095	3443058
1989	53092	178289	1526073	675352	196178	3389374
1990	53629	181877	1618200	676747	191313	3364861
1991	54006	181939	1603344	685759	185872	3371424
1992	54891	183289	1646931	712367	189359	3374556
1993	57005	187966	1760506	727380	189704	3377769
1994	60447	193902	1781787	757931	187871	3364730
1995	61898	203011	1886082	819412	183036	3345848
1996	72496	217235	2118940	917151	183884	3358051
1997	79273	231337	2363108	873688	186382	3402946
1998	102225	234716	2853942	930622	189652	3361484
1999	66649	232674	2979007	989122	190056	3348054
2000	70968					

注：邮路总长度1981年及以前是邮路及农村投递线路长度。

a) Length of postal routes before 1982 included the length of postal routes and rural delivery routes.

15-43 邮电通信电路及长途电信线路（年底数）

Telecommunications Facilities (Year-end)

年份 Year	长话业务电路（路） Long Distance Telephone Lines (line)	#光缆电路 Optical Cable Lines	#数字电路 Digital Lines	长途光缆线路长度（公里） Length of Long Distance Optical Cable Lines (km)	长途微波线路长度（公里） Length of Long Distance Microwave Lines (km)
1978	18801				13958
1979	20307				13958
1980	22011				13958
1981	23909				13958
1982	25937				14129
1983	28637				14358
1984	32354				16380
1985	37551				17275
1986	44085				18940
1987	53416				20282
1988	68460	2717		493	22320
1989	87139	5670		1851	26338
1990	112437	11453		3334	33626
1991	151779	23613		6490	39282
1992	234276	51352	109300	14388	54418
1993	420323	162861	298045	38666	64368
1994	615809	330359	518915	73290	
1995	735545	484231	677672	106882	79634
1996	998287	754143	965263	130159	71503
1997	1146121	935835	1139476	150754	65013
1998	1576483	1351665	1560201	194100	66518
1999	1869671			239735	65228
2000	2201746			286642	121947

15-44 邮电通信水平

Level of Postal and Telecommunication Services

指标	Item	1996	1997	1998	1999	2000
全国邮电通信水平	**National Level**					
平均每人每年发函件数（件）	Annual Average Number of Letters Mailed per Capita	6.62	5.56	5.27	4.90	6.40
平均每百人每年订报刊数（份）	Annual Average Number of Newspaper and Magazine Subscribed per 100 Persons	17.60	17.69	18.42	20.00	16.40
平均每百人拥有电话机部数（部）	Number of Telephone Sets Owned per 100 Persons	6.33	8.11	10.53	13.00	20.10
农村邮电通信水平	**Rural Level**					
设有邮电局、所的乡(镇)比重(%)	Percentage of Townships with Post and Telecommunication Offices	78.2	78.7	77.6	79.4	
通电话的乡(镇)比重（%）	Percentage of Townships with Telephone Communication	95.7	89.2	92.9	97.7	100.0
进入长话自动网的乡(镇)比重(%)	Percentage of Townships with Connected Autoexchange Net of Long Distance Call	71.2	81.7	87.5	100.0	100.0

15-45 邮电通信设备年末拥有量

Telecommunications Facilities at the Year-end

年份 Year	长途自动交换机容量(路端) Capacity of Long-distance Telephone Exchanges (circuit)	本地电话局用交换机容量(万门) Capacity of Local Office Telephone Exchanges (10 000 line)	中央国有 Central State-owned	地方国有 Local State-owned	电话机(万部) Number of Telephone (10 000 sets)	中央国有 Central State-owned	地方国有 Local State-owned
1978	1863	405.88	174.94	230.94	368.82	236.40	132.42
1979	2001	422.03	185.25	236.78	395.01	262.13	132.88
1980	1969	443.20	200.29	242.91	418.64	284.07	134.57
1981	3058	463.36	217.90	245.46	442.51	310.11	132.40
1982	3126	490.71	240.86	249.85	471.23	339.10	132.13
1983	4306	516.07	262.21	253.86	507.15	373.40	133.75
1984	6544	553.57	291.96	261.61	553.89	415.25	138.64
1985	11522	613.44	336.54	276.91	625.98	476.11	149.87
1986	20689	672.36	380.49	291.86	705.91	544.14	161.77
1987	42773	773.93	464.50	309.43	805.72	628.28	177.44
1988	62484	887.22	555.84	331.38	941.79	745.10	196.70
1989	103269	1034.69	667.95	366.74	1089.33	868.38	220.95
1990	161370	1231.82	826.05	405.77	1233.16	1026.10	205.23
1991	286325	1492.18	1033.14	459.03	1459.18	1215.68	238.74
1992	521885	1915.06	1355.50	559.56	1863.65	1544.94	301.02
1993	1206091	3040.78	2210.25	830.53	2631.28	2147.51	419.94
1994	2416296	4926.24	3723.39	1202.86	3958.64	3148.11	653.75
1995	3518781	7203.59	5456.35	1747.24	5762.26	4346.32	1152.06
1996	4162009	9291.22	6923.67	2367.56	7732.03	5537.78	1508.97
1997	4368305	11269.18	8406.80	2862.37	10111.12	6745.23	2042.61
1998	4491595	13823.66	9951.35	3872.31	13123.44	7963.29	2773.86
1999	5032026	15346.13	11094.08	4252.05	17567.44	9505.43	3732.41
2000	5635498	17825.63	13306.16	4519.47	25606.55	12634.36	4518.89

注：电话交换机容量中不包括用户交换机容量。1990年以后，电话机总数中含移动电话。

a)The capacity of exchanges in this table excludes the capacity of exchanges owned by users. Since 1990, total number of telephone sets include mobile phones.

主 要 统 计 指 标 解 释

铁路营业里程　又称营业长度（包括正式营业和临时营业里程），指办理客货运输业务的铁路正线总长度。凡是全线或部分建成双线及以上的线路，以第一线的实际长度计算；复线、站线、段管线、岔线和特殊用途线以及不计算运费的联络线都不计算营业里程。铁路营业里程是反映铁路运输业基础设施发展水平的重要指标，也是计算客货周转量、运输密度和机车车辆运用效率等指标的基础资料。

铁路正线延展里程　指正线第一线、第二线、第三线和其他正线建筑里程之和，不包括站线、段管线、岔线及特殊用途线的延展里程。它是作为计算铁路线上钢轨、枕木及路基砂石需要量的主要依据。

铁路电气化里程　指在全部铁路营业里程中已安装了供电线路及设备，可以供电力机车牵引列车运行的区段的总里程。

铁路自动、半自动闭塞里程　为保证列车安全运行，在一个区间、同一时间内，一般只允许一列列车运行，这种保证列车在这个区间安全间隔运行的技术方法称为“闭塞”。自动和半自动闭塞里程是指装有列车自动或人工完成闭塞状态的铁路设备里程。自动或半自动闭塞里程占铁路营业里程的比重是反映铁路现代化的重要标志之一。

公路里程　指在一定时期内实际达到《公路工程[WTBZ]技术标准 JTJ01－88》规定的等级公路，并经公路主管部门正式验收交付使用的公路里程数。包括大中城市的郊区公路以及通过小城镇街道部分的公路里程和桥梁、渡口的长度，不包括大中城市的街道、厂矿、林区生产用道和农业生产用道的里程。两条或多条公路共同经由同一路段，只计算一次，不得重复计算里程长度。它是反映公路建设发展规模的重要指标，也是计算运输网密度等指标的基础资料。

内河航道里程　也称内河通航里程，指在一定时期内，能通航运输船舶及排筏的天然河流、湖泊水库、运河及通航渠道的长度。包括全年季节性通航累计三个月以上的航道，不包括仅供零散流放竹、木排的河道。它是反映内河水运网规模、水平和发展情况的主要指标。

民用航空航线里程　指民航运输定期班机飞行的航线长度的总和。航线长度按机场之间的距离计算，通常有两种计算方法：一是将每条航线长度相加称为重复计算航线里程；一是将两线或两条以上航线经过同一区段里程，只计算一次航线长度称为不重复计算航线里程。一般常用的是后者，它能确切反映民航运输网的规模，是表明民航事业为国民经济服务和方便人民生活程度的主要指标。

输油(气)管道长度　也称输油(气)里程，指油品(或天然气)的实际输送距离，一般按输油(气)管道的单线长度计算。若包括复线和备用线长度则称为输油(气)管道延展长度，是指管道铺设的实际长度。我们通常使用的是不包括复线的“输油(气)管道里程”，它是反映管道运输发展规模和水平的主要指标。

货(客)运量　指在一定时期内，各种运输工具实际运送的货物(旅客)数量。它是反映运输业为国民经济和人民生活服务的数量指标，也是制定和检查运输生产计划、研究运输发展规模和速度的重要指标。货运按吨计算，客运按人计算。货物不论运输距离长短、货物类别，均按实际重量统计。旅客不论行程远近或票价多少，均按一人一次客运量统计；半价票、小孩票也按一人统计。

货(客)运密度　指在一定时期内某种运输方式在营运线路的某一区段平均每公里线路通过的货物(旅客)运输周转量。计算公式为：

货(客)运密度＝货物(旅客)周转量／营业线路长度

货(客)运密度是反映交通运输线路上货物(旅客)运输量运输繁忙程度的主要指标，是平衡运输线路运输能力和通过能力，规划线路建设及改造、配备技术设备，研究运输网布局的重要依据。

货物(旅客)周转量　指在一定时期内，由各种运输工具运送的货物(旅客)数量与其相应运输距离的乘积之总和。它是反映运输业生产总成果的重要指标，也是编制和检查运输生产计划，计算运输效率、劳动生产率以及核算运输单位成本的主要基础资料。计算货物周转量通常按发出站与到达站之间的最短距离，也就是计费距离计算。计算公式为：

货物(旅客)周转量＝Σ货物(旅客)运输量×运输距离

铁路货车平均静载重　指铁路货车在始发站静止状态下平均每车装载的货物重量，用以分析货车完成装车时车辆载重力的利用情况。计算公式为：

货车平均静载重＝货物发送吨数／装车数

静载重的多少取决于运送货物的性质、种类、车辆的类型和装载技术的高低。根据货车的平均标记载重与静载重进行对比，可以反映货车载重能力的利用程度。计算公式为：

货车载重力利用率(%)＝货车平均静载重／货车平均标记载重×100%

铁路货运机车日产量　指在一定时期内，平均每台货运机车在一昼夜内所完成的总重吨公里数，包括载运货物的重量和车辆本身的自重。它从时间和牵引能力两方面反映了机车运用效率。计算公式为：

货运机车平均日产量＝货运总重吨公里数／货运机车台日数

沿海主要港口货物吞吐量　指经水运进出沿海主要港区范围，并经过装卸的货物数量，包括邮件及办理托运手续的行李、包裹以及补给运输船舶的燃、物料和淡水。货物吞吐量按货物流向分为进口、出口吞吐量，按货物交流性质分为外贸货物吞吐量和国内贸易货物吞吐量。货物吞吐量的货类构成及其流向，是衡量港口生产能力大小的重要指标。

邮电业务总量 指以价值量形式表现的邮电通信企业为社会提供各类邮电通信服务的总数量。邮电业务量按专业分类包括函件、包件、汇票、报刊发行、邮政快件、特快专递、邮政储蓄、集邮、公众电报、用户电报、传真、长途电话、出租电路、无线寻呼、移动电话、分组交换数据通信、出租代维等。计算方法为各类产品乘以相应的平均单价(不变价)之和，再加上出租电路和设备、代用户维护电话交换机和线路等的服务收入。它综合反映了一定时期邮电业务发展的总成果，是研究邮电业务量构成和发展趋势的重要指标。计算公式为：

邮电业务总量 = Σ（各类邮电业务量 × 不变单价）+出租代维及其他业务收入

无线寻呼用户 无线寻呼是指电话用户通过无线寻呼中心，在规定范围内向携带小型寻呼机的用户发出声音、数字或文字显示信息。在寻呼台办理登记手续携带小型寻呼机的用户，称为无线寻呼用户。

移动电话用户 是指通过移动电话交换机进入移动电话网、占用移动电话号码的电话用户。用户数量以报告期末在移动电话营业部门实际办理登记手续进入移动电话网的户数进行计算，一部移动电话统计为一户。

电话用户 指接入国家公众固定电话网，并按固定电话业务进行经营管理的电话用户。1997 年以前，电话用户分为市内电话用户和农村电话用户。“市内电话用户”是指接入县城及县以上城市的电话网上的电话用户；“农村电话用户”是指接入县邮电局农话台及县以下农村电话交换点，以县城为中心（除市话用户外）联通县、乡（镇）、行政村、村民小组的用户。从 1997 年起，电话用户数分组调整为以用户所在区域划分为“城市电话用户”和“乡村电话用户”，与过去的按市内电话和农村电话划分方法不同。而电话用户总数、电话机总部数统计范围不变。

城市电话用户 指直辖市、省辖市、地级市、县级市的市区、市郊区及县城(包括县人民政府所在地的县城关区或行政建制相当于县人民政府所在地的镇)范围内接入局用交换机的电话用户数，包括分布在农村地区的独立工矿区、林区、驻军等接入局用交换机的电话用户数。

乡村电话用户 指县城关区以下的集镇和农村接入局用交换机的电话用户数。

住宅电话用户 是指安装在居民住宅或农民家里并按照住宅电话用户登记注册和收费的电话用户。包括私人付费、单位付费和按规定免费安装的住宅电话用户。

局用交换机容量 是指安装在本地电信运营商内用于接续本地固定电话的电话交换机容量，有倍增设备按倍增后的数量计数。包括现用和备用的人工或自动交换机的全部容量。

Explanatory Notes on Main Statistical Indicators

Length of Railways in Operation refers to the total length of the trunk line under passenger and freight transportation (including both full operation and temporary operation). The calculation is based on the actual length of the first line even if this line has a full or partial double track or more tracks, excluding double tracks, station sidings, tracks under the charge of stations, branch lines, special-purpose lines and the non-payable connecting lines. The length of railways in operation is an important indicator to show the development of the infrastructure for the railway transport, and also the essential data to calculate volume of passenger freight transport, traffic density and utilization efficiency of the locomotives and carriages.

Extenuation Length of Trunk Lines refers to the sum of the first, the second, the third lines and other constructed length of the trunk railways, excluding the extenuation length of the station lines, lines under the jurisdiction of depots, sidings and lines for special purpose. It provides important information for the calculation of the needs for rails, sleepers, sand and stone for the construction of railways.

Length of Electrified Railways refers to the length of the section of railways in operation in which the power supply lines and other equipment are installed for the running of electrified locomotives. The proportion of the length of electrified railways to the total length of railways in operation is an important indicator to show the modernization of railways.

Automatic-blocking and Semi-automatic-blocking Length of Railways Blocking is a spacing technique by which a section of the railway only allows one train to pass at a time, in order to ensure the traffic safety. Automatic (semi-automatic) blocking length of railways refers to railways installed with equipment to perform automatic or manual blocking of trains, the proportion of automatic/semi-automatic blocking length to the total length of railways in operation is an important indicator to show the modernization of railways.

Length of Highways refers to the length of highways which are built in conformity with the grades specified by the highway engineering standard formulated by the Ministry of Communications, and have been formally checked and accepted by the departments of highways and put into use. The length of highways includes that of the suburb highways at large and medium-sized cities, highways passing through streets at small cities and towns, and also the length of bridges and ferries. It does not include the length of streets in big and medium-sized cities and highways built for the production purpose at factories, mines, forest areas and agricultural areas. If two or more highways go the same section of the way, the length of the section is only calculated for once and no duplication is allowed. The length of highways is an important indicator to show the development of the highway construction and to provide essential information to calculate the transport network density.

Length of Navigable Inland Waterways an indicator reflecting the size and development of inland water network, it refers to the length of the natural rivers, lakes, reservoirs, canals, and ditches open to navigation during a given period, which enables the transport by ships and rafts. It includes the channels open to navigation for over an accumulative 3 months in a year, yet this does not include the river courses which are only used to float odd logs and bamboo rafts.

Length of Civil Aviation Routes refers to the length of all routes for regular civil aviation flights. There are usually two ways to calculate the distance between airports connected by the route length: One is to put the length of all air routes together, called duplicated calculation of the length of the routes; the other is not to allow the duplication in calculation when two or more routes passing the same section of aviation routes. The latter is usually used, as it can precisely show the size of the civil aviation network and indicate the extent of civil aviation serving the national economy and the people.

Length of Oil (Gas) Pipelines used as an indicator to show the development, scale and level of the pipeline transportation, it refers to the actual transport distance of oil (or gas) products, and is in general calculated in the length of single pipe line. If the length of the double pipelines and alternate pipeline are included, it is called the extension length of the oil (gas) pipelines, which indicates the actual length of the pipelines built, excluding double pipelines.

Freight (Passenger) Traffic refers to the volume of freight (passenger) transported with various means. Freight transport is calculated in tons and passenger traffic is calculated in the number of persons. Despite the type of freight and travelling distance, the freight transport is calculated in the actual weight of the goods: and despite the travelling distance and ticket price, the passenger traffic is calculated by the principle that one person can be counted only once in one travel. The passenger who travel with a half price ticket or a child ticket is also calculated as one person. The freight (passenger) traffic provides a quantitative measure to show how the transport industry serves the national economy and people, and is also an important indicator for planning the transport industry and for studying the development scale and speed of the transport industry.

Freight (Passenger) Traffic Density refers to the freight (passenger) traffic volume carried by a particular means of transportation during a given period through one kilometer of a specific section of transportation route. The formula is as follows:

Freight (Passenger) Traffic Density=[Freight Ton-kilometers (Passenger-kilometers)] / (Length of Route in Operation)

Measuring unit: ton-kilometer / kilometer (or person-kilometer / kilometer)

Freight (passenger) traffic density reflects the degree of business of freight (passenger) traffic on transportation routes, and therefore provides important information for balancing transport capability, planning construction and upgrading of transport routes and studying the distribution of transport network.

Freight Ton-kilometers (Passenger-kilometers) refer to the sum of the products of the volume of transported cargo (passengers) multiplying by the transport distance, usually using ton-kilometer and passenger-kilometer as units for measurement. Normally, the shortest distance between the departure station and the destination station (i.e., the payable distance) is the basis to calculate the freight ton-kilometers. This is an important indicator to show the total results of the transport industry, to prepare and examine the transport plan and to measure the efficiency, the labour productivity and the unit cost of transport.

The formula is as follows:

Freight Ton-kilometers (Passenger-kilometers) = Σ {Freight (Passenger) Traffic x Distance of Transportation}

Measuring unit: ton-kilometer (person-kilometer)

Static Load of Freight Cars refers to the average cargo weight as loaded by each freight car under the static condition at the departure station. It is used to show the utilization extent of the loading capacity of the freight cars. The formula is:

Static Load (ton) of Freight Car = (Tonnage of Goods Dispatched) / (Number of Freight Cars Loaded)

The static load of freight cars is determined by the nature and type of goods loaded, the type of vehicles, and the technique of loading. The difference between the average marked load and the static load of freight cars reflects the utilization of loading capacity of freight cars. For its calculation the following formula is applied:

Utilization Rate of Capacity of Freight Cars(%)=[(Average Static Load) × 100%] / (Average Marked Load)

Average Daily Haul of Freight Locomotives refers to the average total ton-kilometers accomplished by each freight transport locomotive over day and night during a given period of time. It includes both the weight of the goods carried and the dead weight of the train itself. It is a comprehensive indicator reflecting the locomotive efficiency in terms of both time and the pulling force.

Average Daily Haul of Freight Transport Locomotive (ton-kilometer)=[(Total Ton/(Kilometers of Freight)] / (Daily Number of Freight Transport Locomotive)

Volume of Freight Handled in Major Coastal Ports refers to the volume of cargo passing in and out the harbor area of the major coastal ports and having been loaded and unloaded. The volume includes that of the postal matters, registered luggage and fuels, materials and fresh water as supplies of the ships. The volume of freight handled may be classified by direction of flow as freight for import and freight for export, or by nature of cargo as freight for domestic trade and freight for foreign trade. As an important indicator, the volume of freight handled by type of cargo and by main flow direction reflects the production capacity of ports.

Business Volume of Post and Telecommunications refers to the total amount of post and telecommunications services, expressed in value terms, provided by the post and telecommunications departments for the society. Post and telecommunication services can be classified as letters, parcels, remittance, issue of newspapers and magazines, fast mail service, express mail service, savings deposits, stamps for collection, public and individual telegraph service, facsimiles, long-distance telephone service, leasing of telephone lines, urban paging service, mobile telephone service, data transfer and transmission, etc. The accounting approach is to multiply the service products of all types with their average unit price (constant price) to get sum of business value, plus income from other services such as leasing of telephone lines and equipment, maintenance of telephone switchboards and lines on behalf of customers. This indicator reflects the overall results of post and telecommunications service during a given period, and is important to study the composition of business service and the development of post and telecommunications service.

The formula is as follows:

Business Volume of Post and Telecommunications= Σ (Transaction of Post and Telecommunication Service x Constant Price) + Income from Leasing, Maintenance and other Services

Subscribers of Wireless Paging Services Wireless paging service refers the service by which telephone users send audio, digital or character signals to persons carrying small-size pagers within the designated areas through wireless paging centers. The page carriers who have registered in paging centers are counted as paging subscribers.

Mobile Telephone Subscribers refer to the persons who own mobile telephone numbers and are connected with the mobile telephone communication network through the mobile telephone switchboards. The number of subscribers is calculated by the subscribers who have completed registration at mobile communication business centers and entered into the mobile telephone network. One mobile telephone is taken as a subscriber.

Telephone Subscribers refer to subscribers that are connected to the public line telephone network provided with telephone services. Before 1997, telephone subscribers were classified as city subscribers and village subscribers. City subscribers referred to those connected to city telephone networks in county towns and cities, while village subscribers referred to those connected to village telephone stations at and below counties. Since 1997, the classification of telephone subscribers was modified on the basis of physical location of the subscribers as "urban telephone subscribers" and "rural telephone subscribers", which is different from the previous classification of categorizing "local telephones" and "rural telephones", while the definition of total subscribers and total number of telephones remain unchanged.

Urban Telephone Subscribers refer to subscribers telephone subscribers, located at municipalities, cities under the jurisdiction of province, cities at prefectural level, downtown and suburb of city at county level town and county towns (including country towns where county government located, and towns of county level according to the administrative organizational system), that are connected to the public line telephone network, including rural mineral area, forest area, military area.

Rural Telephone Subscribers refer to telephone subscribers, located at towns under county town and country, that are connected to the public line telephone network.

Household Telephone Subscribers refer to telephone sets installed in the dwelling units of urban or rural residents, and registered as residence subscribers for payment, including 3 types of payment for the service: private payment, public payment and free service.

Capacity of Office Telephone Exchanges refers to the capacity (measured in gate) of telephone exchanges installed in the offices of local telecommunication service providers for communication between fixed telephones. It includes the capacity of both manual and automatic exchanges in use and for stand-by purpose. Equipment with expansion function is to be counted by the expanded capacity.

十六、国内贸易

Domestic Trade

简要说明

一、本篇资料反映我国国内市场发展情况和批发零售贸易业、餐饮业商品经营情况。主要内容有批发零售贸易业商品流通，批发零售贸易企业、餐饮企业财务状况，社会消费品零售总额、国内集市贸易等。

二、本篇资料是国家统计局贸易外经司根据批发零售贸易、餐饮业统计报表制度进行搜集和加工整理而得，城乡集市贸易情况由国家工商行政管理局提供。

三、本篇资料的统计范围和调查方法：财务状况报表为限额以上批发、零售贸易业法人企业和餐饮业法人企业。社会消费品零售总额报表为有零售业务的企业、事业单位以及农业生产者。限额以上企业（单位）逐一调查，自下而上逐级汇总上报，采取全面调查的方法；其他资料有的以抽样调查数据推断，有的利用工商、税务等部门的有关资料推算。

四、本篇资料中各地区社会消费品零售总额相加不等于全国总计，原因是全国总计根据相关核算资料和部门资料进行了修正和调整。

Brief Introduction

I. The data in this chapter show the development of China's domestic market and the sales of the commodities in wholesale and retail sale trades as well as catering trade, including mainly the circulation of commodities in the wholesale and retail sale trades, the financial condition of the wholesale, retail and catering trade enterprises, the total sales of the consumer goods in the whole country and the domestic fair trade, etc.

II. Data in this chapter are collected and processed in accordance with the statistical reporting scheme on wholesale and retail sale trades as well as catering trade, stipulated by the Department of Trade and External Economic Relations of the National Bureau of Statistics. Data on the urban and rural fair trade are provided respectively by the State Administration for Industry and Commerce.

III. Statistical coverage and survey methods: Statistics on financial conditions include all corporate enterprises of wholesale, retail and catering trade that are above the designated size. Statistics on retail sales of consumer goods include all enterprises, institutional units and peasants engaged in retail sale business. The method used in data collection for enterprises (units) above designated size is a complete enumeration, under which all units are covered in the survey and data are reported from lower to higher level statistical offices. For units below the designated size, sample surveys are used, and in some cases, administrative registers from industrial and commercial administration and taxation administration are used in the estimation.

IV. In this chapter, the sum of total retail sales of consumer goods of all provinces is not equal to the national total, as the national total has been adjusted and modified in line with national accounts data and data from other departments.

16-1 国内贸易基本情况

Basic Conditions of Domestic Trade

指 标	Item	1996	1997	1998	1999	2000
法人机构 （个）	**Number of Corporation Unit**					
批发零售贸易业	Wholesale and Retail Trades	592487			27115	25567
餐饮业	Catering Trade	48240			3266	3508
产业活动单位 （个）	**Number of Economic Active Unit**					
批发零售贸易业	Wholesale and Retail Trades				42940	42438
餐饮业	Catering Trade				4966	5363
从业人员 （人）	**Persons Employed (person)**					
批发零售贸易业	In Wholesale and Retail Trade	44991244			4922171	4485335
餐饮业	In Catering Trade	7753108			660850	664749
批发零售贸易业	**Wholesale and Retail Trade**					
商品购进总额 （亿元）	Total Purchases (100 million yuan)	38549.7	39788.3	24297.4	24580.8	29784.1
商品销售总额 （亿元）	Total Sales (100 million yuan)	42546.9	55168.7	56437.7	58780.1	66359.5
商品库存总额 （亿元）	Total Inventory (100 million yuan)	7227.3	7544.8	3789.7	3629.7	3569.9
社会消费品零售总额 （亿元）	**Total Retail Sales of Consumer Goods （100 million yuan）**	**24774.1**	**27298.9**	**29152.5**	**31134.7**	**34152.6**
按销售单位所在地分	By Location of Establishments					
市	City	14951.2	16650.4	17825.2	19091.6	21110.3
县	County	3280.0	3500.1	3681.9	3892.5	4217.2
县以下	Under County Level	6542.9	7148.4	7645.4	8150.6	8825.1
按行业分	By Sector					
批发零售贸易业	Wholesale and Retail Trade	16205.1	18108.3	19185.8	20551.8	23042.3
餐饮业	Catering Trade	2024.9	2433.3	2816.4	3199.6	3752.6
其他行业	Others	6544.1	6757.3	7150.3	7383.3	7357.7
#制造业	Manufacturing	1775.3	1987.9	2037.6	2094.5	2191.8
农业生产者	Farm Producers	3261.9	3744.9	4088.7	4205.0	4035.8

注：1.1998年及以后批发零售贸易业商品购进、库存总额为限额以上批发零售贸易业数据。
2.1997年及以后社会消费品零售总额不含居民购买住房(下表同)。
3.1999年及以后法人机构、产业活动单位和从业人员为限额以上企业。

a) Figures since 1998 on purchase, sales and inventory by wholesale and retail trade refer to units above designated size.
b) Data on total retail sales of consumer goods since 1997 exclude purchase of commodity housing by households.
c) Number of corporation unit, economic active units and persons employed since 1999 refer to those enterprise above designated size.

16-2 全国消费品市场交易情况

Trade of Consumable Markets in Urban and Rural Areas

项 目	Item	1985	1990	1998	1999	2000
消费品市场数(个)	**Number of Free Markets**	**61337**	**72579**	**89177**	**88576**	**88811**
城市市场	Urban Areas	8013	13106	24127	24983	26395
农村市场	Rural Areas	53324	59473	65050	63593	62416
消费品市场成交额(亿元)	**Transaction Value(100 million yuan)**	**632.3**	**2168.2**	**19835.5**	**21707.8**	**24279.6**
城市市场	Urban Areas	120.7	837.8	11042.8	12325.7	13800.4
农村市场	Rural Areas	511.6	1330.4	8792.7	9382.1	10479.2
在成交额中	**Of the Transaction Value:**					
#粮油类	Grain and Oil	49.6	146.8	1464.8	1591.1	1959.5
肉禽蛋类	Meat, Poultry and Eggs	140.1	618.8	3557.4	3802.1	4201.9
水产品类	Aquatic Products	33.2	182.4	1659	1800.7	2073.4
蔬菜类	Vegetables	48.8	264.2	2207	2425.5	2661.8
干鲜果类	Dried and Fresh Fruits	25.5	183.5	1234.7	1398.2	1546.2

注：1.1985年商品分类交易额为农村消费品市场数，1990年及以后为全国消费品市场数。
2.本表资料取自于国家工商行政管理局。

a) The transaction value by category of commodities in 1985 referred to the data of the rural consumable markets, and since 1990 the figures have referred to the data of the consumable markets in both rural and urban areas.
b) Data in this table were obtained from the State Administration of Industry and Commerce.

16-3 社会消费品零售总额（按销售单位所在地分）

Total Retail Sale of Consumer Goods by Location of Retailers

单位：亿元 (100 million yuan)

年份 Year	地区 Region	社会消费品零售总额 Total Retail Sales of Consumer Goods	市 City	县 County	县以下 Under County Level
1952		276.8			
1957		474.2			
1962		604.0			
1965		670.3			
1970		858.0			
1975		1271.1	416.7	350.0	504.4
1978		1558.6	505.2	380.4	673.0
1979		1800.0	584.7	347.5	867.8
1980		2140.0	733.6	399.4	1007.0
1981		2350.0	843.3	431.9	1074.8
1982		2570.0	920.5	471.3	1178.2
1983		2849.4	1057.3	520.8	1271.3
1984		3376.4	1348.7	586.4	1441.3
1985		4305.0	1874.5	737.2	1693.3
1986		4950.0	2018.0	902.0	2030.0
1987		5820.0	2427.0	1030.0	2363.0
1988		7440.0	3260.8	1264.3	2914.9
1989		8101.4	3666.8	1329.5	3105.1
1990		8300.1	3888.6	1337.4	3074.1
1991		9415.6	4529.8	1491.2	3394.6
1992		10993.7	5470.3	1689.8	3833.6
1993		12462.1	7224.9	2039.5	3197.7
1994		16264.7	9661.2	2407.2	4196.3
1995		20620.0	12376.7	2919.6	5323.7
1996		24774.1	14951.2	3280.0	6542.9
1997		27298.9	16650.4	3500.1	7148.4
1998		29152.5	17825.2	3681.9	7645.4
1999		31134.7	19091.6	3892.5	8150.6
2000		34152.6	21110.3	4217.2	8825.1
北京	Beijing	1443.3	1138.5	92.6	212.2
天津	Tianjin	736.6	564.5	58.6	113.5
河北	Hebei	1613.9	749.5	312.8	551.6
山西	Shanxi	629.1	369.2	132.5	127.4
内蒙古	Inner Mongolia	484.0	288.4	117.1	78.5
辽宁	Liaoning	1847.6	1529.9	102.3	215.4
吉林	Jilin	810.9	596.4	55.6	158.9
黑龙江	Heilongjiang	1094.0	785.1	160.6	148.3
上海	Shanghai	1722.3	1398.9	81.2	242.2
江苏	Jiangsu	2604.1	1598.1	187.0	819.0
浙江	Zhejiang	2298.8	1255.2	225.4	818.2
安徽	Anhui	1054.3	499.0	234.5	320.8
福建	Fujian	1372.8	778.0	178.6	416.2
江西	Jiangxi	704.9	333.7	159.8	211.4
山东	Shandong	2545.9	1573.0	243.6	729.3
河南	Henan	1786.7	874.2	381.3	531.2
湖北	Hubei	1789.4	1128.5	177.7	483.2
湖南	Hunan	1364.7	710.1	255.1	399.5
广东	Guangdong	4071.9	2685.7	221.8	1164.4
广西	Guangxi	859.2	416.4	176.4	266.4
海南	Hainan	172.5	113.6	14.8	44.1
重庆	Chongqing	643.4	361.6	88.9	192.9
四川	Sichuan	1523.7	713.1	271.2	539.4
贵州	Guizhou	343.7	197.4	66.8	79.5
云南	Yunnan	583.2	309.3	139.1	134.8
西藏	Tibet	42.9	16.3	18.5	8.1
陕西	Shaanxi	607.6	400.7	103.1	103.8
甘肃	Gansu	362.7	234.0	57.5	71.2
青海	Qinghai	82.1	50.7	19.8	11.6
宁夏	Ningxia	90.2	58.9	16.6	14.7
新疆	Xinjiang	374.5	233.7	65.1	75.7

注：1.1992年及以前为社会商品零售总额（下表同）。
2.各地区相加不等于全国总计，原因是全国数据进行了修正（下表同）。

a) Figures before 1993 refer to retail sales of commodities. Similarly in following tables.
b) The sum of provincial figures do not add up to the national total, as the national total was adjusted. Similarly in following tables.

16-4 社会消费品零售总额（按行业分）

Total Retail Sale of Consumer Goods by Sector

单位:亿元 (100 million yuan)

年份 Year	地区 Region	批发零售贸易业 Wholesale and Retail Trade	餐饮业 Catering Services	其他行业 Others	#制造业 Manufacturing	#农业生产者 Agriculture
1952		211.3	14.1	51.4	37.9	11.8
1957		399.5	24.2	50.5	33.9	13.2
1962		502.1	39.1	62.8	27.9	27.0
1965		594.6	31.2	44.5	24.2	13.0
1970		769.3	29.6	59.1	27.4	17.0
1975		1113.9	45.5	111.7	61.6	25.0
1978		1363.7	54.8	140.1	73.2	31.1
1979		1540.5	63.7	195.8	103.6	47.5
1980		1768.0	80.0	292.0	165.0	69.0
1981		1915.4	87.6	347.0	195.4	89.4
1982		2068.1	98.4	403.5	216.8	110.8
1983		2269.1	112.1	468.2	249.7	133.0
1984		2645.5	137.1	593.8	314.1	170.0
1985		3272.2	196.9	835.9	400.7	291.0
1986		3717.8	232.8	999.4	457.6	375.0
1987		4343.5	283.0	1193.5	537.1	461.0
1988		5544.6	366.5	1528.9	686.1	595.0
1989		6009.5	405.1	1686.8	720.3	698.0
1990		6127.4	419.8	1752.9	699.1	773.3
1991		6903.9	492.0	2019.7	788.0	909.8
1992		7922.2	589.7	2481.8	939.4	1077.4
1993		8726.9	800.1	2935.1	1062.9	1436.2
1994		11039.7	1175.1	4049.9	1272.8	2143.7
1995		13801.3	1579.2	5239.5	1540.7	2777.6
1996		16205.1	2024.9	6544.1	1775.3	3261.9
1997		18108.3	2433.3	6757.3	1987.9	3744.9
1998		19185.8	2816.4	7150.3	2037.6	4088.7
1999		20551.8	3199.6	7383.3	2094.5	4205.0
2000		23042.3	3752.6	7357.7	2191.8	4035.8
北京	Beijing	1025.5	86.4	331.4	86.9	6.4
天津	Tianjin	379.2	79.0	278.4	31.0	61.0
河北	Hebei	1121.1	162.6	330.2	140.4	147.0
山西	Shanxi	423.3	54.3	151.5	36.7	88.4
内蒙古	Inner Mongolia	314.5	48.1	121.4	34.7	66.1
辽宁	Liaoning	1355.1	219.7	272.8	52.4	188.3
吉林	Jilin	674.6	98.7	37.6	12.9	18.7
黑龙江	Heilongjiang	848.6	98.5	146.9	39.7	88.1
上海	Shanghai	1368.2	127.7	226.4	45.4	168.0
江苏	Jiangsu	1905.3	241.4	457.4	182.4	225.2
浙江	Zhejiang	1600.5	214.0	484.3	150.9	260.6
安徽	Anhui	666.2	117.1	271.0	85.3	163.8
福建	Fujian	991.5	157.2	224.1	67.5	93.3
江西	Jiangxi	433.2	60.1	211.6	48.2	139.6
山东	Shandong	1618.7	265.4	661.8	280.3	259.5
河南	Henan	1113.0	209.6	464.1	234.4	168.7
湖北	Hubei	1107.4	192.4	489.6	98.1	307.7
湖南	Hunan	885.0	139.6	340.1	69.8	243.2
广东	Guangdong	2894.3	646.6	531.0	180.1	259.9
广西	Guangxi	590.9	96.3	172.0	44.1	109.0
海南	Hainan	103.9	22.9	45.7	4.5	35.2
重庆	Chongqing	383.2	54.6	205.6	38.3	15.5
四川	Sichuan	885.3	222.4	416.0	89.9	275.8
贵州	Guizhou	232.4	42.3	69.0	18.0	43.1
云南	Yunnan	376.5	74.9	131.8	27.0	90.0
西藏	Tibet	33.9	4.2	4.8	1.8	2.1
陕西	Shaanxi	380.7	63.1	163.8	52.5	97.9
甘肃	Gansu	235.2	46.6	80.9	16.7	46.4
青海	Qinghai	56.9	11.3	13.9	3.6	8.1
宁夏	Ningxia	54.0	10.9	25.3	3.7	19.9
新疆	Xinjiang	242.3	38.2	94.0	22.0	51.2

16-5 限额以上批发零售贸易、餐饮业基本情况（2000年，按登记注册类型分）

Basic Conditions of Enterprises above Designated Size in Wholesale and Retail Trade, Catering Services by Types of Registration (2000)

指 标	Item	法人企业（个）Number of Corporation Unit	产业活动单位数（个）Number of Economic Active Unit	从业人数（人）Persons Employed（person）
总 计	**Total**	**29075**	**47801**	**5150084**
一、批发业合计	**Wholesale Trade**	**15393**	**23956**	**2319248**
内资企业	**Domestic Funded Enterprises**	**15279**	**23780**	**2306312**
国有企业	State-owned Enterprises	9317	14428	1465201
集体企业	Collective-owned Enterprises	2406	3641	373647
股份合作企业	Cooperative Enterprises	355	569	30706
联营企业	Joint Ownership Enterprises	228	259	10510
国有联营企业	State Joint Ownership Enterprises	123	127	4992
集体联营企业	Collective Joint Ownership Enterprises	21	22	834
国有与集体联营企业	Joint State-collective Enterprises	51	69	3630
其他联营企业	Other Joint Ownership Enterprises	33	41	1054
有限责任公司	Limited Liability Corporations	1722	3039	250835
国有独资公司	State Sole Funded Corporations	233	552	48226
其他有限责任公司	Other Limited Liability Corporations	1489	2487	202609
股份有限公司	Share-holding Corporations Ltd.	685	1267	154685
私营企业	Private Enterprises	560	571	20405
私营独资企业	Private-funded Enterprises	36	37	1279
私营合伙企业	Private Partnership Enterprises	17	17	904
私营有限责任公司	Private Limited Liability Corporations	472	482	16598
私营股份有限公司	Private Share-holding Corporations Ltd.	35	35	1624
其他企业	Other Enterprises	6	6	323
港、澳、台商投资企业	**Enterprises with Funds from Hong Kong, Macao and Taiwan**	**47**	**55**	**3330**
合资经营企业（港或澳、台资）	Joint-venture Enterprises (with Funds from Hong Kong, Macao and Taiwan)	22	26	1781
合作经营企业（港或澳、台资）	Cooperative Enterprises (with Funds from Hong Kong, Macao and Taiwan)	6	7	723
港、澳、台商独资经营企业	Enterprises with Sole Investment from Hong Kong, Macao and Taiwan	18	21	806
港、澳、台商投资股份有限公司	Share-holding Corporations Ltd. with Investment from Hong Kong, Macao and Taiwan	1	1	20
外商投资企业	**Foreign Funded Enterprises**	**67**	**121**	**9606**
中外合资经营企业	Joint-venture Enterprises	36	87	6121
中外合作经营企业	Cooperation Enterprises	5	7	1241
外资企业	Enterprises with Sole Foreign Investment	23	24	1737
外商投资股份有限公司	Share-holding Corporations Ltd. with Foreign Investment	3	3	507
二、零售业合计	**Retail Trade**	**10174**	**18482**	**2166087**
内资企业	**Domestic Funded Enterprises**	**9984**	**17786**	**2070449**
国有企业	State-owned Enterprises	4616	7842	909962
集体企业	Collective-owned Enterprises	2505	4375	324048
股份合作企业	Cooperative Enterprises	437	688	65834
联营企业	Joint Ownership Enterprises	123	135	23184
国有联营企业	State Joint Ownership Enterprises	53	53	7733
集体联营企业	Collective Joint Ownership Enterprises	17	17	3129
国有与集体联营企业	Joint State-collective Enterprises	35	44	6313
其他联营企业	Other Joint Ownership Enterprises	18	21	6009
有限责任公司	Limited Liability Corporations	1059	2515	275353
国有独资公司	State Sole Funded Corporations	73	120	25337
其他有限责任公司	Other Limited Liability Corporations	986	2395	250016
股份有限公司	Share-holding Corporations Ltd.	651	1534	392803

16-5 续表 1 continued

指 标	Item	法人企业（个）Number of Corporation Unit	产业活动单位数（个）Number of Economic Active Unit	从业人数（人）Persons Employed（person）
私营企业	Private Enterprises	588	675	78099
私营独资企业	Private-funded Enterprises	61	68	9057
私营合伙企业	Private Partnership Enterprises	23	24	1633
私营有限责任公司	Private Limited Liability Corporations	454	530	61909
私营股份有限公司	Private Share-holding Corporations Ltd.	50	53	5500
其他企业	Other Enterprises	5	22	1166
港、澳、台商投资企业	**Enterprises with Funds from Hong Kong, Macao and Taiwan**	**101**	**221**	**44805**
合资经营企业（港或澳、台资）	Joint-venture Enterprises (with Funds from Hong Kong, Macao and Taiwan)	55	133	25515
合作经营企业（港或澳、台资）	Cooperative Enterprises (with Funds from Hong Kong, Macao and Taiwan)	27	66	16021
港、澳、台商独资经营企业	Enterprises with Sole Funds from Hong Kong, Macao and Taiwan	16	18	2498
港、澳、台商投资股份有限公司	Share-holding Corporations Ltd. with Funds from Hong Kong, Macao and Taiwan	3	4	771
外商投资企业	**Foreign Funded Enterprises**	**89**	**475**	**50833**
中外合资经营企业	Joint-venture Enterprises	57	409	28275
中外合作经营企业	Cooperation Enterprises	26	57	20250
外资企业	Enterprises with Sole Foreign Investment	4	7	1536
外商投资股份有限公司	Share-holding Corporations Ltd. with Foreign Investment	2	2	772
三、餐饮业合计	**Catering Services**	**3508**	**5363**	**664749**
内资企业	**Domestic Funded Enterprises**	**2877**	**4310**	**498998**
国有企业	State-owned Enterprises	895	1574	207046
集体企业	Collective-owned Enterprises	635	915	78127
股份合作企业	Cooperative Enterprises	180	270	26310
联营企业	Joint Ownership Enterprises	40	65	7620
国有联营企业	State Joint Ownership Enterprises	17	30	3498
集体联营企业	Collective Joint Ownership Enterprises	7	13	1153
国有与集体联营企业	Joint State-collective Enterprises	8	12	1603
其他联营企业	Other Joint Ownership Enterprises	8	10	1366
有限责任公司	Limited Liability Corporations	331	553	69119
国有独资公司	State Sole Funded Corporations	7	14	1967
其他有限责任公司	Other Limited Liability Corporations	324	539	67152
股份有限公司	Share-holding Corporations Ltd.	104	171	34586
私营企业	Private Enterprises	689	756	75731
私营独资企业	Private-funded Enterprises	261	286	24015
私营合伙企业	Private Partnership Enterprises	45	48	3535
私营有限责任公司	Private Limited Liability Corporations	343	379	43125
私营股份有限公司	Private Share-holding Corporations Ltd.	40	43	5056
其他企业	Other Enterprises	3	6	459
港、澳、台商投资企业	**Enterprises with Funds from Hong Kong, Macao and Taiwan**	**378**	**581**	**88184**
合资经营企业（港或澳、台资）	Joint-venture Enterprises (with Funds from Hong Kong, Macao and Taiwan)	224	359	50518
合作经营企业（港或澳、台资）	Cooperative Enterprises (with Funds from Hong Kong, Macao and Taiwan)	84	119	24123
港、澳、台商独资经营企业	Enterprises with Sole Funds from Hong Kong, Macao and Taiwan	64	94	11676
港、澳、台商投资股份有限公司	Share-holding Corporations Ltd. with Funds from Hong Kong, Macao and Taiwan	6	9	1867
外商投资企业	**Enterprises With Foreign Investment**	**253**	**472**	**77567**
中外合资经营企业	Joint-venture Enterprises	141	205	41840
中外合作经营企业	Cooperation Enterprises	57	113	18944
外资企业	Enterprises with Sole Foreign Funds	53	150	16262
外商投资股份有限公司	Share-holding Corporations Ltd. with Foreign Investment	2	4	521

16−6 限额以上批发零售贸易、餐饮业法人企业数（2000年，按地区分）

Number of Corporation Units above Designated Size in Wholesale and Retail Trade, Catering Services by Region (2000)

单位:个 (unit)

地区	Region	合计 Total	批发业 Wholesale Trade	零售业 Retail Trade	餐饮业 Catering Service
全国	**National Total**	**29075**	**15393**	**10174**	**3508**
北京	Beijing	2727	1059	1276	392
天津	Tianjin	675	337	262	76
河北	Hebei	1039	638	346	55
山西	Shanxi	682	319	316	47
内蒙古	Inner Mongolia	388	203	150	35
辽宁	Liaoning	1286	688	379	219
吉林	Jilin	463	266	159	38
黑龙江	Heilongjiang	718	365	289	64
上海	Shanghai	1002	445	384	173
江苏	Jiangsu	1781	990	582	209
浙江	Zhejiang	2258	1389	643	226
安徽	Anhui	666	463	188	15
福建	Fujian	1407	850	368	189
江西	Jiangxi	528	358	135	35
山东	Shandong	2015	1047	707	261
河南	Henan	2126	752	1200	174
湖北	Hubei	1076	544	401	131
湖南	Hunan	813	469	287	57
广东	Guangdong	2720	1582	535	603
广西	Guangxi	766	407	274	85
海南	Hainan	129	68	25	36
重庆	Chongqing	490	231	148	111
四川	Sichuan	784	421	244	119
贵州	Guizhou	254	158	76	20
云南	Yunnan	931	568	325	38
西藏	Tibet	19	8	11	
陕西	Shaanxi	385	257	95	33
甘肃	Gansu	328	148	155	25
青海	Qinghai	97	55	36	6
宁夏	Ningxia	127	69	46	12
新疆	Xinjiang	395	239	132	24

16-7 限额以上批发零售贸易、餐饮业产业活动单位数（2000年，按地区分）

Number of Economic Active Units above Designated Size in Wholesale and Retail Trade, Catering Services by Region (2000)

单位:个 (unit)

地 区	Region	合 计 Total	批发业 Wholesale Trade	零售业 Retail Trade	餐饮业 Catering Services
全 国	**National Total**	**47801**	**23956**	**18482**	**5363**
北 京	Beijing	2819	1086	1319	414
天 津	Tianjin	1604	585	759	260
河 北	Hebei	1039	638	346	55
山 西	Shanxi	682	319	316	47
内蒙古	Inner Mongolia	697	362	294	41
辽 宁	Liaoning	1321	693	384	244
吉 林	Jilin	533	270	163	100
黑龙江	Heilongjiang	1946	1063	795	88
上 海	Shanghai	7147	2098	4408	641
江 苏	Jiangsu	3107	1567	1278	262
浙 江	Zhejiang	5159	3072	1638	449
安 徽	Anhui	3442	2489	882	71
福 建	Fujian	1518	870	382	266
江 西	Jiangxi	556	359	140	57
山 东	Shandong	2138	1096	727	315
河 南	Henan	2211	772	1228	211
湖 北	Hubei	1252	632	427	193
湖 南	Hunan	937	520	322	95
广 东	Guangdong	2954	1589	557	808
广 西	Guangxi	839	415	280	144
海 南	Hainan	148	68	25	55
重 庆	Chongqing	512	235	150	127
四 川	Sichuan	828	428	248	152
贵 州	Guizhou	254	158	76	20
云 南	Yunnan	2732	1778	853	101
西 藏	Tibet	19	8	11	
陕 西	Shaanxi	385	257	95	33
甘 肃	Gansu	333	150	156	27
青 海	Qinghai	107	62	37	8
宁 夏	Ningxia	150	70	50	30
新 疆	Xinjiang	432	247	136	49

16-8 限额以上批发零售贸易、餐饮业从业人数（2000年，按地区分）

Number of Persons Employed in Enterprises above Designated Size in Wholesale and Retail Trade, Catering Services by Region (2000)

单位：人 (person)

地 区	Region	合 计 Total	批发业 Wholesale Trade	零售业 Retail Trade	餐饮业 Catering Services
全 国	**National Total**	**5150084**	**2319248**	**2166087**	**664749**
北 京	Beijing	344767	96488	200383	47896
天 津	Tianjin	95267	38911	47204	9152
河 北	Hebei	210939	93499	107510	9930
山 西	Shanxi	132359	50787	73382	8190
内蒙古	Inner Mongolia	49840	20525	25171	4144
辽 宁	Liaoning	244432	101952	106601	35879
吉 林	Jilin	110082	51422	44157	14503
黑龙江	Heilongjiang	157558	72525	77238	7795
上 海	Shanghai	313006	132767	137530	42709
江 苏	Jiangsu	415453	195820	176249	43384
浙 江	Zhejiang	259569	122624	92828	44117
安 徽	Anhui	138025	77595	54577	5853
福 建	Fujian	128316	61319	39279	27718
江 西	Jiangxi	83968	51878	25557	6533
山 东	Shandong	416946	189343	176649	50954
河 南	Henan	357822	163686	174430	19706
湖 北	Hubei	303073	158652	116820	27601
湖 南	Hunan	172575	95917	59015	17643
广 东	Guangdong	404491	162242	107711	134538
广 西	Guangxi	121678	46371	53686	21621
海 南	Hainan	16287	5832	4692	5763
重 庆	Chongqing	89081	39507	30687	18887
四 川	Sichuan	178258	68190	81181	28887
贵 州	Guizhou	45328	26247	15766	3315
云 南	Yunnan	114101	71801	36509	5791
西 藏	Tibet	1879	936	943	
陕 西	Shaanxi	81840	37448	36372	8020
甘 肃	Gansu	54258	25987	24847	3424
青 海	Qinghai	17696	9457	7569	670
宁 夏	Ningxia	17706	5988	8808	2910
新 疆	Xinjiang	73484	43532	22736	7216

16-9 限额以上批发、零售贸易业商品购、销、存总额(2000年，按行业分)

Total Purchases, Sales and Inventory of Enterprise above Designated Size in Wholesale and Retail Trade by Sector(2000)

单位：亿元 (100 million yuan)

指 标	Item	购进总额 Total Purchases	销售总额 Total Sales	批发 Wholesale Trade	零售 Retail Trade	年末库存总额 Inventory (year-end)
总 计	**Total**	**29784.06**	**32265.47**	**25977.87**	**6287.60**	**3569.92**
一、批发企业合计	**Wholesale Trade**	**24979.75**	**26947.40**	**24875.89**	**2071.51**	**2831.10**
食品、饮料、烟草批发业	Wholesale of Food, Beverages and Tobaccos	5685.62	6517.67	6141.42	376.25	890.00
#粮食、食用油批发业	Wholesale of Grains and Edible Oil	754.28	823.46	777.96	45.50	380.71
烟草及其制品批发业	Whole of Tobaccos	3618.54	4258.97	4189.23	69.74	393.56
棉、麻、土畜产品批发业	Wholesale of Cotton, Ambery and Animal Products	791.95	930.32	918.96	11.37	385.69
纺织品、服装和鞋帽批发业	Wholesale of Textiles, Garments, Shoes and Hats	1754.63	1932.57	1908.71	23.85	94.39
日用百货批发业	Wholesale of Daily Consumer Goods	553.89	588.70	514.62	74.08	62.40
日用杂品批发业	Wholesale of Daily Sundry Articles	62.53	70.55	58.21	12.34	7.52
五金、交电、化工批发业	Wholesale of Hardware, Transport, Electric and Chemical Products	991.16	1029.82	918.11	111.71	138.70
药品及医疗器械批发业	Wholesale of Medicines and Medical Appliances	1089.24	1206.00	720.44	485.56	160.66
能源批发业	Wholesale of Energy Products	6269.82	6205.70	5738.20	467.50	295.77
#石油及制品批发业	Wholesale of Petroleum and Related Products	5776.82	5623.00	5215.24	407.76	261.77
煤炭及制品批发业	Wholesale of Coal and Related Products	462.07	525.27	511.98	13.29	26.84
化工材料批发业	Wholesale of Chemical Materials	764.59	807.40	788.06	19.34	67.15
木材批发业	Wholesale of Timber	68.47	74.61	72.72	1.90	7.88
建筑材料批发业	Wholesale of Building Materials	176.01	188.39	177.50	10.89	14.02
矿产品批发业	Wholesale of Mineral Products	140.84	182.23	181.29	0.94	14.99
金属材料批发业	Wholesale of Metal Materials	1818.36	1930.73	1887.78	42.96	151.23
机械、电子设备批发业	Wholesale of Machinery and Electronic Equipment	1296.36	1448.49	1375.91	72.58	124.68
汽车、摩托车及零配件批发业	Wholesale of Motor Vehicles, Motorcycles and Parts	1316.44	1411.54	1149.47	262.08	128.97
#汽车批发业	Wholesale of Motor Vehicles	1094.56	1167.79	978.15	189.64	110.94
再生物资回收批发业	Wholesale of Recycled Materials	139.76	150.44	145.06	5.38	6.87
工艺美术批发业	Wholesale of Arts and Handicraft Products	144.19	156.56	156.06	0.50	8.29
图书报刊批发业	Wholesale of Books, Newspapers and Magazines	287.30	284.00	261.72	22.28	48.55
农业生产资料批发业	Wholesale of Means of Agricultural Production	974.60	1059.79	1016.41	43.39	136.72
其他类未包括的批发业	Other Wholesale not Classified Elsewhere	654.01	771.87	745.25	26.62	86.62
二、零售企业合计	**Retail Trade**	**4804.31**	**5318.07**	**1101.98**	**4216.10**	**738.82**
食品、饮料、烟草零售业	Retail of Food, Beverages and Tobaccos	607.83	679.89	168.42	511.47	125.39
#粮油食品零售业	Retail of Grains and Edible Oil	105.38	105.47	36.28	69.19	54.71
副食品零售业	Retail of Non-staple Food	249.22	267.43	59.60	207.83	35.50
日用百货零售业	Retail of Daily Consumer Goods	2626.74	2943.92	396.90	2547.02	369.55
#百货零售业	Retail of Consumer Goods	2515.54	2807.56	352.69	2454.87	334.40
文化体育用品零售业	Retail of Cultural and Sports Goods	15.67	18.31	4.29	14.02	5.04
纺织品、服装和鞋帽零售业	Retail of Textiles, Garments, Shoes and Hats	103.60	120.70	23.32	97.38	18.29
日用杂品零售业	Retail of Daily Sundry Articles	20.90	24.97	8.84	16.13	3.13
五金、交电、化工零售业	Retail of Hardware, Transport, Electric and Chemical Products	356.11	370.08	103.57	266.51	61.05
药品及医疗器械零售业	Retail of Medicines and Medical Appliances	199.39	241.74	55.66	186.08	41.06
图书报刊零售业	Retail of Books, Newspapers and Magazines	235.76	234.73	51.43	183.30	48.45
其他零售业	Other Retail Trade	653.98	702.05	293.84	408.21	71.91
#家具零售业	Retail of Furniture	12.12	15.10	0.39	14.71	2.91
汽车、摩托车及其零配件零售业	Retail of Motor Vehicles, Motorcycles and Parts	212.99	226.10	52.23	173.87	23.24
计算机及软件、办公设备零售业	Retail of Computers, Software and Office Appliances	47.97	49.96	29.05	20.92	4.73

16-10 限额以上批发零售贸易业商品购、销、存总额(2000年,按地区分)

Total Purchases, Sales and Inventory of Enterprise above Designated Size in Wholesale and Retail Sale Trades by Region (2000)

单位：亿元 (100 million yuan)

地区	Region	购进总额 Total Goods Purchase	销售总额 Total Sales	批发 Wholesale Trade	零售 Retail Trade	年末库存总额 Inventory (year-end)
全国	**National Total**	**29784.06**	**32265.47**	**25977.87**	**6287.60**	**3569.92**
北京	Beijing	2814.22	2969.67	2308.52	661.14	410.30
天津	Tianjin	1011.30	1059.03	906.70	152.34	100.32
河北	Hebei	797.85	861.20	671.86	189.34	97.36
山西	Shanxi	314.31	365.45	261.82	103.63	56.10
内蒙古	Inner Mongolia	196.48	212.70	152.30	60.39	34.76
辽宁	Liaoning	1527.00	1615.46	1378.12	237.34	166.83
吉林	Jilin	293.85	327.90	223.77	104.13	61.02
黑龙江	Heilongjiang	473.27	541.02	404.52	136.50	136.77
上海	Shanghai	2800.77	3116.58	2124.41	992.17	236.46
江苏	Jiangsu	2715.80	2952.54	2381.84	570.69	278.23
浙江	Zhejiang	2834.89	3109.95	2694.40	415.55	205.68
安徽	Anhui	616.99	662.30	556.72	105.58	96.58
福建	Fujian	1356.87	1194.93	1051.51	143.42	81.27
江西	Jiangxi	312.64	330.57	273.49	57.08	44.69
山东	Shandong	1778.11	1941.35	1529.18	412.17	229.70
河南	Henan	928.43	1063.43	864.70	198.73	151.10
湖北	Hubei	921.16	1058.56	830.79	227.77	168.03
湖南	Hunan	614.09	665.65	519.43	146.22	91.86
广东	Guangdong	3410.83	3648.17	3068.50	579.67	207.96
广西	Guangxi	389.06	418.11	307.13	110.98	39.42
海南	Hainan	85.63	88.54	75.67	12.87	7.66
重庆	Chongqing	355.20	393.74	292.18	101.56	86.98
四川	Sichuan	789.12	847.83	682.77	165.05	92.89
贵州	Guizhou	231.31	260.10	225.75	34.36	44.26
云南	Yunnan	987.81	1183.74	1074.02	109.73	213.56
西藏	Tibet	6.58	7.04	3.92	3.12	1.97
陕西	Shaanxi	390.71	419.46	329.53	89.93	39.75
甘肃	Gansu	332.00	365.47	309.61	55.86	41.13
青海	Qinghai	39.06	48.98	33.29	15.69	10.82
宁夏	Ningxia	54.37	57.65	36.15	21.50	15.66
新疆	Xinjiang	404.33	478.35	405.27	73.08	120.80

16-11 限额以上批发零售贸易业主要商品分类销售额

Total Sales of Enterprises above Designated Size in Wholesale and Retail Trade by Category of Main Commodities

单位：亿元 (100 million yuan)

项目	Item	销售合计 Total		批发 Wholesale Trade		零售 Retail Trade	
		1999	2000	1999	2000	1999	2000
食品、饮料、烟酒类	Food, Beverages, Tobacco and Liquor	6881.2	7274.4	5804.3	6040.8	1076.9	1233.6
肉禽蛋类	Meat, Poultry and Eggs	437.5	505.5	301.2	337.9	136.3	167.6
其他食品类	Other Food	1885.9	1872.3	1299.9	1220.0	586.0	652.3
饮料类	Beverages	173.9	228.7	96.8	109.7	77.1	119.0
烟酒类	Tobacco and Liquor	4383.9	4667.9	4106.4	4373.2	277.5	294.7
服装鞋帽、针、纺织品类	Clothing, Shoes, Hats and Textiles	2463.8	2785.1	1593.9	1827.3	869.9	957.8
#针、纺织品类	Knitwear and Textiles	860.4	949.2	664.2	763.0	196.2	186.2
化妆品类	Cosmetics	195.8	217.0	86.6	85.1	109.2	131.9
金银珠宝类	Gold, Silver and Jewelry	210.6	197.3	64.1	50.2	146.5	147.1
日用品类	Articles for Daily Use	737.4	842.4	393.0	439.4	344.4	403.0
#洗涤用品类	Washing Articles	116.0	147.2	66.8	66.7	49.2	80.5
五金、电料类	Hardware and Electrical Materials	241.1	244.6	167.1	176.2	74.0	68.4
体育、娱乐用品类	Sports and Recreation Articles	112.0	113.4	63.4	61.1	48.6	52.3
书报杂志类	Newspapers and Magazines	513.2	528.2	319.5	314.1	193.7	214.1
电子出版物及音像制品类	E-journal and Video Products	34.5	39.3	14.3	14.6	20.2	24.7
家用电器和音像器材类	Household Appliances and Video Appliances	1527.7	1507.5	803.4	722.8	724.3	784.7
中西药品类	Traditional Chinese and Western Medicines	1143.0	1402.6	603.4	742.7	539.6	659.9
文化办公用品类	Cultural and Official Goods	256.6	282.1	146.4	165.1	110.2	117.0
家具类	Furniture	78.5	94.2	30.4	42.0	48.1	52.2
通讯器材类	Communication Appliances	282.5	373.0	249.4	325.0	33.1	48.0
煤炭及制品类	Coal and Related Product	450.8	528.0	428.8	511.9	22.0	16.1
木材及制品类	Wood and Wooden Product	83.3	77.5	77.0	73.0	6.3	4.5
石油及制品类	Petroleum and Related Product	3537.4	5829.0	3233.5	5277.2	303.9	551.8
化工材料及制品类	Raw Chemical Materials	1690.0	1767.1	1658.5	1743.3	31.5	23.8
金属材料类	Metal Materials	1700.3	1778.4	1667.8	1757.0	32.5	21.4
建筑及装潢材料类	Building and Decoration Materials	198.5	180.1	161.2	138.5	37.3	41.6
机电产品设备类	Mechanical and Electrical Products	2517.8	2809.0	2104.7	2269.8	413.1	539.2
#农机类	Agricultural Machinery	217.7	188.0	217.7	188.0		
种子饲料类	Seed and Feedstuff	95.3	81.8	95.3	81.8		
棉麻类	Cotton, Hemp	458.0	634.3	458.0	634.3		

16-12 限额以上批发零售贸易业商品销售数量

Total Sales Number of Enterprises above Designated Size in Wholesale and Retail Trade by Commodities

项目	Item	销售合计 Total		批发 Wholesale Trade		零售 Retail Trade	
		1999	2000	1999	2000	1999	2000
粮食 （万吨）	Grain (10 000 ton)	2889.7	4234.3	2445.4	3883.9	444.3	350.4
食用植物油（万吨）	Edible Vegetable Oil (10 000 ton)	354.1	282.1	289.4	231.6	64.7	50.5
食糖 （万吨）	Sugar (10 000 ton)	369.6	343	349.4	327.6	20.2	15.4
棉花 （万吨）	Cotton (10 000 ton)	328.9	557.1	326.4	553.7	2.5	3.4
电视机 （万台）	Television Set (10 000 units)	2221.0	2039.1	1401.2	1206.8	819.8	832.3
组合音响 （万台）	Hi-Fi Stereo Component System (10 000 units)	121.3	103.5	76.2	42.3	45.1	61.2
摄像机 （万台）	Pickup Camera (10 000 units)	9.7	13.7	1.4	2.4	8.3	11.3
录像机 （万台）	Video-recorder (10 000 units)	21.2	7.2	12.3	1.1	8.9	6.1
影碟机 （万台）	Video Disc Player (10 000 units)	394.9	502	130.0	191.2	264.9	310.8
家用电冰箱（万台）	Household Refrigerator (10 000 units)	988.8	840.2	620.0	463.0	368.8	377.2
家用洗衣机（万台）	Household Washing Machine (10 000 units)	995.9	886.8	617.0	480.5	378.9	406.3
房间空调器（万台）	Room Air Conditioner (10 000 units)	591.6	813.6	363.5	487	228.1	326.6
微波炉 （万台）	Micro-oven (10 000 units)	353.9	527.2	162.3	220.4	191.6	306.8
微型计算机（万台）	Personal Computer (10 000 units)	67.5	72.6	45.4	33.7	22.1	38.9
普通电话机（万台）	Telephone (10 000 units)	468.3	701.7	177.9	299.3	290.4	402.4
移动电话机（万台）	Hand Telephone (10 000 units)	984.6	1389.7	926.1	1276.9	58.5	112.8
寻呼机 （万台）	Beep-Pager (10 000 units)	207.7	150.1	147.0	89.8	60.7	60.3
化学肥料 （万吨）	Chemical Fertilizers (10 000 ton)	6479.7	5994.3	6479.7	5994.3		
化学农药 （万吨）	Chemical Pesticide (10 000 ton)	104.7	90.9	104.7	90.9		
农用薄膜 （万吨）	Farming Pellicle (10 000 ton)	54	33.5	54.0	33.5		
煤炭 （万吨）	Coal (10 000 ton)	18936.5	21841.6	17969.5	20652.4	967.0	1189.2
木材 （万立方米）	Wood (10 000 cu.m)	243.7	259	229.2	253.5	14.5	5.5
汽油 （万吨）	Gasoline (10 000 ton)	4577.8	6429.9	4053.1	5688.6	524.7	741.3
柴油 （万吨）	Diesel Oil (10 000 ton)	7375.0	11471.9	7375	11471.9		
钢材 （万吨）	Steel Products (10 000 ton)	4440.3	4454.1	4440.3	4454.1		
铜 （万吨）	Copper (10 000 ton)	51.2	49.1	51.2	49.1		
铝 （万吨）	Aluminum (10 000 ton)	45.7	54.8	45.7	54.8		
水泥 （万吨）	Cement (10 000 ton)	1221.2	1023.2	1221.2	1023.2		
汽车 （万辆）	Motor Vehicles (10 000 units)	143.8	134.8	112.7	99.5	31.1	35.3
#轿车 （万辆）	Car (10 000 units)	74.1	65.1	57.5	47.7	16.6	17.4
摩托车 （万辆）	Motor (10 000 units)	297.9	259.8	180.5	168.1	117.4	91.7
拖拉机 （万台）	Tractors (10 000 units)	79.1	53.9	79.1	53.9		

16-13 餐饮业营业收入（2000年）

Business Revenue of Catering Services (2000)

单位:亿元 (100 million yuan)

指 标	Item	1998年	1999年	2000年
总 计	**Total**	**3080.3**	**3554.8**	**4123.3**
按限额标准分	By Size of Enterprises			
限额以上企业	Above Designated Size	470.9	442.6	528.5
限额以下企业	Below Designated Size	2609.4	3112.2	3594.8
按地区分	By Region			
北 京	Beijing	96.5	82.4	90.6
天 津	Tianjin	62.8	69.9	82.9
河 北	Hebei	143.1	179.1	184.1
山 西	Shanxi	45.7	51.5	54.0
内蒙古	Inner Mongolia	36.6	43.1	52.6
辽 宁	Liaoning	169.2	198.4	234.4
吉 林	Jilin	67.5	76.5	101.9
黑龙江	Heilongjiang	73.8	83.7	101.2
上 海	Shanghai	101.1	111.3	139.9
江 苏	Jiangsu	203.3	220.5	264.0
浙 江	Zhejiang	136.8	188.8	235.6
安 徽	Anhui	82.8	97.0	110.9
福 建	Fujian	125.4	146.9	158.1
江 西	Jiangxi	54.6	60.7	68.5
山 东	Shandong	218.8	269.0	311.8
河 南	Henan	177.1	184.3	211.8
湖 北	Hubei	164.2	155.4	191.2
湖 南	Hunan	108.6	136.8	155.3
广 东	Guangdong	486.9	576.0	654.8
广 西	Guangxi	83.0	88.1	102.8
海 南	Hainan	19.4	21.9	24.2
重 庆	Chongqing	45.4	50.7	56.2
四 川	Sichuan	161.8	197.2	242.0
贵 州	Guizhou	26.8	33.3	43.8
云 南	Yunnan	42.5	54.5	51.2
西 藏	Tibet	7.7	8.3	6.6
陕 西	Shaanxi	55.3	61.9	71.7
甘 肃	Gansu	38.6	45.2	46.9
青 海	Qinghai	10.8	11.6	12.2
宁 夏	Ningxia	7.2	12.4	11.5
新 疆	Xinjiang	27.0	38.4	50.7

16-14 限额以上批发、零售贸易企业资产及负债情况（2000年，按登记注册类型分）

Assets and Liability of Enterprises above Designated Size in Wholesale and Retail Trade by Types of Registration (2000)

单位:亿元 (100 million yuan)

指标	Item	资产合计 Total Assets	#流动资产 Circulating Funds	#固定资产 Fixed Asset	负债合计 Total Liabilities	#流动负债 Liquid Liabilities	#长期负债 Long-term Liabilities
批发零售贸易业总计	**Total**	**19092.2**	**12705.4**	**3852.3**	**15219.2**	**13145.4**	**1825.4**
一、批发业合计	**Wholesale Trade**	**15141.7**	**10807.2**	**2303.3**	**12336.3**	**10730.0**	**1389.6**
内资企业	**Domestic Funded Enterprises**	**14938.4**	**10645.5**	**2281.7**	**12172.3**	**10580.6**	**1377.0**
国有企业	State-owned Enterprises	9969.0	7171.5	1556.5	8165.9	7193.7	856.6
集体企业	Collective-owned Enterprises	1744.0	1238.9	197.8	1656.3	1338.1	303.2
股份合作企业	Cooperative Enterprises	137.8	100.5	25.7	121.1	114.3	5.1
联营企业	Joint Ownership Enterprises	144.9	107.0	21.2	108.8	99.8	6.4
国有联营企业	State Joint Ownership Enterprises	56.3	41.1	9.8	39.2	34.4	3.1
集体联营企业	Collective Joint Ownership Enterprises	10.3	6.6	2.7	6.6	6.4	0.03
国有与集体联营企业	Joint State-collective Enterprises	46.0	30.8	7.2	36.2	33.2	3.0
其他联营企业	Other Joint Ownership Enterprises	32.3	28.4	1.5	26.8	25.8	0.3
有限责任公司	Limited Liability Corporations	1641.5	1153.0	254.4	1204.0	1058.1	126.0
国有独资公司	State Sole Funded Corporations	597.2	399.5	76.0	433.5	361.5	70.6
其他有限责任公司	Other Limited Liability Corporations	1044.2	753.5	178.4	770.5	696.6	55.4
股份有限公司	Share-holding Corporations Ltd.	1157.5	755.3	212.2	808.9	674.6	76.7
私营企业	Private Enterprises	141.9	117.8	13.6	105.8	100.6	2.9
私营独资企业	Private-funded Enterprises	8.2	6.2	1.1	5.9	5.8	0.1
私营合伙企业	Private Partnership Enterprises	3.4	2.9	0.5	2.5	2.4	0.1
私营有限责任公司	Private Limited Liability Corporations	121.6	101.7	11.1	90.7	86.1	2.2
私营股份有限公司	Private Share-holding Corporations Ltd.	8.6	6.9	0.9	6.8	6.3	0.5
其他企业	Other Enterprises	2.0	1.7	0.2	1.6	1.5	0.006
港、澳、台商投资企业	**Enterprises with Funds from Hong Kong, Macau and Taiwan**	**28.8**	**21.5**	**5.7**	**21.9**	**16.5**	**5.4**
合资经营企业（港或澳、台资）	Joint-venture Enterprises (with Funds from Hong Kong, Macau and Taiwan)	12.6	6.7	4.7	9.0	6.8	2.2
合作经营企业（港或澳、台资）	Cooperative Enterprises (with Funds from Hong Kong, Macau and Taiwan)	4.7	4.0	0.5	3.1	3.0	0.03
港、澳、台商独资经营企业	Enterprises with Sole Funds from Hong Kong, Macau and Taiwan	11.5	10.7	0.6	9.7	6.6	3.1
港、澳、台商投资股份有限公司	Share-holding Corporations Ltd. with Funds from Hong Kong, Macau and Taiwan	0.03	0.03		0.02		
外商投资企业	**Foreign Funded Enterprises**	**174.4**	**140.3**	**15.8**	**142.1**	**132.9**	**7.2**
中外合资经营企业	Joint-venture Enterprises	136.7	113.2	12.9	111.8	102.8	7.0
中外合作经营企业	Cooperation Enterprises	0.9	0.9	0.03	1.2	1.2	
外资企业	Enterprises with Sole Foreign Funds	28.3	21.3	1.0	24.1	23.9	0.2
外商投资股份有限公司	Share-holding Corporations Ltd. with Foreign Funds	8.5	4.9	1.9	5.0	4.9	0.1

16-14 续表1 continued

单位:亿元 (100 million yuan)

指 标	Item	资产合计 Total Assets	#流动资产 Circulating Funds	#固定资产 Fixed Asset	负债合计 Total Liabilities	#流动负债 Liquid Liabilities	#长期负债 Long-term Liabilities
二、零售企业合计	**Retail Trade**	**3950.5**	**1898.2**	**1549.1**	**2882.9**	**2415.5**	**435.9**
内资企业	**Domestic Funded Enterprises**	**3589.2**	**1768.8**	**1398.4**	**2612.5**	**2209.6**	**371.3**
国有企业	State-owned Enterprises	1400.6	728.3	539.5	1125.2	940.8	175.1
集体企业	Collective-owned Enterprises	353.9	194.5	124.0	267.2	235.1	28.8
股份合作企业	Cooperative Enterprises	92.3	46.9	33.4	69.1	58.4	8.3
联营企业	Joint Ownership Enterprises	53.9	28.8	19.3	35.9	27.5	7.6
国有联营企业	State Joint Ownership Enterprises	16.1	9.0	4.8	9.9	9.1	0.9
集体联营企业	Collective Joint Ownership Enterprises	11.2	5.7	5.0	8.6	4.1	4.5
国有与集体联营企业	Joint State-collective Enterprises	12.6	7.8	4.3	7.5	5.0	1.7
其他联营企业	Other Joint Ownership Enterprises	14.0	6.2	5.3	9.8	9.3	0.5
有限责任公司	Limited Liability Corporations	485.4	255.6	169.0	361.0	316.4	38.9
国有独资公司	State Sole Funded Corporations	63.9	35.9	21.3	52.3	48.6	3.6
其他有限责任公司	Other Limited Liability Corporations	421.5	219.7	147.8	308.8	267.9	35.3
股份有限公司	Share-holding Corporations Ltd.	1077.3	435.0	480.0	656.8	541.5	107.1
私营企业	Private Enterprises	124.7	79.1	32.5	96.3	88.8	5.6
私营独资企业	Private-funded Enterprises	17.1	13.4	2.9	14.4	13.9	0.5
私营合伙企业	Private Partnership Enterprises	2.7	1.5	0.6	1.2	1.2	0.1
私营有限责任公司	Private Limited Liability Corporations	94.2	57.7	26.3	73.7	67.3	4.6
私营股份有限公司	Private Share-holding Corporations Ltd.	10.7	6.6	2.8	6.9	6.4	0.4
其他企业	Other Enterprises	1.2	0.5	0.6	1.0	1.0	0.003
港、澳、台商投资企业	**Enterprises with Funds from Hong Kong, Macau and Taiwan**	**181.9**	**70.7**	**71.5**	**146.4**	**115.4**	**31.0**
合资经营企业（港或澳、台资）	Joint-venture Enterprises (with Funds from Hong Kong, Macau and Taiwan)	93.7	29.8	41.0	79.7	60.1	19.7
合作经营企业（港或澳、台资）	Cooperative Enterprises (with Funds from Hong Kong, Macau and Taiwan)	47.3	24.6	15.3	39.7	32.8	6.9
港、澳、台商独资经营企业	Enterprises with Sole Funds from Hong Kong, Macau and Taiwan	5.3	2.9	0.3	2.4	2.3	0.1
港、澳、台商投资股份有限公司	Share-holding Corporations Ltd. with Funds from Hong Kong, Macau and Taiwan	35.6	13.4	14.9	24.6	20.2	4.3
外商投资企业	**Foreign Funded Enterprises**	**179.4**	**58.7**	**79.2**	**124.0**	**90.5**	**33.5**
中外合资经营企业	Joint-venture Enterprises	116.9	34.5	53.9	78.1	52.6	25.4
中外合作经营企业	Cooperation Enterprises	62.2	24.1	25.2	45.7	37.6	8.1
外资企业	Enterprises with Sole Foreign Funds	0.02	0.004	0.02	0.02	0.02	
外商投资股份有限公司	Share-holding Corporations Ltd. with Foreign Funds	0.3	0.1	0.04	0.2	0.2	

16-15 限额以上批发、零售贸易企业资产及负债情况（2000年，按行业分）

Assets and Liability of Enterprises above Designated Size in Wholesale and Retail Trade by Sector (2000)

单位：亿元 (100 million yuan)

指 标	Item	资产合计 Total Assets	#流动资产 Circulating Funds	#固定资产 Fixed Asset	负债合计 Total Liabilities	#流动负债 Liquid Liabilities	#长期负债 Long-term Liabilities
总　计	**Total**	**19092.2**	**12705.4**	**3852.3**	**15219.2**	**13145.4**	**1825.4**
一、批发企业合计	**Wholesale Trade**	**15141.7**	**10807.2**	**2303.3**	**12336.3**	**10730.0**	**1389.6**
食品、饮料、烟草批发业	Wholesale of Food, Beverages and Tobaccos	4052.0	2992.1	693.7	3127.7	2764.1	335.4
#粮食、食用油批发业	Wholesale of Grains and Edible Oil	1425.5	1118.6	182.2	1323.6	1060.2	248.1
烟草及其制品批发业	Whole of Tobaccos	1717.5	1321.3	280.8	1161.0	1129.1	22.8
棉、麻、土畜产品批发业	Wholesale of Cotton, Ambery and Animal Products	1292.3	882.1	109.4	1346.6	1045.1	292.4
纺织品、服装和鞋帽批发业	Wholesale of Textiles, Garments, Shoes and Hats	1147.4	784.5	130.2	848.8	794.7	49.6
日用百货批发业	Wholesale of Daily Consumer Goods	379.1	259.7	79.9	328.0	298.5	26.1
日用杂品批发业	Wholesale of Daily Sundry Articles	41.4	29.9	8.3	38.3	34.3	1.8
五金、交电、化工批发业	Wholesale of Hardware, Transport, Electric and Chemical Products	493.9	370.3	79.3	445.9	417.9	25.1
药品及医疗器械批发业	Wholesale of Medicines and Medical Appliances	628.1	468.5	107.4	505.9	455.5	31.7
能源批发业	Wholesale of Energy Products	1727.7	1088.6	373.8	1405.7	1072.9	228.8
#石油及制品批发业	Wholesale of Petroleum and Related Products	1382.9	857.8	301.7	1168.3	851.1	214.4
煤炭及制品批发业	Wholesale of Coal and Related Products	335.3	224.1	70.6	229.6	214.2	14.3
化工材料批发业	Wholesale of Chemical Materials	393.6	284.2	50.8	302.7	280.0	17.6
木材批发业	Wholesale of Timber	66.7	39.9	16.7	55.9	50.3	4.6
建筑材料批发业	Wholesale of Building Materials	127.4	87.8	23.0	97.2	87.1	7.2
矿产品批发业	Wholesale of Mineral Products	227.1	169.7	18.8	200.2	183.5	15.4
金属材料批发业	Wholesale of Metal Materials	1206.4	850.7	139.9	922.3	845.0	62.3
机械、电子设备批发业	Wholesale of Machinery and Electronic Equipment	1014.8	808.4	99.9	849.0	730.9	114.8
汽车、摩托车及零配件批发业	Wholesale of Motor Vehicles, Motorcycles and Parts	525.5	389.0	72.3	449.4	410.3	36.1
#汽车批发业	Wholesale of Motor Vehicles	366.7	285.0	48.7	339.0	324.0	12.7
再生物资回收批发业	Wholesale of Recycled Materials	57.0	36.8	13.7	44.1	40.5	3.0
工艺美术批发业	Wholesale of Arts and Handicraft Products	135.0	88.1	19.4	108.5	99.7	8.7
图书报刊批发业	Wholesale of Books, Newspapers and Magazines	132.1	88.3	32.1	82.1	78.9	2.9
农业生产资料批发业	Wholesale of Means of Agricultural Production	691.5	527.2	110.1	583.2	550.1	23.5
其他类未包括的批发业	Other Wholesale not Classified Elsewhere	802.7	561.6	124.7	594.8	490.7	102.3
二、零售企业合计	**Retail Trade**	**3950.5**	**1898.2**	**1549.1**	**2882.9**	**2415.5**	**435.9**
食品、饮料、烟草零售业	Retail of Food, Beverages and Tobaccos	486.5	273.9	158.7	387.1	322.2	59.5
#粮油食品零售业	Retail of Grains and Edible Oil	163.3	115.0	39.0	161.6	120.0	38.4
副食品零售业	Retail of Non-staple Food	218.8	102.5	90.2	159.7	140.9	17.6
日用百货零售业	Retail of Daily Consumer Goods	2468.0	1042.0	1077.7	1775.7	1455.4	300.5
#百货零售业	Retail of Consumer Goods	2372.9	986.0	1048.6	1706.2	1394.1	292.6
文化体育用品零售业	Retail of Cultural and Sports Goods	16.8	9.3	5.1	12.8	10.5	2.2
纺织品、服装和鞋帽零售业	Retail of Textiles, Garments, Shoes and Hats	99.2	53.4	35.3	78.0	69.6	8.1
日用杂品零售业	Retail of Daily Sundry Articles	22.9	13.5	5.5	15.5	13.6	1.4
五金、交电、化工零售业	Retail of Hardware, Transport, Electric and Chemical Products	240.8	147.5	71.2	182.0	167.2	13.9
药品及医疗器械零售业	Retail of Medicines and Medical Appliances	130.7	85.6	37.7	99.1	94.1	3.9
图书报刊零售业	Retail of Books, Newspapers and Magazines	159.8	88.9	60.8	92.7	85.3	6.6
其他零售业	Other Retail Trade	341.9	192.8	102.0	252.5	207.7	41.8
#家具零售业	Retail of Furniture	10.9	6.8	2.5	8.8	8.3	0.5
汽车、摩托车及其零配件零售业	Retail of Motor Vehicles, Motorcycles and Parts	104.8	70.1	20.5	77.9	69.8	7.6
计算机及软件、办公设备零售业	Retail of Computers, Software and Office Appliances	15.6	12.2	2.2	10.2	9.8	0.3

16-16 限额以上批发零售贸易企业资产及负债情况（2000年，按地区分）

Assets and Liability of Enterprises above Designated Size in Wholesale and Retail Trade by Region (2000)

单位：万元 (10 000 yuan)

地区	Region	资产合计 Total Assets	#流动资产 Circulating Funds	#固定资产 Fixed Asset	负债合计 Total Liabilities	#流动负债 Liquid Liabilities	#长期负债 Long-term Liabilities
全国	**National Total**	**190922133**	**127054217**	**38523314**	**152192382**	**131454450**	**18254235**
北京	Beijing	28124708	18284625	3116282	19747886	15863298	3884589
天津	Tianjin	4617430	3360410	789029	3924716	3532625	392090
河北	Hebei	5036206	3262672	1212065	4339618	3644253	524861
山西	Shanxi	2746043	1672481	861924	2306434	1910372	280098
内蒙古	Inner Mongolia	1442811	914023	353751	1213266	934826	261782
辽宁	Liaoning	9308137	6002149	2208402	7738706	6893984	716908
吉林	Jilin	3034299	2094330	765654	2872832	2537444	296131
黑龙江	Heilongjiang	4417747	3195651	1028831	3967900	3575476	365820
上海	Shanghai	16879196	10907334	3442242	11941480	10045380	1764716
江苏	Jiangsu	13232565	8874845	3171219	10372471	9021996	1038762
浙江	Zhejiang	11825539	7979311	2468083	8373533	7370086	874282
安徽	Anhui	3788606	2742975	822097	3388718	2954194	405863
福建	Fujian	5955426	3976849	1019629	4014685	3630727	330372
江西	Jiangxi	1995839	1404969	398701	1914245	1651962	235435
山东	Shandong	11687238	7286531	2844783	9986094	8656198	1144023
河南	Henan	6914217	4945279	1351587	6435206	5835583	599623
湖北	Hubei	7416433	4680533	1721354	6693104	5428606	1079626
湖南	Hunan	4736100	2893960	1181994	4206857	3649641	557216
广东	Guangdong	18175169	12021204	3388427	14395878	12446819	1329289
广西	Guangxi	2500986	1465531	776399	2004216	1731123	166655
海南	Hainan	636604	355851	194813	499519	395408	101000
重庆	Chongqing	2342699	1592467	565461	1993172	1827256	133804
四川	Sichuan	4133435	2795973	920676	3384565	3150399	223392
贵州	Guizhou	2235208	1647618	453222	2004767	1814944	130377
云南	Yunnan	8274751	6072698	1410648	6140998	5499065	606700
西藏	Tibet	108423	74052	25621	81367	71015	9897
陕西	Shaanxi	2623996	1724763	608730	2226071	1990397	203878
甘肃	Gansu	1379843	817358	386765	1221023	1005968	203470
青海	Qinghai	396036	259458	117186	350738	272232	72008
宁夏	Ningxia	408511	269289	111969	334185	270817	48498
新疆	Xinjiang	4547935	3479028	805772	4118133	3842359	273071

16-17 限额以上批发贸易企业资产及负债情况（2000年，按地区分）

Assets and Liability of Enterprises above Designated Size in Wholesale Trade by Region (2000)

单位：万元 (10 000 yuan)

地区	Region	资产合计 Total Assets	#流动资产 Circulating Funds	#固定资产 Fixed Asset	负债合计 Total Liabilities	#流动负债 Liquid Liabilities	#长期负债 Long-term Liabilities
全国	**National Total**	**151417114**	**108072294**	**23032712**	**123363167**	**107299663**	**13895585**
北京	Beijing	23850357	15998595	1774905	17020747	13330264	3690484
天津	Tianjin	3587773	2788268	451334	3236738	2920177	316560
河北	Hebei	3619063	2614689	670927	3238071	2739151	338442
山西	Shanxi	1748562	1204668	408916	1568813	1295273	178998
内蒙古	Inner Mongolia	1015742	711458	167294	878989	696990	171173
辽宁	Liaoning	6839473	4929574	1137232	5897644	5434335	368815
吉林	Jilin	2162076	1703224	357300	2143126	1935553	179898
黑龙江	Heilongjiang	3322177	2709272	462716	3119428	2851642	241931
上海	Shanghai	12365600	9041653	1573868	8954368	7694074	1159142
江苏	Jiangsu	10374288	7566166	1907086	8218805	7205173	731468
浙江	Zhejiang	10171536	7195178	1733190	7279390	6430599	731010
安徽	Anhui	3037554	2385014	506374	2790435	2471969	292079
福建	Fujian	5180837	3574209	790526	3495038	3176932	270617
江西	Jiangxi	1686879	1223461	290681	1666780	1441042	201525
山东	Shandong	8773513	5907545	1578338	7752632	6805409	804100
河南	Henan	5393622	4106720	801470	5078566	4709008	369558
湖北	Hubei	5633931	3950747	978369	5398740	4404942	837616
湖南	Hunan	3716610	2459994	739722	3503442	3063766	439676
广东	Guangdong	15073304	10252302	2556630	12037013	10364770	1063201
广西	Guangxi	1680119	1081532	416767	1432067	1250243	90326
海南	Hainan	481313	286489	120449	388853	314830	71333
重庆	Chongqing	1891606	1392105	382883	1691188	1567380	94424
四川	Sichuan	3091367	2264184	562162	2638515	2506912	128637
贵州	Guizhou	1901746	1502586	290735	1751771	1632052	68785
云南	Yunnan	7523493	5671057	1147709	5555571	4995296	537875
西藏	Tibet	60404	46169	9991	48728	45130	3598
陕西	Shaanxi	1926061	1400248	351308	1780007	1612099	150138
甘肃	Gansu	917173	617115	199636	870331	721091	138188
青海	Qinghai	296938	222110	61777	261346	210650	49776
宁夏	Ningxia	273662	205444	56070	239809	197555	27385
新疆	Xinjiang	3820335	3060518	546349	3426217	3275357	148829

16-18 限额以上零售贸易企业资产及负债情况（2000年，按地区分）

Assets and Liability of Enterprises above Designated Size in Retail Trade by Region (2000)

单位：万元 (10 000 yuan)

地区	Region	资产合计 Total Assets	#流动资产 Circulating Funds	#固定资产 Fixed Asset	负债合计 Total Liabilities	#流动负债 Liquid Liabilities	#长期负债 Long-term Liabilities
全国	**National Total**	**39505019**	**18981924**	**15490602**	**28829215**	**24154787**	**4358650**
北京	Beijing	4274351	2286029	1341377	2727139	2533034	194105
天津	Tianjin	1029658	572142	337695	687978	612448	75530
河北	Hebei	1417142	647984	541138	1101548	905102	186419
山西	Shanxi	997481	467814	453007	737622	615099	101099
内蒙古	Inner Mongolia	427069	202565	186458	334276	237835	90609
辽宁	Liaoning	2468664	1072574	1071170	1841062	1459649	348093
吉林	Jilin	872223	391106	408354	729706	601891	116233
黑龙江	Heilongjiang	1095569	486379	566115	848472	723834	123890
上海	Shanghai	4513596	1865680	1868374	2987112	2351305	605574
江苏	Jiangsu	2858277	1308679	1264133	2153666	1816823	307294
浙江	Zhejiang	1654003	784133	734893	1094144	939487	143272
安徽	Anhui	751052	357961	315723	598283	482225	113784
福建	Fujian	774589	402640	229103	519647	453795	59756
江西	Jiangxi	308960	181508	108020	247466	210920	33910
山东	Shandong	2913725	1378986	1266445	2233462	1850789	339923
河南	Henan	1520595	838559	550117	1356640	1126575	230066
湖北	Hubei	1782502	729786	742985	1294364	1023663	242010
湖南	Hunan	1019490	433966	442272	703415	585875	117541
广东	Guangdong	3101865	1768901	831797	2358865	2082049	266088
广西	Guangxi	820866	383999	359632	572149	480880	76329
海南	Hainan	155291	69362	74364	110666	80578	29667
重庆	Chongqing	451093	200362	182578	301984	259876	39380
四川	Sichuan	1042069	531789	358514	746050	643487	94754
贵州	Guizhou	333462	145032	162486	252996	182892	61592
云南	Yunnan	751257	401641	262939	585427	503770	68826
西藏	Tibet	48019	27884	15629	32639	25885	6299
陕西	Shaanxi	697935	324515	257422	446064	378298	53740
甘肃	Gansu	462670	200243	187129	350692	284877	65282
青海	Qinghai	99098	37348	55409	89391	61582	22231
宁夏	Ningxia	134849	63845	55899	94376	73262	21114
新疆	Xinjiang	727600	418510	259423	691916	567003	124242

16-19 限额以上餐饮企业资产及负债情况
(2000年，按登记注册类型和行业分)
Assets and Liability of Enterprises above Designated Size in in Catering Services by Types of Registration and by Sector (2000)

单位：万元 (10 000 yuan)

指标	Item	资产合计 Total Assets	#流动资产 Circulating Funds	#固定资产 Fixed Asset	负债合计 Total Liabilities	#流动负债 Liquid Liabilities	#长期负债 Long-term Liabilities
总计	**Total**	**7642861**	**1807671**	**4572018**	**5086311**	**3489329**	**1514837**
一、按登记注册类型分	**By Types of Registration**						
内资企业	**Domestic Funded Enterprises**	**4865268**	**1196632**	**2924219**	**3043196**	**2177854**	**816707**
国有企业	State-owned Enterprises	2140589	473674	1348309	1342472	946218	368500
集体企业	Collective-owned Enterprises	694335	167101	449249	443827	298929	138756
股份合作企业	Cooperative Enterprises	172289	53791	88819	113375	91461	20049
联营企业	Joint Ownership Enterprises	101483	25197	63330	66105	35298	30797
国有联营企业	State Joint Ownership Enterprises	48241	6515	37150	36281	14526	21745
集体联营企业	Collective Joint Ownership Enterprises	3880	1362	1966	1274	1254	20
国有与集体联营企业	Joint State-collective Enterprises	21608	12170	8141	12058	11430	628
其他联营企业	Other Joint Ownership Enterprises	27754	5151	16075	16492	8089	8404
有限责任公司	Limited Liability Corporations	769899	185743	423548	489779	370942	115150
国有独资公司	State Sole Funded Corporations	65391	19376	30926	30313	29393	920
其他有限责任公司	Other Limited Liability Corporations	704508	166367	392622	459466	341549	114230
股份有限公司	Share-holding Corporations Ltd.	425316	101007	274349	256057	182356	73350
私营企业	Private Enterprises	561065	190067	276380	331542	252611	70106
私营独资企业	Private-funded Enterprises	187531	58264	95416	106324	75423	25430
私营合伙企业	Private Partnership Enterprises	25639	8813	14454	11596	9517	1042
私营有限责任公司	Private Limited Liability Corporations	313396	111221	154917	188259	145582	41150
私营股份有限公司	Private Share-holding Corporations Ltd.	34499	11768	11594	25363	22089	2484
其他企业	Other Enterprises	292	52	235	39	39	
港、澳、台商投资企业	**Enterprises with Funds from Hong Kong, Macau and Taiwan**	**1384189**	**325904**	**812310**	**1065226**	**683726**	**352246**
合资经营企业（港或澳、台资）	Joint-venture Enterprises (with Funds from Hong Kong, Macau and Taiwan)	926677	200982	562929	732583	461420	247919
合作经营企业（港或澳、台资）	Cooperative Enterprises (with Funds from Hong Kong, Macau and Taiwan)	260794	66987	148568	201932	115690	83515
港、澳、台商独资经营企业	Enterprises with Sole Investment from Hong Kong, Macau and Taiwan	154969	46180	73095	91363	67868	20212
港、澳、台商投资股份有限公司	Share-holding Corporations Ltd. with Investment from Hong Kong, Macau and Taiwan	41749	11756	27718	39349	38749	600
外商投资企业	**Foreign Funded Enterprises**	**1393404**	**285134**	**835489**	**977889**	**627749**	**345884**
中外合资经营企业	Joint-venture Enterprises	902413	155111	634800	605130	376163	228473
中外合作经营企业	Cooperation Enterprises	208176	58661	75022	139129	110630	28498
外资企业	Enterprises with Sole Foreign Funds	280234	70939	124973	233496	140822	88914
外商投资股份有限公司	Share-holding Corporations Ltd. with Foreign Investment	2582	423	693	135	135	
二、按国民经济行业分	**By Sector**						
正餐	Dinner	6910311	1592056	4266812	4604184	3110037	1412365
快餐	Snack	606651	185117	221215	382597	326445	55853
其他餐饮业	Other	125899	30498	83990	99530	52846	46619

16-20 限额以上餐饮企业资产及负债情况（2000年，按地区分）

Assets and Liability of Enterprises above Designated Size in Catering Services by Region (2000)

单位：万元 (10 000 yuan)

地区	Region	资产合计 Total Assets	#流动资产 Circulating Funds	#固定资产 Fixed Asset	负债合计 Total Liabilities	#流动负债 Liquid Liabilities	#长期负债 Long-term Liabilities
全国	**National Total**	**7642861**	**1807671**	**4572018**	**5086311**	**3489329**	**1514837**
北京	Beijing	503933	175678	211878	312625	288165	24460
天津	Tianjin	128618	33663	61448	78268	55852	22329
河北	Hebei	118724	31754	68549	88301	67071	21129
山西	Shanxi	43251	14615	23944	29812	16382	13429
内蒙古	Inner Mongolia	107175	17559	61843	46560	39858	6702
辽宁	Liaoning	631697	123516	390906	397177	287495	107701
吉林	Jilin	42208	16680	19505	26614	21397	3784
黑龙江	Heilongjiang	67932	19923	39629	37453	22486	12323
上海	Shanghai	503581	133637	275271	415794	320348	93533
江苏	Jiangsu	672318	137522	444001	436081	304531	131518
浙江	Zhejiang	516272	127075	319391	343923	263114	79711
安徽	Anhui	16659	3528	8582	12085	10932	1153
福建	Fujian	271327	88303	125833	155837	124939	26872
江西	Jiangxi	28756	5256	20241	14123	10927	2771
山东	Shandong	778185	138463	526710	531396	283835	221225
河南	Henan	137441	26301	94960	86977	62316	24661
湖北	Hubei	324796	51318	224903	205126	123303	79179
湖南	Hunan	130258	28196	91435	86856	53337	33519
广东	Guangdong	1273588	353582	648349	844165	612377	218204
广西	Guangxi	157796	35478	108312	105335	68380	36526
海南	Hainan	227679	25419	182347	184668	80422	103646
重庆	Chongqing	257186	58473	164723	170247	88682	80966
四川	Sichuan	295091	68801	191342	180242	137712	41859
贵州	Guizhou	21774	6424	11055	14445	10732	3413
云南	Yunnan	92964	18191	64320	61206	25742	33730
西藏	Tibet						
陕西	Shaanxi	87699	38075	33868	52124	44357	7760
甘肃	Gansu	60756	13178	45054	43261	17719	25541
青海	Qinghai	1591	586	188	1711	1711	
宁夏	Ningxia	7645	2618	4395	7167	3900	2332
新疆	Xinjiang	135964	13861	109038	116734	41307	54861

16-21 限额以上批发零售贸易企业主要财务指标情况（2000年，按登记注册类型分）

Main Financial Indicators of Enterprises above Designated Size in Wholesale and Retail Trade by Registration (2000)

单位：万元 (10 000 yuan)

指 标	Item	商品销售收入 Sales Revenue	商品销售成本 Cost of Sales	经营费用 Management Cost	商品销售税金及附加 Sales Tax and Extra Changes	商品销售利润 Total Profits
批发零售贸易业总计	**Total**	**285918605**	**261411058**	**10078870**	**542000**	**11278707**
一、批发业合计	**Wholesale Trade**	**241841349**	**223649603**	**7512251**	**376008**	**8623787**
内资企业	**Domestic Funded Enterprises**	**238257662**	**220343756**	**7404201**	**375082**	**8456859**
国有企业	State-owned Enterprises	157309727	144948995	4707684	281556	5978740
集体企业	Collective-owned Enterprises	20320975	19093888	566314	24954	515073
股份合作企业	Cooperative Enterprises	2821751	2568639	93391	4443	144748
联营企业	Joint Ownership Enterprises	1920615	1801339	54237	2899	61042
国有联营企业	State Joint Ownership Enterprises	959617	899001	27337	1515	31014
集体联营企业	Collective Joint Ownership Enterprises	165190	157235	2612	416	4928
国有与集体联营企业	Joint State-collective Enterprises	580784	543481	17194	739	19244
其他联营企业	Other Joint Ownership Enterprises	215023	201623	7094	229	5856
有限责任公司	Limited Liability Corporations	29312868	27202551	1041041	29311	915330
国有独资公司	State Sole Funded Corporations	7438694	6822204	345833	6079	186598
其他有限责任公司	Other Limited Liability Corporations	21874173	20380347	695208	23232	728733
股份有限公司	Share-holding Corporations Ltd.	22584562	20966343	822153	27062	751729
私营企业	Private Enterprises	3912785	3689764	117961	4849	89597
私营独资企业	Private-funded Enterprises	220433	210315	5980	287	3420
私营合伙企业	Private Partnership Enterprises	137601	127665	4774	272	4889
私营有限责任公司	Private Limited Liability Corporations	3324460	3134308	98772	4052	77144
私营股份有限公司	Private Share-holding Corporations Ltd.	230291	217476	8435	237	4143
其他企业	Other Enterprises	74381	72235	1420	10	600
港、澳、台商投资企业	**Enterprises with Funds from Hong Kong, Macau and Taiwan**	**535588**	**497585**	**21372**	**400**	**15921**
合资经营企业（港或澳、台资）	Joint-venture Enterprises (with Funds from Hong Kong, Macau and Taiwan)	293381	283997	5172	115	4011
合作经营企业（港或澳、台资）	Cooperative Enterprises (with Funds from Hong Kong, Macau and Taiwan)	100996	81936	12173	274	6614
港、澳、台商独资经营企业	Enterprises with Sole Investment from Hong Kong, Macau and Taiwan	139774	130309	3964	11	5296
港、澳、台商投资股份有限公司	Share-holding Corporations Ltd. with Funds from Hong Kong, Macau and Taiwan	1436	1343	63		
外商投资企业	**Foreign Funded Enterprises**	**3048099**	**2808263**	**86679**	**527**	**151007**
中外合资经营企业	Joint-venture Enterprises	2496954	2305332	76408	208	113738
中外合作经营企业	Cooperation Enterprises	21957	19019	3266	2	-414
外资企业	Enterprises with Sole Foreign Funds	398737	358153	4937	105	35316
外商投资股份有限公司	Share-holding Corporations Ltd. with Foreign Funds	130451	125758	2068	212	2367

16-21 续表 1 continued

单位：万元 (10 000 yuan)

指　标	Item	商品销售收入 Sales Revenue	商品销售成本 Cost of Sales	经营费用 Management Cost	商品销售税金及附加 Sales Tax and Extra Changes	商品销售利润 Total Profits
二、零售企业合计	**Retail Trade**	**44077256**	**37761455**	**2566619**	**165992**	**2654920**
内资企业	**Domestic Funded Enterprises**	**39528271**	**34286922**	**2196212**	**155884**	**2381565**
国有企业	State-owned Enterprises	15088248	12909457	942506	59380	895836
集体企业	Collective-owned Enterprises	4100437	3677703	208982	18210	162288
股份合作企业	Cooperative Enterprises	1172861	1034864	68274	4386	59677
联营企业	Joint Ownership Enterprises	996327	898305	42642	2478	47155
国有联营企业	State Joint Ownership Enterprises	295786	253489	14708	1570	25374
集体联营企业	Collective Joint Ownership Enterprises	138429	124916	6711	218	6054
国有与集体联营企业	Joint State-collective Enterprises	364400	348653	6576	221	7296
其他联营企业	Other Joint Ownership Enterprises	197712	171247	14648	468	8432
有限责任公司	Limited Liability Corporations	6868848	6007540	387167	24451	389051
国有独资公司	State Sole Funded Corporations	647132	551828	39240	2343	44377
其他有限责任公司	Other Limited Liability Corporations	6221716	5455712	347927	22108	344675
股份有限公司	Share-holding Corporations Ltd.	9237963	7921388	420718	40208	754021
私营企业	Private Enterprises	2042141	1818400	123791	6687	73573
私营独资企业	Private-funded Enterprises	267783	241424	14511	1216	10214
私营合伙企业	Private Partnership Enterprises	50692	46418	4446	233	-405
私营有限责任公司	Private Limited Liability Corporations	1524972	1347203	97399	4753	57159
私营股份有限公司	Private Share-holding Corporations Ltd.	198694	183354	7436	486	6604
其他企业	Other Enterprises	21445	19265	2132	83	-35
港、澳、台商投资企业	**Enterprises with Funds from Hong Kong, Macau and Taiwan**	**2223779**	**1531355**	**158581**	**7923**	**136901**
合资经营企业（港或澳、台资）	Joint-venture Enterprises (with Funds from Hong Kong, Macau and Taiwan)	821370	678888	69018	2356	67622
合作经营企业（港或澳、台资）	Cooperative Enterprises (with Funds from Hong Kong, Macau and Taiwan)	1033131	558200	62612	1235	28530
港、澳、台商独资经营企业	Enterprises with Sole Funded from Hong Kong, Macau and Taiwan	69013	53507	10039	274	4669
港、澳、台商投资股份有限公司	Share-holding Corporations Ltd. with Funds from Hong Kong, Macau and Taiwan	300265	240761	16912	4058	36080
外商投资企业	**Foreign Funded Enterprises**	**2325206**	**1943178**	**211826**	**2184**	**136454**
中外合资经营企业	Joint-venture Enterprises	1173222	950309	118369	1315	81861
中外合作经营企业	Cooperation Enterprises	1138522	979905	93097	852	54472
外资企业	Enterprises with Sole Foreign Funds	542	482	26	1	33
外商投资股份有限公司	Share-holding Corporations Ltd. with Foreign Funds	12920	12482	334	16	88

16-22 限额以上批发、零售贸易企业主要财务指标情况（2000年，按行业分）

Main Financial Indicators of Enterprises above Designated Size in Wholesale and Retail Trade by Sector(2000)

单位：万元 (10 000 yuan)

指　标	Item	商品销售收入 Sales Revenue	商品销售成本 Cost of Sales	经营费用 Management Cost	商品销售税金及附加 Sales Tax and Extra Changes	商品销售利润 Total Profits
总　计	**Total**	**285918605**	**261411058**	**10078870**	**542000**	**11278707**
一、批发企业合计	**Wholesale Trade**	**241841349**	**223649603**	**7512251**	**376008**	**8623787**
食品、饮料、烟草批发业	Wholesale of Food, Beverages and Tobaccos	58636778	52072850	2201444	191417	3584206
#粮食、食用油批发业	Wholesale of Grains and Edible Oil	8382658	7946045	486592	4831	-290934
烟草及其制品批发业	Whole of Tobaccos	38679048	33712465	1226150	157421	3322164
棉、麻、土畜产品批发业	Wholesale of Cotton, Ambery and Animal Products	8850571	8302952	237470	9875	288866
纺织品、服装和鞋帽批发业	Wholesale of Textiles, Garments, Shoes and Hats	17573535	16261536	588995	9312	651396
日用百货批发业	Wholesale of Daily Consumer Goods	5480493	5094525	213373	6010	152219
日用杂品批发业	Wholesale of Daily Sundry Articles	594104	548070	27152	1411	15799
五金、交电、化工批发业	Wholesale of Hardware, Transport, Electric and Chemical Products	8657830	8110730	303649	9811	176872
药品及医疗器械批发业	Wholesale of Medicines and Medical Appliances	10022832	8965930	430840	17315	556265
能源批发业	Wholesale of Energy Products	56792584	53839873	1490449	51367	1296393
#石油及制品批发业	Wholesale of Petroleum and Related Products	52094932	49567910	1241178	38266	1141275
煤炭及制品批发业	Wholesale of Coal and Related Products	4629385	4205913	247946	13065	154263
化工材料批发业	Wholesale of Chemical Materials	7633859	7242797	204089	5931	175138
木材批发业	Wholesale of Timber	528138	482815	30759	1991	12341
建筑材料批发业	Wholesale of Building Materials	1437037	1339082	50754	2622	36203
矿产品批发业	Wholesale of Mineral Products	1927829	1794804	89674	8104	34793
金属材料批发业	Wholesale of Metal Materials	17494749	16797382	370874	12583	287126
机械、电子设备批发业	Wholesale of Machinery and Electronic Equipment	12142852	11477714	275331	8875	329264
汽车、摩托车及零配件批发业	Wholesale of Motor Vehicles, Motorcycles and Parts	11218149	10733177	264222	12913	197272
#汽车批发业	Wholesale of Motor Vehicles	7468527	7172710	160885	3243	126274
再生物资回收批发业	Wholesale of Recycled Materials	1323797	1277023	25152	3495	12725
工艺美术批发业	Wholesale of Arts and Handicraft Products	1431523	1301323	64948	559	64665
图书报刊批发业	Wholesale of Books, Newspapers and Magazines	2497981	1643338	112906	4454	152737
农业生产资料批发业	Wholesale of Means of Agricultural Production	10305261	9735127	295306	4929	220673
其他类未包括的批发业	Other Wholesale not Classified Elsewhere	7291445	6628556	234865	13034	378834
二、零售企业合计	**Retail Trade**	**44077256**	**37761455**	**2566619**	**165992**	**2654920**
食品、饮料、烟草零售业	Retail of Food, Beverages and Tobaccos	5292554	4679538	345580	16280	210620
#粮油食品零售业	Retail of Grains and Edible Oil	862868	809672	61060	2793	-18531
副食品零售业	Retail of Non-staple Food	2347855	2059538	165083	8529	100732
日用百货零售业	Retail of Daily Consumer Goods	24541563	20707965	1449386	101247	1643587
#百货零售业	Retail of Consumer Goods	23596483	19886155	1389429	97968	1589789
文化体育用品零售业	Retail of Cultural and Sports Goods	141949	113844	14941	587	10948
纺织品、服装和鞋帽零售业	Retail of Textiles, Garments, Shoes and Hats	934102	775578	61381	5592	82745
日用杂品零售业	Retail of Daily Sundry Articles	174538	157061	10826	635	5244
五金、交电、化工零售业	Retail of Hardware, Transport, Electric and Chemical Products	2989388	2738857	126550	9281	89786
药品及医疗器械零售业	Retail of Medicines and Medical Appliances	1979904	1660443	134165	5474	161842
图书报刊零售业	Retail of Books, Newspapers and Magazines	2013649	1409769	177238	9269	248568
其他零售业	Other Retail Trade	6149863	5630481	261469	18212	212428
#家具零售业	Retail of Furniture	112446	88992	18056	495	4662
汽车、摩托车及其零配件零售业	Retail of Motor Vehicles, Motorcycles and Parts	2084049	1990420	39906	3803	37320
计算机及软件、办公设备零售业	Retail of Computers, Software and Office Appliances	454059	427962	15406	835	9193

16-23 限额以上批发零售贸易企业主要财务指标情况（2000年，按地区分）

Main Financial Indicators of Enterprises above Designated Size in Wholesale and Retail Trade by Region (2000)

单位：万元 (10 000 yuan)

地 区	Region	商品销售收 入 Sales Revenue	商品销售成 本 Cost of Sales	经营费用 Management Cost	商品销售税金及附加 Sales Tax and Extra Changes	商品销售利 润 Total Profits
全 国	**National Total**	**285918605**	**261411058**	**10078870**	**542000**	**11278707**
北 京	Beijing	24464228	22554378	894021	35748	879124
天 津	Tianjin	8803355	8333146	225669	6674	225800
河 北	Hebei	7498985	6900212	273909	9463	259868
山 西	Shanxi	3380141	3039014	175968	17583	115935
内蒙古	Inner Mongolia	1888398	1717380	84038	4672	65409
辽 宁	Liaoning	13818025	12852195	522716	17938	364770
吉 林	Jilin	3167845	2995513	172080	4329	-35941
黑龙江	Heilongjiang	4640327	4270072	193747	8492	144643
上 海	Shanghai	32393458	29454498	936684	44158	1472965
江 苏	Jiangsu	24529139	22123993	917882	37884	1153580
浙 江	Zhejiang	28093011	26004586	791362	38555	1106832
安 徽	Anhui	5854128	5326635	215659	8204	260281
福 建	Fujian	11018343	9919568	347581	28097	460919
江 西	Jiangxi	3043940	2785460	106426	4739	105934
山 东	Shandong	16110669	14685566	682836	28501	571204
河 南	Henan	8895662	8042924	363330	19772	401924
湖 北	Hubei	9248836	8485582	257321	16299	358629
湖 南	Hunan	6032444	5465364	216952	11327	288833
广 东	Guangdong	32910228	30690624	1025402	40240	1100734
广 西	Guangxi	3501034	3172717	142805	7210	151780
海 南	Hainan	816022	735752	27754	2083	42674
重 庆	Chongqing	3318318	2966095	154999	7722	151446
四 川	Sichuan	7120861	6460803	277337	13615	239423
贵 州	Guizhou	2359742	2095281	111180	6895	107681
云 南	Yunnan	10233079	8690908	463565	96659	767466
西 藏	Tibet	103313	88675	7409	242	6191
陕 西	Shaanxi	3787237	3470800	134296	4621	149942
甘 肃	Gansu	3416650	3175675	106389	8869	112583
青 海	Qinghai	435014	371216	26067	775	19759
宁 夏	Ningxia	506599	449805	27124	1679	19993
新 疆	Xinjiang	4529574	4086623	196363	8959	208327

16-24 限额以上批发贸易企业主要财务指标情况
(2000年，按地区分)
Main Financial Indicators of Enterprises above Designated Size in Wholesale Trades by Region (2000)

单位：万元 (10 000 yuan)

地 区	Region	商品销售收入 Sales Revenue	商品销售成本 Cost of Sales	经营费用 Management Cost	商品销售税金及附加 Sales Tax and Extra Changes	商品销售利润 Total Profits
全 国	**National Total**	**241841349**	**223649603**	**7512251**	**376008**	**8623787**
北 京	Beijing	18985560	17790342	488687	17907	609730
天 津	Tianjin	7586605	7252655	156580	3482	166095
河 北	Hebei	6256188	5829553	209019	4712	173413
山 西	Shanxi	2510650	2305656	120345	8492	57795
内蒙古	Inner Mongolia	1577918	1450491	65617	3126	46702
辽 宁	Liaoning	12270783	11574538	426673	8947	232878
吉 林	Jilin	2470355	2365808	139339	2354	-61327
黑龙江	Heilongjiang	3760106	3514221	143713	4317	79171
上 海	Shanghai	26438097	24695836	579400	24334	1098026
江 苏	Jiangsu	20790518	18938084	698321	24945	905798
浙 江	Zhejiang	25803418	23990496	676557	30407	974288
安 徽	Anhui	5121258	4702392	170452	5036	210081
福 建	Fujian	10002777	9025096	291454	22965	409067
江 西	Jiangxi	2716134	2500310	88561	3176	87632
山 东	Shandong	12826896	11809626	534418	20484	387764
河 南	Henan	7317763	6618314	290977	13109	347334
湖 北	Hubei	7574914	7047996	197278	7634	237066
湖 南	Hunan	5105956	4696631	166826	6643	200740
广 东	Guangdong	27973969	26391353	707732	26754	815913
广 西	Guangxi	2794646	2560779	101147	4205	104978
海 南	Hainan	727438	663800	22643	1136	34808
重 庆	Chongqing	2723999	2456371	124134	4947	109419
四 川	Sichuan	6104967	5606051	202471	9085	191130
贵 州	Guizhou	2084453	1853495	94022	5163	93960
云 南	Yunnan	9546286	8108901	420877	93991	730527
西 藏	Tibet	58497	53159	4860	79	-57
陕 西	Shaanxi	3122856	2884962	107758	3012	100546
甘 肃	Gansu	2966082	2778877	83563	6693	85029
青 海	Qinghai	354878	301643	20612	558	16783
宁 夏	Ningxia	362685	331330	18025	1080	10174
新 疆	Xinjiang	3904698	3550838	160192	7233	168328

16-25 限额以上零售贸易企业主要财务指标情况
（2000年，按地区分）
Main Financial Indicators of Enterprises above Designated Size in Retail Trades by Region (2000)

单位：万元 (10 000 yuan)

地区	Region	商品销售收入 Sales Revenue	商品销售成本 Cost of Sales	经营费用 Management Cost	商品销售税金及附加 Sales Tax and Extra Changes	商品销售利润 Total Profits
全国	**National Total**	**44077256**	**37761455**	**2566619**	**165992**	**2654920**
北京	Beijing	5478668	4764036	405335	17841	269394
天津	Tianjin	1216749	1080492	69089	3191	59705
河北	Hebei	1242798	1070658	64890	4751	86456
山西	Shanxi	869491	733358	55622	9090	58140
内蒙古	Inner Mongolia	310480	266889	18421	1546	18708
辽宁	Liaoning	1547241	1277657	96043	8992	131892
吉林	Jilin	697491	629705	32742	1975	25385
黑龙江	Heilongjiang	880221	755851	50035	4175	65472
上海	Shanghai	5955361	4758662	357283	19824	374939
江苏	Jiangsu	3738621	3185909	219561	12939	247782
浙江	Zhejiang	2289593	2014090	114806	8147	132544
安徽	Anhui	732870	624243	45207	3168	50200
福建	Fujian	1015566	894472	56127	5131	51853
江西	Jiangxi	327806	285149	17866	1562	18302
山东	Shandong	3283774	2875940	148418	8017	183441
河南	Henan	1577899	1424610	72353	6662	54590
湖北	Hubei	1673922	1437586	60043	8665	121563
湖南	Hunan	926489	768733	50126	4684	88093
广东	Guangdong	4936259	4299271	317670	13486	284821
广西	Guangxi	706388	611938	41658	3005	46803
海南	Hainan	88584	71952	5111	947	7865
重庆	Chongqing	594319	509724	30865	2775	42028
四川	Sichuan	1015894	854752	74865	4530	48293
贵州	Guizhou	275289	241786	17158	1732	13721
云南	Yunnan	686793	582007	42687	2668	36939
西藏	Tibet	44816	35516	2550	163	6249
陕西	Shaanxi	664382	585838	26539	1609	49396
甘肃	Gansu	450568	396798	22826	2176	27554
青海	Qinghai	80136	69573	5456	217	2975
宁夏	Ningxia	143914	118474	9099	598	9819
新疆	Xinjiang	624876	535785	36172	1726	39999

16-26 限额以上餐饮企业主要财务指标情况
（2000年，按登记注册类型和行业分）
Main Financial Indicators of Enterprises above Designated Size in Catering Services by Types of Registration and by Sector (2000)

单位：万元 (10 000 yuan)

指　标	Item	营业收入 Sales Revenue	营业成本 Cost of Sales	营业费用 Management Cost	商品销售税金及附加 Sales Tax and Extra Changes	经营利润 Profits
总　计	**Total**	**4052445**	**1945662**	**1321533**	**210481**	**574769**
一、按登记注册类型分	**By Types of Registration**					
内资企业	**Domestic Funded Enterprises**	**2620603**	**1327200**	**800649**	**136925**	**355829**
国有企业	State-owned Enterprises	837616	404229	274343	40660	118385
集体企业	Collective-owned Enterprises	408030	205626	129409	21834	51161
股份合作企业	Cooperative Enterprises	153170	84622	42192	7529	18828
联营企业	Joint Ownership Enterprises	34744	14641	12014	2089	6000
国有联营企业	State Joint Ownership Enterprises	12677	4694	5617	707	1660
集体联营企业	Collective Joint Ownership Enterprises	3793	2328	856	231	378
国有与集体联营企业	Joint State-collective Enterprises	10837	4036	3124	704	2972
其他联营企业	Other Joint Ownership Enterprises	7437	3584	2417	447	990
有限责任公司	Limited Liability Corporations	432370	213978	131413	21985	64994
国有独资公司	State Sole Funded Corporations	38342	18669	10303	1716	7654
其他有限责任公司	Other Limited Liability Corporations	394028	195310	121109	20269	57340
股份有限公司	Share-holding Corporations Ltd.	175634	79705	56948	8595	30387
私营企业	Private Enterprises	578082	323746	154181	34166	65990
私营独资企业	Private-funded Enterprises	193790	111917	45458	11120	25296
私营合伙企业	Private Partnership Enterprises	26617	14718	8471	1327	2100
私营有限责任公司	Private Limited Liability Corporations	321351	177157	89595	19511	35088
私营股份有限公司	Private Share-holding Corporations Ltd.	36325	19954	10657	2208	3506
其他企业	Other Enterprises	956	652	150	68	85
港、澳、台商投资企业	**Enterprises with Funds from Hong Kong, Macau and Taiwan**	**562090**	**235623**	**214896**	**29140**	**82431**
合资经营企业（港或澳、台资）	Joint-venture Enterprises (with Funds from Hong Kong, Macau and Taiwan)	346696	140172	125124	17853	63547
合作经营企业（港或澳、台资）	Cooperative Enterprises (with Funds from Hong Kong, Macau and Taiwan)	109944	46954	46398	5605	10986
港、澳、台商独资经营企业	Enterprises with Sole Funds from Hong Kong, Macau and Taiwan	101204	46091	40973	5457	8684
港、澳、台商投资股份有限公司	Share-holding Corporations Ltd. with Funds from Hong Kong, Macau and Taiwan	4246	2405	2402	225	-785
外商投资企业	**Foreign Funded Enterprises**	**869752**	**382839**	**305987**	**44417**	**136509**
中外合资经营企业	Joint-venture Enterprises	435709	193440	145217	21710	75342
中外合作经营企业	Cooperation Enterprises	135720	56500	55418	6849	16952
外资企业	Enterprises with Sole Foreign Funds	293828	131073	104262	15644	42849
外商投资股份有限公司	Share-holding Corporations Ltd. with Foreign Funds	4495	1826	1090	214	1365
二、按国民经济行业分	**By Sector**					
正餐	Dinner	3146884	1539185	989911	165613	452175
快餐	Snack	848384	376871	313566	42540	115406
其他餐饮业	Other	57177	29605	18056	2328	7188

16−27 限额以上餐饮企业主要财务指标情况（2000年，按地区分）

Main Financial Indicators of Enterprises above Designated Size in Catering Services by Region (2000)

单位：万元 (10 000 yuan)

地　区	Region	营业收入 Sales Revenue	营业成本 Cost of Sales	营业费用 Management Cost	商品销售税金及附加 Sales Tax and Extra Changes	经营利润 Profits
全　国	**National Total**	**4052445**	**1945662**	**1321533**	**210481**	**574769**
北　京	Beijing	442251	210791	153256	21523	56681
天　津	Tianjin	100132	50360	32740	5167	11865
河　北	Hebei	39008	21536	10566	2126	4779
山　西	Shanxi	43208	24235	11282	2431	5261
内蒙古	Inner Mongolia	30201	15395	9413	2574	2820
辽　宁	Liaoning	223446	111029	68881	12879	30657
吉　林	Jilin	28666	14320	8511	1518	4317
黑龙江	Heilongjiang	56315	32990	12883	3664	6778
上　海	Shanghai	365044	167020	126458	17144	54422
江　苏	Jiangsu	302266	138734	95884	15347	52301
浙　江	Zhejiang	287844	140359	82935	15322	49228
安　徽	Anhui	13336	7983	4184	746	423
福　建	Fujian	174195	90045	50569	11779	21802
江　西	Jiangxi	24126	13656	5680	1324	3466
山　东	Shandong	247234	114172	73322	12470	47270
河　南	Henan	73222	41363	18275	3136	10448
湖　北	Hubei	121797	60172	39782	6434	15409
湖　南	Hunan	59339	30321	18380	2968	7671
广　东	Guangdong	910686	426567	325764	45669	112686
广　西	Guangxi	58808	29334	18344	2887	8244
海　南	Hainan	37353	11573	15671	2102	8007
重　庆	Chongqing	100677	40877	31800	5140	22860
四　川	Sichuan	126542	60641	43730	6589	15583
贵　州	Guizhou	16947	9240	4448	1058	2201
云　南	Yunnan	46495	26749	15487	1690	2569
西　藏	Tibet					
陕　西	Shaanxi	69298	34124	25381	3703	6090
甘　肃	Gansu	17729	8243	6029	1116	2341
青　海	Qinghai	2009	1204	475	114	216
宁　夏	Ningxia	7967	4338	1869	428	1333
新　疆	Xinjiang	26304	8291	9535	1435	7043

主 要 统 计 指 标 解 释

社会消费品零售总额 指国民经济各行业直接售给城乡居民和社会集团的消费品总额。它是反映各行业通过多种商品流通渠道向居民和社会集团供应的生活消费品总量，是研究国内零售市场变动情况、反映经济景气程度的重要指标。

社会消费品零售总额包括：⑴售给城乡居民作为生活用的商品和修建房屋用的建筑材料；⑵售给社会集团的各种办公用品和公用消费品；⑶售给机关、团体、学校、部队、企业、事业单位的职工食堂和旅店(招待所)附设专门供本店旅客食用，不对外营业的食堂的各种食品、燃料；企业、单位和国营农场直接售给本单位职工和职工食堂的自己生产的产品；⑷售给部队干部、战士生活用的粮食、副食品、衣着品、日用品、燃料；⑸售给来华的外国人、华侨、港澳台同胞的消费品；⑹居民自费购买的中、西药品、中药材及医疗用品；⑺报社、出版社直接售给居民和社会集团的报纸、图书、杂志，集邮公司出售的新、旧纪念邮票、特种邮票、首日封、集邮册、集邮工具等；⑻旧货寄售商店自购、自销部分的商品；⑼煤气公司、液化石油气站售给居民和社会集团的煤气灶具和罐装液化石油气；⑽农民售给非农业居民和社会集团的商品。不包括售给国民经济各部门企业、事业单位(包括国有经济的农场)生产经营用的各种原材料、燃料、设备、工具等和售给批发零售贸易业、餐饮业作为转卖用的商品，旧货寄售商店受托寄售卖出的商品，服务业的营业收入，邮局出售邮票的收入，自来水、电力、煤气生产(供应)单位的产品供应收入，也不包括农民之间的商品销售。

批发零售贸易业商品购、销、存总额 指各种登记注册类型的批发、零售贸易业企业（单位）以本企业（单位）为总体的商品购进、销售、库存总额。

商品购进总额 指从本企业(单位)以外的单位和个人购进(包括从境外直接进口)作为转卖或加工后转卖的商品总额。它反映批发零售贸易业从国内、国外市场上购进商品的总量。商品购进总额包括：⑴从工农业生产者购进的商品；⑵从出版社、报社的出版发行部门购进的图书、杂志和报纸；⑶从各种登记注册类型的批发零售贸易企业(单位)购进的商品；⑷从其他单位购进的商品，如从机关、团体、企业等单位购进的剩余物资，从餐饮业、服务业购进的商品，从海关、市场管理部门购进的缉私和没收的商品，从居民手中收购的废旧商品等；⑸从国(境)外直接进口的商品。不包括企业(单位)为自身经营用和未通过买卖行为而收入的商品以及销售退回、商品升溢等。

商品销售总额 指对本企业(单位)以外的单位和个人出售(包括对境外直接出口)的商品总额。它反映批发零售贸易业在国内市场上销售商品以及出口商品的总量。商品销售总额包括：⑴售给城乡居民和社会集团消费用的商品；⑵售给工业、农业、建筑业、运输邮电业、批发零售贸易业、餐饮业、服务业等作为生产、经营使用的商品；⑶售给批发零售贸易业作为转卖或加工后转卖的商品；⑷对国(境)外直接出口的商品。不包括出售本企业(单位)自用的废旧包装用品；未通过买卖行为付出的商品；经本单位介绍，由买卖双方直接结算，本单位只收取手续费的业务；购货退出的商品以及商品损耗和损失等。

批发零售贸易业库存 指报告期末各种登记注册类型的批发零售贸易企业(单位)已取得所有权的商品。它反映批发零售贸易企业(单位)的商品库存情况和对市场商品供应的保证程度。期末库存包括：⑴存放在批发零售贸易业经营单位(如门市部、批发站、经营处)仓库、货场、货柜和货架中的商品；⑵挑选、整理、包装中的商品；⑶已记入购进而尚未运到本单位的商品，即发货单或银行承兑凭证已到而货未到的部分；⑷寄放他处的商品，如因购货方拒绝承付而暂时存放在购货方的商品和已办完加工成品收回手续而未提回的商品；⑸委托其他单位代销(未作销售或调出)尚未售出的商品；⑹代其他单位购进尚未交付的商品。不包括所有权不属于本单位的商品、拨付除批发零售贸易业以外的其他行业所属独立核算加工厂等加工生产尚未收回成品的商品、代国家物资储备部门保管的商品等。

库存总额采用的计算价格是：农副产品采购单位按购进价计算；批发单位按进货价计算；零售单位按核算价格计算，即按什么价格核算就按什么价格计算。

消费品市场成交额 指从事消费品交易的商品市场的全部商品成交金额。消费品市场包括农副产品市场和工业消费品市场。

Explanatory Notes on Main Statistical Indicators

Total Retail Sales of Consumer Goods refer to the sum of retail sales of consumer goods sold by all sectors of the national economy to urban and rural residents and social groups. This indicator is used to show the supply of consumers goods through various channels to households and institutions, and is very important for the study on changes at the domestic retail market, and on economic cycles.

The retail sales of consumer goods include: (1) commodities sold to urban and rural residents for their daily use and building materials sold to them for the construction or repair of houses; (2) office appliances and supplies sold to institutions; (3) food and fuels sold to canteens of institutions, enterprises, schools, military units and to canteens of hotels and hostels that only serve their guests, and commodities produced by enterprises, institutions or state farms and sold directly to their employees or their canteens; (4) grain and non-staple food, clothing, daily articles and fuels sold to military personnel; (5)consumer goods sold to foreigners, overseas Chinese, and Chinese compatriots from Taiwan, Hong Kong and Macao during their stay in the mainland of China; (6) Chinese and western medicines, herbs and medical facilities purchased by residents; (7) newspapers, books and magazines directly sold to residents and social groups by publishers, new and old commemorative stamps, special stamps, first-day covers, stamp albums and other stamp-collection articles sold by stamp companies; (8) consumer goods purchased and then sold by second-hand shops; (9) stoves and other heating facilities and liquefied gas sold by gas companies to households and institutions; and (10) commodities sold by farmers to non-agricultural residents and social groups. Excluded under this heading are: raw materials, fuels, equipment, tools sold to enterprises, institutions and state farms for production purpose; commodities sold to trade establishments for re-selling; commissioned sales at second-hand shops; operational income of urban public utilities; stamps sold at post offices; income of water, power, gas production and supply establishments from the supply of their products; and sales of commodities among farmers.

Purchase, Sales and Stock of Commodities by Wholesale and Retail Trade refer to the purchase, sales and stock of commodities by wholesale and retail establishments of different status of registration (excluding individual sellers).

Total Purchases of Commodities refer to the total value of purchases of commodities by the establishments from other establishments or individuals (including direct import from abroad) for the purpose of re-selling, either with or without further processing of the commodities purchased. This indicator is used to show the total value of purchases of commodities by wholesale and retail establishments from domestic and overseas markets. The total purchases include: (1) agricultural and industrial products purchased from producers; (2) books, magazines and newspapers purchased from distribution departments of the publishers; (3) commodities purchased from wholesale and retail establishments of different status of registration; (4) commodities purchased from other units, such as surplus materials purchased from government agencies, enterprises or institutions, commodities purchased from catering and service establishments, confiscated goods purchased from customs authorities or market management agencies, second-hand goods and wastes purchased from residents; and (5) commodities directly imported from abroad. Excluded are commodities purchased by establishments (units) for use in their own business operation, commodities obtained without buying or selling procedures, rejected commodities, etc.

Total Sales of Commodities refer to value of commodities sold by the establishments to other establishments and individuals (including direct export). This indicator is used to show the total value of sales of commodities at domestic markets and export. The total sales include: (1) commodities sold to urban and rural residents and social groups for their consumption; (2) commodities sold to establishments in industry, agriculture, construction, transportation, post and telecommunications, wholesale and retail trades, catering trade and public utility for their production and operation; (3) commodities sold to wholesale and retail establishments for re selling, with or without further processing; and (4)commodities for direct export to other countries. Excluded are selling of waste packaging materials used by the establishments (units) themselves, commodities transferred without buying or selling procedures, commission income from brokerage in transactions whose settlement is directly handled by buyers and sellers, rejected commodities in the purchase, loss in commodities, etc.

Commodity Stock of Wholesale and Retail Enterprises refers to total commodities possessed by wholesale and retail enterprises (units) of various types of registration status at the end of the reference period, which reflects the commodity stock level of various wholesale and retail enterprises and the potential for market supply. It includes: (1) commodities located in storage, garages, counters, and shelves of operating units (such as sale stores, wholesale centers, and operating offices) of wholesale and retail enterprises; (2) commodities in the process of selecting, sorting, and packing; (3)commodities not arrived but recorded as purchase in the account, i.e. commodities not arrived but payment receipts for the commodities from the sellers or the banks arrived; (4) commodities deposited in other places rather than places mentioned above, for instance: commodities in the hold of purchasers temporarily due to the refusal of payment and commodities not taken back after going through the formalities; (5) commodities entrusted to other units to sell but not sold yet; (6) commodities purchased for other units but not delivered yet. Commodities not included as stock are those not owned by the enterprises (units), those allocated to financially independent factories rather than wholesale and retail enterprises for processing but not taken back yet, and finally those put in stock by wholesale and retail enterprises on behalf of the state material reserves units.

For the calculation of the value of commodities stock, the value is calculated at purchasing prices in agricultural goods purchasing units and wholesale units, and at the accounting prices in retail units.

Volume of Transaction at Free Markets for Consumer Goods refers to the value of transaction of all goods at the free trade markets for consumer goods, where markets include both free markets for farm and sideline products and for manufactured consumer goods.

十七、对外经济贸易

Foreign Trade and Economic Cooperation

简要说明

一、本篇资料综合反映中国的对外贸易、利用外资、对外承包工程和劳务合作的历年概况数据，重点反映对外经济贸易的近况，是国家统计局贸易外经司根据对外贸易经济合作部、海关总署、国家外汇管理局和国家工商行政管理局的有关资料加工整理的。

二、17－1表综合反映“八五”以来我国对外贸易、利用外资、对外承包工程和劳务合作的总量变化情况。17－2表反映历年人民币对美元、日元、港币的年平均汇价。资料来源于国家外汇管理局，是根据当年国家外汇管理局提供的每日汇价进行加权平均计算而得出的当年年平均汇价。17－3表至17－12表系统反映我国进出口贸易的规模、进出口商品结构、对贸易伙伴国的进出口总额以及各地区三资企业的进出口变化情况。1979年及以前为外贸业务统计数字，来源于对外贸易经济合作部；1980年及以后为海关进出口统计数字，来源于海关总署。17－4表和17－5表的进、出口商品分类按联合国《国际贸易标准分类》(SITC)统计。17－6表的进出口商品则按海关合作理事会制定的《商品名称及编码协调制度》(HS)目录进行分类统计。17－13表至17－18表，资料来源于对外贸易经济合作部，是根据对外贸易经济合作部和国家统计局于1996年11月共同制订的《利用外资统计制度》的全面统计资料加工、整理而成。该制度统计范围是指我国境内所有的利用外资单位和部门，以及经批准在我国境内设立的中外合资经营企业、合作经营企业、外资企业、外商投资股份制企业、合作开发项目等具有法人资格的独立核算企业(包括港澳台地区投资企业)。17－19表和17－20表反映各地区外商投资企业注册登记情况，资料来源于国家工商行政管理局，是根据国家工商行政管理局1994年制订的《工商行政管理系统统计报表制度》进行统计、加工、整理而得。凡经工商行政管理机关核准登记，在中华人民共和国境内的中外合资经营企业、中外合作经营企业、外商独资企业、中外股份公司、在华从事经营活动的外国及港澳台地区企业及外国公司在中国境内设立的分支机构均列入统计范围。该表以开业登记、变更登记、注销登记等管理资料为统计依据。17－21表及17－22表反映历年中国对外承包工程和劳务合作及对外设计咨询的发展状况。资料来源于对外贸易经济合作部，是根据对外贸易经济合作部与国家统计局于1996年7月共同制订的《对外承包工程和劳务合作统计制度》的全面统计资料加工、整理而得。该制度统计单位是经各级对外贸易经济合作部门批准的从事对外承包和劳务合作业务并具有法人地位的对外承包劳务企业。

三、我国对各国(地区)进出口总额表中，出口货物按中华人民共和国关境外最终目的国(地)，进口货物按中华人民共和国关境外原产国(地)统计。各地区进出口商品总值分别按境内经营单位所在地和目的地、货源地列示。经营单位所在地是指中华人民共和国关境内进出口企业报关注册的登记地；境内货源地是指出口货物在中华人民共和国关境内的产地或原始发货地；境内目的地则指进口货物在中华人民共和国关境内的消费、使用地或最终运抵地。

Brief Introduction

I. Data in this chapter show the summary data of China's foreign trade, utilization of foreign capital, contracted projects and labour cooperation with the foreign countries or territories over the years, stressing on the recent situation of foreign trade and economic cooperation.

II. Table 17-1 shows the summary data of the total changes in China's foreign trade, utilization of foreign capital, contracted projects and labour cooperation with the foreign countries or territories since the Eighth Five-year Plan Period. Table 17-2 shows the average exchange rates of RMB yuan to US dollar, Japanese yen and Hong Kong dollar over the years. The data come from the State Administration of Exchange Control. The annual average exchange rate is calculated as the weighted mean of the daily exchange rates provided by the State Administration of Foreign Exchange in the year. Tables from 17-3 to 17-12 show systematically the size of China's imports and exports, composition of import and export commodities, China's foreign trade with the related countries and territories, the changes in the import and export of the foreign-funded enterprises by region. The data in the years prior to 1980 were statistical data of foreign trade and come from the Ministry of Foreign Trade and Economic Cooperation. Since 1980, the data have been the statistical data of customs on imports and exports and come from the General Customs Administration. For Table 17-4 and 17-5, the UN Standard International Trade Classification (SITC) was used for the classification of the import and export commodities. However, the Harmonized Commodity Description and Coding System (HS) stipulated by the Customs Cooperation Council is used in the classification of the import and export commodities as displayed in Table 17-6. Data in tables 17-13 to 17-18 are from the Ministry of Foreign Trade and Economic Cooperation and are tabulated in accordance with the *"Statistical Scheme on the Utilization of Foreign Capital"* designed by the Ministry of Foreign Trade and Economic Cooperation and the National Bureau of Statistics in November of 1996, which are data of complete enumeration. The statistical coverage includes all the units and departments which have utilized foreign capital and all the Sino-foreign joint ventures, Sino-foreign cooperative enterprises, ventures exclusively with foreign investment, foreign-funded stock companies, Sino-foreign cooperative development projects and other corporate enterprises (including the enterprises funded by the entrepreneurs from Hong Kong, Macao and Taiwan) with independent accounting system which have been approved by the Chinese government to set up in the boundary of the People's Republic of China. Tables 17-19 and 17-20 show the registration of the foreign- funded enterprises in various regions. The data come from the State Administration for Industry and Commerce and are tabulated in accordance with the" Statistical Reporting Scheme in the Administrative System of Administration for Industry and Commerce" stipulated by the State Administration for Industry and Commerce in 1994. The statistical coverage includes all the Sino-foreign joint ventures, Sino-foreign cooperative enterprises, ventures exclusively with foreign investment, Sino-foreign share-holding companies, foreign enterprises and enterprises of Hong Kong, Macao and Taiwan engaged in commercial activities and the branch offices of the foreign companies in China, which have been approved by and registered at the State Administration for Industry and Commerce to set up in the boundary of the People's Republic of China. The data in this table are collected on the basis of the registration on opening business, changes and cancellation. Tables 17-21 and 17-22 shows the development of the contracted projects, labour services cooperation and design and consultation service with foreign countries over the years in China. The data come from the Ministry of Foreign Trade and Economic Cooperation and are collected with the method of complete enumeration and are tabulated in accordance with the Table CS-4 in the "Statistical Reporting Scheme on the Contracted Projects and Labour Services Cooperation with Foreign Countries" jointly stipulated by the Ministry of Foreign Trade and Economic Cooperation and the National Bureau of Statistics in July, 1996. The statistical unit in the scheme is the corporate enterprise engaged in contracted projects and labour services cooperation with foreign countries and has been approved by the departments of foreign trade and economic cooperation at various levels.

III. In the table on China's total imports and exports with related countries and territories, the export commodities are calculated as the countries (or territories) of final destination and the import commodities as the countries (or territories) of origin.

The total values of the import and export commodities by region are calculated respectively at the provinces where the import or export corporations are situated and at the provinces of destination or provinces of origin within the boundary of the People's Republic of China. The province where the import or export corporations are situated refers to the province where the import or export corporations have applied to and have been registered at the customs. The province of origin within the boundary of the People's Republic of China refers to the province where the export commodities are produced or originally delivered. The province of destination within the boundary of the People's Republic of China refers to the province where the import commodities are consumed, used or transported to the destination.

17-1 对外经济贸易基本情况

Foreign Trade and Economic Cooperation

指标	Item	1996	1997	1998	1999	2000
进出口总额 （人民币亿元）	**Total Value of Imports and Exports (RMB 100 million yuan)**	**24133.8**	**26967.2**	**26857.7**	**29896.3**	**39274.2**
出口总额	Total Exports	12576.4	15160.7	15231.6	16159.8	20635.2
进口总额	Total Imports	11557.4	11806.5	11626.1	13736.5	18639.0
进出口差额	Balance	1019.0	3354.2	3605.5	2423.3	1996.2
进出口总额 （亿美元）	**Total Value of Imports and Exports (USD 100 million)**	**2898.8**	**3251.6**	**3239.5**	**3606.3**	**4742.9**
出口总额	Total Exports	1510.5	1827.9	1837.1	1949.3	2492.0
初级产品	Primary Goods	219.3	239.5	204.9	199.4	254.6
工业制成品	Manufactured Goods	1291.2	1588.4	1632.2	1749.9	2237.4
进口总额	Total Imports	1388.3	1423.7	1402.4	1657.0	2250.9
初级产品	Primary Goods	254.4	286.2	229.5	268.5	467.4
工业制成品	Manufactured Goods	1133.9	1137.5	1172.9	1388.5	1783.5
进出口差额	Balance	122.2	404.2	434.7	292.3	241.1
对外签订利用外资合同外资项目 （个）	**Number of Projects for Utilization of Foreign Capital in the Signed Agreements & Contracts**	**24673**	**21138**	**19850**	**17022**	
对外借款	Foreign Loans	117	137	51	104	
外商直接投资	Foreign Direct Investments	24556	21001	19799	16918	22347
对外签订利用外资合同外资金额（亿美元）	**Total Amount of Foreign Capital to Be Utilized in the Signed Agreements & Contracts (USD 100 million)**	**816.10**	**610.58**	**632.01**	**520.09**	
对外借款	Foreign Loans	79.62	58.72	83.85	83.60	
外商直接投资	Foreign Direct Investments	732.77	510.04	521.02	412.23	623.80
外商其他投资	Other Foreign Investments	3.71	41.82	27.14	24.26	87.50
实际利用外资额 （亿美元）	**Total Amount of Foreign Capital Actually Used (USD 100 million)**	**548.04**	**644.08**	**585.57**	**526.59**	**593.56**
对外借款	Foreign Loans	126.69	120.21	110.00	102.12	100.00
外商直接投资	Foreign Direct Investments	417.25	452.57	454.63	403.19	407.15
外商其他投资	Other Foreign Investments	4.10	71.30	20.94	21.28	86.41
外商投资企业基本情况	**Registered Foreign-funded Enterprises**					
年底登记户数 （户）	Number of Registered Enterprises	240447	235681	227807	212436	203208
投资总额 （亿美元）	Total Investment (USD 100 million)	7153.22	7534.70	7742.29	7785.68	8246.75
注册资本 （亿美元）	Registered Capital (USD 100 million)	4414.85	4598.14	4672.87	4635.49	4839.50
＃外方	Capital from Foreign Partners	2897.96	3029.87	3137.12	3166.82	3371.99
对外经济合作 （亿美元）	**Economic Cooperation with Foreign Countries & Territories (USD 100 million)**					
合同金额	Contracted Value	102.73	113.56	117.73	130.02	149.43
＃对外承包工程	Contracted Projects	77.28	85.16	92.43	101.99	117.19
对外劳务合作	Labor Services	25.45	28.40	23.90	26.32	29.91
完成营业额	Value of Business Fulfilled	76.96	83.83	101.34	112.35	113.25
＃对外承包工程	Contracted Projects	58.20	60.36	77.69	85.22	83.79
对外劳务合作	Labor Services	18.76	23.47	22.76	26.23	28.13

17-2 人民币对主要外币年平均汇价(中间价)

Average Exchange Rate of RMB Yuan Against Main Convertible Currencies (Middle Rate)

单位：人民币元 (RMB yuan)

年 份 Year	100美元 100 US Dollars	100日元 100 Japanese Yen	100港元 100 Hong Kong Dollars
1981	170.50	0.7735	30.41
1982	189.25	0.7607	31.15
1983	197.57	0.8318	27.36
1984	232.70	0.9780	29.71
1985	293.66	1.2457	37.57
1986	345.28	2.0694	44.22
1987	372.21	2.5799	47.74
1988	372.21	2.9082	47.70
1989	376.51	2.7360	48.28
1990	478.32	3.3233	61.39
1991	532.33	3.9602	68.45
1992	551.46	4.3608	71.24
1993	576.20	5.2020	74.41
1994	861.87	8.4370	111.53
1995	835.10	8.9225	107.96
1996	831.42	7.6352	107.51
1997	828.98	6.8600	107.09
1998	827.91	6.3488	106.88
1999	827.83	7.2932	106.66
2000	827.84	7.6864	106.18

17-3 进出口贸易总额

Total Value of Imports and Exports

本表1979年以前为外贸业务统计数，1980年以后为海关进出口统计数。
Data before 1979 were obtained from the Ministry of Foreign Trade, and the data since 1980 have been obtained from the customs statistics.

年 份 Year	人民币（亿元） 100 million Yuan				美 元（亿元） USD 100 million			
	进出口总额 Total Imports & Exports	出口总额 Total Exports	进口总额 Total Imports	差 额 Balance	进出口总额 Total Imports & Exports	出口总额 Total Exports	进口总额 Total Imports	差 额 Balance
1952	64.6	27.1	37.5	-10.4	19.4	8.2	11.2	-3.0
1957	104.5	54.5	50.0	4.5	31.0	16.0	15.0	1.0
1962	80.9	47.1	33.8	13.3	26.6	14.9	11.7	3.2
1965	118.4	63.1	55.3	7.8	42.5	22.3	20.2	2.1
1970	112.9	56.8	56.1	0.7	45.9	22.6	23.3	-0.7
1975	290.4	143.0	147.4	-4.4	147.5	72.6	74.9	-2.3
1978	355.0	167.6	187.4	-19.8	206.4	97.5	108.9	-11.4
1979	454.6	211.7	242.9	-31.2	293.3	136.6	156.7	-20.1
1980	570.0	271.2	298.8	-27.6	381.4	181.2	200.2	-19.0
1981	735.3	367.6	367.7	-0.1	440.3	220.1	220.2	-0.1
1982	771.3	413.8	357.5	56.3	416.1	223.2	192.9	30.3
1983	860.1	438.3	421.8	16.5	436.2	222.3	213.9	8.4
1984	1201.0	580.5	620.5	-40.0	535.5	261.4	274.1	-12.7
1985	2066.7	808.9	1257.8	-448.9	696.0	273.5	422.5	-149.0
1986	2580.4	1082.1	1498.3	-416.2	738.5	309.4	429.1	-119.7
1987	3084.2	1470.0	1614.2	-144.2	826.5	394.4	432.1	-37.7
1988	3821.8	1766.7	2055.1	-288.4	1027.9	475.2	552.7	-77.5
1989	4155.9	1956.0	2199.9	-243.9	1116.8	525.4	591.4	-66.0
1990	5560.1	2985.8	2574.3	411.5	1154.4	620.9	533.5	87.4
1991	7225.8	3827.1	3398.7	428.4	1356.3	718.4	637.9	80.5
1992	9119.6	4676.3	4443.3	233.0	1655.3	849.4	805.9	43.5
1993	11271.0	5284.8	5986.2	-701.4	1957.0	917.4	1039.6	-122.2
1994	20381.9	10421.8	9960.1	461.7	2366.2	1210.1	1156.1	54.0
1995	23499.9	12451.8	11048.1	1403.7	2808.6	1487.8	1320.8	167.0
1996	24133.8	12576.4	11557.4	1019.0	2898.8	1510.5	1388.3	122.2
1997	26967.2	15160.7	11806.5	3354.2	3251.6	1827.9	1423.7	404.2
1998	26857.7	15231.6	11626.1	3605.5	3239.5	1837.1	1402.4	434.7
1999	29896.3	16159.8	13736.5	2423.3	3606.3	1949.3	1657.0	292.3
2000	39274.2	20635.2	18639.0	1996.2	4742.9	2492.0	2250.9	241.1

注：进出口差额负数为入超。
a)A negative balance indicates an unfavourable balance of foreign trade.

17-4 海关历年出口商品分类金额

Value of Exports by Category of Commodities (Customs Statistics)

单位：亿美元 (USD 100 million)

年份 Year	总额 Total	初级产品 Primary Goods	食品及主要供食用的活动物 Food and Live Animals Used Chiefly for Food	饮料及烟类 Beverages and Tobacco	非食用原料 Non-Edible Raw Materials	矿物燃料、润滑油及有关原料 Mineral Fuels, Lubricants and Related Materials	动、植物油脂及蜡 Animal and Vegetable Oils, Fats and Wax
1980	181.19	91.14	29.85	0.78	17.11	42.80	0.60
1981	220.07	102.48	29.24	0.60	19.48	52.28	0.88
1982	223.21	100.50	29.08	0.97	16.53	53.14	0.78
1983	222.26	96.20	28.53	1.04	18.92	46.66	1.05
1984	261.39	119.34	32.32	1.10	24.21	60.27	1.44
1985	273.50	138.28	38.03	1.05	26.53	71.32	1.35
1986	309.42	112.72	44.48	1.19	29.08	36.83	1.14
1987	394.37	132.31	47.81	1.75	36.50	45.44	0.81
1988	475.16	144.06	58.90	2.35	42.57	39.50	0.74
1989	525.38	150.78	61.45	3.14	42.12	43.21	0.86
1990	620.91	158.86	66.09	3.42	35.37	52.37	1.61
1991	718.43	161.45	72.26	5.29	34.86	47.54	1.50
1992	849.40	170.04	83.09	7.20	31.43	46.93	1.39
1993	917.44	166.66	83.99	9.01	30.52	41.09	2.05
1994	1210.06	197.08	100.15	10.02	41.27	40.69	4.95
1995	1487.80	214.85	99.54	13.70	43.75	53.32	4.54
1996	1510.48	219.25	102.31	13.42	40.45	59.31	3.76
1997	1827.92	239.53	110.75	10.49	41.95	69.87	6.47
1998	1837.09	204.89	105.13	9.75	35.19	51.75	3.07
1999	1949.31	199.41	104.58	7.71	39.21	46.59	1.32
2000	2492.03	254.60	122.82	7.45	44.62	78.55	1.16

17-4 续表 1 continued

单位：亿美元 (USD 100 million)

年份 Year	工业制成品 Manufactured Goods	化学品及有关产品 Chemicals and Related Products	轻纺产品、橡胶制品矿冶产品及其制品 Light and Textile Industrial Products, Rubber Products, Minerals Metallurgical Products	机械及运输设备 Machinery and Transport Equipment	杂项制品 Miscellaneous Products	未分类的其他商品 Products Not Otherwise Classified
1980	90.05	11.20	39.99	8.43	28.36	2.07
1981	117.59	13.42	47.06	10.87	37.25	8.99
1982	122.71	11.96	43.02	12.63	37.05	18.05
1983	126.06	12.51	43.65	12.21	38.04	19.65
1984	142.05	13.64	50.54	14.93	46.97	15.97
1985	135.22	13.58	44.93	7.72	34.86	34.13
1986	196.70	17.33	58.86	10.94	49.48	60.09
1987	262.06	22.35	85.70	17.41	62.73	73.87
1988	331.10	28.97	104.89	27.69	82.68	86.87
1989	374.60	32.01	108.97	38.74	107.55	87.33
1990	462.05	37.30	125.76	55.88	126.86	116.25
1991	556.98	38.18	144.56	71.49	166.20	136.55
1992	679.36	43.48	161.35	132.19	342.34	
1993	750.78	46.23	163.92	152.82	387.81	
1994	1012.98	62.36	232.18	218.95	499.37	0.12
1995	1272.95	90.94	322.40	314.07	545.48	0.06
1996	1291.23	88.77	284.98	353.12	564.24	0.12
1997	1588.39	102.27	344.32	437.09	704.67	0.04
1998	1632.20	103.21	324.77	502.17	702.00	0.05
1999	1749.90	103.73	332.62	588.36	725.10	0.09
2000	2237.43	120.98	425.46	826.00	862.78	2.21

注：1992年、1993年海关统计改用新商品目录，未分类的其他商品已包含在各大类中，下表同。

a)In 1992 and 1993, a new commodity catalogue has been used in the Customs statistics and the products not otherwise classified in the previous years have been classified and included in different categories of commodities. The same as in the following table.

17-5 海关历年进口商品分类金额

Value of Imports by Category of Commodities (Customs Statistics)

单位：亿美元 (USD 100 million)

年 份 Year	总 额 Total	初级产品 Primary Goods	食品及主要供食用的活动物 Food and Live Animals Chiefly for Food	饮料及烟类 Beverages and Tobacco	非食用原料 Non-edible Raw Materials	矿物燃料、润滑油及有关原料 Mineral Fuels, Lubricants and Related Materials	动、植物油脂及蜡 Animal and Vegetable Oils, Fats and Waxes
1980	200.17	69.59	29.27	0.36	35.54	2.03	2.39
1981	220.15	80.44	36.22	2.13	40.27	0.83	0.99
1982	192.85	76.34	42.01	1.30	30.12	1.83	1.08
1983	213.90	58.08	31.22	0.46	24.59	1.11	0.70
1984	274.10	52.08	23.31	1.16	25.42	1.39	0.80
1985	422.52	52.89	15.53	2.06	32.36	1.72	1.22
1986	429.04	56.49	16.25	1.72	31.43	5.04	2.05
1987	432.16	69.15	24.43	2.63	33.21	5.39	3.49
1988	552.75	100.68	34.76	3.46	50.90	7.87	3.69
1989	591.40	117.54	41.92	2.02	48.35	16.50	8.75
1990	533.45	98.53	33.35	1.57	41.07	12.72	9.82
1991	637.91	108.34	27.99	2.00	50.03	21.13	7.19
1992	805.85	132.55	31.46	2.39	57.75	35.70	5.25
1993	1039.59	142.10	22.06	2.45	54.38	58.19	5.02
1994	1156.14	164.86	31.37	0.68	74.37	40.35	18.09
1995	1320.84	244.17	61.32	3.94	101.59	51.27	26.05
1996	1388.33	254.41	56.72	4.97	106.98	68.77	16.97
1997	1423.70	286.20	43.04	3.20	120.06	103.06	16.84
1998	1402.37	229.49	37.88	1.79	107.15	67.76	14.91
1999	1656.99	268.46	36.19	2.08	127.40	89.12	13.67
2000	2250.94	467.39	47.58	3.64	200.03	206.37	9.77

17-5 续表 1 continued

单位：亿美元 (USD 100 million)

年 份 Year	工业制成品 Manufactured Goods	化学品及有关产品 Chemicals and Related Products	轻纺产品、橡胶制品矿冶产品及其制品 Light and Textile Industrial Products, Rubber Products, Minerals and Metallurgical Products	机械及运输设备 Machinery and Transport Equipment	杂项制品 Miscellaneous Products	未分类的其他商品 Products Not Otherwise Classified
1980	130.58	29.09	41.54	51.19	5.42	3.34
1981	139.71	26.06	40.35	58.66	5.58	9.06
1982	116.51	29.36	39.06	32.04	4.86	11.19
1983	155.82	31.83	62.89	39.88	7.82	13.40
1984	222.02	42.37	73.18	72.45	11.82	22.20
1985	369.63	44.69	118.98	162.39	19.02	24.55
1986	372.55	37.71	111.92	167.81	18.77	36.34
1987	363.01	50.08	97.30	146.07	18.78	50.78
1988	452.07	91.39	104.10	166.97	19.82	69.79
1989	473.86	75.56	123.35	182.07	20.73	72.15
1990	434.92	66.48	89.06	168.45	21.03	89.90
1991	529.57	92.77	104.93	196.01	24.39	111.47
1992	673.30	111.57	192.73	313.12	55.88	
1993	897.49	97.04	285.27	450.23	64.95	
1994	991.28	121.30	280.84	514.67	67.68	6.79
1995	1076.67	172.99	287.72	526.42	82.61	6.93
1996	1133.92	181.06	313.91	547.63	84.86	6.46
1997	1137.50	192.97	322.20	527.74	85.50	9.09
1998	1172.88	201.58	310.75	568.45	84.56	7.54
1999	1388.53	240.30	343.17	694.53	97.01	13.52
2000	1783.55	302.13	418.07	919.31	127.51	16.53

17-6 海关进出口商品分类金额

Value of Imports and Exports by Category of Commodities (Customs Statistics)

单位：亿美元 (USD 100 million)

商品类别	Categories of Commodities	1999		2000	
		出口 Exports	进口 Imports	出口 Exports	进口 Imports
总　额	**Total Value**	**1949.31**	**1656.99**	**2492.02**	**2250.94**
活动物；动物产品	**Live Animals & Animal Products**	**38.14**	**17.29**	**43.55**	**22.79**
活动物	Live Animals	3.85	0.65	3.85	0.52
肉及食用杂碎	Meat and Edible Haslets	6.91	4.99	7.53	6.37
鱼、甲壳动物、软体动物及其他水生无脊椎动物	Fish; Shellfish; Molluscs and Other Aquatic Invertebrates	19.47	8.83	22.70	12.12
乳品；蛋品；天然蜂蜜；其他食用动物产品	Dairy Products; Eggs; Natural Honey; Other Edible Animal Products	1.64	1.64	1.88	2.18
植物产品	**Vegetables; Fruits and Cereals**	**45.70**	**26.68**	**52.02**	**43.21**
食用蔬菜、根及块茎	Edible Vegetables; Roots and Stem Tubers	15.19	0.83	15.44	0.82
食用水果及坚果；甜瓜或柑桔属水果的果皮	Edible Fruits and Nuts; Muskmelon and Orange Peels	4.25	2.58	4.17	3.68
咖啡、茶、马黛茶及调味香料	Coffee; Tea and Spices	4.89	0.19	5.06	0.23
谷物	Cereals	11.35	4.97	16.43	5.74
含油子仁及果实；杂项子仁及果实；工业用或药用植物；稻草、秸秆及饲料	Oil Seeds and Kernels and Oleaginous Fruits; Other Seeds and Kernels and Fruits; Plants for Industrial and Medicinal Use; Straws and Forage	8.05	16.38	8.77	30.72
动植物油脂及分解产品；精制食用油脂；动植物蜡	**Animal and Vegetable Oils; Fats and Wax; Refined Edible Oils and Fats**	**1.41**	**13.59**	**1.29**	**10.23**
食品、饮料、酒及醋；烟草及代用品的制品	**Food; Beverages; Liquor and Vinegar; Tobacco and Tobacco Substitutes**	**43.26**	**12.86**	**51.66**	**18.10**
肉鱼甲壳和软体动物及其他水生无脊椎动物制品	Meat; Fish and Shellfish Products Mollusks and Other Aquatic Products	13.86	0.12	18.83	0.12
糖及糖食	Sugar and Sugar Products	1.40	1.82	1.73	1.77
谷物、粮食粉、淀粉或乳的制品；糕饼点心	Cereals; Grain; Starches or Milk and Pastry Products	2.90	0.48	3.60	0.71
蔬菜水果坚果或植物其他部分的制品	Products of Vegetables; Fruits and Nuts	11.26	0.43	13.15	0.60
饮料、酒及醋	Beverages; Liquor and Vinegar	4.57	1.23	4.93	1.61
烟草、烟草及烟草代用品的制品	Tobacco;Products of Tobacco & Tobacco Substitutes	3.36	0.87	3.02	2.04
矿产品	**Minerals**	**58.54**	**115.78**	**92.01**	**245.22**
盐；硫磺；泥土及石料；石膏料、石灰及水泥	Salt; Sulphur; Clay and Rock; Plaster Stone; Lime and Cement	11.18	4.50	12.66	7.07
矿砂、矿渣及矿灰	Ore; Slag and Mortar	0.77	21.98	0.79	31.34
矿物燃料、矿物油及蒸馏产品；沥青物质；矿物蜡	Mineral Fuels; Lubricants; Asphalt; Mineral Wax	46.59	89.30	78.56	206.81
化学工业及其相关工业的产品	**Chemicals and Related Products**	**100.04**	**140.60**	**116.39**	**181.00**
有机化学品	Organic Chemicals	36.24	55.25	41.70	83.27
药品	Medicinal and Pharmaceutical Products	6.23	6.28	6.70	7.99
肥料	Fertilizers	2.30	22.48	3.24	17.30
鞣料和染料浸膏；鞣酸及衍生物；染颜料及其他着色料；油漆清漆；油灰及类似胶粘剂；墨水、油墨	Tanning and Dyeing Extracts; Tannic Acid; Coloring and Dyeing Materials; Paint and Lacquer; Putty; Ink and Printing Ink	9.63	12.98	11.34	16.55
精油及香膏；芳香料制品及化妆盥洗品	Essential Oils and Perfumed Materials; Cosmetics	2.91	1.28	3.51	1.61
塑料及其制品；橡胶及其制品	**Plastics and Related Products;Rubber and Related Products**	**63.00**	**130.78**	**79.49**	**163.62**
塑料及其制品	Plastics and Related Products	51.23	116.09	63.88	144.56
橡胶及其制品	Rubber and Related Products	11.77	14.69	15.61	19.06
生皮、皮革、毛皮及制品；鞍具挽具；旅行用品、手提包及类似物品；动物肠线(蚕胶丝除外)制品	**Raw Hides; Leather; Furs and Related Products; Saddle; Travel Articles; Handbags and Similar Containers**	**58.83**	**25.13**	**75.05**	**31.85**
生皮(毛皮除外)及皮革	Raw Hides and Leather	3.60	23.28	5.44	29.55
皮革制品；鞍具挽具；旅行用品、手提包及类似容器；动物肠线制品	Leather Products; Saddle; Travel Articles; Handbags and Similar Containers	52.36	0.40	65.71	0.54
毛皮、人造毛皮及其制品	Furs; Artificial Furs and Related Products	2.87	1.45	3.90	1.76
木及木制品；木炭；软木及软木制品；稻草、秸秆、针茅或其他编结材料制品；篮筐及柳条编结品	**Wood and Wooden Products; Charcoal; Cork and Related Products; Straws; Plaited Products; Baskets and Wickerwork**	**21.77**	**29.41**	**26.80**	**37.40**
木浆及其他纤维状纤维素浆；纸及纸板的废碎品；纸、纸板及其制品	**Paper Pulp and Cellulose Pulp; Paper and Waste Paper; Paperboard and Related Products**	**12.92**	**59.30**	**18.52**	**69.62**
木浆及其他纤维状纤维素浆；纸及纸板的废碎品	Paper Pulp and Cellulose Pulp; Paper and Paper Board Waste	0.04	16.60	0.10	26.78
纸及纸板；纸浆、纸或纸板制品	Paper and Paperboad; Articles of Paper Pulp or Paper and Paperboad Products	9.25	39.82	14.06	39.63

17-6 续表 1 continued

单位：亿美元 (USD 100 million)

商品类别	Categories of Commodities	1999 出口 Exports	1999 进口 Imports	2000 出口 Exports	2000 进口 Imports
纺织原料及纺织制品	**Textile Materials and Products**	**412.70**	**139.23**	**493.79**	**165.64**
蚕丝	Natural Silk	7.55	1.24	9.28	1.38
羊毛、动物细毛或粗毛；马毛纱线及其机织物	Wool; Wool Yarn and Woolen Woven Fabrics	9.64	12.62	12.03	18.31
棉花	Cotton	32.91	23.56	37.30	27.89
其他植物纺织纤维；纸纱线及其机织物	Other Textile Fiber; Yarn and Related Woven Fabrics	3.83	1.99	5.21	2.74
化学纤维长丝	Chemical Fiber; Continuous Filament	8.32	31.10	13.26	36.42
化学纤维短纤	Chemical Fiber; Staple Fiber	23.08	25.97	27.24	31.10
絮胎毡呢及无纺织物；特种纱线；线绳索缆及制品	Wadding; Felt and Adhesive-Bond Fabrics; Special Yarn; Thread; Rope; Cable and Related Products	2.58	3.55	3.08	3.93
地毯及纺织材料的其他辅地制品	Carpets and Related Products	4.21	0.23	4.71	0.26
特种机织物；簇绒织物；花边；装饰毯；装饰带；刺绣品	Special Woven Fabrics; Lace; Embroidery	6.11	5.76	7.43	6.70
浸渍、涂布、包覆或层压纺织物；工业用纺织制品	Coated Textiles; Textile Products for Industrial Use	2.62	10.47	3.96	11.83
针织物及钩编织物	Knitwear and Crocheted Fabrics	9.77	11.83	12.88	13.39
针织或钩编织的服装及衣着附件	Knitted or Crocheted Garments & Clothing Accessories	117.54	3.34	134.24	3.83
非针织或钩编织的服装及衣着附件	Garments Not Knitted or Crocheted	155.73	7.24	188.65	7.52
其他纺织制成品；成套物品；旧衣着旧纺织品；碎织物	Other Textile Products; Secondhand Garments	28.81	0.33	34.52	0.34
鞋、帽、伞、杖、鞭及其零件；已加工的羽毛及其制品；人造花；人发制品	**Footwear; Headgear; Umbrellas; Canes; Whips; Processed Feather; Artificial Flowers; Wigs**	**105.63**	**3.80**	**119.58**	**4.09**
鞋靴、护褪和类似品及其零件	Parts of Footwear; Gaiters	86.79	3.06	98.50	3.20
帽类及其零件	Headgear And Accessories	5.02	0.05	6.17	0.07
雨伞阳伞、手杖、鞭子马鞭及其零件	Umbrellas; Canes; Whips and Accessories	5.73	0.24	6.02	0.19
已加工羽毛、羽绒及其制品；人造花；人发制品	Processed Feathers and Related Products; Artificial Flowers; Wigs	8.09	0.45	8.89	0.63
石料石膏水泥石棉云母及类似材料的制品；陶瓷产品；玻璃及其制品	**Gypsum; Cement; Asbestos; Mica; Ceramic Glass**	**34.13**	**13.06**	**40.47**	**17.80**
石料、石膏、水泥、石棉、云母及类似材料制品	Gypsum; Cement; Asbestos; Mica and Related Products	8.24	2.32	9.45	2.45
陶瓷产品	Ceramics	17.23	0.97	19.36	1.26
玻璃及其制品	Glass and Glassware	8.66	9.77	11.66	14.09
天然或养殖珍珠、宝石或半宝石、贵金属、包贵金属及其制品；仿首饰硬币	**Natural or Cultivated Pearls; Precious or Semi-Precious Stones; Jewelery of Precious Metal or Rolled Precious Metal; Artificial Jewelery; Coins**	**25.28**	**20.63**	**25.34**	**24.19**
贱金属及其制品	**Base Metals and Related Products**	**125.78**	**150.93**	**166.09**	**206.11**
钢铁	Iron and Steel	20.44	71.63	35.90	95.69
钢铁制品	Iron and Steel Products	43.52	15.90	54.78	16.90
铜及其制品	Copper and Related Products	6.19	30.86	8.29	46.60
镍及其制品	Nickel and Related Products	0.85	1.13	0.89	2.27
铝及其制品	Aluminium and Related Products	8.29	21.39	10.32	32.13
铅及其制品	Lead and Related Products	2.46	0.12	2.33	0.17
锌及其制品	Zinc and Related Products	5.90	1.85	7.13	2.24
锡及其制品	Tin and Related Products	3.60	0.75	4.71	0.93
机器、机械器具、电气设备及零件；录音机及放声机、电视图象声音的录制和重放设备及零附件	**Machinery; Electric Equipment and Accessories; Recorders; Videorecorder and Accessories**	**520.85**	**630.70**	**728.85**	**851.77**
车辆、航空器、船舶及有关运输设备	**Locomotives; Vehicles; Aircraft; Ship and Related Transportation Equipment**	**65.82**	**60.11**	**93.37**	**63.78**
铁道及电车道机车、车辆及零件；铁道及电车轨道固定装置及零附件；各种机械(电动)；交通信号设备	Rail Locomotives; Tramcars and Accessories; Fixed Track Equipment; Signal Equipment for Transportation	16.09	2.10	25.61	2.58
车辆及其零件、附件；但铁道及电车道车辆除外	Vehicles and Related Parts and Accessories	27.87	23.73	46.06	36.13
航空器、航天器及零件	Aircraft; Spacecraft and Parts Thereof	5.68	31.75	5.36	21.71
船舶及浮动结构体	Ships and Related Products	16.18	2.53	16.34	3.36
光学、照相、电影、计量、检验、医疗或外科用仪器设备、精密仪器及设备；钟表；乐器；及其零附件	**Optical; Photographic; Film; Measuring and Checking and Medical Instruments and Equipment; Precision Instruments and Equipment; Clocks; Musical Instruments; Related Parts and Accessories**	**68.84**	**59.04**	**85.36**	**81.91**
其他	**Others**	**146.67**	**8.07**	**182.39**	**12.61**

17−7 我国同各国(地区)海关进出口总额

China's Foreign Trade with Related Countries and Territories (Customs Statistics)

单位：万美元　　(USD 10 000)

国　别（地区）	Country (Territory)	1999			2000		
		进出口总额 Total	出口总额 Exports	进口总额 Imports	进出口总额 Total	出口总额 Exports	进口总额 Imports
总　计	**Total**	**36062998**	**19493087**	**16569911**	**47429628**	**24920255**	**22509373**
亚洲	**Asia**	**20424334**	**10256255**	**10168079**	**27365011**	**13230823**	**14134188**
#阿富汗	Afghanistan	1958	1668	290	2529	1989	540
巴林	Bahrain	7068	3177	3891	12111	4901	7210
孟加拉国	Bangladesh	71514	70089	1425	91844	89959	1885
文莱	Brunei	810	810		7437	1302	6135
缅甸	Myanmar	50821	40653	10168	62126	49644	12482
柬埔寨	Cambodia	16012	10433	5579	22355	16406	5949
塞浦路斯	Cyprus	10253	10201	52	15243	15186	57
朝鲜	Democratic People's Republic of Korea	37041	32870	4171	48801	45080	3721
中国香港	Hong Kong, China	4375463	3686275	689188	5394730	4451829	942901
印度	India	198773	116196	82577	291421	156073	135348
印度尼西亚	Indonesia	482998	177907	305091	746377	306182	440195
伊朗	Iran	134746	66274	68472	248650	71344	177306
伊拉克	Iraq	26407	14795	11612	97490	32726	64764
以色列	Israel	68183	49058	19125	105419	71884	33535
日本	Japan	6617398	3241060	3376338	8316399	4165431	4150968
约旦	Jordan	18026	14931	3095	25310	20180	5130
科威特	Kuwait	28856	13743	15113	61552	31667	29885
老挝	Laos	3172	2216	956	4084	3442	642
黎巴嫩	Lebanon	15740	15732	8	16935	16894	41
中国澳门	Macao, China	73446	63751	9695	80485	70986	9499
马来西亚	Malaysia	527934	167375	360559	804487	256487	548000
马尔代夫	Maldives	93	85	8	136	134	2
蒙古	Mongolia	26310	6883	19427	32261	11054	21207
尼泊尔	Nepal	21536	20702	834	20421	19707	714
阿曼	Oman	66245	2708	63537	332131	5954	326177
巴基斯坦	Pakistan	97061	58061	39000	116250	67032	49218
菲律宾	the Philippines	228681	137928	90753	314173	146441	167732
卡塔尔	Qatar	9112	2786	6326	47218	3122	44096
沙特阿拉伯	Saudi Arabia	185543	94383	91160	309826	114474	195352
新加坡	Singapore	856333	450223	406110	1082067	576104	505963
韩国	Republic of Korea	2503380	780762	1722618	3449977	1129236	2320741
斯里兰卡	Sri Lanka	26809	25891	918	45830	44545	1285
叙利亚	Syria	20833	20334	499	17407	17398	9
泰国	Thailand	421561	143521	278040	662404	224325	438079
土耳其	Turkey	68391	63659	4732	120464	107789	12675
阿联酋	United Arab Emirates	163323	144377	18946	249450	207843	41607
也门共和国	Arab Republic of Yemen	68360	12673	55687	91182	17631	73551
越南	Viet Nam	121815	86386	35429	246641	153726	92915
中国台湾	Taiwan, China	2347668	394986	1952682	3053256	503900	2549356
非洲	**Africa**	**649013**	**411501**	**237512**	**1059708**	**504201**	**555507**
#阿尔及利亚	Algeria	22215	15996	6219	19886	17292	2594
安哥拉	Angola	37203	1638	35565	187643	3374	184269
贝宁	Benin	16526	16284	242	37154	37041	113
布隆迪	Burundi	146	146		475	363	112
喀麦隆	Cameroon	9646	2015	7631	16066	2263	13803
加那利群岛	Canary Islands	2118	2112	6	2450	2448	2
中非	Central Africa	101	101		64	34	30
塞卜泰	Ceuta	196	196		210	210	
刚果(布)	Congo（B）	7073	1080	5993	34206	1834	32372
吉布提	Djibouti	3834	3834		5413	5411	2
埃及	Egypt	75023	71587	3436	90737	80530	10207
赤道几内亚	Eq.Guinea	16960	250	16710	32303	355	31948
埃塞俄比亚	Ethiopia	5422	5345	77	5857	5570	287

17-7 续表 1 continued

单位：万美元 (USD 10 000)

国　别（地区）	Country (Territory)	1999			2000		
		进出口总额 Total	出口总额 Exports	进口总额 Imports	进出口总额 Total	出口总额 Exports	进口总额 Imports
加蓬	Gabon	28564	652	27912	34170	443	33727
冈比亚	Gambia	5719	5719		6163	6163	
加纳	Ghana	11510	11029	481	12092	10593	1499
几内亚	Guinea	5422	4631	791	3404	3402	2
几内亚(比绍)	Guinea-Bissau	338	318	20	480	462	18
科特迪瓦	Cote d'Ivoir	20609	19816	793	23001	22276	725
肯尼亚	Kenya	10570	10079	491	13693	13308	385
利比里亚	Liberia	1237	1237		16129	12600	3529
利比亚	Libya	8162	6475	1687	7737	5231	2506
马达加斯加	Madagascar	4551	4060	491	7768	7123	645
马里	Mali	1986	1850	136	3525	3484	41
毛里塔尼亚	Mauritania	2264	1779	485	2962	2468	494
毛里求斯	Mauritius	6354	7115	2239	11310	8380	2930
摩洛哥	Morocco	30930	25381	5549	33606	27782	5824
莫桑比克	Mozambique	2224	1894	330	3348	2470	878
尼日尔	Niger	1509	1509		702	702	
尼日利亚	Nigeria	57895	39646	18249	85608	54878	30730
留尼汪	Reunion	553	553		580	579	1
卢旺达	Rwanda	349	175	174	605	342	263
塞内加尔	Senegal	3985	3931	54	5281	5128	153
塞舌尔	Seychelles	201	201		172	157	15
塞拉利昂	Sierra Leone	435	435		867	866	1
索马里	Somalia	55	49	6	106	100	6
南非	South Africa	172197	86080	86117	205094	101365	103729
苏丹	Sudan	28265	22935	5330	89011	15838	73173
坦桑尼亚	Tanzania	6970	6396	574	9053	8576	477
多哥	Togo	7034	7028	6	8043	8037	6
突尼斯	Tunisia	12576	9737	2839	9891	9672	219
乌干达	Uganda	1085	1065	20	1524	1440	84
布基纳法索	Burkina Faso	338	138	200	296	296	
刚果（金）	Congo (J)	2006	1874	132	1941	1843	98
赞比亚	Zambia	2602	840	1762	10225	3286	6939
津巴布韦	Zimbabwe	7160	2726	4434	13465	3191	10274
欧洲	**Europe**	**6812664**	**3548172**	**3264492**	**8626564**	**4548156**	**4078408**
#比利时	Belgium	279293	182248	97045	368688	230074	138614
丹麦	Denmark	101534	61513	40021	133419	78202	55217
英国	United Kingdom	787487	488004	299483	990257	631010	359247
德国	Federal Republic of Germany	1611505	777964	833541	1968650	927779	1040871
法国	France	670593	292111	378482	765494	370516	394978
爱尔兰	Ireland	41967	21249	20718	71358	33628	37730
意大利	Italy	560942	292949	267993	688045	380202	307843
卢森堡	Luxembourg	8655	3814	4841	9927	5360	4567
荷兰	Netherlands	642354	541295	101059	792345	668722	123623
希腊	Greece	39109	36787	2322	62677	57870	4807
葡萄牙	Portugal	25827	21996	3831	30777	26082	4695
西班牙	Spain	233740	179593	54147	274718	212421	62297
奥地利	Austria	68537	24718	43819	78118	30883	47235
保加利亚	Bulgaria	6266	5344	922	9430	8083	1347
捷克	Czecho	35676	28462	7214	43702	35407	8295
斯洛伐克	Slovakia	2907	2710	197	6992	5562	1430
芬兰	Finland	219642	36448	183194	318984	83679	235305
直布罗陀	Gibraltar	49	49		1448	1448	
匈牙利	Hungary	62208	55063	7145	99666	89711	9955
冰岛	Iceland	1459	669	790	3175	1761	1414
马耳他	Malta	6069	5074	995	9467	7617	1850
挪威	Norway	82706	34282	48424	109728	48661	61067
波兰	Poland	86023	70244	15779	96002	86041	9961
罗马尼亚	Romania	19127	14564	4563	29783	19239	10544
瑞典	Sweden	276186	61004	215182	350276	82808	267468
瑞士	Switzerland	168599	67478	101121	220915	74778	146137

17-7 续表 2 continued

单位：万美元 (USD 10 000)

国　别（地区）	Country (Territory)	1999			2000		
		进出口总额 Total	出口总额 Exports	进口总额 Imports	进出口总额 Total	出口总额 Exports	进口总额 Imports
南斯拉夫	Yugoslavia	3733	3055	678	6850	6096	754
斯洛文尼亚	Slovenia	5805	4791	1014	6992	5562	1430
克罗地亚	Croatia	5284	4754	530	8503	7996	507
马其顿	Macedonia	440	394	46	710	626	84
波黑共和国	Bosnia and Herzegovina	87	56	31	406	157	249
爱沙尼亚	Estonia	1039	723	316	6689	6179	510
拉脱维亚	Latvia	2111	1436	675	2908	2630	278
立陶宛	Lithuania	2713	2653	60	3870	2901	969
格鲁吉亚	Georgia	373	223	150	389	154	235
亚美尼亚	Armenia	1159	1158	1	524	114	410
阿塞拜疆	Azerbajan	114	99	15	617	219	398
白俄罗斯	Belorussia	2602	533	2069	11362	4111	7251
哈萨克	Kazakhstan	113878	49438	64440	155696	59875	95821
吉尔吉斯	Kirghizia	13487	10290	3197	17761	11017	6744
摩尔多瓦	Moldavia	38	38		812	20	792
俄罗斯	Russia	571993	149729	422264	800324	223335	576989
塔吉克	Tadzhikistan	804	230	574	1717	679	1038
土库曼	Turkmenistan	949	747	202	1616	1210	406
乌克兰	Ukraine	42133	8100	34033	59102	13643	45459
乌兹别克	Uzbekstan	4034	2739	1295	5146	3943	1203
拉丁美洲	**Latin America**	**826186**	**526952**	**299234**	**1259549**	**718521**	**541028**
#阿根廷	Argentina	108691	49612	59079	154029	61030	92999
巴巴多斯	Barbados	203	202	1	305	304	1
玻利维亚	Bolivia	753	506	247	1684	468	1216
巴西	Brazil	184456	87601	96855	284499	122355	162144
智利	Chile	126877	60519	66358	212203	78352	133851
哥伦比亚	Colombia	12501	10433	2068	18813	15597	3216
多米尼加联邦	Commonwealth of Dominica	4077	3937	140	6016	5770	246
古巴	Cuba	28877	23212	5665	31394	23280	8114
库腊索岛	Curacao	1480	1480		3328	3328	
多米尼加共和国	Dominican Republic	5746	5694	52	7630	7541	89
厄瓜多尔	Ecuador	11851	3989	7862	15500	7487	8013
危地马拉	Guatemala	10363	10333	30	14322	13862	460
洪都拉斯	Honduras	6115	6115		6228	6217	11
牙买加	Jamaica	5837	5000	837	7901	4945	2956
墨西哥	Mexico	95094	79169	15925	182353	133525	48828
尼加拉瓜	Nicaragua	1659	1659		4344	4309	35
巴拿马	Panama	103856	103749	107	129118	129016	102
巴拉圭	Paraguay	5881	5698	183	8918	8596	322
秘鲁	Peru	44075	13079	30996	70459	14433	56026
波多黎各	Puerto Rico	6602	5732	870	6863	5721	1142
萨尔瓦多	El Salvador	5171	5170	1	6313	6264	49
苏里南	Surinam	692	690	2	1145	1064	81
特立尼达和多巴哥	Trinidad and Tobago	2842	1747	1095	2718	2674	44
乌拉圭	Uruguay	21282	14236	7046	34436	24302	10134
委内瑞拉	Venezuela	18836	16070	2766	35128	25650	9478
北美洲	**North America**	**6620376**	**4438907**	**2181469**	**8139310**	**5527351**	**2611959**
#加拿大	Canada	476699	243296	233403	690892	315784	375108
美国	United States	6142519	4194691	1947828	7446237	5209922	2236315
大洋洲及太平洋岛屿	**Oceanic and Pacific Islands**	**730387**	**311300**	**419087**	**978757**	**391022**	**587735**
#澳大利亚	Australia	631161	270441	360720	845288	342888	502400
库克群岛	Cook Islands	22	22		25	25	
斐济	Fiji	2099	2009	90	1543	1514	29
新西兰	New Zealand	82419	34285	48134	105430	41603	63827
诺福克岛	Norfolk Islands	5	5		34	34	
巴布亚新几内亚	Papua New Guinea	11474	2923	8551	22559	2486	20073
其　他	**Others**	**38**		**38**	**729**	**181**	**548**

17-8 海关出口主要商品数量和金额

Main Export Commodities in Volume and Value (Customs Statistics)

金额单位：万美元 (USD 10 000)

品名	Item	1999 数量 Volume	1999 金额 Value	2000 数量 Volume	2000 金额 Value
活猪 (万头)	Live Hogs (10 000 heads)	196	23597	203	23045
活家禽 (万只)	Live Poultry (10 000 heads)	4500	9850	4890	10411
鲜冻牛肉 (万吨)	Beef (10 000 tons)	2	2572	2	2354
鲜冻猪肉 (万吨)	Pork (10 000 tons)	5	6738	5	6862
冻鸡 (万吨)	Frozen Chicken (10 000 tons)	30	47375	36	51302
冻家兔肉 (吨)	Rabbit Meat Frozen (ton)	16583	3271	22563	4581
鲜蛋 (百万个)	Fresh Eggs (million units)	466	1228	757	1712
水产品 (万吨)	Aquatic Products (10 000 tons)	109	194464	120	226737
谷物及谷物粉 (万吨)	Cereals and Cereals Flour (10 000 tons)	738	118651	1378	169417
#大米 (万吨)	Rice (10 000 tons)	271	65189	295	56105
玉米 (万吨)	Maize (10 000 tons)	431	45002	1047	105170
大豆 (万吨)	Soybean (10 000 tons)	20	6169	21	6414
花生及花生仁 (万吨)	Peanuts (10 000 tons)	34	19399	40	23175
干豆 (万吨)	Dried Plusles (10 000 tons)	81	27805	57	23112
蔬菜 (万吨)	Vegetables (10 000 tons)	217	142688	245	157688
#鲜蔬菜 (万吨)	Fresh Vegetables (10 000 tons)	130	46118	139	49161
桔、柑、橙 (吨)	Mandarins and Oranges (ton)	166448	3957	191353	4537
苹果 (吨)	Apples (ton)	219196	7594	297651	9656
核桃仁 (吨)	Walnut Meat (ton)	8282	2087	7810	2110
栗子 (吨)	Chestnut (ton)	33729	6426	35414	6779
白果 (吨)	Gingko Nuts (ton)	3327	1042	3809	693
松子仁 (吨)	Pinenut Kernels (ton)	4877	3142	3528	1866
食糖 (万吨)	Sugar (10 000 tons)	37	7819	41	8359
天然蜂蜜 (吨)	Natural Honey (ton)	87188	7476	102888	8412
茶叶 (吨)	Tea (ton)	199608	33834	227662	34714
辣椒干 (吨)	Dried Chillies (ton)	43447	3482	54075	3446
猪肉罐头 (吨)	Canned Pork (ton)	38338	6238	38175	5845
蘑菇罐头 (吨)	Canned Mushroom (ton)	142981	13278	204334	16913
啤酒 (吨)	Beer (ton)	6035	3030	8442	3960
烤烟 (吨)	Flue-cured Tobacco (ton)	109585	19136	93821	13206
猪鬃 (吨)	Bristle (ton)	10103	6771	12398	8396
肠衣 (吨)	Casings (ton)	51356	32988	52316	31512
填充用羽毛及绒 (吨)	Feathers and Dawn for Stuffing (ton)	32066	17538	36882	30710
药材 (吨)	Medical Materials (ton)	150997	20710	175661	21047
未硝毛皮 (吨)	Raw Fur Skins (ton)	97	299	105	506
#水貂皮 (吨)	Raw Mink Skins (ton)		6		
锯材 (立方米)	Wood Sawn (cu.m)	310188	13751	422507	17800
棉花 (吨)	Cotton (ton)	236322	28348	292475	30579
生丝 (吨)	Raw Silk (ton)	12089	23938	12532	27159
山羊绒 (吨)	Cashmere (ton)	5074	23996	3123	25227
兔毛 (吨)	Rabbit Hair (ton)	5185	5489	4990	6177
苎麻 (吨)	Ramie (ton)	1493	580	1288	490
天然石墨 (吨)	Natural Graphite (ton)	205891	3676	333460	5097
镁矿物 (万吨)	Magnesian Ores (10 000 tons)	210	23249	204	26638
氟石 (万吨)	Fluorite (10 000 tons)	122	11542	120	11791
重晶石 (万吨)	Barite (10 000 tons)	129	4707	252	7939
滑石 (万吨)	Talcum (10 000 tons)	71	5848	75	6350

17-8 续表 1 continued

金额单位：万美元 (USD 10 000)

品 名	Item	1999 数量 Volume	1999 金额 Value	2000 数量 Volume	2000 金额 Value
铝矿砂 (万吨)	Aluminum Ores (10 000 tons)		7		
钨矿砂 (吨)	Tungsten Ores (ton)	80	15		
煤 (万吨)	Coal (10 000 tons)	3741	108375	5505	145945
焦炭、半焦炭 (万吨)	Coke and Semi-coke (10 000 tons)	997	55122	1520	91581
原油 (万吨)	Crude Oil (10 000 tons)	717	76528	1031	212801
成品油 (万吨)	Petroleum Products Refined (10 000 tons)	645	109541	827	212808
石蜡 (万吨)	Paraffin Wax (10 000 tons)	45	18757	52	22831
仲钨酸铵 (吨)	Tungstates (ton)	10507	4418	9276	4377
氧化锌 (吨)	Zinc Oxide and Zinc Peroxide (ton)	68540	5114	135022	10116
食用植物油(含棕榈油) (吨)	Edible Vegetable Oil (ton)	96615	7577	111505	6702
糠醛 (吨)	Furfural (ton)	35569	2119	49199	2521
合成有机染料 (吨)	Synthetic Organic Dyestuffs (ton)	155734	46687	179632	54650
医药品 (吨)	Medical and Pharmaceutical Products (ton)	198063	167872	193758	178837
#中式成药 (吨)	Medicaments of Chinese Type (ton)	11034	7386	12322	8468
医用敷料 (吨)	Pharmaceutical Goods (ton)	50342	24001	57092	26147
洗衣粉 (吨)	Detergent (ton)	37628	1656	41675	2347
鞭炮烟花 (吨)	Fireworks and Firecrackers (ton)	210908	31272	201984	25035
松香 (吨)	Resin and Resin Acids (ton)	261060	14168	281420	13877
轮胎 (万条)	Rubber Tyres (10 000 units)	8647	72199	10906	100289
纸及纸板(未切成形) (万吨)	Paper and Paperboard in Rolls (10 000 tons)	21	17990	65	51189
棉纱 (吨)	Cotton Yarn (ton)	173987	52802	210602	63083
麻纱 (吨)	Flax or Ramie Yarn (ton)	20277	8008	28553	11178
棉布 (万米)	Cotton Cloth (10 000 m)	299625	271156	321248	308540
麻布 (万米)	Flax or Ramie Cloth (10 000 m)	18951	27418	24186	37786
涤棉布 (万米)	Polyester Cotton Cloth (10 000 m)	201377	95376	218571	116110
人棉布 (万米)	Rayon Cloth (10 000 m)	57437	22586	52177	24232
真丝绸缎 (万米)	Silk and Satins (10 000 m)	11438	31552	13425	37512
塑料编织袋 (万条)	Bags of PP or PE Strip (10 000 units)	108197	13803	127727	15760
地毯 (万平方米)	Carpets (10 000 sq.m)	2701	42129	3807	47091
棉浴巾 (万条)	Cotton Bath Towels (10 000 units)	13913	18799	18165	23310
水泥 (万吨)	Cement (10 000 tons)	636	20092	606	18996
平板玻璃 (万平方米)	Plate Glass (10 000 sq.m)	4418	10970	5593	14901
玻璃制品	Glass Products		41037		49762
家用陶瓷器 (吨)	Porcelain and Pottery Ware for Household Use (ton)	897863	81569	109669	91121
生、镜铁 (万吨)	Pig Iron and Spiegeleise (10 000 tons)	162	18551	333	39631
硅铁 (万吨)	Ferro-silicon (10 000 tons)	35	17189	49	22910
钢坯及粗锻件 (万吨)	Billet and Crude Fougings (10 000 tons)	173	31721	434	81778
钢材 (万吨)	Rolled Steel (10 000 tons)	370	141640	621	222933
未锻造铜及合金 (吨)	Unwrought Copper and its Alloys (ton)	103058	16469	118739	21564
铜材 (吨)	Rolled Copper (ton)	101974	34362	144484	50797
未锻造铝及合金 (吨)	Unwrought Aluminum and its Alloys (ton)	206601	27319	209111	30386
铝材 (吨)	Rolled Aluminum (ton)	94787	21783	130052	31989
锌及锌合金 (吨)	Zinc and Zinc Alloys (ton)	527142	53905	593336	65027
锡及锡合金 (吨)	Tin and Tin Alloys (ton)	64584	31448	77733	38778
锑 (吨)	Antimony (ton)	44359	4724	44979	4837
锰 (吨)	Manganese (ton)	73633	7025	92971	8524
标准紧固件 (万吨)	Nails, Bolts, etc. (10 000 tons)	38	36470	51	48627
手用或机用工具 (吨)	Hand Tools and Tools for Machines (ton)	417687	91125	511285	110958
搪瓷器 (吨)	Enamelware (ton)	63602	8644	88381	11633

17-8 续表 2 continued

金额单位：万美元 (USD 10 000)

品　名	Item	1999 数量 Volume	1999 金额 Value	2000 数量 Volume	2000 金额 Value
锁 (吨)	Locks (ton)	131310	31387	153670	37021
缝纫机(包括工业用)(万架)	Sewing Machines (Including Industrial Use) (10 000 sets)	442	23706	600	34619
纺织机械	Textile Machinery		17983		29006
电动机及发电机 (万台)	Electric Motors and Generators (10 000 sets)	218987	149183	275442	193092
金属加工机床 (万台)	Machine Tools (10 000 sets)	339	22743	438	29895
轴承 (万套)	Bearings (10 000 units)	108645	43648	146224	54349
静止式变流器 (万个)	Static Converters (10 000 units)	50587	122902	75247	152926
电容器 (吨)	Electrical Capacitors (ton)	23170	56888	32734	77529
半导体器件 (万个)	Semi Conductors (10 000 units)	4982664	85518	6841553	108361
电线电缆 (吨)	Insulated Wire or Cable (ton)	438150	125845	534069	161593
电子计算器 (万台)	Electric Calculator (10 000 sets)	44205	49092	41170	57255
通断保护电路装置	Electrical Apparatus for Switching or Protecting Electrical Circuits		141337		173903
电风扇 (万只)	Fans (10 000 sets)	14010	65085	11245	70368
原电池 (万个)	Primary Cells and Batteries (10 000 units)	1111120	49743	1327192	56649
蓄电池 (万个)	Electric Accumulators (10 000 units)	55240	63410	77997	93153
有线电话机 (万台)	Line Telephone Sets (10 000 sets)	13422	152202	16030	169283
扬声器 (万个)	Loudspeakers (10 000 units)	121571	90123	146375	96533
收录机及组合音响 (万台)	Sound Recording Apparatus (10 000 sets)	16152	233702	20106	281012
收音机 (万台)	Radio (10 000 sets)	12778	29919	16409	30693
电视机 (万台)	TV Sets (10 000 sets)	1298	80309	1944	129735
集装箱 (个)	Containers (unit)	639776	147812	1107032	237664
船舶 (艘)	Ships (unit)	34968	160621	43032	149665
汽车和汽车底盘 (辆)	Motor Vehicles and Chassis (unit)	8060	10244	22779	19374
汽车的零件	Parts of Motor Vehicles		78009		112346
自行车 (万辆)	Bicycles (10 000 units)	2270	77561	3286	102148
手电筒 (万个)	Flashlights (10 000 units)	48229	17048	58064	19061
医疗仪器及器械	Medical Instruments and Appliances		36184		51524
照相机 (万只)	Cameras (10 000 sets)	5951	99031	9073	123708
手表 (万只)	Wrist Watches (10 000 units)	83004	90813	89440	91980
日用钟 (万只)	Clocks (10 000 sets)	47798	40230	46562	38878
家俱	Furniture		270781		356515
服装(针织、钩织的除外)	Garments (Excluding Knitwear and Crochet)		1441579		1747826
针织钩织服装	Garments, Knitted or Crocheted		1101543		1245433
皮鞋 (万双)	Leather Shoes (10 000 pairs)	71967	395762	82896	436895
橡胶或塑料底布鞋 (包括球鞋) (万双)	Cloth Shoes With Outer of Rubber or Artificial Plastic Materials (including Gym Shoes) (10 000 pairs)	63732	100485	73484	117509
塑料制品 (万吨)	Plastic Articles (10 000 tons)	287	391806	347	489432
玩具	Toys		511216		557566
足球、篮球、排球 (万个)	Footballs, Basketballs and Volleyballs (10 000 units)	4749	7315	4605	6964
铅笔	Pencils		7213		8486
伞 (万把)	Umbrellas (10 000 units)	48005	54261	55879	57547
竹编结品 (吨)	Bamboo Products (ton)	57340	8843	70901	11729
藤编结品 (吨)	Rattan Products (ton)	24747	5268	25090	5357
草席及草编结品 (吨)	Straw Mats and Straw Products (ton)	17563	3758	20533	4698
柳编结品 (吨)	Wickerwork (ton)	54607	8526	64861	11138
鬃刷 (万打)	Bristle Brushes (10 000 doz.)	2825	4899	3067	5321
热水瓶 (万个)	Vacuum Flasks (10 000 units)	7947	14049	8124	14934
人造花 (吨)	Artificial Flowers (ton)	152570	50316	165733	51579
机电产品	Mechanical and Electrical Products		7695238		10531284

17-9 海关进口主要商品数量和金额

Main Import Commodities in Volume and Value (Customs Statistics)

金额单位：万美元 (USD 10 000)

品名	Item	1999 数量 Volume	1999 金额 Value	2000 数量 Volume	2000 金额 Value
谷物及谷物粉 (万吨)	Cereals and Cereals Flour (10 000 tons)	339	52414	315	59375
#小麦 (万吨)	Wheat (10 000 tons)	45	8565	88	14737
大米 (万吨)	Rice (10 000 tons)	17	7815	24	11271
玉米 (万吨)	Maize (10 000 tons)	7	825		
食用植物油(含棕榈油) (万吨)	Edible Vegetable Oil (10 000 tons)	208	107434	179	62714
其他植物油 (万吨)	Other Vegetable Oils (10 000 tons)	15	10705	23	12773
食糖 (万吨)	Sugar (10 000 tons)	42	8518	64	11533
动物饲料 (吨)	Prepared Feeding Stuff (ton)	65368	9220	101967	14993
天然橡胶 (万吨)	Natural Rubber (10 000 tons)	43	28188	85	58374
合成橡胶 (万吨)	Synthetic Rubber (10 000 tons)	65	60200	71	72184
原木 (万立方米)	Logs (10 000 cu.m)	1014	124863	1361	165564
纸浆 (万吨)	Paper Pulp (10 000 tons)	310	141457	335	212097
锯材 (立方米)	Wood Sawn (cu.m)	2720149	65866	3575208	97852
棉花(原棉) (万吨)	Cotton, not Carded or Combed (10 000 tons)	5	6692	5	7411
羊毛及条 (吨)	Wool and Wool Tops (ton)	198624	63772	300687	103731
纺织用合成纤维 (万吨)	Synthetic Fibers Suitable for Spinning (10 000 tons)	83	77093	100	109735
#涤纶纤维 (吨)	Polyester Fibers (ton)	530988	40699	622436	54435
腈纶纤维 (吨)	Polyacryolnitr Fibers (ton)	257565	32202	353906	51503
合成纤维纱线 (吨)	Synthetic Fibers, Continuous Filament and Yarn (ton)	600899	103000	747351	135107
#锦纶长丝 (吨)	Polyamide Fiber Yarn (ton)	112467	21503	141567	27035
涤纶长丝 (吨)	Polyester Fiber Yarn (ton)	317330	37702	413629	51627
铁矿砂 (万吨)	Iron Ore (10 000 tons)	5527	137899	6997	185770
锰矿砂 (万吨)	Manganese Ores (10 000 tons)	107	8796	120	9540
铜矿砂 (万吨)	Copper Ores (10 000 tons)	125	47436	181	80578
铬矿砂 (万吨)	Chromium Ores (10 000 tons)	82	7431	111	9683
氧化铝 (万吨)	Aluminum Oxide (10 000 tons)	162	33791	188	63846
煤 (万吨)	Coal (10 000 tons)	167	6086	212	6860
原油 (万吨)	Crude Oil (10 000 tons)	3661	464124	7027	1486066
成品油 (万吨)	Petroleum Products Refined (10 000 tons)	2082	269775	1805	365706
乙二醇 (万吨)	Ethylene Glycol (10 000 tons)	57	24047	105	58270
对苯二甲酸 (吨)	Telephthalic Acid (ton)	1542330	62581	2505390	122517
己内酰胺 (吨)	Carprolactam (ton)	220817	22713	244873	33840
纯碱 (吨)	Soda Ash (ton)	35705	490	134953	1460
合成有机染料 (吨)	Synthetic Organic Dyestuffs (ton)	37659	16451	45273	19772
医药品 (吨)	Pharmaceutical Products (ton)	23618	82076	29720	95253
化学肥料(自然吨) (万吨)	Chemical Fertilizers, Manufactured (Actual Weight) (10 000 tons)	1335	224819	1189	173006

17-9 续表 1 continued

金额单位：万美元 (USD 10 000)

品 名		Item	1999 数量 Volume	1999 金额 Value	2000 数量 Volume	2000 金额 Value
#氯化钾	(万吨)	Potassium Chloride (10 000 tons)	520	60841	599	71572
尿素	(万吨)	Urea (10 000 tons)	7	9364		
复合肥	(万吨)	Compound Fertilizers (10 000 tons)	786	158379	568	97601
原形聚乙烯	(万吨)	Polyethylene in primary Forms (10 000 tons)	260	163155	297	213365
原形聚丙烯	(万吨)	Polypropylene in Primary Forms (10 000 tons)	147	92913	164	114416
ABS树脂	(万吨)	ABS Copolymers (10 000 tons)	133	125420	147	152750
原形聚苯乙烯	(万吨)	Polystyrene in Primary Forms (10 000 tons)	173	128883	175	144253
原形聚氯乙烯	(万吨)	Polyvinyl Chioride in Primary Forms (10 000 tons)	180	107696	192	135280
聚酯切片	(万吨)	Slices or Chips of Polyethylene Terephthalate (10 000 tons)	34	19466	34	24610
农药	(吨)	Pesticides (ton)	47714	24258	41138	19223
纸及纸板	(万吨)	Paper and Paperboard (10 000 tons)	650	336836	595	329553
钢材	(万吨)	Rolled Steel (10 000 tons)	1486	700686	1596	853589
铜及铜合金	(吨)	Copper and Copper Alloys (ton)	547736	88420	812126	150137
铜材	(吨)	Rolled Copper (ton)	631920	159468	740989	199689
铝及铝合金	(吨)	Aluminum and Aluminum Alloys (ton)	534004	67575	914099	132544
铝材	(吨)	Rolled Aluminum (ton)	426945	106189	457032	121933
金属加工机床	(台)	Machine Tools (set)	89384	150631	104794	189027
锅炉	(台)	Boilers (set)	6158	6458	1625	6353
电视机	(万台)	TV Sets (10 000 sets)	26	14378	10	6054
显像管	(万只)	Cathode-ray TV Picture Tube (10 000 sets)	949	89183	954	84712
制冷压缩机	(万台)	Compressors for Refrigerating Equipment (10 000 sets)	737	46316	750	45558
阀门	(万套)	Valves (10 000 sets)	3843	40939	8260	45072
自动数据处理设备	(万台)	Automatic Data Processing Machines (10 000 sets)	4799	325333	7472	451645
电话电报交换机	(台)	Line Telephonic or Telegraphic Switching Apparatus (set)	22020	53526	23712	13864
收录机及组合音响	(万台)	Sound Recording Apparatus (10 000 sets)	122	4217	102	3887
汽车和汽车底盘	(辆)	Motor Vehicles and Chassis (unit)	34906	81096	42371	119311
#小轿车	(辆)	Cars (unit)	19952	32428	21614	48310
卡车	(辆)	Trucks (unit)	2682	7140	3085	9746
自卸车	(辆)	Dump Trucks (unit)	70	1553	130	1373
装有引擎的底盘	(台)	Chassis with Engines (unit)	531	2043	353	1500
汽车的零件		Parts of Motor Vehicles		125253		211281
飞机	(架)	Aircraft (unit)	63	231618	85	162953
船舶	(艘)	Ships (unit)	1409	12809	908	12831
复印机	(台)	Photo or Thermos Copying Apparatus (sets)	72837	6678	75427	5958
医疗仪器及器械		Medical Instruments and Appliances		67855		92171
机电产品		Mechanical and Electrical Products		7758461		10287150

17-10 各地区进出口商品总值(按经营单位所在地分)

Total Value of Import and Export by Location of China's Foreign Trade Managing Units by Region

单位:万美元

(USD 10 000)

地区	Region	1998			1999			2000		
		进出口 Total	出口 Exports	进口 Imports	进出口 Total	出口 Exports	进口 Imports	进出口 Total	出口 Exports	进口 Imports
全国	**National Total**	**32404588**	**18380907**	**14023681**	**36062998**	**19493087**	**16569911**	**47429628**	**24920255**	**22509373**
北京	Beijing	3050608	1051293	1999315	3435951	990352	2445599	4962189	1196813	3765376
天津	Tianjin	1061384	549874	511510	1260094	633134	626960	1715400	862578	852822
河北	Hebei	422732	311617	111115	457995	311914	146081	523862	371000	152862
山西	Shanxi	111113	89321	21792	128750	83951	44799	176438	123687	52751
内蒙古	Inner Mongolia	96294	52579	43715	129415	53460	75955	262205	97017	165188
辽宁	Liaoning	1274402	805499	468903	1371832	819988	551844	1903148	1085632	817516
吉林	Jilin	165191	74809	90382	221234	101877	119357	257042	125683	131359
黑龙江	Heilongjiang	201955	90863	111092	219830	95714	124116	298637	145118	153519
上海	Shanghai	3137623	1594674	1542949	3861812	1879958	1981854	5470802	2535233	2935569
江苏	Jiangsu	2634158	1561997	1072161	3125741	1830582	1295159	4563636	2576683	1986953
浙江	Zhejiang	1485100	1086335	398765	1830561	1287144	543417	2783262	1944275	838987
安徽	Anhui	233149	151214	81935	264844	167607	97237	334684	217198	117486
福建	Fujian	1715296	995794	719502	1761919	1035166	726753	2122046	1290607	831439
江西	Jiangxi	124628	101732	22896	131382	90606	40776	162405	119741	42664
山东	Shandong	1671389	1044385	627004	1826698	1157645	669053	2498976	1552884	946092
河南	Henan	173372	118698	54674	174885	112730	62155	228290	149578	78712
湖北	Hubei	283213	170757	112456	267762	151229	116533	322286	193555	128731
湖南	Hunan	178172	128261	49911	195546	128187	67359	251222	165271	85951
广东	Guangdong	12979804	7561766	5418038	14034241	7768679	6265562	17009888	9191770	7818118
广西	Guangxi	240910	180415	60495	175340	124721	50619	203379	148891	54488
海南	Hainan	174323	76492	97831	121704	74725	46979	128786	80289	48497
重庆	Chongqing	103396	51411	51985	120879	49038	71841	178590	99566	79024
四川	Sichuan	209274	117112	92162	246847	113851	132996	254520	139437	115083
贵州	Guizhou	62761	38787	23974	54758	35775	18983	65998	42056	23942
云南	Yunnan	164380	112214	52166	166011	103455	62556	181276	117509	63767
西藏	Tibet	11959	4758	7201	16645	8627	8018	13031	11334	1697
陕西	Shaanxi	205062	117582	87480	200576	115084	85492	214008	131005	83003
甘肃	Gansu	44788	34475	10313	40627	31703	8924	56953	41495	15458
青海	Qinghai	11774	10405	1369	10785	8686	2099	15973	11200	4773
宁夏	Ningxia	23895	21037	2858	31799	24765	7034	44292	32737	11555
新疆	Xinjiang	152483	74751	77732	176535	102734	73801	226404	120413	105991

17-11 各地区进出口商品总值(按境内目的地、货源地分)

Import and Export Value of Commodities by Places of Destination or Origin in China by Region

单位:万美元 (USD 10 000)

地区	Region	1998			1999			2000		
		进出口 Total	出口 Exports	进口 Imports	进出口 Total	出口 Exports	进口 Imports	进出口 Total	出口 Exports	进口 Imports
全国	**National Total**	**32404588**	**18380907**	**14023681**	**36062998**	**19493087**	**16569911**	**47429628**	**24920255**	**22509373**
北京	Beijing	1577668	649107	928561	1837190	628539	1208651	2424378	766723	1657655
天津	Tianjin	1107729	546525	561204	1341315	637682	703633	1715625	767427	948198
河北	Hebei	424137	261247	162890	452850	266003	186847	548711	327814	220897
山西	Shanxi	211768	171248	40520	230211	150053	80158	279154	209094	70060
内蒙古	Inner Mongolia	92970	52174	40796	126539	68409	58130	238627	111400	127227
辽宁	Liaoning	1376320	762505	613815	1463378	812791	650587	2006747	1058947	947800
吉林	Jilin	220598	110715	109883	255331	121712	133619	298532	148693	149839
黑龙江	Heilongjiang	319045	199316	119729	302483	153962	148521	399259	242393	156866
上海	Shanghai	3120202	1563175	1557027	3805279	1829087	1976192	5470336	2463961	3006375
江苏	Jiangsu	2806925	1592340	1214585	3285953	1857982	1427971	4919437	2637694	2281743
浙江	Zhejiang	1674639	1160203	514436	2026235	1365375	660860	3152170	2048214	1103956
安徽	Anhui	253987	153627	100360	281496	163914	117582	368983	211942	157041
福建	Fujian	1811229	1071698	739531	1839988	1061958	778030	2295726	1362282	933444
江西	Jiangxi	147965	113057	34908	150792	92516	58276	205206	118837	86369
山东	Shandong	1919797	1129409	790388	2079788	1221885	857903	2824997	1609267	1215730
河南	Henan	210749	133762	76987	240420	124035	116385	312389	158683	153706
湖北	Hubei	319339	160442	158897	307495	153555	153940	389264	189977	199287
湖南	Hunan	202637	133188	69449	223371	139814	83557	299226	163190	136036
广东	Guangdong	13144636	7628026	5516610	14339105	7875985	6463120	17548753	9342792	8205961
广西	Guangxi	238801	160389	78412	186875	122023	64852	228496	164048	64448
海南	Hainan	157201	64226	92975	103992	55118	48874	109420	60853	48567
重庆	Chongqing	108628	48418	60210	132406	53429	78977	185107	106048	79059
四川	Sichuan	239150	121424	117726	273238	116479	156759	277752	143360	134392
贵州	Guizhou	66381	42507	23874	66042	39944	26098	85646	48166	37480
云南	Yunnan	158730	100671	58059	172240	92205	80035	188420	109271	79149
西藏	Tibet	9031	2929	6102	16523	8255	8268	14892	10902	3990
陕西	Shaanxi	211621	109372	102249	207679	101853	105826	238754	132693	106061
甘肃	Gansu	55624	38483	17141	56293	37716	18577	69155	42079	27076
青海	Qinghai	17817	11729	6088	18886	12020	6866	22645	13355	9290
宁夏	Ningxia	30195	23529	6666	40290	28488	11802	53211	35426	17785
新疆	Xinjiang	169069	65466	103603	199315	100300	99015	258610	114724	143886

17-12 各地区外商投资企业进出口商品总值

Value of Import and Export Goods of Foreign-Funded Enterprises by Region

单位:万美元 (USD 10 000)

地区	Region	1998			1999			2000		
		进出口 Total	出口 Exports	进口 Imports	进出口 Total	出口 Exports	进口 Imports	进出口 Total	出口 Exports	进口 Imports
全国	**National Total**	**15767938**	**8096189**	**7671749**	**17451127**	**8862766**	**8588361**	**23671390**	**11944121**	**11727269**
北京	Beijing	408045	126273	281772	512711	146514	366197	776847	287108	489739
天津	Tianjin	815622	382367	433255	985555	449079	536476	1369289	637925	731364
河北	Hebei	132808	72029	60779	145673	80044	65629	158147	101240	56907
山西	Shanxi	18212	10567	7645	40929	8088	32841	41876	15209	26667
内蒙古	Inner Mongolia	9934	5861	4073	11309	7468	3841	18157	13799	4358
辽宁	Liaoning	686648	383276	303372	825814	436131	389683	1229698	624464	605234
吉林	Jilin	85086	27875	57211	96018	34709	61309	112274	39197	73077
黑龙江	Heilongjiang	44388	22427	21961	43602	22612	20990	47353	26679	20674
上海	Shanghai	1821775	816461	1005314	2266907	1034641	1232266	3341054	1426102	1914952
江苏	Jiangsu	1663145	804595	858550	1963675	985907	977768	3018082	1445340	1572742
浙江	Zhejiang	470714	268295	202419	566368	332775	233593	938993	534851	404142
安徽	Anhui	61974	26439	35535	83006	29143	53863	94779	39993	54786
福建	Fujian	1062231	544915	517316	1134090	588818	545272	1405740	759713	646027
江西	Jiangxi	17530	8659	8871	28632	9989	18643	31814	16298	15516
山东	Shandong	945594	522517	423077	1018622	585026	433596	1392569	792766	599803
河南	Henan	46833	24677	22156	46103	23679	22424	57695	30889	26806
湖北	Hubei	94529	25428	69101	91289	30986	60303	104686	42956	61730
湖南	Hunan	28326	11504	16822	29860	12900	16960	47717	18250	29467
广东	Guangdong	7091507	3918329	3173178	7331577	3939790	3391787	9203696	4951011	4252685
广西	Guangxi	71293	31925	39368	48384	22044	26340	55339	34112	21227
海南	Hainan	42069	7616	34453	39164	28669	10495	45993	30464	15529
重庆	Chongqing	39097	6905	32192	23566	6213	17353	32389	9666	22723
四川	Sichuan	31360	12476	18884	42982	15805	27177	61524	24517	37007
贵州	Guizhou	6139	4468	1671	4575	3456	1119	5690	4012	1678
云南	Yunnan	14634	3780	10854	13984	4240	9744	19658	8113	11545
西藏	Tibet	1159	159	1000	1070	219	851	634	389	245
陕西	Shaanxi	35211	11082	24129	32824	8914	23910	35433	11611	23822
甘肃	Gansu	6260	3514	2746	4050	2392	1658	5657	3832	1825
青海	Qinghai	605	336	269	103	88	15	925	202	723
宁夏	Ningxia	3652	2935	717	4578	2791	1787	6125	4294	1831
新疆	Xinjiang	11558	8499	3059	14107	9636	4471	11557	9119	2438

17-13 利用外资概况

Utilization of Foreign Capital

项目单位：个；金额单位：亿美元 (USD 100 million)

年份 Year	总计 Total 项目 Number of Projects	总计 Total 金额 Value	对外借款 Foreign Loans 项目 Number of Projects	对外借款 Foreign Loans 金额 Value	外商直接投资 Direct Foreign Investments 项目 Number of Projects	外商直接投资 Direct Foreign Investments 金额 Value	外商其他投资额 Other Foreign Investments
签订利用外资(合同)外资额 Total Amount of Foreign Capital to Be Utilized through the Signed Agreements and Contracts							
1979—1983	1471	239.78	79	150.62	1392	77.42	11.74
1984	1894	47.91	38	19.16	1856	26.51	2.24
1985	3145	98.67	72	35.34	3073	59.32	4.01
1986	1551	117.37	53	84.07	1498	28.34	4.96
1987	2289	121.36	56	78.17	2233	37.09	6.10
1988	6063	160.04	118	98.13	5945	52.97	8.94
1989	5909	114.79	130	51.85	5779	56.00	6.94
1990	7371	120.86	98	50.99	7273	65.96	3.91
1991	13086	195.83	108	71.61	12978	119.77	4.45
1992	48858	694.39	94	107.03	48764	581.24	6.12
1993	83595	1232.73	158	113.06	83437	1114.36	5.31
1994	47646	937.56	97	106.68	47549	826.80	4.08
1995	37184	1032.05	173	112.88	37011	912.82	6.35
1996	24673	816.10	117	79.62	24556	732.77	3.71
1997	21138	610.58	137	58.72	21001	510.04	41.82
1998	19850	632.01	51	83.85	19799	521.02	27.14
1999	17022	520.09	104	83.60	16918	412.23	24.26
2000					22347	623.80	87.50
实际利用外资额 Total Amount of Foreign Capital Actually Used							
1979—1983		144.38		117.55		18.02	8.81
1984		27.05		12.86		12.58	1.61
1985		46.47		26.88		16.61	2.98
1986		72.58		50.14		18.74	3.70
1987		84.52		58.05		23.14	3.33
1988		102.26		64.87		31.94	5.45
1989		100.59		62.86		33.92	3.81
1990		102.89		65.34		34.87	2.68
1991		115.54		68.88		43.66	3.00
1992		192.02		79.11		110.07	2.84
1993		389.60		111.89		275.15	2.56
1994		432.13		92.67		337.67	1.79
1995		481.33		103.27		375.21	2.85
1996		548.04		126.69		417.25	4.10
1997		644.08		120.21		452.57	71.30
1998		585.57		110.00		454.63	20.94
1999		526.59		102.12		403.19	21.28
2000		593.56		100.00		407.15	86.41
1979-2000		5189.20		1473.39		3466.37	249.44

17－14 利用外资额(按方式分)

Amount of Utilization of Foreign Capital and Foreign Investment

本表为对外贸易经济合作部统计资料，下同。

Data in this table are obtained from the Ministry of Foreign Trade and Economic Cooperation. The same as in the following tables.

项目单位：个　金额单位：万美元　(USD 10 000)

指　标	Item	1999			2000		
		项　目 Number of Projects	合同金额 Contract Value	实际使用金额 Used Value	项　目 Number of Projects	合同金额 Contract Value	实际使用金额 Used Value
总　计	**Total**	**17022**	**5200874**	**5265896**			**5935627**
对外借款	**Foreign Loans**	**104**	**836000**	**1021200**			**1000000**
外国政府贷款	Government Loans	104	148800	331600			
国际金融机构贷款	Loans from International Financial Organizations		360400	260600			
出口信贷	Export Loans		20000	102500			
外国银行商业贷款	Commercial Loans		226800	246500			
对外发行债券	External Bonds		80000	80000			
外商直接投资	**Foreign Direct Investments**	**16918**	**4122302**	**4031871**	**22347**	**6237952**	**4071481**
合资经营企业	Joint Ventures Enterprises	7050	1351520	1582729	8378	1964807	1434305
合作经营企业	Cooperative Operation Enterprises	1656	680302	823367	1757	811671	659575
外资企业	Foreign Investment Enterprises	8201	2070637	1554475	12196	3430896	1926388
外商投资股份制企业	Foreign Investment Share Enterprises	3	10285	29233	8	19403	13021
合作开发	Cooperative Development	5	5850	38389	8	11175	38192
其他	Others	3	3708	3678			
外商其他投资	**Other Foreign Investment**		**242572**	**212825**		**875048**	**864146**
对外发行股票	Sale Share		51000	61000		693049	693049
国际租赁	International Lease		10697	18500		2380	3358
补偿贸易	Compensation Trade		4146	1262		1236	1102
加工装配	Processing and Assembly		176729	132063		178383	166637

17-15 实际利用外商直接和其他投资额（按国别、地区分）

Actually Used Foreign Direct and Other Investment by Country or Territory

单位：万美元 (USD 10 000)

国别(地区)	Country (Territory)	1999		2000	
		外商直接投资 Foreign Direct Investment	外商其他投资 Foreign Other Investment	外商直接投资 Foreign Direct Investment	外商其他投资 Foreign Other Investment
总计	**Total**	**4031871**	**212825**	**4071481**	**864146**
亚洲	**Asia**	**2683231**	**132436**	**2548209**	**166146**
#孟加拉国	Bangladesh	43		66	
文莱	Brunei	18			
缅甸	Myanmar	1101		230	
柬埔寨	Cambodia	248		194	
塞浦路斯	Cyprus	189		297	
朝鲜	Democratic People's Republic of Korea	368		956	
中国香港	Hong Kong, China	1636305	103928	1549998	122935
印度	India	49		1044	
印度尼西亚	Indonesia	12917		14694	
伊朗	Iran			20	
伊拉克	Iraq	202		18	
以色列	Israel	327		1491	
日本	Japan	297308	9050	291585	14532
约旦	Jordan			25	
科威特	Kuwait	248		1067	
老挝	Laos			307	
黎巴嫩	Lebanon	20		25	
澳门	Macao	30864	2914	34728	3511
马来西亚	Malaysia	23771	2	20288	
蒙古	Mongolia	6		526	
尼泊尔	Nepal			20	
巴基斯坦	Pakistan	189		102	
巴勒斯坦	Palestine			10	
菲律宾	the Philippines	11728		11112	
沙特阿拉伯	Saudi Arabia	256		2556	
新加坡	Singapore	264249	3	217220	41
韩国	Republic of Korea	127473	552	148961	1081
叙利亚	Syria	11			
泰国	Thailand	14832		20357	2
土耳其	Turkey	385		148	
阿联酋	United Arab Emirates	221		407	
也门	Republic of Yemen	20			
越南	Viet Nam	13		56	
台湾	Taiwan, China	259870	15987	229658	24044
非洲	**Africa**	**19606**		**28771**	
#阿尔及利亚	Algeria	35		40	
贝宁	Benin	7			
博茨瓦纳	Bostswana			5	
喀麦隆	Cameroon	6			
埃及	Egypt	16		67	
加蓬	Gabon			11	

17-15 续表 1 continued

单位：万美元 (USD 10 000)

国别(地区)	Country (Territory)	1999 外商直接投资 Foreign Direct Investment	1999 外商其他投资 Foreign Other Investment	2000 外商直接投资 Foreign Direct Investment	2000 外商其他投资 Foreign Other Investment
几内亚(比绍)	Guinea-Bissan	176			
肯尼亚	Kenya	40			
利比里亚	Liberia	429			
利比亚	Libya	7			
马达加斯加	Madagascar	54			
毛里塔尼亚	Mauritania	156			
毛里求斯	Mauritius	17025		26479	
摩洛哥	Morocco	5			
纳米比亚	Namibia	635		199	
尼日利亚	Nigeria	200		652	
塞舌尔	Seychelles	29			
塞拉利昂	Sierra Leone	105		142	
南非	South Africa	590		919	
苏丹	Sudan			19	
坦桑尼亚	Tanzania	10		65	
多哥	Togo	10		10	
乌干达	Uganda	26		12	
赞比亚	Zambia			10	
津巴布韦	Zimbabwe	15		63	
莱索托	Lesotho			8	
欧洲	**Europe**	**479713**	**16980**	**476539**	**223**
#比利时	Belgium	8322		5616	
丹麦	Denmark	8491		4946	
英国	United Kingdom	104449	45	116405	
德国	Federal Republic of Germany	137326	37	104149	84
法国	France	88429		85316	
爱尔兰	Ireland	305		76	
意大利	Italy	18744		20951	
卢森堡	Luxembourg	422		2344	
荷兰	Netherlands	54168		78948	139
希腊	Greece	3		1289	
葡萄牙	Portugal	831		340	
西班牙	Spain	1754		3400	
奥地利	Austria	2317		2259	
保加利亚	Bulgaria	10		381	
芬兰	Finland	6765		5983	
直布罗陀	Gibraltar	39		3	
匈牙利	Hungary	1204		1065	
冰岛	Iceland	1		24	
列支敦士登	Liechtenstein	416		399	
马耳他	Malta	279		110	
挪威	Norway	1859		2410	
摩纳哥	Monaco	10		3	
波兰	Poland	354		464	
罗马尼亚	Romania	642		772	
瑞典	Sweden	15580	16898	15924	
瑞士	Switzerland	24709		19403	
爱沙尼亚	Estonia	30			
白俄罗斯	Belorussia	7		108	
哈萨克	Kazakhstan			73	

17-15 续表 2 continued

单位：万美元 (USD 10 000)

国别(地区)	Country (Territory)	1999 外商直接投资 Foreign Direct Investment	1999 外商其他投资 Foreign Other Investment	2000 外商直接投资 Foreign Direct Investment	2000 外商其他投资 Foreign Other Investment
俄罗斯	Russia	1954		1623	
乌克兰	Ukraine	24		24	
南斯拉夫	Yugoslavia	112		571	
捷克	Czecho	1407		975	
斯洛伐克	Slovakia	10		46	
拉丁美洲	**Latin America**	**320447**	**1388**	**461658**	**923**
#安提瓜和巴布达	Antigua and Barbuda	7		20	
阿根廷	Argentina	177		1389	
巴哈马	Bahama	4301		6776	
巴巴多斯	Barbados	392		5	
伯利兹	Belize			890	
玻利维亚	Bolivia	38		707	
巴西	Brazil	338		393	
凯曼群岛	Cayman Islands	37795		62373	
智利	Chile	208		44	
哥伦比亚	Colombia	228		50	
哥斯达黎加	Costarica	250		548	
古巴	Cuba			43	
多米尼加联邦	Commonwealth of Dominica	10		2	
多米尼加共和国	Republic of Dominica	2		10	
厄瓜多尔	Ecuador	29			
圭亚那	Guyana			90	
危地马拉	Guatemala			93	
洪都拉斯	Honduras	90		73	
牙买加	Jamiaca	300		49	
墨西哥	Mexico	33		93	
巴拿马	Panama	8951		4263	
巴拉圭	Paraguay	500		30	
秘鲁	Peru	272		7	
圣文森特和格林纳丁斯	Saint Vincent & Grenadines			29	
苏里南	Suriname	45		20	
特克斯和凯科斯岛	Turks and Caicos Islands			322	
乌拉圭	Uruguay			5	
委内瑞拉	Venezuela	565		37	
维尔京群岛	Virgin Islands	265896	1386	383289	923
圣其茨-尼维斯	St. Kitts-Nevis	10			
北美洲	**North America**	**461608**	**676**	**478579**	**3434**
#加拿大	Canada	31442	7	27978	3371
美国	United States	421586	669	438389	63
百慕大	Bermuda	8580		12212	
大洋洲及太平洋岛屿	**Oceanic and Pacific Islands**	**50920**	**345**	**69403**	
#澳大利亚	Australia	26331	345	30888	
库克群岛	Cook Islands	84		25	
斐济	Fiji	85			
新西兰	New Zealand	1839		1822	
巴布亚新几内亚	Papua New Guinea	52		45	
汤加	Tonga	130		120	
萨摩亚	Samoan	20136		28316	
马绍尔群岛	Marshall Islands	159		913	
其他	**Others**	**16346**	**61000**	**8322**	**693420**

17-16 实际利用外商直接和其他投资额（按地区分）

Actually Used Foreign Direct and Other Investment by Region

单位：万美元 (USD 10 000)

地区、部门	Region and Sector	1999 外商直接投资 Foreign Direct Investment	1999 外商其他投资 Foreign Other Investment	2000 外商直接投资 Foreign Direct Investment	2000 外商其他投资 Foreign Other Investment
总　计	**National Total**	**4031871**	**212825**	**4071481**	**864146**
省市合计	**Regional Total**	**3993482**	**151825**	**4033289**	**171097**
北　京	Beijing	197525		168368	
天　津	Tianjin	176399		116601	
河　北	Hebei	104202		67923	371
山　西	Shanxi	39129		22472	
内蒙古	Inner Mongolia	6456		10568	
辽　宁	Liaoning	106173		204446	
吉　林	Jilin	30120		33701	
黑龙江	Heilongjiang	31828		30086	
上　海	Shanghai	283665		316014	
江　苏	Jiangsu	607756		642550	
浙　江	Zhejiang	123262		161266	
安　徽	Anhui	26131		31847	
福　建	Fujian	402403		343191	
江　西	Jiangxi	32080		22724	
山　东	Shandong	225878	20669	297119	5636
河　南	Henan	52135		56403	
湖　北	Hubei	91488	7426	94368	9244
湖　南	Hunan	65374		67833	
广　东	Guangdong	1165750	123488	1128091	155403
广　西	Guangxi	63512		52466	300
海　南	Hainan	48449		43080	
重　庆	Chongqing	23893	242	24436	143
四　川	Sichuan	34101		43694	
贵　州	Guizhou	4090		2501	
云　南	Yunnan	15385		12812	
西　藏	Tibet				
陕　西	Shaanxi	24197		28842	
甘　肃	Gansu	4104		6235	
青　海	Qinghai	459			
宁　夏	Ningxia	5134		1741	
新　疆	Xinjiang	2404		1911	
部门合计	**Total of the Ministries and Other Departments**	**38389**	**61000**	**38192**	**693049**

17-17 按行业分外商直接投资合同外资额

Agreement of Foreign Direct Investment by Sector

行 业	Sector	项 目(个) Number of Projects		金 额(万美元) Amount of Capital (USD 10 000)	
		1999	2000	1999	2000
总 计	**National Total**	**16918**	**22347**	**4122302**	**6237952**
农、林、牧、渔业	Farming, Forestry, Animal Husbandry and Fishery	762	821	147170	148314
采掘业	Mining and Quarrying	130	162	32221	50640
制造业	Manufacturing	12042	15988	2533180	4425430
电力、煤气及水的生产和供应业	Electric Power, Gas and Water Production and Supply	116	107	163519	122686
建筑业	Construction	247	233	109619	83088
交通运输、仓储及邮电通信业	Transport, Storage, Post and Telecommunication Services	205	306	111401	141658
批发和零售贸易餐饮业	Wholesale & Retail Trade and Catering Services	825	852	120413	143514
房地产业	Real Estate Management	669	684	417785	523213
社会服务业	Social Services	1474	2679	301680	425463
卫生体育和社会福利业	Health Care, Sports and Social Welfare	28	31	6727	15428
教育、文化艺术和广播电影电视业	Education, Cuiture and Arts, Radio, Film and Television	29	19	7258	8332
其他行业	Other Sectors	391	465	171329	150186

17-18 按行业分外商实际直接投资额

Actually Used Amount of Foreign Direct Investment by Sector

单位:万美元 (USD 10 000)

行 业	Sector	1999	2000
总计	**National Total**	**4031871**	**4071481**
农、林、牧、渔业	Farming, Forestry, Animal Husbandry and Fishery	71015	67594
采掘业	Mining and Quarrying	55714	58328
制造业	Manufacturing	2260334	2584417
电力、煤气及水的生产和供应业	Electric Power, Gas and Water Production and Supply	370274	224212
建筑业	Construction	91658	90542
交通运输、仓储及邮电通信业	Transport, Storage, Post and Telecommunication Services	155114	101188
批发和零售贸易餐饮业	Wholesale & Retail Trade and Catering Services	96513	85781
房地产业	Real Estate Management	558831	465751
社会服务业	Social Services	255066	218544
卫生体育和社会福利业	Health Care, Sports and Social Welfare	14769	10588
教育、文化艺术和广播电影电视业	Education, Culture and Arts, Radio, Film and Television	6072	5446
其他行业	Other Sectors	96511	159090

17-19 年末登记外商投资企业行业分布情况

Sector Distribution Registered of Foreign Funded Enterprises at the Year-end

行业	Sector	企业数(户) Number of Registered Enterprises		投资总额(百万美元) Total Investment (USD million)		注册资本(百万美元) Registered Capital (USD million)		#外方 Capital Invested by Foreign Partner	
		1999	2000	1999	2000	1999	2000	1999	2000
合计	**National Total**	**212436**	**203208**	**778568**	**824675**	**463549**	**483950**	**316682**	**337199**
农、林、牧、渔业	Farming, Forestry, Animal Husbandry and Fishery	5259	5066	9112	9215	6285	6301	4735	4726
采掘业	Mining and Quarrying	1277	1131	2978	2770	2190	1980	1547	1430
制造业	Manufacturing	150020	142754	410291	453632	271535	289030	182323	198651
电力、煤气及水的生产和供应业	Electricity, Gas and Water Production and Supply	1345	1301	47852	49105	19740	19658	11130	11426
建筑业	Construction	6172	5610	22894	22131	12600	12033	8418	8025
地质勘查和水利管理业	Geological Prospecting and Water Conservancy	137	134	4178	4181	1550	1525	1431	1399
交通运输、仓储及邮电通信业	Transport, Storage, Post and Telecommunication Services	3471	3352	32659	33205	14996	17267	9696	11809
批发和零售贸易餐饮业	Wholesale and Retail Trade & Catering Services	13064	12275	24724	25283	16359	16277	11494	11724
金融、保险业	Finance and Insurance	65	72	1764	1999	1654	1886	1170	1324
房地产业	Real Estate Trade	13395	12732	154890	151247	75962	74303	56964	56085
社会服务业	Social Services	15054	15331	52452	55400	31442	33471	20744	22575
卫生体育和社会福利业	Health Care, Sports and Social Welfare	485	455	2671	2438	1632	1497	1192	1087
教育、文化艺术及广播电影电视业	Education, Culture and Arts, Radio, Film and Television	676	611	1580	1495	1112	1049	753	723
科学研究和综合技术服务业	Scientific Research and Polytechnic Services	975	1189	1921	2673	1369	1672	1023	1281
其他	Others	1041	1195	8602	9901	5123	6001	4062	4934

17-20 各地区外商投资企业年末登记情况

Basic Indicators of Registered Foreign Funded Enterprises by Region at the Year-end

地　区	Region	企 业 数(户) Number of Registered Enterprises		投资总额(万美元) Total Investment (USD 10 000)		注册资本(万美元) Registered Capital (USD 10 000)		#外　方 Capital Invested by Foreign Partner	
		1999	2000	1999	2000	1999	2000	1999	2000
全　国	**National Total**	**212436**	**203208**	**77856752**	**82467505**	**46354938**	**48394975**	**31668235**	**33719912**
北　京	Beijing	8621	8495	3933398	4024578	2098591	2173754	1383035	1479646
天　津	Tianjin	9924	9942	2941212	3308590	1696650	1850961	1284473	1425288
河　北	Hebei	4011	3812	1458345	1400971	860228	829018	467343	455564
山　西	Shanxi	1204	959	470185	482749	253339	255967	127215	129053
内蒙古	Inner Mongolia	919	874	226772	253634	157492	171773	83686	84084
辽　宁	Liaoning	13825	13146	4308454	6554253	2584599	3962628	1524605	2544774
吉　林	Jilin	2931	2747	725728	766098	506102	527717	285978	311979
黑龙江	Heilongjiang	3788	3318	904922	834390	612968	560605	351655	316062
上　海	Shanghai	15059	15930	9073365	9853971	4940130	5334470	3453171	3808408
江　苏	Jiangsu	18843	18060	7290850	7500428	4029616	4065698	2761820	2916728
浙　江	Zhejiang	9646	10002	2748640	2931301	1602594	1712191	960244	1053944
安　徽	Anhui	2439	2216	906091	914400	582506	586788	320714	341328
福　建	Fujian	17965	16013	4942246	4708446	3050255	2758492	2579989	2303206
江　西	Jiangxi	2149	2246	485298	687577	313552	330088	199568	207078
山　东	Shandong	12358	12389	3814482	3895046	2327187	2309717	1303472	1384675
河　南	Henan	3772	3004	1195165	1135854	790302	733653	431165	424649
湖　北	Hubei	5407	5123	1628750	1666978	1016187	1034766	603077	595372
湖　南	Hunan	2513	2316	721367	730585	442332	433837	266023	265101
广　东	Guangdong	53644	49865	21523898	21651026	12893567	12808607	9593830	9674891
广　西	Guangxi	3018	2705	1089032	1084956	640533	626848	400820	409965
海　南	Hainan	6993	7248	2315054	2343595	1366865	1392553	1100250	1121131
重　庆	Chongqing	2150	1708	725845	660201	498381	441940	313228	282396
四　川	Sichuan	3730	3539	1004273	1010651	701051	702808	357784	367479
贵　州	Guizhou	947	715	200569	149349	153188	116635	100574	75936
云　南	Yunnan	1596	1634	436213	481867	279746	310120	160825	186253
西　藏	Tibet	70	78	25648	33547	11552	18825	5839	11973
陕　西	Shaanxi	2604	2761	769359	832224	471904	507107	291090	319651
甘　肃	Gansu	759	826	182533	256455	119222	181717	64779	98581
青　海	Qinghai	83	113	87951	57724	37805	33199	19727	23533
宁　夏	Ningxia	392	408	81855	94032	62402	69627	32961	39227
新　疆	Xinjiang	447	371	127708	114341	83853	74880	46796	39674
国家工商行政管理局	State Administration for Industry and Commerce	629	645	1511544	2047688	1170239	1477986	792499	1022283

17-21 对外经济合作

Economic Cooperation with Foreign Countries or Territories

年 份 Year	签订合同的国家(地区)数 (个) Number of Countries or Territories with Contracts Signed	合同数 (份) Number of Contracts	合同金额 (亿美元) Contracted Value (USD 100 million)	完成营业额 (亿美元) Value of Business Fulfilled (USD 100 million)
总 计 **Total**		**206048**	**1114.12**	**809.33**
1976-1988	103	7534	105.95	60.91
1989	124	3100	22.12	16.86
1990	122	5175	26.04	18.67
1991	147	8438	36.09	23.63
1992	159	9405	65.85	30.49
1993	158	11605	68.00	45.38
1994	171	17491	79.88	59.78
1995	178	19321	96.72	65.88
1996	178	24891	102.73	76.96
1997	181	28442	113.56	83.83
1998	188	25955	117.73	101.34
1999	187	21126	130.02	112.35
2000	181	23565	149.43	113.25
对外承包工程 **Contracted Projects**				
1976-1988		3449	89.00	49.70
1989		776	17.81	14.84
1990		920	21.25	16.44
1991		1171	25.24	19.70
1992		1164	52.51	24.03
1993		1393	51.89	36.68
1994		1702	60.28	48.83
1995		1558	74.84	51.08
1996		1634	77.28	58.21
1997		2085	85.16	60.36
1998		2322	92.43	77.69
1999		2527	101.99	85.22
2000		2597	117.19	83.79
对外劳务合作 **Labor Cooperation**				
1976-1988		4085	16.95	11.21
1989		2324	4.31	2.02
1990		4255	4.78	2.23
1991		7267	10.85	3.93
1992		8241	13.35	6.46
1993		10212	16.11	8.70
1994		15789	19.60	10.95
1995		17397	20.07	13.47
1996		22723	22.80	17.12
1997		25743	25.50	21.65
1998		23191	23.90	22.76
1999		18173	26.32	26.23
对外设计咨询 **Design Consultation**		20474	29.91	28.13
1995		366	1.81	1.33
1996		534	2.65	1.64
1997		614	2.90	1.82
1998		442	1.40	0.89
1999		426	1.71	0.90
2000		494	2.33	1.34

17－22　对外经济合作完成营业额（按国别、地区分）

Turnover of Economic Cooperation with Foreign Countries or Territories

单位:万美元　　　　(USD 10 000)

国别(地区)	Country (Territory)	1999				2000			
		合　计 Total	承包工程 Contracted Projects	劳务合作 Labour Cooperation	设计咨询 Design Consultation	合　计 Total	承包工程 Contracted Projects	劳务合作 Labour Cooperation	设计咨询 Design Consultation
合　计	**Total**	**1123458**	**852232**	**262268**	**8958**	**1132536**	**837897**	**281256**	**13383**
亚洲	**Asia**	**624719**	**450209**	**171100**	**3410**	**673664**	**479477**	**191227**	**2960**
#巴林	Bahrain	3		3		31		31	
孟加拉国	Bangladesh	15535	14491	649	395	23122	22042	959	121
文莱	Brunei	1720	1673	47		996	955	41	
缅甸	Myanmar	19783	19269	429	85	18672	17848	628	196
柬埔寨	Cambodia	4107	1501	2592	14	4982	1866	3004	112
塞浦路斯	Cyprus	856	669	187		1391	1226	165	
朝鲜	Korea, DPR	1349	1209	140		1589	1274	315	
中国香港	Hongkong, China	219212	196653	22468	91	225006	202782	22099	125
印度	India	3351	2642	592	117	1318	919	395	4
印度尼西亚	Indonesia	5490	2240	3207	43	3966	1196	2711	59
伊朗	Iran	20582	20012	25	545	36805	36029	163	613
伊拉克	Iraq	4391	4316		75	7948	7876	72	
以色列	Israel	7540	1048	6492		8834	672	8153	9
日本	Japan	28768	316	28330	122	39722	1513	38118	91
约旦	Jordan	1253	1140	107	6	1973	1300	667	6
科威特	Kuwait	21580	18750	2798	32	6441	5203	1098	140
老挝	Laos	8510	8321	169	20	9371	9077	273	21
黎巴嫩	Lebanon	16		16		28	5	22	1
中国澳门	Macau, China	24932	11824	13084	24	22128	9789	12329	10
马来西亚	Malaysia	10760	8793	1450	517	11073	9478	1587	8
马尔代夫	Maldives	494		492	2	345	1	344	
蒙古	Mongolia	2582	1139	1440	3	2950	1778	1149	23
尼泊尔	Nepal	6425	6360	41	24	5649	5201	46	402
阿曼	Oman	47		46	1	2319	2255	64	
巴基斯坦	Pakistan	30798	30577	86	135	32941	32042	503	396
巴勒斯坦	Palestine	11		5	6	329	315	6	8
菲律宾	Philippines	5876	5558	318		4369	4026	343	
卡塔尔	Qatar	252	203	49		1050	953	97	
沙特阿拉伯	Saudi Arabia	4540	3390	1149	1	3213	1588	1625	
新加坡	Singapore	101864	53085	48732	47	120818	65421	55344	53
韩国	Korea Rep	16740	148	16582	10	21633	37	21552	44
斯里兰卡	Sri Lanka	5079	4645	419	15	6358	5809	276	273
叙利亚	Syrian	806	786	20		469	448	21	
泰国	Thailand	12520	10865	1182	473	9501	8645	836	20
土耳其	Turkey	363	66	274	23	652	473	167	12

17-22 续表 1 continued

单位:万美元 (USD 10 000)

国别(地区)	Country (Territory)	1999				2000			
		合计 Total	承包工程 Contracted Projects	劳务合作 Labour Cooperation	设计咨询 Design Consultation	合计 Total	承包工程 Contracted Projects	劳务合作 Labour Cooperation	设计咨询 Design Consultation
阿联酋	United Arab Emirates	4487	2517	1970		4778	2638	2140	
也门共和国	Republic of Yemen	9668	9467	189	12	9792	9636	140	16
越南	Vietnam	8317	6534	1343	440	8749	6715	1941	93
台湾省	Taiwan, China	14112	2	13978	132	12353	446	11875	32
非洲	**Africa**	**203629**	**182770**	**20312**	**547**	**128721**	**109621**	**18514**	**586**
#阿尔及利亚	Algeria	10667	8962	1705		4710	3843	841	26
安哥拉	Angola	830	827		3	318	315	2	1
贝宁	Benin	294	220	71	3	250	141	86	23
博茨瓦纳	Botswana	5740	5525	214	1	6636	6358	278	
布隆迪	Burundi	43	25	18		87	75	12	
喀麦隆	Cameroon	1809	1648	159	2	1812	1642	170	
佛得角	Cape Verde	101	89		12	188	182		6
中非	Central Africa	261	259	2		69	66	1	2
科摩罗	Comoros	66	62	4		142	142		
刚果（布）	Congo(B)	47	43	4		10	5	5	
吉布提	Djibouti	676	660	15	1	948	888	57	3
埃及	Egypt	1600	1508	61	31	783	720	56	7
赤道几内亚	Eq. Guinea	5189	5084	89	16	578	513	61	4
埃塞俄比亚	Ethiopia	3811	3668	127	16	4760	4624	104	32
加蓬	Cabon	3278	2928	350		1502	1343	159	
冈比亚	Gambia	66	49	17		65	36	29	
加纳	Ghana	1473	978	474	21	2179	1921	216	42
几内亚	Guinea	1633	1085	527	21	4140	3634	495	11
几内亚(比绍)	Guinea Bissau	5016	5000	16		2408	2332	74	2
科特迪瓦	Cote d'Lvoire	4961	4877	77	7	5351	5331	20	
肯尼亚	Kenya	5537	5345	192		6247	6110	121	16
利比里亚	Liberia	2055		2055		1602	160	1442	
利比亚	Libyan	1171	289	878	4	730	204	522	4
马达加斯加	Madagascar	1996	1907	84	5	1996	1849	145	2
马拉维	Malawi	220	220			706	548	158	
马里	Mali	9989	9884	95	10	10505	10214	290	1
毛里塔尼亚	Mauritania	2973	1718	1252	3	3448	2420	1028	
毛里求斯	Mauritius	8193	902	7222	69	9048	820	8228	
摩洛哥	Morocco	1546	123	1420	3	1655	482	1173	
莫桑比克	Mozambique	1070	1019	11	40	1564	1537	24	3
纳米比亚	Namibia	2597	2481	110	6	2442	2326	114	2
尼日尔	Niger	935	905	29	1	533	493	40	

17-22 续表 2 continued

单位:万美元 (USD 10 000)

国别(地区)	Country (Territory)	1999 合计 Total	1999 承包工程 Contracted Projects	1999 劳务合作 Labour Cooperation	1999 设计咨询 Design Consultation	2000 合计 Total	2000 承包工程 Contracted Projects	2000 劳务合作 Labour Cooperation	2000 设计咨询 Design Consultation
尼日利亚	Nigeria	10881	10372	508	1	6139	5504	635	
卢旺达	Rwanda	1634	1523	108	3	1740	1616	103	21
圣多美和普林西比	Sao Tome & Principe	50	50			9	9		
塞内加尔	Senegal	5426	5399	27		2816	2776	40	
塞舌尔	Seychelles	3118	2923	195		2995	2811	184	
塞拉利昂	Sierra Leone	571	466	105		1763	1759	4	
南非	S. Africa	2157	1746	409	2	1145	649	466	30
苏丹	Sudan	74337	72893	1231	213	11882	11466	227	189
坦桑尼亚	Tanzania	3681	3569	80	32	5127	4700	385	42
多哥	Togo	576	552	18	6	538	512	26	
突尼斯	Tunisia	1027	998	29		387	353	34	
乌干达	Uganda	1512	1485	25	2	1945	1905	35	5
布基纳法索	Burkina Faso	250	248	2		31	31		
刚果（金）	Congo(J)	650	648	2		246	242	4	
赞比亚	Zambia	2048	2027	21		3848	3733	10	105
津巴布韦	Zimbabwe	8490	8449	41		8756	8692	64	
莱索托	Lesotho	1013	798	215		1513	1196	314	3
斯威士兰	Swaziland	18		18		31		31	
厄立特里亚	Eritrea	347	334		13	398	393	1	4
欧洲	**Europe**	**30616**	**12593**	**17102**	**921**	**54239**	**35446**	**18398**	**395**
#比利时	Belgium	342	210	132		608	413	172	23
丹麦	Denmark	43		43		93		90	3
英国	United Kingdom	3324	668	2379	277	3188	2076	1094	18
德国	German ,FR	3238	392	2801	45	9557	5494	4012	51
法国	France	1120	2	1087	31	1139		1134	5
爱尔兰	Ireland	8		8		39		39	
意大利	Italy	682	399	253	30	493	178	235	80
卢森堡	Luxembourg	19		19		51		51	
荷兰	Netherlands	449	218	193	38	3800	3491	309	
希腊	Greece	539	5	534		707		707	
葡萄牙	Portugal	10		10		18		18	
西班牙	Spain	453		453		2772	2206	565	1
阿尔巴尼亚	Albania	226	208	2	16	77	60	3	14
奥地利	Austria	393	300	93		225	112	112	1
保加利亚	Bulgaria	352	3	349		542		542	
芬兰	Finland	367	305	62		140	1	139	
匈牙利	Hungary	213		213		144	19	125	

17-22 续表 3 continued

单位:万美元 (USD 10 000)

国别(地区)	Country (Territory)	1999				2000			
		合计 Total	承包工程 Contracted Projects	劳务合作 Labour Cooperation	设计咨询 Design Consultation	合计 Total	承包工程 Contracted Projects	劳务合作 Labour Cooperation	设计咨询 Design Consultation
冰岛	Iceland	1		1					
马耳他	Malta	77	8	69		75		75	
挪威	Norway	901	388	513		880		846	34
波兰	Poland	476	434	42		666	624	42	
罗马尼亚	Romania	802	125	677		320	35	285	
圣马力诺	San Marino	24		24					
瑞典	Sweden	115	10	105		307	63	244	
瑞士	Switzerland	172	15	157		306		306	
拉脱维亚	Latvia	3		3		13		13	
立陶宛	Lithuania	1		1					
格鲁吉亚	Georgia	3		3		263	262	1	
亚美尼亚	Armenia	36	36			7		7	
阿塞拜缰	Azerbaijan	194	15	179		131	99	32	
白俄罗斯	Belorussia	19		19					
哈萨克	Kazakhstan	933	871	55	7	4469	4418	29	22
吉尔吉斯	Kirghizia	50		50		880	825	39	16
摩尔多瓦	Moldavia	99		99		93	43	50	
俄罗斯	Russia	9095	3322	5751	22	11145	4484	6656	5
塔吉克	Tadzhikistan	583	495	88		391	388		3
乌克兰	Ukraine	504	62	442		264	102	161	1
乌兹别克	Uzbekstan	496	495	1		1356	1329	27	
土库曼	Turkmenistan	2197	2191	1	5	3210	3188	20	2
南斯拉夫	Yugoslavia	1978	1416	112	450	1907	1636	155	116
斯洛文尼亚	Slovenia	17		17		6		6	
捷克	Czech	62		62		57		57	
马其顿	Macedonia					3900	3900		
拉丁美洲	**Latin America**	**14366**	**7184**	**6969**	**213**	**23216**	**16820**	**6293**	**103**
#安提瓜和巴布达	Antigua & Barbuda	970	887		83	2574	2528	46	
阿根廷	Argentina	1331	711	620		889	332	557	
巴哈马	Bahamas	29		29		95	39	56	
巴巴多斯	Barbados	311	286	18	7	423	383	40	
伯利兹	Belize	23	1	22		50		50	
玻利维亚	Bolivia	23		23		624	600	22	2
巴西	Brazil	319	238	81		1851	1267	584	
智利	Chile	189	150	39		191	180	11	
哥伦比亚	Colombia	2		2					
多米尼加联邦	Dominica	645	636	9		11		11	
古巴	Cuba	139	90	49		812	771	41	
多米尼加共和国	Dominican Rep	2		2		160	159	1	
厄瓜多尔	Ecuador	834	713	109	12	211	134	73	4

17-22 续表 4 continued

单位:万美元　　(USD 10 000)

国别(地区)	Country (Territory)	1999 合计 Total	1999 承包工程 Contracted Projects	1999 劳务合作 Labour Cooperation	1999 设计咨询 Design Consultation	2000 合计 Total	2000 承包工程 Contracted Projects	2000 劳务合作 Labour Cooperation	2000 设计咨询 Design Consultation
危地马拉	Guatemala	36		36		18		18	
圭亚那	Guyana	183	111	66	6	455	328	119	8
格林纳达	Grenada					292	292		
洪都拉斯	Honduras	59		59		194	49	145	
牙买加	Jamaica	618	9	609		438		404	34
墨西哥	Mexico	187	10	177		1717	1369	348	
尼加拉瓜	Nicaragua	105		105		175		175	
巴拿马	Panama	3407		3407		2053		2053	
巴拉圭	Paraguay	25		25		8		8	
秘鲁	Peru	873	756	111	6	2544	2312	230	2
圣卢西亚	Saint Lucia	1122	993	125	4	951	863	49	39
圣马丁	Saint Martin Is.	1		1					
圣文森特和格林纳丁斯	Saint Vincent & Grenadines	46		46		92	10	82	
萨尔瓦多	EL Salvador	55		55		58		58	
苏里南	Suriname	1331	1131	195	5	1414	1271	139	4
特立尼达和多巴哥	Trinidad & Tobago	415	415			492	472	10	10
乌拉圭	Uruguay	72		72		96	10	86	
委内瑞拉	Venezuela	963	47	826	90	4212	3451	761	
维尔京群岛	Virgin Is.	51		51		116		116	
北美洲	**North America**	**33088**	**10367**	**22534**	**187**	**36421**	**12914**	**23312**	**195**
加拿大	Canada	571	248	323		964	375	584	5
美国	United States	32316	10119	22010	187	35058	12539	22329	190
格陵兰	Greenland	201		201		399		399	
大洋洲及太平洋岛屿	**Oceanic & Pacific Is.**	**18221**	**11950**	**6250**	**21**	**16616**	**12322**	**4253**	**41**
#澳大利亚	Australia	1657	1345	312		1383	1131	251	1
斐济	Fiji	1152	561	585	6	982	428	544	10
盖比群岛	Gambier Is.	2009	158	1851		4101	2792	1309	
马克萨斯群岛	Marquesas Is.	1		1					
瓦努阿图	Vanuatu	105	99	6		14		7	7
新西兰	New Zealand	479		479		323	60	262	1
巴布亚新几内亚	Papua New Guinea	8568	8115	451	2	5130	5003	120	7
所罗门群岛	Solomon Is.	1		1					
汤加	Tonga	4		4		93	55	38	
萨摩亚	Samoa	570	140	428	2	537	141	296	
基里巴斯	Kirbate	19	7	1	11	21	5	1	15
密克罗尼西亚	Micronesia FS	2784	779	2005		2758	1426	1332	
马绍尔群岛	Marshall Is.	19	2	17		18	16	2	
贝劳共和国	Palau	791	744	47		1316	1265	51	
法属波利尼西亚	French Polynesia	62		62		40		40	
其它	**Others**	**5851**	**4414**	**1429**	**8**	**7249**	**3817**	**3432**	
国境内	**Inner Country**	**192968**	**172745**	**16572**	**3651**	**192410**	**167480**	**15827**	**9103**

主 要 统 计 指 标 解 释

进出口总额 海关进出口总额指实际进出我国国境的货物总金额。包括对外贸易实际进出口货物，来料加工装配进出口货物，国家间、联合国及国际组织无偿援助物资和赠送品，华侨、港澳台同胞和外籍华人捐赠品，租赁期满归承租人所有的租赁货物，进料加工进出口货物，边境地方贸易及边境地区小额贸易进出口货物(边民互市贸易除外)，中外合资企业、中外合作经营企业、外商独资经营企业进出口货物和公用物品，到、离岸价格在规定限额以上的进出口货样和广告品(无商业价值、无使用价值和免费提供出口的除外)，从保税仓库提取在中国境内销售的进口货物，以及其他进出口货物。进出口总额用以观察一个国家在对外贸易方面的总规模。我国规定出口货物按离岸价格统计，进口货物按到岸价格统计。

商品经营单位所在地进、出口额 指所在地海关注册登记的有进出口经营权的企业实际进、出口额。

商品目的地进口额和商品货源地出口额 目的地进口额指进口货物的消费、使用或最终抵运地的实际进口额，货源地出口额是指出口货物的产地或原始发货地的实际出口额 。

利用外资 指我国各级政府、部门、企业和其他经济组织通过对外借款、吸收外商直接投资以及用其他方式筹措的境外现汇、设备、技术等。

对外借款 是我国利用外资的重要部分。指通过对外正式签订借款协议，从境外筹措的资金，包括外国政府贷款、国际金融组织贷款、外国银行商业贷款、出口信贷以及对外发行债券等。1996年及以前还包括对外发行股票。

外商直接投资 指外国企业和经济组织或个人(包括华侨、港澳台胞以及我国在境外注册的企业)按我国有关政策、法规，用现汇、实物、技术等在我国境内开办外商独资企业、与我国境内的企业或经济组织共同举办中外合资经营企业、合作经营企业或合作开发资源的投资(包括外商投资收益的再投资)，以及经政府有关部门批准的项目投资总额内企业从境外借入的资金。

外商其他投资 指除对外借款和外商直接投资以外的各种利用外资的形式。包括企业在境内外股票市场公开发行的以外币计价的股票（目前主要是在香港证券市场发行的H股和在境内证券市场发行的B股）发行价总额，国际租赁进口设备的应付款，补偿贸易中外商提供的进口设备、技术、物料的价款，加工装配贸易中外商提供的进口设备、物料的价款。

对外承包工程 指各对外承包公司以招标议标承包方式承揽的下列业务：⑴承包国外工程建设项目，⑵承包我国对外经援项目，⑶承包我国驻外机构的工程建设项目，⑷承包我国境内利用外资进行建设的工程项目，⑸与外国承包公司合营或联合承包工程项目时我国公司分包部分，⑹对外承包兼营的房屋开发业务。对外承包工程的营业额是以货币表现的本期内完成的对外承包工程的工作量，包括以前年度签订的合同和本年度新签订的合同在报告期内完成的工作量。

对外劳务合作 指以收取工资的形式向业主或承包商提供技术和劳动服务的活动。我国对外承包公司在境外开办的合营企业，中国公司同时又提供劳务的，其劳务部分也纳入劳务合作统计。劳务合作营业额按报告期内向雇主提交的结算数(包括工资、加班费和奖金等)统计。

对外设计咨询 指以服务成果向业主收费的技术服务项目。包括承担地形地貌测绘，地质资源勘探与普查，建设区域规划，提供设计文件、图纸、生产工艺技术资料和工程技术经济咨询，工程项目的可行性考察、研究和评估，进行技术指导和培训人员等；也包括承担国（境）内利用外资进行建设的工程项目的上述规定的设计咨询项目的收取外币部分。

Explanatory Notes on Main Statistical Indicators

Total Imports and Exports at Customs refer to the value of commodities imported into and exported from the boundary of China. They include the actual imports and exports through foreign trade, imported and exported goods under the processing and assembling trades and materials, supplies and gifts as aid given gratis between governments and by the United Nations and other international organizations, and contributions donated by overseas Chinese, compatriots in Hong Kong and Macao and Chinese with foreign citizenship, leasing commodities owned by tenant at the expiration of leasing period, the imported and exported commodities processed with imported materials, commodities trading in border areas (excluding mutual exchange goods), the imported and exported commodities and articles for public use of the Sino-foreign joint ventures, cooperative enterprises and ventures exclusively with foreign own investment. Also included are import or export of samples and advertising goods for whose CIF or FOB value are beyond the permitted ceiling (excluding goods of no trading or use value and free commodities for export), imported goods sold in China from bonded warehouses and other imported or exported goods. The indicator of the total imports and exports at customs can be used to observe the total size of external trade in a country. In accordance with the stipulation of the Chinese government, imports are calculated at CIF, while exports are calculated at FOB

Import Export Value by Location of China's Foreign Trade Managing Units refers to actual value of imports and exports carried out by corporations which have been registered by the local customhouse and are vested with right to run import export business.

Import Value of Commodities by the Places of their Destination and Export Value of Commodities by the Places of their Origin in China: The former indicator refers to the value of import commodities of the places of their consumption, utilization or the places of their final destination. The latter indicator refers to the value of export commodities of the places of their origin or the places of the commodities dispatched.

Utilization of Foreign Capital refers to remittance, equipment and technology financed from abroad, by loans, foreign direct investment and other forms undertaken by the Chinese governments at all levels, by various departments, enterprises and other economic units.

Foreign Borrowings an important part of China's utilization of foreign capital, it refer to funds borrowed from abroad through formal signing of borrowing agreements with foreign institutions, including loans of foreign governments, loans of international financial institutions, commercial loans of foreign banks, export credit, and funds raised by Chinese bonds (and shares before 1996) issued abroad.

Direct Investment by Foreign Entrepreneurs refers to the investments inside China by foreign enterprises and economic organizations or individuals (including overseas Chinese, compatriots from Hong Kong and Macao, and Chinese enterprises registered abroad), following the relevant policies and laws of China, for the establishment of ventures exclusively with foreign own investment, Sino-foreign joint ventures and cooperative enterprises or for co-operative exploration of resources with enterprises or economic organizations in China. It includes the re investment of the foreign entrepreneurs with the profits gained from the investment and the funds that enterprises borrow from abroad in the total investment of projects which are approved by the relevant department of the government.

Other Investment by Foreign Entrepreneurs refers to all forms of utilization of foreign capitals other than foreign borrowings and foreign direct investment. It includes the total value of stock shares in foreign currencies issued by enterprises at domestic or foreign stock exchanges (now mainly consisting of H shares issued at Hong Kong Security Market and B shares issued at domestic security markets), rent payable for the imported equipment through international leasing arrangement, cost of imported equipment, technology and materials provided by foreign counterparts in compensation trade and processing and assembly trade.

Contracted Projects with Foreign Countries refer to projects undertaken by Chinese contractors (project contracting companies) through bidding process. They include: (1)overseas civil engineering construction projects financed by foreign investors; (2)overseas projects financed by the Chinese government through its foreign aid programs; (3)construction projects of Chinese diplomatic missions, trade offices and other institutions stationed abroad; (4)construction projects in China financed by foreign investment; (5)sub-contracted projects to be taken by Chinese contractors through a joint umbrella project with foreign contractor(s); (6)housing development projects. The business income from international contracted projects is the work volume of contracted projects completed during the reference period, expressed in monetary terms, including completed work on projects signed in previous years.

Service Cooperation with Foreign Countries refers to the activities of providing technology and labour services to employers or contractors in the forms of receiving salaries and wages.

Labour services providing by contractual joint ventures of Chinese international contracting corporations should be included in the statistics of service co-operation with foreign countries. The business income of labour service co operation is the income in the form of wages and salaries, overtime pay, bonuses and other remuneration received from the employers during the reference period.

Overseas Design and Consultation Service refers to projects with charges for technical services from overseas operators. It includes geographic and topographic mapping, geological resource prospecting and survey, planning of construction areas, provision of design documents, blueprints, materials on production process and techniques, as well as engineering, technical and economic consultation, and feasibility study, research and evaluation of projects. Also included under this category are the above-mentioned services of foreign-financed projects in China that are paid in foreign currencies.

十八、旅游

Tourism

简要说明

一、旅游统计的范围，包括国际旅游和国内旅游。本篇的主要内容有入境国际旅游者(外国人、华侨、港澳同胞和台湾同胞)人数，出境居民人数，国内居民(城镇和农村)旅游人数，有组织接待的旅游人数以及国际、国内旅游收入。

二、本篇资料是国家统计局贸易外经司根据公安部和国家旅游局的资料编制的。资料来源: 入境国际旅游人数和出境居民人数来自公安部出、入境管理资料；各地区接待国际旅游者人数、旅行社接待国际旅游者人数、国内旅游人数和国内旅游收入来自国家旅游局；国际旅游外汇收入1994年以前由国家统计局贸易外经司根据国际旅游者在华花费外汇券统计资料整理提供；1994年及以后由国家旅游局整理提供；旅行社、涉外饭店基本情况来自国家旅游局。

三、旅游统计调查方法：国际、国内旅游收入和国内出游人数等指标采取抽样调查方法，其余指标均为全面调查统计取得。

Brief Introduction

I. Tourist statistics cover international and domestic tourism. The contents of this chapter include total number of international tourists received (foreigners, overseas Chinese, Chinese compatriots from Hong Kong, Macao and Taiwan), Chinese residents going abroad, domestic tourists (from urban and from rural areas), tourists participating in organized tours, and income from international and domestic tourism.

II. Statistics in this chapter are compiled by the Department of Trade and Foreign Economic Relations of the National Bureau of Statistics on the basis of data from the Ministry of Public Security and State Tourism Administration. Sources of data are as follows: number of international tourists entering into China and Chinese residents going abroad is provided by the Frontier Administration of the Ministry of Public Security; number of international tourists received by province, number of international tourists received by travel agency, number of domestic tourists and earnings from domestic tourism are provided by the State Tourism Administration; figures on the earnings from international tourism before 1994 are provided by the Department of Trade and Foreign Economic Relations Statistics of the National Bureau of Statistics using data on the expenditure of Foreign Exchange Certificates by international tourists, and since 1994, by the State Tourism Administration; data on basic situation of travel agencies and tourist hotels are provided the State Tourism Administration.

III. Data collection approaches: data on the earnings from international and domestic tourism and domestic tourists are collected from sample surveys, while statistics on other items are from administrative reports.

18-1 旅游事业发展情况

Development of Tourism

指　　标	Item	1996	1997	1998	1999	2000
旅行社总数　（个）	**Total Number of Travel Agencies**	**4252**	**4986**	**6222**	**7326**	**8993**
国际旅行社	International Travel Agencies	977	991	1312	1256	1268
国内旅行社	Domestic Travel Agencies	3275	3995	4910	6070	7725
旅行社职工人数(人)	**Number of Staff and Workers of Travel Agencies (person)**	**87555**	**94829**	**100448**	**108830**	**164336**
国际旅行社	International Travel Agencies	53093	48881	52290	47153	68093
国内旅行社	Domestic Travel Agencies	34462	45948	48158	61677	96243
涉外饭店总数　（个）	**Total Number of Tourist Hotel**	**4418**	**5201**	**5782**	**7035**	**10481**
入境旅游人数（万人）	**Total Number of International Tourists Arrival to China (10 000 persons)**	**5112.75**	**5758.79**	**6347.84**	**7279.56**	**8344.39**
外国人	Foreigners	674.43	742.80	710.77	843.23	1016.04
华　侨	Overseas Chinese	15.46	9.90	12.07	10.81	7.55
港澳同胞	Compatriots from Hong Kong and Macao	4249.47	4794.33	5407.54	6167.06	7009.94
台湾同胞	Compatriots from Taiwan	173.39	211.76	217.46	258.46	310.86
三大旅行社接待入境旅游人数(万人)	**Number of International Tourists Received by Three Major Travel Service (10 000 persons)**	**171.46**	**189.68**	**167.00**	**205.11**	**223.30**
中国国际旅行社	China International Travel Service	80.80	88.45	77.45	100.25	91.16
中国旅行社	China Travel Service	59.25	66.94	53.79	65.10	88.32
中国青年旅行社	China Youth Travel Service	31.41	34.29	35.76	39.76	43.82
国内居民出境总人数（万人）	**Total Number of Domestic Resident Outbound (10 000 persons)**	**758.82**	**817.54**	**842.56**	**923.24**	**1047.26**
#因私出境人数	For Private Purpose	241.39	243.96	319.02	426.61	563.09
国内旅游人数(万人)	**Total Number of Domestic Tourists (10 000 persons)**	**63900**	**64400**	**69450**	**71900**	**74400**
旅游收入	**Receipts of Tourism**					
国际旅游收入（亿美元）	International Tourism Receipts (USD 100 million)	102.00	120.74	126.02	140.99	162.24
国内旅游收入（亿元）	Domestic Tourism Receipts (100 million yuan)	1638.38	2112.70	2391.18	2831.92	3175.54

18-2 各地区旅行社单位数和职工人数（2000年底）

Number of Travel Agencies and Staff and Workers by Region (End of 2000)

地区	Region	旅行社数（个）Total Number of Travel Agencies	国际旅行社 International Travel Agencies	国内旅行社 Domestic Travel Agencies	旅行社职工人数（人）Number of Staff and Workers of Travel Agencies	国际旅行社 International Travel Agencies	国内旅行社 Domestic Travel Agencies
全　国	**National Total**	**8993**	**1268**	**7725**	**164336**	**68093**	**96243**
北　京	Beijing	452	155	297	9755	6677	3078
天　津	Tianjin	196	19	177	3339	693	2646
河　北	Hebei	384	34	350	4196	812	3384
山　西	Shanxi	198	16	182	3265	574	2691
内蒙古	Inner Mongolia	91	25	66	1232	672	560
辽　宁	Liaoning	504	49	455	5245	1421	3824
吉　林	Jilin	116	35	81	1593	768	825
黑龙江	Heilongjiang	323	51	272	3651	1363	2288
上　海	Shanghai	478	40	438	8504	2496	6008
江　苏	Jiangsu	636	69	567	9262	3232	6030
浙　江	Zhejiang	540	46	494	9362	2426	6936
安　徽	Anhui	333	36	297	3848	873	2975
福　建	Fujian	338	36	302	7155	2943	4212
江　西	Jiangxi	224	19	205	2632	452	2180
山　东	Shandong	667	50	617	8368	1536	6832
河　南	Henan	430	28	402	4894	1122	3772
湖　北	Hubei	294	28	266	6519	3484	3035
湖　南	Hunan	245	29	216	4476	1353	3123
广　东	Guangdong	498	174	324	24212	16328	7884
广　西	Guangxi	260	49	211	5135	2219	2916
海　南	Hainan	152	39	113	4454	2551	1903
重　庆	Chongqing	190	20	170	4201	1420	2781
四　川	Sichuan	384	41	343	7335	2594	4741
贵　州	Guizhou	107	13	94	1459	538	921
云　南	Yunnan	369	41	328	9219	3736	5483
西　藏	Tibet	34	19	15	713	584	129
陕　西	Shaanxi	234	31	203	5278	2464	2814
甘　肃	Gansu	94	20	74	1701	952	749
青　海	Qinghai	62	9	53	674	356	318
宁　夏	Ningxia	29	8	21	414	188	226
新　疆	Xinjiang	131	39	92	2245	1266	979

18-3 各地区按经济类型分的涉外饭店个数（2000年底）

Number of Tourist Hotels by Ownership and Regions (End of 2000)

单位：个 (unit)

地区	Region	涉外饭店个数 Total Number of Tourist Hotels	国有 State-owned	集体 Collective owned	私营 Private	联营 Joint Ownership	有限责任 Ltd. Liability Co.	股份合作 Cooperative	股份有限 Shareholding Co.	其它内资 Other Domestic Funds	外商投资 Foreign Funded	港澳台投资 Funded from Hong Kong, Macao and Taiwan
全国	**National Total**	**10481**	**6646**	**1280**	**324**	**176**	**383**	**69**	**395**	**375**	**414**	**419**
北京	Beijing	522	318	61	5	12	28	10	15	3	35	35
天津	Tianjin	121	66	18	1		1			3	2	30
河北	Hebei	225	209	2						10	2	2
山西	Shanxi	184	113	18	16	1	12	1	9	12	2	
内蒙古	Inner Mongolia	168	155	7					1		1	4
辽宁	Liaoning	431	261	43	13	4	13	1	23	1	33	39
吉林	Jilin	218	174	8	1		1	1	9		3	21
黑龙江	Heilongjiang	196	37	2	2	1	4			146	4	
上海	Shanghai	354	183	59	3	19	30	3	17	21	18	1
江苏	Jiangsu	803	592	73	7	11	18	1	30	28	22	21
浙江	Zhejiang	594	272	114	18	10	34	5	86	21	20	14
安徽	Anhui	274	205	20	5	3	4	1	15	1	10	10
福建	Fujian	401	189	71	12	16	23	4	10	4	42	30
江西	Jiangxi	204	173	12	6				1	1	7	4
山东	Shandong	558	437	40	4	7	9	4	13	5	12	27
河南	Henan	275	209	25	26		4	2	2		5	2
湖北	Hubei	497	399	41	6	4	1		20		14	12
湖南	Hunan	332	226	69		7	2	1	9		4	14
广东	Guangdong	1506	790	257	70	48	66	12	30	50	126	57
广西	Guangxi	403	253	50	6	2	40	2	12	3	18	17
海南	Hainan	379	130	54	48	16	11	4	49	20	9	38
重庆	Chongqing	111	51	8	9		7	1	6	19	3	7
四川	Sichuan	408	240	47	32	4	29	9	19	12	10	6
贵州	Guizhou	80	75				1		1	1	1	1
云南	Yunnan	629	408	98	22	11	39	6	12	11	9	13
西藏	Tibet	61	22	35	3				1			
陕西	Shaanxi	155	135	6	2				2	1	1	8
甘肃	Gansu	94	92									2
青海	Qinghai	27	27									
宁夏	Ningxia	38	34		1					2		1
新疆	Xinjiang	233	171	42	6		6	1	3		1	3

18-4 各地区按规模分的涉外饭店个数（2000年底）

Number of Tourist Hotels by Capacity and Regions (End of 2000)

单位：个 (unit)

地区	Region	涉外饭店个数 Total Number of Tourist Hotel	客房总数500间以上 with 500 Rooms and Over	客房总数300-499间 with 300-499 Rooms	客房总数200-299间 with 200-299 Rooms	客房总数100-199间 with 100-199 Rooms	客房总数99间以下 with Less than 100 Rooms
全　国	**National Total**	**10481**	**129**	**309**	**547**	**1926**	**7570**
北　京	Beijing	522	22	51	51	130	268
天　津	Tianjin	121	1	7	9	35	69
河　北	Hebei	225	1	6	14	45	159
山　西	Shanxi	184		4	3	30	147
内蒙古	Inner Mongolia	168	1	2	3	18	144
辽　宁	Liaoning	431	6	14	20	86	305
吉　林	Jilin	218	2	6	5	33	172
黑龙江	Heilongjiang	196		5	11	37	143
上　海	Shanghai	354	17	31	42	102	162
江　苏	Jiangsu	803	3	19	37	134	610
浙　江	Zhejiang	594	6	14	35	176	363
安　徽	Anhui	274		2	11	74	187
福　建	Fujian	401	4	10	16	54	317
江　西	Jiangxi	204		2	11	35	156
山　东	Shandong	558	5	9	36	119	389
河　南	Henan	275	1		4	44	226
湖　北	Hubei	497	1	9	20	76	391
湖　南	Hunan	332	2	5	8	36	281
广　东	Guangdong	1506	29	42	77	190	1168
广　西	Guangxi	403	4	16	24	72	287
海　南	Hainan	379	5	10	22	37	305
重　庆	Chongqing	111	1	5	8	37	60
四　川	Sichuan	408	1	11	24	106	266
贵　州	Guizhou	80	1	1	6	16	56
云　南	Yunnan	629	7	8	22	63	529
西　藏	Tibet	61	3	1	1	7	49
陕　西	Shaanxi	155	5	6	5	25	114
甘　肃	Gansu	94	1	5	6	25	57
青　海	Qinghai	27		1	2	7	17
宁　夏	Ningxia	38			1	16	21
新　疆	Xinjiang	233		7	13	61	152

18-5 国际旅游外汇收入及构成

Foreign Exchange Earnings and It's Composition

单位：百万美元 (USD 1 million)

指标	Item	1999 数额 Value	1999 比重 Percentage (%)	2000 数额 Value	2000 比重 Percentage (%)
总计	**Total**	**14099**	**100.0**	**16224**	**100.0**
长途交通	Long Distance Transportation	4165	29.6	4880	30.1
民航	Air	3140	22.3	3502	21.6
铁路	Railway	445	3.2	596	3.7
汽车	Highway	382	2.7	596	3.7
轮船	Waterway	198	1.4	186	1.1
游览	Visiting	749	5.3	751	4.6
住宿	Accommodation	2034	14.4	2205	13.6
餐饮	Food and Beverage	1528	10.8	1523	9.4
商品销售	Shopping	2771	19.7	3231	19.9
娱乐	Entertainment	845	6.0	1193	7.3
邮电通讯	Post and Communication Services	411	2.9	503	3.1
市内交通	Local Transportation	533	3.8	534	3.3
其他服务	Other Service	1063	7.5	1404	8.7

18-6 接待外国旅游人数（按性别、年龄和职业分）

Number of International Tourists by Sex, Age and Occupation

单位：万人 (10 000 persons)

指标	Item	1990	1995	1996	1997	1998	1999	2000
总　计	**Total**	**174.73**	**588.67**	**674.43**	**742.80**	**710.77**	**843.23**	**1016.04**
按性别分	**By Sex**							
男	Male	112.17	404.94	463.75	501.39	481.79	553.07	655.97
女	Female	62.56	183.73	211.68	241.41	228.98	290.16	360.07
按年龄分	**By Age**							
14岁及以下	14 and under					24.05	29.03	35.71
15至24岁	15-24					61.70	67.86	82.43
25至44岁	25-44					355.91	413.80	494.44
45至64岁	45-64					229.54	282.44	343.53
65岁以上	65 and over					39.57	50.10	59.93
按职业分	**By Occupation**							
专业技术人员	Technicians	31.50	48.27	48.43	59.95	42.64	48.79	77.17
行政管理人员	Administrators	30.66	45.33	45.42	45.04	65.71	68.45	48.84
商　人	Businessmen	36.96	117.17	117.88	131.45	135.33	151.84	171.10
办事员	Office Clerks		43.09	43.92	50.80	43.93	42.11	47.94
服务人员	Service Clerks		46.86	43.60	49.93	33.53	33.00	54.94
工人、农民	Workers and Farmers	33.34	59.80	57.89	51.97	47.87	51.53	52.49
其他职业人员	Others	23.27	146.06	181.27	228.72	291.77	385.57	500.33
无职业人员	Freemen	19.00	82.09	136.02	124.94	49.99	61.94	63.23

18-7 接待外国旅游人数（按国别分）

Number of International Tourists by Country

单位：万人 (10 000 persons)

国　别	Country	1990	1995	1996	1997	1998	1999	2000
总　计	**Total**	**174.73**	**588.67**	**674.43**	**742.80**	**710.77**	**843.23**	**1016.04**
亚洲	**Asia**	**91.52**	**338.26**	**406.51**	**428.17**	**400.06**	**499.27**	**610.16**
#朝鲜	Democratic People's Republic of Korea	2.79	6.64	6.34	7.14	6.12	6.98	7.64
印度	India	1.43	4.50	5.51	6.05	6.57	8.42	12.09
印度尼西亚	Indonesia	2.69	13.28	13.78	14.73	10.46	18.29	22.06
日本	Japan	46.33	130.52	154.88	158.17	157.21	185.52	220.15
马来西亚	Malaysia	3.68	25.18	29.85	36.13	30.01	37.29	44.10
蒙古	Mongolia	1.79	26.19	28.19	34.29	26.48	35.45	39.91
菲律宾	the Philippines	7.89	21.97	24.37	27.67	25.65	29.83	36.39
新加坡	Singapore	7.17	26.15	28.63	31.68	31.64	35.25	39.94
韩国	Republic of Korea		52.95	69.39	78.11	63.28	99.20	134.47
泰国	Thailand	6.79	17.33	19.33	16.85	14.43	20.64	24.11
非洲	**Africa**	**1.17**	**4.08**	**4.72**	**4.91**	**5.43**	**5.21**	**6.57**
欧洲	**Europe**	**44.63**	**159.06**	**163.30**	**201.83**	**181.33**	**211.27**	**249.05**
#英国	United Kingdom	7.89	18.49	20.52	22.79	24.29	25.89	28.39
德国	Federal Republic of Germany	5.62	16.65	17.90	18.47	19.19	21.76	23.91
法国	France	5.07	11.85	12.33	13.13	13.80	15.56	18.50
意大利	Italy	2.63	6.37	6.21	6.51	7.25	7.22	7.78
荷兰	Netherlands	1.38	3.49	4.13	5.23	5.89	7.01	7.60
葡萄牙	Portugal	0.95	2.56	2.46	3.58	3.85	4.02	2.28
瑞典	Sweden	1.05	3.52	3.42	3.85	4.06	4.68	5.36
瑞士	Switzerland	1.15	3.43	3.34	3.03	2.84	2.99	3.07
哈萨克	Kazakhstan		9.92	8.41	9.49	9.60	6.87	6.71
俄罗斯	Russia	10.98	48.93	55.59	81.37	69.20	83.30	108.02
拉丁美洲	**Latin America**	**2.36**	**5.37**	**7.62**	**7.66**	**7.46**	**7.59**	**8.43**
北美洲	**North America**	**28.08**	**64.36**	**73.30**	**79.05**	**87.33**	**95.01**	**113.27**
#加拿大	Canada	4.76	12.88	15.66	17.41	19.60	21.37	23.65
美国	United States	23.32	51.49	57.64	61.64	67.73	73.64	89.62
大洋洲及太平洋岛屿	**Oceanic and Pacific Islands**	**6.35**	**15.85**	**17.34**	19.35	**22.48**	**24.38**	**28.24**
#澳大利亚	Australia	5.02	12.94	13.27	15.68	18.64	20.35	23.41
新西兰	New Zealand	1.00	2.29	3.02	2.83	3.00	3.14	3.76
其他	**Others**	**0.62**	**1.69**	**1.64**	**1.83**	**0.68**	**0.50**	**0.32**

注：俄罗斯1990年的数据为前苏联数据。

a)The data of Russia in 1990 referred to the data of former USSR.

18-8 各地区国际旅游外汇收入

Foreign Exchange Earnings by Region

单位：百万美元 (USD million)

地　区	Region	1990	1995	1996	1997	1998	1999	2000
北　京	Beijing	658	2182	2252	2248	2384	2496	2768
天　津	Tianjin	23	133	152	180	202	209	232
河　北	Hebei	5	42	74	97	100	124	142
山　西	Shanxi	5	21	27	37	38	43	50
内蒙古	Inner Mongolia	1	91	94	107	126	120	126
辽　宁	Liaoning	69	189	224	260	262	304	383
吉　林	Jilin	6	41	53	59	38	45	58
黑龙江	Heilongjiang	7	61	78	105	121	148	189
上　海	Shanghai	230	939	1171	1317	1218	1364	1613
江　苏	Jiangsu	71	260	317	408	529	620	724
浙　江	Zhejiang	54	236	292	345	361	410	514
安　徽	Anhui	5	31	42	64	51	67	86
福　建	Fujian	101	484	555	614	651	725	894
江　西	Jiangxi	3	25	34	45	43	50	62
山　东	Shandong	36	154	196	204	220	265	315
河　南	Henan	6	60	73	95	101	114	124
湖　北	Hubei	22	73	125	170	88	105	146
湖　南	Hunan	10	65	101	140	156	185	221
广　东	Guangdong	713	2393	2638	2801	2942	3272	4112
广　西	Guangxi	76	121	154	178	156	202	307
海　南	Hainan	27	81	85	102	96	105	109
重　庆	Chongqing				105	88	97	138
四　川	Sichuan	36	125	162	79	84	97	122
贵　州	Guizhou	1	29	38	44	48	55	61
云　南	Yunnan	16	165	221	264	261	350	339
西　藏	Tibet		11	30	32	33	36	52
陕　西	Shaanxi	41	139	198	225	247	272	280
甘　肃	Gansu	6	21	19	28	30	37	55
青　海	Qinghai		2	2	3	3	4	7
宁　夏	Ningxia		1	1	1	1	2	3
新　疆	Xinjiang	12	74	68	71	82	86	95

注：1990年外汇收入是将当年人民币外汇券收入按当年人民币对美元平均汇价折算。

a)Foreign exchange earnings in 1990 were calculated to the RMB Foreign Exchange Certificate by the average exchange rate of the year.

18-9 各地区接待国际旅游人数

Number of International Tourists by Region

单位：万人次 (10 000 person-times)

地区	Region	1990 总计 Total	1990 # 外国人 Foreigners	1995 总计 Total	1995 # 外国人 Foreigners	1999 总计 Total	1999 # 外国人 Foreigners	2000 总计 Total	2000 # 外国人 Foreigners
北京	Beijing	100.07	63.75	206.87	166.52	252.39	205.02	282.09	237.96
天津	Tianjin	5.60	3.55	20.06	16.27	32.08	28.15	35.62	32.14
河北	Hebei	3.19	2.20	16.50	13.59	37.09	32.22	41.43	35.90
山西	Shanxi	4.68	2.70	7.12	5.15	13.78	10.11	16.53	11.66
内蒙古	Inner Mongolia	1.76	1.30	30.09	29.46	36.84	36.35	39.19	38.74
辽宁	Liaoning	11.41	7.48	26.38	21.46	49.13	38.63	61.22	50.05
吉林	Jilin	4.61	2.96	15.61	14.49	15.95	14.11	22.27	19.19
黑龙江	Heilongjiang	5.98	3.38	16.23	13.94	40.71	36.06	55.17	50.47
上海	Shanghai	89.30	46.06	136.79	107.54	165.68	128.73	181.40	143.90
江苏	Jiangsu	72.48	21.92	76.77	48.68	134.41	80.44	160.95	98.15
浙江	Zhejiang	45.58	10.77	67.27	36.65	94.78	50.67	112.59	64.75
安徽	Anhui	8.47	2.06	14.29	7.28	25.12	13.83	31.84	16.79
福建	Fujian	70.79	8.78	90.64	22.41	135.68	35.30	161.33	49.75
江西	Jiangxi	2.50	0.50	7.36	2.34	13.86	4.10	16.31	5.54
山东	Shandong	12.47	6.89	45.09	30.43	62.20	41.79	72.31	48.01
河南	Henan	6.95	2.74	21.84	9.12	30.01	16.03	32.50	18.21
湖北	Hubei	10.04	2.53	27.09	16.83	30.54	22.33	45.08	35.74
湖南	Hunan	8.52	1.65	17.73	7.18	38.58	13.48	45.40	15.79
广东	Guangdong	541.48	56.36	620.68	122.07	876.02	148.77	1198.94	212.85
广西	Guangxi	51.83	15.34	41.85	30.74	77.07	37.07	122.91	50.80
海南	Hainan	18.87	2.46	28.71	5.75	45.65	7.32	48.68	9.37
重庆	Chongqing					18.49	13.36	26.61	19.29
四川	Sichuan	19.39	6.29	37.67	24.51	37.34	17.95	46.20	19.97
贵州	Guizhou	2.41	0.74	13.66	7.79	16.70	6.57	18.39	7.12
云南	Yunnan	14.82	4.98	59.69	47.38	104.00	72.50	100.11	66.59
西藏	Tibet			6.78	6.54	10.08	9.26	15.00	13.58
陕西	Shaanxi	25.88	15.40	44.23	39.73	63.03	50.16	71.28	58.48
甘肃	Gansu	5.20	3.90	9.09	7.07	14.46	9.46	21.31	14.34
青海	Qinghai	0.55	0.41	1.33	0.87	2.05	0.89	3.26	1.46
宁夏	Ningxia	0.20	0.13	0.37	0.28	0.60	0.45	0.78	0.58
新疆	Xinjiang	7.98	6.43	20.36	18.55	22.38	19.02	25.61	20.84

18-10 三大旅行社接待国际旅游人数

Number of International Tourists Received by Major Travel Services

单位：万人 (10 000 persons)

年 份 Year	合 计 Total	中国国际旅行社 China International Travel Service	中国旅行社 China Travel Service	中国青年旅行社 China Youth Travel Service	占接待人数比重(%) Proportion to total (Total=100) 中国国际旅行社 China International Travel Service	中国旅行社 China Travel Service	中国青年旅行社 China Youth Travel Service
1978	68.64	12.46	56.18		18.15	81.85	
1979	97.24	16.59	80.61	0.04	17.06	82.90	0.04
1980	92.39	21.87	69.47	1.05	23.67	75.19	1.14
1981	118.19	26.83	88.59	2.77	22.70	74.96	2.34
1982	120.52	31.62	86.46	2.44	26.24	71.74	2.02
1983	125.68	32.00	90.75	2.93	25.46	22.21	2.33
1984	127.19	39.87	82.58	4.74	31.35	64.93	3.72
1985	129.39	46.88	77.33	5.18	36.23	59.77	4.00
1986	113.36	45.93	59.53	7.90	40.52	52.51	6.97
1987	147.80	50.50	84.77	12.53	34.17	57.35	8.48
1988	177.74	52.62	110.39	14.73	29.60	62.11	8.29
1989	108.07	13.78	84.31	9.98	12.75	78.02	9.23
1990	131.00	11.02	106.46	13.52	8.41	81.27	10.32
1991	170.98	48.79	106.59	15.60	28.54	62.34	9.12
1992	175.91	64.69	96.23	14.99	36.78	54.70	8.52
1993	170.13	74.07	82.02	14.04	43.54	48.21	8.25
1994	165.44	81.02	61.94	22.48	48.97	37.44	13.59
1995	162.86	84.65	47.74	30.47	51.98	29.31	18.71
1996	171.46	80.80	59.25	31.41	47.12	34.56	18.32
1997	189.68	88.45	66.94	34.29	46.63	35.29	18.08
1998	167.00	77.45	53.79	35.76	46.38	32.21	21.41
1999	205.11	100.25	65.10	39.76	48.88	31.74	19.38
2000	223.30	91.16	88.32	43.82	40.82	39.55	19.63

18-11 国内旅游情况

Conditions of Domestic Tourism

年 份 Year	总人次 (百万人次) Total (million person-times) 总计 Total	城镇居民 Urban Residents	农村居民 Rural Residents	总花费 (百万元) Total Expenditure (million yuan) 总计 Total	城镇居民 Urban Residents	农村居民 Rural Residents	人均花费 (元) Per Capita Expenditure (yuan) 总计 Total	城镇居民 Urban Residents	农村居民 Rural Residents
1994	524.00	204.55	319.45	102351	84821	17530	195.33	414.67	54.88
1995	629.00	245.70	383.30	137570	114010	23560	218.71	464.02	61.47
1996	639.50	256.20	383.30	163838	136836	27002	256.20	534.10	70.45
1997	644.00	259.00	385.00	211270	155183	56087	328.06	599.80	145.68
1998	695.00	250.00	445.00	239118	155113	87605	345.00	607.00	197.00
1999	719.00	284.00	435.00	283192	174823	108369	394.00	614.80	249.50
2000	744.00	329.00	415.00	317554	223526	94028	426.60	678.60	226.60

主 要 统 计 指 标 解 释

旅游者人数

⑴入境国际旅游者人数：指来中国参观、访问、旅行、探亲、访友、休养、考察、参加会议和从事经济、科技、文化、教育、宗教等活动的外国人、华侨、港澳同胞和台湾同胞的人数。不包括外国在我国的常驻机构，如使领馆、通讯社、企业办事处的工作人员；来我国常住的外国专家、留学生以及在岸逗留不过夜人员。

⑵出境居民人数：指大陆居民因公务活动或私人事务短期出境的人数。公务活动出境居民人数包括在国际交通工具上的中国服务员工，因私出境居民人数不包括在国际交通工具上的中国服务员工。

⑶国内旅游者人数：指我国大陆居民和在我国常住1年以上的外国人、华侨、港澳台同胞离开常住地在境内其他地方的旅游设施内至少停留一夜，最长不超过6个月的人数。

国际旅游(外汇)收入　指入境旅游的外国人、华侨、港澳同胞和台湾同胞在中国大陆旅游过程中发生的一切旅游支出，对于国家来说就是国际旅游(外汇)收入。

国际旅行社　指经营对外招徕并接待外国人、华侨、港澳同胞和台湾同胞来中国、归国或回内地旅游业务的旅行社。

国内旅行社　指负责经营招徕、组团、接待国内旅客的旅游业务，以及不对外招徕，负责经营接待国际旅行社或其它涉外部门组织的外国人、华侨、港澳同胞和台湾同胞来中国、归国或回内地的旅游业务的旅行社。

涉外饭店　指经有关部门批准，允许接待外国人、华侨、港澳同胞和台湾同胞的饭店。

Explanatory Notes on Main Statistical Indicators

Number of Tourists

(1) International tourists refer to foreigners, overseas Chinese, Chinese compatriots from Hong Kong, Macao and Taiwan coming to China for sight-seeing, visits, tours, family reunions, vacations, study tours, conferences and other activities of a business, scientific and technological, cultural, educational and religious nature. It does not include representatives and employees of resident institutions of foreign countries in China such as embassies, consulates, news agencies and offices of foreign companies and organizations, nor does it include long-term foreign experts or students residing in China, or persons in transition without spending a night in China.

(2) Chinese residents going abroad refer to Chinese residents going abroad for short terms for either public business or private purposes. Chinese employees working on international transport carriers are included in those going abroad for public business purpose, not in those for private purpose.

(3) Domestic tourists refer to residents of the mainland of China who stay for one night at least but no more than 6 months at tourist facilities in other places than their permanent residence within the territory of the mainland China, including foreigners, overseas Chinese and Chinese compatriots from Hong Kong, Macao and Taiwan who have resided in China for over one year.

Foreign Exchange Earnings from International Tourism refer to the total expenditures of foreigners, overseas Chinese, Chinese compatriots from Hong Kong, Macao and Taiwan during their stay in the mainland of China, which are earnings of foreign exchange from international tourism from the point of view from China.

International Travel Agencies refer to travel agencies engaged in the promotion, solicitation, organization and reception of tours to the mainland of China by foreigners, overseas Chinese, Chinese compatriots from Hong Kong, Macao and Taiwan.

Domestic Travel Agencies refer to travel agencies engaged in the promotion, solicitation, organization and reception of domestic tourists, and in the reception of foreigners, overseas Chinese, Chinese compatriots from Hong Kong, Macao and Taiwan organized by international travel agencies or other departments concerned, without their own promotion and solicitation programmes.

Tourist Hotels refer to hotels that are able, with the approval of departments concerned, to accommodate foreigners, overseas Chinese, Chinese compatriots from Hong Kong, Macao and Taiwan Province.

十九、金融和保险

Banking and Insurance

简要说明

一、本篇反映近十年来我国金融、证券和保险业发展情况。有以下五个部分：一是银行系统机构人员，二是金融机构金融活动情况，三是存贷款利率调整情况，四是直接融资情况，五是保险业务情况。

二、各部分资料来源

1.反映金融机构人员情况的表是"19-1银行系统机构、人员数"，由中国人民银行总行人事部门根据有关的行政记录汇总和填报。

2.反映金融机构活动情况的资料包括："19-2金融机构信贷资金平衡表(资金来源)"，"19-3金融机构信贷资金平衡表(资金运用)"，"19-4金融机构现金收入"，"19-5金融机构现金支出"，"19-6金融机构现金投放回笼差额"，"19-7黄金和外汇储备"。金融机构信贷资金平衡表及现金收支表的统计范围包括中国人民银行、国家政策性银行、国有商业银行、其他商业银行、城市信用合作社、农村信用合作社、财务公司、信托投资公司、金融租赁公司、邮政储蓄机构。中国人民银行总行根据金融机构的基层单位全面填报、并按各自系统汇总的资料，进行归并和汇总，最后得到金融机构的信贷收支及现金收支表。黄金和外汇储备表中的资料取自于中国人民银行的资产负债表，由该行有关部门提供。

3.反映存贷款利率调整情况的"19-8金融机构法定存款利率表"和"19-9金融机构法定贷款利率表"，数据来自中国人民银行总行规定的、并对外发布的存贷款利率。

4.反映直接融资情况的"19-10国内有价证券分类发行情况"、"19-11上市公司数量一览表"、"19-12股票发行筹集情况"、"19-13股票交易统计表"，资料取自中国证券管理委员会编制的《中国证券统计年报》。

5.反映保险业务情况的"19-14保险公司业务经济技术指标"、"19-15保险系统机构、人员数"，数据取自中国保险监察管理委员会编制的保险统计资料。

Brief Introduction

I. Data in this chapter show the development of China's banking, securities and insurance, including the following 5 parts: (1) The number of the institutions and personnel in the banking system; (2) The financial activities of banking institutions; (3) The changes of the interest rates of the deposits and loans; (4) The direct financing; (5) The business of insurance.

II.Sources of data:

(1) Table 19-1 showing the number of banking institutions and personnel are prepared by the personnel departments of the Headquarter of the People's Bank of China on the basis of the related administrative registers.

(2) Tables 19-2 to 19-7 shows the banking activities of banks and rural credit cooperatives. The statistics cover the balance table of the credit funds and the tables on the cash revenue and expenditure of the banking institutions include the People's Bank of China, the state policy banks, the state-owned commercial banks, other commercial banks, urban and rural credit cooperatives, financing corporations, trust investment corporations, financing and leasing corporations, and savings deposit institutions under the postal offices. The grassroots units of the above banking institutions fill out the questionnaires and report to the higher authorities. The higher authorities tabulate the data level by level. Finally, the Department of Investigation and Statistics of the Head Office of the People's Bank of China tabulate the data and get the national total. The data in the table on the gold and foreign exchange reserves are extracted from the balance sheet of the People's Bank of China and provided by its concerned department.

(3) Tables 19-8 and 19-9 show the changes of the interest rates. Data are collected from the interest rates of deposits and loans stipulated and published by the Head Office of the People's Bank of China.

(4) Tables 19-10 to 19-13 shows the direct fund raising. The data are collected from the "Annual Statistical Report on China's Securities" compiled by China Securities Regulatory Commission.

(5) Tables 19-14 and 19-15 shows the business of insurance, with data coming from the insurance statistics compiled by China Insurance Regulatory Commission.

19-1 银行系统机构、人员数（2000年底）

Number of Institutions and Employed Persons in Finance System (End of 2000)

项　目	Item	机构数 Number of Institutions	年末人数 Number of Staff and Workers	# 女性 Female
总　计	**Total**	**130170**	**1937136**	**796275**
中国人民银行	The People's Bank of China	2222	169302	53368
中国工商银行	Industrial and Commercial Bank of China	31673	471097	208498
中国农业银行	Agricultural Bank of China	50546	509572	165524
中国银行	Bank of China	12925	192279	86797
中国建设银行	Construction Bank of China	25763	427566	213783
中国农业发展银行	Agricultural Development Bank of China	2241	58833	18059
交通银行	Bank of Communications	2881	47121	22437
中国进出口银行	Export Import Bank of China	1	469	182
浦东发展银行	Shanghai Pudong Development Bank	194	4680	2207
国家开发银行	National Development Bank	30	2995	1145
中信实业银行	CITIC Industrial Bank	293	7733	3459
中国光大银行	China Everbright Bank	32	6456	3084
中国民生银行	China Minsheng Banking Corp., Ltd	74	2124	1034
华夏银行	China Huaxia Bank	17	4480	2093
招商银行	China Merchants Bank	249	11077	4850
广东发展银行	Guangdong Development Bank	541	10352	4632
福建兴业银行	Fujiang Industrial Bank	246	5105	2413
深圳发展银行	Shenzhen Development Bank Co., Ltd	163	4533	1993
烟台住房储蓄银行	Yantai House Saving Bank	79	1362	717

19-2 金融机构信贷资金平衡表(资金来源)

Credit Funds Balance Sheet of Financial Institutions (Sources of Funds)

(年末余额) 单位：亿元　　　　(year-end) (100 million yuan)

项　目	Item	1999	2000
资金来源合计	**All Sources**	**123230.6**	**135483.7**
各项存款	Deposits	108778.9	123804.4
企业存款	Deposits of Enterprises	37182.4	44093.7
财政存款	Treasury Deposits	2128.1	3508.1
机关团体存款	Deposits of Government Agencies and Organizations	1814.5	2224.3
城乡储蓄存款	Urban and Rural Savings Deposits	59621.8	64332.4
农业存款	Agricultural Deposits	2126.3	2642.9
信托类存款	Trusted Deposits	3072.2	2873.6
其他类存款	Other Deposits	2833.7	4129.4
金融债券	Bonds	39.5	30.2
对国际金融机构负债	Liabilities to International Financial Institutions	371.9	368.3
货币流通量	Currency in Circulation	13455.5	14652.7
其　他	Others	584.8	-3371.9

注：金融机构包括人民银行、政策性银行、国有独资商业银行、邮政储蓄机构、其他商业银行、城市合作银行、农村信用社、城市信用社、信托投资公司、租赁公司、财务公司等。

a) Financial Institutions include banks, savings deposit agencies of postal offices, housing saving banks, urban credit cooperative banks, rural credit cooperatives, urban credit banks, financial trust investment agencies and financial companies etc.

19-3 金融机构信贷资金平衡表(资金运用)

Credit Funds Balance Sheet of Financial Institutions (Uses of Funds)

(年末余额) 单位：亿元 (year-end) (100 million yuan)

项目	Item	1999	2000
资金运用合计	**All Uses**	**123230.6**	**135483.7**
各项贷款	Loans	93734.3	99371.1
短期贷款	Short-term Loans	63887.6	65748.1
工业贷款	Industrial Loans	17948.9	17019.3
商业贷款	Commercial Loans	19890.9	17868.5
建筑业贷款	Construction Loans	1476.9	1617.1
农业贷款	Agricultural Loans	4792.4	4889.0
乡镇企业贷款	Loans to Township Enterprises	6161.3	6060.8
私营企业及个体贷款	Loans to Private Enterprises and Individuals	579.1	654.6
三资企业贷款	Loans to Sino-foreign Joint Venture and Cooperative Enterprises and Foreign-funded Enterprises	2985.8	3049.8
其他短期贷款	Other Short-term Loans	10052.4	14589.0
中长期贷款	Medium-term & Long-term Loans	23968.3	27931.2
信托类贷款	Credit Loans	2504.6	2409.7
其他类贷款	Other Loans	3373.8	3282.1
有价证券及投资	Securities & Investment	12505.8	19651.1
在国际金融机构资产	Assets in International Financial Institutions	604.1	576.3
金银占款	Purchase of Gold & Silver	12.0	12.0
外汇占款	Purchase of Foreign Exchanges	14792.4	14291.1
财政借款	Government Debt	1582.1	1582.1

19-4 货币供应量(年底数)

Money Supply at the Year-end

单位:亿元 (100 million yuan)

年份 Year	货币和准货币(M_2) Money and Quasi-Money (M_2)	货币(M_1) Money (M_1)	流通中现金(M_0) Currency in Circulation (M_0)
1990	15293.4	6950.7	2644.4
1991	19349.9	8633.3	3177.8
1992	25402.2	11731.5	4336.0
1993	34879.8	16280.4	5864.7
1994	46923.5	20540.7	7288.6
1995	60750.5	23987.1	7885.3
1996	76094.9	28514.8	8802.0
1997	90995.3	34826.3	10177.6
1998	104498.5	38953.7	11204.2
1999	119897.9	45837.2	13455.5
2000	134610.3	53147.2	14652.7

注:1.1992年以前为国家银行与农村信用社统计口径。
2.1992年以后统计范围为《银行概览》统计口径。

a)The statistics coverage is according to China National Bank and Rural Credit Union before 1992.
b)The statistics coverage is according to *Banking Survey* since 1992.

19-5 金融机构现金收入

Cash Income of Financial Institutions

单位：亿元 (100 million yuan)

项目	Item	1999	2000
收入总计	**Total Income**	**233399.0**	**277067.1**
商品销售收入	Income from Commodity Sales	27731.1	32593.1
服务业收入	Income from Service Trade	11387.6	13316.4
税款收入	Income from Taxes	1387.3	1585.8
城乡个体经营收入	Income from Urban and Rural Individual Business	9068.0	10651.9
储蓄存款收入	Income from Savings Deposits	154778.3	183022.8
其他金融机构收入	Income from Other Financial Institutions	2391.8	3059.5
居民归还贷款收入	Income from Repayment of Loans by Residents	3597.3	4077.8
汇兑收入	Income from Remittances	4577.4	5935.3
有价证券收入	Income from Securities	1421.5	1917.5
其他收入	Other Income	17058.8	20907.0
#兑换外币收入	Income from Exchange of Foreign Currencies	178.8	207.0

19-6 金融机构现金支出

Cash Expenditures of Financial Institutions

单位：亿元 (100 million yuan)

项　　目	Item	1999	2000
支出合计	**Total**	**235650.4**	**278264.3**
工资性支出	Wages	19001.9	20397.9
农副产品采购支出	Purchases of Agricultural and Sideline Products	5863.4	7126.0
工矿及其他产品采购支出	Expenditure for Purchases of Industrial and Mineral Products	3962.6	4653.2
行政企事业管理费支出	Government and Enterprises Overhead	12901.7	15298.2
城乡个体经营支出	Expenditure for Individual Business	11438.1	13318.5
储蓄存款支出	Expenditure for Savings Deposits	154844.1	184907.0
其他金融机构支出	Expenditure for Other Financial Institutions	1977.4	2105.6
居民提取贷款支出	Expenditure for Loans by Residents	3396.1	3977.1
汇兑支出	Expenditure for Remittances	3080.5	3789.8
有价证券支出	Expenditure for Securities	1126.5	1303.7
其他支出	Other Expenditure	18058.3	21387.2

19-7 金融机构现金投放回笼差额

Cash Statistics of Financial Institutions

单位：亿元 (100 million yuan)

年　　份 Year	现金收入 Cash Income	现金支出 Cash Expenditures	投　　放 Currency Issuance
1957	516.7	512.2	-4.5
1962	633.2	614.0	-19.2
1965	675.7	686.5	10.8
1970	812.8	799.3	-13.5
1975	1128.2	1134.2	6.0
1978	1336.0	1352.6	16.6
1979			
1980	2033.2	2111.7	78.5
1981			
1982			
1983			
1984			
1985	5499.1	5694.8	195.7
1986	6613.3	6843.9	230.6
1987	8779.6	9015.7	236.1
1988	12810.5	13490.0	679.5
1989	15057.6	15267.6	210.0
1990	17171.1	17471.4	300.4
1991	21465.1	21998.5	533.4
1992	31248.0	32406.2	1158.2
1993	48883.8	50412.5	1528.7
1994	71247.1	72671.0	1423.9
1995	96725.5	97322.3	596.8
1996	120263.3	121179.9	916.6
1997	141612.6	142988.3	1375.7
1998	203966.5	204993.1	1026.6
1999	233399.0	235650.37	2251.3
2000	277067.1	278264.27	1197.2

注：投放栏中的负数表示现金回笼。

a)The negative amount in currency issuance indicates the amount of cash withdrawn.

19-8 黄金和外汇储备

Gold and Foreign Exchange Reserves

年份 Year	黄金储备 (万盎司) Gold Reserve (10 000 Ounces)	外汇储备 (亿美元) Foreign Exchange Reserve (USD 100 million)	年份 Year	黄金储备 (万盎司) Gold Reserve (10 000 ounces)	外汇储备 (亿美元) Foreign Exchange Reserve (USD 100 million)
1978	1280	1.67	1990	1267	110.93
1979	1280	8.40	1991	1267	217.12
1980	1280	-12.96	1992	1267	194.43
1981	1267	27.08	1993	1267	211.99
1982	1267	69.86	1994	1267	516.20
1983	1267	89.01	1995	1267	735.97
1984	1267	82.20	1996	1267	1050.49
1985	1267	26.44	1997	1267	1398.90
1986	1267	20.72	1998	1267	1449.60
1987	1267	29.23	1999	1267	1546.75
1988	1267	33.72	2000	1267	1655.74
1989	1267	55.50			

19-9 金融机构法定存款利率

Nominal Interest Rates on Deposits of Financial Institutions

单位：年利率% (annual interest rate %)

项目	Item	1996.8.23 Aug. 23, 1996	1997.10.23 Oct. 23, 1997	1998.3.25 Mar. 25, 1998	1998.7.1 Jul. 1, 1998	1998.12.7 Dec. 7, 1998	1999.6.10 Jun. 10,1999
个人人民币储蓄存款	**Household Deposits**						
活期	Demand	1.98	1.71	1.71	1.44	1.44	0.99
定期	Time						
三个月	3 Months	3.33	2.88	2.88	2.79	2.79	1.98
半年	6 Months	5.40	4.14	4.14	3.96	3.33	2.16
一年	1 Year	7.47	5.67	5.22	4.77	3.78	2.25
二年	2 Year	7.92	5.94	5.58	4.86	3.96	2.43
三年	3 Year	8.28	6.21	6.21	4.95	4.14	2.70
五年	5 Year	9.00	6.66	6.66	5.22	4.50	2.88
企业单位	**Enterprises Deposits**						
活期	Demand	1.98	1.71	1.71	1.44	1.44	0.99
定期	Time						
三个月	3 Months	3.33	2.88	2.88	2.79	2.79	1.98
半年	6 Months	5.40	4.14	4.14	3.96	3.33	2.16
一年	1 Year	7.47	5.67	5.22	4.77	3.78	2.25
二年	2 Year	7.92	5.94	5.58	4.86	3.96	2.43
三年	3 Year	8.28	6.21	6.21	4.95	4.14	2.70
五年	5 Year	9.00	6.66	6.66	5.22	4.50	2.88
大额可转让定期存单	**CDs**						
1个月	1 months	2.70					
3个月	3 months	3.33	2.88	2.88	2.79	2.79	
6个月	6 months	5.40	4.14	4.14	3.96	3.33	
9个月	9 months	6.66					
12个月	12 months	7.47	5.67	5.22	4.77	3.78	

19-10 金融机构法定贷款利率表

Nominal Interest Rates on Loans of Financial Institutions

单位：年利率%　　(annual interest rate %)

项　　目	Item	1996.8.23 Aug. 23, 1996	1997.10.23 Oct. 23, 1997	1998.3.25 Mar. 25, 1998	1998.7.1 Jul. 1, 1998	1998.12.7 Dec. 7, 1998	1999.6.10 Jun. 10, 1999
流动资金贷款	**Working Capital Loans**						
一般流动资金	Ordinary						
六个月	6 Months	9.18	7.65	7.02	6.57	6.12	5.58
一年	1 Year	10.08	8.64	7.92	6.93	6.39	5.85
个体工商户贷款	Individuals Enterprise	①	②				
固定资产投资贷款	**Fixed Asset Investment Loans**						
技术改造贷款	Technical Innovation	③	③	③	③	③	③
基本建设贷款	Capital Construction						
一年以内及一年	1 Year or Less	10.08	8.64	7.92	6.93	6.12-6.39	5.58-5.85
一年以上至三年	3 Year or Less	10.98	9.36	9.00	7.11	6.66	5.94
三年以上至五年	5 Years or Less	11.70	9.90	9.72	7.65	7.20	6.03
五年以上	More than 5 Years	12.42	10.53	10.35	8.01	7.56	6.21

注：1．①指个体工商户贷款在10.08%基础上上浮10%。
　　2．②指个体工商户贷款在8.64%基础上上浮10%。
　　3．③指技术改造贷款与同档次基本建设贷款相同。

a)① Loan rates to self-employed persons in industry and commerce can be 10 higher than 10.08%.
b)② Loan rates to self-employed persons in industry and commerce can be 10 higher than 8.64%.
c)③ Loan rates of investment in innovation are same as loan rates on capital construction loans with corresponding maturity.

19-11 国内有价证券分类发行情况（2000年）

Issuance of Domestic Securities (2000)

单位：亿元　　(100 million yuan)

种　类	Kind	发行额 Total Value of Issued Securities	兑付额 Total Value of Redemption	年末余额 Balance (Year-end)
国债	National Debt	4657	1525	13674
#国库券	Treasury Bonds			
财政证券	Fiscal Bonds			
政策性金融债券	Policy Financial Bonds			
其他金融债	Other Financial Bonds			
企业债	Corporate Bonds	83	0	862
国家投资债	Government Investment Bonds			
国家投资公司债	Bonds Issued by Government Investment Company			
股票	Shares	117	979	

注：股票是指A种股票(不含A股可转换债券)，股票兑付额是指筹资额。
a)Shares refer to A shares. The figure shown under the column "total value of redemption" for shares refers to the capital raised.

19-12 上市公司数量一览表

Summary for Number of Listed Companies

单位：个　　(unit)

年份 Year	全国合计 National	上交所 Shanghai Stock Exchange	深交所 Shenzhen Stock Exchange	仅发A股公司 A share Only	发A、H股公司 A&H Share	发A、B股公司 A&B Share	仅发B股公司 B Share Only
1990	10	8	2	10			
1991	14	8	6	14			
1992	53	29	24	53		18	
1993	183	106	77	183	3	34	6
1994	291	171	120	227	6	54	4
1995	323	188	135	242	11	58	12
1996	530	293	237	431	14	69	16
1997	745	383	362	627	17	76	25
1998	851	438	413	727	18	80	26
1999	949	484	465	822	19	82	26
2000	1088	572	516	955	19	86	28

19-13 股票发行筹资情况

Issuing Summary for Stocks

年份 Year	股票发行量 (亿股) Amount Issued (billion shares)	A 股 A Shares	H股，N股 H,N Shares	B 股 B Shares	股票筹资额 (亿元) Raised Capital (billion yuan)	A 股 A Shares	H股,N股 H & N Shares	B 股 B Shares	AB股配股筹资 A&B Shares Rights Issued
1991	5.00	5.00			5.00	5.00			
1992	20.75	10.00		10.75	94.09	50.00		44.09	
1993	95.79	42.59	40.41	12.79	375.47	194.83	60.93	38.13	81.58
1994	91.26	10.97	69.89	10.40	326.78	49.62	188.73	38.27	50.16
1995	31.60	5.32	15.38	10.90	150.32	22.68	31.46	33.35	62.83
1996	86.11	38.29	31.77	16.05	425.08	224.45	83.56	47.18	69.89
1997	267.63	105.65	136.88	25.10	1293.82	655.06	360.00	80.76	198.00
1998	105.56	86.30	12.86	9.90	841.52	443.05	37.95	25.55	334.97
1999	122.93	98.11	23.05	1.77	944.56	572.63	47.17	3.79	320.97
2000	512.03	145.68	7.10	359.25	2103.08	1007.41	562.21	13.99	519.46

19-14 股票交易统计表

Trading Summary for Stocks

项 目	Item	1994	1995	1996	1997	1998	1999	2000
会员总数	**No. of Members**	**1046**	**1085**	**1066**	**840**	**659**	**628**	**631**
上市公司数目	No. Of listed Companies	291	323	530	745	851	949	1088
上市股票数目	No. Of listed Stocks	345	381	599	821	931	1029	1174
A股	A Shares	287	311	514	720	825	922	1060
B股	B Shares	58	70	85	101	106	108	114
股票总发行股本（亿股）	**Total Issued Capital (100 million share)**	**684.54**	**848.42**	**1219.54**	**1942.67**	**2526.79**	**3088.95**	**3791.71**
A股	A Shares	592.63	704.08	1025.01	1646.13	2203.96	2757.88	3439.60
B股	B Shares	47.01	61.55	85.49	125.29	141.37	150.96	173.79
流通股本（亿股）	**Negotiable Shares (100 million share)**	**226.04**	**301.46**	**429.85**	**671.44**	**861.94**	**1079.65**	**1354.26**
A股	A Shares	144.40	178.98	267.14	443.24	607.01	810.45	1078.17
B股	B Shares	45.99	46.00	78.41	117.57	133.91	141.88	151.57
股票市价总值(亿元)	**Total Market Capitalization (100 million yuan)**	**3691**	**3474**	**9842**	**17529**	**19506**	**26471**	**48091**
A股	A Shares	3516	3311	9449	17154	19299	26168	47456
B股	B Shares	175	164	394	375	206	304	635
股票流通市值(亿元)	**Negotiable Market Capitalization (100 million yuan)**	**969**	**938**	**2867**	**5204**	**5746**	**8214**	**16088**
A股	A Shares	814	791	2514	4856	5550	7937	15524
B股	B Shares	155	147	353	348	196	276	563
股票成交金额(亿元)	**Total Turnover (100 million yuan)**	**8128**	**4036**	**21332**	**30722**	**23544**	**31320**	**60827**
A股	A Shares	8003	4319	21052	30295	23418	31050	60279
B股	B Shares	125	78	280	427	127	270	548
总成交股数（亿股）	**Trading Volume (100 million share)**	**101.33**	**705.31**	**2533.14**	**2560.02**	**2154.11**	**2932.39**	**4758.36**
A股	A Shares	98.80	681.07	2464.93	2471.30	2092.50	2809.75	4558.00
B股	B Shares	25.32	24.24	68.21	89.49	61.60	122.64	200.36
深证综合指数	**Shenzhen Composite Index**							
最高	High	242.06	169.66	473.02	517.91	441.04	525.14	654.37
最低	Low	96.56	112.63	105.34	305.81	317.10	310.65	414.69
收盘	Close	140.63	113.24	327.45	381.29	343.85	402.18	635.73
上证综合指数	**Shanghai Composite Index**							
最高	High	1052.94	926.41	1258.69	1510.18	1422.98	1756.18	2125.72
最低	Low	325.89	524.43	512.83	870.18	1043.02	1047.83	1361.21
收盘	Close	647.87	555.29	917.01	1194.10	1146.70	1366.58	2073.48

19−15 保险公司业务经济技术指标(2000年)

Economic and Technical Indicators of Insurance Companies Funded with Chinese and Foreign Capital (2000)

项　　目	Item	保险金额（亿元） Amount Insured (100 million yuan)	保　费（亿元） Premium (100 million yuan)	赔款及给付（亿元） Claim and Payment (100 million yuan)
合计	**Total**	**508579**	**1598**	**526**
财产保险公司	**Property Insurance Companies**	**161521**	**608**	**308**
企业财产险	Enterprise Property Insurance	69603	118	51
家庭财产险	Family Property Insurance	5829	13	4
机动车辆险	Motor Vehicle Insurance	34041	373	203
船舶险	Ship Insurance	9834	11	9
货物运输险	Freight Transport Insurance	17735	36	16
卫星及核能险	Satellite and Nuclear Energy Insurance	2667	3	2
建筑、安装工程保险及责任保险	Construction and Installation Projects Insurance and Related Liability Insurance	3357	6	2
责任险	Liability Insurance	6682	21	11
保证保险	Guarantee Insurance	541	2	1
出口信用险	Export Credit Insurance	388	3	1
农业险	Agriculture Insurance	499	4	3
其他险	Other Insurance	10345	18	5
人寿保险公司	**Life Insurance Companies**	**347058**	**990**	**218**
寿险	Life Insurance	69282	882	174
健康险	Health Insurance	27277	28	12
人身意外伤害险	Unforeseen Human Injury Insurance	250499	80	32

19−16 保险系统机构、人员数（2000年底）

Number of Institutions and Employed Persons in Insurance System (End of 2000)

项　　目	Item	机构数（个） Number of Institution	职工人数（人） Employees	# 女职工 Female
总计	**Total**	**8828**	**166602**	**61893**
一、中资保险公司	**Domestic Funded Insurance Institutions**	**13**	**164170**	**60534**
(一)国有公司	**State-owned**			
#总公司	National Corporations	4	1047	415
省级分公司	Provincial Branches	63	6960	2284
计划单列市	Branches at Separate Planning Cities	28	1457	641
省会城市营业部	Business Departments at Provincial Capitals	24	2865	1111
地市级分公司	Prefecture/City Branches	910	34675	12811
地市级营业部	Prefecture/City Business Departments	103	1720	747
县级支公司	County Branches	4313	57204	18883
县级营业部	County Business Departments	915	10157	3237
办事处或营业部	Business Offices or Departments	1892	3142	1250
保险院校	Colleges and Schools	4	427	186
其他	Others	29	586	198
(二)股份制公司	**Share-holding Corporations**			
#总公司	National Corporations	9	3000	1231
一级分公司	First Level Filiales	86	24522	10897
二级分公司	Second Level Filiales	34	5074	2155
支公司	Branches	197	9789	3881
办事处或营业部	Offices or Business Departments	185	1474	597
其他	Others	11	71	28
二、外资保险公司营业性机构	**Business Institutions of Foreign Funded Insurance Co.**	**21**	**2432**	**1359**
#中外合资公司	Joint-venture with Foreign Investment	7	688	409
外资分公司	Foreign Funded Insurance Filiales	12	1659	899
外资支公司	Foreign Funded Insurance Branches	2	85	51

注：职工人数不包括营销、代理人员。

a) Number of employed persons exclude the marketing persons and agent persons.

主要统计指标解释

信贷资金　指金融机构以信用方式积聚和分配的货币资金。金融机构信贷资金的来源有各项存款、对国际金融机构负债、流通中货币、银行自有资金及当年结益等；信贷资金的运用有各项贷款、黄金占款、外汇占款、财政借款及在国际金融机构中的资产等。

存款　指企业、机关、团体或居民根据资金必须收回的原则，把货币资金存入银行或其他信用机构保管并取得一定利息的一种信用活动形式。根据存款对象的不同可划分为企业存款、财政存款、机关团体存款、基本建设存款、城镇储蓄存款、农村存款等科目。它是银行信贷资金的主要来源。

贷款　指银行或其他信用机构根据资金必须归还的原则，按一定利率，为企业、个人等提供资金的一种信用活动形式。我国银行贷款分为流动资金贷款、固定资产贷款、城乡个体工商户贷款以及农业贷款等科目。

保险公司　在中国境内的、经过保险监督部门批准设立，并依法登记注册的各类商业保险公司。

保险金额　指保险人承担赔偿或者给付保险金责任的最高限额。

保费　指投保人为取得保险人在约定范围内所承担赔偿责任而支付给保险人的费用。

赔款　指保险人根据保险合同的规定，向被保险人支付的赔偿保险责任损失的金额。

给付　包括死伤医疗给付和满期给付。死伤医疗给付是指保险人根据人寿保险及长期健康保险合同的规定，因被保险人在保险期内发生保险责任范围内的保险事故支付给被保险人（或受益人）的金额。满期给付是指被保险人生存期满，保险人按人寿保险合同规定支付给被保险人的满期保险金额。

Explanatory Notes on Main Statistical Indicators

Credit Funds refer to the funds issued as loans by banking institutions. The sources of credit funds of the banking institutions included deposits, liabilities to international financial institutions, currency in circulation, self-owned funds and current retained profits, etc. The credit funds can be used in forms of loans, gold, foreign exchange, government debt and assets in the international financial institutions.

Deposit is a form of credit by which enterprises, institutions, organizations or households can put money into banks and other credit institutions for safekeeping and interest earning under the principle of free withdrawal. According to different depositors, deposits are divided into enterprise deposits, treasury deposits, deposits of government agencies and organizations, capital construction deposits, urban savings deposits, rural deposits and other deposits. Deposits are major sources of the credit funds of banks.

Loan is a form of credit by which banks and other credit institutions provide funds at certain interest rate to enterprises and individuals in the light of the principle of unconditional repayment. Loans from Chinese banks include circulating capital loans, fixed assets loans, loans to urban and rural individuals engaged in industrial and commercial business and agricultural loans.

Insurance Companies refer to commercial insurance companies of various forms registered by law and established in China with the approval of insurance regulatory agencies.

Amount Insured refers to the maximum that the insurant will get for the claim of the case insured.

Premium is the fee paid by the insurant to the insurer to obtain the obligation of compensation from the insurance within the agreed terms.

Settled Claim is the compensation paid by the insurer to the insurant in accordance with the insurance contract.

Payment includes payment for death, injury or medical treatment and mature payment. Payment for death, injury or medical treatment refers to the money paid to the insurant (or the beneficiary) in accordance with the life or health insurance contract when the insurant encounters accidents within the insured period covered in the contract. Mature payment refers to the mature payment to the insurant in accordance with the life insurance contract at the end of the insured period.

二十、教育和科技

Education, Science and Technology

简要说明

一、本篇反映我国教育事业的发展情况和科学技术活动的基本情况。

二、教育部分包括高等教育(大专院校及研究生院)、中等教育(中等专业学校、技工学校、普通中学、职业中学和工读学校)、初等教育(小学)、幼儿教育、特殊教育(盲聋哑和弱智儿童学校等)、各级各类成人教育(成人高校、成人中等学校和成人初等学校)以及教育经费等资料，主要指标有学校数、在校学生数、招生数、毕业生数、教职工数和教师数、教育经费来源和支出以及国家财政性教育经费等。

教育统计资料主要由教育部发展规划司提供，其资料来源是通过教育部制定的教育统计报表制度搜集加工整理而成；教育经费资料由教育部财务司提供；技工学校的资料来源于劳动和社会保障部。

三、科学技术部分主要包括了我国科技活动的规模、构成、布局和发展状况的资料，收录了全国和省、自治区、直辖市及国务院有关部门的科技统计数据。全国科技活动基本情况，综合地反映科技机构、大中型工业企业和高等学校三大科技活动主体单位的机构数、人员数和经费收支等情况，根据科技部、教育部、国防科工委和国家统计局科技统计综合年报汇总。

专业技术人员人数由组织部提供，其统计对象和范围是：在事业、国有企业单位中，专职从事专业技术工作的人员以及原评有专业技术职务(职称)而现从事行政管理工作的人员。

科技成果、科技奖励、技术市场、开发区高新技术企业的统计数据及登记数，由科技部提供。

科协系统科技活动情况数据，由中国科协提供。

测绘、气象、技术监督等科技服务部门发展情况资料，分别由国家测绘局、中国气象局、国家质量监督检验检疫总局提供。

专利申请受理量和批准量由国家知识产权局提供。

由中国统计出版社出版的国家统计局和科学技术部合作编印了《中国科技统计年鉴》，提供了1991年以来各年度科技活动和发展趋势更为详细的统计资料。

Brief Introduction

I. The data in this chapter show the development of China's education and the basic conditions of the activities of China's science and technology.

II. The data on education cover the situations on higher education (universities and colleges as well as college of postgraduates), secondary education (specialized secondary schools, regular secondary schools, vocational secondary schools and schools for juvenile delinquents), primary education (primary schools), kindergarten education, special education (schools for the blind, deaf-mutes, and the retarded), adult education of various levels and categories (adult universities and colleges, adult secondary schools, and adult primary schools), and expenditure on education. The main indicators cover the number of schools, the number of students enrolled, the number of new students enrolled, the number of graduates, the number of staff and workers, the number of teachers, sources and outlay of education fund, education expenditure from the state budget.

Statistical data on education are mainly provided by the Department of Planning and Development, Ministry of Education. The data are collected and tabulated in accordance with the reporting scheme on educational statistics stipulated by the Ministry of Education. Date on education expenditure are provided by the Department of Financial Management of the Ministry of Education. In addition, data on the technical training schools are provided by the Ministry of Labour and Social Security.

III. The data on science and technology cover mainly the scale, composition, distribution and development of the scientific and technological activities, including the statistical data of the provinces, autonomous regions and municipalities directly under the central government as well as the departments concerned under the State Council on science and technology. Data on the basic conditions of the scientific and technological activities show in a summary way the number of institutions and personnel in scientific and technological institutions, large and medium-sized industrial enterprises and universities and colleges, the three main bodies engaged in the scientific and technological activities as well as their income and expenditure. The data are collected and tabulated in accordance with the annual reporting scheme on science and technology statistics of the Ministry of Science and Technology, Ministry of Education, Commission of Science, Technology and Industry for National Defence and the National Bureau of Statistics.

The data on the number of scientific and technological personnel are provided by the Bureau of Deployment, Department of Organization of the Central Committee of the Communist Party of China. The statistical coverage includes the full-time persons engaged in the scientific and technological work and the persons with technical titles but now engaged in administrative or managerial work in the institutions or state-owned enterprises.

The data on scientific and technological results, encouragement and reward on scientific and technological achievements, technical market and the high-tech enterprises in the developed areas are provided by the Ministry of Science and Technology.

The data on the scientific and technological activities of the associations for science and technology are provided by the China Association for Science and Technology.

The data on the development of the mapping, meteorology, technological supervision and other service departments for science and technology are provided separately by the National Bureau of Surveying and Mapping, China Meteorological Administration and State Administration of Technical Supervision and Quarantine.

The data on the number of patent applications examined and certified are provided by State Bureau of Intellectual Properties.

"China Statistical Yearbook on Science and Technology", jointly compiled by the National Bureau of Statistics and the Ministry Science and Technology and published by China Statistics Press, provides more detailed statistical data on the scientific and technological activities and the trend of development since 1991.

20-1 教育事业基本情况

Basic Statistics on Education

指 标	Item	1985	1990	1995	1999	2000
学校数 （所）	**Number of Schools**					
普通高等学校	Regular Institutions of Higher Education	1016	1075	1054	1071	1041
普通中等学校	Secondary Schools	104848	100777	95216	95255	93935
#中等专业学校	Specialized Secondary Schools	3557	3982	4049	3962	3646
中等技术学校	Technical Secondary Schools	2529	2956	3135	3147	2963
中等师范学校	Teacher Secondary Schools	1028	1026	897	815	683
普通中学	Regular Secondary Schools	93221	87631	81020	77213	77268
高中	Senior Secondary Schools	17318	15678	13991	14127	14564
初中	Junior Secondary Schools	75903	71953	67029	63086	62704
职业中学	Vocational Secondary Schools	8070	9164	10147	9636	8849
小学	Primary Schools	832309	766072	668685	582291	553622
幼儿园	Kindergartens	172262	172322	180438	181136	175836
特殊教育	Special Schools	375	746	1379	1520	1539
专任教师（万人）	**Number of Full-time Teachers (10 000 persons)**					
普通高等学校	Regular Institutions of Higher Education	34.4	39.5	40.1	42.6	46.3
普通中等学校	Secondary Schools	296.7	349.2	388.3	459.6	473.4
#中等专业学校	Specialized Secondary Schools	17.4	23.4	25.7	27.4	25.6
中等技术学校	Technical Secondary Schools	12.8	17.6	19.5	21.2	20.4
中等师范学校	Teacher Secondary Schools	4.6	5.9	6.2	6.2	5.3
普通中学	Regular Secondary Schools	265.2	303.3	333.4	384.1	400.5
职业中学	Vocational Secondary Schools	14.1	22.4	29.2	33.6	32.0
小学	Primary Schools	537.7	558.2	566.4	586.1	586.0
幼儿园	Kindergartens	55.0	75.0	87.5	87.2	85.6
特殊教育	Special Schools	0.7	1.4	2.5	3.1	3.2
招生数（万人）	**New Student Enrollment (10 000 persons)**					
普通高等学校	Regular Institutions of Higher Education	61.9	60.9	92.6	159.7	220.6
普通中等学校	Secondary Schools	1789.8	1815.8	2354.1	2963.3	3103.2
#中等专业学校	Specialized Secondary Schools	66.8	73.0	138.1	163.4	132.6
中等技术学校	Technical Secondary Schools	45.4	50.3	107.3	134.3	111.6
中等师范学校	Teacher Secondary Schools	21.5	22.7	30.8	29.1	21.0
普通中学	Regular Secondary Schools	1606.9	1619.6	2025.9	2546.0	2736.0
高中	Senior Secondary Schools	257.5	249.8	273.7	396.3	472.7
初中	Junior Secondary Schools	1349.4	1369.9	1752.3	2149.7	2263.3
职业中学	Vocational Secondary Schools	116.1	123.2	190.0	194.1	182.7
小学	Primary Schools	2298.2	2064.0	2531.8	2029.5	1946.5
幼儿园	Kindergartens			1972.4	1617.5	1531.1
特殊教育	Special Schools	0.9	1.6	5.6	5.0	5.3
在校学生（万人）	**Student Enrollment (10 000 persons)**					
普通高等学校	Regular Institutions of Higher Education	170.3	206.3	290.6	413.4	556.1
普通中等学校	Secondary Schools	5092.6	5105.4	6191.5	8002.7	8518.5
#中等专业学校	Specialized Secondary Schools	157.1	224.4	372.2	515.5	489.5
中等技术学校	Technical Secondary Schools	101.3	156.7	287.4	425.0	412.5
中等师范学校	Teacher Secondary Schools	55.8	67.7	84.8	90.5	77.0
普通中学	Regular Secondary Schools	4706.0	4586.0	5371.0	6771.3	7368.9
高中	Senior Secondary Schools	741.1	717.3	713.2	1049.7	1201.3
初中	Junior Secondary Schools	3964.8	3868.7	4657.8	5721.6	6167.6
职业中学	Vocational Secondary Schools	229.5	295.0	448.3	533.9	503.2
小学	Primary Schools	13370.2	12241.4	13195.2	13548.0	13013.3
幼儿园	Kindergartens	1479.7	1972.2	2711.2	2326.3	2244.2
特殊教育	Special Schools	4.2	7.2	29.6	37.2	37.8
毕业生数（万人）	**Graduates (10 000 persons)**					
普通高等学校	Regular Institutions of Higher Education	31.6	61.4	80.5	84.8	95.0
普通中等学校	Secondary Schools	1279.1	1497.5	1636.9	2229.2	2302.3
#中等专业学校	Specialized Secondary Schools	42.9	66.1	83.9	140.1	150.7
中等技术学校	Technical Secondary Schools	26.2	42.8	59.4	109.3	119.6
中等师范学校	Teacher Secondary Schools	16.7	23.4	24.5	30.9	31.1
普通中学	Regular Secondary Schools	1194.9	1342.1	1429.0	1852.7	1908.6
高中	Senior Secondary Schools	196.6	233.0	201.6	262.9	301.5
初中	Junior Secondary Schools	998.3	1109.1	1227.4	1589.8	1607.1
职业中学	Vocational Secondary Schools	41.3	89.3	124.0	167.8	176.3
小学	Primary Schools	1999.9	1863.1	1961.5	2313.7	2419.2
特殊教育	Special Schools	0.4	0.5	1.9	3.8	4.3

注：1.1999年普通高等学校招生数和在校学生数包括成人高等学校中招收的"新高职"学生数。

a)New student enrollment and student enrollment of regular institutions of higher education in 1999 include the new enrollment student of higher vocational student in adult institutions of higher education.

20-2 各级各类学校数

Number of Schools by Level and Type of School

单位：所 (unit)

年 份 Year	普通高等学校 Regular Institutions of Higher Education	中等学校 Secondary Schools	中等专业学校 Specialized Secondary Schools	中等技术学校 Technical Secondary Schools	中等师范学校 Teacher Secondary Schools	普通中学 Regular Secondary Schools	高中 Senior Secondary Schools	初中 Junior Secondary Schools	职业中学 Vocational Secondary Schools	小学 Primary Schools	幼儿园 Kinder-gartens	盲、聋哑学校 Blind, Deaf, Deaf-mute Schools
1978	598	165105	2760	1714	1046	162345	49215	113130		949323	163952	292
1979	633	147266	3033	1980	1053	144233	40289	103944		923532	165629	289
1980	675	124760	3069	2052	1017	118377	31300	87077	3314	917316	170419	292
1981	704	112505	3132	2170	962	106718	24447	82271	2655	894074	130296	302
1982	715	107829	3076	2168	908	101649	20874	80775	3104	880516	122107	312
1983	805	105045	3090	2229	861	96474	18876	77598	5481	862165	136306	318
1984	902	104017	3301	2293	1008	93714	17847	75867	7002	853740	166526	326
1985	1016	104848	3557	2529	1028	93221	17318	75903	8070	832309	172262	350
1986	1054	104936	3782	2741	1041	92967	17111	75856	8187	820846	173376	387
1987	1063	105151	3913	2854	1059	92857	16930	75927	8381	807406	176775	414
1988	1075	104468	4022	2957	1065	91492	16524	74968	8954	793261	171845	446
1989	1075	102732	3984	2940	1044	89575	16050	73525	9173	777244	172634	483
1990	1075	100777	3982	2956	1026	87631	15678	71953	9164	766072	172322	555
1991	1075	99348	3925	2977	948	85851	15243	70608	9572	729158	164465	651
1992	1053	97784	3903	2984	919	84021	14850	69171	9860	712973	172506	754
1993	1065	96744	3964	3046	918	82795	14380	68415	9985	696681	165197	824
1994	1080	96562	3987	3093	894	82358	14242	68116	10217	682588	174657	871
1995	1054	95216	4049	3152	897	81020	13991	67029	10147	668685	180438	933
1996	1032	94115	4099	3206	893	79967	13875	66092	10049	645983	187324	980
1997	1020	92832	4143	3251	892	78642	13880	64762	10047	628840	182485	1015
1998	1022	92071	4109	3234	875	77888	13948	63940	10074	609626	181368	1062
1999	1071	95255	3962	3147	815	77213	14127	63086	9636	582291	181136	1102
2000	1041	93935	3646	2963	683	77268	14564	62704	8849	553622	175836	1108

注：1999年起中等学校中包括技工学校和工读学校数（下表同）。

a) Number of secondary schools since 1999 includes various technical schools and schools for juvenile delinquents.The same as in the following table

20-3 各级各类学校教职工数

Number of Teachers and Staff by Level and Type of School

单位：万人 (10 000 persons)

年 份 Year	普通高等学校 Regular Institutions of Higher Education	中等学校 Secondary Schools	中等专业学校 Specialized Secondary Schools	中等技术学校 Technical Secondary Schools	中等师范学校 Teacher Secondary Schools	普通中学 Regular Secondary Schools	职业中学 Vocational Secondary Schools	小学 Primary Schools	幼儿园 Kinder-gartens	盲、聋哑学校 Blind, Deaf, Deaf-mute Schools
1952	7.2	26.0	8.1	3.9	4.2	17.6		152.8	1.9	
1957	15.5	53.4	13.6	10.6	3.0	39.4		198.1	10.1	0.1
1962	33.5	77.8	13.7	11.1	2.6	62.2	2.0	262.0	16.1	0.3
1965	33.3	110.5	12.2	10.1	2.1	67.7	30.6	407.5	16.2	0.4
1970	31.2	153.3	7.9	5.6	2.3	145.4		390.9		
1975	40.8	282.1	17.7	12.8	4.5	264.4		554.3	37.8	0.6
1978	51.8	415.4	23.7	17.6	6.1	391.7		562.0	46.9	0.7
1980	63.2	423.6	29.8	22.3	7.5	389.7	4.1	605.4	61.0	0.8
1985	87.1	417.6	40.3	31.3	9.0	355.7	21.6	602.1	79.8	1.1
1986	93.1	437.7	43.6	33.9	9.7	368.9	25.2	606.5	88.1	1.2
1987	96.9	455.3	45.9	35.7	10.2	381.3	28.1	608.5	94.1	1.3
1988	99.4	468.1	47.6	37.0	10.6	389.7	30.8	614.2	97.9	1.4
1989	100.4	473.9	48.2	37.6	10.6	393.1	32.6	619.5	101.2	1.5
1990	100.6	482.6	49.2	38.5	10.7	399.1	34.3	624.0	105.2	1.6
1991	100.9	490.6	49.4	38.8	10.6	405.4	35.8	619.4	106.2	1.9
1992	101.4	499.2	50.3	39.7	10.6	411.3	37.6	619.9	112.1	2.1
1993	102.1	504.1	51.1	40.3	10.8	413.3	39.7	621.8	112.6	2.3
1994	104.0	512.3	51.7	40.7	11.0	419.1	41.5	627.1	114.9	3.3
1995	104.1	525.9	53.0	41.8	11.2	429.5	43.4	632.4	116.0	2.7
1996	103.6	541.9	54.3	43.0	11.3	442.4	45.2	638.6	117.4	2.8
1997	103.2	556.2	55.4	44.0	11.4	454.1	46.7	643.6	117.3	3.0
1998	103.0	564.6	54.7	43.5	11.2	462.1	47.8	644.6	115.8	3.1
1999	106.5	606.7	52.9	42.1	10.7	475.4	47.2	647.1	115.8	3.1
2000	111.3	611.8	48.8	39.8	39.8	491.1	44.7	645.5	114.4	3.2

20-4　各级各类学校教师数

Number of Teachers by Level and Type of School

单位：万人　(10 000 persons)

年份 Year	普通高等学校 Regular Institutions of Higher Education	中等学校 Secondary Schools	中等专业学校 Specialized Secondary Schools	中等技术学校 Technical Secondary Schools	中等师范学校 Teacher Secondary Schools	普通中学 Regular Secondary Schools	高中 Senior Secondary Schools	初中 Junior Secondary Schools	职业中学 Vocational Secondary Schools	小学 Primary Schools	幼儿园 Kinder-gartens	盲、聋哑学校 Blind, Deaf, Deaf-mute Schools
1978	20.6	328.1	9.9	6.9	3.0	318.2	74.1	244.1		522.6	27.7	0.4
1979	23.7	319.1	11.3	7.9	3.4	307.8	66.8	241.0		538.2	29.5	0.5
1980	24.7	317.1	12.8	9.1	3.7	302.0	57.1	244.9	2.3	549.9	41.1	0.5
1981	25.0	300.9	13.6	9.8	3.8	284.4	49.4	235.0	2.9	558.0	40.1	0.5
1982	28.7	287.1	15.0	11.0	4.0	268.1	46.6	221.5	4.0	550.5	41.5	0.5
1983	83.3	282.6	15.6	11.6	4.0	259.7	45.1	241.6	7.3	542.5	43.3	0.6
1984	31.5	282.2	16.1	11.9	4.3	255.7	45.9	209.7	10.4	537.0	49.1	0.6
1985	34.4	296.7	17.4	12.8	4.6	265.2	49.2	216.0	14.1	537.7	55.0	0.7
1986	37.2	311.5	19.3	14.3	5.0	275.8	51.8	223.9	16.4	541.4	60.5	0.7
1987	38.5	326.6	21.0	15.6	5.4	287.0	54.4	232.7	18.5	543.4	65.1	0.8
1988	39.3	338.9	22.5	16.8	5.7	296.0	55.7	240.3	20.3	550.1	67.0	0.9
1989	39.7	342.3	22.9	17.1	5.8	298.0	55.4	242.7	21.4	554.4	70.9	0.9
1990	39.5	349.2	23.4	17.6	5.8	303.3	56.2	247.0	22.4	558.2	75.0	1.1
1991	39.1	355.7	23.2	17.5	5.7	309.0	57.3	251.7	23.5	553.2	76.9	1.2
1992	38.8	362.4	23.5	17.8	5.7	314.1	57.6	256.5	24.8	552.7	81.5	1.3
1993	38.8	366.8	23.9	18.1	5.8	316.7	55.9	260.8	26.2	555.2	83.6	1.5
1994	39.6	375.7	24.7	18.7	6.0	323.4	54.7	268.7	27.7	561.1	86.2	1.6
1995	40.1	388.3	25.7	19.5	6.2	333.4	55.1	278.4	29.2	566.4	87.5	1.8
1996	40.3	404.0	26.7	20.4	6.3	346.5	57.2	289.3	30.8	573.6	88.9	1.9
1997	40.5	418.6	27.6	21.2	6.4	358.7	60.5	298.2	32.2	579.4	88.4	2.0
1998	40.7	431.2	27.9	21.5	6.4	369.7	64.2	305.5	33.6	581.9	87.5	2.1
1999	42.6	459.6	27.4	21.2	6.2	384.1	69.2	314.8	33.6	586.1	87.2	2.2
2000	46.3	473.4	25.6	20.4	5.3	400.5	75.7	324.9	32.0	586.0	85.6	2.3

20-5　各级各类学校在校学生数

Number of Students Enrollment by Level and Type of School

单位：万人　(10 000 persons)

年份 Year	普通高等学校 Regular Institutions of Higher Education	中等学校 Secondary Schools	中等专业学校 Specialized Secondary Schools	中等技术学校 Technical Secondary Schools	中等师范学校 Teacher Secondary Schools	普通中学 Regular Secondary Schools	高中 Senior Secondary Schools	初中 Junior Secondary Schools	职业中学 Vocational Secondary Schools	小学 Primary Schools	幼儿园 Kinder-gartens	盲、聋哑学校 Blind, Deaf, Deaf-mute Schools
1978	85.6	6637.2	88.9	52.9	36.0	6548.3	1553.1	4995.2		14624.0	787.7	3.1
1979	102.0	6024.9	119.9	71.7	48.5	5905.0	1292.0	4613.0		14662.9	879.2	3.2
1980	114.4	5677.8	124.3	76.1	48.2	5508.1	969.8	4538.3	45.4	14627.0	1150.8	3.3
1981	127.9	5014.6	106.9	63.2	43.7	4859.6	715.0	4144.6	48.1	14332.8	1056.2	3.3
1982	115.4	4702.8	103.9	62.8	41.1	4528.5	640.5	3888.0	70.4	13972.0	1113.1	3.4
1983	120.7	4637.7	114.3	68.8	45.5	4397.8	629.0	3768.8	122.0	13578.0	1140.3	3.6
1984	139.6	4860.9	132.2	81.1	51.1	4554.2	689.8	3864.3	174.5	12557.1	1294.7	3.6
1985	170.3	5092.6	157.1	100.9	56.2	4706.0	741.1	3964.8	229.5	13370.2	1479.7	3.8
1986	188.0	5321.6	175.7	114.6	61.1	4889.9	773.4	4116.6	256.0	13182.5	1629.0	4.1
1987	195.9	5403.1	187.4	122.3	65.1	4948.1	773.7	4174.4	267.6	12835.9	1807.8	4.3
1988	206.6	5246.1	205.2	136.8	68.3	4761.5	746.0	4015.5	279.4	12535.8	1854.5	4.5
1989	208.2	5054.0	217.7	149.3	68.5	4554.0	716.1	3837.9	282.3	12373.1	1847.7	4.7
1990	206.3	5105.4	224.4	156.7	67.7	4586.0	717.3	3868.7	295.0	12241.4	1972.2	5.1
1991	204.4	5226.8	227.7	161.6	66.1	4683.5	722.9	3960.6	315.6	12164.2	2209.3	5.6
1992	218.4	5354.4	240.8	174.3	66.6	4770.8	704.9	4065.9	342.8	12201.3	2428.2	6.1
1993	253.6	5383.7	282.0	209.8	72.2	4739.1	656.9	4082.2	362.6	12421.2	2552.5	6.4
1994	279.9	5707.1	319.8	241.4	78.4	4981.7	664.9	4316.7	405.6	12822.6	2630.3	7.2
1995	290.6	6191.5	372.2	287.4	84.8	5371.0	713.2	4657.8	448.3	13195.2	2711.2	8.3
1996	302.1	6635.7	422.8	334.8	88.0	5739.7	769.3	4970.4	473.3	13615.0	2666.3	9.0
1997	317.4	6995.2	465.4	374.3	91.1	6017.9	850.1	5167.8	511.9	13995.4	2519.0	9.5
1998	340.9	7340.7	498.1	406.0	92.1	6301.0	938.0	5363.0	541.6	13953.8	2403.0	9.8
1999	413.4	8002.7	515.5	425.0	90.5	6771.3	1049.7	5721.6	533.9	13548.0	2326.3	10.1
2000	556.1	8518.5	489.5	412.5	77.0	7368.9	1201.3	6167.6	503.2	13013.3	2244.2	10.3

20-6 各级各类学校招生数

Number of New Students Enrollment by Level and Type of School

单位：万人 (10 000 persons)

年份 Year	普通高等学校 Regular Institutions of Higher Education	中等学校 Secondary Schools	中等专业学校 Specialized Secondary Schools	中等技术学校 Technical Secondary Schools	中等师范学校 Teacher Secondary Schools	普通中学 Regular Secondary Schools	高中 Senior Secondary Schools	初中 Junior Secondary Schools	职业中学 Vocational Secondary Schools	小学 Primary Schools	盲、聋哑学校 Blind, Deaf, Deaf-mute Schools
1978	40.2	2743.6	44.7	26.8	17.9	2698.9	692.9	2006.0		3315.4	0.6
1979	27.9	2391.0	49.1	26.5	22.6	2341.9	614.1	1727.8		3101.7	0.6
1980	28.1	2011.8	46.8	25.3	21.5	1934.3	383.4	1550.9	30.7	2942.3	0.6
1981	27.9	1810.5	43.3	23.8	19.5	1740.5	327.8	1412.7	26.7	2749.2	0.6
1982	31.5	1726.9	41.9	24.1	17.8	1642.4	279.3	1363.1	42.6	2671.7	0.6
1983	39.1	1700.4	47.8	28.7	19.1	1576.9	259.8	1317.1	75.7	2544.0	0.6
1984	47.5	1713.4	54.6	35.1	19.5	4564.9	262.3	1302.5	93.9	2472.9	0.7
1985	61.9	1789.8	66.8	45.2	21.6	1606.9	257.5	1349.4	116.1	2298.2	0.7
1986	57.2	1824.4	67.7	45.0	22.7	1643.9	257.3	1386.6	112.8	2258.2	0.9
1987	61.7	1834.2	71.5	48.5	23.0	1649.5	255.2	1394.3	113.2	2094.6	0.9
1988	67.0	1781.9	77.6	54.1	23.6	1584.8	244.3	1340.5	119.5	2123.3	0.9
1989	59.7	1743.3	73.5	50.8	22.7	1551.5	242.1	1309.4	118.3	2151.5	0.9
1990	60.9	1815.8	73.0	50.3	22.7	1619.6	249.8	1369.9	123.2	2064.0	1.0
1991	62.0	1871.0	78.0	55.1	22.9	1655.2	243.8	1411.3	137.8	2072.7	1.2
1992	75.4	1939.8	87.9	63.8	24.1	1699.7	234.7	1465.0	152.1	2183.2	1.3
1993	92.4	1983.7	114.9	86.5	28.4	1707.3	228.3	1479.0	161.5	2353.5	1.2
1994	90.0	2157.6	122.5	93.5	29.1	1859.8	243.4	1616.4	175.3	2537.0	1.4
1995	92.6	2354.1	138.1	107.3	30.8	2025.9	273.6	1752.3	190.1	2531.8	1.7
1996	96.6	2384.2	152.3	120.8	31.6	2042.9	282.2	1760.7	188.9	2524.7	1.8
1997	100.0	2501.5	162.1	129.6	32.5	2128.2	322.6	1805.6	211.2	2462.0	1.8
1998	108.4	2705.4	166.8	134.9	31.9	2321.0	359.6	1961.4	217.6	2201.4	1.7
1999	159.7	2963.3	163.4	134.3	29.1	2546.0	396.3	2149.7	194.1	2029.5	1.7
2000	220.6	3103.2	132.6	111.6	21.0	2736.0	472.7	2263.3	182.7	1946.5	1.8

20-7 各级各类学校毕业生数

Number of Graduates by Level and Type of School

单位：万人 (10 000 persons)

年份 Year	普通高等学校 Regular Institutions of Higher Education	中等学校 Secondary Schools	中等专业学校 Specialized Secondary Schools	中等技术学校 Technical Secondary Schools	中等师范学校 Teacher Secondary Schools	普通中学 Regular Secondary Schools	高中 Senior Secondary Schools	初中 Junior Secondary Schools	职业中学 Vocational Secondary Schools	小学 Primary Schools	盲、聋哑学校 Blind, Deaf, Deaf-mute Schools
1978	16.5	2398.5	23.2	11.9	11.3	2375.3	682.7	1692.6		2287.9	0.3
1979	8.5	2402.5	18.1	7.9	10.2	2384.4	726.5	1657.9		2087.9	0.3
1980	14.7	1629.9	41.0	20.1	20.9	1581.0	616.2	964.7	7.9	2053.3	0.4
1981	14.0	1710.2	60.5	36.5	24.0	1640.3	486.1	1154.2	9.4	2075.7	0.4
1982	45.7	1400.4	44.6	24.2	20.4	1342.7	310.6	1032.2	13.1	2068.9	0.4
1983	33.5	1254.5	37.5	23.0	14.5	1195.4	235.1	960.3	21.6	1980.7	0.3
1984	28.7	1205.6	37.6	23.8	13.8	1140.2	189.8	950.4	27.8	1995.0	0.4
1985	31.6	1279.1	42.9	26.1	16.8	1194.9	196.6	998.3	41.3	1999.9	0.4
1986	39.3	1388.5	49.6	32.1	17.5	1281.0	224.0	1057.0	57.9	2016.1	0.5
1987	53.2	1496.9	57.8	38.9	18.9	1364.1	246.8	1117.3	75.0	2043.0	0.4
1988	55.3	1548.4	59.6	39.2	20.4	1407.8	250.6	1157.2	81.0	1930.3	0.4
1989	57.6	1520.9	59.1	36.5	22.6	1377.5	243.2	1134.3	86.3	1857.1	0.5
1990	61.4	1497.5	66.1	42.8	23.4	1342.1	233.0	1109.1	89.3	1863.1	0.5
1991	61.4	1477.0	74.0	49.6	24.4	1308.5	222.9	1085.5	94.5	1896.7	0.5
1992	60.4	1499.4	74.3	50.7	23.6	1328.4	226.1	1102.3	96.7	1872.4	0.5
1993	57.1	1541.9	73.6	50.7	22.8	1365.9	231.7	1134.2	102.5	1841.5	0.6
1994	63.7	1542.4	72.9	50.4	22.6	1361.9	209.3	1152.6	107.6	1899.6	0.7
1995	80.5	1636.9	83.9	59.4	24.5	1429.0	201.6	1227.4	124.0	1961.5	0.7
1996	83.9	1725.4	101.9	73.8	28.1	1484.0	204.9	1279.0	139.6	1934.1	0.8
1997	82.9	1929.8	115.7	86.3	29.4	1664.0	221.7	1442.4	150.1	1960.1	0.8
1998	83.0	2124.1	129.3	98.7	30.6	1832.0	251.8	1580.2	162.8	2117.4	1.0
1999	84.8	2229.2	140.2	109.3	30.9	1852.7	262.9	1589.8	167.8	2313.7	1.1
2000	95.0	2302.3	150.7	119.6	31.1	1908.6	301.5	1607.1	176.3	2419.2	1.2

20-8 研究生和留学生数

Number of Postgraduates and Students Studying Abroad

单位：人 (person)

年份 Year	研究生数 Number of Postgraduates			出国留学人员 Number of Students Studying Abroad	学成回国留学人员 Number of Returned Students
	在学人数 Student Enrollment	招生数 New Student Enrollment	毕业生数 Graduates		
1952	2763	1785	627	231	
1957	3178	334	1723	529	347
1962	6130	1287	1019	114	980
1965	4546	1456	1665	454	199
1975				245	186
1978	10934	10708	9	860	248
1979	18830	8110	140	1777	231
1980	21604	3616	476	2124	162
1981	18848	9363	11669	2922	1143
1982	25847	11080	4058	2326	2116
1983	37166	15642	4497	2633	2303
1984	57566	23181	2756	3073	2290
1985	87331	46871	17004	4888	1424
1986	110371	41310	16950	4676	1388
1987	120191	39017	27603	4703	1605
1988	112776	35645	40838	3786	3000
1989	101339	28569	37232	3329	1753
1990	93018	29649	35440	2950	1593
1991	88128	29679	32537	2900	2069
1992	94164	33439	25692	6540	3611
1993	106771	42145	28214	10742	5128
1994	127935	50864	28047	19071	4230
1995	145443	51053	31877	20381	5750
1996	163322	59398	39652	20905	6570
1997	176353	63749	46539	22410	7130
1998	198885	72508	47077	17622	7379
1999	233513	92225	54670	23749	7748
2000	301239	128484	58767	38989	9121

20-9 高等学校分科在校学生数

Student Enrollment in Institutions of Higher Education by Field of Study

单位：人 (person)

项目	Item	1999			2000		
		合计 Total	本科 Regular College Course	专科 Specialized Subject (Three Years)	合计 Total	本科 Regular College Course	专科 Specialized Subject (Three Years)
合计	**Total**	**4085874**	**2724421**	**1361453**	**5560900**	**3400181**	**2160719**
哲学	Philosophy	4892	4272	620	5608	4917	691
经济学	Economics	614028	385525	228503	876452	484579	391873
法学	Law	174496	115687	58809	272016	147963	124053
教育学	Education	167145	97316	69829	236208	130533	105675
文学	Literature	563698	307059	256639	818568	413974	404594
历史学	History	55652	35055	20597	62246	40288	21958
理学	Science	421048	278259	142789	536776	363637	173139
工学	Engineering	1612200	1144396	468904	2148329	1382357	765972
农学	Agriculture	142415	105486	36929	181828	126949	54879
医学	Medicine	329200	251366	77834	422869	304984	117885

20-10 高等学校分科招生数

New Student Enrollment in Institutions of Higher Education by Field of Study

单位：人 (person)

项 目	Item	1999 合计 Total	1999 本科 Regular College Course	1999 专科 Specialized Subject (Three Years)	2000 合计 Total	2000 本科 Regular College Course	2000 专科 Specialized Subject (Three Years)
合 计	**Total**	**1548554**	**936690**	**611864**	**2206072**	**1160191**	**1045881**
哲 学	Philosophy	1763	1386	377	1847	1530	317
经济学	Economics	237129	131459	105670	363379	165173	198206
法 学	Law	69048	42765	26283	114682	51467	63215
教育学	Education	67257	35163	32094	107259	49143	58116
文 学	Literature	230175	117599	112576	343418	151461	191957
历史学	History	19070	11043	8027	22003	12803	9200
理 学	Science	155880	99870	56010	202466	131539	70927
工 学	Engineering	607597	386458	221139	832124	465508	366616
农 学	Agriculture	52251	35834	16417	68966	42099	26867
医 学	Medicine	108384	75113	33271	149928	89468	60460

20-11 高等学校分科毕业生数

Graduates of Institutions of Higher Education by Field of Study

单位：人 (person)

项 目	Item	1999 合计 Total	1999 本科 Regular College Course	1999 专科 Specialized Subject (Three Years)	2000 合计 Total	2000 本科 Regular College Course	2000 专科 Specialized Subject (Three Years)
合 计	**Total**	**847617**	**440935**	**406682**	**949767**	**495624**	**454143**
哲 学	Philosophy	1067	852	215	916	775	141
经济学	Economics	134258	67611	66647	159299	78205	81094
法 学	Law	31500	16363	15137	44124	19806	24318
教育学	Education	40271	15479	24792	42052	17939	24113
文 学	Literature	120957	44285	76672	146997	53826	93171
历史学	History	13374	6097	7277	13661	6755	6906
理 学	Science	90395	42351	48044	98200	49214	48986
工 学	Engineering	326180	195354	130826	354291	212905	141386
农 学	Agriculture	28070	17453	10617	30370	19154	11216
医 学	Medicine	61545	35090	26455	59857	37045	22812

20-12 高等学校分科专任教师数（2000年）

Number of Full-time Teachers by Field of Study in Regular Higher Educational Institutions (2000)

单位：人 (person)

项 目	Item	合计 Total	教授 Professors	副教授 Asso. Prof.	讲师 Lecturers	助教 Assistants	教员 Instructors
合 计	**Total**	**462772**	**43674**	**138820**	**166607**	**89090**	**24581**
哲 学	Philosophy	15669	1301	5051	6251	2530	536
经济学	Economics	37772	3041	10588	15169	7199	1775
法 学	Law	14097	1003	3642	5752	2875	825
教育学	Education	44416	1797	11552	18233	10123	2711
文 学	Literature	84009	5191	21106	31004	20433	6275
历史学	History	8387	1041	2656	3201	1193	296
理 学	Science	78904	8660	26955	26500	13253	3536
工 学	Engineering	127758	14567	41212	43935	21875	6169
农 学	Agriculture	15494	2069	5042	5224	2493	666
医 学	Medicine	36266	5004	11016	11338	7116	1792

20-13 中等专业学校分科学生数

Number of Students by Field of Study in Specialized Secondary Schools

单位：人 (person)

项 目	Item	1999 毕业生数 Graduates	1999 招生数 New Student Enrollment	1999 在校学生数 Student Enrollment	2000 毕业生数 Graduates	2000 招生数 New Student Enrollment	2000 在校学生数 Student Enrollment
合 计	**Total**	**1401451**	**1633761**	**5154984**	**1507237**	**1325870**	**4895159**
工 科	Engineering	406832	543010	1797589	463022	461400	1765751
农 科	Agriculture	50926	68168	207115	58584	47138	192618
林 科	Forestry	11732	17305	52455	12700	12548	49085
医药卫生科	Health	135794	173754	526507	129893	178810	568101
财 经	Economics and Finance	211571	182290	621729	217054	128301	523468
管 理	Administration	153615	190723	578299	169308	142896	540025
政 法	Politics and Law	45197	62311	141755	47534	48471	144693
艺 术	Art	45132	78782	231419	58184	73566	244855
体 育	Physical Culture	19125	26712	75160	20474	25404	76433
师 范	Teacher Training	321527	290706	922956	330484	207336	790130

20-14 中等专业学校分类别专任教师数（2000年）

Full-time Teachers in Specialized Secondary Schools by Field of Study (2000)

单位：人 (person)

项 目	Item	合 计 Total	高级讲师 Senior Lecturers	讲 师 Lecturers	助理讲师 Assistant Lecturers	教 员 Instructors
合 计	**Total**	**256419**	**48411**	**112743**	**86522**	**8743**
中等技术学校	Secondary Technical Schools	203843	39668	91084	66609	6482
工业学校	Industry	76925	15234	34562	24820	2309
农业学校	Agriculture	23951	4117	10440	8700	694
林业学校	Forestry	3868	895	1743	1198	32
医药学校	Health	30203	7138	13857	8456	752
财经学校	Economics and Finance	33564	6402	15708	10576	878
政法学校	Politics and Law	6621	1080	2904	2335	302
体育学校	Physical Culture	8123	1432	3836	2555	300
艺术学校	Arts	11096	1980	4320	4156	640
其他学校	Others	9492	1390	3714	3813	575
中等师范学校	Secondary Teacher Training Schools	52576	8743	21659	19913	2261

20-15 技工学校数和学生数

Number of Technical Schools, Students, Staff and Teachers

年 份 Year	学 校 数 (所) Schools	在校学生数 (万人) Student Enrollment (10 000 persons)	毕业生数 (万人) Graduates (10 000 persons)	招生数 (万人) New Student Enrollment (10 000 persons)	教职工数 (万人) Staff and Teachers (10 000 persons)
1985	3548	74.2	22.6	35.5	21.5
1986	3765	89.2	23.3	39.4	24.4
1987	3952	103.1	26.5	42.3	26.2
1988	3996	116.1	31.1	46.1	28.0
1989	4102	125.8	36.8	47.0	29.6
1990	4184	133.2	41.3	50.6	30.8
1991	4269	142.2	45.4	54.4	32.5
1992	4392	155.6	45.7	60.2	33.6
1993	4477	171.7	49.7	66.4	33.5
1994	4430	187.1	55.7	71.4	34.0
1995	4521	188.6	68.1	74.0	33.7
1996	4467	191.8	68.1	72.7	33.5
1997	4395	193.1	69.9	73.4	31.0
1998	4362	181.3	68.2	59.4	31.0
1999	4098	156.0	66.2	51.5	26.9
2000	3792	140.1	64.6	50.4	24.0

20-16 各类技工学校情况 （2000年）

Statistics on Various Technical Schools (2000)

指　　标	Item	合计 Total	国务院各部门 Ministries of the State Council	省、自治区、直辖市 Provinces, Autonomous Regions and Municipalities
学校数 （所）	Number of Schools	3792	474	3318
在校学生数 （万人）	Number of Students （10 000 persons）	140.1	13.2	126.9
教职工数 （万人）	Teachers and Staff （10 000 persons）	24.0	3.9	20.1
＃文化技术理论课指导教师（万人）	Classroom Teachers （10 000 persons）	10.5	1.5	9.0
生产实习课指导教师 （万人）	Practical Training Teachers (10 000 persons)	3.5	0.6	2.9

20-17 初中毕业生和小学毕业生升学率及小学学龄儿童入学率

Percentage of Graduates of Junior Secondary Schools and Primary Schools Entering Higher Level Schools, Percentage of School-Age Children Enrolled

年份 Year	初中毕业生升学率 Percentage of Graduates of Junior Secondary Schools Entering Senior Secondary Schools			小学毕业生升学率 Percentage of Graduates of Primary Schools Entering Junior Secondary Schools			小学学龄儿童入学率 Percentage of School-age Children Enrolled		
	初中毕业生数（万人） Graduates of Junior Secondary Schools (10 000 persons)	高级中等学校招生数（万人） Students Entering Senior Secondary Schools (10 000 persons)	升学率(%) Percentage of Graduates of Junior Secondary Schools Entering Senior Secondary Schools	小学毕业生数（万人） Graduates of Primary Schools (10 000 persons)	初级中等学校招生数（万人） Students Entering Junior Secondary Schools (10 000 persons)	升学率(%) Percentage of Graduates of Primary Schools Entering Junior Secondary Schools	学龄儿童数（万人） School-Age Children (10 000 persons)	已入学学龄儿童数（万人） School-Age Children Enrolled in Schools (10 000 persons)	入学率 Enrollment Rate (%)
1952	18.5	31.2	168.6	149.0	143.0	96.0	6642.4	3268.1	49.2
1957	111.2	44.2	39.7	498.0	219.9	44.2	8077.7	4986.6	61.7
1962	158.4	47.5	30.0	559.0	253.3	45.3	10836.0	6082.0	56.1
1965	173.8	121.6	70.0	667.6	550.7	82.5	11603.2	9829.1	84.7
1970	618.9	239.0	38.6	1652.5	1176.3	71.2	…	…	…
1975	1047.7	633.1	60.4	1999.4	1810.5	90.6	12261.9	11868.5	96.8
1978	1692.6	692.9	40.9	2287.9	2006.0	87.7	12131.3	11585.4	95.5
1979	1657.9	623.3	37.6	2087.9	1727.8	82.8	12323.1	11580.1	93.0
1980	964.7	442.8	45.9	2053.3	1557.6	75.9	12219.6	11478.2	93.9
1981	1154.2	364.1	32.5	2075.7	1417.6	68.3	12018.5	11175.5	93.0
1982	1032.2	333.3	32.3	2068.9	1370.1	66.2	11762.7	10958.0	93.2
1983	960.3	340.5	35.5	1980.7	1333.8	67.3	11251.2	10577.8	94.0
1984	950.4	364.5	38.4	1995.0	1321.1	66.2	10669.0	10169.8	95.3
1985	998.3	416.2	41.7	1999.9	1367.0	68.4	10362.3	9942.8	96.0
1986	1057.0	429.2	40.6	2016.1	1402.0	69.5	10067.5	9702.1	96.4
1987	1117.3	437.0	39.1	2043.0	1410.9	69.1	9750.9	9477.2	97.2
1988	1157.2	439.6	38.0	1930.3	1359.0	70.4	9623.9	9351.4	97.2
1989	1134.3	434.6	38.3	1857.1	1328.4	71.5	9699.1	9450.7	97.4
1990	1109.1	450.4	40.6	1863.1	1389.2	74.6	9740.7	9529.7	97.8
1991	1085.5	462.9	42.6	1896.7	1435.1	75.7	9806.6	9594.8	97.8
1992	1102.3	478.1	43.4	1872.4	1491.7	79.7	11156.2	10845.5	97.2
1993	1134.2	500.5	44.1	1841.5	1505.6	81.8	11432.0	11170.9	97.7
1994	1166.4	541.1	46.4	1899.6	1644.9	86.6	11949.6	11758.2	98.4
1995	1244.3	601.6	48.3	1961.5	1781.1	90.8	12375.4	12192.5	98.5
1996	1297.8	633.4	48.8	1934.1	1791.4	92.6	12876.5	12723.3	98.8
1997	1463.3	721.6	44.3	1960.1	1836.5	93.7	13346.7	13202.5	98.9
1998	1603.1	812.2	50.7	2117.4	1996.3	94.3	13369.3	13226.8	98.9
1999	1613.9	807.0	50.0	2313.7	2183.4	94.4	12991.4	12872.8	99.1
2000	1633.5	834.6	51.1	2419.2	2295.6	94.9	12445.3	12333.9	99.1

注：1.1952年的初中升学率高于100%，是因为当年毕业的初中学生数少于当年高级中等学校的招生人数。
2.1994年以后各年的初中毕业生数包括职业初中毕业生数。

a)The percentage of graduates of junior Secondary schools entering senior Secondary schools in 1952 was higher than 100% because the number of students graduated from junior Secondary schools was less than the number of students enrolled in senior Secondary schools.

b)The number of the graduates of junior Secondary schools since 1994 has included the graduates of vocational schools.

20-18 平均每万人口在校学生数和大中小学学生构成
Student Enrollment per 10 000 Population and Composition of Students Enrolled

年 份 Year	各级学校在校学生数占全国人口% Students as Percentage of Total Population	平均每万人口中 Number of Students per 10 000 Population			大、中、小学学生占学生总数(%) Students of Different Level as Percentage of Total Students (%)		
		大学生(人) University and College Students	中学生(人) Secondary School Students	小学生(人) Primary School Students	大学生 University and College Students	中学生 Secondary School Students	小学生 Primary School Students
1952	9.47	3.3	55	889	0.4	5.8	93.9
1957	11.11	6.8	110	994	0.6	9.9	89.5
1965	18.09	9.3	197	1602	0.5	10.9	88.6
1978	22.18	8.9	690	1519	0.4	31.1	68.5
1979	21.41	10.5	621	1510	0.5	29.0	70.5
1980	20.69	11.6	575	1482	0.6	27.8	71.6
1981	19.55	12.8	503	1439	0.7	25.7	73.6
1982	18.58	11.4	465	1381	0.6	25.0	74.4
1983	17.91	11.8	453	1326	0.6	25.3	74.1
1984	17.93	13.5	470	1310	0.7	26.2	73.1
1985	17.60	16.1	481	1263	0.9	27.3	71.8
1986	17.39	17.5	495	1226	1.0	28.5	70.5
1987	16.87	17.9	494	1174	1.1	29.3	69.6
1988	16.20	18.6	473	1129	1.1	29.2	69.7
1989	15.65	18.5	448	1098	1.2	28.7	70.2
1990	15.35	18.0	447	1071	1.2	29.1	69.7
1991	15.19	17.6	451	1050	1.2	29.7	69.1
1992	15.17	18.6	457	1041	1.2	30.1	68.7
1993	15.24	21.4	454	1048	1.4	29.8	68.8
1994	15.69	23.4	476	1070	1.5	30.3	68.2
1995	16.25	24.0	511	1089	1.5	31.5	67.1
1996	16.95	24.7	542	1112	1.5	32.3	66.2
1997	17.24	25.7	566	1132	1.5	32.8	65.7
1998	17.33	27.3	588	1118	1.6	33.9	64.5
1999	17.50	32.8	636	1076	1.9	36.4	61.7
2000	17.43	43.9	672	1027	2.5	38.6	58.9

20-19 各级学校教师负担学生数
Student-teacher Ratio by Level of School

年 份 Year	高等学校 Institutions of Higher Education		中等学校 Secondary Schools		小 学 Primary Schools	
	教师数(万人) Number of Teachers (10 000 persons)	平均每个教师负担学生数(人) Student-teacher Ratio	教师数(万人) Number of Teachers (10 000 persons)	平均每个教师负担学生数(人) Student-teacher Ratio	教师数(万人) Number of Teachers (10 000 persons)	平均每个教师负担学生数(人) Student-teacher Ratio
1952	2.7	7.1	13.0	24.2	143.5	35.6
1957	7.0	6.3	29.4	24.1	188.4	34.1
1965	13.8	4.9	70.9	20.2	385.7	30.1
1978	20.6	4.2	328.1	20.2	522.6	28.0
1979	23.7	4.3	319.1	18.9	538.2	27.2
1980	24.7	4.6	317.1	17.9	549.9	26.6
1981	25.0	5.1	300.9	16.7	558.0	25.7
1982	28.7	4.0	287.1	16.4	550.5	25.4
1983	30.3	4.0	282.7	16.4	542.5	25.0
1984	31.5	4.4	282.1	17.2	537.0	25.2
1985	34.4	5.0	296.7	17.2	537.7	24.9
1986	37.2	5.1	311.5	17.1	541.4	24.3
1987	38.5	5.1	326.6	16.5	543.4	23.6
1988	39.3	5.3	338.9	15.5	550.1	22.8
1989	39.7	5.2	342.3	14.8	554.4	22.3
1990	39.5	5.2	349.2	14.6	558.2	21.9
1991	39.1	5.2	355.7	14.7	553.2	22.0
1992	38.8	5.6	362.4	14.8	552.7	22.1
1993	38.8	6.5	366.8	14.7	555.2	22.4
1994	39.6	7.1	375.7	15.2	561.1	22.9
1995	40.1	7.2	388.3	15.9	566.4	23.3
1996	40.3	7.5	404.0	16.4	573.6	23.7
1997	40.5	7.8	418.6	16.7	579.4	24.2
1998	40.7	8.4	431.2	17.0	581.9	23.9
1999	42.6	9.7	459.6	17.4	586.1	23.1
2000	46.3	12.0	473.4	18.0	586.0	22.2

20–20 各级学校女学生和女教师数

Number of Female Students and Teachers by Level of School

单位：万人 (10 000 persons)

项目	Item	1980	1985	1990	1995	1999	2000
女学生数	**Number of Female Students**	**8778.3**	**8086.5**	**7880.8**	**9156.8**	**10268.4**	**10339.6**
高等学校	Institutions of Higher Education	26.8	51.1	69.5	102.9	162.1	227.9
中等专业学校	Specialized Secondary Schools	39.2	60.7	102.0	187.1	287.5	277.3
普通中学	Regular Secondary Schools	2180.1	1893.1	1920.1	2407.5	3109.2	3402.4
职业中学	Vocational Secondary Schools	14.8	95.4	133.7	218.2	254.7	237.4
小　学	Primary Schools	6517.4	5986.2	5655.5	6241.1	6454.9	6194.6
女学生占学生总数的百分比（%）	**Percentage of Female Students to Total Students(%)**	**43.0**	**43.4**	**44.9**	**46.5**	**47.1**	**47.1**
高等学校	Institutions of Higher Education	23.4	30.0	33.7	35.4	39.2	41.0
中等专业学校	Specialized Secondary Schools	31.5	38.6	45.4	50.3	55.8	56.6
普通中学	Regular Secondary Schools	39.6	40.2	41.9	44.8	45.9	46.2
职业中学	Vocational Secondary Schools	32.6	41.6	45.3	48.7	47.7	47.2
小　学	Primary Schools	44.6	44.8	46.2	47.3	47.6	47.6
女教师数	**Number of Female Teachers**	**288.9**	**305.6**	**364.0**	**417.9**	**488.3**	**505.3**
高等学校	Institutions of Higher Education	6.3	9.2	11.5	13.2	15.9	17.7
中等专业学校	Specialized Secondary Schools	3.4	5.7	8.9	10.7	12.2	11.5
普通中学	Regular Secondary Schools	75.0	74.4	95.6	119.2	155.0	165.7
职业中学	Vocational Secondary Schools	0.3	3.5	10.7	10.8	14.2	13.7
小　学	Primary Schools	203.9	212.8	240.9	264.0	291.0	296.7
女教师占教师总数的百分比（%）	**Percentage of Female Teachers to Total Teachers(%)**	**32.4**	**35.2**	**38.4**	**42.0**	**45.5**	**46.3**
高等学校	Institutions of Higher Education	25.5	26.7	29.1	32.9	37.6	38.2
中等专业学校	Specialized Secondary Schools	26.6	32.8	38.0	41.6	44.6	44.9
普通中学	Regular Secondary Schools	24.8	28.1	31.5	35.8	40.4	41.4
职业中学	Vocational Secondary Schools	13.0	24.8	31.5	37.0	42.3	42.9
小　学	Primary Schools	37.1	39.6	43.2	46.6	49.7	50.6

20–21 各级各类成人学校基本情况（2000年）

Student Enrollment in Adult Schools by Level and Type (2000)

单位:所、万人 (unit,10 000 persons)

项目	Item	学校数 Schools	毕业生数 Graduates	招生数 New Student Enrollment	在校学生数 Student Enrollment	教职工数 Teachers and Staff	#专任教师 Full-time Teachers
总计	**Total**	**655423**	**10138.31**	**8789.20**	**7516.54**	**107.93**	**46.88**
成人高等学校	**Adult Education Schools**	**772**	**88.04**	**156.15**	**353.64**	**18.70**	**9.34**
广播电视大学	Radio and TV Universities	45	9.90	15.91	34.70	5.68	2.83
职工、农民高等学院	Schools of Higher Education for Staff, Workers and Peasants	469	9.90	14.22	33.32	7.40	3.82
管理干部学院	Colleges for Management Cadres	117	6.41	7.35	16.70	2.84	1.20
教育学院	Pedagogical Colleges	138	6.25	13.19	25.78	2.71	1.44
独立函授学院	Independent Correspondence Colleges	3	0.44	0.59	1.27	0.08	0.05
普通高等学校办	Run by Institution of Higher Education		55.16	104.88	241.87		
函授部	Correspondence Divisions		31.00	60.00	141.28		
夜大学	Evening Schools		10.60	19.09	48.64		
成人脱产班	Short-cycle Courses for Adults		13.55	25.79	51.96		
成人中等学校	**Secondary Schools for Adults**	**494111**	**9545.77**	**8179.30**	**6677.66**	**73.16**	**32.93**
中等专业学校	Specialized Secondary Schools for Adults	4634	111.40	74.94	240.28	20.85	11.84
广播电视中等专业学校	Radio and TV Specialized Secondary Schools	148	20.30	13.43	48.30	1.88	0.95
干部中等专业学校	Specialized Secondary Schools for Cadres	1807	29.67	19.27	65.09	7.83	4.26
职工中等专业学校	Specialized Secondary Schools for Staff	213	3.84	1.99	7.10	1.10	0.56
农民中等专业学校	Specialized Secondary Schools for Peasants	381	6.99	5.87	16.48	1.81	1.17
函授中等专业学校	Specialized Correspondence Secondary Schools	77	5.92	4.09	10.48	0.96	0.46
教师进修学校	Teacher Training Schools	2008	12.60	8.73	21.81	7.27	4.44
成人中学	Secondary Schools for Adults	3921	38.15	44.92	50.73	2.91	1.76
职工中学	Secondary Schools for Staff and Workers	1299	18.65	26.34	25.56	1.62	0.94
农民中学	Secondary Schools for Peasants	2622	19.50	18.57	25.17	1.29	0.82
成人技术培训学校	Technical Training Schools for Adults	485556	9396.22	8059.44	6386.65	49.40	19.33
职工技术培训学校	Technical Training Schools for Staff and Workers	10630	588.89	542.88	364.07	8.89	4.74
农民技术培训学校	Technical Training Schools for Peasants	474926	8807.33	7516.56	6022.58	40.51	14.59
成人初等学校	**Primary Schools for Adults**	**160540**	**504.49**	**453.76**	**485.24**	**16.07**	**4.62**
职工初等学校	Primary Schools for Staff and Workers	627	10.97	11.18	11.78	0.19	0.09
农民初等学校	Primary Schools for Peasants	159913	493.52	442.58	473.46	15.88	4.53
#扫盲班	Literacy Courses	107501	258.04	214.01	252.99	10.87	2.84

20-22 各地区高等学校分类别学校数（2000年）

Number of Institutions of Higher Education by Region and Type (2000)

单位：所 (unit)

地区	Region	合计 Total	综合大学 Comprehensive Universities	理工院校 Science and Engineering	农业院校 Agriculture	林业院校 Forestry	医药院校 Medicine
全国	**National Total**	**1041**	**83**	**239**	**44**	**6**	**100**
北京	Beijing	58	3	19	2	1	3
天津	Tianjin	21	1	6	1		2
河北	Hebei	51	1	15	3		5
山西	Shanxi	24	1	4	1		4
内蒙古	Inner Mongolia	18	1	2	1		2
辽宁	Liaoning	64	4	19	2		6
吉林	Jilin	34	4	9	2		2
黑龙江	Heilongjiang	35	5	7	2	1	5
上海	Shanghai	37	2	12	1		2
江苏	Jiangsu	69	4	23	1	1	7
浙江	Zhejiang	35	2	6	1	1	3
安徽	Anhui	42	1	7	1		4
福建	Fujian	28	2	4	1		2
江西	Jiangxi	32	6	6	1		5
山东	Shandong	47	7	10	2		7
河南	Henan	52	2	14	4		3
湖北	Hubei	54	5	12	2		4
湖南	Hunan	52	2	14	1	1	4
广东	Guangdong	52	13	4	3		5
广西	Guangxi	30	1	4			4
海南	Hainan	5	1		1		1
重庆	Chongqing	22	2	7	2		1
四川	Sichuan	42	2	12	2		3
贵州	Guizhou	23	1	1			4
云南	Yunnan	24	1	2	1	1	3
西藏	Tibet	4	1		1		1
陕西	Shaanxi	39	3	15	1		2
甘肃	Gansu	18	1	3	1		2
青海	Qinghai	7	1				1
宁夏	Ningxia	6	1		1		1
新疆	Xinjiang	16	2	2	2		2

20-22 续表 1 continued

单位：所 (unit)

地区	Region	师范院校 Teacher Training	语言院校 Linguistics and Literacy	财经院校 Economics and Finance	政法院校 Politics and Law	体育院校 Physical Culture	艺术院校 Art Institutes	民族院校 Nationality Academy	职业技术学院 Short-cycle Vocational Colleges
全 国	**National Total**	**221**	**15**	**68**	**26**	**14**	**29**	**12**	**184**
北 京	Beijing	3	6	4	4	1	7	1	4
天 津	Tianjin	2	1	2		1	2		3
河 北	Hebei	12		2	1	1			11
山 西	Shanxi	8		2	1				3
内蒙古	Inner Mongolia	6	1	1					4
辽 宁	Liaoning	13	1	4	2	1	2	1	9
吉 林	Jilin	6		4	1	1	1		4
黑龙江	Heilongjiang	6		3		1			5
上 海	Shanghai	2	1	6	2	1	2		6
江 苏	Jiangsu	10		3	1	1	1		17
浙 江	Zhejiang	7	1	3	2		1		8
安 徽	Anhui	13		3					13
福 建	Fujian	8	1	1	1				8
江 西	Jiangxi	7		2	1				4
山 东	Shandong	10		3	1	1	2		4
河 南	Henan	12		3	1				13
湖 北	Hubei	7		4	1	1	2	2	14
湖 南	Hunan	13		3	1				13
广 东	Guangdong	4	1	2	1	1	2		16
广 西	Guangxi	10		3		1	1	1	5
海 南	Hainan	2							
重 庆	Chongqing	4	1	1	1		1		2
四 川	Sichuan	12		2	1	1	1	1	5
贵 州	Guizhou	10		2				1	4
云 南	Yunnan	11		1	1		1	1	1
西 藏	Tibet							1	
陕 西	Shaanxi	8	1	2	1	1	2		3
甘 肃	Gansu	6		1	1			1	2
青 海	Qinghai	3						1	1
宁 夏	Ningxia	1						1	1
新 疆	Xinjiang	5		1			1		1

20−23 各地区高等学校教职工数（2000年）

Number of Teachers and Staff in Institutions of Higher Education by Region (2000)

单位：人 (person)

地 区	Region	教职工总数 Total	校本部教职工 Number of Staff and Workers	专任教师 Full-time Teachers	教辅人员 Auxiliary Teaching Staff	行政人员 Administrative Personnel	工勤人员 Logistics Personnel
全 国	**National Total**	**1112776**	**930068**	**462772**	**138859**	**182948**	**145489**
北 京	Beijing	105154	81704	34863	18578	14793	13470
天 津	Tianjin	25952	21622	10137	3778	4453	3254
河 北	Hebei	46327	39836	19414	5035	8046	7341
山 西	Shanxi	24950	20899	10466	3062	4072	3299
内蒙古	Inner Mongolia	19228	17576	8856	2579	3499	2642
辽 宁	Liaoning	61707	53313	27508	7726	10579	7500
吉 林	Jilin	41813	36519	17476	5676	6984	6383
黑龙江	Heilongjiang	43120	33944	16169	4746	6906	6123
上 海	Shanghai	60799	44775	20491	8164	8929	7191
江 苏	Jiangsu	78850	64758	33085	9376	12599	9698
浙 江	Zhejiang	35083	29638	16057	3863	5844	3874
安 徽	Anhui	31860	28321	15065	3569	5281	4406
福 建	Fujian	21826	18744	9779	2424	4195	2346
江 西	Jiangxi	25573	20429	10380	2555	4262	3232
山 东	Shandong	54910	47499	24764	5883	10133	6719
河 南	Henan	44378	39068	20239	5326	7438	6065
湖 北	Hubei	72265	58902	30363	8204	12031	8304
湖 南	Hunan	46642	39745	20317	5137	7561	6730
广 东	Guangdong	46827	39975	20433	6401	8614	4527
广 西	Guangxi	19304	17141	9326	2591	3164	2060
海 南	Hainan	3848	3333	1571	442	698	622
重 庆	Chongqing	24970	20371	10449	3182	3914	2826
四 川	Sichuan	46092	39271	18418	5799	7763	7291
贵 州	Guizhou	14884	13892	7240	2021	2623	2008
云 南	Yunnan	19847	18352	9237	2473	3882	2760
西 藏	Tibet	1673	1607	813	153	392	249
陕 西	Shaanxi	52220	41037	20723	5440	7078	7796
甘 肃	Gansu	16557	14081	7208	1998	2341	2534
青 海	Qinghai	4229	3883	2107	429	714	633
宁 夏	Ningxia	3996	3645	1894	387	715	649
新 疆	Xinjiang	17892	16188	7924	1862	3445	2957

20－24 各地区中等专业学校数（2000年）

Number of Specialized Secondary Schools by Region and Type (2000)

单位：所 (unit)

地区	Region	合计 Total	中等技术学校 Technical Secondary Schools	工业学校 Engineering	农业学校 Agriculture	林业学校 Forestry	医药学校 Medicine	财经学校 Economtics and Finance	政法学校 Politics and Law	体育学校 Physical Culture	艺术学校 Art	其他学校 Others	中等师范学校 Secondary Teacher Training Schools
全国	**National Total**	**3646**	**2963**	**957**	**313**	**47**	**489**	**535**	**126**	**176**	**168**	**152**	**683**
北京	Beijing	108	92	29	1	1	35	8	4	7	6	1	16
天津	Tianjin	80	70	23	1	1	8	8	3	5	4	17	10
河北	Hebei	149	117	31	15	1	20	23	7	9	6	5	32
山西	Shanxi	127	105	25	14	1	15	23	4	7	11	5	22
内蒙古	Inner Mongolia	86	81	23	12	2	16	15	6	1	4	2	5
辽宁	Liaoning	133	124	40	10	1	20	16	4	14	13	6	9
吉林	Jilin	98	81	16	9	3	10	9	4	6	2	22	17
黑龙江	Heilongjiang	109	83	24	10	6	16	16	5	3	2	1	26
上海	Shanghai	83	82	38	3	1	18	10	2	3	6	1	1
江苏	Jiangsu	187	160	76	9		17	29	3	11	11	4	27
浙江	Zhejiang	86	85	24	6	1	8	18	5	6	5	12	1
安徽	Anhui	138	104	44	12	1	18	21	2	2	3	1	34
福建	Fujian	119	94	33	12	2	15	18	4	3	6	1	25
江西	Jiangxi	97	76	25	12	2	13	14	3	3	3	1	21
山东	Shandong	243	187	68	17		28	35	8	16	10	5	56
河南	Henan	176	135	41	6	3	22	31	7	8	14	3	41
湖北	Hubei	203	180	71	9	4	22	31	9	10	15	9	23
湖南	Hunan	144	118	44	21	1	11	24	3	5	5	4	26
广东	Guangdong	244	198	63	13	2	37	36	9	17	13	8	46
广西	Guangxi	127	98	34	9	3	18	20	4	1	4	5	29
海南	Hainan	34	26	7	5		4	6	2	1	1		8
重庆	Chongqing	62	41	10	7		10	6	1	1	3	3	21
四川	Sichuan	194	128	41	16	1	25	26	4	2	4	9	66
贵州	Guizhou	104	79	18	15	2	14	19	4	2	2	3	25
云南	Yunnan	127	108	24	19	2	18	23	5	6	4	7	19
西藏	Tibet	12	11		1			1	1			8	1
陕西	Shaanxi	111	89	28	11	2	14	15	4	9	4	2	22
甘肃	Gansu	113	91	27	13	2	14	15	2	10	2	6	22
青海	Qinghai	15	8	4	1		1			1	1		7
宁夏	Ningxia	25	21	5	3	1	3	4	2	1	1	1	4
新疆	Xinjiang	112	91	21	21	1	19	15	5	6	3		21

20-25 各地区中等专业学校教职工数（2000年）

Number of Teachers and Staff in Specialized Secondary Schools by Region (2000)

单位：人 (person)

地 区	Region	教职工总数 Total	校本部教职工 Number of Teachers and Staff in Central Campus	专任教师 Full-time Teachers	教辅人员 Auxiliary Teaching Staff	行政人员 Administrative Personnel	工勤人员 Logistics Personnel
全 国	**National Total**	**488083**	**462739**	**256419**	**44138**	**87076**	**75106**
北 京	Beijing	10468	9879	4648	1201	2173	1857
天 津	Tianjin	10716	10240	5548	898	2099	1695
河 北	Hebei	27030	25860	14091	2320	4821	4628
山 西	Shanxi	18600	18016	9823	1601	3468	3124
内蒙古	Inner Mongolia	11645	11296	6216	1269	2104	1707
辽 宁	Liaoning	18651	17582	9285	1903	3401	2993
吉 林	Jilin	14639	13924	7748	1169	2968	2039
黑龙江	Heilongjiang	16443	15283	7358	1507	3162	3256
上 海	Shanghai	12673	11381	5242	1238	2208	2693
江 苏	Jiangsu	25014	23618	13686	2198	4108	3626
浙 江	Zhejiang	9662	9182	5285	920	1531	1446
安 徽	Anhui	16034	15408	8815	1437	2791	2365
福 建	Fujian	12412	11903	6920	1114	2154	1715
江 西	Jiangxi	13304	12500	7213	1287	2125	1875
山 东	Shandong	37241	35417	20409	3349	6863	4796
河 南	Henan	30355	28238	16640	2479	4925	4194
湖 北	Hubei	28816	27238	15549	2593	5303	3793
湖 南	Hunan	21078	19755	10775	1903	3826	3251
广 东	Guangdong	24579	23963	14131	2456	4155	3221
广 西	Guangxi	17206	15379	8800	1525	2474	2580
海 南	Hainan	3284	3165	1809	233	558	565
重 庆	Chongqing	8168	7587	4125	825	1383	1254
四 川	Sichuan	25608	24205	12732	2519	4803	4151
贵 州	Guizhou	11617	11317	6628	751	2570	1368
云 南	Yunnan	14084	13782	7750	1053	2439	2540
西 藏	Tibet	1255	1221	742	54	188	237
陕 西	Shaanxi	16535	15134	7979	1683	3030	2442
甘 肃	Gansu	12775	12455	6779	1098	2153	2425
青 海	Qinghai	2398	2376	1363	178	409	426
宁 夏	Ningxia	3000	2878	1544	266	523	545
新 疆	Xinjiang	12793	12557	6786	1111	2361	2299

20−26 各地区高等学校和中等专业学校学生数（2000年）

Enrollment of Institutions of Higher Education and Specialized Secondary Schools by Region (2000)

单位：人 (person)

地区	Region	高等学校 Institutions of Higher Education			中等专业学校 Specialized Secondary Schools		
		毕业生数 Number of Graduates	招生数 New Student Enrollment	在校学生数 Student Enrollment	毕业生数 Number of Graduates	招生数 New Student Enrollment	在校学生数 Student Enrollment
全国	**National Total**	**949767**	**2206072**	**5560900**	**1507237**	**1325870**	**4895159**
北京	Beijing	51931	97736	280282	28113	27816	119427
天津	Tianjin	20112	45468	119117	23325	20209	89505
河北	Hebei	43473	111033	252571	72519	61751	235228
山西	Shanxi	20657	49428	125023	42356	67975	196494
内蒙古	Inner Mongolia	12218	33456	71868	24099	30195	106407
辽宁	Liaoning	53353	113319	307931	35843	30399	148905
吉林	Jilin	30480	67807	181019	42018	22569	118238
黑龙江	Heilongjiang	35180	79970	210146	38157	35473	115489
上海	Shanghai	40929	81328	226798	38556	29978	118906
江苏	Jiangsu	75643	172491	451844	144900	106369	436216
浙江	Zhejiang	32477	77608	192371	50834	35425	148010
安徽	Anhui	29830	80204	191824	60437	49191	191891
福建	Fujian	24307	53267	137859	33130	34819	129041
江西	Jiangxi	25903	57921	148589	45776	45379	160022
山东	Shandong	58355	135185	325317	103629	93493	333184
河南	Henan	45709	122896	273404	112019	99713	334790
湖北	Hubei	56566	142237	357728	125593	62418	278602
湖南	Hunan	47426	105237	265849	73076	63625	258342
广东	Guangdong	51432	123338	306019	83030	68358	256875
广西	Guangxi	21858	49432	123729	41688	40990	158671
海南	Hainan	4021	8181	19193	8613	10951	30722
重庆	Chongqing	22187	49951	126279	29381	23095	84524
四川	Sichuan	42672	100965	245648	77620	60854	232481
贵州	Guizhou	13739	33718	79833	35003	38447	119991
云南	Yunnan	18573	33879	95893	37651	37636	119199
西藏	Tibet	764	2320	5475	1895	2957	6585
陕西	Shaanxi	36587	97209	244723	43730	44352	146614
甘肃	Gansu	14255	33825	82577	19921	29898	82259
青海	Qinghai	2202	6176	13485	4093	4781	13406
宁夏	Ningxia	3154	7207	17463	4390	7973	19880
新疆	Xinjiang	13774	33280	81043	25842	38781	105255

20−27 各地区普通中学分城乡学校和在校学生数（2000年）

Number of Regular Secondary Schools and Student Enrollment by Urban and Rural Areas and by Region (2000)

地区	Region	学校数（所） Number of Regular Secondary Schools (unit)							
		合计 Total	#高中 Senior Secondary Schools	城市 Urban Areas	#高中 Senior Secondary Schools	县镇 Counties and Towns	#高中 Senior Secondary Schools	农村 Rural Areas	#高中 Senior Secondary Schools
全国	**National Total**	**77268**	**14564**	**14473**	**5760**	**20853**	**6175**	**41942**	**2629**
北京	Beijing	760	302	370	206	235	83	155	13
天津	Tianjin	690	215	342	123	157	72	191	20
河北	Hebei	4910	716	725	257	1425	373	2760	86
山西	Shanxi	3346	443	486	201	490	157	2370	85
内蒙古	Inner Mongolia	1707	377	385	177	430	157	892	43
辽宁	Liaoning	2401	461	787	277	361	127	1253	57
吉林	Jilin	1710	288	473	160	640	124	597	4
黑龙江	Heilongjiang	2674	463	789	241	684	177	1201	45
上海	Shanghai	875	333	514	199	318	124	43	10
江苏	Jiangsu	3675	859	585	213	1967	500	1123	146
浙江	Zhejiang	2940	620	526	224	1815	391	599	5
安徽	Anhui	3767	674	499	224	399	190	2869	260
福建	Fujian	1921	477	262	130	877	281	782	66
江西	Jiangxi	2792	506	341	172	990	287	1461	47
山东	Shandong	4575	714	864	288	459	185	3252	241
河南	Henan	6217	761	897	313	1405	301	3915	147
湖北	Hubei	3261	583	1128	371	300	111	1833	101
湖南	Hunan	4505	712	642	265	1392	305	2471	142
广东	Guangdong	3964	947	703	337	1114	301	2147	309
广西	Guangxi	3019	464	281	113	610	227	2128	124
海南	Hainan	503	93	47	17	69	39	387	37
重庆	Chongqing	1568	281	527	142	536	129	505	10
四川	Sichuan	4321	783	535	258	1694	488	2092	37
贵州	Guizhou	1953	305	269	89	328	128	1356	88
云南	Yunnan	2236	418	223	111	566	241	1447	66
西藏	Tibet	98	15	19	8	78	7	1	
陕西	Shaanxi	2599	579	577	268	795	233	1227	78
甘肃	Gansu	1689	419	233	130	236	142	1220	147
青海	Qinghai	448	165	68	47	145	88	235	30
宁夏	Ningxia	433	107	63	28	80	45	290	34
新疆	Xinjiang	1711	484	313	171	258	162	1140	151

20-27 续表 1 continued

地 区	Region	在校学生数（人） Student Enrollment (person) 合 计 Total	#高中 Senior Secondary Schools	城 市 Urban Areas	#高中 Senior Secondary Schools	县 镇 Counties and Towns	#高中 Senior Secondary Schools	农 村 Rural Areas	#高中 Senior Secondary Schools
全 国	**National Total**	**73689101**	**12012643**	**14970220**	**4623869**	**22856105**	**5810662**	**35862776**	**1578112**
北 京	Beijing	691353	179002	357050	121085	227052	53568	107251	4349
天 津	Tianjin	570577	124147	263378	72712	141047	38831	166152	12604
河 北	Hebei	4817454	700396	761349	221823	1626857	416054	2429248	62519
山 西	Shanxi	1997500	337163	454412	145567	473960	153020	1069128	38576
内蒙古	Inner Mongolia	1307251	266394	403069	125343	449471	126056	454711	14995
辽 宁	Liaoning	2167017	429393	876538	239746	401107	154647	889372	35000
吉 林	Jilin	1431195	262681	541757	166727	524941	94563	364497	1391
黑龙江	Heilongjiang	2487437	328765	786521	188626	698562	119784	1002354	20355
上 海	Shanghai	803480	241351	494475	158897	288647	79423	20358	3031
江 苏	Jiangsu	3736462	801815	611097	175532	2065826	497306	1059539	128977
浙 江	Zhejiang	2495527	554343	568712	203876	1625812	346588	301003	3879
安 徽	Anhui	3583191	541417	489656	158198	527912	212499	2565623	170720
福 建	Fujian	2335032	372400	305745	99803	1315850	236769	713437	35828
江 西	Jiangxi	2592189	385287	351159	122629	1160177	239734	1080853	22924
山 东	Shandong	6786003	1086363	1297197	441694	826447	371588	4662359	273081
河 南	Henan	6381450	751508	847784	260038	1634326	397640	3899340	93830
湖 北	Hubei	3509318	698409	1196566	424406	404508	171592	1908244	102411
湖 南	Hunan	3917326	625719	608591	197265	1411957	311826	1896778	116628
广 东	Guangdong	4606890	725276	848971	235893	1433648	313784	2324271	175599
广 西	Guangxi	2856320	369286	301030	79259	664368	228964	1890922	61063
海 南	Hainan	435789	59857	44488	11986	121585	37796	269716	10075
重 庆	Chongqing	1477861	210858	466678	93945	597361	108249	413822	8664
四 川	Sichuan	3919813	563110	537987	187032	1712996	360641	1668830	15437
贵 州	Guizhou	1572025	191059	219974	62397	322088	104528	1029963	24134
云 南	Yunnan	1859651	222076	185001	63265	580299	139169	1094351	19642
西 藏	Tibet	55232	12111	17836	7581	37219	4530	177	
陕 西	Shaanxi	2305168	427224	538693	155245	901311	235955	865164	36024
甘 肃	Gansu	1314710	229500	231339	76637	280614	112326	802757	40537
青 海	Qinghai	224660	49391	47261	12621	84712	30349	92687	6421
宁 夏	Ningxia	318308	67703	54725	17438	104638	41076	158945	9189
新 疆	Xinjiang	1132912	198639	261181	96603	210807	71807	660924	30229

20–28 各地区普通中学分城乡招生数和毕业生数（2000年）

Number of New Student Enrollment and Graduates of Regular Secondary Schools by Urban and Rural Areas and Region (2000)

单位：人 (person)

地区	Region	招生数 New Student Enrollment							
		合计		城市		县镇		农村	
		Total	#高中 Senior Secondary Schools	Urban Areas	#高中 Senior Secondary Schools	Counties and Towns	#高中 Senior Secondary Schools	Rural Areas	#高中 Senior Secondary Schools
全国	**National Total**	**27359900**	**4726861**	**5468321**	**1764846**	**8589208**	**2318434**	**13302371**	**643581**
北京	Beijing	249074	65890	125265	43652	84934	20723	38875	1515
天津	Tianjin	194353	45116	87066	25323	51500	14724	55787	5069
河北	Hebei	1772213	262226	283758	81521	603504	157183	884951	23522
山西	Shanxi	726669	137662	169123	58836	172901	62496	384645	16330
内蒙古	Inner Mongolia	477260	109322	147920	51544	164681	51492	164659	6286
辽宁	Liaoning	830026	152354	310784	84514	153140	55013	366102	12827
吉林	Jilin	532233	96073	197341	59895	196721	35695	138171	483
黑龙江	Heilongjiang	780271	118418	256248	68548	221235	43333	302788	6537
上海	Shanghai	267248	79046	163130	51980	97166	26172	6952	894
江苏	Jiangsu	1414377	299301	227094	64600	791902	184567	395381	50134
浙江	Zhejiang	925094	207631	213872	75958	602177	130260	109045	1413
安徽	Anhui	1297505	219633	183680	62593	202738	86876	911087	70164
福建	Fujian	818116	151798	110788	38778	459248	97916	248080	15104
江西	Jiangxi	966221	160494	130584	49190	433400	101244	402237	10060
山东	Shandong	2341830	425643	455211	173340	306450	150954	1580169	101349
河南	Henan	2464595	314818	331330	104878	640629	167840	1492636	42100
湖北	Hubei	1352592	277065	450189	168541	157420	68314	744983	40210
湖南	Hunan	1518734	260515	235890	78537	546832	132230	736012	49748
广东	Guangdong	1711562	286825	313575	90734	526477	122898	871510	73193
广西	Guangxi	1098409	153372	112015	31528	253577	93891	732817	27953
海南	Hainan	159425	22886	16265	4455	42667	13942	100493	4489
重庆	Chongqing	545615	82011	162457	35144	228538	42969	154620	3898
四川	Sichuan	1527602	224216	200382	68657	677520	148849	649700	6710
贵州	Guizhou	641859	84393	84771	25191	130975	46619	426113	12583
云南	Yunnan	698372	88214	66289	23868	219557	56312	412526	8034
西藏	Tibet	25662	5289	7247	3247	18335	2042	80	
陕西	Shaanxi	889446	181652	203506	62425	347725	102159	338215	17068
甘肃	Gansu	508648	90840	83659	28861	108470	45134	316519	16845
青海	Qinghai	86540	19791	18254	4733	31855	12143	36431	2915
宁夏	Ningxia	119559	27623	20815	6534	38528	16452	60216	4637
新疆	Xinjiang	418790	76744	99813	37241	78406	27992	240571	11511

20-28 续表 1 continued

单位：人 (person)

地区	Region	毕业生数 Number of Graduates 合计 Total	#高中 Senior Secondary Schools	城市 Urban Areas	#高中 Senior Secondary Schools	县镇 Counties and Towns	#高中 Senior Secondary Schools	农村 Rural Areas	#高中 Senior Secondary Schools
全国	**National Total**	**19085957**	**3015089**	**3810082**	**1164590**	**5845920**	**1458461**	**9429955**	**392038**
北京	Beijing	186501	47569	104657	33197	55734	12988	26110	1384
天津	Tianjin	157481	33584	88292	20148	36218	10049	32971	3387
河北	Hebei	1315824	181626	192078	57241	420844	108773	702902	15612
山西	Shanxi	561751	78622	120923	32814	131068	37111	309760	8697
内蒙古	Inner Mongolia	339789	67474	97518	29446	120113	33430	122158	4598
辽宁	Liaoning	551157	118892	227469	62385	105490	46479	218198	10028
吉林	Jilin	396333	70225	146857	43589	147574	26239	101902	397
黑龙江	Heilongjiang	578390	91419	179908	51583	166972	34430	231510	5406
上海	Shanghai	231455	72547	145862	44236	80144	27243	5449	1068
江苏	Jiangsu	959944	229852	155082	49156	504609	144251	300253	36445
浙江	Zhejiang	668356	139549	145221	48961	439259	89397	83876	1191
安徽	Anhui	1023077	131453	126839	37544	137378	51907	758860	42002
福建	Fujian	690377	78423	85357	22038	379787	48637	225233	7748
江西	Jiangxi	737954	91925	93365	30515	314068	55851	330521	5559
山东	Shandong	1679560	276377	306616	110703	200171	91169	1172773	74505
河南	Henan	1621556	174719	203944	62318	408961	94234	1008651	18167
湖北	Hubei	883828	165813	296755	98353	103291	41382	483782	26078
湖南	Hunan	1000980	145587	150450	48241	358743	71052	491787	26294
广东	Guangdong	1318199	182354	227082	61577	412033	78747	679084	42030
广西	Guangxi	740654	81936	76545	19190	167276	50507	496833	12239
海南	Hainan	118797	14010	11768	2923	33898	9035	73131	2052
重庆	Chongqing	295270	51793	103031	22732	119243	27423	72996	1638
四川	Sichuan	818595	143038	127179	50787	368826	88815	322590	3436
贵州	Guizhou	377175	45846	52335	15632	80907	24737	243933	5477
云南	Yunnan	475426	56504	48945	16661	153075	35115	273406	4728
西藏	Tibet	12124	2458	4133	1499	7947	959	44	
陕西	Shaanxi	562489	98128	135082	37949	210566	51692	216841	8487
甘肃	Gansu	327787	56479	61385	19503	70656	27038	195746	9938
青海	Qinghai	57812	14156	11172	3608	23308	8718	23332	1830
宁夏	Ningxia	89091	17746	15205	4822	29039	11141	44847	1783
新疆	Xinjiang	308225	54985	69027	25239	58722	19912	180476	9834

20-29 各地区普通中学按城乡和主办部门分的教职工数（2000年）

Number of Staff and Full-time Teachers in Regular Secondary Schools by Urban and Rural Areas, by Department and by Region (2000)

单位：人 (person)

地 区	Region	教职工数 Number of Teachers and Staff in Regular Secondary Schools							
			按主办部门分 By Departments				按城乡分 By Urban and Rural Areas		
		合计 Total	教育部门办 Schools Run by Educational Departments	其他部门办 Schools Run by Other Departments	集体办 Schools Run by Collective Units	民办 Run by Private and Other Social Sources	城市 Urban Areas	县镇 Counties and Towns	农村 Rural Area
全 国	**National Total**	**4910968**	**4462585**	**307670**	**41352**	**99361**	**1249134**	**1590535**	**2071299**
北 京	Beijing	73492	67030	4203		2259	41097	21461	10934
天 津	Tianjin	53618	49436	3198	33	951	27865	13463	12290
河 北	Hebei	300842	274573	13958	394	11917	63428	110097	127317
山 西	Shanxi	157870	129937	16226	5893	5814	41107	38248	78515
内蒙古	Inner Mongolia	108125	87868	15856	1682	2719	34568	36544	37013
辽 宁	Liaoning	175455	158211	10461	4939	1844	69439	35745	70271
吉 林	Jilin	117239	99405	15367	478	1989	47480	45153	24606
黑龙江	Heilongjiang	182246	129652	44274	3825	4495	67617	54976	59653
上 海	Shanghai	77452	71986	1785		3681	47495	27893	2064
江 苏	Jiangsu	275736	259500	6546	3614	6076	56330	152027	67379
浙 江	Zhejiang	165200	157428	1657	491	5624	42667	104039	18494
安 徽	Anhui	187610	176252	8502	408	2448	36166	33136	118308
福 建	Fujian	146363	142886	507	268	2702	24941	79330	42092
江 西	Jiangxi	159242	146117	9258	1190	2677	27901	70382	60959
山 东	Shandong	430754	398900	14431	9476	7947	103002	57334	270418
河 南	Henan	360847	337619	16083	1907	5238	69471	99632	191744
湖 北	Hubei	237500	216338	15483	2316	3363	97054	28889	111557
湖 南	Hunan	259989	241639	11905	1600	4845	50037	93313	116639
广 东	Guangdong	275686	262578	6281	853	5974	64210	87259	124217
广 西	Guangxi	165753	153654	7573	486	4040	21479	46353	97921
海 南	Hainan	29461	23421	4810	50	1180	3642	8439	17380
重 庆	Chongqing	103198	97168	4662	143	1225	37828	40702	24668
四 川	Sichuan	265449	250528	13001	363	1557	46180	122667	96602
贵 州	Guizhou	94670	86699	6212	125	1634	17081	23640	53949
云 南	Yunnan	128994	121467	5909	7	1611	16275	44073	68646
西 藏	Tibet	5176	5107	63		6	1760	3382	34
陕 西	Shaanxi	149267	129316	15180	353	4418	40193	56960	52114
甘 肃	Gansu	86072	75823	9585		664	18670	19996	47406
青 海	Qinghai	19378	17013	2125	43	197	4455	8182	6741
宁 夏	Ningxia	23782	20791	2649	76	266	4516	8050	11216
新 疆	Xinjiang	94502	74243	19920	339		25180	19170	50152

20−29 续表 1 continued

单位：人 (person)

地区	Region	专任教师数 Number of Full-time Teachers 合计 Total	按主办部门分 By Department 教育部门办 Schools Run by Educational Departments	其他部门办 Schools Run by Other Departments	集体办 Schools Run by Collective Units	民办 Run by Private and Other Social Sources	按城乡分 By Urban and Rural Areas 城市 Urban Areas	县镇 Counties and Towns	农村 Rural Areas
全国	**National Total**	**4005458**	**3683270**	**230655**	**25140**	**66393**	**944165**	**1274967**	**1786326**
北京	Beijing	48903	44812	2725		1366	25572	15107	8224
天津	Tianjin	39197	36207	2414		576	18748	9783	10666
河北	Hebei	253706	234895	10406	229	8176	48162	90031	115513
山西	Shanxi	127582	106974	12665	4297	3646	30305	29732	67545
内蒙古	Inner Mongolia	79999	66263	11131	747	1858	25023	26980	27996
辽宁	Liaoning	139731	126350	8043	3494	1844	54629	27106	57996
吉林	Jilin	90007	76881	11590	157	1379	35251	34787	19969
黑龙江	Heilongjiang	144399	106205	31978	2908	3308	51902	43087	49410
上海	Shanghai	50676	47075	1201		2400	31330	17943	1403
江苏	Jiangsu	215914	206866	4782	209	4057	40685	120759	54470
浙江	Zhejiang	139256	134153	1267	31	3805	33114	89542	16600
安徽	Anhui	158146	149559	6975	110	1502	28777	26193	103176
福建	Fujian	120667	118455	372	48	1792	19410	65674	35583
江西	Jiangxi	139138	129438	7405	567	1728	23176	60748	55214
山东	Shandong	350353	326727	10868	7186	5572	78039	42250	230064
河南	Henan	308634	291061	12332	1690	3551	52708	82451	173475
湖北	Hubei	198486	183077	12183	1198	2028	77415	23474	97597
湖南	Hunan	223693	210199	9598	529	3367	38733	79404	105556
广东	Guangdong	228602	219971	4577	500	3554	49091	72578	106933
广西	Guangxi	126660	118565	5203	229	2663	16268	33540	76852
海南	Hainan	22776	18849	3125	39	763	2846	6171	13759
重庆	Chongqing	81766	77362	3524	82	798	29062	31588	21116
四川	Sichuan	217039	205983	9913	181	962	34900	98115	84024
贵州	Guizhou	81156	74844	4985	96	1231	13705	18971	48480
云南	Yunnan	105620	100483	4285		852	12208	34622	58790
西藏	Tibet	4306	4261	39		6	1415	2862	29
陕西	Shaanxi	122279	107080	11969	290	2940	31017	46732	44530
甘肃	Gansu	74082	66327	7345		410	14575	16250	43257
青海	Qinghai	16645	14815	1705	2	123	3482	6783	6380
宁夏	Ningxia	20145	17782	2153	74	136	3624	6466	10055
新疆	Xinjiang	75895	61751	13897	247		18993	15238	41664

20-30 各地区小学分城乡学校数和在校学生数（2000年）

Basic Statistics on Primary Schools by Urban and Rural Areas and by Region (2000)

地 区	Region	学校数 (所) Number of Primary Schools (unit)	城市 Urban Areas	县镇 Counties and Towns	农村 Rural Areas	在校学生数 (人) Student Enrollment (person)	城市 Urban Areas	县镇 Counties and Towns	农村 Rural Areas
全 国	**National Total**	**553622**	**32154**	**81184**	**440284**	**130132548**	**18166507**	**26928904**	**85037137**
北 京	Beijing	2169	627	663	879	743109	323762	233779	185568
天 津	Tianjin	2323	443	452	1428	717146	277422	180602	259122
河 北	Hebei	36465	1639	3973	30853	8137268	888237	1253914	5995117
山 西	Shanxi	37451	802	2193	34456	3436044	553794	485352	2396898
内蒙古	Inner Mongolia	10147	599	681	8867	2015076	423300	331942	1259834
辽 宁	Liaoning	13356	1297	706	11353	3444172	999878	422599	2021695
吉 林	Jilin	9435	740	1376	7319	2415858	605145	537538	1273175
黑龙江	Heilongjiang	13995	1082	1019	11894	2830578	757951	482825	1589802
上 海	Shanghai	1034	486	298	250	797512	416808	306165	74539
江 苏	Jiangsu	19110	1545	9768	7797	7185458	888348	3686838	2610272
浙 江	Zhejiang	11841	998	7519	3324	3537556	629724	2327824	580008
安 徽	Anhui	24281	1026	1431	21824	6442405	666678	587830	5187897
福 建	Fujian	13935	671	3662	9602	3691003	421916	1477033	1792054
江 西	Jiangxi	21082	467	7291	13324	4226750	323582	1681404	2221764
山 东	Shandong	26017	2040	1183	22794	7748822	1101761	557319	6089742
河 南	Henan	41269	1811	5309	34149	11306260	1102786	1832510	8370964
湖 北	Hubei	23372	3319	1155	18898	6677422	1585037	457132	4635253
湖 南	Hunan	34521	1640	9261	23620	6639289	776719	2030583	3831987
广 东	Guangdong	24202	2104	1962	20136	9299314	1580904	1460299	6258111
广 西	Guangxi	16109	855	1432	13822	5367949	430582	635935	4301432
海 南	Hainan	4167	128	137	3902	1035810	92484	119069	824257
重 庆	Chongqing	14730	2773	4137	7820	2761308	659439	920462	1181407
四 川	Sichuan	43326	714	3776	38836	8026506	527531	1591598	5907377
贵 州	Guizhou	17985	706	1410	15869	5002082	325695	513954	4162433
云 南	Yunnan	22151	338	1590	20223	4720611	210729	618454	3891428
西 藏	Tibet	842	26	91	725	313807	21674	43530	248603
陕 西	Shaanxi	33336	2173	6948	24215	4809315	773417	1404165	2631733
甘 肃	Gansu	21557	497	824	20236	3164603	293470	298438	2572695
青 海	Qinghai	3429	102	365	2962	504750	78689	100092	325969
宁 夏	Ningxia	3267	96	115	3056	657352	76070	86663	494619
新 疆	Xinjiang	6718	410	457	5851	2477413	352975	263056	1861382

20-30 续表 1 continued

地区	Region	毕业生数（人）Number of Graduates (persons)	城市 Urban Areas	县镇 Counties and Towns	农村 Rural Areas	招生数（人）New Student Enrollment (person)	城市 Urban Areas	县镇 Counties and Towns	农村 Rural Areas
全国	**National Total**	**24191773**	**3478149**	**5037549**	**15676075**	**19464653**	**2891190**	**4035987**	**12537476**
北京	Beijing	185059	79077	58062	47920	92002	42851	27826	21325
天津	Tianjin	155253	62634	36974	55645	100453	33690	29071	37692
河北	Hebei	1549252	175713	231214	1142325	1070513	136476	171790	762247
山西	Shanxi	640894	97785	90048	453061	631942	99540	93384	439018
内蒙古	Inner Mongolia	432930	83443	72978	276509	327021	74922	56318	195781
辽宁	Liaoning	722325	221179	88158	412988	508907	151823	66347	290737
吉林	Jilin	486000	126041	111452	248507	313295	90143	72451	150701
黑龙江	Heilongjiang	698124	177835	114883	405406	442988	132628	80212	230148
上海	Shanghai	189754	110967	61955	16832	104092	49479	44568	10045
江苏	Jiangsu	1147774	166557	590561	390656	955262	130689	490630	333943
浙江	Zhejiang	718471	119257	475124	124090	615772	106823	404545	104404
安徽	Anhui	1211986	112043	109573	990370	1165995	106712	107711	951572
福建	Fujian	686385	72511	280928	332946	493384	63707	211648	218029
江西	Jiangxi	856148	68694	334748	452706	677872	60358	276378	341136
山东	Shandong	1951160	262330	136406	1552424	1044775	182033	79449	783293
河南	Henan	2255704	209841	386204	1659659	1711119	173143	269010	1268966
湖北	Hubei	1160203	281706	84207	794290	904559	239984	75192	589383
湖南	Hunan	1302004	146813	409130	746061	717496	105176	212304	400016
广东	Guangdong	1484833	221932	221904	1040997	1557286	287450	246412	1023424
广西	Guangxi	1036978	81350	117101	838527	767579	62842	90361	614376
海南	Hainan	154099	12659	20369	121071	156735	14806	17501	124428
重庆	Chongqing	496681	130154	162394	204133	466086	111669	152939	201478
四川	Sichuan	1397579	96879	304769	995931	1256880	92467	250169	914244
贵州	Guizhou	732301	50732	80897	600672	810492	54575	82571	673346
云南	Yunnan	721486	35627	100337	585522	702017	34806	96045	571166
西藏	Tibet	37039	3562	7007	26470	57969	3705	7207	47057
陕西	Shaanxi	769965	138925	228522	402518	682226	117395	198515	366316
甘肃	Gansu	459255	49712	46466	363077	552740	49822	53653	449265
青海	Qinghai	75615	12885	16780	45950	93584	12723	18115	62746
宁夏	Ningxia	104758	13523	15280	75955	119419	11527	15466	92426
新疆	Xinjiang	371758	55783	43118	272857	364193	57226	38199	268768

20-31 各地区小学按城乡和主办部门分的教职工数（2000年）

Number of Staff and Full-time Teachers in Primary Schools by Urban and Rural Areas, by Department and by Region (2000)

单位：人 (person)

地区	Region	教职工数 Number of Teachers and Staff in Primary Schools							
		合计 Total	按主办部门分 By Department				按城乡分 By Urban and Rural Areas		
			教育部门办 Schools Run by Educational Departments	其他部门办 Schools Run by Other Departments	集体办 Schools Run by Collective Units	民办 Run by Private and Other Social Sources	城市 Urban Areas	县镇 Counties and Towns	农村 Rural Areas
全国	**National Total**	**6454862**	**5774093**	**319044**	**292340**	**69385**	**1075403**	**1396831**	**3982628**
北京	Beijing	71701	68612	2297		792	32266	20445	18990
天津	Tianjin	56948	54225	2395	3	325	25153	15375	16420
河北	Hebei	353278	329813	12754	5619	5092	51987	61453	239838
山西	Shanxi	196165	145590	19222	29426	1927	34615	27816	133734
内蒙古	Inner Mongolia	149283	125276	16294	6634	1079	27423	24886	96974
辽宁	Liaoning	216677	190346	9194	16534	603	59245	27230	130202
吉林	Jilin	173182	153890	16608	2224	460	41132	41070	90980
黑龙江	Heilongjiang	221859	162764	47237	10307	1551	52585	39017	130257
上海	Shanghai	62145	59503	1513		1129	30456	25848	5841
江苏	Jiangsu	319959	308710	6696	2475	2078	51143	164790	104026
浙江	Zhejiang	175662	171779	1016	38	2829	32596	111145	31921
安徽	Anhui	289125	271387	10441	6246	1051	34320	28035	226770
福建	Fujian	197272	194892	728	97	1555	23631	73538	100103
江西	Jiangxi	234242	199180	9673	23785	1604	18362	91096	124784
山东	Shandong	440161	356105	11645	69377	3034	75371	35409	329381
河南	Henan	489530	445585	15815	24511	3619	60613	83451	345466
湖北	Hubei	299994	226291	15794	55718	2191	84877	23515	191602
湖南	Hunan	324199	305723	13733	2292	2451	44019	100764	179416
广东	Guangdong	420835	390313	8173	7980	14369	76981	66127	277727
广西	Guangxi	230492	216794	7869	1973	3856	24088	37753	168651
海南	Hainan	56307	41769	9833	3090	1615	4742	6917	44648
重庆	Chongqing	133451	124793	4222	2797	1639	40377	42182	50892
四川	Sichuan	369525	350417	10698	5270	3140	31630	84397	253498
贵州	Guizhou	187305	171442	6240	5444	4179	17052	26639	143614
云南	Yunnan	225293	216995	6946	248	1104	12003	33415	179875
西藏	Tibet	13936	12174	66	1674	22	1615	3002	9319
陕西	Shaanxi	199395	176529	13102	6796	2968	40476	57329	101590
甘肃	Gansu	131298	119937	8423	156	2782	16028	14315	100955
青海	Qinghai	29371	26173	1930	1063	205	4052	6518	18801
宁夏	Ningxia	36586	33102	3144	204	136	4182	5645	26759
新疆	Xinjiang	149686	123984	25343	359		22383	17709	109594

20-31 续表 1 continued

单位：人 (person)

地区	Region	专任教师数 Number of Full-time Teachers in Primary Schools 合计 Total	按主办部门分 By Department 教育部门办 Schools Run by Educational Departments	其他部门办 Schools Run by Other Departments	集体办 Schools Run by Collective Units	民办 Run by Private and Other Social Sources	按城乡分 By Urban and Rural Areas 城市 Urban Areas	县镇 Counties and Towns	农村 Rural Areas
全国	**National Total**	**5860316**	**5262497**	**269835**	**277207**	**50777**	**927155**	**1255146**	**3678015**
北京	Beijing	58002	55523	1911		568	24961	16658	16383
天津	Tianjin	46697	44538	2025		134	19519	12721	14457
河北	Hebei	329525	309438	10845	5519	3723	45678	56191	227656
山西	Shanxi	180362	133789	16441	28849	1283	30022	25100	125240
内蒙古	Inner Mongolia	129242	109222	13155	6004	861	23132	20575	85535
辽宁	Liaoning	185884	162108	7614	15559	603	48863	23675	113346
吉林	Jilin	150291	134456	13439	2059	337	33850	33735	82706
黑龙江	Heilongjiang	193113	145466	36682	9906	1059	43334	32661	117118
上海	Shanghai	44955	42952	1172		831	22187	18021	4747
江苏	Jiangsu	289030	280016	5917	1721	1376	45741	148136	95153
浙江	Zhejiang	160396	157901	881	23	1591	29059	102138	29199
安徽	Anhui	273745	257547	9374	6012	812	31700	26207	215838
福建	Fujian	183547	181793	649	84	1021	21614	66915	95018
江西	Jiangxi	223047	189867	8907	22915	1358	16889	86829	119329
山东	Shandong	408200	328634	10010	67300	2256	65834	32156	310210
河南	Henan	459277	419658	13559	23576	2484	53714	77474	328089
湖北	Hubei	274979	207562	13875	51925	1617	75377	21459	178143
湖南	Hunan	306387	290393	12388	1893	1713	39455	95449	171483
广东	Guangdong	364118	340013	6793	7539	9773	64469	58484	241165
广西	Guangxi	198977	187362	6619	1865	3131	21118	33011	144848
海南	Hainan	50339	38004	8311	2976	1048	3952	5965	40422
重庆	Chongqing	119014	111338	3648	2683	1345	35310	37794	45910
四川	Sichuan	331551	316132	9235	3298	2886	27282	73146	231123
贵州	Guizhou	174822	160304	5515	5298	3705	15140	24549	135133
云南	Yunnan	210507	203618	5960	248	681	10588	30472	169447
西藏	Tibet	13181	11424	64	1674	19	1476	2685	9020
陕西	Shaanxi	182297	162351	11534	6647	1765	35070	52396	94831
甘肃	Gansu	125172	115009	7454	156	2553	14370	13338	97464
青海	Qinghai	27706	24766	1751	1040	149	3725	6119	17862
宁夏	Ningxia	34694	31595	2813	191	95	3815	5283	25596
新疆	Xinjiang	131259	109718	21294	247		19911	15804	95544

20-32 各地区职业中学基本情况（2000年）

Basic Statistics on Vocational Secondary Schools by Region (2000)

单位：人 (person)

地区	Region	学校数（所）Number of Schools	毕业生数 Number of Graduates	招生数 New Student Enrollment	在校学生数 Student Enrollment	教职工数 Number of Staff and Teachers	#专任教师 Full-time Teachers
全国	**National Total**	**8849**	**1762836**	**1826648**	**5032062**	**446863**	**320016**
北京	Beijing	144	35667	21965	90283	11975	7067
天津	Tianjin	124	22583	20995	74618	7550	4778
河北	Hebei	463	151104	134336	416143	32634	23782
山西	Shanxi	339	48364	52476	136231	13997	10343
内蒙古	Inner Mongolia	425	55826	74798	207600	19400	14821
辽宁	Liaoning	383	70175	50470	170517	17858	12517
吉林	Jilin	241	52148	52518	128021	12168	8355
黑龙江	Heilongjiang	240	44527	31417	105060	12009	8396
上海	Shanghai	60	39859	24433	84819	6558	3886
江苏	Jiangsu	362	72470	58655	167074	27850	20597
浙江	Zhejiang	506	87847	116921	295840	20237	15411
安徽	Anhui	716	148326	155988	452846	23915	19362
福建	Fujian	262	57863	74985	184902	14233	10382
江西	Jiangxi	278	46151	53136	127129	10665	7056
山东	Shandong	492	153347	149690	430996	41492	28294
河南	Henan	609	186514	165199	479550	33600	24899
湖北	Hubei	290	52549	52411	148770	15105	11047
湖南	Hunan	539	68800	93447	213898	22375	15795
广东	Guangdong	414	65343	86076	217458	19248	15005
广西	Guangxi	240	40815	47251	125321	9877	6532
海南	Hainan	41	3134	3563	8459	1354	1027
重庆	Chongqing	172	31058	31307	77707	9240	6073
四川	Sichuan	349	59976	65013	159309	19400	13556
贵州	Guizhou	258	24438	31824	79937	7082	5368
云南	Yunnan	199	46112	47670	141991	9987	7091
西藏	Tibet		174	81	386		
陕西	Shaanxi	367	57075	78691	182041	13987	9165
甘肃	Gansu	170	15210	21461	52573	6230	4549
青海	Qinghai	31	4645	4069	8331	946	709
宁夏	Ningxia	29	3395	5775	12982	1321	1049
新疆	Xinjiang	106	17341	20027	51270	4570	3104

20−33 各地区幼儿园基本情况（2000年）

Basic Statistics on Kindergartens by Region (2000)

地　区	Region	园　数（所）Number of Kindergartens (unit)	班　数（个）Number of Classes (unit)	幼儿数（人）Student Enrollment (person)	教职工数（人）Number of Staff and Teachers (person)	#教　师 Teachers
全　国	**National Total**	**175836**	**771512**	**22441806**	**1144297**	**856455**
北　京	Beijing	2047	8636	229012	27257	12595
天　津	Tianjin	240	4586	137445	6941	3762
河　北	Hebei	4476	37085	1004186	46306	40291
山　西	Shanxi	10856	37973	1025982	51694	42565
内蒙古	Inner Mongolia	1960	14002	335667	19666	14680
辽　宁	Liaoning	9990	29549	835542	52422	36383
吉　林	Jilin	4407	17236	439184	26189	17609
黑龙江	Heilongjiang	4503	22429	470317	32840	24221
上　海	Shanghai	977	7931	243825	25652	15286
江　苏	Jiangsu	13832	50190	1457445	89438	72298
浙　江	Zhejiang	15073	41271	1124527	67773	51168
安　徽	Anhui	3932	32257	1161911	31676	26470
福　建	Fujian	11885	27454	786387	47492	39409
江　西	Jiangxi	6573	19384	620624	26472	21154
山　东	Shandong	27258	65645	1613045	105727	86057
河　南	Henan	2937	48582	1563655	35959	24369
湖　北	Hubei	3748	25004	726712	40484	29889
湖　南	Hunan	5473	29896	628744	39790	31987
广　东	Guangdong	12027	65447	2141789	129060	83552
广　西	Guangxi	3846	24768	728381	30538	22942
海　南	Hainan	706	4217	128139	6921	4843
重　庆	Chongqing	6659	19866	640804	28249	22598
四　川	Sichuan	12780	54690	1892626	71622	58128
贵　州	Guizhou	1435	13867	496044	17655	14204
云　南	Yunnan	1770	18921	603534	25849	19164
西　藏	Tibet	21	160	4491	322	196
陕　西	Shaanxi	2803	25156	603562	22132	15767
甘　肃	Gansu	2249	13733	427960	14890	10782
青　海	Qinghai	201	2332	63711	2721	2115
宁　夏	Ningxia	340	2855	93117	3820	2672
新　疆	Xinjiang	832	6390	213438	16740	9299

20−34 各地区特殊教育情况（2000年）

Basic Statistics on Special Education by Region (2000)

单位：人 (person)

地区	Region	学校数(所) Number of Schools (unit)	毕业生数 Number of Graduates	招生数 New Student Enrollment	在校学生数 Student Enrollment	教职工数 Number of Staff and Teachers	#专任教师 Full-time Teachers
全 国	**National Total**	**1539**	**43430**	**52939**	**377599**	**43678**	**31983**
北 京	Beijing	24	1347	824	7807	894	644
天 津	Tianjin	24	503	276	2567	658	461
河 北	Hebei	95	1121	1507	9669	2203	1467
山 西	Shanxi	39	604	856	4265	1170	856
内蒙古	Inner Mongolia	29	210	476	3245	974	754
辽 宁	Liaoning	74	818	916	7939	2754	2043
吉 林	Jilin	52	685	709	6306	1882	1331
黑龙江	Heilongjiang	77	1025	1146	7684	2962	2221
上 海	Shanghai	34	868	1141	8893	1584	943
江 苏	Jiangsu	123	3591	3902	35889	3670	2742
浙 江	Zhejiang	62	3701	2445	19749	1396	1139
安 徽	Anhui	70	1907	2223	18346	1262	960
福 建	Fujian	76	7483	6279	40708	1512	1261
江 西	Jiangxi	33	1073	3421	13142	392	329
山 东	Shandong	141	1734	2163	16818	5035	3389
河 南	Henan	121	3353	4529	29744	2929	2289
湖 北	Hubei	74	1310	1655	9739	1676	1231
湖 南	Hunan	57	1138	2090	12179	1203	918
广 东	Guangdong	61	2819	2770	27507	1329	1053
广 西	Guangxi	49	1792	1629	14755	1715	1149
海 南	Hainan	3	159	317	2086	98	70
重 庆	Chongqing	42	1515	4105	21160	731	569
四 川	Sichuan	63	1190	1182	8224	1377	1113
贵 州	Guizhou	28	960	2225	15845	2080	1482
云 南	Yunnan	24	727	1603	15526	589	448
西 藏	Tibet	1	47	78	10	7	
陕 西	Shaanxi	35	666	898	6869	683	485
甘 肃	Gansu	12	948	1094	6438	363	269
青 海	Qinghai	7	78	233	3334	126	97
宁 夏	Ningxia	3	35	101	414	120	80
新 疆	Xinjiang	6	70	177	674	301	183

注：特殊教育指盲、聋、哑和弱智儿童的教育。

a)Special education refers to the education for the blind, deaf, deaf-mute and the mentally retarded.

20−35 各地区盲、聋哑学校基本情况（2000年）

Enrolled Basic Statistics on Schools for the Blind and Deaf-mute by Region (2000)

单位：人 (person)

地区	Region	学校数(所) Number of Schools (unit)	毕业生数 Number of Graduates	招生数 New Student Enrollment	在校学生数 Student Enrollment	教职工数 Number of Staff and Teachers	#专任教师 Full-time Teachers
全国	**National Total**	**1108**	**11558**	**17792**	**103124**	**31641**	**22683**
北京	Beijing	7	291	263	1272	367	252
天津	Tianjin	9	152	137	684	335	226
河北	Hebei	81	478	896	4804	1610	1210
山西	Shanxi	28	349	594	2920	953	666
内蒙古	Inner Mongolia	18	125	252	1737	654	507
辽宁	Liaoning	50	467	576	4933	1911	1399
吉林	Jilin	24	244	326	3348	1361	882
黑龙江	Heilongjiang	65	632	618	4311	2466	1751
上海	Shanghai	14	319	371	1417	792	421
江苏	Jiangsu	73	1055	1208	6974	2643	1784
浙江	Zhejiang	44	616	653	3900	1054	836
安徽	Anhui	57	480	779	4936	1123	836
福建	Fujian	37	819	941	5746	871	692
江西	Jiangxi	25	283	805	2372	306	251
山东	Shandong	118	1175	1524	9946	4317	2863
河南	Henan	100	1180	1554	10333	2639	2042
湖北	Hubei	68	477	867	4253	1563	1141
湖南	Hunan	54	383	872	4598	1155	888
广东	Guangdong	23	481	585	4180	661	515
广西	Guangxi	23	275	466	3128	713	435
海南	Hainan	2	47	107	519	84	58
重庆	Chongqing	41	156	562	2493	533	418
四川	Sichuan	57	218	580	3048	1065	823
贵州	Guizhou	21	134	654	3002	520	399
云南	Yunnan	14	232	473	2878	518	383
西藏	Tibet	1		47	56	10	7
陕西	Shaanxi	29	100	353	2380	600	440
甘肃	Gansu	10	247	325	1480	322	237
青海	Qinghai	7	56	156	554	102	81
宁夏	Ningxia	2	30	82	359	99	64
新疆	Xinjiang	6	57	166	563	294	176

20-36 各地区教育经费情况

Basic Statistics on Educational Funds by Region

单位：万元 (10 000 yuan)

年份 地区 Year Region	合计 Total	国家财政性教育经费 Government Appropriation for Education	# 预算内教育经费 Budgetary	社会团体和公民个人办学经费 Funds of Social Organizations and Citizens for Running Schools	社会捐资和集资办学经费 Donations and Fund-raising for Running Schools	学费和杂费 Tuition and Miscellaneous Fee	其他教育经费 Other Educational Funds
1991	7315028.2	6178286.0	4597308.1		628209.7	323475.6	185056.9
1992	8670490.5	7287505.8	5387381.7		696285.2	439319.3	247380.2
1993	10599374.4	8677618.3	6443914.0	33322.7	701856.1	871476.9	315100.4
1994	14887812.6	11747395.6	8839794.7	107795.2	974487.1	1469228.1	588906.6
1995	18779501.1	14115233.3	10283930.0	203671.5	1628414.0	2012422.5	819759.8
1996	22623393.5	16717045.5	12119133.6	261998.9	1884189.5	2610391.2	1149798.4
1997	25317325.7	18625416.3	13577262.1	301746.4	1706587.6	3260792.0	1422783.4
1998	29490592.0	20324526.0	15655917.0	480314.0	1418537.0	3697474.0	3569741.0
1999	33490416.4	22871756.1	18157597.3	628957.1	1258694.2	4636107.9	4094901.1
北 京 Beijing	1930682.1	1351040.3	1215707.3	27879.7	59651.3	156558.1	335552.7
天 津 Tianjin	579702.8	378038.1	312684.2	24774.0	7995.1	66548.7	102346.9
河 北 Hebei	1382481.6	979261.1	734078.9	38242.9	50243.6	232593.7	82140.3
山 西 Shanxi	694615.7	494727.2	383246.2	15153.8	40132.8	93789.2	50812.7
内蒙古 Inner Mongolia	533015.7	424876.5	327781.9	4859.5	5969.7	61058.8	36251.2
辽 宁 Liaoning	1252493.0	925731.4	740488.2	13745.7	9056.0	164576.1	139383.8
吉 林 Jilin	837866.3	614027.4	483691.0	7098.9	36424.2	105577.3	74738.5
黑龙江 Heilongjiang	1044767.3	789124.0	534222.7	17788.5	10828.7	141628.6	85397.5
上 海 Shanghai	1744475.7	1211291.5	1013799.1	53690.2	55831.4	180052.7	243609.9
江 苏 Jiangsu	2617051.4	1697212.6	1341304.3	39844.9	127053.1	340528.2	412412.6
浙 江 Zhejiang	1828190.9	1111919.9	754905.5	102456.3	116915.4	200811.8	296087.5
安 徽 Anhui	1034183.8	703397.2	568487.5	5869.9	21208.9	198009.0	105698.8
福 建 Fujian	1042181.7	735496.4	646322.6	21232.6	40629.4	114516.4	130306.9
江 西 Jiangxi	658618.3	439787.6	358056.0	3910.8	12682.6	114356.2	87881.1
山 东 Shandong	2087357.0	1482785.2	1123022.9	26397.8	60062.1	308456.7	209655.2
河 南 Henan	1531727.2	1038857.2	806748.0	21042.7	100604.3	245601.6	125621.4
湖 北 Hubei	1538420.6	873787.6	659990.8	12710.6	83102.7	294998.9	273820.8
湖 南 Hunan	1397292.1	800694.3	596317.7	18661.9	71783.6	321074.6	185077.7
广 东 Guangdong	3144558.4	1868329.5	1574511.7	111354.0	175376.7	615607.7	373890.5
广 西 Guangxi	840142.7	576463.2	441202.9	6582.0	22801.4	107068.6	127227.5
海 南 Hainan	212244.1	142904.2	109806.9	4843.9	8546.7	34733.3	21216.0
重 庆 Chongqing	601278.1	387028.6	320873.0	5318.0	27080.6	64760.2	117090.7
四 川 Sichuan	1375095.2	967090.3	748879.1	8776.3	38173.2	129239.0	231816.4
贵 州 Guizhou	433565.9	348292.3	288349.3	2703.8	7166.3	48028.8	27374.7
云 南 Yunnan	900880.6	755374.0	663114.7	10268.3	26209.8	52661.5	56367.0
西 藏 Tibet	76981.0	74104.0	72992.0		2400.0	121.9	355.1
陕 西 Shaanxi	852509.0	605862.4	501509.5	14867.3	21555.1	126343.0	83881.2
甘 肃 Gansu	476792.9	385206.3	313533.7	2905.7	11858.7	46171.6	30650.6
青 海 Qinghai	106626.5	92794.6	82427.7	239.4	1022.3	7226.0	5344.2
宁 夏 Ningxia	128222.1	102230.6	84555.6	284.5	2338.7	14216.3	9152.0
新 疆 Xinjiang	606396.7	514020.6	354986.4	5453.2	3989.8	49193.4	33739.7

20-37 各类学校教育经费情况（1999年）

Educational Funds in Various School (1999)

单位：万元 (10 000 yuan)

学校类别	Type of Schools	合计 Total	国家财政性教育经费 Government Appropriation for Education	#预算内教育经费 Budgetary	社会团体和公民个人办学经费 Funds of Social Organizations and Citizens for Running Schools	社会捐资和集资办学经费 Donations and Fund-Raising for Running Schools	学费和杂费 Tuition and Miscellaneous Fee	其他教育经费 Other Educational Funds
全国总计	**National Total**	**33490416.4**	**22871756.1**	**18157597.3**	**628957.1**	**1258694.2**	**4636107.9**	**4094901.1**
#中央	Central Government	4227406.2	2766078.3	2153961.0		116522.4	449375.3	895430.2
地方	Local Government	29263010.2	20105677.8	16003636.3	628957.1	1142171.8	4186732.6	3199470.9
按学校类别分组	**Grouped by Type of Schools**							
高等学校	Institutions of Higher Education	7646450.3	4728311.9	4444956.8	39083.0	163891.0	1378830.9	1336333.5
普通高等学校	Regular Institutions of Higher Education	7087280.0	4431601.2	4226112.2	32565.1	161676.6	1207835.5	1253601.6
成人高等学校	Institutions of Higher Education for Adults	559170.3	296710.7	218844.6	6517.9	2214.4	170995.4	82731.9
中等专业学校	Specialized Secondary Schools	2473986.6	1360576.9	1216931.4	19121.4	23103.8	794065.9	277118.6
中等技术学校	Technical Schools	1651712.1	902594.6	822182.7	10416.0	10788.7	571488.8	156424.0
中等师范学校	Teacher Training Schools	447778.7	245920.8	222491.5		8383.2	129704.4	63770.3
成人中专学校	Specialized Secondary Schools for Adults	374495.8	212061.5	172257.2	8705.4	3931.9	92872.7	56924.3
技工学校	Technical Schools	342343.8	273278.0	95450.6		819.9	44912.0	23333.9
中学	Secondary Schools	9848874.7	6671228.9	4863612.0	353184.4	552386.7	1180676.4	1091398.3
普通中学	Regular Secondary Schools	9818888.9	6658801.6	4856432.5	344947.8	552197.8	1176271.8	1086669.9
高级中学	Senior Secondary Schools	1636004.5	866169.5	617045.5	67774.8	130722.5	293220.2	278117.5
完全中学	Whole Secondary Schools	2665420.1	1667596.6	1233096.3	140002.9	162098.1	325634.4	370088.1
初级中学	Junior Secondary Schools	5517464.3	4125035.5	3006290.7	137170.1	259377.2	557417.2	438464.3
#农村	Rural	2885042.8	2208547.8	1710254.3		146980.0	329767.1	199747.9
成人中学	Secondary Schools for Adults	29985.8	12427.3	7179.5	8236.6	188.9	4404.6	4728.4
职业中学	Vocational Schools	1124704.9	700239.8	539429.4	44721.9	25417.6	228777.1	125548.5
小学	Primary Schools	9948143.0	7711763.9	5875623.5	172846.4	442076.4	928366.6	693089.7
普通小学	Regular Primary Schools	9939983.1	7704708.3	5870219.0	172370.0	441972.8	928213.2	692718.8
#农村	Rural Areas	5735693.6	4548153.3	3620974.2		277933.8	608566.7	301039.8
成人小学	Primary Schools for Adults	8159.9	7055.6	5404.5	476.4	103.6	153.4	370.9
特殊教育学校	Special Education Schools	93157.0	81966.6	70601.1		1965.3	1973.0	7252.1
幼儿园	Kindergartens	455440.3	275445.9	252127.7		14045.5	78506.0	87442.9
其它	Others	1557315.8	1068944.2	798864.8		34988.0		453383.6

20-38 全国科技活动基本情况

Basic Statistics on National Scientific and Technological Activities

指　　标	Item	1996	1997	1998	1999	2000
科技活动	**Scientific and Technological Activities**					
科技机构数（个）	**Number of Scientific Technological Research Institutions**	**23610**	**22531**	**22151**	**22223**	**28461**
科技活动人员（万人）	**Number of Persons Engaged in Scientific and Technological Activities (10 000 persons)**	**290.3**	**288.6**	**281.4**	**290.6**	**319.0**
#科学家与工程师	Scientists and Engineers	168.8	166.8	149.0	159.5	200.4
研究与试验发展全时人员（万人年）	**Number of Persons Engaged in Research and Development (10 000 person year)**	**80.4**	**83.1**	**75.5**	**82.2**	**89.3**
#科学家与工程师	Scientists and Engineers	54.8	58.9	48.5	53.1	67.5
科技经费筹集额（亿元）	**Funding for Scientific and Technological Activities (100 million yuan)**	**1043.2**	**1181.9**	**1289.8**	**1460.6**	**2370.0**
#政府资金	Government Funds	272.0	310.0	353.8	473.0	594.8
企业资金	Funds Self-raised by Enterprises	434.2	527.1	655.1	745.9	1319.5
银行贷款	Bank Loans	149.8	155.2	171.0	123.0	194.9
科技经费内部支出（亿元）	**Expenditures for Scientific and Technological Activities (100 million yuan)**	**933.0**	**1065.2**	**1128.5**	**1284.9**	**2064.1**
#劳务费	Service Fees	187.1	211.5	236.2	270.2	476.5
固定资产购建费	Purchases of Fixed Assets	269.1	293.4	304.6	357.4	619.6
#研究与试验发展经费支出	Research and Development Expenses	404.5	481.5	551.1	678.9	897.7
基础研究	Fundamental Research	20.2	27.4	28.9	33.9	44.8
应用研究	Applied Research	99.1	130.6	124.6	151.5	147.1
试验发展	Experimental Development	285.1	323.4	397.5	493.5	705.8
研究与试验发展经费支出占国内生产总值比重（%）	**Proportion of Research and Development Expenses to GDP (%)**	**0.6**	**0.6**	**0.7**	**0.8**	**1.0**
技术成果和国家奖励	**Achievements in Scientific and Technological Research and National Prizes Won**					
重大科学技术成果（项）	Number of Major Achievements in Science and Technology	**31000**	**30566**	**28584**	**31060**	**32858**
国家发明奖（项）	Number of National Invention Prizes Awarded	111	100	72	69	23
国家科学技术进步奖（项）	Number of National Scientific and Technological Progress Prizes Awarded	536	475	471	476	250
技术市场成交额(亿元)	**Transaction Value in Technical Market by Region (100 million)**	**300**	**351**	**436**	**523**	**651**
专利	**Patent**					
专利申请受理量（件）	**Total Patent Applications Examined**	**102735**	**114208**	**121989**	**134239**	**170682**
发明	Creation and Inventions	28517	33669	35960	36694	51747
实用新型	Utility Models	49604	50129	51397	57492	68815
外观设计	Designs	24614	30413	34632	40053	50120
专利申请批准量（件）	**Total Patent Applications Certified**	**43780**	**50992**	**67889**	**100156**	**105345**
发明	Creation and Inventions	2976	3494	4733	7637	12683
实用新型	Utility Models	27171	27338	33902	56368	54743
外观设计	Designs	13633	20160	29254	36151	37919

注：2000年数据为全社会R&D资源清查初步数。

a) Data in 2000 are the primary data of survey on all R&D resources.

20-39 全国县级以上政府部门属研究与开发机构及科技信息与文献机构、人员数（2000年）

State-owned Research and Development Institutions and Information and Literature Institutions at and Above County Level and Employed Persons (2000)

地 区	Region	合计 Total Number 机构（个） Institutions (unit)	合计 Total Number 从业人员(人) Employees (person)	自然科学技术领域 Field of Natural Sciences and Technology 机构（个） Institutions (unit)	自然科学技术领域 从业人员(人) Employees (person)	自然科学技术领域 #科技活动人员 S & T Personnel
全 国	**National Total**	**5064**	**702673**	**4317**	**662354**	**443309**
北 京	Beijing	412	128617	308	114165	77710
天 津	Tianjin	107	18904	93	17731	12182
河 北	Hebei	122	14282	109	13322	9534
山 西	Shanxi	192	16777	160	15646	10457
内蒙古	Inner Mongolia	136	10588	109	9692	6556
辽 宁	Liaoning	276	32063	248	30759	22002
吉 林	Jilin	162	20753	132	19808	12503
黑龙江	Heilongjiang	215	16526	188	15739	10016
上 海	Shanghai	227	51509	187	48788	31448
江 苏	Jiangsu	285	37482	258	36517	26174
浙 江	Zhejiang	144	12149	128	11608	8418
安 徽	Anhui	170	14937	142	14168	10855
福 建	Fujian	125	6738	107	6157	4678
江 西	Jiangxi	127	15362	113	14848	7530
山 东	Shandong	304	26972	266	25346	16201
河 南	Henan	173	22457	143	21468	14490
湖 北	Hubei	245	33261	218	32357	22525
湖 南	Hunan	164	17309	148	16787	9974
广 东	Guangdong	262	20966	229	19663	12296
广 西	Guangxi	155	11949	125	11221	5739
海 南	Hainan	43	2071	36	1978	1125
重 庆	Chongqing	56	10214	48	9576	5976
四 川	Sichuan	208	56854	169	55269	34879
贵 州	Guizhou	107	8007	96	7682	4867
云 南	Yunnan	141	11095	120	10422	6830
西 藏	Tibet	13	795	11	673	403
陕 西	Shaanxi	160	56607	142	55715	40947
甘 肃	Gansu	123	13558	106	12627	8808
青 海	Qinghai	38	2709	32	2497	1774
宁 夏	Ningxia	38	2659	28	2290	881
新 疆	Xinjiang	134	8503	118	7835	5531

20−39 续表 1 continued

地区	Region	社会、人文科学技术领域 Field of Social Sciences and Humanities 机构(个) Institutions (unit)	从业人员(人) Employees (person)	#科技活动人员 S & T Personnel	科技信息和文献机构 Scientific-Technical Information and Literature Institutions 机构(个) Institutions (unit)	从业人员(人) Employees (person)	#科技活动人员 S & T Personnel
全国	**National Total**	**333**	**18283**	**15240**	**414**	**22036**	**16954**
北京	Beijing	65	5115	4488	39	9337	6690
天津	Tianjin	3	403	295	11	770	569
河北	Hebei	2	545	386	11	415	354
山西	Shanxi	20	796	619	12	335	298
内蒙古	Inner Mongolia	13	559	394	14	337	276
辽宁	Liaoning	12	641	535	16	663	559
吉林	Jilin	18	650	555	12	295	265
黑龙江	Heilongjiang	11	467	385	16	320	283
上海	Shanghai	27	1166	928	13	1555	1059
江苏	Jiangsu	11	392	365	16	573	473
浙江	Zhejiang	4	225	207	12	316	248
安徽	Anhui	10	419	369	18	350	314
福建	Fujian	4	236	207	14	345	305
江西	Jiangxi	1	159	129	13	355	318
山东	Shandong	13	691	556	25	935	798
河南	Henan	13	579	474	17	410	347
湖北	Hubei	13	340	300	14	564	511
湖南	Hunan	3	259	219	13	263	221
广东	Guangdong	16	780	661	17	523	442
广西	Guangxi	9	340	313	21	388	336
海南	Hainan	1	17	17	6	76	72
重庆	Chongqing	4	235	177	4	403	234
四川	Sichuan	13	727	528	26	858	627
贵州	Guizhou	1	149	125	10	176	138
云南	Yunnan	14	470	425	7	203	169
西藏	Tibet	1	95	81	1	27	25
陕西	Shaanxi	4	378	285	14	514	399
甘肃	Gansu	9	645	541	8	286	247
青海	Qinghai	4	163	132	2	49	43
宁夏	Ningxia	6	241	202	4	128	91
新疆	Xinjiang	8	401	342	8	267	243

20-40 全国县级以上政府部门属研究与开发机构及科技信息与文献机构科技经费筹集和支出总额（2000年）

Total Funds and Total Expenditures of State-owned Research and Development Institutions and Information and Literature Institutions at and above County Level (2000)

单位：万元 (10 000 yuan)

地区	Region	合计 Total		自然科学技术领域 Field of Natural Sciences and Technology			
		经费筹集总额 Funds	经费支出总额 Expenditures	经费筹集总额 Funds	#政府拨款 Government Appropriations	经费支出总额 Expenditures	#基本建设支出 For Capital Construction
全国	**National Total**	**5679234**	**5154704**	**5398617**	**3583679**	**4889296**	**868303**
北京	Beijing	1883831	1591280	1755777	1198908	1472037	238568
天津	Tianjin	132168	116187	126311	57517	109104	20999
河北	Hebei	119771	102239	110478	90332	95073	8487
山西	Shanxi	68418	59076	64512	40721	55388	8419
内蒙古	Inner Mongolia	29587	26545	27474	20733	24354	2364
辽宁	Liaoning	234284	227326	229253	156472	222393	45321
吉林	Jilin	105066	102005	100539	61047	97461	18171
黑龙江	Heilongjiang	81245	68578	77391	41879	64875	6433
上海	Shanghai	482723	460333	451681	261049	430618	83375
江苏	Jiangsu	388099	331475	380712	225010	324564	50362
浙江	Zhejiang	94856	95658	91216	58222	92356	17304
安徽	Anhui	80759	92213	77367	51439	89109	18261
福建	Fujian	48287	41722	43996	24128	37600	7918
江西	Jiangxi	47368	44647	45919	30662	43494	14213
山东	Shandong	149110	151968	139833	69374	142502	31559
河南	Henan	121303	126391	116526	87036	122264	40227
湖北	Hubei	197488	195954	193187	141018	191484	41722
湖南	Hunan	90177	84864	86630	31719	81816	10022
广东	Guangdong	194313	187144	181991	86785	175325	30407
广西	Guangxi	40984	41117	37937	24045	38431	6542
海南	Hainan	15179	12262	14606	31050	11715	1875
重庆	Chongqing	55951	57412	53232	307951	54550	10771
四川	Sichuan	424693	366260	417810	46443	359636	50271
贵州	Guizhou	27595	23370	26501	30161	22331	2736
云南	Yunnan	75744	64392	72778	289592	61487	11036
西藏	Tibet	3341	3124	2626	10142	2382	151
陕西	Shaanxi	356200	363665	352503	31978	360192	70355
甘肃	Gansu	72301	64404	66251	42112	57757	13985
青海	Qinghai	12136	10959	11568	8045	10393	1325
宁夏	Ningxia	7212	7204	6048	4116	6133	735
新疆	Xinjiang	39048	34933	35966	23995	32473	4390

20-40 续表 1 continued

单位：万元 (10 000 yuan)

地区	Region	社会、人文科学技术领域 Field of Social Sciences and Humanities				科技信息和文献机构 Scientific-Technological Information and Literature Institutions			
		经费筹集总额 Funds	#政府拨款 Government Appropriations	经费支出总额 Expenditures	#基本建设支出 For Capital Construction	经费筹集总额 Funds	#政府拨款 Government Appropriations	经费支出总额 Expenditures	#基本建设支出 For Capital Construction
全 国	**National Total**	**110000**	**88422**	**103060**	**15717**	**170618**	**120823**	**162347**	**47640**
北 京	Beijing	38108	30848	33166	2904	89946	62017	86077	24890
天 津	Tianjin	1387	1244	2511	1195	4470	3571	4572	549
河 北	Hebei	7889	7873	5779	2070	1405	931	1388	197
山 西	Shanxi	2921	1650	2807	102	984	692	881	88
内蒙古	Inner Mongolia	1398	1371	1508	168	715	651	683	48
辽 宁	Liaoning	2455	2263	2369	45	2576	2219	2564	306
吉 林	Jilin	3578	3239	3642	863	949	822	902	116
黑龙江	Heilongjiang	2476	2277	2473	426	1378	983	1230	117
上 海	Shanghai	6458	5531	5996	430	24585	19539	23719	12363
江 苏	Jiangsu	3596	1789	3431	310	3791	1851	3480	320
浙 江	Zhejiang	1542	1443	1494	183	2097	1477	1808	328
安 徽	Anhui	1879	1231	1741	108	1513	955	1363	263
福 建	Fujian	1543	1489	1443	179	2748	2297	2680	1155
江 西	Jiangxi	696	551	430	17	754	665	723	68
山 东	Shandong	3120	2518	3261	607	6157	4116	6205	2566
河 南	Henan	2792	1631	2311	137	1985	1576	1816	505
湖 北	Hubei	1708	1273	2165	636	2594	1679	2305	674
湖 南	Hunan	1710	838	1784	245	1837	1533	1264	230
广 东	Guangdong	6662	5908	6650	1769	5660	2883	5169	576
广 西	Guangxi	1328	1232	1167	94	1720	1187	1520	314
海 南	Hainan	73	73	73	1	500	441	474	145
重 庆	Chongqing	1069	725	1083	62	1650	937	1778	218
四 川	Sichuan	3774	3673	3754	1792	3109	2548	2869	628
贵 州	Guizhou	495	495	510	31	598	475	529	22
云 南	Yunnan	1784	1779	1718	99	1183	909	1188	78
西 藏	Tibet	537	537	555	42	177	177	187	0
陕 西	Shaanxi	2057	1390	1797	372	1640	1283	1676	102
甘 肃	Gansu	4432	1369	5106	698	1618	1203	1540	621
青 海	Qinghai	410	367	431	31	158	128	135	5
宁 夏	Ningxia	679	664	667	28	485	364	405	25
新 疆	Xinjiang	1447	1150	1241	75	1635	716	1219	137

注：科技经费筹集和支出分别扣除生产性经营收入和支出。

a)Science and technology funds and expenditure excludes income from and expenditure for production activities.

20-41 大中型工业企业技术开发基本情况

Basic Statistics on Technical Development of Large and Medium-sized Industrial Enterprises

指标	Item	1998	1999	2000
有技术开发机构的企业 （个）	Number of Enterprises Having Institutions for Technical Development	7220	7120	6275
有技术开发机构的企业占全部企业的比重 (%)	Percentage to Total Number of Enterprises	30.6	32.0	28.5
技术开发机构数 （个）	Institutions for Number of Technical Development	10926.0	11237.0	7667.0
企业技术开发人员总数(万人)	Number of Personnel Engaged in Technical Development in Enterprises (10 000 persons)	141.0	145.3	139.8
＃科学家和工程师	Scientists and Engineers	63.7	66.8	77.7
技术开发机构科技活动人员数（万人）	Number of Personnel in Institutions for Technical Development (10 000 persons)	41.1	42.0	44.2
＃科学家和工程师	Scientists and Engineers	24.0	26.1	27.7
技术开发经费筹集额 （亿元）	Funds of Technical Development (100 million yuan)	556.4	665.4	936.9
＃上级拨款	Appropriations from Higher Authorities	44.0	49.7	43.9
＃企业自筹	Funds Self-raised by Enterprises	402.5	510.3	755.1
技术开发经费支出额 （亿元）	Expenditures for Technical Development (100 million yuan)	478.7	567.2	849.3
＃开发新产品用款	Expenditure for New Product Development	246.5	304.5	393.5
技术开发经费支出占产品销售收入的比重 (%)	Technical Development Funds as Percentage of Sales Revenue (%)	1.28	1.35	1.49
技术开发项目数 （项）	Number of Projects for Technical Development	83143	84830	100794
＃新产品项目	Projects for New Product Development	51763	52292	56338

注：2000年数据为全社会R&D资源清查初步数，含国家级高新技术开发区划分的大中型工业企业。

a) Data in 2000 is the primary data of survey on all R&D resources, including large and medium-sized industrial enterprises classified as national hi-tech developing zones.

20-42 高等学校科技活动情况

Basic Statistics on Higher Education for Scientific and Technological Activities

指标	Item	1996	1997	1998	1999	2000
科技活动人员 （人）	**S&T Personnel (person)**	**332008**	**326202**	**345159**	**341910**	**305908**
＃科学家工程师	Scientists and Engineers	316354	311622	311417	328991	265466
研究与试验发展机构 （个）	**R&D Institutions (unit)**	**3398**	**3306**	**3241**	**3124**	**3509**
研究与试验发展人员全时当量 （万人年）	**Full-time Equivalent of R&D Personnel (10,000man.year)**	**14.8**	**16.6**	**16.9**	**17.6**	**16.2**
＃科学家与工程师	Scientists and Engineers	13.2	15.7	16.1	16.8	15.1
＃基础研究	Fundamental Research	4.1	4.3	4.6	4.7	5.2
应用研究	Applied Research	8.0	9.2	9.3	9.8	8.8
试验发展	Experimental Development	2.7	3.0	3.0	3.1	2.2
科技经费筹集额 （万元）	**Sources of Funds for S&T (10,000 yuan)**	**565380**	**730763**	**849566**	**1029460**	**1663956**
＃政府拨款	Government Funds	258241	364700	411494	492174	971013
自筹资金	Self-raised	17138	18248	392490	501908	621890
银行贷款	Bank Loans	8302	7126	-	4509	13796
科技经费内部支出额 （万元）	**Intramural Expenditure for S&T (10,000 yuan)**	**511824**	**629892**	**731542**	**850978**	**1367805**
＃劳务费	Labor Expenses	66018	80622	70565	89185	277411
固定资产购建费	Expenses on Fixed Assets	95645	125786	131629	170262	274199
＃研究与试验发展经费支出(亿元)	R&D Expenditure (100 million yuan)	47.8	57.7	57.2	63.5	76.5
基础研究	Fundamental Research	7.5	9.7	9.5	11.4	16.4
应用研究	Applied Research	26.7	31.6	31.4	37.7	37.1
试验发展	Experimental Development	13.7	16.4	16.3	14.4	17.3

注：2000年数据为全国R&D资源清查初步数。

a) Data in 2000 are the primary data of survey on all R&D resources.

20-43 中国科协系统科技活动情况（2000年）

项目	Item	科协合计 Total Number of Associations for Science & Technology	中国科协 China Associations
机构数　（个）	**Number of Associations or Learned Societies**	**421**	**1**
直属单位	Enterprises and Non-profit Organizations Attached to Associations or Learned Societies	953	26
#院校	Universities and Colleges	138	2
人员数　（人）	**Personnel (person)**		
机关	Associations	6927	173
#科学家与工程师	Scientists and Engineers	2916	149
直属单位	Enterprises and Non-profit Organizations Attached to Associations or Learned Societies	10919	1271
学会理事	Members of Boards of Directors		
#高级职称	Members with Senior Titles		
学术活动	**Academic Activities**		
国内学术会议	Domestic Academic Meetings		
次数　（次）	Number (time)	2773	33
参加人数　（人次）	Number of Participants (person-time)	274277	5915
交流论文数　（篇）	Number of Papers Presented	49257	3908
国际学术会议	International Meetings Held in China		
次数　（次）	Number	116	13
参加人数　（人次）	Number of Participants (person-time)	46018	34744
交流论文数　（篇）	Number of Papers Presented	6569	1685
国际民间科技交流	International Folk Exchange of S&T		
接待来访科技团组(个)	International Group on S&T Received Home(unit)	612	71
接待总人数　（人次）	Person Received (person-time)	6544	970
外派科技团组　（个）	Number of Study Tours Sent Aboard (unit)	352	38
外派总人数　（人次）	Total People Sent Aboard (person-time)	3192	731
#访问考察	Number of People Sent for Study Tours	1983	256
外派研修生	Number of Trainees Sent Abroad	492	157
科技培训	**Training Program**		
院校培训人数　（人次）	Number of Persons Trained in Universities and Colleges (person-time)	23381	0
培训班培训人数　（人次）	Number of Persons Trained in Training Classes (person-time)	706187	4011
科普活动	**Activities for Popular Science**		
讲座次数　（次）	Number of Lectures	22154	95
听讲座人数　（人次）	Number of Participants (person-time)	4311233	54000
展览次数　（次）	Number of Exhibitions	5316	9
参观展览人数　（人次）	Number of Participants (person-time)	21634407	1289000
青少年科技竞赛次数(次)	Number of Teenagers Participating in Science and Technology Competitions	2034	3
咨询活动	**Consultative Activities**		
完成合同　（项）	Number of Consultative Contracts Completed	47616	40
决策咨询　（项）	Number of Consultation for Decision-making	2858	0
合同实现金额　（万元）	Revenue from Fulfillment of Consultative Contracts (10 000 yuan)	126249	800
出版	**Publications**		
科技期刊总数　（种）	Number of Academic Journals (kind)	195	10
论文集种数　（种）	Number of Collections of Articles (kind)	135	5
论文集发行量　（册）	Number of Copies Distributed (copies)	95335	11800
科技报纸种数　（种）	Number of Scientific & Technological Newspapers (kind)	85	1

Basic Statistics on Scientific and Technological Activities of China Associations for Science and Technology (2000)

省科协 Provincial Associations	地(市)科协 Prefectural(city) Associations	学会合计 Total Number of Learned Societies	全国性学会 National Learned Societies	省学会 Provincial Learned Societies
31	**389**	**3638**	**168**	**3470**
237	690	893	74	819
20	116	71	7	64
1320	5434	9686	1901	7785
717	2050			
4725	4923	6659	628	6031
			20238	141821
			18294	104811
252	2488	9476	2206	7270
79527	188835	899471	262021	637450
13256	32093	359110	155899	203211
32	71	508	202	306
4575	6699	87769	50594	37175
2323	2561	35851	26834	9017
278	263	2043	414	1629
2815	2759	13676	2779	10897
221	93	822	356	466
1661	800	8814	3979	4835
1137	590	3508	1055	2453
243	92	473	143	330
5238	18143	34259	14584	19675
99385	602791	769163	220098	549065
570	21489	11490	979	10511
174567	4082666	3011468	236970	2774498
297	5010	2193	255	1938
5527974	14817433	8269747	2091657	6178090
134	1897	584	24	560
11858	35718	4118	441	3677
347	2511	1938	181	1757
60899	64550	12144	277	11867
73	112	1748	726	1022
40	90	2103	772	1331
34250	49285	760080	30011	730069
29	55	98	16	82

20-44 国有企事业单位年底专业技术人员数

Number of Scientific and Technical Personnel in State-owned Enterprises and Institutions at the Year-end

单位：人 (persons)

年份 地区	Year Region	合计 Total	工程技术人员 Engineering	农业技术人员 Agriculture	科学研究人员 Scientific Research	卫生技术人员 Health Care	教学人员 Teaching
	1978.6.30	4345000	1571000	294000	310000	1276000	894000
	1979	4705400	1666900	324600	316800	1396400	1000700
	1980	5276000	1862000	311000	323000	1530000	1250000
	1981	5714000	2077000	328000	338000	1680000	1291000
	1982	6264000	2354000	362000	372000	1807000	1369000
	1983	6852000	2802000	405000	328000	1934000	1383000
	1984	7466000	3162000	435000	335000	2078000	1456000
	1985	7817000	3404000	451000	336000	2161000	1465000
	1990	10808572	5100773	550954	291314	2719864	2145667
	1991	17168413	5024000	463050	341934	2757993	8581436
	1992	17596532	5204950	476853	337146	2827599	8749984
	1993	18124140	5363632	496279	333851	2916255	9014123
	1994	18658689	5535329	519827	321036	2995940	9286557
	1995	19133834	5625850	535731	302879	3035335	9634039
	1996	19856213	5680795	579157	303177	3130788	10162296
	1997	20495006	5719337	611458	302684	3213762	10647765
	1998	20913343	5656735	635929	290537	3254958	11075184
	1999	21430140	5654863	654138	283532	3329706	11507901
	2000	21650807	5551098	670105	274506	3371966	11783132
北京	Beijing	356902	114354	5064	3974	68021	165489
天津	Tianjin	275793	88110	2760	2305	57824	124794
河北	Hebei	931231	161423	23951	3167	122883	619807
山西	Shanxi	568207	121751	17074	3681	83886	341815
内蒙古	Inner Mongolia	418120	77348	19076	2002	68954	250740
辽宁	Liaoning	880232	246033	27167	7305	165385	434342
吉林	Jilin	557323	113307	26485	3814	97256	316461
黑龙江	Heilongjiang	737890	182346	31134	5252	135295	383863
上海	Shanghai	362743	125467	3097	5776	77929	150474
江苏	Jiangsu	1117458	269126	40364	6193	166843	634932
浙江	Zhejiang	635233	125710	19183	4075	117971	368294
安徽	Anhui	713794	125050	22814	3262	93282	469386
福建	Fujian	516439	86683	14495	3798	56703	354760
江西	Jiangxi	573612	91360	19470	2333	99631	360818
山东	Shandong	1443745	296845	50699	7997	234810	853394
河南	Henan	1149116	150991	26645	4337	156191	810952
湖北	Hubei	892680	164752	30109	5760	186488	505571
湖南	Hunan	881417	137905	24711	5006	137884	575911
广东	Guangdong	1071537	180223	15083	4705	175521	696005
广西	Guangxi	657274	128462	23630	2815	104160	398207
海南	Hainan	101960	13226	3577	479	16009	68669
重庆	Chongqing	370097	61187	12109	1754	55464	239583
四川	Sichuan	1023838	166627	42473	5049	161776	647913
贵州	Guizhou	459818	67299	25833	1724	70667	294295
云南	Yunnan	611566	98066	36713	3622	100304	372861
西藏	Tibet	30924	4093	1852	352	7304	17323
陕西	Shaanxi	517000	106620	18966	2328	76737	312349
甘肃	Gansu	346805	59786	17847	1742	49398	218032
青海	Qinghai	88846	15264	5821	609	16351	50801
宁夏	Ningxia	113612	22328	7070	725	19864	63625
新疆	Xinjiang	370694	58730	27769	2542	62505	219148

注：分地区数据中不含中央属国有企事业单位人数。

a)The regional data exclude the personnel in the state-owned enterprises and institution under the central government.

20−45 全国技术市场成交额

Transaction Value in Technical Market by Region

单位：万元　　　　(10 000 yuan)

地　区	Region	1994	1995	1996	1997	1998	1999	2000
全　国	**National Total**	**2288696**	**2683447**	**3002045**	**3513718**	**4358228**	**5234123**	**6507519**
北　京	Beijing	371821	411681	458152	543192	815591	921889	1402871
天　津	Tianjin	95188	121200	133475	150074	200298	220296	262581
河　北	Hebei	68371	84278	97853	115256	139090	153795	94143
山　西	Shanxi	10723	18454	11644	10284	9758	3955	5258
内蒙古	Inner Mongolia		12601	16044	28958	31332	29348	60287
辽　宁	Liaoning	215709	228615	242570	250372	280977	301546	347817
吉　林	Jilin	60485	51217	76492	85793	93167	103498	71390
黑龙江	Heilongjiang	95107	110522	114177	145752	152569	157121	152382
上　海	Shanghai	220927	230409	256499	287568	314060	366324	738952
江　苏	Jiangsu	138057	181563	238126	284473	330684	416683	449568
浙　江	Zhejiang	71966	97768	107293	133232	162275	188496	276275
安　徽	Anhui	11531	21853	24904	29585	39545	48544	61012
福　建	Fujian	25117	30550	46205	57454	69363	80868	172601
江　西	Jiangxi	14176	21555	24929	31058	38332	51444	69299
山　东	Shandong	166977	185946	222509	241583	261922	275121	288135
河　南	Henan	106797	122798	142122	157766	176492	201661	211621
湖　北	Hubei	115265	125912	105576	145733	187596	230161	276000
湖　南	Hunan	94955	105434	140209	161392	220189	246605	286833
广　东	Guangdong	95885	125972	131112	195993	248122	344528	482104
广　西	Guangxi	13543	20622	25181	17293	37021	25344	17741
海　南	Hainan			27878	35645	41533	82407	
重　庆	Chongqing				60628	92951	325345	296594
四　川	Sichuan	201929	221882	200630	158004	152000	125931	104150
贵　州	Guizhou	582	9561	53397	1150	14071	762	620
云　南	Yunnan	11927	39125	1606	54515	127222	172339	187742
西　藏	Tibet							
陕　西	Shaanxi	32173	55501	44756	71782	57765	82537	92560
甘　肃	Gansu	21513	25157	24180	26427	28137	25816	26413
青　海	Qinghai	692	1375	7886	12035	2917	4283	
宁　夏	Ningxia	1630	1822	2121	2351	2643	4654	6402
新　疆	Xinjiang	18252	20074	24519	18370	30606	42822	66168

20-46 开发区高新技术企业主要经济指标（2000年）

Main Economic Indicators of High-tech Enterprises in Development Areas (2000)

开发区	Development Area	企业数（个）Number of Enterprises	职工人数(人) Number of Staff & Workers (person)	总产值（万元）Gross Output Value (10000 yuan)	总收入（万元）Total Income (10000 yuan)	出口总额(千美元) Exports (1000 US dollars)
全国	**National Total**	**20796**	**2350679**	**79419852**	**92092631**	**18581751**
北京	Beijing	6181	219857	9103777	14326050	1816922
天津	Tianjin	1987	105480	2746140	2969890	912691
石家庄	Shijiazhuang	393	38635	840178	1154644	242271
保定	Baoding	118	42211	612831	615111	73552
太原	Taiyuan	325	49943	699719	767336	56794
包头	Baotou	173	29390	368539	432130	73391
沈阳	Shenyang	391	43778	1583028	2619483	459094
大连	Dalian	844	78770	1057837	1509541	406190
鞍山	Anshan	212	31910	494140	485321	41702
长春	Changchun	578	97319	2235639	2576548	193667
吉林	Jilin	393	83993	2159749	2134163	60783
哈尔滨	Harbin	355	71860	1521966	1646103	199165
大庆	Daqing	175	14489	501935	516284	2287
上海	Shanghai	438	85146	6747683	7513625	2327534
南京	Nanjing	144	49846	4440674	4348592	644515
常州	Changzhou	205	30160	765378	774714	191756
无锡	Wuxi	250	31110	2277521	2747891	1270308
苏州	Suzhou	236	67084	3462132	3390873	2249153
杭州	Hangzhou	277	21710	1554179	1777900	231898
合肥	Hefei	138	41997	1033379	1092336	60476
福州	Fuzhou	106	23020	1266229	1200030	251861
夏门	Xiamen	54	23957	1136441	1107928	552140
南昌	Nanchang	102	30199	640501	722056	28580
济南	Ji'nan	227	40288	1000368	1043071	57237
青岛	Qingdao	84	36711	3014540	3650773	405398
淄博	Zibo	110	40096	1013689	1028201	61334
潍坊	Weifang	43	12745	394223	418407	48000
威海	Weihai	90	33702	842362	853100	366634
郑州	Zhengzhou	236	32936	837067	915807	115396
洛阳	Luoyang	225	33510	430841	563361	50738
武汉	Wuhan	484	81012	2133578	2523851	135290
襄樊	Xiangfan	68	37441	582128	650348	10959
长沙	Changsha	469	50579	1753031	2034903	109815
株洲	Zhuzhou	112	20904	424449	493656	105273
广州	Guangzhou	689	31474	824966	1519985	73636
深圳	Shenzhen	122	61452	4563637	4257679	2085795
珠海	Zhuhai	96	22556	805459	813504	344776
惠州	Huizhou	60	21013	1487623	1358234	728246
中山	Zhongshan	210	45969	1165380	1013130	742061
佛山	Foshan	42	20617	1524528	1599166	171153
南宁	Nanning	214	19260	454658	623494	18629
桂林	Guilin	177	27677	586037	605362	74910
海南	Hainan	66	8589	263583	274163	31803
重庆	Chongqing	254	45975	1574076	1666994	34938
成都	Chengdu	262	74346	1254647	1601409	154995
绵阳	Mianyang	72	32777	1498038	1331715	34603
贵阳	Guiyang	45	22291	306767	313467	11033
昆明	Kunming	104	26317	559846	675275	104030
西安	Xi'an	1590	93608	1916251	2741984	104079
宝鸡	Baoji	107	32500	414480	405974	21674
杨凌	Yangling	21	2042	27733	30714	2000
兰州	Lanzhou	336	22692	428419	504122	9569
乌鲁木齐	Urumqi	106	7736	87853	152237	21017

20−47 测绘部门生产完成情况（2000年）

Statistics on Projects Completed by Surveying and Mapping Departments by Region (2000)

地区	Region	大地测量 Geodesy 平面控制测量（点） Horizontal Control Survey (point)	高程控制测量（公里） Vertical Control Survey (kilometer)	测图合计（幅） Mapping	地图数字化（幅） Digital Maps	地图编制 地形图（幅） Topographic Maps	专题地图（幅） Special Maps	地图集（册） Atlas
全　国	**National Total**	**20448**	**24875**	**121840**	**78560**	**4104**	**1243775**	**123303**
北　京	Beijing	2217	300	1279	4054	104	144400	34230
天　津	Tianjin	24	2022	14025	537		8	
河　北	Hebei	1686	2673	4424	8474		32	
山　西	Shanxi	403		3298	702		58	10
内蒙古	Inner Mongolia	495	1592	1779	192	556	27	6
辽　宁	Liaoning	5922	1439	5649	4006	126	19	2
吉　林	Jilin	263	2400	1051	283			1
黑龙江	Heilongjiang	235	472	7319	6972	57	37000	59000
上　海	Shanghai			7588	6196		1060400	
江　苏	Jiangsu	781	1831	4514	2213	4	255	1
浙　江	Zhejiang	2142	830	2603	3455			
安　徽	Anhui	50		4987	2146	8	132	2
福　建	Fujian	98	755	2783	2286		16	6
江　西	Jiangxi	230	460	586	637	840	25	
山　东	Shandong	250	372	5939	1499	152	57	9
河　南	Henan	618	1500	3754	948	87	46	2
湖　北	Hubei	100		1931	2752		27	
湖　南	Hunan	832	1060	5908	1360	101	22	5
广　东	Guangdong	530	2377	4477	1907	761	27	8
广　西	Guangxi	140		2921	953	193	43	2
海　南	Hainan	20		97	1145	49	1	
重　庆	Chongqing	210	87	3280	2710	19	14	
四　川	Sichuan	87		4291	4172	34	34	
贵　州	Guizhou	304	1524	2133	389		189	
云　南	Yunnan	254	359	934	787	321		
西　藏	Tibet			92			2	
陕　西	Shaanxi	1136	949	13147	5258			
甘　肃	Gansu	110	35	2092	1553		124	
青　海	Qinghai	297	129	1244	197	583	83	
宁　夏	Ningxia	638	695	434	90	5		2
新　疆	Xinjiang	308	1014	1945	2600	70		
国家基础地理信息中心	National Geomatics Center of China	68		1116	880	34	666	3
中国测绘科学研究院	China Academy of Surveying and Mapping Science			4220	7207		68	30000
中国地图出版社	China Atlas Publishing House							14

20—48 各地区测绘资料提供情况（2000年）

Statistics on Output of Surveying and Mapping Materials by Region (2000)

地 区	Region	地形图合计（张） Topographic Maps	1:10000 (scale)	1:50000 (scale)	大地成果（点） Geodetic Results (point)	航摄成果（片） Aerial Photograph (piece)	挂图（张） Wall Maps	地图集（册） Atlas
全 国	**National Total**	**1023936**	**190233**	**122961**	**53639**	**128287**	**34399**	**26975**
北 京	Beijing	46774	3106	637			783	900
天 津	Tianjin	1185	641	504	109		1185	
河 北	Hebei	4976	1964	2193	1086	6840	99	60
山 西	Shanxi	13882	10860	2959	1087	22546	5692	27
内蒙古	Inner Mongolia	10003	2250	5232	2281	70	410	92
辽 宁	Liaoning	4235	3062	1003	148		2164	91
吉 林	Jilin	9892	3680	2807	4600	4100	983	1362
黑龙江	Heilongjiang	24347	13415	8733	541	20148	1071	552
上 海	Shanghai	601077	1077		1230	2500	1724	
江 苏	Jiangsu	8222	5521	2323	1076	16	352	510
浙 江	Zhejiang	20195	15645	3281	2246	19440		
安 徽	Anhui	9745	7011	2085	6307	3		
福 建	Fujian	8095	5301	2102	3680	2077		
江 西	Jiangxi	9190	7266	1638	377	281	33	17
山 东	Shandong	15819	12806	2193	833	300	128	392
河 南	Henan	4425	3491	734	376	340		
湖 北	Hubei	9750	6876	2619	453	671	300	500
湖 南	Hunan	14617	10823	3384	521		358	178
广 东	Guangdong	18474	13951	3568	3283	6119		
广 西	Guangxi	17273	12960	3511	10113	2878		
海 南	Hainan	2366	1634	488	57	38	804	133
重 庆	Chongqing	7600	100		130		100	
四 川	Sichuan	22562	10372	8483	1218	5500	565	35
贵 州	Guizhou	12583	8890	2970	918	2504	753	109
云 南	Yunnan	21383	3954	11021	6625	2028	1999	7
西 藏	Tibet	4452	123	530			2890	20242
陕 西	Shaanxi	13431	11009	1935	68	328		
甘 肃	Gansu	14188	7184	4222	1377	5002	1194	124
青 海	Qinghai	8432	725	3668	339	2100	260	245
宁 夏	Ningxia	5126	2745	1995	442		110	7
新 疆	Xinjiang	9725	1791	5600	764		10442	205
国家基础地理信息中心	National Geomatics Center of China	49912		30543	1354	22458		1097

20−49 气象台站数和卫星云图接收、使用情况（2000年）

Meteorological Observatories, Stations and The Reception and Use of Satellite Cloud Images (2000)

地区和单位	Region, City and Units	气象台站总数（个）Number of Meteorological Observatories and Stations (unit)	#气象台 Meteorological Observatories	#气象台 Meteorological Stations	#独立农区气象试验站 Independent Agro-Meteorological Experimental Stations	#大气本底特种观测站 Atmosphere Background Special Observation Stations	卫星云图接收站点数（个）Number of Satellite Cloud Images Receiving Stations	#极轨卫星 Polar Orbiting Meteorological Satellites	#同步卫星 Geostationary Meteorological Satellites	使用卫星云图资料单位数（个）Number of Units Using Satellite Cloud Images
全　国	**National Total**	**2620**	**356**	**2206**	**55**	**3**	**319**	**44**	**295**	**531**
北　京	Beijing	23	2	21			2	1	1	
天　津	Tianjin	15	3	12			4	1	3	
河　北	Hebei	147	12	135			9	2	8	16
山　西	Shanxi	117	12	105			7	1	6	4
内蒙古	Inner Mongolia	124	13	105	6		5	2	3	14
辽　宁	Liaoning	63	14	46	3		4	2	4	35
吉　林	Jilin	65	9	53	3		3	1	3	3
黑龙江	Heilongjiang	87	13	72	1	1	7	2	6	15
上　海	Shanghai	11	1	10			8	1	7	10
江　苏	Jiangsu	79	13	64	2		47	1	46	61
浙　江	Zhejiang	78	11	66		1	45	1	44	121
安　徽	Anhui	82	16	65	1		12	1	11	5
福　建	Fujian	74	9	62	3		20	1	20	
江　西	Jiangxi	92	12	79	1		3	1	2	10
山　东	Shandong	119	17	101	1		19	1	19	25
河　南	Henan	128	19	106	3		12	1	11	13
湖　北	Hubei	85	13	70	2		9	2	9	59
湖　南	Hunan	103	14	86	3		6	1	5	5
广　东	Guangdong	95	19	75	1		18	3	16	34
广　西	Guangxi	107	12	90	5		3	2	2	
海　南	Hainan	0					3	1	2	48
重　庆	Chongqing	40	5	35			2		2	
四　川	Sichuan	182	21	159	2		2	1	1	8
贵　州	Guizhou	87	10	76	1		10	1	9	3
云　南	Yunnan	135	17	115	3		3	1	3	2
西　藏	Tibet	41	8	32	1		4	2	3	
陕　西	Shaanxi	109	12	95	2		9	1	8	15
甘　肃	Gansu	97	13	80	4		13	1	12	4
青　海	Qinghai	55	9	44	1	1	5	1	4	1
宁　夏	Ningxia	25	5	19	1		2	2	2	
新　疆	Xinjiang	126	16	106	4		10	4	10	
大连市	Dalian	9	2	7			1		1	
宁波市	Ningbo	9	1	8			8		8	5
青岛市	Qingdao	7	1	6			1		1	1
厦门市	Xiamen	2	1	1			1		1	4
国家气象中心	National Meteorological Center	1	1							
国家卫星气象中心	National Satellite Meteorological Center						2	1	2	10
气象科学研究院	Chinese Academy of Meteorological Science	1			1					

20−50 农气观测站和农业气象预报台站数（2000年）

Agro-Meteorological Observation Stations and Forecast Observatories and Stations (2000)

单位：个 (unit)

地区和单位	Region, City and Units	农气观测站点数 Agro-Meteorological Observation Stations and Sub-stations				农业气象预报台站 Agro-Meteorological Forecast Observatories and Stations	农业气象情报业务站点 Agro-Meteorological Information Services Stations
		开展农气观测站数 Agro-Meteorological Observation Stations	农作物观测点 Agricultural Observation Points	土壤湿度测定点 Soil Moisture Measurement Points	物候观测点 Phonological Observation Points		
全　国	**National Total**	**1125**	**772**	**832**	**564**	**1249**	**1415**
北　京	Beijing	7	7	7	7	2	1
天　津	Tianjin	7	7	7	7	1	1
河　北	Hebei	145	27	143	30	30	30
山　西	Shanxi	44	35	44	35	45	36
内蒙古	Inner Mongolia	39	28	39	35	40	57
辽　宁	Liaoning	45	23	43	22	56	56
吉　林	Jilin	46	22	46	22	46	46
黑龙江	Heilongjiang	35	34	34	34	41	41
上　海	Shanghai	1	1	0	0	1	11
江　苏	Jiangsu	36	28	33	11	35	57
浙　江	Zhejiang	11	11	0	10	61	61
安　徽	Anhui	22	22	15	22	22	22
福　建	Fujian	23	16	1	23	38	23
江　西	Jiangxi	79	79	2	5	89	89
山　东	Shandong	57	18	57	16	111	111
河　南	Henan	116	45	116	30	96	110
湖　北	Hubei	28	28	25	16	32	56
湖　南	Hunan	22	22	4	22	30	22
广　东	Guangdong	25	25	1	25	90	90
广　西	Guangxi	24	22	11	24	86	86
海　南	Hainan	6	6	0	6	1	6
重庆市	Chongqing	20	20	10	12	36	36
四　川	Sichuan	66	63	33	47	84	99
贵　州	Guizhou	18	18	5	18	9	18
云　南	Yunnan	21	21	7	17	24	27
西　藏	Tibet	4	4	4	2	4	4
陕　西	Shaanxi	32	18	32	18	22	32
甘　肃	Gansu	28	21	28	19	17	44
青　海	Qinghai	24	19	24	17	1	24
宁　夏	Ningxia	16	11	16	8	16	19
新　疆	Xinjiang	62	60	35	0	62	79
大连市	Dalian	5	2	5	2	6	6
宁波市	Ningbo	7	7	1	0	7	7
青岛市	Qingdao	3	1	3	1	7	7
气象科学研究院	Chinese Academy of Meteorological Science	1	1	1	1	1	1

20-51 地震监测情况（2000年）

Situation of Earthquake Monitoring (2000)

单位：个 (unit)

地区	Region	地震台数 总数 Total Number of Earthquake Stations	基本台 Standard	综合台 Comprehensive	观测台 Monitoring	地方台站 Local	企业台站 Enterprises Managing	强震观测点 Number of Observation for Spot Strong Earthquake	骨干测报点 Number of Main Observation Spots	一般测报点 Number of Normal Observation Spots
全国	**National Total**	**1245**	**38**	**157**	**186**	**651**	**213**	**252**	**1666**	**4597**
北京	Beijing	46	2	9		32	3		53	59
天津	Tianjin	17		8	1	4	4		40	32
河北	Hebei	96	1	10	17	50	18		137	433
山西	Shanxi	93	1	6	6	40	40	10	54	419
内蒙古	Inner Mongolia	60	1	4	16	31	8		63	237
辽宁	Liaoning	60	2	6	10	35	7		70	547
吉林	Jilin	12	2	7	1	2			3	32
黑龙江	Heilongjiang	15	1	2	7	5		142	18	24
上海	Shanghai	19	1	1		17		2	14	
江苏	Jiangsu	59	1	14		31	13	6	69	113
浙江	Zhejiang	19	1	4	1	11	2		3	24
安徽	Anhui	29	1	8	3	11	6		67	171
福建	Fujian	34	1	10	3	20			27	167
江西	Jiangxi	9	1	2		6			2	8
山东	Shandong	60	1	6	18	26	9		171	497
河南	Henan	42	1	2	9	18	12		79	395
湖北	Hubei	36	2		7	19	8		48	42
湖南	Hunan	31	1		6	16	8		27	2
广东	Guangdong	30	1	4	11	14		10	46	103
广西	Guangxi	25	1	6		17	1		75	153
海南	Hainan	17	1		4	12			6	3
重庆	Chongqing	4				4			9	3
四川	Sichuan	84	1	10	15	33	25	7	114	282
贵州	Guizhou	5				5			1	
云南	Yunnan	97	2	5	20	63	7	12	10	60
西藏	Tibet	8	2		6					
陕西	Shaanxi	45	1	4	9	18	13		103	74
甘肃	Gansu	89	3	7	9	47	23	28	316	654
青海	Qinghai	17	1	4	2	8	2	8	6	1
宁夏	Ningxia	40	1	2	4	31	2	3	4	47
新疆	Xinjiang	47	3	16	1	25	2	24	31	15

20-52 国家监督抽查产品质量情况
Results of Sampling Check on Product Quality Under State Supervision

年 份 Year	抽查企业 (个) Number of Enterprises Selected	无不合格品企业数(个) Number of Enterprises without Products Unqualified	抽查产品 Products Selected in Sampling (类) Number of Types	(种) Number of Kinds	合格产品 (种) Number of Products Qualified (kind)	样品合格率 (%) Rate of Sample Products Qualified(%)
1988	2983		181	4031	3072	76.2
1989	3948	2795	180	5437	4092	75.3
1990	2495	1838	131	3457	2657	76.9
1991	2845	2186	138	3902	3122	90.0
1992	6845	4477	231	9007	6312	70.1
1993	8110	5509	281	9915	6980	70.4
1994	4640	3090	164	6036	4216	69.8
1995	5288	3851	185	6713	5061	75.4
1996	6779	5052	217	8318	6420	77.2
1997	5441	4116	187	6590	5162	78.3
1998	5431	4056	176	6770	5269	77.8
1999	7131	5440	207	8345	6562	78.6
2000	8142	6254	235	9705	7655	78.9

20-53 各地区产品质量情况（2000年）
Quality of Products by Region (2000)

单位：% (%)

地 区	Region	产品质量等级品率 Rates of Grade Products: 优等品率 Rate of Products with Excellent Quality	一等品率 Rate of Products with First Grade Quality	合格品率 Rate of Products with Qualified Quality	新产品产值率 Rate of New Products	质量损失率 Rate of Loss Due to Bad Quality
全 国	**National Total**	**21.81**	**42.67**	**34.39**	**16.97**	**0.62**
北 京	Beijing	33.94	20.80	45.26	15.31	0.49
天 津	Tianjin	14.58	48.45	31.10	20.54	0.36
河 北	Hebei	27.35	37.12	35.49	10.26	0.49
山 西	Shanxi	10.71	42.69	46.60	3.11	2.09
内蒙古	Inner Mongolia	27.64	25.28	47.07	5.38	1.04
辽 宁	Liaoning	26.60	46.91	26.16	12.14	0.62
吉 林	Jilin					
黑龙江	Heilongjiang	21.23	44.50	34.26	7.34	1.31
上 海	Shanghai	11.98	60.71	27.31	38.58	0.65
江 苏	Jiangsu	25.16	38.22	36.27	16.65	0.38
浙 江	Zhejiang	14.48	38.72	46.80	24.17	0.68
安 徽	Anhui	23.90	46.25	29.86	17.87	0.56
福 建	Fujian	23.64	51.62	24.74	23.79	0.34
江 西	Jiangxi	4.80	38.50	56.70	14.86	0.84
山 东	Shandong	17.06	48.78	33.95	14.67	0.44
河 南	Henan	25.80	36.84	37.36	6.74	0.82
湖 北	Hubei	44.23	29.75	25.96	20.31	0.42
湖 南	Hunan	25.70	31.31	34.47	8.01	0.72
广 东	Guangdong	29.73	19.02	51.03	14.70	0.62
广 西	Guangxi	25.96	41.16	32.88	12.32	0.75
海 南	Hainan					
重 庆	Chongqing	16.74	53.08	29.92	31.62	1.58
四 川	Sichuan	28.68	29.60	36.35	3.71	0.38
贵 州	Guizhou	4.54	60.72	34.74	25.20	2.28
云 南	Yunnan	0.03	17.53	82.18	3.83	0.67
西 藏	Tibet					
陕 西	Shaanxi	2.51	24.86	72.63	10.45	0.14
甘 肃	Gansu	7.16	30.73	62.10	12.36	0.66
青 海	Qinghai		35.59	64.23	13.86	
宁 夏	Ningxia					
新 疆	Xinjiang					

注：本资料由73个重点工业城市抽样数据汇总而成。
a)Sampling data in this table are collected from 73 main industrial cities.

20−54 全国产品、商品质量监督检查情况（2000年）

Results of Sampling Check on The Quality of Products and Commodities under State Supervision (2000)

项目	Item	产品质量 Product Quality 监督检验企业数（个） Number of Enterprises Supervised & Checked	有不合格产品企业所占比例（%） Proportion of Enterprises with Products Unqualified	批次合格率（%） Rate of Batch-time Qualified (%)	商品质量 Commodity Quality 检查商业企业数（个） Number of Commercial Enterprises	批次合格率（%） Rate of Batch-time Qualified (%)
全国总计	**Total**	**389675**	**20.13**	**80.87**	**392346**	**70.11**
农用产品	**Agricultural Products**	**20232**	**20.21**	**82.38**	**62399**	**71.24**
拖拉机	Tractors	270	18.15	83.67	191	57.79
农用化肥	Chemical Fertilizers	7649	20.64	79.90	25829	70.60
化学农药	Chemical Pesticides	819	11.60	89.87	10715	81.94
饲料	Forages	7700	19.53	84.07	6974	72.33
农用薄膜	Agricultural Films	754	27.72	72.30	1604	73.56
种子	Seeds	518	26.83	85.38	3739	82.66
加工食品和饮料	**Food and Beverage**	**170044**	**23.98**	**77.18**	**145799**	**75.63**
食用植物油	Edible Vegetable Oil	16585	11.20	88.04	6526	80.62
糕点糖果	Cake	36929	22.63	77.63	18613	76.59
乳制品	Dairy Products	2369	20.47	83.54	3100	78.60
罐头	Canned Food	1655	26.77	75.99	4625	79.80
白酒	White Spirit	26722	23.18	78.83	32820	76.35
啤酒	Beer	1425	9.75	92.47	9285	85.01
冷冻饮料	Frozen Beverage	7729	35.81	67.40	4738	67.58
家用电器	**Household Electric Appliances**	**3983**	**19.26**	**82.85**	**12350**	**61.47**
收录机、音响设备	Radio and Cassette Players, Hi-fi Stereo Component Systems	233	19.31	84.13	856	70.96
电视机、录像机	TV Sets, Videocorders	55	10.91	81.33	417	71.41
洗衣机	Washing Machines	47	14.89	86.27	121	90.56
电风扇	Electric Fans	287	26.83	79.20	1072	57.96
电话机	Telephone Sets	189	38.62	76.04	1980	60.15
冰箱、冷藏冷冻箱	Refrigerators, Freezers	56	3.57	95.45	114	92.86
电热器具	Electric Heating Appliances	877	20.52	79.80	1402	58.97
厨房电器具	Electric Cooking Utensils	413	.17.68	85.52	1096	63.41
抽油烟机	Smoke Absorbers	84	22.62	79.35	361	76.06
轻工产品	**Light Industry Products**	**34601**	**20.00**	**81.69**	**40563**	**67.41**
纸	Paper	1971	24.61	77.46	489	66.08
纸制品	Paper Products	7307	20.99	81.48	1110	28.84
玩具	Toys	531	18.83	82.63	736	47.49

20-54 续表 1 continued

项目	Item	产品质量 Product Quality 监督检验企业数(个) Number of Enterprises Supervised & Checked	有不合格产品企业所占比例(%) Proportion of Enterprises with Products Unqualified	批次合格率(%) Rate of Batch-time Qualified (%)	商品质量 Commodity Quality 检查商业企业数(个) Number of Commercial Enterprises	批次合格率(%) Rate of Batch-time Qualified (%)
家具	Furniture	5682	19.85	76.82	2319	54.6
铝制品压力锅	Aluminum Products	186	23.66	74.45	574	72.50
眼镜(架、片)	Spectacles (Glass & Frame)	2785	24.99	78.03	5735	69.98
灯泡灯管	Electric Bulbs & Fluorescence Tubes	551	20.15	81.97	1695	50.73
镇流器	Ballast	177	15.82	82.38	234	34.84
电热、燃气热水器	Water Heaters	290	7.59	93.29	444	77.76
纺织、鞋类产品	**Textile and Shoes**	**20315**	**16.67**	**84.92**	**16970**	**59.99**
布(印染、色织、坯布)	Cloth	1949	7.34	93.91	265	53.58
毛织品	Wool Fabrics	870	10.46	90.52	993	58.04
丝麻织品	Silk & Fabrics	494	5.47	94.77	197	53.28
针织品	Knit Goods	1484	20.49	81.24	1336	61.03
鞋	Shoes	5826	24.36	77.07	5695	64.13
化工产品	**Chemical Products**	**9873**	**16.01**	**86.13**	**7604**	**61.14**
涂料、油漆	Paint	3784	21.06	81.81	4904	63.91
化学试剂	Chemical Reagent	593	11.47	89.96	337	67.44
建材产品	**Building Raw Materials**	**84992**	**14.56**	**85.56**	**23119**	**65.30**
水泥	Cement	12023	6.45	94.30	5467	76.09
水泥预制构件	Cement Prefabricated Components	20783	9.81	89.88	1685	76.45
砖瓦	Bricks & Tiles	35659	16.63	83.49	1751	70.09
油毡油纸	Asphalt Felts & Oilpaper	771	38.78	49.86	753	56.78
平板玻璃	Plate Glass	128	26.56	67.93	343	51.62
水暖管件	Waterpipe	1642	28.38	71.28	3558	48.48
机械、电器产品	**Mechanical and Electrical Products**	**17692**	**13.61**	**87.29**	**35068**	**63.91**
轴承	Bearings	475	14.32	87.86	2467	69.99
阀门、泵	Valves	1716	14.86	86.38	2975	50.83
电线	Electric Wire	3017	20.15	82.57	10055	55.73
低压电器元件	Low-voltage Electric Elements	1980	10.00	88.08	4332	60.23
电动工具	Electric Tools	382	12.57	88.01	1249	62.53
消防器材	Fire-fighting Equipment & Materials	338	16.27	84.92	113	58.16
电动机柴油机	Motors & Diesel Engines	538	9.67	91.50	212	73.87
冶金产品及金属制品	**Metallurgical and Metal Products**	**7077**	**25.51**	**77.43**	**9626**	**63.28**
线材	Wire Rod	2342	31.47	71.09	4053	71.99
型材	Section Steel	1584	25.25	77.70	3308	57.11
其他产品	**Others**	**5654**	**21.86**	**75.22**	**6748**	**73.17**

20-55 三种专利申请受理量

Three Types of Patent Applications Examined

单位：项 (item)

指标	Item	1985	1990	1995	1999	2000
申请受理量合计	**Total Applications Examined**	**14372**	**41469**	**83045**	**134239**	**170682**
1. 发　明	**Creations and Inventions**	**8558**	**10137**	**21636**	**36694**	**51747**
国　内	Domestic	4065	5832	10018	15596	25346
职　务	Service	2545	2482	2993	6009	12609
大专院校	Universities and Colleges		509	574	988	1942
科研单位	Research Institutions		805	865	1413	2228
工矿企业	Industrial and Mineral Enterprises		816	1086	3490	8316
机关团体	Government Agencies and Organizations		352	468	118	123
非职务	Non-service	1520	3350	7025	9587	12737
国　外	Foreign	4493	4305	11618	21098	26401
职　务	Service	4111	4018	11045	20245	25334
非职务	Non-service	382	287	573	853	1067
2. 实用新型	**Utility Models**	**5174**	**27615**	**43741**	**57492**	**68815**
国　内	Domestic	5077	27488	43429	57214	68461
职　务	Service	1711	7424	8727	14053	17792
大专院校	Universities and Colleges		811	771	747	965
科研单位	Research Institutions		1521	1376	1465	1616
工矿企业	Industrial and Mineral Enterprises		3830	4739	11512	14912
机关团体	Government Agencies and Organizations		1262	1841	329	299
非职务	Non-service	3366	20064	34702	43161	50669
国　外	Foreign	97	127	312	278	354
职　务	Service	74	55	190	201	259
非职务	Non-service	23	72	122	77	95
3. 外观设计	**Designs**	**640**	**3717**	**17668**	**40053**	**50120**
国　内	Domestic	269	3265	15433	37148	46532
职　务	Service	77	1713	8193	17894	22974
大专院校	Universities and Colleges		13	18	34	17
科研单位	Research Institutions		64	104	170	278
工矿企业	Industrial and Mineral Enterprises		1310	6031	17634	22634
机关团体	Government Agencies and Organizations		326	2040	56	45
非职务	Non-service	192	1552	7240	19254	23558
国　外	Foreign	371	452	2235	2905	3588
职　务	Service	325	418	2013	2742	3432
非职务	Non-service	46	34	222	163	156

注：1985年是从4月1日开始统计的。

a)Data in 1985 referred to the period from April 1 to the end of the year.

20-56 三种专利申请批准量

Three Types of Patent Applications Granted

单位：项 (item)

指　　标	Item	1985	1990	1995	1998	2000
批准量合计	**Total Applications Certified**	**138**	**22588**	**45064**	**100156**	**105345**
1．发　明	**Inventions**	**40**	**3838**	**3393**	**7637**	**12683**
国　内	Domestic	38	1149	1530	3097	6177
职　务	Service	32	908	932	1685	2824
大专院校	Universities and Colleges	18	326	258	425	652
科研单位	Research Institutions	11	331	304	543	910
工矿企业	Industrial and Mineral Enterprises	3	206	205	462	1016
机关团体	Government Agencies and Organizations		45	165	255	246
非职务	Non-service	6	241	598	1412	3353
国　外	Foreign	2	2689	1863	4540	6506
职　务	Service	1	2496	1748	4295	6222
非职务	Non-service	1	193	115	245	284
2．实用新型	**Utility Models**	**60**	**16952**	**30471**	**56368**	**54743**
国　内	Domestic	56	16744	30195	56094	54407
职　务	Service	32	5100	6766	14603	15519
大专院校	Universities and Colleges	21	698	623	848	868
科研单位	Research Institutions	6	1280	1025	1860	1529
工矿企业	Industrial and Mineral Enterprises	5	2249	2627	11519	12821
机关团体	Government Agencies and Organizations		873	2491	376	301
非职务	Non-service	24	11644	23429	41491	38888
国　外	Foreign	4	208	276	274	336
职　务	Service	3	132	154	185	261
非职务	Non-service	1	76	122	89	75
3．外观设计	**Designs**	**38**	**1798**	**11200**	**36151**	**37919**
国　内	Domestic	17	1411	9523	32910	34652
职　务	Service	5	751	5344	17627	17789
大专院校	Universities and Colleges		7	10	31	28
科研单位	Research Institutions	2	35	156	170	248
工矿企业	Industrial and Mineral Enterprises	3	598	2554	17360	17482
机关团体	Government Agencies and Organizations		111	2624	66	31
非职务	Non-service	12	660	4179	15283	16863
国　外	Foreign	21	387	1677	3241	3267
职　务	Service	20	336	1402	3111	3108
非职务	Non-service	1	51	275	130	159

注：1985年是从4月1日开始统计的。

a)Data in 1985 referred to the period from April 1 to the end of the year.

20-57 各地区三种专利申请受理和批准量（2000年）
Three Types of Patent Applications Examined and Granted by Region (2000)

单位：项 (item)

地 区	Region	申请受理量 合 计 Number of Patent Applications Examined	发 明 Inventions	实用新型 Utility Models	外观设计 Designs	批准量合计 Number of Patent Applications Granted	发 明 Inventions	实用新型 Utility Models	外观设计 Designs
全 国	**National Total**	**140339**	**25346**	**68461**	**46532**	**95236**	**6177**	**54407**	**34652**
北 京	Beijing	10344	3409	4984	1951	5905	1074	3463	1368
天 津	Tianjin	2789	470	1492	827	1611	163	994	454
河 北	Hebei	3848	601	2429	818	2812	221	1917	674
山 西	Shanxi	1475	338	861	276	968	173	627	168
内蒙古	Inner Mongolia	1138	234	602	302	775	60	530	185
辽 宁	Liaoning	7151	1299	4970	882	4842	458	3703	681
吉 林	Jilin	2501	585	1460	456	1650	154	1142	354
黑龙江	Heilongjiang	3106	666	2019	421	2252	208	1663	381
上 海	Shanghai	11337	4713	2760	3864	4050	304	2083	1663
江 苏	Jiangsu	8211	1160	4590	2461	6432	341	4095	1996
浙 江	Zhejiang	10316	859	4439	5018	7495	184	3439	3872
安 徽	Anhui	1877	301	1080	496	1482	104	894	484
福 建	Fujian	4211	377	1516	2318	3003	93	1074	1836
江 西	Jiangxi	1557	267	806	484	1072	67	690	315
山 东	Shandong	10019	1245	5731	3043	6962	363	4627	1972
河 南	Henan	3823	655	2551	617	2766	209	2113	444
湖 北	Hubei	3486	771	2102	613	2198	156	1573	469
湖 南	Hunan	4117	814	2465	838	2555	197	1759	599
广 东	Guangdong	21123	1760	6033	13330	15799	261	4797	10741
广 西	Guangxi	1762	252	1059	451	1191	99	730	362
海 南	Hainan	502	101	123	278	320	15	90	215
重 庆	Chongqing	1780	231	930	619	1158	56	677	425
四 川	Sichuan	4496	759	1954	1783	3218	248	1699	1271
贵 州	Guizhou	986	173	503	310	710	65	377	268
云 南	Yunnan	1710	341	737	632	1217	140	606	471
西 藏	Tibet	28	5	7	16	17	4	4	9
陕 西	Shaanxi	2080	435	1307	338	1462	188	1022	252
甘 肃	Gansu	798	221	412	165	493	82	326	85
青 海	Qinghai	174	36	90	48	117	16	67	34
宁 夏	Ningxia	341	112	154	75	224	21	166	37
新 疆	Xinjiang	1088	179	699	210	717	66	475	176
香 港	Hong Kong	1374	152	204	1018	1285	28	207	1050
澳 门	Macao	13	2	4	7	13	0	1	12
台 湾	Taiwan	10778	1823	7388	1567	8465	359	6777	1329

20−58 按国别(地区)分的三种专利申请受理量及批准量（2000年）

Three Types of Patent Applications Examined and Granted by Country (Territory) (2000)

单位：项 (item)

国别（地区）	Country (Territory)	申请受理量 合计 Number of Patent Applications Examined	发明 Inventions	实用新型 Utility Models	外观设计 Designs	批准量合计 Number of Patent Applications Grant	发明 Inventions	实用新型 Utility Models	外观设计 Designs
总　　计	**Total**	**30343**	**26401**	**354**	**3588**	**10109**	**6506**	**336**	**3267**
日　　本	Japan	9888	8300	87	1501	3594	2206	78	1310
马来西亚	Malaysia	13	6	2	5	11	1	2	8
新 加 坡	Singapore	54	27	4	23	24	5	3	16
泰　　国	Thailand	26	7	3	16	15	0	0	15
中国香港	Hong Kong, China								
中国澳门	Macao, China								
台　　湾	Taiwan								
韩　　国	Republic of Korea	1861	1579	63	219	608	390	48	170
塞普路斯	Cyprus	4	4	0	0	0	0	0	0
印　　度	India	19	14	0	5	9	2	1	6
摩 纳 哥	Monaco	6	5	0	1				
南　　非	South Africa	37	35	0	2	11	9	0	2
德　　国	Germany	2787	2578	9	200	871	707	2	162
荷　　兰	Holland	993	900	0	93	311	183	1	127
英　　国	England	802	697	14	91	304	193	16	95
瑞　　士	Switzerland	867	753	1	113	408	275	11	122
丹　　麦	Denmark	229	195	1	33	59	32	1	26
匈 牙 利	Hungary	19	15	0	4	12	8	0	4
奥 地 利	Austria	122	91	0	31	64	53	0	11
比 利 时	Belgium	126	118	0	8	42	33	0	9
法　　国	France	1387	1195	1	191	537	385	2	150
挪　　威	Norway	75	68	0	7	29	26	0	3
俄罗斯联邦	Russia	42	41	1	0	15	11	1	3
卢 森 堡	Luxembourg	54	34	10	10	18	7	0	11
列支敦士登	Liechtenstein	32	32	0	0	26	15	0	11
西 班 牙	Spain	62	33	5	24	37	13	3	21
捷　　克	Czech	1	1	0	0				
波　　兰	Poland	1	1	0	0				
爱 尔 兰	Ireland	22	20	1	1	6	5	1	0
芬　　兰	Finland	378	357	1	20	100	53	0	47
意 大 利	Italy	382	332	2	48	181	114	3	64
瑞　　典	Sweden	768	708	0	60	183	125	0	58
以 色 列	Israel	162	152	1	9	18	12	2	4
巴　　西	Brazil	27	19	1	7	5	2	0	3
美　　国	United States	8418	7503	128	787	2332	1475	134	723
加 拿 大	Canada	235	216	7	12	100	68	8	24
新 西 兰	New Zealand	33	26	0	7	16	6	0	10
澳大利亚	Australia	232	204	2	26	82	65	5	12

20-59 按国际专利标准分类的发明、实用新型专利申请量和批准量

Two Types of Patent Applications Examined and Granted by International Patent Classifications and Utility Models

单位：项 (item)

分 类	Item	1999		2000	
		申请量 Applications Examined	批准量 Applications Granted	申请量 Applications Examined	批准量 Applications Granted
合 计	**Total**	**97753**	**64005**	**116769**	**67426**
A 部(人类生活需要)	**Section A: Personal Use Items**	**24988**	**16094**	**26255**	**16677**
农、林、牧、渔	Agriculture, Forestry, Animal Husbandry and Fishery	3534	2163	3420	2235
烘烤、食用面团	Baking and Edible Doughs	206	127	202	130
屠宰、加工	Butchering and Meat Processing	36	33	36	33
食品、食物及处理	Foods or Foodstuffs and their Treatment	2166	568	1891	789
烟类及用品	Tobacco, Cigars and Cigarettes	323	223	303	247
服 装	Clothing	639	544	780	532
帽类制品	Headwear	94	93	168	91
鞋 类	Footwear	753	565	828	554
男用服饰用品、珠宝	Haberdashery and Jewelry	246	162	257	163
手携及旅行用品	Hand or Traveling Articles	905	759	1042	747
刷类用品	Brushware	257	197	277	193
家具、家庭日用品或设备	Furniture, Domestic Articles and Appliances	5146	4359	5235	4264
医学、兽医学、卫生学	Medical or Veterinary Science and Hygiene	8757	4865	9296	5285
救生、消防	Life-saving and Fire-fighting	293	233	312	230
医学、游戏、娱乐活动	Sports, Games, and Recreation	1633	1203	2208	1184
B 部(作业、运输)	**Section B: Industrial and Transportation**	**18504**	**14519**	**23323**	**15026**
物理或化学的方法或装置	Physical or Chemical Processes or Apparatus	1887	1121	1873	1320
破碎、研磨、粉碎	Crushing, Pulverizing, or Disintegrating	396	358	400	353
分选、分离	Separation of Solid Materials, Electrostatic Separation	174	135	153	139
离心装置、离心机	Centrifugal Apparatus or Equipment	56	62	68	61
喷射、雾化	Spraying or Atomizing General	398	348	670	352
机械振动的产生和传递	Generation or Transmission of Mechanical Vibrations	19	16	22	16
固体分离、分选	Separating Solids from Solid Wastes	166	150	178	151
清 洁	Janitorial	164	137	155	135
固体废料的处理	Disposal of Solid Waste	69	17	111	19
金属加工、冲裁	Mechanical Metal-working and Stamping	439	522	595	559
铸造、粉末冶金	Casting and Powder Metallurgy	337	193	327	236
机床、其他金属加工	Machine Tools	878	823	1143	873
磨削、抛光	Grinding and Polishing	232	246	296	241
简单工具	Hand Tools, Portable Power Tools, and Workshop Equipment	533	562	698	571
手工、切割工具、切断	Hand Cutting Tools, Cutting, and Severing	233	232	337	240
木材加工、保存、钉钉机	Wood Preservation and Nailing or Stapling Machines	283	226	471	238
加工水泥、粘土和石料	Cement, Clay or Stone	323	268	355	296
塑料制品的加工	Plastics	648	421	836	456
压力机	Presses	107	98	106	97
纸品制作、纸的加工	Paper Making and Processing Paper	57	88	76	86
叠层产品	Layered Products	331	143	438	157
印刷、打字机、印刷机	Printing, Lining Machines, and Typewriters	468	260	594	270
装订、图册、文件夹	Bookbinding, Albums, and Files	439	246	406	247

20-59 续表 1 continued

单位：项 (item)

分类	Item	1999 申请量 Applications Examined	1999 批准量 Applications Granted	2000 申请量 Applications Examined	2000 批准量 Applications Granted
绘图具、办公附属用品	Writing or Drafting Devices	902	639	1030	627
装饰艺术	Decorative Arts	362	196	468	206
一般车辆	Vehicles in General	2181	1803	3704	1808
铁 路	Railways	212	192	391	192
无轨陆用车牌	Land Vehicles other than Rail	1840	1483	1900	1479
船舶、船只、有关设备	Ships and Related Equipment	236	224	374	238
飞行器、航空、宇宙航行	Aircraft and Aviation	159	47	177	47
输送、包装、存贮、搬运	Conveying and Packing Inflammatory Materials	3314	2675	4280	2709
卷扬、提升、牵引	Hoisting, Lifting, and Hauling	486	429	540	446
液体的贮运	Opening or Closing Bottles, Jars or Similar Containers	161	148	138	151
鞍具、室内装璜	Saddlery ; Upholstery	14	11	13	10
C 部(化学、冶金)	**Section C: Chemistry and Metallurgy**	**10407**	**3640**	**13683**	**5139**
无机化学	Inorganic Chemistry	543	218	468	330
水、废污水、泥浆的处理	Treatment of Water, Waste Water, Sewage or Sludge	847	576	1021	589
玻璃、石棉和渣棉	Glass; Mineral of Slag Wool	241	141	243	175
水泥、陶瓷等、隔音材料	Cement, Concrete, Artificial Stone; Ceramics, Refractories	601	128	445	207
肥料及制造	Fertilizers and Related Products	357	59	254	85
炸药、火柴	Explosives and Matches	51	24	33	31
有机化学	Organic Chemistry	1685	745	4208	1200
有机高分子化合物	Organic Macromolecular Compounds	1225	308	1545	492
染料、涂料、抛光剂等	Dyes, Paints, Polishes, Resins, and Adhesives	1058	192	887	299
石油、煤气及炼焦工业	Petroleum, Gas or Coke Industries, Inert Gases	917	292	794	403
动植物油、脂类	Animal or Vegetable Oils, Fats	289	119	389	164
生化、酒、醋、酶、遗传工程	Biochemistry, Beer, Spirits, Wine, Vinegar, Microbiology, Benzymology, Mutation or Genetic Engineering	1352	188	2237	259
糖或淀粉工业	Sugar Industry	13	18	18	22
大小原皮、毛皮、皮革	Skins, Hides, Pelts, Leather	44	29	37	35
黑色冶金	Metallurgy of Iron	234	182	247	232
冶金学、合金或有色合金	Metallurgy, Ferrous or Nonferrous Alloys	406	182	311	289
金属加工涂料、防腐防锈	Coating Metallic Materials	268	90	297	126
电解电泳方法及设备	Electrolytic or Electrophoretic Processes	212	128	198	168
晶体生长	Crystal Growth	64	21	51	33
D 部(纺织、造纸)	**Section D: Textiles and Papers Making**	**1720**	**1125**	**2054**	**1261**
线、纤维、纺纱	Natural or Artificial Threads or Fibers, Spinning	197	132	276	166
纺纱、整经或络经	Yarns, Mechanical Finishing of Yarns or Rope	42	33	57	40
织 造	Weaving	110	124	139	150
编带、花边、针织、整理	Braiding, Lace-Making, Knitting	181	123	274	136
缝纫、锈花、簇绒	Sewing, Embroidery, Tufting	130	127	150	151
织物等的处理、洗涤	Treatment of Textiles, Laundering	722	418	782	435
绳、除电缆外的缆绳	Ropes and Cables, other than Electric	27	19	26	22
造纸、纤维素的生产	Paper making, Production of Cellulose	311	149	350	161
E 部(固定建筑物)	**Section E: Fixed Construction**	**6649**	**5983**	**7513**	**5958**
道路、铁路和桥梁的建筑	Construction of Roads, Railways, or Bridges	546	418	613	416
水利工程、基础、运土	Hydraulic Engineering, Foundations, Soil-shifting	595	438	548	468
给水、排水	Water Supply, Sewage	791	719	1161	707

20–59 续表 2 continued

单位：项 (item)

分类	Item	1999 申请量 Applications Examined	1999 批准量 Applications Granted	2000 申请量 Applications Examined	2000 批准量 Applications Granted
建筑物	Building	1600	1576	1775	1576
锁、钥匙、门窗、保险箱	Locks, Keys, Windows or Door Fittings; Safes	1431	1307	1434	1278
一般门、窗、百叶窗、梯子	Doors, Windows, Shutters, or Roller Blinds in General; Ladders	963	885	1178	868
钻井、采矿	Well Drilling, Mining	723	640	804	645
F 部(机械工程)	**Section F: Mechanical Engineering**	**12591**	**10918**	**14979**	**10912**
一般机器、发动机、蒸汽机	Machines or Engines in General; Engine Plants in General; Steam Engines	416	308	524	306
内燃机等	Combustion Engines	933	849	929	874
液力机械和其他发动机	Machines or Engines for Liquids	292	129	319	126
液体变容机械、泵	Positive-displacement Machines for Liquids; Pumps for Liquid or Elastic Fluids	1170	1109	1343	1099
液压调节器、液压技术	Fluid-pressure Acuators; Hydraulic or Pneumatics in General	90	61	173	61
工程元件或部件	Engineering Elements or Units; General Measures for Producing and Maintaining Effective Functioning of Machines or Installations; Thermal Insulation in General	3171	2713	3632	2764
气体或液体的贮藏或分配	Storage or Distribution of Gases or Liquids	123	121	132	123
照　明	Lighting	549	643	739	624
蒸汽的生产	Steam Generation	94	91	148	91
燃烧设备、燃烧技术	Combustion Apparatus; Combustion Processes	757	675	1361	680
采暖、炉灶、通风	Stoves, Ranges, Ventilation	3493	2909	3886	2854
制冷气体的液化和固化	Refrigeration or Cooling, Heat Pump Systems	537	389	654	385
干　燥	Drying	153	164	160	168
炉、窑、灶、罐	Furnaces, Kilns, Ovens	176	175	237	186
一般热交换	Heat Exchange in General	408	450	490	440
武　器	Weapons	127	48	134	48
弹药、爆破	Ammunition, Blasting Caps	102	84	118	83
G 部(物理)	**Section G: Physics**	**11189**	**5795**	**14097**	**6035**
测量、测试	Measurements, Testing	2923	2129	3790	2192
光学技术	Optics	701	387	1147	416
照相术、电影术、电刻术	Photography, Cinematography, Electrography	506	205	637	222
测时技术	Horology	228	200	273	208
控制、调节技术	Controlling, Regulating	272	241	232	253
计算、推算、计数技术	Computing, Calculating, Counting	3169	778	4263	863
核算装置	Measurement Devices	274	141	273	141
信号装置	Signaling	526	355	501	355
教育、密码、显示、广告等	Education, Cryptography, Advertising, Seals	1311	853	1360	842
乐器、声学	Musical Instruments, Acoustics	209	152	332	155
信息的存储	Information Storage	980	293	1189	324
仪器的零部件	Instrument Details	24	45	23	44
核物理、核工程	Nuclear physics, Nuclear Engineering	66	16	77	20
H 部(电学)	**Section H: Electricity**	**11705**	**5931**	**14865**	**6418**
基本电器元件	Basic Electric Elements	4956	2937	5769	3137
电力的发电、变电或配电	Generation, Conversion, or Distribution of Electric Power	1874	1261	2110	1354
基本电子电路	Basic Electronic Circuitry	473	141	695	159
电信技术	Telecommunications Techniques	3649	1125	5338	1276
其他类不包括的电技术	Electric Techniques Not Otherwise Provided for	753	467	953	492

注：此表不包括外观设计分类。

a)Designs patents are excluded in this table.

主 要 统 计 指 标 解 释

普通高等学校 指按照国家规定的设置标准和审批程序批准举办，通过国家统一招生考试，招收高中毕业生为主要培养对象，实施高等教育的全日制大学、独立设置的学院和高等专科学校、短期职业大学。

成人高等学校 指按照国家有关规定审批，招收通过全国成人高教统一招生考试的具有高中毕业或同等学历的在职从业人员，利用脱产、半脱产、业余或函授等多种形式对其实施高等学历教育，培养高等教育专科或本科毕业水平的专门人才，修业年限、课程设置和总学时数均按高等学历教育要求付诸实施的学校。包括广播电视大学、职工高等学校、农民高等学校、管理干部学院、教育学院、独立设置的函授学院等。

小学学龄儿童入学率 指调查范围内已入小学学习的学龄儿童占校内外学龄儿童总数(包括弱智儿童，不包括盲聋哑儿童)的比重。计算公式为：

小学学龄儿童入学率＝已入学的小学学龄儿童数／校内外小学学龄儿童总数×100%

独立研究与开发机构 指有明确的任务和研究方向，有一定学术水平的业务骨干和一定数量的研究人员，具有研究、开发、开展学术工作的基本条件，主要进行科学研究与技术开发活动，并且在行政上有独立的组织形式，财务上独立核算盈亏，有权与其他单位签订合同，在银行有单独户头的单位。包括国务院各部门、中国科学院、中国社会科学院和各省、自治区、直辖市以及地(市)以上〔含地(市)〕各部门所属的国有科学研究与技术开发机构。

独立研究与开发机构职工 指在独立研究与开发机构工作，并由其支付工资的人员。包括长期职工、临时职工和招聘人员，不包括编制以外的离休、退休人员和停薪留职人员。

研究与发展经费支出 指用于研究与发展课题活动(基础研究、应用研究、实验发展)的全部实际支出，包括用于研究与发展课题活动的直接支出和间接用于研究与发展活动的支出（如研究院、所管理费，维持研究院、所正常运转的必需费用和与研究发展有关的基本建设支出)。

科学家和工程师 指具有大学本科及以上学历和不具备上述学历但有高、中级职称的人员。

其他科技人员 指大专、中专毕业和具有初级职称的从事科技活动人员。

专业技术人员 指已取得科学技术职称，或大学、中专的理、工、农、医科系毕业，以及国民经济各部门从工作实践中提拔，从事理、工、农、医等自然科学技术的研究、教学、生产的专业人员和在机关、企业、事业中从事科学技术业务管理工作的专业人员。

工程技术人员 指在国民经济各行业中从事工程技术工作的自然科学技术专业人员，包括高级工程师、工程师、助理工程师、技术员和未评定职称的技术人员。

农业技术人员 指在国民经济各行业中从事农业技术工作的自然科学技术专业人员，包括高级农艺师、农艺师、助理农艺师、技术员和未评定职称的技术人员。

卫生技术人员 指在国民经济各行业中从事卫生医务工作的自然科学技术专业人员，包括正副主任医师、主治医师、医师、医(护)士和未评定职称的技术人员。

科学研究人员 指在国民经济各行业中从事科学技术活动的自然科学技术专业人员，包括正副研究员、助理研究员、研究实习员、技术员和未评定职称的技术人员。

自然科学教学人员 指在国民经济各行业中从事自然科学技术教学活动的专业人员，包括正副教授、讲师、助教、教师和在中学从事自然科学技术教学活动的人员。

发明 是专利法及其实施细则所称的发明，指对有关产品、方法或其改进所提出的新的技术方案。

实用新型 是专利法及其实施细则所称的实用新型，指对产品的形状、构造或者其结合所提出的适于实用的新的技术方案。

外观设计 是专利法及其实施细则所称的外观设计，指对产品的形状、图案、色彩或者其结合所作出的富有美感并适于工业上应用的新设计。

Explanatory Note's on Main Statistical Indicators

Regular Institutions of Higher Learning refer to educational establishments set up according to the government evaluation and approval procedures, enrolling graduates from senior secondary schools and providing higher education courses and training for senior professionals. They include full-time universities, colleges, high professional schools and short-term professional universities.

Institutions of Higher Learning for Adults refer to educational establishments, set up in line with relevant rules approved by the government, enrolling staff and workers with senior secondary school or equivalent education ,and providing higher education courses in many forms of full time, part time, spare time, or correspondence for adults. Professionals thus trained receive a qualification equivalent to graduates studying regular courses at regular universities, colleges and professional colleges. Institutions of higher learning for adults include Radio and TV universities, schools of high education for staff and workers and peasants, colleges for management cadres, pedagogical colleges, independent correspondence colleges.

Enrollment Rate of Primary School Age Children refers to the proportion of school age children enrolled at schools to the total number of school age children both in and outside schools (including retarded children ,but excluding blind, deaf and mute children). The formula is:

Enrollment Rate of Primary School-age Children = (Total Primary School-age Children at Schools)÷ (Total Primary School age Children Both at and Outside Schools) ×100%

Independent Research and Development Institutions refer to the state owned institutions which have direct mission and research purpose, a certain number of core member with higher research level and a certain number of research personnel, necessary conditions for R & D activities and engaging in scientific research and technological development. The institutions also have their own independent organization and finance, authority to sign contracts with other units, with their own accounts in banks. Independent research and development institutions include the institutions attached to central government agencies, Chinese Academy of Sciences. Chinese Academy of Social Sciences and the institutions attached to local governments.

Personnel of Independent Research and Development Institutions refers to the persons working in and receiving payment from research and development institutions. It includes regular full-time and temporary staff and workers and employees working on contracts, but excludes retirees and persons leaving their work without payment but still retaining their posts, who are not on the employee list.

Total Expenditure on Research and Development refers to all actual expenditure made for R&D (basic research, applied research and experimental development)in reference period. It includes direct expenditure on R&D and indirect expenditure on R&D(including management and necessary administrative expenses of research institutes, investment in capital construction relating to R&D).

Scientists and Engineers refer to persons who have completed university or higher education or obtained titles of senior and middle level professional positions.

Other Technical Personnel refers to persons involved in science and technology with secondary specialized education or three-year college education and persons with junior professional titles.

Natural Scientific and Technical Personnel refers to those professionals holding scientific and technical titles or taking such positions, or being graduated from departments of science, engineering, agriculture and medicine, and/or having been promoted in practice in different sectors of the national economy and working on research, teaching and production technique in the scientific and technological fields such as science, engineering, agriculture and medicine, etc. and the professionals doing administrative work related to science and technology in government agencies, enterprises and institutions.

Engineering Professionals refer to the persons who are engaged in engineering science and technology in different sectors of the national economy, including senior engineers, engineers, assistant engineers, technicians and technical personnel without professional titles.

Agricultural Professionals refer to the persons who are working on the science of agriculture in different sectors of the national economy, including senior agronomists, agronomists, assistant argonomists, technicians and technical personnel without professional titles.

Public Health Professionals refer to the persons who are engaged in medical and health work in different sectors of the national economy, including director doctors and their deputies, doctors in charge, doctors, paramedics, nurses and technical personnel without professional titles.

Scientific Research Personnel refers to those personnel engaged in scientific and technical activities in different sectors of the national economy, including research fellows and their deputies, assistant research fellows, research trainees, technicians and technical personnel without professional titles.

Professionals engaged in the teaching of natural science and technology in different sectors of the national economy, including professors, associate professors, lecturers, teaching assistants, teachers and teaching personnel in science and technology in middle schools.

Inventions refer to the inventions as specified by the patent law and its detailed rules and regulations for implementation. They refer to the new technical proposals to the products or methods or their modifications.

Utility Models refer to the utility models as specified by the patent law and its detailed rules and regulations for implementation. They refer to the practical and new technical proposals on the shape and structure of the product or the combination of both.

Designs refer to the designs as specified by the patent law and its detailed rules and regulation for implementation. They refer to the aesthetics and industry applicable new designs for the shape, pattern and color of the product, or their combinations.

二十一、文化、体育和卫生

Culture, Sports and Public Health

简要说明

一、本篇主要反映文化、体育和卫生事业的发展情况。

二、文化部分主要包括艺术表演团体和艺术表演场所、图书馆、群众文化、文物、广播、电影、电视、新闻出版等文化事业的机构、人员和业务活动情况。

1.艺术事业、图书馆事业、群众文化事业的资料主要来自文化部。

2.文物资料来自国家文物局。

3.广播、电影、电视资料主要来源于国家广播电影电视总局。

4.新闻出版有关资料主要来自国家新闻出版总署。

三、体育部分主要包括群众体育和竞技体育，内容有体育系统职工、运动员、教练员和裁判员等人数，体育场地数，竞技体育成绩，体育锻炼达标人数，与国外体育交往次数和人数等。体育部分的资料主要来自国家体育总局

四、卫生部分主要内容有卫生机构、人员、床位数，医院诊疗人次及入院人数，主要疾病死亡原因及构成，传染病的发病及死亡情况等。卫生部分的资料主要来自卫生部。

上述资料都是根据各部门制定的统计报表制度进行汇总加工整理而成，一般是逐级汇总上报。这些统计报表制度包括文化、文物统计报表制度，广播、电影、电视统计报表制度，新闻出版统计报表制度，体育事业统计报表制度和卫生事业统计报表制度。

Brief Introduction

I. Data in this chapter mainly show the development of culture, sports and public health undertakings.

II. Data on culture cover mainly the situations on institutions, personnel and business activities of arts (performing groups and venues), libraries, mass culture, cultural relics, broadcasting, films, televisions, news and publication.

(1) The data on the causes of arts, libraries, mass culture are provided by the Ministry of Culture.

(2) The data on cultural relics are provided by the State Bureau of Cultural Relics.

(3) The data on broadcasting, film and television are mainly provided by the State Administration of Broadcasting, Film and Television.

(4) The data on news and publication are mainly provided by the State Agency of News and Publication.

III. Data on sports cover mass sports (sports for all) and athletics sports, including mainly the number of staff and workers in sports departments, number of athletes, coaches and referees, number of stadiums and gymnasiums, achievements in athletic sport events, number of persons who have come up to the "National Physical Training Program Standards" and the international exchanges of sport delegations. Data on sports are mainly from the State Sports Administration.

IV. Data on public health include mainly the number of institutions, personnel, hospital beds, number of patients treated and in-patients, major diseases as the causes of death and the proportion to the total deaths, the incidence of, and the deaths caused by infectious diseases. Data on public health are mainly from the Ministry of Public Health.

The above-mentioned are collected and tabulated in accordance with the statistical reporting schemes stipulated by the departments concerned, in most cases reported to the higher authorities level by level. They include the statistical reporting schemes on culture, on cultural relics, on radio and television broadcasting and film-making, on news and publication, on sports and on public health.

21-1 文化艺术和文物事业机构、人员情况（2000年）

Number of Institutions and Personnel in Culture, Art and Cultural Relics (2000)

机构类别	Category of Institution	机构数（个） Number of Institutions	从业人数（人） Number of Persons Engaged (person)
文化事业合计	**Culture**	**282784**	**1476176**
艺术事业	Art Institutions	5120	190032
#艺术表演团体	Art Performance Troupes	2630	141440
话剧、儿童剧、滑稽剧团	Drama, Children, Plays and Comedy Troupes	86	7160
歌剧、舞剧、歌舞剧团	Opera, Ballet and Dance Troupes	79	9038
歌舞团、轻音乐团	Song and Dance Troupe, Light Music Troupe	289	22025
文工团、文宣队、乌兰牧骑	Cultural and Performance Troupes and Ulanmuchi (equestrian art troupes)	419	12335
戏曲剧团	Local Opera Troupes	1531	79120
#京剧	Local Beijing Opera Troupes	109	9583
曲艺、杂技、木偶、皮影团	Recitation and Ballad Troupes, Acrobatics and Circus Troupes, Puppet Show Troupes and Shadow Play Troupes	209	9969
艺术表演场所	Art Centers	1912	42177
剧场、影剧院	Theaters and Music Halls	1877	41187
书场、曲艺场	Storytelling Places, Recitation and Ballad Places	20	198
杂技、马戏场	Acrobatics, Circus Places	3	74
音乐厅	Concert Halls	12	718
公共图书馆事业	Public Libraries	2677	51368
群众文化事业	Mass Culture	45321	128420
群众艺术馆	Mass Art Centers	390	11620
文化馆	Cultural Centers	2907	43246
文化站	Cultural Stations	42024	73554
#乡文化站	Township Cultural Stations	39348	61675
艺术教育事业	Culture and Education	220	15578
其他文化事业	Other Cultural Units	225972	1021645
艺术创作机构	Art Creation Institutions	407	3006
艺术研究机构	Art Research Institutions	185	3150
艺术展览机构	Art Exhibition Institutions	49	1380
#美术馆	Art Gallery	26	799
文化艺术经纪与代理业	Brokers and Agents for Cultural and Arts Activities	264	2307
其他	Others	225067	1011802
文物事业合计	**Cultural Relics**	**3618**	**68038**
文物保护管理机构	Agency of Historical Relics Preservation	1984	24051
文物科研机构	Scientific and Research Historical Relics Agency	57	2800
其他文物机构	Other Historical Relics Agency	68	4051
博物馆	Museums	1392	34199
综合性博物馆	Comprehensive Museum	829	17998
专门性博物馆	Special Museum	283	10352
纪念性博物馆	Memorial Museum	280	5849
文物商店	Cultural Relics Agencies	117	2937

21-2 各地区文化艺术、文物事业单位数

Number of Institutions for Culture, Art and Cultural Relics by Region

单位：个 (unit)

地　区	Region	艺术表演团体 Art Performance Troupes	艺术表演场所 Art Performance Places	文化馆 Cultural Centers	公共图书馆 Public Libraries	博物馆 Museums
	1978	3150	1095	2748	1218	349
	1979	3482	1255	2892	1651	344
	1980	3533	1444	2912	1732	365
	1981	3483	1415	2803	1787	383
	1982	3460	1424	2925	1889	409
	1983	3444	1688	2946	2038	467
	1984	3397	1684	3016	2217	618
	1985	3317	1673	2965	2344	711
	1986	3195	2036	2993	2406	777
	1987	3094	2094	2973	2440	827
	1988	2985	2042	2975	2485	903
	1989	2850	2011	2955	2512	967
	1990	2805	2011	2955	2527	1013
	1991	2772	2024	2894	2535	1075
	1992	2753	2037	2900	2565	1106
	1993	2707	2024	2886	2579	1130
	1994	2698	1998	2887	2596	1161
	1995	2682	1972	2886	2615	1194
	1996	2664	1934	2892	2631	1219
	1997	2663	1947	2901	2661	1282
	1998	2652	1929	2901	2731	1339
	1999	2632	1911	2905	2767	1364
	2000	2630	1912	2907	2677	1392
北　京	Beijing	20	25	22	25	25
天　津	Tianjin	16	32	18	31	14
河　北	Hebei	138	101	166	145	43
山　西	Shanxi	159	49	118	121	76
内蒙古	Inner Mongolia	116	30	104	108	25
辽　宁	Liaoning	77	71	102	128	30
吉　林	Jilin	65	52	89	60	16
黑龙江	Heilongjiang	91	56	118	97	41
上　海	Shanghai	29	43	45	31	11
江　苏	Jiangsu	133	142	107	101	86
浙　江	Zhejiang	79	95	84	83	65
安　徽	Anhui	92	104	103	84	37
福　建	Fujian	96	80	80	81	81
江　西	Jiangxi	79	62	101	104	81
山　东	Shandong	118	105	140	133	59
河　南	Henan	205	166	191	134	70
湖　北	Hubei	101	78	129	103	94
湖　南	Hunan	91	94	125	115	71
广　东	Guangdong	138	76	119	125	131
广　西	Guangxi	118	32	99	94	39
海　南	Hainan	21	18	18	19	15
重　庆	Chongqing	38	25	43	42	14
四　川	Sichuan	98	94	171	129	50
贵　州	Guizhou	28	14	85	89	8
云　南	Yunnan	129	40	127	148	30
西　藏	Tibet	26	20	52	1	2
陕　西	Shaanxi	118	112	111	114	67
甘　肃	Gansu	76	46	83	91	65
青　海	Qinghai	14	2	43	38	14
宁　夏	Ningxia	15	19	22	22	4
新　疆	Xinjiang	88	23	92	80	23

21-3 艺术表演团体演出情况（2000年）

Basic Statistics on Performance of Art Troupes (2000)

种类	Item	演出场数（万场） Number of Performances (10 000 shows)	#到农村演出 Shows in Rural Areas (10 000)	观众人数（万人次） Number of Spectators(10 000 person-times)
总计	**Total**	**43**	**26**	**46168**
国有剧团	Troupes Sponsored by State-owned Units	28	14	30946
集体经营剧团	Troupes Sponsored by Collective Units	15	11	15213
按剧种分:	**Art Troupes**			
话剧、儿童剧、滑稽剧团	Drama, Children's Play and Comedy Troupes	0.8		1162.2
歌舞剧团	Song and Dance Drama Troupes	0.8	0.3	1259.4
歌舞团、轻音乐团	Song and Dance, Light Music	3.5	0.9	5082.1
文工团、宣传队、乌兰牧骑	Cultural and Performance Troupes and Ulanmuchi (equestrian art troupes)	4	2.1	3916.5
乐团、合唱团	Philharmonic and Chorus Troupes	-	-	-
戏曲剧团	Local Opera Troupes	23.8	18.3	31465.2
#京　剧	Local Beijing Opera Troupes	1	0.3	1458.3
曲艺、杂技、木偶、皮影团	Recitation and Ballad Troupes, Acrobatics and Circus Troupes, Puppet Show Troupes, and Shadow Play Troupes	6.7	2.9	3097.2

注：歌舞剧团包括歌剧、舞剧、歌舞剧团(下表同)。

a)Song and dance drama troupes include opera, dance and light music troupes. The same as in the following table.

21-4 艺术表演团体收支情况（2000年）

Income and Expenditures of Art Troupes (2000)

种类	Item	补贴团数（个） Number of Troupes Receiving Government Subsidies (unit)	总收入（万元） Total Income (10 000 yuan)	#财政补助收入（万元） Government Subsidies (10 000 yuan)	#演出收入 Income from Perform	总支出（万元） Total Expenditures (10 000 yuan)	经费自给率（%） Total Income/ Total Expenditures Ratio (%)
总计	**Total**	**2464**	**263664**	**172864**	**51650**	**268886**	**31.5**
国有剧团	Troupes Sponsored by State-owned Units	1839	233046	157263	41369	238380	29.3
集体经营剧团	Troupes Sponsored by Collective Units	624	30600	15590	10281	30488	48.0
按剧种分:	**Art Troupes**						
话剧、儿童剧、滑稽剧团	Drama, Children's Play and Comedy Troupes	83	21089	14395	2807	21153	28.6
歌舞剧团	Song and Dance Drama Troupes	72	23371	15125	4001	23663	33.3
歌舞团、轻音乐团	Song and Dance, Light Music	279	47171	32146	8848	48175	27.4
文工团、宣传队、乌兰牧骑	Cultural and Performance Troupes and Ulanmuchi (equestrian art troupes)	399	12886	10799	1178	12819	15.6
乐团、合唱团	Philharmonic and Chorus Troupes	15	9716	5556	2201	8990	43.6
戏曲剧团	Local Opera Troupes	1435	124176	81457	24224	124234	32.6
#京　剧	Local Beijing Opera Troupes	106	24388	17542	2666	24369	26.7
曲艺、杂技、木偶、皮影团	Recitation and Ballad Troupes, Acrobatics and Circus Troupes, Puppet Show Troupes and Shadow Play Troupes	181	25255	13386	8391	29852	36.9

注：本表各项指标仅指文化部系统内的。

a)The data in this table only refer to those under the administration of the cultural departments.

21-5 群众艺术馆、文化馆站业务活动及经费情况（2000年）
Basic Statistics on Activities and Expenditures of Mass Art Centers and Cultural Centers (2000)

项目	Item	总计 Total	群众艺术馆 Mass Art Centers	文化馆 Cultural Centers	文化站 Cultural Stations
单位数（个）	Number of Units (unit)	45321	390	2907	42024
举办展览（个）	Number of Exhibitions (unit)	91670	1837	14440	75393
组织文艺活动（次）	Art Performances and Story-Telling Sessions (times)	276574	8462	60157	207955
举办训练班	Training Courses				
班次（次）	Number of Classes (times)	143370	7045	29432	160893
结业人次（万人次）	Number of Persons Completing Courses (10 000 person-times)	494	21	89	384
群众艺术馆、文化馆负责指导单位	Units Responsible for Guiding Mass Art Centers and Cultural Centers				
农村集镇文化中心（个）	Cultural Centers in County Towns (unit)	22171	1613	20558	
文化俱乐部、室（个）	Cultural Clubs (unit)	104587	3200	101387	
文化户（户）	Households Specializing in Cultural Activities (household)	180470	4622	175848	
群众业余演出团(队)（个）	Part-time Art Groups (unit)	36151	1892	34259	
总支出（万元）	Total Expenditures (10 000 yuan)	188437	33010	78871	76557
#业务费（万元）	Professional Expenditures (10 000 yuan)	27909	6986	10065	10858
修缮费（万元）	Maintenance Expenses (10 000 yuan)	10147	1571	3731	4845

注：本表各项指标仅指文化部系统内的。
a)The data in this table only refer to those under the administration of the cultural departments.

21-6 公共图书馆业务活动及经费情况（2000年）
Facilities, Services and Expenditures of Public Libraries (2000)

项目	Item	总计 Total	#省级公共图书馆 Public Libraries at Provincial Level	#县级公共图书馆 Public Libraries at County Level
总藏量（万册、件）	Total Collections (10 000 volumes)	40953	13158	14524
书架总长度（万米）	Total Length of Bookshelves (10 000 m)	978	284	330
发放借书证数（万个）	Number of Library Cards Distributed (10 000 units)	623	98	288
图书流通情况	Circulation of Books			
总流通人次（万人次）	Total Number of Circulation (10 000 person-times)	18854	2163	9953
书刊外借册次(万册次)	Number of Books Borrowed by the Readers (10 000 volume-times)	16913	1508	9266
为读者服务举办各种活动	Service Activities Provided for Readers			
次数（次）	Number of Activities (times)	40448	6953	25077
参加人数（万人次）	Number of Readers Involved (10 000 person-times)	1802	368	764
总支出（万元）	Total Expenditures (10 000 yuan)	157173	44422	43659
#藏量购置费（万元）	Purchase Expenses (10 000 yuan)	40575	16878	5269
本年新购藏量（万册）	Number of Books Purchased During the Year (10 000 volumes)	975	271	320
公用房屋建筑面积（万平方米）	Floor Space of Public Buildings / Floor Space of Buildings (10 000 sq.m)	598	79	343
#书库（万平方米）	Stack Rooms (10 000 sq.m)	139	30	63
阅览室座席（万个）	Seating Capacity of Reading Rooms (10 000 seats)	42	3	27

21-7 博物馆、文物机构业务活动及经费情况（2000年）

Facilities, Services and Expenditures of Museums and Cultural Relic Agencies (2000)

项 目	Item	文物保护管理机构 Protection and Management Agencies	文物科研机构 Scientific and Research Historical Relics Preservation	其他文物机构 Other Agencies	博物馆 Museums
藏 品 （件）	Number of Collections (piece)	2038940	570276	68392	9813923
#一级品 （件）	Grade One (piece)	6377	1208	159	43939
业务活动	Operations				
陈列展览 （个）	Number of Displays and Exhibitions				17752
参观人数 （万人次）	Number of Visitors (10 000 person-times)	4319			8340
经费支出 （万元）	Total Expenditures (10 000 yuan)	84759	17597	15524	144543
#业务费 （万元）	Professional Expenditures (10 000 yuan)		3155	1046	25656
#考古发掘费 （万元）	Archaeology and Excavation Expenses (10 000 yuan)	1230	3855	428	765
修缮费 （万元）	Maintenance Expenses (10 000 yuan)	4725		1712	12685
增加值 （万元）	Value Added (10 000 yuan)	34264	22466	4377	63078

21-8 摄制电影片产量

Film Production

年 份 Year	电影故事片厂（个） Number of Feature Film Studios	故事片（部） Feature Films (film)	美术片（本） Cartoons (reel)	科学教育片（本） Popular Science Films (reel)	纪录片（本） Documentary Films (reel)
1952	4	4	2	41	157
1957	11	40	5	84	272
1962	16	34	17	94	133
1965	16	52	21	240	378
1975	15	27	11	214	313
1978	12	46	26	289	202
1979	17	65	25	349	317
1980	17	82	32	337	242
1981	19	105	33	277	276
1982	19	112	33	284	259
1983	19	127	37	343	299
1984	20	144	37	387	337
1985	20	127	45	357	419
1986	20	134	46	383	417
1987	22	146	45	353	347
1988	22	158	38	344	350
1989	22	136	53	334	259
1990	22	134	51	326	296
1991	22	130	46	351	283
1992	22	170	56	354	307
1993	22	154	47	252	300
1994	22	148	32	182	22
1995	30	146	37	40	111
1996	30	110	58	33	39
1997	31	88	28	34	95
1998	31	82	9	30	54
2000	31	91	1	49	10

注：本表电影故事片厂只包括国务院批准的厂。

a)The number of feature film studios in this table only includes those approved by the State Council.

21-9 广播、电视事业发展情况

Basic Statistics on Broadcasting and Television Stations

项　目	Item	1999	2000	2000年为1999年% 2000 as Percentage of 1999
广播电视系统职工人数(人)	Number of Staff and Workers (person)	453405	494566	109.00
广播电台 (座)	Number of Broadcasting Stations (set)	296	304	102.70
广播发射台及转播台 (座)	Number of Broadcast Transmission Stations and Relaying Stations (set)	767	737	96.09
广播发射机功率 (千瓦)	Broadcast Power of Transmitters (kw)	45535.9	46210.4	101.48
县级广播电视台 (座)	Number of Wire Broadcast Stations in Counties and Cities (set)	1562	1446	92.57
广播人口覆盖率 (%)	Listener Rating (%)	90.5	92.47	102.18
电视台 (座)	Number of Television Stations (set)	357	354	99.16
电视发射台及转播台(座)	Television Transmission Stations and Relaying Stations (set)	42094	51436	122.19
电视发射机功率 (千瓦)	Power of Transmitters (kw)	8021.8	8862.1	110.47
电视人口覆盖率 (%)	Viewer Rating (%)	92	93.65	101.79

注：广播电台、电视台未包括县级数。

a) Number of Broadcasting and Television stations excludes that in county level.

21-10 广播、电视节目制作时间

Basic Statistics on Broadcasting and Television

单位：小时 (hour)

项　目	Item	1985	1990	1995	1999	2000
广播节目制作	Production of Broadcasting	280799	647762	2332164	2931682	3381466
#新闻	News Programs	65955	135550	353368	413120	449582
专题	Special Subject Programs	51603	123741	565464	717224	821031
教育	Educational Programs	26336	39590	91240	88078	171057
文艺	Programs of Entertainment	84926	235766	924656	979047	1087252
服务性	Service Programs	51979	113115	397436	478943	554219
电视节目制作	Production of TV Programs	38056	91572	383513	526483	585007
#新闻	News Programs	7444	28593	80800	128036	147239
专题	Special Subject Programs	4752	15739	81146	94863	105257
教育	Educational Programs	15810	5365	11630	10920	19255
文艺	Programs of Entertainment	6957	22096	109322	125320	133084
服务性	Service Programs	3093	19779	100615	76510	75104

21-11 广播、电视宣传基本情况（2000年）

Basic Statistics on Broadcasting and Television (2000)

项　目	Item	节目套数(套) Number of Programs (set)	平均每日(周)播出时间(小时) Broadcasting Hours Per Day/Week(hour)	自办节目时间(小时) Self-Produced Programs (hour)	新闻节目 News Programs	专题节目 Special Subject Programs	教育节目 Educational Programs	文艺节目 Entertainment Programs	服务性节目 Service Programs
无线广播合计	**All Radio Broadcasting Stations**	**1934**	**20317**	**14738**	**1906**	**3112**	**722**	**5649**	**2069**
中央台和国际台	China Central Broadcasting and China International Broadcasting	59	366	366	108	126	17	91	16
地方台	Local	1875	19951	14372	1798	2986	705	5558	2053
电视播映合计	**All Television Stations**	**1206**	**83373**	**61556**	**5969**	**6065**	**1239**	**36838**	**5259**
中央电视台	China Central Television	9	1086	1086	178	328	28	418	82
地方台	Local Television	1197	82287	60470	5791	5737	1211	36420	5177

注：自办节目时间，无线广播为平均每日，电视播映为平均每周。

a)The data on program hours refer to the number of hours per day for radio broadcasting and the number of hours per week for television broadcasting.

21-12 各地区新闻出版事业机构和人员数（2000年）

Number of Institutions and Persons Engaged in News and Publishing Undertakings by Region (2000)

地区	Region	书刊出版社 Publishing Houses 机构数（个）Institutions (unit)	书刊出版社 Publishing Houses 从业人员（人）Personnel (person)	国家定点书刊印刷厂 Printing Houses 机构数（个）Institutions (unit)	国家定点书刊印刷厂 Printing Houses 从业人员（人）Personnel (person)	书店 Book Stores 机构数（个）Institutions (unit)	书店 Book Stores 从业人员（人）Personnel (person)
全　国	**National Total**	**565**	**46408**	**301**	**146399**	**13633**	**152219**
中　央	National Publishing House	220	20788	38	16183	15	2327
地　方	Local Publishing House	345	25620	263	130216	13618	149892
北　京	Beijing	16	809	9	4053	192	4318
天　津	Tianjin	12	1105	7	4136	116	2048
河　北	Hebei	7	719	15	7327	582	8018
山　西	Shanxi	8	470	4	2291	438	4209
内蒙古	Inner Mongolia	7	504	5	2062	295	2589
辽　宁	Liaoning	18	1175	13	7897	248	5995
吉　林	Jilin	14	843	7	3225	179	4447
黑龙江	Heilongjiang	12	752	7	4632	252	4935
上　海	Shanghai	37	3666	17	5377	295	4471
江　苏	Jiangsu	16	1092	13	6007	972	8922
浙　江	Zhejiang	13	757	9	2952	513	5352
安　徽	Anhui	9	499	7	3444	615	4672
福　建	Fujian	11	699	6	2833	350	3887
江　西	Jiangxi	7	485	10	7027	370	4662
山　东	Shandong	17	1101	19	10926	1023	10398
河　南	Henan	12	664	14	8530	1460	11526
湖　北	Hubei	15	1397	16	6699	681	7565
湖　南	Hunan	12	977	13	6073	590	6814
广　东	Guangdong	19	1360	16	5632	548	9407
广　西	Guangxi	8	802	8	4321	350	4496
海　南	Hainan	4	240	2	620	66	1289
重　庆	Chongqing	3	512	3	2195	274	3950
四　川	Sichuan	16	1234	11	5436	782	8495
贵　州	Guizhou	4	339	3	2137	489	2269
云　南	Yunnan	8	482	4	2299	544	3725
西　藏	Tibet	2	75	2	461	72	245
陕　西	Shaanxi	15	1363	8	4991	446	4526
甘　肃	Gansu	9	344	6	3439	396	2507
青　海	Qinghai	2	100	3	774	144	1178
宁　夏	Ningxia	3	127	2	505	81	735
新　疆	Xinjiang	9	928	4	1915	255	2242

注：全国出版社565家，其中含副牌37家。

a)There are 565 publishing houses in mainland, including 37 publishing houses with secondary names.

21-13 全国图书、杂志和报纸出版情况

Number of Books, Magazines and Newspaper Published in China

年份 地区	Year Region	图书 Books Published 种数（种）Number of Publications (kind)	#新出版 New Publications	总印数（亿册、张）Printed Copies (100 million copies)	总印张数（亿印张）Printed Sheets (100 million sheets)	杂志 Magazines Published 种数（种）Number of Publications (kind)	每期平均印数（万册）Average Printed Copies per Issue (10 000 copies)	总印数（亿册）Total Printed Copies (100 million copies)	总印张数（亿印张）Printed Sheets (100 million sheets)	报纸 Newspapers Published 种数（种）Number of News Publish-ed (kind)	每期平均印数（万份）Average Printed Copies per Issue (10 000 copies)	总印数（亿份）Total Printed Copies (100 million copies)	总印张数（亿印张）Printed Signatures (100 million sheets)
	1978	14987	11888	37.7	135.4	930	6200	7.6	22.7	186	4280	127.8	113.5
	1979	17212	14007	40.7	172.5	1470	7960	11.8	30.1		4762	130.8	123.0
	1980	21621	17660	45.9	195.7	2191	10298	11.3	36.7	188	6236	140.4	141.7
	1981	25601	19854	55.8	217.7	2801	13096	14.6	45.4	242	7152	140.7	133.6
	1982	31784	23445	58.8	222.0	3100	13885	15.1	15.1	277	8074	140.0	129.1
	1983	35700	25826	58.0	232.4	3415	15995	17.7	52.5	340	9611	155.1	142.7
	1984	40072	28794	62.5	260.6	3907	20440	21.8	64.3	458	16246	180.8	162.3
	1985	45603	33743	66.7	282.8	4705	23952	25.6	77.3	1445	19107	246.8	202.8
	1986	51798	39426	52.0	220.3	5248	21980	24.0	68.1	1574	18387	242.7	203.5
	1987	60213	42854	62.5	261.3	5687	24375	25.9	72.7	1611	20275	264.5	223.6
	1988	65962	46774	62.3	269.0	5865	23275	25.5	71.2	1537	19788	267.8	231.3
	1989	74973	55475	58.6	243.6	6078	17145	18.4	50.7	1576	15288	207.0	179.5
	1990	80224	55245	56.4	232.1	5751	16156	17.9	48.1	1444	14670	211.3	182.8
	1991	89615	58467	61.4	266.1	6056	18216	20.6	54.4	1524	16393	236.5	205.8
	1992	92148	58169	63.4	280.4	6486	20506	23.6	62.7	1657	18031	257.9	238.8
	1993	96761	66313	59.3	282.3	7011	20780	23.5	64.2	1788	18478	263.8	287.1
	1994	103836	69779	60.1	297.2	7325	19763	22.1	63.9	1953	17736	253.2	310.8
	1995	101381	59159	63.2	316.8	7583	19794	23.4	67.0	2089	17644	263.3	359.6
	1996	112813	63647	71.6	360.5	7916	19300	23.1	68.1	2163	17877	274.3	392.4
	1997	120106	66585	73.1	364.0	7918	20046	24.4	73.3	2149	18259	287.6	459.8
	1998	130613	74719	72.4	373.6	7999	20928	25.4	79.9	2053	18211	300.4	540.0
	1999	141831	83095	73.2	391.4	8187	21845	28.5	96.8	2038	18632	318.4	636.7
	2000	143376	84235	62.7	376.2	8725	21544	29.4	100.0	2007	17914	329.3	799.8
北　京	Beijing	2691	1519	0.5	3.8	158	374	0.5	3.9	34	479.7	9.0	37.8
天　津	Tianjin	2744	1543	0.6	4.3	234	469	0.5	1.7	26	366.0	6.0	10.4
河　北	Hebei	2014	1090	3.1	14.6	214	450	0.5	1.4	66	469.8	9.0	16.5
山　西	Shanxi	1532	1240	1.0	6.2	165	232	0.3	0.9	59	708.9	6.3	8.1
内蒙古	Inner Mongolia	1545	904	0.7	4.5	154	136	0.2	0.5	63	114.4	1.8	2.0
辽　宁	Liaoning	5008	2752	1.7	10.8	301	901	1.2	2.9	87	825.6	12.6	31.9
吉　林	Jilin	3581	1926	1.3	8.9	225	444	0.6	1.7	55	554.1	5.5	7.6
黑龙江	Heilongjiang	2099	1352	1.0	5.0	319	609	0.8	2.5	75	432.4	7.3	11.9
上　海	Shanghai	12683	6926	2.5	19.0	613	1490	1.9	7.4	72	1119.3	16.7	44.5
江　苏	Jiangsu	5143	2794	3.5	20.1	423	635	1.1	3.3	92	1230.9	23.3	43.0
浙　江	Zhejiang	4106	1842	2.7	12.7	201	724	0.9	2.1	87	856.3	17.4	32.6
安　徽	Anhui	2326	1088	3.1	14.7	151	622	0.8	2.0	50	407.9	7.6	11.5
福　建	Fujian	2634	1515	2.0	9.7	187	372	0.4	1.5	47	369.0	6.9	13.5
江　西	Jiangxi	1726	1115	2.0	9.0	181	637	0.9	1.9	40	236.1	4.0	6.6
山　东	Shandong	3883	2151	4.1	21.5	270	802	1.3	3.9	97	891.2	20.1	47.2
河　南	Henan	2419	1204	3.5	17.0	250	867	1.1	3.3	81	819.7	12.9	21.2
湖　北	Hubei	4529	2445	2.9	15.4	393	1227	2.2	7.5	98	549.9	13.4	33.9
湖　南	Hunan	3112	1734	2.4	12.1	245	966	1.1	2.1	54	590.5	8.3	12.8
广　东	Guangdong	4374	2534	2.7	14.8	337	1596	2.6	9.2	101	1631.0	34.6	176.7
广　西	Guangxi	2739	1500	2.4	11.5	191	412	0.5	1.5	60	294.2	5.6	8.3
海　南	Hainan	726	485	0.3	2.4	41	61	0.1	0.3	19	69.8	1.2	2.8
重　庆	Chongqing	1706	869	1.1	5.7	123	287	0.3	1.4	31	247.8	4.9	15.6
四　川	Sichuan	3907	2146	2.7	15.6	273	440	0.5	1.6	81	759.7	15.0	42.6
贵　州	Guizhou	827	348	1.0	4.4	98	91	0.1	0.4	35	127.9	2.9	5.8
云　南	Yunnan	1644	1002	1.3	6.6	125	236	0.3	0.9	47	173.3	3.6	6.8
西　藏	Tibet	301	53	0.1	0.3	25	9			16	13.3	0.2	0.3
陕　西	Shaanxi	3433	2080	1.6	8.3	260	353	0.5	1.9	48	346.5	7.0	21.7
甘　肃	Gansu	769	601	0.7	3.2	127	428	0.8	3.0	52	138.6	2.5	4.7
青　海	Qinghai	209	98	0.1	0.4	43	13			18	24.6	0.4	0.4
宁　夏	Ningxia	390	183	0.2	0.9	30	16		0.1	16	39.2	0.6	1.0
新　疆	Xinjiang	3446	1911	0.7	3.8	174	110	0.1	0.4	94	163.1	2.9	5.3

21-14 全国图书出版分类构成情况（2000年）

Composition of Books Published in China (2000)

类别	Category	种数（种） Number of Publications	印数（万册） Printed Copies (10 000 copies)	印张（千印张） Printed Sheets (1 000 sheets)
总计	**Total**	**143376**	**627449**	**37621440**
使用“中国标准书号”合计	Publications with "China International Standard Book Number"	141291	622965	37448385
马列主义、毛泽东思想	Marxism-Leninism, Mao Zedong Thought	236	531	53747
哲学	Philosophy	1461	1099	140523
社会科学总论	General Social Sciences	1731	1251	158815
政治、法律	Politics and Law	5509	7475	859800
军事	Military Affairs	425	318	35666
经济	Economics	9107	8842	1116981
文化、科学、教育、体育	Culture, Science, Education and Sports	58513	539671	27529245
语言、文字	Languages	6301	10067	1400103
文学	Literature	10756	10594	1290704
艺术	Arts	7577	9970	553507
历史、地理	History and Geography	4402	3564	404239
自然科学总论	General Natural Sciences	926	3883	200574
数理科学、化学	Mathematics and Chemistry	2530	2613	345437
天文学、地球科学	Astronomy and Geology	630	188	20847
生物科学	Biology	514	299	41728
医学、卫生	Medicine and Health Care	6329	4639	723488
农业科学	Agricultural Science	3384	2821	222177
工业技术	Industrial Technology	16267	11014	1858094
交通运输	Transportation	1161	1153	143705
航空、航天	Aeronautics and Aerospace	90	38	5340
环境科学	Environmental Science	400	251	23725
综合性图书	General Books	3042	2684	319940
不使用“中国标准书号”图书	Publications without "China International Standard Book Number"	2085	4484	118004
#年画	New Year's Pictures	156	152	1231

21-15 各地区少年儿童读物类图书和课本出版情况 （2000年）

Number of Books Published for Children and Textbooks by Region (2000)

地 区	Region	种 数(种) Number of Publications		总 印 数（万册） Printed Copies (10 000 copies)		总 印 张(千印张) Printed Sheets (1 000 sheets)	
		儿童读物 Books for Children	课本 Textbooks	儿童读物 Books for Children	课本 Textbooks	儿童读物 Books for Children	课本 Textbooks
全 国	**National Total**	**7004**	**23694**	**16890**	**355988**	**635341**	**19464771**
中 央	National Publishing House	1053	9009	1876	27623	111850	2140929
地 方	Local Publishing House	5951	14685	15014	328365	523491	17323842
北 京	Beijing	264	374	247	2481	15223	142060
天 津	Tianjin	189	597	570	3737	18732	262949
河 北	Hebei	147	386	204	21714	6575	990680
山 西	Shanxi	132	116	503	6495	9399	397535
内蒙古	Inner Mongolia	109	433	288	5450	14790	304444
辽 宁	Liaoning	231	927	606	9486	17697	607729
吉 林	Jilin	272	907	919	7536	47492	410459
黑龙江	Heilongjiang	79	402	135	7274	3226	366978
上 海	Shanghai	1212	1862	1845	7838	120074	593389
江 苏	Jiangsu	371	1004	1370	18970	41557	1080190
浙 江	Zhejiang	370	625	1385	10900	47654	565976
安 徽	Anhui	235	109	372	19539	14215	904167
福 建	Fujian	112	270	627	10855	9538	557528
江 西	Jiangxi	209	149	639	10441	13645	583981
山 东	Shandong	166	486	762	26011	23052	1298137
河 南	Henan	160	166	507	24936	10832	1327214
湖 北	Hubei	127	881	97	16982	3094	910896
湖 南	Hunan	158	389	380	17524	12008	871187
广 东	Guangdong	106	717	323	18292	6839	989839
广 西	Guangxi	308	274	1092	15499	27575	734520
海 南	Hainan	20	5	41	1944	2157	98218
重 庆	Chongqing	102	501	720	7254	11448	383866
四 川	Sichuan	213	570	302	15740	9378	914254
贵 州	Guizhou	52	42	229	6742	3234	324992
云 南	Yunnan	164	180	381	9344	9327	436430
西 藏	Tibet	10	230	20	448	1155	21786
陕 西	Shaanxi	166	609	196	11909	10981	585719
甘 肃	Gansu	24	36	47	5884	3117	276784
青 海	Qinghai	1	62	1	438	98	24806
宁 夏	Ningxia	24	12	21	1244	427	71322
新 疆	Xinjiang	218	1364	185	5458	8952	285807

21-16 全国课本出版情况(2000年)
Publication of Textbooks (2000)

项　目	Item	种数(种) Number of Publication (kind)	#新出版 New Publication	总印数(万册) Printed Copies (10 000)	总印张(千印张) Printed Sheets (1 000)	定价总金额(万元) Total Priced Value (10 000 yuan)
总计	**Total**	**23694**	**7057**	**355988**	**19464771**	**1808108**
大专及以上课本	Textbooks for Colleges and Universities	9250	3817	11469	1776194	202759
中专、技校课本	Textbooks for Secondary Technical Schools	2759	857	4745	581088	58762
中学课本	Textbooks for Secondary Schools	3488	620	136463	9993433	739591
小学课本	Textbooks for Primary Schools	4440	705	198857	6702410	768822
业余教育课本	Textbooks for Spare-time Education	818	402	965	115061	14260
扫盲课本	Textbooks for Eliminating Illiteracy	3	1	3	241	10
教学用书	Teaching Materials	2936	655	3486	296344	23904

21-17 各地区图书发行流转情况 (2000年)
Basic Statistics on Distribution and Circulation of Books by Region (2000)

单位：万册、万元　　(10 000 copies) (10 000 yuan)

地区	Region	图书购进 Purchases		图书销售 Sales		图书库存 Stock	
		册数 Copies	金额 Value	册数 Copies	金额 Value	册数 Copies	金额 Value
全　国	**National Total**	**1606794**	**8882160**	**1580402**	**8478848**	**364712**	**2726813**
中　央	National Publishing House	95829	1349161	88994	1179041	57454	831838
地　方	Local Publishing House	1510965	7532999	1491408	7299807	307258	1894975
北　京	Beijing	19569	179342	18295	166364	5208	72289
天　津	Tianjin	13570	110271	13728	106067	3245	35626
河　北	Hebei	100783	374671	99714	364172	20063	75358
山　西	Shanxi	35803	170245	34619	166999	4485	26965
内蒙古	Inner Mongolia	15821	81429	15494	81519	2323	14387
辽　宁	Liaoning	53453	281142	55668	285093	13289	68567
吉　林	Jilin	25428	148171	23814	140619	5991	42494
黑龙江	Heilongjiang	29315	146160	29926	144853	6182	35182
上　海	Shanghai	50729	518304	47596	464494	14612	214270
江　苏	Jiangsu	117240	681328	119762	672121	20128	140387
浙　江	Zhejiang	62259	356230	60176	339527	12113	108711
安　徽	Anhui	76247	304515	75249	299645	10014	56504
福　建	Fujian	46173	231417	44994	226189	5222	31179
江　西	Jiangxi	52487	211825	49831	201314	8078	43753
山　东	Shandong	119836	512899	115339	498772	22824	124769
河　南	Henan	156706	531801	168025	535956	18489	73590
湖　北	Hubei	42526	337542	42681	327262	21635	104105
湖　南	Hunan	74312	338109	74620	332143	11775	67564
广　东	Guangdong	85669	469815	74478	433409	29622	158433
广　西	Guangxi	48440	231026	48173	226460	6869	51709
海　南	Hainan	10528	51917	10949	52290	2060	8371
重　庆	Chongqing	33879	141706	30233	140457	8549	27672
四　川	Sichuan	78444	393825	77425	387233	17919	120885
贵　州	Guizhou	26073	100799	27396	101817	4122	11277
云　南	Yunnan	35999	161433	34295	148437	9850	54696
西　藏	Tibet	536	3014	480	2329	305	2305
陕　西	Shaanxi	46679	230274	46022	224395	12590	75363
甘　肃	Gansu	24503	106957	24510	105627	2952	18490
青　海	Qinghai	1784	11362	1756	12546	1151	4549
宁　夏	Ningxia	4874	19877	4847	19960	1350	5640
新　疆	Xinjiang	21300	95593	21313	91738	4243	19885

21-18 各地区图书纯销售情况(2000年)

Net Sales of Books by Region (2000)

单位：万元 (10 000 yuan)

地区	Region	总计 Total Sales	对居民和社会集团零售 Retail Sales to Households and Institutions				批发 Wholesale		出口 Export
			合计 Total	市 Cities	县 Counties	县以下 Below Counties	供销社 Supply & Marketing Coops	集体和个体 Collectives and Individuals	
全国	**National Total**	**3768592**	**2850840**	**1326568**	**754018**	**770254**	**313787**	**593538**	**10427**
中央	National Publishing House	266822	86423	83299	2394	730	8189	164055	8155
地方	Local Publishing House	3501770	2764417	1243269	751624	769524	305598	429483	2272
北京	Beijing	105160	88112	76072	10224	1816	78	16970	
天津	Tianjin	50731	42222	25706	14438	2078	1	8380	128
河北	Hebei	176541	171322	46419	64783	60120	915	4304	
山西	Shanxi	85856	77452	28142	18365	30945	610	7794	
内蒙古	Inner Mongolia	45600	43314	19436	20080	3798	155	2131	
辽宁	Liaoning	99560	80155	62514	13725	3916	3094	16311	
吉林	Jilin	48926	46744	27728	13414	5602	262	1920	
黑龙江	Heilongjiang	66721	62077	39402	19747	2928	1079	3565	
上海	Shanghai	140220	120256	105167	9827	5262	7950	10655	1359
江苏	Jiangsu	305195	263133	90627	15096	157410	5122	36830	110
浙江	Zhejiang	170228	122765	70317	26580	25868	23562	23636	265
安徽	Anhui	160393	125117	43615	37458	44044	7799	27477	
福建	Fujian	118545	82695	43359	21203	18133	23867	11904	79
江西	Jiangxi	105236	99632	25670	68413	5549	846	4758	
山东	Shandong	273900	235438	86269	55256	93913	3338	35124	
河南	Henan	207063	152323	44309	23363	84651	23892	30848	
湖北	Hubei	132433	75640	30761	21608	23271	15699	41094	
湖南	Hunan	167649	155839	49589	61049	45201	200	11558	52
广东	Guangdong	300246	132611	119706	10217	2688	139310	28061	264
广西	Guangxi	77419	51427	26779	13764	10884	5348	20629	15
海南	Hainan	25714	7306	4912	2383	11	11904	6504	
重庆	Chongqing	75664	57615	24542	24345	8728	5181	12868	
四川	Sichuan	189959	150334	59651	56173	34510	20637	18988	
贵州	Guizhou	46356	34636	11154	13820	9662		11720	
云南	Yunnan	77930	74774	17242	27462	30070	935	2221	
西藏	Tibet	83	69	69				14	
陕西	Shaanxi	125323	98888	18203	50896	29789	1475	24960	
甘肃	Gansu	57419	51059	15077	13819	22163	202	6158	
青海	Qinghai	6975	6589	3185	3324	80		386	
宁夏	Ningxia	11449	10746	5563	4522	661	4	699	
新疆	Xinjiang	47276	44127	22084	16270	5773	2133	1016	

21-19 各地区录像制品出版情况(2000年)
Publication of Video Products (2000)

地区	Region	录像带 Videotapes 种数(种) Kind	录像带 Videotapes 数量(盒) Volume (cassette)	数码激光视盘 VCD 种数(种) Kind	数码激光视盘 VCD 数量(张) Volume (disk)	高密度激光视盘 DVD-V 种数(种) Kind	高密度激光视盘 DVD-V 数量(张) Volume (disk)
全　国	**National Total**	**1271**	**711351**	**7101**	**78803183**	**294**	**1309881**
中　央	National Publishing House	977	311668	2221	29364013	65	314314
地　方	Local Publishing House	294	399683	4880	49439170	229	995567
北　京	Beijing	6	2120	161	6627505	4	35000
天　津	Tianjin	18	15524	144	1132000	47	43350
河　北	Hebei			145	592000		
山　西	Shanxi	26	39000	120	335000		
内蒙古	Inner Mongolia			13	41970		
辽　宁	Liaoning	15	27600	267	4247000	5	148000
吉　林	Jilin	11	96000	79	260800		
黑龙江	Heilongjiang	8	10200	26	49000		
上　海	Shanghai	39	35351	329	3387555		
江　苏	Jiangsu			73	561200		
浙　江	Zhejiang	21	59000	205	1024590	18	26000
安　徽	Anhui			86	422800		
福　建	Fujian			237	4048867	16	80000
江　西	Jiangxi			233	1178300		
山　东	Shandong	2	5000	83	545650	1	3000
河　南	Henan	26	22766	173	2089900	1	20000
湖　北	Hubei			513	2192300	3	9000
湖　南	Hunan	114	82042	337	2171100		
广　东	Guangdong	5	1200	1045	12634707	107	501217
广　西	Guangxi			115	917750		
海　南	Hainan			5	128000		
重　庆	Chongqing			34	376544		
四　川	Sichuan			172	977200		
贵　州	Guizhou			41	2103100	24	117000
云　南	Yunnan			73	447500	2	10000
西　藏	Tibet			3	90000		
陕　西	Shaanxi	1	380	98	617530		
甘　肃	Gansu			14	69300		
青　海	Qinghai			1	3000		
宁　夏	Ningxia	1	500				
新　疆	Xinjiang	1	3000	55	167002	1	3000

21-20 各地区录音制品出版情况(2000年)

Publication of Audio Products by Region (2000)

地 区	Region	录音带 Audio-tapes 种数(种) Kind	录音带 Audio-tapes 数量(万盒) Volume (10 000 cassettes)	激光唱盘 CDs 种数(种) (Kind)	激光唱盘 CDs 数量(万张) Volume (10 000 pieces)	高密度激光唱盘 DVD-A 种数(种) (Kind)	高密度激光唱盘 DVD-A 数量(万张) Volume (10 000 pieces)
全 国	**National Total**	**6175**	**11128.4**	**2799**	**1032**	**8**	**1.2**
中 央	National Publishing House	2198	5442.3	948	281		
地 方	Local Publishing House	3977	5686.2	1851	751	8	1.2
北 京	Beijing	211	136.3	43	65		
天 津	Tianjin	27	490.8	78	22		
河 北	Hebei	38	70.4	75	34	7	0.7
山 西	Shanxi	31	27.9				
内蒙古	Inner Mongolia	12	4.8	5	2		
辽 宁	Liaoning	50	226.0	38	44		
吉 林	Jilin	16	5.1	11	2		
黑龙江	Heilongjiang	4	0.4	2	1		
上 海	Shanghai	1563	2589.0	419	80		
江 苏	Jiangsu	70	163.2	129	45		
浙 江	Zhejiang	117	173.9	129	50		
安 徽	Anhui	89	110.7				
福 建	Fujian	18	74.9	37	37		
江 西	Jiangxi	74	116.9	32	12		
山 东	Shandong	11	3.4	9	5		
河 南	Henan	30	8.5	4	2		
湖 北	Hubei	124	91.7	116	54		
湖 南	Hunan	400	189.9	29	10		
广 东	Guangdong	674	967.9	517	195		
广 西	Guangxi	68	41.4	64	29		
海 南	Hainan			2	1		
重 庆	Chongqing	96	35.2	4	3		
四 川	Sichuan	40	37.7	52	26		
贵 州	Guizhou	1	0.3	17	8	1	0.5
云 南	Yunnan	16	6.4	15	12		
西 藏	Tibet			2	6		
陕 西	Shaanxi	149	97.0	5	1		
甘 肃	Gansu	13	6.2	1			
青 海	Qinghai	4	2.0	3	2		
宁 夏	Ningxia	5	0.3	13	2		
新 疆	Xinjiang	26	8.0				

21-21 各地区两级定点书刊印刷企业主要产品产量(2000年)

Production of Designated Book Printing Enterprises by Region (2000)

地区	Region	机构数(个) Number of Enterprises	书刊排字(万字) Typesetting (10 000 characters)	书刊印刷(万令) Printing of Books (10 000 reams)	胶印印刷(万色令) Off-set Printing (10 000 color-reams)	零件印刷(万千印) Printing of Loose Sheets (10 000 k-prints)	书刊装订(万令) Binding of Books (10 000 reams)
全 国	**National Total**	**1152**	**1770219**	**5789**	**11935**	**1836**	**4575**
中 央	National Publishing House	82	245122	600	770	68	287
地 方	Local Publishing House	1070	1525097	5189	11165	1768	4288
北 京	Beijing	151	180201	909	854	504	392
天 津	Tianjin	46	35586	105	262	17	75
河 北	Hebei	82	106445	346	579	108	338
山 西	Shanxi	18	14901	60	166	4	94
内蒙古	Inner Mongolia	18	29334	32	133	16	42
辽 宁	Liaoning	30	69228	150	265	8	161
吉 林	Jilin	25	27386	112	108	7	101
黑龙江	Heilongjiang	21	30618	78	205	23	90
上 海	Shanghai	45	60332	139	863	126	72
江 苏	Jiangsu	60	78898	273	680	201	245
浙 江	Zhejiang	33	59428	128	505	29	114
安 徽	Anhui	41	20477	222	291	74	198
福 建	Fujian	27	30509	100	398	22	98
江 西	Jiangxi	26	21210	99	340	40	113
山 东	Shandong	65	217680	443	933	134	465
河 南	Henan	61	62837	347	475	76	217
湖 北	Hubei	45	49452	206	406	19	247
湖 南	Hunan	41	79211	258	327	24	184
广 东	Guangdong	58	52069	344	1211	55	341
广 西	Guangxi	25	51524	195	362	57	140
海 南	Hainan	10	5216	15	253	9	5
重 庆	Chongqing	6	6209	57	100	1	37
四 川	Sichuan	22	23027	113	351	45	116
贵 州	Guizhou	13	31111	68	192	49	62
云 南	Yunnan	24	55584	92	202	34	72
西 藏	Tibet	2	4103	4	14	1	3
陕 西	Shaanxi	25	31128	164	396	33	129
甘 肃	Gansu	11	19286	71	108	14	68
青 海	Qinghai	9	22763	9	52	26	18
宁 夏	Ningxia	8	8346	13	17	2	7
新 疆	Xinjiang	22	40999	38	119	12	46

21-22 各地区国家定点书刊印刷企业主要财务经济指标(2000年)

Key Financial Indicators of State-designated Book Printing Enterprises by Region(2000)

单位：万元 (10 000 yuan)

地区	Region	产品销售收入 Revenue From Sales	产品销售成本 Cost of Sales	产品销售费用 Expenses of Sales	产品销售税金 Taxes From Sales	管理费用 Management Expenses	财务费用 Financial Expenses	利润总额 Total Profit	产成品存货 Stock of Finished Products	工业增加值 Industrial Value-added
全国	**National Total**	**675370**	**507621**	**12812**	**5306**	**140221**	**21234**	**45093**	**114575**	**317742**
中央	National Publishing House	63809	51726	814	453	21757	927	3211	6624	33372
地方	Local Publishing House	611562	455895	11998	4853	118464	20307	41882	107952	284370
北京	Beijing	19301	14050	170	131	5479	177	779	2335	9894
天津	Tianjin	60368	35058	842	413	6099	615	22731	6036	30411
河北	Hebei	21790	15939	269	217	6152	384	360	3541	10791
山西	Shanxi	9246	6814	77	108	2393	363	63	1073	5351
内蒙古	Inner Mongolia	3748	2386	64	32	1385	174	9	6205	1717
辽宁	Liaoning	26392	18868	1022	287	6251	1857	747	4974	12632
吉林	Jilin	9793	6969	99	93	1981	183	1047	12170	4541
黑龙江	Heilongjiang	11536	8963	930	87	2451	226	207	3096	4068
上海	Shanghai	43343	34891	560	274	8246	1497	1311	4744	16399
江苏	Jiangsu	36212	27054	581	322	6222	833	2197	5998	18484
浙江	Zhejiang	25794	20597	227	154	3965	34	1346	2091	9907
安徽	Anhui	12352	8856	84	128	2837	535	508	596	4483
福建	Fujian	19802	15083	284	203	3265	389	1277	233	5893
江西	Jiangxi	22257	17079	361	135	3916	1406	62	2974	9159
山东	Shandong	61076	47115	1393	465	8956	3386	972	10628	16510
河南	Henan	29176	22897	406	254	6364	855	1089	6653	17042
湖北	Hubei	26472	18405	594	180	6550	865	2015	2811	13937
湖南	Hunan	23499	17873	383	242	5104	690	355	2841	13829
广东	Guangdong	40337	33677	1207	209	7548	879	1952	4807	17775
广西	Guangxi	13779	10237	448	112	3217	730	387	2855	6554
海南	Hainan	4972	3639	10	19	340		1013	1304	5436
重庆	Chongqing	5510	4077	64	97	1611	302	103	708	3292
四川	Sichuan	17944	12749	518	136	4148	934	262	7124	8197
贵州	Guizhou	4936	3320	12	54	1580	97	159	1499	3781
云南	Yunnan	7186	4470	63	88	2269	662	229	2113	3293
西藏	Tibet	1912	1572	34	13	355	71	22	84	1216
陕西	Shaanxi	29624	24178	826	107	3592	1422	177	4788	11370
甘肃	Gansu	11357	10010	265	220	2309	313	183	2136	13961
青海	Qinghai	2385	1808	64	13	708	23	24	527	992
宁夏	Ningxia	1511	1378	4	9	367	98	158	85	835
新疆	Xinjiang	7951	5883	141	56	2806	309	139	924	2620

21-23 体委系统职工人数(2000年)

Number of Staff and Workers in Sports Commissions (2000)

单位：人 (person)

人员分类	Category of Personnel	合计 Total	#优秀运动队 Excellent Sports Teams	#体育运动学校 Physical Education and Sports Schools	#重点业余体校 Key Spare-time Sports Schools
总计	**Total**	**153599**	**34571**	**15742**	**11530**
运动员	Athletes	18659	18659		
专职教练员	Full-time Coaches	25087	3989	3919	5257
专职文化教师	Full-time Teachers	12369	480	4893	1632
科技人员	Scientific and Technical Personnel	1766	107	135	
医务人员	Medical Personnel	2128	835	316	118
管理人员	Administrative Personnel	49073	5840	3191	2277
其他	Others	44517	4661	3288	2246

21-23 续表 1 continued

单位：人 (person)

人员分类	Category of Personnel	#体育中学 Physical Education Middle Schools	#普通业余体校 Popular Spare-time Sports Schools	#公共体育场馆 Public Stadiums and Gymnasiums	#训练基地 Training Bases
总计	**Total**	**2406**	**19407**	**17288**	**4590**
运动员	Athletes				
专职教练员	Full-time Coaches	761	11011		
专职文化教师	Full-time Teachers	1006	2062		
科技人员	Scientific and Technical Personnel			100	31
医务人员	Medical Personnel	20	98	76	122
管理人员	Administrative Personnel	299	3179	7427	1560
其他	Others	320	3057	9685	2877

21-24 等级运动员、等级裁判员人数（2000年）

Number of Athletes and Referees in Grades by Type of Sports (2000)

单位：人 (person)

运动项目	Item	等级运动员 Number of Athletes in Grades	#国际级运动健将 International Master of Sports	#运动健将 Master of Sports	#一级运动员 First Grade Sportsman	等级裁判员 Number of Referees in Grades	#国际裁判 International Referees	#国家级裁判 National Referees	#一级裁判 First Grade Referees
总计	**Total**	**97011**	**51**	**1221**	**2837**	**60053**	**32**	**713**	**3569**
#田径	Track and Field	53745	2	113	309	21075	9	176	848
游泳	Swimming	4334	9	108	301	1215		1	169
跳水	Diving	387	3	25	10	37			7
水球	Water Polo	47		2	26	6			5
举重	Weightlifting	1632	14	84	134	321			29
体操	Gymnastics	884		78	56	209		12	73
艺术体操	Artistic Gymnastics	324	5	24	46	14		3	7
射击	Shooting	848	3	31	148	236			64
射箭	Archery	169		7	37	103			26
国际式摔跤	Wrestling	591		41	106	220		2	29
柔道	Judo	963		20	106	265			55
自行车	Cycling	196	3	27	8	62			22
击剑	Fencing	154		30	41	19			12
赛艇	Rowing	178		21	8	22			8
皮划艇	Canoeing	257		21	16	24			13
帆船	Sailing	12		1		11			10
帆板	Wind Surfing	130		3	6	24			6
冰球	Ice Hockey	6				1			
速度滑冰	Speed Skating	271		41	98	84		17	9
篮球	Basketball	5162		40	131	14061	1	2	485
排球	Volleyball	1987		23	82	2019			124
足球	Football	3204		46	174	3414	15	350	153
乒乓球	Table Tennis	4365	2	42	151	3352		1	159
羽毛球	Badminton	650	2	28	36	761		3	77
网球	Tennis	134		2	21	299			47
手球	Handball	185	3	36	39	19		5	9
棒球	Baseball	193		14	66	21		8	6
垒球	Softball	166		34	14	27		12	9
台球	Billiards	133				253			14
技巧	Acrobatic Gymnastics	85		27	49	40		1	38
国际象棋	International Chess	152			27	86		1	12
中国象棋	Chinese Chess	747	1	1	9	741		15	34
围棋	Weiqi	271			6	289			7
桥牌	Bridge	13				170			17
武术	Wu Shu	3839		47	221	2554	2	54	318
摩托车	Motorcycling	20				22	1	12	2
无线电测向	Radio Goniometry	204		2	36	76			1
蹼泳	Web Swimming	51		2	12	10		1	5
航海模型	Model Ship Sailing	132		4	23	36			9
航空模型	Model Airplane	292		2	99	198			36

21-25 新建体育场地数

Newly-Built Stadiums and Gymnasiums

单位：个

项　　目	Item	1980	1985	1990	1998	1999
总　计	**Total**	**709**	**700**	**3681**	**307**	**572**
#体育场	Stadiums	10	47	27	11	6
体育馆	Gymnasiums	9	29	34	16	14
游泳馆	Natatoriums		1	4		
室内外游泳池	Indoor and Outdoor Swimming Pools	44	135	105	32	15
有固定看台的灯光球场	Illuminated Fields with Fixed Seating	96	137	60	13	14

注：从1996年起新建体育场地数为部分省（市）汇总数据。

a)Starting from 1996, data on newly-built stadiums and gymnasiums refer to statistics from selected provinces.

21-26 我国运动员创世界纪录情况

World Records Chalked up by Chinese Athletes

单位：项、人、次　　(item, person/team, time)

年　份 Year	项　数 Number of Events	#女　子 Female	人、队数(人/队) Number of Persons (person/team)	#女　子 Female	次　数 Number of Times	#女　子 Female
1956	1		1		3	
1957	3	1	3	1	3	1
1963	13	7	14	6	20	13
1965	28	12	66	28	41	20
1970	1		1		1	
1975	6	6	7	7	12	12
1978	3	3	6	6	3	3
1979	13	3	32	5	26	
1980	7		17		15	
1981	8	2	15	3	18	3
1982	11	4	16	8	15	4
1983	13	1	25	1	18	1
1984	12	6	17	10	17	10
1985	5	1	6	1	9	1
1986	7	4	12	4	12	6
1987	22	6	28	6	41	12
1988	33	20	16	13	34	29
1989	36	25	25	14	47	35
1990	14	9	17	10	16	9
1991	31	26	29	24	50	44
1992	42		31/4	27	106	102
1993	57	47	38/7	28/7	124	109
1994	41	39	26/4	24/4	72	69
1995	13	11	14/2	12/2	24	22
1996	22	15	17/1	13/1	30	22
1997	29	24	29/2	24/2	43	38
1998	31	27	30/3	26/3	68	64
1999	24	21	16	13	50	46
2000	22	17	14/2	10/1	30	25

注：1991年以前各年集体项目的队数折合在人数中。

a)The number of teams in the years before 1991 was converted into the number of persons.

21-27 我国运动员分项创世界纪录情况（2000年）

World Records Chalked up by Chinese Athletes by Event (2000)

单位：项、人、次 (item, person, time)

项目	Item	项数 Number of Events	#女子 Female	人数 Number of Persons	#女子 Female	次数 Number of Times	#女子 Female
总计	**Total**	**22**	**17**	**14**	**10**	**30**	**25**
举重	Weightlifting	14	13	8	7	21	20
射击	Web Swimming	5	4	3	3	6	5
航海模型	Shooting	3		3		3	

21-28 我国运动员获得世界冠军情况

World Championships Won by Chinese Athletes

单位：项、人、个 (item, person, number)

年份 Year	项数 Number of Events	#女子 Female	人数 Number of Persons	#女子 Female	个数 Number of Times	#女子 Female
1959	1		1		1	
1963	4		7		4	
1965	5	2	9	4	5	2
1971	4	2	7	2	4	2
1975	2	1	9	4	2	1
1978	4	2	4	2	4	2
1979	12	6.5	20	11	12	6.5
1980	3		3		3	
1981	25	12.5	53	32	25	12.5
1982	12	2	31	15	13	2
1983	37	15	50	24	39	17
1984	33	10	46	26	37	10
1985	42	20	70	41	46	23
1986	26	14	56	34	26	14
1987	64	39	72	34	69	41.5
1988	54	36.5	59	30	54	36.5
1989	80	49	83	48	82	50
1990	54	33.5	61	30	54	33.5
1991	88	57.5	86	51	93	61.5
1992	86	69.5	68	52	89	72.5
1993	101	66.5	106	70	103	68.5
1994	79	53.5	86	45	79	53.5
1995	98	49.5	187	86	102	51.5
1996	72	55	58	42	75	57
1997	87	46	96	46	92	50.5
1998	75	49	89	59	83	55
1999	91	43	129	72	92	44
2000	92	52	109	60	110	66.5

注：男女混合运动项目，女子按半项和半个计算。

a)Mixed doubles table tennis champions count 0.5 for females.

21-29 我国运动员分项获得世界冠军情况（2000年）

World Championships Won by Chinese Athletes by Item (2000)

单位：项，人 (item, person)

项　目	Item	项　数 Number of Events	#女　子 Female	人　数 Number of Persons	#女　子 Female	个　数 Number of Times	#女　子 Female
总　计	**Total**	**92**	**52**	**109**	**60**	**110**	**66.5**
跳　水	Diving	11	4.5	13	7	15	6
举　重	Weightlifting	5	4	5	4	5	4
乒乓球	Table Tennis	6	3	11	5	8	4
技　巧	Acrobatic Gymnastics	4	0	6		4	0
游　泳	Swimming	2	2	2	2	2	2
射　击	Shooting	8	4	8	5	9	5
体　操	Gymnastics	4	2	8	2	4	2
柔　道	Judo	2	2	2	2	2	2
航空模型	Model Ship Sailing	2		3		2	
蹼　泳	International Chess	16	12	11	7	22	18
航海模型	Model Ship Sailing	4		4		4	
国际象棋	International Chess	2	2	4	4	2	2
短道速划	Short Skating	11	6	8	4	16	11
羽毛球	Badminton	5	3	12	10	5	3
田　径	Track and Field	1	1	1	1	1	1
跆拳道	Kickboxing	3	3	3	3	3	3
无线电测向	Radio Goniometry	5	3	6	3	5	3
花样滑冰	Figure Skating	1	0.5	2	1	1	0.5

注：男女混合运动项目，女子按半项和半个计算。

a)The number of events and times of mixed doubles is counted 0.5 for females.

21-30 我国运动员分项创全国纪录情况（2000年）

National Records Chalked up by Chinese Athletes (2000)

单位：项、人、队、次 (item, person, team, time)

项　目	Item	项　数 Number of Events	#女　子 Female	人　数 Number of Persons	#女　子 Female	队　数 Number of Teams	#女　子 Female	次　数 Number of Times	#女　子 Female
总　计	**Total**	**60**	**25**	**49**	**25**	**11**	**4**	**73**	**35**
田　径	Track and Field	5	3	7	5			9	7
室内田径	Indoor Track and Field	3	2	6	5			6	5
短池游泳	Short Pool Swimming	16	5	8	3	3	1	16	5
举　重	Weightlifting	7	3	6	3			7	3
射　箭	Archery	1		1				1	
射　击	Shooting	12	4	8	4	7	2	17	7
自行车	Cycling	6	3	5	2	1	1	7	3
航海模型	Model Ship Sailing	2		2				2	
速度滑冰	Speed Skating	7	4	5	2			7	4
游　泳	Swimming	1	1	1	1			1	1

注：人数栏中是个人单项创全国纪录的运动员人数，队数栏中是集体项目创全国纪录的队数，队中人数未计算在人数中。

a)The number of persons refers to the number of persons who have chalked up the national records in single events. The number of teams refers to the number of teams which have chalked up the national records in the collective events. The number of persons in the teams is excluded in the "number of persons".

21-31 我国与外国体育活动交往情况

Visits between Chinese and Foreign Sports Delegations

项　目	Item	1985	1990	1995	1999	2000
来我国的体育团体	Foreign Sports Delegations Visiting China					
次数　(次)	Number of Times　(time)	466	364	1929	1671	1000
人数　(人次)	Persons-Times　(person-time)	3537	3171	38700	23859	20320
我国派出的体育团体	Chinese Sports Delegations Visiting Foreign Countries					
次数　(次)	Number of Times　(time)	476	607	2787	3963	3880
人数　(人次)	Persons-Times　(person-time)	5381	5227	18033	20799	22789

注：自1995年起，来华、出访次数、人数包括地方各级体委组办数。

a)The data have included the visits organized by the local sports commissions since 1995.

21-32 群众体育活动情况

Activities of Mass Sports

项　目	Item	1985	1990	1995	1999	2000
《国家体育锻炼标准》达标人数　(万人)	Number of Persons Who Have Come up to *the State Physical Training Standards* (10 000 persons)	4362	7478	10608	14316	15202
优秀级　(万人)	Excellent　(10 000 persons)	647	1414	1888	2644	2787
良好级　(万人)	Good　(10 000 persons)	1553	2746	3586	4922	5366
及格级　(万人)	Pass　(10 000 persons)	2161	3318	5135	6750	7048
县以上体委举办运动会次数　(次)	Number of Sports Meets Held by Sports Commissions at and Above County Level　(time)	26949	30158	24880	26816	26196
参加运动会的运动员人数　(万人)	Number of Athletes Attending Sports Meets　(10 000 persons)	742	1076	1345	1424	1272

21-33 卫 生 机 构 数

Number of Health Institutions

单位：个 (unit)

年份 Year	总计 Total	医院、卫生院 Hospitals	#县及县以上医院 At and Above County level	疗养院、所 Sanatoriums	门诊部、所 Clinics	专科防治所、站 Specialized Prevention & Treatment Centers or Stations
1949	3670	2600	2600	30	769	11
1952	38987	3540	3540	270	29050	188
1957	122954	4179	4179	835	102262	626
1962	217985	34379	5300	1266	172708	678
1965	224266	42711	5445	887	170430	822
1970	149823	64822	6030	359	79600	607
1975	151733	62425	7757	297	80739	683
1978	169732	64421	8841	389	94395	887
1979	176793	65009	9254	440	99643	1066
1980	180553	65450	9478	470	102474	1138
1981	190126	65911	9825	538	111189	1197
1982	193438	66149	10073	593	113916	1272
1983	196017	66662	10466	606	115826	1326
1984	198256	67169	10935	599	117028	1458
1985	200866	59614	11497	640	126604	1566
1986	203139	59693	11940	638	127575	1635
1987	204960	60429	12348	652	128459	1697
1988	205988	61383	12795	652	128422	1727
1989	206724	61929	13248	651	128112	1747
1990	208734	62454	13489	650	129332	1781
1991	209036	63101	13638	642	128665	1818
1992	204787	61352	13917	639	125873	1845
1993	193586	60784	14713	600	115161	1872
1994	191742	67857	14762	587	105984	1905
1995	190057	67807	14771	582	104406	1895
1996	188803	67964	15056	528	103472	1887
1997	315033	67911	15219	506	229474	1893
1998	314097	67081	15277	503	229349	1889
1999	310996	66935	15413	503	226588	1877
2000	324771	66509	15446	471	240934	1839

21-33 续表 1 continued

单位：个 (unit)

年份 Year	卫生防疫机构 Sanitation and Antiepidemic Agencies	妇幼保健所、站 Maternity and Child Care Centers	药品检验所、站 Medicines and Chemical Reagent Test Labs	医学科学研究机构 Research Institutes of Medical Science	其他卫生机构 Other Institutions
1949		9	1	3	247
1952	147	2379	12	3	3398
1957	1626	4599	28	38	8761
1962	2208	2636	93	171	3746
1965	2499	2795	131	94	3897
1970	1714	1058	98	72	1493
1975	2912	2025	310	141	2201
1978	2989	2459	844	219	3129
1979	3047	2559	1159	295	3575
1980	3105	2610	1213	282	3811
1981	3202	2630	1182	285	3992
1982	3271	2645	1186	294	4112
1983	3274	2649	1191	301	4182
1984	3339	2716	1258	307	4382
1985	3410	2724	1420	323	4565
1986	3475	2775	1534	333	5481
1987	3512	2792	1647	340	5432
1988	3532	2793	1756	332	5391
1989	3591	2796	1854	328	5716
1990	3618	2820	1892	337	5850
1991	3652	2854	1927	335	6042
1992	3673	2841	1953	339	6272
1993	3609	2791	1976	436	6357
1994	3611	2857	1990	437	6514
1995	3629	2832	1995	427	6484
1996	4000	2764	2000	427	5761
1997	4012	2748	2014	426	6049
1998	4018	2724	2020	423	6090
1999	4023	2630	1927	421	6092
2000	4065	2598	1790	405	6160

注：1.1997年开始，原不列入卫生机构的"个体开业人员"，改称"私人办诊所"后计入门诊部所中。

2.1995年以前各年份卫生防疫机构数据仅为卫生防疫站数。

a)"Individual practitioners" that were not included in health institutions before 1997 were reclassified as "private clinics" in 1997, and were included in the number of clinics.

b)Data on sanitation and antiepidemic agencies before 1995 referred only to the number of sanitation and antiepidemic stations.

21-34 卫生机构的人员数
Number of Employed Persons in Health Institutions

单位：万人　　(10 000 persons)

年份 Year	总计 Total	卫生技术人员 Medical Technical Personnel	#医生 Doctors	#中医 Doctors of Traditional Chinese Medicine	#西医师 Doctors of Western Medicine	#西医士 Paramedics of Western Medicine	#护师、护士 Senior and Junior Nurses	每千人口医生数(人) Number of Doctors per 1 000 Population (person)
1949	54.1	50.5	36.3	27.6	3.8	4.9	3.3	0.67
1952	81.9	69.0	42.5	30.6	5.2	6.7	6.1	0.74
1957	125.4	103.9	54.7	33.7	7.4	13.6	12.8	0.85
1962	168.5	141.4	68.8	34.4	12.0	22.4	20.0	1.02
1965	187.2	153.2	76.3	32.1	18.9	25.3	23.5	1.05
1970	179.3	145.3	70.2	22.5	22.1	25.6	29.5	0.85
1975	259.4	205.7	87.8	22.9	29.3	35.6	38.0	0.95
1978	310.6	246.4	103.3	25.1	35.9	42.3	40.7	1.07
1979	340.4	264.2	108.8	25.8	39.5	43.5	42.1	1.12
1980	353.5	279.8	115.3	26.2	44.7	44.4	46.6	1.17
1981	379.6	301.1	124.4	29.0	51.6	43.6	52.5	1.25
1982	395.8	314.3	130.7	30.3	55.7	44.5	56.4	1.29
1983	409.0	325.3	135.3	31.3	58.8	45.0	59.6	1.33
1984	421.4	334.4	138.1	32.4	59.7	45.8	61.6	1.34
1985	431.3	341.1	141.3	33.6	60.2	47.3	63.7	1.33
1986	444.6	350.7	144.4	34.1	61.9	48.2	68.1	1.34
1987	456.4	360.9	148.2	34.6	64.5	48.7	71.8	1.36
1988	467.8	372.4	161.7	36.2	89.9	35.2	82.9	1.46
1989	478.7	380.9	171.8	37.0	102.3	32.1	92.2	1.52
1990	490.6	389.8	176.3	36.9	105.8	33.1	97.5	1.54
1991	502.5	398.5	178.0	36.3	106.5	34.7	101.2	1.54
1992	514.0	407.4	180.8	36.4	107.9	36.0	104.0	1.54
1993	521.5	411.7	183.2	35.8	111.5	35.1	105.6	1.55
1994	530.7	419.9	188.2	36.1	115.9	35.4	109.4	1.57
1995	537.3	425.7	191.8	35.9	118.6	36.5	112.6	1.58
1996	541.9	431.2	194.1	34.8	120.7	37.5	116.3	1.59
1997	551.6	439.8	198.5	34.6	123.6	39.2	119.8	1.61
1998	553.6	442.4	200.0	34.0	124.7	40.2	121.9	1.60
1999	557.0	445.9	204.5	33.7	129.3	40.3	124.5	1.67
2000	559.1	449.1	207.6	33.7	133.0	39.5	126.7	1.68

21-35 卫生机构床位数
Number of Beds in Health Institutions

单位：万张　　(10 000 units)

年份 Year	总计 Total	医院、卫生院 Hospitals	#县及县以上医院 At and Above County Level	疗养院、所 Sanatoriums	其他卫生机构 Other Health Institutions	每千人口医院、卫生院床位数(张) Number of Hospital Beds per 1 000 Population (unit)
1949	8.5	8.0	8.0	0.4	0.1	0.15
1952	23.1	16.0	16.0	2.0	5.1	0.28
1957	46.2	29.5	29.5	6.9	9.8	0.46
1962	93.3	69.0	57.7	10.5	13.8	1.03
1965	103.3	76.6	62.1	9.8	16.9	1.06
1970	126.2	110.5	71.2	4.8	10.9	1.33
1975	176.4	159.8	94.8	3.7	12.9	1.73
1978	204.2	185.6	109.3	5.1	13.5	1.93
1979	212.8	193.2	114.8	6.0	13.6	1.99
1980	218.4	198.2	119.2	6.8	13.4	2.01
1981	223.4	201.7	123.9	8.1	13.6	2.02
1982	228.0	205.4	128.5	8.8	13.8	2.03
1983	234.2	211.0	134.7	9.2	14.0	2.07
1984	241.2	216.6	141.5	9.5	15.1	2.10
1985	248.7	222.9	148.7	10.6	15.2	2.11
1986	256.3	229.7	155.9	11.1	15.5	2.14
1987	268.5	240.5	164.8	11.9	16.2	2.20
1988	279.5	250.3	173.1	12.2	16.9	2.25
1989	286.7	256.8	179.7	12.3	17.6	2.28
1990	292.5	262.4	184.7	12.3	17.8	2.30
1991	299.2	268.9	190.1	12.5	17.8	2.32
1992	304.9	274.4	195.3	12.5	18.0	2.34
1993	309.9	279.5	201.7	11.9	18.5	2.36
1994	313.4	283.1	205.1	11.8	18.4	2.36
1995	314.1	283.6	205.3	11.6	18.8	2.34
1996	310.0	286.6	208.3	10.9	12.5	2.34
1997	313.5	290.3	210.9	10.4	12.8	2.35
1998	314.3	291.4	212.4	10.2	12.7	2.33
1999	315.9	292.8	213.9	9.8	13.2	2.39
2000	317.7	294.8	215.5	9.7	13.2	2.38

21-36 按市县分的医院床位和专业卫生技术人员
Hospital Beds and Medical Technical Personnel By City and County Areas

年份 Year	医院、卫生院床位(万张) Number of Hospital Beds (10 000 units)		专业卫生技术人员(万人) Number of Medical Technical Personnel (10 000 persons)		# 医生 Doctors		# 护师、护士 Senior and Junior Nurses	
	市 City	县 County	市 City	县 County	市 City	县 County	市 City	县 County
1952	12.1	3.9	22.5	46.5	8.1	34.3	4.3	1.8
1957	22.1	7.4	38.2	65.7	13.8	40.8	10.0	2.8
1962	43.7	25.3	57.1	84.3	21.4	47.4	15.5	4.5
1965	45.8	30.8	65.2	88.0	26.9	49.4	17.6	5.9
1970	51.0	59.5	59.6	85.7	24.1	46.1	18.0	11.6
1975	63.7	96.1	95.7	110.0	36.7	51.0	24.0	14.0
1980	76.8	121.4	131.3	148.5	52.7	62.6	30.0	16.6
1981	80.3	121.4	143.5	157.6	58.6	65.8	33.4	19.1
1982	83.2	122.1	150.9	163.4	62.8	67.9	35.4	21.0
1983	86.9	124.0	157.4	167.9	66.5	68.7	37.3	22.3
1984	91.9	124.7	164.2	170.2	69.4	68.8	39.3	22.3
1985	96.2	126.7	167.7	173.4	70.9	70.4	39.2	24.5
1986	103.3	126.4	177.4	173.3	74.9	69.5	42.9	25.2
1987	112.7	127.7	188.2	172.6	79.3	68.9	46.1	25.7
1988	125.5	124.8	202.8	169.6	88.6	73.2	53.7	29.2
1989	133.5	123.3	212.1	168.8	95.0	76.8	59.9	32.2
1990	138.7	123.7	218.5	171.3	97.8	78.5	63.4	34.1
1991	144.8	124.0	226.4	172.1	100.3	77.7	66.6	34.6
1992	152.4	122.0	236.3	171.1	104.3	76.5	69.5	34.5
1993	159.6	119.9	243.3	168.5	107.7	75.5	71.5	34.1
1994	170.7	112.4	258.9	161.0	115.0	73.2	76.2	33.2
1995	174.0	109.7	265.9	159.8	118.4	73.4	79.0	33.5
1996	179.1	107.5	272.2	159.0	120.3	73.8	82.3	34.0
1997	184.2	106.1	279.5	160.3	123.5	75.0	85.3	34.6
1998	187.2	104.2	281.9	160.5	124.2	75.7	87.0	34.9
1999	188.7	104.2	283.0	162.9	126.1	78.4	88.6	35.9
2000	191.4	103.4	283.5	165.6	126.8	80.8	89.8	36.9

21-37 医院、卫生院平均每院床位和人员数
Average Number of Beds and Persons Engaged Per Hospital

项目	Item	1999			2000		
		床位(张) Beds (unit)	人员(人) Personnel (person)	#卫生技术人员 Medical Technical Personnel	床位(张) Beds (unit)	人员(人) Personnel (person)	#卫生技术人员 Medical Technical Personnel
医院合计	**Hospitals**	**131.2**	**186.0**	**145.2**	**131.9**	**186.2**	**145.8**
县及县以上医院	Hospitals at County and Higher Levels	138.8	196.8	153.6	139.5	197.2	154.4
其他医院	Other Hospitals	39.2	53.9	40.2	39.9	54.1	42.8
卫生院合计	**Township Hospitals**	**14.7**	**23.4**	**20.5**	**14.9**	**23.9**	**20.9**
城市街道卫生院	Urban Township Hospitals	10.5	31.4	25.3	11.7	32.1	27.2
农村乡(镇)卫生院	Rural Township Hospitals	14.8	23.3	20.5	14.9	23.8	20.8

21-38 各地区卫生机构、床位数（2000年）

Number of Health Institutions, Beds and Employed Persons by Region (2000)

地　区	Region	机构合计（个）Health Institutions	#医院 Hospital	#卫生院 Health Center	#诊所、医务室 Clinics	#卫生防疫站 Sanitation and Antiepidemic Agencies	#妇幼保健机构 Maternity and Child Care Centers	床位合计（万张）Beds Total	#医院 Hospital	卫生院 Health Center
全　国	**National Total**	**324771**	**16732**	**49777**	**237256**	**3602**	**2598**	**317.7**	**220.7**	**74.1**
北　京	Beijing	6176	458	216	5061	21	8	7.1	6.5	0.4
天　津	Tianjin	2983	257	231	2249	24	18	4.0	3.7	0.2
河　北	Hebei	20663	779	3680	15357	199	161	16.9	10.8	4.1
山　西	Shanxi	13736	716	1915	10463	145	136	11.2	7.7	2.6
内蒙古	Inner Mongolia	7852	473	1515	5200	148	108	6.7	4.8	1.5
辽　宁	Liaoning	12564	992	1151	9236	129	108	19.1	15.0	2.2
吉　林	Jilin	5544	542	850	3699	82	58	8.9	7.0	1.3
黑龙江	Heilongjiang	8038	901	1112	5250	229	159	12.0	10.1	1.3
上　海	Shanghai	5136	291	168	4501	28	14	7.5	6.4	0.9
江　苏	Jiangsu	12813	634	1877	9533	137	112	17.3	10.0	6.2
浙　江	Zhejiang	17034	433	2736	13219	97	67	11.4	8.1	2.6
安　徽	Anhui	6705	492	2461	3012	128	110	12.4	7.4	4.1
福　建	Fujian	9807	333	990	7982	95	73	9.0	5.9	2.4
江　西	Jiangxi	8048	599	1683	5083	117	119	9.1	6.2	2.1
山　东	Shandong	17118	973	2177	13061	166	127	21.5	14.7	5.6
河　南	Henan	10764	966	2061	6856	179	136	19.9	13.3	5.1
湖　北	Hubei	11065	530	1511	8216	119	94	14.3	8.8	4.2
湖　南	Hunan	24678	697	2642	20392	161	125	14.3	9.3	3.9
广　东	Guangdong	13499	746	1680	9749	155	31	16.8	11.2	4.5
广　西	Guangxi	13707	553	1315	11328	110	12	8.5	6.4	1.9
海　南	Hainan	2689	180	312	2012	30	21	2.1	1.5	0.5
重　庆	Chongqing	9375	299	1951	6402	49	41	6.6	4.0	1.9
四　川	Sichuan	33351	888	6777	23309	208	188	19.1	11.1	6.0
贵　州	Guizhou	8992	408	1470	6477	101	88	5.9	4.1	1.4
云　南	Yunnan	13356	602	1521	10381	151	142	9.8	6.6	2.3
西　藏	Tibet	1237	105	705	303	81	32	0.6	0.4	0.2
陕　西	Shaanxi	10737	734	2045	7323	122	82	9.7	7.4	1.9
甘　肃	Gansu	7191	365	1502	4789	102	90	5.9	4.4	1.3
青　海	Qinghai	1847	161	416	1139	58	39	1.7	1.4	0.2
宁　夏	Ningxia	1361	97	283	879	27	25	1.4	1.2	0.2
新　疆	Xinjiang	6705	528	824	4795	204	74	7.1	5.3	1.3

21-39 各地区卫生机构人员数（2000年）

Number of Employed Persons in Health Institutions by Region(2000)

单位：万人 (10 000 persons)

地区	Region	人员合计 Total	#卫生技术人员 Medical Technical Personnel	#医生 Doctors	#医师 Physician	#护师、护士 Senior and Junior Nurses
全国	**National Total**	**559.1**	**449.1**	**207.6**	**160.3**	**126.7**
北京	Beijing	16.0	11.6	5.2	4.7	4.0
天津	Tianjin	8.5	6.5	3.0	2.7	2.1
河北	Hebei	27.7	22.9	11.1	8.0	5.2
山西	Shanxi	19.5	16.5	8.3	6.7	4.2
内蒙古	Inner Mongolia	13.1	10.7	5.6	4.3	2.7
辽宁	Liaoning	29.6	22.8	10.0	8.2	7.5
吉林	Jilin	16.8	13.2	6.0	4.6	4.1
黑龙江	Heilongjiang	22.2	17.1	7.8	6.3	5.1
上海	Shanghai	14.6	10.7	5.0	4.2	3.7
江苏	Jiangsu	32.2	25.4	11.4	9.2	7.4
浙江	Zhejiang	20.0	15.8	7.4	5.5	4.0
安徽	Anhui	18.8	15.4	7.0	5.3	4.1
福建	Fujian	11.8	9.8	4.1	3.2	2.9
江西	Jiangxi	15.2	12.3	5.4	4.3	3.6
山东	Shandong	38.3	31.5	14.5	11.7	9.2
河南	Henan	33.5	26.8	11.1	8.8	6.3
湖北	Hubei	30.0	23.9	10.3	8.3	7.5
湖南	Hunan	27.2	22.8	10.1	7.0	5.7
广东	Guangdong	32.7	26.5	11.1	8.4	8.3
广西	Guangxi	15.9	12.7	6.1	4.6	4.0
海南	Hainan	3.9	3.1	1.3	1.0	1.0
重庆	Chongqing	10.8	8.9	4.5	3.2	2.1
四川	Sichuan	31.0	25.3	13.0	9.2	6.0
贵州	Guizhou	10.2	8.5	4.6	3.3	2.2
云南	Yunnan	15.2	12.4	6.3	4.6	3.6
西藏	Tibet	1.1	0.9	0.5	0.4	0.2
陕西	Shaanxi	16.4	13.3	6.4	4.9	3.6
甘肃	Gansu	9.5	7.9	3.8	2.8	2.2
青海	Qinghai	2.6	2.2	1.0	0.8	0.6
宁夏	Ningxia	2.7	2.1	1.0	0.8	0.7
新疆	Xinjiang	12.1	9.7	4.5	3.4	3.1

21-40 卫生机构各类人员数

Employed Persons in Health Care Institutions by Type of Occupation

单位：万人　　(10 000 persons)

人员分类	Type of Personnel	1985	1990	1995	1999	2000
总　计	**Total**	**431.3**	**490.6**	**537.3**	**557.0**	**559.1**
卫生技术人员	Medical Technical Personnel	341.1	389.8	425.7	445.9	449.1
其他技术人员	Other Technical Personnel	4.6	8.6	12.1	15.0	15.8
管理人员	Managerial Personnel	35.9	39.7	45.0	43.4	42.8
工勤人员	Logistics Workers	49.7	52.6	54.5	52.6	51.6
卫生技术人员	**Medical Technical Personnel**	**341.1**	**389.8**	**425.7**	**445.9**	**449.1**
中医师	Doctors of Traditional Chinese Medicine	12.0	24.0	26.0	25.7	26.0
西医师	Doctors of Western Medicine	60.2	105.8	118.6	129.3	133.0
中西医结合高级医师	Senior Doctors Who Integrate Traditional Chinese Therapeutics with Western Therapeutics in Practice	0.2	0.5	0.8	1.1	1.3
护师	Senior Nurses	6.8	43.2	63.4	78.7	81.9
药剂师	Pharmacists of Chinese Medicine	4.7	16.4	21.2	24.0	24.3
检验师	Laboratory Technicians	2.4	8.1	11.0	12.8	13.1
其他技师	Other Technicians	2.1	6.8	9.2	10.6	10.9
中医士	Paramedics of Chinese Medicine	15.0	9.1	7.5	6.8	6.6
西医士	Paramedics of Western Medicine	47.3	33.1	36.5	40.3	39.5
护士	Junior Nurses	56.9	54.3	49.2	45.8	44.8
助产士	Midwives	7.6	5.8	4.9	4.4	4.4
药剂士	Junior Pharmacists of Chinese Medicine	14.5	16.2	13.5	12.5	12.2
检验士	Junior Laboratory Technicians	7.5	7.0	5.9	5.6	5.4
其他技士	Other Junior Technicians	5.8	6.0	5.4	4.8	4.6
其他中医	Other Doctors of Chinese Medicine	6.6	3.8	2.3	1.2	1.1
护理员	Assistant Nurses	25.9	12.7	11.8	8.5	7.7
药剂员	Assistant Pharmacists of Chinese Medicine	17.3	8.0	7.1	5.3	4.9
检验员	Assistant Laboratory Technicians	4.7	2.0	2.0	1.7	1.6
其他初级卫生技术人员	Other Junior Medical Technical Personnel	43.6	27.1	29.1	26.6	25.7
平均每千人口有卫生技术人员(人)	**Number of Medical Technical Personnel per 1,000 Population**	**3.2**	**3.4**	**3.5**	**3.5**	**3.6**

21-41 医院、卫生院诊疗人次及入院人数（2000年）

Number of Hospital Patients (2000)

医院类别	Type of Hospital	诊疗人次（亿人次） Total Number of Patients Treated (100 million person-times)	#门、急诊 Out-patients and Emergency Patients	入院人数（万人） Hospital Admissions (10 000 patients)	每百诊次的入院人数(人) Hospital Admissions per 100 Patient-Times (person)	每百门、急诊次的入院人数（人） Hospital Admissions per 100 Out-Patient times and Emergency Patient-Times (person)
医院、卫生院合计	**Total**	**21.23**	**19.67**	**5297**	**2.5**	**2.7**
县及县以上医院合计	Hospitals at and above County Level	12.40	11.40	3543	2.9	3.1
#卫生部门	Health Departments	8.76	8.32	2862	3.3	3.4
工业及其他部门	Industrial and Other Departments	3.37	2.83	632	1.9	2.2
集体所有制	Collective Owned Units	0.24	0.23	41	1.7	1.8
其他医院	Other Hospitals	0.46	0.43	41	0.9	1.0
卫生院	Rural Township Hospitals	8.37	7.84	1713	2.0	2.2

21-42 县及县以上医院病床使用情况

Utilization of Hospital Beds at and above County Level

医院类别	Type of Hospital	病床周转次数（次） Turnover of Beds (times)	病床工作日（日） Number of Days per Bed in Use in a Year (days)	病床使用率(%) Utilization Rate of Beds	出院者平均住院日(日) Average Hospital-ization Period (days)
1985 合计	**Total in 1985**	**18.1**	**301.9**	**82.7**	**15.8**
卫生部门	Health Departments	19.8	320.8	87.9	15.4
工业及其他部门	Industrial and Other Departments	14.2	253.7	69.5	16.5
集体单位	Collective Owned Units	13.9	297.5	81.5	19.4
1990 合计	**Total in 1990**	**17.6**	**295.3**	**80.9**	**15.9**
卫生部门	Health Departments	19.2	312.4	85.6	15.5
工业及其他部门	Industrial and Other Departments	13.8	254.8	69.8	17.0
集体单位	Collective Owned Units	13.8	253.7	69.5	16.9
1995 合计	**Total in 1995**	**15.5**	**244.2**	**66.9**	**14.7**
卫生部门	Health Departments	17.1	256.2	70.2	14.2
工业及其他部门	Industrial and Other Departments	11.8	216.1	59.2	16.7
集体单位	Collective Owned Units	12.4	199.7	54.7	13.9
1998 合计	**Total in 1998**	**15.8**	**219.7**	**60.2**	**13.1**
卫生部门	Health Departments	17.5	230.3	63.1	12.6
工业及其他部门	Industrial and Other Departments	11.7	194.2	53.2	15.1
集体单位	Collective Owned Units	11.7	190.5	52.2	16.0
1999 合计	**Total in 1999**	**16.3**	**218.3**	**59.8**	**12.6**
卫生部门	Health Departments	18.2	230.3	63.1	12.1
工业及其他部门	Industrial and Other Departments	11.5	187.6	51.4	14.8
集体单位	Collective Owned Units	11.7	184.7	50.6	14.3
2000 合计	**Total in 2000**	**17.3**	**222.0**	**60.8**	**12.1**
卫生部门	Health Departments	19.5	235.5	64.5	11.6
工业及其他部门	Industrial and Other Departments	11.5	187.6	51.4	14.4
集体单位	Collective Owned Units	12.7	187.6	51.4	13.1

21-43 城市前十位疾病死亡原因及构成（2000年）

Death Rate of 10 Major Diseases in Urban Areas (2000)

顺位 No.	疾病死亡原因	Cause of Death	占死亡总人数的% As % of Total Deaths
	十种死因合计	**Total**	**92.18**
1	恶性肿瘤	Malignant Tumour	24.38
2	脑血管病	Cerebrovasular Disease	21.28
3	心脏病	Heart Trouble	17.74
4	呼吸系病	Respiratory Disease	13.29
5	损伤和中毒	Trauma and Toxicosis	5.91
6	消化系病	Digestive Disease	3.06
7	内分泌、营养、代谢及免疫疾病	Internal System, Nutrition, Metabolite and Immunity Disease	2.99
8	泌尿、生殖系病	Urinary Disease	1.5
9	精神病	Mental Disease	1.11
10	神经病	Neuropathy	0.92
	男性十种死因合计	**Male Total**	**93.02**
1	恶性肿瘤	Malignant Tumour	27.23
2	脑血管病	Cerebrovasular Disease	20.81
3	心脏病	Heart Trouble	16.49
4	呼吸系病	Respiratory Disease	12.77
5	损伤和中毒	Trauma and Toxicosis	6.69
6	消化系病	Digestive Disease	3.37
7	内分泌、营养、代谢及免疫疾病	Internal System, Nutrition, Metabolite and Immunity Disease	2.26
8	泌尿、生殖系病	Urinary Disease	1.48
9	神经病	Neuropathy	0.96
10	精神病	Mental Disease	0.96
	女性十种死因合计	**Female Total**	**91.15**
1	脑血管病	Cerebrovasular Disease	21.86
2	恶性肿瘤	Malignant Tumour	20.88
3	心脏病	Heart Trouble	19.27
4	呼吸系病	Respiratory Disease	13.93
5	损伤和中毒	Trauma and Toxicosis	4.96
6	内分泌、营养、代谢及免疫疾病	Internal System, Nutrition, Metabolite and Immunity Disease	3.89
7	消化系病	Digestive Disease	2.68
8	泌尿、生殖系病	Urinary Disease	1.52
9	精神病	Mental Disease	1.3
10	神经病	Neuropathy	0.86

注：统计范围包括北京等36个市全市或部分市区资料。

a)Statistics in the table cover full or partial areas of 36 cities including Beijing.

21-44　农村前十位疾病死亡原因及构成（2000年）

Death Rate of 10 Major Diseases in Rural Areas (2000)

顺位 No.	疾病死亡原因	Cause of Death	占死亡总人数的% As % of Total Deaths
	十种死因合计	**Total**	**91.46**
1	呼吸系病	Respiratory Disease	23.11
2	恶性肿瘤	Malignant Tumour	18.40
3	脑血管病	Cerebrovasular Disease	18.40
4	心脏病	Heart Trouble	12.37
5	损伤和中毒	Trauma and Toxicosis	11.03
6	消化系病	Digestive Disease	3.98
7	泌尿、生殖系病	Urinary Disease	1.51
8	肺结核	Pulmonary Tuberculosis	1.19
9	新生儿病	Newborn Baby Disease	1.14
10	内分泌、营养、代谢及免疫疾病	Internal System, Nutrition, Metabolite and Immunity Disease	1.11
	男性十种死因合计	**Male Total**	**92.57**
1	呼吸系病	Respiratory Disease	21.46
2	恶性肿瘤	Malignant Tumour	20.82
3	脑血管病	Cerebrovasular Disease	18.57
4	损伤和中毒	Trauma and Toxicosis	11.77
5	心脏病	Heart Trouble	10.78
6	消化系病	Digestive Disease	4.20
7	泌尿、生殖系病	Urinary Disease	1.55
8	肺结核	Pulmonary Tuberculosis	1.36
9	新生儿病	Newborn Baby Disease	1.05
10	传染病(肺结核除外)	Infectious Disease (Excluding Pulmonary Tuberculosis)	1.01
	女性十种死因合计	**Female Total**	**90.15**
1	呼吸系病	Respiratory Disease	25.18
2	脑血管病	Cerebrovasular Disease	18.93
3	恶性肿瘤	Malignant Tumour	15.12
4	心脏病	Heart Trouble	13.39
5	损伤和中毒	Trauma and Toxicosis	9.01
6	消化系病	Digestive Disease	3.48
7	泌尿、生殖系病	Urinary Disease	1.46
8	内分泌、营养、代谢及免疫疾病	Internal System, Nutrition, Metabolite and Immunity Disease	1.37
9	新生儿病	Newborn Baby Disease	1.24
10	肺结核	Pulmonary Tuberculosis	0.97

注：统计范围包括北京等90个县的资料。

a)Statistics in the table cover full or partial areas of 90 counties, including counties in Beijing.

21-45 全国法定报告传染病发病及死亡情况（2000年）

Incidence and Death from Infectious Diseases (2000)

病　　名	Item	发病率 (1/10万) Incidence Disease Rate (per 100 000 persons)	死亡率 (1/10万) Death Rate (per 100 000 persons)	病死率 (%) Mortality Rate per 100 Infectious Disease Patients
总计	**Total**	**185.98**	**0.26**	**0.14**
鼠疫	The Plague	0.02		0.80
霍乱	Cholera	0.15		0.48
病毒性肝炎	Viral Hepatitis	63.04	0.04	0.07
痢疾	Dysentery	39.65	0.01	0.03
伤寒副伤寒	Typhoid and Paratyphoid Fever	3.90		0.08
艾滋病	AIDS	0.01	0.01	42.24
淋病	Gonorrhea	18.31		
梅毒	Syphilis	4.73		0.02
脊髓灰质炎	Poliomyelitis			
麻疹	Measles	5.74	0.01	0.17
百日咳	Pertussis	0.45		0.13
白喉	Diphtheria			
流脑	Epidemic Encephalitis	0.19	0.01	4.62
猩红热	Scarlet Fever	1.03		0.04
出血热	Hemorrhage Fever	2.89	0.02	0.74
狂犬病	Hydrophobia	0.04	0.04	93.94
钩端螺旋体病	Leptospirosis	0.31	0.01	2.73
布氏杆菌病	Brucellosis	0.14		0.06
炭疽	Anthrax	0.05		1.87
斑疹伤寒	Typhus Fever	0.46		
乙脑	Encephalitis B	0.93	0.03	2.86
黑热病	Kala-Azar	0.01		
疟疾	Malaria	1.94		0.16
登革热	Dengue Fever	0.03		
新生儿破伤风	Newborn Baby Tetanus	15.85	0.03	12.60
肺结核	Pulmonary Tuberculosis	41.68	0.04	0.11

主 要 统 计 指 标 解 释

文化事业机构 指从事专业文化工作和为专业文化工作服务的独立建制的单位。不包括这些单位另外举办独立核算的其他机构和各部门的业余文化组织。

艺术表演团体 指从事戏曲、音乐、舞蹈、杂技等专业艺术表演，有独立帐户的单位，不包括半工半艺、半农半艺和民间职业剧团。

电影放映单位 指具有放映机器设备、固定或不固定的放映场所与专职或兼职的放映技术人员，经有关部门登记批准，经常为一定的观众对象放映电影的机构。包括经批准对外开放进行营业，并与电影发行放映管理机构分帐的专用放映单位和军委系统租片单位。

艺术表演观众人数(人次) 指售票、包场演出或民族地区免费演出的艺术表演观众人次数，不包括彩排审查和内部观摩演出的观看人次数。

图书纯销售 指向读者直接销售的图书以及直接向国外出口的图书。

书刊排字 指用手工排字和激光排版生产的、可供印刷的排字产量。

书刊印刷 指铅印和胶印印书。

胶印印刷 指用胶印机完成的单色或多色印刷产品。

零件印刷 指单张小件印品。

等级运动员人数 指经考核正式批准授予等级运动员称号的人数。运动员等级分为国际级运动健将、运动健将、一级运动员、二级运动员、三级运动员、少年级运动员。

等级裁判员人数 指经考核正式批准授予等级裁判员称号的人数。裁判员等级分为国际裁判、国家级裁判、一级裁判、二级裁判、三级裁判。

体育场 指有400米跑道(中心含足球场)，有固定道牙，跑道6条以上，并有固定看台的室外田径场地。体育场按看台容纳观众人数分为：甲级25000人以上，乙级15000-25000人，丙级5000-15000人，丁级5000人以下。

体育馆 指有固定看台，可供篮球、排球、羽毛球、乒乓球、体操等项目训练比赛活动用的室内运动场地。体育馆按看台容纳观众人数分为：甲级6000人以上，乙级4000-6000人，丙级2000-4000人，丁级2000人以下。

医院 指设有固定床位，能收容病人住院并能为病人提供医疗、护理服务的医疗机构，包括县及县以上医院、农村乡卫生院和其他医院三部分。医院按所属性质不同分为卫生部门、工业及其他部门和集体经济单位三类。县及县以上医院按业务性质不同分为综合医院和专科医院。

卫生技术人员 指卫生事业机构支付工资的全部职工中现任职务为卫生技术工作的专业人员，包括中医师、西医师、中西医结合高级医师、护师、中药师、西药师、检验师、其他技师、中医士、西医士、护士、助产士、中药剂士、西药剂士、检验士、其他技士、其他中医、护理员、中药剂员、西药剂员、检验员和其他初级卫生技术人员。

医生 指经卫生部门审查合格，从事医疗工作的专业人员。分为中医医生和西医医生。包括卫生技术人员中的中医师、西医师、中西医结合高级医师、中医士、西医士和其他中医。

Explanatory Notes on Main Statistical Indicators

Cultural Institutions refer to units which have their own organizational system and independent accounting system and specialize in or serve cultural development. They exclude other establishments run by these cultural institutions and amateur cultural groups established by various departments.

Art Troupe refers to the troupe which is engaged in drama, opera, music, dance, acrobatics or other art performance, opens independent accounts with banks and has self-supporting accounting system; excluding the troupes which are engaged partly in industrial or agricultural activities, partly in art performance and the professional troupes organized by the people.

Film Projection Units refer to units with film projection equipment, full or part time projectionists, permanent or non permanent places, approved by related administrative departments to show films regularly for certain groups of audience, including those film projection units which have been approved to give commercial shows and run business with independent accounting system as well as those film-renting units of the military system.

Number of Spectators at Art Performance refers to the number of attendants at commercial shows, completely booked shows or free shows given in minority national areas, and does not include the number of spectators at rehearsals for examination and internal shows for study.

Net Sales of Books refers to books sold directly to readers and directly exported.

Typesetting of Books refers to the volume of work (characters) of manual or laser typesetting ready for printing.

Printing of Books refers to printing of books by stereotype or offset printing method.

Offset Printing refers to mono or multi color materials printed by offset press.

Small Piece Printing refers to printing of single-sheet products in small quantity.

Number of Athletes in Grades refers to the number of athletes who have been given titles through examination. The titles of athletes include international masters of sports, masters of sports, first-grade, second-grade and third-grade sportsmen and young athletes.

Number of Referees in Grades refers to the number of referees who have been given titles after examination. They are classified as international referees, national referees and referees of the first, second and third grades.

Stadiums refer to stadiums for track and field events with six lane 400-meter tracks around soccer fields, permanent track marks and permanent bleachers. Stadiums are classified according to seating capacity. They include: Class A stadiums seating 25000 people each. Class B stadiums seating 15000 to 25000 people each. Class C stadiums seating 5000 to 15000 people each, and Class D stadiums seating fewer than 5000 people.

Gymnasiums refer to indoor sports grounds with permanent seats in which basketball, volleyball. badminton, table tennis and gymnastics competitions can be held. Gymnasiums are classified according to seating capacity. They include Class A gymnasiums seating over 6000 people. Class B gymnasiums seating 4000 to 6000 people. Class C gymnasiums seating 2000 to 4000 people, and Class D gymnasiums seating fewer than 2000 people.

Hospitals refer to medical institutions with permanent hospital beds, which are able to take in patients and provide them with medical and nursing services. Hospitals are classified into three categories: hospitals at or above the county level, hospitals of rural townships, and other hospitals. According to their ownership, hospitals can be classified into three categories: hospitals under the public health departments, hospitals under industrial and other departments and collective-owned hospitals. Hospitals at or above county level are divided into comprehensive and specialized hospitals.

Medical Technical Personnel refers to all medical staff and workers employed by medical institutions, including doctors of Chinese and Western medicine, senior doctors who integrate traditional Chinese therapeutics with Western therapeutics in practice, senior nurses, pharmacists of Chinese and Western medicine, laboratory specialists, other specialists, paramedics of Chinese and Western medicine, nurses, midwives, druggists in Chinese and Western medicine, laboratory technicians, other technicians, other practitioners of Chinese medicine, nursing attendants, pharmacological workers of Chinese and Western medicine, laboratory workers, and other primary medical personnel.

Doctors refer to qualified professional medical workers approved to practice by public health departments. They are classified into doctors of Chinese medicine, doctors of Western medicine, senior doctors who integrate traditional Chinese therapeutics with Western therapeutics in practice, paramedics of Chinese medicine and Western medicine, and other specialists of Chinese medicine.

二十二、其他社会活动及环境保护

Other Social Activities and Environment Protection

简要说明

本篇主要包括社会活动参与、公检法司、民政事业、劳动保障、环境保护和残疾人情况等内容。

一、社会活动参与的内容主要包括历届全国人大代表、历届全国政协委员情况和全国工会组织情况，资料由全国人大、全国政协、全国总工会分别提供。

二、公检法司的内容由公安部、最高人民检察院、最高人民法院和司法部提供的资料组成。主要包括公安机关的刑事案件立案情况和治安案件查处情况，交通、火灾事故情况，检察机关的办案情况，人民法院审理案件和收结案情况，以及律师、公证、调解工作的情况等。

三、民政事业和劳动保障统计资料分别由民政部、劳动和社会保障部提供。主要包括社会福利企事业机构、人员、经费情况、优抚情况、社会救济、城镇社区服务及农村社会保障网络、婚姻登记、离退休人员及费用和劳动争议仲裁等情况。

四、环境保护统计资料由国家环保局提供。主要包括：

1.“三废”排放与处理：根据有污染的县及县以上工业企业的数据汇总而成，反映各地区、各工业行业“三废”排放与处理的情况。

2.环境保护与管理：反映各地区环境污染事故的发生和环境保护区建设方面的情况。

3.环保系统自身建设：反映地方各级环保部门的基本情况，不包括国家环境保护局及其直属单位和国务院各有关部门的资料。

五、残疾人资料由残联提供，主要包括残疾人康复、教育、就业、扶贫和残联组织建设等情况。

公安部、最高人民检察院、最高人民法院、司法部、民政部、劳动和社会保障部、国家环境保护总局、全国总工会和中国残疾人联合会等资料，主要是依据各部门的定期统计报表制度逐级汇总上报整理而成的。

Brief Introduction

Data in this chapter show statistics on participation in social activities, public security, procuratorial, legal and judicial affairs, civil affairs, labor protection, environment protection and disabled population.

I. Data on participation cover mainly information on representatives to the National People's Congress (NPC), members of the Chinese People's Political Consultative Conference (CPPCC) and trade unions, which are provided by NPC, CPPCC and All-China Federation of Trade Unions.

II. Data on public security, procuratorial, legal and judicial affairs are provided by the Ministry of Public Security, the Supreme People's Procuratorate, the Supreme People's Court and the Ministry of Justice. They cover information such as criminal cases registered and offense cases handled by the public security agencies, traffic or fire accidents, cases handled by procurator's offices, cases accepted and settled by the people's courts, and statistics on lawyers, notarization and mediation.

III. Data on civil affairs and labor protection are provided by the Ministry of Civil Affairs and the Ministry of Labor and Social Security. They cover information such as institutions and personnel, budget, social welfare relief, urban welfare facilities, rural network of social security, marriage registration, retirement pensions, arbitration of labor disputes, etc..

IV. Data on environment protection are provided by the State Environment Protection Administration. They cover the following:

(1) The discharge and treatment of waste water, waste gas and solid wastes: The summary data are tabulated from the data of industrial enterprises at county and higher levels, which discharge pollutants. They show the discharge and treatment of waste water, waste gas and solid wastes in various regions and various industrial sectors.

(2) The protection of environment: The data show the incidence of pollution of environment and the development of environment protection zones in various regions.

(3) The improvement of the departments of environment protection: The data show the basic conditions of the local departments of environment protection, excluding the data on the State Environment Protection Administration and its directly subordinate units as well as the departments under State Council.

V. Data on disabled persons are provided by the All-China Federation of Disabled Persons, covering information on the rehabilitation, education, employment and poverty alleviation of disabled persons and institutions serving the needs of disabled persons.

Data from the Ministry of Public Security, the Supreme People's Procuratorate, the Supreme People's Court and the Ministry of Justice, the Ministry of Civil Affairs, the Ministry of Labor and Social Security, the State Environment Protection Administration, All-China Federation of Trade Unions and All-China Federation of Disabled Persons are collected and tabulated in accordance with the regular statistical reporting systems of the departments concerned.

22-1 历届全国人民代表大会的代表人数

Number of Deputies to All the Previous National People's Congresses

单位：人 (person)

项　目	Item	一 届 First Congress (1954)	二 届 Second Congress (1959)	三 届 Third Congress (1964)	四 届 Fourth Congress (1975)	五 届 Fifth Congress (1978)	六 届 Sixth Congress (1983)	七 届 Seventh Congress (1988)	八 届 Eighth Congress (1993)	九 届 Ninth Congress (1998)
代表总数	**Total Number of All Deputies**	**1226**	**1226**	**3040**	**2885**	**3497**	**2978**	**2978**	**2978**	**2979**
在代表总数中	Of Which									
女代表	Female Deputies	147	150	542	653	742	632	634	626	650
占代表总数%	As Percentage to Total	12.0	12.2	17.8	22.6	21.2	21.2	21.3	21.0	21.8
在代表总数中	Of Which									
少数民族代表	Deputies from National Minorities	178	179	372	270	381	403	445	439	428
占代表总数%	As Percentage to Total	14.5	14.6	12.2	9.4	10.9	13.5	14.9	14.8	14.4

22-2 历届全国政治协商会议的委员人数

Number of Deputies to All the Previous Chinese People's Political Consultative Conferences

单位：人 (person)

项　目	Item	一 届 First Congress (1954)	二 届 Second Congress (1959)	三 届 Third Congress (1964)	四 届 Fourth Congress (1975)	五 届 Fifth Congress (1978)	六 届 Sixth Congress (1983)	七 届 Seventh Congress (1988)	八 届 Eighth Congress (1993)	九 届 Ninth Congress (1998)
委员总数	**Total Number of Deputies**	**198**	**729**	**1071**	**1199**	**1988**	**2039**	**2083**	**2093**	**2196**
在委员总数中	Of Which									
中国共产党代表	Deputies from the Communist Party of China		40	60	61	76	76	90	91	92
占委员总数%	As Percentage to Total		5.5	5.6	5.1	3.8	3.7	4.3	4.3	4.2
在委员总数中	Of Which									
少数民族代表	Deputies from National Minorities	19	61	78	81	143	185	225	241	258
占委员总数%	As Percentage to Total	9.6	8.4	7.3	6.8	7.2	9.1	10.8	11.5	11.7

22-3 工会组织情况

Basic Statistics on Trade Unions

年 份 Year	工会基层组织数（万个） Number of Grassroots Unions (10 000 units)	全国已建工会组织的基层单位的职工与会员人数（万人） Membership and Number of Staff and Workers in Grassroots Unions (10 000 persons)				工会专职工作人员人数(万人) Number of Full-time Personnel of Unions(10 000 persons)
		职工人数 Number of Staff and Workers	#女职工 Female	会员人数 Membership	#女会员 Female	
1952	20.7	1393.2		1002.3		5.3
1957	16.5	2158.3		1746.7		
1962	16.5	2667.1		1922.0		8.6
1978						
1979	32.9	6897.2	2171.7	5147.3		17.9
1980	37.6	7448.2	2518.6	6116.5		24.3
1981	41.1	8183.0	2902.0	6843.9	2412.8	29.1
1982	43.3	8586.6	3065.9	7331.6	2629.3	32.2
1983	44.7	8845.7	3191.8	7693.4	2771.4	33.7
1984	46.6	9243.9	3370.3	8029.1	2950.3	41.9
1985	46.5	9643.0	3596.7	8525.8	3149.2	38.1
1986	50.2	9949.6	3664.3	8908.5	3309.2	45.9
1987	53.6	10411.8	3900.4	9336.5	3486.9	47.0
1988	56.4	10747.4	4434.9	9628.9	3647.0	47.4
1989	58.9	10998.6	4178.7	9909.2	3777.7	48.8
1990	60.6	11156.9	4291.0	10135.6	3897.7	55.6
1991	61.4	11351.4	4394.8	10389.1	3991.6	58.0
1992	61.7	11223.9	4377.1	10322.5	3974.0	58.0
1993	62.7	11103.8	4359.9	10176.1	3949.6	55.4
1994	58.3	11269.6	4483.2	10202.5	4018.1	56.0
1995	59.3	11321.4	4515.3	10399.6	4116.5	46.8
1996	58.6	11181.4	4500.0	10211.9	4093.1	60.5
1997	51.0	10111.5	4004.8	9131.0	3579.4	57.7
1998	50.4	9716.5	3882.0	8913.4	3546.7	48.4
1999	50.9	9683.0	3797.9	8689.9	3406.2	49.7
2000	85.9	11472.1	4534.5	10361.5	3917.3	48.2

22-4 律师、公证、调解工作基本情况
Basic Statistics on Lawyers, Notarization and Mediation

项　目	Item	1996	1997	1998	1999	2000
律师工作	**Lawyers**					
律师事务所 (个)	Number of Law Offices	8265	8441	8946	9144	9541
律师工作人员 (人)	Number of Lawyers (persons)	100198	98902	101220	111433	117260
#专职律师 (人)	Full-time Lawyers (persons)	47879	47574	51008	61761	69117
兼职律师 (人)	Part-time Lawyers (persons)	20243	18695	17958	17082	15639
聘请担任常年法律顾问的单位 (处)	Number of Units with Permanent Legal Advisors	223043	232434	235676	238576	247160
民事诉讼代理 (件)	Agent of Civil Cases (cases)	353840	454273	526633	592455	640610
经济诉讼代理 (件)	Agent of Economic Cases (cases)	360224	403337	414229	426358	438672
刑事辩护 (件)	Defender of Criminal Cases (cases)	245877	275188	296668	309767	317108
行政诉讼代理 (件)	Agent of Administrative Action(cases)	19360	29618	35865	39006	41785
非诉讼法律事务 (件)	Agent of Non-Litigious Legal Affairs (cases)	435483	1222239	851433	716287	770087
涉外及涉港澳台法律事务 (件)	Agent of Foreign-related, Hong Kong, Macao & Taiwan Legal Affairs (cases)	27730	24765	21618	18793	30531
解答法律询问 (万件)	Agent of Legal Advisory Services (10 000 cases)	186.5	425.9	489.9	419.2	457.4
代写法律事务文书(万件)	Agent of Legal Documents Written on Behalf of Clients (10 000 cases)	52.3	95.9	125.9	96.6	111.3
公证工作	**Notarization**					
公证处 (个)	Number of Notary Offices	3167	3162	3179	3189	3189
公证人员 (人)	Notarial Personnel (persons)	17019	17431	18159	18654	19211
#公证员 (人)	Notaries (persons)	11322	11749	13006	13083	12849
公证员助理 (人)	Assistant Notaries (persons)	1925	1741	1428	1584	2103
办理公证文书 (万件)	Number of Notarized Documents (10 000 cases)	792.7	982.8	1022.9	1644.6	1249.7
人民调解工作	**Number of People's Mediation**					
专职司法助理员 (人)	Number of Full-time Judicial Assistants (persons)	56173	57029	52875	54987	54638
人民调解委员会 (万个)	Number of People's Mediation Committees (10 000 units)	100.2	98.5	98.4	97.4	96.4
调解人员 (万人)	Number of Mediators (10 000 persons)	1035.4	1027.4	917.5	880.3	844.5
调解民间纠纷 (万件)	Number of Civil Disputes Mediated (10 000 cases)	580.2	554.3	526.7	518.9	503.1

22-5 国内公证文书分类

Domestic Notarial Documents by Type

分类	Item	1999 办证件数(件) Number of Notarial Documents Issued (pieces)	1999 比重(%) Percentage	2000 办证件数(件) Number of Notarial Documents Issued (pieces)	2000 比重(%) Percentage
经济公证	**Notarized Documents on Economic Affairs**				
合计	Total Documents	8004578	100.00	4233306	100.00
购销	Purchases and Sales of Products	145491	1.82	152499	3.60
联营	Joint Business	8732	0.11	7118	0.17
拍卖	Auctions	34844	0.44	32344	0.76
贷款	Loans	757148	9.46	1109888	26.22
担保	Guarantees	97869	1.22	101507	2.40
招标、投标	Bidding	46067	0.58	76243	1.80
技术合作	Scientific and Technological Contracts	3005	0.04	17023	0.40
供用电	Supply and Use of Electric Power	40936	0.51	253243	5.98
劳务合同	Labor Contracts	298531	3.73	214677	5.07
建筑工程承包	Construction Project Contracts	20529	0.26	19653	0.46
工商服务业承包	Industrial and Commercial Service Contracts	28820	0.36	20929	0.49
农林牧副渔业承包	Farming, Forestry, Animal Husbandry, Sideline Production and Fishery Contracts	3545075	44.29	656390	15.51
乡镇企业承包	Township Enterprise Contracts	12500	0.16	7569	0.18
财产租赁	Property Leases	35714	0.45	30037	0.71
企业租赁	Leases of Enterprise	10561	0.13	9469	0.22
资产经营协议	Asset Business Contracts	7563	0.09	4219	0.10
还款协议	Payment Contracts	73844	0.92	86791	2.10
土地使用权出让、转让	Selling or Transfer of Right of Land Utilization	70206	0.88	72934	1.72
其他经济合同	Other Business Contracts	782142	9.77	395756	9.77
法人(代表人)资格	Legal Person (agent) Identification	10785	0.13	8465	0.20
法人委托书	Legal Person Trust Deeds	16399	0.20	22295	0.53
公司章程	Corporation Constitutions	5811	0.07	4789	0.11
执行许可证明	Operating Permits	6800	0.08	7023	0.17
提存	Consignation	18078	0.23	13527	0.32
抵押登记	Mortgage Registration	58242	0.73	48819	1.15
公司会议记录	Minutes of Corporation Meetings	34100	0.43	3853	0.09
其他	Others	1834786	22.92	821561	19.41
民事法律关系公证	**Notarized Documents on Civil Legal Relations**				
合计	Total	6197295	100.00	5591412	100.00
收养	Child Adoption	16506	0.27	15556	0.28
解除收养	Adoption Renouncements	979	0.02	1886	0.03
继承权	Rights of Inheritance	83423	1.35	109315	1.96
遗嘱	Testaments	45952	0.74	58571	1.05
产权	Property Rights	70526	1.14	53636	0.96
亲属关系	Kinship Confirmation	29961	0.48	44641	0.80
死亡	Death Certificates	9318	0.15	8416	0.15
房屋买卖	Purchases and Sales of Houses	451864	7.29	503505	9.00
房屋租赁	House Leases	57287	0.92	37848	0.68
留学协议	Foreign Study Contracts	7608	0.12	7628	0.14
遗赠扶养协议	Donations and Family Fostering	6952	0.11	7920	0.14
委托书	Trust Deeds	71001	1.15	240509	4.30
赠与书	Presentation Documents	100753	1.63	94246	1.69
声明书	Declarations	96443	1.56	118588	2.12
现场监督	Field Supervision	124686	2.01	116975	2.09
签名印鉴属实	Confirmation of Signatures and Seals	26991	0.44	31594	0.57
副本等与原本相符	Confirmation of Copies and Photo-offset Copies to Originals	12526	0.20	17079	0.31
宅基地使用权	Rights to Housing Site	66066	1.07	87073	1.56
证据保全	Evidence Preservation	19388	0.31	28560	0.51
拆迁协议	Housing Demolition Agreements	124624	2.01	104496	1.87
计划生育	Family Planning	1281153	20.67	1383137	24.74
赡养协议	Agreements on Supporting Parents	46813	0.76	30054	0.54
合伙协议	Partnership Agreements	11248	0.18	7208	0.13
夫妻财产协议	Property Agreements Between Spouses	85282	1.38	94428	1.69
其他民事协议	Other Civil Agreements	593443	9.58	454379	8.13
其他	Others	2756502	44.48	1934104	34.59

22-6 涉外公证文书分类（2000年）

Foreign-Related Notarial Documents by Type (2000)

分 类	Item	办证件数（件） Number of Notarial Documents Issued (pieces)	比 重 (%) Percentage	分 类	Item	办证件数（件） Number of Notarial Documents Issued (pieces)	比 重 (%) Percentage
合 计	**Total**	**2514485**	**100.00**	委托书	Proxy	14578	0.58
收 养	Child Adoption	8803	0.35	营业证书	Shop Card	13523	0.54
遗 嘱	Testaments	1026	0.04	公司章程	Corporation Constitutions	3296	0.13
出 生	Births	396150	15.75	其他法律文书	Other Legal Documents	34111	1.36
死 亡	Deaths	13467	0.54	职 称	Professional Certificates	20876	0.83
生存、居住	Survival and Residence	14362	0.57	法人资格	Legal Person Identification	3351	0.13
学 历	Schooling	282585	11.24	商标注册	Trademark Registrations	1765	0.07
经 历	Personal Histories	66897	2.66	贷 款	Loans	1354	0.05
国 籍	Nationality	34422	1.37	担 保	Guarantees	3384	0.13
婚姻状况	Marital Status	239209	9.51	其他经济合同	Other Business Contracts	20761	0.83
亲属关系	Kinship Confirmation	262172	10.43	副本等与原本相符	Confirmation of Copies and Photo-offset Copies to Originals	331506	13.18
继承权	Rights of Inheritance	3046	0.12	签名印鉴属实	Confirmation of Copies and Photo-offset Copies to Originals	151132	6.01
受、未受刑事处分	Criminal Records	286396	11.39				
声明书	Announcement	39320	1.56	其 他	Other	267002	10.62

22-7 调解民间纠纷分类

Number of Civil Disputes Mediated by Type

项 目	Item	调解纠纷（件） Civil Disputes (cases) 1999	2000	各类纠纷所占比重(%) Percentage 1999	2000
合 计	**Total**	**5188646**	**5030619**	**100.00**	**100.00**
婚姻家庭	Family Disputes	1923175	1951114	37.07	38.78
婚 姻	Marriages	868585	871710	16.74	17.33
继 承	Rights of Inheritance	270751	276601	5.22	5.50
赡抚扶养	Family Fostering	372193	390002	7.17	7.75
其 他	Others	411646	412801	7.93	8.21
房屋、宅基地	Housing and Housing Sites	538843	532656	10.39	10.59
债 务	Debts	480341	451049	9.26	8.97
生产经营	Business	529318	495783	10.20	9.86
邻 里	Neighbor Disputes	764541	740161	14.73	14.71
损害赔偿	Compensation for Damages	387208	364585	7.46	7.25
其 他	Others	565220	495271	10.89	9.85

22-8 劳动争议处理情况(2000年)

项 目	Item	合 计 Total	国 有 企 业 State-owned Enterprises	城镇集体 企 业 Urban Collective-owned Enterprises
上期未结案数 (件)	**Number of Cases Left Over from Last Period (case)**	**6374**	**2435**	**1117**
案件受理情况	**Cases Accepted**			
案件数 (件)	Number of Cases (case)	135206	32715	23203
用人单位申诉案件	Number of Cases Appealed by Units	5985	1887	1162
劳动者申诉案件数	Number of Cases Appealed by Labourers	120043	29613	21683
#集体劳动争议数	Number of Collective labour Disputes	8247	2203	1262
劳动者当事人数 (人)	Number of Persons Involved (person)	422617	108457	65821
#集体争议劳动者当事人数	Number of Persons Involved in Collective Disputes	259445	70942	37482
争议原因 (件)	Cause of the Disputes (case)			
劳动报酬	Labour Remuneration	41671	8105	6422
保险福利	Social Insurance and Welfare	31350	8389	6307
劳动保护	Labour Protecting	13008	2222	2051
职业培训	Occupation Training	834	197	104
变更劳动合同	Change the labour Contract	3829	1195	575
解除劳动合同	Relieve the labour Contract	21149	6305	3167
终止劳动合同	End the labour Contract	10816	3519	1739
其他	Others	12549	2783	2838
本期结案数 (件)	**Number of Cases Settled (case)**	**130688**	**32121**	**22087**
按处理方式分	by Manners of Settlement			
仲裁调解	by Mediation	41877	10445	7660
仲裁裁决	by Arbitrition Lawsuit	54142	15356	9510
其他方式	Others	34669	6320	4917
按处理结果分	by Result of Settlement			
用人单位胜诉	Won by Units	13699	4750	1975
劳动者胜诉	Lawsuit Won by Labourers	70544	15940	12364
双方部分胜诉	Lawsuit Partly by Both Parties	37247	10474	6692
本期未结案数 (件)	**Number of Cases Dissettled (case)**	**10892**	**3029**	**2233**
其他方式调解案件数(件)	**Number of the Arbitrated cases throught Other Forms (case)**	**72399**	**16654**	**15154**
用人单位调解 (件)	**Mediated by Units**			
受理争议案件数	Number of Cases Accepled (case)	31193	21159	6071
调解成功案件数	Number of Cases Successful Mediated (case)	27114	18802	4886

The Disposal of Labor Disputes (2000)

乡村集体企业 Rural Collective Owned Enterprises	外商投资及港澳台投资企业 Foreign Funded and Hong Kong, Macao and Taiwan Chinese Funded Enterprises	私营企业 Private Enterprises	联营及股份制企业 Joint Owned and Share-Holding Enterprises	个体工商户 Individual Economy	机关社团事业单位 State Organs and Institutions	其他 Others
237	**937**	**565**	**511**	**116**	**190**	**266**
3927	20930	20128	14521	4098	4289	11395
165	595	826	821	139	178	212
3965	20326	19138	13655	3892	4058	3983
181	1576	1430	998	161	156	280
13780	88223	54598	40655	8637	8348	34098
9863	63060	36663	22005	3641	2937	12852
1134	7414	7539	3984	1842	933	4298
1384	2727	4375	3273	776	1044	3075
372	2437	3351	1394	707	121	353
2	224	113	152	10	21	11
46	328	291	521	42	64	767
259	4621	2340	2212	297	777	1171
143	1712	725	1281	108	283	1306
587	1467	1394	1704	316	1046	414
3559	**20844**	**19184**	**13783**	**3986**	**4000**	**11124**
1303	4443	7788	4362	1942	1184	2750
1649	6783	5735	5884	1037	1264	6924
607	9618	5661	3537	1007	1552	1450
340	2132	1451	1750	213	668	390
2125	12628	11814	8614	2712	2135	2212
1025	6073	5756	3371	991	1144	1721
605	**1023**	**1509**	**1249**	**228**	**479**	**535**
2071	**10132**	**9971**	**5797**	**2549**	**778**	**9293**
1185	447	251	888	98	126	968
1101	251	212	717	67	81	997

22-9 公安机关立案的刑事案件情况
Criminal Cases Registered in Public Security Organs

案件类别	Category of Cases	立案（起） Number of Cases Registered (case)		构成（%） Composition (%)	
		1999	2000	1999	2000
合计	**Total**	**2249319**	**3637307**	**100.00**	**100.00**
杀人	Homicide	27426	28429	1.22	0.78
伤害	Injury	92772	120778	4.13	3.32
抢劫	Robbery	198607	309818	8.83	8.52
强奸	Rape	39435	35819	1.75	0.98
拐卖妇女儿童	Abducting Women or Children	7257	23163	0.32	0.64
盗窃	Larceny	1447390	2373696	64.35	65.26
诈骗	Fraud	93192	152614	4.14	4.20
走私	Smuggling	1205	1993	0.05	0.05
伪造、变造货币,出售、购买、运输、持有、使用假币	Forging Coin, and Selling, Buying, Transporting, Using the False Coin	10047	15863	0.45	0.44
其他	Others	331988	575134	14.76	15.81

22-10 公安机关受理查处治安案件情况
Offense Cases Against Public Order Handled by Public Security Organs

单位：起 (case)

案件类别	Category of Cases	1999		2000	
		受理 Number of Cases Accepted to be Treated	查处 Number of Cases Investigated and Treated	受理 Number of Cases Accepted to be Treated	查处 Number of Cases Investigated and Treated
合计	**Total**	**3356083**	**3105940**	**4437417**	**3823011**
扰乱工作、公共秩序	Disturbing Work or Public Order	268747	267119	272113	264865
结伙斗殴、寻衅滋事	Gang Fighting or Picking Quarrels and Making Troubles	103178	98808	135930	121290
侮辱妇女及其他流氓活动	Acting Indecently Towards Women	34192	33538	32341	30791
阻碍国家工作人员执行职务	Obstructing the Government Workers to Perform Their Duty	47640	46909	50490	48504
违反枪支管理规定	Violating Regulations on Management of Firearms	24734	24434	26456	26081
违反爆炸物品管理规定	Violating Regulations on Management of Explosives	49304	48832	62819	61410
殴打他人	Beating Other Body	576712	536009	837778	695294
偷窃财物	Robbing Other People of Their Valuables	517277	351066	732633	399436
骗取、抢夺、敲榨勒索财物	Defrauding, Snatching or Extorting and Racketeering Valuables	90494	79449	117594	87948
哄抢公私财物	Making Stirs and Then Robbing Public or Private Valuables	4529	4254	6048	5320
故意损坏公私财物	Intentionally Damaging Public or Private Valuables	54492	51465	82159	66250
伪造倒卖票券、证件	Forging and Fraudulently Selling Bills or Certificates	23075	22863	18131	17911
利用迷信扰乱秩序或骗财	Disturbing Public Order or Defrauding People of Their Valuables by Making Use of Their Superstition	10134	10001	17539	16765
卖淫、嫖娼	Prostitution or Going Whoring	216660	215128	225693	222132
赌博	Gambling	382272	379039	413846	402588
违反户口、居民身份证管理	Violating Regulations on Management of Residence or Identity Cards	306111	305002	561719	557131
其他	Others	646532	632024	844128	799295

22-11 交通事故情况（2000年）

Basic Statistics on Traffic Accidents (2000)

类别	Type	发生数(起) Number of Traffic Accidents (case)	死亡人数(人) Number of Deaths (person)	受伤人数(人) Number of Injuries (person)	损失折款(万元) Losses Coverted into Cash (10 000 yuan)
总计	**Total**	**616971**	**93853**	**418721**	**266890.4**
#重大事故	Extraordinarily Serious	85637	86432	45547	46021.7
特大事故	Serious	3014	7421	8445	23825.3
机动车	Motor-driven Vehicles	577282	81562	388027	262333.8
#汽车	Automobiles	450896	55298	267575	237332.1
摩托车	Motorcycles	80426	16261	82475	11342.8
拖拉机	Tractors	15953	3194	12170	3931
非机动车	Non-motor-driven Vehicles	19677	4563	16053	2054.3
#自行车	Bicycles	15467	3720	12340	1542
行人乘车人	Pedestrians and Passengers	18659	7014	13069	1817.3

注：损失折款指直接损失(下表同)。

a)Losses converted into cash refer to direct losses (the same as in the following table).

22-12 火灾事故情况（2000年）

Basic Statistics on Fires (2000)

项目	Item	合计 Total	按事故发生程度分 By Serious Degree of Fires 特大 Extraordinarily Serious	重大 Serious	一般 Ordinary
发生（起）	Fires (case)	189185	61	384	188740
死亡（人）	Deaths (person)	3021	529	497	1995
受伤（人）	Injuries (person)	4404	191	250	3963
损失折款（万元）	Losses Converted into Cash (10 000 yuan)	152217.3	20013.9	16664.9	115538.5
平均每起事故损失（元）	Average Loss per Fire (yuan)	8046	3280967	433982	6122

22-13 各地区交通事故情况（2000年）

Basic Statistics on Traffic Accidents by Region(2000)

地　区	Region	合计 Total				#城　区 Urban Areas		
		发生数（起） Number of Traffic Accidents (case)	死亡人数（人） Number of Deaths (person)	受伤人数（人） Number of Injuries (person)	损失折款（万元） Losses Coverted into Cash (10000 yuan)	发生数（起） Number of Traffic Accidents (case)	死亡人数（人） Number of Deaths (person)	受伤人数（人） Number of Injuries (person)
全　国	**National Total**	**616971**	**93853**	**418721**	**266890.4**	**385171**	**21232**	**132850**
北　京	Beijing	33057	1470	10963	14272.7	20241	943	3262
天　津	Tianjin	8102	1177	5291	5294.9	924	226	3610
河　北	Hebei	30614	5168	25283	11616.7	8518	1028	6335
山　西	Shanxi	11364	2254	9229	4415.9	3330	419	2489
内蒙古	Inner Mongolia	9526	1882	7331	2540.0	4305	614	2981
辽　宁	Liaoning	18959	3522	10631	9875.0	8803	1052	3905
吉　林	Jilin	13950	2238	7982	4512.8	8440	661	3360
黑龙江	Heilongjiang	12091	2189	10066	4037.4	7332	851	5697
上　海	Shanghai	41219	1494	16117	20377.5	33898	917	12188
江　苏	Jiangsu	50368	7782	29169	23696.9	17256	1359	7480
浙　江	Zhejiang	56938	6044	32051	35910.1	156884	998	7485
安　徽	Anhui	20870	3397	17891	6479.0	7764	676	5479
福　建	Fujian	29987	3855	22606	12833.7	10876	593	6002
江　西	Jiangxi	17105	3223	14006	7065.5	4161	545	2986
山　东	Shandong	47461	7617	37151	15117.2	14373	1604	9374
河　南	Henan	19724	3841	17270	8721.5	7313	868	5833
湖　北	Hubei	20130	3784	16500	7038.2	9575	1037	6642
湖　南	Hunan	20314	3056	18821	8470.5	7248	498	5653
广　东	Guangdong	39527	7333	22800	16382.1	15709	1856	9728
广　西	Guangxi	14000	3389	13951	6100.6	2823	571	2233
海　南	Hainan	1476	263	1219	779.4	845	80	548
重　庆	Chongqing	6851	634	5029	1889.4	3475	187	1863
四　川	Sichuan	33837	5731	27412	11015.9	11550	1140	6828
贵　州	Guizhou	2593	1251	1725	1899.6	880	256	375
云　南	Yunnan	16842	2694	9004	8661.1	4271	304	1252
西　藏	Tibet	980	360	773	709.3	322	165	351
陕　西	Shaanxi	11391	2264	8486	3853.5	4549	510	3012
甘　肃	Gansu	10484	2044	6902	2953.6	3030	342	1646
青　海	Qinghai	1534	584	1361	642.7	448	114	351
宁　夏	Ningxia	6163	887	4075	1865.6	2243	172	1188
新　疆	Xinjiang	9514	2425	7624	4262.1	3785	646	2711

注：损失折款指直接损失。

a)Losses converted into cash refer to direct losses.

22-14 36个大中城市交通事故情况（2000年）

Basic Statistics on Traffic Accidents in 36 Major Cities(2000)

城市	City	合计 Total 发生数（起）Number of Traffic Accidents (case)	死亡人数（人）Number of Deaths (person)	受伤人数（人）Number of Injuries (person)	损失折款（万元）Losses Coverted into Cash (10 000yuan)	#城区 Urban Areas 发生数（起）Number of Traffic Accidents (case)	死亡人数（人）Number of Deaths (person)	受伤人数（人）Number of Injuries (person)
合　计	**Total**	**207659**	**20480**	**109396**	**91133.6**	**123173**	**7851**	**55060**
北　京	Beijing	33057	1470	10963	14272.7	20241	943	3262
上　海	Shanghai	41219	1494	16117	20377.5	33898	917	12188
天　津	Tianjin	8102	1177	5291	5294.9	924	226	3610
南　京	Nanjing	5803	527	1553	4396.2	3477	188	646
杭　州	Hangzhou	9742	847	5971	6299.8	4072	241	2334
合　肥	Hefei	3349	352	2181	971.9	2394	120	1361
南　昌	Nanchang	1984	321	1416	641.9	1111	139	636
福　州	Fuzhou	6733	685	4100	2994.5	3903	159	1871
济　南	Jinan	1150	352	840	328.6	493	106	389
徐　州	Xuzhou	2699	709	2436	1150.4	659	99	546
青　岛	Qingdao	14220	1277	7815	4517.7	4135	122	1150
石家庄	Shijiazhuang	3748	612	2658	998.5	1442	140	830
太　原	Taiyuan	2214	256	1792	730.7	1523	172	1230
包　头	Baotou	2006	170	1259	223.8	1623	114	1020
沈　阳	Shenyang	5875	703	3353	2745.4	2839	199	1475
长　春	Changchun	7173	756	3128	2338.3	5418	390	1544
哈尔滨	Harbin	2701	536	2227	1475.5	1569	210	1243
大　连	Dalian	4369	645	940	3425.0	2626	274	222
鞍　山	Anshan	667	192	402	211.0	222	53	91
广　州	Guangzhou	8414	1221	4570	3868.7	4156	421	2386
南　宁	Nanning	906	340	952	419.0	232	79	196
长　沙	Changsha	4626	256	3585	886.1	3373	116	2409
武　汉	Wuhan	5351	669	3226	1926.9	4168	348	2394
郑　州	Zhengzhou	3662	418	3179	1614.2	1943	113	1650
成　都	Chengdu	4865	1193	4171	1338.7	2385	445	2189
重　庆	Chongqing	6851	634	5029	1889.4	3475	187	1863
渡　口	Dukou	561	70	841	117.1	358	37	523
西　安	Xi'an	4061	587	2851	1109.3	3083	341	1948
兰　州	Lanzhou	3143	434	1744	1233.8	2310	196	1175
银　川	Yinchuan	2452	179	1176	577.0	1532	88	591
昆　明	Kunming	1468	358	597	1140.7	676	169	248
贵　阳	Guiyang	921	253	452	819.8	597	127	236
呼和浩特	Hohhot	1021	245	754	316.0	435	73	258
西　宁	Xining	511	208	373	148.7	246	87	213
乌鲁木齐	Urumqi	1768	274	1368	413.1	1433	187	1071
拉　萨	Lhasa	268	60	86	102.7	202	25	62

注：损失折款指直接损失。

a)Losses converted into cash refer to direct losses.

22-15 各地区火灾事故情况（2000年）

Basic Statistics on Fires by Region (2000)

地 区	Region	发生数（起）Number of Traffic Accidents (case)	死亡人数（人）Number of Deaths (person)	受伤人数（人）Number of Injuries (person)	直接经济损失（万元）Losses Coverted into Cash (10 000 yuan)	人口火灾发生率（1/10万人）Average Number of Fires per 100 Thousand People
全 国	**National Total**	**189185**	**3021**	**4404**	**152217.3**	**15.4**
北 京	Beijing	6875	41	106	2355.4	62.1
天 津	Tianjin	7519	43	46	1683.7	82.1
河 北	Hebei	7627	102	177	5174.6	11.6
山 西	Shanxi	2844	45	65	4737.6	9.0
内蒙古	Inner Mongolia	2022	25	59	1395.4	8.7
辽 宁	Liaoning	14836	138	229	8083.3	36.2
吉 林	Jilin	13420	95	94	4581.1	51.3
黑龙江	Heilongjiang	9498	95	148	6928.5	25.9
上 海	Shanghai	5164	40	57	1944.3	39.3
江 苏	Jiangsu	11156	164	356	9482.3	15.9
浙 江	Zhejiang	14207	167	273	16266.3	31.8
安 徽	Anhui	6099	79	148	6819.4	9.8
福 建	Fujian	3839	99	175	6923.4	11.7
江 西	Jiangxi	5317	92	137	4267.0	12.9
山 东	Shandong	18783	215	313	9372.7	21.1
河 南	Henan	10050	523	302	8281.4	10.6
湖 北	Hubei	6780	54	106	3933.7	11.4
湖 南	Hunan	3440	102	165	5227.2	5.3
广 东	Guangdong	8622	261	386	12980.5	11.8
广 西	Guangxi	3189	102	181	4083.5	6.8
海 南	Hainan	591	7	24	547.1	8.0
重 庆	Chongqing	3712	56	116	2718.2	12.1
四 川	Sichuan	5718	102	243	4410.1	6.8
贵 州	Guizhou	1606	68	97	3256.2	4.5
云 南	Yunnan	2890	107	132	6223.3	7.2
西 藏	Tibet	122	15	8	314.7	4.9
陕 西	Shaanxi	3818	77	60	3852.7	10.8
甘 肃	Gansu	2212	25	57	2555.6	8.8
青 海	Qinghai	670	9	10	479.3	14.2
宁 夏	Ningxia	2893	16	35	966.5	53.2
新 疆	Xinjiang	3666	57	99	2372.2	20.8

注：全国总计数据包括发生在铁道、交通、军队的火灾情况。

a)The national data include the fires which happen in railways and other transport process.

22-16 全国检察机关直接立案侦查案件情况（2000年）

Cases under Direct Investigation by Procurator's Offices(2000)

案件分类	Case Item	受案(件) Cases Accepted (Case)	立案合计 Total Number of Cases Registered		#大案(件) Large Cases (Case)	#要案(人) Key Cases (Person)	结案合计 Total Number of Cases Settled	
			件 (Case)	人 (Person)			件 (Case)	人 (Person)
合计	**Total**	**104427**	**45113**	**50784**	**18284**	**2872**	**40770**	**45720**
贪污贿赂案件小计	**Sub-total of Cases on Corruption and Bribery**	**83461**	**37183**	**41377**	**16121**	**2556**	**34085**	**37868**
贪污	Corruption	44874	16765	19428	6736	683	15129	17553
贿赂	Bribery	20771	9872	10367	3658	1279	9082	9530
挪用公款	Misappropriation of Public Funds	14958	10170	11068	5623	540	9472	10258
集体私分	Collective Illegal Possession of Public Funds	901	277	393	70	43	257	365
巨额财产来源不明	Unstated Source of Large Properties	281	30	32	23	8	30	30
其他	Others	1676	69	89	11	3	115	132
渎职案件小计	**Sub-total of Cases on Abuse and Dereliction of Duty**	**20966**	**7930**	**9407**	**2163**	**316**	**6685**	**7852**
滥用职权	Abuse of Power	3808	1620	1788	524	83	1347	1456
玩忽职守	Dereliction of Duty	4497	2625	2914	1044	188	2213	2440
徇私舞弊	Fraudulent Practice	6593	1791	2048	318	33	1492	1678
其他	Others	6068	1894	2657	277	12	1633	2278

22-17 全国检察机关审查批准、决定逮捕犯罪嫌疑人和提起公诉被告人情况（2000年）

Arrests of Criminal Suspects and Defendants Under Public Prosecution Approved by Procurator's Offices (2000)

案件分类	Item	批捕、决定逮捕合计 Total of Arrests		决定起诉合计 Total of Public Prosecutions	
		件 (Case)	人 (Person)	件 (Case)	人 (Person)
合计	**Total**	**473864**	**715833**	**480119**	**708836**
公安、安全、监狱机关提请小计	**Sub-total of Requests by Departments of State and Public Security and Prisons**	**456084**	**696265**	**456376**	**681254**
危害国家安全案	Offences Against State Security	313	690	270	683
危害公共安全案	Offences Against Public Security	31427	38182	39249	45022
破坏社会主义市场经济秩序案	Offences Against Socialist Economic Order	17375	27666	15401	25257
侵犯公民人身、民主权利案	Offences Against Citizens' Personal and Democratic Rights	116268	153875	119130	153107
侵犯财产案	Offences Against Properties	230110	374098	224415	361964
妨害社会管理秩序案	Offences Against Social Management of Order	60451	101512	57754	94947
危害国防利益案	Offences Against National Defense	132	234	148	262
军人违反职责案	Offences on Dereliction of Duty by Servicemen	8	8	9	12
检察机关直接立案侦查案件小计	**Sub-total of Cases Handled by Procuratorates**	**17780**	**19568**	**23743**	**27582**
贪污贿赂案	Offences on Corruption and Bribery	16522	18055	21585	24854
渎职案	Offences on Abuse and Dereliction of Duty	1258	1513	2158	2728

22-18 全国检察机关处理申诉案件情况（2000年）

Appeals Handled by Procurator's Offices (2000)

单位：件次 (case)

案件分类	Item	受理 Cases Accepted	立案复查 Cases Registered for Reinvestigation	结案 Cases Settled	#改变原决定 Original Decision Changed
合计	**Total**	**148343**	**9674**	**4831**	**760**
不服刑事拘留	Appeals Against Criminal Detention	2599	52	33	8
不服不立案	Appeals Against Rejection of the Case	7080	1371	699	212
不服逮捕	Appeals Against Arrest	3940	230	136	21
不服不批捕	Appeals Against Rejection of Arrest	3263	849	542	34
不服不起诉	Appeals Against Rejection of Prosecute	4294	1503	742	93
不服撤案	Appeals Against Withdrawal of the Case	1126	225	130	23
不服原免于起诉	Appeals Against Original Exemption of Lawsuit	2336	403	239	69
不服刑事判决	Appeals Against Judgment of Criminal Case	29469	1563	706	32
不服劳教	Appeals Against Judgment of Reeducation Through Labor	820	13	8	1
其他	Others	93416	3465	1596	267

22-19 人民法院刑事一审案件收结案情况（2000年）

First Trial Criminal Cases Accepted and Settled by Courts(2000)

单位：件 (case)

项 目	Item	收 案 Cases Accepted	结 案 Cases Settled
合 计	**Total**	**560432**	**560111**
危害公共安全罪	Offences Against Public Security	40119	39988
破坏社会主义市场经济秩序罪	Offences Against Socialist Economic Order	17023	16940
侵犯公民人身权利民主权利罪	Offences Against Citizens' Personal and Democratic Rights	187331	187416
侵犯财产罪	Offences Against Properties	321169	231397
妨害社会管理秩序罪	Offences Against Social Management of Order	61452	61236
危害国防利益罪	Offences Against National Defense	116	116
贪污贿赂罪	Offences on Corruption and Bribery	21431	21249
渎职罪	Offences on Dereliction of Duty	1473	1445
其他	Others	318	324
合计中含自诉案件	Private Prosecution of Total	58976	58318

注：结案中含上年旧存。

Note: Cases settled include cases turned over from the previous year.

22-20 人民法院审理一审案件情况

First Trial Cases by Courts

单位：件　　　　　　　　　　　　　　　　　　　　　　　　　　　　　　(case)

年份 Year	收案 Cases Accepted	刑事 Criminal	民事 Civil	经济纠纷 Economic Disputes	行政 Administrative	海事海商 Maritime Law and Affairs
1978	447755	146968	300787			
1979	513789	123846	389943			
1980	763535	197856	565679			
1981	906051	232125	673926			
1982	1024160	245219	778941			
1983	1343164	542648	756436	43553	527	
1984	1355460	431357	838307	84813	983	
1985	1319741	246655	846391	225541	916	238
1986	1611282	299720	989409	321220	632	301
1987	1875229	289614	1213219	366110	5940	346
1988	2290624	313306	1455130	513046	8573	569
1989	2913515	392564	1815385	694907	9934	725
1990	2916774	459656	1851897	591462	13006	753
1991	2901685	427840	1880635	566592	25667	951
1992	3051157	422991	1948786	650601	27125	1654
1993	3414845	403267	2089257	892580	27911	1830
1994	3955475	482927	2383764	1051742	35083	1959
1995	4545676	495741	2718533	1275959	52596	2847
1996	5312580	618826	3093995	1515848	79966	3945
1997	5288379	436894	3277572	1478822	90557	4534
1998	5410798	482164	3375069	1450049	98350	5166
1999	5692434	540008	3519244	1529877	97569	5736
2000	5356294	560432	3412259	1290867	85760	6976

注：一审案件指人民法院按照诉讼级别管辖按第一审程序审理的案件。历年经济纠纷数据未包括海事海商案件数。

Note: First trial cases refer to cases accepted by people's courts according to the first trial proceedings. Cases concerning maritime law and affairs over the years were not included in the cases of economic disputes.

22-21 人民法院刑事案件中青少年犯罪情况

Juvenile Delinquency Among Criminal Cases

单位：人　　　　　　　　　　　　　　　　　　　　　　　　　　　　　　(case)

年份 Year	刑事罪犯总数 Offenders	# 青少年罪犯 Young Offenders	不满18岁 Less Than 18	18岁至25岁 Between 18 to 25	青少年罪犯占刑事罪犯% Proportion to Total
1997	526312	199212	30446	168766	37.9
1998	528301	208076	33612	174464	39.4
1999	602380	221153	40014	181139	36.7
2000	639814	220981	41709	179272	34.5

22-22 人民法院民事一审案件收结案情况（2000年）

First Trial Civil Cases Accepted and Settled by Courts(2000)

单位：件 (case)

项 目	Item	收案 Cases Accepted	结案 Cases Settled	调解 Mediation	判决 Judgement	驳回 Reject	撤诉 With-drawal	其他 Other
合 计	**Total**	**3412259**	**3418481**	**1336002**	**1328510**	**31914**	**669166**	**52889**
婚姻家庭	Marriages and Family Affairs	1347027	1347808	627061	451732	5207	253795	10013
继承	Inheritance	14114	14244	4082	7112	142	2659	249
房屋	Housing	165799	166225	34194	80713	4156	44643	2519
土地等不动产	Real Estates(Land etc)	31376	31368	7260	13933	1527	7966	682
相邻关系	Neighbourhood Affairs	27775	27598	6249	13026	672	7373	278
赔偿	Compensation	387069	388168	117255	199906	5049	61060	4898
债	Debts	1322658	1327763	510062	512943	12473	264524	27761
知识产权	Intellectual Rights	1496	1534	243	685	55	452	99
人身权	Personal Rights	11763	11596	2219	5857	316	2932	272
特别程序	Special Proceedings	3184	2987	_	1893	_	327	767
其他	Others	99998	99190	27377	40710	2317	23435	5351

注：结案中含上年旧存。

Note: Cases settled include cases turned over from the previous year.

22-23 人民法院经济纠纷一审案件收结案情况（2000年）

First Trial Cases of Economic Disputes Accepted and Settled by Courts(2000)

单位：件 (case)

项 目	Item	收案 Cases Accepted	结案 Cases Settled	调解 Mediation	判决 Judgement	驳回 Reject	撤诉 With-drawal	其他 Other
合 计	**Total**	**1297843**	**1315405**	**449558**	**524928**	**17676**	**273905**	**49338**
经济合同	Economic Contracts	1184613	1203410	416039	484959	15518	248859	38035
损害赔偿	Compensation for Damages	4491	4428	704	2081	147	1205	291
经济权属	Economic Rights	797	758	167	335	20	176	60
企业破产	Bankruptcy of Enterprises	7219	5255	188	217	119	173	4558
铁路运输	Railway Transport	1352	1329	391	491	47	361	39
航空运输	Aviation Transport	488	479	135	192	26	107	19
公路运输	Highway Transport	4194	4222	1275	1872	78	880	117
水路运输	Waterway Transport	334	329	127	127	3	58	14
海事海商	Maritime Affairs	6645	6995	1784	2494	89	1187	1441
其 他	Other	87710	88200	28748	32160	1629	20899	4764

注：结案中含上年旧存。

Note: Cases settled include cases turned over from the previous year.

22-24 人民法院行政一审案件收结案情况（2000年）

First Trial Administrative Cases Accepted and Settled by Courts(2000)

单位：件 (case)

项 目	Item	收 案 Cases Accepted	结 案 Cases Settled	维 持 Affirmation of Original Judgement	撤 消 Cancel Lation	驳 回 Reject	撤 诉 With-drawal	单独赔偿 Separate Compen-sation	其 他 Other
合计	**Total**	**85760**	**86614**	**13431**	**13635**	**11146**	**31822**	**2502**	**14078**
土地	Land	13357	13640	2643	2938	1858	3834	275	2092
公安	Public Security	13173	13173	2940	1879	1520	4792	680	1362
城建	City Construction	8184	8234	1743	1429	890	2914	201	1057
交通运输	Traffic and Transportation	2658	2650	325	228	211	1144	104	638
工商	Industry and Commerce	2897	2858	472	401	316	1196	105	368
环保	Environment Protection	909	1040	91	31	185	484	6	243
林业	Forest	1738	1757	340	473	111	688	45	100
税务	Tax	2055	2025	157	183	164	1200	54	267
卫生	Health	1144	1182	160	212	191	419	48	152
其他	Other	39645	40055	4560	5861	5700	15151	984	7799

注：结案中含上年旧存。

Note: Cases settled include cases turned over from the previous year.

22-25 社会福利事业、企业单位和工作人员数

Number of Social Welfare Institutions and Enterprises and Persons Engaged

项 目	Item	机 构（个） Number of Institutions or Enterprises 1999	2000	工 作 人 员（人） Number of Persons Engaged (person) 1999	2000
全 国 总 计	**National Total**	**99569**	**101222**	**2139268**	**2033808**
收养性福利事业单位	Adopting Social Welfare Institutions	40430	40491	196757	193166
国家办	Run by Governments	2561	2816	68902	69253
集体	Run by Communities	37419	37295	125651	119547
民办		453	380	2204	4366
社会福利企业	Social Welfare Enterprises	44628	40670	1802165	1658359
国有	Run by Governments	1486	2726	118260	142295
集体	Run by Communities	43142	28854	1683905	1235211
其他			9090		280853
优抚事业单位	Administration Agencies for Martyrs	2538	2646	29452	29887
收容遣送单位	Collecting and Repatriation Units	745	857	12487	18450
殡葬事业单位	Funeral and Interment Institutions	2344	2521	42512	46244
募捐单位	Collecting Purse Units	1261	1363	4295	5472
社区服务单位	Community Service Institutions	7623	12674	51600	82230

22-26 收养收容类社会福利事业单位基本情况（2000年）

Basic Statistics on Social Welfare Institutions (2000)

项　目	Item	院　数（个）Number of Homes (unit)	工作人员（人）Number of Staff and Workers	床　位（张）Number of Beds	年末收养收容人数（人）Number of Persons Housed (year-end)
全国总计	**Total Social Welfare Institutions**	**41348**	**211616**	**1191543**	**884816**
收养类福利事业单位	**Adopting Social Welfare Institutions**	**40491**	**193166**	**1130407**	**854304**
国家办	Run by Government	2816	69253	221152	171685
集体办	Run by Collective Units	37295	119547	878315	663168
民　办	Run by Private Units	380	4366	30940	19451
优抚休、疗养院	Convalescent Homes	127	14284	22117	15089
光荣院	Homes for Disabled Veterans	1332	9592	43202	30453
社会福利院	Social Welfare Homes	1175	26539	109582	86739
儿童福利院	Baby Welfare Homes	126	5030	18284	18039
精神病福利院	Psychopathy Welfare Homes	130	12371	27883	22782
城镇老年性福利机构	Urban Elderly Welfare Units	11182	46782	327902	240286
农村老年性福利机构	Rural Elderly Welfare Units	25576	74124	555782	428108
其他收养机构	Other Adopting Units	843	4444	25655	18208
收容类福利事业单位		**857**	**18450**	**61136**	**30512**

22-27 社会福利救济主要费用情况

Basic Statistics on Social Welfare Relief Funds

单位：万元　　(10 000 yuan)

项　目	Item	1996	1997	1998	1999	2000
全国总计	**National Total**	**930792**	**1077496**	**1180121**	**1430062**	**1680327**
国家支出	Government Funds	411864	461710	496573	727024	880349
集体供给	Collective Funds	518928	615786	683548	703038	799978
优抚对象补助金额	Funds for Family Members of Martyrs and Disabled Veterans	518797	615411	680148	914443	1076605
国家支出	Government Funds	266998	293670	323735	511444	607550
集体供给	Collective Funds	251799	321741	356413	402999	469055
农村困难户得救济金额		71227	75088	88177	89316	97143
国家支出	Government Funds	36707	36127	41092	62626	68037
集体供给	Collective Funds	34520	38961	47085	26690	29106
农村散居孤老残幼供养	Funds for Orphans, Disabled, Elderly and Young Persons in Society	185668	196951	209341	195737	219917
国家支出	Government Funds	25393	26545	28702	16091	15163
集体供给	Collective Funds	160275	170406	180639	179646	204754
城乡各种福利院支出	Funds for Urban and Rural Welfare Homes of All Types	155100	190046	202455	230566	286662
国家支出	Government Funds	68162	89402	87824	118659	189599
集体供给	Collective Funds	71221	83549	98375	92429	97063
#光荣院	Homes for the Disabled Veterans	15717	17095	16257	19478	21882
国家支出	Government Funds	14604	15966	15220	18204	20561
集体供给	Collective Funds	1113	1129	1037	1274	1321

22-28 享受补助、救济人员情况

Persons Receiving Subsidies or Relief Funds

单位：万人、万户 (10 000 persons 10 000 households)

项目	Item	1996	1997	1998	1999	2000
城乡居民最低生活保障人数	**Number of Persons Receiving Lowest Cost-of-living in Urban Area and Rural Area**			**184.1**	**531.7**	**702.8**
城镇居民最低生活保障人数	Number of Persons Receiving Lowest Cost-of-living in Urban Area				265.9	402.6
农村居民最低生活保障人数	Number of Persons Receiving Lowest Cost-of-living in Rural Area				265.8	300.2
传统救济情况	**Traditional Relief**					
农村贫困户得到临时救济人数	Number of Rural Poor Persons Receiving Temporary Almsgiving	3079.2	2602.2	2691.7	1659.8	1667.6
农村散居五保户人数	Number of Persons in Rural Households with Livelihood Guaranteed in Five Aspects	267.5	279.1	282.8	303.7	270.6
#得到国家定期定量救济人数	Number of Persons Receiving Periodical and Fixed Government Relief Funds	25.6	21.8	21.7	52.5	62.5
#得到集体给予补助人数	Number of Persons Receiving Collective Subsidies	213.0	200.3	200.9	195.4	208.1
城镇困难户得到临时救济人次数	Number of Urban Poor Persons Receiving Temporary Almsgiving	261.1	268.3	332.2	157.1	155.6
#得到国家定期定量救济人数	Number of Persons Receiving Periodical and Fixed Government Relief Funds	20.0	14.0	16.4	23.2	22.3
精减退职老弱残职工得到救济人数	Number of Laid-Off, Retired, Elderly and Disabled Staff and Workers Receiving Relief Funds	53.5	53.1	54.9	51.5	49.7
享受原工资40%救济人数	Persons Receiving 40% of Their Original Wages	23.6	23.3	24.9	22.5	22.1
享受定期定量救济人数	Persons Receiving Periodical and Fixed Government Relief Funds	29.9	29.8	29.9	28.7	27.6

22-29 社会福利企业基本情况

Basic Statistics on Social Welfare Enterprises

年份 Year	国有和集体 State-owned and Collective-owned			其他 Other		
	单位（个）Number of Units (unit)	职工（人）Number of Staff and Workers (person)	#残疾职工 Disabled Persons	单位（个）Number of Units (unit)	职工（人）Number of Staff and Workers (person)	#残疾职工 Disabled Persons
1985	2214	219189	83051	12554	448829	151250
1986	2551	236371	89421	17211	637747	225708
1987	2976	250329	96605	24714	875974	337944
1988	3692	282947	106095	36701	1180589	875974
1989	4595	310345	119626	36864	1192179	494182
1990	5208	325461	124630	36517	1245072	512941
1991	6329	352112	136183	37889	1342064	565139
1992	6798	373412	142473	42985	1528266	635700
1993	7232	390619	147211	49649	1672141	695046
1994	7373	382519	151523	52805	1800262	757307
1995	7734	368636	148551	52503	1845838	790671
1996	7364	355864	141831	52033	1811820	794003
1997	8024	351354	141778	47485	1747143	767980
1998	7527	322522	133389	42987	1630654	722656
1999	7819	207271	132330	36809	1594894	657955
2000	31580	1377506	605592	9090	280853	123899

注：2000年的统计口径有变化。1999年以前的国有和集体办仅指民政系统办的福利企业，2000年是指全社会范围国有和集体办的福利企业。

a) The statistical coverage in 2000 have been adjusted. The state-owned and collective-owned social welfare enterprises before 2000 refer to those managed by the system of civil administration, and those in 2000 refer to all state-owned and collective-owned social welfare enterprises.

22-30 各地区城镇社区服务设施和农村社会保障网络基本情况（2000年）

Basic Statistics on Urban Welfare Facilities and Rural Social Security Network (2000)

单位：个 (unit)

地区	Region	城镇社区服务设施数 Number of Urban Welfare Facilities	#社区服务单位个数 Number of Community Service	城镇便民、利民服务网点 Number of Urban Service Points for Civilian	农村社会保障网络数 Rural Social Security Network
全国	**National Total**	**181444**	**12674**	**451567**	**18855**
北京	Beijing	813	198	8857	118
天津	Tianjin	1922	89	7933	61
河北	Hebei	10559	1340	18923	992
山西	Shanxi	1392	56	5148	399
内蒙古	Inner Mongolia	3817	819	18524	465
辽宁	Liaoning	6144	847	43693	846
吉林	Jilin	11016	1451	18318	852
黑龙江	Heilongjiang	11246	274	38979	803
上海	Shanghai	14614	92	16508	164
江苏	Jiangsu	18065	794	42503	1351
浙江	Zhejiang	20696	143	38052	808
安徽	Anhui	7868	695	17334	660
福建	Fujian	3453	95	10215	730
江西	Jiangxi	1066	263	4107	518
山东	Shandong	9413	349	28797	1943
河南	Henan	2367	186	8170	1892
湖北	Hubei	9026	175	12629	918
湖南	Hunan	9533	1246	25219	548
广东	Guangdong	4983	787	11337	1536
广西	Guangxi	1262	419	2441	479
海南	Hainan	1121	347	1850	
重庆	Chongqing	1739	20	3401	280
四川	Sichuan	6818	1140	21144	1299
贵州	Guizhou	3450	45	8179	20
云南	Yunnan	148	11	1448	77
西藏	Tibet	10	10	28	
陕西	Shaanxi	9682	485	18551	510
甘肃	Gansu	2852	39	12874	365
青海	Qinghai	943		976	75
宁夏	Ningxia	4212	170	1973	97
新疆	Xinjiang	1214	89	3456	49

22-31 分地区离休、退休、退职人员年底人数（2000年）

Number of Retired and Resigned Persons by Region at the Year-end (2000)

单位：万人 (10 000 persons)

地区	Region	总计 Total				#企业 Enterprises			
		合计 Total	离休人员 Retired Veterans	退休人员 Retired Persons	退职人员 Resigned Persons	合计 Total	离休人员 Retired Veterans	退休人员 Retired Persons	退职人员 Resigned Persons
全国	**National Total**	**3875.8**	**169.7**	**3621.0**	**85.1**	**2977.9**	**86.7**	**2821.6**	**69.7**
北京	Beijing	179.6	9.9	164.2	5.5	140.7	4.5	131.2	5.0
天津	Tianjin	92.9	2.5	88.5	1.9	77.7	1.3	74.8	1.6
河北	Hebei	150.9	10.0	138.6	2.4	111.9	4.3	105.6	2.0
山西	Shanxi	100.3	7.4	91.5	1.4	79.5	3.9	74.6	1.1
内蒙古	Inner Mongolia	75.8	3.5	71.3	1.1	53.1	1.5	50.7	0.9
辽宁	Liaoning	299.7	13.9	278.5	7.3	254.0	8.1	239.3	6.6
吉林	Jilin	113.4	6.3	105.2	2.0	89.3	3.3	84.4	1.6
黑龙江	Heilongjiang	186.7	10.4	171.5	4.8	156.8	6.1	146.4	4.3
上海	Shanghai	234.7	3.8	227.9	3.1	202.7	2.0	197.8	2.9
江苏	Jiangsu	247.4	9.0	230.4	8.0	195.4	4.1	184.5	6.8
浙江	Zhejiang	131.8	3.8	124.1	3.9	100.1	1.6	95.5	3.0
安徽	Anhui	122.7	6.3	113.8	2.6	91.0	3.0	85.9	2.2
福建	Fujian	71.0	2.5	67.0	1.5	48.5	0.9	46.5	1.0
江西	Jiangxi	84.9	2.6	81.2	1.1	62.0	1.2	59.9	0.9
山东	Shandong	182.3	14.9	160.7	6.7	135.2	6.7	124.3	4.3
河南	Henan	175.8	11.7	161.4	2.6	127.5	5.2	120.1	2.3
湖北	Hubei	175.6	5.7	166.8	3.0	136.4	3.1	130.9	2.4
湖南	Hunan	154.3	4.0	147.7	2.5	109.5	2.1	105.3	2.1
广东	Guangdong	197.7	6.6	188.9	2.3	148.0	3.2	143.1	1.7
广西	Guangxi	76.8	2.0	73.5	1.3	51.0	0.9	49.1	1.0
海南	Hainan	29.7	0.8	26.9	2.0	24.5	0.4	22.1	1.9
重庆	Chongqing	93.1	1.6	89.6	1.9	71.9	0.8	69.4	1.7
四川	Sichuan	202.1	4.8	193.6	3.7	146.9	2.8	141.2	2.9
贵州	Guizhou	62.6	2.3	59.7	0.7	41.4	1.0	39.9	0.5
云南	Yunnan	89.3	3.6	84.4	1.3	60.1	1.5	57.7	0.9
西藏	Tibet	4.1	0.1	4.0	...	1.9	...	1.9	...
陕西	Shaanxi	96.8	5.2	89.1	2.4	72.1	2.6	67.9	1.6
甘肃	Gansu	58.9	2.8	54.6	1.5	43.3	1.5	40.8	0.9
青海	Qinghai	20.1	0.8	18.6	0.6	12.9	0.3	12.3	0.3
宁夏	Ningxia	18.2	1.2	16.4	0.6	12.7	0.5	11.8	0.3
新疆	Xinjiang	143.2	9.8	128.0	5.4	119.9	8.1	106.7	5.0

22-32 离休、退休、退职费

Pensions for Retired and Resigned Persons

年 份 Year	费用总额(亿元) Total Pensions (100 million yuan)	民政部门支付 Paid by Civil Affairs Departments	总后事业单位支付 Paid by Units Under the General Logistics Departments of PLA	国有单位 Funds of State-Owned Units	单位支付 Paid by Employer Units	城镇集体单位 Funds of Urban Collective Owned Units	其他单位 Funds of Other Ownership Units	平均每人(元) Per Capita Funds (yuan)	#国有单位 State-Owned Units
绝对数 Absolute Figure									
1980	50.4	3.3		43.4	40.1	7.0		714	781
1981	62.3	3.3		53.3	50.0	9.0		706	774
1982	73.1	3.2		62.1	58.9	11.0		709	774
1983	87.3	3.2		74.0	70.8	13.3		726	787
1984	106.1	3.0		84.6	81.6	21.2	0.3	766	815
1985	145.6	3.7		116.1	112.4	29.1	0.4	935	1043
1986	172.2	3.3		140.6	137.3	31.0	0.6	1001	1139
1987	208.1	4.0		171.9	167.9	35.3	0.8	1103	1261
1988	275.1	6.6		220.5	213.9	53.2	1.4	1346	1486
1989	319.4	7.5		258.9	251.4	59.1	1.4	1478	1632
1990	396.2	7.2		319.7	312.5	74.7	1.8	1760	1907
1991	467.5	7.6		380.7	373.1	84.5	2.3	1975	2141
1992	578.5	9.2		474.3	465.1	100.8	3.4	2300	2493
1993	759.3	12.0		623.2	611.2	123.9	12.2	2824	3029
1994	1043.6	17.5		875.9	858.4	146.2	21.5	3656	3989
1995	1305.6	19.4		1093.1	1073.7	182.4	30.1	4335	4701
1996	1552.2	20.1		1308.2	1288.1	204.0	40.0	4923	5321
1997	1790.8	22.7	1.9	1517.6	1493.0	225.2	48.0	5458	5890
1998	2073.7	26.1	3.6	1726.0	1696.3	229.0	114.8	5972	6369
1999	2420.9	29.6	3.1					6614	
2000	2733.3	36.4	3.4					7190	
比上年增长(%) Increase over Preceding Year (%)									
1981	23.6			22.8	24.7	28.6		-1.1	-0.9
1982	17.3	-3.0		16.5	17.8	22.2		0.4	
1983	19.4			19.2	20.2	20.9		2.4	1.7
1984	21.5	-6.3		14.3	15.3	59.4		5.5	3.6
1985	37.2	23.3		37.2	37.7	37.3	33.3	22.1	8.0
1986	18.3	-10.8		21.1	22.2	6.5	50.0	7.1	9.2
1987	20.8	21.2		22.3	22.3	13.9	33.3	10.2	0.7
1988	32.2	65.0		28.3	27.4	50.7	75.0	22.0	17.8
1989	16.1	13.6		17.4	17.5	11.1		9.8	9.8
1990	24.0	-4.0		23.5	24.3	26.4	28.6	19.1	16.9
1991	18.0	5.6		19.1	19.4	13.1	27.8	12.2	12.3
1992	23.7	21.1		24.6	24.7	19.3	47.8	16.5	16.4
1993	31.3	30.4		31.4	31.4	22.9	258.8	22.8	21.5
1994	37.4	45.8		40.5	40.4	18.0	76.2	29.5	31.7
1995	25.1	10.9		24.8	25.1	24.8	40.0	18.6	17.8
1996	18.9	3.6		19.7	20.0	11.8	32.9	13.6	13.2
1997	15.4	12.9		16.0	15.9	10.4	20.0	10.9	10.7
1998	15.8	15.0	89.5	13.7	13.6	1.7	139.2	9.4	8.1
1999	16.7	13.4	-13.9					10.8	
2000	12.9	23.0	9.7					8.7	

注：1.本表数字不包括离休、退休、退职职工的医疗卫生费。

2.本表1985—1988年的数字不包括根据1985年有关规定发给离休、退休、退职职工的肉类等价格补贴。

a)Figures in this table exclude medical expenditures of retired and resigned workers and staff.

b)Figures of 1985-1988 in this table exclude subsidies on meat, etc. delivered to retired and resigned workers and staff in accordance with relevant regulations issued in 1985.

22-33 历年全国离休、退休、退职人员保险福利费用构成情况

Historic Figures of Total Social Insurance and Welfare Fund of Retirees

年　份 Year	合　计 Total	离休金 Pensions for Termination	退休金 Retirement Pensions	退职生活费 Resignation Allowances for Living Expenses	医　疗 卫生费 Medical Care Expenses	其　他 Others
一、绝对数（亿元） **Absolute Figure (100 million yuan)**						
1990	465.2	34.6	239.4	5.0	76.2	110.0
1991	554.4	38.6	271.5	5.7	94.5	144.1
1992	685.6	47.1	338.8	6.7	116.3	176.7
1993	901.7	57.1	435.5	8.6	154.3	246.2
1994	1218.9	103.2	766.5	12.4	192.8	144.0
1995	1522.4	121.9	986.3	15.3	236.3	162.6
1996	1797.7	137.7	1199.3	17.1	265.6	178.0
1997	2043.8	162.6	1423.9	23.5	277.6	156.2
1998	2330.9	167.7	1708.5	24.1	286.9	143.7
1999	2708.3	186.1	2035.2	27.2	320.1	139.7
2000	3040.5	201.1	2305.7	30.3	346.9	156.5
二、比上年增长（%） **Increase over Preceding Year (%)**						
1991	19.2	11.6	13.4	14.0	24.0	31.0
1992	23.7	22.0	24.8	17.5	23.1	22.6
1993	31.5	21.3	28.5	28.4	32.7	39.3
1994	35.2	80.7	76.0	44.2	25.0	-41.5
1995	24.9	18.1	28.7	23.4	22.6	12.9
1996	18.1	13.0	21.6	11.8	12.4	9.5
1997	13.7	18.1	18.7	37.4	4.5	-12.2
1998	14.0	3.1	20.0	2.6	3.4	-8.0
1999	16.2	11.0	19.1	12.9	11.6	-2.8
2000	12.3	8.1	13.3	11.4	8.4	12.0
三、构成(以合计为100) **Composition (Total=100)**						
1990	100.0	7.4	51.5	1.1	16.4	23.6
1991	100.0	7.0	49.0	1.0	17.0	26.0
1992	100.0	6.9	49.4	1.0	17.0	25.8
1993	100.0	6.3	48.3	1.0	17.1	27.3
1994	100.0	8.5	62.9	1.0	15.8	11.8
1995	100.0	8.0	64.8	1.0	15.5	10.7
1996	100.0	7.7	66.7	1.0	14.8	9.9
1997	100.0	8.0	69.7	1.1	13.6	7.6
1998	100.0	7.2	73.3	1.0	12.3	6.2
1999	100.0	6.9	75.1	1.0	11.8	5.2
2000	100.0	6.6	75.8	1.0	11.4	5.2

注：本表不包括民政部门支付的离休、退休、退职费。

a) Included retired and resigned staff and workers Paid by the civil administration organs.

22-34 分地区失业保险基本情况(2000年)

单位:千人

地　区	Region	企业应参保职工人数 Nominal Contri-butors	本年参保人数 Contributors This Year 合　计 Total	一、企业 Enterprises	国有企业 State-owned Enterprises	#中央直属企业 Enterprises Directly under Central Government	集体企业 Collected-owned Enter-prises	外商投资企业 Foreign Funded Enterprises	其他企业 Other Enterprises
全　国	**National Total**	**134091**	**103262.7**	**84021.3**	**59131.1**	**8315.2**	**14454.0**	**4459.9**	**5976.2**
北　京	Beijing	4153	3062.0	2440.0	1819.0		205.0	116.0	300.0
天　津	Tianjin	2613	2168.7	1826.3	1294.3	116.0	290.2	223.9	17.8
河　北	Hebei	6007	5421.7	4184.3	2987.9	678.9	722.2	115.4	358.8
山　西	Shanxi	4079	2547.4	2283.3	2029.7	262.3	241.8	9.6	2.2
内蒙古	Inner Mongolia	2936	2204.2	1642.1	1272.8	216.6	212.2	14.8	142.3
辽　宁	Liaoning	8590	6480.8	6256.8	4128.4	571.4	1645.1	278.5	204.8
吉　林	Jilin	4373	2793.0	2467.0	2017.0		377.0	34.0	39.0
黑龙江	Heilongjiang	7120	5387.2	4895.3	3694.2	418.2	1058.9	130.3	12.0
上　海	Shanghai	4227	4349.0	3523.0	1746.0	440.0	591.0	530.0	656.0
江　苏	Jiangsu	8368	7570.7	6110.5	3496.0	452.3	1766.5	500.8	347.3
浙　江	Zhejiang	4636	3924.5	2295.6	1265.0	75.9	704.5	210.3	745.7
安　徽	Anhui	4614	3649.3	2870.4	1959.4	220.0	684.3	32.9	193.8
福　建	Fujian	3555	1657.2	1420.6	873.9	85.0	202.4	296.6	47.7
江　西	Jiangxi	3687	2315.9	1828.0	1588.0	235.2	180.1	16.0	43.9
山　东	Shandong	9192	7150.0	5799.0	4158.0	749.0	1204.0	204.0	233.0
河　南	Henan	7738	6776.1	5165.6	3769.5	366.0	882.4	54.6	459.1
湖　北	Hubei	6653	4596.0	3692.9	3124.5	470.3	436.1	62.8	69.5
湖　南	Hunan	5564	3463.0	2727.0	2306.0	508.0	371.0	25.0	25.0
广　东	Guangdong	8675	7484.9	6543.9	2728.0	45.8	966.7	1438.2	1411.0
广　西	Guangxi	3063	2246.2	1523.6	1303.6	118.6	150.2	27.3	42.5
海　南	Hainan	935	498.1	329.4	248.0	11.1	41.7	13.8	25.9
重　庆	Chongqing	2634	2103.9	1828.5	1275.9	178.3	370.0	39.5	43.2
四　川	Sichuan	5875	4386.9	3301.8	2628.8	556.7	425.5	28.7	218.9
贵　州	Guizhou	2039	1266.5	934.5	827.0	289.3	41.3	0.2	66.0
云　南	Yunnan	2758	1960.3	1380.8	1116.7	152.5	175.9	17.0	71.2
西　藏	Tibet	121	63.0	32.0	32.0	6.0			
陕　西	Shaanxi	3892	3090.3	2798.7	2529.6	524.0	199.0	24.1	46.0
甘　肃	Gansu	2183	1720.1	1360.0	1119.6	203.0	172.2	5.8	62.4
青　海	Qinghai	524	437.7	317.4	257.9	100.0	56.2		3.3
宁　夏	Ningxia	652	341.7	293.6	233.9	46.5	19.1	0.3	40.2
新　疆	Xinjiang	2641	1786.7	1419.6	1300.6	218.3	61.8	9.6	47.7

Basic Conditions of Unemployment Insurance by Region (2000)

(1000 persons)

事业单位 Institutions	其他单位 Others	覆盖率 (%) Coverage Rate	本年月平均领取失业保险金人数 Persons Attained Unemployment Insurance per-mouth	领取失业保险金人数 Persons Attained Unemployment Insurance this Year	# 下岗转失业人数 Laid-off workers	# 当年再就业人数 Reemployed this Year
18434.2	**807.2**	**77.0**	**22547.3**	**3297.5**	**330.1**	**610.3**
573.0	49.0	73.7	664.7	109.1	3.2	31.8
342.4		83.0	820.3	110.5	15.2	0.7
1166.9	70.5	90.3	1072.1	72.4	4.6	14.0
260.1	4.0	62.5	109.1	33.0	1.2	19.4
527.8	34.4	75.1	684.9	64.0	11.7	19.0
579.1	4.9	75.4	1755.2	238.5	8.7	17.9
323.0	3.0	63.9	615.2	51.3	14.4	0.3
428.8	63.1	75.7	309.7	60.0	8.2	28.5
747.0	79.0		3439.5	386.5	16.3	3.3
1440.5	19.7	90.5	3743.4	438.2	63.7	115.5
868.2	130.7	84.7	2227.0	345.5	21.2	44.0
770.9	8.0	79.1	526.6	144.4	23.8	10.9
235.8	0.9	46.6	434.9	69.9	15.6	15.8
484.6	3.2	62.8	58.0	8.1	3.2	0.6
1334.0	17.0	77.8	1312.3	185.9	6.8	37.8
1546.3	64.2	87.6	434.1	95.8	6.7	33.4
889.1	14.0	69.1	790.5	165.2	22.8	27.1
727.0	9.0	62.2	250.3	47.2	6.4	23.0
817.0	124.0	86.3	980.6	273.1	27.3	29.8
707.2	15.4	73.3	189.1	38.1	7.1	16.8
131.7	37.0	53.3	33.2	9.0	0.3	1.9
367.2	8.2	79.9	361.6	48.5	3.5	19.9
1069.6	15.5	74.7	801.5	161.6	24.6	40.4
324.1	7.9	62.1	34.8	5.7	0.1	0.2
569.1	10.5	71.1	365.0	52.4	3.1	30.9
31.0		52.1	0.4			
286.0	5.6	79.4	139.1	22.8	3.5	3.7
357.9	2.2	78.8	94.5	22.4	1.3	9.1
120.1	0.2	83.5	37.9	12.1	0.3	5.7
46.7	1.4	52.4	23.0	7.0	1.0	3.7
362.2	5.0	67.7	238.7	19.3	4.4	5.1

22-35 分地区基本养老保险情况（2000年）

Conditions of Basic Endowment Insurance(2000)

单位:人 (person)

地区	Region	本年参保职工 Number of Staff and Workers with Health Insurant						
		合计 Total	企业 Enterprises	国有企业 State-owned Enterprises	集体企业 Collective-owned Enterprises	其他企业 Other Enterprises	机关事业 Undertaking Units	其他 Other Units
全国	**National Total**	**104474965**	**91241831**	**64665589**	**14699286**	**6981904**	**9776410**	**3456724**
北京	Beijing	2753282	2686643	2013598	262986	160727	66627	12
天津	Tianjin	2080771	2014448	1323782	280126	191210	66323	
河北	Hebei	4969507	4162250	3145309	654938	271174	767355	39902
山西	Shanxi	3380747	2824694	2285951	448648	73575	512343	43710
内蒙古	Inner Mongolia	2326475	1897880	1455114	185573	248746	324051	104544
辽宁	Liaoning	7489204	6479206	4404304	1604669	172972	649376	360622
吉林	Jilin	2938988	2828418	2408664	360044	31830	86797	23773
黑龙江	Heilongjiang	4664077	4511277	3915110	395602	133075	66321	86479
上海	Shanghai	4410852	3565239	1846279	590418	598456	747415	98198
江苏	Jiangsu	6899794	6301067	3408829	1800802	611580	431261	167466
浙江	Zhejiang	4473727	3480414	1689283	655018	957775	301253	692060
安徽	Anhui	3219157	2978757	2132196	639959	170319	184548	55852
福建	Fujian	1747132	1646112	877505	273913	127745	15494	85526
江西	Jiangxi	2548530	2366254	1980038	308271	65953	161206	21070
山东	Shandong	8285757	6418703	4068004	1472959	586006	1797263	69791
河南	Henan	5944659	5272573	4491375	669052	86666	667859	4227
湖北	Hubei	4655997	4448177	3269767	895027	218567	86485	121335
湖南	Hunan	3273701	3168195	2590723	501356	49461	68931	36575
广东	Guangdong	9983374	7767970	3330657	1047665	1653321	1336638	878766
广西	Guangxi	1848839	1802460	1637151	111428	36263	21241	25138
海南	Hainan	991416	759727	649549	41943	43374	229277	2412
重庆	Chongqing	1921536	1790094	1333100	382821	43318	41868	89574
四川	Sichuan	4121685	3606820	2790718	516456	258016	210218	304647
贵州	Guizhou	1249324	1002267	923380	49255	24443	244091	2966
云南	Yunnan	1840538	1500058	1316460	147260	17678	293930	46550
西藏	Tibet	51873	43575	43452	123		7907	391
陕西	Shaanxi	2183180	2168349	1954554	159792	40797		14831
甘肃	Gansu	1437091	1360670	1213864	105473	37845	55163	21258
青海	Qinghai	364266	333622	305093	26583	1892	18215	12429
宁夏	Ningxia	444926	411073	360392	32404	13436	28984	4869
新疆	Xinjiang	1757187	1644839	1501388	78722	55684	70597	41751

22-36 残疾人事业基本情况

Basic Conditions of People with Disabilities

项　　目	Item	1996	1997	1998	1999	2000
康复	**Rehabilitation**					
白内障复明	Re-light of Cataract					
白内障复明手术(万例)	Operation (10 000 Cases)	25.7	34.8	36.3	41.7	48.1
人工晶体植入率(%)	Embedded Rate of Artificial Crystal (%)			52.4	60.4	71.3
低视力配用助视器(人)	Low-eyesight Matched with Eyesight-aid Apparatus (persons)	15808	20691	21084	22079	21701
聋儿康复	Rehabilitation of Deaf Children					
年收训聋儿　(人)	Annual Adoptive Deaf Children (persons)	13420	14479	16087	17030	16904
聋儿入普幼普小率(%)	Enrollment Rate to General Infant School or Elementary School (%)					19.4
培训家长　(人)	Patriarch Trained (persons)	4352	10940	12520	13998	13568
精神病防治康复	Prevention, Cure and Rehabilitation of Psychosis(units)					
开展精神病防治康复工作市县数(个)	Number of Counties Carried on the Works of Prevention, Cure and Rehabilitation (units)	235	235	235	243	243
综合防治康复精神病人数(万人)	Number of Psychosis Sicks Synthetically Prevented, Cured and Rehabilitated (10 000 persons)		87.21	103.10	103.29	122.55
监护率　(%)	Warding Rate (%)		85.8	93.2	91.5	93
显好率　(%)	Rate of Getting Better (%)		72.5	71.8	73.6	71.6
社会参与率　(%)	Social Participation Rate (%)		60.3	62.6	64.9	62.7
肇事率　(%)	Rate of Causing Trouble (%)		0.86	0.37	0.21	0.21
救济贫困患者数(人)	Number of Poor Sufferer Relieved (persons)		55887	74032	96173	130295
用品用具供应件数(万件)	Number of Appliances Supplied (10 000 units)	50.4	77.5	80.7	82.0	85.0
康复训练与服务　(人)	Rehabilitation Training and Service (persons)					
肢体残疾康复训练数	Rehabilitation Training of Body Disabilities (persons)	29468	41300	47406	54263	52538
智力残疾儿童康复训练数	Rehabilitation Training of Mental Disabilities Children (persons)	21819	19405	20879	23213	24009
教育	**Education**					
未入学适龄残疾儿童少年　(万人)	Number of Uneducated Children (10 000 persons)				43.33	39.06
职业教育与培训	Vocational Education and Training					
机构数	Number of Institutions					
独立建制　(个)	Self Help (units)	350	401	879	998	970
依托社会　(个)	Supported by Society (units)	1864	2186	2821	3001	3194
教育与培训人数(万人)	Number of Educated and Trained (10 000 persons)	26.27	45.85	56.33	57.92	65.38
就业	**Employment**					
城镇残疾人就业状况	Employment of Urban Handicappeds					
当年安排就业 (万人)	Persons Employed in the Year (10 000 persons)	16.22	16.12	24.85	26.05	26.58
#按比例就业	Employment by Proportion	2.50	4.67	5.24	5.90	7.15
集中就业	Centralized Employment	5.24	4.36	6.34	6.23	7.11
个体就业	Individual Employment	8.45	7.09	13.27	13.93	12.31
未安排就业	Un-arranged Handicappends		123.69	166.10	116.11	96.25
农村残疾人就业状况	Employment of Rural Handicapped					
就　业　(万人)	Employed (10 000 persons)	1472.11	1423.99	1562.41	1568.76	1616.08
未就业　(万人)	Unemployed (10 000 persons)	586.58	671.77	506.77	467.62	358.22
残疾人就业服务机构(个)	Number of Institutions Engaging in Handicappeds Employment (units)	1280	1970	2612	2880	3012
省	Provinces		29	29	31	30
地	Prefectures		89	158	85	73
市(含县级市)	Cities (Cities at County Level)		469	518	610	632
县	County		1016	1427	1497	1550
市辖区	Districts under the Jurisdiction of Cities		367	480	653	727
实施分散按比例就业的地区数 (个)	Number of Regions Implemented the Policy of the Disperse Employment by Proportion (units)					
省	Provinces		24	29	29	29
地	Prefectures		68	164	84	77
市(含县级市)	Cities (Cities at County Level)		385	461	590	623
县	County		733	999	1302	1381
市辖区	Districts under the Jurisdiction of Cities		354	455	613	702
扶贫	**Poverty Alleviation**					
扶贫开发解决温饱 (万人)	Number of Handicappeds Have Lived with Warmth Fill-bellies (persons)	60.58	166.49	246.24	251.00	231.57
尚未解决温饱贫困残疾人　(万人)	Number of Handicappeds Have Lived without Warmth Fill-bellies yet (persons)	1673.34	1205.78	1177.80	649.47	978.93
#可扶持贫困残疾人 (万人)	Number of Handicappeds Can Be Supported (10 000 persons)		876.64	821.09	445.22	682.54
残联组织建设	**Organization Building of Handicappeds Association**					
残疾人工作者数　(万人)	Number of Workers for Handicappeds (persons)	5.81	6.63	6.46	8.21	8.04

补充资料：根据1987年全国残疾人抽样调查的结果推算，全国各类残疾人的总数共有6000万人。

a) According to the calculation from the handicappeds survey in 1987, total handicappeds in China will be 600 million persons.

22-37 婚姻登记和离婚情况

Number of Marriages and Divorces

年份 Year	内地居民登记结婚(对) Registered Marriages (couples)	初婚(人) First Marriages (persons)	再婚(人) Remarriages (persons)	离婚(对) Divorces (couples)	离婚率(‰) Divorce Rate (‰)
1985	8290588	16076337	504839	457938	0.9
1986	8822935	17075107	570763	505675	0.9
1987	9247372	17880856	613888	581484	1.1
1988	8971750	17285077	658423	658551	1.2
1989	9351915	17959680	744150	752914	1.3
1990	9486870	18191303	782437	800037	1.4
1991	9509849	18203226	816472	829449	1.4
1992	9545047	18320957	769137	849611	1.5
1993	9121622	17470092	773152	909195	1.5
1994	9290027	17793306	786748	980980	1.6
1995	9297061	17760657	833465	1055196	1.8
1996	9339615	17817240	861990	1132215	1.8
1997	9090571	17259504	921638	1197759	1.9
1998	8866593	16753749	979437	1190214	1.9
1999	8799079	16593593	1004565	1201541	1.9
2000	8420044	15813933	1026155	1212863	1.9

22-38 各地区婚姻登记和离婚情况（2000年）

Number of Marriages and Divorces by Region (2000)

地区	Region	内地居民登记结婚(对) Registered Marriages (couples)	初婚(人) First Marriages (persons)	再婚(人) Remarriages (persons)	离婚(对) Divorces (couples)
全国	**National Total**	**8420044**	**15813933**	**1026155**	**1212863**
北京	Beijing	79516	135620	23412	26616
天津	Tianjin	61416	107228	15604	13356
河北	Hebei	475153	881891	68415	53340
山西	Shanxi	164639	313195	16083	23788
内蒙古	Inner Mongolia	151947	283092	20802	32483
辽宁	Liaoning	272644	482897	62391	81647
吉林	Jilin	175425	320661	30189	51057
黑龙江	Heilongjiang	217750	384399	51101	74878
上海	Shanghai	89876	150833	28919	31818
江苏	Jiangsu	496899	944270	49528	55907
浙江	Zhejiang	384032	727576	40488	43168
安徽	Anhui	491959	956560	27358	36335
福建	Fujian	246171	475552	16790	28787
江西	Jiangxi	294249	570202	18296	24229
山东	Shandong	675602	1266917	84287	61085
河南	Henan	661793	1278245	45341	64870
湖北	Hubei	353781	673294	34268	47418
湖南	Hunan	383092	717676	48508	54875
广东	Guangdong	550388	1058051	42725	47521
广西	Guangxi	318563	614337	22789	28765
海南	Hainan	38145	73840	2450	3935
重庆	Chongqing	190184	344931	35437	44176
四川	Sichuan	470351	864833	75869	100622
贵州	Guizhou	279402	543331	15473	25874
云南	Yunnan	311312	595405	27219	36290
西藏	Tibet	4087	7613	561	1211
陕西	Shaanxi	203173	382458	23888	31979
甘肃	Gansu	127799	244975	10623	19081
青海	Qinghai	34535	65853	3217	6693
宁夏	Ningxia	35711	67550	3872	6163
新疆	Xinjiang	180450	280648	80252	55076

22-39 各地区环保系统机构、人员数（2000年）

Environmental Protection Agencies and Persons Engaged by Region (2000)

地 区	Region	机构总数 (个) Number of Agencies (unit)	人员总数 (人) Total Number of Staff & Workers (person)	# 科技人员 Scientific and Technical Personnel	# 监测人员 Monitoring Personal	# 监理人员 Supervising and Administrative Personnel
全 国	**National Total**	**11115**	**131092**	**6394**	**40674**	**31228**
北 京	Beijing	69	1448	223	489	80
天 津	Tianjin	75	1423	178	547	89
河 北	Hebei	517	9155	219	1705	1689
山 西	Shanxi	496	7493	136	2315	2043
内蒙古	Inner Mongolia	504	3167	160	996	293
辽 宁	Liaoning	458	7201	659	2162	1659
吉 林	Jilin	285	4601	201	1359	1705
黑龙江	Heilongjiang	410	4098	174	1466	1002
上 海	Shanghai	88	1996	228	785	386
江 苏	Jiangsu	873	7433	341	2574	1714
浙 江	Zhejiang	292	3867	241	1846	740
安 徽	Anhui	361	4104	166	1442	987
福 建	Fujian	334	3089	193	1088	741
江 西	Jiangxi	344	3338	169	996	862
山 东	Shandong	596	10618	321	3282	2831
河 南	Henan	648	12421	315	3315	4153
湖 北	Hubei	423	6491	189	1946	2192
湖 南	Hunan	495	6186	253	2105	1542
广 东	Guangdong	1041	7013	265	1841	1253
广 西	Guangxi	257	2934	139	1104	407
海 南	Hainan	76	1073	21	345	223
重 庆	Chongqing	306	1939		697	430
四 川	Sichuan	540	4236	142	1717	773
贵 州	Guizhou	272	1790	98	577	438
云 南	Yunnan	356	2671	198	931	407
西 藏	Tibet	22	163		50	
陕 西	Shaanxi	352	4154	114	1252	1172
甘 肃	Gansu	245	2210	87	655	775
青 海	Qinghai	70	538	19	189	115
宁 夏	Ningxia	62	630	52	147	111
新 疆	Xinjiang	224	1965	110	654	416

22-40 县及县以上工业企业“三废”排放及治理情况

Discharge and Treatment of Waste Water, Waste Gas and Solid Wastes by Industry Enterprises at and Above County Level

项 目	Item	1995	1999	2000
废水	**Waste Water**			
工业废水排放总量 (万吨)	Total Volume of Industrial Waste Water Discharged (10 000 tons)	2218943	1607678	1530558
工业废水排放达标量 (万吨)	Volume of Industrial Waste Water up to the Standards for Discharge (10 000 tons)	1228680	1158703	1257294
工业废水排放达标率 (%)	Percentage of Industrial Waste Water up to the Standards for Discharge (%)	55.4	72.1	82.1
工业废水处理量 (万吨)	Total Volume of Industrial Waste Water Treated (10 000 tons)	2156615	2778021	3137881
工业废水处理率 (%)	Percentage of Industrial Waste Water Treated (%)	76.8	91.1	95.0
工业废水处理排放达标量 (万吨)	Volume of Treated Industrial Waste Water up to the Standards for Discharge (10 000 tons)	481428	719927	914610
废气	**Waste Gas**			
工业废气排放总量 (亿标立方米)	Total Volume of Industrial Waste Gas Emission (100 million cu.m)	107478	114721	123151
工业二氧化硫排放量 (万吨)	Volume of Sulphur Dioxide Emission (10 000 tons)	1405	1078	1149
烟尘排放量 (万吨)	Volume of Soot Emission (10 000 tons)	838	557	517
工业粉尘排放量 (万吨)	Volume of Industrial Dust Emission (10 000 tons)	639	458	404
固体废物	**Solid Wastes**			
工业固体废物产生量 (万吨)	Volume of Industrial Solid Wastes Produced (10 000 tons)	64474	64905	66599
工业固体废物综合利用量 (万吨)	Volume of Industrial Solid Wastes Utilized (10 000 tons)	28511	33240	34482
工业固体废物综合利用率(%)	Percentage of Industrial Solid Wastes Utilized (%)	42.9	51.7	51.8
工业固体废物贮存量 (万吨)	Volume of Industrial Solid Wastes Accumulated (10 000 tons)	24779	24811	27456
工业固体废物处置量 (万吨)	Volume of Industrial Solid Wastes Treated (10 000 tons)	14204	9747	8232
工业固体废物排放量 (万吨)	Volume of Industrial Solid Wastes Discharged (10 000 tons)	2242	1154	1040
工业固体废物历年贮存占地面积 (万平方米)	Areas Occupied by Industrial Solid Wastes Accumulated (10 000 sq.m)	55440	62010	57763
“三废”综合利用产品产值 (万元)	Output Value of Products Made from Waste Gas, Waste Water and Solid Wastes (10 000 yuan)	2036052	2180111	2628477
“三废”综合利用产品利润 (万元)	Profits Obtained from Use of Waste Gas, Waste Water and Solid Wastes (10 000 yuan)	527223	465334	539070
污染治理	**Pollution Treatment**			
当年安排污染治理项目数(个)	Number of Projects for Pollution Treatment in the Year	21644	19866	27243
污染治理项目本年完成投资额 (万元)	Actual Investment in Implementation of the Project for Pollution Treatment in the Year (10 000 yuan)	987376	1527307	2394391
#治理废水	Treatment of Waste Water	455909	688302	1095897
治理废气	Treatment of Waste Gas	331560	509847	909242
治理固体废物	Treatment of Solid Wastes	140769	83354	114673
治理噪声	Noise Abatement	21528	9213	60189
治理其他	Others	37611	235075	214390
排污收费及使用	**Fee for Discharging Waste and Fines for Pollution**			
排污费交纳单位 (个)	Number of Units Charged levied	368213	722375	739193
排污费征收额 (万元)	Amount of Pollution Charges (10 000 yuan)	371280	554513	579607
排污费支出额 (万元)	Outlays of Pollution Levy Charges (10 000 yuan)	345812	545870	613630

22-41 各地区工业废水排放及处理情况（2000年）

Discharge and Treatment of Industrial Waste Water by Region (2000)

单位：万吨 (10 000 tons)

地 区	Region	汇总工业企业数(个) Number of Industrial Enterprises (unit)	工业废水排放总量 Total Volume of Waste Water Discharged	#工业废水排放达标量 Volume of Industrial Waste Water up to the Discharge Standards	废水治理设施数(套) Number of Facilities for Treatment of Waste Water (set)	工业废水处理量 Volume of Industrial Waste Water Treated	#工业废水处理回用量 Volume of Industrial Waste Water Recovered After Treatment	工业废水处理排放达标量 Volume of Treated Industrial Waste Water up to the Discharge Standards
全 国	**National Total**	**70944**	**1942405**	**1493277**	**64453**	**3482625**	**2441945**	**914610**
北 京	Beijing	1122	23164	21456	779	107409	92934	13271
天 津	Tianjin	1277	17604	17186	842	27697	18822	8392
河 北	Hebei	2888	89600	63649	3177	409277	365129	41348
山 西	Shanxi	2800	32406	20056	2468	95031	80686	11372
内蒙古	Inner Mongolia	1016	21844	14116	665	47367	36853	6764
辽 宁	Liaoning	2466	109044	87196	2350	178348	123054	49413
吉 林	Jilin	1057	37386	24626	853	38978	23472	14194
黑龙江	Heilongjiang	1780	52644	44152	1310	106807	82395	22078
上 海	Shanghai	1968	72446	67553	2174	138657	102117	34185
江 苏	Jiangsu	6461	201923	185653	4761	240670	141230	95354
浙 江	Zhejiang	5530	136433	115680	5087	137929	57027	77018
安 徽	Anhui	1812	63106	53355	1612	133507	102487	29638
福 建	Fujian	3783	57617	46574	3347	71119	33715	33962
江 西	Jiangxi	1069	41956	28796	1338	64926	38122	20574
山 东	Shandong	5433	110324	102743	3946	324239	239883	81469
河 南	Henan	3631	109210	88297	3586	271622	199473	66029
湖 北	Hubei	2172	106733	80591	2120	168784	121792	40825
湖 南	Hunan	2891	112563	74396	3034	141641	80701	45647
广 东	Guangdong	7592	114055	88271	7273	160545	81151	65997
广 西	Guangxi	1906	81571	51287	2251	102954	62002	30303
海 南	Hainan	286	7064	6134	264	6096	2825	2834
重 庆	Chongqing	1296	84344	63612	1235	112792	79402	36427
四 川	Sichuan	3530	116979	69596	3642	148205	93574	41606
贵 州	Guizhou	1687	20598	9766	1261	42397	34357	5399
云 南	Yunnan	1376	35117	16245	1609	86987	75079	9422
西 藏	Tibet	58	1006		17	981	296	
陕 西	Shaanxi	1694	30903	19749	1745	42217	26162	12986
甘 肃	Gansu	1225	23795	16973	851	45670	31517	9980
青 海	Qinghai	204	4661	3777	101	2082	986	907
宁 夏	Ningxia	233	10942	3867	330	12898	7891	2301
新 疆	Xinjiang	701	15365	7923	425	14792	6811	4915

22-42 工业分行业废水排放及处理情况（2000年）

Discharge and Treatment of Waste Water by Branch of Industry (2000)

单位：万吨 (10 000 tons)

行业 Branch	汇总工业企业数（个） Number of Industrial Enterprises (unit)	工业废水排放总量 Total Volume of Industrial Waste Water Discharged (10 000 tons)	#工业废水排放达标量 Volume of Industrial Waste Water up to the Discharge Standards	废水治理设施数（套） Number of Facilities for Treatment of Waste Water (set)	工业废水处理量 Volume of Industrial Waste Water Treated	#工业废水处理回用量 Volume of Industrial Waste Water Recovered After Treatment	工业废水处理排放达标量 Volume of Treated Industrial Waste Water up to the Discharge Standards
采掘业 Mining and Quarrying	4312	127952	105781	6334	330624	244948	76782
食品、饮料和烟草制造业 Food, Beverage and Tobacco Industry	8283	164304	94459	6713	131953	57123	59316
纺织业 Textile Industry	6077	125649	97891	5134	84815	5186	73224
皮革毛皮羽绒及其制品业 Leather, Furs, Down and Related Products	994	13008	6513	838	6775	391	5669
造纸及纸制品业 Papermaking & Paper Products	4119	352876	189620	5629	324352	102220	173950
印刷业记录媒介的复制 Printing & Record Medium Reproduction	643	1749	1549	157	544	75	463
石油加工及炼焦业 Petroleum Processing & Coking	720	48500	45817	1240	54098	14251	38285
化学原料及化学制品制造业 Raw Chemical Materials and Chemical Products	6449	337346	276507	9343	793400	627144	145562
医药制造业 Medical and Pharmaceutical Products	1886	34381	27942	1515	17834	2974	13688
化学纤维制造业 Chemical Fiber	269	53134	43151	354	31133	5446	22580
橡胶制品业 Rubber Products	640	8124	7792	379	9451	6435	2953
塑料制品业 Plastic Products	952	2994	2883	274	1573	572	986
非金属矿物制品业 Nonmetal Mineral Products	12174	42422	35652	4726	42975	29940	11890
#水泥制造业 Cement Manufacturing	4635	24115	21109	1395	15724	11332	3998
黑色金属冶炼及压延加工业 Smelting and Pressing of Ferrous Metals	1698	220528	198944	2888	1026950	921318	100757
有色金属冶炼及压延加工业 Smelting and Pressing of Nonferrous Metals	1257	32871	25847	1607	72221	53014	16039
金属制品业 Metal Products	4500	11817	10699	4204	11692	3016	8028
机械、电气、电子设备制造业 Machine Building, Electric Machinery, & Electronic Equipment Manufacturing	9154	91779	82247	7790	52374	18239	32207
电力煤气及水生产供应业 Production & Supply of Electric Power, Gas & Water	1756	186594	171364	2389	403201	303683	89318
其他 Other Industries	5061	37525	31944	2939	28397	4950	21669

22-43 各地区工业废气排放及处理情况（2000年）

Emission and Treatment of Industrial Waste Gas by Region (2000)

地 区	Region	汇总工业企业数(个) Number of Industrial Enterprises (unit)	废气治理设施数(套) Number of Facilities for Treatment of Waste Gas (set)	工业废气排放总量(亿标立方米) Total Volume of Industrial Waste Gas Emission (100 million cu.m)	燃料燃烧过程中废气排放量 Volume of Waste Gas in the Process of Fuel Burning	# 经过消烟除尘的 Volume of Gas with Soot & Dust Removed	生产工艺过程中废气排放量 Volume of Waste Gas from the Process of Production	# 经过净化处理的 Volume of Gas Purified
全 国	**National Total**	**70944**	**145534**	**138145**	**81970**	**74928**	**56032**	**47000**
北 京	Beijing	1122	3318	3227	1864	1691	1363	1315
天 津	Tianjin	1277	2431	1749	1341	1284	408	345
河 北	Hebei	2888	9263	9858	4847	4519	5011	4639
山 西	Shanxi	2800	7050	6635	4203	3894	2432	1273
内蒙古	Inner Mongolia	1016	3178	4768	3252	2983	1516	1204
辽 宁	Liaoning	2466	7377	9432	5925	5295	3507	2961
吉 林	Jilin	1057	3654	3082	2172	2055	910	547
黑龙江	Heilongjiang	1780	4786	4326	3517	3434	809	728
上 海	Shanghai	1968	4276	5755	3282	2879	2474	2264
江 苏	Jiangsu	6461	9860	9078	6522	6294	2557	2218
浙 江	Zhejiang	5530	9905	6509	4262	3736	2246	1891
安 徽	Anhui	1812	3449	3945	2282	2035	1663	1501
福 建	Fujian	3783	5051	2828	1297	1190	1531	1424
江 西	Jiangxi	1069	2252	2220	1218	999	860	708
山 东	Shandong	5433	10813	12179	7438	7215	4741	4555
河 南	Henan	3631	8008	7436	4408	4174	3029	2383
湖 北	Hubei	2172	5248	5674	2468	2400	3206	2672
湖 南	Hunan	2891	5493	3569	1718	1529	1851	1658
广 东	Guangdong	7592	10901	8326	5169	4646	3157	2926
广 西	Guangxi	1906	5112	4607	1787	1662	2820	2567
海 南	Hainan	286	543	434	226	221	208	208
重 庆	Chongqing	1296	2321	1908	1130	969	778	665
四 川	Sichuan	3530	5609	4779	2332	1757	2447	1835
贵 州	Guizhou	1687	2265	3882	2326	1639	1555	918
云 南	Yunnan	1376	3581	2749	1402	1104	1347	1176
西 藏	Tibet	58	35	15	8	3	7	3
陕 西	Shaanxi	1694	3831	2379	1503	1418	876	651
甘 肃	Gansu	1225	2533	2800	1523	1406	1277	828
青 海	Qinghai	204	559	607	163	154	444	271
宁 夏	Ningxia	233	760	1445	995	979	449	175
新 疆	Xinjiang	701	2072	1944	1389	1364	554	493

22-43 续表 1 continued

地区	Region	工业二氧化硫排放量(吨) Volume of Sulphur Dioxide Emission (ton)	工业二氧化硫去除量(吨) Volume of Sulphur Dioxide Removed (ton)	工业烟尘排放量(吨) Volume of Industrial Soot Emission (ton)	工业烟尘去除量(吨) Volume of Industrial Soot Removed (ton)	工业粉尘排放量(吨) Volume of Industrial Dust Emission (ton)	工业粉尘去除量(吨) Volume of Industrial Dust Romoved (ton)
全国	**National Total**	**16153200**	**5750600**	**9533292**	**107173542**	**10920000**	**44795560**
北京	Beijing	146431	9748	51842	1357227	93681	996605
天津	Tianjin	241815	41355	112234	2312175	37891	234231
河北	Hebei	1133599	175177	672176	7195272	812663	2979927
山西	Shanxi	902681	166120	791300	6416287	504133	1771044
内蒙古	Inner Mongolia	506309	104883	303292	4528710	175644	587030
辽宁	Liaoning	705672	665676	547223	8610888	429231	3087312
吉林	Jilin	201688	50251	283006	4544264	123792	1161732
黑龙江	Heilongjiang	221670	20907	409337	6428612	103853	502422
上海	Shanghai	326804	37687	83153	3083548	26941	2180813
江苏	Jiangsu	1140991	187240	374737	7254087	256790	2104759
浙江	Zhejiang	561847	101562	247096	4195609	489627	2049220
安徽	Anhui	350625	552684	243493	3362890	284977	1352453
福建	Fujian	214338	23102	103539	1320414	187076	1346911
江西	Jiangxi	288108	528701	234059	2893533	343351	1223416
山东	Shandong	1460902	320352	543067	9027355	745589	5059711
河南	Henan	747384	139081	690618	7182665	817734	2927880
湖北	Hubei	508218	356553	321461	2215959	410286	2331507
湖南	Hunan	626494	483946	381268	2007277	639667	1737738
广东	Guangdong	881558	151546	264453	5704256	579895	2517735
广西	Guangxi	800485	309499	590999	2435335	567717	2668408
海南	Hainan	20178	963	18078	231497	13470	121642
重庆	Chongqing	664240	167562	121783	1457313	220127	446098
四川	Sichuan	994064	198682	798910	2284428	559794	1852488
贵州	Guizhou	642490	84712	342453	2780444	406234	480781
云南	Yunnan	323853	352301	232566	1496724	122818	1073720
西藏	Tibet	756		1150	613	2114	14
陕西	Shaanxi	553738	43331	371908	2477843	377237	410829
甘肃	Gansu	311878	437063	124768	1499372	146347	820292
青海	Qinghai	20177	78	63810	318724	41658	110119
宁夏	Ningxia	174155	18408	125537	1677833	132781	120093
新疆	Xinjiang	187689	21431	84000	872389	112574	538630

22-44 工业分行业废气排放及处理情况（2000年）

Emission and Treatment of Waste Gas by Branch of Industry (2000)

行业 Branch	汇总工业企业数（个） Number of Industrial Enter-prises (unit)	废气治理设施数(套) Number of Facilities for Treat-ment of Waste Gas (set)	工业废气排放总量（亿标立方米） Total Volume of Waste Gas Emission (100 million cu.m)	燃料燃烧过程中废气排放量 Volume of Waste Gas from the Burning Pro-cess of Fuels	#经过消烟除尘的 Volume of Gas with Soot and Dust Removed	生产工艺过程中废气排放量 Volume of Waste Gas from the Process of Production	#经过净化处理的 Volume of Gas Purified
采掘业 Mining and Quarrying	4312	10222	3541	2403	2069	1138	970
食品、饮料和烟草制造业 Food, Beverage and Tobacco Industry	8283	10294	3218	2964	2668	255	229
纺织业 Textile Industry	6077	7451	1577	1534	1409	44	38
皮革毛皮羽绒及其制品业 Leather, Furs, Down and Related Products	994	805	125	86	64	40	37
造纸及纸制品业 Papermaking & Paper Products	4119	5032	2553	2131	1991	422	263
印刷业记录媒介的复制 Printing & Record Medium Reproduction	643	342	49	31	26	19	10
石油加工及炼焦业 Petroleum Processing & Coking	720	1811	3915	2177	1514	1738	814
化学原料及化学制品制造业 Raw Chemical Materials and Chemical Products	6449	12745	8787	4969	4565	3818	3020
医药制造业 Medical and Pharmaceutical Products	1886	2398	473	437	407	36	30
化学纤维制造业 Chemical Fiber	269	580	2750	990	754	1759	813
橡胶制品业 Rubber Products	640	1090	476	254	233	222	192
塑料制品业 Plastic Products	952	833	193	97	82	96	80
非金属矿物制品业 Nonmetal Mineral Products	12174	45635	27336	5545	3952	21791	19842
#水泥制造业 Cement Manufacturing	4635	37189	22850	2990	2639	19860	18489
黑色金属冶炼及压延加工业 Smelting and Pressing of Ferrous Metals	1698	7611	21343	6452	5012	14891	13565
有色金属冶炼及压延加工业 Smelting and Pressing of Nonferrous Metals	1257	3641	8533	1624	1497	6908	5007
金属制品业 Metal Products	4500	2262	425	185	144	240	228
机械、电气、电子设备制造业 Machine Building, Electric Machinery, & Electronic Equipment Manufacturing	9154	17912	3586	1583	1429	2003	1428
电力煤气及水生产供应业 Production & Supply of Electric Power, Gas & Water	1756	7257	48028	47552	46234	333	184
其他 Other Industries	5061	7613	1236	956	877	280	249

22-44 续表 1 continued

行业 Branch	工业二氧化硫排放量(吨) Volume of Sulphur Dioxide Emission (ton)	工业二氧化硫去除量(吨) Volume of Sulphur Dioxide Removed (ton)	工业烟尘排放量(吨) Volume of Industrial Soot Emission (ton)	工业烟尘去除量(吨) Volume of Industrial Soot Removed (ton)	工业粉尘排放量(吨) Volume of Industrial Soot Emission (ton)	工业粉尘去除量(吨) Volume of Industrial Dust Removed (ton)
采掘业 Mining and Quarrying	330648	163727	215467	1655379	91715	1004377
食品、饮料和烟草制造业 Food, Beverage and Tobacco Industry	405648	71780	259855	1255696	14456	66328
纺织业 Textile Industry	254094	54915	119069	657646	2557	11884
皮革毛皮羽绒及其制品业 Leather, Furs, Down and Related Products	12765	1312	8503	18869	631	82
造纸及纸制品业 Papermaking & Paper Products	335238	67629	209454	2119467	37298	24349
印刷业记录媒介的复制 Printing & Record Medium Reproduction	4987	450	2358	8874	667	726
石油加工及炼焦业 Petroleum Processing & Coking	375009	256744	247596	1052490	54238	126832
化学原料及化学制品制造业 Raw Chemical Materials and Chemical Products	819386	663088	420744	3599665	103298	512574
医药制造业 Medical and Pharmaceutical Products	64212	23425	38058	274577	204	623
化学纤维制造业 Chemical Fiber	150034	39312	55272	969219	14756	140859
橡胶制品业 Rubber Products	46623	9618	15050	167590	442	2787
塑料制品业 Plastic Products	14612	1127	8785	23496	28217	3170
非金属矿物制品业 Nonmetal Mineral Products	2333138	241650	2423926	2479675	8241758	29166560
#水泥制造业 Cement Manufacturing	1001611	188184	409552	2123910	7682081	28385848
黑色金属冶炼及压延加工业 Smelting and Pressing of Ferrous Metals	753357	142363	289663	2216228	853460	10811449
有色金属冶炼及压延加工业 Smelting and Pressing of Nonferrous Metals	714168	3183286	217654	2224449	115473	2182243
金属制品业 Metal Products	72450	3872	29384	71627	93952	6249
机械、电气、电子设备制造业 Machine Building, Electric Machinery, & Electronic Equipment Manufacturing	214177	58395	117813	776460	32857	252729
电力煤气及水生产供应业 Production & Supply of Electric Power, Gas & Water	7072292	745803	3013124	86876648	24577	211173
其他 Other Industries	1397555	22105	1841447	725486	55155	270565

22-45 各地区工业固体废物产生及处理利用情况（2000年）

Discharge, Treatment and Utilization of Industrial Solid Wastes by Region (2000)

地区	Region	汇总工业企业数（个） Number of Industrial Enterprises (unit)	工业固体废物产生量（万吨） Volume of Industrial Solid Wastes Produced (10 000 tons)	#危险废物产生量 Dangerous Wastes	工业固体废物综合利用量（万吨） Volume of Industrial Solid Wastes Utilized in a Comprehensive Way(10 000 tons)	工业固体废物贮存量（万吨） Volume of Industrial Solid Wastes Accumulated (10 000 tons)	工业固体废物处置量（万吨） Volume of Industrial Solid Wastes Treated (10 000 tons)
全　国	**National Total**	**70944**	**81608**	**830**	**37451**	**28921**	**9152**
北　京	Beijing	1122	1139	11	839	223	9
天　津	Tianjin	1277	470	5	457	14	25
河　北	Hebei	2888	7028	31	2877	3057	441
山　西	Shanxi	2800	7695	7	1734	817	2875
内蒙古	Inner Mongolia	1016	2376	45	552	1524	182
辽　宁	Liaoning	2466	7563	89	2573	4067	252
吉　林	Jilin	1057	1604	19	779	688	53
黑龙江	Heilongjiang	1780	2694	7	1847	430	483
上　海	Shanghai	1968	1355	28	1516	2	91
江　苏	Jiangsu	6461	3038	77	2598	359	56
浙　江	Zhejiang	5530	1386	13	1099	142	103
安　徽	Anhui	1812	2815	70	2015	490	949
福　建	Fujian	3783	2191	4	912	1037	165
江　西	Jiangxi	1069	4796	2	702	3861	99
山　东	Shandong	5433	5407	64	4173	1050	219
河　南	Henan	3631	3625	17	2016	1122	469
湖　北	Hubei	2172	2818	7	1514	791	128
湖　南	Hunan	2891	2355	45	1106	534	137
广　东	Guangdong	7592	1694	54	1144	360	841
广　西	Guangxi	1906	2108	42	1058	682	227
海　南	Hainan	286	95		54	33	9
重　庆	Chongqing	1296	1305	32	626	225	38
四　川	Sichuan	3530	4714	1	1689	2015	121
贵　州	Guizhou	1687	2272	46	689	842	363
云　南	Yunnan	1376	3187	25	1152	1144	157
西　藏	Tibet	58	17			17	
陕　西	Shaanxi	1694	2625	6	381	1595	227
甘　肃	Gansu	1225	1704	16	397	1141	45
青　海	Qinghai	204	337	1	458	242	2
宁　夏	Ningxia	233	479		199	215	297
新　疆	Xinjiang	701	718	67	296	201	92

22-45 续表 1 continued

地区	Region	工业固体废物排放量（万吨）Volume of Industrial Solid Wastes Discharged (10 000 tons)	#危险废物排放量 Dangerous Wastes	工业固体废物历年贮存量（万吨）Total Volume of Industrial Solid Wastes Accumulated (10 000 tons)	工业固体废物占地面积（万平方米）Areas Occupied by Industrial Solid Wastes (10 000 sq.m)	"三废"综合利用产品产值（万元）Output Value of Products Made from Comprehensive Utilization of Waste Gas, Waste Water & Solid Wastes (10 000 yuan)	"三废"综合利用产品利润（万元）Profits Obtained from Comprehensive Utilization of Waste Water & Solid Wastes (10 000 yuan)
全　国	**National Total**	**3186**	**3**	**633631**	**58364**	**3104793**	**793828**
北　京	Beijing	32		11830	291	85530	18382
天　津	Tianjin	17		921	1078	25075	2380
河　北	Hebei	119		71163	8151	128914	134910
山　西	Shanxi	646		25868	1951	62338	7688
内蒙古	Inner Mongolia	81		27789	2431	29992	5865
辽　宁	Liaoning	84		110699	4605	164388	34933
吉　林	Jilin	22		14751	3211	201748	24770
黑龙江	Heilongjiang	-		21246	2895	105976	20359
上　海	Shanghai			281	111	91630	54387
江　苏	Jiangsu	5		9525	2584	218723	47396
浙　江	Zhejiang	6		4132	1455	123462	32244
安　徽	Anhui	2		24660	2231	74921	14554
福　建	Fujian	9		4376	211	92695	24157
江　西	Jiangxi	29		54869	3132	40456	6465
山　东	Shandong	1		30744	3213	405626	118352
河　南	Henan	31		26206	2131	196527	42882
湖　北	Hubei	16		12406	2041	128351	21709
湖　南	Hunan	139	-	23294	1978	116153	25722
广　东	Guangdong	12	-	17943	1772	161439	23167
广　西	Guangxi	127	1	8609	963	84856	14441
海　南	Hainan			2032	325	1149	193
重　庆	Chongqing	238	-	7568	773	59593	10963
四　川	Sichuan	321	-	32797	854	236510	57623
贵　州	Guizhou	411	-	18955	727	46457	8920
云　南	Yunnan	530		22350	1672	70088	11768
西　藏	Tibet	17		33	5	31	11
陕　西	Shaanxi	127	-	17963	921	41792	9403
甘　肃	Gansu	58	1	19968	2021	42862	5788
青　海	Qinghai			1941	181	1613	344
宁　夏	Ningxia	13		4484	4038	17926	2832
新　疆	Xinjiang	93		4227	412	47974	11224

22-46 工业分行业工业固体废物产生及处理利用情况（2000年）

Production, Treatment and Utilization of Industrial Solid Wastes by Branch of Industry (2000)

行业 Branch	汇总工业企业数(个) Number of Industrial Enterprises (unit)	工业固体废物产生量(万吨) Volume of Industrial Solid Wastes Produced (10 000 tons)		工业固体废物综合利用量(万吨) Volume of Industrial Solid Wastes Utilized (10 000 tons)	工业固体废物贮存量(万吨) Volume of Industrial Wastes Accumulated (10 000 tons)	工业固体废物处置量(万吨) Volume of Industrial Solid Wastes Treated (10 000 tons)
			#危险废物产生量 Dangerous Wastes			
采掘业 Mining and Quarrying	4312	39203	167	8827	18830	5234
食品、饮料和烟草制造业 Food, Beverage and Tobacco Industry	8283	2050	-	1880	52	76
纺织业 Textile Industry	6077	437	1	385	1	40
皮革毛皮羽绒及其制品业 Leather, Furs, Down and Related Products	994	52	1	30	11	8
造纸及纸制品业 Papermaking & Paper Products	4119	763	5	619	46	85
印刷业记录媒介的复制 Printing & Record Medium Reproduction	643	13	-	10	-	2
石油加工及炼焦业 Petroleum Processing & Coking	720	895	42	591	121	166
化学原料及化学制品制造业 Raw Chemical Materials and Chemical Products	6449	4920	429	3750	1054	382
医药制造业 Medical and Pharmaceutical Products	1886	183	7	167	2	14
化学纤维制造业 Chemical Fiber	269	329	6	296	39	9
橡胶制品业 Rubber Products	640	77	-	71	-	4
塑料制品业 Plastic Products	952	27	-	25	1	1
非金属矿物制品业 Nonmetal Mineral Products	12174	1504	1	1330	109	106
＃水泥制造业 Cement Manufacturing	4635	815		727	93	28
黑色金属冶炼及压延加工业 Smelting and Pressing of Ferrous Metals	1698	12072	38	8191	3250	842
有色金属冶炼及压延加工业 Smelting and Pressing of Nonferrous Metals	1257	2949	60	987	1132	833
金属制品业 Metal Products	4500	69	2	55	-	14
机械、电气、电子设备制造业 Machine Building, Electric Machinery, & Electronic Equipment Manufacturing	9154	786	14	627	52	107
电力煤气及水生产供应业 Production & Supply of Electric Power, Gas & Water	1756	13274	-	9131	4129	1156
其他 Other Industries	5061	2005	54	478	91	72

22-46 续表 1 continued

行业 Branch	工业固体废物排放量（万吨） Volume of Industrial Solid Wastes Discharged (10 000 tons)	#危险废物排放量 Dangerous Wastes	工业固体废物历年贮存量（万吨） Total Volume of Industrial Solid Wastes Accumulated (10 000 tons)	工业固体废物占地面积（万平方米） Areas Occupied by Industrial Solid Wastes (10 000 sq.m)	“三废”综合利用产品产值（万元） Output Value of Products Made from Comprehensive Utilization of Waste Gas, Waste Water & Solid Wastes (10 000 yuan)	“三废”综合利用产品利润（万元） Profits Obtained from Comprehensive Utilization of Waste Water & Solid Wastes (10 000 yuan)
采掘业 Mining and Quarrying	2556	1	426021	16604	221487	36757
食品、饮料和烟草制造业 Food, Beverage and Tobacco Industry	44		469	57	282584	108393
纺织业 Textile Industry	10		25	2	26709	5510
皮革毛皮羽绒及其制品业 Leather, Furs, Down and Related Products	3		66	5	2044	660
造纸及纸制品业 Papermaking & Paper Products	15		612	74	174739	175379
印刷业记录媒介的复制 Printing & Record Medium Reproduction	1				1696	711
石油加工及炼焦业 Petroleum Processing & Coking	20	1	10769	1213	227876	48045
化学原料及化学制品制造业 Raw Chemical Materials and Chemical Products	133	-	11725	2765	431743	105466
医药制造业 Medical and Pharmaceutical Products	4		11	3	23007	6684
化学纤维制造业 Chemical Fiber	8		906	148	31223	3540
橡胶制品业 Rubber Products	1		15	1	6205	827
塑料制品业 Plastic Products					5778	1134
非金属矿物制品业 Nonmetal Mineral Products	69		2384	189	681372	81997
#水泥制造业 Cement Manufacturing	10		1056	119	565434	70355
黑色金属冶炼及压延加工业 Smelting and Pressing of Ferrous Metals	155		63860	2516	393505	107831
有色金属冶炼及压延加工业 Smelting and Pressing of Nonferrous Metals	32	1	31217	3047	192504	56181
金属制品业 Metal Products	2	-	63	7	11891	2698
机械、电气、电子设备制造业 Machine Building, Electric Machinery, & Electronic Equipment Manufacturing	19	-	2208	151	193523	21544
电力煤气及水生产供应业 Production & Supply of Electric Power, Gas & Water	48		80803	31394	141410	21726
其他 Other Industries	154	-	2476	186	55501	8746

22–47 各地区环境污染与破坏事故情况（2000年）
Pollution Accidents by Region (2000)

地 区	Region	环境污染与破坏事故次数（次） Number of Pollution Accidents (times)	按事故类型分（次） Pollution Accidents by Type(times)					污染直接经济损失（万元） Losses Coverted into Cash (10 000 yuan)	污染事故赔、罚款总额（万元） Amount of Reparations and Fines (10 000 yuan)
			水污染 Water Pollution	大气污染 Air Pollution	固体废物污染 Solid Wastes Pollution	噪声与振动危害 Noise and Vibration Pollution	其他 Others		
全国	**National Total**	**2411**	**1138**	**864**	**103**	**266**	**40**	**17807.9**	**3682.65**
北京	Beijing								
天津	Tianjin	1	1					60.0	
河北	Hebei	14	14					17.4	6.3
山西	Shanxi	33	22	9	1	1		139.6	111.3
内蒙古	Inner Mongolia	9	3	3	3			67.9	61.9
辽宁	Liaoning	94	39	34	16	4	1	130.4	140.2
吉林	Jilin	5		1	3	1		2.3	2.3
黑龙江	Heilongjiang	5		2	1	1	1	3.5	3.7
上海	Shanghai	8	5	2	1			10.4	
江苏	Jiangsu	98	67	31				9140.2	250.5
浙江	Zhejiang	179	118	51	4	3	3	483.7	563.5
安徽	Anhui	66	43	23				802.1	170.3
福建	Fujian	32	23	9				42.2	27.1
江西	Jiangxi	122	70	24	7	14	7	147.5	117.1
山东	Shandong	89	51	35	2	1		156.4	139.7
河南	Henan	21	9	11			1	21.1	26.1
湖北	Hubei	30	19	8	1	2		28.9	23.2
湖南	Hunan	317	125	113	25	53	1	763.9	473.4
广东	Guangdong	127	92	30	2		3	193.1	199.3
广西	Guangxi	242	88	137	12	5		568.2	596.6
海南	Hainan	4	2	1			1	6.2	0.7
重庆	Chongqing	34	24	9		1		57.6	59.3
四川	Sichuan	470	120	175	3	162	10	753.4	133.5
贵州	Guizhou	54	26	27	1			39.8	27.3
云南	Yunnan	139	49	68	9	10	3	193.0	178.1
西藏	Tibet	2	2					250.0	
陕西	Shaanxi	79	55	19	2	2	1	236.7	143.9
甘肃	Gansu	114	63	33	6	6	6	3414.4	127.5
青海	Qinghai	5	2	3				16.6	20.5
宁夏	Ningxia	9	3	3	3			45.6	51.2
新疆	Xinjiang	9	3	3	1		2	16.0	25.8

22-48 各地区生活污染物排放情况（2000年）

Discharge of Pollutants from Daily Life by Region (2000)

地区	Region	生活污水排放量（万吨） Volume of Waste Water Discharged From Daily Life (10000 tons)	生活污水中化学需氧量排放量（吨） Absorption of Oxygen by Waste Water From Daily Life (ton)	生活二氧化硫排放量（吨） Emission of Sulfur Dioxide From Daily Life (ton)	生活烟尘排放量（吨） Emission of Dust from Daily Life (ton)
全　国	**National Total**	**2209152**	**7404562**	**3825827**	**2121047**
北　京	Beijing	66317	156997	77544	48465
天　津	Tianjin	23170	115851	116160	59400
河　北	Hebei	58290	214174	187693	115837
山　西	Shanxi	58626	158768	298939	193841
内蒙古	Inner Mongolia	24348	127412	157510	180357
辽　宁	Liaoning	96578	373925	226775	250035
吉　林	Jilin	49220	258785	83971	79801
黑龙江	Heilongjiang	61070	354355	74911	98492
上　海	Shanghai	121217	249391	138105	58053
江　苏	Jiangsu	147407	412439	60787	21263
浙　江	Zhejiang	76883	267688	30985	7347
安　徽	Anhui	80189	275104	44639	37166
福　建	Fujian	64478	195954	10700	11498
江　西	Jiangxi	54017	303863	34951	6001
山　东	Shandong	118679	487162	335017	129498
河　南	Henan	118433	376673	129496	44246
湖　北	Hubei	126353	435937	52148	41927
湖　南	Hunan	98662	350440	146047	60099
广　东	Guangdong	333488	669510	23103	11509
广　西	Guangxi	82453	268306	29792	7482
海　南	Hainan	16740	57883	196	16
重　庆	Chongqing	43953	141701	175200	91761
四　川	Sichuan	123350	413812	228976	105087
贵　州	Guizhou	34789	176438	807578	163291
云　南	Yunnan	32410	119699	62040	53400
西　藏	Tibet	4197	37304		
陕　西	Shaanxi	35795	164451	69602	39226
甘　肃	Gansu	16637	80584	56653	41961
青　海	Qinghai	7336	29346	11840	17795
宁　夏	Ningxia	4083	34164	31664	25514
新　疆	Xinjiang	29984	96444	122805	120679

22-49 各地区工业污染治理项目及投资情况（2000年）

Investment in Anti-Industrial Pollution Projects(2000)

地区	Region	汇总工业企业数（个）Number of Industrial Enterprises	施工项目数（个）Projects Under Construction	治理废水 Treatment of Waste Water	治理废气 Treatment of Waste Gas	治理固体废物 Treatment of Solid Wastes	治理噪声 Treatment of Noise Pollution	治理其他 Treatment of Other Pollution
全　国	**National Total**	**20459**	**27243**	**11894**	**12840**	**803**	**551**	**791**
北　京	Beijing	234	337	123	167	3	7	37
天　津	Tianjin	427	433	167	227	11	15	13
河　北	Hebei	747	979	312	612	22	20	13
山　西	Shanxi	882	1291	358	802	67	32	32
内蒙古	Inner Mongolia	726	863	134	341	14	6	9
辽　宁	Liaoning	576	797	350	359	35	13	40
吉　林	Jilin	344	447	160	255	5	11	16
黑龙江	Heilongjiang	564	737	259	451	12	8	7
上　海	Shanghai	444	713	371	271	14	21	36
江　苏	Jiangsu	1623	2343	929	1188	68	96	62
浙　江	Zhejiang	2241	2681	1596	962	30	34	59
安　徽	Anhui	673	861	444	368	15	12	22
福　建	Fujian	1234	1641	861	653	36	34	57
江　西	Jiangxi	250	394	161	186	26	3	14
山　东	Shandong	1181	1557	488	946	62	18	43
河　南	Henan	632	846	325	446	29	23	23
湖　北	Hubei	583	851	384	361	27	31	48
湖　南	Hunan	670	994	407	482	68	17	20
广　东	Guangdong	2115	2543	1611	797	32	50	53
广　西	Guangxi	796	1270	524	670	41	7	28
海　南	Hainan	102	109	85	21			3
重　庆	Chongqing	449	561	238	288	6	13	16
四　川	Sichuan	1124	1483	669	671	60	33	50
贵　州	Guizhou	256	366	100	229	13	8	16
云　南	Yunnan	569	826	319	443	37	7	19
西　藏	Tibet	17	17	8	7		1	1
陕　西	Shaanxi	475	627	274	272	33	15	33
甘　肃	Gansu	272	337	128	169	24	7	9
青　海	Qinghai	16	24	7	16			1
宁　夏	Ningxia	83	112	35	63	7	2	5
新　疆	Xinjiang	154	203	67	117	6	7	6

22-49 续表 1 continued

地 区	Region	污染治理项目 本年完成投资（万元） Investment Completed in Anti-pollution Projects (10000 yuan)	治理废水 Treatment of Waste Water	治理废气 Treatment of Waste Gas	治理固体废物 Treatment of Solid Waste	治理噪声 Treatment of Noise Pollution	治理其他 Treatment of Other Pollution	本年竣工项目数（个） Number of Projects Completed
全 国	**National Total**	**2394391**	**1095897**	**909242**	**114673**	**60189**	**214390**	**20749**
北 京	Beijing	58204	10950	33740	14	474	13026	
天 津	Tianjin	76993	22793	5329	1130	46595	1145	304
河 北	Hebei	74834	39936	33591	665	298	344	910
山 西	Shanxi	97845	28144	58485	5927	126	5163	935
内蒙古	Inner Mongolia	55939	14106	37923	3490	36	384	403
辽 宁	Liaoning	120195	61765	42489	8857	373	6711	662
吉 林	Jilin	111697	21074	28916	3129	125	58453	400
黑龙江	Heilongjiang	110972	72338	32306	5335	91	903	628
上 海	Shanghai	109429	39087	21174	5375	463	43330	495
江 苏	Jiangsu	131036	65323	54781	7939	1441	1553	1577
浙 江	Zhejiang	223064	120725	74150	2610	910	24670	2362
安 徽	Anhui	56470	26389	25621	2165	375	1920	576
福 建	Fujian	56700	32292	19828	1382	920	2279	1002
江 西	Jiangxi	26190	10449	9322	4437	7	1975	339
山 东	Shandong	252855	119633	93823	20449	274	18677	1442
河 南	Henan	80553	34724	40138	3984	190	1517	716
湖 北	Hubei	85238	45653	26668	6072	644	6201	692
湖 南	Hunan	54462	22668	28215	2979	149	451	892
广 东	Guangdong	167110	109854	52085	1220	1168	2782	1438
广 西	Guangxi	73659	40020	26895	2716	102	3927	1060
海 南	Hainan	7107	6364	677			66	97
重 庆	Chongqing	33524	11458	18232	283	169	3382	520
四 川	Sichuan	84116	47751	28594	3790	418	3563	1181
贵 州	Guizhou	23671	8017	10301	1192	100	4060	325
云 南	Yunnan	68593	24639	38828	4028	417	682	650
西 藏	Tibet	600	450	125		25		1
陕 西	Shaanxi	44053	26762	13762	1617	140	1772	550
甘 肃	Gansu	64347	12144	36218	12439	49	3497	292
青 海	Qinghai	4083	548	3285			250	19
宁 夏	Ningxia	18541	11313	4624	1102	3	1498	83
新 疆	Xinjiang	22311	8528	9116	349	4109	209	198

22-50 各地区自然保护工作基本情况（2000年）

Basic Situation of Natural Protection Work by Region (2000)

地区	Region	自然保护区个数（个）Number of Nature Reserves	保护区面积（公顷）Area of Nature Reserves	保护区面积占辖区面积(%) Percentage of Nature Reserves in the Region	珍稀濒危动物繁殖场(个) Number of Farms To Breed Rare and Dying out Animals	珍稀植物引种栽培场(个) Cultivating Farms of Rare Plants	生态示范区个数(个) Number of Demonstration Zone of Ecology
全国	**National Total**	**1227**	**98207967**	**9.85**	**992**	**50**	**220**
北京	Beijing	13	68107	4.05	80		2
天津	Tianjin	8	129199	11.40			2
河北	Hebei	12	117391	0.63			13
山西	Shanxi	12	113188	0.72			
内蒙古	Inner Mongolia	80	6642634	5.61			2
辽宁	Liaoning	45	2020632	7.58	1		12
吉林	Jilin	28	1846267	10.20	6	5	18
黑龙江	Heilongjiang	122	3187111	7.00	58	20	23
上海	Shanghai	3	44145	6.96			1
江苏	Jiangsu	20	523137	5.10	7	3	28
浙江	Zhejiang	27	123399	1.21	1	2	19
安徽	Anhui	28	342406	2.63			
福建	Fujian	45	282752	1.83			11
江西	Jiangxi	38	252457	1.51			
山东	Shandong	35	450222	2.71	20	7	24
河南	Henan	19	226336	1.36			9
湖北	Hubei	30	554510	2.98			6
湖南	Hunan	60	825594	3.90			6
广东	Guangdong	72	741291	3.49	810	5	3
广西	Guangxi	62	1612242	6.66			
海南	Hainan	75	2694166	5.11			
重庆	Chongqing	26	474767	5.76			
四川	Sichuan	90	5536823	11.30			12
贵州	Guizhou	60	342594	1.95	4	2	4
云南	Yunnan	112	2198212	5.58	2	4	3
西藏	Tibet	17	39087172	32.60			1
陕西	Shaanxi	16	354020	1.71			2
甘肃	Gansu	35	5045713	11.10	3	2	13
青海	Qinghai	7	5351960	7.44			1
宁夏	Ningxia	8	204836	3.95			
新疆	Xinjiang	22	15943733	9.96			5

主 要 统 计 指 标 解 释

社会福利事业单位 指集中收养社会孤老、残、幼的机构，包括由民政部门管理的社会福利院、儿童福利院、精神病人福利院和城镇集体举办的福利院及农村集体举办的敬老院。

社会福利事业单位收养人数 包括民政部门管理和城镇、农村集体举办的社会福利事业单位中收养的老人、少年儿童、缺乏生活自理能力的残疾人员和精神病人。

社会福利企业单位 指以安置城镇有一定劳动能力的盲、聋、哑和肢体残疾人员就业为目的，享受国家减免税待遇的国有或集体企业。包括福利工厂、福利商业和服务业、假肢厂和安置农场等单位。

农村五保户 指农村中既无劳动能力，又无经济来源的老、弱、孤、残的农民，其生活由集体供养，实行保吃、保穿、保住、保医、保葬(孤儿保教)，简称"五保"。享受五保待遇的家庭叫五保户。

双扶户 包括被扶持的优抚户和贫困户。主要是对具有一定劳动能力且生活困难的两户给予一定的救济金以扶持其通过生产自救达到脱贫的目的。

律师 指受聘参加法律顾问处工作，担任法律顾问、刑(民)事代理人、刑事辩护人，办理非诉讼事件、解答法律询问，代写法律事务文书等主要从事律师业务的专职法律工作者和兼职律师。

公证人员 指在国家公证机关依法办理公证事务的司法人员，包括公证员、助理公证员和在公证处工作的其他人员。

办理公证文书 指公证处在一定时期内办结的公证文书件数。公证文书按司法部规定或批准的格式制作，包括国内公证和涉外公证两部分。国内公证分为经济合同公证和民事法律关系公证两大类。

调解人员 指在人民调解委员会担负调解民间一般民事纠纷和轻微违法行为引起纠纷的工作人员，包括调解委员会的委员和调解小组的调解员。

调解民间纠纷 指调解委员会依照法律规定，根据自愿原则，用说服教育的方法调解民间发生的有关民事权利和义务的争执，促成当事双方达到协议和谅解，解决纠纷。包括婚姻家庭纠纷，财产权益纠纷等，不包括法院受理调解的民事案件数。

受理劳动争议案件数 指劳动争议仲裁委员会根据国家有关规定，对劳动争议当事人的申请予以审查，符合受理条件而正式立案、准备处理的劳动争议案件数。

立案 指检察机关对犯罪线索进行初步调查后，认为存在职务犯罪事实并需要追究刑事责任时，依法决定作为刑事案件进行侦查的诉讼活动，是追究犯罪的开始。

大案 贪污贿赂犯罪案件指贪污、贿赂数额在5万元以上，挪用公款案在10万元以上，其他案件在50万元以上。渎职犯罪大案一般为直接经济损失5万元以上，死亡1人以上或者重伤3人以上的案件；或虽然没有造成经济损失和伤亡，但犯罪情节恶劣或造成严重后果的案件。

要案 指县、处级以上干部的犯罪案件。

决定逮捕 指检察机关对直接受理、自行侦查的案件，认为需要逮捕犯罪嫌疑人时，依据法律作出的逮捕决定。

批准逮捕 指检察机关对公安机关、国家安全机关、监狱管理机关提出逮捕的犯罪嫌疑人进行审查，根据事实，依法作出逮捕决定。

决定起诉 指检察机关对公安机关、国家安全机关、监狱管理机关和检察机关内设机构反贪污贿赂部门移送起诉的刑事犯罪嫌疑人进行审查，根据事实，依法向人民法院提起公诉。

离休、退休、退职人员 指正式办理了离休、退休、退职手续，并享受相应的离休、退休、退职待遇的人员。

保险福利费用 指企业、事业、机关单位在工资以外实际支付给职工和离休、退休、退职人员个人以及用于集体的劳动保险和福利费用。

(1)职工保险福利费用包括：

①医疗卫生费：指实行公费医疗企业的职工及其供养的直系亲属的医疗费、医务经费、职工因工负伤就医路费以及住院伙食补助费等；卫生部门开支的事业及机关单位职工的公费医疗经费；未参加公费医疗的企业、事业和机关单位职工的医药费。

②文体宣传费：指企业、事业和机关单位实际支付的文体宣传费，不包括学习费。

③集体福利事业补贴费：指对职工浴室、理发室、洗衣房、哺乳室、托儿所等集体福利设施各项支出与收入相抵后的差额补助费。

④集体福利设施费：指按照国家规定开支的集体福利设施费用，如职工食堂炊事用具的购置费、修理费、职工宿舍的修缮费用。不包括由企业、事业、机关单位自筹经费开支的职工福利设施的基本建设费用。

⑤其他：指上述费用以外，单位支付给职工的保险福利费。

(2)离休、退休、退职人员保险福利费用包括：

①离休金：指发给离休人员的工资和按1982年国务院发布的"关于老干部离职休养制度的几项规定"，发给符合规定的离休干部相当于1-2个月标准工资的生活补贴及1988年增发的生活补贴费。

②退休金：指按照国家有关规定发给退休人员的退休费及1988年增发的生活补贴费。

③退职生活费：指按照1978年国务院《关于工人退休、退职的暂行办法》规定，定期发给退职人员的生活费

及1988年增发的生活补贴费。

④其他：指上述费用以外，单位支付给离休、退休、退职人员的保险福利费。

工业废水排放量 指经过企业厂区所有排放口排到企业外部的工业废水量。包括生产废水、外排的直接冷却水、超标排放的矿井地下水和与工业废水混排的厂区生活污水，不包括外排的间接冷却水(清污不分流的间接冷却水应计算在内)。

工业废水排放达标量 指各项指标都达到国家或地方排放标准的外排工业废水量，包括未经处理外排达标和经过处理后外排达标两部分。

工业废水处理量 指报告期内各种水治理设施实际处理的工业废水量，包括处理后外排和处理后回用的工业废水量和虽经处理但未达到国家或地方排放标准的废水量。如车间和厂排放口均有治理设施，并对同一废水分级处理时，不应重复计算工业废水处理量。

工业废气排放量 指企业厂区内燃料燃烧和生产工艺过程中产生的各种排入空气的含有污染物的气体总量，按标准状态〔273K，101325Pa〕计算。

工业二氧化硫排放量 指企业在燃料燃烧和生产工艺过程中排入大气的二氧化硫数量。

烟尘排放量 指企业厂区内燃料燃烧产生的烟气中夹带的颗粒物数量。

工业粉尘排放量 指企业在生产工艺过程中排放的颗粒物重量，如钢铁企业的耐火材料粉尘、焦化企业的筛焦系统粉尘、烧结机的粉尘、石灰窑的粉尘、建材企业的水泥粉尘等。不包括电厂排入大气的烟尘。

工业固体废物产生量 指企业在生产过程中产生的固体状、半固体状和高浓度液体状废弃物的总量，包括危险废物、冶炼废渣、粉煤灰、炉渣、煤矸石、尾矿、放射性废物和其他废物等；不包括矿山开采的剥离废石和掘进废石(煤矸石和呈酸性或碱性的废石除外)。酸性或碱性废石指采掘的废石其流经水、雨淋水的pH值小于4或pH值大于10.5者。

危险废物 指列入国家危险废物名录或根据国家规定的危险废物鉴别标准和鉴别方法认定的，具有爆炸性、易燃性、易氧化性、毒性、腐蚀性、易传染疾病等危险特性之一的废物。

工业固体废物综合利用量 指通过回收、加工、循环、交换等方式，从固体废物中提取或者使其转化为可以利用的资源、能源和其他原材料的固体废物量(包括当年利用往年的工业固体废物累计贮存量)，如用作农业肥料、生产建筑材料、筑路等。综合利用量由原产生固体废物的单位统计。

工业固体废物贮存量 指以综合利用或处置为目的，将固体废物暂时贮存或堆存在专设的贮存设施或专设的集中堆存场所内的数量。专设的固体废物贮存场所或贮存设施必须有防扩散、防流失、防渗漏、防止污染大气、水体的措施。

工业固体废物处置量 指将固体废物焚烧或者最终置于符合环境保护规定要求的场所，并不再回取的工业固体废物量(包括当年处置往年的工业固体废物累计贮存量)。处置方法有填埋(其中危险废物应安全填埋)、焚烧、专业贮存场(库)封场处理、深层灌注、回填矿井等。

工业固体废物排放量 指将所产生的固体废物排到固体废物污染防治设施、场所以外的数量，不包括矿山开采的剥离废石和掘进废石(煤矸石和呈酸性或碱性的废石除外)。

“三废”综合利用产品产值 指利用“三废”(废液、废气、废渣)作为主要原料生产的产品价值(现行价)；已经销售或准备销售的应计算产品价值，留作生产自用的不应计算产品价值。

“三废”综合利用产品利润 指利用“三废”(废液、废气、废渣)生产的产品，销售后所得到的利润。

环境污染与破坏事故 指由于违反环境保护法规的经济、社会活动与行为，以及意外因素的影响或不可抗拒的自然灾害等原因，致使环境受到污染，国家重点保护的野生动植物、自然保护区受到破坏，人体健康受到危害，社会经济和人民财产受到损失，造成不良社会影响的突发性事件。

聋儿入普幼普小率 指本年度内进入普通幼儿园、普通小学的聋儿数与在训聋儿数（不含当年新收训聋儿数）之比。

综合防治康复精神病人数 是指在开展精神病防治康复工作地区，采取不同形式，接受综合性防治康复措施、开放式管理的精神病人数。

监护率 是指通过监护小组、家庭病床、工疗站、社会就业以及精神卫生机构，接受社会化，综合性、开放式治疗与康复的精神病人占经调查摸底、登记在册的精神病人数的百分比。

社会参与率 是指生活能自理，并参加生产劳动和社会生活的精神病人数占监护精神病人数的百分比。

未入学适龄残疾儿童少年 指根据义务教育法规定应接受义务教育，但因各种原因未能入学的适龄视力残疾、听力与言语残疾、智力残疾、肢体残疾、精神残疾、多重残疾儿童少年。适龄残疾儿童少年的年龄段参照各省级人民政府依照义务教育法规定的入学年龄。

实施分散按比例就业 是指机关、团体、企业事业组织、城乡经济组织，按照所在地有关法规规定的具体比例分散安排残疾人就业，并为其选择适当工种和岗位。实施分散按比例就业的地区应具备四个条件：一是当地出台实施分散按比例就业的政府文件；二是残疾人就业服务机构建立；三是开展了残疾人口的普查登记工作；四是按比例就业的实施面地市达到100%，县区达到90%，社会覆盖面要达到90%。

Explanatory Notes on Main Statistical Indicators

Social Welfare Institutions refer to institutions taking care of old people without children, handicapped people and orphans. They include social welfare institutions run by civil affairs departments, children welfare institutions, social welfare institutions for mental patients, and collective-owned old peoples homes in rural areas.

Number of People Taken in by Social Welfare Institutions refers to the number of old people, children, totally dependent handicapped people and mental patients taken in by social welfare institutions run by civil affairs departments and those run by collective units in urban and rural areas.

Social Welfare Enterprises are collective owned enterprises which employ the blind, deaf-mute, and other handicapped people who are able to work in cities and towns and enjoy exemption from state taxes, including welfare plants, welfare commercial services, artificial limb plants and farms, etc.

Rural Households with Livelihood Guaranteed in Five Aspects refer to the households in which there are old people without child, orphans and handicapped people who are unable to work and without financial resources in rural areas. They are taken care of by the collective units and their food, clothing, housing, medical care, funeral expenses (or schooling for orphans) are guaranteed to be provided for.

Households in the Poor Household Support Program refer to the households of martyrs and disabled servicemen, and poor households, who are able to work but in poor conditions, receiving government or collective relief funds. In this way, the households can get to work and make themselves break away from poverty.

Lawyers are legal workers who are employed full time by legal counseling firms to act as legal advisers, agents in criminal or civil lawsuits, or defenders in criminal lawsuits, or to handle non-litigious legal affairs, to advise on matters of law or to write legal papers for others. Both full-time and part time lawyers are included.

Notary Personnel refers to judicial workers of the state notary offices handling notarization work according to law. They include notaries, assistant notaries, and other people working for notary offices.

Notarized Documents refer to the documents settled by notary offices in a year. The notary documents are drawn up in accordance with the regulations of the Ministry of Justice, including domestic documents and foreign-related documents. Domestic documents are divided into two major categories, documents on economic contracts and documents on civil legal relations.

Mediators refer to workers on peoples mediation committees responsible for mediating in civil disputes and cases of slight infraction of the law. They include members of the mediation committees and mediators of mediation groups.

Mediation of Civil Disputes refers to mediation committees work in mediating in civil disputes concerning civil rights and duties through persuasion and education in accordance with the provisions of law on a voluntary basis, so as to solve disputes by helping the parties involved come to an agreement and understanding. These disputes include divorce cases and disputes over property ownership, but exclude the civil cases to be handled by the court.

Number of Labour Dispute Cases Accepted refers to the number of cases of labour dispute submitted that, after being reviewed by the labour dispute arbitration committees in line with the relevant state regulations, are accepted and registered for treatment.

Acceptance of Case refers to the decision made by the procurators office to confirm the act of crime after initial investigation and to start legal proceedings of the case as criminal case.

Large Case In case of corruption and bribery, it refers to the case involves a bribery of over 50,000 yuan, or a misappropriation of over 100,000, or other cases involving 500,000 yuan. In case of offence on dereliction of duty, it refers to the case that causes an economic loss of over 50,000, loss of one life, or severe injury of 3 persons; or a case that displays extremely disgusting behavior of the offender or results in grave aftermath.

Key Case refers to a case committed by government officials with a ranking of division director or county administrator.

Decision on Arrest refers to decision made by procurators office, in accordance with laws, to arrest the suspect(s) in the cases that are accepted and to be investigated by procurators office.

Approval for Arrest refers to the decision made by procurators office, in accordance with laws and relevant facts, to approve the arrest of the suspect(s) that is proposed by the public security departments, state security departments or authority of prisons .

Decision on Prosecution refers to the decision made by procurators office, in accordance with laws and relevant facts, to institute proceedings to the peoples court against the suspect(s) of criminal cases handed over by the public security departments, state security departments or authority of prisons, or by the anti-corruption departments within the procurators office .

Retired or Resigned Personnel refers to the persons who have formally gone through the formalities for their retirement or quitting work and enjoy the corresponding treatments.

Insurance and Welfare Funds refers to labour insurance and welfare fund paid by enterprises, organizations and institutions to their staff and workers as well as retired and resigned persons in addition to their wages and salaries.

(1) Insurance and Welfare Funds for Staff and Workers include:

Medical Care Allowance: It refers to the cost of medical care of staff and workers and their dependent family members who are covered by the medicare system of enterprises, travelling expenses of injured employees to hospital and their per diem subsidies during hospitalization, cost of medical care of employees who are covered by the medicare system of institutions and organizations, as well as cost of medicine of employees of enterprises and institutions who are not covered by the medicare system.

Expenses for Recreational, Sports and Publicity Activities: They refer to actual payment made by enterprises and institutions in recreational, sports and publicity activities, excluding training cost.

Subsidies to Collective Welfare Undertakings: They refer to subsidies to the operation of welfare undertakings that can not fully cover their cost, such as public bath rooms, barbershops, laundries, nurseries and kindergartens.

Expenses for Collective Welfare Facilities: They refer to expenses for collective welfare facilities that are spent in line with state regulations, such as the purchase and repair of cooking utensils for canteens, and repair of living quarters of staff and workers, but excluding the expenses for welfare projects that are constructed with self-raised funds.

Others: They refer to their insurance and welfare funds paid to staff and workers.

(2)Insurance and Welfare Funds for Retired and Resigned Staff and Workers

Pensions for retired veteran cadres: They refer to pensions, other subsidies, and additional allowances paid to retired in line with relevant government documents.

Pensions for Retirement: They refer to living allowance, other subsidies and additional allowances paid to retired staff and workers in line with the relevant government documents.

Resignation Allowances for Living Expenses: They refer to living allowance, and additional allowances subsidies paid to resigned staff and workers in line with relevant government instructions.

Others: They refer to other expenses, including moving and settlement allowance, allowance for difficult families, book and newspaper allowance, subsidy for non staple foods, housing subsidy, water and electricity subsidy, special allowance for staff and workers of national minorities, travelling cost for senior retired staff, etc.

Volume of Industrial Waste Water Discharged refers to the volume of industrial waste water discharged, through all outlets, to the outside of industrial enterprises, including waste water produced, direct-cooling water, underground water from mines that does not meet the standard of discharge, and the domestic sewage mixed up with industrial waste water when discharged, but excluding discharged indirect-cooling water.

Volume of Waste Water up to the Standard for Discharge refers to the volume of discharged industrial waste water that, with or without treatment, has come up to the national or local standards for discharge.

Volume of Treated Industrial Waste Water refers to the volume of industrial waste water after being treated and purified through various water treatment facilities in the reference period, including the volume discharged or recovered after being treated. The volume of waste water that fails to meet the national or local standards after treatment is also included. If there are treatment facilities both at the outlets of workshops and at the outlets of the factory, and the same volume of waste water has been treated twice, duplication should be avoided in the calculation of the volume of treated industrial waste water.

Volume of Waste Industrial Gas Emission refers to waste gas emitted from burning of fuels and from production process in the area of the factory, and is measured by 10000 standard cubic meters each year under normal condition.

Volume of Industrial Sulphur Dioxide Discharged refers to the volume of sulphur dioxide discharged to the air in the process of fuel burning or in the production process.

Volume of Industrial Soot Discharged refers to the volume of solid soot in the smoke discharged in the process of fuel burning in the area of the factory.

Industrial Dust Discharged refers to the total weight of solid dust discharged by industrial enterprises in the production process, such as dust of refractory materials from iron plants, dust from coke-screening system or from sintering machines of coking plants, dust from lime kilns, cement dust from building material enterprises, etc., but excluding smoke and dust discharged by power plants.

Volume of Industrial Solid Wastes Produced refers to the total volume of solid, semi-solid or high concentration liquid residue produced by industrial enterprises in their production process, including dangerous wastes, residues from melting, slag, powdered coal ash, gangue, chemical residues, tailings, radioactive residues and other residues, but excluding stripped or dug stones in mining (except gangue and acid or alkali stones which are stones washed or soaked by water with a pH value smaller than 4 or larger than 10.5)

Dangerous Wastes refers to the wastes which are listed by the government as the dangerous wastes or the wastes which are explosive, inflammable, oxidizable, poisonous, corrosive or liable to cause infectious diseases or have other dangerous characteristics specified in accordance with the standards or methods stipulated by the government for identifying the dangerous wastes.

Volume of Industrial Solid Wastes Utilized in a Comprehensive Way refers to the volume of solid wastes from which useful materials can be extracted or which can be changed to be utilizable resources, energy or other materials, including the volume of industrial solid wastes stored up in the previous years and utilized in the current year, such as the solid wastes utilized as fertilizers, building materials, for making roads or for other purpose. Statistical data on utilization of industrial solid wastes are collected by solid wastes producing units.

Volume of Industrial Stored up Solid Wastes refers to the volume of industrial solid wastes temporarily stored up or piled with special facilities or piled in the special sites for the purpose of utilization or treatment in future. The special facilities or special sites for storing up solid wastes should have the measures against spreading or being washed away to other places, permeating the soil or causing air pollution or water contamination.

Volume of Industrial Solid Wastes Treated refers to solid wastes disposed of in a non-recoverable place that meet the requirement of environmental protection, such as burying (The dangerous wastes should be buried safely), burning, piling in designated sites, pouring water into the deep strata, filling of old mines, etc. (including treatment of solid wastes piled up in the previous years).

Volume of Industrial Solid Wastes Discharged refers to the volume of industrial solid wastes produced and discharged at the places outside the special facilities or special sites for preventing against pollution, excluding stripped or dug stones in mining (except gangue and acid or alkali waste stones).

Output Value of Products Made from Utilization of Waste Gas, Waste Water and Industrial Solid Wastes refers to the value of products (calculated at current prices) made by industrial enterprises using recovered waste water, waste gas or solid wastes as main raw materials. Only the value of the products which have been sold or are ready to be sold should be included. The value of the products which will be used in the production of the enterprises should not be included.

Profit Obtained from Utilization of Waste Gas, Waste Water and Industrial Solid Wastes refers to profit obtained from selling or own-consumption of products made by industrial enterprises using recovered waste water, waste gas or solid wastes as main raw materials.

Accidents of Environment Pollution and Destruction refer to sudden accidents, due to economic and social behavior or activities in contrast with environment protection legislation, unexpected factors or irresistible natural disasters, that cause the pollution of environment, the destruction of natural protection zones, wild plants and animals, the danger to the health of people, and the loss in the property of the society and people.

Proportion of Deaf Children Enrolled in Ordinary Preschool and Primary Education refers to the proportion of deaf children who are enrolled in ordinary kindergartens or primary schools during the year in the total number of deaf children under rehabilitation programs (not including new comers into the rehabilitation programs during the year).

Number of Mental Patients under Integrated Prevention and Rehabilitation Program refers to mental disease patients receiving integrated prevention and rehabilitation treatment of various forms under open environment in areas with mental disease rehabilitation programs.

Supervision Rate refers to the percentage of patients among the total number of registered mental disease patients, who participate in social integrated and open treatment and rehabilitation programs through various forms such as supervision groups, family treatment, employment or guidance from psychiatric institutions.

Social Participation Rate refers to proportion of mental disease patients who are able to manage their daily life and participate in economic activities to the total number of mental disease patients under supervision.

School-age Disabled Children not in Schools refer to children with disability in sight, listening, speaking, mentality, limbs or multi-disability who are obliged to compulsory education by law but have not been enrolled in schools due to various reasons. The definition of school age for disabled children is decided by the definition of school age as specified by provincial governments in line with the local laws on compulsory education.

Proportional Employment Programs refer to the programs implemented by government agencies, social organizations, enterprises, institutions or other economic entities in line with the proportions specified by local laws for decentralized employment of disabled persons with proper jobs and posts. Provinces eligible for the decentralized proportional employment programs should meet the 4 criteria: a) issue of relevant local government decrees, b) establishment of employment agencies for the disabled, c) conduct of census and registration for the disabled population, and d) proportional employment programs are implemented in 100 percent of prefectures/cities and 90 percent of counties/districts in the province, covering 90 percent of the disabled persons.

二十三、香港特别行政区主要社会经济指标

Main Social and Economic Indicators of Hong Kong Special Administrative Region

简要说明

一、本章资料反映香港特别行政区主要社会、经济发展情况。内容包括：土地、人口、就业、国民收入、国际收支平衡表、工业、能源、建筑、交通、对外贸易、财政金融、教育、房屋、卫生、社会保障等方面。

二、本章涉及的1996年及以前数据均指原列名为“香港地区”的数据。

三、载于本期年鉴的人口数字及其它在编制过程中涉及应用人口数字的统计数字，可能与本年鉴前几期所载的数字有所不同，这是由于以下原因中的一项或两项因素所致：

(1) 自2000年8月起，“居住人口”方法已取代“广义时点”方法以编制香港的人口数字。追溯至1996年的修订人口数字已编制。根据新方法编制的人口数字，更能反映香港人口的居住和流动形态。

(2)香港特别行政区在2001年3月进行了人口普查。该普查除了是细小分区及人口分组资料的重要来源外，亦提供一个基准，用作修订自1996年中期人口统计以来编制的人口数字。于较早以前公布的由1996年至2000年的人口数字，已根据2001年人口普查于2001年8月底公布的初步结果作出修订。同样地，在合适的情况下，其它在编制过程中要利用人口数字的统计数字亦已作出相应的修订。

四、本章由香港特别行政区政府统计处提供所有数据，国家统计局国际统计信息中心负责整理、编辑。

五、在统计工作方面，按中华人民共和国“香港特别行政区基本法”的有关原则，香港特别行政区保留其单独运作的统计系统，并负责编制和发布反映香港特别行政区情况的统计数据。由于香港和内地在使用统计名词及概念方面会有所不同，读者在比较两地数据时，请参考以下资料：

(1)本章内的“《中国统计年鉴》与香港特别行政区统计刊物中使用的指标对照表”列出两地概念相近但名称不同的词汇。

(2)本章末的“主要统计指标解释”，载有一些重要概念的解释。

六、香港特别行政区是单独的关税地区，香港与内地之间的贸易，亦需办理进出口报关。在贸易统计方面，香港特别行政区对外贸易统计数据亦包括香港特别行政区与内地的贸易。

七、在外汇统计及与之有关的各方面，港币是香港特别行政区的法定货币，因此，除港币以外的货币(包括人民币)均视作外币。

八、更详细的统计资料及有关的技术细节，可参阅香港特别行政区政府统计处出版的《香港统计月刊》、《香港统计年刊》及各专题统计出版物。

九、本章节表中的符号使用说明：

“－”表示不适用；“N.A.”表示没有数字。

Brief Introduction

I. Data in this chapter show main social and economic developments of the Hong Kong Special Administrative Region, including data on land, population, employment, national income, Balance of Payments account, industry, energy, construction, transportation, external trade, finance and banking, education, housing, health and social security.

II. Data of 1996 and previous years in this chapter refer to data of the former Hong Kong region.

III. Population figures presented in the present edition may be different from those presented in earlier editions of this Yearbook. The same applies to other statistics which in the process of their compilation have involved the use of population figures. The differences may be due to one or both of the following reasons:

1. Since August 2000, the "resident population" approach has been adopted in place of the "extended de facto" approach for compiling Hong Kong population figures. Revised population figures backdated to 1996 have been compiled. Population figures compiled based on the new approach will better reflect the residency and mobility patterns of Hong Kong people.

2. A Population Census was conducted in March 2001 in the Hong Kong Special Administrative Region. Apart from serving as the prime source of data for small areas and population sub-groups, the 2001 Population Census provides a benchmark for revising the population figures compiled since the 1996 Population By-census. With the release of the preliminary results of the 2001 Population Census in end August 2001, population figures released in earlier periods for 1996 to 2000 have been revised accordingly. Similarly, other statistics which in the process of their compilation have involved the use of population figures have also been revised where appropriate.

IV. All data in this chapter are provided by the Census and Statistics Department, the Government of the Hong Kong Special Administrative Region, and further tabulated or edited by the International Statistical Information Centre of the National Bureau of Statistics.

V. According to the Basic Law of the Hong Kong Special Administrative Region of the People's Republic of China, Hong Kong Special Administrative Region maintains its independent statistical system, and compiles and disseminates statistics on the Region. As Hong Kong and the mainland of China use different statistical concepts, definitions and terminologies, users are advised to make reference of the following materials when using and comparing data of the mainland of China and the Hong Kong Special Administrative Region:

1. A Comparison of Common Statistical Terms Used in China Statistical Yearbook and Publications Compiled by the Census and Statistics Department, the Government of the Hong Kong Special Administrative Region, which listed similar statistical concepts using different terms.

2.The Explanatory Note at the end of this chapter which gives explanation on important statistical indicators.

VI. As Hong Kong is a separate custom territory, trade between Hong Kong and the mainland of China needs customs declaration procedures. In terms of trade statistics, data on Hong Kong's imports and exports include Hong Kong's trade with the mainland of China.

VII. As HK dollar is the legal tender in the Hong Kong Special Administrative Region, all other currencies (including Renminbi) are regarded as foreign currencies in compiling foreign exchange statistics and related statistics.

VIII. For more detailed statistics and technical details, users are advised to read the Hong Kong Monthly Digest of Statistics, the Hong Kong Annual Digest of Statistics and other publications compiled by the Census and Statistics Department, the Government of the Hong Kong Special Administrative Region.

IX. Notations used in this chapter:

"-" indicates not applicable; "N.A." indicates not available.

23-1 主要统计指标概览

Summary of Key Statistics

项目	Item	1996	1997	1998	1999	2000
人口及生命事件	**Population and Vital Events**					
年中人口@ (万人)	Mid-year Population@ (10000 persons)	643.6	648.9	654.4	660.7	666.5
粗出生率@ (‰)	Crude Birth Rate@ (‰)	9.9	9.1	8.1	7.8	8.1
粗死亡率@ (‰)	Crude Death Rate@ (‰)	5.0	4.9	5.0	5.0	5.1
劳工	**Labour**					
劳动人口@ (万人)	Labour Force@ (10000 persons)	316.1	323.5	327.6	332.0	337.4
劳动人口参与率@ (%)	Labour Force Participation Rate@ (%)	61.6	61.3	61.3	61.3	61.4
失业率@ (%)	Unemployment Rate@ (%)	2.8	2.2	4.7	6.2	4.9
就业不足率@ (%)	Underemployment Rate@ (%)	1.6	1.1	2.5	2.9	2.8
选定行业的就业人数@（人）	Number of Employed Persons in Selected Industries @(person)					
(i) 制造业	(i) Manufacturing	489900	443000	379600	353900	333700
(ii) 建筑业	(ii) Construction	273100	303100	306600	286800	301700
(iii)批发、零售、进出口贸易、饮食及酒店业	(iii) Wholesale, Retail and Import/Export Trades, Restaurants and Hotels	907800	960800	953500	935100	981700
(iv)运输、仓库及通讯业	(iv) Transport, Storage and Communications	336200	343400	349200	339400	356600
(v)金融、保险、地产及商用服务业	(v) Financing, Insurance, Real Estate and Business Services	363800	405100	410300	437700	452700
(vi)社区、社会及个人服务业	(vi) Community, Social and Personal Services	667900	678200	695600	732900	754700
实际工资指数 (1992年9月=100)	Real Wage Index (September 1992=100)	102.8	104.5	104.4	109.0	112.8
对外贸易	**External Trade**					
进口 (百万港元)	Imports (HKD million)	1535582	1615090	1429092	1392718	1657962
港产品出口 (百万港元)	Domestic Exports (HKD million)	212160	211410	188454	170600	180967
转口 (百万港元)	Re-exports (HKD million)	1185758	1244539	1159195	1178400	1391722
贸易价格比率指数(1990=100)	Terms of Trade Index (1990=100)	99.7	100.4	101.6	100.8	99.9
工业生产	**Industrial Production**					
工业生产指数(1986=100)	Index of Industrial Production(1986=100)	121.5	120.6	110.1	103.1	102.5
工业电力耗用 (万亿焦耳)	Industrial Electricity Consumption (terajoules)	19934	18965	18489	17547	17769
工业煤气耗用 (万亿焦耳)	Industrial Gas Consumption (terajoules)	918	911	888	914	982
经销贸易业、运输业、服务业	**Distributive Trades, Transport Services and Other Services**					
增加价值 (百万港元)	Value Added (HKD million)					
批发业	Wholesale	16100	15760	13076	13789	N.A.
零售业	Retail	38491	38409	26368	27094	N.A.
进出口贸易业	Import/Export	222922	232828	206548	198618	N.A.
运输及有关服务	Transport and Related Services	70444	71596	73816	80315	N.A.
仓库、通讯、财务(银行除外) 及商用服务业	Storage, Communications, Financing (Except Banking) and Business Services	81476	100836	84565	86332	N.A.
土地、楼宇、建筑	**Land, Building and Construction**					
建筑工程完成名义总值 (百万港元)	Gross Value of Construction Work in Nominal Terms (HKD million)	116290	131500	133316	126437	122071
获批准可动工兴建私人居住单位 (个)	Private Residential Flats with Consent to Commence Work (number)	22113	40962	33843	44323	31366
送达土地注册处登记的文件涉及的价值 (百万港元)	Consideration of Documents Received for Registration in the Land Registry (HKD million)					
楼宇及地段买卖合约	Agreements for Sale and Purchase of Building Units and Land	517767	937806	364612	287010	242996
楼宇转让契约	Assignments of Building Units	412420	790408	348352	300059	273040
地段转让契约	Assignments of Land	38098	93750	24311	35670	19921
房屋	**Housing**					
新落成房屋委员会租住单位① (个)	Housing Authority Rental Flats Newly Completed① (number)	14946	17917	9759	31806	47552
新落成居者有其屋计划的居住单位①②(个)	Home Ownership Scheme Residential Flats Newly Completed①② (number)	13188	12040	3320	13778	23542

23-1 续表 1 continued

项目	Item	1996	1997	1998	1999	2000
运输、通讯、旅游	**Transport,Communications and Tourism**					
进出香港货运车辆 (辆)	Inward/Outward Movement of Goods Vehicle (vehicle)	8191994	8543130	8543123	8874750	9379793
进出香港货物	Inward and Outward Movements of Cargo					
总卸下 (千吨)	Total Discharged(thousand tonnes)	119689	127223	126414	127940	130349
总装上 (千吨)	Total Loaded (thousand tonnes)	75272	80913	78999	81754	86919
货柜吞吐量③ (千标准货柜单位)	Container Throughput ③ (thousand TEUs)	13460	14567 (14386)	14582	16211	18098
领牌车辆 (辆)	Motor Vehicles Licensed (vehicle)	475115	500228	500673	503974	516782
电话线 (千条)	Telephone Lines (thousand lines)	3402	3624	3708	3839	3946
访港旅客④ (万人次)	Visitor Arrivals④ (10000 persons)	1297.4	1127.3	1016.0	1132.8	1305.9
酒店入住率 (%)	Hotel Room Occupancy Rate (%)	88	76	76	79	83
政府收支、货币、金融 (百万港元)	**Public Accounts, Money and Finance (HKD million)**					
政府储备结余①	Government's Reserve Balances①	173605	457543	434302	444254	430278
政府收入总额①	Total Government Revenue①	208358	281226	216115	232995	225060
政府开支及证券投资总额①	Total Government Expenditure and Equity Investments①	182680	194360	239356	223043	232893
货币供应(定义三)#	Money Supply (definition 3)#					
港币⑤	Hong Kong Dollar⑤	1520461	1670379	1826233	1922962	1999152
外币⑥	Foreign Currency⑥	1091176	1155230	1296112	1438843	1649322
总计	Total	2611636	2825609	3122345	3361805	3648473
在港使用的贷款及垫款#	Loans and Advances for Use in Hong Kong#	1637191	2037278	1960371	1819792	1861465
港币汇率指数⑦ (贸易总值加权) (1983年11月=100)	Effective Exchange Rate Indices for the Hong Kong Dollar⑦ (trade-weighted)(November 1983=100)	125.0	130.3	137.5	134.2	135.0
消费物价指数 (1999年10月至2000年9月=100)	**Consumer Price Indices (Oct. 99-Sept.2000 =100)**					
综合消费物价指数	Composite Consumer Price index	98.8	104.5	107.5	103.2	99.4
甲类消费物价指数	Consumer Price Index(A)	97.6	103.2	105.9	102.5	99.5
乙类消费物价指数	Consumer Price Index(B)	99.7	105.5	108.5	103.4	99.4
丙类消费物价指数	Consumer Price Index(C)	98.6	104.6	107.9	103.9	99.3
教育	**Education**					
日校小学学生人数 (人)	Student Enrolment in Primary Day School (person)	466507	461911	476802	491851	493979
日校中学学生人数 (人)	Student Enrolment in Secondary Day School (person)	465658	458118	455872	453465	456693
教资会资助院校学生人数(人)	Student Enrolment in UGC-funded Institutions (person)	85550	86202	84538	83754	81472
医疗卫生	**Medical and Health**					
登记死亡人数 (人)	Registered Deaths (person)	32049	32079	32680	33387	33993*
死于心脏病人数 (人)	Deaths from Heart Diseases (person)	4844	4806	5060	5220	5315*
死于恶性肿瘤人数 (人)	Deaths from Malignant Neoplasms (person)	10134	10373	10691	10977	11176*
婴儿死亡率(按每千名登记活产婴儿计算)	Infant Mortality Rate (per 1 000 Registered Live Births)	4.0	4.0	3.2	3.2	2.9*
社会福利	**Social Welfare**					
综合社会保障援助①	Comprehensive Social Security Assistance①					
个案数目⑧ (个)	Number of Cases⑧ (case)	166720	195645	232819	228015	228263
发放款项 (百万港元)	Amount (HKD million)	7127.8	9441.3	13028.7	13623.4	13559.8+
公共福利金①	Social Security Allowances①					
个案数目⑧ (个)	Number of Cases⑧ (case)	510091	517865	526742	535452	550585
发放款项 (百万港元)	Amount (HKD million)	4041.6	4420.2	4737.3	4883.3	5129.6+
交通意外伤亡援助①	Traffic Accident Victims Assistance①					
获批个案数目 (个)	Number of Cases Authorized for Payment (case)	5558	5655	5809	5797	5998
发放款项 (百万港元)	Amount (HKD million)	122.8	137.4	164.8	133.5	130.0
治安	**Law and Order**					
举报罪案合计 (件)	Overall Reported Crime (case)	79050	67367	71962	76771	77245
暴力罪案总计 (件)	Total Violent Crime (case)	15191	13749	14682	15705	14812
犯罪被捕人数总计 (人)	Total Offenders Arrested (person)	47157	41714	40422	40745	40930
国内生产总值⑨	**Gross Domestic Product (GDP)⑨**					
以固定(1990年)价格计算	**At Constant (1990) Market Prices**					
支出法国内生产总值	Expenditure-based GDP					
年增长率 (%)	Annual Growth Rate (%)	4.5	5.0	-5.3	3.0#	10.5#
国内生产总值(百万港元)	Total GDP (HKD million)	789753	829017	785073	808826#	893537#
按人口平均计算的国内生产总值@ (港元)	Per Capita GDP@ (HKD)	122718	127751	119974	122429#	134064#

23-1 续表 2 continued

项　目	Item	1996	1997	1998	1999	2000
以现价计算	**At Current Market Prices**					
支出法国内生产总值	Expenditure-based GDP					
年增长率　(%)	Annual Growth Rate　(%)	10.7	11.1	-4.9	-2.5#	3.2#
国内生产总值(百万港元)	Total GDP　(HKD million)	1191890	1323862	1259306	1227658#	1267175#
按人口平均计算的国内生产总值@ (港元)	Per Capita GDP@　(HKD)	185206	204007	192446	185826#	190124#
生产法国内生产总值(百万港元)	Production-based GDP (HKD million)	1192656	1318035	1231602	1195209#	N.A.
国民生产总值⑩	**Gross National Product (GNP) ⑩**					
以现价计算的国民生产总值(百万港元)	GNP at Current Market Prices (HKD million)	1192078	1334337	1288068	1262435#	1288715#
按人口平均计算的国民生产总值@ (港元)	Per Capita GNP@　(HKD)	185235	205621	196841	191090#	193356#
对外要素收益流动净值总计(百万港元)	Total Net External Factor Income Flows　(HKD million)	188	10475	28762	34777	21540#
国际收支平衡表	**Balance Of Payments Account**					
经常帐⑾ (百万港元)	Current Account⑾(HKDmillion)	-	-	30238	89109#	68784#
资本及金融帐⑾ (百万港元)	Capital and Financial Account⑾ (HKDmillion)	-	-	-31514	-83374#	-59369#
净误差及遗漏⑿ (百万港元)	Net errors and omissions⑿(HKD million)	-	-	1276	-5735#	-9415#
整体的国际收支 (百万港元)	Overall Balance Of Payments(HKD million)	-	-	-52581 (赤字) (in deficit)	77867# (盈余) (in surplus)	76798# (盈余) (in surplus)

注：①数字是以相应的财政年度为根据。例如1996年的数字代表1996至1997财政年度数字。
②不包括私人机构参建居屋计划。
③1998年开始，一系列新的货柜吞吐量数字已经开始编制。为方便比较，按新系列编制的1997年数字于括号内展示。
④访港旅客数字包括经澳门访港的非澳门居民。
⑤所列数字已包括外币掉期存款。
⑥所列数字已扣除外币掉期存款。《中华人民共和国香港特别行政区基本法》说明，港币是香港特别行政区的法定货币。外币指港币以外的其他货币，因而人民币亦视作外币。
⑦数字是电汇或现钞收市中间兑换价年内平均数。
⑧于财政年度终结时的数字。
⑨香港特别行政区出版物中称为"本地生产总值"。
⑩香港特别行政区出版物中称为"本地居民生产总值"。
⑾经常帐差额的正数显示盈余而负数则显示赤字。在资本及金融帐方面，正数显示净资金流入而负数则显示净资金流出。由于对外资产的增加是属于借方帐目而减少则属贷方帐目，因此负数的储备资产变动净值显示储备资产的增加，而正数则显示减少。
⑿原则上，贷方和借方各项帐目的净总和应相等于零。但实际上，贷方和借方帐目的资料是透过不同的来源搜集，基于各种原因会有差异。为了令贷方和借方帐目的总和相等，便须加进一个余额项目，以反映平衡表的"净误差及遗漏"。
— 不适用。
* 临时数字。
# 日后会作出修订。
N.A.没有数字。
@载于本表内的人口数字及其它在编制过程中涉及应用人口数字的统计数字，与载于本年鉴前几期的数字或有不同，这是由于以下其中一项或两项因素所致：
(1)自2000年8月起编制人口数字的方法有所改变。
(2)2001年人口普查结果为人口数据提供最新基准资料。
有关详情，请参阅本章节的"简要说明"第三点。
+包括2001年4月1日所发放的款项。

Notes: ①Figures are for the corresponding financial year. For example, figures for 1996 would represent the figures for financial year 1996/97.
②Excluding Private Sector Participation Scheme .
③Starting from 1998, a new series of container thoughput statistics has been compiled. To facilitate comparison, figure for 1997 under the new series are presented in brackets.
④Figures include arrival of non-Macau residents via Macau.
⑤Figures are adjusted to include foreign currency swap deposits.
⑥Figures are adjusted to exclude foreign currency swap deposits. Hong Kong dollar is the legal tender in the Hong Kong Special Administrative Region, as stated in "The Basic Law of the Hong Kong Special Administrative Region of the People's Republic of China". Foreign currency refers to any currency other than the Hong Kong currency. Accordingly Chinese Renminbi is also treated as foreign currency
⑦Figures are based on average of the closing middle-market telegraphic transfer rates or notes rates for the year.
⑧Figures are as at end of the financial year.
⑨The Chinese term used in the publications of the Hong Kong Special Administrative Region is "本地生产总值".
⑩The Chinese term used in the publications of the Hong Kong Special Administrative Region is "本地居民生产总值".
⑾A postive value for the balance figure in the current account represents a surplus whereas a negative value represents a deficit. For the capital and financial account, a positive value indicates a net capital and financial inflow and a negative value indicates a net outflow. As increases in external assets are debit entries and decreases are credit entries, a negative value for net change in reserve assets represents a net increase and a positive value represents a net decrease.
⑿In principle, the net sum of credit entries and debit entries is zero. In practice, discrepancies between the credit and debit entries may however occur for various reasons as the data are collected from many sources. Equality between the sum of credit entries and debit entries is brought about by the inclusion of a balancing item which reflects net errors and omissions.
- not applicable.
* Provisional figure.
# Subject to revision later on.
N.A. Not available.
@ Population figures presented in this table may be different from those presented in earlier editions of this Yearbook. The same applies to other statistics which in the process of their compilation have involved the use of population figures. The differences may be due to one or both of the following reasons :
1. The change in the approach for compiling population figures since August 2000.
2. The availability of up-to-date benchmark population data based on the results of the 2001 Population Census.
For details, please see Note III in the "Brief Introduction" of this chapter.
+Includes the payments for 1 April 2001.

23-2 按区议会分区划分的香港地区面积

Area of Hong Kong by District Council District

单位：平方公里 (sq. km)

区议会分区	District Council District+	1997	1998	1999	2000	2001
总计	**Total**	**1096**	**1097**	**1098**	**1098**	**1099**
香港岛	**Hong Kong Island**					
中西区	Central and Western	13	13	13	12	12
湾仔	Wan Chai	10	10	10	10	10
东区	Eastern	19	19	19	19	19
南区	Southern	39	39	39	39	39
小计	Sub-total	80	80	80	80	80
九龙	**Kowloon**					
九龙城	Kowloon City	10	10	10	10	10
观塘	Kwun Tong	11	11	11	11	11
深水土步	Sham Shui Po	9	9	9	9	9
黄大仙	Wong Tai Sin	9	9	9	9	9
油尖旺	Yau Tsim Mong	7	7	7	7	7
小计	Sub-total	47	47	47	47	47
新界	**New Territories**					
离岛	Islands	175	175	175	175	175
北区	North	137	137	137	137	137
西贡	Sai Kung	135	136	136	136	136
沙田	Sha Tin	69	69	69	69	69
大埔	Tai Po	147	147	147	147	148
荃湾	Tsuen Wan	61	61	61	61	61
葵青	Kwai Tsing	22	22	22	22	22
屯门	Tuen Mun	84	84	84	84	84
元朗	Yuen Long	138	138	138	139	139
小计	Sub-total	969	970	971	971	971

注：1997年的数字是6月份的数据。1998至2001年的数字则是5月份的数据。
2000年及以后的数字是根据1999年区议会选举界线计算。

Notes: Figures for 1997 are as at June of the year. Figures for 1998 to 2001 are as at May of the year.
Figures from 2000 onwards are based on 1999 District Council electoral boundaries.
+ Before 2000, District Council District was known as 'District Board District'.

23-3 土地用途分布情况

Land Usage

单位：平方公里 (sq. km)

类　别	Class	2000
私人住宅①	Private Residential①	24
公屋②	Public Residential②	16
乡郊居所③	Rural Settlements③	27
商业/商贸和办公室	Commercial/Business and Offices	3
工业	Industrial	5
工业企业	Industrial Estates	3
货仓和贮物处④	Warehouse and Storage④	11
政府、机构和社区设施	Government, Institution and Community Facilities	20
道路	Roads	35
铁路	Railways	1
机场	Airport	13
休憩用地⑤	Open Space⑤	20
空置发展/正在进行建筑工程的土地	Vacant Development Land/Construction in Progress	27
坟场和火葬场	Cemeteries and Crematoriums	5
公用事业设施	Public Utilities	6
其他用途	Other Uses	14
农地	Agricultural	57
鱼塘/基围	Fish Ponds/Gei Wais	13
林地	Woodland	190
灌丛	Shrubland	241
草地	Grassland	310
红树林和沼泽	Mangrove and Swamp	6
劣地	Badland	16
石矿场	Quarries	3
石岸	Rocky Shore	5
水塘	Reservoirs	24
河道和明渠	Streams and Nullahs	4
总计	**Total**	**1099**

注：由2000年起，规划署采用了新的测量方法，利用遥感技术和新的土地用途分类法作出测量。测量结果就土地用途，特别是未建设乡郊地区的土地用途，提供更详细的分类。因此，本表所载的数字不能与1999年及之前的数字作严格比较。

数字是当年12月的数据。

①由私人发展商发展的住宅用地（乡村屋宇、居屋计划/私人参建计划屋苑和临时房屋区除外）。

②包括居屋计划/私人参建计划屋苑和临时房屋区。

③包括临时构筑物。

④包括露天贮物用地。

⑤包括公园、体育馆和运动场。

Notes: From 2000, a new survey method by using remote sensing technology and a new classification of land uses has been adopted. The results of the survey provide a set of more detailed land uses, particularly in the rural non-built-up areas. Hence, figures presented above are not strictly comparable with those for years 1999 and before.

Figures are as at December of the year.

①Residential land developed by private developers except village houses, Home Ownership Scheme (HOS)/Private Sector Participation Scheme (PSPS) and temporary housing areas.

②Include HOS/PSPS and temporary housing areas.

③Include temporary structures.

④Include open storage areas.

⑤Include parks, stadiums and playgrounds.

23-4 人口主要指标

Main Indicators of Population

项　目	Item	1996	1997	1998	1999	2000
年中人口① (万人)	Mid-year Population① (10 000 persons)	643.6	648.9	654.4	660.7	666.5
粗出生率① (‰)	Crude Birth Rate① (‰)	9.9	9.1	8.1	7.8	8.1
粗死亡率① (‰)	Crude Death Rate① (‰)	5.0	4.9	5.0	5.0	5.1
婴儿死亡率 (‰)	Infant Mortality Rate (‰)	4.1	3.9	3.2	3.1	3.0
自然增长率① (‰)	Rate of Natural Increase① (‰)	4.8	4.2	3.1	2.7	3.1
总和生育率①②③	Total Fertility Rate①②③	1166	1095	990	965	1024
登记结婚数 (对)	Registered Marriages (couple)	37045	37593	31673	31287	30879
离婚判令 (对)	Divorce Decrees (couple)	9473	10492	13129	13408	13048
出生时平均预期寿命① (岁)	Expectation of Life at Birth① (years)					
男	Male	76.1	76.4	76.3	76.7	77.0
女	Female	81.7	81.8	81.7	81.8	82.2

注：①载于本表内的人口数字及其它在编制过程中涉及应用人口数字的统计数字，与载于本年鉴前几期的数字或有不同，这是由于以下其中一项或两项因素所致：

(1)自2000年8月起编制人口数字的方法有所改变。

(2)2001年人口普查结果为人口数据提供最新基准资料。

有关详情，请参阅本章节的“简要说明”第三点。

②按每千名15至49岁女性人口计算。

③此数字是以没有包括女性外籍家庭佣工的人口作分母编制。

Notes: ①Population figures presented in this table may be different from those presented in earlier editions of this Yearbook. The same applies to other statistics which in the process of their compilation have involved the use of population figures. The differences may be due to one or both of the following reasons :

1. The change in the approach for compiling population figures since August 2000.
2. The availability of up-to-date benchmark population data based on the results of the 2001 Population Census.

For details, please see Note III in the "Brief Introduction" of this chapter.

②Per 1000 women aged 15-49.

③These figures have been compiled using a population denominator which has excluded female foreign domestic helpers.

23-5 劳动人口及失业状况

Labour Force and Unemployment

项　目	Item	1996	1997	1998	1999	2000
劳动人口数目(万人)	Labour Force (10 000 persons)	316.1	323.5	327.6	332.0	337.4
男	Male	192.5	195.5	195.8	195.7	196.4
女	Female	123.6	128.0	131.8	136.2	141.0
就业人数 (万人)	Employed Persons (10 000 persons)	307.3	316.4	312.2	311.2	320.7
失业人数 (万人)	Unemployed Persons(10 000 persons)	8.7	7.1	15.4	20.7	16.7
失业率 (%)	Unemployment Rate (%)	2.8	2.2	4.7	6.2	4.9

注：载于本表内的数字与载于本年鉴前几期的数字或有不同，这是由于以下其中一项或两项因素所致：

(1)自2000年8月起编制人口数字的方法有所改变。

(2)2001年人口普查结果为人口数据提供最新基准资料。

有关详情，请参阅本章节的“简要说明”第三点。

Note: Figures presented in this table may be different from those presented in earlier editions of this Yearbook due to one or both of the following reasons:

1. The change in the approach for compiling population figures since August 2000.
2. The availability of up-to-date benchmark population data based on the results of the 2001 Population Census.

For details, please see Note III in the "Brief Introduction" of this chapter.

23-6 按行业划分的就业人数

Number of Employed Persons by Industry

单位：人 (person)

行业	Industry	1996	1997	1998	1999	2000
制造业	Manufacturing	489900	443000	379600	353900	333700
建筑业	Construction	273100	303100	306600	286800	301700
批发、零售、进出口贸易、饮食及酒店业	Wholesale, Retail and Import/Export Trades, Restaurants and Hotels	907800	960800	953500	935100	981700
运输、仓库及通讯业	Transport, Storage and Communications	336200	343400	349200	339400	356600
金融、保险、地产及商用服务业	Financing, Insurance, Real Estate and Business Services	363800	405100	410300	437700	452700
社区、社会及个人服务业	Community, Social and Personal Services	667900	678200	695600	732900	754700
其他	Others	34600	30000	27200	26500	26200
总计	**Total**	**3073300**	**3163600**	**3122000**	**3112100**	**3207300**

注：有关就业统计数字，可分别按"综合住户统计调查"及"雇佣及职位空缺按季统计调查"的结果编制。此两套数字用于反映有关就业情况时，各有优点和局限。上表载列了"综合住户统计调查"的估计数字，是由于其包括的就业人口范围较全面。再者，个别人士，包括有多过一份工作的职位持有者，都只计算一次。但"综合住户统计调查"的就业估计数字有一个主要局限，就是被访者有困难准确地提供其本身所属行业的资料，尤以制造业员工为甚。随着香港制造业机构将部分工序移往中国内地，这些机构在香港的传统运作模式已有改变。就一些已将大部分工序移往中国内地的机构而言，他们应归类为进出口贸易业。不过，由于有关机构的员工，尤其是技师及技工级等员工，未必全部都能清楚理解这个统计分类上的改变，有些被访者仍认为他们是属于制造业而非进出口贸易业，因而使"综合住户统计调查"的有关制造业估计就业人数有高估的现象。

载于本表内的数字与载于本年鉴前几期的数字或有不同，这是由于以下其中一项或两项因素所致：

(1)自2000年8月起编制人口数字的方法有所改变。

(2)2001年人口普查结果为人口数据提供最新基准资料。

有关详情，请参阅本章节的"简要说明"第三点。

Notes: Employment statistics are compiled separately based on the General Household Survey (GHS) and the Quarterly Survey of Employment and Vacancies. Each source has its own merits and limitations in reflecting the employment situation. The GHS estimates are presented here because the omission in terms of coverage of the employed population is negligible. Besides, individual persons, including multiple job holders, are counted only once. However, a major limitation of the GHS estimates is that the respondents might not have reported accurately the industry to which they belong, especially for workers in the manufacturing sector. With the relocation of some production processes to the mainland of China, there is a change in the mode of operation of the traditional manufacturing establishments in Hong Kong. As a result, some of these establishments are more appropriately classified as import/export establishments if the majority of the production activities are carried out in the mainland of China. However, this change in statistical classification may not be readily recognized by all the employed persons, particularly the technicians and craftsmen, of the establishments concerned. Hence, the GHS employment estimate in respect of the manufacturing sector will be overstated to the extent that some respondents mistakenly regard themselves as still being engaged in the manufacturing sector instead of the import/export trades.

Figures presented in this table may be different from those presented in earlier editions of this Yearbook due to one or both of the following reasons :

1. The change in the approach for compiling population figures since August 2000.
2. The availability of up-to-date benchmark population data based on the results of the 2001 Population Census.

For details, please see Note III in the "Brief Introduction" of this chapter.

23-7 国内生产总值
Gross Domestic Product

年份 Year	国内生产总值①（按现价计算） Gross Domestic Product①(GDP) At Current Market Prices		国内生产总值与上年比较的实际增长%② GDP Real Growth Rate over the Preceding Year% ②	人均国内生产总值（按现价计算）③ Per Capita GDP③ At Current Market Prices	
	（亿港元） (HKD 100 million)	（亿美元） (USD 100 million)		（港元） (HKD)	（美元） (USD)
1988	4550	583	8.0	80855	10358
1989	5239	672	2.6	92128	11811
1990	5825	748	3.4	102121	13111
1991	6685	860	5.1	116223	14956
1992	7793	1007	6.3	134357	17357
1993	8975	1160	6.1	152087	19660
1994	10109	1308	5.4	167493	21674
1995	10771	1392	3.9	174972	22618
1996	11919	1541	4.5	185206	23947
1997	13239	1710	5.0	204007	26351
1998	12593	1626	-5.3	192446	24848
1999④	12277	1582	3.0	185826	23953
2000④	12672	1626	10.5	190124	24403

注：①香港特别行政区出版物中称为"本地生产总值"。
②增长率是按固定(1990年)价格计算的国内生产总值计算而得。
③载于本表内的数字与载于本年鉴前几期的数字或有不同，这是由于以下其中一项或两项因素所致：
(1)自2000年8月起编制人口数字的方法有所改变。
(2)2001年人口普查结果为人口数据提供最新基准资料。
有关详情，请参阅本章节的"简要说明"第三点。
④数字在日后得到更多资料时会作出修订。

Notes: ①The Chinese term used in the publications of the Hong Kong Special Administrative Region is "本地生产总值".
②The growth rates are calculated based on GDP at constant (1990) market prices.
③Figures presented in this table may be different from those presented in earlier editions of this Yearbook due to one or both of the following reasons :
1. The change in the approach for compiling population figures since August 2000.
2. The availability of up-to-date benchmark population data based on the results of the 2001 Population Census.
For details, please see Note III in the "Brief Introduction" of this chapter.
④Figures are subject to revisions later on as more data become available.

23-8 生产法国内生产总值①
Production-based Gross Domestic Product①

单位：百万港元 (HKD million)

经济活动	Economic Activity	1996	1997	1998	1999*
农业及渔业	**Agriculture and Fishing**	**1444**	**1464**	**1530**	**1171**
工业	**Industry**	**175127**	**181184**	**174632**	**166542**
采矿及采石业	Mining and Quarrying	311	272	301	307
制造业	Manufacturing	82769	80049	70849	65767
电力、燃气及水务业	Electricity, Gas and Water	26989	29212	33546	34358
建筑业	Construction	65058	71650	69937	66111
服务业	**Services**	**953642**	**1050386**	**992902**	**971650**
批发、零售、进出口贸易、饮食及酒店业	Wholesale, Retail and Import/Export Trades, Restaurants and Hotels	301277	313270	288081	282194
运输、仓库及通讯业	Transport, Storage and Communications	111087	112829	107958	108957
金融、保险、地产及商用服务业	Financing, Insurance, Real Estate and Business Services	284119	322618	282686	267017
社区、社会及个人服务业	Community, Social and Personal Services	198967	220451	232963	245647
楼宇业权	Ownership of Premises	147547	171383	170660	162415
非直接计算的金融中介服务调整	Adjustment for Financial Intermediation Services Indirectly Measured	-89356	-90164	-89446	-94580
以生产面编制的本地生产总值（以要素成本计算）	**Production-based GDP at Factor Cost**	**1130212**	**1233034**	**1169064**	**1139363**
生产及入口税	**Taxes on Production and Imports**	**62443**	**85001**	**62538**	**55846**
以生产面编制的本地生产总值（以市价计算的）	**Production-based GDP at Market Prices**	**1192656**	**1318035**	**1231602**	**1195209**
以开支面编制的本地生产总值（以市价计算）	**Expenditure-based GDP at Market Prices**	**1191890**	**1323862**	**1259306**	**1227658**
统计差额	**Statistical Discrepancy**	**0.1%**	**-0.4%**	**-2.2%**	**-2.6%**

注释：①香港特别行政区出版物中称为"以生产面编制的本地生产总值"。
* 数字在日后得到更多资料时会作出修订。

Notes: ①The Chinese term used in the publications of the Hong Kong Special Administrative Region is "以生产面编制的本地生产总值"
* Figures are subject to revisions later on as more data become available.

23-9 支出法国内生产总值①

Expenditure-based Gross Domestic Product ①

单位：百万港元 (HKD million)

国内生产总值组成部份	GDP Components	1996	1997	1998	1999*	2000*
以现价计算	**At Current Market Prices**					
私人消费开支	Private Consumption Expenditure	722098	798450	762234	733575	736204
政府消费开支	Government Consumption Expenditure	104385	113749	117760	121465	121834
国内固定资本形成总额	Gross Domestic Fixed Capital Formation	372327	444963	381079	316960	332965
存货增减	Changes in Inventories	9762	12313	-15651	-10637	16194
货物出口(离岸价)	Exports of Goods(f.o.b.)	1397917	1455949	1347649	1349000	1572689
减:货物进口(到岸价)	Less:Imports of Goods(c.i.f.)	1539851	1619468	1432423	1395521	1661404
服务输出	Exports of Services	296188	298176	280756	288574	327969
减:服务输入	Less:Imports of Services	170936	180270	182098	175758	179276
支出法国内生产总值	**Expenditure-based GDP**	**1191890**	**1323862**	**1259306**	**1227658**	**1267175**
按人口平均计算的国内生产总值②（港元）	**Per Capita GDP② (HKD)**	**185206**	**204007**	**192446**	**185826**	**190124**
以固定(1990年)价格计算	**At Constant (1990) Market Prices**					
私人消费开支	Private Consumption Expenditure	471766	501015	463695	466906	492395
政府消费开支	Government Consumption Expenditure	60162	61629	62124	64203	65529
本地固定资本形成总额	Gross Domestic Fixed Capital Formation	270146	304569	281554	232397	255267
存货增减	Changes in Inventories	9608	10927	-14781	-10824	14791
货物出口(离岸价)	Exports of Goods(f.o.b.)	1322954	1404124	1343716	1392823	1631144
减:货物进口(到岸价)	Less:Imports of Goods(c.i.f.)	1430864	1533705	1424031	1425939	1683831
服务输出	Exports of Services	218000	217818	213892	226042	257924
减:服务输入	Less:Imports of Services	132019	137360	141096	136782	139682
支出法国内生产总值	**Expenditure-based GDP**	**789753**	**829017**	**785073**	**808826**	**893537**
按人口平均计算的国内生产总值②（港元）	**Per Capita GDP② (HKD)**	**122718**	**127751**	**119974**	**122429**	**134064**

注：①香港特别行政区出版物中称为"以开支面编制的本地生产总值"。

②载于本表内的数字与载于本年鉴前几期的数字或有不同，这是由于以下其中一项或两项因素所致：

(1)自2000年8月起编制人口数字的方法有所改变。

(2)2001年人口普查结果为人口数据提供最新基准资料。

有关详情，请参阅本章节的"简要说明"第三点。

Notes: ①The Chinese term used in the publications of the Hong Kong Special Administrative Region is "以开支面编制的本地生产总值"

②Figures presented in this table may be different from those presented in earlier editions of this Yearbook due to one or both of the following reasons :

1. The change in the approach for compiling population figures since August 2000.
2. The availability of up-to-date benchmark population data based on the results of the 2001 Population Census.

For details, please see Note III in the "Brief Introduction" of this chapter.

23-10 香港国际收支平衡表

Hong Kong's Balance of Payments Account

单位：百万港元 HKD million

标准组成部分①	Standard Components①	1998	1999#	2000#
经常帐②	**Current Account②**	**30238**	**89109**	**68784**
货物	Goods	-60667	-24501	-64021
服务	Services	74507	90776	123976
收益	Income	28762	34777	21540
经常转移	Current Transfers	-12364	-11943	-12712
资本及金融帐②	**Capital and Financial Account②**	**-31514**	**-83374**	**-59369**
资本转移	Capital Transfers	-18445	-13812	-11829
直接投资	Direct Investment	-17016	40737	11005
有价证券投资	Portfolio Investment	171052	256812	226852
金融衍生工具	Financial Derivatives	25374	78999	-4648
其他投资	Other Investment	-245059	-368243	-203952
储备资产(变动净值)③	Reserve Assets (Net Change)③	52581	-77867	-76798
净误差及遗漏④	**Net Errors and Omissions④**	**1276**	**-5735**	**-9415**
整体的国际收支	**Overall Balance of Payments**	**-52581** (赤字) (in deficit)	**77867** (盈余) (in surplus)	**76798** (盈余) (in surplus)

注：①根据国际收支平衡表的核算常规，某标准组成部分的净贷方数字以正数显示，而净借方则以负数显示。

②经常帐差额的正数显示盈余而负数则显示赤字。在资本及金融帐方面，正数显示净资金流入而负数则显示净资金流出。由于对外资产的增加是属于借方帐目而减少则属贷方帐目，因此负数的储备资产变动净值显示储备资产的增加，而正数则显示减少。

③在国际收支平衡架构下储备资产变动净值的估计是指交易数字。因计价方式改变（包括价格变动及汇率变动）及分类重组所导致的影响并不包括在内。

④原则上，贷方和借方各项账目的净总和应相等于零。但实际上，贷方和借方账目的资料是透过不同的来源搜集，基于各种原因会有差异。为了令贷方和借方账目的总和相等，便须加进一个余额项目，以反映平衡表的「净误差及遗漏」。

#日后会作出修订。

Notes:①In accordance with the Balance of Payments accounting rules, a net credit for a standard component is represented by a positive value, and a net debit a negative value.

②A positive value for the balance figure in the current account represents a surplus whereas a negative value represents a deficit. For the capital and financial account, a positive value indicates a net capital and financial inflow and a negative value indicates a net outflow. As increases in external assets are debit entries and decreases are credit entries, a negative value for net change in reserve assets represents a net increase and a positive value represents a net decrease.

③The estimates on net change in reserve assets under the Balance of Payments framework are transaction figures. Effects from valuation changes (including price changes and exchange rate changes) and reclassifications are excluded.

④In principle, the net sum of credit entries and debit entries is zero. In practice, discrepancies between the credit and debit entries may however occur for various reasons as the data are collected from many sources. Equality between the sum of credit entries and debit entries is brought about by the inclusion of a balancing item which reflects net errors and omissions.

Subject to revision later on.

23-11 电力、煤气、水消费量

Electricity, Gas and Water Consumption

用　途	Use	1996	1997	1998	1999	2000
电力　(万亿焦耳)	**Electricity　(Terajoules)**					
住宅	Domestic	29194	28937	32793	31400	32234
商业	Commercial	64465	67849	73857	76028	80347
工业	Industrial	19934	18965	18489	17547	17769
街灯	Street lighting	287	311	307	312	325
出口往中国内地	Export to the Mainland of China	1910	2014	2197	2279	4253
总计	Total	115790	118077	127643	127566	134928
煤气　(万亿焦耳)	**Gas　(Terajoules)**					
住宅	Domestic	11986	12465	12519	13064	13866
商业	Commercial	10085	10529	10536	10709	11209
工业	Industrial	918	911	888	914	982
总计	Total	22989	23906	23943	24687	26057
水　(百万立方米)	**Water　(Million Cubic Meters)**	**928**	**913**	**916**	**911**	**924**

23-12 工业生产指数
Index of Industrial Production

(1986年=100) (1986=100)

工业组别/组别内选定工业	Industry Group/Selected Component Industry	1996	1997	1998	1999	2000
所有制造行业	**All Manufacturing Industries**	**121.5**	**120.6**	**110.1**	**103.1**	**102.5**
食品、饮品及烟草制品业	Food, Beverages and Tobacco	159.0	158.3	143.9	141.6	137.2
服装制品业(鞋类除外)	Wearing Apparel, Except Footwear	109.7	105.6	99.2	99.2	102.1
纺织制品业(包括针织)	Textiles(Including Knitting)	103.8	106.4	95.1	89.9	93.3
纸品及印刷业①	Paper Products and Printing①	264.2	269.7	248.8	224.9	229.4
化学产品、橡胶制品、塑胶制品及非金属矿产制品业	Chemical, Rubber, Plastic and Non-metallic Mineral Products	63.1	63.9	55.5	47.2	40.4
塑胶制品业	Plastic Products	36.2	34.1	27.4	22.3	19.9
基本金属及金属制品业	Basic Metals and Fabricated Metal Products,	85.2	80.4	72.3	58.1	51.6
金属制品业(机械及设备除外)	Fabricated Metal Products, Except Machinery and Equipment	81.1	76.8	63.1	49.7	40.5
电器及电子制品、机械、专业设备及光学用品制造业	Electrical and Electronic Products,Machinery, Professional Equipment and Optical Goods	170.3	166.0	154.7	151.7	153.0
电器及电子制品制造业	Consumer Electrical and Electronic Products	103.4	93.4	81.0	78.8	77.9
机械、设备、仪器及零件制造业	Machinery, Equipment, Apparatus, Parts and Components	274.6	294.2	298.7	301.5	322.4
其他产品制造行业	Miscellaneous Manufacturing Industries	82.6	84.3	74.4	65.7	68.5

: ①由1996年开始，纸品及印刷业的数字亦包括了从事出版而不负责自行印刷的机构。

Note: ①As from 1996, the paper products and printing industry also included establishments engaged in publishing without printing.

23-13 按楼宇种类划分的新落成私人楼宇
Private Buildings Newly Completed by Type of Building

年份 Year	住宅楼宇 Residential: 楼宇数目(栋) Number of Blocks	住宅楼宇 Residential: 实用楼面面积(千平方米) Usable Floor Area (1000 sq.m.)	商住两用楼宇 Residential/Commercial: 楼宇数目(栋) Number of Blocks	商住两用楼宇: 实用楼面面积(千平方米) Usable Floor Area (1000 sq.m.) 住宅 Residential	商住两用楼宇: 实用楼面面积 非住宅 Non-residential	商业楼宇 Commercial: 楼宇数目(栋) Number of Blocks	商业楼宇 Commercial: 实用楼面面积(千平方米) Usable Floor Area (1000 sq.m.)
1996	608	429	97	302	67	65	353
1997	328	416	81	180	90	57	451
1998	453	536	59	294	80	61	792
1999	304	524	115	672	235	50	371
2000	373	783	46	272	42	26	118

23-13 续表 1 continued

年份 Year	工业楼宇 Industrial: 楼宇数目(栋) Number of Blocks	工业楼宇 Industrial: 实用楼面面积(千平方米) Usable Floor Area (1000 sq.m.)	其他用途楼宇 Others: 楼宇数目(栋) Number of Blocks	其他用途楼宇: 实用楼面面积(千平方米) Usable Floor Area(1000 sq.m.) 住宅 Residential	其他用途楼宇: 实用楼面面积 非住宅 Non-residential	总计 Total: 楼宇数目(栋) Number of Blocks	总计: 实用楼面面积(千平方米) Usable Floor Area(1000 sq.m.) 住宅 Residential	总计: 实用楼面面积 非住宅 Non-residential
1996	51	426	165	38	218	986	769	1065
1997	43	392	295	116	204	804	712	1137
1998	45	399	189	45	380	807	875	1652
1999	26	195	146	99	482	641	1295	1283
2000	28	104	133	7	150	606	1062	414

23-14 按楼宇种类划分的获批准可动工兴建私人楼宇
Private Buildings with Consent to Commence Work by Type of Building

年份 Year	住宅楼宇 Residential		商住两用楼宇 Residential/Commercial			商业楼宇 Commercial	
	楼宇数目（栋）Number of Blocks	实用楼面面积（千平方米）Usable Floor Area (1000 sq.m.)	楼宇数目（栋）Number of Blocks	可用楼面面积（千平方米）Usable Floor Area (1000 sq.m.) 住宅 Residential	非住宅 Non-residential	楼宇数目（栋）Number of Blocks	可用楼面面积（千平方米）Usable Floor Area (1000 sq.m.)
1996	778	532	174	419	94	84	912
1997	712	1107	148	502	99	72	500
1998	869	937	107	471	70	37	326
1999	244	777	98	881	91	16	196
2000	468	699	57	402	99	32	239

23-14 续表 1 continued

年份 Year	工业楼宇 Industrial		其他用途楼宇 Others			总计 Total		
	楼宇数目（栋）Number of Blocks	实用楼面面积（千平方米）Usable Floor Area (1000 sq.m.)	楼宇数目（栋）Number of Blocks	实用楼面面积（千平方米）Usable Floor Area(1000 sq.m.) 住宅 Residential	非住宅 Non-residential	楼宇数目（栋）Number of Blocks	实用楼面面积（千平方米）Usable Floor Area(1000 sq.m.) 住宅 Residential	非住宅 Non-residential
1996	45	530	166	107	376	1247	1058	1912
1997	41	462	189	23	259	1162	1631	1320
1998	35	69	180	64	201	1228	1472	667
1999	18	85	113	34	126	489	1693	498
2000	20	129	131	43	240	708	1143	707

23-15 按类型划分的永久性屋宇单位数量（3月底的数字）
Number of Permanent Quarters by Type (as at End March of the Year)

年份 Year	总计 Total	公营租住房屋① Public Rental Housing①	补助出售单位① Subsidized Sale Flats①	私人房屋② Private Housing②
1996	2004900	708200	211300	1085400
1997	2021800	703400	224000	1094400
1998	2060100	708000	239300	1112800
1999	2104500	705800	270300	1128400
2000	2177200	691200	324700	1161300

注：①香港特别行政区政府以优惠条件提供土地及拨款，以便兴建单元住宅，并以低于市场价格的定价，出租或出售给有需要的家庭。家庭入息低于指定入息限额的家庭，即有资格申请这些单位。公营租住单位所采用的入息限额，是较各类补助出售单位所用的为低。
②由私人发展商建造的单元住宅。

Notes: ①Units built on land and finance provided by the SAR Government on concessionary terms for letting or sale to the needy households at below market rent or price. Households with household income below the specified income limits are eligible to apply for these units. The income limit for public rental flats is lower than the limit(s) for various kinds of subsidized sale flats.
②Units built for residential purposes by the private sector developers.

23-16 按居处租住权划分的家庭住户数目
Domestic Households by Tenure of Accommodation

单位：户 (Households)

项目	Item	1981	1986	1991	1996
总计①	**Total①**	**1237643**	**1445689**	**1580072**	**1853248**
自置	Owner-occupier	345026	506926	673067	824184
全租	Sole Tenant	545158	657818	719954	842236
合租	Co-tenant	68910	85274	63683	62733
二房东	Main Tenant	48634	24353	12209	9205
三房客	Sub-tenant	145382	73570	41505	28424
免租	Rent Free	30534	31486	16969	22631
由雇主提供	Provided by Employer	53999	66262	52685	63835

注：①数字不包括住在船上的家庭住户。

Note: ①Figures exclude domestic households living on board vessels.

23-17 进出香港货物
Inward and Outward Movements of Cargo

单位:千吨 (1000 tons)

项目	Item	1996	1997	1998	1999	2000
卸下	**Discharged**					
空运	By Air	734	840	775	841	953
水运①	By water①	100928	107513	106851	106305	106935
海运①	By Ocean①	86694	91950	90104	88621	88003
河运①	By River①	14235	15563	16747	17684	18932
道路运输	By Road	17343	18333	18465	20500	22142
铁路运输②	By Rail②	684	537	324	293	318
总计	Total	119689	127223	126414	127940	130349
装上	**Loaded**					
空运	By Air	830	947	854	1133	1288
水运①	By water①	56371	61716	60319	62533	67707
海运①	By Ocean①	39145	41351	37378	39601	42934
河运①	By River①	17226	20365	22941	22932	24773
道路运输	By Road	17817	18075	17688	17915	17791
铁路运输	By Rail	255	175	138	173	133
总计	Total	75272	80913	78999	81754	86919

注：①水运包括海运及河运。自1993年开始，海运的定义已修订为越过内河航限操作的船只运输，而河运的定义则已修订为仅于内河航限以内操作的船只运输。
②数字不包括家畜。

Notes: ①Transport by water includes transport by ocean and by river.Starting from 1993, ocean has been redefined to refer to transport by all vessels operating beyond the river trade limits whereas river has been redefined to refer to transport by all vessels operating exclusively within the river trade limits.
②Figures exclude livestock.

23-18 按主要货物装卸地点划分的货柜吞吐量
Container Throughput by Main Cargo Handling Location

单位：千标准货柜单位 Thousand TEUs

项目	Item	1996	1997		1998	1999	2000
货柜吞吐量	Container Throughput	13460	14567	(14386)	14582	16211	18098
货柜码头	Container Terminals						
抵港	Inward						
载货货柜	Laden Container	3328	3708	(3698)	3432	3584	3862
空货柜	Empty Container	819	856	(856)	1214	1251	1644
港	Outward						
载货货柜	Laden Container	4148	4474	(4558)	4470	5072	5747
空货柜	Empty Container	391	451	(451)	439	389	349
货柜码头以外	Other than Container Terminals						
海	Ocean						
抵港	Inward						
载货货柜	Laden Container	1401	1374	(1326)	1258	1360	1528
空货柜	Empty Container	224	258	(258)	200	182	171
港	Outward						
载货货柜	Laden Container	1220	1270	(1063)	874	1037	1128
空货柜	Empty Container	201	253	(253)	309	259	205
河	River						
抵港	Inward						
载货货柜	Laden Container	406	439	(439)	599	765	861
空货柜	Empty Container	475	545	(545)	582	885	912
港	Outward						
载货货柜	Laden Container	601	666	(666)	856	983	1121
空货柜	Empty Container	248	272	(272)	349	444	568

注：1998年开始，一系列新的货柜吞吐量数字已经开始编制。为方便比较，按新系列编制的1997年数字于括号内展示。
标准货柜单位是20英尺x8英尺x8英尺的标准货柜为根据。

Notes:Starting from 1998, a new series of container throughput statistics has been compiled. To facilitate comparison, figures for 1997 under the new series are presented in brackets.
TEU refers to Twenty-Foot Equivalent Units (based on a standardized container size of 20 ft. x 8 ft. x 8 ft.).

23-19 通讯服务

Communications Services

项　　目	Item	1996	1997	1998	1999	2000
邮递服务	**Postal Services**					
信件邮件（百万件物品）	Letter Mail (million articles)	1175	1273	1257	1269	1341
包裹（千件）	Parcels (thousands)	1678	1425	1125	1027	975
电话服务①（千条操作线路）	**Telephone Services① (thousand working lines)**					
住宅	Residential	2028	2098	2159	2190	2210
商用	Business	1374	1526	1549	1649	1736
总计	Total	3402	3624	3708	3839	3946
图文传真①（千条操作线路）	**FAX① (thousand working lines)**	**308**	**343**	**360**	**384**	**404**
对外电话通讯量（千分钟）	**External Telephone Traffic Volume (thousand minutes)**					
拨出②③	Outgoing②③	1737513	1738236	1718519	2550112	3074885
拨入④	Incoming④	1844556	2120480	1957619	1679222	1858045
对外专用电报通讯量（千分钟）	**External Telex Traffic Volume (thousand minutes)**					
发出	Outward	15637	8652	6119	4073	3047
收到	Inward	11652	8724	5758	4129	3230
转接	Transit	9697	10976	7713	5348	3628
本港电报机电讯（千分钟）	**Internal Telex Traffic(thousand minutes)**	**18641**	**17148**	**13131**	**9832**	**7289**
电报（千件）	**Public Telegram Traffic (thousand messages)**					
发出	Outward	72	52	37	27	21
收到	Inward	49	34	20	12	8
本港电报（千件）	**Inland Telegram (thousand messages)**	**14**	**11**	**9**	**15**	**1**
公共无线电传呼接收器①（户）	**Public Radio Paging Receivers①(numbers)**	**1089904**	**932854**	**571800**	**342058**	**327768**
公共流动无线电话用户系统①⑤（户）	**Public Mobile Radiotelephone Subscriber Units①⑤ (numbers)**	**1210680**	**2085600**	**2767941**	**3650238**	**4173318**
		(-)	**(2127935)**	**(2898077)**	**(3989750)**	**(5234370)**

注：①数字为该年年底数字。
②包括图文传真及数据。
③1999年以前的数字只计话音通讯。
④估计数字。
⑤数字不包括储值智能卡。包括储值智能卡的数字于括号内展示。

Notes: ①Figures are as at end of the year.
②Figures include facsimile and data.
③Figures prior to 1999 refer to voice traffic only.
④Estimated figures.
⑤Excluding pre-paid SIM cards. Figures including prepaid SIM cards are presented in brackets.

23-20 进出口贸易总额

Total Imports and Exports

单位：百万港元　　(HKD million)

贸易种类	Type of Trade	1996	1997	1998	1999	2000
进口	Imports	1535582	1615090	1429092	1392718	1657962
港产品出口	Domestic Exports	212160	211410	188454	170600	180967
转口	Re-exports	1185758	1244539	1159195	1178400	1391722
贸易总额	Total Trade	2933499	3071040	2776741	2741717	3230652
商品贸易差额	Merchandise Trade Balance	-137664	-159141	-81443	-43718	-85273

23-21 主要商品进口供应地和出口去向

Imports and Exports by Supplier or Destination

单位：百万港元 (HKD million)

贸易种类/主要国家/地区	Type of Trade/Main Country/Territory	1996	1997	1998	1999	2000
进口(供应地)	**Imports (Supplier)**	**1535582**	**1615090**	**1429092**	**1392718**	**1657962**
中国内地	The Mainland of China	570442	608372	580614	607546	714987
日本	Japan	208239	221646	179947	162652	198976
中国台湾	Taiwan, China	123202	124547	104075	100426	124172
美国	United States of America	121058	125381	106537	98572	112801
韩国	Republic of Korea	73302	73226	68836	65432	80600
港产品出口(目的地)	**Domestic Exports (Destination)**	**212160**	**211410**	**188454**	**170600**	**180967**
美国	United States of America	53860	55073	54842	51358	54438
中国内地	The Mainland of China	61620	63867	56066	50414	54158
英国	United Kingdom	10597	10723	10058	10392	10681
德国	Federal Republic of Germany	11388	10321	9805	8543	9294
中国台湾	Taiwan, China	6705	7029	6505	5101	6104

23-22 商品转口的主要来源和去向

Re-Exports by Origin or Destination

单位：百万港元 (HKD million)

贸易种类/主要国家/地区	Type of Trade/Main Country/Territory	1996	1997	1998	1999	2000
转口(目的地)	**Re-exports (Destination)**	**1185758**	**1244539**	**1159195**	**1178400**	**1391722**
中国内地	The Mainland of China	417752	443878	407366	399188	488823
美国	United States of America	242342	261372	259856	269444	311047
日本	Japan	80154	77724	64194	67506	82050
英国	United Kingdom	35991	39066	42259	45541	52356
德国	Federal Republic of Germany	47216	46336	42161	44122	50599
转口(来源地)	**Re-exports (Origin)**	**1185758**	**1244539**	**1159195**	**1178400**	**1391722**
中国内地	The Mainland of China	683514	723416	691219	720126	849517
日本	Japan	129292	133825	123879	121265	137338
中国台湾	Taiwan, China	82177	83341	71782	71957	87942
美国	United States of America	62192	62633	54530	56737	65465
韩国	Republic of Korea	38049	39672	39637	38822	46057

23-23 发往中国内地加工的贸易额

Trade Involving Outward Processing in the Mainland of China

项　目	Item	1996	1997	1998	1999	2000
涉及外发加工贸易的估计货值　（百万港元）	**Estimated Value of Outward Processing Trade　(HKD million)**					
输往中国内地的港产出口货品	Domestic Exports to the Mainland of China	43089	47078	42184	37696	39304
输往中国内地的转口货品	Re-exports to the Mainland of China	179235	197809	179089	197890	242929
由中国内地进口的货品	Imports from the Mainland of China	452890	491142	477743	487507	567000
原产地为中国内地经香港输往其他地方的转口货品	Re-exports of the Mainland of China Origin to Other Places	552822	595511	559726	570126	647338
涉及外发加工贸易的估计比率　（%）	**Estimated Proportion of Outward Processing Trade　(%)**					
输往中国内地的港产出口货品	Domestic Exports to the Mainland of China	72.8	76.1	77.4	75.9	72.7
输往中国内地的转口货品	Re-exports to the Mainland of China	43.2	44.7	44.1	49.7	49.7
由中国内地进口的货品	Imports from the Mainland of China	79.9	81.2	82.7	80.5	79.3
原产地为中国内地经香港输往其他地方的转口货品	Re-exports of the Mainland of China Origin to Other Places	86.0	88.4	87.6	86.6	85.1

23-24 按主要投资者国家／地区划分的外来直接投资头寸及流动

Position and Flow of Inward Direct Investment by Major Investor Country/Territory

单位：十亿港元　　(HKD billion)

主要投资者国家／地区①	Major Investor Country/Territory①	以市值计算的外来直接投资 Inward Direct Investment at Market Value			
		年底头寸 Position at end of year		年间流入 Inflow in year	
		1998	1999	1998	1999
英属维尔京群岛	British Virgin Islands	542.6	924.7	30.3	48.8
中国内地	The Mainland of China	213.7	814.8	20.2	38.6
百慕大	Bermuda	202.0	280.6	20.7	24.6
荷兰	Netherlands	124.5	207.0	13.2	24.3
英国	The United Kingdom	153.4	196.1	8.3	2.0
美国	The United States	115.5	170.5	6.6	19.1
新加坡	Singapore	43.3	143.1	0.5	5.9
日本	Japan	108.8	111.5	0.6	6.7
开曼群岛	Cayman Islands	86.2	99.3	5.3	1.3
瑞士	Switzerland	13.7	20.7	0.8	5.3
其他	Others	140.3	181.3	8.0	14.1
总计	**Total**	**1744.0**	**3149.8**	**114.4**	**190.8**

注：①国家／地区是指直接来源经济体系。此分类未必反映最初资金流出的国家／地区。

Note:①Country/territory refers to the immediate source economy. It does not necessarily reflect the country/territory in which the funds are initially mobilised.

23-25 按主要接受投资国家／地区划分的向外直接投资头寸及流动

Position and Flow of Outward Direct Investment by Major Recipient Country/Territory

单位：十亿港元 (HKD billion)

主要接受投资国家／地区①	Major Recipient Country/Territory①	以市值计算的向外直接投资 Outward Direct Investment at Market Value			
		年底头寸 Position at end of year		年间流出② Outflow in year②	
		1998	1999	1998	1999
英属维尔京群岛	British Virgin Islands	720.2	1395.6	57.4	33.1
中国内地	The Mainland of China	547.7	620.6	54.1	78.6
百慕大	Bermuda	92.1	93.2	2.3	6.0
开曼群岛	Cayman Islands	97.9	86.1	8.4	1.4
新西兰	New Zealand	36.8	31.5	4.6	0.5
巴拿马	Panama	22.8	30.9	-4.0	0.4
英国	The United Kingdom	56.6	26.0	3.8	-23.3
德国	Germany	0.9	23.2	**	22.6
美国	The United States	20.4	22.5	1.3	1.1
新加坡	Singapore	15.6	18.9	-8.4	4.0
其他	Others	123.4	151.4	12.0	25.6
总计	**Total**	**1734.4**	**2499.9**	**131.5**	**150.0**

注：①国家／地区是指首个目的地经济体系。此分类未必反映资金最终被使用的所在国家／地区。
②负流出不一定指撤走资金。负流出可指境外联营公司归还借款。
**少于5亿港元

Notes: ①Country/territory refers to the immediate destination economy. It does not necessarily reflect the country/territory in which the funds are ultimately used.
②Negative outflow does not necessarily mean equity withdrawal. It may be the result of repayment of loans by non-resident affiliates.
** Less than 0.5 HKD billion

23-26 按母公司注册国家/地区划分的在香港的地区总部公司数目

Number of Companies in Hong Kong that are Regional Headquarters by Country/Territory of Incorporation of Parent Company

单位：在香港的地区总部公司数目 (Number of companies in Hong Kong that are regional headquarters)

母公司的注册国家/地区	Country/territory of incorporation of parent company	1996	1997	1998	1999	2000
美国	The United States	188	219	194	205	212
日本	Japan	122	119	109	114	127
英国	United Kingdom	90	84	95	82	81
中国内地	The Mainland of China	85	113	70	69	69
德国	Germany	40	51	59	55	50
荷兰	Netherlands	30	25	27	32	31
瑞士	Switzerland	27	25	28	32	29
法国	France	26	35	38	36	28
维尔京群岛	British Virgin Islands	16	20	9	17	22
加拿大	Canada	12	16	13	19	21
新加坡	Singapore	10	18	17	20	21
中国台湾	Taiwan,China	25	28	26	28	21
其他	Others	158	161	144	139	149
总计①	**Total①**	**829**	**914**	**829**	**848**	**861**
		(816)	**(903)**	**(819)**	**(840)**	**(855)**

注：指有关年度6月1日的数字。
地区总部是指一个有权管理所属地区内的其他办事处或附属公司的运作而毋须经常请示或咨询母公司的办事处。
①由于部分公司是由两个或以上的投资者经营，此表内按母公司注册国家/地区划分的地区总部公司的总数可能较实际的数目为大。括号内数字为有关年份的实际数目。

Notes: Figures refer to 1 June of the year.
A regional headquarters is an office which controls the operation of other offices or branches of the company in the region, and manages the business in the region without frequent referrals to its parent company.
① The total number of companies that are regional headquarters by country/territory of incorporation of parent company in this table may be greater than the actual number because some companies are joint ventures undertaken by two or more investors. The actual number for respective years is given in brackets.

23–27 按母公司注册国家/地区划分的在香港的地区办事处公司数目

Number of Companies in Hong Kong that are Regional Offices by Country/Territory of Incorporation of Parent Company

单位：在香港的地区办事处公司数目 (Number of companies in Hong Kong that are regional offices)

母公司的注册国家/地区	Country/territory of incorporation of parent company	1996	1997	1998	1999	2000
日本	Japan	338	379	347	368	492
美国	The United States	226	261	285	278	358
中国内地	The Mainland of China	128	130	135	136	160
英国	United Kingdom	123	130	128	124	155
中国台湾	Taiwan,China	59	49	85	97	113
德国	Germany	85	78	74	76	93
法国	France	31	65	76	74	88
新加坡	Singapore	35	44	37	39	76
韩国	Republic of Korea	60	80	66	56	71
瑞士	Switzerland	57	42	54	50	69
其他	Others	360	358	350	357	474
总计①	**Total①**	**1502**	**1616**	**1637**	**1655**	**2149**
		(1491)	**(1611)**	**(1630)**	**(1650)**	**(2146)**

注：指有关年度6月1日的数字。

地区办事处是指一个有权协调及管理其所在的城市以及区内其他城市的办事处的运作但须经常请示或咨询母公司或地区总部的办事处。

①由于部分公司是由两个或以上的投资者经营，此表内按母公司注册国家/地区划分的地区办事处公司的总数可能较实际的数目为大。括号内数字为有关年份的实际数目。

Notes: Figures refer to 1 June of the year.

A regional office is an office which coordinates offices/operations elsewhere in the region in addition to the city in which it is located, and manages the business but with frequent referrals to its parent company or a regional headquarters.

① The total number of companies that are regional offices by country/territory of incorporation of parent company in this table may be greater than the actual number because some companies are joint ventures undertaken by two or more investors. The actual number for respective years is given in brackets.

23–28 政府储备结余(一般收入帐目及各基金)

Government's Reserve Balances (General Revenue Account and Funds)

单位：百万港元 (HKD million)

项　目	Item	1996/1997	1997/1998	1998/1999	1999/2000	2000/2001
期初储备结余	Opening Reserve Balances	147927	370677#	457543	434302	444254
收入①	Revenue①	208358	281226	216115	232995	225060
开支①	Expenditure①	182680	194360	239356	223043	232893
盈余/(赤字)	Surplus/(Deficit)	25678	86866	-23241	9952	-7833
存放在外汇基金的财政储备投资市值下降而作出的储备	Provision for Fall in Market Value of Investment with the Exchange Fund	-	-	-	-	-6143
期末储备结余	Closing Reserve Balances	173605	457543	434302	444254	430278

注：①数额不包括"政府一般收入帐目与各基金之间的转拨"。

#包括于1997年7月1日，从先前的香港特别行政区政府土地基金受托人接收的资产净值共1970.72亿元。

Notes: ①Figures exclude 'transfers between the General Revenue Account and Funds'.

Including net worth of $197072 million received from Trustee of the former Hong Kong SARG Land Fund at 1 July 1997.

23-29 政府收入(一般收入帐目及各基金)

Government Revenue (General Revenue Account and Funds)

单位：百万港元 (HKD million)

项目	Item	1996/1997	1997/1998	1998/1999	1999/2000	2000/2001
经营收入	**Operating Revenue**					
直接税	Direct Taxes					
入息税及利得税	Earnings and Profits Tax	83966	91524	75746	66914	73870
间接税	Indirect Taxes					
博彩及彩票税	Bets and Sweeps Tax	12191	13453	12228	11938	12630
酒店房租税	Hotel Accommodation Tax	580	511	219	182	223
印花税	Stamp Duties	20461	29097	10189	12116	10911
飞机乘客离境税	Air Passenger Departure Tax	1121	1002	573	499	537
海底隧道使用税	Cross Harbour Tunnel Passage Tax	199	200	195	97	-
应课税品税项	Duties	8450	8465	7698	7377	7293
一般差饷	General Rates	6285	6258	3614	7132	14428
车辆税	Motor Vehicle Taxes	3249	4246	2237	2613	3025
专利税及特权税	Royalties and Concessions	1755	1889	1286	1577	1767
其他收入	Other Revenue					
罚款、没收及罚金	Fines,Forfeitures and Penalties	1592	1566	1333	1093	1061
物业及投资	Properties and Investments	2926	7159	8335	6986	7579
贷款、偿款、供款及其他收入	Loans, Reimbursements, Contributions and Other Receipts	5044	6042	6517	5672	4210
公用事业	Utilities	6608	6735	4400	3326	3297
各项收费	Fees and Charges	10766	11279	10565	10896	10973
投资收入	Investment Income					
政府一般收入帐目	General Revenue Account	5616	8976	21568	15390	6835
土地基金①	Land Fund①	-	6006	10080	21388	12681
经营收入总额	Total Operating Revenue	170809	204408	176783	175196	171320
非经常收入	**Capital Revenue**					
直接税	Direct Taxes					
遗产税	Estate Duty	1510	1588	1237	1272	1503
间接税	Indirect Taxes					
出租车专营权税	Taxi Concessions	-	23	-	-	-
其他收入	Other Revenue					
土地交易②	Land Transactions②	451	17864	-	-	-
其他	Others	282	1076	982	1384	10525
从房屋委员会收回的款项	Recovery from Housing Authority	805	1188	1471	640	2067
基金	Funds					
基本工程储备基金③(不包括债券收入)	Capital Works Reserve Fund③ (exclude proceeds of bond issue)	29057	48067	25686	39111	32183
资本投资基金	Capital Investment Fund	3023	3888	6329	2665	2949
赈灾基金	Disaster Relief Fund	1	2	3	4	3
贷款基金	Loan Fund	1919	2475	2533	11515	3612
公务员退休金储备基金	Civil Service Pension Reserve Fund	501	647	1091	1016	602
创新及科技基金	Innovation and Technology Fund	-	-	-	192	296
非经常收入总额	Total Capital Revenue	37549	76818	39332	57799	53740
政府收入总额	**Total Government Revenue**	**208358**	**281226**	**216115**	**232995**	**225060**

注：①包括截至1998年10月31日为止的投资净值的变动。

②在1985年5月27日至1997年6月30日期间，这个总目只包括其所带来利益于1997年6月30日或之前届满的土地交易。至于1997年7月1日至1997年12月31日期间，即基本工程储备基金决议修订前，所有土地收入均记入这个总目。

③由1985年5月27日至1997年6月30日，这个总目包括香港政府根据中英《联合声明》附件三的规定所摊分得的土地收入。由1998年1月1日起，所有土地交易的收入，均记入这个总目。

Notes: ①Including the change in the net worth of the investments up to 31 October 1998.

②From 27 May 1985 up to 30 June 1997 this head included only land transactions conferring a benefit that expired on or before 30 June 1997. From 1 July 1997 to 31 December 1997, pending amendment of the Capital Works Reserve Fund resolution, all land revenue was credited to this head.

③From 27 May 1985 up to 30 June 1997 this head included the former Hong Kong Government share of land revenue distributed in accordance with Annex III of the Sino-British Joint Declaration. From 1 January 1998 this head has been credited with all revenue from land transactions.

23-30 政府开支(一般收入帐目及各基金)

Government Expenditure (General Revenue Account and Funds)

单位：百万港元 (HKD million)

项　目	Item	1996/1997	1997/1998	1998/1999	1999/2000	2000/2001
经营开支	**Operating Expenditure**					
经常开支	Recurrent Expenditure					
个人薪酬	Personal Emoluments	37404	40114	44092	46488	50497
与员工有关联的开支	Personnel Related Expenses	4129	4345	4708	5035	5116
退休金	Pensions	8724	9272	7395	8254	9381
部门开支	Departmental Expenses	7062	8067	8935	10184	12934
其他费用	Other Charges	21147	24139	28568	29590	30355
资助金	Subventions					
教育	Education	17179	18877	21082	22282	23860
卫生	Health	20930	24040	26562	27609	28221
社会福利	Social Welfare	3207	4598	5419	6065	6453
大学及理工学院	Universities and Polytechnics	10723	11792	13189	13711	13131
职业训练局	Vocational Training Council	1668	1806	1968	2116	2039
杂项	Miscellaneous	2564	2336	2359	2579	2535
其他非经常开支	Other Non-recurrent	1116	11180	13129	2008	2164
经营开支总额	**Total Operating Expenditure**	**135853**	**160566**	**177406**	**175921**	**186686**
非经常开支	**Capital Expenditure**					
机器、设备及工程	Plant, Equipment and Works	616	852	790	1372	853
资助金	Subventions					
教育	Education	416	409	322	385	464
卫生	Health	339	17	380	411	371
职业训练局	Vocational Training Council	14	21	46	19	67
杂项	Miscellaneous	1274	618	706	139	110
基金	Funds					
基本工程储备基金①	Capital Works Reserve Funds①	29168	28772	31267	29490	30577
资本投资基金(证券投资)②	Capital Investment Fund (Equity Investments)②	9036	119	20545	8510	8102
贷款基金②	Loan Fund②	5944	2948	7856	6580	5310
赈灾基金③	Disaster Relief Fund③	20	38	38	32	43
创新及科技基金④	Innovation and Technology Fund④	-	-	-	184	310
非经常开支及证券投资总额	**Total Capital Expenditure and Equity Investments**	**46827**	**33794**	**61950**	**47122**	**46207**
政府开支及证券投资总额	**Total Government Expenditure and Equity Investments**	**182680**	**194360**	**239356**	**223043**	**232893**

注：①基本工程储备基金于1982年1月20日经前立法局决议成立，目的是为工务计划、征用土地及债券支付利息提供资金。

②资本投资基金及贷款基金于1990年4月1日经前立法局决议成立，以承担前发展贷款基金、地下铁路基金及学生贷款基金原有的功能。

③赈灾基金在1993年12月1日经前立法局决议成立，目的是对香港以外发生的灾难给予人道援助。

④创新及科技基金是由立法会于1999年6月30日决议通过成立，以资助那些有助促进制造业和服务业创新及提升科技水平的项目。

Notes: ①The Capital Works Reserve Fund was established on 20 January 1982 by Resolution of the former Legislative Council for the purpose of financing the Public Works Programme, acquisition of land and payment for interest on bond.

②The Capital Investment Fund and the Loan Fund were established on 1 April 1990 by Resolution of the former Legislative Council. These funds assumed the functions of the former Development Loan Fund, the Mass Transit Fund and the Student Loan Fund.

③The Disaster Relief Fund was established on 1 December of 1993 by Resolution of the former Legislative Council for purpose of humanitarian aid in relief of disasters that occur outside Hong Kong.

④The Innovation and Technology Fund was established on 30 June 1999 by Resolution of the Legislative Council to finance projects to help promote innovation and technology upgrading in manufacturing and service industries.

23－31 外币兑换率及港币汇率指数

Exchange Rates and the Effective Exchange Rate Indices

(一单位外币兑换的港元) (HK dollars to one unit of foreign currency)

项　目	Item	1996	1997	1998	1999	2000
年内平均数字①	Average for the year①					
澳元	Australian Dollar	6.06	5.76	4.88	5.01	4.53
比利时法郎	Belgian Franc	0.252	0.218	0.215	0.205	0.178
加拿大元	Canadian Dollar	5.67	5.59	5.23	5.22	5.25
人民币	Chinese Renminbi	107.49	107.07	106.87	106.67	106.17
德国马克	Deutsche Mark	5.14	4.47	4.41	4.23	3.68
荷兰盾	Dutch Guilder	4.59	3.97	3.91	3.75	3.27
法国法郎	French Franc	1.51	1.33	1.32	1.26	1.10
印尼卢比	Indonesian Rupiah	0.0034	0.0029	0.0008	0.0010	0.0009
意大利里拉	Italian Lira	0.0050	0.0046	0.0045	0.0043	0.0037
日圆	Japanese Yen	0.0712	0.0641	0.0595	0.0685	0.0723
马来西亚林吉特	Malaysian Ringgit	3.08	2.81	1.99	2.04	2.04
新台币	New Taiwan Dollar	0.274	0.263	0.230	0.240	0.248
菲律宾比索	Philippine Peso	0.2949	0.2703	0.1943	0.2011	0.1797
英镑	Pound Sterling	12.08	12.69	12.83	12.55	11.81
韩圆	Republic of Korea Won	0.0096	0.0083	0.0056	0.0065	0.0069
新加坡元	Singapore Dollar	5.49	5.23	4.64	4.58	4.52
瑞士法郎	Swiss Franc	6.26	5.34	5.35	5.17	4.62
泰铢	Thai Baht	0.307	0.262	0.190	0.205	0.194
美元	US Dollar	7.734	7.742	7.745	7.758	7.791
欧元③	Euro③	-	-	-	8.27	7.20
特别提款权	SDR	11.22567	10.65346	10.50555	10.60666	10.27532
港币汇率指数 (1983年11月=100)	Effective Exchange Rate Indices for the Hong Kong dollar (November 1983=100)					
贸易总值(进口及整体出口)加权	Trade (import and export)-weighted	125.0	130.3	137.5	134.2	135.0
进口货值加权	Import-weighted	115.7	121.7	131.2	126.1	125.7
整体出口货值加权④	Export-weighted④	135.6	139.9	144.5	143.2	145.4
年底数字②	As at end of year②					
澳元	Australian Dollar	6.17	5.06	4.76	5.06	4.35
比利时法郎	Belgian Franc	0.243	0.211	0.227	0.194	0.182
加拿大元	Canadian Dollar	5.65	5.41	5.00	5.35	5.20
人民币	Chinese Renminbi	107.19	106.85	106.86	106.61	106.04

23-31 续表 1 continued

(一单位外币兑换的港元) (HK dollars to one unit of foreign currency)

项 目	Item	1996	1997	1998	1999	2000
德国马克	Deutsche Mark	4.97	4.33	4.62	4.00	3.76
荷兰盾	Dutch Guilder	4.43	3.84	4.10	3.55	3.33
法国法郎	French Franc	1.48	1.29	1.38	1.19	1.12
印尼卢比	Indonesian Rupiah	0.0034	0.0015	0.0010	0.0011	0.0008
意大利里拉	Italian Lira	0.0051	0.0044	0.0047	0.0040	0.0038
日圆	Japanese Yen	0.0666	0.0597	0.0682	0.0761	0.0682
马来西亚林吉特	Malaysian Ringgit	3.07	2.01	2.04	2.04	2.04
新台币	New Taiwan Dollar	0.274	0.231	0.244	0.245	0.238
菲律宾比索	Philippine Peso	0.2975	0.2005	0.2015	0.1935	0.1675
英镑	Pound Sterling	13.07	12.85	12.86	12.59	11.64
韩圆	Republic of Korea Won	0.0092	0.0045	0.0064	0.0069	0.0062
新加坡元	Singapore Dollar	5.54	4.62	4.69	4.66	4.50
瑞士法郎	Swiss Franc	5.73	5.33	5.62	4.88	4.84
泰铢	Thai Baht	0.303	0.170	0.211	0.207	0.180
美元	US Dollar	7.736	7.746	7.746	7.771	7.796
欧元③	Euro③	-	-	-	7.82	7.34
特别提款权	SDR	11.12406	10.45129	10.90660	10.65370	10.16140
港币汇率指数	Effective Exchange Rate Indices					
(1983年11月=100)	for the Hong Kong dollar					
	(November 1983=100)					
贸易总值(进口及整体出口)加权	Trade (import and export)-weighted	125.3	137.9	131.8	131.5	136.0
进口货值加权	Import-weighted	116.5	132.0	124.0	122.4	127.7
整体出口货值加权④	Export-weighted④	135.3	144.4	140.6	141.8	145.3

注：《中华人民共和国香港特别行政区基本法》说明，港币是香港特别行政区的法定货币。外币指港币以外的其他货币，因而人民币亦视作外币。

①所列数字是电汇或现钞收市中间兑换价的年内平均数。

②所列数字是该年最后一个交易日的电汇或现钞收市中间兑换价。

③于1999年1月1日推出。

④包括转口和港产品出口。

Notes: Hong Kong dollar is the legal tender in the Hong Kong Special Administrative Region, as stated in "The Basic Law of the Hong Kong Special Administrative Region of the People's Republic of China". Foreign currency refers to any currency other than the Hong Kong currency. Accordingly Chinese Renminbi is also treated as foreign currency.

①Figures are based on average of the closing middle-market telegraphic transfer rates or notes rates for the year.

②Figures are based on closing middle-market telegraphic transfer rates or notes rates as at the last trading day of the year.

③Launched on 1 January 1999.

④Including re-exports and domestic exports.

23-32 货 币 供 应

Money Supply

单位：百万港元(年底数字) (HKD million,As at end of year)

项目	Item	1996	1997	1998	1999	2000
法定纸币及硬币的流通量	Legal Tender Notes and Coins in Circulation					
由商业银行发行	Commercial Bank Issues	82575	87015	86465	118195	99265
由政府发行	Government Issues	4538	5651	6030	6029	6170
总计	Total	87113	92666	92495	124224	105435
由认可机构持有的法定纸币及硬币	Authorized Institutions' Holdings of Legal Tender Notes and Coins	10597	12077	11321	24705	13674
由公众持有的法定纸币及硬币	Legal Tender Notes and Coins in Hands of Public	76516	80589	81174	99519	91761
货币供应：就外币掉期存款作出调整	Money Supply: Adjusted for Foreign Currency Swap Deposits					
货币供应(定义一)	Money Supply (Definition 1)					
港币	Hong Kong Dollar	198311	188135	178260	205339	203966
外币	Foreign Currency	19149	19958	19406	19818	39881
总计	Total	217460	208093	197666	225156	243847
货币供应(定义二)	Money Supply (Definition 2)					
港币①	Hong Kong Dollar①	1503603	1652473	1814100	1910972	1984756
外币②	Foreign Currency②	1028633	1090520	1251989	1402562	1620457
总计	Total	2532236	2742993	3066089	3313534	3605213
货币供应(定义三)	Money Supply (Definition 3)					
港币①	Hong Kong Dollar①	1520461	1670379	1826233	1922962	1999152
外币②	Foreign Currency②	1091176	1155230	1296112	1438843	1649322
总计	Total	2611636	2825609	3122345	3361805	3648473
货币供应：未就外币掉期存款作出调整	Money Supply: Unadjusted for Foreign Currency Swap Deposits					
货币供应(定义二)	Money Supply (Definition 2)					
港币	Hong Kong Dollar	1465100	1610141	1784812	1882630	1980430
外币	Foreign Currency	1067135	1132852	1281277	1430904	1624783
总计	Total	2532236	2742993	3066089	3313534	3605213
货币供应(定义三)	Money Supply (Definition 3)					
港币	Hong Kong Dollar	1481959	1628047	1796944	1894620	1994825
外币	Foreign Currency	1129678	1197562	1325401	1467185	1653648
总计	Total	2611636	2825609	3122345	3361805	3648473

注：《中华人民共和国香港特别行政区基本法》说明，港币是香港特别行政区的法定货币。外币指港币以外的其他货币，因而人民币亦视作外币。

①所列数字已包括外币掉期存款。

②所列数字已扣除外币掉期存款。

Notes: Hong Kong dollar is the legal tender in the Hong Kong Special Administrative Region, as stated in "The Basic Law of the Hong Kong Special Administrative Region of the People's Republic of China". Foreign currency refers to any currency other than the Hong Kong currency. Accordingly Chinese Renminbi is also treated as foreign currency.

①Figures are adjusted to include foreign currency swap deposits.

②Figures are adjusted to exclude foreign currency swap deposits.

23-33 证券交易成交额、市场总值及股票价格指数

Value of Stock Exchange Turnover, Market Capitalization and Index of Share Prices

项　目	Item	1996	1997	1998	1999	2000
主板	**Main Board**					
股票价格指数	Index of Share Prices					
恒生指数(1964.7.31=100)	Hang Seng Index (31.7.1964=100)	11646.6	13294.7	9484.5	12859.9	15838.3
分类指数	Sectoral Sub-indices:					
金融	Finance	11411.8	16039.2	13383.2	18736.1	20229.5
公用	Utilities	10243.4	11722.6	11868.8	14877.8	18896.9
地产	Properties	21926.0	22495.3	11713.4	15677.0	16558.3
工商	Commerce and Industry	8647.5	8857.6	5421.5	7589.1	10640.9
恒生100指数① (1998.1.2=100)	Hang Seng 100 Index① (2.1.1998=100)	-	-	79.7@	112.0	138.2
恒生中国企业指数② (1994.7.8=1000)	Hang Seng China Enterprises Index② (8.7.1994=1000)	838.2	1043.4	475.6	466.1	409.2
恒生香港中资企业指数③ (1993.1.4=1000)	Hang Seng China-Affiliated Corporations Index③ (4.1.1993=1000)	-	2872.6#	1071.8	1019.2	1239.7
新恒生50中型股指数① (1998.1.2=1000)	New Hang Seng MidCap 50 Index① (2.1.1998=1000)	-	-	745.5@	881.4	814.3
所有普通股指数 (1986.4.2=1000)	All Ordinaries Index (2.4.1986=1000)	5586.3	6702.4	4264.7	5385.0	6607.2
成交金额(百万港元)	Turnover (HKD million)	1412242	3788960	1701112	1915941	3047565
市场总值④ (百万港元)	Market Capitalisation④ (HKD million)	3475965	3202630	2661713	4727527	4795150
创业板⑤	**Growth Enterprise Market⑤**					
创业板指数	Growth Enterprise Index	-	-	-	-	472.4+
成交金额(百万港元)	Turnover(HKD million)	-	-	-	3604.7	84287.1
市场总值④ (百万港元)	Market capitalisation④ (HKD million)	-	-	-	7236.8	67290.1

注：按年指数是该年内12个月，每月最后一日的收市指数的平均数字。
①在1998年4月20日首次公布，取代恒生50中型股指数。
②1994年8月8日推出。
③于1997年6月16日推出。
④年末数字。
⑤于1999年11月25日推出。创业板指数于2000年3月20日起开始编制。
@该年数字由1998年4月至12月的平均指数编制而成。
#该年数字由1997年6月至12月的平均指数编制而成。
+该年数字由2000年3月至12月的平均指数编制而成。

Notes: Annual indices are averages of the closing indices of the last day of the 12 months.
①Launched on 20 April 1998, this index replaces the Hang Seng MidCap 50 Index.
②Launched on 8 August 1994 .
③Launched on 16 June 1997 .
④Year-end figures.
⑤Launched on 25 November 1999. Growth Enterprise Index has been compiled since 20 March 2000.
@Yearly figure compiled on average from April to December 1998.
#Yearly figures compiled on average from June to December 1997.
+ Yearly figure compiled on average from March to December 2000.

23–34 消费物价指数(1999年10月至2000年9月=100)

Consumer Price Indices (October 1999-September 2000=100)

项 目	Item	权数 Weight	1996	1997	1998	1999	2000
综合消费物价指数	**Composite Consumer Price Index**						
总指数	**All Items**	100.00	98.8	104.5	107.5	103.2	99.4
食品	Food	26.67	98.3	101.9	103.8	101.9	99.7
外出用餐	Meals Bought away from Home	-16.39	96.0	99.9	102.1	100.8	99.9
食品(不包括外出用餐)	Food, Excluding Meals Bought away from Home	-10.28	102.2	105.3	106.9	103.8	99.4
住房	Housing	29.91	98.9	108.0	113.1	107.3	98.5
电力、燃气及水	Electricity, Gas and Water	2.98	91.7	96.2	97.6	97.3	100.7
烟酒	Alcoholic Drinks and Tobacco	0.94	88.7	93.7	99.9	101.1	100.1
服装、鞋	Clothing and Footwear	4.13	127.6	138.3	137.2	109.2	97.9
耐用物品	Durable Goods	6.24	107.8	110.1	110.3	103.7	98.7
杂项物品	Miscellaneous Goods	5.70	92.8	97.8	100.4	99.6	100.5
交通	Transport	9.01	91.5	95.2	98.9	99.4	100.3
杂项服务	Miscellaneous Services	14.42	94.6	98.8	101.4	100.2	99.9
甲类消费物价指数	**Consumer Price Index (A)**						
总指数	All Items	100.00	97.6	103.2	105.9	102.5	99.5
食品	Food	31.88	98.8	102.4	104.3	102.0	99.7
外出用餐	Meals Bought away from Home	-17.94	95.6	99.7	102.1	100.7	99.9
食品(不包括外出用餐)	Food, Excluding Meals Bought away from Home	-13.94	103.0	105.9	107.1	103.8	99.4
住房	Housing	29.13	98.0	106.9	110.2	105.3	98.8
电力、燃气及水	Electricity, Gas and Water	3.99	91.9	96.4	97.6	97.0	100.7
烟酒	Alcoholic Drinks and Tobacco	1.50	88.6	93.7	99.8	101.0	100.1
服装、鞋	Clothing and Footwear	3.36	126.7	138.2	138.3	111.5	97.6
耐用物品	Durable Goods	4.96	106.0	108.4	108.8	103.3	98.7
杂项物品	Miscellaneous Goods	5.25	89.6	96.0	99.4	99.4	100.9
交通	Transport	8.23	91.5	95.1	99.2	99.6	100.2
杂项服务	Miscellaneous Services	11.70	91.8	96.3	100.3	99.7	99.7
乙类消费物价指数	**Consumer Price Index (B)**						
总指数	All Items	100.00	99.7	105.5	108.5	103.4	99.4
食品	Food	25.94	98.2	101.9	104.0	101.8	99.7
外出用餐	Meals Bought away from Home	-17.20	96.4	100.4	102.6	100.8	99.9
食品(不包括外出用餐)	Food, Excluding Meals Bought away from Home	-8.74	101.8	104.9	106.7	103.8	99.4
住房	Housing	29.68	101.7	110.4	115.2	107.3	98.5
电力、燃气及水	Electricity, Gas and Water	2.81	91.6	96.2	97.6	97.3	100.7
烟酒	Alcoholic Drinks and Tobacco	0.86	88.4	93.5	99.9	101.3	100.1
服装、鞋	Clothing and Footwear	4.47	128.4	140.6	140.7	111.5	97.9
耐用物品	Durable Goods	6.93	108.0	110.5	110.7	103.9	98.5
杂项物品	Miscellaneous Goods	5.58	93.0	97.9	100.1	99.6	100.5
交通	Transport	9.05	92.1	95.9	99.3	99.6	100.3
杂项服务	Miscellaneous Services	14.68	94.0	98.5	101.7	100.3	99.9
丙类消费物价指数	**Consumer Price Index (C)**						
总指数	All Items	100.00	98.6	104.6	107.9	103.9	99.3
食品	Food	21.38	97.4	100.6	102.5	101.7	99.8
外出用餐	Meals Bought away from Home	-13.28	95.6	98.9	100.8	100.8	99.9
食品(不包括外出用餐)	Food, Excluding Meals Bought away from Home	-8.10	101.6	104.8	106.7	103.9	99.6
住房	Housing	31.22	96.4	106.2	113.0	108.9	98.2
电力、燃气及水	Electricity, Gas and Water	2.02	90.9	95.5	97.6	97.7	100.6
烟酒	Alcoholic Drinks and Tobacco	0.39	89.3	93.9	99.9	101.3	100.2
服装、鞋	Clothing and Footwear	4.55	127.3	135.2	131.6	104.2	98.2
耐用物品	Durable Goods	6.73	109.1	111.1	111.3	103.7	98.8
杂项物品	Miscellaneous Goods	6.43	96.6	100.2	101.9	100.1	100.1
交通	Transport	9.94	90.6	94.2	97.8	98.7	100.5
杂项服务	Miscellaneous Services	17.34	97.6	101.2	102.0	100.3	100.1

注：以上的权数是根据1999至2000年间进行的住户开支统计调查结果计算出来。

Note: The weights are derived from the results of the 1999/2000 Household Expenditure Survey.

23-35 按四分位开支组别及商品或服务类别划分的住户每月平均开支

Average Monthly Household Expenditure by Commodity/Service Section by Quartile Expenditure Group

商品或服务类别	Commodity/Service Section	四分位开支组别 Quartile Expenditure Group									
		总数 Overall		最低四分位 The Lowest 25%		第二四分位 The Second 25%		第三四分位 The Third 25%		最高四分位 The Highest 25%	
		绝对值 Value	百分比 (%)	绝对值 Value	百分比 (%)	绝对值 Value	百分比 (%)	绝对值 Value	百分比 (%)	绝对值 Value	百分比 (%)
食品	Food	5612	25.7	2917	36.3	4650	31.5	5929	27.9	8953	20.8
住房	Housing	7009	32.2	2275	28.3	4539	30.7	6413	30.1	14813	34.4
电力、燃气及水	Electricity, Gas and Water	631	2.9	402	5.0	559	3.8	659	3.1	906	2.1
烟酒	Alcoholic Drinks & Tobacco	226	1.0	150	1.9	211	1.4	213	1.0	331	0.8
服装、鞋	Clothing & Footwear	958	4.4	211	2.6	538	3.6	933	4.4	2150	5.0
耐用物品	Durable Goods	988	4.5	226	2.8	553	3.7	1036	4.9	2136	5.0
杂项物品	Miscellaneous Goods	1053	4.8	397	4.9	715	4.8	1029	4.8	2073	4.8
交通	Transport	2009	9.2	598	7.4	1146	7.8	1869	8.8	4424	10.3
杂项服务	Miscellaneous Services	3310	15.2	851	10.6	1866	12.6	3194	15.0	7329	17.0
总数（港元）	**All Sections (HKD)**	**21797**	**100.0**	**8026**	**100.0**	**14778**	**100.0**	**21275**	**100.0**	**43114**	**100.0**
住户总数（户）	**Number of Households (household)**	**1624000**	**100.0**	**406000**	**25.0**	**406000**	**25.0**	**406000**	**25.0**	**406000**	**25.0**

注：从1999年10月至2000年9月进行的住户开支统计调查获取的结果。

Note: Results are obtained from the Household Expenditure Survey carried out from October 1999 to September 2000.

23-36 15岁及15岁以上人口教育程度

Educational Attainment of Population Aged 15 and Above

项目	Item	1981		1986		1991		1996	
		人数(人) Number of Persons (person)	百分比 (%)	人数(人) Number of Persons (person)	百分比 (%)	人数(人) Number of Persons (person)	百分比 (%)	人数(人) Number of Persons (person)	百分比 (%)
总计	**Total**								
男	**Male**	**1961803**	**52.3**	**2122826**	**51.2**	**2212947**	**50.6**	**2511854**	**49.6**
女	**Female**	**1787250**	**47.7**	**2026224**	**48.8**	**2157418**	**49.4**	**2554664**	**50.4**
未受教育/幼稚园	No Schooling/Kindergarten								
男	Male	148670	4.0	148943	3.6	157473	3.6	128395	2.5
女	Female	455953	12.2	436948	10.5	399824	9.1	352457	7.0
小学	Primary								
男	Male	721146	19.1	653927	15.9	576381	13.1	569431	11.2
女	Female	562247	15.0	558987	13.4	524218	12.0	577451	11.4
初中	Lower Secondary								
男	Male	418758	11.2	464708	11.2	506431	11.6	569097	11.2
女	Female	260773	7.0	290585	7.0	331299	7.6	389148	7.7
高中	Upper Secondary								
男	Male	434905	11.6	524736	12.6	576058	13.2	667664	13.2
女	Female	361498	9.6	499149	12.0	593213	13.6	735547	14.5
预科	Matriculation								
男	Male	79161	2.1	105147	2.5	109345	2.5	148683	2.9
女	Female	56395	1.5	89383	2.2	105232	2.4	160125	3.2
专上教育	Tertiary								
非学位课程	Non-degree Courses								
男	Male	69998	1.9	105784	2.5	126489	2.9	128246	2.5
女	Female	53755	1.4	90608	2.2	108423	2.5	114758	2.3
学位课程	Degree Courses								
男	Male	89165	2.4	119581	2.9	160770	3.7	300338	5.9
女	Female	36629	1.0	60564	1.5	95209	2.2	225178	4.4

23-37 按院校类别划分的学生人数

Student Enrolment by Type of Educational Institution

单位：人 (person)

类　别	Type	1996	1997	1998	1999	2000
幼稚园	Kindergarten	180771	177462	175073	171138	160921
小学	Primary School					
日校	Day School	466507	461911	476802	491851	493979
夜校	Evening School	-	98	342	-	-
中学	Secondary School					
日校	Day School	465658	458118	455872	453465	456693
初中	Lower Secondary	260574	246713	238877	235874	241616
高中	Upper Secondary	151979	157068	160430	159343	155518
中六及中七	Secondary 6 and Secondary 7	53105	54337	56565	58248	59559
夜校	Evening School	11950	10871	12095	11785	10017
特殊教育学校	Special Education School					
日校	Day School	8697	8956	9667	9687	9387
特殊学校	Special School	8542	8825	9513	9499	9181
普通学校内的特殊班	Special Classes in Ordinary School	155	131	154	188	206
香港专业教育学院①	Hong Kong Institute of Vocational Education①	-	-	-	54781	53734
全日制	Full-time					
技工级课程②	Craft Level Course②	-	-	-	1640	1977
技术员级课程③	Technician Level Course③	-	-	-	8019	12808
高级技术员/技术员级课程④	Higher Technician/Technician Level Course④	-	-	-	6298	420
高级技术员级课程③	Higher Technician Level Course③	-	-	-	3803	7074
兼读制	Part-time					
技工级课程②	Craft Level Course②	-	-	-	10941	8835
技术员级课程③	Technician Level Course③	-	-	-	14286	12941
高级技术员级课程③	Higher Technician Level Course③	-	-	-	9794	9679
工业学院①	Technical Institute①	48832	48907	47747	-	-
全日制	Full-time					
技工级课程②	Craft Level Course②	5616	5206	5043	-	-
技术员级课程③	Technician Level Course③	8531	8595	10161	-	-
兼读制	Part-time					
技工级课程②	Craft Level Course②	16192	16033	14850	-	-
技术员级课程③	Technician Level Course③	18493	19073	17693	-	-
科技学院①⑤	Technical College①⑤	13872	14444	14974	-	-
全日制	Full-time					
高级技术员级课程③	Higher Technician Level Course③	5141	5265	5520	-	-
兼读制	Part-time					
高级技术员级课程③	Higher Technician Level Course③	8731	9179	9454	-	-
认可专上学院	Approved Post-secondary College					
全日制	Full-time	2434	2383	2346	2361	2707
其他专上学院	Other Post-secondary College					
日间课程	Day Course	2213	2281	3084	3632	4203
夜间课程	Evening Course	848	969	1219	991	1098

23-37 续表 1 continued

单位：人 (person)

类别	Type	1996	1997	1998	1999	2000
教资会资助院校⑥	UGC-funded Institution⑥	85550	86202	84538	83754	81472
全日制	Full-time					
副学位程度	Sub-degree	10701	11220	11081	10887	10284
学士学位程度	Undergraduate	44302	44225	43885	44031	44241
研究院修课课程	Taught Postgraduate	1069	1229	1374	1480	1593
研究院研究课程	Research Postgraduate	2952	3113	3188	3363	3290
兼读制	Part-time					
副学位程度	Sub-degree	12165	11758	10835	10029	8365
学士学位程度	Undergraduate	4223	4120	3759	3436	3365
研究院修课课程	Taught Postgraduate	9470	9827	9729	9870	9662
研究院研究课程	Research Postgraduate	668	710	687	658	672
香港演艺学院	The Hong Kong Academy for Performing Arts					
全日制	Full-time	638	697	748	704	712
非学位程度⑦	Non-degree⑦	430	448	485	433	438
学位程度	Degree	208	249	263	271	274
香港公开大学⑧	The Open University of Hong Kong⑧					
兼读制	Part-time	20451	22904	24318	25654	25722
成人教育院校⑨	Adult Education Institution⑨					
日间课程	Day Courses	33359	36588	48905	64281	76596
夜间课程	Evening Courses	59211	62948	76724	77871	100226

注：表内列载有关幼稚园、小学、中学及特殊教育学校的数字是截至该年9月为止。认可专上学院、成人教育院校、其他专上学院课程、香港演艺学院及香港公开大学的数字，是截至该年10月为止。香港专业教育学院的数字是截至该年11月为止。教资会资助院校的数字是截至该年12月为止。

①香港专业教育学院于1999年成立，属下有九间分校，包括两间前科技学院和七间前工业学院。九间分校包括柴湾分校、黄克竞分校、葵涌分校、观塘分校、李惠利分校、摩理臣山分校、沙田分校、青衣分校及屯门分校。柴湾分校及青衣分校前身为两间科技学院，其余七间分校前身为七间工业学院。

②技工级课程为中三以上程度课程。

③高级技术员及技术员级课程为中五以上程度课程，而高级技术员级课程则为较高程度课程。

④高级技术员/技术员级课程为中五以上程度课程，首年须修读共同科目。

⑤香港科技学院（柴湾）及香港科技学院（青衣）于1993年成立。

⑥数字只包括教资会资助课程的学生人数。1996年及以后的数字包括香港教育学院。该学院自1996年7月1日起成为大学教育资助委员会资助院校。

⑦数字包括证书、深造证书、专业证书、文凭、深造文凭及专业文凭课程的学生。

⑧香港公开进修学院于1989年成立。并于1997年5月30日正名为香港公开大学。

⑨“成人教育院校”是指由官立夜校及各间提供各类科目（包括商科班）的私立学校所开办的课程。

Notes: Figures for kindergarten, primary, secondary and special education school are as at September of the year. Figures for approved post-secondary college, institutions offering adult education and courses offered by other post-secondary college, the Hong Kong Academy for Performing Arts and the Open University of Hong Kong are as at October of the year. Figures for the Hong Kong Institute of Vocational Education are as at November of the year. Figures for UGC-funded institutions are as at December of the year.

①The Hong Kong Institute of Vocational Education was established in 1999 and was composed of nine campuses of which two are the former Technical Colleges and seven are the former Technical Institutes. The nine campuses are Chai Wan, Haking Wong, Kwai Chung, Kwun Tong, Lee Wai Lee, Morrison Hill, Sha Tin, Tsing Yi, and Tuen Mun. The Chai Wan and Tsing Yi campuses were the two former Technical Colleges whereas the other campuses were the seven former Technical Institutes.

②Craft level courses are post-secondary 3 courses.

③Higher technician and technician level courses are post-secondary 5 courses but higher technician level courses are more advanced courses.

④Higher technician/technician level courses are post-secondary 5 courses with common first year curricula.

⑤The Hong Kong Technical College (Chai Wan) and the Hong Kong Technical College (Tsing Yi) started operation in 1993.

⑥Figures refer to students of UGC-funded programmes only. Figures from 1996 onwards include those for the Hong Kong Institute of Education, which came under the aegis of the University Grants Committee (UGC) with effect from 1 July 1996.

⑦Figures include students in certificate, advanced certificate, professional certificate, diploma, advanced diploma and professional diploma courses.

⑧The Open Learning Institute of Hong Kong was established in June 1989. It was retitled The Open University of Hong Kong on 30 May 1997.

⑨'Adult education institution' refers to courses in Government evening institutes and various private schools offering a variety of subjects including commercial classes.

23-38 教育方面的开支

Expenditure on Education

单位：千港元 (HKD thousand)

项　目	Item	1996/1997	1997/1998	1998/1999	1999/2000
经常开支	**Recurrent**				
教育署①	Education Department①				
小学学前服务	Pre-primary Services	427342	487289	590393	600600
小学	Primary	6880003	7493274	8357530	8972013
中学	Secondary	10654336	11725568	13104435	13720626
特殊教育	Special Education	1024683	1165292	1331533	1430020
专上程度②	Post-secondary②	13244	20842	23327	23804
其他教育服务	Other Education	190732	207818	241599	245178
行政费用(非拨款金额)	Administrative (non-allocated)	842081	946898	1065629	1111904
职业训练局	Vocational Training Council				
工业教育及训练	Technical and Vocational	2047602	2237087	2437368	2435667
大学教育资助委员会③	University Grants Committee③				
给予教资会资助院校的补助费	Subvention to UGC-funded Institutions	10722820	11791777	13188520	13710719
教资会及秘书处开支	UGC and Secretariat Expenses	29523	33080	39926	45370
学生资助办事处	Student Financial Assistance Agency				
学生经济补助－助学金④	Student Finance-grants④	968373	1034111	886973	843637
学生车船津贴计划④⑤	Student Travel Subsidy Scheme④⑤	244207	244185	272263	284571
香港公开大学⑥	The Open University of Hong Kong⑥	321931	369304	399456	434438
非经常开支	**Non-recurrent**				
教育署	Education Department	1940774	2681594	4179296	4896895
职业训练局	Vocational Training Council				
工业教育及训练	Technical and Vocational	56341	67015	131353	126860
大学教育资助委员会③	University Grants Committee③	390510	1135687	929843	919111
香港公开大学⑥	The Open University of Hong Kong⑥	9796	19325	50831	15296

注：①开支已包括教育补助额。

②由1992至1993年起，这项开支不再包括拨予学生贷款／津贴的款项，计有本地专上学生资助计划、英国及香港政府联合拨款资助计划(3.3247亿元)、英联邦奖学金(85万元)。

③包括给予教资会资助院校的资助。香港教育学院自1997年4月1日起取得工程及设备资助，而经常性资助则由1996年12月1日起提供资助。

④自1990至1991年开始,此计划正式由学生资助办事处管理。

⑤自1991／1992年起，学生车船津贴计划，采用入息审查制度来评估个别学校学生的申请。

⑥香港公开进修学院于1993年4月1日开始以自负盈亏方式运作，并于1997年5月30日正名为香港公开大学。

Notes: ①Subventions on education are included.

②Excludes provisions for student loans/grants related to Local Student Finance Scheme,UK/HK Government Joint Funding Scheme ($332.47 million) and Commonwealth Scholarship($0.85 million) as from 1992/1993.

③Grants to the UGC-funded institutions are included. The Hong Kong Institute of Education started to receive capital grants from 1.4.1997 and recurrent grants from 1.12.1996.

④Student finance-grants and student travel subsidy scheme are administered by the Student Financial Assistance Agency as from 1990/1991.

⑤A means test was introduced to student travel subsidy scheme as from 1991/1992 to assess the application of individual school students.

⑥The Open Learning Institute of Hong Kong became self-financing starting from 1 April 1993. It was retitled the Open University of Hong Kong on 30 May 1997.

23-39 医疗卫生条件
Conditions of Public Health

项　目	Item	1996	1997	1998	1999	2000
注册医护人员①　　(人)	Number of Registered Medical Personnel①(person)					
医生	Doctors	8976	9289	9527	9818	10130
牙医	Dentists	1654	1684	1724	1779	1826
药剂师	Pharmacists	1067	1143	1212	1273	1315
护士	Nurses	36395	37880	39250	38960	40388
按每千名人口计算的医生数②	Doctors Per Thousand Population②	1.4	1.4	1.4	1.5	1.5
医疗机构和病床	Number of Medical Institutions and Hospital Beds					
医疗机构　　(个)	Medical Institutions　　(number)	92	96	102	105	102
病床　　(张)	Hospital Beds　　(bed)	29955	30800	32836	34286	35100
按每千名人口计算的病床数②	Beds Per Thousand Population②	4.6	4.7	5.0	5.2	5.2

注：年底的数字。
①注册医护人员的统计资料取自不同的资料来源。医务委员会提供医生的资料，牙医管理委员会提供牙医的资料，护士管理局提供护士的资料，及药剂业及毒药管理局提供药剂师的资料。医生、牙医及药剂师需要每年重新申请执业证书。医生／牙医的数字包括本地及海外名册的正式注册医生／牙医。
②载于本表内的数字与载于本年鉴前几期的数字或有不同，这是由于以下其中一项或两项因素所致：
(1)自2000年8月起编制人口数字的方法有所改变。
(2)2001年人口普查结果为人口数据提供最新基准资料。
有关详情，请参阅本章节的"简要说明"第三点。

Notes: Figures are as at end of the year.
①Statistics on the registered medical personnel are maintained by the Medical Council for doctors, Dental Council for dentists, Nursing Council for nurses and Pharmacy and Poisons Board for pharmacists. Annual renewal of practising certificate is required for doctors, dentists and pharmacists. Figures for doctors/dentists refer to the doctors/dentists with full registration on both the local and overseas lists.
②Figures presented in this table may be different from those presented in earlier editions of this Yearbook due to one or both of the following reasons :
1. The change in the approach for compiling population figures since August 2000.
2. The availability of up-to-date benchmark population data based on the results of the 2001 Population Census.
For details, please see Note III in the "Brief Introduction" of this chapter.

23-40　社会保障
Social Security

社会保障计划	Social Security Scheme	1996/1997	1997/1998	1998/1999	1999/2000	2000/2001
综合社会保障援助	Comprehensive Social Security Assistance					
处理中的个案数目①	Number of Active Cases①　(case)					
年老	Old Age	98765	112067	124304	133070	135409
失明	Blind	495	522	550	283	295
听觉受损	Deaf	195	218	210	215	253
肢体疾残	Physically Disabled	3209	3680	4313	2836	3485
精神病患	Mentally Ill	7913	8735	9668	8380	8584
健康欠佳	Temporary disability/Ill Health	17948	21364	25041	19979	18917
单亲家庭	Single Parent Family	13303	17161	25613	25146	26078
低收入	Low Earnings	3102	4714	7562	8002	8319
失业	Unemployment	14964	19108	31942	26185	23250
其他	Others	6826	8076	3616	3919	3673
总计	Total	166720	195645	232819	228015	228263
发放款项（百万港元）	Amount(HKD million)	7127.8	9441.3	13028.7	13623.4	13559.8+
公共福利金	Social Security Allowance					
处理中的个案数目①	Number of Active Cases①　(case)					
伤残津贴	Disability Allowance	72264	77051	81741	89617	96851
高龄津贴	Old Age Allowance	437827	440814	445001	445835	453734
总计	Total	510091	517865	526742	535452	550585
发放款项　(百万港元)	Amount(HKD million)	4041.6	4420.2	4737.3	4883.3	5129.6+
暴力及执法伤亡赔偿	Criminal and Law Enforcement Injuries Compensation					
获批个案数目　　(个)	Number of Cases Authorized for Payment (case)	568	604	557	447	427
交通意外伤亡援助	Traffic Accident Victims Assistance					
获批个案数目　　(个)	Number of Cases Authorized for Payment (case)	5558	5655	5809	5797	5998
紧急救济	Emergency Relief					
受助灾民人数　　(人)	Number of Victims Assisted (person)	807	1082	1097	2643	868

注：①于财政年度终结时的数字。财政年度是由4月1日至3月31日。处理中的个案包括新申请个案，正在复查中的个案，正领取援助款项的个案和已停止领取援助款项等待覆查的个案。
＋包括2001年4月1日所发放的款项。

Notes: ①Figures are as at end of the financial year. Financial year is from 1 April to 31 March. Active cases refer to cases being handled which include new applications, cases being reviewed, cases being paid and cases suspended for payment pending review.
+Includes the payments for 1 April 2001.

《中国统计年鉴》与香港特别行政区统计刊物中使用的指标对照表

A Comparison of Common Statistical Terms Used in *China Statistical Yearbook* and Publications Compiled by the Census and Statistics Department，the Government of the Hong Kong Special Administrative Region

对应表号 Table Number	中国内地统计名词 Statistical Terms Used in China Statistical Yearbook	香港特别行政区统计名词及对应英文 Statistical Terms Used in Publications of the Hong Kong Special Administrative Region
1	实际工资指数	实质工资指数 Real wage index
1	国民生产总值	本地居民生产总值 Gross National Product(GNP)
1, 7, 8, 9	国内生产总值	本地生产总值 Gross Domestic Product(GDP)
1, 7, 8, 9	以现价计算（按现行价格计算）	以当时市价计算 At current market prices
1, 9	以固定价格计算（按不变价格计算）	以固定市价计算 At constant market prices
1, 9	支出法国内生产总值	以开支面编制的本地生产总值 Expenditure-based GDP
1	增加值	增加价值 Value added
1	批发贸易业	批发业 Wholesale
1	零售贸易业	零售业 Retail
6, 8	建筑业	建造业 Construction
9	居民消费	私人消费支出 Private consumption expenditure
9	政府消费	政府消费开支 Government consumption expenditure
9	国内固定资本形成总额	本地固定资本形成总额 Gross domestic fixed capital formation
9	存货变动(存货增加)	存货增减 Changes in inventories
1, 8	生产法国内生产总值	以生产面编制的本地生产总值 Production-based GDP
8	生产及进口税	生产及入口税 Taxes on production and imports
8	电力、煤气及水的生产和供应业	电力、燃气及水务业 Electricity, gas and water
11	水	食水 Water
21, 22, 27	韩国	大韩民国 Republic of Korea
24, 25	百慕大	百慕达 Bermuda
31	澳元	澳洲元 Australian Dollar
31	马来西亚林吉特 Malaysian Ringgit	马来西亚元 Malaysian Dollar
31	韩圆	南韩圆 Republic of Korea Won
31	泰铢	泰国铢 Thai Baht
31	菲律宾比索	菲律宾披索 Philippine Peso
34	居民消费价格指数	消费物价指数 Consumer Price Indices
34	外出用餐	外出用膳 Meals bought away from home
34	服装、鞋	衣履 Clothing and footwear
34	住房	住屋 Housing

主 要 统 计 指 标 解 释

粗出生率 是指某一年内的活产婴儿数目与年中人口的比率，一般按每千人口表示。

粗死亡率 是指某一年内的死亡人数与年中人口的比率，一般按每千人口表示。

出生时平均预期寿命 是指某年出生的男、女性，若其一生经历的死亡情况，正如该年的年龄性别死亡率所反映，他／她预期能活的年数。

年中人口 在1996年前是以“广义时点”方法编制，数字包括在统计时点身在香港的永久性居民、非永久性居民和旅客，亦包括暂时离港前往中国内地及澳门的香港永久性居民。自2000年8月起，“居住人口”方法已取代“广义时点”方法用以编制香港的人口数字。追溯至1996年的修订人口数字已经编制。利用“居住人口”方法所编制的人口估计，称“居港人口”。“居港人口”包括“常住居民”和“流动居民”。“常住居民”指两类人士：(一) 在统计时点之前的6个月内，在港逗留最少3个月，又或在统计时点之后的6个月内，在港逗留最少3个月的香港永久性居民，不论在统计时点他们是否身在香港； 及 (二) 在统计时点身在香港的香港非永久性居民。至于“流动居民”，是指在统计时点之前的6个月内，在港逗留最少一个月但少于3个月，又或在统计时点之后的6个月内，在港逗留最少1个月但少于3个月的香港永久性居民，不论在统计时点他们是否身在香港。根据新的编制方法，旅客并不包括在香港人口内。

总和生育率 是指某年的每一千名妇女，若他们在生育龄期(即15至49岁)的生育率依循该年的年龄别生育率，一生中活产子女的平均数目。

婴儿死亡率 是以一年内，年龄一岁以下死亡人数与同年出生的每千名活产婴儿的比率。

劳动人口 是指15岁及以上陆上非住院人口，并符合就业人口或失业人口定义的人士。

劳动人口参与率 是指劳动人口占所有15岁及以上陆上非住院人口的比例。

就业人口 包括在统计前7天内有做工赚取薪酬或利润或有一份正式工作的15岁及以上人士。无酬家庭从业员及在统计前七天内正休假的就业人士亦包括在内。

失业人口 包括所有在统计前30天内有找寻工作，而在统计前7天内并无职位，且并无为赚取薪酬或利润而工作，并随时可工作的15岁及以上人士。失业人口亦包括那些并无职位，有找寻工作，但由于暂时生病而不能工作的人士；及并无职位，可随时工作，但由于下列理由而没有找寻工作的人士：(Ⅰ)已为于稍后时间担当的新工作或开展的业务作出安排；或(Ⅱ)正期待返回原来的工作岗位；或(Ⅲ)相信没有工作可做（第Ⅲ类为“因灰心而不求职的人士”）。

失业率 是指失业人士在劳动人口中所占的比例。

就业不足人口 包括在统计前7天内在非自愿情况下工作少于35小时，而在统计前30天内有找寻更多工作，或即使没有找寻更多工作，但在统计前七天内可担任更多工作的就业人士。

就业不足率 是指就业不足人士在劳动人口中所占的比例。

实质工资指数 是从名义工资指数中，按甲类消费物价指数的变幅，扣除通胀的影响而得出，显示督导级及以下雇员所赚取工资金额购买力的转变。

国内生产总值 香港特别行政区刊物中称为“本地生产总值”。是指一国家或地区的所有常住生产单位，在一个指定的期间内，未扣除固定资本消耗的生产总值。

一个国家或地区的人均国内生产总值是指该国家或地区在某统计年的国内生产总值除以该国家或地区在该年的人口总数而得的数字。

国民生产总值 香港特别行政区刊物中称为“本地居民生产总值”。是指一个国家或地区的居民从事各项经济活动而赚取的收益，不论该经济活动是否在该国家或地区的经济领域内进行。换言之，编制国民生产总值应包括本地居民在经济领域内或领域以外从事各类经济活动的收益，而扣除非本地居民在经济领域内从事经济活动的收益。

计算国民生产总值，可用以下方程式：

国民生产总值=国内生产总值+本地居民从经济领域外所赚取的要素收益−非本地居民从经济领域内所赚取的要素收益

一个国家或地区的人均国民生产总值是指该国家或地区在某统计年的国民生产总值除以该年的人口总数而得的数字。

要素收益组成部分主要分为投资收益及雇员报酬，而投资收益包括了直接投资收益、有价证券投资收益及其他投资收益。

以下指标(“国际收支平衡表”至“储备资产”)适用于国际收支平衡表（表22−10)：

国际收支平衡表 是有系统地载录，在指定期间内，某经济体系与世界各地的各类经济交易的统计表。完整的国际收支平衡表包括以下两个主要核算帐：（甲）经常帐；（乙）资本及金融帐。

经常帐 是主要量度实质资源的流动，包括货物的进出口、服务的输入及输出、从外地应收及应付予外地的收益，以及从外地及往外地的经常转移。

货物 包括所有可移动的货物，其拥有权由本地居民转至非本地居民(出口)及由非本地居民转至本地居民(进口)。

服务 包括由本地居民向非本地居民(出口)和由非本地居民向本地居民(进口)所提供的服务。

收益 是提供生产要素而赚取的所得，包括本地居民从非本地居民(应收收益)或非本地居民从本地居民(应付收益)所赚取的所得。

经常转移 是指一个经济体系，在无同等经济价值回报的情况下，对其他经济体系所提供的实质或金融资源，而且该资源在转移后会被立刻或于短时间内消耗。

资本帐 是用来量度资本转移及非生产／非金融资产的对外交易。

资本转移 是指在无报偿下，固定资产的转移或债务的减免。

金融帐 记录本地居民与非本地居民之间的金融资产及负债交易。它显示某经济体系如何融资以进行其对外交易。金融帐内的交易可归类为直接投资、有价证券投资、金融衍生工具、其他投资及储备资产。

直接投资 是指一个经济体系内的某投资者购买设立在另一经济体系内的企业，兼且对该企业有持久利益和在管理方面具有效的控制权。

有价证券投资 是指对非居民的股本证券及债务证券（例如中长期债券、货币市场工具）所作的投资，而投资者对投资于该企业并无持久的利益或在管理方面具影响力。

金融衍生工具 是一种与某种特定的金融工具、指标或商品有连系的金融工具，使特定的金融风险本身能透过这种工具而进行交易（包括在交易所内及场外）。

其他投资 是指不属于直接投资、有价证券投资、金融衍生工具或储备资产，而对非居民的其他金融申索及负债。

储备资产 是指一个经济体系的金融当局(在香港是指香港金融管理局)可直接用来支付对外收支赤字，且可用于干预外汇市场以影响汇率从而间接调节该赤字的对外资产。

工业生产指数 量度本地制造业生产量的实质变动，即撇除价格调整因素后的本地生产量变动。

楼宇转让契约 是指订明不可分割业权(即楼宇单位)转让的文件。

获批准可动工兴建楼宇 是指获屋宇署签发《同意书》动工兴建的楼宇。这种《同意书》是发给私人发展计划（包括香港房屋协会的计划）及香港房屋委员会的私人机构参建居屋计划，但建于新界区小型屋宇则毋需获取这种《同意书》。

实用楼面面积 指各层楼面面积总和，但不包括楼梯、公共通道空间、升降机(指电梯，下同)等候处、盥洗室、厕所、厨房、及为楼宇提供升降机、空调系统、或类似服务而安装的机器所占用的空间。

居处租住权 是指居所是由住户自置或租用，或是由雇主提供等。所包括的各项定义如下：

自置 是指住户拥有其居住的屋宇单位。

全租 是指住户向不在该屋宇单位居住的人士租住整个屋宇单位，但不与其他住户同住或分租。

合租 是指两个或以上的住户，每户分别向不在该屋宇单位居住的人士租住屋宇单位的部分地方。

二房东 是指住户向不在该屋宇单位居住的人士租住整个屋宇单位，及再将屋宇单位的部分地方分租予其他住户。

三房客 是指住户向居住在同一屋宇单位内的人士租住该屋宇单位的部分地方。

免租 是指住户在已获得或未获得业主同意情况下免费居住在一屋宇单位，但不包括由雇主提供屋宇单位的住户。

由雇主提供 是指住户居住在由其成员之一的雇主提供的屋宇单位，包括以象征式租金向雇主租住屋宇单位的住户。假如住户使用由雇主提供的房屋津贴租住屋宇单位，则租住权不属于“由雇主提供”类。

进出香港的客运火车 是指由九广铁路公司经营来往香港与中国内地的直通火车服务。

进出香港的车辆 是指经落马洲、文锦渡及沙头角出入境管制站往返中国内地的陆路交通。

车辆牌照 给予车辆在道路上行驶的权利，有效期分为4个月及一年两种。领牌车辆总数指年底的数字。

酒店入住率 数字的编制是根据每日可供出租房间数目计算，正在维修或翻新之房间并不包括在内。

港产品出口货物 是指香港的天然产品或在香港经过制造工序，以致其基本原料的形状、性质、式样或用途受到永久改变的产品。其货值是以离岸价计算。

转口货品 是指输出曾经自外地输入香港的货品，而这些货品并没有在香港经过任何制造工序，以致永久改变其形状、性质、式样或用途。其货值是以离岸价计算。

进口货品 是指在香港以外出产或制成的货品，输入香港供本地使用或转口，以及再进口的香港产品。其货值是以到岸价计算。

输往中国内地作外发加工用途的出口货品 是指那些由香港或经香港出口往中国内地加工的原料或半制成品，经加工后成为制成品，并以合约安排再进口香港。

由中国内地进口与外发中国内地加工有关的货品 是指那些加工后进口香港的货品，其中全部或部分原料或半制成品是以合约安排由香港或经香港出口往中国内地加工。

原产地为中国内地而涉及外发中国内地加工、并经香港输往其他地方的转口货品 是指那些经香港转口的制成品，其中全部或部分原料或半制成品是以合约安排由香港或经香港出口往中国内地加工，而加工后的货品再进口香港。

以下项目（“直接投资”至“直接投资流动”）适用于直接投资(表22-24，22-25)：

直接投资 是指一个经济体系的投资者在另一经济体系的企业所作的投资，而此等投资令该投资者能长期有效地影响有关企业的管理经营决定。在统计上，若投资者持有某一企业10%或以上的股权，便被视为能长期有效地影响有关企业的管理经营决定。直接投资包括股本资本、再投资收益及其他资本。股本资本包括所持有分行的股本，附属及联营公司的股票。再投资收益是指投资者从其附属或联营公司应得但未以股息形式分发的利润。其他资本涉及公司之间长期或短期的债务交易，包括母公司与其附属公司、联营公司及分行之间的借贷。

外来直接投资 是指境外居民在香港的企业所作的直接投资。跨国企业在香港经营的分行或附属公司，是外来直接投资的典型例子。

向外直接投资 是指香港居民投资者在境外的企业所作的直接投资。

直接投资头寸 是指某一特定日子香港居民在境外投

资的价值及接受外来投资的价值。

直接投资流动 是指某一时段内香港居民于境外的投资或接受境外的投资的投入或撤走。

地区总部 是指一个有权管理所属地区内的其他办事处或附属公司的运作而毋须经常请示或咨询母公司的办事处。

地区办事处 是指一个有权协调及管理其所在的城市以及区 其他城市的办事处的运作但须经常请示或咨询母公司或地区总部的办事处。

贷款基金 为香港特别行政区政府贷款计划，例如房屋贷款和学生贷款，提供资金。基金收入主要来自政府一般收入帐目转拨的款项、偿还的贷款及贷款利息。

港币汇率指数（EERI） 量度港元与香港主要贸易伙伴的货币的平均加权汇率变动情况。

外币兑换率 指外币电汇或现钞平均收市中间兑换价。

认可机构 包括持牌银行、有限制牌照银行及接受存款公司。

持牌银行 可以接受任何数额和期限的存款。在1994年10月1日之前，期限少于15个月的港币50万元以下存款利率，是受香港银行公会的《利率规则》管制。但这种管制已自该日起分期放宽。自1995年11月2日起，此规则只适用于来往帐户、储蓄帐户与及7日以下的定期存款。

有限制牌照银行 可接受金额不少于港币50万元的任何期限的定期存款，而存款利率并无任何限制。

接受存款公司 可接受金额不少于港币10万元而期限不少于3个月的定期存款，而存款利率并无任何限制。

外币掉期存款 是指顾客在现货市场购买外币，然后存入认可机构，但同时订下远期合约，将该笔外币(本金加利息)在存款到期时售予认可机构。从分析角度来看，这类掉期存款应当作港元定期存款。

货币供应定义一 是指市民持有的法定纸币和硬币加上持牌银行的活期存款。

货币供应定义二 是指货币供应定义一所包括的项目，加上持牌银行客户的储蓄及定期存款，再加上持牌银行发行而由非认可机构持有的可转让存款证。

货币供应定义三 是指货币供应定义二所包括的各项，再加上有限制牌照银行及接受存款公司客户的存款，再加上以上两类认可机构发行而由非认可机构持有的可转让存款证。

恒生指数 于1969年11月24日推出，是香港股票市场的主要指标，用以反映股价的一般变动，以及股市的整体表现。

消费物价指数 反映住户一般所购买的消费商品和服务价格水平变动情况。指数的变动反映购买一个固定篮子的消费品和服务的总值的变动。消费物价指数的按年变动率是一个重要指标，用以量度通胀对消费者的影响。按年变动率是指当期指数比较早一年同期指数的上升或下降的百分率。

香港特别行政区政府统计处编制不同的消费物价指数数列，以反映消费物价变动对不同开支范围的住户的影响。甲类、乙类及丙类消费物价指数分别根据较低、中等及较高开支范围的住户消费模式编制而成。而综合消费物价指数是根据整体住户开支模式而编制，反映消费物价转变对全体住户的影响。

消费物价指数的开支权数每五年更新一次，现时采用的权数是根据1999至2000年间进行的住户开支统计调查的结果计算出来的。

教育程度 是指某人在学校或其他教育机构修读达到的最高教育水平，无论他是否已完成该项课程。计算教育程度时，只包括正式课程。正式课程最少为期一学年，入学有特定的学历资格规定(香港公开进修学院即现时的香港公开大学主办的学位、副学士及副学位课程除外)，课程必须包括考试或指定评核成绩的程序。

幼稚园 包括所有幼稚园班级。

非学位课程 包括工业学院／科技学院（工业学院及科技学院于1999年已合并为香港专业教育学院）／理工学院(现已改制为大学)的所有高级文凭／增修证书院士课程、理工学院(现已改制为大学)及其他专上学院的院士衔和其他非学位课程。教育学院及工商师范学院的证书／文凭课程及护士训练课程亦包括在内。

学位课程 包括所有在香港及海外专上学院的学士学位课程及研究院课程。

社会保障计划 旨在帮助社会上需要经济或物质援助的人士，应付基本及特别需要。这个毋须供款的社会保障制度，包括综合社会保障援助计划、公共福利金计划、暴力及执法伤亡赔偿计划、交通意外伤亡援助计划和紧急救济。

综合社会保障援助计划 （1993年7月1日前为公共援助计划)是向有需要的个人或家庭提供经济援助，使他们的入息达到一定的水平，以应付生活上的基本需要。申请人须接受经济状况调查。

公共福利金计划 （1993年7月1日前为特别需要津贴计划)包括高龄津贴及伤残津贴。本计划为65岁或以上人士及严重残疾人士发放每月津贴，以应付因年老或残疾而引致的特别需要。

暴力及执法伤亡赔偿计划 提供现金援助给暴力罪行或执法行动中受害的人士或其遗属。申请人毋需接受经济状况调查。

交通意外伤亡援助计划 为交通意外受害人或其遗属迅速提供经济援助。申请人毋需接受经济状况调查，亦不论交通意外是因何人的过失而引致。援助金只按当事人伤亡情况支付，但不包括补偿财物损失。

紧急救济 是为天灾或其他灾祸的受害人提供物资援助，包括供应热饭或干粮及其他必需的救济物品。

犯罪被捕人数 是指因干犯罪行而被拘捕的人，不论有否遭起诉。其中年龄介乎7至15岁因犯罪而被捕的人士称为少年罪犯；而16至20岁的则称为青年罪犯。

Explanatory Notes on Main Statistical Indicatiors

Crude birth rate refers to the number of live births occurred during a calendar year to the mid-year population of that year. It is usually expressed in terms of 1000 population.

Crude death rate refers to the number of deaths occurred during a calendar year to the mid-year population of that year. It is usually expressed in terms of 1000 population.

Expectation of life at birth refers to the average number of years of life that a male/female born in a given year can expect to live if he/she were subjected to the prevalent mortality conditions as reflected by the set of age sex specific mortality rates for that year.

Mid-year population before 1996 was compiled using the "extended de facto" approach. It includes Hong Kong Permanent and Non-permanent Residents and visitors who are in Hong Kong at the reference time-point. Hong Kong Permanent Residents temporarily away to the mainland of China and Macau are also included. Since August 2000, the "resident population" approach has been adopted in place of the "extended de facto" approach for compiling Hong Kong population figures. Revised population figures backdated to 1996 have been compiled. The population estimate compiled under the "resident population" approach is referred to as the "Hong Kong Resident Population". The "Hong Kong Resident Population" comprises "Usual Residents" and "Mobile Residents". "Usual Residents" refer to two categories of people : (1) Hong Kong Permanent Residents who have stayed in Hong Kong for at least three months during the six months before or for at least three months during the six months after the reference time-point, regardless of whether they are in Hong Kong or not at the reference time-point; and (2) Hong Kong Non-permanent Residents who are in Hong Kong at the reference time-point. As for "Mobile Residents", they are Hong Kong Permanent Residents who have stayed in Hong Kong for at least one month but less than three months during the six months before or for at least one month but less than three months during the six months after the reference time-point, regardless of whether they are in Hong Kong or not at the reference time-point. Under the new approach, visitors are not included in the Hong Kong Population.

Total fertility rate refers to the average number of children that would be born alive to 1000 women during their lifetime if they were to pass through all their childbearing years following the age-specific fertility rates of a given year.

Infant mortality rate refers to the number of deaths aged under one occurred during a calendar year per 1000 live births in the same year.

Labour force refers to the land-based non-institutional population aged 15 and over who satisfy the criteria for inclusion in the employed population or the unemployed population.

Labour force participation rate refers to the proportion of labour force in the land-based non-institutional population aged 15 and over.

Employed population consists of persons aged 15 and over who have been at work for pay or profit during the seven days before enumeration or who have had formal job attachment. Unpaid family workers and persons who were on leave/holiday during the seven days before enumeration are included.

Unemployed population comprises all those persons aged 15 and over who have not had a job, have not performed any work for pay or profit, have been available for work during the seven days before enumeration and have sought work during the thirty days before enumeration. It also includes persons without a job who have sought work but unavailable for work because of temporary sickness; and persons without a job who have been available for work but have not sought work because they (I) have made arrangements to take up a new job or to start business at a subsequent date; or (II) were expecting to return to their original jobs; or (III) believed that work was not available to them (discouraged workers).

Unemployment rate refers to the proportion of unemployed persons in the labour force.

Underemployed population comprises those employed persons who have involuntarily worked less than thirty-five hours during the seven days before enumeration and have sought additional work during the thirty days before enumeration, or have not sought additional work but have been available for additional work during the seven days before enumeration.

Underemployment rate refers to the proportion of underemployed persons in the labour force.

Real wage index indicates changes in the purchasing power of the amount of money earned as wages by employees up to supervisory level and is obtained by deflating the nominal wage index by the Consumer Price Index(A).

Gross Domestic Product (GDP) is a measure of the total value of production of all resident producing units of a country or territory in a specified period, before deducting allowance for consumption of fixed capital.

Per capita GDP of a country or territory is obtained by dividing total GDP in a year by the population of that country or territory in the same year.

Gross National Product (GNP) refers to the total income

of the residents of a country or region from engaging in various economic activities, irrespective of whether the economic activities are carried out in the economic territory of the country or region or not. In other words, the gross national product should include the income of the residents engaged in various economic activities within or outside the economic territory of the country or region, but exclude the income of non-residents engaged in economic activities in the economic territory of the country or region. The following formula is used in the calculation of the gross national product:

GNP = Gross Domestic Product

+Factor income earned by residents from outside the economic territory of the country or region

- Factor income earned by non-residents from within the economic territory of the country or region.

Per capita GNP of a country or a region refers to the gross national product of the country or region in a year divided by the total population in the same year.

The components of factor income are mainly classified into investment income and compensation of employees. Investment income includes direct investment income, portfolio income and other investment income.

The items "Balance of Payments accounts" until "Reserve assets" are applicable to balance of payments account (Table 22-10):

Balance of Payments (BOP) account is a statistical statement that systematically summarizes, for a specific time period, the economic transactions of an economy with the rest of the world. A complete BoP account comprises two broad accounts: (a) Current Account; (b) Capital and Financial Account.

Current account largely measures flow of real resources, including exports and imports of good and services, income receivable and payable abroad, and current transfers from and to abroad.

Goods comprise all movable goods that change ownership from residents to non-residents (exports) and from non-residents to residents (imports).

Services include services rendered by residents to non-residents (exports) and by non-residents to residents (imports).

Income consists of earnings by residents from non-residents (income receivable) and by non-residents from residents (income payable) for the provision of factors of production.

Current transfers are those transactions in which an economy provides to other economies real or financial resources, that are immediately or shortly consumed, without receiving equivalent values in return.

Capital account measures external transactions in capital transfers, and in acquisition or disposal of non-produced, non-financial assets.

Capital transfers are transfers of ownership of a fixed asset or the forgiveness of a liability without receiving any economic value in return.

Financial account records transactions in financial assets and liabilities between residents and non-residents. It shows how an economy's external transactions are financed. Transactions in the financial account are classified into direct investment, portfolio investment, financial derivatives, other investment and reserve assets.

Direct investment refers to external investment in which an investor of an economy acquires a lasting interest and an effective control over the management of an enterprise located in another economy.

Portfolio investment refers to investment in non-resident equity securities and debt securities (e.g. bonds and notes, money market instruments), for which the investors have no lasting interest or influence in the management of the companies they invest.

Financial derivatives are financial instruments that are linked to a specific financial instrument or indicator or commodity, and through which specific financial risks can be traded in financial markets (including on Exchange and over the counter) in their own right.

Other investment refers to other financial claims on and liabilities to non-residents that are not classified as direct investment, portfolio investment, financial derivatives or reserve assets.

Reserve assets consist of external assets that are readily available to and controlled by monetary authorities of an economy (in the case of Hong Kong, the Hong Kong Monetary Authority) for directly financing payment imbalances and for indirectly regulating the magnitude of such imbalances through intervention in foreign exchange markets to affect the currency exchange rate of that economy.

Index of industrial production measures the changes in local manufacturing output in real terms, i.e. changes in the volume of local production after discounting the effect of price changes.

Assignments of building units refer to documents which effect the transfer of ownership of property of undivided shares of a lot, i.e. building units.

Buildings with consents to commence work refer to buildings with consents to commence building works issued by the Buildings Department. Such "consents" are issued to private development projects (including Hong Kong Housing Society's projects) and Hong Kong Housing Authority's development projects under the Private Sector Participation Scheme, except small houses in the New Territories where "consents" are not required.

Usable floor area is defined as the aggregate of the areas of the floor or floors in a storey or a building excluding any staircases, public circulation space, lift landings, lavatories, water-closets, kitchens and any space occupied by machinery for any lift, air-conditioning system or similar service provided for the building.

Tenure of accommodation refers to the terms or conditions under which accommodation is held by a household. The different terms are defined as follows:

Owner-occupier refers to a household which owns the quarters it occupies.

Sole tenant refers to a household which rents the whole quarters it occupies from someone who lives outside the quarters without sharing it with other household(s) or subletting.

Co-tenant refers to two or more households each of which rents part of a quarters from someone who lives outside the quarters.

Main tenant refers to a household which rents the whole quarters it occupies from someone who lives outside the quarters and sublets part of it to other household(s).

Sub-tenant refers to a household which rents part of a quarters from someone who lives in the same quarters.

Rent free refers to a household which occupies an accommodation free, with or without the owner's permission. This excludes households occupying accommodation provided by employers.

Provided by employer refers to a household which occupies an accommodation provided by the employer of one of the household members. This also includes households occupying quarters leased from employers at a nominal rent. If a household member uses housing allowance given by his employer for renting accommodation, the tenure is not considered as provided by employer.

Inward and outward movements of passenger trains refer to the through train services operated by the Kowloon-Canton Railway Corporation (KCRC) between Hong Kong and the mainland of China.

Inward and outward movements of motor vehicles refer to traffic through the Control Points at Lok Ma Chau, Man Kam To and Sha Tau Kok to and from the mainland of China.

Motor vehicle licensing conveys the right for a vehicle to be driven on a road. The valid period is either four months or a year. The total vehicles licensed figure refers to end of the year position.

Hotel room occupancy rate is compiled based on daily number of rooms available for sale only. Rooms under repair or being refurbished are excluded.

Domestic exports are the natural produce of Hong Kong or the products of a manufacturing process in Hong Kong which has changed permanently the shape, nature, form or utility of the basic materials used in manufacture. Their values are recorded on f.o.b (free-on-board) basis.

Re-exports are products which have previously been imported into Hong Kong and which are re-exported without having undergone in Hong Kong a manufacturing process which has changed permanently the shape, nature, form or utility of the product. Their values are recorded on f.o.b (free-on-board) basis.

Imports are goods which have been produced or manufactured in places outside the jurisdiction of Hong Kong and brought into Hong Kong for domestic use or for subsequent re-export as well as Hong Kong products re-imported. Their values are recorded on c.i.f. (cost, insurance and freight) basis.

Exports to the mainland of China for outward processing refer to raw materials or semi-manufactures exported from or through Hong Kong to the mainland of China for processing with a contractual arrangement for subsequent re-importation of the processed goods into Hong Kong.

Imports from the mainland of China related to outward processing refer to processed goods imported from the mainland of China of which all or part of the raw materials or semi-manufactures have been under contractual arrangement exported from or through Hong Kong to the mainland of China for processing.

Re-exports of the mainland of China origin to other places involving outward processing in the mainland of China refer to processed goods re-exported through Hong Kong of which all or part of the raw materials or semi-manufactures have been exported from or through Hong Kong to the mainland of China for processing with a contractual arrangement for subsequent re-importation of the processed goods into Hong Kong.

The items "Direct investment" until "Flow of direct investment" are applicable to direct investment (Table 22-24 and 22-25):

Direct investment represents investment which allows investors in one economy, on a long term basis, to influence or have an effective voice in the management of an enterprise in another economy. For statistical purpose, an effective voice is taken as equivalent to a holding of 10% or more of the equity in an enterprise. Direct investment comprises equity capital, reinvested earnings and other capital. Equity capital means equity in branches, stock and shares in subsidiaries and associates. Reinvested earnings consist of investors' share of earnings of their subsidiaries or associates not distributed as dividends. Other capital involves inter-company debt transactions. These include short-term or long-term borrowing and lending of funds between parent companies and their subsidiaries, associates and branches.

Inward direct investment refers to direct investment in a Hong Kong enterprise by a non-Hong Kong resident. Typical examples of inward direct investment are multinational corporations' branches and subsidiaries operating in Hong Kong.

Outward direct investment refers to direct investment by a Hong Kong resident in a non-resident enterprise.

Position of direct investment refers to the value of investment abroad and investment received from abroad of Hong Kong residents at a specified date.

Flow of direct investment refers to the additions/withdrawal of investment abroad or investment received from abroad of Hong Kong residents during a period.

A regional headquarters is an office which controls the operation of other offices or branches of the company in the region, and manages the business in the region without frequent referrals to its parent company.

A regional office is an office which coordinates offices/ operations elsewhere in the region in addition to the city in which it is located, and manages the business but with frequent referrals to its parent company or a regional headquarters.

The Loan Fund is used to finance schemes of the HKSAR Government loans, such as housing loans and students loans. The main sources of income are appropriations from the General Revenue Account, loan repayments and interest on loans.

Effective exchange rate indices(EERI) measure movements in the weighted average of the exchange rate of Hong Kong Dollar (HKD)against the currencies of major trading partners of Hong Kong.

Exchange rates between Hong Kong Dollar and other currencies refer to the average closing middle market telegraphic transfer rates or notes rates.

Authorized institutions include licensed banks, restricted licence banks and deposit-taking companies.

Licensed banks can accept deposits of any size and maturity. Before 1 October 1994, interest rates payable to HK dollar time deposits of less than HK$500,000 for a maturity under fifteen months, were governed by the Interest Rate Rules of the Hong Kong Association of Banks. However, the Interest Rate Rules have been liberalized by phases since then. As from 2 November 1995, the rules only apply to current accounts, savings accounts and time deposits with a maturity below seven days.

Restricted licence banks can accept time deposits in amounts of not less than HK$500,000 with any term of maturity. There is no restriction on interest rate payable.

Deposit-taking companies can accept time deposits in amounts of not less than HK$100, 000 with a term of maturity of at least three months. There is no restriction on interest rate payable.

Foreign currency swap deposits refer to deposits involving customers buying foreign currencies in the spot market and placing them as deposits with authorized institutions, while at the same time entering into a contract to sell such foreign currencies (principal plus interest) forward in line with the maturity of such deposits. For most analytical purpose, they should be regarded as Hong Kong dollar time deposits.

Money supply definition 1 (M1) refers to the sum of legal tender notes and coins held by the public plus customers' demand deposits placed with licensed banks.

Money supply definition 2 (M2) refers to the sum of M1 plus customers' savings and time deposits with licensed banks, plus negotiable certificates of deposits issued by licensed banks held by non-authorized institutions.

Money supply definition 3 (M3) refers to the sum of M2 plus customer deposits with restricted licence banks and deposit-taking companies plus negotiable certificates of deposits issued by restricted licence banks and deposit-taking companies held by non-authorized institutions.

Hang Seng Index launched on 24 November 1969, is the key barometer of the Hong Kong stock market and reflects general price movements and the performance of the market as a whole.

Consumer Price Index (CPI) summarizes changes in the price level of consumer goods and services purchased by households. Its change measures the change over time in the total cost of a given basket of goods and services. Its year-on-year rate of change is an important indicator of inflation affecting consumers. The year-on-year rate of change is the percentage increase or decrease in the current index compared to that in the same period of preceding year.

Different CPIs are compiled by the Census and Statistics Department of the HKSAR to reflect the impact of consumer price changes on households in different expenditure ranges. The CPI(A), CPI(B) and CPI(C) are compiled based on the expenditure patterns of households in the relatively low, medium and relatively high expenditure ranges. A Composite CPI is compiled based on the expenditure patterns of all households taken together to reflect the impact of consumer price changes on the household sector as a whole.

The expenditure weights of the CPIs are updated once every five years. The expenditure weights currently in use are derived from the results of the Household Expenditure Survey conducted in 1999/2000 .

Educational attainment refers to the highest level of education ever attained by a person in school or other educational institution, regardless of whether he/she had completed the course. Only formal courses are counted as educational attainment. A formal course shall be one that lasts for at least one academic year, requires specific academic qualification for entrance (except degree, associate degree and sub-degree course offered by the Open Learning Institute of Hong Kong, i.e. the present Open University of Hong Kong) and includes examinations or specific academic assessment procedures.

Kindergarten refers to all classes in kindergarten.

Non-degree course refers to all higher diploma/endorsement certificate courses in technical institutes/technical colleges (technical institutes and technical colleges were merged as the Hong Kong Institute of Vocational Education in 1999)/polytechnics (the present universities), associateship and other non-associateship courses in polytechnics (the present universities) and other post-secondary colleges. Certificate/diploma courses in colleges/institute of education and in the Hong Kong Technical Teachers' College and nurse training courses are also included in his category.

Degree course refers to all first degree courses and post-graduate courses in tertiary educational institutions in Hong Kong and overseas.

Social Security Schemes aim to provide for the basic and special needs of the members of our community who are in need of financial or material assistance. The non-contributory social security system comprises: the Comprehensive Social Security Assistance Scheme, the Social Security Allowance Scheme, the Criminal and Law Enforcement Injuries Compensation Scheme, the Traffic Accident Victims Assistance Scheme and Emergency Relief.

The Comprehensive Social Security Assistance (CSSA) Scheme (known as Public Assistance (PA) Scheme before 1 July 1993), which is means-tested, is designed to provide financial assistance to bring the income of needy individuals or families up to a prescribed level to meet their basic needs.

The Social Security Allowance (SSA) Scheme (known as Special Needs Allowance (SNA) Scheme before 1 July 1993) comprises Old Age Allowance (OAA) and Disability Allowance (DA). It provides monthly allowance to elderly persons aged 65 or above and severely disabled persons to meet special needs arising from old age or disability.

The Criminal and Law Enforcement Injuries Compensation (CLEIC) Scheme provides cash assistance to victims of crimes of violence and law enforcement acts (or to their dependants in case of death) on a non-means-tested basis.

The Traffic Accident Victims Assistance (TAVA) Scheme provides speedy cash assistance to road traffic accident victims (or their dependants in the case of death). It is a non-means-tested scheme which does not take into account the element of fault in causing the accident. Payments cover only personal injury and death but not damage to property.

Emergency relief is to help victims of natural and other disasters by means of material aid, including cooked meals or dry rations and other essential relief articles.

Offenders arrested refer to persons arrested for crime, whether or not they are prosecuted. Persons arrested for crime who are between the ages of 7 and 15 are called juvenile offenders and those of the ages between 16 and 20 are called young offenders.

二十四、澳门特别行政区主要社会经济指标

Main Social and Economic Indicators of Macao Special Adminstrative Region

简要说明

一、本章资料反映澳门特别行政区主要社会、经济发展情况。内容包括：土地、人口、就业、国民经济核算、工业、能源、建筑、交通通讯、对外贸易、财政金融、物价、教育、卫生、房屋、社会保障等方面。

二、本章涉及的1999年及以前数据均指原名为“澳门地区”的数据。

三、本章由澳门特别行政区政府统计暨普查局提供所有数据，国家统计局国际统计信息中心负责整理、编辑。

四、在统计工作方面，按中华人民共和国“澳门特别行政区基本法”的有关原则，澳门特别行政区保留其单独运作的统计系统，并负责编制和发布反映澳门特别行政区情况的统计数据。由于澳门和内地在使用统计名词及概念方面会有所不同，读者在比较两地数据时，请参考本章末的“主要统计指标解释”。

五、澳门特别行政区是单独的关税地区，澳门与内地之间的贸易，亦需办理进出口报关。在贸易统计方面，澳门特别行政区对外贸易统计数据亦包括澳门特别行政区与内地的贸易。

六、在外汇统计及与之有关的各方面，澳门元是澳门特别行政区的法定货币，因此，除澳门元以外的货币(包括人民币)均视作外币。

七、更详细的统计资料及有关的技术细节，可参阅澳门特别行政区政府统计处出版的《澳门统计月刊》、《澳门统计年鉴》及各专题统计出版物。

八、本章节表中的符号使用说明：“..”为不适用；“_”为绝对数值为零；“…”为未能提供；“r”为更正资料。“p”为临时性数字；“×”为估计数字；“o”为数据小于本表最小单位半数；“~”为没有数字。

Brief Introduction

I. Data in this chapter show main social and economic developments of the Macao Special Administrative Region, including data on land, population, employment, national accounts, industry, energy, construction, transportation, communication, external trade, public finance and banking, prices, education, health, housing and social security.

II. Data of 1999 and previous years in this chapter refer to data of the former Macao region.

III. All data in this chapter are provided by the Statistics and Census Services, the Government of the Macao Special Administrative Region, and further tabulated or edited by the International Statistical Information Centre of the National Bureau of Statistics.

IV. According to the Basic Law of the Macao Special Administrative Region of the People's Republic of China, Macao Special Administrative Region maintains its independent statistical system, and compiles and disseminates statistics on the Region. As Macao and the mainland of China use different statistical concepts, definitions and terminologies, users are advised to make reference of the Explanatory Note at the end of this chapter when using and comparing data of the mainland of China and the Macao Special Administrative Region.

V. As Macao is a separate custom territory, trade between Macao and the mainland of China needs customs declaration procedures. In terms of trade statistics, data on Macao's imports and exports include Macao's trade with the mainland of China.

VI. As Pataca (MOP) is the legal tender in the Macao Special Administrative Region, all other currencies (including Renminbi) are regarded as foreign currencies in compiling foreign exchange statistics and related statistics.

VII. For more detailed statistics and technical details, users are advised to read Macao Monthly Bulletin of Statistics, Macao Yearbook of Statistics and other publications compiled by the Statistics and Census Services, the Government of the Macao Special Administrative Region.

VIII. Notations used in this chapter:

".." indicates not applicable; "-" indicates magnitude zero; "..." indicates not available; "r" indicates rectified data; "p" indicates provisional data; "x" indicates estimate; "o" indicates less than half of the unit employed;"~" indicates no figure provided.

24-1 主要统计指标概况

Principal Statistical Indicators

项目	Items	1990	1997	1998	1999	2000
人口及生命事件	**Population and Demographics Characteristics**					
年中人口估计（千人）	Mid-year Estimates Population (1000 persons)	335	419	426	434	438
出生率（‰）	Crude Birth Rate (‰)	20.5	12.0	10.4	9.6	8.8
死亡率（‰）	Crude Mortality (‰)	4.4	3.1	3.2	3.2	3.1
劳工	**Labour**					
经济活动人口（千人）	Active Population (1000 persons)	168.6	207.1	210.7	216.2	214.6
劳动力参与率（%）	Labour Force Participation Rate (%)	66.6	65.8	65.3	64.7	63.4
失业率（%）	Unemployment Rate (%)	3.2	3.2	4.6	6.4	6.8
就业不足率（%）	Underemployment Rate (%)	2.3	0.8	1.5	1.3	2.9
就业人口（千人）①	Employed Population (1000 persons) ①	163.3	200.6	201.0	202.5	200.1
制造业	Manufacturing	53.2	41.4	41.5	44.5	39.3
零售及批发业	Wholesale and Retail Trade	35.2	31.3	33.5	31.3	30.9
餐厅及酒店业	Restaurants and Hotels		21.9	23.2	21.7	21.6
团体、社会及个人服务业	Community, Social and Personal Services	45.0	62.5	52.3	56.6	57.9
对外贸易	**External Trade**					
出口（百万澳门元）	Exports (Million MOP)	13638	17129	17084	17580	20380
本地产品出口（百万澳门元）	Domestic Exports (Million MOP)		15048	14904	15044	17081
再出口（百万澳门元）	Reexports (Million MOP)		2081	2180	2536	3300
进口（百万澳门元）	Imports (Million MOP)	12343	16603	15596	16300	18098
贸易条件指数（1996 = 100）	Terms of Trade Index (1996=100)	100.7	98.9	102.2	103.1	100.7
工业生产	**Industrial Production**					
工业电力消耗量（百万千瓦小时）	Electricity Consumption (Million kwh)		150.6	176.7	165.6r	146.8
建筑(私人部门)	**Construction (Private Sector)**					
新建及扩建私人房屋单位数目（个）	Units Completed and Expanded (No.)	11574	9096	8321	5389	3146
新建及扩建私人房屋总面积（平方米）	Gross Floor Area Completed and Expanded (m^2)	1056671	1149961	969192	668778	370315
新动工的私人房屋单位数目（个）	Units Newly Commenced Work (No.)		7684	3825	3619r	1167
新动工的私人房屋总面积（平方米）	Gross Floor Area Newly Commenced Work (m^2)		853251	569987	417225r	202776
房屋单位买卖数目　（个）	Number of Units Sold (No.)	8463	14304	12776	11039	10211
不动产买卖契约数目（宗）	Deed of Real Estate Transacted (No.)	8559	12255	13361	12230	12484
不动产按揭贷款数目（宗）	Real Estate Mortgage Loans (No.)	6610	8511	8696	7363	7367
运输、通讯、旅游	**Transport, Communications, Tourism**					
进出澳门货运车辆数目（千辆）	Lorries Entering and Leaving Macao (1000 units)	264.3	291.0	243.1	241.9	454.1*
登记车辆（千辆）	Licensed Vehicles (1000)	51.2	96.3	107.3	114.2	114.2
电话线（千条）	Telephone Lines (1000)	96.4	222.5	251.1	300.1	320.9
访澳旅客（千人次）	Visitors (1000)	5942.2	7000.4	6948.5	7443.9	9162.2
酒店入住率（%）	Hotel Occupancy Rate (%)	69	50	51	54r	58
财政收支、货币、金融（百万澳门元）	**Government Accounts, Monetary and Finance (Million MOP)**					
财政总收入②	Total Government Revenue②	6015r	15001	15548	16943	15339
财政总支出②	Total Government Expenditure②	5507r	14241	15506	16636	15024
货币供应（广义货币供应量M2）	Money Supply (M2)					
澳门元③	MOP③	6947	24180	25796	28169	23824
港元	HKD	14990	41599	45530	46702	47391
其他货币	Other Currencies	8652	12579	14891	15268	18980
总计	Total	30589	78358	86217	90140	90194
本地机构及私人贷款及垫款	Loans/advances to Resident Firms & Individuals	15743	47804	47271	45941r	43867

24-1 续表1 Continued

项　　目	Items	1990	1997	1998	1999	2000
居民消费物价指数	**Consumer Price Index**					
（1995年7月至1996年6月=100）	**(Jul/95 - Jun/96=100)**					
综合消费物价指数	Composite Consumer Price Index			101.83	98.56	96.98
甲类消费物价指数	Consumer Price Index (A)			103.08	100.00	98.59
乙类消费物价指数	Consumer Price Index (B)			102.44	99.34	97.78
房屋（期末值）	**Housing (End of period balance)**					
社会房屋（个）	Social Housing (No.)	4871	7420	7824	9084	9084
教育④	**Education ④**					
学前教育学生（人）	Pre-primary Education (No. of Students)	20814	18291	17354	16083	
小学生（人）	Primary Education (No. of Students)	34972	47235	48269	47059	
中学生（人）	Secondary Education (No. of Students)	17601	28280	31782	34761	
高等教育学生（人）	Higher Education (No. of Students)	7425	7409r	8444r	7094	
医疗卫生	**Health**					
死亡登记人数（人）	Registered Deaths (No.)	1482	1293	1356	1374	1338
死于心脏病人数（人）	Deaths of Heart Diseases (No.)		304	292	274	357
死于癌症人数（人）	Deaths of Cancers (No.)	283	325	335	366	370
婴儿死亡率	Infant Mortality Rate	8.4	5.4	6.1	4.1	2.9
（按每千名出生登记活产婴儿计算）	(per 1000 registered live births)					
社会保障	**Social Security**					
供款人数目（人）	Contributors		7066	7360	7609	8451
总发放援助次数	Number of Payments Granted		107779	129742	157889	163363
总发放金额（千澳门元）	Amount of Payments Granted (1000 MOP)		89981	111461	147164	201912
治安	**Criminality**					
罪案数目（宗）	Number of Crimes	5514	8162	8487	9262	8925
囚犯数目（期末值,人）	Number of Prisoners (as at end of year)	719	657	711	788	868
国内生产总值②⑤	**Gross Domestic Product (GDP) ②⑤**					
以固定（1996年）价格计算	At Constant (1996) Prices					
支出法国内生产总值实际增长率(%)	Expenditure-based GDP Real Growth Rate(%)	8.0	-0.3	-4.6	-3.0r	4.6
国内生产总值（百万澳门元）	GDP (Million MOP)	41738	55139	52580	51028r	53385
人均国内生产总值（澳门元）	GDP per Capita (MOP)	124606	131613	123341	117576r	121974
以现价计算	At Current Prices					
支出法国内生产总值名义增长率(%)	Expenditure-based GDP Nominal Growth Rate(%)	18.6	1.1	-7.1	-5.5r	1.5
国内生产总值（百万澳门元）	GDP (Million MOP)	26175	55894	51902	49071r	49828
人均国内生产总值（澳门元）	GDP per Capita (MOP)	78144	133416	121750	113067r	113847

注：①1990年的资料，参考期为5月。"零售及批发业"和"餐厅及酒店业"共同组成一项分类，故未能分列。有关就业人数行业分类方面，1997年及以前是根据"澳门行业分类第一版"分类。自1998年起，采用"澳门行业分类第一修订版"。其中较显著的差异在于，室内装修工程在前分类中被归入"团体、社会及个人服务"；而此后分类则被归入"建筑"一项。

②2000年数字在日后得到更多资料时会作出修订。

③"中华人民共和国澳门特别行政区基本法"说明，澳门元是澳门特别行政区的法定货币。

④不包括特殊教育学生。第n年的学生人数是指n/n+1学年年终学生人数。

⑤澳门特别行政区出版刊物中称为"本地生产总值"。

* 包括关闸及路氹城边检站

Notes: ①Data of 1990 refer to May and in the same year "Wholesale and Retail Trade"and "Hotels and Restaurants"were grouped as one category. Data on employment by industry of 1997 and earlier were classified according to "Classification of Economic Activities of Macao, Version 1"while "Classification of Economic Activities of Macao, Revision 1"has been applied since 1998.The major difference between the two versions is the classification of "Interior Decoration",which was categorized under "Community, social and personal services"in the Version 1 and in "Construction"in Revision 1.

②Figures of 2000 are subject to revisions as more data become available.

③Pataca (MOP) is the legal tender in the Macao Special Administrative Region, as stated in "The Basic Law of the Macao Special Administrative Region of the People's Republic of China".

④Excluded students of special education. The number of students of year N refer to the students at the end of academic year N/N+1.

⑤The Chinese term used in the publications of the Macao Special Administrative Region is "本地生产总值".

*Include the Border Gate and the Checkpoint of CoTai.

24-2 按堂区划分的澳门面积

Land Area of Macao by Parish

单位：平方公里 (km²)

分　区	Sub-division	1990	1997	1998	1999	2000
总面积	**Total Land Area**	**17.4**	**21.4**	**23.6**	**23.8**	**25.4**
澳门	**Macao Peninsula**	**6.5**	**7.8**	**7.8**	**7.8**	**8.5**
圣安多尼堂区	Santo Antonio		1.1	1.1	1.1	1.1
望德堂区	Sao Lazaro		0.6	0.6	0.6	0.6
风顺堂区	Sao Lourenco		0.9	0.9	0.9	0.9
大堂区	Se		2.1	2.2	2.2	2.9
花地玛堂区	N.S. de Fatima		3.1	3.0	3.0	3.0
氹仔	**Island of Taipa**	**3.8**	**5.8**	**6.2**	**6.2**	**6.2**
路环	**Island of Coloane**	**7.1**	**7.8**	**7.6**	**7.6**	**7.6**
路氹填海区	**Reclaimed Land between the Islands of Taipa and Coloane**			**2.0**	**2.2**	**3.1**

24-3 人口主要指标

Main Demographic Indicator

项　目	Item	1990	1997	1998	1999	2000
年中人口估计（千人）	Mid-year Estimates of Population (1000)	335.0	418.9	426.3	434.0	437.7
出生率（‰）	Crude Birth Rate (‰)	20.5	12.0	10.4	9.6	8.8
死亡率（‰）	Crude Mortality (‰)	4.4	3.1	3.2	3.2	3.1
婴儿死亡率（‰）	Infant Mortality Rate (‰)	8.4	5.4	6.1	4.1	2.9
自然增长率（‰）	Natural Growth Rate (‰)	16.1	8.9	7.2	6.4	5.7
总和生育率	Total Fertility Rate	1.8	1.2	1.0	1.0	0.9
登记结婚数（宗）	No. of Registered Marriages	1794	1678	1451	1367	1222
离婚数目（宗）	No. of Registered Divorces	95	304	260	283	335
出生时平均预期寿命（1995-1998）（岁）	Life Expectancy at Birth (years)					
男	Male			75.52		
女	Female			79.92		

24-4 经济活动人口及失业状况

Active Population and Unemployment

项　目	Item	1997	1998	1999	2000
经济活动人口（千人）	Active Population (1000)	207.1	210.7	216.2	214.6
男	Male	115.1	116.4	115.7	113.7
女	Female	92.0	94.3	100.5	100.9
就业人口（千人）	Employed Population (1000)	200.6	201.0	202.5	200.1
失业人口（千人）	Unemployed Population (1000)	6.5	9.6	13.8	14.5
失业率(%)	Unemployment Rate (%)	3.2	4.6	6.4	6.8

24-5 按行业划分的就业人口

Employed Population by Industry

单位：千人 (Thousands)

行业	Industry	1999	2000
总数	**Total**	**202.5**	**200.1**
农业、畜牧业、狩猎及林业	Agriculture, Farming of Animals, Hunting and Forestry	0.1	0.1
捕渔业	Fishery	0.1	0.3
采矿业	Mining and Quarrying	o	o
制造业	Manufacturing	44.5	39.3
电力、煤气及水的生产与供应业	Production and Distribution of Electricity, Gas and Water	1.2	0.8
建筑	Construction	16.3	16.2
批发及零售业	Wholesale and Retail Trade	31.3	30.9
住宿、餐厅、酒楼及同类场所	Hotels, Restaurants and Similar Activities	21.7	21.6
运输、仓储及邮电通信业	Transport, Storage and Communications	15.0	15.0
金融、保险业	Financial Activities	6.0	7.1
房地产业务、租赁及向企业提供的服务	Real Estate, Leasing and Commercial Services	9.7	10.8
公共行政、防卫及强制性社会保障	Public Administration, Defence and Mandatory Social Security	16.7	16.7
教育	Education	9.2	8.3
医疗卫生及社会福利	Health and Social Welfare	5.2	5.3
团体、社会及个人的其他服务	Other Community, Social and Personal Services	19.8	22.2
雇用佣人的家庭	Households with Domestic Helpers	5.6	5.5
国际组织及其他领土以外的机构	International Organizations and Other Extra-territorial Institutions	0.1	0.1
不详	Unknown	0.1	0.1

24-6 按行业划分的每月工资中位数

Median Monthly Employment Income

单位：澳门元 (MOP)

行业	Industry	1999	2000
总数	**Total**	**4889**	**4792**
农业、畜牧业、狩猎及林业	Agriculture, Farming of Animals, Hunting and Forestry		
捕渔业	Fishery		
采矿业	Mining and Quarrying		
制造业	Manufacturing	2911	2944
电力、煤气及水的生产与供应业	Production and Distribution of Electricity, Gas and Water	11674	11587
建筑	Construction	4656	4337
批发及零售业	Wholesale and Retail Trade	4699	4502
住宿、餐厅、酒楼及同类场所	Hotels, Restaurants and Similar Activities	4401	4055
运输、仓储及邮电通信业	Transport, Storage and Communications	5651	5637
金融、保险业	Financial Activities	7442	7673
房地产业务、租赁及向企业提供的服务	Real Estate, Leasing and Commercial Services	4367	3939
公共行政、防卫及强制性社会保障	Public Administration, Defence and Mandatory Social Security	13711	13692
教育	Education	9444	9003
医疗卫生及社会福利	Health and Social Welfare	7796	9119
团体、社会及个人的其他服务	Other Community, Social and Personal Services	6415	6113
雇用佣人的家庭	Households with Domestic Helpers	2966	2819
国际组织及其他领土以外的机构	International Organizations and Other Extra-territorial Institutions		

24-7 国内生产总值（以现价计算）

Gross Domestic Product (Current Prices)

年份 Year	国内生产总值① GDP① （百万澳门元） (Million MOP)	（百万美元） (Million USD)	国内生产总值与上年比较的实际增长率(%)② GDP Real Growth Rate Over the Preceding Year (%)②	人均国内生产总值 GDP per Capita （澳门元） (MOP)	（美元） (USD)
1989	22061	2746	5.0	67861	8446
1990	26175	3263	8.0	78144	9740
1991	30327	3789	3.7	86242	10775
1992	39519	4957	13.3	106555	13365
1993	45193	5672	5.2	117695	14772
1994	50114	6296	4.3	126303	15867
1995	55333	6946	3.3	135190	16970
1996	55294	6940	-0.4	133096	16705
1997	55894	7009	-0.3	133416	16729
1998	51902	6505	-4.6	121750	15259
1999	49071r	6140r	-3.0r	113067r	14148r
2000③	49828	6208	4.6	113847	14185

注：①澳门特别行政区出版刊物中称为“本地生产总值”。
②实际增长率是按不变(1996年)价格估算的国内生产总值计算而得。
③估算数字在日后得到更多资料时会作出修订。

Notes:①The Chinese term used in the publications of the Macao Special Administrative Region is “本地生产总值”.
②The real growth rates are calculated based on GDP at constant (1996) prices.
③The estimates are subject to revisions as more data become available.

24-8 支出法国内生产总值①

Gross Domestic Product (Expenditure-based Estimates)①

单位：百万澳门元 (Million MOP)

国内生产总值组成部份	GDP Components	1997	1998	1999	2000②
以现行价格计算	**At Current Prices**				
居民消费支出	Private Consumption Expenditure	20997	20685	20403r	20512
政府最终消费支出	Government Final Consumption Expenditure	5732	6029	6772r	5704
固定资本形成总额	Gross Fixed Capital Formation	11837	9667	8668r	5916
存货增加	Changes in Inventories	113	-72	83r	74
货物出口	Exports of Goods	17129	17084	17580	20380
减:货物进口	Less: Imports of Goods	20126	19132	20170r	22457
服务出口	Exports of Services	25226	22696	21539r	26103
减:服务进口	Less: Imports of Services	5013	5056	5804r	6404
支出法国内生产总值	**Expenditure-based GDP**	**55894**	**51902**	**49071r**	**49828**
人均国内生产总值（澳门元）	**GDP per Capita (MOP)**	**133416**	**121750**	**113067r**	**113847**
以固定(1996年)价格计算	**At Constant (1996) Prices**				
居民消费支出	Private Consumption Expenditure	20490	20299	20604r	20976
政府最终消费支出	Government Final Consumption Expenditure	5416	5547	6406r	5589
固定资本形成总额	Gross Fixed Capital Formation	12018	10497	9669r	6937
存货增加	Changes in Inventories	107	-70	83r	70
货物出口	Exports of Goods	16503	17084	17831	20234
减:货物进口	Less: Imports of Goods	19167	18966	20624r	21940
服务出口	Exports of Services	24580	22963	22639r	27695
减:服务进口	Less: Imports of Services	4808	4774	5580r	6177
支出法国内生产总值	**Expenditure-based GDP**	**55139**	**52580**	**51028r**	**53385**
人均国内生产总值（澳门元）	**GDP per Capita (MOP)**	**131613**	**123341**	**117576r**	**121974**

注：①澳门特别行政区出版刊物中称为“以支出法估算的本地生产总值”。
②估算数字在日后得到更多资料时会作出修订。

Notes:①The Chinese term used in the publications of the Macao Special Administrative Region is “以支出法估算的本地生产总值”.
②The estimates are subject to revisions as more data become available.

24-9 生产法国内生产总值①

Gross Domestic Product(Production-Based Estimates)①

单位：百万澳门元 (Million MOP)

经济活动	Economic Activities	1996	1997	1998	1999②
第二产业	**Secondary Industry**	**7073**	**7248**	**6999**	**6775**
采矿业	Mining and Quarrying	10	12	12	7
制造业	Manufacturing	3781	3928	4028	3911
电力、煤气及水的生产和供应	Electricity, Gas and Water Supply	1180	1229	1363	1359
建筑业	Construction	2101	2079	1596	1498
第三产业	**Tertiary Industry**	**41853**	**42623r**	**39720r**	**37049**
批发零售、维修、酒店、餐厅及酒楼业	Wholesale, Retail, Repair, Hotels and Restaurants	5822	4832	4303	4037
交通运输、仓储及邮电通信业	Transport, Storage and Communications	2147	3092	2963	2995
金融保险、房地产、租赁及商业服务	Financial Intermediation, Real Estate, Renting and Business Activities	11787	12255	11885r	10848
公共行政、社会服务及个人服务（包括博彩业）	Public Administration, Other Community, Social and Personal Services (Including the gambling)	22096	22443r	20568r	19170
减调整项：间接计算的金融中介服务	**Less: Adjustment for Financial Intermediation Services Indirectly Measured (FISIM)**	**-2211**	**-2563**	**-2758r**	**-2273**
以基本价格按生产法估算的国内生产总值	**Production-based GDP at Basic Prices**	**46714**	**47308r**	**43961r**	**41552**
加产品税	Add: Taxes on Products	6314r	6743	6603	5541
以现行价格按生产法估算的国内生产总值	**Production-based GDP at Current Prices**	**53028r**	**54050r**	**50564r**	**47093**
以现行价格按支出法估算的国内生产总值	**Expenditure-based GDP at Current Prices**	**55294**	**55894**	**51902**	**49071**
统计差额（%）	Statistical Discrepancy (%)	-4.1	-3.3r	-2.6r	-4.0

注：①澳门特别行政区出版刊物中称为“以生产法估算的本地生产总值”。
②估算数字在日后得到更多资料时会作出修订。

Notes:①The Chinese term used in the publications of the Macao Special Administrative Region is “以生产法估算的本地生产总值”.
②The estimates are subject to revisions as more data become available.

24-10 生产法国内生产总值结构①

Structure of Gross Domestic Product (Production-Based Estimates)①

单位：% (%)

经济活动	Economic Activities	1996	1997	1998	1999②
第二产业	**Secondary Industry**	**15.1**	**15.3r**	**15.9r**	**16.3**
采矿业	Mining and Quarrying				
制造业	Manufacturing	8.1	8.3r	9.2r	9.4
电力、煤气及水的生产和供应业	Electricity, Gas and Water Supply	2.5	2.6	3.1	3.3
建筑业	Construction	4.5	4.4	3.6r	3.6
第三产业	**Tertiary industry**	**89.6**	**90.1r**	**90.4r**	**89.2**
批发零售、维修、酒店、餐厅及酒楼业	Wholesale, Retail, Repair, Hotels and Restaurants	12.5	10.2r	9.8r	9.7
运输、仓库及通讯业	Transport, Storage and Communications	4.6	6.5r	6.7r	7.2
金融、保险、房地产、租赁及商业服务	Financial Intermediation, Real Estate, Renting and Business Activities	25.2	25.9r	27.0r	26.1
公共行政、社会服务及个人服务（包括博彩业）	Public Administration, Other Community, Social and Personal Services (Including the gambling)	47.3	47.4r	46.8	46.1
减调整项：间接计算的金融中介服务	**Less: Adjustment for Financial Intermediation Services Indirectly Measured (FISIM)**	**-4.7**	**-5.4r**	**-6.3r**	**-5.5**
以基本价格按生产法估算的国内生产总值	**Production-based GDP at Basic Prices**	**100.0**	**100.0**	**100.0**	**100.0**

注：①澳门特别行政区出版刊物中称为“以生产法估算的本地生产总值”。
②估算数字在日后得到更多资料时会作出修订。

Notes:①The Chinese term used in the publications of the Macao Special Administrative Region is “以支出法估算的本地生产总值”.
②The estimates are subject to revisions as more data become available.

24–11 电力、燃料及水消耗量

Consumption of Electricity, Fuels and Water

项目	Item	1990	1997	1998	1999	2000
电力（百万千瓦小时）	**Electricity (Million kwh)**					
住户	Domestic		461.2	520.8	507.4r	517.1
工业	Industrial		150.6	176.7	165.6r	146.8
商业	Commercial		792.6	815.4	836.8	888.8
公共照明	Public Lighting		8.1	10.0	10.8	11.9
燃料	**Fuels**					
重油（千公升）	Fuel Oil (1000 l)	203914	281189	313195	304241	315775
轻柴油（千公升）	Gas Oil and Diesel (1000 l)	101769	94731	90241	81102	95965
汽油（千公升）	Gasoline (1000 l)	22639	41168	42785	42868	41087
液化石油气（吨）	L.P.G. (tons)	11929	21384	22644	24902	24466
水（百万立方米）	**Water (Million m^3)**	**34.6**	**46.7**	**48.1**	**48.0**	**48.9**

24–12 按用途划分的建成私人房屋单位及建筑面积

Units and Gross Floor Area Completed by End-use

年份 Year	住宅 Residential		商业及写字楼 Commercial and Offices		工业 Industrial		其他用途 Other Uses		总计 Total	
	单位数目（个） No. of Units	建筑面积（千平方米） Gross Floor Area (1000 m^2)	单位数目（个） No. of Units	建筑面积（千平方米） Gross Floor Area (1000 m^2)	单位数目（个） No. of Units	建筑面积（千平方米） Gross Floor Area (1000 m^2)	单位数目（个） No. of Units	建筑面积（千平方米） Gross Floor Area (1000 m^2)	单位数目（个） No. of Units	建筑面积（千平方米） Gross Floor Area (1000 m^2)
1990	9488	686.1	1748	122.9	281	102.8	57	144.8	11574	1056.7
1996	14693	1247.7	2055	265.4			118	395.2	16866	1908.3
1997	6191	576.9	2540	363.4			365	209.6	9096	1150.0
1998	6695	559.5	1562	174.6	4	39.6	60	195.5	8321	969.2
1999	4252	307.7	1085	128.6	2	33.9	50	198.5	5389	668.8
2000	2747	230.1	368	54.8			31	85.4	3146	370.3

24–13 按用途划分的获批准新动工私人房屋单位及建筑面积

Units and Gross Floor Area Newly Commenced Work by End-use

年份 Year	住宅 Residential		商业及写字楼 Commercial and Offices		工业 Industrial		其他用途 Other Uses		总计 Total	
	单位数目（个） No. of Units	建筑面积（千平方米） Gross Floor Area (1000 m^2)	单位数目（个） No. of Units	建筑面积（千平方米） Gross Floor Area (1000 m^2)	单位数目（个） No. of Units	建筑面积（千平方米） Gross Floor Area (1000 m^2)	单位数目（个） No. of Units	建筑面积（千平方米） Gross Floor Area (1000 m^2)	单位数目（个） No. of Units	建筑面积（千平方米） Gross Floor Area (1000 m^2)
1996	6702	506.5	1517	115.9	1	0.5	33	135.7	8253	758.6
1997	6299	508.5	1347	124.6	4	40.9	34	179.3	7684	853.2
1998	3308	382.6	482	40.3	2	26.2	33	120.9	3825	570.0
1999	3157r	250.1r	442r	97.2	1	3.5	19r	66.5r	3619r	417.2r
2000	1038	99.1	111	21.6	3	5.8	15	76.3	1167	202.8

24-14 外地进出澳门货物

External Trade by Mode of Transport

单位：吨 (Tons)

项 目	Mode of Transport	1990	1997	1998	1999	2000
卸下①	**Unload ①**					
海路	Sea	4894881	2036203	2635363	1567602	1365302
空路	Air	53	11371	17393	11467	13416
陆路	Land	475786	290656	219526	237703	438599
其他②	Others ②	41314964	53048010	54220836	57171497	58511473
总数	**Total**	**46685684**	**55386241**	**57093118**	**58988269**	**60328790**
装上①	**Load ①**					
海路	Sea	547948	695322	560175	479472	441190
空路	Air	7891	31808	31332	32794	39367
陆路	Land	48822	124554	187328	171893	164458
其他②	Others ②	22	36307	38645	36450	48618
总数	**Total**	**604683**	**887992**	**817481**	**720609**	**693633**

注：①包括直接转运货物。
②包括邮递及以管道运输方式进出澳门的货物。

Notes: ①Includes quantities of direct transit.
②Includes quantities of external trade in Macao by postal parcels and pipelines.

24-15 货柜流量

Container Movement

单位：次数 (No.)

项 目	Item	1990	1997	1998	1999	2000
入境	Inward	21737	44823	44357	33983	34327
出境	Outward	24371	49720	51701	36106	36934
转口	Trans-shipment		11299	12369	13218	12012

24-16 通讯服务

Communications Service

项 目	Item	1990	1997	1998	1999	2000
邮递服务	**Postal Service**					
信件邮件（百万件）	Mail (Millions)	6.7	11.5	13.0	14.3	15.9
包裹（千件）	Parcels (1000)	8.3	9.3	9.1	9.7	6.4
电话服务（千条操作线路）	**Telephone Service (1000 Telephone Lines)**					
固定电话线	Fixed Lines	96.4	169.6	173.9	178.4	176.8
移动电话	Mobile Telephone Lines		50.7	67.0	92.1	121.0
数码式储值卡	Stored Value GSM Cards		2.2	10.2	29.5	23.1
对外电话通讯量（百万分钟）	**International Calls (Million Minutes)**					
拨出	Outgoing	52.0	119.0	125.2	132.8	152.1
拨入	Incoming		93.6	97.1r	97.9r	94.4
电报（件）	**Telex (No.)**					
发出	Transmitted	21108	1905	1145	1449	638
收到	Received		3162	2304	1279r	41
无线寻呼用户（户）	**Pagers (No.)**				**19312**	**9390**
国际互联网	**Internet Service**					
登记用户	Registered Users		5846	9516	17034	27346
总使用时数（千小时）	Total Hours Used (1000)		1105.6	2360.0	3377.9	10817.2

24-17 主要商品进出口总额

Values of Major Merchandise Trade

单位：百万澳门元 (Million MOP)

贸易种类	Trade Type	1990	1997	1998	1999	2000
出口	Exports	13638	17129	17084	17580	20380
本地产品出口	Domestic Exports		15048	14904	15044	17081
再出口	Reexports		2081	2180	2536	3300
进口	Imports	12343	16603	15596	16300	18098
进出口总额	Total Trade	25981	33733	32680	33880	38478
进出口差额	Trade Balance	1295	526	1487	1280	2283
出口/进口比率（%）	Exports/Imports Ratio(%)	110.5	103.2	109.5	107.9	112.6

24-18 主要商品进口原产地和出口目的地

Values of Imports and Exports by Major Country/Region

单位：百万澳门元 (Million MOP)

贸易种类 主要国家/地区	Trade Type Major Country/Region	1990	1997	1998	1999	2000
进口（原产地）	**Imports (Country or Region of Origin)**					
中国内地	Mainland China	2194	4741	5092	5809	7429
中国香港	Hong Kong SAR	5210	4176	3697	2945	2758
欧洲联盟	European Union	1036	2052	1641	2103	1738
日本	Japan	1423	1417	1208	1084	1142
中国台湾	Taiwan, China	878	1537	1537	1550	1720
美国	United States of America	634	1042	733	831	820
出口（目的地）	**Exports (Country or Region of Destination)**					
美国	United States of America	4931	7747	8141	8249	9837
欧洲联盟	European Union	4679	5632	5210	5304	5790
中国内地	Mainland China	616	1111	1157	1617	2080
中国香港	Hong Kong SAR	1770	1315	1301	1195	1330

24-19 财政收入

Government Revenue

单位：百万澳门元 (Million MOP)

项　目	Items	1990	1997	1998	1999	2000
经常收入	**Current Revenue**					
直接税	Direct Tax	2587	7591	6355	5987	6895
间接税	Indirect Tax	454	553	489	496	533
费用、罚款及其他金钱制裁	Compulsory Fees, Fines and Penalties	118	301	293	255	228
财产收益	Property Income	776	674	992	2059	545
转移	Transfers	111	829	358	165	163
耐用品的出售	Sales of Durable Goods		1		1	1
劳务及非耐用品的出售	Sales of Services and Non-durable Goods	56	39	40	46	35
其他经常收入	Other Current Receipts	12	48	131	65	41
资本收入	**Capital Receipts**					
投资资产的出售	Sales of Invested Property	16	17	14	68	8
转移	Transfers	40		193	279	19
财务资产	Financial Assets	537		4	9	4
财务负债	Financial Liabilities	260				
其他资本收入	Other Capital Receipts		400	1570	400	306
非从支付中扣减的退回	Reimbursements Not Deducted from Payments	5	21	18	29	37
指定帐目	**Specific Accounts**	**1044r**	**4528**	**5091**	**7084**	**6523**
总数	**Total**	**6015r**	**15001**	**15548**	**16943**	**15339**

24-20 财政支出

Government Expenditure

单位：百万澳门元 (Million MOP)

项目	Items	1990	1997	1998	1999	2000
经常支出	**Current Expenditure**					
人员	Personnel	1453	2815	2979	2927	2649
物品及劳务	Goods and Services	486	591	574	686	525
利息	Interest	6	74	51	5	0
经常转移	Current Transfers	1121	4113	4520	4232	4258
其他经常支出	Other Current Expenditure	27	122	209	302	52
资本支出	**Capital Payments**					
投资	Investment	990	1474	1598	1128	870
资本转移	Capital Transfers	321	113	38	47	37
财务活动	Financial Transactions	60	411	447	225	110
其他资本支出	Other Capital Expenditure					
指定帐目	**Specific Accounts**	**1044r**	**4528**	**5091**	**7084**	**6523**
总数	**Total**	**5507r**	**14241**	**15506**	**16636**	**15024**

24-21 货币供应

Money Supply

单位：百万澳门元（年底数字） (Million MOP(as at end of year))

项目	Items	1990	1997	1998	1999	2000
狭义货币供应量M1	**Money Supply (M1)**	**8979**	**18953**	**20171**	**21045**	**21021**
分类一：澳门元	Classification 1: MOP	3213	8279	8477	9223	8674
港元	HKD	4243	8577	9693	9600	10089
其他货币	Other Currencies	1523	2098	2001	2222	2258
分类二：流通货币（澳门元）	Classification 2: Currency in Circulation (MOP)	699	1518	1555	1820	1740
活期存款	Demand Deposits	1879	3965	4106	3334	2669
储蓄存款	Savings Deposits	6401	13469	14510	15892	16612
广义货币供应量M2	**Money Supply (M2)**	**30589**	**78358**	**86217**	**90140**	**90194**
分类一：澳门元	Classification 1: MOP	6947	24180	25796	28169	23824
港元	HKD	14990	41599	45530	46702	47391
其他货币	Other Currencies	8652	12579	14891	15268	18980
分类二：狭义货币供应量M1	Classification 2: Money Supply (M1)	8979	18953	20171	21045	21021
通知存款	Notice Deposits	492	670	881	888	773
定期存款	Time Deposits	21104	58734	65165	68206	68401
存款证明书	Certificates of Deposits	13				

注：《中华人民共和国澳门特别行政区基本法》说明，澳门元是澳门特别行政区的法定货币。

Notes: Pataca (MOP) is the legal tender in the Macao Special Administrative Region, as stated in "*The Basic Law of the Macao Special Administrative Region of the People's Republic of China*".

24-22 外币兑换率

Exchange Rates

(一单位外币兑换的澳门元) (MOP to one unit of foreign currency)

项　目	Items	1990	1997	1998	1999	2000
年内平均数字	**Average for the Year**					
澳元	Australian Dollar	6.2674	5.9341	5.0203	5.1574	4.6739
欧元①	Euro ①	10.2280	9.0177	8.9532	8.5277	7.4183
韩圆	South Korean Won	0.0118	0.0086	0.0057	0.0067	0.0071
西班牙比塞塔	Spanish Peseta	0.0789	0.0545	0.0535	0.0513	0.0446
美元	US Dollar	8.0230	7.9749	7.9788	7.9918	8.0260
新台币	Taiwan Dollar	0.2973	0.2788	0.2384	0.2477	0.2574
法国法郎	French Franc	1.4767	1.3679	1.3537	1.3000	1.1309
英镑	Pound Sterling	14.3239	13.0709	13.2203	12.9284	12.1663
港元	Hong Kong Dollar	1.0300	1.0300	1.0300	1.0300	1.0300
日圆	Japanese Yen	0.0556	0.0661	0.0611	0.0704	0.0745
马来西亚林吉特	Malaysian Ringgit	2.9674	2.8954	2.0387	2.1031	2.1121
新西兰元	New Zealand Dollar	4.7901	5.2849	4.2816	4.2315	3.6684
葡萄牙埃斯库多	Portuguese Escudo	0.0564	0.0456	0.0443	0.0425	0.0370
德国马克	Deutsche Mark	4.9750	4.6049	4.5381	4.3601	3.7929
人民币	P.R. China Renminbi	1.6879	0.9620	0.9637	0.9654	0.9695
新加坡元	Singapore Dollar	4.4293	5.3851	4.7720	4.7160	4.6553
瑞士法郎	Swiss Franc	5.8021	5.5020	5.5090	5.3278	4.7590
年底数字	**As at End of Year**					
澳元	Australian Dollar	6.2043	5.2075	4.9001	5.2096	4.4888
欧元①	Euro ①	10.9054	8.8196	9.3113	8.0489	7.5665
韩圆	South Korean Won	0.0112	0.0046	0.0067	0.0070	0.0064
西班牙比塞塔	Spanish Peseta	0.0837	0.0527	0.0559	0.0484	0.0455
美元	US Dollar	8.0340	7.9815	7.9799	8.0049	8.0337
新台币	Taiwan Dollar	0.2963	0.2448	0.2476	0.2546	0.2426
法国法郎	French Franc	1.5776	1.3327	1.4164	1.2271	1.1535
英镑	Pound Sterling	15.4655	13.2297	13.2586	12.9559	11.9951
港元	Hong Kong Dollar	1.0300	1.0300	1.0300	1.0300	1.0300
日圆	Japanese Yen	0.0598	0.0614	0.0695	0.0782	0.0702
马来西亚林吉特	Malaysian Ringgit	2.9767	2.0518	2.0999	2.1066	2.1141
新西兰元	New Zealand Dollar	4.7220	4.6392	4.2234	4.1682	3.5629
葡萄牙埃斯库多	Portuguese Escudo	0.0601	0.0436	0.0463	0.0401	0.0377
德国马克	Deutsche Mark	5.3784	4.4596	4.7478	4.1153	3.8688
人民币	P.R. China Renminbi	1.5385	0.9640	0.9639	0.9669	0.9706
新加坡元	Singapore Dollar	4.6212	5.5692	5.1533	4.8054	4.6344
瑞士法郎	Swiss Franc	6.2962	5.4865	5.7721	5.0165	4.9865

注：《中华人民共和国澳门特别行政区基本法》说明，澳门元是澳门特别行政区的法定货币。外币指澳门元以外的其他货币，因而人民币亦视作外币。

①1999年1月1日之前汇率为欧洲货币单位的兑换率。

Notes:Pataca (MOP) is the legal tender in the Macao Special Administrative Region, as stated in "The Basic Law of the Macao Special Administrative Region of the People's Republic of China". Foreign currency refers to any currency other than the Pataca. Accordingly P.R. China Renminbi is also treated as foreign currency.

①Quotations before 1/1/1999 referred to the ECU of the European Union.

24-23 居民消费物价指数（房租除外）

（1995年7月至1996年6月=100）

Consumer Price Index(Excluding Rent)

(July/95 - June/96=100)

项　目	Items	权数 Weight	1990	1997	1998	1999	2000
综合消费物价指数	**Composite Consumer Price Index**						
总指数	**Global Index**	**75.52**	**65.25**	**102.82**	**103.00**	**99.71**	
		(100.00)			(101.83)	(98.56)	(96.98)
粮食及不含酒精饮品	Foodstuff and Non-alcoholic Beverages	31.31	*	103.69	104.32	99.73	98.24
衣履	Clothing and Footwear	5.74	*	100.42	101.43	99.22	93.82
（租金）、维修及住屋开支	(Rent), Maintenance and Housing Expenses	5.78	*	107.80	109.21	107.04	
		(30.26)	*		(100.31)	(97.33)	(95.63)
烟酒	Alcoholic Drinks and Tobacco	1.42	*	101.96	105.49	105.28	104.50
家居用品	Household Goods	4.09	*	99.87	98.95	96.28	94.75
药物及医疗	Health	1.84	*	107.49	109.24	106.47	107.13
交通及通讯	Transport and Communications	10.12	*	103.05	99.96	97.91	96.30
教育、文化及消闲	Education, Culture and Leisure	9.22	*	102.35	104.66	101.92	101.03
其他物品及服务	Other Goods and Services	6.01	*	97.64	94.49	91.59	91.77
甲类消费物价指数	**Consumer Price Index (A)**						
总指数	**Global Index**	**67.74**		**104.25**	**105.40**	**102.37**	
		(100.00)			(103.08)	(100.00)	(98.59)
粮食及不含酒精饮品	Foodstuff and Non-alcoholic Beverages	35.60		103.87	104.31	99.59	98.07
衣履	Clothing and Footwear	3.40		100.05	101.27	99.29	94.21
（租金）、维修及住屋开支	(Rent), Maintenance and Housing Expenses	7.51		108.51	109.82	107.60	
		(39.76)			(100.40)	(97.41)	(95.70)
烟酒	Alcoholic Drinks and Tobacco	1.96		101.30	105.49	105.59	104.93
家居用品	Household Goods	1.59		99.60	99.78	97.11	95.35
药物及医疗	Health	1.52		106.20	107.18	104.88	105.07
交通及通讯	Transport and Communications	5.39		105.08	106.48	106.53	104.30
教育、文化及消闲	Education, Culture and Leisure	7.81		106.61	110.20	109.22	109.78
其他物品及服务	Other Goods and Services	2.98		98.38	99.43	99.74	103.04
乙类消费物价指数	**Consumer Price Index (B)**						
总指数	**Global Index**	**75.15**		**103.28**	**103.84**	**100.76**	
		(100.00)			(102.44)	(99.34)	(97.78)
粮食及不含酒精饮品	Foodstuff and Non-alcoholic Beverages	32.47		103.68	104.41	99.86	98.31
衣履	Clothing and Footwear	5.94		100.94	102.14	100.06	94.93
（租金）、维修及住屋开支	(Rent), Maintenance and Housing Expenses	6.02		107.12	108.55	106.44	
		(30.87)			(100.23)	(97.26)	(95.58)
烟酒	Alcoholic Drinks and Tobacco	1.33		101.95	105.71	105.45	104.44
家居用品	Household Goods	3.69		99.59	98.53	95.58	93.78
药物及医疗	Health	2.16		107.64	109.60	107.43	109.35
交通及通讯	Transport and Communications	8.98		103.37	101.21	99.45	97.72
教育、文化及消闲	Education, Culture and Leisure	9.79		104.27	106.90	105.23	104.84
其他物品及服务	Other Goods and Services	4.77		97.81	95.69	93.62	93.63

注：括号内为包括租金权数及指数，由1998年1月开始公布。
房租除外的消费物价指数已于2000年底停止公布。
* 当时分类与现在分类不同。

Notes: Figures in parenthesis refer to the CPI series including rent, published since January 1998.
Consumer Price Index excluding rent is discontinued since 2000.
* Current classification of goods and services is different from the previous series.

24-24　14岁及14岁以上人口教育程度

Education Level of Population Aged 14 and Over

项　目	Item	1997		1998		1999		2000	
		人数(千) No.(1000)	百分比 %	人数(千) No.(1000)	百分比 %	人数(千) No.(1000)	百分比 %	人数(千) No.(1000)	百分比 %
总计	**Total**	**314.7**	**100.0**	**322.8**	**100.0**	**334.0**	**100.0**	**338.6**	**100.0**
男	**Male**	**147.0**	**46.7r**	**150.2**	**46.5**	**153.2**	**45.9**	**154.9**	**45.6**
女	**Female**	**167.7**	**53.3**	**172.6**	**53.5**	**180.8**	**54.1**	**183.8**	**54.3**
从未入学/学前教育	No Education/Pre-primary Education	59.7	19.0	58.8	18.2	59.4	17.8	60.2	17.8
男	Male	21.8	6.9	21.3	6.6	21.3	6.4	21.9	6.5
女	Female	37.9	12.0	37.5	11.6	38.0	11.4	38.3	11.3
小学	Primary Education	96.5	30.7	97.1	30.1	98.3	29.4	98.6	29.1
男	Male	46.8	14.9	46.3	14.3	47.1	14.1	47.7	14.1
女	Female	49.7	15.8	50.8	15.7	51.2	15.3	50.9	15.0
初中	Junior Secondary Education	93.8	29.8	99.4	30.8	105.2	31.5	102.8	30.4
男	Male	45.4	14.4	48.8	15.1	49.3	14.8	48.0	14.2
女	Female	48.4	15.4	50.7	15.7	55.9	16.8	54.8	16.2
高中	Senior Secondary Education	43.9	13.9	44.3	13.7	44.3	13.3	47.6	14.1
男	Male	21.8	6.9	21.9	6.8	22.2	6.6	22.9	6.8
女	Female	22.1	7.0	22.5	7.0	22.1	6.6	24.7	7.3
高等教育	Higher Education								
高等专科	Non-university Degree	5.8	1.8	5.9	1.8	6.4	1.9	6.9	2.0
男	Male	2.4	0.8	2.6	0.8	2.4	0.7	2.9	0.9
女	Female	3.4	1.1	3.2	1.0	4.0	1.2	4.0	1.2
大学	University	15.0	4.8	17.1	5.3	20.1	6.0	22.1	6.5
男	Male	8.8	2.8	9.2	2.9	10.7	3.2	11.2	3.3
女	Female	6.2	2.0	7.9	2.4	9.4	2.8	10.9	3.2
不详	Unknown			0.1		0.2	0.1	0.4	0.1
男	Male			0.1		0.2	0.1	0.3	0.1
女	Female					0.1		0.1	

24-25　按各类型教育机构学生人数①

Students by Type of Educational Institutes①

单位：人

(No. of Students)

类　别	Type	1990/1991	1997/1998	1998/1999	1999/2000
正规教育	**Regular Education**	**80812**	**102187**	**107419**	**104997**
学前教育	Pre-Primary Education	20814	18291	17354	16083
小学	Primary Education	34972	47235	48269	47059
中学	Secondary Education	16911	26406	28543	30685
技术及职业中学	Vocational Technical College	690	1874	3239	4076
高等教育 ②	Higher Education ②	7425	8381	10014	7094*
特殊教育	**Special Education**	**182**	**442**	**494**	**563**
学前	Pre-Primary Education	61	22	19	19
小学	Primary Education	117	46	49	49
中学	Secondary Education	4	13	18	18
特殊班	Special Classes in Ordinary School		361	408	408
成人教育	**Adult Education**	**38399**	**46571**	**47504**	**46432**

注：①学生人数为学年终人数。

②包括师范及护理训练的学生。

*只计算政府认可的高等教育机构。

Notes: ①No. of students as at the end of the school-year.

②Includes students of teachers and nurses trainings.

*Includes only the higher education institution recognized by the government.

24-26 医疗卫生条件

Medical and Health Conditions

项　目	Items	1990	1997	1998	1999	2000
医护人员（人）	**Medical Personnel in Health Care**					
医生	Doctors	537	859	869	896	997
牙科技术员	Odontologists		2	2	2	2
护士	Nurses	864	905	895	897	943
诊断及治疗助理员	Diagnostic and Therapeutic Technical		175	181	212	206
卫生服务助理员	Health Service Assistants		355	356	360	381
按每千名人口计算的医生数	Number of Doctors per 1000 Population	1.58	2.04	2.02	2.05	2.28
医疗机构和病床	**Health Care Establishments and Beds**					
医院（所）	Hospitals	2	2	2	2	2
病床（张）①	Beds (No.) ①	974	864	858	855	923
按每千名人口计算的病床数	Number of Beds per 1000 Population	3.49	2.05	1.99	1.95	2.11

注：　①包括普通住院及深切治疗部的病床。

Notes: ①Includes beds of general hospitalization and intensive care.

24-27 按住所租住权划分的家庭住户数目

Number of Households by Tenure of Accommodation

单位：户　　(No. of households)

项　目	Item	1993/1994	1998/1999
自置	Owner of Housing Unit	68599	87887
租客	Tenant	20335	21248
二房东	Main tenant	348	233
三房客	Sub-tenant	440	269
合租者	Co-tenant	4528	6355
由雇主提供	Provided by Employer	4051	2721
免租	Rent-free	8745	9140

24-28 社会保障基金发放次数及金额

Number of Payments and Amounts Granted by Social Security Fund

形　式	Type	1997 次数 No. of Payments	1997 金额 千澳门元 Amount (1000MOP)	1998 次数 No. of Payments	1998 金额 千澳门元 Amount (1000MOP)	1999 次数 No. of Payments	1999 金额 千澳门元 Amount (1000MOP)	2000 次数 No. of Payments	2000 金额 千澳门元 Amount (1000MOP)
总计	**Total**	**107779**	**89981**	**129742**	**111461**	**157889**	**147164**	**163363**	**201912**
养老金	Old Age Pension	34974	34922	45668	45580	60775	58890	66558	76431
伤残津贴	Disability Pension	5551	5516	7281	7234	8213	7963	7930	9074
救济金	Social Security Pension	56330	33553	59159	35206	64772	38642	59923	44501
特别给付	Special Allowance	7630	5712	8821	6833	9926	7855	10842	10377
失业津贴	Unemployment Allowance	1664	3198	4870	9594	8581	17059	7950	17867
疾病津贴	Illness Allowance	613	818	579	900	616	875	708	971
出生津贴	Maternity Allowance	501	506	2118	2125	2201	2227	2032	2052
结婚津贴	Marriage Allowance	126	126	789	789	926	926	794	794
丧葬津贴	Funeral Allowance	182	199	244	315	264	343	326	424
因肺尘埃沉着病的给付	**Payments for Pneumoconiosis**	**8**	**1927**	**2**	**316**	**3**	**698**	**5**	**1474**
因劳动关系产生的债权的担保	**Guarantee of Liabilities Resulted from Work Relation**	**200**	**3504**	**185**	**2477**	**123**	**5789**	**276**	**5966**
根据23/07/97博彩合同修订版第三条款规定给予援助失业人士的款项	Subsidy to the Unemployed as Stipulated in the Third Clause of the Revision of Gambling Contract of 23/07/97			26	92	1489	5897	6019	31981

主 要 统 计 指 标 解 释

国内生产总值 澳门特区称作本地生产总值，反映每年在澳门特区生产的货物和提供各种服务的总量。本年鉴中的国内生产总值用支出法及生产法估算，支出法等于私人消费支出、政府最终消费支出、固定资本形成总额、库存变化和货物及服务出口净值（出口减进口）的总和。而生产法等于各经济行业的增加值总额的总和，这种方法可以评估澳门特区的产业结构。

婴儿死亡率 参考期内年龄在1岁或以下的死亡人数与出生活婴数目的千分比。

自然增长率 参考期内出生人数和死亡人数差额与平均人口之千分比。

出生率 参考期内出生活婴数目与平均人口之千分比。

死亡率 参考期内死亡人数与平均人口之千分比。

正规教育 指有系统的，且主要为儿童及青少年开办的，由学前教育至大学教育之学制课程。学制课程必须符合下列三个条件：

— 课程最少为期一学年；

— 入学有特定的学历资格规定；

— 有考试或指定程序评核成绩。

学前教育 由两阶段组成：相等于学前教育第一年及第二年之幼儿教育及相等于学前教育第三年之小学教育预备班。

1）幼儿教育 对象是年龄3-4岁的儿童。在报名当年的12月31日年满3岁的幼儿皆可报读。而晋升方面，则无须进行知识的考核。

2）小学教育预备班 在报名当年的12月31日年满5岁的儿童可报读预备班。为晋升之目的，只设有进度测验。在某些教育机构，小学教育预备班仍被称为学前教育第三年。

小学教育 为期6年，完成小学教育预备班或在报名当年的12月31日年满6岁的儿童可报读小学教育第一年。就读小学的最高年龄为15岁。

中学教育 由两个阶段组成：初中教育及高中教育。大学预科亦被视为中学教育。

1）初中教育 为期3年，合格完成小学教育者可以入读。就读初中最大年龄为18岁，但在特别情况下，经教育机构决定，可以逾越此年限。

2）高中教育 为期最少2年，最多3年，合格完成初中教育者可以入读。就读高中最大年龄为21岁，但在特别情况下，经教育机构决定，可以逾越此年限。

技术及职业教育 以培训初级及中级程度的技术及专业人员为目的之课程。

高等教育 由大学、理工学院及相等之学院开办之学位或非学位课程。

特殊教育 指专为有精神缺陷，失聪及肢体残障之人士所开办的课程。

成人教育 指正规教育系统以外之为一般人士开办的应用课程，学生年龄一般为15岁或以上。

劳动人口 在参考期间，可参与生产商品或／及提供服务的14岁或以上人口。包括就业人口和失业人口。

就业人口 在参考期间，为了金钱或物质报酬、利润或家庭收入而工作至少1小时的14岁或以上人口。包括被雇用而没有上班，但与雇主保持正式联系和拥有1家公司但因特别原因暂时没有上班的人口。

失业人口 在参考期间，年龄在14岁或以上，没有工作或与雇主没有联系，但随时可接受有酬工作或自己做生意，并在过去30日内寻找过工作的人口。

就业不足人口 在参考期间，不论其职业身份，非自愿地工作少于35小时，但随时可接受更多工作或寻找更多工作的就业人口。

劳动力参与率 劳动人口占14岁或以上的澳门特区居住人口的比例。

失业率 指失业人口在劳动人口中所占的比例。

就业不足率 指就业不足人口在劳动人口中所占的比例。

访澳旅客 指任何非以澳门特区为常居地的人士，其连续逗留时间自2000年8月开始由原来少于3个月改为少于12个月，旅客之旅游目的并非在澳门特区参与任何有偿活动。

酒店入住率 入住客房数量与可供应客房数量之百分比。

进口 指将产自外地的货物输入澳门特区，但再进口和直接转运制度下输入者除外。

出口 指将货物输出澳门特区，但暂时出口和直接转运制度下输出者除外。

本地产品出口 指将产地为澳门特区的货物输出澳门特区。

再出口 指原进口的货物未经加工输出澳门特区，或虽加工，但不能取得澳门特区产地资格的。

直接转运 指仅为运输之目的，货物在澳门特区经过或转船，且其下目的地应于附同之文件中列明。

原产地 指农产品种植之国家或地区、矿业开采之国家或地区以及工业产品全部或部份生产之国家或地区。若生产产品之部份，负责产品变成确定形式进入澳门特区前的最后一个生产工序之国家或地区，都可被视为原产地。而再包装、再分类及混合不被视为生产工序。

目的地 目的地是指货物实际最后到达的国家或地区（不论在运输途中有或没有中断）。如有中间国家，只要不在中间国家内进行商业交易，都可被视为目的地国家。

贸易条件指数 即出口单位价格指数与进口价格指数

之比率。

单位　指永久性楼宇之一个或多个间格及其附属建筑物。每一个单位具有独立入口与楼宇内之公用地方相通，具有合法条件进行分层物业登记和作独立转让。

楼宇建筑面积　相等于所有层数之面积总和。楼面面积的计算方法是从外墙起量度，同时亦包括大堂面积、升降机所占面积以及所有公用地方面积(两个或以上单位合用)。

消费物价指数　反映澳门特区家庭于购买一篮子之指定商品或服务时，在不同时间该等商品或服务之价格变动。

狭义货币供应量M1　为流通货币、活期存款及储蓄存款之和。

广义货币供应量M2　指狭义货币供应量M1加上准货币负债。准货币负债指定期存款、通知存款和存款证明书。

财务活动　由财务资产及财务负债组成。

Explanatory Notes on Main Statistical Indicatiors

Gross Domestic Product (GDP) Reflects the total of goods produced and services provided annually in Macao SAR. The GDP in this statistical yearbook is estimated by using the expenditure and production approaches. The expenditure-based GDP is measured as the sum of private consumption expenditure, government final consumption expenditure, gross fixed capital formation, changes in inventories, and net exports of goods and services (exports less imports). The production-based GDP, which is measured as the sum of gross value added of all economic activities, can be used to evaluate the structure of the industrial sectors in Macao SAR.

Infant Mortality Rate Deaths of infants under one year old per 1,000 live births.

Natural Growth Rate Excess of births over deaths per 1, 000 inhabitants. (average population)

Crude Birth Rate Live births per 1,000 inhabitants. (average population)

Crude Mortality Rate Deaths per 1,000 inhabitants. (average population)

Regular Education Systematic academic programmes designed in principle, for children and juveniles to access / progress from pre-primary education to university. Three pre-conditions are set up:

- At least with a duration of one academic year,
- Specific academic qualification for entrance,
- Examination on specific academic assessment procedures included.

Pre-primary Education Composed of 2 stages: infant education, equivalent to the first and second year of pre-primary education, and the preparatory year for access to primary education or the third year of pre-primary education

(1) Infant education Designed for children aged between 3-4 years old. Children aged 3 as at 31st December of the year of enrolment are eligible. No knowledge tests are required for progression.

(2) Preparatory classes to primary education Designed for children of 5 years old as at 31st December of the year of enrolment. Progress examination is a pre-requisite for advancement access. This type of preparatory class is also called the third year of pre-primary education in some educational institutes.

Primary Education Lasts for 6 years. Children completed the preparatory class or of 6 years old as at 31st December of the year of enrolment are eligible to the first year of primary education. The maximum age for primary education is 15.

Secondary Education It is divided into 2 stages: Junior secondary and senior secondary. Pre-university courses are also considered secondary education.

(1) Junior Secondary Education For a duration of 3 years. Students successfully completed the primary education are eligible. The maximum age for this level is 18 years old. However, under certain circumstances, the educational institutes can exercise their discretion to accept enrolment beyond the age limit.

(2) Senior Secondary Education For a duration of 2-3 years. Students successfully completed the junior secondary level are eligible. The maximum age for this level is 21. However, under certain circumstances, the educational institutes can exercise their discretion to accept enrolment beyond the age limit.

Vocational technical college Programmes aim to train vocational technical personnels in elementary and middle levels.

Higher Education Degree or non-degree programmes offered by universities, polytechnic institutes or equivalent.

Special Education Programmes designed for students with mental, hearing and physical problems.

Adult Education Practical programmes or courses, outside the regular education, organized for general participants. Usually, the students are 15 years old or above.

Active Population (Labour Force) Individuals aged 14 or over who, during the reference period, are available to participate in the production of goods and/or services. This comprises both the employed population and the unemployed population.

Employed Population Individuals aged 14 or over who have worked for at least 1 hour during the reference period, for pay, profits or family gain in cash or in kind. It also includes individuals who have a job and are absent from work but maintain a formal job attachment, and owners of a company, temporarily not at work because of specific reasons.

Unemployed Population Individuals aged 14 or over who, during the reference period, do not have a job or formal job attachment, but are available to work for pay or run a business at any time and have sought work during the last 30 days.

Underemployed Population Employed population, irrespective of the status in employment, who have worked involuntarily for less than 35 hours during the reference period, but are available for or have sought additional work.

Labour Force Participation Rate The proportion of labour force in the population aged 14 and over.

Unemployment Rate The proportion of unemployed in the labour force.

Underemployment Rate The proportion of underemployed in the labour force.

Visitor Any person travelling to Macao SAR other than his/her usual environment and whose main purpose of travel is other than the exercise of an activity remunerated from within Macao SAR. The maximum length of stay has been amended from 3 consecutive months to 12 consecutive months since August 2000.

Hotel Occupancy Rate Number of rooms occupied by guests over total number of available rooms, expressed in percentage.

Imports The entry of any commodities into Macao SAR, except Reimports and Direct Transit.

Exports The outgoing from Macao SAR of any commodities, excluding Temporary Exports and Direct Transit.

Domestic Exports The outgoing from Macao SAR of any commodities with the origin of Macao SAR.

Reexports The outgoing from Macao SAR of any commodities previously imported, without any transformation, or even with transformation, the commodities did not qualify for the origin of Macao SAR.

Direct Transit Commodities passing through or transhipped in Macao SAR for the exclusive purpose of transportation and with their next destination mentioned in the attached documents.

Country of origin The country or territory where the crops were grown, the minerals were mined and the articles were manufactured wholly or partly. If partly, the origin is considered the country or territory responsible for the last phase of manufacture before the merchandise took its final form. Repacking, sorting or mixing is not considered a manufacture operation.

Country of destination The final country or territory to which the goods are delivered, whether or not the transport has been interrupted, and without any commercial transaction in the transit country or territory.

Terms of Trade Index The ratio of the unit value index for exports to that of imports.

Housing Unit Division(s) or annex of a permanent building. Each housing unit has independent entrance to access to the common area of the building, can be legally registered with the property registry and can be independently transacted.

Gross Floor Area The sum of the area of each floor of the building measured to the outer surface of the outer walls including the area of lobbies, lift landings and communal space (shared by 2 or more housing units).

Consumer Price Index Reflects the price change of a representative "basket" of goods and services consumed by families of Macao SAR.

Money supply (M1) Refers to the sum of currency in circulation, demand deposits and savings deposits.

Money supply (M2) Refers to the sum of money supply M1 and quasi-monetary liabilities that consist of time deposits, notice deposits and certificates of deposits.

Financial transactions Comprise financial assets and financial liabilities.

附录一、台湾省主要社会经济指标

APPENDIX I. Main Social and Economic Indicators of Taiwan Province

附录1-1 面积和人口主要指标

Main Indicators of Area and Population

项目	Item	1996	1997	1998	1999	2000
面积 (万平方公里)	Area (10 000 sq.km)	3.6	3.6	3.6	3.6	3.6
年底人口数 (万人)	Year-end Population (10 000 persons)	2152.5	2174.3	2192.9	2209.2	2227.7
男	Male	1106.6	1116.4	1124.3	1131.3	1139.2
女	Female	1046.0	1057.9	1068.5	1078.0	1088.5
出生率 (‰)	Crude Birth Rate (‰)	15.20	15.10	12.40	12.89	13.80
死亡率 (‰)	Crude Death Rate (‰)	5.7	5.6	5.6	5.7	5.7
婴儿死亡率 (‰)	Infant Mortality Rate (‰)	5.75	5.68	6.30		
妇女生育率 (‰)	Fertility Rate (‰)	54	53	43	45	
人口自然增长率 (‰)	Natural Population Growth Rate (‰)	9.50	9.50	6.80	7.16	8.10
结婚率 (‰)	Marriage Rate (‰)	7.90	7.70	6.70	7.87	8.20
离婚率 (‰)	Divorce Rate (‰)	1.70	1.80	2.00	2.23	2.40
平均期望寿命 (岁)	Life Expectancy at Birth (years)					
男	Male	73.72	73.90	73.14		
女	Female	79.73	79.86	79.18		
人口的年龄构成 (%)	Age-specific Distribution (%)					
0-14岁	0-14	23.20	22.60	22.00	21.43	21.10
15-64岁	15-64	69.00	69.30	69.80	70.13	70.30
65岁及以上	65 and Over	7.90	8.10	8.30	8.44	8.60
非农户人口占总人口比率 (%)	Non-agricultural Population as % of Total Population (%)	82.7	82.8	83.0		
人口密度(人/平方公里)	Population Density (persons/sq.km)	594.9	600.8	606.0	610.5	615.6

附录1-2 劳动力和就业状况

Labor Force and Employment

项目	Item	1996	1997	1998	1999	2000
劳动力总人数 (万人)	Labor Force (10 000 persons)	931.0	943.2	954.6	966.8	978.4
男	Male	566.2	573.1	578.0	581.2	586.7
女	Female	364.8	370.1	376.7	385.6	391.7
就业人数 (万人)	Employment (10 000 persons)	906.8	917.6	928.9	938.5	949.1
男	Male	550.8	556.2	561.0	562.4	567.0
女	Female	356.0	361.3	367.9	376.1	382.1
就业人数部门构成 (%)	Distribution of Employment by Industry (%)	100.0	100.0	100.0	100.0	100.0
农、林、渔、猎业	Agriculture, Forestry, Fishery and Hunting	10.1	9.6	8.8	8.3	
工业	Industry					
采矿业	Mining and Quarrying	0.2	0.1	0.1	0.1	
制造业	Manufacturing	26.7	28.0	28.1	27.7	
电、煤气、水	Electricity, Gas, Water	0.4	0.4	0.4	0.4	
建筑业	Construction	10.2	9.6	9.3	9.0	
服务业	Services					
批发、零售及餐饮业	Wholesale and Retail Trade and Catering Services	21.8	21.7	22.0	22.7	
运输、仓储和通信业	Transport, Storage, Communications	5.2	5.1	5.1	5.1	
金融、保险和不动产业	Financing, Insurance & Real Estate	3.7	3.8	4.1	4.3	
工商服务业	Business Services	2.6	2.6	2.8	3.0	
公共行政、社会和个人服务业	Public Administration, Community, Social and Personal Services	19.1	19.0	19.1	19.4	
失业人数 (万人)	Unemployment (10 000 persons)	24.2	25.6	25.7	28.3	29.3
失业率 (%)	Unemployment Rate (%)	2.6	2.7	2.7	2.9	3.0

附录1-3 国民生产总值

Gross National Product

年份 Year	国民生产总值 Gross National Product			人均国民生产总值 Per Capita Gross National Product	
	新台币亿元 (NT $100 million)	比上年增长%① Annual Growth Rate over the Preceding Year %①	亿美元 (USD 100 million)	新台币元 NT $	美元 USD
1991	49278	6.0	1837	240909	8982
1992	54598	7.3	2170	264338	10506
1993	60322	6.7	2286	264196	10011
1994	65710	6.8	2483	286191	10812
1995	71291	6.3	2691	308086	11630
1996	77876	5.9	2836	333948	12161
1997	84174	6.3	2933	357503	12457
1998	90066	4.3	2692	379202	11333
1999	93758	5.6	2905	390466	12100
2000	98203	6.4	3144	404763	12961

注:①按1991年价格计算。

①At 1991 constant prices.

附录1-4 国内生产总值支出构成

Expenditures on Gross Domestic Product

单位:% (%)

年份 Year	国内生产总值(新台币亿元) Gross Domestic Product (NT$ 100 million)	居民消费 Household Consumption Expenditure	政府消费 Government Consumption Expenditure	存货增加 Change in Stocks	固定资本形成 Gross Fixed Capital Formation	货物及服务输出 Exports of Goods and Services	减：货物及服务输入 Minus:Imports of Goods and Services
1991	48107.05	54.80	17.39	1.12	22.17	47.41	42.87
1992	53376.93	56.00	17.01	1.67	23.24	43.38	41.28
1993	59183.76	56.57	15.63	1.01	25.17	44.08	42.46
1994	64636.00	58.30	14.57	0.80	24.58	43.65	41.98
1995	70179.33	58.77	14.24	0.38	24.95	47.98	46.32
1996	76781.26	59.13	14.30	0.70	22.50	47.41	44.04
1997	83287.80	59.70	14.38	1.45	22.76	48.26	46.20
1998	89389.67	59.67	14.32	1.37	23.54	47.81	46.71
1999	92899.29	60.73	13.15	0.50	22.87	48.29	45.54
2000	96859.39	62.17	13.03	-0.52	23.30	54.20	52.18

附录1-5 国内生产总值及部门构成

Gross Domestic Product by Kind of Economic Activity

单位:% (%)

年份 Year	国内生产总值(新台币亿元) Gross Domestic Product (NT$ 100 million)	农业 Agriculture Forestry, Hunting and Fishery	工业 Industry			
				制造业 Manufacturing	水、电、煤气业 Electricity Gas & Water	建筑业 Construction
1991	48107.1	3.8	41.1	33.3	2.7	4.7
1992	53376.9	3.6	39.9	31.7	2.7	5.0
1993	59183.8	3.6	39.4	20.6	2.7	5.3
1994	64636.0	3.5	37.7	29.0	2.6	5.6
1995	70179.3	3.4	36.4	27.9	2.6	5.4
1996	76781.3	3.2	35.7	27.9	2.5	4.9
1997	83287.8	2.6	35.3	27.8	2.4	4.7
1998	89389.7	2.5	34.6	27.4	2.3	4.4
1999	92899.3	2.6	33.2	26.6	2.2	3.9
2000	96859.4	2.1	32.4	26.3	2.1	3.5

附录1-5 续表 1 continued

单位：%　(%)

年份 Year	服务业 Services	商业 Wholesale and Retail Trade, and Hotels Restaurants	运输仓储及通信业 Transport, Storage & Communications	金融保险不动产及工商服务业 Finance, Insurance, Real Estate & Business Services	政府部门服务业 Government Services
1991	55.14	14.61	6.19	17.85	11.06
1992	56.53	14.98	6.29	18.66	11.02
1993	57.01	15.30	6.40	17.56	10.49
1994	58.78	15.61	6.55	18.96	10.27
1995	60.15	16.80	6.65	19.26	10.35
1996	61.09	16.80	6.78	19.50	10.36
1997	62.14	17.23	6.74	20.56	10.90
1998	62.97	17.77	6.96	20.36	10.02
1999	64.25	18.49	6.73	20.35	10.19
2000	65.57	19.16		20.50	10.20

附录1-6 农 业 生 产 指 数
Index of Agricultural Production

(1996年=100)　(1996=100)

年份 Year	总指数 Total	种植业 Crops	林业 Forestry	畜牧业 Livestock	渔业 Fishery
1986	84.5	96.6	642.8	59.9	100.9
1990	94.5	97.0	233.5	74.3	120.4
1991	95.9	99.5	218.7	80.9	111.4
1992	93.6	95.4	132.0	82.9	107.5
1993	99.3	101.9	137.8	86.5	114.2
1994	96.3	98.3	104.0	91.4	100.7
1995	99.8	100.3	121.4	96.0	104.9
1996	100.0	100.0	100.0	100.0	100.0
1997	98.7	101.6	112.5	92.6	102.1
1998	93.3	93.2	142.5	85.7	101.6
1999	94.4	99.6	119.7	82.6	99.9

附录1-7 主 要 农 产 品 产 量
Output of Major Crops

单位：万吨　(10 000 ton)

年份 Year	稻谷 Rice	小麦(吨) Wheat(ton)	玉米 Maize	大豆 Soy Beans	土豆 Potato	茶叶 Tea	甘蔗 Sugarcane	烟叶 Tobacco
1990	180.7	2932	33.9	0.8	3.1	2.2	558.1	1.9
1991	181.9	3581	32.1	0.8	3.6	2.1	453.6	2.1
1992	162.8	4326	33.9	0.9	4.9	2.0	585.8	1.6
1993	182.0	4921	34.6	1.3	3.7	2.1	480.3	1.7
1994	167.9	4440	39.7	1.2	3.6	2.4	550.4	1.9
1995	168.7	4429	37.6	0.9	3.4	2.1	486.2	1.3
1996	157.7	193	39.5	1.0	3.9	2.3	419.0	1.1
1997	166.3	85	33.8	0.5	5.2	2.4	390.2	1.0
1998	148.9	66	24.4	0.1	3.9	2.3	355.9	1.0
1999	155.9	88	20.1	-	3.6	2.1	325.6	0.9

附录1-8 工业生产指数

Index of Industrial Production

(1996年=100) (1996=100)

年份 Year	总指数 General	矿业 Mining	制造业 Manufacturing	电、煤气、水 Electricity, Gas & Water	建筑业 Construction
1990	75.39	126.81	76.37	65.10	65.61
1991	80.97	115.33	82.04	71.26	67.92
1992	84.54	110.55	85.23	75.78	79.56
1993	87.80	109.49	87.37	82.75	101.99
1994	93.60	109.94	92.37	89.24	126.36
1995	98.01	106.29	97.17	94.78	121.06
1996	100.00	100.00	100.00	100.00	100.00
1997	107.43	99.71	108.69	106.12	83.73
1998	110.26	77.99	111.25	114.23	84.17
1999	118.76	77.28	120.29	118.48	89.73

附录1-9 主要工业产品产量

Output of Major Industrial Products

年份 Year	棉布 (亿米) Cotton Fabrics (100 million sq.m)	聚胺丝织物 (亿米) Nylon Fabrics (100 million sq.m)	塑料皮布(亿米) Plastic Leather Clothes (100 million m)	电风扇 (万台) Electric Fan (10 000 units)	收录音机 (万台) Radio Cassette Player (10 000 units)	自行车 (万辆) Bicycle (10 000 units)	电冰箱 (万台) Refrigerator (10 000 units)	电子计算器 (万台) Electronic Calculator (10 000 units)
1991	11.78	15.90	7.66	3639.17	928.35	878.00	38.88	3513.82
1992	11.32	16.41	7.38	3220.67	715.54	807.38	39.55	1820.81
1993	10.30	17.19	7.40	2284.76	619.33	826.04	45.98	1288.32
1994	10.83	18.15	6.84	2105.71	643.25	791.43	47.11	1063.06
1995	8.95	15.64	5.59	1993.86	697.47	803.91	52.25	638.17
1996	9.41	15.39	5.76	2219.71	656.23	782.41	46.58	295.10
1997	9.71	15.84	5.66	2132.48	604.42	767.23	43.23	114.62
1998	9.84	15.90	4.91	2034.74	536.12	904.29	45.54	85.54
1999	10.62	17.17	4.65	2380.00	462.06	722.83	41.39	55.66

附录1-9 续表 1 continued

年份 Year	电脑 (万台) Computer (10 000 units)	电话机 (万台) Telephone Set (10 000 units)	电视机 (万台) T.V. Set (10 000 units)	照相机 (万台) Camera (10 000 units)	煤 (万吨) Coal (10 000 tons)	天然气 (亿立方米) Natural Gas (100 million cu.m)	发电量 (亿千瓦小时) Electric Power (100 million K.W.H.)
1991	300.70	1121.44	353.89	1216.38	40.26	9.28	896.39
1992	324.30	1097.52	262.82	1024.25	33.48	8.72	938.85
1993	375.10	1068.18	210.69	680.37	32.81	8.26	1017.84
1994	483.20	872.92	190.29	761.38	28.51	8.67	1102.76
1995	703.60	801.00	142.31	704.89	23.50	8.89	1178.59
1996	891.50	623.58	104.45	482.66	14.75	8.74	1249.73
1997	989.80	858.44	102.07	388.58	9.82	8.49	1322.48
1998	1170.80	773.66	98.84	322.26	7.93	8.70	1429.64
1999	1295.90	662.95	102.15	280.66	9.17	8.48	1457.61

附录1-9 续表 2 continued

年份 Year	摩托车 (万辆) Motorcycle (10 000 units)	钢筋 (万吨) Steel Bar (10 000 tons)	水泥 (万吨) Cement (10 000 tons)	制成材 (万立方米) Lumber (10 000cub.m)	聚氯乙烯 (万吨) PVC (10 000 tons)	平板玻璃 (万标准箱) Plate Glass (10 000 Std.Cases)	纸板 (万吨) Paper Board (10 000 tons)	小汽车 (万辆) Car (10 000 units)
1991	117.41		1939.86	75.78	97.84	850.35	285.60	39.79
1992	134.50	655.03	2146.37	56.50	104.26	938.07	295.04	42.83
1993	148.71	755.09	2397.08	39.88	107.85	925.28	283.66	38.92
1994	163.33	741.24	2272.17	37.81	111.37	1080.45	304.55	40.95
1995	169.51	655.32	2247.80	32.09	97.59	1120.00	303.03	38.97
1996	141.42	595.70	2153.73	34.99	110.53	972.91	321.32	36.34
1997	150.88	632.00	2152.24	21.01	114.86	969.56	325.38	36.98
1998	126.64	686.70	1965.15	19.59	115.80	960.75	297.54	39.72
1999	113.55	607.35	1828.30	19.59	139.71	951.20	307.35	34.50

附录1-10 能源生产和消费
Production and Consumption of Energy

项目	Item	1996	1997	1998	1999	2000
供给量总计 (亿升标准油)	**Total Supply (100 000 kl oil equivalent)**	**833.0**	**882.8**	**924.6**	**988.8**	**1062.3**
供给量比重(%)	Distribution of Supply (%)	100.0	100.0	100.0	100.0	
煤炭	Coal	27.0	29.6	28.9	29.9	
石油	Petroleum	53.4	51.3	51.4	51.5	
天然气	Natural Gas	5.6	6.2	7.0	6.7	
水力发电	Hydraulic Power	2.8	2.7	2.9	2.3	
核能发电	Nuclear Energy Source	11.3	10.2	9.8	9.7	
消费量总计 (亿升标准油)	**Total Consumption (100 000 kl oil equivalent)**	**722.6**	**768.5**	**808.0**	**852.6**	**909.1**
分部门消费比重(%)	Distribution of Consumption (%)	100.0	100.0	100.0	100.0	
运输	Transportation	17.7	17.0	17.0	17.1	
工业	Industry	54.3	55.9	54.9	54.6	
农业	Agriculture	2.1	1.9	1.5	1.5	
住宅	Residence	12.3	11.9	12.5	12.2	
商业	Commerce	5.0	5.1	5.7	5.8	
其他	Other	6.4	6.2	6.0	6.2	
非能源消费	Non-energy Use	2.0	1.9	2.4	21.7	
平均每人能源消费量 (千升标准油)	Per Capita Energy Consumption (kl oil equivalent)	3.4	3.6	3.1	3.8	

附录1-11 按用途分的批准动工的建筑面积

Floor Space of Authorized Construction Projects by the Purpose

单位:万平方米 (10 000 sq.m.)

年份 Year	总计 Total	住宅用 Residential	商业用 Stores & Mercantile	工业用 Industrial	机关学校用 Office & School	其他用 Other
1992	3692	1566	898	464	251	153
1993	4754	2177	1264	482	237	203
1994	5816	2858	1536	539	216	236
1995	5526	2646	1534	440	229	268
1996	4571	2063	1086	393	249	345
1997	3846	1459	964	378	290	342
1998	3868	1392	922	461	247	406
1999	4124	1356	899	681	409	360

附录1-12 铁路和公路客货运量

Railway and Highway Passenger and Freight Traffic

年份 Year	铁路 Railway				公路 Highway			
	客运量(万人) Passenger Traffic (10 000 persons)	客运周转量(万人公里) Passenger Kilometers (10 000p-km)	货运量(万吨) Freight Traffic (10 000 tons)	货物周转量(万吨公里) Freight Ton-kilometers (10 000ton-km)	客运量(万人) Passenger Traffic (10 000 persons)	客运周转量(万人公里) Passenger-Kilometers (10 000 p-km)	货运量①(万吨) Freight Traffic① (10 000 tons)	货物周转量①(万吨公里) Freight Ton-kilometers① (10 000 ton-km)
1991	13778	862101	2626	196114	150248	2532946	25430	1181376
1992	14987	935740	2819	213996	142089	2422747	26796	1221989
1993	15803	955227	3058	201778	135556	2327504	30167	1286684
1994	16099	951518	3123	200674	128921	2151583	31340	1309140
1995	16092	949939	3012	189954	120345	1938868	29100	1249150
1996	17100	903200	2741	158486	116716	1850225	28940	1199090
1997	19700	950700	2657	151385	116280	1750926	27700	1216500
1998	23300	1030500	2656	140434	115483	1739795	36000	1742600
1999	31000	1102000	2600	131400	114900	1751800	35000	1847000
2000	46000	1260600	2230	117900	110400	1756900	34200	1813100

注:①仅为民营汽车公司数。

①Data only refer to private truck companies.

附录1-13 邮　电　业　务　量

Telecommunication Services

项　目	Item	1996	1997	1998	1999	2000
省内电信	**Domestic**					
电报　（万封）	Telegrams　(10 000 Messages)	0.14	0.06			
长途电话(万次)	Long Distance Calls (10 000 Calls)	933	1019	925		
市内电话(万户)	Number of Local Telephone Subscribers (10 000 subscribers)	1001	1086	1150	1204	1264
海外电信	**International**					
电报　（万封）	Telegrams　(10 000 Messages)	2.93	2.28			
电话（万分钟）	Telephone Call　(10 000 Minutes)	70050	78906	86088	95826	105838
邮政(投递数)	**Postal Services　(Pieces Delivered)**					
函件　（亿件）	Correspondence　(100 million PCs)	25.63	27.51	29.16	30.52	34.09
包裹　（万件）	Parcels　(10 000 pieces)	1868	1874	1735	1654	1784

附录1-14 商品进出口贸易总额

Total Imports and Exports

年份 Year	按新台币计算（十亿元） (NT $ billion)			按美元计算（十亿美元） (USD billion)		
	进出口总额 Total	出口额 Exports	进口额 Imports	进出口总额 Total	出口额 Exports	进口额 Imports
1987	2821	1708	1114	89	54	35
1988	3155	1732	1423	110	61	50
1989	3134	1748	1386	119	66	52
1990	3275	1803	1472	122	67	55
1991	3732	2041	1691	139	76	63
1992	3865	2048	1817	153	81	72
1993	4274	2239	2035	162	85	77
1994	4718	2456	2262	178	93	85
1995	5692	2950	2743	215	112	104
1996	5992	3177	2815	218	116	102
1997	6758	3482	3276	237	122	114
1998	7197	3693	3504	216	111	105
1999	7493	3917	3576	233	122	111
2000	8985	4616	4369	288	148	140

附录1-15 商品进口来源和出口去向

Origin of Imports and Destination of Exports

单位：百万美元 (US $ 1 million)

项目	Item	1996	1997	1998	1999	2000
商品进口来源	**Imports (Major Origin)**					
中国香港	Hong Kong,China	1705	1996	1952	2093	2187
日　本	Japan	27493	29022	27001	30591	38558
韩　国	Korea,Rep.of	4162	5024	5669	7193	8988
新加坡	Singapore	2789	3150	2697	3312	5014
马来西亚	Malaysia	3565	4228	3623	3882	5325
泰　国	Thailand	1672	1927	1968	2383	2768
法　国	France	4061	4726	5329	1887	1830
德　国	Germany	5023	5369	5149	5313	5542
意大利	Italy	1558	1605	1482	1308	1391
英　国	United Kingdom	1805	1953	1684	1720	1937
加拿大	Canada	1357	1587	1160	1125	1276
美　国	United States	19972	23234	19679	19693	25126
澳大利亚	Australia	2845	3217	2913	2957	3501
印度尼西亚	Indonesia	1884	2185	2101	2291	3015
菲律宾	Philippines	840	1375	1823	2173	3594
越　南	Viet Nam	317	391	343	388	469
阿　曼	Oman	197	125	50	328	399
沙特阿拉伯	Saudi Arabia	1763	1904	1204	1384	2690
荷　兰	Netherlands	1471	1638	1565	1706	2087
商品出口去向	**Exports (Major Destination)**					
中国香港	Hong Kong,China	26788	28688	24820	26012	31336
日　本	Japan	13659	11691	9324	11900	16599
韩　国	Korea,Rep.of	2662	2366	1486	2605	8988
新加坡	Singapore	4573	4895	3256	3818	5014
马来西亚	Malaysia	2954	3035	2286	2848	5325
泰　国	Thailand	2790	2562	1926	2104	2768
法　国	France	1306	1394	1376	1584	1638
德　国	Germany	3644	3691	4084	4077	4891
意大利	Italy	1080	1130	1344	1327	1484
英　国	United Kingdom	2807	3278	3280	3830	4509
加拿大	Canada	1397	1598	1573	1751	1882
美　国	United States	26866	29552	29376	30902	34815
澳大利亚	Australia	1837	1873	1632	1847	1828
印度尼西亚	Indonesia	1955	2134	1049	1299	1734
菲律宾	Philippines	1931	2242	1934	2611	3036
越　南	Viet Nam	1175	1297	1213	1342	1664
阿　曼	Oman	17	18	16	16	20
沙特阿拉伯	Saudi Arabia	468	491	418	382	351
荷　兰	Netherlands	3823	4298	4369	4214	4934

附录1-16 出口与进口商品分类

Composition of Exports and Imports

单位:百万美元 (US $ 1 million)

年份 Year	出口 Exports 出口额 Total	农产品 Agricultural Products	农产加工品 Processed Agricultural Products	工业产品 Industrial Products	进口 Imports 进口额 Total	原材料 Agricultural & Industrial Raw Materials	资本货物 Capital Goods	消费品 Consumer Goods
1991	76178	525	3046	72608	62861	45501	10532	6828
1992	81470	509	2975	77987	72007	49868	12868	9271
1993	85091	471	3013	81607	77061	54143	13006	9913
1994	93049	460	3348	89241	85349	60301	13611	11438
1995	111659	482	3802	107375	103550	74561	16872	12118
1996	115942	465	3619	111858	102370	70636	18355	13379
1997	122081	382	2169	119529	114425	77132	21735	15558
1998	110582	324	1632	108627	104665	66773	24301	13592
1999	121591	381	1572	119638	110690	70978	29239	10473
2000	148321	358	1748	146215	140011	89778	39256	10976

附录1-17 旅　游　人　数

Visitor Arrivals and International Tourists

单位:万人 (10 000 persons)

项　目	Item	1993	1994	1995	1996	1997	1998	2000
总　计	**Total**	**185.0**	**212.7**	**233.2**	**235.8**	**237.2**	**229.9**	**262.4**
华　侨	Overseas Chinese	24.9	27.1	26.6	27.0	25.7	26.7	31.3
外国人	Foreign Tourists	160.1	185.7	206.6	208.9	211.6	203.2	231.1

附录1-18 消 费 物 价 指 数

Consumer Price Indices

(1996年=100) (1996=100)

年份 Year	总指数 General Index	食品类 Food	衣着 Clothing	居住 Housing	交　通 Transportation	医　药 保　健 Medicines and Medical Care	教　育 娱　乐 Education and Entertainment	杂　项 Miscellaneous
1993	89.9	86.9	94.8	90.8	95.8	95.0	85.2	92.9
1994	93.6	92.5	94.3	94.6	96.2	96.8	89.6	95.4
1995	97.0	96.4	97.6	97.9	98.7	98.3	93.7	98.3
1996	100.0	100.0	100.0	100.0	100.0	100.0	100.0	100.0
1997	100.9	99.1	100.7	101.2	101.2	102.4	103.4	102.1
1998	102.6	103.5	95.6	102.4	100.1	103.3	106.5	103.9
1999	102.8	103.0	94.3	102.5	99.3	106.9	104.5	104.5
2000	104.1	103.1	94.6	103.1	102.7	110.9	111.7	106.2

附录1-19 各级政府财政收入净额

Net Revenue of Treasury

单位:新台币百万元 (NT $ 1 million)

项 目	Item	1996	1997	1998	1999
总 计	**Total**	**2023977**	**2074064**	**2325350**	**2218135**
经常性收入小计	**Sub-total of Current Revenues**	**1550943**	**1629420**	**1960620**	**1867081**
直接税	Direct Tax	620386	692493	779555	779998
一般间接税	Indirect Tax	521452	520781	560049	563864
专卖收益	Revenue from Monopoly	55959	58179	57448	55322
财产利息收入	Revenue from Profit of Public Properties	16346	19570	41483	25416
企业所得	Surplus and Revenue of Public Enterprises	181094	180797	361574	324851
各项费用收入	Fees	59939	65894	68946	61555
罚款和赔款收入	Revenue from Fines & Indemnities	31918	32557	38140	38705
捐赠收入	Receipts from Donations and Contributions	875	1492	1644	1508
工程受益费收入	Special Assessments	666	645	220	135
杂项收入	Miscellaneous Revenues	62309	57013	51561	54225
资本收入小计	**Sub-total of Capital Revenues**	**473034**	**444644**	**364730**	**351054**
财产售卖收入	Sales of Public Properties	40221	67179	45630	63187
财产收回	Return of Properties	13019	8159	47208	74115
公债收入	Proceeds from Issues of Public Debts	115769	136265	59904	77558
借贷收入	Receipts from Loans	249676	199991	176262	112444
移用以前年度盈余	Moving Budgetary Surplus of Prior Year	54348	33049	35726	23739

注:本表按财政年度计算。各级政府财政收入净额为各级政府实际或计划收入扣除了政府间转移和划拨后的净额之和。

a)The data in this table are calculated in fiscal year. Net revenue shows the sum of receipts recorded or planned by all levels of governments, and net of all the duplicated parts of inter-government transfers and intro-governmental appropriations.

附录1-20 各级政府财政支出净额

Net Expenditures of Treasury

单位:新台币百万元 (NT $ 1 million)

项 目	Item	1996	1997	1998	1999
总 计	**Total**	**2005897**	**2066751**	**2204658**	**2217846**
经常性支出小计	**Sub-total of Current Expenditures**	**1383725**	**1463449**	**1545052**	**1554405**
一般行政支出	General Administration	216466	217772	232114	244013
防务支出	National Defense	272808	278778	299738	272935
教育科学文化支出	Expenditures on Education, Science and Culture	279647	284604	324227	340309
经济发展支出	Economic Development	71888	76143	74766	80194
社会安全支出	Social Security	426743	478261	482993	490921
债务支出	Obligations	106061	115630	115896	140910
杂项支出	Miscellaneous	10110	12260	15331	11789
资本性支出小计	**Sub-total of Capital Expenditures**	**622172**	**603302**	**659606**	**663441**
一般行政支出	General Administration	27507	26985	25151	35099
防务支出	National Defense	12118	13141	12548	13636
教育科学文化支出	Expenditures on Education, Science and Culture	94754	91218	87286	88818
经济发展支出	Economic Development	257246	218893	260246	270909
社会安全支出	Social Security	68412	65057	62296	60362
债务支出	Obligations	162111	187988	212065	167842
杂项支出	Miscellaneous	25	20	14	46

注:本表按财政年度计算。各级政府财政支出净额为各级政府实际或计划支出扣除了政府间转移和划拨后的净额之和。

a)The data in this table are calculated in fiscal year. Net expenditure shows the sum of disbursements recorded or planned by all levels of governments, and net of all the duplicated parts of inter-government transfers and intro-governmental appropriations.

附录1-21 公　债　发　行　情　况

Government Bonds

单位:新台币亿元　　(NT $ 100 million)

年份 Year	总计 Total			台湾省级 Taiwan Provincial			省级及"院"辖市级 Sub-provincial and Municipal Gov't		
	发行额 Issues	偿还额 Redemption	余额 Outstanding	发行额 Issues	偿还额 Redemption	余额 Outstanding	发行额 Issues	偿还额 Redemption	余额 Outstanding
1992	2504	466	5514	2250	341	4511	254	125	1003
1993	2373	665	72223	2100	475	6135	273	189	1087
1994	1480	725	7976	1480	514	7102		211	876
1995	1250	556	8671	1250	300	8051		256	620
1996	2450	1159	9963	2250	940	9361	200	219	601
1997	1740	1354	10348	1600	1208	9754	140	147	594
1998	1460	1369	10439	1200	1260	9694	260	109	745
1999	2828	815	12452	2828	703	11819		112	633
2000	3625	1274	14803	3465	1194	14090	160	80	713

附录1-22 主 要 金 融 指 标

Principal Financial Indicators

年份 Year	货币供应额 (新台币亿元) Money Supply (NT $100 million)	流动性负债 (新台币亿元) Liquid Liabilities (NT $100 million)	储备货币 (新台币亿元) Reserve Money (NT $100 million)	存款 (新台币亿元) Deposits (NT $100 million)	放款与投资 (新台币亿元) Loans & Investments (NT $100 million)	再贴现率 (年息%) Rediscount Rate (% annum)	汇率(卖出价) (新台币/美元) Exchange Rates of Selling (NT $/US $)
1990	19237	69874	11564	64701	50613	7.75	27.11
1991	21562	82829	12653	75728	61970	6.25	25.80
1992	24259	97497	14119	90767	79521	5.63	25.47
1993	28051	113601	15014	104638	95093	5.50	26.72
1994	31412	129964	16688	120405	109565	5.50	26.26
1995	31680	142738	16381	131469	121003	5.50	27.32
1996	34287	156420	16525	142606	130518	5.00	27.54
1997	37153	170145	16413	154213	142358	5.25	32.62
1998	38548	185767	16651	166969	153118	4.75	32.26
1999	45072	203015	16433	180642	157984	4.50	31.44

附录1-23 股　票　交　易

Transactions of Listed Stock

单位:新台币十亿元　　(NT $ billion)

年份 Year	上市股票 Listed Stock				股票成交额 Total Trading Value	股票指数(年平均) (1966年=100) Stock Price Index (1966=100) (year average)
	公司数(家) Number	种类(种) Kind	总面值 Total Par Value	总市值 Total Market Value		
1991	221	234	617	3184	9683	4928.83
1992	256	286	736	2546	5917	4271.63
1993	285	325	891	5145	9057	4214.78
1994	313	354	1071	6502	18812	6252.99
1995	347	383	1325	5108	10152	5543.75
1996	382	425	1627	7524	12908	6003.72
1997	404	470	2066	9696	37241	8410.56
1998	437		2690	8377	29619	7737.68
1999	462		3054	11787	29292	7426.68
2000	531		3630	8191	30527	7847.21

附录1-24 入学率和教育经费

Net Enrollment Rate and Public Expenditures for Education at Current Market Prices

单位：% (%)

年份 Year	粗入学率(6-21岁) Gross Enrollment Rate (age 6-21) 初等教育(6-11岁) Primary Education (age 6-11)	中等教育(12-17岁) Secondary Education (age 12-17)	高等教育(18-21岁) Higher Education (age 18-21)	每千人口高等教育学生数 Higher Education Student per 1000 Population	15岁以上人口识字率 Percentage of Literate Aged 15 and Over	教育经费 Public Expenditure for Education 总计(新台币亿元) Total (NT $100 million)	占国民生产总值% As % of GNP
1991	101.0	95.4	37.9	26.8	92.9	3009.7	6.5
1992	101.3	95.6	42.0	28.9	93.2	3530.9	6.8
1993	101.8	95.3	45.0	30.5	93.4	4031.9	7.1
1994	100.9	95.9	45.3	31.7	93.7	4303.7	6.9
1995	101.4	95.7	46.4	32.7	94.0	4524.7	6.8
1996	101.1	95.8	47.7	34.3	94.3	5039.2	7.0
1997	100.6	97.2	51.1	37.6	94.7	5371.9	6.9
1998	99.8	98.6	56.1	40.7	94.9	5545.2	6.5
1999	99.7	99.6	61.0	44.6	95.3	5864.2	6.6
2000				49.4	95.6		

附录1-25 科技人员数和科研开发经费

Number of Scientists, Engineers and Technicians and Expenditures for R & D

年份 Year	科技人员数(人) Number of Scientists, Engineers and Technicians Engaged in Research and Experimental Development (Headcount) 总计 Total	科学家和工程师 Scientists & Engineers	技术员 Technicians	辅助人员 Assistant	科研开发经费 Expenditures for Research and Experimental Development 总计(新台币亿元) Total (NT $100 million)	占国民生产总值% As % of GNP	占科研开发经费比重(%) As % of Expenditures for Research and Development 政府经费 Government	民间经费 Private
1991	82436	46173	22844	13419	818	1.70	52.1	47.9
1992	77750	48356	22117	7277	948	1.78	52.2	47.8
1993	90918	54905	23720	12293	1036	1.76	49.5	50.5
1994	95088	58156	24067	12865	1147	1.77	48.2	51.8
1995	105822	66478	25635	13709	1250	1.78	45.9	54.1
1996	116853	71611	28987	16255	1380	1.80	42.7	57.7
1997	129165	76588	34021	18556	1563	1.88	40.8	59.2
1998	129305	83209	30535	15561	1765	1.98	38.3	61.7
1999	136323	88708	31674	15941	1905	2.05	37.9	62.1

附录1-26 医院、病床和医务人员情况

Medical Facilities and Health Personnel

年份 Year	医疗机构 (所) Number of Medical Care Facilities	平均每一机构服务人数 (人) Population Served per Medical Care Facility (person)	病床数 (床) Beds (bed)	每万人病床数 (床) Beds per 10 000 Population	从业医务人数 (人) Health Personnel (person)	每万人拥有医务人员 (人) Health Personnel per 10 000 Population
1987	12199	1613	86328	43.88	77246	39.27
1988	12215	1629	88572	44.50	83045	41.72
1989	12267	1639	86693	43.12	85599	42.57
1990	12902	1578	89151	43.80	91153	44.79
1991	13661	1505	92785	45.14	96921	47.15
1992	14468	1434	96084	46.30	102977	49.62
1993	15062	1392	100570	47.90	109538	52.17
1994	15752	1342	103733	48.98	114076	53.87
1995	16109	1326	112379	52.62	118248	55.37
1996	16645	1293	114923	53.39	123829	57.53
1997	17398	1250	121162	55.73	137829	66.72
1998	17731	1237	124564	56.80	144070	65.71
1999	17770	1243	122937	55.65	152385	68.98

附录1-27 家 庭 设 备 普 及 率

Percent of Families Owning Household Appliances

单位:% (%)

年份 Year	彩色电视机 Color T.V. Sets	冰箱 Refrigerators	空调 Air Conditioners	洗衣机 Washing Machines	电话机 Telephone Sets	汽车 Automobiles	家用电脑 Family Computers
1985	92.31	96.67	23.95	77.84	82.12	11.91	2.32
1986	94.42	97.11	25.45	79.49	85.25	13.63	2.92
1987	95.78	97.41	28.66	81.33	87.20	15.54	3.55
1988	97.34	97.93	34.29	83.97	89.11	19.21	3.95
1989	97.80	98.25	41.74	86.82	91.51	24.90	5.42
1990	98.26	98.37	47.26	88.79	93.08	29.07	6.77
1991	99.16	98.96	52.37	89.53	94.75	33.67	9.57
1992	99.30	98.93	56.14	90.38	95.13	38.94	11.76
1993	99.25	99.14	60.69	91.51	96.00	41.05	13.56
1994	99.36	99.14	64.01	92.31	96.53	45.54	15.29
1995	99.29	99.19	67.08	92.83	96.70	47.95	18.54
1996	99.32		71.65	93.00	97.49	51.16	22.56
1997	99.47		73.83	93.99	97.54	53.79	28.39
1998	99.17		76.20	93.86	97.63	54.52	32.31
1999	99.31		78.89	94.74	98.00	54.33	38.92

附录二、我国经济、社会统计指标同世界主要国家比较

APPENDIX II. A Comparison of Indicators of Economy and Society Among the People's Republic of China and Other Countries

附录2-1 国 土 面 积 和 人 口

Territory and Population

国外资料来源：联合国《统计月报》2001年2月；联合国粮农组织数据库；世界银行《世界发展报告》2000/2001年。

Sources: United Nations "*Monthly Bulletin of Statistics*" February 2001; FAO Database;
The World Bank "*World Development Indicators*" 2000/2001.

国家和地区	Country or Territory	国土面积 (万平方公里) Area (10 000 sq.km)	1999 年中人口数 (万人) Mid-year Population (10 000 persons)	1991-1999年 人口年均增长率(%) Annual Average Growth Rate(%)	1999 人口密度 (人/平方公里) Population Density (persons/sq.km)
世界总计	**World**	**13381.6①**	**597840**	**1.4**	**45**
亚　洲	**Asia**	**3174.8**	**363428**		**114**
#中　国②	China②	960.0	125909	1.1	131
日　本	Japan	37.8	12651	0.3	335
印　度③	India③	297.4	97753	1.8	329
印度尼西亚	Indonesia	190.5	20926	1.7	110
菲律宾	Philippines	30.0	7475	2.3	249
泰　国	Thailand	51.3	6181	1.2	120
马来西亚	Malaysia	33.0	2271	2.5	69
新加坡	Singapore	0.06	389	1.9	6483
巴基斯坦	Pakistan	79.6	13451	2.5	169
缅　甸	Myanmar	67.7	4506	1.2	67
孟加拉国	Bangladesh	14.4	12695	1.6	882
土耳其	Turkey	78.0	6439	1.5	83
蒙　古	Mongolia	156.7	262	1.9	2
朝　鲜	Korea, D.P.Rep.	12.3	2370		193
韩　国	Korea, Rep. of	9.9	4686	1.0	473
越　南	Viet Nam	33.0	7871	1.8	239
非　洲	**Africa**	**3031.2**	**76673**		**25**
#埃　及	Egypt	100.2	6723	1.9	67
尼日利亚	Nigeria	92.4	10895	2.8	118
欧　洲	**Europe**	**2298.8**	**72893**		**32**
#德　国	Germany	35.7	8209	0.4	230
英　国	United Kingdom	24.2	5874	0.3	243
法　国	France	55.2	5910	0.5	107
意大利	Italy	30.1	5734	0.2	190
捷　克	Czech Rep.	7.9	1028	-0.1	130
波　兰	Poland	31.3	3865	0.2	123
匈牙利	Hungary	9.3	1007	-0.3	108
罗马尼亚	Romania	23.8	2246	-0.4	94
保加利亚	Bulgaria	11.1	821	-0.7	74
南斯拉夫	Yugoslavia F.R.	10.2	1064		104
俄罗斯	Russian Fed.	1707.5	14556	-0.1	9
北美洲	**North America**	**2239.1**	**47779**		**21**
#美　国	United States	937.3	27313	1.0	29
加拿大	Canada	997.1	3049	1.1	3
墨西哥	Mexico	196.7	9737	1.8	50
南美洲	**South America**	**1783.2**	**34075**		**19**
#巴　西	Brazil	854.7	16537	1.4	19
阿根廷	Argentina	277.7	3658	1.3	13
大洋洲	**Oceania**	**853.6**	**3001**		**4**
#澳大利亚	Australia	768.2	1897	1.2	2
新西兰	New Zealand	27.1	381	1.2	14

注：①是指有定居人口的各大洲面积，未包括尚无定居人口的南极洲。如包括南极洲，全世界陆地面积为 14950万平方公里。原资料各大洲面积以百万平方公里为单位，其和与世界总计略有出入。②中国为年末人口数。③不包括查谟、克什米尔和锡金等地区。

①The data exclude the Antarctic Continent. If included, it would be 149.50 million sq.km. ②The population of China refers to the population of the year-end. ③Excluding Jammu, Kashmir and Sikkim.

附录2-2 生　命　统　计(1999年)

Vital Statistics (1999)

国外资料来源：世界银行《世界发展指标》2001年。

Sources: World Bank "*World Development Indicators*" 2001.

单位：‰ (‰)

国家和地区	Country or Territory	人口自然增长率 Natural Growth Rate	人口出生率 Crude Birth Rate	人口死亡率 Crude Death Rate	婴儿死亡率 Infant Mortality Rate	平均预期寿命(岁) Life Expectancy at Birth (Years)		
						总计 Total	男 Male	女 Female
世界总计	**World**	**12.7**	**21.8**	**9.1**	**54.3**	**66.5**	**64.6**	**68.6**
中　国	China	8.4	15.6	7.2	30.0①	71.0①		
阿根廷	Argentina	11.6	19.2	7.7	18.4	73.6	70.1	77.2
澳大利亚	Australia	6.2	13.1	7.0	4.9	78.8	76.0	81.7
孟加拉国	Bangladesh	18.9	28.0	9.1	61.2	60.7	60.3	61.2
巴　西	Brazil	12.6	20.0	7.4	32.2	67.2	63.3	71.2
加拿大	Canada	4.0	11.1	7.1	5.3	79.0	76.1	82.1
捷　克	Czech Republic	-2.0	8.7	10.7	4.6	74.6	71.3	78.2
埃　及	Egypt, Arab Rep.	18.6	25.5	6.9	47.3	66.8	65.3	68.4
法　国	France	3.5	12.7	9.2	4.8	78.5	74.9	82.3
德　国	Germany	-0.9	9.4	10.3	4.8	77.0	74.0	80.2
匈牙利	Hungary	-4.8	9.4	14.2	8.4	70.6	66.3	75.1
印　度	India	16.7	25.8	9.1	70.9	63.2	62.4	63.9
印度尼西亚	Indonesia	14.9	22.4	7.5	41.9	65.7	63.9	67.6
意大利	Italy	-0.6	9.3	9.9	5.4	78.3	75.0	81.8
日　本	Japan	1.7	9.6	7.9	3.6	80.6	77.3	84.1
韩　国	Korea, Rep. of	8.2	14.1	5.8	8.4	72.9	69.4	76.5
马来西亚	Malaysia	20.0	24.4	4.4	7.9	72.3	69.9	74.9
墨西哥	Mexico	21.5	26.6	5.1	29.4	72.1	69.2	75.2
蒙　古	Mongolia	14.6	21.1	6.4	58.0	66.6	65.1	68.1
缅　甸	Myanmar	15.7	25.8	10.1	77.4	59.7	58.1	61.5
新西兰	New Zealand	7.8	14.9	7.1	5.2	77.4	74.7	80.2
尼日利亚	Nigeria	24.1	39.8	15.7	83.3	47.5	46.8	48.2
巴基斯坦	Pakistan	26.5	34.5	7.9	89.8	62.5	61.5	63.6
菲律宾	Philippines	21.8	27.4	5.6	31.5	68.9	67.1	70.8
俄罗斯	Russian Federation	-4.9	9.1	14.0	16.0	65.8	59.8	72.2
罗马尼亚	Romania	-1.8	10.4	12.2	19.8	69.5	65.7	73.4
新加坡	Singapore	8.3	12.8	4.5	3.2	77.6	75.6	79.6
南　非	South Africa	12.1	26.3	14.1	61.5	48.5	47.3	49.7
泰　国	Thailand	9.8	17.0	7.2	28.3	68.6	66.5	70.8
土耳其	Turkey	14.4	20.8	6.4	36.2	69.5	67.0	72.1
英　国	United Kingdom	0.9	11.8	10.9	5.7	77.2	74.7	79.9
美　国	United States	6.1	14.7	8.6	6.9	76.9	73.9	80.0
委内瑞拉	Venezuela, RB	19.9	24.3	4.4	20.2	73.2	70.4	76.1
南斯拉夫	Yugoslavia, FR	0.8	11.6	10.8	12.5	72.3	69.9	74.9

注：①1996年数。

①Data refer to 1996.

附录2-3　就　业　状　况

Employment

国外资料来源：国际劳工组织《劳工统计年鉴》2000年。

Source: International Labour Office "*Yearbook of Labour Statistics*" 2000.

国家和地区	Country or Territory	年份 Year	就业人数（万 人） Employment (10 000 persons)					
				农林牧渔业 Agriculture Forestry Hunting and Fishing	矿业、采掘业 Mining and Quarrying	制造业 Manufac-turing	水、电、煤气业 Electri-city, Gas and Water	建筑业 Construc-tion
中　国	China	1999	70586.0	33493.0	667.0	8109.0	285.0	3412.0
美　国	United States	1999	13348.8	341.6	56.5	2007.0	146.8	898.7
日　本	Japan	1999	6462.0	335.0	6.0	1345.0	38.0	657.0
德　国	Germany	1999	3640.2	102.6	16.1	853.2	31.1	314.6
英　国	United Kingdom	1999	2744.2	42.5	10.1	488.6	18.8	192.9
法　国	France	1994	2211.0	104.8	6.6	416.2	20.4	144.3
意大利	Italy	1999	2086.4	113.4	7.0	492.8	17.6	157.5
加拿大	Canada	1999	1453.1	52.2	15.6	221.7	11.6	76.9
澳大利亚	Australia	1999	874.7	42.3	7.0	107.5	6.4	66.3
俄罗斯	Russian Fed	1997	6463.9		115.0	1207.5	138.0	534.2
捷　克	Czech Rep.	1999	476.5	24.2	7.5	130.2	8.0	44.4
波　兰	Poland	1998	1535.4	294.6	38.1	320.5	26.5	107.1
匈牙利	Hungary	1999	381.2	27.0	2.4	92.9	9.0	25.3
罗马尼亚	Romania	1999	1077.6	449.9	18.6	216.5	22.4	39.7
印　度①	India①	1989	2596.2	142.8	106.4	625.7	90.9	122.0
印度尼西亚	Indonesia	1998	8767.2	3941.5	67.5	993.4	14.8	352.2
菲律宾	Philippines	1999	2900.3	1134.2	8.9	277.8	14.5	150.6
泰　国	Thailand	1999	3208.7	1556.4	5.2	439.5	15.8	128.6
新加坡	Singapore	1999	188.6	0.6	0.1	39.6	0.9	13.1
马来西亚	Malaysia	1999	883.8	162.4	3.8	199.1	5.0	72.3
巴基斯坦	Pakistan	1997	3418.0	1509.1	3.5	379.3	33.4	230.7
缅　甸	Myanmar	1998	1835.9	1150.7	12.1	166.6	4.8	40.0
韩　国	Korea,Rep. of	1999	2028.1	234.9	2.0	400.6	6.1	147.6
巴　西	Brazil	1998	6996.3	1633.8	86.2	823②		498.0

附录2-3 续表 1 continued

国家和地区	Country or Territory	年份 Year	就业人数(万 人) Employment (10 000 persons) 商业、饭店业、旅店业 Wholesale Retail Trade, Hotel, Restaurant	运输、仓储及通信业 Transport Storage and Communication	金融、保险不动产及产业服务 Finance Insurance Real Estate Business Services	社会服务及个人服务 Community Social and Personal Services	其他 Other	失业率 (%) Rate of Unemployment
中国	China	1999	4751③	2022.0	535.0	4248④	4969.0	3.1⑤
美国	United States	1999	2757.2	808.6	1605.4	4727.1		4.2
日本	Japan	1999	1483.0	406.0	599.0	1552.0	41.0	4.7
德国	Germany	1999	639.6	195.3	402.9	1084.8		8.8
英国	United Kingdom	1999	542.8	181.3	416.5	843.0	7.9	6.0
法国	France	1994	371.6	139.7	234.0	773.4		12.4
意大利	Italy	1999	404.7	113.3	200.7	579.3		11.4
加拿大	Canada	1999	343.8	110.4	227.2	393.8		7.6
澳大利亚	Australia	1999	226.0	57.0	129.8	231.6		7.2
俄罗斯	Russian Fed	1997	906.5	512.0	503.4	1615.2		11.8
捷克	Czech Rep.	1999	79.6	37.0	36.1	109.2	0.1	9.0
波兰	Poland	1998	233.6	95.8	81.4	337.4	-	10.5
匈牙利	Hungary	1999	65.1	30.8	26.5	102.1	-	7.0
罗马尼亚	Romania	1999	105.0	45.0	22.8	152.7	-	6.8
印度①	India①	1989	44.1	303.8	135.0	1030.7		
印度尼西亚	Indonesia	1998	1681.4	415.4	61.8	1239.4	-	5.5
菲律宾	Philippines	1999	461.9⑥	200.9	71.6	578.9	1.0	9.4
泰国	Thailand	1999	473.6⑦	98.9		489.2	1.5	3.0
新加坡	Singapore	1999	40.0	20.4	30.1	43.6	0.2	3.2
马来西亚	Malaysia	1999	166.1	42.0	46.6	186.5		3.4
巴基斯坦	Pakistan	1997	499.6	195.0	33.6	532.4	1.4	4.6
缅甸	Myanmar	1998	178.1	49.5	59.7	174.4		
韩国	Korea, Rep. of	1999	572.4	120.2	192.5	351.7		6.3
巴西	Brazil	1998	941.7	278.7	130.9	2604.0		9.0

注：①只包括国营部门和10人及10人以上的非农业私人机构。②包括水、电、煤气业。③商业和餐饮业。④包括卫生、体育和社会福利事业、教育、文化艺术和广播电视事业以及科学研究和综合技术服务事业、国家机关、政党机关和社会团体。⑤指城镇登记失业率。⑥饭店、旅馆业包含在社会服务及个人服务业中。⑦包括金融、保险、不动产及产业服务。

①Only public sector and establishments of non-agricultural private sector with 10 or more persons employed are included.②Including electricity, gas and water.③Refering to wholesale retail trade and food services.④Including social services, health care, sports and social welfare, education, culture, arts, radio and television, broadcasting, scientific research and polytechnic services' government agencies,party agencies and social organizations.⑤Data refer to registered unemployment rate in urban areas.⑥Restaurants and hotels are included in community social and personal services.⑦Including finance,insurance, real estate business services.

附录2-4 国内生产总值及其增长率

Gross Domestic Product and its Growth Rate

国外资料来源：国际货币基金组织《国际金融统计月报》2001年5月，《IMF经济展望》2001年5月。

Sources: International Monetary Fund "*International Financial Statistics*" May 2001.

"*IMF Economy Outlook*"May 2001.

国家和地区		Country or Territory		1999 国内生产总值(亿本币) GDP (national currency 100 million)	国内生产总值增长率(比上年增长%) GDP Growth Rate over the Preceding Year (%)			
					1997	1998	1999	2000③
中国	(人民币元)	China	(Yuan Renminbi)	82068	8.8	7.8	7.1	8.0
美国	(美元)	United States	(US Dollar)	92992	4.4	4.4	4.2	5.0
日本	(日元)	Japan	(Yen)	4953750	1.9	-1.1	0.8	1.7
德国	(欧元)	Germany	(Euro)	19823	1.4	2.1	1.6	3.0
英国	(英镑)	United Kingdom	(Pound)	8910	3.5	2.6	2.3	3.0
法国	(欧元)	France	(Euro)	13443	1.9	3.3	3.2	3.2
意大利	(里拉)	Italy	(Euro)	10991	2.0	1.8	1.6	2.9
加拿大	(加元)	Canada	(Dollar)	9579	4.4	3.3	4.5	4.7
澳大利亚	(澳元)	Australia	(Dollar)	6107	3.8	5.6	4.7	3.7
俄罗斯	(卢布)	Russian Fed.	(Rouple)	45455	0.9	-4.9	3.2	7.5
捷克	(克朗)	Czech Rep	(Koruna)	18330	-1.0	-2.2	-0.8	3.1
波兰	(兹罗提)	Poland	(Zloty)	6156	6.8	4.8	4.1	4.1
匈牙利	(福林)	Hungary	(Forint)	100874①	4.6	4.9	4.5	5.3
罗马尼亚	(列伊)	Romania	(Lei)	5217350	-6.1	-5.4	-3.2	2.0
印度	(卢比)	India	(Rupee)	195700	4.9	6.0	6.6	6.4
印度尼西亚	(卢比)	Indonesia	(Rupiah)	11099800	4.5	-13.1	0.8	4.8
菲律宾	(比索)	Philippines	(Peso)	29964	5.2	-0.6	3.3	3.9
泰国	(铢)	Thailand	(Baht)	46154	-1.4	-10.8	4.2	4.3
马来西亚	(林吉特)	Malaysia	(Ringgit)	2997	7.3	-7.4	5.8	8.5
新加坡	(新加坡元)	Singapore	(Dollar)	1440	8.4	0.3	5.9	9.9
巴基斯坦	(卢比)	Pakistan	(Rupee)	30257	1.8	2.6	4.3	5.1
缅甸	(缅元)	Myanmar	(Kyat)	21903	5.7	5.8	10.9	5.5
孟加拉国	(塔卡)	Bangladesh	(Taka)	17376	5.3	5.0	5.2	5.0
土耳其	(里拉)	Turkey	(Lira)	829255000	7.5	3.1	-4.7	7.2
韩国	(韩圆)	Korea,Rep.of	(Won)	4837780	5.0	-6.7	10.9	8.8
埃及	(埃镑)	Egypt	(Pound)	3023	5.3	5.7	6.0	5.1
尼日利亚	(奈拉)	Nigeria	(Naira)	12371②	3.1	1.9	1.1	2.8
墨西哥	(新比索)	Mexico	(New peso)	45838	6.8	4.9	3.8	6.9
巴西	(雷亚尔)	Brazil	(Reai)	9609	3.3	0.2	0.8	4.2
阿根廷	(比索)	Argentina	(Peso)	2833	8.1	3.8	-3.4	-0.5

注：①1998年数。②1994年数。③估计数(中国除外)。

①Data refer to 1998. ②Data refer to 1994. ③Estimates(except China).

附录2-5　主要农产品产量

Output of Major Agricultural Products

国外资料来源：联合国粮农组织数据库。

Sources: United Nations FAO database.

单位：万吨　　(10 000 tons)

国家和地区	Country or Territory	2000	国家和地区	Country or Territory	2000
谷　物	**Cereals**		**棉　花**	**Cotton Lint**	
世界总计	**World**	**204941**	**世界总计**	**World**	**1884**
中　国	China	40522	中　国	China	442
美　国	USA	34387	美　国	USA	375
印　度	India	23981	印　度	India	206
法　国	France	6654	巴基斯坦	Pakistan	191
俄罗斯	Russian Federation	6409	乌兹别克斯坦	Uzbekistan	95
印度尼西亚	Indonesia	6017	土耳其	Turkey	79
加拿大	Canada	5132	澳大利亚	Australia	71
巴　西	Brazil	4660	巴　西	Brazil	63
德　国	Germany	4530	希　腊	Greece	42
阿根廷	Argentina	3811	叙利亚	Syrian Arab Republic	32
大　豆	**Soybeans**		**花　生**	**Groundnuts in Shell**	
世界总计	**World**	**16199**	**世界总计**	**World**	**3451**
美　国	USA	7538	中　国	China	1444
巴　西	Brazil	3269	印　度	India	610
阿根廷	Argentina	2020	尼日利亚	Nigeria	278
中　国	China	1541	美　国	USA	149
印　度	India	540	印度尼西亚	Indonesia	100
巴拉圭	Paraguay	275	苏　丹	Sudan	99
加拿大	Canada	270	塞内加尔	Senegal	83
玻利维亚	Bolivia	123	缅　甸	Myanmar	64
印度尼西亚	Indonesia	120	阿根廷	Argentina	60
意大利	Italy	94	刚果(金)	Congo, Dem Rep. of	38
油菜籽	**Rapeseed**		**黄　麻**	**Jute & Jute-like Fibres**	
世界总计	**World**	**4019**	**世界总计**	**World**	**402**
中　国	China	1138	孟加拉国	Bangladesh	185
加拿大	Canada	712	印　度	India	174
印　度	India	612	中　国	China	13①
德　国	Germany	358	泰　国	Thailand	5
法　国	France	357	俄罗斯	Russian Federation	5
澳大利亚	Australia	180	缅　甸	Myanmar	3
英　国	United Kingdom	113	乌兹别克斯坦	Uzbekistan	2
波　兰	Poland	96	尼泊尔	Nepal	2
美　国	USA	92	越　南	Viet Nam	1
捷　克	Czech Republic	84	智　利	Chile	1

附录2-5 续表1 continued

单位：万吨 (10 000 tons)

国家和地区	Country or Territory	2000	国家和地区	Country or Territory	2000
甘　蔗	**Sugar Cane**		**甜　菜**	**Sugar Beets**	
世界总计	**World**	**127809**	**世界总计**	**World**	**24478**
巴　西	Brazil	32467	法　国	France	3145
印　度	India	31510	美　国	United States of America	2950
中　国	China	6828	德　国	Germany	2522
泰　国	Thailand	5121	土耳其	Turkey	1685
墨西哥	Mexico	4927	俄罗斯	Russian Federation	1404
巴基斯坦	Pakistan	4633	乌克兰	Ukraine	1319
澳大利亚	Australia	3834	波　兰	Poland	1313
哥伦比亚	Colombia	3700	意大利	Italy	1175
古　巴	Cuba	3600	英　国	United Kingdom	934
菲律宾	Philippines	3373	西班牙	Spain	834
茶　叶	**Tea**		**烟　叶**	**Tobacco Leaves**	
世界总计	**World**	**299**	**世界总计**	**World**	**694**
印　度	India	75	中　国	China	255
中　国	China	68	印　度	India	70
斯里兰卡	Sri Lanka	29	巴　西	Brazil	59
肯尼亚	Kenya	24	美　国	United States of America	50
土耳其	Turkey	18	土耳其	Turkey	26
印度尼西亚	Indonesia	17	津巴布韦	Zimbabwe	23
日　本	Japan	9	印度尼西亚	Indonesia	14
伊　朗	Iran, Islamic Rep of	8	意大利	Italy	13
越　南	Viet Nam	7	希　腊	Greece	13
格鲁吉亚	Georgia	6	马拉维	Malawi	12
肉　类②	**Meat②**		**牛　奶⑤**	**Cow Milk⑤**	
世界总计	**World**	**23322**	**世界总计**	**World**	**48490**
中　国	China	6125	美　国	United States of America	7629
美　国	United States of America	3764	俄罗斯	Russian Federation	3156
巴　西	Brazil	1441	印　度	India	3090
法　国	France	636	德　国	Germany	2842
德　国	Germany	622	法　国	France	2489
西班牙	Spain	494	巴　西	Brazil	2213
印　度	India	483	英　国	United Kingdom	1446
墨西哥	Mexico	450	乌克兰	Ukraine	1240
俄罗斯	Russian Federation	430	新西兰	New Zealand	1201
阿根廷	Argentina	420	意大利	Italy	1174
水　果	**Fruit**		**羊　毛④**	**Wool, Greasy④**	
世界总计	**World**	**47514**	**世界总计**	**World**	**233**
中　国	China	6225	澳大利亚	Australia	67
印　度	India	4920	中　国	China	33
巴　西	Brazil	3991	新西兰	New Zealand	26
美　国	United States of America	3257	伊　朗	Iran, Islamic Rep of	7
意大利	Italy	1941	阿根廷	Argentina	7
西班牙	Spain	1497	英　国	United Kingdom	6
墨西哥	Mexico	1236	乌拉圭	Uruguay	5
伊　朗	Iran, Islamic Rep of	1155	南　非	South Africa	5
法　国	France	1114	苏　丹	Sudan	5
土耳其	Turkey	1061	印　度	India	4

附录2-5 续表2 continued

单位：万吨 (10 000 tons)

国家和地区	Country or Territory	2000	国家和地区	Country or Territory	2000
水 产 品③	**Fishery③**		**天然橡胶**	**Natural Rubber**	
世界总计	**World**	**12214**	**世界总计**	**World**	**669**
中　国	China	3602	泰　国	Thailand	224
日　本	Japan	669	印度尼西亚	Indonesia	149
智　利	Chile	608	马来西亚	Malaysia	77
印　度	India	538	印　度	India	62
印度尼西亚	Indonesia	440	中　国	China	48
挪　威	Norway	322	越　南	Viet Nam	29
韩　国	Korea, Rep.of	260	科特迪瓦	Cote d'Ivoire	12
冰　岛	Iceland	221	尼日利亚	Nigeria	11
丹　麦	Denmark	187	斯里兰卡	Sri Lanka	10
墨西哥	Mexico	153	利比里亚	Liberia	9

注：①包括红麻。②包括牛肉、羊肉、猪肉、马肉、家禽肉以及其他家养和野生动物肉。③1997年数字。 ④未洗羊毛。
⑤包括水牛奶。

Notes: ①Including apocynum. ②Including beef and veal, buffalo meat, mutton and lamb, goat meat, pork, horse meat, poultry meat and meats of all other domestic or wild animals such as camels, rabbits and game animals. ④Contained 30 to 50 percent of impurities.
⑤ Including buffalo milk.

附录2-6 我国农业主要产品产量居世界位次

Changes in the Order of Precedence of Output of Major Agricultural Products

国外资料来源：联合国粮农组织数据库。

Sources: United Nations FAO database.

项目	Item	1949	1978	1980	1985	1990	1995	1999	2000
谷　物	Cereals		2	1	2	1	1	1	1
肉　类①	Meat①	3	3	3	2	1	1	1	1
棉　花	Cotton Lint	4	3	2	1	1	1	1	1
大　豆	Soybeans	2	3	3	3	3	3	4	4
花　生	Groundnuts in Shell	2	2	2	2	2	1	1	1
油菜籽	Rapeseeds	2	2	2	1	1	1	1	1
甘　蔗	Sugar Cane		9	9	4	4	3	3	3
茶　叶	Tea	3	2	2	2	2	2	2	2
水　果	Fruit			10	8	4	1	1	1

注：①1993年以前为猪、牛、羊肉产量的位次。

①Data refer to pork, beef and mutton prior to 1993.

附录2-7 主要工业产品产量(1999年)

Output of Major Industrial Products (1999)

国外资料来源：联合国《统计月报》2001年3月、《工业产品统计年鉴》1997年；联合国粮农组织数据库；英国汽车生产商和贸易商协会《世界汽车统计》2000年。

Sources: United Nations "*Monthly Bulletin of Statistics*" March 2001, "*Industrial Commodity Statistics Yearbook*" 1997; FAO database; The United Kingdom "*World Automotive Statistics*" 2000.

国家和地区	Country or Territory	1999	国家和地区	Country or Territory	1999
钢(万吨)	**Crude Steel (10 000 tons)**		**煤炭④(万吨)**	**Coal ④ (10 000 tons)**	
世界总计	**World**	**77192**	**世界总计②**	**World②**	**390517**
中国	China	12426	中国	China	104500
美国	USA	10740	美国	USA	99245
日本	Japan	9420	印度	India	29219
德国	Germany	4402	俄罗斯	Russian Fed.	24703
俄罗斯①	Russian Fed.①	4367	澳大利亚⑾	Australia⑾	22501
韩国	Korea, Rep. of	4068	南非	South Africa	22032
巴西	Brazil	2496	德国	Germany	20640
意大利	Italy	2473	波兰	Poland	17245
乌克兰	Ukraine	2245	乌克兰	Ukraine	8165
法国①	France ①	2012	印度尼西亚	Indonesia	7070
原油(万吨)	**Crude Petroleum (10 000 tons)**		**电(亿千瓦小时)**	**Electricity (100 million kwh)**	
世界总计②	**World②**	**328339**	**世界总计②**	**World②**	**140737**
沙特阿拉伯	Saudi Arabia	36773	美国	USA	37076
俄罗斯	Russian Fed.	30475	中国	China	12393
美国	USA	29663	日本	Japan	9211
伊朗	Iran	17660	俄罗斯	Russian Fed.	8473
中国	China	16000	德国	Germany	5517
委内瑞拉	Venezuela	15623	加拿大	Canada	5419
墨西哥	Mexico	15108	法国	France	5006
挪威	Norway	14873	印度	India	4772
英国	United Kingdom	12836	英国	United Kingdom	3364
伊拉克	Iraq	12439	巴西	Brazil	3323
水泥(万吨)	**Cement (10 000 tons)**		**化肥①(万吨)**	**Fertilizer ① (10 000 tons)**	
世界总计②	**World②**	**15091**	**世界总计**	**World**	**14725**
中国	China	57300	中国	China	3010
美国	USA	10693	美国	United States of America	2452
印度	India	9826	印度	India	1366
日本	Japan	8020	加拿大	Canada	1270
韩国	Korea, Rep. of	4858	俄罗斯	Russian Federation	920
巴西	Brazil	4027	德国	Germany	494
德国①	Germany①	3656	白俄罗斯	Belarus	402
意大利	Italy	3372	印度尼西亚	Indonesia	313
土耳其	Turkey	3222	巴西	Brazil	242
墨西哥	Mexico	3205	法国	France	241

附录2-7 续表1 continued

国家和地区	Country or Territory	1999	国家和地区	Country or Territory	1999
合成橡胶(万吨)	**Synthetic Rubber (10 000 tons)**		**汽车(万辆)⑥**	**Motor Vehicles ⑥ (10 000)**	
世界总计	**World**	**945**	**世界总计**	**World**	**5072**
美　国	USA	235	美　国	USA	1303
日　本	Japan	158	日　本	Japan	990
俄罗斯①	Russian Fed.①	74	法　国	France	318
中　国	China	73	德　国	Germany	569
德　国①	Germany ①	72	加拿大	Canada	305
韩　国	Korea, Rep. of	66	西班牙	Spain	285
法　国	France	57	韩　国	Korea, Rep. of	284
巴　西	Brazil	37	英　国	United Kingdom	197
比利时	Belgium	33	中　国	China	183
英　国	United Kingdom	28	意大利	Italy	170
天然气(千万亿焦耳)	**Natural Gas (10 000 terajoules)**		**轮胎⑧(万条)**	**Tires⑧ (10 000)**	
世界总计②	**World②**	**90198**	**世界总计②**	**World②**	**95445**
俄罗斯	Russian Fed.	21688	美　国	USA	26765
美　国	USA	20230	日　本	Japan	16225
加拿大	Canada	6712	中　国	China	10970
英　国	United Kingdom	4146	法　国①	France ①	6746
印度尼西亚	Indonesia	3345	韩　国	Korea, Rep. of	6712
荷　兰	Netherlands	2240	德　国①	Germany ①	5921
墨西哥	Mexico	2191	意大利①	Italy ①	3436
挪　威	Norway	2092	巴　西③	Brazil ③	3323
乌兹别克斯坦	Uzbikstan	1897	英　国①	United Kingdom ①	3266
阿根廷	Argentina	1711	印度尼西亚②	Indonesia②	2417
新闻纸(万吨)	**Newsprint (10 000 tons)**		**原木⑦(万立方米)**	**Roundwood ⑦(10 000cum)**	
世界总计②	**World②**	**3612**	**世界总计**	**World**	**327508**
加拿大	Canada	920	美　国	United States of America	50075
美　国	USA	652	印　度	India	30279
日　本	Japan	330	巴　西	Brazil	19790
瑞　典	Sweden	250	印度尼西亚	Indonesia	19060
韩　国	Korea, Rep. of	174	加拿大	Canada	18566
德　国①	Germany ①	163	俄罗斯	Russian Federation	11100
芬　兰	Finland	149	尼日利亚	Nigeria	10064
俄罗斯①	Russian Fed. ①	139	瑞　典	Sweden	5870
中　国	China	113	芬　兰	Finland	5385
英　国①	United Kingdom ①	104	中　国	China	5237

附录2-7 续表2 continued

国家和地区	Country or Territory	1999	国家和地区	Country or Territory	1999
糖（万吨）	**Sugar (10 000 tons)**		**电视机②⑤（万台）**	**TV Sets ②⑤ (10 000)**	
世界总计	**World**	**13397**	**世界总计**	**World**	**13013**
巴　西	Brazil	2106	中　国	China	3637
印　度	India	1744	韩　国③	Korea, Rep. of③	1872
中　国	China	861	美　国③	United States③	1144
美　国	USA	820	巴　西	Brazil	789
澳大利亚	Australia	578	马来西亚	Malaysia	777
泰　国	Thailand	563	日　本	Japan	756
法　国	France	491	西班牙	Spain	539
墨西哥	Mexico	476	土耳其	Turkey	466
德　国	Germany	430	印　度	India	237
巴基斯坦	Pakistan	379	德　国③	Germany③	197

注：①1998年数字。②1997年数字。③1996年数字。④中国为原煤，国外为商品煤。⑤包括彩色电视机和黑白电视机。美国为交货量。⑥包括商用车和乘用车。⑦指采伐所得的全部木材量，其中包括工业用圆木、薪炭材、从采伐中回收的木材。中国为木材产量，包括原木和薪材，同其他国家的原木产量不完全可比。⑧国外为汽车轮胎。⑨仅指硬煤。

Notes: ①Data refer to 1998.②Data refer to 1997.③Data refer to 1996.④The figures relate to all grades of anthracite and bituminous coal, lignite and brown coal, but exclude recovered slurries. Chinese data refers to the raw coal including lignite and waste.⑤Including color TV sets and black and white TV sets. ⑥Including commercial vehicles and passenger cars. ⑦All wood obtained from wood logging, including log for industrial use, fuel wood and wood recovered from logging losses. But Chinese data refer to log and fuel wood.⑧Data of foreign countries refer to rubber tires for automobiles. ⑨ Lithoid only.

附录2-8 我国工业主要产品产量居世界位次

Changes in the Order of Precedence of Output of Major Industrial Products

国外资料来源：联合国《统计月报》2001年3月、《工业产品统计年鉴》1997年；联合国粮农组织数据库。

Sources: United Nations "*Monthly Bulletin of Statistics*" March 2001, "*Industrial Commodity Statistics Yearbook*" 1997; FAO Database.

产品名称	Item	1949	1957	1965	1978	1980	1985	1990	1995	1998	1999③
钢	Crude Steel	26	9	8	5	5	4	4	2	1	1
煤	Coal	9	5	5	3	3	2	1	1	1	1
原　油	Crude Petroleum	27①	23	12	8	6	6	5	5	5	5
发电量	Electricity	25	13	9	7	6	5	4	2	2	2
水　泥	Cement		8	8	4	4	1	1	1	1	1
化　肥	Fertilizer		33	8	3	3	3	3	2	1	1
化学纤维	Chemical Fibre		26②		7	5	4	2	2	2	2
棉　布	Woven Cotton Fabrics			3	1	1	1	1	1	2	2
糖	Sugar			8	8	10	6	6	4	3	3
电视机	Television				8	5	3	1	1	1	1

注：①1950年数字。②1960年数字。③估计数。

①Data refer to 1950.②Data refer to 1960.③Estimates.

附录2-9 消 费 物 价 指 数

Consumer Price Indices

国外资料来源：联合国《统计月报》2001年4月。

Source: United Nations "*Monthly Bulletin of Statistics*" April 2001.

1990年=100 (1990=100)

国家和地区	Country or Territory	总指数 General Index			其中：食品 Of which Food		
		1998	1999	2000	1998	1999	2000
中国	China	202.4	199.6	200.4	214.7	205.7	200.4
美国	United States	124.8	122.5	131.7	122.0	124.6	127.5
日本	Japan	109.7	109.4	108.6	109.4	108.9	106.8
德国⑨	Germany⑨	119.7	120.4	122.7	103.0	101.7	101.2
英国	United Kingdom	129.2	131.2	135.0		120.4	121.2①
法国	France	116.0	116.9②	118.6	110.7	111.5②	113.7
意大利⑧	Italy⑧	138.0	140.3	144.0	132.4	132.9	135.0
加拿大	Canada	116.4	118.5	121.7	114.1	115.6	117.2
澳大利亚	Australia	117.3	119.1	124.4	122.3	126.4	129.5
俄罗斯⑩	Russian Fed.⑩	416814	773814	1000825②	412044	810254	1012695②
捷克	Czech Rep.	329.7	336.7	352.9③	273.3	258.0	264.5③
波兰(11)	Poland(11)	857.5	936.0	1030.2	670.9	102.0	101.9
匈牙利	Hungary	517.7	569.5	625.3	479.8	493.7	539.1
印度(14)	India(14)	217.7	228.0	239.8①	228.8	232.5	237.2①
印度尼西亚(11)	Indonesia(11)	100.0	120.5	125.9⑤	100.0	125.0	143.1⑤
菲律宾(12)	Philippines(12)	204.0	217.6	227.0	190.8	200.8	204.9
泰国(曼谷)	Thailand (Bangkok)	152.7	153.2	154.8	168.4	166.9	164.0
马来西亚	Malaysia	135.8	139.5	141.7	151.4	158.3	161.4
新加坡	Singapore	117.0	117.1	118.7	114.5	114.7	115.7
巴基斯坦	Pakistan	221.9	231.1	247.8②	229.0	237.9	254.0②
缅甸(仰光)	Myanmar (Yangon)	754.6	893.4	896.4③	834.6	997.0	972.0③
孟加拉国(达卡)(13)	Bangladesh (Dhaka)(13)	128.7	136.6	141.6②	130.1	141.3④	145.7②
土耳其(12)(13)	Turkey(12)(13)	1163.0	1917.5	2970.4	1162.0	1997.2②	2907.3①
韩国	Korea,Rep. of	159.2	160.5	164.2	164.3	168.9	170.3
埃及	Egypt	207.5	218.4	224.4	190.9	203.4	207.7⑦
尼日利亚	Nigeria	1075.5		1202.8⑥	984.6		1022.7⑥
墨西哥(12)	Mexico(12)	422.0	491.9	538.6	408.9	473.6	503.4
巴西(13)	Brazil(13)	212.0	222.4	238.0	173.8	179.8	193.3①
阿根廷(布宜诺斯艾利斯)	Argentina (Buenos Aires)	410.7	405.9	402.7	393.0	378.6	369.7

注：①12月份数字。②11月份数字。③10月份数字。④9月份数字。⑤8月份数字。⑥5月份数字。⑦4月份数字。⑧总指数不包括烟草业。⑨总指数1991年为100；食品中包含饮料和烟草业，1995年=100。⑩ 1991年=100。(11)1998年为100。其中波兰是从1999年开始。(12)食品中包括烟草。(13)1994年=100。(14)产业工人。

①Data refer to December.②Data refer to November.③Data refer to October.④Data refer to September.⑤Data refer to August.⑥Data refer to May.⑦Data refer to April.⑧Excluding tobacco:All items only⑨General index:1991=100. Food includes beverages and tobacco: 1995=100. (11)Base:1998=100, Among which, only food for Poland beginning 1999. (12)Food includes tobacco.(13)Base:1994=100.(14)Industrial workers.

附录2-10 中央政府财政收入构成

Types of Revenue as Percentage of Total Central Government Revenue

国外资料来源：国际货币基金组织《政府财政统计年鉴》2000年。

Source: International Monetary Fund "*Government Finance Statistics Yearbook*"2000.

单位：% (%)

国家和地区	Country or Territory	年 份 Year	公司利润和资本所得税 Taxes on Income, Profits & Cap. Gains	社会保险缴款 Social Security Contrib.	工资税 Taxes on Payroll and Work Force	财产税 Taxes on Property	货物和服务税 Domestic Taxes on Goods & Services	国际贸易税 Taxes on Internatl. Trade & Transact.	其他税 Other Taxes	非税收收入 Non-tax Revenue
美　　国	United States	1999	55.80	31.84		1.46	3.61	1.04		6.14
日　　本	Japan	1993	36.16	26.48		4.05	14.43	1.24	1.60	15.45
德　　国	Germany	1998	14.50	47.58		0.03	20.04			15.94
英　　国	United Kingdom	1999	39.71	17.02		7.21	31.02			4.89
法　　国	France	1997	19.34	41.16	1.41	1.97	28.23		0.63	6.07
加 拿 大	Canada	1997	53.87	18.73			16.77	1.48		9.15
澳大利亚	Australia	1998	67.14		2.26		20.24	2.56		6.33
捷　　克	Czech Rep.	1999	13.85	44.11		1.09	35.88	1.93	0.02	3.07
罗马尼亚	Romania	1997	29.15	25.84			25.99	5.57	2.40	7.71
印　　度	India	1999	23.60			0.07	27.00	20.23	0.13	24.59
印度尼西亚	Indonesia	1999	57.79	2.12		0.58	22.71	2.46	0.07	14.23
泰　　国	Thailand	1999	28.87	2.34		0.59	45.38	9.20	0.41	13.19
马来西亚	Malaysia	1997	36.32	1.23		0.65	26.39	12.63	4.68	17.92
新 加 坡	Singapore	1998	22.13			3.55	13.34	1.04	6.67	33.20
缅　　甸	Myanmar	1998	17.68				26.49	4.64		51.12
韩　　国	Korea,Rep.of	1997	26.41	9.25		1.73	33.32	6.30	8.26	13.38
埃　　及	Egypt	1997	20.04			0.74	15.89	11.62	10.03	34.19
墨 西 哥	Mexico	1998	36.26	11.58			58.81	4.29	1.57	10.11
巴　　西	Brazil	1997	16.10	35.27	4.89	0.12	21.97	2.41		16.45
阿 根 廷	Argentina	1998	15.83	25.82		0.96	41.72	6.57	0.46	8.43

附录2-11 中央政府财政支出构成

Types of Expenditure as Percentage of Total Central Government Expenditure

国外资料来源：国际货币基金组织《政府财政统计年鉴》2000年。

Source: International Monetary Fund "*Government Finance Statistics Yearbook*" 2000.

单位：% (%)

国家和地区	Country or Territory	年 份 Year	一般公务支出 Gen. Pub. Service and Public Order	国　防 Defense	教　育 Education	卫　生 Health	社会保障及福利 Social Security and Welfare	住房和公共环境 Housing and Community Amenities
美　　国	United States	1999	10.98	15.22	1.80	20.41	28.75	2.88
日　　本	Japan	1993	3.63	4.11	6.03	1.60	36.80	13.76
英　　国	United Kingdom	1999	7.67	7.10	3.73	15.42	36.50	2.24
加 拿 大	Canada	1997	8.61	5.51	1.83	0.71	46.09	1.57
澳大利亚	Australia	1998	7.93	7.00	7.64	14.81	35.46	1.22
捷　　克	Czech Rep.	1999	7.78	5.02	10.13	17.90	37.76	2.99
罗马尼亚	Romania	1997	6.09	7.25	9.42	6.83	31.00	0.79
印　　度	India	1999		15.41	2.99	1.80		5.66
印度尼西亚	Indonesia	1999	17.45	3.48	6.66	2.39	5.71	13.56
泰　　国	Thailand	1999	8.15	6.64	17.30	6.48	3.27	4.10
马来西亚	Malaysia	1997	16.30	11.14	22.80	6.26	7.20	7.31
新 加 坡	Singapore	1998	10.91	27.94	18.20	7.16	0.74	12.10
缅　　甸	Myanmar	1998	12.10	31.94	7.72	2.61	1.29	0.25
韩　　国	Korea, Rep. of	1997	11.12	16.66	20.51	0.78	10.79	2.26
埃　　及	Egypt	1997	7.87	9.43	14.76	3.29	0.47	5.30
巴　　西	Brazil	1997	19.64	3.99	4.46	7.45	44.86	0.72
阿 根 廷	Argentina	1998	13.18	4.40	5.80	2.28	50.44	2.32

附录2-11 续表 1 continued

单位:%　　(%)

国家和地区	Country or Territory	年 份 Year	文化、娱乐和宗教 Recreational, Cultural and Relg. Affairs	燃料和能源 Fuel and Energy	农林牧渔 Agric., Forestry, Fishing, & Hunting	矿产、制造和建筑 Mining, Manufc. & Construc.	交通通讯 Transport and Communica-tion	其 他 Other Economic Affairs and Services
美　国	United States	1999	0.54	0.13	1.66	0.07	2.42	1.62
日　本	Japan	1993	0.14		1.09	1.64	0.30	0.32
英　国	United Kingdom	1998	0.29	0.12	0.36	0.15	0.86	2.85
加拿大	Canada	1997	1.50	0.03	1.51	0.08	1.69	3.17
澳大利亚	Australia	1998	0.97	0.71	1.39	0.28	1.43	2.27
捷　克	Czech Rep.	1999	1.16	0.45	2.72	0.41	4.85	3.86
罗马尼亚	Romania	1997	1.12	1.21	4.59	2.13	4.53	1.86
印　度	India	1999			6.02	1.66	1.85	6.14
印度尼西亚	Indonesia	1999	1.56	0.19	4.47	0.55	2.26	2.70
泰　国	Thailand	1999	0.87	0.21	6.13	0.72	9.06	29.30
马来西亚	Malaysia	1997			4.65		9.89	7.07
新加坡	Singapore	1998	0.05		0.19	0.01	7.88	11.23
缅　甸	Myanmar	1998	1.70	0.02	14.44	0.16	17.86	0.57
韩　国	Korea,Rep.of	1997	0.85	0.71	7.97	2.57	10.41	2.02
埃　及	Egypt	1997	8.07	0.36	5.27	0.14	4.55	0.48
巴　西	Brazil	1997	0.08	0.16	2.58	0.14	1.53	1.44
阿根廷	Argentina	1998	0.29	1.05	0.93	0.25	3.56	0.96

附录2-12 进 出 口 贸 易 额
Total Imports and Exports

国外资料来源：国际货币基金组织《国际金融统计月报》2001年5月。

Source: IMF "*International Financial Statistics*" May 2001.

单位:亿美元　　(US$ 100 million)

国家和地区	Country or Territory	1990		2000	
		进　口 Imports	出　口 Exports	进　口 Imports	出　口 Exports
世界总计	**World**	**35171**	**34229**	**57422①**	**62201**
中　国	China	534	621	2251	2492
美　国	United States	5170	3936	12576	7811
日　本	Japan	2354	2876	3795	4792
德　国②	Germany ②	3462	4101	4978	5496
英　国	United Kingdom	2244	1853	3344	2815
法　国	France	2344	2166	3044	2977
意大利	Italy	1820	1703	2366	2383
加拿大	Canada	1232	1276	2202①	2766
澳大利亚	Australia	420	398	715	639
俄罗斯	Russian Fed.	1207	1042	445	1048
捷　克	Czech Rep.			295①	268①
波　兰	Poland	84	136	459①	274①
匈牙利	Hungary	87	95	279①	250①
罗马尼亚	Romania	98	58	131	104
保加利亚	Bulgaria	47	48	54①	39①
印　度	India	236	180	505	423
印度尼西亚	Indonesia	218	257	240①	487①
菲律宾	Philippines	130	81	338	398
泰　国	Thailand	330	231	619	691
马来西亚	Malaysia	293	295	650①	845①
新加坡	Singapore	608	527	1345	1379
巴基斯坦	Pakistan	74	56	110	92
缅　甸	Myanmar	3	3	24	14
孟加拉国	Bangladesh	36	17	77①	39
土耳其	Turkey	223	130	535	266
韩　国	Korea, Rep. of	698	650	1605	1723
埃　及	Egypt	168	50	160①	36①
尼日利亚	Nigeria	56	136	100③	97③
墨西哥	Mexico	435	407	1486①	1364①
巴　西	Brazil	225	314	585	551
阿根廷	Argentina	41	124	251	263

注：①1999年数字。②1991年以前数字仅指原联邦德国。③1998年数字。

①Data refer to 1999. ②Data prior to 1991 refer to the former Federal Rep. of Germany. ③Data refer to 1998.

附录2-13 国　际　收　支（1999年）

Balance of Payments (1999)

国外资料来源：国际货币基金组织《国际金融统计月报》2001年5月。

Source: International Monetary Fund "*International Financial Statistics*" May 2001.

单位:亿美元　　　　(US$ 100 million)

国家和地区	Country or Territory	经常帐户 Current Account — 商品贸易 Merchandise — 出口 Exports F.o.b	进口 Imports F.o.b	差额 Trade Balance	服务贸易 Services — 收入 Credit	支出 Debit	要素收入 Factor Income — 收入 Credit	支出 Debit	经常帐户收支盈余 Current Account Balance	资本帐户收支盈余 Capital Account Balance	金融帐户收支盈余 Financial Account Balance	国际收支总盈余 Overall Balance
中　国	China	1947.2	-1585.1	362.1	237.8	-312.9	105.7	-285.5	156.7	-0.3	76.7	86.5
美　国	United States	6866.6	-10299.2	-3432.6	2695.8	-1913.0	2761.7	-2946.5	-3314.8	-35.0	3146.2	-87.3
日　本	Japan	4036.9	-2803.7	1233.3	610.0	-1151.6	1882.7	-1384.3	1068.7	-164.7	-311.1	762.6
德　国	Germany	5429.6	-4709.6	720.0	830.7	-1343.4	859.0	-986.1	-193.1	-1.2	-338.9	-141.1
英　国	United Kingdom	2689.4	-3112.8	-423.5	1048.4	-865.9	1802.9	-1654.7	-159.8	13.0	174.8	-10.4
法　国	France	2982.2	-2788.3	193.9	837.9	-646.7	678.7	-568.2	365.8	14.7	-411.6	-14.5
意大利	Italy	2308.3	-2104.5	203.8	614.6	-586.7	459.4	-574.3	63.0	29.3	-179.3	-80.5
加拿大	Canada	2428.2	-2200.6	227.6	348.5	-389.2	212.8	-429.2	-22.7	34.3	-18.7	59.3
澳大利亚	Australia	561.0	-658.3	-97.3	172.9	-183.0	69.1	-192.1	-230.7	8.1	272.6	67.1
捷　克	Czech Rep.	262.6	-281.6	-19.0	69.3	-58.3	16.7	-24.1	-10.3	0.0	25.0	16.4
波　兰	Poland	300.6	-451.3	-150.7	84.6	-70.8	18.4	-28.5	-124.9	0.6	104.6	1.6
匈牙利	Hungary	218.5	-240.4	-21.9	56.5	-42.7	7.8	-24.2	-21.0	0.3	46.7	23.4
罗马尼亚	Romania	85.0	-96.0	-10.9	13.7	-17.9	1.5	-5.6	-13.0	0.5	7.0	2.4
印　度	India	375.3	-455.6	-80.3	144.4	-174.1	19.2	-56.3	-27.8		91.5	66.6
印度尼西亚	Indonesia	512.4	-306.0	206.4	45.8	-115.5	18.9	-116.9	57.9		-59.4	19.7
菲律宾	Philippines	342.1	-292.5	49.6	48.0	-75.2	80.8	-29.1	79.1	-0.1	-9.4	36.6
泰　国	Thailand	567.8	-427.6	140.1	146.4	-135.8	30.9	-60.8	124.3		-110.7	13.9
新加坡	Singapore	1156.4	-1043.4	113.0	236.9	-188.8	154.2	-91.2	212.5	-1.9	-173.7	41.9
巴基斯坦①	Pakistan①	83.6	-107.6	-24.0	16.3	-26.6	1.5	-23.7	-17.1		23.2	5.4
韩　国	Korea, Rep. of	1451.6	-1167.9	283.7	265.3	-271.8	32.4	-84.0	244.8	-3.9	127.1	332.6
埃　及	Egypt	52.4	-151.6	-99.3	94.9	-64.5	17.9	-10.4	-16.3		-14.2	-46.1
尼日利亚	Nigeria	128.8	-85.9	42.9	9.8	-34.8	2.4	-28.2	5.1	-0.5	-40.0	-35.4
墨西哥	Mexico	1363.9	-1419.7	-55.8	117.3	-143.0	48.9	-172.3	-141.7		192.6	42.8
巴　西	Brazil	480.1	-492.2	-12.1	77.3	-144.3	39.3	-227.9	-250.7	3.4	72.2	-167.7
阿根廷	Argentina	233.3	-241.0	-7.7	44.1	-84.9	61.0	-138.4	-123.1		147.0	20.1

注：①1997年数字。

①Data refer to 1997.

附录2-14 国际储备和黄金储备（年底数）

International Reserves and Gold Reserves (Year-end)

国外资料来源：国际货币基金组织《国际金融统计月报》2001年5月。

Source: IMF "*International Financial Statistics*"May 2001.

国家和地区	Country or Territory	国际储备(不包括黄金，百万美元) International Reserves (minus gold,USD million)			黄金储备(百万盎司) Gold Reserves (fine troy ounces, million)		
		1998	1999	2000	1998	1999	2000
中国	China	144960	154675	165574	12.67	12.67	12.67
美国	United States	70715	60500		261.61	261.67	
日本	Japan	215471	286916	354902	24.23	24.23	24.55
德国	Germany	74024	61039	56890	118.98	111.52	111.52
英国	United Kingdom	32212	35870	43891	23.00	20.55	15.67
法国	France	44312	39701	37039	102.37	97.24	97.25
意大利	Italy	29888	22421	25566	83.36	78.83	78.83
加拿大	Canada	23308	28126	31924	2.49	1.81	1.18
澳大利亚	Australia	14641	21212	18118	2.56	2.56	2.56
波兰	Poland	27325	26355	25657	3.31	3.31	3.31
匈牙利	Hungary	9319	10954	11190	0.10	0.10	0.10
罗马尼亚	Romania	2867	2687	3922	3.22	3.32	3.37
印度	India	27341	32667	37902	11.49	11.50	11.50
印度尼西亚	Indonesia	22713	26445	22548	3.10	3.10	3.10
菲律宾	Philippines	9226	13230	13054	5.43	6.20	7.23
泰国	Thailand	28825	34063	32016	2.47	2.47	2.37
马来西亚	Malaysia	25559	30588	29523	2.35	1.18	1.17
新加坡	Singapore	74928	76843	80127			
巴基斯坦	Pakistan	1028	1511	1513	2.08	2.09	2.09
缅甸	Myanmar	315	265		0.23	0.23	
孟加拉国	Bangladesh	1905	1604	1486	0.11	0.11	0.11
土耳其	Turkey	19489	23340	19952	3.75	3.74	3.74
韩国	Korea, Rep. of	51975	73987	96131	0.43	0.44	0.44
埃及	Egypt	18124	14484	13118	2.43	2.43	2.43
墨西哥	Mexico	31799	31782	35509	0.22	0.16	0.25
巴西	Brazil	42580	34796	32488	4.60	3.17	1.89
阿根廷	Argentina	24752	26252	25147	0.36	0.34	0.02

附录2-15 货　币　汇　率（年末中间价）

Exchange Rates (Mid-Point Rates in the Year-end)

国外资料来源：联合国《统计月报》2001年4月。

Source: UN "*Monthly Bulletin of Statistics*" April 2001.

一美元合该国货币数　　(Unless otherwise stated national currency per U.S.dollar)

国家和地区	货币名称	Country or Territory	Currencies	1985	1990	1995	1999	2000
中　国	（人民币元）	China	(Renminbi Yuan)	3.20	5.22	8.32	8.28	8.28
美　国	（美　元）	United States	(Dollar)	1.00	1.00	1.00	1.00	1.00
日　本	（日　元）	Japan	(Yen)	200.21	134.65	102.59	102.20	114.90
德　国①	（德国马克）	Germany①	(Deutsche Mark)	2.46	1.50	1.43	1.00	1.07
英　国	（英　镑）	United Kingdom	(Pound)	0.69	0.52	0.64	0.62	0.67
法　国①	（法　郎）	France①	(Franc)	7.55	5.14	4.89	1.00	1.07
意大利①	（里　拉）	Italy①	(Lire)	1676.09	1132.27	1580.99	1.00	1.07
加拿大	（加　元）	Canada	(Dollar)	1.40	1.16	1.36	1.44	1.50
澳大利亚	（澳　元）	Australia	(Dollar)	1.47	1.30	1.34	1.53	1.81
俄罗斯	（卢　布）	Russian Fed.	(Rouple)			4.63	27.00	28.16
捷　克	（克　朗）	Czech.Rep.	(Koruna)			26.54	35.98	37.81
波　兰	（兹罗提）	Poland	(Zloty)	0.01	0.95	2.46	4.15	4.14
匈牙利	（福　林）	Hungary	(Forint)	47.28	61.56	139.14	252.52	284.73
罗马尼亚	（列　伊）	Romania	(Lei)	15.71	34.78	2571.93	18255.00	25926.00
保加利亚	（列　弗）	Bulgaria	(Leva)			0.07	1.95	2.10
南斯拉夫	（第纳尔）	Yugoslavia,FR	(Dinar)		10.66	5.32	11.18	70.00
印　度	（卢　比）	India	(Rupee)	12.15	18.11	35.10	43.49	46.75
印度尼西亚	（卢　比）	Indonesia	(Rupiah)	1123.38	1904.56	2302.56	7085.00	9595.00
菲律宾	（比　索）	Philippines	(Peso)	19.00	28.05	26.15	40.31	50.00
泰　国	（　铢　）	Thailand	(Baht)	26.61	25.34	25.13	37.47	42.27
马来西亚	（林吉特）	Malaysia	(Ringgit)	2.42	2.71	2.54	3.80	3.80
新加坡	（新加坡元）	Singapore	(Dollar)	2.10	1.75	1.41	1.67	1.73
巴基斯坦	（卢　比）	Pakistan	(Rupee)	15.92	21.89	34.08	51.78	58.03
缅　甸	（缅　元）	Myanmar	(Kyat)	7.73	5.99	5.71	6.27	6.60
孟加拉国	（塔　卡）	Bangladesh	(Taka)	30.96	35.86	40.65	51.00	54.00
土耳其	（里　拉）	Turkey	(Lira)	576.03	2935.56	59509.46	541400.00	673385.00
蒙　古	（图格里克）	Mongolia	(Tugrik)		14.00	473.62	1072.37	1097.00
韩　国	（韩　圆）	Korea,Rep.of	(Won)	888.92	717.74	772.87	1138.00	1264.50
埃　及	（埃　镑）	Egypt	(Pound)	0.70	2.00	3.38	3.41	3.69
尼日利亚	（奈　拉）	Nigeria	(Naira)	1.00	9.02	21.84	97.95	109.55
墨西哥	（新比索）	Mexico	(New Peso)	0.37	2.95	7.62	9.51	9.57
巴　西	（雷亚尔）	Brazil	(Reai)			0.97	1.79	1.96
阿根廷	（比　索）	Argentina	(Peso)		0.56	1.00	1.00	1.00

注：①1999年以后为欧元兑美元汇率。1999年1月1日欧元启动，各成员国货币与欧元汇率锁定，其中1欧元分别可兑换1.95583德国马克、6.55957法国法郎和1936.27意大利里拉。

① From 1999, data refer to Euro per US Dollar. Euro was launched on Jan. 1, 1999, which fixed the central rates between Euro and the currencies participating in the exchange rate mechanism. For example, one Euro equals to 1.95583 Deutsche Mark or 6.55957 French Franc or 1936.27 Italian Lire.

附录2-16 居民文化程度构成

Educational Attainment of Population of 25 Years Old and Over

国外资料来源：联合国教科文组织《统计年鉴》1999年。

Source: United Nations Educational, Scientific and Cultural Organization "*Statistical Yearbook*" 1999.

单位：% (%)

国家和地区	Country or Territory	年 份 Year	25岁和25岁以上人口总计（万人） Total Population of 25 Years Old & over (10 000 persons)	大 学 Post-secondary	中 学 Entered Second Level		小 学 First Level		文盲及文化程度不明确者 No Schooling and Not Otherwise Included
					初 中 First Stage	高 中 Second Stage	肄 业 Incompleted	毕 业 Completed	
美 国	United States	1994	16451	46.5	44.6	⑤	8.2	⑥	0.6
日 本	Japan	1990	8199	20.7	43.7	⑤	33.6	⑥	0.3
德 国	Germany								
前联邦德国	Fed.Rep.	1970	3886	4.3	④	18.0	④	④	77.7
前民主德国	Former DR	1981	1072	17.3	52.6	⑤	30.1	⑥	
英 国①	United Kingdom①	1976		11.0	④	④	④	④	89
意大利⑦	Italy⑦	1991		3.8	30.7	18.6	12.2	32.5	2.1
加拿大	Canada	1991	1747	21.4	34.3	27.7	4.0	11.7	1.0
澳大利亚	Australia	1971	688	21.5	48.3	⑤	29.3	⑥	0.9
俄罗斯	Russian Federation	1989	8602	14.1	49.0	⑤	36.9	⑥	...
捷克共和国	Czech Republic	1991	658	8.5	58.6	⑤	31.4	⑥	0.3
波 兰	Poland	1988	2299	7.9	47.8	⑤	5.6	37.2	1.5
匈牙利	Hungary	1990	680	10.1	②	30.7	24.3	33.6	1.3
罗马尼亚⑧	Romania⑧	1996	1907	5.6	69.4	⑤	20.7	⑥	4.3
原南斯拉夫	Former Yugoslavia	1981	1308	6.8	23.4	⑤	53.9	⑥	15.8
印 度	India	1991	36800	7.3	7.2	⑤	28.0	⑥	57.5
印度尼西亚	Indonesia	1990	7850	2.3	16.8	⑤	26.4	⑥	54.5
菲律宾⑨	Philippines⑨	1995	4270	21.9	17.2	21.2	20.7	15.1	3.7
泰 国	Thailand	1990	4908	5.1	13.7	⑤	69.6	⑥	10.7
马来西亚	Malaysia	1996	965	6.8	19.3	23.5	13.0	20.6	16.7
新加坡	Singapore	1995	186	7.6	36.8	13.7	11.2	16.5	14.3
巴基斯坦	Pakistan	1990		2.5	5.8	8.2	9.7	⑥	73.8
缅 甸	Myanmar	1983	1395	2.0	14.5	⑤	27.7	⑥	55.8
孟加拉国	Bangladesh	1981	3159	1.3	7.4	4.2	16.7	⑥	70.4
土耳其	Turkey	1993		⑤	21.9	⑤	6.6	40.6	30.6
韩 国	Korea,Rep.of	1995	2622	21.1	15.7	36.2	0.9	17.3	8.7
埃 及	Egypt	1986	1944	4.6	14.8	⑤	16.5	⑥	64.1
墨西哥	Mexico	1990	3119	9.2	12.7	10.7	28.6	19.9	18.8
巴 西⑩	Brazil⑩	1989	11016	③	11.9	5.5	57.0	6.9	18.7
阿根廷	Argentina	1991	1734	12.0	25.3	⑤	22.3	34.6	5.7

注：①25-69岁人口的文化构成。②包括在"小学毕业"栏内。③包括在"高中"栏内。④包括在"文盲及文化程度不明确者"栏内。⑤包括在"初中"栏内。⑥包括在小学"肄业"栏中。⑦6岁以上人口的文化构成。⑧12岁以上人口的文化构成。⑨15岁以上人口的文化构成。⑩10岁以上人口的文化构成。

①Only refer to 25-69 age group.②Included in the column " Completed of first level".③Included in the column of second stage.④Included in the column of no schooling.⑤Included in the column of first stage. ⑥Included in the column of incompleted of first level.⑦Refer to the age group "6 years and over". ⑧Refer to the age group "12 years and over".⑨Refer to the age group "15 years and over". ⑩Refer to the age group "10 years and over".

附录2-17 公共教育经费占国民生产总值比重

Public Expenditures on Education as Percentage of GNP

国外资料来源：联合国教科文组织《统计年鉴》1999年。

Source: United Nations Educational,Scientific and Cultural Organization "*Statistical Yearbook*" 1999.

单位：%　　　　　　　　　　　　　　　　　　　　　　　　　　　　　　　　　　　　(%)

国家和地区	Country or Territory	1980	1985	1990	1995	1996
世界总计	**World**	**4.8**	**4.8**	**4.8**	**5.2**	
中　　国②	China②	2.5	2.5	2.5	2.5	2.5
美　　国③	United States③		4.9	5.2	5.4⑧	
日　　本③	Japan③	5.8	5.0	4.7	3.6⑧	
德　　国①	Germany ①	4.7	4.5		4.8	4.8
英　　国③	United Kingdom③	5.6	4.9	4.9	5.3	
法　　国③	France③	5.0	5.8	5.4	6.1	6.0
意 大 利③	Italy③	4.4⑥	5.0		4.7	4.9
加 拿 大③	Canada③	6.9	6.5	6.8	6.9⑧	
澳大利亚③	Australia③	5.5	5.6	5.3	5.5	
俄 罗 斯③	Russian Fed.③	3.5	3.2	3.5	3.5	
捷　　克③	Czech Rep.③	4.0	4.2	4.6	5.4	5.1
波　　兰③	Poland③		4.9		5.2	7.5
匈 牙 利③	Hungary③	4.7	5.5	6.1	5.3	4.6
罗马尼亚	Romania	3.3	2.2	2.8		3.6
保加利亚	Bulgaria	4.5	5.5	5.6	3.9	3.2
原南斯拉夫	Former Yugoslavia	4.7	3.4	6.1		
印　　度	India	3.0	3.5	3.9	3.3	3.2
印度尼西亚	Indonesia	1.7	1.4	1.0⑤	1.4⑨	1.4⑨
菲 律 宾	Philippines	1.7	1.4	2.9	3.0	3.2
泰　　国	Thailand	3.4	3.8	3.6	4.1	4.8
马来西亚	Malaysia	6.0	6.6	5.5	4.7	5.2
新 加 坡	Singapore	2.8	4.4	3.0	3.0	
巴基斯坦	Pakistan	2.1	2.9	2.7	2.8	3.0
孟加拉国⑨	Bangladesh⑨	1.1	1.4	1.5		2.2
土 耳 其	Turkey	2.2	1.8	2.1⑩	2.2	
韩　　国③	Korea,Rep.of③	3.7	4.5	3.5	3.7	
埃　　及	Egypt	5.7④	6.3	3.8	4.8	
尼日利亚⑨	Nigeria⑨		1.2	1.0	0.7	
墨 西 哥③	Mexico③	4.7	3.9	3.7	4.9	
巴　　西	Brazil	3.6	3.8	4.5⑦	5.1	
阿 根 廷	Argentina	2.7	2.7⑾	3.4⑿	3.8⑧	3.5

注：①1991年以前为原联邦德国。②国家财政性教育经费占GNP比重。③1990年起，统计口径有所调整。④1981年数字。⑤仅指教育部支出。⑥1979年数字。⑦1989年数字。⑧1994年数字。⑨仅指中央政府支出。⑩不包括大学经费支出。⑾1984年数字。⑿1991年数字。

①Data prior to 1991 refer to the former Federal Republic of Germany. ②Data refer to the proportion of budgetary expenditure for education to GNP ③Starting from 1990, the data is not comparable with those for the past years. ④Data refer to 1981.⑤Ministry of Education only.⑥Data refer to 197 ⑦Data refer to 1989. ⑧Data refer to 1994. ⑨Central government only.⑩Not including expenditure on tertiary education. ⑾Data refer to 1984. ⑿Data refer to 1991.

附录2-18 研究与开发经费

Expenditures on Research and Experimental Development

国外资料来源：联合国教科文组织《统计年鉴》1999年。

Source: United Nations Educational, Scientific and Cultural Organization "*Statistical Yearbook*" 1999.

单位：各国本币 (national currency units)

国家和地区		Country or Territory		年份 Year	研究与开发经费占国民生产总值的比重 As % of GNP (%)	按人口平均的研究与开发费用 per Capita Expenditure on R & D	每一研究人员年平均费用 Annual Average Expenditure per R & D Scientist or Engineer
美国	(美元)	United States	(Dollar)	1996	2.64	720	177625①
日本	(日元)	Japan	(Yen)	1996	2.80	112549	22928184
德国	(马克)	Germany	(Mark)	1997	2.41	1061	344051①
英国	(英镑)	United Kingdom	(Pound)	1996	1.95	246	100278
法国	(法郎)	France	(Franc)	1997	2.25	3140	1184090①
意大利	(里拉)	Italy	(Lire)	1997	2.21	358271	236495195①
加拿大	(加元)	Canada	(Dollar)	1997	1.66	446	154838①
澳大利亚	(澳元)	Australia	(Dollar)	1996	1.80	480	142768
俄罗斯	(卢布)	Russian Federation	(Rouple)	1996	0.88	131150	34504406
捷克	(克朗)	Czech Rep.	(Koruna)	1997	1.20	1891	1548283
波兰	(兹罗提)	Poland	(Zloty)	1996	0.77	72	52625
匈牙利	(福林)	Hungary	(Forint)	1996	0.68	4404	4312971
罗马尼亚	(列伊)	Romania	(Lei)	1995	0.72	22442	10652279③
保加利亚	(列弗)	Bulgaria	(Leva)	1996	0.57	1083	620162
南斯拉夫	(第纳尔)	Yugoslavia F.R.	(New dinar)	1995			43912
印度	(卢比)	India	(Rupee)	1994	0.73	75	499698
印度尼西亚	(卢比)	Indonesia	(Rupiah)	1995	0.10	2156	8092983⑤
菲律宾	(比索)	Philippines	(Peso)	1992	0.22①	47	295236
泰国	(铢)	Thailand	(Baht)	1996	0.13	94	915558
马来西亚	(林吉特)	Malaysia	(Ringgit)	1996	0.24	27	290069
新加坡	(新加坡元)	Singapore	(Dollar)	1995	1.13	412	177592
巴基斯坦	(卢比)	Pakistan	(Rupee)	1987	0.92	51	840050④
土耳其	(里拉)	Turkey	(Lira)	1996	0.45	1070526	3688259065
韩国	(韩圆)	Korea, Rep.of	(Won)	1996	2.82	239896	109400803
埃及	(埃镑)	Egypt	(Pound)	1996	0.22	8	36164②
尼日利亚	(奈拉)	Nigeria	(Naira)	1987	0.09	2	75809
墨西哥	(比索)	Mexico	(New peso)	1995	0.33	63	292645
巴西	(雷亚尔)	Brazil	(Reai)	1995	0.84	33	194140
阿根廷	(比索)	Argentina	(Peso)	1995	0.38	30	44914

注：①1995年。②1991年。③1994年数。④估计数。⑤1988年。

①Data refer to 1995. ②Data refer to 1991. ③Data refer to 1994. ④Estimate. ⑤Data refer to 1988.

中国统计出版社最新资料书简目

《中国统计年鉴-2001》
《中国统计摘要-2001》
《中国发展报告-2001》
《国际统计年鉴-2001》
《中国农村统计年鉴-2001》
《中国城市统计年鉴-2000》
《中国人口统计年鉴-2001》
《中国能源统计年鉴-2001》
《中国劳动统计年鉴-2001》
《中国基本单位统计年鉴-2001》
《中国市场统计年鉴-2001》
《中国价格及城镇居民家庭收支调查统计年鉴-2001》
《如何使用统计年鉴》
《中国民政统计年鉴-2001》
《中国食品工业年鉴-1999》
《北京统计年鉴-2001》
《天津统计年鉴-2001》
《河北经济年鉴-2001》
《山西统计年鉴-2001》
《内蒙古统计年鉴-2001》
《辽宁统计年鉴-2001》
《吉林统计年鉴-2001》
《黑龙江统计年鉴-2001》
《上海统计年鉴-2001》
《江苏统计年鉴-2001》
《浙江统计年鉴-2001》
《安徽统计年鉴-2001》
《福建统计年鉴-2001》
《江西统计年鉴-2001》
《山东统计年鉴-2001》
《河南统计年鉴-2001》
《湖北统计年鉴-2001》
《湖南统计年鉴-2001》
《广东统计年鉴-2001》
《广西统计年鉴-2001》
《海南统计年鉴-2001》
《四川统计年鉴-2001》
《重庆统计年鉴-2001》
《贵州统计年鉴-2001》
《云南统计年鉴-2001》

《西藏统计年鉴-2001》
《陕西统计年鉴-2001》
《甘肃年鉴-2001》
《青海统计年鉴-2001》
《宁夏统计年鉴-2001》
《新疆统计年鉴-2001》
《新疆生产建设兵团统计年鉴-2001》
《石家庄统计年鉴-2001》
《唐山统计年鉴-2001》
《衡水统计年鉴-2001》
《邯郸统计年鉴-2001》
《廊坊统计年鉴-2001》
《太原统计年鉴-2001》
《呼和浩特经济统计年鉴-2001》
《沈阳年鉴-2001》
《长春统计年鉴-2001》
《延吉统计年鉴-2001》
《四平统计年鉴-2001》
《吉林市社会经济统计年鉴-2001》
《齐齐哈尔经济统计年鉴-2001》
《哈尔滨统计年鉴-2001》
《黑龙江垦区统计年鉴-2001》
《牡丹江社会经济统计年鉴-2001》
《上海浦东新区统计年鉴-2001》
《南京统计年鉴-2001》
《苏州统计年鉴-2001》
《常州统计年鉴-2001》
《无锡统计年鉴-2001》
《徐州统计年鉴-2001》
《南通统计年鉴-2001》
《盐城统计年鉴-2001》
《连云港统计年鉴-2001》
《张家口统计年鉴-2001》
《杭州统计年鉴-2001》
《绍兴统计年鉴-2001》
《宁波统计年鉴-2001》
《舟山统计年鉴-2001》
《温州统计年鉴-2001》
《台州统计年鉴-2001》
《福州年鉴-2001》
《厦门经济特区年鉴-2001》

《福州经济技术开发区年鉴-2001》
《南昌统计年鉴-2001》
《九江经济统计年鉴-2001》
《济南统计年鉴-2001》
《青岛统计年鉴-2001》
《泰安统计年鉴-2001》
《郑州统计年鉴-2001》
《洛阳统计年鉴-2001》
《三门峡统计年鉴-2001》
《平顶山统计年鉴-2001》
《南阳经济统计年鉴-2001》
《武汉统计年鉴-2001》
《宜昌统计年鉴-2001》
《十堰统计年鉴-2001》
《广州统计年鉴-2001》
《东莞统计年鉴-2001》
《惠州统计年鉴-2001》
《珠海统计年鉴-2001》
《深圳统计信息年鉴-2001》
《桂林经济社会统计年鉴-2001》
《南宁地区统计年鉴-2001》
《南宁统计年鉴-2001》
《柳州地区统计年鉴-2001》
《柳州经济统计年鉴-2001》
《海口统计年鉴-2001》
《成都统计年鉴-2001》
《攀枝花统计年鉴-2001》
《广安统计年鉴-2001》
《贵阳统计年鉴-2001》
《昆明统计年鉴-2001》
《西安统计年鉴-2001》
《兰州年鉴-2001》
《天水统计年鉴-2001》
《西宁统计年鉴-2001》
《乌鲁木齐统计年鉴-2001》
《吐鲁番统计年鉴-2001》
《巴音郭楞统计年鉴-2001》
《伊克昭盟统计年鉴-2001》
《石河子统计年鉴-2001》

编辑部电话：(010) 63262276　63266600—30605
欲购以上图书请与中国统计出版社发行部联系。电话：(010) 63459084　同榉行书店电话：68585978
通讯地址：北京市西城区三里河月坛南街75号。邮政编码：100826

New Published Statistical Yearbook by China Statistics Press

China Statistical Yearbook -2001
China Statistical Abstract -2001
China Development Report -2001
International Statistical Yearbook-2001
China Rural Statistical Yearbook-2001
China Urban Statistical Yearbook-2000
China Population Statistical Yearbook-2001
China Energy Statistical Yearbook-2001
China Labour Statistical Yearbook-2001
China Basic Statistical Units Yearbook-2001
China Market Statistical Yearbook-2001
China Statistical Yearbook of Price and Urban Household Survey-2001
How to Use Statistical Yearbook
China Civil Affairs's Statistical Yearbook -2001
China Food Industrial Statistical Yearbook-2000
Beijing Statistical Yearbook-2001
Tianjin Statistical Yearbook-2001
Hebei Economic Statistical Yearbook-2001
Shanxi Statistical Yearbook-2001
Inner Mongolia Statistical Yearbook-2001
Liaoning Statistical Yearbook-2001
Jilin Statistical Yearbook-2001
Helongjiang Statistical Yearbook -2001
Shanghai Statistical Yearbook-2001
Jiangsu Statistical Yearbook-2001
Zhejiang Statistical Yearbook-2001
Anhui Statistical Yearbook-2001
Fujiang Statistical Yearbook-2001
Jiangxi Statistical Yearbook-2001
Shandong Statistical Yearbook-2001
Henan Statistical Yearbook-2001
Hubei Statistical Yearbook-2001
Huann Statistical Yearbook-2001
Guangdong Statistical Yearbook-2001
Guangxi Statistical Yearbook-2001
Hainan Statistical Yearbook-2001
Sichuan Statistical Yearbook-2001
Chongqing Statistical Yearbook-2001
Guizhou Statistical Yearbook-2001
Yunnan Statistical Yearbook-2001
Tibet Statistical Yearbook-2001
Shaanxi Statistical Yearbook-2001
Gansu Yearbook-2001
Qinghai Statistical Yearbook-2001
Ningxia Statistical Yearbook-2001
Xinjiang Statistical Yearbook-2001
Xinjiang Production & Construction Group Statistical Yearbook-2001
Shijiazhuang Statistical Yearbook-2001
Tangshan Statistical Yearbook-2001
Hengshui Statistical Yearbook-2001
Handan Statistical Yearbook-2001
Langfang Statistical Yearbook-2001
Taiyuan Statistical Yearbook-2001
Hohhot Economic Statistical Yearbook-2001
Shenyang Yearbook-2001
Changchun Statistical Yearbook-2001
Yanji Statistical Yearbook-2001
Siping Statistical Yearbook-2001
Jilin City Social Economic Statistical Yearbook-2001
Qiqihrer Economic Statistical Yearbook-2001
Harbin Statistical Yearbook-2001
Heilongjiang Assarting District Statistical Yearbook-2001
Mudanjiang Social Economic Statistical Yearbook-2001
Statistical Yearbook of Shanghai Pudong New Area -2001
Nanjing Statistical Yearbook-2001
Suzhou Statistical Yearbook-2001
Changzhou Statistical Yearbook-2001
Wuxi Statistical Yearbook-2001
Xuzhou Statistical Yearbook-2001
Nantong Statistical Yearbook-2001
Yancheng Statistical Yearbook-2001
Lianyungang Statistical Yearbook-2001
Zhangjiakou Statistical Yearbook-2001
Hangzhou Statistical Yearbook-2001
Shaoxing Statistical Yearbook-2001
Ningbo Statistical Yearbook-2001
Zhoushan Statistical Yearbook-2001
Wenzhou Statistical Yearbook-2001
Taizhou Statistical Yearbook-2001
Fuzhou Yearbook-2001
Xiamen Special Economic Zoon Statistical Yearbook-2001
Statistical Yearbook of Fuzhou Economic &Technical Development District -2001
Nanchang Statistical Yearbook-2001
Jiujiang Economic Statistical Yearbook-2001
Jinan Statistical Yearbook-2001
Qingdao Statistical Yearbook-2001
Tai'an Statistical Yearbook-2001
Zhengzhou Statistical Yearbook-2001
Luoyang Statistical Yearbook-2001
Sanmenxia Statistical Yearbook-2001
Pingdingshan Statistical Yearbook-2001
Nanyang Economic Statistical Yearbook-2001
Wuhan Statistical Yearbook-2001
Yichang Statistical Yearbook-2001
Shiyan Statistical Yearbook-2001
Guangzhou Statistical Yearbook-2001
Dongguan Statistical Yearbook-2001
Huizhou Statistical Yearbook-2001
Zhuhai Statistical Yearbook-2001
Shenzhen Statistical and Information Yearbook-2001
Guilin Economic Social Statistical Yearbook-2001
Nanning Prefectural Statistical Yearbook-2001
Nanning Statistical Yearbook-2001
Liuzhou Prefecture Statistical Yearbook-2001
Liuzhou Economic Statistical Yearbook-2001
Haikou Statistical Yearbook-2001
Chengdu Statistical Yearbook-2001
Pangzhihua Statistical Yearbook-2001
Guang'an Statistical Yearbook-2001
Guiyang Statistical Yearbook-2001
Kunming Statistical Yearbook-2001
Xi'an Statistical Yearbook-2001
Lanzhou Yearbook-2001
Tianshui Statistical Yearbook-2001
Xining Statistical Yearbook-2001
Urumqi Statistical Yearbook-2001
Tulufan Statistical Yearbook-2001
Bayinguoleng Statistical Yearbook-2001
Yikezhaomeng Statistical Yearbook-2001
Shihezi Statistical Yearbook-2001

Address: No 75 Yuetan Nanjie, Sanlihe, Beijing 100826, P. R. China
China Statistics Press
E-mail: yearbook@stats.gov.cn
Tel: 8610-63459084, 68585978